www.wadsworth.com

www.wadsworth.com is the World Wide Web site for
Thomson Wadsworth and is your direct source to dozens
of online resources.

At *www.wadsworth.com* you can find out about supple-
ments, demonstration software, and student resources.
You can also send e-mail to many of our authors and pre-
view new publications and exciting new technologies.

www.wadsworth.com
Changing the way the world learns®

The Practice of Macro Social Work

THIRD EDITION

William G. Brueggemann

Kyushu University of Health and Welfare
Nobeoka, Japan

THOMSON

BROOKS/COLE

Australia • Brazil • Canada • Mexico • Singapore • Spain
United Kingdom • United States

THOMSON

BROOKS/COLE

The Practice of Macro Social Work, Third Edition
William G. Brueggemann

Executive Editor, Social Work: Lisa Gebo
Assistant Editor: Alma Dea Michelena
Editorial Assistant: Sheila Walsh
Executive Marketing Manager: Caroline Concilla
Marketing Assistant: Rebecca Weisman
Senior Marketing Communications Manager: Tami Strang
Project Manager, Editorial Production: Brenda Ginty
Creative Director: Rob Hugel
Art Director: Vernon Boes

Print Buyer: Doreen Suruki
Permissions Editor: Joohee Lee
Production Service: Melanie Field, Strawberry Field Publishing
Compositor: International Typesetting and Composition
Photo Researcher: Sue Howard
Copy Editor: Kay Mikel
Cover Designer: Lisa Henry
Cover Image: Johner/Photonica
Cover and Text Printer: Transcontinental Printing/Louiseville

© 2006 Thomson Brooks/Cole, a part of The Thomson Corporation. Thomson, the Star logo, and Brooks/Cole are trademarks used herein under license.

Printed in Canada
1 2 3 4 5 6 7 09 08 07 06 05

Thomson Higher Education
10 Davis Drive
Belmont, CA 94002-3098
USA

For more information about our products, contact us at:
Thomson Learning Academic Resource Center
1-800-423-0563

For permission to use material from this text or product,
submit a request online at
http://www.thomsonrights.com.

Any additional questions about permissions can be
submitted by e-mail to
thomsonrights@thomson.com

Library of Congress Control Number: 2005927097

ISBN 0-534-57585-4

*In Memory of William John
and Blanch Lena Clarke Brueggemann
and Keiko Kimura Inaba*

BRIEF CONTENTS

CONTENTS

PART II
Social Work Practice With Communities   111

Chapter 8 THE PRACTICE OF COMMUNITY ORGANIZATION 200

Chapter 11 THE PRACTICE OF SOCIAL WORK ADMINISTRATION 311

Chapter 12 THE PRACTICE OF ORGANIZATION DEVELOPMENT 338

PART IV
Social Work Practice at the National and International Levels   369

Chapter 13 THE PRACTICE OF SOCIAL WORK POLICY ADVOCACY   372

Epilogue   Macro Social Work: A Profession of Heroes   495

The only thing necessary for the triumph of evil is for good men to do nothing.

Edmund Burke (1729–1797)

The original mission and purpose of social work was the eradication of social problems, but in the past several decades social work has drifted away from its historical mission, concentrating on clinical practice. The first and second editions of this textbook were written to support the efforts of macro social workers in reversing that drift. Today macro social work is beginning to experience a revival, which is reflected in this third edition.

MISSION AND PURPOSE OF SOCIAL WORK

At the turn of the 20th century, the field of social work was peopled by leaders of enormous vision and energy whose goal was nothing less than eradication of the overwhelming social problems of the day—grinding poverty, political corruption, abusive working conditions, exploited women and immigrants, and dangerous and unhealthy slums. These macro social workers wanted to create a wholesome, safe, and equitable social environment in which the American dream would be a reality not just for the rich, but for everyone. Jane Addams, Florence Kelly, Homer Folks, Graham Taylor, Harriet Tubman, Mary Simkhovitch, W. E. B. Du Bois, the Abbott sisters, Mary Parker Follett, Clara Barton, Lillian Wald, and many other macro social work heroes displayed altruism and compassion, courage and character that we rarely see at the turn of the 21st century. The pioneering efforts of macro social workers such as these laid the groundwork for many of the social advances we continue to benefit from today.

MAGNITUDE OF SOCIAL PROBLEMS

Despite their efforts, social problems continue to plague people in North America and around the world. Crime still haunts our neighborhoods, poverty continues to abound, and even after years of legislation, civil rights abuses still occur. Even though our economic and political systems offer opportunity for many, it is becoming increasingly clear that the choices that matter most to us are not made by ordinary citizens but by a few at the top. Rather than generating social capital such as social involvement, caring, and commitment, many of our economic and government organizations create alienation, dehumanization, and social passivity.

DOMINANCE OF CLINICAL SOCIAL WORK PRACTICE

Not only has the modern project failed to eradicate most of our social problems, but the social work profession itself has retreated from whole-hearted engagement in community organization, community development and planning, and other arenas of macro practice. In its effort to achieve professional status, social work has, by and large, come to be dominated by the education and practice of psychotherapy. Relatively few graduate social work students are engaged in the study of macro social work practice in comparison to those specializing in clinical practice. The profession of social work today is comprised of more clinicians in private practice than all other psychotherapeutic professions combined.

REVIVAL OF MACRO SOCIAL WORK

Recently, macro social work has experienced a revival, especially with regard to community social work. Community development corporations have increased in number and have expanded globally. Community organization has become more consensually oriented and has often combined with community development corporations and community planning in a three-pronged approach. New social organizational forms have arisen, creating a new social sector and comprising an unprecedented third force in government. New social movement organizations have grown in North America and globally, promising a revolution in social thinking.

Most important, in the 21st century it has become increasingly clear that our society is at the beginning of a new postmodern era in which the social will become our most compelling and prominent concern. Even as the ideology of the market economy, individualism, and modern functional reason seems to be triumphant, the seeds of its demise have already been sown. A new era is emerging that is altering the way we think about social problems, re-creating community, providing alternatives to market-centered organizations, and transforming modern politics. These developments are occurring in the least likely of places—in the slums and barrios of the most poverty-stricken areas of the globe. Significant changes are being brought about by the forgotten ones—the members of North America's inner cities and the landless peasants of Guatemala, the homeless beggars of India and the grandmothers of Plaza de Mayo. The poorest people of the earth who bear the brunt of the world's problems are constructing a social revolution, and they are doing it mostly without the help of mainstream North American social work.

It should not be surprising that fundamental social change is arising from those who have been locked out of the benefits of modernity, who experience the violence that sustains it, the poverty that supports it, and the oppression that results from it. Fundamental social change will never come from the powerful who are at the center of the modern project. Rich politicians and influential corporate bosses are helpless to change the basic structures on which their power and wealth depend. Social problems will never be solved by clinical social work practice or the individualism on which it is based.

THIRD EDITION OF THE PRACTICE OF MACRO SOCIAL WORK

It is this awareness that inspires the content of this third edition of *The Practice of Macro Social Work*. This third edition is intended to help you—the macro social workers of the 21st century—bring about the new postmodern era and to assist you in a renewal of the profession of social work that reflects its original mission and heritage. The third edition challenges you to examine your motivations for being a social worker, the premises of the social work profession, and learn about a world of opportunity and social promise far beyond the conventional wisdom of today.

Format

Each chapter begins with quotations that summarize the spirit of the chapter, followed by a story that illustrates the chapter's content. The key ideas of the chapter are then presented in summary form. Each chapter provides a short exploration of the chapter's principle concept, followed by a brief history of the theoretical component, social setting, or practice method described in the chapter. A detailed, practical, step-by-step exploration of how to practice the method, theory, or social setting follows. Where possible I have included a section on the use of the Internet. Each chapter ends with a conclusion, a list of key concepts, questions for discussion, and an additional reading list. The conclusion provides a quick review of the chapter content. If you can identify and define all the key concepts, you can be assured that you will have adequately prepared for most examinations. Your instructor may use the questions for discussion as topics for written or oral reports or as a means to engage you to think more deeply about some of the issues in class. You will find the extensive lists of additional reading at the end of each chapter useful to expand your understanding of particular topics or as a place to begin to research written reports.

Individual and Group Levels

In this third edition, the role of individuals and groups in working with community, organization, society, and international social work has been expanded, placing the practice of macro social work in a generalist framework. For example, Chapter 1 has a more complete definition of macro social work that includes the reciprocal relationship between individuals, groups, and macro systems in the process of social change. In many of the chapters that follow, you will discover how macro social workers make connections between individuals, groups, community, organizations, and society as a whole.

Historical Context

Macro social workers practice in a social environment that is rapidly changing. To maintain touch with our roots while working in our evolving present, we need to have a clear understanding of the way we have come. The history of macro social work practice was included in previous editions, but this discussion is expanded in the third edition. Each chapter has a new or significantly expanded historical background of the theory, social setting, or practice method to help you understand its place in macro social work.

Theory and Practice

Theory and practice components have been thoroughly reviewed and reshaped to make the information as clear, relevant, and up to date as possible. In addition, many new components have been added to deepen and expand the presentations. Among the new material is a new definition and description of the place of macro practice in the field of social work in Chapter 1; new sections on approaches to problem solving in Chapter 2; rational problem solving in Chapter 3; and task group leadership in Chapter 4.

In Part Two, on community social work, Chapter 5 contains revised and expanded information about the history, theory, and kinds of communities with which social workers practice; Chapter 6 stresses the foundational practice principles of community social planning; Chapter 7 includes an expanded description of community development history and practice; and

Chapter 8 describes the new consensual model of community organization.

In Part Three, the practice of social work with organizations, Chapter 9 has a revised description of social and modern organizations; Chapter 10 has an expanded section on training and orienting the board and parliamentary procedure; Chapter 11 features a new section on administrative law and an expanded section on decision-making techniques; and Chapter 12 has a completely reorganized approach to organization development.

In Part Four, macro social work at the societal and international levels, you will find a new critique of conventional policy-making models in Chapter 13, a revised section on how to engage in social action in Chapter 14, and a new section on international social problems and a history and description of international social organizations in Chapter 15. The Epilogue includes additional information and resources about heroes of macro social work.

A Wealth of Information Is Now on the Book's Website

On the book's companion website at http://socialwork .wadsworth.com/Brueggemann. I have included many exercises and checklists that will help you think critically about social issues, improve your skills, and develop your self-understanding. In addition, material previously in the appendixes of the book is now on the website, and you may link directly to the URLs of social organizations that will help you obtain volunteer experiences, internships, or jobs. There is also a list of many social organizations from which you can learn more about the practice of macro social work. Finally, you will also find useful information about the Internet and web addresses for sites of interest to macro social workers at the book's website.

A CHALLENGE

Macro social work presents a compelling opportunity to become involved at the grassroots level where it really matters and to assist people with issues about which they are vitally concerned. It offers an array of possibilities to use your skills, expand your horizons, and deepen your life experiences as your journey leads you onward. There is an arena in macro social work waiting for you to seek new challenges and find new ways to help people and to create a better world.

If you accept the challenge that this book presents, align yourself with the oppressed, identify with the outcast, the poor, the alienated of this world, and disengage yourself from modern thinking, you may be among those social workers who will play a crucial role in helping the poor people of the earth reshape our global society.

ACKNOWLEDGMENTS

I would like to offer my deep thanks to Dr. Miyako Kake, General President of the Takahashi Educational Institution, and to the faculty and administrative staff of Kyushu University of Health and Welfare (KUWH), Nobeoka, Japan, for their support, encouragement, and the opportunity to be part of their learning community. Everyone at KUWH has been extraordinarily generous and understanding, particularly the faculty and staff of the Doctoral Program and Graduate School of Social Welfare, providing the opportunity for me to engage in research at the University of the Philippines and the time to complete this third edition.

Writing, researching, and living in a non-English-speaking country can be an isolating experience. I was extremely fortunate to have the assistance of Miss Mayumi Kamobayashi, whose excellent skills in English helped me in the various aspects of teaching and writing, especially in maintaining communication with the graduate school and my students while I was in the Philippines. In addition, her advice and friendship continually made my life easier and more enjoyable. Vergilio "Vee" David is a good friend whose ideas and friendship were helpful to me.

The staff of Brooks/Cole, particularly Lisa Gebo, managing editor, and Alma Dea Michelena, assistant editor helped me keep this project on track along with Joohee Lee, permissions editor, Melanie Field, production manager, Sue Howard, photo researcher, and especially Kay Mikel copy editor.

The staff and faculty at the College of Social Work and Community Development, University of the Philippines, Diliman generously provided an appointment as a visiting research fellow and use of the college library. I would especially like to acknowledge Chancellor Ermelinda Roman; Romeo C. Quieta, Dean of the College; Lily Mangubat, former Director of Social Work; and Leonida A. de la Cruz, Director of the College Library, for their help and support. A number of faculty and students have taken time to give suggestions or advice to improve the third edition, Michael R. Daley, Stephen F. Austin State University; Kenneth Millar, Aurora University; Irene Quiero-Tajali, Indiana University-Purdue University, Indianapolis; Vanessa Robinson-Dooley, The University of Georgia; and Raymie Wayne, University at Albany (SUNY). I thank them for their efforts, especially Alice Kitchen who reviewed Chapter 13.

As always, Lorraine Inaba Brueggemann and our three children, Jennifer Saeko, William Masato, and Sarah Lena Keiko, provided support and encouragement, especially while I was in Japan and the Philippines, but also kept me connected to my roots and to what matters most.

William G. Brueggemann
Puerto Galera
Oriental Mindoro, Philippines

The Practice of Macro Social Work

THIRD EDITION

1

Overview of the Practice of Macro Social Work

My Brother's Keeper

If anything human is foreign to me, I am myself, by just so much, less human. . . . It is a fact of man's makeup . . . that I am indeed my brother's keeper; the voice of my brother's blood cries out to me from the ground, because, in the most significant sense, his blood is my very own.

As the range of our fellow-feeling contracts, the boundaries of the self close in, and become at last the walls of a prison. As we withdraw from the problems of the aged, the young, the poor, from suffering humanity in any part of the world, it is our own individualities that shrink.

Abraham Kaplan[1]

A Challenge

The dogmas of the quiet past are inadequate to the stormy present. The occasion is piled high with difficulty, and we must rise to the occasion. Just as our case is new, so we must think anew and act anew.

Abraham Lincoln, President of the United States
Annual Message, December 1862

Ideas in This Chapter

One of the most important roles of macro social workers is to help build communities of people.

DEATH COMES TO FRANCISCO

Francisco Martinez is dead. One of millions of faceless and insignificant laborers of our country, his passing will scarcely make a ripple in the course of world affairs. But "when his friends chew over the events of that morning, they taste the bile of being strangers in a strange land, the mules pulling agriculture's plow," writes Alex Pulaski. To his friends, Francisco's death is symbolic of the hypocrisy of American culture. Searching for a better life, Francisco, a young Triqui Indian, came to the United States from the state of Oaxaca, Mexico, but as Filemon Lopez, an advocate for the Mixteco Indians said, "the end of all this, for many, is death." Each year the numbers of Mixteco Indians swell in California when summer farmwork calls. The many who remain in the United States often must live in caves or in the open. Francisco, however, was more fortunate than most. Part of a vine-pruning crew, he was one of 14 men and their wives and children who shared an unheated brick shed owned by rancher Russell Scheidt.

On the morning of January 17, 1993, however, Francisco's fortune changed. Waking for work at about 5:00 a.m., Augustin Ramirez found Francisco on the floor, his breathing labored, appearing near death. Augustin woke two of Francisco's friends, who ran to the ranch house to ask Scheidt to use the phone. Rousted out of bed, Russell Scheidt was exhausted, having just returned at midnight from a Caribbean vacation in Jamaica. Mario Ramirez told him in Spanish that Francisco was dying and they needed to call the police. Scheidt's response, according to Ramirez, was that they had cars, and they could take him to the hospital if they wished. Then he shut the door in their faces. Later Scheidt said "I can't really remember what I told them. . . . I was kind of incoherent, to tell the truth."

Desperate for help, Francisco's friends sped into Kerman, a nearby town. Stopping at a service station, they talked an attendant into calling the Kerman police. They explained their problem to the officer, who asked several questions and then called the Sheriff's department. The friends waited for 22 minutes for the Sheriff's deputies to arrive. Wasting more precious time, the deputies drove to the shed, where they found Francisco at 6:15 a.m. already dead. Finally, they called the ambulance.

Francisco died of acute alcohol poisoning, which caused his brain to shut down his lungs. Tom Stoeckel, manager of the Valley Medical Center's emergency unit in Fresno, said that paramedics often can revive victims of alcohol poisoning by simply giving them oxygen. However, death can result if the supply of oxygen to the brain has stopped for even a few minutes. The official report makes no mention of Scheidt or his refusal to allow the workers to call an ambulance. It stated that Francisco was already dead when the workers found him that morning.

The afternoon Francisco died, Scheidt returned with a translator and told the Mixteco men, women, and children to leave the property. The translator reportedly told them that housing inspectors were coming and the shed was not fit for human habitation. Scheidt said later that the men had finished their work and were basically squatters.

Francisco was buried February 17, 1993, a victim of human indifference, powerlessness, and poverty. His friends, now unemployed and homeless, gave him the best funeral they could buy with the $861 they collected. Four of his friends attended the service. Russell Scheidt did not come.[2]

WHAT YOU WILL LEARN IN THIS CHAPTER

Francisco Martinez died a victim of alcohol poisoning. But his death was ultimately brought on by the social conditions of poverty, racism, indifference, and exploitation against an entire group of people. Even in the United States, many are impoverished economically and socially for the benefit of a few. When social abuse occurs, our entire society is diminished and degraded.

This overview introduces you to the practice of macro social work. You will discover who macro social workers are and explore a short history of macro social work. Then you will look at definition of the practice of macro social work and discover how different aspects of macro social work practice are covered in this book. You will be challenged to consider your own role as a macro social worker. As you read this overview, think about how macro social work and its particular methods could have made a difference to the Triqui Indians and to others like them in our world.

THE PLACE OF MACRO PRACTICE IN THE FIELD OF SOCIAL WORK

Social workers are professionals mandated to protect and enhance people's social welfare. Social workers provide direct and indirect social services. At the BSW level, social workers are general social work practitioners. At the MSW level, social workers specialize in either micro or macro social work.

People's Social Welfare

The word "welfare" means well-being. Social workers are professionals committed to improving the welfare of the poor, the homeless, women, children, the elderly, those who are burdened with disabilities, and those who are ill. We are concerned with the welfare of people in developing nations and of anyone who is disadvantaged or lacks the resources to live a full and productive life. Many social workers apply their concern at the individual or family levels, assisting one person at a time, but other social workers apply their concern to the welfare of people as a whole, especially when the social systems on which they depend create social problems that interfere with people's well-being.

Social Work Services

Social workers assist in improving people's welfare by providing direct and indirect social services.

Direct Social Work Practice   Social workers provide *direct social services* for people who have personal problems, lack resources, or are unable to make use of the resources available to them. The practice of providing direct social work service is also called *micro social work.* The word "micro" comes from the Greek *mikros,* meaning small. Direct or micro social work practitioners offer social case management, social casework, and social work counseling services to individuals, couples, families, and groups.

Indirect Social Work Practice   Social workers provide *indirect social services* for people who experience social problems such as economic or political inequality, exploitation, oppression, discrimination, injustice, and a host of issues that prevent people from using their potential. The practice of indirect social work is also called *macro social work.* The word "macro" comes from the Greek *makros,* meaning large. Macro social workers use nine different methods to improve the welfare of people at the community and organizational levels, within our entire society, and even at the international level, especially assisting people in developing countries.

Undergraduate and Graduate Social Work

Social workers who have BSW degrees practice general social work. Those with graduate degrees practice specialized social work.

BSW Level
Just as many physicians are general practitioners, sometimes called family doctors, social workers who graduate with a BSW degree are also general practitioners. A general practitioner learns and practices skills at all levels and applies them to treating people. A general social work practitioner is an expert in the field of social welfare; he or she needs to understand the entire range of personal and social problems that people encounter in their daily lives. Most general social workers are employed in agencies engaged in direct social work practice with children, the elderly, those who have disabilities, and others. But a general practitioner also needs to understand the range of macro social work practice, services, and methods and how macro social workers help people become strengthened and empowered to improve their social environment.

MSW Level
At the MSW level, social workers have an opportunity to build on their generalist base and engage in more specialized education in either micro or macro social work. Graduate level social workers who specialize in macro social work practice learn how community social workers assist people in community social work planning, community development, and community organization. At the organizational level, macro social workers provide assistance with program development services, social welfare administration, and organization development. At the societal level, macro social workers become involved with social policy advocacy and social activism. Macro social workers may be active in international social work, including refugee and relief social work, international community development, social policy, social action, and human rights social work.

A BRIEF HISTORY OF MACRO SOCIAL WORK

From the beginning of the social work profession, the welfare of the social environment has been our primary concern, and macro social work has been one way social workers have engaged in that effort. Many early social workers concerned themselves with strengthening communities, making government organizations more democratic, working at city, state, and national levels to create better social policies, being active in social movements, and extending themselves to international concerns as well.

Gradually, however, social work became specialized and professionalized, moving away from macro social work practice and concentrating increasingly on individual psychotherapy instead. Recently, however, a shift has begun at both the bachelor's and master's level, and social work has begun slowly to return to its original mission. At the bachelor's level social work reclaimed its heritage of general practice, and at the master's level macro social work practice began to regain the central position in social work that it has always claimed for itself.

Progressive Era (1885–1915)

Early macro social workers saw the entirety of society as their arena of practice, and they advocated for social change wherever and whenever the necessity arose. Progressive social workers engaged individuals and groups, but more important, they conducted research, helped improve communities and organizations, and engaged in social change at the local, state, and national levels. A few even became involved in international issues.

Individuals and Groups
Social workers in the *Charity Organization Society* and *Settlement House movement* engaged individuals in their own neighborhoods. Friendly visitors of the Charity Organization Society, for example, experimented with and invented social casework to assist individuals, many of whom were impoverished immigrants trying to raise families in slums, young men who could not find work, and others who were struggling to adapt to conditions in the new country.

Settlement House social workers invited individuals to join Settlement activities, programs, and services. They understood the value of groups in empowering people. They pioneered the use of social clubs, task groups, and discussion groups to address citizenship issues, promote educational and arts classes to build character, develop leadership, form relationships, and solve common problems.

Research Early social workers realized that they needed to base their efforts at changing the social conditions that created personal problems on a scientific foundation. Charity Organization and Settlement House social workers used social research to examine the extent and effects of social conditions in people's lives. Charity Organization social workers examined the way charity was distributed, the extent of poverty in cities, and the causes and correction of impoverishment.

Settlement House social workers collected, analyzed, and based their solutions on empirical evidence, exemplified in the "3 Rs" of the Settlement House movement: residence, research, and reform. They examined the health conditions of tenements, contaminated food, and crowded slums, among others. They correlated these conditions with tuberculosis and other diseases and used that research to advocate for improvements in health care, housing, and consumer protection.

Community Social Work Charity Organization social workers pioneered community social work, creating the field of community social welfare planning, rationalizing philanthropy, and improving the effectiveness and efficiency of social service delivery. Settlement House social workers initiated community organization social work, bringing neighbors together and using their "evidence-based" research to press local government to improve sanitation, create playgrounds, and correct unhealthy conditions in tenements.

Organizational Social Work Charity and Settlement House social workers were simultaneously active in organizational social work as well. Charity Organization societies pioneered local social service administration, establishing agency networks, organizing new councils of social agencies to coordinate services citywide, and creating community chests, the precursor of the United Way. Settlement House social workers became experts in public administration and government. They knew that public administration must be placed on a neutral foundation that

eliminated favoritism. They advocated for local government reform and designed a new city manager form of government that was adopted by many cities across the nation. Early social workers along with others pressed government to eliminate organizational corruption at the national level, and they succeeded in obtaining passage of the Pendleton Act of 1883, creating the Civil Service Commission, eliminating nepotism in federal administration. Mary Parker Follett, a Settlement House social worker, was then and remains today one of the outstanding pioneers in organizational theory.

Societal Social Work Early social workers actively engaged in politics at the local, state, and national levels, working to ensure that government was more democratic, just, and fair. They advocated for more humane social policies and engaged in social movements.

Democratic Political Process At the local level, social workers helped break the back of political machines in local government that colluded with business to distort the democratic process by means of bribery and favoritism. Progressive social workers pressed for more direct democratic participation in political choice by advocating for laws mandating citizen-sponsored initiatives, the referendum, and the recall of ineffective politicians at the state level. Along with other social activists at the national level, they won the right of people to participate in choosing presidential candidates by means of the direct primary and for direct election of senators.

Social Policy and Social Movements Early social workers continued to advocate for and propose changes in social policy, particularly in the areas of working conditions for women, child labor, juvenile criminal justice, and consumer protection. Social workers engaged in social protest and were active in some of the momentous social movements of the time, including the labor movement, woman's suffrage, temperance, and the peace movement, helping to win amendments to the U.S. Constitution allowing women to vote, and later prohibiting alcohol consumption.

Methodological Separation and Division (1915–1955)

In the 40 years following the Progressive outpouring of broad-based social work, the profession of social work struggled to define and refine its practice methods and grappled with identifying itself as a profession. Gradually social work became divided into three separate but related areas: casework, group work, and community organization.

Social Casework   Many social workers emulated the medical model and identified with the theories of psychoanalysis propounded by Sigmund Freud, and with psychologists who captured the imagination of healing individuals with emotional disabilities. Psychotherapy gained immense popularity, and social workers devised the method of social casework as their own version of individual helping. Social caseworkers, supported by the burgeoning interest and research in individual therapy, formed specialties in medical social work, school social work, and psychiatric social work. They worked in the criminal justice field in probation and parole, in family and child welfare, and also in the arena of public financial assistance.

Social Group Work   Social workers who identified themselves with social group work continued to be concerned with prevention rather than remediation, and they helped strengthen character education, socialization, and leadership development among children, adolescents, and adults in Settlement Houses, neighborhood houses, community centers, and social group work agencies such as the YMCA, YWCA, and the Boy Scouts. Settlement Houses also continued their emphasis on broad-based practice despite the declining support by the profession of social work as a whole.

Community Organization   The practice of macro social work was termed "community organization," which, in general, was the practice of working at the neighborhood and societal levels to bring about social reform. Settlement social workers were the main providers of community organization services, and, according to Robert Fisher, until the 1930s Settlement House community organizing was the most effective means by which people connected with each other to deal with the issues that affected their neighborhoods.

Community Organizing and the Great Depression (1929–1939)   During the Depression years from 1929 to 1940, the crisis in the national economy spurred many social workers to increased activity, especially at the national level. Social work associations pressured government to reverse its laissez-faire (hands off) policies and to provide programs to assist the many destitute families with jobs, relief, and protection from fluctuations in the economy. Many macro social workers were recruited by the Roosevelt administration to formulate plans and carry out those policies. As a result of these efforts, the Social Security Act of 1935 was passed, along with many other programs intended to provide for the social welfare of the nation. Some social workers began to become involved in consciously expanding their skills beyond community organizing to include planning, program development, administration, and policy advocacy.

Faced with the extent of desperation the nation experienced, the Settlement House neighborhood organizing approach began to lose its effectiveness. Saul Alinsky, a research sociologist working in the Back of the Yards neighborhood in Chicago, devised a new and more assertive style of community organization that was to revolutionize how people achieved power.

Community Organizing in the Conservative 1940s and 1950s   Some social workers engaged in planning, administration, and social policy, but an integrated arena of macro social work practice had not been clearly identified, and the field of indirect social work practice continued to be viewed primarily as community organization despite the limited uses to which that approach was often put. The Alinsky style of organizing expanded in community after community, but because of its radical nature, many social work professionals who identified with a less confrontive style of neighborhood social work tended to avoid it. Numerous new social service programs were developed after World War II to care for increasing areas of need, including financial assistance, housing, people with physical disabilities, and those with emotional or developmental disabilities. Some social workers began to understand the need for administrative planning in these arenas as these programs were increasingly being recognized as an important arena of practice.

Professionalization and Specialization (1955–1970)

In 1955 the National Association of Social Work (NASW) was formed, officially recognizing casework and group work as two of its methods, and in 1962 NASW officially included community organization as its third specialty. Soon schools of social work began offering coursework in each of these three methods. Social work specialization continued in the decade of the '60s as more and more caseworkers identified with the practice of clinical psychotherapy and pressed for legislation to allow them to become licensed clinicians on a par with psychiatry and psychology.

Even though community organization had been adopted by social workers in the midst of an era of major social reform in the 1960s, its methods and style were not congruent with the radical nature of the era. Community organization social workers had arrived too late to have a great deal of impact on social changes that were occurring. Social group work was transformed into clinical group therapy or absorbed into community organization as task group work, and as a specialty, it gradually disappeared.

Generalist and Specialist Social Work (1970–1990s)

Clinical social work continued to grow rapidly in the '70s and '80s as local NASW chapters pressed for legislation allowing master's level clinical social workers to establish private clinical practice and to receive third party payments from insurance companies and government providers. So successful were these efforts that in state after state MSW clinical social workers became licensed practitioners, and within a few years social work dominated the field of psychotherapy, a position it continues to hold today.

Other social workers, concerned about social problems, gained skills and increasing competency in macro social work through specialization at the master's level. Macro social work moved beyond its previous identification as community organization and, as described by Jack Rothman and John Tropman,[3] was popularly defined as including locality (community) development, social planning, and community organizing. Macro social work practice was beginning to develop into a comprehensive field of practice.

At the same time, however, a reaction to increased specialization was occurring. A number of social work educators and practitioners were concerned about the bifurcation of social work into individual psychotherapy and social reform.[4] Gradually, the practice of social work, particularly at the BSW level, was reconceptualized as general social work practice. Even though most general social work practitioners concentrated at the micro level, an expectation was established that all social workers at the bachelor's

level should be knowledgeable about the role played by macro social workers and should apply macro social work methods where possible in the larger scope of social work practice.

Expansion and Integration (1990s to the Present)

In the 1990s the field of macro social work continued to grow. While Tropman et al. explored three methods of macro social work, the original edition of this text was the first to identify macro social work as including eight methods in three distinct levels of practice: community social work, organization social work, and societal social work. In the second edition, international social work was added as a fourth practice level for a total of nine methods, and the text explored how practitioners were adding new styles and approaches to many of these arenas.

This third edition demonstrates that macro social work continues to expand and is becoming more integrated. Building on social work's generalist base, this text explores macro social work's increasingly comprehensive approach, which integrates social work planning, community development, community organization, and program development in a continuum of practice, or by piecing together various components of practice as the situation demands. The text shows how the fields of social work administration and organization development are also becoming stronger and more integrated. Although international social work lags, North American social workers inevitably will be drawn into the global arena of practice as awareness of the interrelated nature of social problems expands.

WHAT IS THE PRACTICE OF MACRO SOCIAL WORK?

Macro social work is the practice of helping individuals and groups solve social problems and make social change at the community, organizational, societal, and global levels. Let's look at this definition in more detail.

Help Individuals and Groups

The way large systems in society affect individuals and groups is a concern of all macro social workers. Where those systems disempower people, create injustice, or threaten to overwhelm the individual, macro social workers help individuals and groups understand their collective strengths and resources. These resources can aid efforts to establish countervailing community networks, social organizations, social policies, and social movements. However, when macro social workers assist individuals and groups in changing social structures, they do more than improve their social environment. When people shape society, they change themselves. When individuals change themselves, they become more capable of shaping society. Macro social work is interactive and reciprocal. Macro social workers help individuals and groups change themselves and society by empowering, connecting, training, engaging in practice, and helping people integrate their skills.

Change Themselves

When people become agents in constructing civil society, they change themselves, develop meaning, and create individual character. According to John Ehrenreich,

> Numerous observers . . . have noted the association between involvement in social action and improved "mental health." For example, it was reported that crime among black youths in Montgomery, Alabama declined sharply during the year of the bus boycott. . . . Students involved in the sit-in movement used that experience of "prosocial acting out" to serve in constructive developmental tasks.
>
> Later in the decade, some outstanding successes in the treatment of drug addiction were achieved by the Black Muslims and by militant community groups such as the Black Panther party and the (Puerto Rican) Young Lords organization, who found that participation in militant movements for social change provided the motivation and context for startling personality change. Participation in the women's liberation movement at the very end of the decade was to prove a powerful vehicle for personal change as well as for helping achieve social reform. Maximum feasible participation was central to bridging the traditional gap between "macro" and "micro" approaches for dealing with social problems.[5]

Community organizer Dara Silverman asserts, "Ultimately, organizing is the development of people. If you see that, support it. Organizing elevates people. . . . I believe in myself and I can make a difference."[6]

Shape Society

When people make changes in their personal lives and relationships, they concurrently create a ripple effect across society, simultaneously generating social goods and producing social capital. When people become empowered, they discover they can overcome the emotional inertia characteristic of imposed dependency, reclaiming their anger and the hope that change is possible. When macro social workers challenge community members to think critically about social issues, they find their collective voice and begin to speak out against the forces that have deceived them. When they join with others, they find the strength to shrug off the passivity on which oppressors depend and take united action on their own behalf to create a better world.

Interactive and Reciprocal

Macro social workers understand that helping individuals change and use those changes to shape society does not come automatically, nor does the process flow easily or naturally. People who have been affected by social problems bear the wounds in their emotions, thinking, and behavior. Many have few resources and are burdened with more than the average number of responsibilities. As a result, to be effective in bringing about change, macro social workers help individuals and groups become empowered. We help connect people with one another, provide them with training, engage them in practice, and help them integrate new ways of being.

Empower   One of the first and most important roles of macro social workers is to assist people who have been denied opportunity, excluded from using their capabilities, never been challenged to utilize their resources, or been intimidated by massive corporate and government structures. Before people can begin to undertake the massive challenges of changing their social environment, which has often placed them in an inferior and dependent position, they must be awakened and provided with the tools to help them take on wealthy, resource rich, sophisticated, and powerful systems. Macro social workers empower individuals and groups to control their life chances and create a social environment that reflects their values, establishing a just, equitable, and sustainable society for themselves and others.

Connect   Macro social workers help people who have been isolated and separated to connect in groups and work together to resolve the issues that confront them.

Macro social workers have helped establish a number of social groups, associations, and organizations that challenge and defeat the dehumanization, demoralization, and disenfranchisement that many private and public organization and control systems foster.

If macro social workers do nothing else, we help connect people to community planning councils, community development corporations, community and neighborhood organizations, and coalitions. We engage community members, social workers, and community boards in developing multitudes of social organizations in every community in the United States and Canada to work for the social good and to develop resources that enhance the human condition.

We help citizens engage in local and societal policy advocacy groups to change the rules and premises of social decisions for the better. Macro social workers participate and encourage others to become involved in the major social movements of the day: to work for a clean environment, social justice, against war and gun violence, to overcome poverty, for better health care, and so on. We support and advocate for international social movements and causes that advocate political self-determination, authentic economic freedom, and an end to corporate oppression and domination of citizens in underdeveloped nations.

Train   We help members develop community, organizational, political skills and learn how to engage in international social change. For example, we teach members to use rational problem solving and social thinking to develop solutions to issues that plague them. We help all members develop leadership skills and work closely with particular members to learn how to lead task groups and become active in organizing coalitions and exerting leadership in organizations.

We assist citizens in forming groups and community associations that can work to their benefit, including community planning councils, community development corporations, program development groups, and social agencies. We help members learn how to begin a social organization, help with the incorporation process, train the board, and develop skills for recruiting employees, funding the organization, and maintaining the organization.

We help community members in the change effort find answers to questions for themselves through research and analyzing data. We teach people how to perform needs assessments, resource and assets assessments, and policy analysis.

We help community members understand the change process and train them in the use of strategies, tactics, and techniques of social action that involve direct confrontation. In addition, we engage people in underdeveloped nations and teach them how to use their own strengths to gain empowerment and social justice and to bring about a better world for themselves.

Practice   The more often people engage in social change, the stronger and more capable they become. Macro social workers rarely, if ever, carry out activities for people that they can do for themselves. Our role is to motivate, train, reflect, support, encourage, and help members move to action. We help members sharpen their skills and strengthen their capacities, and we critique their performance to help them learn from their mistakes, strategize, and try again.

Integrate   As we work closely with individual members and their groups, we observe how they have learned, changed, and developed. We help them see how their efforts have improved the social environment and how the ongoing processes they have initiated create indigenous leaders who continue to recruit members, inspire action, train others, engage in practice, and reintegrate the skills they have learned. We help members become consciously aware of how the processes they construct not only change society but themselves in an ongoing upward spiral of development.

Solve Social Problems and Make Social Change

Solving social problems and making social change by means of macro social work practice is the heritage, the present responsibility, and the future promise of the social work profession. It is social work's commitment to social betterment at all levels that ensures its continued impact in our world today.

People who initiate social change are change agents. Change agents come from a variety of disciplines and work at resolving different kinds of social issues. Change agents may come from many walks of life and any number of professions, but macro social work claims change agent practice as its own. Macro social workers need to understand how social systems work to design systems that are better, fix them when they become dysfunctional, challenge those models that are failing, and infuse with integrity and goodness those that are unethical. Macro social workers see the spectrum of communities, organizations, society, and global cultures as arenas of our concern and involvement. In Part One of this book you will learn the basic principles of how macro social workers solve social problems and initiate social change. You will learn about social problems, problem solving, and leadership.

Social Problems
In Chapter 2 you will have an opportunity to consider your own definition of social problems and compare it with conventional definitions as well as one that the author provides. You will explore the history of a social problem and consider nine modern assumptions theorists offer to explain why social problems exist. You will be invited to critique these theories and develop your own working definition of social problems.

In addition, you will discover four general approaches people take in relation to social problems. You will learn that the interactivist approach, which is based on an ecological perspective, symbolic interactionist premises, social thinking, and strengths and assets and social enhancement, is most often utilized by macro social workers.

Rational Problem Solving and Social Thinking
In Chapter 3 you will learn that the most common method by which social workers have approached both personal and social problems is rational problem solving (RPS), whose origins can be traced to the Enlightenment movement in the early 17th century. Most social work continues to be based on the RPS model, but social workers are beginning to recognize and use another way of thinking, called social reason, in which people use the strengths and empowerment perspective to take advantage of social opportunities to initiate social change.

Social thinking is a means by which communities of people, members of social organizations, those engaged in societal movements, and people in underdeveloped nations envision a new future, access hope, and discover new ways to construct themselves and create the kind of social environment that embodies their shared values and hopes. You will learn how to use social thinking as people engage one another on the common journey of fulfilling meaning and completing the purpose of their lives together.

Develop Leaders
The heart of helping individuals and groups utilize social opportunities is leadership. In Chapter 4 you will explore both task group and

social leadership. You will look at the history of how both kinds of leadership have emerged in social work. You will learn how to lead a task group and how to help others become social leaders who take charge of the social, economic, and political conditions that affect their lives and contribute to the process of social betterment.

The Spectrum of Macro Social Work
This text covers the entire range of the practice of macro social work: social work with communities, organizations, society, and in the international arena.

Community Social Work
Macro social workers help communities strengthen relationships between people and mediate between individuals and the organizational megastructures of society.[7] Part Two of this book is devoted to the practice of community social work.

Communities   In Chapter 5 you will examine a definition of community and explore the role of community in people's lives and in society. You will learn a brief history of community in America and review several communities in which macro social workers have become engaged. You will be introduced to community social planning, community development, and community organization.

Community Social Planning   Community social workers assist local community groups in developing plans for their own communities and acting on those plans. In Chapter 6 you will explore what community planning is, review a short history of social welfare and community planning, explore a number of planning tools and techniques that you can apply to community projects, and explain how to carry out a community planning project.

Community Development   Macro social workers who help make communities better places for individuals and families engage in *community development*. Community developers work in inner cities, barrios, migrant work camps, on reservations, and in housing projects, bringing people together to build strong human relationships and organize community development corporations (CDCs). CDCs develop new housing, open banks, form co-ops, and sponsor many community projects, bringing new possibilities and opportunity to people. In Chapter 7 you will explore a history of community development, and you will learn how to establish a community development corporation. You will also explore how community development and community organizations work together in a triple-pronged approach to community empowerment.

Community Organizing   Some community social workers help overcome the estrangement imposed by large megastructures of corporate and public life. These macro social workers are called *community organizers.* Community organization is a process by which neighborhoods and coalitions of neighborhoods work over the long term for community betterment and political empowerment. Chapter 8 explains how community organizers have assisted people in overcoming economic and political inequality throughout American history. You will learn how to do community organizing and how to use four kinds of community organization practice models to strengthen neighborhoods.

Organizational Social Work
Robert Presthus and others have observed that we live in an organizational society.[8] In Part Three of this book, you will learn how macro social work enhances the social welfare of people in organizations through program development, social administration, and organization development.

Organizations   In Chapter 9 you will explore the dynamics of organizational systems. You will learn that macro social workers and others have been developing a new form of social organization by which social problems can be resolved. You will explore a history of these new social organizations and how they are structured. You will learn about their purpose, diversity, scope and size, clients, and staff. Macro social workers and others have been forging these new social organizations into a third, relatively new social sector without which government and the economy could not exist.

You will also learn about a second and even more prominent organizational form: modern complex organizations. You will learn a definition of modern organizations, explore their size, power, and the principles by which they function, and review a brief history of modern complex organizations. You will learn how macro social workers use an organization deviance model to help solve some of the social problems that complex organizations create in our modern society.

Program Development   Chapter 10 describes *program development social work.* As social entrepreneurs, these social workers help people in communities construct social organizations. You will learn what program development is and review a short history of some of the social organizations macro social workers have assisted in developing. You will discover that, as a macro social worker, you can help members of a community develop one of these new social organizations. You will discover, for example, how to form a community group, help the group become incorporated, form a board, develop funding, and hire staff and recruit clients.

Social Work Administration   Social organizations require skilled social work administrators to implement change over the long term. *Social work administration* is a complex arena of macro social work practice, which includes supervision, decision making, budgeting, personnel, and planning. Chapter 11 describes the differences between management and administration and how macro social workers are redefining administration and returning it to its original meaning of service. You will explore a brief history of administrative laws and discover how social work supervisors help their units and workers increase their effectiveness. You will learn how administrators arrive at decisions and how to use a variety of decision-making tools. You will read about administering an agency's budgeting and finances. One important area of administration is assisting employees and personnel administrators engage in employee recruitment and selection, ensuring diversity, and assisting workers who have difficulties. You will learn about the important process of collective bargaining. You will explore the role of the chief social work administrator and how the administrator goes about planning, relating to the board of directors, and evaluating the social agency.

Organization Development   Sometimes business and government organizations fail to adapt to their rapidly changing social environment and become dysfunctional. When this occurs, corporate and government administrators may call upon macro social work consultants, called *organization developers,* to help bring their systems back to effective functioning. In Chapter 12 you will learn several roles organization developers play and explore a short history of organization development. You will learn step by step how management consultants use conventional organization development techniques to bring about organizational change. For example, you will learn several approaches to organization development, a number ways to diagnose an organization, and a variety of treatment techniques to use at the individual, group, and intergroup levels and with the organization as a whole.

You will also discover a second social approach to organization development that social workers can use to assist the social organizations in which they are employed to become more effective and congruent with the principles and values of the social work profession. You will learn each of the steps in carrying out social organization development.

Societal Social Work   Social workers are concerned with the welfare of our national society, particularly how the economic, political, and social sectors interrelate. In Part Four, you will see how macro social workers get involved in politics, policy advocacy, become active in social movements at the societal level, and engage in international social work at the global level.

Social Policy and Politics   Macro social workers are concerned when the political process becomes distorted or social policies favor one group over another. We work to ensure that government operates fairly and justly on behalf of all citizens. We recommend social policies and advocate for those whose voices are often ignored.

In Chapter 13 you learn what social policy and politics is and discover that some macro social workers become elected officials. Some prominent social work elected officials are highlighted in this chapter. You will learn a number of theories that political scientists believe describe how people arrive at social policies and explore a brief history of social policy in America. You will discover how macro social workers lobby, give testimony before state legislative bodies and Congress, and work as watchdogs over regulatory commissions to ensure that laws, once enacted, are carried out.

You will learn all of the necessary steps to help community members devise their own social policy to build their own communities and engage the political process at the local level, where it really belongs. You will discover how to assist your members as they gather facts, decide among various policy alternatives, and choose the best policy, and you will learn

how to help your community group implement that policy.

Social Action and Social Movements   As important as they are, political processes are sometimes ineffective in bringing about social change. When social problems remain unattended for long periods of time, people organize themselves into mass *social movements* to shift the direction of social policy and practice. Macro social workers who either lead or become involved in these societal movements are called *social activists*. Chapter 14 explores the history of some prominent social movements including the Progressive movement, the abolition and labor movements, and the social movements of the 1960s. You will learn about modern social movements as well as new, postmodern social movements, and you will examine how macro social work activists organize a modern social movement. You will discover how to use a number of strategies, tactics, and techniques to influence the political process and bring about changes in social policy.

International Social Work   Macro social workers not only want to make their own societies better but reach out to poverty-stricken, war-torn areas of undeveloped and developing countries in Central and South America, Africa, and Southeast Asia. In Chapter 15, you will discover how *international macro social workers* engage social problems including poverty, slavery, displaced persons, and the violence that exists on a scale unknown in the West. You will explore theories of modernization and development, the history of international social work, and learn how international macro social workers help people develop stronger communities, engage in economic development projects, and provide relief and assistance to refugees who are homeless due to natural disasters, war, and famine.

You will learn how indigenous peoples are transforming their own social world by means of new international social movements. New social organizations, including grassroots organizations (GROs), nongovernmental organizations (NGOs), and nongovernmental support organizations (NGSOs), are bringing about a better, more humane global society. You will learn the fundamentals of how to practice international social work and find out how you too can be part of this exciting world of global social change.

Epilogue   Many macro social workers have been heroes of social change who not only practiced change but also wrote about it. The epilogue of this book provides you with a list of resources written by and about many of these macro social work heroes.

RESOURCES

You will find three appendixes on the book's website that will help you expand your understanding of macro social work opportunities.

Become a Volunteer   One way that you can get involved in social change is to volunteer in a social organization. Domestic as well as international volunteer organizations are listed on the book's website. Contact them for more information on how you can get valuable experience in macro social work.

Join a Social Organization   Another way to gain more understanding is to join a social organization or find out more about what they do. The book's website lists many social organizations in each of the arenas of social work described in this book. Write to them for more information, visit, or invite a macro social worker to your class. As you review the wide variety of social organizations that macro social workers have developed, administer, and serve, you might discover an area to explore for your internship.

Macro Social Work and the Internet   Worldwide information is available on the Internet. The book's website explains how to use your computer to access information about macro social work through user and newsgroups as well as locating resources about macro social work issues and links to agencies of the federal government. This information can be useful in researching a paper or making a report to your class.

A CHALLENGE TO YOU

Modernity has directed the bulk of human intellectual and creative effort at overcoming physical and biological problems that plague humanity. Nearly every day another medical or physical science breakthrough is announced that astounds our imagination. These developments hold the key to extending life and making existence more prosperous, comfortable, and enjoyable.

Yet the genuine wonder of these accomplishments pale in comparison to the social problems that stretch before us. Science and technology promise a world increasingly free of disease and disability, but the social science professions have abysmally failed to develop a world free of poverty, conflict, violence, hunger, homelessness, crime, oppression, injustice, and ethnic intolerance. Instead of reinvigorating efforts to find new approaches and new solutions to these social problems, many social workers today have retreated entirely from the social arena. They are content to deal with people's personal problems, avoiding the vast social issues under which our global civilization groans.

Mainstream social workers sometimes fail to understand that the genuine technological accomplishments of the modern age do not constitute the real revolution that is occurring around them. They do not recognize that we are living in one of the pivotal moments in history, the hallmark of which is a revitalization of the social sphere. Social theorists are even now recognizing that the struggle for authentic social equality, which has eluded mankind for millennia, and the power to construct social reality is beginning to occur as a major turning point in the history of the human condition.

Even our most perceptive theorists often do not recognize that many of the most important of these developments are occurring in the most unsuspecting places and by the least likely people. It is gradually becoming evident that the new, postmodern society is emerging from the slums, jungles, migrant labor camps, refugee centers, barrios, rancherias, and shanty towns in the underdeveloped nations of the world. Those who are bringing it about are the landless peasants, the homeless refugees, and the exiles who are shut out, left out, and kept out of the luxuries of modern, developed nations. The simple quest by the least influential of the world for their own humanity is quietly and often unintentionally undermining the foundations of modern instrumental reason, individualism, modern complex organization, the managerial hierarchy of modern corporations, and the paternalistic government bureaucracy.

The practice of macro social work is committed to a society free of social problems. Social work is a profession that calls you to creatively use your social intelligence, your social ideals, and your social leadership in constructing a truly humane society. The practice of macro social work is and ought to be a profession that calls forth actions of the greatest humanity of which we are capable. It is also a calling in which you construct yourself and simultaneously help build your community just as you assist others in constructing themselves and developing a better world. Social workers who engage in the practice of generalist-based macro social work will have a lasting impact on our social environment, helping to make fundamental changes in the way we live and guiding the future direction of our society.

CONCLUSION

Macro social workers want to make a difference in people's lives where injustice, oppression, and intolerance exist. We try to see beyond the distortions that those in power sometimes use to justify their positions. We challenge illusions that lead nowhere and contest false answers that only prolong the status quo. Macro social workers take a fresh look at social conditions and try new ways to resolve old problems. We try to correct social conditions that create human suffering and misery. Macro social workers struggle to get at the root of social problems by calling attention to inequity and exposing conditions that cause personal troubles for people. We engage individuals and groups to become active and creative agents in challenging the difficulties that megastructures of society create in their lives.

This textbook explores assumptions underlying social problems along with how macro social workers use those assumptions as a basis of their practice. In this book you will learn theories of problem solving, leadership, community, organization, social policy, societal movements, and modernization, among others. You will discover the heritage of macro social work practice at each of four levels and the nine arenas in which social workers at the macro level work to bring about a healthier social environment. Most important, you will discover how to use the knowledge macro social workers have developed in more than a century of creative, innovative engagement with social change.

There is no one best way to practice macro social work. You will find that there is no best method, way of solving problems, way of thinking, or ultimate answer to the process of constructing a good community, organization, or society. The practice of macro social work requires skill, understanding, and competence, but it also demands ingenuity and creativity that come from your own insight and personal development. Above all, you may learn that in the process of helping people grow and develop you will grow to become the person you were meant to be.

KEY CONCEPTS

macro social work
social welfare
social work services
direct social work practice
micro social work
indirect social work practice
macro social work
BSW level social work
generalist social work
MSW level social work
specialized social work
Charity Organization Society
Settlement House movement
research
social casework
social group work
help individuals and groups
solve social problems
make social change
rational problem solving (RPS)

social thinking
develop leaders
community social work
community
community social planning
community development
community organization
organizational social work
modern organization
social organization
program development
social administration
organization development
societal social work
social policy and politics
social action
social movements
social activists
international social work

QUESTIONS FOR DISCUSSION

1. What are the characteristics of a good person, a good neighborhood, a good organization, or a good society?
2. Do you think the social sphere has become eroded in today's society? Why or why not?
3. What are some indicators that our society has a strong sense of social responsibility? What are

indicators that our society has a weak sense of the social sphere?

4. What is the responsibility of social work for the social good? How do social workers produce the social good?

5. Consider the following statement: The trend in the social work profession in the past 30 years has been to concentrate on clinical helping—individual counseling, family therapy, and group work—rather than macro level helping. In this way social workers often serve people who have already been damaged by the effects of social problems rather than work toward the eradication of the causes and conditions of social decay itself. In this sense, social work is reactive rather than proactive.

Do you believe this assessment is correct? Why or why not? If you believe it is true, comment on the implications of this trend for the practice of social work today.

6. Macro level social workers must often take a moral or ethical stance against people or social systems that perpetuate injustice. In what ways is the stance of a macro social worker similar or different from the ethical stance that micro social workers take in working with individual clients?

ADDITIONAL READING

Social Compassion

Bach, George and Laura Torbet. *A Time for Caring.* New York: Delacourte, 1982.

Clark, Margaret S., ed. *Prosocial Behavior.* London: Sage, 1991.

Coles, Robert. *The Call of Service: A Witness to Idealism.* New York: Houghton Mifflin, 1993.

Luks, Allen and Peggy Payne. *The Healing Power of Doing Good.* New York: Fawcett, 1992.

Margolis, Howard. *Selfishness, Altruism & Rationality: A Theory of Social Change.* Chicago: University of Chicago Press, 1982.

Monroe, Kristen Renwick. *Heart of Altruism: Perceptions of a Common Humanity.* Princeton, NJ: Princeton University Press, 1996.

Wuthnow, Robert. *Acts of Compassion: Caring for Others and Helping Ourselves.* Princeton, NJ: Princeton University Press, 1991.

Oliner, Samuel P. and Pearl M. Oliner. *The Altruistic Personality: Rescuers of the Jews in Nazi Europe.* New York: Free Press, 1988.

Social Problems

Pharr, Suzanne. *Homophobia: A Weapon of Sexism.* Inverness, CA: Chardon Press, 1988.

McWilliams, Cary. *Brothers Under the Skin.* Boston: Little, Brown, 1951.

McWilliams, Cary. *Factories in the Field: The Story of Migratory Farm Labor in California.* Santa Barbara: Penguin, 1971.

Freedman, Jonathan. *From Cradle to Grave: The Human Face of Poverty.* New York: Atheneum, 1993.

Reiman, Jeffrey. *The Rich Get Richer and the Poor Get Prison: Ideology, Crime and Criminal Justice*, 4th ed. Boston: Allyn and Bacon, 1990.

Kozo, Jonathan. *Rachel and Her Children: Homeless Families in America.* New York: Fawcett Columbine, 1988.

Greider, William. *Who Will Tell the People? The Betrayal of the American Democracy.* New York: Simon and Schuster, 1992.

Social Thinking

Minnech, E. K. *Transforming Knowledge.* Philadelphia: Temple University Press, 1990.

Schon, Donald. *The Reflective Practitioner: How Professionals Think in Action.* New York: Basic Books, 1985.

Marcuse, Herbert. *One-Dimensional Man: Studies in the Ideology of Advanced Industrial Society.* Boston: Beacon Press, 1964.

Social Leadership

Block, Peter. *Stewardship: Choosing Service Over Self-Interest.* San Francisco: Berrett-Koehler, 1993.

Oakley, Edward and Douglas Krug. *Enlightened Leadership: Getting to the Heart of Change.* New York: Simon and Schuster, 1993.

Community

Boyte, Harry C. *Community Is Possible: Repairing America's Roots.* New York: Harper and Row, 1984.

Hallman, Howard W. *Neighborhoods: Their Place in Urban Life,* Vol. 154. Beverly Hills: Sage Library of Social Research, 1984.

Community Social Planning

Wildavsky, Aaron. *Speaking Truth to Power.* Boston: Little, Brown, 1979.

Forester, John. *Planning in the Face of Power.* Berkeley: University of California Press, 1989.

Community Development

Perry, Stewart E. *Communities on the Way.* New York: State University of New York Press, 1987.

Perkins, John M. *Let Justice Roll Down.* Glendale, CA: G/L Books, 1976.

Community Organizing

Alinsky, Saul. *Reveille for Radicals.* New York: Vintage, 1969.

Alinsky, Saul. *Rules for Radicals.* New York: Random House, 1971.

Kahn, Si. *How People Get Power: Organizing Oppressed People for Action.* New York: McGraw Hill, 1978.

Burghardt, Steve. *Organizing for Community Action.* Beverly Hills: Sage, 1982.

Organization

Weber, Max. "Bureaucracy." In *From Max Weber: Essays in Sociology,* H. H. Gerth and C. Wright Mills, eds. New York: Oxford University Press, 1958.

Ramos, Alberto. *Reconceptualization of the Wealth of Nations.* Toronto: University of Toronto Press, 1981.

Hummel, Ralph. *The Bureaucratic Experience.* New York: St. Martin's Press, 1977.

Program Development

Heskett, James L., W. Earl Sasser Jr., and Christopher W. L. Hart. *Service Breakthroughs: Changing the Rules of the Game.* New York: Freedom Press, 1990.

Crane, Jonathan D., ed. *Social Programs That Work.* New York: Russell Sage Foundation, 1998.

Social Administration

Bellone, Carl J. *Organization Theory and the New Public Administration.* Boston: Allyn and Bacon, 1980.

Follett, Mary Parker. In *Dynamic Administration: The Collected Papers of Mary Parker Follett,* Elliot M. Fox and L. Urwick, eds. New York: Hippocrene Books, 1977.

Harmon, Michael M. *Action Theory for Public Administration.* New York: Longman, 1981.

Organization Development

Schaef, Anne Wilson and Diane Fassel. *The Addictive Organization: Why We Overwork, Cover Up, Pick Up the Pieces, Please the Boss, and Perpetuate Sick Organizations.* San Francisco: Harper and Row, 1990.

Social Policy and Politics

Carson, Rachel. *The Silent Spring.* Boston: Houghton Mifflin, 1962.

Cloward, Richard and Frances Fox Piven. *The Politics of Turmoil.* New York: Vintage, 1975.

Harrington, Michael. *The Other America: Poverty in the United States.* Baltimore: Penguin Books, 1962.

Harris, Richard. *A Sacred Trust: The Story of Organized Medicine's Multi-Million Dollar Fight Against Public Health Legislation,* Rev. ed. Baltimore: Penguin Books, 1969.

Withorn, Ann. *Serving the People: Social Services and Social Change.* New York: Columbia University Press, 1984.

Social Action and Social Movements

King Jr., Martin Luther. *Stride Toward Freedom: The Montgomery Story.* New York: Ballantine, 1958.

Harding, Vincent. *There Is a River: The Black Struggle for Freedom in America.* New York: Harcourt Brace Jovanovich, 1981.

Piven, Frances Fox and Richard Cloward. *Poor People's Movements: Why They Succeed, How They Fail.* New York: Random House, 1987.

Jones, Mary Harris. *The Autobiography of Mother Jones.* Chicago: Charles H. Kerr, 1990.

International Social Work

La Pierre, Dominique. *The City of Joy.* Garden City, NY: Doubleday, 1995.

Social History

Commager, Henry Steele. *The American Mind: An Interpretation of American Thought and Character Since the 1880s.* New York: Bantam, 1950.

Hofstadter, Richard. *The Age of Reform: From Bryan to F.D.R.* New York: Vintage, 1955.

Hofstadter, Richard. *The American Political Tradition and the Men Who Made It.* New York: Vintage, 1954.

Zinn, Howard. *A People's History of the United States.* New York: Harper and Row, 1980.

Flacks, Richard. *Making History: The American Left and the American Mind.* New York: Columbia University Press, 1990.

Evans, S. M. *Born for Liberty: A History of Women in America.* New York: Free Press, 1989.

Lerner, G. *The Majority Finds Its Past: Placing Women in History.* New York: Oxford University Press, 1979.

Social Critique

Bartlett, Donald and James Steele. *America: What Went Wrong.* Kansas City, MO: Andrews and McMeel, 1992.

Memmi, Albert. *The Colonizer and the Colonized.* Boston: Beacon Press, 1967.

Freire, Paulo. *Pedagogy of the Oppressed.* New York: Herder and Herder, 1970.

Malcolm X. *The Autobiography of Malcolm X.* New York: Ballantine, 1987.

Schaper, Donna. *A Book of Common Power: Narratives Against the Current.* San Diego, CA: Lura Media, 1989.

PART One

Solving Social Problems and Making Social Change

Social Meaning

People's action towards external objects, as well as relationships between people and social institutions can be understood only in terms of what humans think about them. Society as we know it, is built up from concepts and ideas held by the people; and social phenomena can be recognized and have meaning for us only as they are reflected in the minds of human beings.[1]

Friedreich A. Hayek

Who Can End Oppression?

Dehumanization, although a concrete historical fact, is *not* a given destiny but the result of an unjust order that engenders violence in the oppressor, which in turn dehumanizes the oppressed.

It is only the oppressed, who, by freeing themselves, can free their oppressors. Oppressors can free neither others nor themselves. It is essential, therefore, that the oppressed wage the struggle to resolve the contradiction in which they are caught.[2]

Paulo Freire

FOUNDATIONAL IDEAS OF MACRO SOCIAL WORK

Part One introduces you to some of the ideas that shape a macro social work perspective. Among the foundations of macro social work practice is the person as an active, social creature who joins with others to solve social problems, enhance community, and make social change by means of rational problem solving, social thinking, and task group and social leadership.

People as Active, Social Creatures

Throughout this book you will discover that macro social workers affirm that humans are active, social creatures who continually form the bases of their lives together by engaging one another in projects to build their social environments.

Active   "Active" means that individuals engage in and take responsibility for themselves. They are active and creative agents in the construction of social reality, not subject to a deterministic existence ruled by laws derived from physics, biology, or the social sciences. We are not passive creatures who wait to be enlightened by a leader's vision or who compliantly carry out decisions made by others.

Social   Humans are irrevocably and irrefutably social creatures. The self is a social self, and the world that people construct is a social world. The propensity of people to create their humanity by shaping their culture and developing society is one of the permanent and ineradicable characteristics of the human condition without which people cannot live rich meaningful lives. "This means that people have a measure of autonomy in determining their actions, which are at the same time bound up by a social context . . . and focused on subjective meanings that people attach to their own actions and to the actions of others."[3]

Social Problems and Social Change

People take action together to solve their own social problems and make social change in communities, social organizations, and the world at large, and macro social work is centered in helping people assume that responsibility. Social change does not come from outside, no matter how compelling; or from the top, no matter how powerful; or from experts, no matter how brilliant. It does not happen by professionals acting on people. Change happens when people engage their own visions, carry out their own decisions, exert their own leadership, and bring about the society that they construct themselves. Macro social work, as you will discover in Chapter 2, is unrelentingly oriented to assisting people identify their own social problems, decide on how to solve those problems, and bring about social change by their own actions.

Rational Problem Solving and Social Thinking

Rational problem solving is the most common form of thinking in our modern world. Macro social workers need to be conscious of this way of thinking, its origins, its strengths and limitations, and the way modern reason has shaped our world.

Social thinking, on the other hand, begins in the here and now, in the lived experience of the world, and in the vision of macro social workers who not only understand social work techniques and possess knowledge but who are committed to their own growth, openness to change, and to the making of a better world. In Chapter 3 you will discover that social thinking is a process of rebirth in relationship with others who are also on a path of discovering ideas, shaping their values, and applying that learning to constructing a social world.

Task Group and Social Leadership

Macro social workers are dedicated to assisting others to become skilled leaders. Macro social workers assert that authentic leadership is always the right, the duty, and the privilege of each person, never the prerogative of one or a few at the top, no matter how skilled or well intentioned.

In Chapter 4 you will learn that to deny or diminish the leadership potential of even those who seem weakest is to eliminate a human quality that is indispensable. You will discover that one of the key leadership skills of macro social workers occurs by means of task groups. In addition, you will discover that social leadership is the capacity of people to have their own ideas, exert their own abilities, and help one another move in a journey of self-discovery to become the people they were meant to become. Social leadership does not stress how fast we achieve a goal, how effective or efficient our drive to accomplish our objectives, or how straight the path that leads to the future. What is important is the path that we choose ourselves, no matter how slow, inefficient, or convoluted.

ADDITIONAL READING

Social Model of the Self

Barrett, William. *Irrational Man: A Study in Existential Philosophy.* Garden City, NY: Doubleday, 1958.

Berdyaev, Nikolai. *Slavery and Freedom.* New York: Scribner, 1944.

Buber, Martin. *I and Thou,* 2d. ed. New York: Scribner, 1958.

Frankl, Viktor E. *Man's Search for Meaning: An Introduction to Logotherapy.* New York: Washington Square Press, 1963.

Social Critique

Berger, Peter and Thomas Luckman. *The Social Construction of Reality.* Garden City, NY: Doubleday, 1967.

Ellul, Jacques. *The Technological Society.* New York: Vintage, 1967.

Horkheimer, Max. *The Eclipse of Reason.* New York: Oxford University Press, 1947.

Mannheim, Karl. *Man and Society in an Age of Reconstruction.* New York: Harcourt, Brace and World, 1940.

Niebuhr, Reinhold. *The Children of Light and the Children of Darkness.* New York: Scribner, 1944.

Niebuhr, Reinhold. *Moral Man and Immoral Society: A Study in Ethics and Politics.* New York: Scribner, 1960.

Polanyi, Karl. *The Great Transformation.* Boston: Beacon Press, 1957.

Ramos, Alberto Guerreiro. *The New Science of Organization: A Reconceptualization of the Wealth of Nations.* Toronto: University of Toronto Press, 1981.

Rauschenbusch, Walter. *A Theology for the Social Gospel.* Nashville: Abingdon, 1945.

Slater, Philip. *The Pursuit of Loneliness: American Society at the Breaking Point.* Boston: Beacon Press, 1971.

Toffler, Alvin. *The Third Wave.* New York: William Morrow, 1980.

Voegelin, Eric. *The New Science of Politics: An Introduction.* Chicago: University of Chicago Press, 1952.

Weisskopf, Walter. *Alienation and Economics.* New York: Dell, 1971.

2 Social Problems: The Challenge of Macro Social Work

The Challenge of Being a Macro Social Worker

Let us not forget, when we talk of violence, that the death of a young mother in childbirth is violent; that the slow starvation of the mind and body of a child is violent; let us not forget that hunger is violent, that pain is violent, that oppression is violent, that early death is violent; and that the death of hope is the most violent of all. The organizer brings hope to the people.[1]

Si Kahn

The Origin of Injustice

In the final analysis, however, we must realize that social injustice and unjust social structures exist only because individuals and groups of individuals deliberately maintain or tolerate them. It is these personal choices, operating through structures that breed and propagate situations of poverty, oppression, and misery.[2]

Pope John Paul II

Ideas in This Chapter

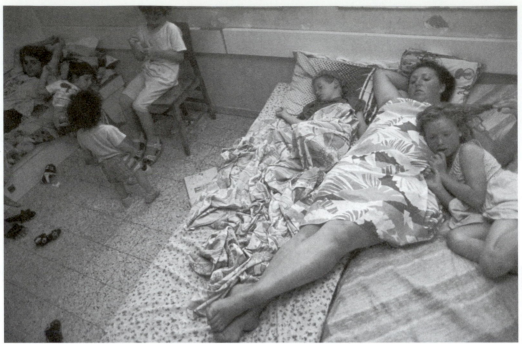

Social problems such as poverty and homelessness take a toll and a dreadful one.
People's lives are diminished or destroyed.

OUR MODERN SOCIETY

Even though the American economy was booming in 2003, prosperity had not filtered down to the 36.8 million poor people in the United States including 12.9 million children. While millions of dollars in stock options helped the earnings of corporate CEOs soar in the last few years, those same employers terminated the jobs of many workers through corporate "downsizing" that left "millions of children without health insurance plans at their parents' workplaces."[3] In the United States in 2003, 12.5% of the population lived below the threshold of meeting their basic needs—an increase of 1.3 million people since 2002.

Even more people lacked health insurance. Forty-five million people, or 15.6% of the population, had no medical coverage, an increase of 1.5 million people over 2002. In 2002 16.7% of all children lived in poverty. That number increased in 2003 by 800,000 to 17.6% of the under age 18 population.[4]

A report by the Children's Defense Fund indicates that the gap between rich and poor continues to increase. Since 1989, for example, the poorest fifth of families in America *lost* $587 and the richest 5% gained an average of $29,533.[5] In 1995 *Fortune* 500 CEOs averaged $7.8 million in total compensation, exceeding the combined average salaries of 226 school teachers in a year. In 2003 American CEOs were paid an average of $9.2 million, an annual raise of $220,000 according to the AFL/CIO's Paywatch. More than 100 of those same corporations, however, paid their CEOs $10 million or more in salary, not including stock options. Jeff Greenberg of Marsh and McLennon is the highest paid CEO in America, earning nearly $328 million. The top 5 CEOs averaged $123.2 million in 2003; 27 CEOs earned between $25 million and $50 million and 72 had incomes between $10 million and $25 million.[6]

The burden of poverty falls most heavily on our children. America cut its child poverty rate in half in the 1960s primarily as a result of Johnson's "War on Poverty," but it began to rise again as poverty programs were cut during the Nixon administration. The number of poor children reached a peak of 15.7 million in 1993 in the Reagan/Bush years, then fell for eight years during the Clinton administration, but rose again in 2002 and 2003 during the second Bush administration.

Today the United States has the highest child poverty rate of any wealthy nation on the globe. In 2003 an American child is more likely to live without the resources to meet its basic needs than a child in 17 other wealthy industrialized nations according to a cross-national Luxembourg Income Study.[7] If the U.S. government lifted low-income children out of poverty in the same proportion as we currently lift low-income seniors, three out of four poor children would no longer be poor.[8]

Not only is this pattern commonplace in the United States, but it is also occurring with even more ferocity throughout the remainder of the world. At the extreme, more than 1 billion people in underdeveloped nations have incomes below the poverty line and 1.2 billion people live beneath the threshold of basic needs. The gap dividing the rich from the poor has never been wider: the top fifth of the world's population on the global economic ladder enjoys 60 times the goods and services of the lowest fifth.[9] As Ronald Frederico observes, social problems such as poverty "take a toll and a dreadful one. People's lives are diminished or destroyed. Society is disrupted by the behavior of those who no longer care, or are so damaged that they cannot function in acceptable ways. Our society continues to suffer from serious problems, some of them longstanding and others more recent."[10]

The field of "social work may be thought of as a profession concerned with social problems, their remedy and control,"[11] asserts H. Wayne Johnson. If you are like many others, you are drawn to the profession of social work by a "passion for social justice and a desire to help those most in need."[12] All social workers should be involved in solving social problems such as racism, sexism, economic injustice, urban decay, and dysfunctional political systems. We must have the ability to understand and diagnose social problems and take a stance. More than ever, our society is desperate for people of stature, vision, and resolve who can assist in helping eradicate the most pressing social problems of the day. It is an endeavor that not only this nation but our entire global society cannot afford to ignore.

WHAT YOU WILL LEARN IN THIS CHAPTER

In this chapter you will explore a conventional definition of social problems, learn how to critique it, and arrive at your own definition. You will explore a brief history of a social problem, helping you to understand the scope and the size that social problems often acquire. You will learn a number of the most common assumptions people have about why social problems exist and several approaches people take when confronted by social problems. You will particularly explore the interactionist approach that has been adopted by many macro social workers. Finally, you will discover the reasons people sometimes give that deny, avoid, or perpetuate social problems.

DEFINING SOCIAL PROBLEMS

Although modern sociologists have developed a generally accepted conventional definition of social problems, and this textbook presents an alternative one, as a social worker, one of your skills is to be able to examine such definitions, critique them, and arrive at your own working definition. Before reading either the conventional definition or the one that this text offers, exercise your "sociological imagination" and complete Exercise 2.1. You will then have an opportunity to develop your own definition of social problems and compare it with the others.

EXERCISE 2.1

Define Social Problem

In this exercise you will consider the characteristics that distinguish social problems. Choose a social problem that concerns you such as poverty, crime, gun violence, or ethnic intolerance, and answer the following questions. When you have finished, form into groups of five and compare your definition with those of your classmates. In class come up with a composite definition.

Dimensions of Social Problems

Size: How many people do social problems affect? Do they primarily affect single individuals or become global in nature?

Location: Do social problems tend to be localized in particular geographical areas, or are they dispersed throughout a sector or locality? Can they be confined to one population group, or can social problems cross cultural, ethnic, and political boundaries?

Time orientation: Consider the length of time required to solve social problems. How long, for example, have people in North America been trying to resolve major social problems such as ethnic intolerance, crime, or economic inequality? Is the time orientation of resolving many social problems a few months, a few years, a few generations, a few centuries, longer than a few centuries?

Cost: What is the cost of social problems to the victims, to the perpetrators, and to the nation as a whole? Try to estimate the costs of the social problem you have chosen.

Problem-Solving Orientation

Diagnosing the problem: Who is responsible for identifying and defining social problems? Is defining a social problem the responsibility of professionals such as sociologists, psychologists, or social workers? Is it the role of government, including politicians and governmental employees? Are identifying social problems the domain of those who are particularly affected by them, or is it the responsibility of every citizen to call attention to the problems that plague us?

Treating the problem: Once a social problem is identified, who should be charged with resolving it? Should social problems be resolved by professional social workers applying expert evidence-based solutions? Is it the responsibility of the nonprofit social sector to deal with social problems? Are remedies for social problems best developed by policy makers, politicians, or governmental bureaucrats? Is it the job of ordinary citizens in civic society to volunteer their time and energy to the common good, or should we expect the victims of social problems to rise above their difficulties and resolve them? Should the perpetrators of social ills be required to resolve the problems they have created? Is a combination of some or all of these the best way to resolve our social problems?

Paying for the problem: Who should pay the costs of social problems? Should those who are identified as the perpetrators pay for the damage they create? Should victims of a social problem be expected to pay the costs of social problems? Should citizens make voluntary contributions to pay for the cost of social problems? Should all citizens be forced to pay in the form of higher taxes?

Methods of solving social problems: What kinds of strategies have been used to solve social problems in the past? Have these methods been aimed at changing people's behavior or the social environment? Which of these methods have been successful?

Conventional Definitions

Sullivan and Thompson assert that a "social problem exists when an influential group defines a social condition as threatening its values, the condition affects a large number of people, and it can be remedied by collective action," a definition echoed by Charles Zastrow.[13] Robert K. Merton and Robert Nisbet, two influential sociologists, have defined social problems as "the substantial, unwanted discrepancies between what is in a society and what a functionally significant collectivity within that society seriously . . . desires to be in it."[14]

Many sociologists agree that social problems have the following components:

1. The problem must have a *social* cause rather than be an issue of individual behavior.

2. It must *affect* a large number of people.

3. It must be judged by an *influential* number of people to be undesirable.[15]

4. It must be *collectively* solvable rather than solvable by individual action.

A Social Work Definition of Social Problems

A social problem is experienced collectively by an identifiable group or community of people, caused by a source external to them that harms their welfare in specific ways, and can only be resolved by people themselves in partnership with the public and private sectors of society.

Compare this definition with the conventional definition of social problems and the one you and your classmates developed. How is it the same? How is it different? Let's look at this definition in more detail and use it to critique the conventional definition.

Social Problems Are Experienced Collectively by an Identifiable Group or Community of People

Recall that in the conventional definition a social problem must *affect* a large number of people and be judged by an *influential* number of people to be undesirable.

Affect a Large Number of People It is true that poverty, crime, or drug abuse often includes many people, but social problems are not mere statistical abstractions that occur in amorphous mass society. A social problem is real and significant to the community of people experiencing it even if it is relatively inconsequential in the aggregate. For example, the low wages in the Colonias of San Antonio, Texas, is an important problem to the people who live there even though many others do not consider it to be an important issue.

Macro social workers accept people's perceptions of social reality as valid. We insist on the right of people to own their feelings and values in relation to those experiences. It is the lived experience that people encounter in their own day-to-day reality that we value, not the experience or perceptions of those external to them, no matter how powerful those people may be.

Influence The conventional definition of social problems is ruled by a qualitative criterion of influence. An "influential" group of people is required to judge whether an issue is a social problem. Social problems, however, are most often experienced by people who are not at all influential, and they alone are the best ones to judge whether issues in their social environment are problematical. Moreover, social problems interfere, disrupt, or disadvantage people whether those conditions are recognized or acknowledged by those who are influential or powerful, or by anyone else.

THE COST OF A SOCIAL PROBLEM

Economists Philip J. Cook of Duke University and Jens Ludwig of Georgetown University made a comprehensive assessment of the costs of gun violence in America as reported in their book, *Gun Violence: The Real Costs,* Oxford University Press 2000. The two economists estimated that the price the United States pays for criminal shootings, gun accidents, and suicides committed with guns is $100 billion a year. This price was obtained by estimating losses in the workplace and jury awards to determine the statistical value of life and costs of nonfatal injuries. The cost also involved emotional damage experienced by relatives and friends of the victims, the fear and a general reduction in quality of life that the threat of gun violence imposes on everyone in America, and included people who are not victimized such as time lost waiting in metal detection lines and the differences in property values in neighborhoods with high and low rates of violence.[16]

Empowered to Define Social Reality   Macro social workers maintain that the essence of being human lies in the ability of people to jointly examine and define the dilemmas of existence for themselves rather than allowing the influential to define social reality for them. People who experience injustice, intolerance, or economic or political oppression must define their own issues on their own terms and in their own way, regardless of the size of their group, their influence, or the approval or recognition of the majority of the population. When the influential usurp this right, they not only steal a part of people's humanity but also assume that victims of social problems are incapable of understanding their own social situation. The presumption that the influential should define and decide for others what is important is the beginning of social problems and the heart of oppression.

People become empowered when they share experiences with one another, confirm their perceptions, reflect on the meaning of those experiences, gain deeper insights into the causes of those conditions, and make decisions about what to do about them. Claiming the right to own one's reality is the first step toward breaking the cycle of oppression. Macro social workers are people who "continually translate personal troubles into public issues and public issues into terms of human meaning."[17]

Social Problems Are Caused by a Source External to People and Harm Their Welfare in Specific Ways
Macro social workers observe the effects that social problems cause. We must be careful to see the source of problems as located in the conditions people must endure and not in themselves.

Effects of Social Problems   The effects of social problems are often seen in the lives of people who experience them and who have had to adapt to the conditions that these problems impose. The effects of social problems, for example, may be seen in people's attitudes, values, and social behavior. They may be seen in the lessened ability of parents to provide advantages that help their children grow into physically strong, emotionally healthy, and socially engaged individuals or the opportunity to live in safe, clean neighborhoods. Social problems may be exhibited in the inability of communities to sustain themselves or provide resources or tools for their members to achieve the potential that is inherent in their nature.

Source of Social Problems   While individuals, groups, or communities often display the effects of social problems in their living conditions, behavior, or attitudes, the source of those problems is often, if not entirely, external to those experiencing them. We social workers must guard ourselves from confusing the effects of social problems with their causes. Simply because groups of people must live in low-income neighborhoods, receive poor education and inadequate wages, experience stressful or dangerous working environments, or obtain little or no health care does not mean that they are the causes of those conditions.

Locate Problems at Their Source   Macro social workers place the locus of social problems where they belong. Social workers observe how social problems occur when economic institutions such as financial, sales, commercial, and manufacturing industries use the resources of communities and export their benefits for their own profit. We see how social problems grow when school systems, police systems, or others are unresponsive to the problems in the community. Social workers perceive how social problems develop when institutionalized discrimination occurs in housing, loan practices, and in the criminal justice system. We understand how social problems arise when society not only condones but also systematically perpetuates economic, social, and political inequality. We see the origin of social problems in the attitudes and values of a society that keeps some people poor and excluded while handing privilege and benefits to others.

Social Problems Can Only Be Resolved by the People Themselves in Partnership With the Public and Private Sectors of Society
The insidious nature of social problems often lies in their ability to separate and disengage people. However, macro social workers understand that grassroots communal action, especially when combined with the private and public sectors of society, is one of the most powerful and compelling devices that people have for overcoming the social problems that work to defeat them. Joining with the power brokers of society, however, may mean that their self-perceptions and roles must be reshaped.

Delusions of Alienation and Apathy   Because of modern problems of alienation and apathy, many people suffer from the desperation of bearing social problems alone, believing they are helpless to change things. Others may live with the delusion that the powerful and influential will disentangle the problems in which they are enmeshed, that government or big business will bring about equality or "trickle down" prosperity. Many people fail to act collectively because they are convinced that their problems are either lodged internally in their psyches or exist externally in social megastructures over which they have little control.

Strength in Grassroots Action Macro social workers understand that solutions rarely come if people allow themselves to be separated in apathetic individualism, rely on experts or large institutional systems to solve problems for them, or despair in social passivity. Before action can take place, people must be connected in a recognizable group in which the "personal troubles of each become public problems of all."[18] Only when people refuse to allow themselves to be separated and alone can they break the bonds of individualism. When people resist the temptation to let others create economic and political structures for them, they begin to see through the deception that patriarchy fosters. As they confront their common situation together, they break the shackles of dependency, gain power and mastery, and forge themselves into a people.

Community Oriented Many macro social workers believe community "is the only possible form of social organization that can meaningfully reconnect people to their world and provide them with some degree of control over its political directions."[19] Empowered and engaged communities of people do not rely on the powerful to solve problems for them. They do not ask for permission. They do not wait until those in positions of influence take notice. Community members take action on their own behalf, on their own terms, and in their own time. The social environment is theirs to define, shape, and construct.

Partnership With Economy and Government Even when acting together, however, citizen groups cannot change the conditions that confront them entirely by themselves. They engage and must, in fact, connect with other sectors of society in the economy and in government to make lasting change. People who are affected by social problems demand that those in positions of power and responsibility take notice. Once they take notice, community members expect the influential to be accountable and live up to their commitments and responsibilities.

The modern economic and public sectors of society, which often make unilateral decisions out of their own interests, must be compelled to make room for communal and social organizations of people united to solve their own social problems. Ordinary citizens who have the most at stake will refuse to play the role of respectful listeners or interested spectators in the affairs that affect them. The community of citizen problem solvers will be full partners and leaders, not invited guests, at the table of decision-making. It is the community of an engaged citizenry who will be the catalysts of change, who will write the agendas, develop solutions, and present them to corporate and governmental leaders—not for permission or approval but for assistance with action.

Resocialize Decision Makers Macro social workers know that government and corporate managers are not used to sharing power or leaving control to others. They are not familiar with agreeing to decisions others make, helping with plans others create, or following the vision others see. These managers will need to be resocialized to their new role as partners. It is in this process of helping people redefine and restructure social reality and reformulate the relationship between community, government, and corporate America that macro social workers may make their most substantial contribution toward shaping our new postmodern society.

ETHNIC INTOLERANCE: A BRIEF HISTORY OF A SOCIAL PROBLEM

Social problems often begin with a small, sometimes insignificant event or activity. But once entrenched in the fabric of a community or society and unless checked, a social problem may grow in size and scope until it affects everyone in that society. As you think more deeply about the issue of defining social problems, consider the following brief history of one social problem, that of ethnic intolerance. Think about its causes, who it has affected, its costs, and its solutions.

Early Beginnings

The first English settlement in America originated in April 1607 with the landing of three ships in Chesapeake Bay. The men and women from these ships laid out the colony of Jamestown and claimed the territory as English soil. By 1619 the colony of Virginia comprised no more than 2,000 people. "In that year, however, two events occurred that were to set a pattern for the emerging society in America for the next several centuries. On July 30, the first legislative assembly on the continent met, initiating representative government in America. In August, a Dutch ship arrived with African slaves, twenty of whom were sold to the settlers."[20]

These two contradictory impulses—freedom, independence, and democracy for some; slavery, exploitation, and even extermination for others—were to run like scarlet threads throughout the American experience. Beginning with Africans and Native Americans, exploitation and subsequent fear of immigrants and strangers waxed and waned with the particular insecurities and instabilities of the times. The foreigner and the stranger, especially but not exclusively non-Whites, were often victimized and blamed for conditions brought on by the greed and ambition of the majority population.

Eastern, Midwestern, and Southern Native Americans

One overriding motive, the self-interested pursuit of wealth, guided many early settlers of America. To that end, they appropriated with impunity land that had been the domain of Native American inhabitants for 10,000 years. The early frontiersmen presumed that the continent was not yet possessed by anybody at all. It was theirs for the taking "to exploit and despoil or to use to build a new society."[21] Native Americans were a mere impediment to the inevitable process of exploitation of the wilderness. The solution was extermination or removal of these undesirables from the East, Midwest, and southern United States.

Eastern Native Americans   As early as 1637, the Pequot War in New England ended in the complete destruction of the Pequot Tribe inhabiting the Connecticut Valley. The conflict between Virginia settlers and Powhatan's tribes resulted in the annihilation of the Native Americans in the northeastern United States.

Midwest   In the fall of 1794, on the heels of American Independence, "Mad Anthony" Wayne defeated Chief Tecumseh's followers at the Battle of Fallen Timbers on the Maumee River, not far from present day Ft. Wayne, Indiana. The Black Hawk Wars, several years later, were particularly brutal affairs. Under threat of force to relinquish his claim to 50 million acres of prime forest in the Midwest, Black Hawk and his tribes, the Sauk and Fox Indians, withdrew from their traditional corn farming lands in Illinois to the west bank of the Mississippi. Suffering from hunger, they recrossed the river to join the friendly Winnebago in Wisconsin to grow their corn there. They were immediately attacked. Black Hawk retreated, making offers of peace, which were ignored by the 2,000-soldier militia. Driven mercilessly through southern Wisconsin to the west bank of the Mississippi, Black Hawk and his followers were slaughtered as they tried to cross the river. "Although they were of the savage enemy," wrote one rifleman, "it was a horrid sight to witness little children, wounded, and suffering the most excruciating pain" as they were gunned down.[22] Hungry for land, claiming unfettered rights to exercise their own interests, the white settlers "constantly encroached on Indian lands in defiance of treaties, . . . destroyed the game on which the Indians depended for food and clothing; and many were ready to slay any redskin on sight. When the Indians tried to defend themselves, war ensued."[23]

South   In the same year that "Mad Anthony" Wayne was decimating Tecumseh's tribes in one of the most "bloodcurdling wars with the Creeks in the South, Andrew Jackson won a bloody victory."[24] Later, the Seminoles were slaughtered in the Florida swamps. For those Native Americans who had survived, an "Indian Country" was established beginning at the Mississippi River and running from Canada to Texas. This area, part of the Great Plains and including the badlands of the Dakotas, was thought to be worthless and uninhabitable by White men. The entire Native American population was to be removed, forcibly if necessary, with little consideration for how these people, who were forest hunters and farmers, would survive on the plains of the West.

The "Five Civilized Tribes"—the Creeks, Choctaws, Chickasaws, Cherokees, and Seminoles—offered stubborn resistance. They loved their homeland, and "many of them, especially the Creeks and Cherokees, had learned to be thrifty farmers, built good homes and towns, acquired herds of cattle, erected gristmills, and educated their children in missionary schools. They clung to their lands to the last."[25]

Between 1838 and 1842 the entire population of these tribes were brutally rounded up by soldiers at gunpoint and herded on foot from Georgia and Florida across the Mississippi. About half of the Creek Nation died, and many members of the Cherokee Nation, particularly the children and women, failed to survive this removal along the "trail of tears." Even after this forced removal, captive Native Americans continued to be expendable. Tribes were removed again and again to less desirable areas whenever settlers laid stake to the land. Between 1829 and 1866, for example, the Winnebago were forced to move six times.[26]

French, Irish, and German Americans

French Americans In 1798 a pathological xenophobia against French Americans resulted in the passage of the Alien, Sedition, and Naturalization Acts, giving the president a blank check to repress "dangerous aliens" by fines, deportation, or imprisonment, particularly recent immigrants who opposed him politically or criticized the government.

Irish and German Americans Xenophobia appeared in eastern cities directed at Irish and German Americans as their numbers increased in the 1840s and 1850s. Irish Americans, who fled to the United States in increasing numbers because of the "potato famine" of the 1840s in Ireland were particularly vulnerable. Men were used for the most backbreaking labor laying rails and in mines. Out of desperation, even children were forced to labor in mines and factory sweatshops. Marked by the burning of an Irish convent in New England and "beer riots" against German Americans in Columbus, New York, and Louisville, this period was the most violent in terms of abuse of immigrants in our nation's history. One result was a residence requirement of 21 years before citizenship could be obtained by these immigrants, and there were severe restrictions against holding political office.

During World War I, nearly anything associated with German culture was considered suspect. Many Germans anglicized their names, especially German Jews who bore a double stigma. German Lutherans were viewed with suspicion for holding worship services in their native language and maintaining private parochial schools in which classes were taught in German. So strong were the feelings against all things German that playing German music such as Wagnerian operas was considered unpatriotic, and even the innocuous German "frankfurter" on a bun, an American favorite at baseball games, shed its German roots, becoming a "hot dog" out of deference to the patriotic sensibilities of sports fans.

Mexican Americans

As early as 1503, one of the first groups of European settlers in America, many of whom were Catholic missionaries, staked a claim to the land that stretched north along the California coast nearly to Oregon and eastward into Texas. They brought with them Mexican culture, a mixture of Native American and Spanish immigrants, and established the first towns and cities in this country, predating those on the east coast by more than 100 years. This northern half of Mexico was sparsely populated with farmers and ranchers who, for the most part, maintained a peaceful relationship with the Native American population and did not despoil its land for mineral wealth or destroy its natural environment.

By the time James Polk became president in 1845, the principle that the United States had a "Manifest Destiny" to acquire all the land from the Atlantic to the Pacific Ocean had become a foregone conclusion. The drive to annex the entire southwestern part of North America began a year later, when on April 25, 1846, the United States sent troops to support its claim over Texas. By the end of the Mexican American War, the United States had spent $100 million, and the lives of 13,780 soldiers and even more lives of Mexicans were lost.[27]

On February 2, 1848, when the United States signed the Treaty of Guadalupe Hidalgo, Mexico ceded the northern half of its country to the United States, including the states of Texas, California, Nevada, Arizona, New Mexico, and Utah, on condition that the U.S. government would guarantee citizenship, religious freedom, and honor the personal and property rights of Mexican nationals living in the southwest. Shortly after the Civil War, however, settlers from the east, hungry for California gold, rescinded the rights of Mexican Americans to vote and deprived them of their property. Mexican Americans, who had called the southwest their home for nearly 350 years, were treated as foreigners and interlopers who had no rights or entitlements to the territory they owned and on which they had lived for generations.[28]

African Americans

By 1765 slavery existed in law and fact in each of the 13 colonies. Out of a population that numbered 1.85 million, 400,000 were African Americans, fully seven-eights of whom lived in the southernmost colonies. In South Carolina, African Americans outnumbered the White population by two to one. Hardly considered human, slaves were the machinery that drove the economy of the South, and until the days of the Revolution, this situation was considered "natural."[29]

> [Slavery] exalted a few whites, degraded many more, permitted sinfully wasteful agriculture, created a miasma of fear in areas where [African Americans] were plentiful, hardened class lines, stunted the growth of the Southern middle class, cheapened respect for labor, and dehumanized man's sympathy for man in an age already inhuman enough. . . . As for the slave himself, the sin against him was so colossal as to give most Americans the chills even to this day.[30]

By 1800 most northern states had ended slavery, but the antislavery movement was generally weak and "conciliatory to the master." In 1831, however, agitation against slavery began to grow. William Lloyd Garrison, a young native of Newburyport, Massachusetts, published the first issue of the *Liberator,* a rabid antislavery newspaper. The very next year, the New England Anti-Slavery Society was founded, and by 1833 delegates from several states founded the American Anti-Slavery Society, which was dedicated to immediate emancipation. In 1837 the abolitionists began to agitate for social legislation, circulating petitions directed at Congress. Speakers were recruited to spread the message of abolition and to engage the "formation of town, country, and state antislavery groups. By 1838, the Anti-Slavery Society claimed a membership of 250,000 with over 1,300 auxiliaries."[31]

The success of this movement inspired active and vengeful retaliation. In 1835 a mob in Charleston, South Carolina, broke into the post office and stole and burned antislavery publications. President Andrew Jackson applauded the riot along with southern and a few northern public officials. In the same year, rioters in Boston led Garrison through the streets on a rope, and two years later Elijah Lovejoy, an antislavery editor, was murdered while defending his press in Alton, Illinois.

From 1850 onward events began to escalate. The Fugitive Slave Act required northerners to assist in capturing and returning ex-slaves. African Americans resisted and protested slavery by escaping from bondage, by day-to-day resistance, and by staging occasional insurrections. Engaging in civil disobedience, abolitionists and many African Americans including Frederick Douglass, Sojourner Truth, and Harriet Tubman fought slave-catchers. They rescued fugitives from courtrooms and jails, inspiring the single most effective piece of antislavery propaganda, *Uncle Tom's Cabin* by Harriet Beecher Stowe, published in 1852.

In 1857, despite the moral and human rights issues involved, the U.S. Supreme Court rendered the *Dred Scott* decision, ruling that ownership of people was constitutionally legal and that Congress had no authority to ban it from the territories. In October 1859 John Brown, an antislavery supporter from Kansas, and a small band of African American and abolitionist followers attacked the federal arsenal at Harper's Ferry, Virginia.

A little over a year later, on December 20, 1860, South Carolina seceded from the Union over the issue of slavery and the Civil War began, the bloodiest conflict this nation has ever experienced. By its end in 1865 almost 500,000 Americans had died in the struggle, and hundreds of thousands more were maimed for life.

Even though the Emancipation Proclamation of August 22, 1862, ended slavery in the United States, state governments throughout the South instituted the infamous "Black Codes," the most repressive measures this country has ever seen, denying African Americans equal rights and equal justice in nearly every area of life. In 1896 in *Plessy v. Ferguson,* the Supreme Court concluded that the Fourteenth Amendment could be interpreted as maintaining "separate but equal" facilities, particularly schools. In one stroke the Supreme Court ensured that segregation was not only tacitly permitted but also enforceable as the law of the land. Schools and other facilities for African Americans were to be separate, but they would inevitably become unequal. Discrimination became the official policy in the United States.

Effectively excluded from the mainstream of American culture and opportunity, African Americans, for all intents and purposes, remained socially, economically, and politically enslaved. Even the Constitution was used against them. The institution of racism would exist in fact and as the policy of our country for the next 68 years.[32]

Western Native Americans

By 1851 the policy of maintaining "one big reservation" for the Native Americans in the desert badlands and the Great Plains had ended. White settlers, hungry for more and more land, came into increasing conflict with the Indians. Native Americans were pushed onto ever-shrinking sites, across which the government was permitted to build roads and railroads.

The Great Plains, which had been the traditional home of the Plains Indians, was carved up into ranches. The buffalo were slaughtered, in part to make way for cattle and sheep but primarily to destroy the food supply of the Native Americans, forcing them to give up their freedom and succumb to a life of dependency on government aid. The prairie sod was plowed so that wheat and corn could be planted. In a period of about four decades, the ecology of the great American plains, which had existed as a self-sustaining system since the last Ice Age, supporting animals, plants, as well as humans, was almost completely destroyed.

Following the Civil War, the U.S. Cavalry turned its attention to exterminating the remaining Native Americans of the western plains or rounding them up and forcing them onto reservations. Desperate to maintain their freedom, Native Americans engaged the cavalry in hundreds of battles between 1865 and 1880. On June 25, 1876, for example, General George Custer made his "last stand" against Crazy Horse and Sitting Bull at the Battle of the Little Big Horn. Native American victories, however, were rare. Ten years later, led by Geronimo, a Chiraquahua Apache, the last of the free Native Americans finally surrendered.

Chinese Americans

Actively recruited by many large U.S. companies, particularly the railroads, Chinese males were imported in large numbers in the 1840s to perform the most grueling and dangerous labor imaginable, labor that even Irish Americans refused. They worked hard for pitiful wages, often losing their lives or becoming maimed for life blasting tunnels and carving roadbeds from the sides of California's Sierra Nevada Mountains. When the economy soared during the California gold rush of 1848–1850, Chinese were sought to provide a variety of menial tasks such as cooking and laundering in mining and logging camps. By 1860 more than 50,000 Chinese, mostly men, were living in California.[33]

When prosperity began to wane after the Civil War and the need for gold, mercury, lumber, and other goods lessened, "the Chinese were cavalierly blamed for job shortages."[34] In the election of 1867, anti-Chinese sentiment emerged as a major California campaign issue. Those who had previously benefited from their labor treated the Chinese with suspicion, distrust, and even hatred. Angry men formed Anti-Chinese Coolie Associations and actively protested the Burlingame Treaty of 1868, which allowed Chinese immigration. What made these protests so irrational was the reality that the railroads and San Francisco's mining industries were dependent on the bravery, skills, and labor of Chinese Americans, qualities that no others were willing to provide.[35]

William Brock asserts that the importation of Chinese coolies "produced an explosion of racial hatred and mob violence. 'The Chinese,' said the governor of California in 1869, 'are a stream of filth and prostitution pouring in from Asia, whose servile competition tends to cheapen and degrade labor.'"[36] By the 1870s violence directed at Chinese Americans was intensified by an economic depression. A frenzied Los Angeles mob shot and killed 20 Chinese Americans in one incident alone on October 24, 1871.[37] A grand jury indicted 150 men, but only 6 stood trial. Several years later, in 1877, a mob invaded Chinatown in San Francisco and spent two days destroying and looting property. "The Chinese must go" was the most popular slogan of the newly formed Workingmen's party.[38]

By 1880, 75,000 Chinese Americans were living in California, with more than half concentrated in San Francisco. The San Francisco Board of Supervisors, in response to demands of Anti-Coolie Associations, *taxed* Chinese immigrants for the privilege of performing backbreaking and dangerous work in California's mines. They were denied citizenship and suffrage, and they were restricted in their use of the courts and schools. Governor William Irwin, a keynote speaker at one anti-Chinese rally, claimed that the Chinese were the enemy of American civilization.

Anti-Chinese agitation became so powerful that in 1882 the federal government persuaded China to surrender her most-favored-nation status and to agree to the exclusion of her nationals from the United States. Congress enacted the Chinese Exclusion Act, preventing Chinese immigration and effectively isolating and disenfranchising those Chinese people who had chosen to live in America.

In 1890 the California legislature was authorized to protect the state from "dangerous and detrimental aliens," a euphemism for Chinese Americans. Chinese Americans were not to be employed on public works or by corporations. The legislature discouraged immigration and delegated power to cities and towns to remove Chinese Americans or locate them "within prescribed areas,"[39] reminiscent of the treatment of Native Americans. The result was the establishment of "Chinatowns" throughout California.

This forced segregation required Chinese Americans to fall back on their own resources for mutual support and self-protection. They formed their own cultural associations and social groups, carrying with them their own traditions, language, and religion. In 1892 the Chinese Exclusion Act was renewed, and in 1902 it became permanent.[40]

Japanese Americans

The ink was barely dry on the Chinese Exclusion Act, cutting off this labor resource, when large agribusinesses began looking for another source of cheap, expendable labor. Japanese farmers were actively recruited by large companies to work on the sugar and pineapple plantations in Hawaii and in the fields of California. Between 1890 and 1924, lured by promises of good wages and working conditions, about 200,000 Japanese came to the United States as laborers.

Little thought was given to the social climate into which these Asians were being imported or the impact that immigration would have on them. Unlike the experience of the Chinese, for whom females were not part of the labor force, migration of young Japanese women was encouraged. As a result, the industrious and hard working Japanese began to raise families and save money. Many Japanese quietly began to cultivate areas of the Sacramento–San Joaquin Valley, becoming prosperous farmers.

Anti-Japanese sentiment, however, began to show up almost immediately. By 1911 a variety of proposals to exclude Japanese immigrants had been introduced to Congress by Californians. In 1912 a wave of hysteria was touched off by the news that a group of Japanese American immigrants was about to buy land in Baja, California. Other newspapers carried headlines such as "Jap Puts on Airs" and "Yellow Peril in College Town" when Japanese Americans, after careful saving, had the temerity to purchase homes or attempt to buy land on which to farm.[41] Fully 34 bills curbing Japanese rights were introduced in the 1913 California state legislature, resulting in the Alien Land Act. Not only were Japanese "aliens ineligible for citizenship," but it also became illegal for them to purchase land in California. Land could be leased for only 3 years, and land already owned or leased could not be willed to other persons, preventing parents from passing farms to their own children, a law that remained in effect until 1952.

The hysteria that occurred against the Japanese in the years before World War I was renewed with a vengeance after the bombing of Pearl Harbor on December 7, 1941. Executive Order 3906 gave permission for the mass removal of nearly the entire Japanese American population to "relocation camps," a euphemism for concentration camps, on the pretext that the Japanese Americans, many of whom had become established as farmers in California's Central Valley, were sympathetic to Japan and were potential or even actual spies.

Not only was there no evidence that any Japanese Americans committed an act of treason against the United States during the war, but Japanese Americans went to extreme lengths to demonstrate loyalty. Hundreds of young men volunteered as translators and interpreters in the Pacific, providing invaluable service to allied troops intercepting and translating Japanese messages. In Europe the famed 442 Regiment of the 100th Infantry Battalion became the most decorated regiment in the war. While their parents were imprisoned in concentration camps, these *nisei* (second generation Japanese Americans) suffered more casualties than any other battalion, accomplishing feats of bravery unmatched by any other American combat group.

Other Ethnic Groups

In the 1900s many new arrivals to the United States experienced ethnic intolerance, often covert but invariably demeaning, particularly for those who lived in their own neighborhoods such as Jews, Italians, Poles, Russians, and other Eastern Europeans. During the later half of the 1950s, African Americans brought about some of the most conclusive shifts in American thinking about race relations, culminating in passage of the Civil Rights Act of 1964, destruction of miscegenation laws, and voting rights legislation, and equal employment opportunity laws. Despite these impressive achievements, the most recent groups of immigrants—Koreans, Vietnamese, and other South East Asian refugees, and most recently Iranians, Iraqis, and other Muslims from the Middle East—all have experienced their share of ethnic intolerance in the new land, which has been exacerbated, in part, by the government's efforts to demonize Iraq, North Korea, and others as "rogue nations."

ASSUMPTIONS ABOUT SOCIAL PROBLEMS

Some people see social problems as originating in complex organizations, in the conflicts created as interest groups struggle for dominance, or in society's large political and economic institutions. Others see social problems as originating in defective social systems or in the inherent premises on which our modern market society it is based. Still others see the massive social problems for 80% of the people in the world's developing nations as a result of the economic dominance of the West. Where in society do you assume social problems primarily originate? Are social problems mainly located at one of these levels, in more than one, or is there a common theme in all of them?

Organizational Deviance Model

Modern complex organizations are among the wealthiest, most powerful, and important social systems that exist in our world today. Yet for all of their importance and necessity in our advanced culture, some writers locate many of the problems in our modern society at the level of these large, often transnational organizations, especially but not exclusively those in the economic sphere of our society. Modern complex organizations, they assert, are often deceptive, distort the democratic process, dominate the economy, transform communal relationships, and become our society.

Deceptive Modern complex organizations supply us with nearly all the goods, services, and employment in our society. Because they are so much a part of our social world, we tend to perceive these organizational systems, particularly large corporate structures, as beneficent instruments for social good or as neutral technological apparatuses under the benign management of their owners. The more that we become dependent on organizations, the more we are induced to believe that life would be unthinkable and survival impossible without them.[42] We tie our futures to these systems and work to help them increase our prosperity.

In reality, however, organizations are not socially benevolent systems. Complex modern organizations are artificial economizing tools used to maximize the goals of their owners, whether the owner is a group of stockholders, an interest group, a legislature, or the Congress. "Organizations in today's market society," says Alberto Ramos, "are necessarily deceitful." They tend to "deceive both their members and their clients, inducing us to believe not only that what they produce is desirable, but also that their existence is vital to the interest of the society at large."[43] The products of organizations are an incidental means to their ultimate ends. The ends of complex organizations are their own survival and maximizing the power of their owners. To the extent that employees are no longer useful to the owners of these systems, they are expendable as are the goods that they produce.

Distort the Democratic Process The United States was founded on ideals of social equality, in which people could claim ownership of the political process that would operate on their behalf. Large modern organizations were nonexistent when the Constitution was framed, but today they sometimes destroy equality and create power centers that usurp the power that citizens were intended to command.

Destruction of Equality Sheldon Wolin asserts that reliance on hierarchy and top-down decision making permeates the country so profoundly that every one of its primary institutions is antidemocratic, including the school system. Equality is lessened, and a blend of antidemocratic managerial practices and ideology adopted from private corporations infiltrates governmental institutions, making them more and more similar to corporations. As a result, most North Americans feel powerless; they are not allowed to become involved in the process of controlling their own lives. Their lack of participation in the country's major institutions generates a sense of futility and helplessness.[44]

Power Instruments Organizations, as Max Weber commented, "are power instruments of the first order for one who controls the bureaucratic apparatus."[45] Bureaucracy generates an enormous degree of unregulated and often unperceived social power, comments Charles Perrow, and this power is "placed in the hands of very few leaders who are prone to use it for ends we do not approve of, for ends we are generally not aware of, and more frightening still for ends we are led to accept because we are not in a position to conceive alternative ones."[46]

Transformation of Communal Relationships

Modern organizations are not natural human associations. They were not designed to provide social goods, implement social values, or provide social capital as part of their mechanisms. Complex organizations, instead, systematically engage in the commodification, objectification, and dehumanization of people and encourage reification of the organizational machine tool.

Commodification Organizations shape our mentality, transforming people into economic beings. Where people have not been "socialized to adopt the collective orientation" of organization, asserts Victor Thompson, they "must be changed so that they will not only want more things, but will have the skills necessary to produce them."[47] Organizations induce humans to become factors of production, "commodities" that behave according to utilitarian constraints of the marketplace.[48] "Students become the 'products' of universities. Workers become the 'tools' of management, and individuals become functionaries"[49] who perform their organizational duties and do what they are told in the interest of the owner's goal for the organization. People come to think of themselves in terms of the value they have to the system of organization rather than the intrinsic values of being human. "Each person treats the other primarily as a means to his or her end . . . to seek to make him or her an instrument of one's purposes by adducing whatever influences or considerations will in fact be effective."[50]

Objectification Organizations require people to treat themselves and one another objectively, impartially,

neutrally, and impersonally. "Objective" discharge of business primarily means a discharge of business according to calculable rules and "without regard for persons," asserts Max Weber.[51] If we bring social values, altruistic attitudes, or relationally oriented behaviors into the organization, we must be induced to give them up and accept efficiency, productivity, and task behaviors instead.[52] People are taught to "live comfortably within a contrived reality"[53] as if that reality were authentic and meaningful for human life.

This "structure of objectification (transforming life and a person partly into a thing, partly into a calculating machine) penetrates all realms of life and all spiritual functions."[54] Organizations treat people as "cogs in a wheel," as if they are interchangeable parts in the overall social mechanism.[55] Machinelike qualities become part of the human psyche, and those qualities that personalize individual action and are contrary to calculations that maximize the owner's goals become devalued and discarded.

Dehumanization Complex organizations are specifically aimed at driving out natural social relationships and transforming them into impersonal, artificial, instrumental relationships. In organizational life we tend to be denied "opportunities for engaging in full social relationships, in we relationships, and in the mutual construction of new solutions to individual problems."[56] Ultimately the organizational individual tends to be *unable* to function as a full-fledged human being.

Modern complex organizations are systems that systematically deprive people of their humanity. Modern organizations have inverted social processes once considered horrific into higher social goods. Max Weber, the most perceptive analyst of complex organization, explains in the clearest and starkest terms how that occurs:

> Bureaucracy develops the more perfectly, the more it is "dehumanized," the more completely it succeeds in eliminating from official business love, hatred, and all personal, irrational, and emotional elements which escape calculation . . . and this is apprised as its *special virtue*[57] (emphasis added).

Reification Many thinkers have become so socialized to the organizational culture that they embed objectification of relationships into their common understanding of social life. These writers often engaged in organizational reification, a process that endows organizations with attributes more compelling and powerful than the human beings who compose them, and for many people there is little consciousness that this transformation has occurred. Ralph Hummel observes, for example, that the process of reification, treating an artificial object as if it is a natural, social being as organizations often pretend, leads to a "dwindling of consciousness to the point where humans forget they have made their world."[58] One can often observe reification in the way writers describe organizations. For example, they often talk about abstract organizations as if they are enlarged versions of human beings that have personalities, think, make decisions, and plan. People begin to accept organizational systems as more intelligent, with a higher claim to economic and political resources, and entitled to more rights and privileges than the individuals who constructed them or on whose behalf these tools are presumed to function.

Definer of Society

The organization must be seen today as "defining, creating and shaping its environment,"[59] not the other way around. Society adapts to the large, powerful organizations controlled by a few, often overlapping leaders. To see these organizations as adapting to a turbulent, dynamic, ever-changing environment, says Charles Perrow, is to indulge in fantasy. In fact, Perrow asserts,

> the most significant failure of all organization theory [is] its failure to see *society* as adaptive to organizations. The dominant organizations . . . institutionalize on their own terms to create the environments they desire, shape the existing ones, and define which sections of [society] they will deal with.[60]

Bureaucracy replaces society, says Ralph Hummel. *Fortune* magazine, for example, reminds us that the General Motors Corporation in the 1950s was "a leviathan whose wake touched every American. It wasn't a question of what was good for General Motors being good for the country: General Motors *was* the country."[61]

Domination of the Organized Economy

The dominance of large business organizations has transformed North America into a market-centered society. The social has been reduced to an enclave constrained by and captured within the forces of economic organizations. Transnational corporations have extended their hegemony throughout the developed and developing world, creating a global market society as well.

The transformation of society into a category of the economy is a unique phenomenon in the history of mankind. In all social systems preceding our own, says Karl Polanyi, "the economic order [was] merely a function of the social order in which it was contained. Neither under tribal, or feudal or mercantile conditions was there . . . a separate economic system in society."[62] This state of affairs has come to be viewed by many as only natural. Many modern theorists lead us to believe that our modern rational society is "historically typical";[63] that is, human life has always been organized and rationalized. In reality, however, "it is only in our Western societies that quite recently turned man into an economic being," says Marcel Mauss. People often do not understand that "modern society is unprecedented because no other society uses the criterion of economizing as the standard of human existence."[64]

Those who control these organizations often determine the quality of our lives. They shape our mentality, affect our life chances, and define our humanity. They are our cultural, social, and interpersonal frame of reference.[65] Organization, as Robert Presthus has commented, *is* our social environment.[66]

The Organizational Deviance Model and Macro Social Work

Understanding modern complex organizations is one of the key components of macro social work practice about which you will learn more in Part Three of this book. Social workers use organizations as tools to deliver social services to people. We develop social programs and social agencies, administer organizations, and when those organizations become dysfunctional, we work to improve their effectiveness. However, when large corporate or public organizations become so powerful that they trample on the public interest, social workers and others work to make them accountable and change their practices. Macro social workers use the organizational model of social deviance to understand how large corporate structures dominate our social environment, appropriate power, and control the individual. We use the ideas inherent in this model to confront organizations both in business and government.

Macro social workers who are aware of the extent to which modern complex organizations thrive on commodification, objectification, and dehumanization help promote community and social organizations that act as countervailing centers of *gemeinschaft* relationships and authentic "we relations." Many community organizations actively confront individual corporate organizations. You will learn in Chapter 8, for example, how the Association for Community Organizations for Reform Now (ACORN) challenges financial institutions such as Wells Fargo Bank and others that "redline" poor neighborhoods, denying people access to loans by which they can purchase or improve their homes, thereby ensuring the further decline of a neighborhood, and how other community organizations press large corporations and municipalities to provide living wages for employees.

In addition, using their understanding of organizational deviance, macro social workers promote community development corporations as alternative sources of economic strength for communities, enabling them to become independent of large corporate structures. We rely on the organization deviance model when challenging organizations that seek policy entitlements that distort the public interest. We use our understanding of organizational deviance when we challenge the efforts of transnational organizations that exploit natural and human resources in the developing world that keep people in conditions of poverty, sickness, and misery. Understanding the organizational deviance model is key to much macro social work practice.

Intergroup Conflict Model

The framers of our Constitution were wary of centralizing all political power in one office. Therefore, they divided power into three branches and, within those branches, divided government among local, regional, state, and national levels, a structure called federalism. By fragmenting power over a broad spectrum of society, the framers ensured that those interest groups who attempted to control public affairs would compete among themselves; government would play the role of mediator to keep power in check and guarantee that everyone would at least have a "piece of the pie."[67] In this way, many powerful interest groups find access to power at one or another level of government. They press for policy concessions and preferential treatment by which their interests can find a sympathetic voice. The theory that helps explain this process is called interest group liberalism.

According to interest group liberalism, because the interests of these groups do not normally coincide,

competition among them results in conflict between groups occupying different levels within the overall federalist hierarchy. This conflict may create "a variety of social problems, since policies enacted to further the interests of some . . . create effects that work against the interests of others."[68]

Today, however, modern industrialized society has become so large, Ralf Dahrndorf asserts, that while interest groups continue to manipulate government for preferential treatment, many now carry out economic, political, educational, and other important institutionalized activities on their own. They no longer try to adapt to the conditions established by government. "Interest groups direct and control the activities of other organized groups seizing as much of society's resources for themselves as they can, and in the process exploit the less powerful, often creating social problems such as poverty, discrimination, and oppression," Jim Henslin states. "As the exploited react to their oppression, still other problems emerge such as crime, drug abuse, and various forms of violence such as riots and suicide." According to Henslin, "conflict theorists view social polices that benefit the less privileged as concessions from the powerful . . . (as well as) actions designed to keep the privileged in their positions of power." At the intergroup level, therefore, "social problems occur when powerful interest groups exploit the less powerful and as the less powerful resist, rebel, or appeal to higher values of justice."[69]

Intergroup Conflict Model and Macro Social

Macro social workers have used ideas from the intergroup conflict model to help bring about a better society since the beginning of the social work profession. Today macro social workers make use of the intergroup conflict model to help ordinary citizens become empowered to learn about the processes by which private interest groups work for preferential treatment from government. Community organizers understand that special interests often engage in practices that work to their own advantage but disadvantage others at the same time. When special interests use their influence to obtain preferential treatment or appropriate community resources by using the power of eminent domain, special zoning variances, tax breaks, or subsidies from local government that threaten the integrity of the community, for example, community organizers mobilize communities to act as countervailing power systems to expose those practices.

We assist community members as they confront businesses that want to erect office buildings or shopping centers that will destroy a community. We challenge city governments that want to give subsidies to corporations without guarantees for living wages or other concessions that will benefit community members.

In addition, macro social workers who engage in social policy advocacy use intergroup conflict theory to understand how private interests often work to bend the rules in their favor, and we work to establish equitable social policies that further the public good. We challenge government when it establishes policies that funnel resources to powerful interests while neglecting the interests of citizens who lack the same access to government. We advocate on behalf of the interests of people with low incomes, children, single mothers, and persons with disabilities whose voices are not often heard in the hallways of power.

Macro social workers participate in social movements to ensure that the interests of the public as well as the welfare of the natural environment are protected. Social activists who understand the nature of interest group politics are familiar with the way in which private interests feed from the public trough. Private commercial interests are often eager to use public land as sites to dispose of toxic waste. Large mining conglomerates press for the right to use public land to extract mineral wealth at low cost to themselves, afterward leaving behind gaping scars on the landscape or denuded mountains. Agribusiness pressures government for cheap water rights for irrigation. Large ranching interests lobby for the right to graze their cattle on public land, and lumber industries push for permission to harvest public forests. Social activists press government to protect the interests of the public as well as the irreplaceable ecology of wilderness areas from private exploitation.

Institutional Deviance Model

When health care is unevenly distributed, when poverty persists for millions, "when tax laws permit a business to write off 80% of a $100 luncheon but prohibit a truck driver from writing off a bologna sandwich; when government is run by a few for the profit of the few, when businesses supposedly in competition fix prices to gouge the consumer, then society is permitting what is called *institutional deviance*."[70] Institutional deviance occurs when social problems become officially embedded in the major

ideologies, culture, or structures of society and often become the operating premises on which social decisions are based. Ethnic intolerance in the United States, for example, was institutionalized in social, economic, legal, and governmental structures from its inception. Racism was one of the foundational principles that guided business, government, and legal decisions. Bribery, spoils, nepotism, and other forms of corruption were institutionalized in business and politics immediately after the Civil War until the reforms of Progressive Era social workers such as Florence Kelley, Lillian Wald, Jane Addams, and others.

Characteristics of Institutional Deviance   Institutional deviance occurs when officially mandated structures of society devise rules that disadvantage segments of the population. Institutional deviance is not an aberration, but it seems to be a permanent structure in American society. While at times the goals of large institutions become deviant, some institutions serve antisocial purposes under the guise that they are socially permissible. Other institutions of society overtly engage in social harm.

Institutions Define Rules   According to Eitzen and Baca-Zinn, social workers must keep in mind that powerful agencies of government and business make rules that may disadvantage large segments of the population. They may define social reality in a way that manipulates public opinion and controls behaviors that threaten the status quo and their power. During the first 75 years of the American experience, for example, "slavery on large plantations was not considered to be a social problem at all. Instead, slaves who revolted were the problem. Racism was not a social problem of the Jim Crow South, but pushy blacks were. From the standpoint of U.S. pubic opinion, forcibly dispossessing Native Americans from their lands was not a social problem, but it became a problems when Native Americans refused to be relocated, resisted the destruction of their culture, and their own extermination."[71]

A Perennial Reality   Eitzen and Baca-Zinn assert that institutional deviance is a perennial reality in the American corporate and political culture that create "conditions in society such as poverty and institutional racism that induce material or psychic suffering for certain segments of the population." They assert that "there *are* sociocultural phenomena that prevent a significant number of society's participants from developing and using their full potential; there *are* discrepancies between those principles for which the United States is presumed to stand such as equality of opportunity, justice, and democracy and the actual conditions under which many people live."[72]

Diverge From Goals   Sometimes social institutions, even those created by well-intentioned people for good purposes, may diverge from their original goals and become deviant. For example, the Second Amendment, which in 1783 permitted states to maintain armed militias to keep order, has been reinterpreted by many today as a license for nearly anyone to own handguns and other weapons, resulting in catastrophic violence to children and teenagers.

Antisocial Purposes Masquerading as Socially Permissible   Under the guise of lawful or socially permissible premises, many transactions may intentionally serve antisocial purposes. The defense industry obtains legal sanctions and subsidies from our government to sell weapons to developing countries for profit, ostensibly to promote "a balance of power" or to protect our "national interests." In reality, however, selling weapons of war to poor countries steals the lives of impoverished citizens, often guaranteeing that dictators will be able to continue to oppress their own people and perpetrate violence against their neighbors, and even go to war against our own country.

Do Social Harm   Some businesses do not even have the guise of nobility of purpose behind which to hide their exploitative self-interests. After years of deceit and evasion, for example, the American tobacco industry, having finally been deflected from marketing its products to adolescents in the United States, has now developed the lucrative global market with full realization that it is endangering the health of the world's children and creating enormous health care costs for people who cannot afford to pay.

Macro Social Work and the Institutional Deviance Model

Social workers apply the institutional deviance model of social problems when we become involved in politics and work through the political process. Early social workers including Jane Addams, Florence Kelly, Dorothea Dix, and many others lobbied government for reform. They challenged the laissez-faire principles of government that allowed corporations to monopolize business, fix prices, and artificially manipulate supply and demand

in their favor. They contested political machines that distorted democracy and dominated Congress and the office of the presidency. Social workers used their political and policy skills to reform government corrupted by bribery, graft, and favoritism. Social workers used the premises of the institutional deviance model to advocate for reform of labor laws, to protect women and children against exploitation, to institute governmental agencies such as the Children's Bureau, and to establish a juvenile justice system.

Macro social workers use their understanding of how institutional deviance is a perennial issue in government and corporate structures. When social workers look for objective causes of social problems, therefore, "we must . . . guard against the tendency to accept the definitions of social problems provided by those in power"[73] who may tend to protect the distortions that institutions develop. We struggle with how to hold such large institutions accountable and forge social policies that are morally good and socially just.[74]

Systems Deviance Model

One of the more popular assumptions of how social problems occur is the systems deviance model. Sometimes systems develop defects that result in social problems. At other times social problems occur because of unintended consequences of decisions. The systems deviance model can assist macro social workers in understanding why social systems are difficult to correct, how they can be corrected, and how to avoid illusions of systems blame that managers sometimes perpetuate.

What Are Social Systems?

Martin and O'Connor state that "a *system* is something with interrelated parts."[75] K. Berrien defines a system as "a set of components interacting with each other [within a boundary that] . . . possesses the property of filtering both the kinds and rate of flow of inputs and outputs to and from the system."[76]

Martin and O'Connor assert that all systems have five characteristics: (1) Its component parts are linked or interrelated in some form of organization. (2) Events that happen to one part of a system affect all parts in mutual causality. (3) The component parts are related together in a time period long enough for them to display constancy or stability. (4) Systems take up physical space and are tangible realities that can be observed and measured. (5) Systems have boundaries that set them off from other systems and from their environment.[77] Many systems theories use ideas and terminology derived from physical or mechanical systems and biological systems concepts. However, it is important to understand that social systems differ from mechanical or biological systems.

Mechanical Systems   The social systems perspective is based on the idea that society operates in ways that are similar to the hierarchy of mechanical systems that extend from the smallest atom to gigantic galaxies. Just as clockworks, each social system is presumed to operate by laws of physics including inertia, entropy, and synergy as well as utilizing input, output, and feedback processes. For example, *inertia* is the principle that an object will remain in its current state. If an object is moving, it will continue to move. If it is not moving, it will tend to remain in its immobile state. Systems theorists assert that inertia explains why social systems are difficult to change or to stop. *Entropy* means that every object will tend to reach its lowest point of energy. Systems are prone to eventually wearing out or breaking down. Entropy presumes to help us understand that social systems need fresh inputs and new energy to prevent breakdown. *Synergy* means that the whole is more than the sum of its parts. Systems once established are capable of combining parts that create an entirely different set of characteristics than those that remain separate. In the same way, when people combine together, they generate ideas, activities, and power that individuals acting alone cannot.

In addition, just as physical systems need inputs, provide outputs, and use feedback, social system needs *input* in the form of information, resources, abilities, and skills. They also provide *outputs* such as relationships, social capital, and social goods. *Feedback* helps the system regulate itself and correct errors. Social systems provide feedback by communication.

Biological Systems Model   Social ecology is systems theory derived from biology that helps explain how people interact in their social environment. In addition to being subject to the laws of physics, biological systems experience growth, adaptation, and interaction with their environment. Homeostasis, for example, "suggests that most living systems seek a balance to maintain and preserve the system."[78] Just as biological systems, social systems are assumed to

develop according to relatively predictable patterns often called a "life cycle." You will discover in Chapter 4, for example, that groups move through a life cycle of change, and in Chapter 14 that social movements also follow a cyclic pattern of development.

Many who adopt social ecological theory tend to see people as responding organisms who adapt to and are determined by systems processes in their wider social environment. They believe systems concepts are useful because they "give us a method of conceptualizing a great deal of complexity."[79] For example, systems theory provide a perception that people are products of social stimuli that cause them to react in often similar and predictable ways.[80]

Social Systems Model   Although social systems are presumed to share certain properties of mechanical and biological systems, they also have their own unique characteristics. For example, Martin and O'Conner assert that, "unlike biological systems, social systems are disorderly, loosely organized, and rarely governed by obvious principles or rational goals. Social systems can change in more fundamental ways than biological systems can."[81] Social systems are "open systems" that "exchange continuously with other systems and their environments."[82] Social systems accept inputs such as members and information from their environment and continuously generate outputs such as products, services, and ideas. Social systems are always in a process of interaction, change, and adaptation.

Systems Defects   Systems theorists view defects that occur in social systems including mechanical breakdown, inadequate response to change, slowness in adaptation, and the unintended consequences of decisions as potential causes of social problems.

Systems Breakdown   Systems theorists assume that although society is generally good and healthy, it sometimes develops defects such as when a system experiences entropy or when one component gets out of sync with other system components. Sometimes the feedback loops break down. For example, one of the causes of the Great Depression was the belief that it was not the function of government to regulate the economy. When the economy went into a tailspin, government had few feedback tools at its disposal to diagnose and prevent market failure. Since then, however, government has initiated many feedback mechanisms that continually monitor economic indicators and regularly adjust interest rates, tax rates, and money supply for the effects of inflation and recession.

Inadequate Response to Change   Social ecologists see social problems as malfunctions that occur in one part or another of social systems as they attempt to adjust to growth in their environments. For example, because of improvements in technology, people's job skills may become outmoded. This puts pressure on society to continually provide the means for people to upgrade their abilities and adjust to changing job markets. If this does not happen adequately enough, pools of unemployed and unemployable people will become a continual drain on the economy, creating economic slowdown and increasing social welfare costs.

Slowness of Adaptation   The rapidity of changes in the environment of a social system may outstrip its ability to adjust. The more quickly change occurs, the shorter the amount of time people in systems have to forecast all of the possible outcomes of change strategies. Employees in organizational systems that undergo many changes in rules or policies in a short time may experience a breakdown in communication. Feedback may be unable keep pace with change, leading to ineffective service delivery and employee stress. Certain areas of cities that experience the most rapid changes may have disproportionately high rates of vice, crime, family breakdown, and people with emotional disabilities.

The deinstitutionalization of large psychiatric hospitals and institutions for persons with developmental disabilities in the 1970s in many parts of the United States flooded cities with so many people with handicapping conditions in a short period of time that social workers and service providers were unable to accommodate them all, creating a crisis for clients, service providers, and social workers alike. Societies that are unable to adapt quickly enough to immigration, urbanization, industrialization or globalization, for example, may begin to develop social breakdown.[83]

Unintended Consequences of Decisions   Systems problems also occur because decision makers fail to understand all of the consequences of decisions they make. These latent social problems occur because decision makers may lack complete information or because they cannot predict all of the possible outcomes of systems processes.[84] Medical science, for example, is increasingly able to decrease infant mortality.

Physicians are now able to prevent many premature infant deaths. Some of these infants with birth defects and genetic disorders who otherwise may have died now survive. The ability of medical science to save lives is paradoxically contributing to the unintended consequence of increasing the number of children with severe handicapping conditions.

Systems Deviance Model and Social Work   The systems deviance model can be very useful to macro social workers. Systems theories help us understand why social systems resist change and are often difficult to correct. The systems deviance model can assist macro social workers in pinpointing early signs of systems dysfunction and help us understand the process by which systems defects can be corrected. However, social workers must also realize that organizational managers may use systems theory to disguise authentic causes of social problems. Social workers must not be naïve when managers blame systems defects for causing social problems.

Resist Change   When working with social systems, macro social workers must understand that the forces of inertia, homeostasis, and entropy work against systems change. In addition, "what makes definitive change so enormously difficult," Perry states, is that "each system from the richest to the poorest, is constructed out of networks of interlocking forces and institutions that maintain it, and keep it in its recognizable form."[85] Furthermore, "a poor community is maintained in its impoverished form by a network of self-reinforcing processes and practices, and any attempt to change one part of the network is opposed by the other forces that keep the community the way it is and neutralize the attempted improvement.[86]

Difficult to Correct   Social systems are difficult to fix when problems occur. Perry says, for example, "[a] strategy for change that selects just one part of the community as a focus for improvement . . . is likely to be neutered in the long run by the rest of the community influences. . . . Any effective strategy has to consider many parts of the network of interlocking community influences and deal with them more or less simultaneously or at least in interconnected phases so that the different parts no longer neutralize improvements but actually reinforce the change."[87]

Warning Signs   Social problems are to some extent inevitable, but they are also correctable. Problems that occur in a part of a system are warning signs that tell us where we need to focus our efforts in making that system work better. If system entropy occurs, for example, social workers look for systems dysfunction in the input system, the processing system, or system outputs. When lack of information makes decision making difficult or leads to incorrect decisions, systems managers often look for defects in the feedback system. They scan the environment for sources of increased information inputs and review the feedback systems for communication breakdown or the effectiveness of passing information quickly throughout the system.

Systems Change Strategies　　Change agents use systems theory to devise strategies for change. One strategy based on systems theory that you will learn about in Chapter 14, for example, includes unfreezing dysfunctional system patterns, changing them into new, more effective patterns and then refreezing the new processes.

Disguise Real Causes of Problems　　Social workers must be aware that those who are in charge of the megastructures of society sometimes use systems theory to disguise the real causes of social problems. Some social theorists, for example, propose that what appear to be mere "latent" or unintended consequences of social systems may actually be *intentionally* constructed components of the system. Charles Perrow, for example, reports that once a social system is in place, it sustains the values and goals of those in control of that social system.[88] In our society, those in positions of power are rational and goal maximizing. They mobilize their values and seek advantage by calculating the benefits and costs of achieving their goals. Social problems do not always occur because social change has outstripped the ability of social systems to adjust, because a feedback loop has broken down, or because systems components fail to fit properly. Neither do negative systems outcomes occur because owners or managers lack information, are unaware of the consequences of their decisions, or are unable to predict outcomes.

Ecological problems such as air pollution or pesticide poisoning in a community water supply, for example, are not merely the unintentional consequences of technology that have occurred as well-meaning corporate managers provide us with goods and services. Powerful owners and managers are very well aware of the consequences of the social systems

they command and intentionally create the conditions under which they operate.[89] They anticipate all of the possible outcomes of every decision they make. They calculate the financial costs of decisions such as lawsuits, court costs, fines, taxes, and penalties and include them in the costs of doing business. If the projected cost-benefit ratio is favorable to corporate profits, they may continue to follow policies that harm the environment, maintain poor working conditions, fail to pay living wages, or exploit laborers even if those decisions may be harmful to the public at large.

Avoid Naiveté　　Social workers who do not understand that systems can be and often are used for inhuman purposes will be unable to solve the real social problems that systems create. Social workers must not be naive about the systems they are trying to correct. The claim that corporations are beyond reproach because something goes wrong with otherwise well-intentioned decisions or that social problems are the result of the failure of social systems in adjusting to social conditions beyond their control is often a mask for simple denial or an attempt to evade responsibility.[90] Owners of large corporations or managers of governmental systems may claim ignorance or blame systems problems for the harm they do. More insidiously, they may hold society hostage to processes that are socially harmful because we are socialized to believe we cannot do without the benefits they provide for us.

The challenge for macro social workers using a systems model to solve social problems is to be sensitive in observing whom the system serves and protects. Is the system serving a latent function that advantages some at the expense of others? Are intentional patterns of exploitation, greed, or injustice masquerading as unintended consequences or as mere ignorance? Is there an implication that the system is its own justification and is beyond criticism?

Social Cultural Premises Model

The social cultural premises model assumes that society can be best understood as a conscious, planned construct. People intentionally create societal structures, laws, and governance out of common understandings about meaning and the values that they want to maintain. People are not helpless or determined beings molded by natural societal forces to which they are subject or over which they have little control. Rather, as the social pragmatists argue, although a person's "situation confronts him with limitations and problems, he is the one who struggles to understand his situation, to master it, and to utilize it for the realization of his interests."[91] "Human behavior involves the interpretation of events or phenomena and the sharing of those interpretations with others,"[92] and human society "rests upon a basis of consensus, i.e., the sharing of meanings in the form of common understanding and expectation."[93]

"The cultural perspective assumes that human behavior is guided by patterns of basic assumptions, expectations, and customs that develop over time and slowly drop out of people's conscious awareness,"[94] Holland states. These patterns become habits that continue to influence people even when the social environment changes. Society, therefore, reflects the key ideologies and ways of thinking that were built into it in the first place, and those premises become interpreted and reinterpreted by succeeding generations. Today's modern culture is based, for the most part, on ideas generated out of the European Enlightenment, but for many thinkers, the premises of Enlightenment philosophy have led to a false consciousness.

Enlightenment Philosophy   Frank Coleman asserts that the social failures of American political institutions are "a permanent blindness fixed in the nature of the institutions and the social philosophy used to design them."[95] The social philosophy to which Coleman refers is contained in the heritage of Enlightenment philosophy and cherished social ideologies of modernity that have shaped "the consciousness of a whole people through our national inheritance" and manifest themselves "in characteristic and unvarying ways related to the American constitutional philosophy."[96] Among the staple tenets of American political belief, Richard Hofstadter says, are the powerful legacies of possessive individualism, radical self-interest, and the value of competition, and the substitution of the public good for allegiance to the rights of property.[97]

False Consciousness   The modern culture many people have internalized tends to be a "false consciousness" that presents a massive presence of such strength, according to Peter Berger, that it is often difficult to change. Coleman and Hofstadter claim that the fundamental beliefs that most Americans cherish

are, in reality, the causes of permanent social failure in our political and institutional landscape, which, says Coleman, has become a "total ideology that could not be challenged or even questioned."[98]

Social Work Activism and the Social Cultural Premises Model   Social workers make use of the social cultural premises model to change the premises on which many governmental decisions are made by means of social activism and mass social movements. For example, the green movement and the ecology movement attempt to sensitize people about the endangered natural environment. They work to shift people's thinking from viewing the earth's ecosystems as a source of plunder and exploitation to a sustainable environment that protects the world's resources for future generations. Peace activists work to change the mentality of nations who purchase arms and engage in international conflict. Social workers and others try to change people's attitudes about handguns, urging them to see that the damage to human life they cause is far more destructive than the feelings of security that weapons may provide for people who own them.

Globalization: The Developmental Model

A major cause of social problems in underdeveloped nations is the prevalence of modernization ideology combined with Western political and economic power. According to Mansour Fakih, "the ideas of modernization and developmentalism create a hegemony of thinking that distorts human consciousness."[99] Modernization hegemony is an organizing principle or worldview diffused by modern complex organizations, including universities, corporations, and governments, that supports the rationalization of world processes and inserts premises of ideological control, domination, and patriarchy into every area of human life. The modernization or developmentalist worldview has created a climate in which people incorporate into their consciousness the pretense that economic growth, representative democracy, wealth accumulation, interest-group liberalism, and a host of other modern premises are the epitome of civilization.

Modernization Theory   Modernization is an approach to comparative history that emerged in the

1960s as the dominant explanation of societal change. Modernization theory proposes that the progressive development of history moves in a straight line from the past to the present, involving the replacement of premodern economies, ways of thinking, and modes of communal human association with market economies, rational thinking, and modern complex organizations. Social evolution is believed to be an inevitable sequential process in which all urban and modern societies converge as a single societal type, exemplified by liberal democratic capitalist nations of the West.[100] Popular interpreters of this idea, such as Walt Whitman Rostow, assert that society progresses from uncivilized to civilized, from undeveloped to developed, from east to west, culminating in the most modern nations of North America.[101]

Modernization theorists assume that problems of poverty, poor health, and lack of education among "underdeveloped" people lay in their "primitive," less technological, and often agrarian cultures and not in the social conditions they had been forced to accept. The solution to underdevelopment is to change these people's thinking and their premodern economic and political systems by bringing them into the rational modern world as rapidly as possible. Led by the United States, economically developed nations during the 1950s and 1960s attempted to improve "the living standards of the poor in 'stagnant' and 'backward' regions" by massive transfers of capital, technology, and doling out development aid. They tried to "modernize" nations by supporting political regimes that claimed to encourage free enterprise capitalism, industrialization, and urbanization.[102] The cumulative effect of these improvements was expected to automatically "trickle down" to those at the bottom, or else be handed down in an administrative fashion. Public and private material accumulation, along with formal democratic elections, was expected to solve other social problems of the world's impoverished people.[103]

John F. Kennedy, inspired by the modernization model and the success of the Marshall Plan that helped rebuild European economies after World War II, launched the Alliance for Progress in 1961, which pumped billions of dollars into Latin America and was expected to create markets for U.S. products. This top-down development in South America and other regions, however, was an unequivocal failure.[104] "Despite a number of development efforts," asserts Mansour Fakih, "both the absolute number and percentage of the world's people who lived in utter poverty continued to increase."[105] Economic and political experts created poverty instead of eradicating it, and they increased the dependence of these countries within an inequitable global order.[106]

International Social Work and the Globalization Model

Many social workers today are concerned about the massive social problems that exist in developing nations. In spite of the pretense that modernization is the ultimate solution to the world's social problems, social workers understand that it is the cause of them instead. Among these problems is the deterioration of the environment, particularly the destruction of rain forests, oceans, rivers, and lakes. Economic inequality is a major social problem in the global society in which collusion between international economic institutions of the International Monetary Fund and the World Bank, transnational corporations, and national governments develop policies that result in poverty and exploitation of underdeveloped nations. Poverty results in enormous social problems including hunger, disease, homeless children living on the streets in urban areas, trafficking in children and adults, exploitation of child labor, and using children as soldiers. Armed conflict results in millions of refugees who seek help in neighboring countries. AIDS destroys populations and leaves millions of orphans in its wake.

International social workers challenge modernization theory and its underlying premises of racism, patriarchal rule, dominance, and control. We claim the rights of people everywhere to be free from economic oppression and oppose the power of transnational corporations that exploit people in underdeveloped nations. We respect the integrity and the rights of people to develop their own cultures free from the self-interests of corporate capitalism or the imperialism of nation-states. Social workers and many others work with indigenous grassroots organizations (GROs), nongovernmental organizations (NGOs), and others to assist people in strengthening their communities. We assist refugees fleeing from international conflict. We work to eradicate trafficking in humans, especially children. We engage in social movements that help bring about a different way of thinking and being than that offered by the modernization theory of the West.

FOUR APPROACHES TO SOLVING SOCIAL PROBLEMS

Social change often depends on the attitude that leaders and the populace take toward the necessity of solving problems and making social change. Understanding these approaches can assist a macro social worker not only in understanding the positions that differing people take but in clarifying the best stance to take on the issues that confront people in a locality or in larger segments of society. Most people face the social issues that confront them in one of four ways:

1. Reactive problem solving to restore the past

2. Inactive problem solving to preserve the present

3. Proactive problem solving to accelerate the future

4. Interactive problem solving to create a just society[107]

Reactive Approach

Reactive problem solving is often linear, sequential, and tries to solve problems that occur one at a time. Much modern problem solving is reactive in nature. For example, reactive problem solvers often use a mechanistic systems model to "try to re-create a previous state of the system by unmaking changes that have converted the system state into one that they find less desirable."[108] They spend a great deal of energy fixing what is broken in social systems by identifying problems and designing solutions that restore the system's stable state. Once the system is repaired, they are satisfied if it continues to run as smoothly as it did before the breakdown occurred.

Critics of the Reactive Approach to Problem Solving
Critics of reactive problem solving point out that this approach focuses only on fixing problems after the fact, looks to the past, uses simplistic thinking, employs moral blame, or blames technological progress.

After the Fact Reactive problem solving engages in issues after the fact. Reactive problem solving assumes that the current system function is simply in need of repair, ignoring the fact that the social environment may have changed and that the solution is not repair but adaptation. The process of diagnosing a social problem long after its inception is often impossible. Correcting a problem after it has become entrenched in the social and cultural environment is not only costly but difficult and time consuming.

Look to the Past Reactivists tend to look to a simpler, less complicated past, which becomes their operative reality. As a result, they may tune out significant aspects of the causes of social problems, pretending that by holding onto an imaginary past they can exclude the pain of the present and minimize the struggles of the future. Reactivists in the Old South, for example, contended that African Americans were happy and contented as slaves. Disturbing this equilibrium would only cause disharmony and conflict. Things should be left as they were.

Simplistic Thinking Reactivists utilize thinking that is simplistic, sequential, and unidirectional in nature. Rational problem solving, about which you will learn in Chapter 3, is a sequential model that uses one mode of thinking, that of cognition. Mechanistic systems metaphors are also dominated by sequential processes that progress from past to the future. People whose thinking is dominated by these processes tend to see social issues one by one, as if they were highly discrete and operate independently of each other. They fail to see that just as social systems are interactive in nature, social problems are the result of systems interactions as well. One cannot simply solve one problem and then go on to the next. Instead, "action taken to resolve one problem may render ineffective or harmful the actions taken to resolve another. . . . Because the causes of social problems interact synergistically, the focus of solving social problems should be on their interactions, not just on their separate reactions."[109]

Moral Blame Reactivists sometimes assume that behaviors of the present are the result of abandonment of values of the past. When reactivists see social problems as the eradication of the social evil that contaminates society, they sometimes become obsessed with moral blame rather than practical reality. Attacking social evil sometimes results in entrenching the very problems that reactivists want to eliminate. Prohibitionists, for example, attempted to destroy saloons, cripple alcohol manufacture, outlaw alcohol consumption, and interdict illicit trafficking in alcohol. Rather than resolving the problem of alcoholism in the United States, prohibition not only failed to curb drinking but also criminalized a large percentage of the American population, created a lucrative market for illicit alcohol products, and ultimately resulted in the rise of organized crime.

Blame Technology Reactivists sometimes have blamed technology for less than desirable conditions. During the early years of the Industrial Revolution in England, the Luddites attacked new factories being built because they were convinced that technology was destroying the quality of life.

Macro Social Work and the Reactive Approach

Macro social workers who take a reactivist approach should ask themselves whether a return to a previous state is needed or even desirable. When social workers or other problem solvers concentrate only on getting rid of what they do not want, what they consider to be morally wrong, what does not work, or become suspicious of progress, they "may not get what they do want, but may, instead, get something much worse, . . . [The] removal or suppression of a problem or dysfunction in the present state does not guarantee a return to a previous state."[110] Rather than merely eradicate or eliminate aspects of current reality that are creating difficulty, solutions need to include reshaping or changing systems to more desirable patterns.

Inactive Approach

Unlike reactivists who want to restore a past state of affairs, inactivists work hard at preventing change. Inactivists seek to maintain the status quo and keep things just as they are. Inactivists face the future by putting on the brakes. The inactive approach conserves the present by preventing change. The world may not be perfect, but it is good enough. Implicit in the inactivist approach is a kind of social Darwinism that assumes that social systems naturally "evolve" by means of the laws of natural selection and survival of the fittest. It is not only easier but actually better, in the long run, so proponents claim, to let "nature take its course," to leave things alone, particularly though not exclusively, in the economy. Inactivists believe that meddling with the natural course of events creates most of our problems. Inactivists try to prevent change in the political process, economy, and society as a whole.

Political Inactivism

Inactivism does not mean "not acting." Political inactivists work very hard to

prevent social action that results in change. A large number of people must be kept busy without actually accomplishing anything, or they must be kept busy keeping others from doing something. Inactivist policy makers, for example, set up commissions and committees that study problems, then do nothing, giving the illusion of progress while delaying it at the same time. Inactivist administrators use bureaucracy to wrap processes in red tape, obfuscating and delaying decisions. Inactivist presidents use the veto to stop the work of Congress, delaying what may have taken congressional committees and the joint action of the Senate and the House months of work. Inactivist politicians waste time by blaming others for problems and by engaging in endless and fruitless debates about what went wrong, the object of which is to diffuse the problem and to justify their own inaction.

Economic Inactivism

Economic inactivists claim that government intervention in the economy by regulation, taxation, and redistributing wealth only distorts natural laws of supply and demand. In the aggregate, economic inactivists argue, while some may be disadvantaged in the short run, society is better off when the free market is allowed to control itself.

Social Inactivism

This laissez-faire inactivist approach also extends into the social sector. Inactivists recommend that government should not play a role in social intervention including social planning, funding and operating social programs, or providing social services. If people want or need such services, they should be provided voluntarily. Money that is appropriated by taxation for social programs only distorts the economy and artificially diverts resources to support those who drain the economy. Moreover, public schools, libraries, parks, and other public services are best provided by the private sector and paid for by those who use them rather than by all taxpayers.

Critics of Inactivist Approach

Critics of the inactivist approach claim that inactivism is incapable and even opposed to making fundamental changes in the social environment. Instead inactivists tend to perpetuate a social system in the direction it is headed or make modest improvements in it. They blame victims or activists for social problems. Inactivists react to problems by law and order solutions or by crisis management.

Person or Activist Blame   Burdened by the consequences of their perspective, many inactivists blame victims such as those in poverty as the cause of problems and those who protest social injustice as destroyers of the social fabric. Inactivist power figures punish people who threaten the existing social order or who act out defiantly against its rules and practices. Officials in the segregationist South blamed "agitators" from the North for civil rights demonstrations. Others harassed and even murdered African American protestors as if activists rather than political disenfranchisement, discrimination, and the unfair labor practices that racism created were the cause of citizen unrest.

Law and Order Solutions   Inactivist politicians and policy makers see social problems in simplistic and synoptic ways. Their perspective often limits them to "law and order" solutions in the form of more laws, harsher penalties for lawbreakers, larger police forces, increased military budgets, and larger and more numerous prisons. They tend to be incapable of recognizing that these remedies, rather than solving, may add to problems and prevent solutions.

Crisis Management   Inactivist decision makers allow unattended social problems to pile up to the point where they cannot be ignored. Because inactivist decision makers try to put off decisions, they tend to respond to serious threats by engaging in what has come to be known as "crisis management." Inactivists act when necessary for survival or stability but do no more than is required to "turn off the heat." "Crisis management focuses on suppressing symptoms rather than on curing ailments."[111]

Macro Social Work and the Inactivist Approach

Inactivist governmental and corporate managers relegate social welfare services to a subsidiary maintenance role of "filling in the gap" where the market has failed. The welfare system and social planners are expected to clean up the damage such as unemployment and poverty that the market economy has left in its wake. Rather than get at the roots of social problems, social welfare from an inactivist perspective simply "picks up the pieces" by treating or remediating people who are the fallout of systems processes, allowing the system to continue on its course. Inactivists often seen social work as an adjunct to the economy, "balancing social welfare resources to meet social welfare needs"[112] to keep the system going.

Macro social workers, however, tend to reject placing the profession of social work in the role of colluding with oppression or collaborating in maintaining an unequal and unjust system. Rather than appeasement, macro social workers empower people whom the economy disadvantages and join with them to change social structures that create social problems. Macro social workers assist people in making social change rather than prevent it.

Understanding the inactivist approach, however, can assist macro social workers become sensitive to the ways that public officials and those in the corporate sector attempt to coopt social workers, using them and social service programs to further system maintenance rather than system change.

Proactive Approach

Proactivists are not satisfied with reverting to a less complicated past like reactivists or keeping things as they are like inactivists. The watchwords of proactivists are "future oriented." They are invested in growth and technology and often see politics as an exciting game whose goal is to win.

Future Oriented   Proactivists are forward looking. Not content merely to seek "good enough" solutions, proactivists want to optimize. They try to solve rather than resolve, accelerate movement into the future rather than slow it down, and encourage change instead of resist it. For them, the future is filled with opportunity. Change is virtually synonymous with progress.

Proactive leaders attempt to forecast alternative futures and spend considerable time researching and anticipating. They tend to ride a precarious wave of future events. Proactivists approach the future by predicting and preparing. Of the two, the most crucial is prediction, because they know that if their calculations are wrong, "then the preparation, no matter how good, is either ineffective or harmful. On the other hand, even if preparation for a correctly predicted future is less than perfect, one is likely to be better off with [the calculations] than without them."[113] Proactivist problem solvers "try harder to avoid missing opportunities (acts of omission) than doing something wrong."[114] It is better, claim proactivists, to ask forgiveness than permission.

Growth and Technology   Proactivists encourage and facilitate technology as a crucial weapon in the game and tend to be enamored with its possibilities. Proactivists also become excited by growth for its own sake. "Growth is the ultimate objective of proactivists: to become the largest, wealthiest, strongest."[115] Proactivist problem solvers attempt to squeeze growth out of the economy, shaping its confines to political and social goals of survival and dominance rather than letting the economy shape the society as inactivists tend to do.

Politics as a Game

Proactivists as political "gamespersons" enjoy using social and political systems in contests of power and progress, quickly moving systems further into modernity. In the calculus of winning, proactive gamespersons focus on indicators such as the standard of living, wealth accumulation, and acquisition of power to reach a goal first with the most. To the extent that social problems create a drag on the system, proactivists engage in social problem solving with some gusto, employing progressive examination and active social experimentation, particularly if there is evidence of a clear payoff for them.

Macro Social Work and the Proactivist Approach

Proactivist problem solvers are excited by change, progress, and its attendant components of power, success, and achievement for their own sakes. In this sense, proactivists are authentic modernists who revel in technology, speed, wealth, and size. Although much good can come through progress and change, macro social workers also understand that what some consider to be progress others may view as overriding their interests, particularly when progress is imposed from the top and ultimately benefits those in power.

Many macro international social workers have seen the effects of so-called progress in developing nations. In India they have watched as massive systems of dams have left many homeless, deprived them of their livelihood, their land and culture, and destroyed the environment. The citizens of Bhopal continue to suffer the ravages of progress as pesticides poison their land and water. Indians in Bolivia have seen how progress has stolen their natural resources and left them destitute. Social workers support social change when those changes occur from the bottom up, are in service of the people who make those changes, and when the benefits of social change accrue to all citizens equally.

Interactive Approach

Persons using the interactivist approach borrow concepts from social ecology that assert that individuals, groups, communities, and society interact together synergistically to form a whole. In this interaction, each part is interconnected, necessary, and essential. Interactivists also use ideas from symbolic interaction theory, such as that the glue that binds people together comprises the social goods of relationship, honesty, trust, responsibility, genuineness, compassion, and caring generated by *gemeinschaft,* or we relations.

Interactivists do not resolve problems as do reactivists or solve problems as do proactivists. They want to *dissolve* problems. Dissolving social problems requires changing the institution, community, organization, system, or culture in which the problem is embedded in such a way as to eliminate the issue.

In the same way, rather than looking to the past to discover what went wrong as do reactivists, interactivists look ahead to see what is possible as do proactivists. Unlike proactivists, however, interactivists move beyond simple prediction and preparation. Interactivist macro social workers want to create a sustainable, equitable future, shaping not only its design but also its internal culture.

Interactive social workers seek technical solutions where possible, as do proactivists, but infuse social change with value content, consciously applying social reason to scan social systems and adjusting plans as the situation changes. Interactivists aim to not only achieve a goal but also to make quality decisions. Interactive problem solving uses a strengths and assets perspective and is participation oriented, flexible, and value centered.

Strengths and Assets Perspective

Ann Weick and Dennis Saleeby assert that, in fundamental ways, "the strength perspective changes the modernist heritage of psychopathology and problem solving which has permeated social work practice for a significant part of this century."[116] Rather than perceive themselves as "problems" or their communities as deficit laden, people see themselves as having multitudes of possibilities and opportunities they can use to construct themselves and build a civic society. Instead of weaknesses, pathologies, and problems, people are seen as having strengths, being growth enhancing, and having solutions with which to build their own futures. Instead of assuming communities are arenas of neglect, crime, and poverty, the community is perceived as full of resources and assets that can be used to make a better society.

The strengths approach, like the interactivist approach, harnesses nonmaterial assets and resources such as people's participation, community support, and naturally occurring social networks and combines these strengths into organized community programs around issues of common concern. Both focus on the development of human and social capital and recognize the importance of involving people in their own development. Social workers using the strengths approach begin with the premise that members of the community know best. They are the experts, not the professionals. Both models maintain an inherent faith in people and their propensity to find their own solutions to life's challenges. Just as in the interactive approach, the social work strengths model provides the critical edge for empowerment practice.[117]

Each approach recognizes the resilience of people to rise above their surroundings and hope. Weick and Saleeby claim that "to examine the strengths and resiliencies of people in their everyday lives signals . . . an important shift in our thinking."[118] When this happens, often with the help of a macro social worker, people begin to gain power. The assets-based strength approach often begins with a process of community engagement where the community worker is a facilitator and partner in helping the community unleash its collective potential. Both focus on assets and resources rather than needs and problems.

Participation Oriented
Networking is extremely important to the interactivist perspective, bringing together people with similar interests, talents, skills, and knowledge to work cooperatively. Interactive macro social work is based on the idea that "all those who are intended to benefit from solving social problems should be given an opportunity to participate in it . . . that more development takes place by engaging in problem solving than as a result of the implementation of solutions."[119] Democratic, participatory, and people centered, the interactive approach stems from a view that social justice requires that people be given equal access to society's resources and self-determination in making decisions that affect them and their communities.

Flexible
Interactive problem solving takes into account that plans, even those based on technology, never work out exactly as expected. Interactivists recognize that there are often both good and bad unintended consequences of decisions. Implementation requires, therefore, that the critical assumptions on which any plan is based be explicitly formulated, checked frequently, and changed when necessary. For example, as a group moves toward meeting its goals using a planned strategy of action, they will inevitably encounter difficulties and learn how to overcome obstacles. As they talk together about their common experiences, new tactics or different strategies may occur to them that may be more successful. Rather than continuing with their original plan, they may change directions or try new approaches.

Dangers of Sunk Costs
Because organizations are powerful systems, there is always a tendency to allow previous decisions and sunk costs to determine future action. (Sunk costs are money, time, and effort already sunk into projects.) Sometimes projects that have negative outcomes are continued merely because of the resources already expended on them. One of the reasons for the government's resistance to ending the futile war in Vietnam was the perception that victory could still be achieved by just a little more effort, a bit more progress, and then all of the expense and the lives lost would be justified. People using interactive problem solving, on the other hand, are flexible, learn from the challenges they face, and adapt to new and changing conditions.

Value Centered
Social welfare decisions inevitably include values and ethics. Unlike reactivists who are committed to values of the past, inactivists who are bound to values of the present, or proactivists who are enamored by values inherent in growth, power, and technology, social workers using the interactive approach accept certain values as of overall importance but shift the way those values are implemented. Interactivists believe that social problem solving must be morally acute and that the values implicit in decisions be sensitive to the changing social climate. In the 1850s, for example, killing a whale was socially sanctioned, but now it is a morally contentious issue. Technologically improved ways to kill whales, increased demand for whale products, and the near extinction of whale species have occurred, requiring people to shift their perspective.

Hazards of Growth Unlimited growth may have been a worthy goal at one point in our history. But unless mediated by other worthy ends, such as environmental quality, growth becomes self-defeating or even disastrous. Interactivist social workers desire growth only if it contributes to the development of people and is consistent with the welfare of the entire social and sustainable ecological milieu.

ANSWERS THAT WON'T WORK

Sometimes the answers people arrive at to our social problems may delude, blind, or prevent us from solving them. Sometimes those mechanisms are so strong that people, especially those in positions of power, condone or perpetuate the very problems they pretend to solve.

Macro social workers must seek answers that work. We must be honest with ourselves and with others when we look for answers. We must be aware that in spite of our good intentions, we may subscribe to a range of illusions about social problems that exacerbate rather than solve them. We must learn to recognize these escapes to illusion. Among these are social denial, avoidance, blaming, moralizing, and the quick fix.

Social Denial

Denial takes many forms. We refuse to acknowledge the existence of social problems. When we do admit their existence, we look at them as "personal" problems instead of "social" problems. We also deny their existence by excluding problem people from our lives, or by rationalizing our inaction.

Refuse to Admit the Problem Exists A major form of denial in our society is our refusal to admit that social problems exist. Many people in the United States did not consider economic exploitation and ethnic intolerance to be social problems at all. If anything, the exploitation of women, children, and immigrants, the extermination of Native Americans, and the enslavement of Africans were seen as necessary adjuncts to the economic development of North America. How many social problems can you think of whose seriousness or existence people, especially those in positions of leadership, have either denied or

justified as necessary for a higher purpose? What processes or techniques would you recommend when corporate or governmental organizations engage in social denial or rationalize social harm for the common good?

Exclude Reality Excluding reality operates by the maxim "out of sight, out of mind." What we do not see and experience is not part of our reality, and therefore not our problem. We relocated Native Americans to reservations, Chinese to Chinatowns, and Japanese Americans to concentration camps. We effectively banished intellectually, developmentally, and emotionally disabled people from our awareness by placing them in large institutions. Segregation in the South before the Civil Rights Act attempted to use this form of denial as a way of dealing with race relations.

Rationalize One form of rationalizing is the "yes, but" game. Some rationalizations are: "Yes, gangs are rampant, but more social programs will not make them go away." "Yes, there are few services for children, but throwing more money at social problems is not the answer." "Yes, our cities are deteriorating, but we tried community development in the 1960s and we still have the problem." "Yes, poor people need medical care, but a national health care system will only make inefficient medical care worse and cost too much money."

Avoidance

We tend to avoid responsibility for social problems because it may be in our own interests to do so, because they are too difficult to face, or because we are implicated in the social milieu that creates or condones them. Sometimes we avoid social problems by ignoring them, hoping they will go away or waiting until people adjust to their condition.

Avoid Responsibility Corporations tend not to see themselves as a cause of poverty but rather as a cause of prosperity. In addition, the political system sees itself not as preventing change but as developing solutions to society's problems. To the contrary, however, as Coleman states, "The political system in America is marvelously well designed to enable actors to evade responsibility for events such as energy waste and widespread pollution, even when these events are the products of decisions they have made."[120]

Society Heal Thyself   One form of avoidance is to insist that if you ignore problems eventually they will go away. It is easy to delude ourselves that by waiting long enough social problems will either diminish on their own or become someone else's problem. This laissez-faire approach to social problems expects the powerless to turn down the lamp of reason and rely on the operation of a benevolent social system that will ultimately work things out in their interest.

Time Heals All Wounds   If we give things time, some argue, the naturally self-correcting mechanisms of the social body will cure the problem. Although there may be short-term pain or difficulties for certain groups, they say, if we have faith in economic and political systems, everything will work out in the long run.

Social Adaptation   A more subtle variation of the time heals all wounds strategy is the idea that the longer society puts things off, the more people will adapt and accept their lot. They will eventually forget injustices and learn to live with their social condition. As they adjust, however, they form a culture of victimization in which powerlessness becomes part of their milieu. The more people act the role of victims, the more they reinforce their stereotyped roles, becoming unwilling or unable to gain resources for themselves. Delaying and avoiding dealing with social problems always works in favor of those in power.

Blaming

Blaming others is a way of deflecting responsibility from those who create social problems to those who bear their effects. Those in power have honed this strategy to a fine point. There is no dearth of targets of blame. We can blame the victim, we can blame the providers, we can blame the reformers, among other targets. These strategies always result in a dead end.

Blame the Victim   Sometimes people blame the victim for problems beyond his or her control and then try to change the individual's behavior to conform to social norms. They say that it is the fault of the poor that they are poor: The poor are lazy, undisciplined, and lack personal initiative. Peter Breggin asserts, for example, that many mental health social workers have participated in blaming child victims by diagnosing them as having histories of neglect or abuse and then drugging and hospitalizing them, taking "the pressure off the parents, the family, the school and the society."[121]

Blame the Provider   People charged with the responsibility of solving problems are sometimes blamed for their cause. "We have too many bureaucrats." "There is too much inefficiency, too much red tape, too much regulation, too much interference, too much government." These games beg the question of the real locus of social problems.

Blame the Reformers   Sometimes social change agents are blamed for causing social problems. Socialists, pacifists, social activists, protesters, union organizers, community organizers, and a host of social reformers have been vilified as malcontents and subversives who disturb social stability and undermine the social order. Many of these reformers have been harassed, jailed, and even murdered.

Pass the Buck   Sometimes those wanting to exonerate themselves for their complicity with oppression or to further their own ambitions use social problems as a means for their ends. Crimes, welfare, or racial intolerance often become the focus of political campaigns. One politician blames another for being "soft on crime" or for the "welfare mess." The president blames Congress, or Congress blames the president. One political party blames the other. Social problems become political footballs. After an election has been won, however, and one politician or political party gains power, concern for resolving the social problem often seems to evaporate.

Scapegoating   A social group may be blamed for the existence of a social problem even when they are its victims. You have discovered by reading the short history of a social problem how any number of ethnic groups have been unfairly targeted as "problems" and blamed for situations caused by conditions in the social environment over which they had no control. The French, for example, were blamed for subversion, Native Americans for impeding the onward march of opening the West to settlement, African Americans for resisting enslavement, Chinese for causing recessions, and Japanese for threatening national security. Racially identifiable groups who have little power and few resources can easily become targets of scapegoating and racial hysteria.

Moralizing

Those people who do not meet the moral standards of people in power may be perceived as not deserving help. People who are destitute, for example, have been divided into the "deserving" poor and the "undeserving" poor. Those we consider deserving will receive help; those not worthy will receive little or nothing. Retribution sometimes follows this way of thinking. In the retribution game, those enmeshed in social problems are made to pay. Punish welfare recipients by reducing payments, passing residency requirements, and increasing restrictions as incentives for people to get off welfare. Punish criminals by longer, harsher sentences. Once freed, label them so that they will find it even more difficult to find a job or succeed in overcoming the issues that led to being imprisoned.

The Quick Fix

Most social problems are perpetuated by years of reinforcement, neglect, and denial. Those who propose one-shot, short-term, stop-gap solutions and expect an immediate turnaround set up social change efforts for failure. Johnson's War on Poverty, begun in the 1960s, was dismantled by the Nixon administration after only a few years and has been blamed for problems plaguing our cities 30 years later. The illusion that long-standing social problems can be solved by a quick fix ultimately leads to discouragement and anger.

CONCLUSION

In this chapter you examined several definitions of social problems and arrived at your own perceptions of them. You explored the history of one social problem and discovered that ethnic intolerance has been a permanent fixture in the history of the American experience. You discovered that while suspicion and discrimination were specifically targeted at some groups for relatively short periods of time, intolerance was expressed without letup against Native Americans, Hispanic Americans, and African Americans wherever they lived and throughout the entirety of their history in American society. Against these citizens

intolerance was invariably ruthless, mostly overt, and at times violent.

You have explored nine assumptions about why social problems occur, reviewed four different approaches people take to solving social problems, and looked at a number of solutions that will not work. Macro social workers understand that for social problems to be solved, we must have an adequate understanding of society's role in creating social problems, and we must not be naive about the ways decision makers justify, minimize, evade, deny, and even perpetuate them.

Macro social workers assert that elimination of many of our social problems requires the active social engagement of people in the processes that contribute to the construction of social reality. We work with communities of people who are building on their hopes and dreams, their visions, and their strengths to make better neighborhoods and a better society. We see communities in terms of their resources and assets rather than in terms of their deficits and weaknesses. People can move ahead and construct a world that is theirs to achieve, and macro social workers stand beside them in the struggle for a better life.

KEY CONCEPTS

conventional definition of social problems

macro social work definition of social problems

ethnic intolerance

trail of tears

Alien, Sedition, and Naturalization Act of 1798

manifest destiny

Mexican American War

Treaty of Guadalupe Hidalgo (1848)

William Lloyd Garrison

American Anti-Slavery Society

Fugitive Slave Act

Dred Scott decision of 1857

John Brown

Civil War

Emancipation Proclamation of 1862

black codes

Plessy v. Ferguson

Anti-Chinese Coolie Association

Chinese Exclusion Act

Alien Land Act, 1913

Executive Order 3906

assumptions about social problems

organizational deviance model

commodification

objectification

dehumanization

reification

intergroup conflict
  model

federalism

interest group liberalism

institutional deviance
  model

systems deviance model

mechanical systems
  model

inertia

entropy

synergy

input

output

feedback

biological systems
  model

social ecology

social systems model

open systems

systems defects

unintended
  consequences

social cultural premises
  model

enlightenment

false consciousness

globalization

developmental model

modernization theory

approaches to solving
  social problems

reactive approach

inactive approach

political inactivism

economic inactivism

social inactivism

law and order solutions

crisis management

proactive approach

interactive approach

sunk costs

strength and assets
  approach

answers that won't work

refusing to admit
  problems exist

personalizing problems

excluding reality

rationalizing

avoiding responsibility

society heal thyself

time heals all wounds

social adaptation

blaming the victim

blaming providers

blaming reformers

passing the buck

scapegoating

moralizing

retribution

quick fix

QUESTIONS FOR DISCUSSION

1. Why do social problems persist?
2. Ann Schaef says that society is deteriorating at an alarming rate. Do you agree or disagree? If you agree, to what do you attribute this deterioration?
3. Eric Voegelin claims that society is both progressing and regressing at the same time. Do you agree with this assessment? If you disagree, provide your perspective on societal change. If you

agree, describe the areas in which are we progressing. In what areas are we regressing?

4. Technological solutions to problems have increased a great deal over time, but many of the solutions for social problems have not changed from those used even in the distant past. For example, the most common solutions to crime—incarceration, physical punishment, or execution—have not changed in well over 2,000 years despite the fact that many criminologists assert that these methods may sometimes create more crime than they solve. Our responses to poverty still rely on the principles of the Elizabethan Poor Law enacted 400 years ago, yet poverty continues to plague us. Our responses to drug abuse—criminalizing drug use, incarceration, interdiction, and confiscation—were found unworkable more than 70 years ago during Prohibition, yet we continue to use those same remedies today. Why do we seem incapable of arriving at better ways of solving the social troubles that have plagued the human condition for millennia?

ADDITIONAL READING

Social Problems Textbooks

Eitzen, D. Stanely and Maxine Baca-Zinn. *Social Problems,* 6th ed. Boston: Allyn and Bacon, 1994.

Henslin, James M. *Social Problems,* 4th ed. Upper Saddle River, NJ: Prentice Hall, 1996.

Kornblum, William and Joseph Julian. *Social Problems,* 9th ed. Saddle River, NJ: Prentice Hall, 1998.

Soroka, Michael P. and George J. Brayjak. *Social Problems: A World at Risk.* Boston: Allyn and Bacon, 1995.

Theory of Social Problems

Baker, Paul J., Louis E. Anderson, and Dean S. Dorn. *Social Problems: A Critical Thinking Approach,* 2d ed. Belmont, CA: Wadsworth, 1993.

Dewey, John. *The Public and Its Problems: An Essay in Political Inquiry.* Chicago: Gateway Books, 1946.

Freire, Paulo. *Pedagogy of the Oppressed.* New York: Herder and Herder, 1970.

Horton, Paul G., Gerald R. Leslie, Richard F. Larson, and Robert L. Horton. *The Sociology of Social Problems,* 12th ed. Upper Saddle River, NJ: Prentice Hall, 1997.

Manis, Jerome G. *Analyzing Social Problems.* New York: Praeger, 1976.

Mills, C. Wright. *The Sociological Imagination*. London: Oxford University Press, 1959.

Seidman, Edward and Julia Rappaport, eds. *Redefining Social Problems*. New York: Plenum Press, 1986.

Simon, David R. and Joel H. Henderson. *Private Troubles and Public Issues: Social Problems in the Postmodern Era*. Fort Worth: Harcourt Brace, 1997.

Individualist Approach

Dawes, R. M. *House of Cards: Psychology and Psychotherapy Built on Myth*. New York: Free Press, 1994.

Means, Richard L. *The Ethical Imperative: The Crisis in American Values*. Garden City, NY: Anchor Books, Doubleday, 1970.

Winslow, Robert. *The Emergence of Deviant Minorities, Social Problems and Social Change*. San Ramon, CA: Consensus Publishers, 1972.

Ryan, William. *Blaming the Victim*. New York: Vintage Books, 1976.

Social Pathology

Hofstadter, Richard. *Social Darwinism in American Thought, 1860–1915*. Boston: Beacon Press, 1959.

Merton, Robert K. and Robert Nisbet. *Contemporary Social Problems*, 2d ed. New York: Harcourt Brace, 1966.

Parent–Family Approach

Harris, Judith Rich. *The Nurture Assumption: Why Children Turn Out the Way They Do*. New York: Simon and Schuster, 1998.

Society as Inherently Defective

Coleman, Frank M. *Hobbes and America: Exploring the Constitutional Foundations*. Toronto: University of Toronto Press, 1977.

Reik, Charles A. *The Greening of America*. New York: Bantam Books, 1970.

Social Systems Approach

Ackoff, Russell L. *Redesigning the Future: A Systems Approach to Societal Problems*. New York: Wiley, 1974.

Special Problems

Allport, Gordon. *The Nature of Prejudice*. Reading, MA: Addison-Wesley, 1954.

McWilliams, Carey. *Prejudice, Japanese Americans: Symbol of Racial Intolerance*. Hamden, CT: Archon Books, 1971.

Billingsley, Andrew and J. Giovannoni. *Children of the Storm: Black Children and American Child Welfare*. New York: Harcourt, Brace and Jovanovich, 1972.

Riis, Jacob. *Children of the Tenements*. New York: MacMillan, 1903.

Steinbeck, John. *Grapes of Wrath*. New York: Viking, 1939.

Bean, Walton. *Boss Reuf's San Francisco: The Story of the Union Labor Party, Big Business and Graft Prosecution*. Berkeley: University of California Press, 1952.

Norris, Frank. *The Pit: A Story of Chicago*. New York: Doubleday, 1903.

Myrdal, Gunnar. *An American Dilemma*. New York: Harper, 1944.

Strengths Approach

McKnight, John and John Kretzmann. *Mapping Community Capacity*. Evanston, IL: Institute for Policy Research, 1966.

Saleebey, Dennis, ed. *The Strengths Perspective in Social Work Practice*, 2d ed. New York: Longman, 1997.

Research

Young, Ted I. K. and William R. A. Freudenburg, eds. *Research in Social Problems and Public Policy*, Vol. 6. Greenwich, CT: JAI Press, 1997.

Journals

Economy and Society. Routledge Subscriptions, ITPS, North Way, Andover, New Hampshire.

Journal of Aging and Social Policy. Hayworth Press.

Social Problems. UC Press for the Society for Study of Social Problems, Journal Dept. UC Press, 2120 Berkeley Way, Berkeley, CA 94720.

Theory and Society: Renewal and Critique in Social Theory. Kluwer Academic Publishers, 3300 Alt Dordrecht, The Netherlands.

3 Rational Problem Solving and Social Thinking

Modern Reason

When a man *reasoneth* he does nothing else but conceive a sum total.... For reason, in this sense, is nothing but *reckoning,* that is, adding and subtracting of the consequences ... agreed upon. The use and end of reason is not finding the sum and truth of one, or a few consequences ... but to begin at these and proceed from one consequence to another.[1]

Thomas Hobbes

Idiocy and the Public Good

Ancient Greeks defined idiots as citizens who are so concerned with their private lives and preferences that they fail to attend to or even comprehend, the common good. Idiots are persons who refuse to simultaneously be both private and public citizens, as democracy requires. They put personal freedom to do as they please way out in front of the common good, thus undermining the community that secures those freedoms. They fail to see that freedom and community are not opposing forces, but deeply interdependent.

Walter Parker, Idiocy and Education

Ideas in This Chapter

A problem-solving group identifies issues by listing the specific problems confronting them.

THOMAS HOBBES AND MODERN REASON

Sitting at his desk in an upper room in Paris in 1650, golden light streaming through a window, Thomas Hobbes (1588–1679) contemplated the destructive turmoil of social and political relationships that have occurred since the dawn of history. The natural propensity of people to fight over power, quarrel over religious dogma, and dispute morality, thought Hobbes, had kept humankind in a perpetual "war of all against all" where "every man is enemy to every man . . . and the life of man, solitary, poor, nasty, brutish and short."[2] Was there some other way political and social relationships could be fashioned that would place society on a less turbulent and more rational foundation?

Galileo, Roger Bacon, and others were engaged in the exciting task of discovering the laws that governed the physical universe. Hobbes's friend Galileo, whom he had visited in 1635, suggested that the physical world, based on Euclidean geometry, was nothing but a set of moving parts. Hobbes reasoned that since society was also nothing more than a system of interrelated components[3] were there not universal principles by which social and political relationships could be constructed? By applying rational calculation, Hobbes thought, could not humankind devise ways of regulating and ordering human relationships?[4]

Published in 1651, Hobbes's *Leviathan* attempted nothing less than to remake the entire world of thinking up to that time. Borrowing from principles of mechanics, Hobbes conceptualized society as an artificially constructed *system* that operated by means of natural physical laws. He believed humans no longer had to be at the mercy of irrational emotions, religious dogma, or metaphysics; nor did people need to be subject to the whims of fortune or human passions that so often led to turmoil and conflict.

Science not only would control physical nature but would achieve a rational human world whose outcomes could be predicted and controlled as well. In fact, once a framework was established, systems would operate automatically, just as other mechanical devices, because of the principles and rules built into them. In a single stroke was born the idea of modern reason, rational problem solving and, along with systems theory, the fields of political and social science.

For the first time modern reason was defined. Modern reason, asserts Hobbes is "nothing but reckoning of consequences"[5] in which a person adds up the benefits and costs of any alternative to determine which of them maximizes one's interests to the highest degree. Modern reason is a skill of economic calculation that one learns by "industry," not an inborn component of the human character. "In any matter whatsoever where there is a place for *addition* and *subtraction,* there is also a place for *reason;* and where they have no place, there *reason* has nothing at all to do."[6] It is irrational then to base decisions on personal values, emotions, or beliefs that cannot be calculated. "When man reasoneth," Hobbes asserted, "he does nothing else but conceive a sum total."[7]

Our society has become modern, therefore, not only because of the scientific method devised by the giants of the Enlightenment such as Galileo, Tyco Brahe, and Nikolaus Copernicus, but also because of modern instrumental reason defined by Thomas Hobbes along with John Locke (1632–1704), who applied Hobbes's ideas of rationality to society; Adam Smith (1723–1790), who applied rational thinking to economics; and James Madison (1751–1836),[8] who applied modern reason to politics.

Modern reason has become the way we think, the way Western society has come to be. So ubiquitous has rational calculation become that it is used in every sphere of human transaction, particularly in the economy, in complex corporate and public organizations, and as the common denominator in global society as well. Whenever you purchase goods, plan a trip, choose a college, or decide on a career, you use rational problem solving. It is so common that it has probably become second nature to you. Modern Western society is, without a doubt, a rational society.

WHAT YOU WILL LEARN IN THIS CHAPTER

Macro social workers help people create a more humane social environment, solve social problems, and make social change. In this chapter you will be introduced to two different but related methods of approaching social work practice. The first method, *modern rational problem solving* (RPS), is the conventional way by which people make decisions today. You will also discover that people working to enhance the human condition are conceptualizing a different way of thinking called *social reason* or *thinking socially*. You will learn that social workers need to understand both modern rational problem solving and social thinking. Each has its place as a way to think about the world. Macro social workers need to be adept at understanding the differences between the two, in what contexts each is appropriate, and how to use both of them.

You will explore a short history of modern reason, and how it has shaped our modern worldview. You will explore how rational problem solving is used in social work and how to apply it step by step to solving social problems. Once you understand how to use rational problem solving, you have a powerful tool at your disposal when you intervene to improve people's social environment.

In addition to rational problem solving, you will learn that social reason includes broad-based, multiple ways of thinking compatible with generalist-based macro social work. Instead of focusing on social problems, dysfunctions, or needs, social thinking focuses on the resources, assets, and strengths of people in a community. Social thinking looks ahead to what people can accomplish by using their collective values, combined vision, and communal action. You will learn how to make social change step by step using social thinking, and you will be invited to explore its utility in working with groups, building community, and creating a better social world.

WHAT IS MODERN RATIONAL PROBLEM SOLVING?

Rational problem solving helps a person maximize his or her interests.[9] It is practical and can be used even by large groups. Because it is an economic tool, it has become a nearly universal way of thinking today.

Maximize One's Interests

Rational problem solving is often used when a person chooses between several options to maximize his or her interests. When you choose an alternative that gives you more rather than less, higher rather than lower quality, less rather than more expensive, faster rather than slower, more rather than less efficient, or some combination of these values, you are being rational. For example, when you make a rational choice, you first decide on the goal you want to accomplish or the preferences you want to maximize. Then you gather as much information as you can about the choices you want to make. You test each alternative solution against your experience and the information you have collected and calculate its benefits and costs. You then rank the alternative choices and choose the one that gives you the most benefits at the least cost.[10] Rational problem solving is simply a way of computing a *ratio* of pros to cons or benefits to costs that maximizes the value you receive from your decision.[11]

Practical

The rational problem-solving method is logical and simple, straightforward, and direct. It is systematic and sequential and helps you achieve your purposes quickly and cheaply. Because it deals with facts, RPS easily lends itself to issues that can be quantified. When you use rational problem solving, you are less likely to miss crucial issues or to skip over things that need to be considered.

Unitary Decision Maker

Furthermore, one person, a group, or people in organization can use rational problem solving if they act together in a unitary way. The rational model of foreign policy, for example, often assumes that entire nations act rationally in maximizing their self-interests in competition with other nations, who are assumed to also act rationally. By making that assumption, governmental decision makers calculate how a nation might respond to challenges from our government and can plot strategies based on those calculations.[12]

Reason at Large

RPS is universally used for making economic decisions, but it has become so generalized that rational calculation is commonly understood to be "reason at large." Karl Polyani and others have observed that modern thinking has become so conditioned by a market mentality because ours is the first society in history that "uses the criterion of economizing as the standard of human existence."[13] RPS explains the behavior studied by nearly all social science disciplines from political philosophy to psychology. The range of human behavior that RPS explains encompasses "government decision making, individual consumer decisions, collective economic agents, social institutions such as the criminal justice system or the family,"[14] and provides "a framework applicable to *all* human behavior—to all types of decisions and to persons from all walks of life."[15]

It is not at all surprising then, that along with almost all other arenas of our society, social workers have adopted the calculative logic of modern reason and rational problem solving and applied them to solving the problems of the human condition.

RATIONAL PROBLEM SOLVING AND SOCIAL WORK

The Council on Social Work Education (CSWE) has adopted rational problem solving as the method by which social workers engage in practice. CSWE, for example, officially recommends that social work students learn this method: (1) define issues, (2) collect and assess data, (3) identify alternative interventions, (4) select, (5) implement courses of action, and (6) monitor and evaluate outcomes.[16]

The rational problem solving method is a unifying core that underlies social work practice at the micro, mezzo, and macro levels. Macro social workers use RPS successfully with task group decision making. We engage in rational thinking when we practice community planning, in community development and community organization. It is the foundation on which administration, organization development, and social policy analysis are based, and it is synonymous with social work research.[17]

A BRIEF HISTORY OF RPS IN SOCIAL WORK

Prior to 1850**,** proto-social workers helped rationalize services to persons with intellectual and emotional disabilities, and during Reconstruction and the Progressive Era, social workers applied rational thinking to the way private charity was provided and helped place government on a more rational basis. Rational thinking was extended in the 1930s and 1940s, and in the 1950s and 1960s it was explicitly applied to social work methods. Today it is used in many arenas of social intervention.

Prior to 1850

As early as 1845, Dorothea Dix (1802–1887) worked to rationalize services for persons with intellectual and emotional disabilities by gathering data and using evidence based on problem-solving research and policy analysis. By employing rational arguments based on these data and persistent lobbying, Dix was able to persuade government officials to reform and develop services on behalf of persons with intellectual and emotional disabilities.

Reconstruction (1865–1880)

During Reconstruction Charity Organization Societies (COS) pioneered in placing philanthropy on a rational, efficient, and impartial basis known as "scientific charity." Fabricant and Fisher, for example, assert that "the 'scientific approach' of the COS sought to bring business principles of efficiency, management and consolidation to the administration of charity."[18] COS workers devised the social casework process as a rational, systematic way of helping people make the most effective choices for themselves and their families. COS social workers turned their attention to community issues and developed rational social planning process by which charitable organizations would assess needs, avoid duplication and waste, and work together to raise and distribute funding through efficient, modern, cost-effective service delivery.

Progressive Era (1880–1915)

In an era rife with political corruption and the overextension of the economy in many areas of society, Settlement House workers of the Progressive Era and others pressed for "good government," advocating for a rational basis to ensure fairness, equality, and an end to spoils and bribery. Social workers championed the Pendleton Act, which in 1883 established the Civil Service Commission and the principle of hiring the most qualified person for government office using clear, consistent, rational, job-related criteria rather than hiring on the basis of favoritism, nepotism, and amicism (giving preference to one's friends). Social workers used the power of rational bureaucracy in government as a countervailing force to keep government decision making formal, unbiased, value neutral, and free from the influences of political bargaining.

In 1890 Max Weber (1864–1920), without doubt one of the greatest sociologists, provided the theoretical understanding for the role of rational thinking as a basis for the rise of the modern complex organization in his classic essay on "Bureaucracy," developed an assessment of how governmental bureaucracy uses rational, impersonal, decision making in his essay "Politics as a Vocation," and explored the differences between instrumental reason and substantive or value-laden reason in his classic *Economy and Society* at the turn of the 19th century.[19]

1930s and 1940s

Rational problem solving was described by John Dewey (1864–1952) in his 1933 book *How We Think* as the way people universally make decisions,[20] and in 1945 Nobel Prize winner Herbert Simon (1916–2001), in his influential book *Administrative Behavior,* explored the use of modern rational problem solving as the means by which rational decision making occurs in modern complex organizations.[21]

Social Work Problem Solving in the 1950s and 1960s

The first person to explicitly link social work with rational problem solving was Helen Harris Perlman (1906–2004) who in 1957 described the social casework method as a problem-solving process based on rational problem solving and outlined its steps.[22] Rational problem solving was the basis of many Kennedy administration policies and programs. Graham Allison shows, for example, how Kennedy used rational problem solving in the Cuban Missile Crisis.[23]

Rational Problem Solving Today

Today politicians use rational problem solving to make political and public policy decisions. Complex computer programs are based on this approach as are modern statistical decision theory and game theory.[24] Rational problem solving is the basis of organization and administrative decision making.[25] It is called, for good reason, the "systems approach" by Churchman[26] and is the basis for management science in public policy analysis.[27] Rational problem solving has been described in many social work texts as the universal model by which social workers assist clients in resolving personal and social problems[28] and has became a conscious part of the core understanding of social work.

HOW TO USE RATIONAL PROBLEM SOLVING

Most social workers agree that rational problem solving in social work involves the following steps (see Figure 3.1):

1. Decide on a goal or target
2. Gather information about the problem
3. Generate a number of alternative solutions
4. Assess and compare alternatives
5. Select the best or most cost-beneficial solution
6. Develop a strategy or plan of action
7. Carry out or implement the solution
8. Evaluate the results

Decide on a Goal or Target

Deciding on a social goal or target is the most important part of the problem-solving process. It is also the lengthiest. There are three parts to deciding on a target: recognizing that a problem exists, identifying it, and choosing it.

Recognize the Problem or Issue   A social issue, as troublesome as it may be, is not a "problem" until a person or group recognizes and labels it as such. Often social pain and dysfunction exist, but people ignore or deny their existence. Racial discrimination against African Americans, for example, began when the first slaves were brought to this country. Racism was accepted as a normal, even necessary, way of life among many members of society, and it was perpetuated even after the Civil War until the community of African Americans decided to actively resist. In the same way, the problem of drunken drivers was not a nationally recognized issue until the mother of a child killed by a drunk driver organized MADD—Mothers Against Drunk Drivers.

Identify the Problem   Once your community or organizational group recognizes that a problem exists, the members need to identify the specific problem or

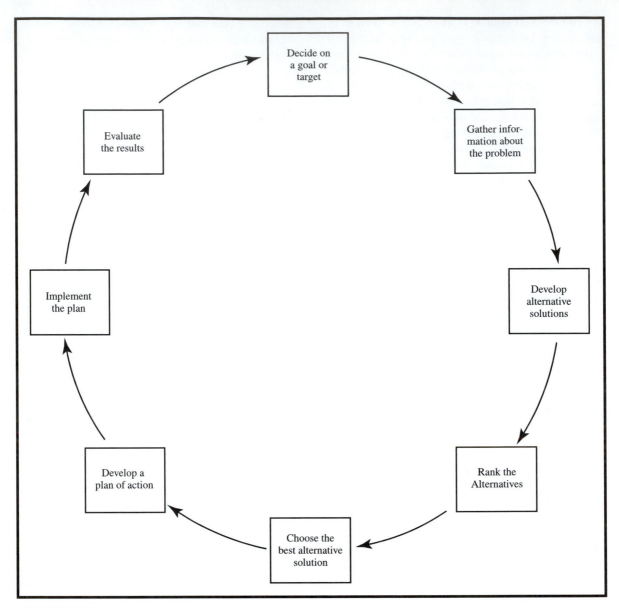

FIGURE 3.1 Rational Problem-Solving Cycle

issues on which they want to work. Make a list of the problems or issues confronting your community or group, and compare your list with the following criteria to narrow your choice to one. The problem chosen should be one that can be resolved successfully, that has legitimacy, and over which the group has some control. The problem should be meaningful, and solving it should have beneficial effects.

Successful Resolution Choose an issue that your group has a good chance of resolving successfully.

Consider the amount of energy, time, and money available to your group. Do not choose a problem that is beyond your group's resources. Rather than tackling a large issue, choose a smaller problem that your group has a good chance of solving.

Legitimacy Select a problem over which your group has some legitimacy. Most community problems can be seen as legitimate. For example, your group can legitimize itself by publicly declaring its intention to cope with the social problem, developing a mission statement, choosing a name that identifies its concern with the problem, and becoming incorporated as a legally recognized organization to address the issue. If your group is dependent on an agency's financial support, however, make sure that your work falls under the agency's mandate, otherwise your source of support may disappear or you may be in conflict with the agency. Sometimes the problem being addressed crosses the boundaries of several agencies or existing groups. In this case you might develop a coalition of agencies and groups from a number of arenas and join together in the change effort.

Control   Choose a problem that is potentially under the control of your group or one in which control needs to be established. Consider, for example, a group of low-income residents concerned about the inadequate schooling their children are receiving. They may have little control over the school board or its policies. They may have no input into the amount of funding available for their children. This does not mean, however, that they cannot become empowered to gain control or change school policies. They can strategize to gain seats on the board or put pressure on local government to make funding more equitable. They can gain control over the forces that affect the lives of their children.

Meaning   Choose a problem that is pressing and current. It should have meaning to your group members, be deeply felt, and be one that can excite and energize them. Its solution should be important to the community as a whole, and the members should have a vested interest in having the situation resolved.

Beneficial Effects   Select a problem that, when resolved, will have far-reaching beneficial effects. By changing one piece of a problem, your group may begin a process that can bring changes in an entire system. In this way, you can initiate a series of events that can cause an entire facade to crumble. At the very least, your group can prevent future problems from occurring. The effort and energy you and your group expend should pay off in tangible benefits.

Choosing the Problem   If your group has misgivings about any of these issues, resolve them before you commit yourself to working on the problem. Your group needs to be fully invested in the issue on which it will be working. After you have chosen the problem on which you will work, write down a tentative statement of the problem as it appears to your group.

Gather Information About the Problem

There are a number of ways of gathering data about a social problem. The people of the community or organization are the best source of information about what is wrong, and you will spend lots of time talking to them. On a more formal level, your group can administer surveys to community or organization members or interview key leaders. Your group may also collect information about the problem from agency records, newspapers, or other existing sources. Macro social workers bring people together in focus groups to discuss the problem from various points of view. (You will learn more about ways of gathering information in Chapter 6.) Regardless of the method you use, however, your group will need to ask the questions *why, when, who, where,* and *how*.

Asking Why: Observing Patterns   Asking "why" gets at causation, helping you form a social diagnosis of the problem. Once you understand why a social condition exists, you have some control over it. Look at your problem definition and then ask "why" until you can go no further. Suppose, for example, you are working with a community about lack of police protection. Encourage group members to ask these "why" questions:

> "Why is there a lack of police involvement?" Because the city's priorities are elsewhere.

> "Why are they elsewhere?" Because neighborhood residents lack input to decision making.

> "Why do residents lack input?" Because they have no effective voice in the process.

> "Why do residents have no voice?" Because the system does not provide for citizen input.

> "Why not?" Because those in power don't want input and have excluded people from the process.

Asking "why" helps your members focus on one possible cause and allows them to see patterns that you can use to correct the problem.

Your problem-solving group might want to track down the ultimate cause of a social problem. Practically speaking, however, this may be a waste of time. Like the ripples in a pond, one problem creates multiple effects, each of which spreads out from its source, touching more and more systems in its wake. Furthermore, the ultimate cause of a social problem, even if known, may be irrelevant to its effects. The series of events leading up to the Civil War in the United States, for example, began with the importation of the first slave into this country. Knowing this fact added nothing to resolving the eventual conflict and resultant racial discrimination that this act set in motion. Causation cannot be undone, but the effects of causation can be understood and dealt with. For the most part, therefore, spend your time understanding the *effects* of social problems and discovering *where* in the system the problem is most acute.

Where: Locating the Pain   The "where" may be a physical location. Where in a city or community do the homeless congregate? Where are the slums developing? The social pain may not be located in a geographical place, however, but may be with particular groups of people who experience the problem. In the past, for example, very few services nationwide were provided for persons with developmental disabilities. Parents, friends, and professionals joined together, identified themselves as a community, and pressed for changes in education, housing, and access to facilities. Bit by bit, attitudes changed and services improved.

THINKING IT THROUGH

At the first meeting the group reviewed the literature prepared by the urban redevelopment agency and began to analyze it point by point. The question was asked, "Why did the city decide on urban redevelopment?" There was little response to this question. When the leader asked, "What groups are supporting urban redevelopment?" answers came forth readily: the Chamber of Commerce, labor (because the building trades would get jobs), and the Church. "Who will lose by it?" Goat Valley residents.

What would happen if the project went through? Everyone would get something except the residents, 65 percent of whom owned their homes. Only a very few who had incomes of $400 or more per month could transfer any equity and get a loan for the balance. And those who had received welfare payments in the past would have these deducted from any equity they might receive. The leader asked, "Is this fair?" At this point, Dolores Huerta asked, "What are we going to do about it? How could we win? What is the best we could get?" It was decided the Community Services Organization must fight.

Who: Discovering Victims and Perpetrators
By asking "who," your group pinpoints victims and perpetrators. Victims are those who are damaged by a social problem. For example, a bank may have an unwritten rule to not approve home loans in certain areas of the city that it assesses as risky—usually areas with low-income residents. Such policies, called *redlining,* tend to discriminate against people in poor neighborhoods, making it next to impossible for people to purchase or improve their homes, resulting in rundown neighborhoods. Redlining makes victims of almost everyone who lives in a targeted neighborhood.

Perpetrators are those who cause, condone, or provide conditions enabling a social problem to exist. The individual acts of specific leaders of businesses or organizations formalize and institutionalize problems in our social system. Target the individuals in charge: the leaders, administrators, policy makers, executives, or others who have control over and can make changes in the system. For example, if redlining policies exist, find out which bank owners, officers, and trustees formulate and carry out those policies. The process of identifying those responsible for instigating or perpetuating social problems helps provide the victims with tangible, personal targets for change.

When: The Time Frame   When did the problem arise, and how did it develop over time? Has the problem been increasing over the last six months or year? Answers to these questions help your community or group understand the history, severity, and patterns of the problem. What specific events triggered the problem, and when did they occur? Establishing a chronology of the problem will also tell you about decisions that were made, who made them, and possibly why they were made.

How the Problem Occurred   If you can understand how a problem developed, you have come some way toward changing it. For instance, you may find that organizational decisions that once made sense are now outmoded. A system has failed to adjust to changing conditions. Perhaps mistakes were made that have not been corrected, and a defective system is being perpetuated. When decision makers defend the current system by saying "We've always done it this way," or "don't ask questions; these are the rules," there is a good chance that they are allowing system inertia to carry them along. Understanding how organizational or government policies and practices came about can help extricate people from dysfunctional patterns in the social system.

On the other hand, you may find that a consciously planned series of events were construed to deprive people of power, control, or resources, keeping them in a position of subservience for the benefit of others. A city council allows a corporation to dump waste in a low-income neighborhood, colludes to keep wages low, and gives tax breaks with a promise of jobs that never materialize. Discovering this history can uncover patterns of systematic abuse and give your members evidence they can use in their struggle to restore justice.

Generate Alternative Solutions

Help your group generate several possible ways to solve the problem, while avoiding the hazards of decision making.

How to Develop Alternatives

If the problem has been well researched, generating solutions should be relatively easy. They should flow naturally from the data. Generate as many alternatives as you can that would legitimately solve the problem. One way of opening up the group to consider all possible alternatives is to list every possible aspect of the problem that can be changed, eliminating those that cannot be changed. Then combine these change variables together into various solutions. Eliminate the ones that do not help accomplish at least some of your goals. The ones that remain are viable possibilities. Your group should now have several innovative solutions to consider.

How to Avoid Hazards

There are some hazards in developing solutions that you should be aware of, however. For example, there is a tendency for individuals or groups to jump to solutions before they have explored the problem in depth. If your group does this, they may be fitting the problem to their own particular solutions. Sometimes people have pet solutions they use to fit any situation, or they may have a tendency to accept the first solution that occurs to them. Try to avoid these pitfalls because you will be prematurely limiting your search for the solution that can best remediate the social problem.

Assess and Compare Alternatives

Herbert Simon asserts, "Rational decision making always requires the comparison of alternative means in terms of the respective ends to which they will lead."[29] Assess each alternative using specific criteria that will allow your group to compare them in a standard way. Two of the more common models are force field analysis and benefit-cost analysis. You will discover other models based on rational choice theory in Chapters 6, 11, and 13.

Force Field Analysis

Kurt Lewin (1890–1947), one of the most prominent social psychologists of his day, developed force field analysis. It is based on the idea that with every potential solution there are *restraining forces* and *driving forces*.[30] Restraining and driving forces are constraints—conditions or boundaries your group decides a solution must meet before it can be accepted.

Restraining Forces Constraints, also called disadvantages or costs, are those forces that tend to keep things the way they are and prevent social change. Decision makers try to minimize restraining forces. Your members may decide that the most important constraints are the amount of time, money, or manpower it will take to solve the problem. Some solutions will be more time consuming, cost more money, or require more manpower than others. Assign each of the restraining forces a weight or number.

Driving Forces Driving forces are the benefits or advantages an alternative will offer that helps you overcome restraining forces and provides incentives for your group to make social change. Your group may decide that each alternative must provide an acceptable quantity of service, meet a level of quality, and be effective.

How to Use Force Field Analysis Decide on a standard set of restraining and driving forces that your group can use to compare alternatives and assign them a weight or number. You need to estimate the strength of these restraining and driving forces on a scale and array them on a force field analysis table such as the one in Figure 3.2. In this hypothetical example, I have used a scale of 0 to 5. After you array all of your alternatives on tables, your group can see how the alternative solutions compare with one another and how each of them meets your criteria.

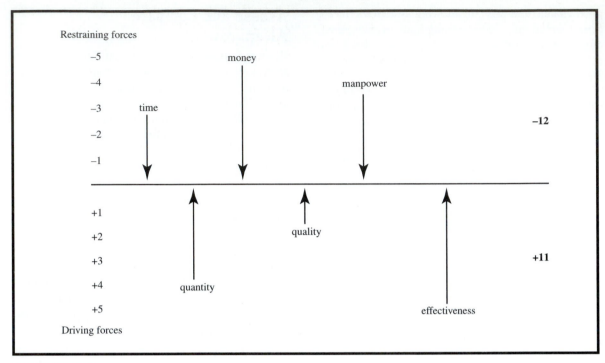

FIGURE 3.2   Force Field Analysis Hypothetical Alternative

As your group assesses the alternatives, they may discover ways to increase the effectiveness of their solutions. For example, perhaps your group can manipulate an alternative's driving or restraining forces by developing more effective services or by reducing costs to make the alternative more attractive. Finally, add up the driving forces and subtract this number from the restraining forces. The alternative with the highest positive number is the solution that has the most power.

Benefit-Cost Analysis

Another way to compare alternatives is to compute a benefit-cost ratio. When calculating benefit-cost ratios, ignore negative numbers. Compute the ratio by dividing the sum of the weighted benefits (B) by the sum of the weighted costs (C). A benefit-cost ratio that is equal to or above 1 (B/C ≥ 1) will provide your group with at least an even chance of being successful. It also shows you whether the benefits are worth the costs of the project. The higher the benefit-cost ratio is, the better its chances for success.

The benefit-cost ratio of the alternative shown in Figure 3.2 is B/C = 11/12, or .916. Would you seriously consider that alternative? Why or why not? Another alternative has a benefit-cost ratio of 12/14, and a third is 10/9. Compute these ratios to see which of these three scores would give the highest return. Which would give the least? Why do decision makers always choose an alternative whose benefit-cost ratio equals or exceeds 1?

Choose the Best Solution

The solution that shows the most powerful driving forces compared to its restraining forces, and has the most favorable benefit-cost ratio, would be the most rational choice for your group. Sometimes a less rational alternative might be the best one, however. The restraining forces aligned against your group, for example, may seem overwhelming, and it may appear irrational to proceed. But the importance of your cause and your commitment to it, although difficult to quantify, may tip the balance in your favor.

Sometimes the most rational solution may fail. The "best and brightest" decision makers in the Kennedy-Johnson administration, for example, calculated that the United States would win the war in Vietnam.

Their rational calculations were ultimately wrong, and in spite of the superiority of weapons and technology the United States lost the war. Rational problem solving is only a tool, not an infallible measure of success. Along with making a rational calculation, your group needs to assess which alternative aligns with its vision, values, and purpose.

Develop a Plan of Action

Deciding how to implement the solution that your group chooses is called a strategy for change. In many cases your strategy will flow directly from the problem solution and almost be self-evident. However, there is a more formal way of developing a strategic plan, which includes developing goals, objectives, tasks, tactics, and targets. You then review your strategy and finalize the plan.

Goals   Planning for action begins with setting goals. Begin with one or two ultimate or long-range goals. On a chalkboard or newsprint, place a long-range goal on the far right. Now work backward, identifying intermediate goals and immediate, short-term objectives. List all of the events that should occur that might precede accomplishing each long-range goal.

Objectives   What specific things need to be accomplished to reach the mid-range goals? These become objectives. Each objective should meet three criteria. It should be (1) time limited, (2) specific, and (3) measurable. For example, "The police department will provide one additional patrol officer on Elm Street by June 1, 2006." Branch these objectives off from the mid-range goals. You may have several objectives preceding each goal.

Tasks   Break down each objective into tasks. Tasks are specific duties or steps members must take to reach objectives. Tasks may be printing information, calling meetings, contacting the media, meeting with perpetrators, or other actions.

Tactics   Tactics tell you how to carry out tasks, especially activities that are politically sensitive or that are complex and require coordination of members. Community organization tactics may include holding public hearings, meeting with government or political officials, or lobbying, among others.

When deciding on specific tactics, be sure that the group members give thought to the kinds of resistance they might encounter from power figures and how they might overcome resistance.

Targets   Often your tactics will include identifying specific targets. Targets are the key power figures in business, government, or the community that your group wants to influence, change, coopt, or whose support is crucial to the project.

Review Your Strategy   There may be duplication. Some issues may be irrelevant or subsidiary. New ideas may have occurred to your group. Revise the plan to eliminate duplication or irrelevant items or to add new ideas. Try to anticipate what could go wrong with your strategy. For example, what if you do not meet your objectives? What alternative objectives are there? What if your tactics backfire? What other tactics or targets should be considered? Think through these issues so that you will not be caught off guard. Then develop a backup or *contingency* plan to use in case things do not go the way you expect.

Finalize the Plan   After reviewing the strategy, your group is ready to finalize the plan. Decide on the sequence of events that need to be orchestrated to accomplish your group's goals. Do certain events, tasks, or activities need to precede others? Which things do the members need to do first, second, or third? Create timelines. Then assign individuals to those tasks and get a commitment from the members to carry them out. Make a list of the assignments and deadlines.

Implement the Solution

Implementation means carrying out the strategy on which your group has decided. Members of your group become the nucleus around which the community becomes organized, a program is developed, or a social plan is implemented. Community meetings, for example, inform people about the problem and the proposed solutions. Members also promote community involvement, soliciting help from other community members, and begin organizing the change effort. Your group members may chair committees or lead task forces committed to carrying out the goals of the project. They may even join the board of a social service organization.

Evaluate the Results

Throughout the change process, you need to monitor its progress. Perhaps the easiest, most useful, and most immediate evaluation is feedback. Spend time "debriefing" after meetings or after carrying out a strategy or tactic. Debriefing gives members a chance to share stories, let off steam, get recognition, enjoy triumphs, and obtain support when things have not gone well. Debriefing also allows members to critique the process, ask questions, and consciously reflect on why they did what they did.

Debriefing empowers your group and provides a learning tool for the members. The group has acquired valuable information about resistance, system dynamics, and power structures. Members learn about change and the change process by sharing and involving themselves with one another. Learning takes place as people talk about problems, share perceptions, and wrestle with what to do next. Debriefing helps group members determine whether their predictions about what would happen were correct. Armed with this new information, your group can reassess the situation, modify its strategy, plan, and move ahead.

In addition to debriefing, more formal evaluation processes may be used. For example, keep records of meetings and activities and refer to them, particularly reviewing progress toward objectives. This will help members shift strategy, keep track of events, and make sense of what has occurred. Writing often helps develop ideas and gain insights. This information also can be helpful in developing a history of the change effort.

LIMITATIONS OF RATIONAL PROBLEM SOLVING

The rational problem-solving approach is effective in helping calculate which of several alternative solutions is logically the most efficient and beneficial, but it also has some limitations for social work. Rational problem solving may not automatically include particular values that people believe are important, and it tends to be a unidimensional way of thinking.[31]

Values

Two kinds of values are embedded in rational problem solving: those that are implicit in the method itself and those that the problem solver wishes to maximize. These pre-given ends tend to be assumed and are rarely questioned.

Values in the Method Itself   Decision makers give higher precedence to problem situations that are logical, straightforward, and contain a clear set of preference orderings, that possess most of the information on which to base a decision, and that can be easily quantified. Values that escape calculation include compassion, altruism, and selflessness, which are considered to be irrational and tend to be disregarded in RPS.

Maximize Interests of Decision Makers   Macro social workers should understand that RPS tends to skew decision making in favor of those whose goal is to maximize their interests, often considered in economic terms. RPS is most useful when calculating how to make a profit or benefit from resources invested in a project. Because corporations are rational economizing tools to achieve the purposes of their owners, the logic of RPS is particularly compatible with large corporations and those who own and operate them.

Pre-Given Ends   The ends or purposes that a decision maker wishes to maximize tend to be inherent in the way the problem is defined. For example, if the end is to increase the tax base of a deteriorating urban inner city neighborhood, RPS can assist in deciding which among such alternatives as a parking lot, a high-rise office building, a park, or a shopping mall is the most cost-beneficial means to increase city revenue. Because they meet the economic constraints chosen by decision makers, these alternatives may be the only ones considered.

The interests of the community members who live in the neighborhood tend to be left out of the calculations. No one asks whether the tax base should be strengthened at the expense of residents of the neighborhood partly because the existing slum has a negative or at best zero utility, and its preservation or renovation will further decrease city revenue. In addition, RPS cannot calculate the cost to people of losing their roots, their relationships, or their attachments to a social network. These intangible costs are often ignored in rational problem solving.

The ends of the decision tend to be foregone conclusions and are generally not considered or even open to discussion. The economic constraints tend to bind decision making to a narrow choice of pre-given ends, any one of which will tend to benefit the decision makers.

Macro social workers must look beyond rival alternatives and assess the values implied in the choices offered. Is minimizing cost or gaining financial benefit, for example, the most important value to be maximized, or should other values take precedence or be equally considered? Whose preferences or values should be maximized? Those of decision makers who speak on behalf of a public or private organization or community members who will bear the cost of the decision? Maximizing the preferences of those who are normally left out of the decision-making process or who bear the costs is a continual challenge for social workers when using rational problem solving.

Unidimensional

Because economic decisions are clear, specific, narrow, and quantifiable, decision makers can nearly always find a means to rationally maximize their preferences. However, in the field of social work decision making, a clear set of preference orderings rarely exists. In fact, there often may be as many preferences as there are stakeholders in any decision. It may be difficult to obtain anywhere near perfect information about a social issue on which to base a decision. It may be difficult to calculate the relative benefits and costs of various alternatives when people's social welfare is at stake, and it may be nearly impossible to frame an alternative in quantifiable, monetary terms. How, for example, does one calculate the benefits of educating children with developmental disabilities? How does one calculate the costs of ethnic intolerance or the benefits of eradicating it?

While rational problem solving is often very valuable, its limitations challenge social workers to think more broadly about social decision making. One way of reaching beyond instrumental reason is to employ social thinking.[32]

COMPONENTS OF SOCIAL THINKING

Social work is based on an understanding of the dynamics of social relationships, social meaning, and the necessity for constructing one's own social reality. A kind of thinking and deciding that is congruent with these tasks is *social reasoning* or *social thinking.*

Social thinking is an ordinary and simple way of knowing that we use in natural human engagement with one another. Even though social thinking is so common, it is barely recognized as a way of thinking at all. But in spite of its unpretentiousness, social reasoning has the power to help people solve some of the most difficult and important issues of the human condition.

Social thinking is change oriented, uses a citizenship approach, is the basis of civic consciousness, utilizes collective effort, and is interdependent, borderless, and nonmanaged. It is democratically based, interdependent, direct and immediate, empowering, rooted in practice, and utilizes multiple thinking.

Change Oriented

The essence of social change lies with an aggrieved group of people who organize themselves into a community, collectively engage in political discourse to identify the root causes of their grievances, and then strategize together to overcome those conditions. Dara Silverman asserts, for example, "when given the opportunity most people have tons of great ideas. Asking people what they would like to see change is the first step. After that it is a matter of helping people create a tangible plan where they can see short term gains, work with others to become empowered and see themselves as having an important role in making change happen."[33]

Citizenship Approach

Social thinking characterizes what Harry Boyte calls the citizenship approach to social change, which contrasts with the institutional approach that often uses top-down expert decision making. A citizenship approach, says Boyte, places respect, responsibility, and control in the hands of citizens in considering ideas that are relevant to their own particular situations and putting them into action. People engaged in social thinking understand that their mission is social renewal from the grassroots based on a "covenant" relationship, in which people come together for a common purpose. It is a solemn commitment made by two or more individuals to do something.[34]

Civic Consciousness

Social thinking is the basis for civic consciousness. As people engage with others, they develop a sense of themselves and begin to exercise their values and judgment, which brings out ideas for social betterment in ways that generate action.

Collective Effort

Social thinking begins with and is centered in the mutual interaction of community members as they work out the meaning of events they encounter, arrive at an understanding of themselves and their social world, and devise the social goods and social reality within which their lives take shape.[35] Thinking socially is based on mutual decision making. "The motive or normative expression of our sociality is mutuality in primary face-to-face relationships," Harmon states, and the motives underlying responsible action are "a function of the *commitment* of one person to the other—as persons."[36]

SOCIAL THINKING IN ACTION

Even though many of the members of the Community Service Organization (CSO) had little formal education, the Stockton CSO used training sessions called "educationals" that showed it had impact. The information officer of the Stockton Planning Commission asked Huerta at the time of the fight over eliminating Goat Valley: "Where do your people learn to ask these questions? They sure are educated people."[37]

Community members who carry out decisions to affect changes in the social environment not only bear responsibility for their own actions, but they benefit from the power of deciding and accepting the consequences of those decisions. By taking charge of their own destiny, by deciding *and* doing, community members actively engage those in power who impose functional and dependency roles upon them. They challenge the assumption that they cannot or ought not decide and act on their own behalf but must leave deciding in the hands of the powerful.

Interdependent

Social thinking is interdependent. It is based on participation and personal engagement with others. Members come to understand who they are and where they are going. They come to rely on one another and to provide support for others as well. Out of interdependence people who have had few opportunities find their voices and rediscover their ideas, dreams, and visions. They share thoughts and feelings, and with others they generate new ideas by means of a synergy that comes from multiplying idea upon idea, feeling upon feeling, dream upon dream.

Borderless and Nonmanaged

In the framework of community-based social thinking, a few people do not organize others in order to control them, as often occurs in large corporate organizations, governmental systems, and universities. Nor do some determine the outcomes by which others do the work. Social thinking is free of the confines of mass education, structured decision-making arrangements, and institutional processes that limit thinking to produce tangible results such as profit as its main objective. Social thinking, instead, maintains the capacity for each person to reflect on his or her unique experience, history, and social understanding and to impute those perceptions into a milieu of social construction in mutual dialogue with other community members.

Direct and Immediate

Social thinking is not dependent on others to think for us or plan for us. Nor does it rest on the judgment of institutional systems through which ideas must be channeled and receive approval. Social thinking is direct and immediate. People do not need permission to put projects into action, nor do they need to wait for approval of large systems. They can autonomously, independently, and immediately act on those ideas that they believe are best for their communities, and they can generate the resources themselves from the assets and strengths in their own communities without relying on systems outside of the community.

Empowering

People engaging in social thinking who feel helpless, separated, and defeated in the presence of massive institutional structures, whose logic stacks the rules against them and narrows thinking to the logic of the marketplace, begin to think anew and act anew. They become an empowered people who conceive and construct the world out of new perceptions. Members understand that people without many financial resources or plentiful alternatives do not need to be captured by calculation that gives preference to economic values. Instead, they realize that the ideas and

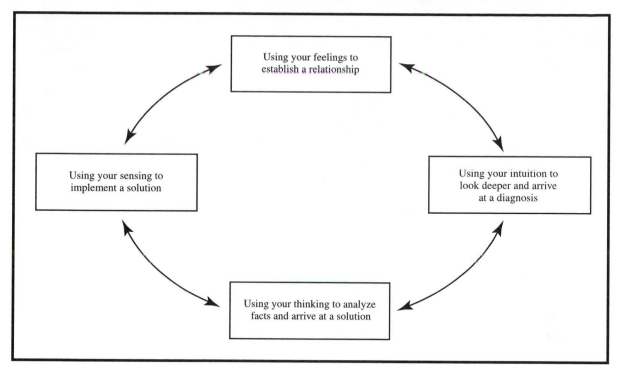

FIGURE 3.3 Whole-Mind Thinking

plans that they conceive together allow them to discard competitive, acquisitive, self-interest.

Acting together for the common good gives people power that calculative logic can never possess. What may have seemed like a problematic and even self-defeating situation when viewed from a rational perspective becomes transformed into an opportunity for rebirth and renewal as members share their feelings, values, hopes, and dreams. According to the calculative logic of the marketplace, it is irrational for a person to join with others to pursue a social cause such as saving the environment, protesting military weapons, or saving an endangered species. It was irrational for labor leaders, civil rights activists, and others to risk their lives fighting injustice. It is seemingly irrational for a group to fight against the construction of a shopping mall in a poor neighborhood. But for each of these struggles, the benefits of giving of oneself to achieve social and civil goods that cannot be calculated outweighed their personal costs.

Rooted in Practice

Social thinking theorists claim that knowledge is derived from experience and validated in practice.

Knowledge is not static; rather, it is forever changing. There is no "one best way" or one solution to a problem at which any rational person will arrive. Ideas are enriched or modified by lessons drawn from practice, which in turn are applied to new ideas as people reflect on the results of their actions.[38]

Multiple Ways of Knowing

Carl Jung (1865–1961) was perhaps the first person to observe that people have four general ways of relating to their environment and making decisions: feeling/valuing, intuiting, thinking, and doing (see Figure 3.3). Social thinking uses each of these four ways of understanding. Heus and Pincus assert that all social workers should exercise multiple ways of thinking that they call "whole-mind thinking."[39] Chris Valley, Program Development Director of Families First, illustrates this kind of whole-mind thinking: "[M]y basic professional 'tools' are intellect (thinking) and imagination (intuition). I am a thinker who is also a doer (sensing). Underlying what I 'think' and 'do' is a belief (feeling/valuing) in the capacity of people to address and resolve their problems."[40]

A BRIEF HISTORY OF SOCIAL THINKING

Social thinking has its origins in the classical reasoning of early Greek philosophers, and developed through the pragmatist tradition of John Dewey, the social psychology of Kurt Lewin, ideas about community organization of social worker Murray Ross, ideas of symbolic interactionists, the conscientization of Paulo Freire, and the work of liberation theologians.

Classical Greeks

Social thinking is often assumed to have originated with the classical Greeks who asserted that when people talk together and mutually deliberate about what is best they can arrive at ideas that inform community with ethical goods or "virtue." This kind of reasoning socially about the nature of a good society has also been called "classical or substantive reason." The Greeks understood that substantive thinking reciprocally constructs a good society and simultaneously creates human character. They believed the most important qualities of citizenship were the ability to understand excellence and to impute it into one's daily life and into the ideas that formed the community or polis. The process of thinking socially about the content and character of the polis became known as "politics."

A fully developed human, in fact, was a *politikon zoon,* a political animal who exercised his humanity by contributing to the foundational principles or policies on which Greek community was constructed. Those unable to distinguish between their private interests and the public good or who allowed their interests to override the public good were "idiots" and were not considered to be fully rational beings. All citizens, therefore, had a duty to their own development and to their communities to infuse their various ideals in the public arena by mutual dialogue and action. In this way, the conjoint acts of social thinking became transformed into "democracy," or the rule of the people.

Pragmatism and Social Psychology

Social thinking was heavily influenced by the pragmatism of John Dewey during the 1930s. Dewey stressed "learning by doing" in which the search for truth was to start in the community among neighbors who explored new ways, leaving behind the old.[41]

The tradition of social thinking continued with Kurt Lewin, who argued that true learning involves restructuring one's relations with the world, a process that called for a personal reeducation of one's self. In the early 1940s Lewin argued that this could be done best in groups because groups form the life space in which most people move about and develop as persons, workers, and citizens.

Researchers in the field of group dynamics found that when members go though the experience of being "acting subjects" and collectively act on their environment, they are often successful in changing their own attitudes and behaviors. Social thinking in groups, Lewin discovered, is a powerful means by which people not only change their social environment but change themselves as well, a principle that macro social workers have also discovered to be important.[42]

Murray Ross and Community Organization

Murray Ross, professor at University of Toronto's school of social work in the early 1950s, applied social thinking to community work. He viewed the role of the social worker as a "guide" in helping people use their understanding and as an "enabler" who facilitates the process of mutual decision making. For Ross a guide is one who helps community members think through the process and move effectively in the direction they choose. The choice of direction must be that of the community. Community organization is a like a university in which people, through mutual dialogue, come to an understanding about who they are, learn how to construct their own social reality, and develop their own culture. For many people this process is one of the highest and most important forms of human reflection.[43]

Symbolic Interactionists

In the 1960s and 1970s a group of social psychologists known as symbolic interactionists pioneered in developing theories of meaning creation and communication, a social model of man, and a theory of social thinking. Among these thinkers were psychiatrist George Herbert Mead, phenomenologist Alfred Schultz, social psychologists Robert Lauer and

Henry Blumer, and philosopher Martin Buber. Symbolic interactionists see the person as a social self and view thinking as a social process that includes meaning and communication (see Chapters 2 and 5 for more on this).

Social Self

Symbolic interactionists, in agreement with macro social workers, assert that the self is never a unitary, isolated being but a social self whose primary source of understanding comes from interaction with others. The idea of radical individualism is tantamount to a deceptive and false conception of a human person. In addition, contrary to modern Western culture, Alberto Ramos says "symbolic interactionists assume that society is essentially social" rather than economic or material. They propose "a multicentric society in which a variety of social forms exist, each of which is deliberately constructed by people to fulfill human needs."[44]

Meaning Creation and Communication

Likewise, their understanding of thinking is that values, perceptions, and understanding are not the possession of solitary persons but arise out of the interaction of people with one another as members of groups and communities share their understanding and the meaning of events they encounter. For symbolic interactionists, meaning creation is a central component of being human. People gain authenticity by attachments they make to events, experiences, and relationships that give meaning to their lives. Meaning is represented by symbolic acts and events and is communicated by language, song, dance, theater, and interactions with others.

Multiple Ways of Knowing

Symbolic interactionists, in agreement with Carl Jung, "rely on the principle that there are multiple ways of knowing."[45] All people, as part of the human family, interact and share their perceptions, experiences, feelings, and values and engage in action to create a universe of social meaning. Humans are "active and creative agents in the construction of social reality."[46] We not only solve problems but develop our social world as we interact with others and engage in "we relations." Thinking and doing are not private endeavors, nor is creative genius limited to gifted individuals. The entire community of persons engaging one another in mutual learning, exploration, and discovery creates the context in which

society is born and forges the conditions and commitments that give it substance.

Paulo Freire's Pedagogy of the Oppressed

Paulo Freire's (1921–1997) ideas on oppression and "critical consciousness" revolutionized social practice. Rather than concentrating on what social actors must "do" to bring about change in their social reality, Freire asserted that *conscientization* (consciousness raising) practice concerns itself with the person, with who the participants will "be." *Conscientization* is a mutual search for knowledge, a critical reflection on reality that carries an ideological option up to and including the transformation of one's own world.

Freire believed that alienation and isolation generate a state of dependency and domination by established powers. *Conscientization* involves a process of unmasking the oppressive condition of institutional practice through action and reflection. Actors who act and reflect acquire the capacity for conscious and creative intervention to change the situation in which they find themselves.[47] Freire, in agreement with Berger and Luckmann, asserts that in the process of autonomously organizing alternative projects based on horizontal interactions that involve dialogue of mutual learning humans construct society and culture emerges. The community is converted into a subject of educational process and collective organizational expression.[48] It is the task of *conscientization,* says Freire, to liberate not only the oppressed from their oppression but to liberate their oppressors as well.

Liberation Theology

Social thinking and learning continued to be developed by contributors to liberation theology in the 1960s and early 1970s. Liberation will only occur when the poor assume responsibility for their own liberation. People are subjects of their own transformation and engage themselves actively and mutually in formulating the kind of culture and truth they are seeking. These are not abstract ideas: They come out of the experience of people, and they affect and change those who are acted upon. Thinking socially is a means by which such liberation can come about.

HOW TO ENGAGE THE SOCIAL THINKING PROCESS

Social thinking often occurs as people experience a social situation that may cause dissonance. As people gather together, they share their mutual feelings about that dissonance and filter it through their values to make sense of it. They engage in mutual reflection by means of their intuition and begin to generate common understanding about what that dissonance means. They use cognition to examine the facts and develop a strategy of action. Once a strategy is in place, people test themselves in the fires of experience, putting their new understandings into action and then reflecting on those experiences to deepen their understanding. These different steps are not sequential; rather, they are reciprocal and build on one another.

Sensing/Experiencing: Cognitive Dissonance

In many situations of everyday life "action proceeds automatically, without any consciousness of meaning."[49] Often, when some difficulty arises in the course of an action or experience, a person may be prompted to a "consciousness of meaning, thought, and a disruption of mechanical repetition."[50] This disruption of our normal thoughts is called *cognitive dissonance*. Many people, for example, experience some events as tragic, wrong, or unjust, and a gap exists between what is and what ought to be. People are jolted out of their ordinary activities and are confronted with trying to understand the meaning that the discontinuity creates. They try to cope with their feelings and wrestle with their values as they struggle to make sense of what has happened. The result is often a reorientation of consciousness and an attempt to establish a new meaning for the self.

Macro social workers are very familiar with these experiences as we often encounter people who have experienced difficult life crises. Dissonance occurs during times of crisis, such as when a loved one dies, a person loses his or her job, or a tragedy suddenly occurs. Social workers apply social thinking to help people cope with these personal crises and wrestle with the inevitable process of working through grieving and putting their lives back together.

Some people are burdened with an ongoing, chronic sense of dissonance due to their life situation.

For people who experience social problems such as institutionalized ethnic intolerance, gender discrimination, prejudice because of sexual orientation, or economic injustice, dissonance is an ongoing, chronic, daily experience that saps their energy, destroys their identity, and injures their spirit. Unlike grieving over a death or a particular injustice, their experience is so generalized that their entire life is sometimes experienced as tragic, and there is often no one specific incident or experience onto which grieving can be attached.

Such social dissonance throws the meaning of one's whole existence into question. Unlike personal tragedies, the common dissonance people feel who share injustice and oppression cannot be resolved individually but requires an act of community. The experience of common troubles often brings people together into community, and community reciprocally becomes the means by which those troubles can be overcome.

Shared Interaction: Feelings and Values

The experience of oppression and injustice that massive impersonal institutions impose on the human condition is inevitably alienating, asserts Peter Berger.[51] Oppression and injustice creates a sense of isolation, disengagement, and guilt. It drives out the social, destroys the basis of communality, and undermines people's resolve to transcend their distress. In modern society where the normal mode of human life is individualism, oppression and injustice are easily exacerbated, and people are often left with few places to turn.

However, most macro social workers understand that the way people can begin to reclaim their lives is by rejecting alienation and its effects and forming groups and communities where they can reestablish their sense of themselves and become reoriented to the puzzle that alienation presents to them. Rather than a self-perpetuating and defeating life of desperation, sharing memories of injustice and stories of oppression becomes a cohesive force that cements people together.

Sharing feelings is not simply a "therapeutic" technique by which macro social workers help people adapt to an alienating life situation or learn to accept the reality of their situation, however. As people begin to face their feelings and examine the events that brought those feelings about, the depression and hopelessness and guilt that once enveloped them begin to give way to anger. Anger helps people translate their apathy into action.

Intuitive Reflection

Harry Blumer asserts that a community of persons who experience dissonance confront a world that they must interpret in order to act. Communities of people use intuition as a means of active reflection to understand events. Active reflection means setting yourself aside momentarily to allow new perceptions of reality to enter your consciousness. When this happens, you transcend ordinary reality and open yourself to alternative perceptions of the world. When people in community generate these new ways of looking at things, often assisted by a macro social worker, they obtain new understandings, new ideas, and new ways of being and becoming.[52]

FRED ROSS AND INTUITIVE REFLECTION

By the end of a meeting of California migrant farm workers, community organizer Fred Ross could see that by turning the questions back to the group, their thinking had penetrated a complex thicket of considerations; they had come to realize where their interests lay and could form a conclusion about what action they should take based on exploration of alternatives. As he jokingly remarked later, "I stopped being a two-bit Messiah and became a two-bit Socrates instead."[53]

Active intuitive reflection is very different from scientific thinking or rational problem solving. Social problems cannot be solved by top-down solutions or by experts who provide ready-made synoptic solutions to people. Instead, people refuse to accept the conventional or presumed definition of things or to take at face value what those in power assert is true. As your community sees what a situation means for them, they begin to understand what may only be implicit in a situation. Their intuitive social consciousness helps them understand the meaning behind the reality that presents itself.

As members begin to understand that their situation is not tragic, they are compelled to rise above their own solitary interests and the alienation that separates them. As Lauer and Handel point out, meaning

is not an external phenomenon imposed on an individual; rather, "meaning emerges from the interaction process."[54] According to Kaufman,

> The values of *human* life never come about automatically. While a human being can lose his own being by his own choices, for example, a tree or stone cannot. Affirming one's own being creates the values of life. . . . Individuality, worth, and dignity are not *gegeben;* given to us as data by nature, but *aufgegeben*—given or assigned to us as a task which we ourselves must solve.[55]

This task of forging our humanity and infusing meaningfulness into our lives can occur only in community as people mutually reflect on their common experiences.

Cognitive Thinking: Developing a Strategy

Your members now begin to look clearly at the facts of the situation they confront. Unlike emotion and intuition, facts help people deal with the concrete reality. Facts help identify perpetrators and opportunities for action. Members put facts together to form a pattern. This helps them understand cognitively and empirically and confirm what their feelings and intuition have already told them. Community members use cognition to relate to the meaning of the situation and to think through the issues that confront them, not accounting for the least cost or most efficient solution.[56] "New possibilities emerge in the process of interaction between individuals as they cooperate in common."[57]

Any number of strategies can be used. If one strategy does not work, community members can try another. Members use information to learn and, if necessary, change direction, modify their plans, and shift their strategies as the situation changes.

The failure of a strategy is just as important as its success. If one "response is unsuccessful, we become consciously concerned with meaning until we arrive at a solution and satisfactory meaning is achieved."[58] It is the meaning of events that is important, not whether your members win the immediate struggle once and for all. In fact, the struggles against oppression and injustice are never won completely. They must be refought again and again. Neither will everything go according to plan. Learning how to cope with failure, imperfection, and incompleteness is a sign of maturity, and it enables your members to refine their plan's direction.

When your members combine cognition with intuition, they can imagine alternative strategies that they can put into action. Consider, for example, a problematic situation in which several alternative actions exist, only one of which can be implemented. Members review their joint past experiences with each different type of response and *imagine* the consequences of implementing them. As members intuitively place themselves in an action framework, they visualize themselves and their feelings. With practice they will be able to grasp the consequences of their strategies and choose those that are not only successful but are right.

Moving to Action: Thinking as Doing

The experience of putting yourself into the arena of action is crucial.[59] You invest yourself personally along with others who likewise commit themselves to a cause, a goal, or an idea.[60] George Herbert Mead asserts:

> [W]hen we respond to an act, we generate meaning. Meaning is not in the objects or in the event that impinges on us, but in the response that *we* make to the event. . . . We generate meaning when we take action about an event in our lives. The meaning that the event has for us becomes part of our repertoire of behaviors which we have generated."[61]

The very act of doing is the means by which thought is engaged. Putting values, feelings, intuition, and cognition into action is a rehearsal for testing out other new ways of action, which generate new experiences and pave the way for more value generation, intuitive reflection, meaning generation, and more action.

CONCLUSION

Two ways of thinking are available to you and the members of your group: Rational problem solving and social reasoning. Rational problem solving is a "thought" process, not a rigid model. As a thought process, it is helpful in its own domain. Once you have mastered its steps, you have a tool at your disposal that you can adapt to a number of situations. Process, however, is a tool, not a master. You learn a particular process to gain mastery. Like any other tool

or process, rational problem solving must be molded, adapted, and modeled to the contours of the people with whom and for whom you are working.

Social reasoning (also called substantive or classical reason) or thinking socially is a process uniquely congruent with macro social work. Social reasoning explicitly includes the search for higher values, civic consciousness, social goods, and social meaning. Substantive reasoning helps people decide on those values that aim people toward a "continuous, responsible, and arduous effort to subdue one's passions and inferior inclinations and achieve that excellence of character (moral virtue) which is potential to one's nature."[62] Social thinking enables people to utilize whole-mind thinking, which moves people to develop maturity and completeness; and through mutual interaction become creative actors who construct their own social reality.

Macro social workers need to use both rational problem solving based on modern calculative reason as well as social thinking based on values, feelings, cognition, intuition, and action.

KEY CONCEPTS

Thomas Hobbes

Enlightenment

modern reason

rational choice theory (RTC)

Dorothea Dix

Charity Organization Societies (COS)

scientific charity

Settlement Houses

Pendleton Act (1883)

Civil Service Commission

Max Weber

John Dewey

Herbert Simon

Helen Harris Perlman

rational problem solving (RPS)

rational problem-solving cycle

decide on a problem

gather information

generate alternative solutions

assess and compare alternatives

force field analysis

Kurt Lewin

driving forces

restraining forces

benefit-cost analysis

choose the best solution

develop a plan of action

goals

objectives

tasks

tactics

targets

review the strategy

contingency plan

finalize the plan

evaluate the results

debriefing

substantive reason

social thinking

multiple ways of
knowing

Carl Jung

feeling/valuing

intuiting

thinking

doing

whole-mind thinking

classical or substantive
reason

pragmatism

Murray Ross

symbolic interactionists

social self

Paulo Freire

conscientization

liberation theology

sensing/experiencing

cognitive dissonance

shared interaction

intuitive reflection

cognitive thinking

moving to action

meaning

QUESTIONS FOR DISCUSSION

1. What are the strengths of rational problem solving? What are its weaknesses?
2. What are the strengths of social thinking? What are its weaknesses?
3. It was asserted that modern reason is value neutral. Why is being value neutral important in some circumstances? Why might it be problematic for social workers? Should social workers be value neutral in helping people solve problems? Should social workers understand and be engaged in the values that attend social issues?

ADDITIONAL READING

Schon, Donald. *The Reflective Practitioner: How Professionals Think in Action.* New York: Basic Books, 1985.

Learning Theory

Blanco, Hilda. *How to Think About Social Problems: American Pragmatism and the Idea of Planning.* New York: Greenwood Press, 1994.

Dewey, John. *How We Think.* Chicago: Heath, 1933.

Kolb, David A. *Experiential Learning: Experience as the Source of Learning and Development.* Englewood Cliffs, NJ: Prentice Hall, 1984.

Kolb, David A. *Learning Style Inventory.* Boston: McBer and Company, 1981.

Kolb, David A. and R. Fry. "Toward an Applied Theory of Experiential Learning." In *Theories of Group Processes,* C. Cooper, ed. London: Wiley, 1975.

Jungian Personality Theory

Briggs Myers, Isabel. *Introduction to Type.* Palo Alto, CA: Consulting Psychologists Press, 1987.

Briggs Myers, Isabel. *Gifts Differing.* Palo Alto, CA: Consulting Psychologists Press, 1980.

Rational Problem Solving

Allison. Graham T. *The Essence of Decision*: *Explaining the Cuban Missile Crisis.* Boston: Little, Brown, 1971.

Brody, Ralph. *Problem-Solving: Concepts and Methods for Community Organizations.* New York: Human Sciences Press, 1982.

Cook, Karen S., and Margaret Levi, eds. *The Limits of Rationality.* Chicago: University of Chicago Press, 1990.

Elster, Jon. *Rational Choice.* New York: New York University Press, 1986.

4

Leadership: The Hallmark of Macro Social Work

Leadership Formation

The purpose of Communities Organized for Public Service (COPS) is not issues; the purpose of COPS is leadership formation.

Reverend Rosendo Urrabazo, former co-chair of COPS[1]

Ideas in This Chapter

A leader provides training and information so that group members can understand what is possible.

JANE ADDAMS (1860–1935), SOCIAL LEADER

Year after year during her lifetime, Jane Addams was voted the greatest woman in the United States, the greatest in the world, and on one occasion, the greatest in history.[2] Even today, in a survey of 100 professors of history she was second only to Eleanor Roosevelt as the most influential woman of the 20th century. Publicist and persuader, social reformer, crusader, and social activist in the causes of progressive education, housing reform, child labor legislation, criminology, labor organizing, recreation, direct democracy, feminism, treatment of the immigrant, pacifism, and more, she was vitally engaged in almost every important issue of her day. Laura Jane Addams was one of the great pioneers of the Progressive Era in American history, winner of the Nobel Peace Prize, and macro social worker.

Born on September 6, 1860, 2 months before Abraham Lincoln was elected to the presidency, she

was valedictorian and president of her senior class at Rockford Female Seminary. At that time, there were no clearly defined roles for young college-educated women, most of whom were thought of primarily as homemakers. Addams was clearly out of the mainstream. Intensely sensitive, wealthy, and a born leader, but with no clear arena in which to expend her gifts, she entered a period of 7 years of deep personal suffering, incapacitating back pain, and depression.

Except for a brief period in medical school, these apparently fruitless and painful years were a period of gestation in which her character, determination, and sense of mission and purpose were being formed. Restless and unhappy, Addams had no thought of entering social work when at the age of 27 she landed at Southampton three days before Christmas, 1887. She had, however, come into direct contact with the poor for the first time on an earlier trip to Europe. Now, she and her companion, Ellen Starr, investigated social work in the slums of London and met Canon Samuel A. Barnett, founder of the first Settlement

House, Toynbee Hall. For the next 6 weeks Addams and Starr lived at Toynbee Hall. It was an experience that would change Addams's life forever. Like Barnett, she saw how the absence of leadership in the poorer districts had allowed local government to fall into disrepair.

Guilt at the desertion of duty by those who had been trained to lead impelled her to absorb the milieu of Toynbee Hall, its philosophy, ideals of service, leadership, community, and culture in the face of massive urban disorganization and poverty. It was this experience that ended her desperate years of struggle. Addams had finally found her mission in life.

She not only conceptualized a new way of life but lived it. Upon returning to the United States, Addams and Starr bought Hull House, a large mansion on Halstead Street in the middle of a Chicago slum, and turned it into a social settlement. For the next 40 years Addams lived not as an observer of social causes but as a resident in one of the poorest sections of Chicago. She engaged people where they were, immersing herself in their sorrows and joys amid the garbage and dirt. Unafraid to get her hands soiled by the squalor around her, she was determined to learn from the homeless poor, the immigrants, working-class women, children, and the elderly. But most of all, she learned from experience, from trying things out. Wherever there was a need, she was open to experiment, establishing programs, building relationships, improving neighborhoods, and forging community. "She had the kind of mind which could tolerate and even thrive on uncertainty and new experiences."[3]

Addams was a visionary, a part of the radical tradition in America. Ahead of her time in numerous issues, she planted the seeds of reform, many of which were to bear fruit years later. "The poor were poor," she said, "because of misconstructed social environment, not because of a defect in themselves,"[4] but Americans in general proved resistant to this idea. She advocated for the rights of women and laborers, and was "concerned with the poor, immigrants, and children simultaneously. . . . She seemed to regard all of them as sources of the social salvation which she continuously sought."[5] She was convinced it was the outcasts of society who could "bring to reality the social vision which she had been formulating. . . . She wanted to enfold the poor, immigrants, children, blacks and women to full participation in American life not only because as a matter of right they deserved it, but because all of society would be redeemed by their inclusion."[6]

Concrete experience and envisioning the future, however, were only the beginning. As she reflected on the misery she saw around her she "effectively convinced Americans . . . of the seriousness of the problems the nation faced, and of the need for change."[7] Publicist for almost every social cause in her time, the author of 12 books and hundreds of articles and speeches, Addams became a master at persuading people to take up the cause of reform. But even more than simply reflecting and writing about human misery, Addams put her words into action, clearly pointing the direction these changes should take. As a leader of the Settlement House movement, she was instrumental in developing day care, kindergartens, adult education, group work and recreation, immigrant education, sanitation, public health and labor research, unions, child welfare and child labor legislation, programs to combat juvenile delinquency, neighborhood playgrounds, probation services, food safety, the eradication of sweatshops, and improvement of sewage disposal.

She supported and was active in the Illinois Equal Suffrage Association, Christian Socialists, the Chicago Peace Society, the National Consumer's League, the Legal Aid Society, the Juvenile Protective Association, and many labor unions. She had a vision of an "America in which women not only had the vote but . . . would aspire and have opportunity to become college professors, legislators, policy makers in the executive departments of government."[8]

Even before World War I, Addams was a fervent advocate for peace, nearly destroying her reputation and credibility. Her unwavering efforts were finally recognized in 1931 when she was awarded the Nobel Peace Prize. She died in 1935 in the midst of the great reforms of Franklin Roosevelt and Harry Hopkins, both of whom followed her legacy—that the role of government in social welfare was not only practical but necessary. Jane Addams, macro social worker, was without doubt one of the great social leaders of our time.

WHAT YOU WILL LEARN IN THIS CHAPTER

In this chapter you will discover that there are two kinds of leadership in macro social work: social leadership and task group leadership. You will explore a brief history of each of these two kinds of leadership.

Like Jane Addams, you will discover that each step of a social leader's personal journey is a challenge in exercising four leadership functions: thinking, intuiting, feeling/valuing, and sensing. You will learn how to put your social leadership functions into action and how to assist members in the exercise of their own social leadership.

You will explore the nature of a task group, learn about different kinds of task groups with which macro social workers associate themselves, learn how to compose a task group, and learn how to assist group members as they move through the various stages of the group's life cycle.

SOCIAL AND TASK GROUP LEADERSHIP

Developing a working relationship is the key by which social workers help individuals, couples, and families at the micro level. Leadership is the hallmark by which macro social workers assist people in groups, communities, organizations, and society as a whole. One of your first and continuing goals as a macro social worker is to help develop social and task group leadership among the members in the systems with which you are working.

Social Leadership

Social leadership is a means by which community members grasp a vision, chart a direction, and take initiative to utilize social opportunity and make social change. Social leadership builds the capacity of individuals and groups to change their communities and social organizations by shaping positive social values and relationships.

Social leadership occurs when community members engage in neighborhood planning, forming community development corporations and community organizations. Reaching beyond local communities, social leadership enables citizens to construct a civil society infused with ideals of public service, citizenship, cooperation, and participatory democracy.

THADDEUS STEVENS (1792–1868), SOCIAL LEADER

Thaddeus Stevens, one of the great social leaders of his time, was born in Danville, Vermont. He suffered many hardships during his childhood, including a clubfoot. His father was an alcoholic who was unable

to hold a steady job and who abandoned the family before dying in the War of 1812. His mother worked as a maid or housekeeper to support her children. Stevens graduated from Dartmouth College in 1814 and then moved to York, Pennsylvania, where he taught school and studied law. After admission to the bar, he established a successful law practice, first in Gettysburg and later in Lancaster, Pennsylvania.

Stevens served for several years in the Pennsylvania state legislature before his election to Congress in 1848 as an antislavery Whig. He opposed the fugitive slave law and the Compromise of 1850. In 1856 Stevens was reelected to Congress as a member of the new antislavery Republican party, and he soon wielded power as the chair of the important House Ways and Means Committee. A passionate believer in the principles of Radical Republicanism, the "Great Commoner," as he was known, pushed for emancipation and black suffrage.

Stevens encouraged strong, sweeping action by the federal government to revolutionize the racist institutions and culture that bolstered White supremacy in the South. He supported the Fourteenth Amendment, which granted suffrage and civil rights to former slaves, and advocated for an unsuccessful plan to confiscate plantations and redistribute the land to former slaves. As a member of Congress's joint committee on Reconstruction, he opposed the notorious Black Codes, which were used to continue the oppression of African Americans in the South. Stevens was a stalwart defender of the Freedmen's Bureau, the federal government's first social welfare program, dedicated to providing assistance, training, education, and other services to African American farmers, enabling emancipated slaves to benefit from their newly won freedom.[9]

Social leadership is present as people join social movements for social change, laborers form unions, persons with disabilities press for equal treatment, and peace activists join together to end international conflict.[10] Social leadership extends itself into our global society, affirming the capacity and right of all people, but especially impoverished people, to become empowered in their struggle to reclaim their common heritage and have a life free of war, disease, poverty, injustice, and oppression.

Social leadership is based on social, not private, goods. It is a joint venture, not an individual enterprise. Social leadership works in partnership with others, not through condescension or control. Social leadership facilitates empowerment, not patriarchy, and meaning over self-interest.

Social Goods and Social Capital

Leadership is a social good "owned by everyone," not a private good that resides in or is owned by one person who exercises authority over others. It is the common property of all community members. The more social leadership is shared, the more community members achieve joint ownership over their common affairs and are able to exert power in the community. If leadership is hoarded as if it were the solitary property of one or a few people, it is diminished and degraded, ultimately devolving to command and control.

People begin to exert social leadership when they express their feelings, volunteer their ideas, take initiative, assume responsibility, and extend themselves in ways they believe can make a difference. In so doing, community members build a fund of social capital in neighborhoods where citizens are increasingly capable, engaged, and committed to the welfare of all.

IMPORTANCE OF LEADERSHIP

Cesar Chavez pointed out the critical importance of leadership in the barrio, where most Mexican Americans had virtually no awareness of their rights. There was no *functioning* leadership. He began organizing among people who had no experience in community work. They did not know there was a simple way to bring people together and to fan a spark to do something for the community, not only for themselves but also for everyone.

Previously, they would just "cuss the cops," but they soon began to understand that there was something they could do themselves. They also learned that the struggle is unending. Years later Chavez could see that people who "got the bug" continued to work to get others to care and to act. "There have never been such people in the Mexican-American community" the people said.[11]

Joint Enterprise

Unlike unidirectional paternalistic management in which everyone is obliged to follow the lead of the boss, social leadership is a multidirectional collective endeavor in which each member has the opportunity to contribute his or her own unique gifts, skills, and insights. Even those who may be considered the most insignificant members of a community can participate in the shared process of reciprocal learning and teaching, following and leading, giving assistance and receiving help. In this joint enterprise, true community occurs. If leadership is limited to "the best and brightest," those who are most skilled in rational problem solving and are gifted in exacting compliance, social leadership becomes distorted, masquerading as benevolent social control.

Partnership

Social leadership expects that community members will become partners with one another, but they also must become partners with people in the corporate world and in government. Community social leaders never accept corporate or governmental structures as superordinate entities that exist above community members and command compliance from them. We may treat corporate officials and the companies that operate in our localities as respected guests who may sometimes be permitted to use community resources, but with qualifications. Corporate managers may be partners in the joint venture of community prosperity, but they do not have peremptory rights that supercede those of citizens at large nor proprietary permission to siphon resources out of the community for their own benefit.

WHO IS A LEADER?

Cesar Chavez, at the beginning of the organizing effort in San Jose, asked Fred Ross "Why look for leaders among us? If you're trying to find the hotshots in the barrio you're looking in the wrong place."[12]

Fred replied, "No, they're the last ones I'm looking for. What I want are just the plain, ordinary working people who've been pushed around all their lives like you have. While I'm with them I know that somewhere along the line they'll lead me to the second thing I'm always on the lookout for—the man among men. A person the people look up to and trust. A person who'll really bear down and work and stand up and fight. . . . If I can find such a person, that's the one the people will probably choose later on to lead the organization. And that person will keep after them when I'm gone. That's what I mean when I say 'leader.'"[13]

In the same way, government officials, agency bureaucrats, and politicians are viewed as partners not bosses. They are welcomed only when they deliver on their promises. They are expected to be honest, trustworthy, and reliable in carrying out their responsibilities as public *servants*.

Partnership between officials of business and governmental megastructures and members of a community is not tantamount to condescension of the powerful toward those with less power, or benevolence on the part of the economically wealthy to the less advantaged. Partnership is not "maximum feasible participation" granted by those who dole out the gift of inclusion. Citizens are already included. Inclusion, rather, is a gift that community members offer to corporate managers or government officials who keep their promises. Partnership is a commitment to a dialogue between equals—community members and managers who participate in a joint venture of service, through cooperation not concession. A social leader acts as a partner, not a boss; offers encouragement, not control; and requires service, not subservience.

Empowerment Social leadership empowers us, stands beside us, and affirms that we can act on our own behalf to create the kind of society we desire. Authentic social leaders affirm that power belongs to everyone in the social community and, therefore, are "concerned with *increasing the power of others, rather than seeking their submission.*"[14] Social leadership asserts that we already have authority to act and to speak, to think and to plan, to decide and to do, to share and to serve. We do not "need permission from others to have feelings or approval from those in authority to take what matters into our own hands,"[15] Peter Block states. It is everybody's right and duty to create a vision and translate that vision into concrete practice. "We do not need sponsorship from above to do the right thing. . . . The only reliable leadership is our own."[16] Social leadership upholds our rights to own our own visions, claim our future, and construct the community of which we are a part.

Meaning Social leadership helps community members define the premises that guide them toward their common goals. Members come to understand that they can contribute to the cumulative life of others beyond their own self-interest. Members grasp meaning and pass it on. In this way the life of the entire community is enhanced. Each person becomes a leader because every person mutually contributes to the meaning and direction of the community. It is the talking and sharing, envisioning and dreaming, acting and doing that give the community a sense of itself: its voice, its direction, and its strength.

COURAGE, WISDOM, AND DEDICATION

When the pastor of his church criticized him for spending all his time with the Community Service Organization (CSO), Cirillo Lopez replied, "A man must be himself, must be responsible for his own actions. He must be free to do what he thinks is right and what is good for others. One man is a good thing, two are better and three still better. *Hombre sin hombre no vale nada.* [A man alone accomplishes nothing.]" So he works for the CSO.

Cirillo Lopez was not an educated man. . . . But without his qualities of courage, wisdom and dedication, the CSO would not have been revived. These were qualities of which any organization might have been proud. It was men like Lopez whom Fred Ross was always on the lookout for when he came into a community to organize.[17]

Task Group Leadership

All macro social workers must be able to assist a task group accomplish its purposes. We need to understand what task groups are. Macro social workers use task groups in community, organizational, societal, and international social work.

What Is a Task Group? A task or work group is an artificially formed gathering of people designated by others to solve a problem, make a decision, or carry out a goal. Task groups are functional groups. A person in authority needs a particular job accomplished and formally designates a task group to carry out that function. This formal group follows specific procedures and often requires members to carry out designated roles. Members are often chosen because they fit the requirements of the purpose for which the group is formed. Task groups are also instrumental. They are tools or instruments by which people carry out the functions of the social system.

Community Task Groups Macro social workers use task groups in community settings. We may help citizen planners form community planning boards, focus groups, community forums, and ad hoc committees to assess needs or community strengths, devise strategies or plans, educate the community about the plan, and implement the plan. Community organizers use task groups to establish a formal organizational structure, conduct educational and leadership training groups, decide on targets, devise strategies and tactics, review the effectiveness of strategies, raise funds, and recruit new members. Community development corporations use task groups to devise business and economic development plans, obtain funds, develop housing, create jobs, oversee and manage projects, engage in public relations and community education, and review and evaluate the effectiveness of its activities.[18]

Organizational Task Groups

Macro social workers use task groups to decide if a new social organization is needed. A social worker may form community members into a task group to gather information and assess needs, to write articles of incorporation and by-laws. The task group members may form a Board of Directors and divide their work among various standing and ad hoc task groups to raise funds, hire staff, oversee the program, set policy, and perform other tasks.

Leaders of the resulting social agency will often form groups of employees into task groups to carry out various organizational projects. Social workers engage task groups in case conferences and participate as members of an interdisciplinary team or a project management group, for example. Social workers may also use task groups to devise agency policies, decide how to distribute workloads, and establish procedures to streamline agency processes. Most social workers form task group units led by a supervisor who meets regularly with members to review the unit's progress, share information, make decisions, and solve problems.

Agency administrators often use task groups to disseminate information and discuss concerns at agency-wide and departmental staff meetings. Social work administrators may ask some of the more senior members of the agency to form an executive group to help plan the agency's direction, coordinate operations, and make budgeting and personnel decisions. Administrators also may be task group members in groups formed by the agency board of directors and may also become members of community and professional task groups.

If an organization becomes dysfunctional, macro social workers use a variety of task groups including integrated work teams, project management teams, conflict management groups, quality circles, and problem-solving task forces to help improve organizational effectiveness.

Societal and International Task Groups

Macro social workers who engage in social policy advocacy or politics will engage people in a policy task force, action research groups, advocacy groups, and policy implementation task groups. Macro social workers help activist movements strategize, plan tactics, and carry out strategies in groups. At the international level, macro social workers may work with non-governmental organizations (NGOs) to carry out community or economic development projects, forming educational groups, planning groups, advocacy groups, and others. Macro social workers must be familiar with and capable of working with many kinds of task groups.

A BRIEF HISTORY OF SOCIAL AND TASK GROUP LEADERSHIP

Social leadership and task group leadership have followed parallel but sometimes intertwined paths. Macro social workers must understand these two different strains of practice and how each has utilized and often borrowed ideas from the other.

Social Leadership: The Early Years

Numbers of outstanding social leaders worked to bring about innovative solutions to social conditions at the founding of the nation, during the mid-1800s, and again at the turn of the 20th century.

Founding of the Nation

The early years before and after the founding of the United States and Canada witnessed the efforts of many dedicated social and civic-minded leaders who worked to enhance civil society, including Benjamin Franklin (1706–1790) in program development, Thomas Gallaudet (1787–1851) with the deaf, Horace Mann (1796–1859) in education, and Samuel Gridley Howe (1801–1876) with persons with developmental and emotional disabilities.

Mid-1800s: Group Work, Advocacy, and Child Saving

As early as the 1850s, social leaders concerned about the lack of socialization opportunities developed character-building group work programs including the Young Men's Christian Association (YMCA) and the Young Women's Christian Association

(YWCA). Social leader Dorothea Dix (1802–1887) pioneered in the field of policy advocacy for persons with developmental and emotional disabilities, and Charles Loring Brace (1826–1938) provided leadership in child welfare reform for homeless children.

Turn of the 20th Century   At the turn of the 20th century, group work and social activism were two ways in which social workers exerted efforts in social leadership.

Group Work   "Social group work ranks among the earliest practice efforts to realize the potentials inherent in the small group experience to maximize the well being of individuals and improve social conditions"[19] says Alissi. It was one of the first of what may now be termed the "process disciplines whose ultimate purpose was to assist in individual character development, citizenship, civic responsibility, encourage skills in leadership and contribute to more just and equitable civil society."[20]

Social group work grew in the 1880s, encouraged by the development of "groups in settlement houses, the recreation movement, labor unions, adult education, brotherhoods, Jewish community centers."[21] Settlement Houses, for example, assisted poor and immigrant families while learning the American way of life, provided children and youth with character-building activities, and engaged in neighborhood improvement by means of social groups, clubs, recreation, adult education classes, theater, and arts groups. Jewish Community Centers, YMCA, Boy Scouts and later Girl Scouts, and Boys and Girls Clubs encouraged self-reliance and responsibility through camping and as a way for children to escape the long hours and 7-day workweek spent in relatively dark, poorly ventilated, and otherwise unhealthy factory settings.[22]

Social Leaders and Social Activism   In addition to building character and civil society, the late 1800s saw an explosion of social leaders, including Thadeus Stevens, Sophonisba Breckenridge, Booker T. Washington, Web Dubois, Ida Wells Barnett, Florence Kelley, Grace and Edith Abbot, Mother Jones, Homer Folks, Carrie Chapman Catt, Susan B. Anthony, Josephine Shaw Lowell, and Clara Barton, who rose to the challenge of combating a host of social ills arising from slavery, racial inequality, poverty, government and political corruption, lack of workers' rights and women's suffrage, child labor, and alcoholism, to name just a few.

FLORENCE KELLY (1859–1932)

Born in Philadelphia on September 12, 1859, Florence Kelly was the daughter of Caroline and William "Pig Iron" Kelly, a member of Congress. Because no American Law School would accept women, Kelly studied law at the University of Zurich, where she published a translation of Friedrich Engels's *The Conditions of the Working Class in England in 1844* for which Engels himself wrote a preface. In 1891 Kelly joined Jane Addams at Hull House. Because of her intense interest in women's and children's labor, she was commissioned by Illinois Governor Altgeld to survey the Chicago slums and report on the employment of children in sweatshops. Kelly's analysis resulted in a new state child-labor law, including the development of a Department of Factory Inspection, to which she was appointed its first chief.

When the district attorney refused to cooperate with her, she decided to conduct her own court battles on behalf of children. She obtained an LLB in 1894 and, as a lawyer, worked through the legal system to improve policies and conditions of the poor. So vivid and compelling were her demands for better protection of children at work that she succeeded in obtaining another child-labor law in 1897.

In 1899 Kelly moved to Henry Street Settlement in New York City to become General Secretary of the National Consumers League. For the next 25 years Kelly built a distinguished pattern of social reforms, including minimum wage laws, women's suffrage, and federal aid to mothers and babies, and radical reforms in the employment and education of children, working conditions for women, and factory hygiene. In 1903 when a challenge to the state's 10-hour workday law was coming before the Supreme Court, Kelly and her associates compiled the brief for Justice Brandeis that provided the basis for the historic Supreme Court decision ratifying the 10-hour law.

Kelly was a courageous advocate of women and children and workers and consumers, and as a legal scholar and policy analyst, she authored many reforms and laws. She was ahead of her time in her belief that the cause of destitution was modern industrialism and that industry must be controlled by the state. Florence Kelly, social worker, lawyer, and policy advocate by profession, a Quaker by religion, a socialist by politics, was one of the great humanitarians at the turn of the century. She died in Germantown, Pennsylvania on February 17, 1932, at the age of 73.[23]

Leadership in the 1920s

In the 1920s several group work theorists began exploring the connection between group process and democracy while early psychologists sought a trait theory of task group leadership.

Social Group Work and Democracy

By the 1920s, social group workers were applying their ideas of leadership to education, recreation, and religious institutions, but especially to the role of group work as a foundation of the democratic process. Social worker Eduard Lindeman (1885–1953), for example, "explored more deeply than others"[24] the principle that leadership should be conducted according to democratic processes and values. In 1921 he asserted that democracy was "an attempt on the part of people who live in small compact local groups to assume their own responsibilities and to guide their own destinies."[25] A democratic society, he asserted, would not only provide the means for the expression of group differences but also provide for the common good as people were integrated into the whole.

Building on Lindeman's work, social worker and administrative theorist Mary Parker Follett (1868–1933) began organizing small groups for political action. In 1926 she developed ideas about social thinking and democracy that she expressed in her book *The New State*. She wrote, for example, "the group process contains the secret of collective life. It is the key to democracy, and is the master lesson for every individual to learn. It is our chief hope for the political, the social, and the international life of the future."[26] Follett believed neighborhood and occupational groups were important elements in the new democratic state and that the group method of building a foundation of participation, expression of ideas, and shared leadership were crucial to the democratic process.[27]

Early Task Group Leadership: The Search for Traits

Early psychologists attempted to define leadership by means of personality traits. Hundreds of traits such as intelligence, maturity, drive, and friendliness were thought to be associated in some way with leadership. However, these psychologists were unable to agree on a definitive listing or discover a clear positive relationship between specific traits and leadership ability. Reviewing this research in 1961, Eugene E. Jennings concluded, "Fifty years of study have failed to produce one personality trait or set of qualities that can be used to discriminate leaders and non-leaders."[28]

Social and Task Group Leadership in the 1930s

In the 1930s social group workers continued to develop social leadership theory and practice. Social work leaders made contributions to social improvement during the Depression, and social group workers expanded the idea of group leadership in a democracy.

Social Leadership Theory and Practice

Drawing on the work of social scientists who had studied subgroups and community and on Charles Cooley's concept of the looking-glass self, in 1930 group worker Grace Coyle (1892–1962) formulated a unified theory of small group leadership. In *Social Process in Organized Groups,* she amplified her many experiences with groups in the YWCA, industry, and the adult education and Settlement House movements. In spite of her efforts, social group workers of the 1930s realized that experience-based generalizations were of limited value. To further their understanding of groups, they needed to engage in systematic investigation. As a result, group dynamics began to emerge as a distinct field.

Group dynamics theorists collaborated with group workers on various research projects and developed a taxonomy of common group work terms, including group purpose, structure, social process, status, roles, and stages of group development. The importance of social leadership and group work were recognized in 1935 when a section for social group work was added to the National Conference of Social Work. Social workers Wilbur Newstetter and Grace Coyle outlined the philosophy and practice knowledge of group work leadership. By the following year enough belief in and commitment to the use of small groups had been generated for social group workers to form their own association, the American Association for the Study of Group Work, which promoted the study of all aspects of working with groups.

Social Leadership During the Depression

During the Depression many social workers served in ranking positions in the Roosevelt administration: Ewan Clague, administrator of the Social Security Administration; Jane Hoey, Director of the Bureau of

Pubic Assistance; Frances Perkins, Secretary of Labor; Wilbur J. Cohen, "Mr. Social Security," author of the social security law and later Secretary of HEW; Harry Hopkins, Director of the Federal Emergency Relief Administration (FERA), the Works Progress Administration (WPA), and Secretary of Commerce; as well as Grace and Edith Abbott, Eduard Lindeman, Henry Morgenthau Jr., and Adolph A. Berle; I. M. Rubinow, father of social insurance in America; and Paul Kellog, editor of *Survey* magazine. In addition "the American Public Welfare Association and the American Association of Social Workers lobbied hard in the early 1930s for federal public works and employment relief. . . . Social workers never showed more interest in public welfare than they did in the Depression years," says James Patterson.[29]

Social Leadership and Democracy

During the 1930s a number of social work practitioners and behavioral scientists sought refuge from the horrors of Nazi Europe by fleeing to the United States. Among them were S. R. Slavson, Giselle Konopka, and Kurt Lewin. They described democracy not only as an ideal model on which group processes should be based but also as a pragmatic and effective style of leadership. Social worker Samuel R. Slavson contributed to the idea of democratic social leadership in his book, *Character Education in a Democracy,* and later Grace Coyle wrote *Group Experience and Democratic Values,* which emphasized the use of small groups in a democratic framework.[30]

Kurt Lewin and Democratic Task Group Leadership
Kurt Lewin and his associates expanded the idea of democratic leadership to include task groups. In 1938 Kurt Lewin, Ronald Lippett, and Robert White conducted the single most influential study of task group leadership. Of the hundreds of traits that seemed to characterize good leadership, Lewin and his colleagues identified three clusters of traits, each forming a type of leadership style. The researchers instructed volunteer leaders to adopt one of these three styles in leading groups of 10-year-old boys: (1) An *authoritarian* leader is directive and does not allow much participation from members in decision making. (2) The *democratic* leader encourages group discussion, sharing, and decision making. (3) The *laissez-faire* leader is highly nondirective and provides very little overt direction to the group. Each of these styles was experimentally manipulated to understand how it affected

such variables as member satisfaction and frustration and aggression.

Although the overall results were inconclusive, the study did suggest that different styles produced different reactions among group members. Groups having autocratic leaders generated high degrees of hostility or apathy in members. Laissez-faire leaders also produced aggressive reactions in some members. Leaders displaying democratic leadership, however, generally produced fewer negative reactions than either autocratic or laissez-faire leaders.

The Lewin, Lippitt, and White study provided an advance over trait theory. Reducing traits to several clearly defined styles provided a model that was simpler and easier to understand. The idea of "style" implied that leadership is not a fixed characteristic of one's personality but is more fluid. A style is something that one can "put on" and adapt. The extremes of either laissez-faire permissiveness or autocratic domineering leadership were seen as less effective, but a democratic leadership style was seen as the "best" style, at least for some groups.[31]

The 1940s and 1950s: Professionalizing Social Leadership

During the 1940s and 1950s the practice of group work developed its theoretical and practice base, and many group workers published textbooks to educate students in the method.

Professional Organizations

Entrusted with teaching and practicing social leadership during the 1940s and 1950s social group work continued to emphasize building character, developing leadership skills, and empowering people for social change within the framework of a democratic group process. By 1946, for example, members of American Association for the Study of Group Work had affirmed the centrality of group work content, as well as group work's common knowledge and theory base in working with small groups.[32] A new organization, the American Association of Group Workers, was established, published its own journal, *The Group,* and disseminated a broad array of ideas and experiences about group work leadership. Gradually hospitals, family agencies, correctional agencies, and schools began to make use of group work leadership methods. When the National Association of Social Workers (NASW) formed in 1955, social group work was included as one of the three primary methods of social work.

Educational Materials   In the late 1940s group workers wrote several seminal books. In 1948 Grace Coyle published *Group Work With American Youth* and Harleigh Trecker provided one of group work's first textbooks, *Social Group Work: Principles and Practice*. A year later, a major textbook, *Social Group Work Practice,* written by Gertrude Wilson and Gladys Ryland, appeared. Wilson and Ryland merged their differing experiences in working with groups and described how to lead social groups as well as the principles of task group leadership, including how to use task groups in social work administration and supervision. In 1951 Helen U. Phillips published *Essentials of Social Group Work Skill,* focusing on the worker's leadership skill as a primary means for fulfilling social values and purposes.[33]

Task Group Leadership From 1945 to 1960

After World War II, a diverse group of organizational scholar/practitioners began a 15-year process of experimentation, interaction, and theorizing to find ways of improving leadership effectiveness in large organizations. Among the first was the Research Center for Group Dynamics (RCGD), founded in 1945 under the direction of Kurt Lewin, who had emerged as one of the most prolific theorists, researchers, and practitioners in interpersonal, group, intergroup, and community relationships.[34] These efforts led to the development of the National Training Laboratory (NTL) in Bethel, Maine, founded by associates of Kurt Lewin, who died in early 1947. Research/practitioners from NTL including Douglas McGregor, Rensis Likert, Robert Blake, Jane Mouton, and Warren Bennis became consultants with corporations such as Exxon, Union Carbide, General Mills, and the U.S. military. Their work led to an explosion of task group leadership theorizing and the experimental use of groups in improving human relations in large organizations. These research/practitioners created a new field called organization development, which is discussed in Chapter 12.

Social and Task Group Leadership in the 1960s

The turbulent 1960s caught social workers unprepared to make a significant contribution to the fertile social changes that were occurring around them. For organizational task group theorists, however, this period saw a rich harvest of theory and practice, reaped from the experiences and research often inspired by former staff of the NTL.

The Decline of Social Leadership in Professional Social Work   Three developments contributed to the decline of social work leadership in the 1960s: the changing role of social casework, the undeveloped position of community organization practice, and the dissolution of group work.

Changing Role of Social Casework   Social caseworkers, by far the largest and most prominent group of social workers, challenged the dominance of psychiatry and psychology in the field of psychotherapy. As social caseworkers shifted from helping people resolve social problems of poverty to providing clinical treatment for personal, relationship, and family problems, their interest in providing leadership for larger social concerns dwindled.

Undeveloped Position of Community Organization Practice   In 1962 the Council on Social Work Education formally recognized community organization as a social work method comparable to casework and group work. The role of social reform and generating social leadership that social group work had played for nearly a century was shifted to this new social work specialty.[35] During the 1960s, however, most schools of social work lagged in providing coursework in community practice due to a "lack of resources to teach this material and a lack of awareness on the part of potential students."[36] In addition, the relatively few students interested in community organization were often placed in group work classes, many of which emphasized therapeutic group work, creating major limitations for those who wanted to develop skills in promoting social change and community leadership.[37]

Dissolution of Group Work   In 1963 the National Group Work Practice Committee of the National Association of Social Workers formally eliminated from social group work its foundational emphases on social growth, personal enhancement, and citizen participation. The principles on which social group work had been based since its inception in the mid-1800s were stripped from its core. Bereft of its role in social reform and deprived of its socialization and character-building function, social group work as a distinct field of practice was effectively destroyed.[38]

Effects on Social Work Leadership Because of these developments, the profession of social work, in general, stood on the sidelines at the very time when some of the 20th century's most momentous struggles for civil rights, welfare rights, women's liberation, human potential, gay liberation, and peace were occurring. "It is ironic," asserts Fatout and Rose, that "while social work was busily dismantling social and task group leadership, Johnson's War on Poverty was working to encourage community social action, emphasized group process though Head Start, and supported citizen participation by community based planning through the Model Cities program and others."[39] Unlike the Progressive Era and the Great Depression, when social workers played an important and creative role, few social workers rose to significant roles of social leadership in the 1960s either in social sector agencies or in government.[40]

The Rise of Task Group Leadership in the 1960s

The 1960s was a seminal decade of task group leadership theory and practice. Task group research, including that of Douglas MacGregor, Rensis Likert, Robert Blake, Jane Mouton, A. K. Korman, Fred Fiedler, Paul Hershey, and Kenneth Blanchard, laid a foundation for almost all subsequent theories of leadership and management.[41]

MacGregor's Theory X and Theory Y In 1960 Douglas MacGregor wrote one of the most influential books in the field of leadership, *The Human Side of Enterprise,*[42] in which he proposed two theories of leadership based on the nature of man and work. One of these he called Theory X, and the other Theory Y.

Theory X assumes that the average human has an inherent dislike of work and will avoid it. Individuals must be coerced, controlled, directed, or threatened to produce. People avoid responsibility and take the path of least resistance. Theory Y, on the other hand, asserts that people want to accept responsibility, learn,

and work. External inducements, punishment, and coercion are not always effective. Instead, people have the capacity for self-direction, growth, independence, and self-reliance. Commitment results from people being rewarded for their achievements.[43]

Although MacGregor emphasized that these two theories are not polar opposites, most managers accepted the implicit message that "'good leadership' is generally described as democratic rather than authoritarian, and employee-centered rather than production-centered, concerned with human relations rather than with bureaucratic rules."[44] MacGregor's concepts, therefore, lent themselves to the notion that two different variables are basic to leadership. These two aspects are a people orientation, as expressed in Theory Y, and task or productivity orientation, as expressed in Theory X.

Rensis Likert's University of Michigan Studies Rensis Likert of the University of Michigan's Institute for Social Research empirically verified that the twin variables of people orientation and task orientation were key components of leadership. Likert found that many high-performing supervisors tended to focus on the "human aspects of their subordinate's problems, and on endeavoring to build effective work groups with high performance goals."[45] Likert called these supervisors "employee-centered" (Theory Y).

Task or "job-centered" (Theory X) supervisors, on the other hand, who kept constant pressure on workers to produce, were more often found to have low-performing work groups. Likert's research also showed a statistically reliable variation between the effects of the two leadership styles: 85% of supervisors with a task/job-oriented (Theory X) leadership style led work groups with poor performance, but surprisingly 15% had high performance. Although 70% of the supervisors who used a people-centered (Theory Y) leadership style led work groups with high productivity, an equally surprising 30% consistently led work groups with poor performance.[46]

Ohio State Studies Ohio State University researchers verified Likert's conclusion that leadership styles vary considerably from leader to leader. Some leaders liked to structure activities of followers in terms of task accomplishments. Others concentrated on providing employee centered, socioemotional support by means of personal relationships, and still others provided little structure at all. No one style appeared dominant. They concluded, "task and relationship are

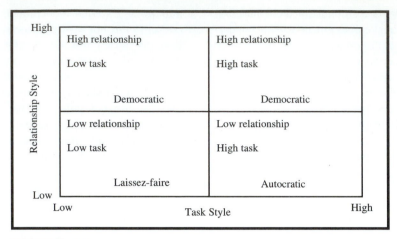

FIGURE 4.1   Ohio State Leadership Model

not either/or leadership styles as the authoritarian-democratic-laissez-faire continuum suggests." These styles can be considered as "typologies" and plotted on two separate axes, where one axis represents task style and the other relationship style, resulting in four different variations in leadership style (see Figure 4.1).

Low relationship/high task orientation was similar to an authoritarian style, low relationship/low task orientation was equivalent to a laissez-faire leadership style. The two middle-range styles, high relationship/high task and low relationship/high task were different types of democratic leadership styles.[47]

Blake and Mouton's Leadership Grid   In 1964 Robert R. Blake and Jane S. Mouton, utilizing the typology developed by the Ohio State group, clarified the definitions of relationship and task leadership.[48] Task behavior, they asserted, is the extent to which a leader decides on member roles, defines the task, provides clear structures, establishes boundaries, provides channels of communication, and demonstrates ways of getting the job done. Relationship behavior, on the other hand, is the extent to which a leader is likely to maintain personal relationships with members of the group and provides socioemotional support, often characterized by friendship, mutual trust, and respect for followers' ideas.[49]

Blake and Mouton theorized that these behavioral leadership factors may be combined so that under differing conditions leaders may be required to adapt *both* people- and task-oriented styles at the same time (see Figure 4.2). A leader who has a low relationship orientation and a low task orientation (1, 1) would be effective under conditions where little direct leadership intervention effort is required. A leader with a high relationship orientation and a low task orientation (1, 9) would do best in situations where there is a strong need to sustain relationships with group members. A leader who possessed a low relationship orientation and a high task orientation (9, 1) would be effective when human elements interfere with accomplishing tasks. Finally, a high relationship combined with a high task leadership style (9, 9) would be useful under conditions in which people need help in becoming independent and task oriented.

A. K. Korman and One Best Way   In 1966 A. K. Korman published some of the most convincing evidence dispelling the idea of a single "best" style of leadership. Korman suspected that both task and relationship were not independent variables inherent in leaders but were *affected by something else as situations changed*. It was this something else that was the key determinant of leadership, not leadership style itself.

Korman reviewed all of the studies examining the relationship between the two leadership dimensions—task orientation and relationship orientation—as well as a variety of intermediate variables such as salary, performance under stress, absenteeism, and turnover. Korman did not definitively discover the conditions under which the two variables interacted, but he did show that there was no one "best" style. Instead, any number of effective leadership styles may be appropriate under different circumstances. After Korman, researchers no longer sought a "one size fits all" leadership style.[50]

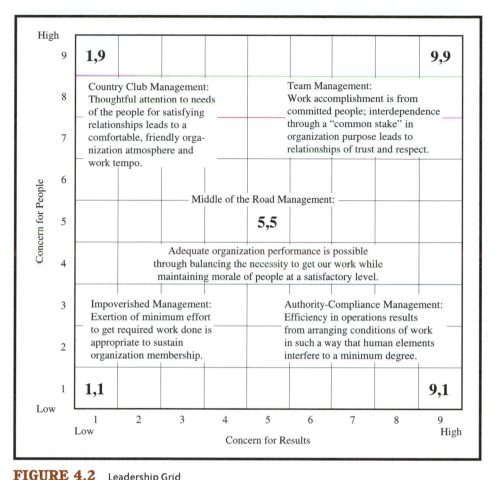

FIGURE 4.2 Leadership Grid

Source: Robert R. Blake and Anne Adams McCanse, *Leadership Dilemmas-Grid Solutions* (Houston, TX: Gulf, 1974), p. 29.

Fiedler's Contingency Theory From 1951 to 1966, Fred Fiedler, an organizational psychologist, struggled to create a model that could verify the relationship between people orientation and task orientation, and in 1967 Fiedler succeeded by inverting the whole leadership paradigm that had been accepted until then.[51]

Relationship- and task-oriented leadership styles are not constants that apply, as Blake and Mouton thought, to any group. Instead, an appropriate leadership style must be adapted to the "situation." One style may work for one group situation, but as soon as the situation changes, that style may become dysfunctional and a different leadership style congruent with the new situation must be used. Among the situational factors, Fiedler asserted, are the needs of the group members and the climate of the group.[52] *"Diffferent leadership situations, therefore, require different leadership styles."*[53]

Fiedler's theory explained in part why the Lewin, Lippitt, and White study found that leaders who used autocratic, democratic, and laissez-faire leadership styles experienced differing degrees of effectiveness and why Likert's empirical work found that leaders who used employee- and task-centered styles could predict that their styles would vary consistently in their effectiveness. Fiedler, however, was not able to demonstrate how leadership varied with group climate nor able to define *climate* in a way that showed what kinds of groups matched the variety of leadership styles. In addition, Fiedler assumed that personal leadership styles were fixed in an individual's personality, and that it would be easier to find a correct fit by placing a leader in a situation that matched his or her own leadership style rather than expect the leader to adapt his or her style to each new leadership situation.[54]

Implications of Contingency Theory The implications of contingency theories of leadership are very significant for both leadership theory and social work education. The fact that leadership effectiveness is not dependent on a single set of traits an individual is born with or acquires at a young age should provide a sense of relief to many people in leadership positions and to educators helping develop leadership. Success in leadership can be attained by almost any individual, assuming that the situation is proper or that a person can modify his or her behavior to fit the situation required by the members of the group. If leaders must "fit their style to the situation," therefore, an understanding of both leadership styles and of various situations in which they find themselves must be at the core of the study of task group leadership. The importance of contingency theories of leadership cannot be overestimated.[55]

Hersey and Blanchard's *Situational Leadership Model*

In 1969 Paul Hersey and Kenneth Blanchard, two organizational psychologists, developed a leadership model that they called "3-D Leader Effectiveness Theory,"[56] which was later renamed "situational leadership." Hersey and Blanchard assumed that individuals in groups go through various phases of learning. As people develop their abilities, they need different styles of leadership. A leader must modify the amount of direction and the intensity of socioemotional support offered depending on the readiness level of the members.

Hersey and Blanchard defined four levels of individual readiness (see Figure 4.3). Some individuals, particularly those in a recently formed group or who are unwilling (lack motivation) and are unable (lack skills), will display low readiness to successfully complete a task, engage in group problem solving, or work on a community project. Hersey and Blanchard recommend that a leader of a group that expresses low readiness should adopt a high-task/low-relationship (HT/LR) "telling" stance characteristic of a directive leader. As group members become more motivated and skilled (struggling but still uncertain), the leader should shift to the high-task/high-relationship (HT/HR) "selling" stance of a democratic leader. When members reach a stage where their skills have progressed but they still need reassurance and encouragement (more capable, but lack practice), a leader should adopt a high-relationship/low-task (HR/LT) "participating" style characteristic of a supportive leader. Finally, when group members are highly capable and self-motivated (willing and able), the leader takes a low-relationship/low-task (LR/LT) "delegating" style similar to that of a laissez-faire leader.[57]

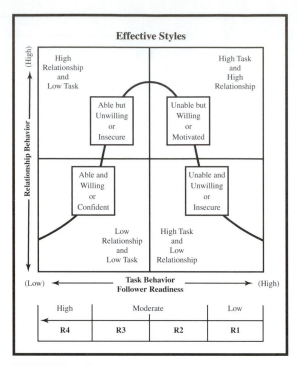

FIGURE 4.3 Situational Leadership*

Source: Paul Hersey, *The Situational Leader* (Escondido, CA: The Center for Leadership Studies, 1984, p. 63). Reprinted with permission; all rights reserved.

*Situational Leadership® is a registered trademark of the Center for Leadership Studies, Escondido, California.

Social Leadership From 1970 to the Present

Social work methods continued to be split in the 1970s, resulting in a further decline of social leadership. Group work, however, was instrumental in bringing about a change in how social work was conceived.

Bifurcation of Social Work in the 1970s

In the 1970s, because of the demise of group work, social work was divided into clinical and community practice. Social workers who remained committed to group work practice tended to link with one or the other of these two methods. Some gravitated to using groups for individual remediation and treatment. Social worker Samuel R. Slavson, for example, became one of the fathers of the group psychotherapy movement and founded the International Association of Psychoanalytic Group Psychotherapy. Virgina Satir became a leading social worker in the field of family therapy. Others joined the emerging field of social work practice with communities. A journal of group work in the social work profession, first published in 1978, reflects this dichotomy, bearing the title *Social Work With Groups: A Journal of Community and Clinical Practice.*[58]

De-emphasis in Social Leadership

By the late 1980s and early 1990s, the problems created by the split in social work between clinical treatment and social reform were increasingly being recognized.[59] One of the casualties in this split was in the area of social leadership.[60] "The role assigned to leadership by the social work profession has declined in recent years," reported Burton Gummer in 1990.[61] The de-emphasis of social work leadership has been the result of an intraprofessional "struggle for primacy between individual intervention and social change to improve the quality of life."[62] The resultant retreat of social work leadership is "in sharp contrast to fields like business and public administration, where the preparation of graduates to assume leadership positions is given high priority."[63]

A New Role in Social Work

Concerned about the consequences of this rivalry, social workers who recognized the importance of task group and social leadership began to have an impact on the profession of social work in a way that would begin to shift its direction. These social workers perceived that the "group is a bridging concept in social work between individuals and . . . communities."[64] They believed the practice of social work with groups is "important enough to have its unique context preserved and developed for continued enrichment of professional practice as a whole."[65]

Rather than continue the false dichotomy in which social workers were forced to choose between clinical or community practice, group workers began advocating for a new way of conceptualizing social work practice. "It was the particular genius of social group work," asserted Pernell in 1986, "to bring together into one concept, into one group, and sometimes into one action concerns for the individual, concerns for the group, and concern for society, and to do this through activities that range from play to social action."[66] Three years later, Lewis commented that "we are reaching for a philosophy base which will

bring greater integration of practice—a more holistic approach which makes possible both personal development and attention to the development of humane societal conditions within one practice."[67]

This one practice has now become understood as generalist social work in which social workers apply their skills at any level of intervention. In the center of this process, mediating between the individual and the community or between the individual and the organization, are generalist social work skills in social and task group leadership. Working with groups had returned to its role as a central component in generalist social work practice, linking social work methods into a unified whole.[68]

HOW TO HELP PEOPLE BECOME SOCIAL LEADERS

Social leadership development doesn't just happen. It is the process of building people with power rather than power over people.[69] A generalist-based macro social worker is a facilitator, adviser, and consultant who help members become leaders. You actively engage people and assist members in building whole-mind thinking and leadership skills.

You use your feeling function to help create community and assist members in using their thinking function to develop strength, their intuition to envision, and their sensing function to help the community move to action (see Figure 4.4).

Feeling to Build Community

You gather people together. You invite your members to get in touch with their own feelings, express their anger, and create meaning.

Gather People Together

You engage others, connect people, and help bind your members together. Going out into the neighborhood, you bring people in. You help members find that common thread that weaves them together in a fabric of commitment and consensus. You foster collaboration, strengthening, and enlisting them in capturing the future that your members were meant to have. You help members form themselves into block clubs, neighborhood associations, community organizations, community planning boards, community development corporations, and social organizations.

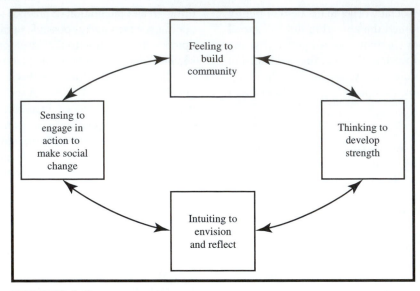

FIGURE 4.4 Social Leadership and the Four Functions

When committee members said, "Let's get started," Fred Ross asked, "What's the best way to get people interested?" It was quickly agreed that strangers starting out to ring doorbells to get signatures on petitions would probably not be successful. Instead, they decided to ask certain people to hold house meetings.

Ross and the chairman headed for the bar and a beer to review what had happened. Ross complemented him for continuing to ask questions, but he continued, "You missed a few opportunities to encourage others to talk. But just remember, whenever you're not sure of something admit it. Members will respect you more for being honest about it. And besides, if they get the idea you think you know it all, they'll turn against you. . . . But the best move of all was that idea of yours about holding a house meeting. That way we'll not only have the people themselves deciding what they want, and working for what they get, but we'll probably wind up with a flock of new members."[70]

Express Their Feelings By having passion for your members' cause and being genuine and real to others, you develop an atmosphere in which members are free to express their feelings. You set a tone of engagement and accessibility in which your members can reach out to one another. You begin where people are, understanding that people frequently carry insecurities about having adequate experience, being skilled enough, or having something worthwhile to say. You ask questions and invite them to share their difficulties and disappointments, successes and failures; you listen as they recount their stories, and you affirm their feelings. You enable and encourage members to respond to their mutual feelings, building a sense of commonality.

Stir Up Anger If your members are unsure, lack hope, or seem afraid or uncertain, you help stir up their indignation, their sense of outrage. As they begin to relate their personal experiences and share their feelings, your members will develop a sense of unity and shared concern. Your members will identify with their common issues and feel united in a cause that gives them a sense of power.

Discover Meaning You assist your members to seek out the brewing consensus among themselves. They will begin to listen carefully for quiet whisperings and attend to subtle cues. They will watch faces and begin to get a sense of what they want and what their friends and neighbors want, what they value, what they dream about. They will develop a deep understanding of their collective yearnings.[71]

You help members articulate those yearnings in a common purpose. You "act as a channel of expression between the down-to-earth followers and their other worldly dreams,"[72] not only communicating but *creating* meaning that gives your people a sense of identity, their own particularity, which sets them apart from all others. This "differentness," cherished and prized among people, fosters pride and self-respect.

Thinking to Develop Strength

You assist your members to become strong thinkers and to confront the past and make sense of the dissonance they feel. Members learn to cement their perceptions with facts and information. They become consistent, confident, and committed in their thinking.

Confront the Past   You help members use their thinking function to gain a sense of the injustices that have been perpetrated against them. Your members confront the way things have been done in the past that create troubles in the present. They challenge the way things are done today to bring about a better tomorrow. Dolores Huerta, an organizer of Mexican American farm laborers in California, said, "You try to crank up your brain. You ask questions to get back to what is basic. You start with: 'What's hurting?' and push on to: 'What's wrong?' and 'Why?'"[73] You help people develop a sense of shared perceptions and feelings that shape and improve their lives.

Obtain Facts and Information   Cognition means adding facts to perceptions and feelings. Without information on which to confirm your members' collective understanding, members may lack the tools that can strengthen their cause. You help members sharpen their thinking, increase their fund of knowledge, and learn more about the conditions that have created problems for them. You conduct an educational session to gain knowledge and understanding: How is the problem affecting people in your community? Who is being affected by it? How many people are affected? How did this situation come about? Who is causing this problem? How long has it been occurring? Who is responsible for resolving it? What are the consequences of the problem to your community? How much will it cost to resolve the problem?

LEADERSHIP TRAINING IN ACTION

The committee chair was encouraged, through the questions put to him by Ross, to anticipate possible difficulties and to consider how he was going to get the group to think about them and solve them. Training

---

did not deal with abstractions. It was conducted in the course of action, encouraging the chairman and members to apply their own experience to dealing with novel problems as they occurred in very real situations. Their judgments as to what to do were quickly tested in action, providing guidance for the next steps.

Action means that community people must take the responsibility and have the opportunity to exercise it. Training in this mode places great demands on the staff worker. He or she must be alert to opportunities, ask questions, encourage the group to consider the consequences of proposals, see new possibilities, take increasing responsibilities, and at the same time be ready if necessary to step in and avert a problem. Until the leaders have learned to cope, the staff must be close at hand to forestall a disaster that could destroy the organization and the confidence of the leader in his or her ability.[74]

Build Confidence   Your members' thinking function helps them become confident in their ability to make things happen and helps you access members' confidence as well.[75] You help your members develop a set of intentions, outcomes, goals, and directions for themselves. If they are firm in their thinking function, they will stand up for their beliefs and assist others to become firm in their beliefs. Help your members practice what they preach and live by the values that they profess. Your members are not simply committed to truth and justice in the abstract; they exemplify the truth in their own lives and actions.

Develop Consistency   Your members' thinking function builds stability and consistency. "It is consistency between words and actions that build your credibility."[76] Edgar Shein adds, "I learned that my own consistency sends clear signals to the audience about my priorities, values, and beliefs. It is the consistency that is important, not the intensity of attention."[77]

Commitment   The more your members cognitively understand the issues that confront them, the firmer will become their resolve, the clearer will be their ability to think through concerns, and the stronger will be their convictions about their cause. They will display commitment and encourage others to become committed as well. Burton Gummer asserts, "People who present clear and convincing arguments for taking action in situations where knowledge is limited or absent will be influential in shaping the thinking and behavior of others."[78]

Intuition to Envision

You help members use their intuition to inspire a shared vision, develop a direction, and articulate their dreams. You assist members as they engage in imagination and reflection to become consciously aware of what they have learned.

Inspire a Shared Vision   The members of your community must have a vision to effect social change. "Every organization, every social movement begins with a dream. The dream or vision is the force that invents the future."[79] This dream gives shape and meaning to people's lives. Dr. Martin Luther King Jr. combined his thinking function, challenging injustice, with an intuited vision. He "envisioned the future 'gazing across the horizon of time' and imagining that greater things were ahead. [He] foresaw something out there, vague as it might appear from the distance, that others did not. [He] imagined that extraordinary feats were possible . . . that the ordinary could be transformed into something noble."[80]

FRED ROSS AND LEADERSHIP

From the start of talking with the chairman about how he was going to conduct the meeting, to encouraging him to keep others involved in the discussion, to raising a question when it was necessary to encourage the group to reflect on the probable consequences of a proposal, to looking back over what happened, praising the good points and warning about the others in all of this process, Fred Ross, a community organizer with migrant workers, was teaching the leader's art so that when he moved on, there would be leaders able to cope with the task.[81]

Sense of Direction   Community members who have a clear sense of direction are best able to lead themselves and help others develop an idea of where they want to go. According to Theodore Hesburgh, president of the University of Notre Dame, "Vision is the key to leadership."[82] Unless your members have a vision of where they are going, they are not going to get there. Your community members "begin with imagination and with the belief that what is merely an image can one day be made real."[83]

Articulate Their Dreams   As you talk with the members and affirm their perceptions, you help members gather their hopes and dreams about what is possible. You help articulate those dreams and assist your members to rekindle inside themselves what is theirs—a future possibility, even though few may see it clearly. You assist your members to envision the outcome and help them head toward it. You reflect their vision back to your members so that they see themselves and their purposes anew; they see their common future and the possibilities of what they can do and be. The community becomes the vehicle by which the shared vision is transmitted.

Reflect on Their Experiences   Learning does not occur from raw experience alone; members must spend time using their imagination and intuition to reflect on those experiences. After an encounter, a meeting, discussion, or confrontation, you create space for reflection. You assist members as they exercise conscious reflection about what occurred, what they did, and why they did it: "What did you learn from that experience?" "What was good and what could have been better about that meeting?" "What could you have done differently?"[84] You assist members in making connections between the actions they have taken and the outcomes that have occurred.

As you play the role of adviser, you attend to the arena of discussion, but you imaginatively place yourself outside of it. For example, you listen to what each member is saying while looking for patterns of interaction that can help the group as a whole move ahead.

You reflect back to members the issues they have been describing, picking up themes and messages, ideas and insights. You pay attention to the content of discussion but look more deeply into what the members may be implying. You think about the problem at hand but try to understand the meaning behind the issues that the members present, and you assist members in seeing underlying issues that can help them understand their own motives, feelings, and actions.

Sensing to Move to Action

You help your members build concrete skills, engage in action, and move ahead one step at a time.

Build Concrete Skills   Your members may have to acquire particular skills in research, leading meetings, speaking at public hearings, organizing committees, writing proposals, seeking funding, hiring staff, training a board, proposing policy, or carrying out services. You assist your members in learning these skills by conducting educational sessions to answer questions like these: What is a meeting? How is a meeting different from a get-together? What about parliamentary procedure? How does it help? Why do we have majority rule? What makes a leader?[85]

Engaging in Action   You help people learn by engaging in action. You offer people different levels of responsibility to increase capabilities. You provide experiences that require them to work with others. You recognize the skills people already have and provide opportunities for them to develop further. You stretch them by placing them in situations to discover talents they did not realize they had, and they put those talents to use in meaningful work that contributes to the common good. You give them specific jobs to do, breaking these down into tasks and concrete steps people can take. You challenge them to think, plan, and engage in action. You offer encouragement and support and facilitate, train, and model social leadership. You consciously use yourself as one who "commits people to action, who converts followers to leaders, and who converts leaders into agents of change."[86]

ALINSKY TEACHES LEADERSHIP IN ACTION

Alinsky asked Fred Ross why he stayed outside and let the council president go in by herself. "Because I wanted her to get in the habit of standing up on her own and demand her rights without my help," I replied.

Alinsky went on to ask why he slipped in later, while she was talking to the board. "Well, that was the first time in her life she had ever gone up before a public official of any kind; and she was very nervous. I wanted to be on hand to help her out in case she got stage fright and started to muff the thing." And Saul is right on me:

"And what difference would it have made if she had muffed it?"

"It would have been a terrible blow to the organization."

"Certainly," Saul nods his head, "and that's so obvious you'd think that anyone could see it, wouldn't you? What all of us have got to remember is that, while it's the function of the organizer to constantly push responsibilities on the people, and to assume right up until the last minute that they will carry them out, still he must always be ready to jump in and take over, himself, in case the people, for some reason or other, fail to follow through.

"Oh, of course, many times it's OK to let them drop the ball and fumble around with it for awhile, so they'll learn. But very often you aren't allowed that luxury. Crisis situations develop, and you've got to move in fast; otherwise the whole program—or a vital phase of it—may be destroyed.

"But it's not only the possible destruction of the program that's involved here and that's the effect on the individual. For instance, how do you think this council president we're discussing would have felt if she had dropped the ball, and you hadn't been around to help her pick it up!"

"Oh," I answer, "she would probably have been so discouraged she'd never be able to face that kind of situation again for the rest of her life."

"Right!" says Saul, "but by being there yourself, the moment you see she's going to muff it, you take over and give her the backing she needs. Even more important you give an example in action, the 'on the spot' leadership training she has to have to be able to meet the same or similar situations in the future. In this field, no real learning takes place unless it's tied right into an action program."[87]

Move Ahead One Step at a Time   The real flesh and blood encounters with one another add substance to members' dreams, and a reality forms as people engage one another in mutuality and trust. You keep your eye on the larger picture as your community moves ahead one step at a time. You help break larger problems into small units, and the community gains with small wins. "The magic in small wins is the experimentation process, or setting up little tests that continually help you learn something."[88] You work with your members as they develop programs, build community development corporations, form community organizations, confront injustice, engage in political activities, and devise social policies.[89] By developing tangible services and programs, community members discover strength in action.

MARJORIE BUCHOLZ DEVELOPS SOCIAL LEADERSHIP

In Marjorie Bucholz's leadership of Chelsea Community Council, one can see [social] leadership at its best. The patience with which she went over agendas with chairmen before they were to perform, not to tell them what to do, but instead to brief them on the issues and their significance is a delight.

The counsel she gave when leaders were perplexed on procedures showed a high level of skill. "The staff worker serves to interpret the worth of a council, to suggest alternatives on how things are done and to handle the feelings and attitudes which play so prominent a part in people working together. The worker must have . . . 'a passion for anonymity,'" she said.[90]

Closing the Circle

The social leadership process now comes full circle. You help members challenge injustice with their thinking function, apply their intuition to hold onto their dream in the face of challenges, draw on their feeling/valuing function to strengthen the community in times of stress, and use their sensing functions to immerse themselves in strategizing and planning.

HOW TO HELP A TASK GROUP ACCOMPLISH ITS PURPOSE

You begin your work by engaging in pregroup planning, helping members conduct the first meeting, and assisting the group as it proceeds through the forming, norming, storming, and performing stages of its life cycle.

Pregroup Planning

The pregroup stage occurs before the group is formed. The success of a task group is based initially on how you define your role, the purpose and process of the group, and its size, composition, and structure.

Role of the Social Worker   The role of macro social workers in a task group is most often as staff. For example, you carry out many of the administrative and household tasks to assist the group in its work such as arranging for a meeting place, sending minutes, arranging for refreshments, taking minutes, following up on assignments and tasks between meetings, and obtaining information and resources for the group.

You provide consultation to the leader by meeting regularly to offer critiques of the chairperson's leadership. You raise questions, point out issues and

concerns, and give advice. You ensure the leader thinks through his or her leadership style, process, and interactions. You may assist members by teaching, giving information, and acting as a liaison to government or other agencies.

Purpose and Process   As you think through the purpose and process, you will more than likely ask yourself a number of questions. Why is this task group important, and what do you expect to accomplish? What roles, tasks, and duties will you expect members to carry out? What will potential members expect from the group, from you, and from the experience as a whole? What will be the role and responsibility of the sponsoring organization? Try to write out answers to these questions in the form of a proposal. This effort will assist you in clarifying what you are trying to accomplish.

Size   "The group should be small enough to allow it to accomplish its purpose, and yet large enough to permit members to have a satisfying experience."[91] The optimal size depends on the purpose of the group and the attributes of the members. Various theorists have recommended groups of from 5 to 9 members as optimal. Herbert Thelen, however, recommends the principle of "the least group size," which states that the proper size of the group is the "smallest group that represents all of the social and achievement skills required for its particular activity."[92]

Composing the Group   When you consider possible membership of the task group, take into consideration member characteristics, knowledge, and skill.

Member Characteristics   Member characteristics affect task group interaction and influence outcomes. The best group members are those who are personally committed to the group project and who bring with them skills, experience, or influence that will enhance the group process. A rule of thumb is to choose people who are homogenous in personal characteristics such as beliefs, values, and commitment to the group, but heterogeneous in demographic characteristics such as life experiences, gender, ethnicity, age, and nationality. Members who share personal ties will ensure stability and help the group become cohesive and motivated. If they also come from different backgrounds, they will increase vitality of the group, add creative perspectives, and devise unique solutions to problems.[93]

CHAPTER 4 Leadership: The Hallmark of Macro Social Work **99**

Ephross and Vassil note that one principle of diversity is the "Law of Optimum Distance." This law states that it is not a good idea to have just one of anything in a group if it can be avoided. The group member who has a unique characteristic may be scapegoated or treated as a token.[94] Try to have a mixture of experienced members and those who are less experienced, those who are verbal, and those who are less verbal. A group with many less verbal members will tend to drag; a group with many highly verbal people may become competitive.

Knowledge and Skill   Another important factor in composing a task group is the knowledge and skill of the potential members. Members of a task group should jointly "possess all the information necessary to the performance of their task plus the ability to interpret and use it."[95] Members should also have the capacity to interact well with others, form relationships, and be able to carry out their commitments responsibly and on time.

Structure   When you plan the task group, think through such administrative matters as the duration of the group, timing and frequency of meetings, meeting time and place, the length of the individual meetings, room arrangement, meeting format, and the resources your group will need, including funding, supplies, and staff support.

Duration of the Group   The time duration of your task group will often affect the quality and quantity of your members' involvement in the project. Members of time-limited temporary groups often take more risks and endure more discomforts than members of long-term groups. If people have reservations about joining a group, serving on a committee, or working with others who are not necessarily to their liking, they may agree to serve if they know they can escape in a short time. In contrast, "members who participate in long-term task groups are more inclined to invest themselves in group membership, develop relationships, and be more cautious."[96]

Time, Place, and Frequency of Group Meetings
Potential members often have constraints on their ability to participate. Make your meetings as convenient as possible for your members. Choose a meeting time and place that is easily accessible for members. For example, for professionals working in government or private agencies, a noon hour near the center of town might be a good choice. Neighborhood residents who

have small children might want to meet at a member's home before children return from school. Others may prefer an evening meeting at a local church. At your first meeting, find out if the meeting time and place are good ones, and if not help members decide on different ones.

Match the frequency of your meetings with the task and availability of members. For example, if there is a demand for intensity in the work, your members may want to meet more often. Otherwise they may meet on a regularly scheduled basis. Your members might appreciate an understanding that the task group will meet 12 times, once a month for a year, with the possibility of one or more additional meetings. With this information, members can plan their schedules, and they may be more willing to commit themselves.

Resources   Try to arrange for a meeting room that is attractive for members. A facility with a large table, comfortable chairs, white or chalk boards, easily accessible telephones and restrooms, convenient parking, and facilities for serving refreshments may add to members' satisfaction.

Leading the First Meeting

Sometimes you may lead a task group. If you are in a position of administrative leadership, for example, you will often provide leadership to your unit or department yourself. You may be asked to serve on the board of a social agency and chair a standing or ad hoc committee.[97] In addition, in a task group where you expect members to lead the group, you may need to assume formal leadership for the first meeting or two and train your members until they can take over effectively.

Keep in mind the principles of good meetings. Make preparations before your first meeting. At your first meeting make introductions, review and modify the agenda, discuss the purposes and structure of the group, work on accomplishing a task, decide on next steps, and bring the meeting to a close. After the meeting, send minutes and an agenda for the next meeting, and between meetings work with members to accomplish their assignments.

Principles of Good Meetings   When you lead or train others in leading a task group, keep the following principles in mind.

1. Begin and end meetings on time.
2. Limit meetings to no more than 1 to 1.5 hours. Shorter meetings are always better.

3. Have an agenda prepared and distribute it to the members in advance.

4. Arrange seating and meeting room facilities to enhance accomplishment of group goals.

5. At the beginning of the meeting, ask members to review the agenda and, if necessary, change, add, or rearrange items.

6. In general, first dispense with short, informational or quick action items that require little or no discussion. Save more complicated issues requiring discussion for the end. If an issue requires more discussion or time than you anticipated, draw the discussion to a close and assign the topic to an ad hoc committee to review and make recommendations to the group at its next session. If the issue is controversial, ask two groups to take opposing views and each present their position at a follow-up meeting to facilitate decision making.

7. After the meeting serve refreshments and ensure that members were satisfied that the meeting was beneficial.

8. Follow up meetings with minutes of what occurred including assignments, deadlines, and a tentative schedule of the next agenda, including place and time of the next meeting.

9. Between meetings follow up with members who have been given specific assignment to ensure that they have been able to carry them out.

10. Keep a quadrifocal vision: Simultaneously focus on individual group members, subgroups, the group as a whole and its stage in the group life cycle, and the purposes for which the group has been formed.[98]

Premeeting Preparation   Send a reminder letter and agenda, and make sure the meeting room is prepared.

Meeting Reminder   About a week before your first meeting, send a letter to each of your members thanking them for their willingness to serve on the task group and reminding them of the location, date, and time of the meeting. List the other members of the task group and include an agenda for the first meeting. Tropman and Morningstar suggest that you divide agenda items into three parts: information items, decision items, and items for discussion. Indicate the action you want taken next to each item.

Leave enough space between items to enable members to take notes or record motions.

Room Preparation   Before the first meeting of your task group, place name cards, an agenda for each member, a pad of paper and pencil, and any other information the group might need on the table. Table arrangements can facilitate power and interaction objectives in meetings. For the first meeting, a square table arrangement is best because it places members in equal proximity to one another. Later you may decide to choose other table arrangements depending on your objectives. For example, a rectangular table places members directly opposite one another, facilitating interaction with leadership directed at the head of the table. Make sure you have coffee and some refreshments prepared and that the room lighting and temperature are comfortable.[99]

Make Introductions   Introduce the purpose of the meeting, the members, and attend to member concerns.

Introduce the Purpose   As members arrive, greet each one by name and introduce members to one another. Begin the meeting on time, even if some members are late. This will establish a norm that members should not be late. Welcome everyone and announce the name and general purpose of the group. You are not only giving information but beginning to establish socioemotional connections.

Introduce Members   Ask members to introduce themselves to one another in relation to the purpose of the task group. For example, if the purpose of the group is to extend transportation services to a particular community, ask members to describe how their lives or the lives of others are affected by the current lack of transportation and explain their interest in or involvement in transportation issues. Such commonalities help members connect with one another and learn about their backgrounds and mutual interests. Make a brief summary statement after a member has introduced him- or herself, such as, "Joe, you, like Sally and John, are interested in attaining bus services so your clients can reach health care services."

Attend to Member Concerns   As individuals come to the meeting, they may have concerns about the mission of the group, how it will be accomplished, where they will fit within this process, and how they will relate to and be accepted by the other members in the group. As you lead members through the first meeting, help them resolve these concerns and assist them in feeling committed to and a part of the group process.

Review and Modify the Agenda
After the introductions, ask members to look at and review the agenda, add items to it, or submit items for a future time. You are establishing your expectation that your members will contribute items for the meeting. You are encouraging them to participate directly in the meeting's content, and you validate each person's worth in the group. If members suggest items, make adjustments to the agenda.

Discuss Purposes and the Structure of the Group
Review the group's purposes, structure of the group, and the roles of members. You are helping members understand how they will participate, assisting them in thinking about how they can contribute, and showing how they can make changes in the group's structure and function to better fit their expectations. When you encourage members to shape the group, you are planting the seeds for group ownership. You demonstrate that they have the power to influence the content and process in the group. If the purpose of the group is to improve their community, develop a plan, or start a new program, help them see how they can make a real difference in making social change.[100]

HELPING MEMBERS DECIDE

Fred Ross was talking with a committee chairman about an upcoming meeting on how to help residents escape the mud by getting the city to pave several blocks of sidewalks in the barrio. Ross asked the chairman how he would handle those who had other problems to bring up. The chairman decided the group should be asked to assign priorities to the various problems.

"But how are you going to decide which comes first?"

"Probably I'll have to help them a little on that. Maybe I'll just keep asking them questions the way you're doing now."

A useful lesson had been learned.[101]

Work on Accomplishing a Task
After everyone is satisfied with the purpose of the group, engage your members in a task on which they can begin to work, such as defining the group's goals. Often the social agency or organization already will have established

the primary goal or purpose of the group. Your group, however, will need to decide how they will accomplish that larger purpose, identify more specific goals and objectives, and look at their priorities.

Members Who Are Unable or Unwilling
You want members to feel excited and motivated by the group. Becoming part of the task group is exciting for some members, but it can create anxiety for others. Sometimes members are hesitant or reluctant to participate. You may present several ideas, but members may be unwilling or unable to discuss them. They may not be sure what is expected of them, what behaviors are appropriate, or that others will accept their ideas in the group. Members may need a way to participate that presents them in a positive way that will add to their self-esteem.[102]

When you ask for feedback, therefore, use a brainstorming or round robin technique in which you go around the table and ask each member for input on goals and ideas. Help the group stay focused. If the group gets off track, redirect the group by restating the purpose and clarifying the direction of the group.

Decide on the Next Steps
When members come to some agreement about the group's goals, ask them to make a list. Have members decide on the next steps in accomplishing the group's purpose and attach tentative time lines to them. Then ask members to volunteer to work on accomplishing one or more goals by the next meeting. Suppose, for example, the purpose of your agency task group is to improve relations between teenagers and the local police department. Your members decide that one goal is to gather information. One member, Mr. Samuels, agrees to discover police policies for stopping and searching juveniles. He will interview the chief of police and attempt to get the procedures in writing by the next meeting. Ask each member to accomplish a task such as this, making the task assignments specific so that you and your members will be able to see the extent to which they have been accomplished.[103]

Bring the Meeting to a Close
After each of your members has agreed to a task assignment, obtain commitment by asking members to structure the agenda for the next meeting. Ask members if the time and place of the next meeting are acceptable; if not,

engage members in making different arrangements. At the end of the meeting, summarize the meeting's accomplishments, the task assignments, the goals of the next meeting, and its time and place. Thank the members for their participation and interest. Serve refreshments and chat personally with members, helping them to relax, enjoy one another's company, and feel more deeply connected to the group.

As you interact with members, both in the meeting and in informal chatting, observe who talks with whom, who are the more silent members, and who are the more talkative members. Watch to see if subgroups form. This will give you clues about how to structure interaction assignments in the future. For example, if certain subgroups seem to form, have those members work together on a project. Pair a more verbal member with a less verbal member to promote mutual communication.

Distribute Minutes and an Agenda for the Next Meeting

Minutes are a record of the decisions made by the task group. In large task groups such as agency boards of directors, one member, usually the secretary, takes minutes. In other task groups you should perform this role. Although there are differing points of view regarding the content of the minutes, a very clear, succinct method should be used that follows the agenda items exactly. You may write your minutes on the agenda if you have left enough space after each agenda item. This way, the minutes are completed as the meeting progresses.

Record the name of the group, the date, time, and place of the meeting, and the names of the members who attended. Record the information that was provided for each information item on the agenda, decisions reached for each decision item, usually with the exact wording of the motion, along with the name of the person making the motion, and the name of the person seconding the motion. Provide a summary of discussion items and any agreements or decisions that result from it. Sign and date the minutes, and send a copy to each member with the agenda for the next meeting.

Work Between Meetings

You follow up with members and committees and work with the chairperson.

Follow Up Although you will accomplish much of your work during group sessions, there are many functions that you will carry out before the next meeting.

For example, you should follow up with members or committees regarding their progress on tasks that they have agreed to accomplish, and make sure that they are prepared to participate effectively at the next meeting. Keep in close touch with your members to ensure that they are learning, growing, and feeling positive about the group and with their participation. Call members on the phone, meet with subcommittees, coordinate work between subgroups, and contact other resources. You also may maintain contact with the administrators, staff, boards of directors, or other significant groups in the community and carry out assignments that you have agreed to.[104]

Meet With the Chairperson After the group chooses a formal leader of the task group, one of your more important roles will be to meet regularly with this chairperson to review the task group meeting, critique his or her performance, give suggestions, help construct the next agenda, and carry out any other tasks that will help the chairperson or the group accomplish its purposes.

Leading the Group Through Its Life Cycle

You focus on individual member development while you attend to the group as a whole.

Developing Member Capacity

Help members move though the stages of the group so they become competent and fully functioning. Ephross and Vassil assert that "as a group matures, so does each member. In a mature group all group members share responsibility for the group's executive function, which can be defined loosely as 'making the group's wheels go 'round.'"[105]

Developing the Group Life Cycle

Not only do your members change and develop as they learn to work with others in a group, but the group itself goes through a cycle of change. Many group theorists have described variations of this cycle. The life cycle stages that seem most useful for task groups were developed by Bruce Tuchman and modified by Linda Yael Schiller.[106] The forming stage occurs in the beginning of group life, the norming and storming stages are middle stages, and the performing stage occurs when group members are fully functioning (see Figure 4.5).[107]

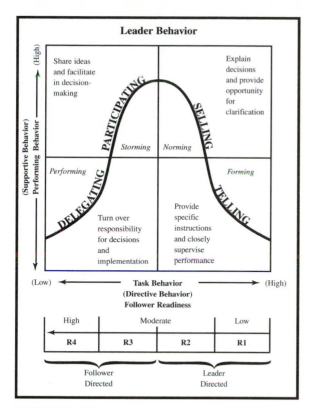

FIGURE 4.5   Group Life Cycle and Leadership Model

Source: Adapted from Paul Hersey and Kenneth Blanchard, *Management of Organization Behavior: Utilizing Human Resources,* 5th ed. (Englewood Cliffs, NJ: Prentice-Hall, 1988), p. 171. Reprinted with permission. All rights reserved.

Each of these stages corresponds to a different leadership style as described by Hersey and Blanchard.

It is important to remember that groups often do not move through these stages in a lockstep fashion. Instead, some groups may skip stages, and others may resolve issues at one stage only to return to those issues again later. Still others, as Bruce Tuchman asserts, may engage in the storming stage before the norming stage. Groups may move through some stages slowly or very quickly. A group may move through issues involving several stages sequentially in one meeting. Other groups may work on issues at several stages simultaneously.

In working with the group as a whole, first informally or formally assess the readiness level of your members. Then adopt a directive leadership style if the group is new or help the chairperson take on this leadership style to help members form the group, shift to a selling stance as members adapt to the group's rules and boundaries at the norming stage, adjust your

role again to a participating style to assist members in developing smooth working relationships in the storming stage, and finally change to a delegating style to enable members to reach a point where they are accomplishing the purpose of the group in the performing stage.

Assessing the Readiness Level of Member

Checklist 4.1 will help you make a formal assessment of the level of readiness and skills of members at each stage of the group's life. Each section relates to a different stage of the group. A high score of 22–28 indicates that a member is clearly operating at that stage. A medium score of 15–21 indicates that a member is in transition from one stage to another. A score of 7–14 indicates that a particular member is not operating at that stage.

CHECKLIST 4.1

Member Readiness Assessment

This assessment will help you identify readiness of members of a task group. Answer as honestly as you can to help the leader and other members understand the level at which the group is functioning. Circle one of the following that most closely matches your feeling about each statement:

1 *Strongly Disagree* **2** *Disagree* **3** *Agree* **4** *Strongly Agree*

If you agree with only part of a question, mark it disagree. After you have finished one section, add up the points and enter the total next to Score_____.

Section I: Forming Stage

a. I need to know what is expected of me in this group.
 1 *Strongly Disagree* **2** *Disagree* **3** *Agree* **4** *Strongly Agree*

b. I need to understand what this group is supposed to accomplish.
 1 *Strongly Disagree* **2** *Disagree* **3** *Agree* **4** *Strongly Agree*

c. I need to know when the group is supposed to accomplish its goals.
 1 *Strongly Disagree* **2** *Disagree* **3** *Agree* **4** *Strongly Agree*

d. I need to get to know members of this group.
 1 *Strongly Disagree* **2** *Disagree* **3** *Agree* **4** *Strongly Agree*

e. I need to know what the members of this group are supposed to do.
 1 *Strongly Disagree* **2** *Disagree* **3** *Agree* **4** *Strongly Agree*

f. I need to know how to proceed in this group.

1 *Strongly Disagree* 2 *Disagree* 3 *Agree* 4 *Strongly Agree*

g. The leader of this group needs to give us clear directions about how this group is to go about its business.

1 *Strongly Disagree* 2 *Disagree* 3 *Agree* 4 *Strongly Agree*

Score:_____

Section II: Norming Stage

a. I know what is expected of me but am not sure how to do it.

1 *Strongly Disagree* 2 *Disagree* 3 *Agree* 4 *Strongly Agree*

b. I am uncomfortable about some of the procedures in this group.

1 *Strongly Disagree* 2 *Disagree* 3 *Agree* 4 *Strongly Agree*

c. I disagree with some of the rules in this group.

1 *Strongly Disagree* 2 *Disagree* 3 *Agree* 4 *Strongly Agree*

d. I am sometimes confused about the direction the group is going.

1 *Strongly Disagree* 2 *Disagree* 3 *Agree* 4 *Strongly Agree*

e. I think we are wasting time in this group.

1 *Strongly Disagree* 2 *Disagree* 3 *Agree* 4 *Strongly Agree*

f. I don't think we are accomplishing everything we could.

1 *Strongly Disagree* 2 *Disagree* 3 *Agree* 4 *Strongly Agree*

g. I have feelings about how the leader is conducting the group.

1 *Strongly Disagree* 2 *Disagree* 3 *Agree* 4 *Strongly Agree*

Score:_____

Section III: Storming Stage

a. This group has internal conflicts it needs to work out.

1 *Strongly Disagree* 2 *Disagree* 3 *Agree* 4 *Strongly Agree*

b. I find myself disagreeing with members in this group.

1 *Strongly Disagree* 2 *Disagree* 3 *Agree* 4 *Strongly Agree*

c. Some members in this group need to be more forthright.

1 *Strongly Disagree* 2 *Disagree* 3 *Agree* 4 *Strongly Agree*

d. Some members in this group dominate discussion.

1 *Strongly Disagree* 2 *Disagree* 3 *Agree* 4 *Strongly Agree*

e. Some members in this group tend to get off track.

1 *Strongly Disagree* 2 *Disagree* 3 *Agree* 4 *Strongly Agree*

f. Some members in this group waste too much time.

1 *Strongly Disagree* 2 *Disagree* 3 *Agree* 4 *Strongly Agree*

g. The leader needs to help group members work through interpersonal issues.

1 *Strongly Disagree* 2 *Disagree* 3 *Agree* 4 *Strongly Agree*

Score:_____

Section IV: Performing Stage

a. Members of this group demonstrate that they know what to do and are able to do it.

1 *Strongly Disagree* 2 *Disagree* 3 *Agree* 4 *Strongly Agree*

b. Rules in this group are jointly worked out with everyone.

1 *Strongly Disagree* 2 *Disagree* 3 *Agree* 4 *Strongly Agree*

c. This group is well on its way to accomplishing its goals.

1 *Strongly Disagree* 2 *Disagree* 3 *Agree* 4 *Strongly Agree*

d. The procedures in this group are clear and workable.

1 *Strongly Disagree* 2 *Disagree* 3 *Agree* 4 *Strongly Agree*

e. Leadership in this group is shared by all the members.

1 *Strongly Disagree* 2 *Disagree* 3 *Agree* 4 *Strongly Agree*

f. Conflicts in this group are resolved internally.

1 *Strongly Disagree* 2 *Disagree* 3 *Agree* 4 *Strongly Agree*

g. Members need only occasional assistance from the leader.

1 *Strongly Disagree* 2 *Disagree* 3 *Agree* 4 *Strongly Agree*

Score:_____

Ask members to compare scores from each section. When scoring for the group as a whole, ask whether members received low, medium, or high scores for each section. Do most members rank one or two sections higher than the others? This will tell you at what stage the group members are operating and what issues the leader needs to resolve before moving to the next stage.

If some members scored high on one section and others scored high on a different section, group members are operating at different levels. This tells you that members are experiencing differing levels of maturity. If members are evenly split, aim you leadership style at the higher level, expecting that the members who are less ready will catch up. In fact, it is probably a good idea to have some members at a lower stage and others at a higher stage so that the higher stage members can assist the lower stage members. However, if several members are two or more stages ahead or behind the others, the higher stage members may feel bored and out of place or the lower stage members may appear to be a drag on the group.

Leading the Task Group Through the Forming Stage

At the beginning of a task group, members will display characteristics of being in the forming stage. They may be anxious and uncertain or appear unwilling (lack motivation) or unable (lack skills) to successfully complete a task. Group members may be unsure about the extent to which other members will personally accept them. Although your members will most certainly come with a variety of skills and experiences that are relevant to the group, members may not yet have a clear understanding of their roles, know the particular rules or boundaries of this group, or know what specific behaviors will be expected of them. They may be wondering how their abilities will be utilized or recognized, and they may attempt to determine their relative power and competence in relation to other members. Members may look to the leader to explain what to do, how to do it, and when and where to do it. They will expect the leader to get things started, provide structure, and give guidance along the way until they get enough experience to begin functioning on their own. Members may direct questions and most of the discussion to the leader.

When members express uncertainty, inability, or anxiety, the most effective leadership stance is to be clear, structured, and organized using a low-relationship/high-task (LR/HT) style characterized by "telling" or directive leadership. Focus on the tasks to be accomplished, provide structure, answer questions, make assignments, and establish the rules, boundaries, and time lines. Acknowledge the socio-emotional concerns of members, but do not focus on them nor encourage or reinforce dependency, anxiety, or uncertainty.

As members begin to exercise their skills, engage in discussion, and place themselves socially in the context of the group, they will soon feel more confident and excited about the group. As members become more comfortable with each other, a few people will begin to try out their ideas. Others may quietly observe to determine what happens to risk takers. As they discover that verbalizing their ideas is valued, they too will begin to participate more freely. Cohesion will increase, and the group members will develop readiness to move into the middle stages of the group.[108]

The Middle Stages: Norming and Storming

During the middle stages of the group, members need to accomplish two major tasks: owning the group and relating with one another. Members need to test or shape the rules and processes to make the group their own. Members who are working through boundary and structure issues of the group are "norming." Norming comes from the word *norms,* which means rules or boundaries. When members are working through personal relationships in the group, they are "storming." In the middle stage of the group you gradually decrease your directiveness and increase your employee-centeredness by adopting a more democratic leadership style.

At times an entire group will work through norming concerns together to get clarity and then move on to the business of developing deeper relationships. At other times members may choose to work on relationships and then engage in boundary concerns. A leader must recognize that what may appear to be dissention or conflict is, in reality, a necessary process by which members develop group ownership and cohesion before they can move ahead to "participate in decision making, move toward task accomplishment, and regulating the group maintenance processes, especially in conflict resolution."[109]

Norming Members in the norming stage have become more motivated and skilled (struggling but still uncertain). They will sometimes test the boundaries of the group, test your leadership style, and struggle with performance anxiety. Your leadership task is to shift to a high-task/high-relationship (HT/HR) "selling" stance of a democratic leader to provide members with reassurance and confidence.

Boundary testing: Although members may understand the rules, boundaries, and structure intellectually, they may need to assure themselves that they are firm, but not rigid, integrate them into their own experience, and make sure they are practical. Members who express confusion about the rules or boundaries are attempting to reduce anxiety and develop a sense of security within the framework of the group.

Testing the leader: In addition, members who are engaging in norming behavior may still be somewhat dependent on you for direction but are struggling against their own dependency in their desire for mastery. Members may need to assure themselves that the leader has consistency, stability, and honesty and can be trusted. Don't be surprised if some or all of your members test themselves against you.

Performance anxiety: Members want to perform but may not know how to do it successfully. Members may know something about what to do but may not be able to do it yet. At this stage, members will inevitably make mistakes because they lack skills. Members may experience cycles of success and productivity while at other times they confront barriers that limit their ability to succeed. They may go too far in one direction or another.

Leadership Tasks at the Norming Stage   When members express anxiety about the group's structure, your leadership, or their own performance, your most effective stance is to remain task-oriented, confident and firm, but supportive, encouraging and accepting members' feelings, which is characteristic of a "selling" high-relationship/high-task (HR/HT) leadership style. You expect members to achieve their purpose, integrate the group's rules and processes, decide on their own rules, and develop mastery, while at the same time you show you are willing to help members overcome barriers.[110]

You watch for verbal and nonverbal cues that indicate misunderstanding, unsureness, or unwillingness on the part of members. Listen carefully for themes or patterns in which members express confusion. While holding to the rules, boundaries, and to your own decisions, respond to your members' needs for more information, clarity, or structure. Welcome these questions, affirm them, and validate members who are willing to challenge you. These are indications that your members are ready to take ownership of the group and are working through dependency to gain mastery.

If members express concern about their ability to perform, keep them on track and give encouragement, but at the same time hold to the goals and deadlines. Give advice, guidance, and assistance, but do not encourage dependency by doing things for members. If things go wrong, step in only to avert failure. Engage members in critiquing what happened so they can learn from the experience.

Storming   At the storming stage, your members have gained task skill. They are more confident and capable but lack practice. To accomplish their goals,

they need to rely on one another and find a comfortable level of cooperation. Their main challenge is to develop good working relationships with other members.

They will work to establish their member roles and responsibility, work to accommodate themselves with one another, and develop effective communication with other members of the group. The task of the leader is to shift to a more supportive leadership stance.

Member roles and responsibility: Members may direct their testing toward other members to develop a deeper relationship or to discover the extent to which they can trust one another. As members become increasingly dependent on one another for information, cooperation, and mutual support, they need to develop trust. They need to show the extent to which they can be counted on and display responsibility. If members are untrustworthy, unreliable, or irresponsible, they will damage the capacity of the group to meet its objectives. Anger and conflict will develop among members.

Accommodation: Members will struggle to find their own style of working, discover how their style fits with others in the group, and work to accommodate themselves with others in the group. At times personality styles may cause conflict. Members who rely primarily on their thinking function and focus on facts may not be comfortable with members who emphasize feelings and make decisions based on relationships or the meaning behind the facts. Members who are intuitive and look at the big picture may become impatient with those who focus on the small details of issues. Some members may be overly dominant or assertive. Others may be submissive and fail to assert themselves adequately.

Communication: Members may have poorly developed communication skills. Some members may interrupt others, fail to listen carefully, or react defensively. Others may overdisclose or withhold information. Members who are poor communicators tend to misunderstand what is being said and are misunderstood by others. These misunderstandings can lead to ineffective performance and cause conflicts.

Leadership Tasks at the Storming Stage   Adopt a high-relationship/low-task (HR/LT) "participating" style characteristic of a supportive leader. Rather than focusing on tasks, you engage members personally, focus on member behavior, help resolve misunderstandings, and resolve issues that are creating difficulty for members. You engage in conflict resolution, develop members' communication skills, and help resolve dysfunctional patterns.

Conflict resolution: You encourage members to express differing learning styles and viewpoints to gain greater understanding of one another. You validate the importance of the variety of problem-solving styles and encourage those with different functions to work with one another. For example, if people who look at the big picture develop conflicts with those who focus on details, help these members understand their differences in style, see that by combining rather than conflicting they can add to their problem solving and learn from one another.

When conflicts occur, you help develop a conflict resolution process. Ask members to elaborate on thinking that led to their positions. Ensure that members listen carefully and ask questions *before* they react. Help members refrain from evaluating ideas or suggestions until all ideas have been generated. As members respond, point out areas of consensus and mutual interest as they arise.[111] Build on agreements, rather than disagreements, promoting consensus rather than discord.

Communication skills: Help members learn good communication skills. Encourage members to keep comments brief, listen attentively to what others are saying, wait until the speaker is finished, and to always include silent members. Encourage members to use "I" statements in which people assume responsibility for their own ideas and feelings rather than "you" statements, which tend to be judgmental, block communication, and often project blame. Assist members to engage in perception checking by asking for clarification about another person's position, paraphrase in their own words what they heard the other person say, and obtain affirmation before they respond.

Ensure that everyone is included in the decision-making process, has time to present his or her ideas fully, and that all ideas count. Build on suggestions, affirming individual contributions. Work toward a clear understanding of the topic and make sure it is relevant to everyone. Frequently summarize progress, check for understanding on issues that need clarification, and review issues that members did not fully discuss.

Resolve dysfunctional patterns: As the group struggles with communicating openly, resolving conflicts, and working toward shared decision making and equal participation, you may observe dysfunctional patterns emerging. If members avoid issues that they must face, point this out. If they are reverting to previous behaviors in the struggle for adaptation, explore this pattern and help members deal with it. If members need information, resources, or assistance, help them process how they can obtain them without doing it for them. Make sure members keep track of their process so that important ideas or decisions are not forgotten. The result of navigating through the channels of the storming stage will mean that members accept one another's differences and learn to use those differences in problem solving. They will have learned skills in communication and conflict resolution and be able to share differences without being afraid of rejection. They cooperate, discuss alternatives, and reach their own decisions.[112]

The Performing Stage   Performing is the final stage of the life cycle of the group. Your members are now self-motivated and capable. Members understand the group's task; they know what to do and how to do it. They have skills, experience, and confidence in their abilities. They own the group and have made its rules and boundaries their own. They have developed working relationships with one another and resolved conflicts that may have gotten in the way of accomplishing their task. They have learned skills in problem solving, group process, and interpersonal relationships. They are working as a cohesive unit with high motivation. Relatively little energy is required to maintain the group as a unit. A member has emerged who serves as the formal leader who facilitates the meetings. Other members also take on leadership roles as necessary. Members spend most of their time solving problems and accomplishing the purposes for which the group was formed.[113]

A good strategy when working with highly independent and motivated members is to take a "hands off" low-relationship/low-task (LR/LT) stance, characteristic of a laissez-faire or "delegating" style of leadership. You encourage, observe, and monitor, but you don't give direction, persuade, or interfere with the group process. If you insert yourself into the process at this point, you will more than likely disrupt a smoothly working group. When you are present, attend carefully to the group and its members, listen and remain silently involved with the process. Maintain eye contact and express interest. Offer support, encouragement, and give input only when asked. After meetings, take notes on the points you have seen and meet with the formal leader. Give support and encouragement. Raise questions, clarify, or summarize, and review the process so that he or she becomes more effective.

Ending the Group

When the group has achieved its goals, members may feel a real sense of accomplishment and satisfaction. Involve the sponsoring agency or organization in celebrating their success with a party acknowledging their achievements, growth, and contributions. Provide awards as a symbol of appreciation. When the group ends, the relationships and interpersonal attraction of members may be carried over into the community outside, between coworkers in an agency, or volunteers in another setting or into other areas of life. You may want to build on these relationships by inviting members to contribute again in the future.[114] You may also assess the group's effectiveness by evaluating its process.

CONCLUSION

Social leadership is a substantive approach based on respect for the self-determination of the members of the group and the community and on the rights of the members to decide, to have a vision of their future, to act on that vision, and to take responsibility for the outcomes of their actions. Social leadership rejects paternalism, unobtrusive controls, implied threats, subtle deceitfulness, and other forms of management in which people are induced to conform or give up their autonomy, values, or right to construct their own social reality.

Rosabeth Moss Kanter observed that "powerlessness corrupts and absolute powerlessness corrupts absolutely."[115] People who have little power tend to hoard the power they do have and lord it over others. Social leaders enrich and empower their followers. They "use their power to transform their followers into leaders."[116] As a social leader, you help members use thinking, feeling, intuition, and sensing to develop whole-mind leadership. Your goal is that your followers will move ahead on a journey to find their dreams. By struggling and working together, they will learn to overcome obstacles, achieve goals, and become the kind of people they want to become. Macro social work "leaders make heroes of other people."[117]

When you assist task groups, your major role is to enable members of a group to develop their own internal leadership and become self-directing and independently functioning. You plan and organize the group before it begins. You help lead members in the first meeting or two until they can conduct the task group themselves. Then you use situational group leadership in which you adjust your style to the readiness of the members as the group as a whole moves through its life cycle.

KEY CONCEPTS

Jane Addams

leadership

social leadership

Thaddeus Stevens

social goods

social capital

joint enterprise

partnership

empowerment

meaning

task group leadership

community task groups

organizational task groups

societal task groups

international task groups

social group work

Florence Kelly

Eduard Lindeman

Mary Parker Follett

trait theory of leadership

Grace Coyle

Samuel R. Slavson

leadership triad

democratic leadership

authoritarian leadership

laissez-faire leadership

National Training Laboratories (NTL)

social casework

community organization

Macgregor's Theory X and Theory Y

Rensis Likert's Michigan State studies

Ohio State studies

Blake and Mouton's managerial grid

A. K. Korman and one best way

Fred Fiedler's contingency theory

Hersey and Blanchard's situational leadership

member maturity

task behavior

relationship behavior

LR/HT

HR/HT

HR/LT

LR/LT

telling leadership style

selling leadership style

participating leadership style

delegating leadership style

de-emphasis in social leadership

generalist social work

feeling to build community

thinking to develop strength

working between meetings

intuiting to empower

group life cycle

sensing to move to action

assessing member readiness

pregroup planning

forming stage

composing the group

norming stage

duration of the group

storming stage

leading the first meeting

performing stage

ending the group

QUESTIONS FOR DISCUSSION

1. Just as developing a working relationship is the key by which micro social workers help individuals, couples, and families, social leadership is the hallmark by which macro social workers work with groups and communities as well as organizations and society as a whole. Is this statement accurate? What is your perspective on the most important components of generalist social work practice at the micro and macro levels?

2. Have you ever lead a task group, social group, or therapeutic group? What did you learn about yourself? What did you learn about leadership?

3. Do you have a vision for helping to improve a social situation in your school, work, church, or community? Have you considered trying to become a social leader with a group in your social environment? How would you go about doing it?

4. Look over the story of Jane Addams at the beginning of this chapter.
   a. What leadership preferences did she exhibit?
   b. What does this tell you about social leadership?

5. Kouzas and Posner say that "leaders take us on journeys where we have never been before."
   a. What is your perspective of this statement? As a social leader would you take people on a journey to where they have never been? Why or why not?
   b. Would you help people decide on their own journeys to where they want to go and accompany them as partners? Why or why not?
   c. Is something lost when an individual's journey has little or no affect on others in a community? If so, what loss occurs? Is this

something that generalist social workers should be concerned about? Why or why not?
   d. Can the journey of a community inform the personal journeys of its members? If so, how?
   e. Is something lost when the journey of a community has little or no effect on its individual members? If so, what loss occurs? Is this something that generalist social workers should be concerned about? Why or why not?
   f. Can all members of a community also be its leaders?

6. Compare the two statements below. What are the strengths and weaknesses of each statement?
   a. "Developing and promulgating . . . a vision . . . is the highest calling and truest purpose of leadership."—Burt Nanus
   b. "The purpose of social leadership is to help people become social leaders."—William Brueggemann

7. Should social work train selected people to be leaders as does business management, or should social work assist as many people as possible to exercise leadership?

8. The heritage of social work is full of people who, in the words of Elenore Brilliant, "manifested leadership both within and outside the profession. We have had leaders of great significance in the development of the [social work] profession and . . . we have had some who achieved a prominent place in the community at large. . . . Jane Addams, Edward T. Devine, Florence Kelly, Edith Abbot, . . . earned reputations beyond the social work community, influencing the course of social welfare and the quality of life in our country in a broader sense."[118]

   Burton Gummer, one of the influential writers in macro social work, asserts that in recent years social leadership has declined.
   a. What is your opinion about these statements?
   b. Is generalist social work leadership on the decline?
   c. If you believe it is, to what do you attribute this?
   d. Is this something about which generalist social work ought to be concerned? Why or why not?
   e. If you believe it is a concern, what proposals can you make to reverse this decline?

ADDITIONAL READING

Social Leadership

Block, Peter. *Stewardship: Choosing Service Over Self-Interest*. San Francisco: Berrett-Koehler, 1993.

Lakey, B., G. Lakey, R. Napier, and J. Robinson. *Grassroots and Nonprofit Leadership: A Guide for Organizations in Changing Times*. Philadelphia: New Society, 1995.

Greenleaf, Robert K. *Servant Leadership: A Journey Into the Nature of Legitimate Power and Greatness*. New York: Paulist Press, 1977.

Portnoy, A. *Leadership: What Every Leader Should Know About People*. Englewood Cliffs, NJ: Prentice Hall, 1986.

Conventional Managerial Leadership

Bennis, Warren G., and Burt Nanus. *Leaders: Strategies for Taking Charge*. New York: Harper and Row, 1986.

Bethel, Sheila. *Making a Difference: Twelve Qualities That Make You a Leader*. New York: Putnam, 1990.

Burns, James MacGregor. *Leadership*. New York: Harper and Row, 1978.

Flores, Ernest. *The Nature of Leadership for Hispanics and Other Minorities*. Saratoga, CA: Century Twenty One, 1981.

Gardner, John. *On Leadership*. New York: Free Press, 1990.

Hersey, Paul. *The Situational Leader: The Other 59 Minutes*. New York: Warner Books, 1985.

Hitt, William. *The Model Leader: A Fully Functioning Person*. Columbus, OH: Battelle Press, 1993.

Kouzes, James, and Barry Posner. *The Leadership Challenge: How to Get Extraordinary Things Done in Organizations*. San Francisco: Jossey-Bass, 1987.

Followership

Bellman, Goeffrey. *Getting Things Done When You Are Not in Charge: How to Succeed From a Support Position*. New York: Simon and Schuster, 1992.

Kelly, Robert. *The Power of Followership: How to Create Leaders, People Who Want to Follow and Followers Who Lead Themselves*. New York: Doubleday, 1992.

Small Group Leadership

Cartwright, Dorwin, and Alvin Zander. *Group Dynamics: Research and Theory*. 3d ed. New York: Harper and Row, 1968.

Forsyth, Donelson R. *Group Dynamics*. 2d ed. Pacific Grove, CA: Brooks/Cole, 1990.

Koestenbaum, Peter. *Leadership: The Inner Side of Greatness*. San Francisco: Jossey-Bass, 1987.

Toseland, Ronald W., and Robert F. Rivas. *An Introduction to Group Work Practice*. 2d ed. Boston: Allyn and Bacon, 1995.

Tubbs, Stewart. L. *A Systems Approach to Small Group Interaction*. 4th ed. New York: McGraw-Hill, 1992.

Zander, Alvin. *Making Groups Effective*. San Francisco: Jossey-Bass, 1983.

PART Two

Social Work Practice With Communities

Community social work *is* social work.[1]

Hans Falck

A Time for Community

It's time to look toward the small but vigorous civic community based on grassroots initiatives. It is time to focus on the churches, voluntary associations and grassroots groups that are rebuilding America's civil society one family, one block, one neighborhood at a time.[2]

William A. Schambra

The Mission of Social Work

Social work's mission should be to build a meaning, a purpose and a sense of obligation for the community. It is only by creating a community that we establish a basis for commitment, obligation, and social support. We must build communities that are excited about their child care systems, that find it exhilarating to care for the mentally ill and the frail aged, and make demands upon people to contribute, and to care for one another.[3]

Harry Specht and Mark Courtney

COMMUNITY SOCIAL WORK

Part Two focuses on social work with the community. In this section, you will explore how people are mobilizing themselves for action and taking responsibility for the life of their communities. When we become a part of these changes, people become determiners of their own future rather than passive recipients of a future handed to them by others. We develop the power to critically examine the social world in which we find ourselves. We come to see society not as a static, impenetrable presence but as a reality in the process of transformation.

You will discover how you can become engaged in this community revolution and make a lasting impact on many people's lives. You will find that you can become a part of a renewed social work reclaiming its original heritage, building meaning, purpose, and a sense of obligation for the community and revitalizing the lives of people from the bottom up.

This section begins with an exploration of community and how to practice community planning, community development, and community organizing.

Community

In Chapter 5 you will explore what macro social workers mean by "community." You will learn what community is and review a brief history of community in North America. You will discover several kinds of communities with which generalist community social workers engage. You will learn how we empower communities of people to take responsibility for their own neighborhoods.

Community Social Planning

In Chapter 6 you will discover how community planning is becoming an important means by which individuals implement grassroots democracy, become engaged in fundamental decisions about their communities, and learn planning skills. You will explore a brief history of social planning in North America and learn how social planning is connected with community development and community organizing.

Community Development

In Chapter 7 you will learn how community development has emerged as a new mode of community effort in the past 50 years, conceived and developed not by professionals but primarily by African American community members using social thinking and social leadership to improve their own communities. You will discover that community development has become a major force for community empowerment and change, and that it has spread throughout the United States and Canada and our global society as well. You will discover how community development corporations have revolutionized the field of community development and how they combine community planning and community organizing. You will learn how to organize a community development corporation.

Community Organization

In chapter 8 you will discover that community organizations, coalitions, and federations are slowly reshaping the social landscape of North America by pursuing political empowerment. You will learn what community organizing is and what a community organization is. You will explore a brief history of community organizing and learn how to create a community organization.

ADDITIONAL RESOURCES

Alliance for National Renewal, http://www.ncl.org/anr/index.htm.

National Association for Community Leadership, http://www.communityleadership.org/.

National Community Building Network, http://www.ncbn.org/welcome.html.

Chronicle of Philanthropy, *Non-Profit Handbook,* 1255 23rd St., Washington, DC 20037; Phone: 202-466-1227.

Community

A Cosmion Illuminated With Meaning

Human society is not merely a fact or an event in the external world to be studied by an observer like natural phenomenon. Although it has externality as one of its important components, it is a whole little world. [It is] a cosmion, illuminated with meaning from within by the human beings *who continuously create and bear it as the mode and condition of their self realization* (emphasis added).[1]

Eric Voegelin

Relational Community

We must delight in each other, make other's conditions our own, rejoyce together, mourn together, labor and suffer together, always having before our eyes our community as members of the same body.[2]

John Winthrop, first governor of Massachusetts Bay Colony

Ideas in This Chapter

© Tom Carter-mga/Photri

Community development aims at the active participation of community members and the fullest reliance on the community's initiative.

THE MIRACLE OF LE CHAMBON

A plague was sweeping through the Western world. In the name of progress it produced a holocaust that wiped out one third of the entire Jewish population with the complicity of established religion and occupied governments. In 1940 France fell to Nazi Germany, and by 1941 the puppet Vichy government began systematic deportation of Jews. The Nazis appeared triumphant.

To the people of Le Chambon Sur Lignon in southwestern France, a poor farming community 350 miles south of Paris, that was beside the point. Here, over the course of 4 long years, 5,000 Christians sheltered 5,000 Jews. Outwardly the people of Le Chambon were much like those of any other small French village. Most were peasants and villagers descended from Huguenots, the first Protestants in Catholic France. Once they, too, had been persecuted for their beliefs, their rights were abolished, their men were deported to slave in galleys, and their women were imprisoned in towers where they left notes to their families that said "resist." The persecution they called "the wilderness" lasted for 100 years.

In spite of this, the people of Le Chambon clung to their beliefs, their land, and their community. The memory of their past was the key to their survival. In every challenge there would be an echo of their forebears' faith and struggle. It was not only their religious beliefs but the persecution they had endured that made them different. At the beginning of the 20th century, when industry exploited women and children in mass numbers, Le Chambon welcomed sickly working-class women and children from neighboring cities and took them in. In the 1930s they sheltered refugees from the Spanish Civil War, and in 1940 they took in "guests," offering them hospitality because "it was only a natural thing to do." Nothing that occurred during the war years was unfamiliar to the people of Le Chambon.

In the beginning, only a few Jews made their way to this tiny corner of the world. At great risk to themselves, villagers took in the Jews. The Jews kept coming, and the people of Le Chambon kept taking them in: individuals, couples, families, children, the elderly, those who could pay, and those who could not—doctors, merchants, intellectuals, and homemakers from Paris and Warsaw, Vienna and Prague.

One day during a church service a man came into the congregation. "I have," said he, "three old testaments," meaning three Jews who needed shelter. Without hesitation, an old farmer raised his hand. "I'll take them," he said. Never once did the people of Le Chambon ask if the strangers were Jews, even though they knew that they were. To them it did not matter. They took in the strangers, protected them, and helped them on their way.

The day before the Nazis threatened the people of Le Chambon with occupation, Rev. Trocme delivered a sermon that exemplified their resolve and the roots of their resistance. "The duty of Christians is to resist the violence that will be brought to bear on their consciences through the weapons of the spirit. We will resist whatever our adversaries demand of us that are contrary to the orders of the Gospel. We will also fear, but without pride and without hate."[3] It was a conspiracy of compassion.

The people of Le Chambon started schools for the refugees, boarded the Jews, and even helped them observe their own religious services. They began a center for forging documents, identification cards, and passports, giving the Jews false identities. Even when Nazis occupied Le Chambon, they continued to hide the Jews, once in a hotel directly across the street from where soldiers were bivouacked. Le Chambon became a center of the French resistance.

The community of Le Chambon and the Jewish people were anchored in community. The Jews were the people of God, and the Huguenots of Le Chambon were also a people of God. The Nazis, on the other hand, considered themselves the epitome of progress, modernity, and technological efficiency. How they despised and attempted to destroy community! And yet the community of compassion and resistance survived, while only a few short years later, all that remained of the Third Reich was the memory of appalling death and destruction.[4]

WHAT YOU WILL LEARN IN THIS CHAPTER

Our society is building a culture in which a sense of community seems lacking.[5] For a large number of people in North America, community exists in only marginal ways, in increasingly diminished form, and comprises little existential space in our lives. The result is that many people live lonely, isolated, and alienated lives. Children and adolescents have fewer opportunities for healthy social group engagement.

Most adults find their main source of meaning in career-oriented pursuits, often in large impersonal organizational systems.

Yet, as you will discover in this chapter, community is one of our most important social structures, if not our most necessary and vital social form. In this chapter you will discover characteristics of community and learn about several kinds of community with which macro social workers engage. You will explore a brief history of community. You will learn how community is the means by which your individual self comes into being. You will discover how community supports your self in the midst of personal, social, and political crises that megastructures of society impose on it. You will find that community is the way that we are transformed into a people who solve our common problems and generate a culture that is transferred from generation to generation.

You will discover that macro social workers use community both as a means and an end of social work practice through community social planning, community development, and community organization. Most important, you will find that although community relationships *seem* to be disappearing, community is a perennial and universal component of the human condition. The presumed triumph of modern rational artificial systems based on impersonal social relations, or what Ferdinand Toennies called "gesellschaft," is a phyrric victory.

WHAT IS COMMUNITY?

Communities are natural human associations based on ties of intimate personal relationships and shared experiences in which each of us mutually provide meaning in our lives, meet our needs for affiliation, and accomplish interpersonal goals. Every one of us needs community. Community arises spontaneously because of the innate sociality of the human condition. With relatively rare exceptions, community has been *the* form of human social life throughout history. Your individual self cannot, in fact, reach its full realization in isolation but *only* as you are nurtured, guided, and suffused with the life of the communal social relationships in which you exist. Our predisposition to community ensures that we become the persons we were meant to become, discover who we are as people, and construct a culture that would be impossible for single, isolated individuals to accomplish alone.

Wherever humans exist, we spontaneously seek and form community. Community is an indelible component of the human condition and is not relative to a particular historical era, place, or time. Neither is community unique to one race, national, or cultural group. Community transcends history and cannot be contained by mere history. Deeply rooted in our nature, the social engagement by which we form ourselves into and relate in a community is a universal characteristic of the human condition, which is not contingent on circumstances or bound by culture or location.[6] When macro social workers talk about community, we talk about two things simultaneously. Community is a locality in space and time, but community also exists as a form of relationships.

Community as a Locality

Community needs to be embodied to have existence. To have permanence, communities often become identified with a physical space the community claims as its own. This could be a territory or a neighborhood that we provide with a name and that includes homes, schools, and shops. For other communities, the locality is a structure such as a union hall, church, or temple. The visible, formal structure or building symbolizes the community for its members as well as for others who are not community members. Sociologists and social workers have often stressed the importance of "the territorial factor, the place, or locality" in which community is said to exist. Bell and Newby assert that "when sociologists talk about community they almost always mean a place in which people have some, if not complete solidarity relations."[7] Thus it is appropriate to talk about community as a neighborhood or a building that exists in space and time and that has permanence and structure. Macro social workers engage themselves with several different kinds of community localities: inner cities, inner ring suburbs, suburbs, and rural communities.

Inner Cities   Following World War II, many White Americans moved out of the inner cities and into the suburbs. At the same time, many African Americans, discouraged by racial inequality and lack of opportunity in the rural South, migrated to the congested inner cities of the North in the hope of a better life, creating one of the most significant population movements in our history.[8] A unified government policy subsidized suburbia with government-insured mortgages and tax breaks for the primarily White middle and upper strata of American society while providing bulldozer urban renewal and government housing in depleted inner cities for low-income, primarily African American citizens.

In the 1970s and into the 1980s, development of massive suburban shopping malls, industrial complexes, and office parks far removed from downtown areas resulted in a further decline in the numbers of jobs in inner city areas. Corporations often used their accumulated capital to purchase locally owned industries and businesses, transferring community wealth from inner cities to national and even transnational conglomerates.[9] Even those cities that transformed their downtowns into administrative and financial centers for service industries were unable to stem the growing tide of poverty in inner cities.

Devastated cities such as Youngstown, Detroit, Flint, Newark, Camden, Hartford, Bridgeport, and Gary were left with large populations of poor, new immigrants, working-class ethnics, and others whose traditional blue-collar jobs began disappearing, making it almost impossible for city governments to raise necessary revenues to provide basic services. To avert fiscal collapse, many of these cities closed schools, hospitals, health centers, and police and fire stations.

> No other major industrial nation has permitted the level of destitution and decay found in America's cities. We see the consequences every day: deadly levels of crime and violence; Third World levels of infant mortality; a growing army of homeless people sleeping on park benches and in vacant buildings.[10]

Inner-Ring Suburbs   Today, according to Peter Dreier, a growing number of middle-income Americans find themselves trapped in older inner-ring suburbs that look more and more like troubled cities.[11] Inner cities and their inner-ring suburbs have much in common. Many face a number of the same problems: crime and violence, high rates of infant mortality, crumbling infrastructure, inadequate housing, and chronic fiscal crises. In fact, when older communities are taxed to fund the massive supporting infrastructure for new, more exclusive development, the poor are further enervated, the process accelerates, and injustice increases. As polarization continues, the concentration of poverty creates waves of socioeconomic decline that roll onward at an astonishingly fast pace.[12]

Suburbs   In 1960 the per capita income of the central cities was 5% greater than the surrounding suburbs. By 1989 income in the cities had fallen to 84% of suburban income. In every region of the country, even where city populations were increasing, the fastest growing parts of the metropolitan areas were the surrounding suburbs. During the 1980s, for example, Los Angeles grew by 17.4%, while its suburbs grew by 29.5%. Baltimore lost 6.4% of its population while its suburbs grew by 16.5%.

The 1992 presidential election campaign was the first in which an absolute majority of voters came from the suburbs. Even more important, the number of Congresspersons representing cities has been declining while the number representing suburban areas is increasing. After the 1992 redistricting, the House had 98 urban districts, 170 suburban districts, and 88 rural districts. The rest were a mix of urban-suburban or rural-suburban populations. In 1996 more than three quarters of all Americans lived in metropolitan areas, two thirds of whom—about half the nation's population—live in the suburbs.[13]

Rural Communities   In spite of the urbanization and globalization brought on by the increased domain and size of public and economic organizations in Europe and North America today, Hassinger and Pinkerton assert that the agricultural village continues to be the most prevalent form of settlement in the world today. Even in the United States, rural communities persist despite predictions to the contrary.

The most important kinds of rural communities exist in countries as the last remnants of a precolonial and premodern era. It is not the teeming cities of India but its rural villages where the bulk of the population of that subcontinent lives. Although "modernization has occurred in all but the most isolated areas,"[14] many people live in rural communities in the "developing" or "least developed" nations of Africa and Central and South America side by side with modern culture. Even though their customs, culture, and attachments are alien to Western industrialized society, people in these villages often attempt to maintain their uniqueness, cultural integrity, and historical identity.[15]

Relational Community

Community is a form of relationships that transcends time, structure, and location. Community is a form of social action and we relations in which people take

others into account. But it is also a means by which compassion and caring are shared. Community creates public goods and social capital.

A Form of Relationships   Although a community can be found in a locality or be embodied by a structure, community is never simply a static physical location as social ecologists sometimes assert; nor is it merely a structure or mechanical process as systems theorists may suggest. Community is always comprised of social relationships in which people naturally and inevitably connect with one another.

> From this view, a community exists because of values, sentiments, and feelings of identification and commitment that are held in common by a collective of individuals. This can occur in a locality, such as a town or city, but can also occur independently of locale. . . . The defining quality is that the members share common sentiments that unite them.[16]

Personal face-to-face relations are the frame of reference in which life occurs in community, and the shared perceptions of its members are the glue that holds communities together.

Transcends Location   Community relationships transcend location. As people in community move from place to place, they carry their community with them. When the nation of Israel was destroyed and most of her people were exiled to Babylon in 597 B.C., they lost their land, their nation, and their political identity, but the Jews never lost themselves, their community. They were then, and 2,600 years later remain, a people, a community, regardless of where they are located.

Transcends Structure   Community relationships transcend its structure. The original group that called themselves "people of the Way" 2,000 years ago was a small amorphous group whose members met in the Temple at Jerusalem, in one another's homes, and who owned everything in common.[17] Today people who belong to the Christian religion structure themselves in a great diversity of forms, from informal associations to highly structured hierarchies, from small groups that continue to meet in homes to massive denominations. Yet they remain communities united in a common belief and heritage.

Transcends Time   Community relationships transcend time. A community existed before we were born and will live on after we die. We develop a shared memory and obtain a sense of ourselves by means of our common history together. The symbols and meaning that community incorporates, while originating in time, become timeless. There is not just one model of community or one community ideal. Each community is a unique blending of the people of which it is composed. The many communities that come into being add to the shape and texture of human existence. The more communities that develop and diversify, therefore, the more opportunities there are to explore alternative ways of being in the world and different ways of achieving richness of character.

Social Action   In its purest sense, community is the *act* by which we engage one another, experience close, personal relationships, and become a people. In "Some Categories of a Sociology of Understanding," Max Weber defined the word *Gemeinschaftshandeln* as social action or "action based on mutual understanding." Action, said Weber, is "social insofar as, by virtue of the subjective meaning attached to it by the acting individual (or individuals), it takes account of the behavior of others and is thereby oriented in its course."[18]

When I "act," I attach some sort of meaning to my action. Such action does not occur as I act individually but as I take into account the meaning that other people attach to my actions. "When I so design my actions that I take into account how others might react, I have begun to transform action, with its purely personal meaning, into social action."[19] When two or more people attempt to direct their actions toward each other, they engage in a social relationship. People "become communities only with this sense of relationships, this shared *Gemeinschaft*."[20]

We Relations   A deeper way of looking at social action is the idea of we relations as expressed by phenomenologist Alfred Schutz. "In the pure we-relationship I create my social life with others who have intentions similar to mine."[21] Furthermore,

> what makes social life appear human is a kind of intimacy I gain from interacting in depth with my consociates—the members of the little world whose center I am and which I enlarge by including you in the we-relationship. In fact, the more I make an effort to understand you in your complexity and the closer to you I feel, the more meaningful and satisfying life in the social world appears to me.[22]

Compassion and Caring   In exemplary communities we do more than simply take others into account, however. We engage in loving, friendly, compassionate, and caring relationships. We engage others by providing support, healing, and helping to those in difficulty and trouble. Our humanity is extended when we offer a milieu of safety and protection to those least able to care for themselves.

Exemplary communities become warm, nurturing, and supportive environments in which personal growth and development take place. A "person as a fully developed individual self is impossible without other fully developed selves,"[23] says Paul Tillich. They provide a safe and healthy social atmosphere by which we can find many points of access to relate to others.

Macro social workers are committed to helping develop such exemplary communities of relationships in which people can become fully developed. From the beginning of our profession, social workers have been providers and developers of community in the form of social settlements, community centers, and neighborhood houses that help communities revitalize the social life of their members.

Social Capital   The product of the economy is monetary and physical capital. The product of a community is social capital. Friendship, for example, is a form of social capital that comes into being as a result of relationships that are formed in groups and communities. A community "is above all a network of friends," say Robert Bellah and colleagues. From the very beginning of American and Canadian society, friendship was an important component of early communities. "In such small communities, it was obvious that people not only helped one another and enjoyed one another's company but also participated mutually in enterprises that furthered the common good."[24] Community produces many kinds of social capital in addition to friendship, including public spirit, social engagement, intimacy, nurture, and support, without which people would live shallow and lonely existences.

Social Goods   The basis of the economic sector is private goods that can be priced, bought and sold, divided, consumed, and from which other people can be excluded. Social goods, on the other hand, are created exclusively in the social sector where communities exist. Social goods, such as communal relationships, cannot be priced, bought, or sold. Community relationships cannot be divided into portions or privately consumed. Once community is created, it is available to all. No one can be excluded from the benefits community provides. While the amount of a private good a person owns is lessened when it is shared, communal social goods multiply the more they are shared with others. Conversely, when communal goods are not given away, they are diminished.

Benefits of Social Capital and Social Goods

Communities and the social goods and social capital they produce shelter us from the "getting and getting all the more" mode of being. Community can be a place of refuge from the market society in which everything has a price, buying and selling become the preeminent activity of human beings, and humans become commodities in the marketplace. Community mediates between our need for intimate, personal connection with others and the emptiness that market structures impose on social life. Without civic friendship, for example, a city may degenerate into a struggle of contending interest groups unmediated by any public solidarity. In community we are prized, appreciated, and valued for ourselves, not for what we produce. By fostering caring and committed social relationships, communities become centers of sociality, helping overcome impersonality, alienation, and emptiness so common in today's modern market society.

Kinds of Relational Communities

Communities that are primarily relational in character include community, civic, and service associations, communities of diversity, and faith-based communities.

Community, Civic, and Service Associations Community associations, civic associations, and fraternal and sororal service associations are a means by which people often maintain identity and connection in today's modern society. The Japanese Cultural Association, for example, is a center of meaning for the Japanese community in many cities. Often supported by the Buddhist Temple, these community associations provide schools, evening classes, summer youth programs, and cultural events such as Bon dances and Taiko drum and Kendo demonstrations, all of which keep the spirit and culture of the Japanese community alive. The Knights of Columbus, founded by Irish Americans in New England in 1882 as a fraternal insurance society, spread nationwide and eventually

became the largest Catholic layperson's group in the world. The Sons of Italy provides an arena in which Italian Americans can share and celebrate their culture, and Chinese, Hispanic, Laotian, Hmong, Vietnamese, Asian, Korean, and other associations help keep their cultures alive.

Civic associations abound. The League of Women Voters is committed to the enhancement of the political process by providing fair and impartial information about issues and candidates. The National Association for the Advancement of Colored People (NAACP) is dedicated to social justice in race relationships, equality, and an end to discrimination. The Junior Chamber of Commerce (Jaycees) exists to promote business interests and connections among people seeking to establish themselves in the world of commerce.

Fraternal and sororal organizations such as the Lions Club, Shriners, Ys Men's Association, Rotary, Junior League, Soroptimists, Kiwanis, Veterans of Foreign Wars, and others provide arenas in which people come together for mutual interaction but also to perform community service and voluntary projects to improve their communities.

Communities of Diversity Many communities of diversity exist today that are active in civic affairs. Some of these resist assimilation, causing conflict with the majority group. Community, however, can be a means of reconciliation for these conflicts.

Ubiquity of ethnic community: Today, North America is probably more ethnically diverse than any society that has ever existed. In any large city, hundreds of languages are spoken, and representatives from almost every nation of the globe can often be found. Many people from ethnically diverse backgrounds tend to be close to their communal roots. For people who identify with their ethnic heritage, community is a place of refuge, a reminder of their past, a place where their traditional language is spoken, foods eaten, rituals celebrated, and relationships formed in a milieu suffused with meaning and substance. They understand, as many do not, the vital necessity, the healing power, and the strength that community offers.

Participants in civic affairs: Members of ethnically diverse neighborhoods have become active participants in the civic life of society. African American communities in every major U.S. city have organized community development corporations (CDCs) to strengthen their social environments. West Oakland,

California, has attacked the drug problem head on, with many community leaders making themselves visible enemies of major dealers. Nearby, an African American teacher has promised to help pay for the college education of her first-grade class if they maintain a "C" average and go on to college. The teacher annually saves $10,000 from her modest salary for this fund. In the rural mountains of Eastern Puerto Rico, there is an exciting revitalization of the community through an energetic community development program. Southeast Asian communities in Boston, New York, Houston, and San Francisco have organized legal immigration and refugee task forces to help fight the arbitrary deportation of undocumented workers, as have Hispanic, Puerto Rican, and other ethnic groups.

Native American tribes are attacking problems of alcoholism through indigenous healing rituals that have the sweat lodge ceremony as its core. Success rates are often dramatic, as in the village of Ahiok, Alaska, where 90% of the adults were chronically drunk, but at least 80% were able to sustain sobriety after treatment. The Latino community in Boston has a very successful grassroots health program called "*Mujeres Latinas en Accion*," which has successfully integrated third world health models that include the extended family in health care delivery systems, and a culture- and gender-sensitive model of community organization is used to reach women in the barrios.

Resistance to assimilation: Many people from ethnically diverse backgrounds are no longer willing to surrender their heritage and cultural roots in the hopes of security, economic betterment, or becoming "Americanized." They understand that freedom "prescribes not only individual liberty, but also a democratic society, respect for human rights, and a process where citizens effect changes."[25] Many Southeast Asian Americans, for example, have come to the realization that "we could accommodate and acculturate, but we can never assimilate. The maintenance of one's culture and language is fast becoming a source of pride rather than a cause for embarrassment."[26]

Despite the American traditions of freedom and justice, White Americans sometimes see the gift of ethnic community in negative terms. The languages, traditions, and social mores of those who are culturally different from the mainstream are often systematically degraded and disparaged, as if it is impossible for members of ethnically diverse communities to be authentic citizens in America or Canada while retaining their rich heritage, the roots of their past. For many, ethnic diversity adds to the texture and creativity of community life, but for others, ethnic differences can lead to misunderstanding, distrust, and fear. In this climate, ethnic diversity becomes the focus for conflict.

Community and conflict resolution: Community, the repository of social capital, can also be a means by which misunderstanding and conflicts are resolved. McCoy and Sherman assert, "the process of overcoming bias must begin in communities where people interact and daily face the consequences of racial, ethnic and class antagonisms."[27] Study circles have become a powerful vehicle for helping people come together to obtain a new understanding of one another. By providing opportunities for safe, respectful dialogue, study circles on race offer a way for people to overcome stereotypes, learn about each other's cultures, and discover commonalities.

Study circles have been used in Lima and Springfield, Ohio, to foster interethnic dialogue, assisted by the Study Circles Resource Center. In Lima, for example, supported by the mayor and Ohio State University, 1,000 community members participated in groups of 10 to 15 members each, meeting for several 2-hour sessions. They experienced new interracial friendships and bonds as well as new interracial networks for addressing community issues.

In phase two of the project, the mayor formed a "study circle council," and organizers reached out to organize businesses, neighborhood associations, and schools to participate in another round of study circles. In April 1994, conference organizers and leaders shared their experiences with community leaders from around the Midwest. As of mid-1994, study circle programs on race relations had been established in Baton Rouge, New Orleans, Albuquerque, Portsmouth, Virginia, and Columbus, Ohio; and 15 other cities were planning study circle programs.[28]

Role of social work: Macro social workers can actively promote programs such as study circles, recognizing that engaging people in groups and personal renewal and community change go hand in hand. In addition, social workers must recognize that all communities, but particularly ethnic communities, need to maintain rights to their own heritage, language, culture, religion, and other expressions of uniqueness, to engage wider society on their own terms, and to be guaranteed freedom and independence. Just as government protects individual rights, it is the duty of government to honor, protect, nurture, and support the rights of communities of people to establish themselves, to be free from exploitation, and to have resources available for growth. Community self-determination means that people ought not to be coerced into giving up their central culture as the cost of inclusion, survival, or the hope of material well-being.

As professional social workers identify and link closely with ethnically diverse people and position themselves as champions of the oppressed, they will have an opportunity to learn a wealth of lessons about social and communal relationships. Speaking of Puerto Ricans, for example, social worker Julio Morales says, "the collective humanism of Puerto Rican society is . . . a culturally sanctioned pattern that enhances community organizing. It appeals to a sense of justice and fairness, an important guiding principle for community social work practice."[29]

Faith-Based Communities Religious institutions form the largest network of voluntary associations in North American society by far. There are close to 500,000 local churches, temples, synagogues, and mosques voluntarily supported by the American people, and many others can be found in Canada. On any given Sunday more people are in churches than the total number of people who attend professional sports events in a whole year, says Berger and Neuhaus.[30] Faith-based communities are important arenas of communality. They encourage the development of civil society, guide values and public discourse, are repositories of historical remembrance, and encourage community building.

Central arena of communality: For many people, faith-based communities are among the more important arenas in which community survives today.[31] The Jewish synagogue is not only a center of religion and worship but also a cultural, social, intellectual, and ethnic center of life for the Jewish community. Mosques provide similar identity for Muslim immigrants, as does the Buddhist Temple for many East and Southeast Asians. For African Americans, Wynetta Devore says, "The church stands out as a center of community life providing spiritual, social, and economic resources."[32] Community developer John Perkins recalls that

> the black church . . . was *ours.* Before the Civil war slave masters appointed white preachers to pastor their slaves, making the church just one more tool of domination. . . . But with Emancipation,

the number of black churches in the South mushroomed. At least we had one social institution that was ours. This newly independent church was the one place where we enjoyed true freedom of speech. It was the one place where, for a few hours a week, we could feel really free. So we often spent the whole day at church.

Naturally, then, the black church came to be not only the center of spiritual life but also the focus of social life and culture for the religious and not-so-religious blacks alike. Because the church provided the only setting where black leadership could arise, the preacher quickly became the central figure in the black community. It was to the church, then, that the black community turned for leadership. If change was to take place, it would start there. The church, and only the church, held within its grasp the means to bring to fruition the hopes and dreams of black America.[33]

Civil society: Church-affiliated groups, says William Galston and Peter Levine, "are the backbone of civil society in America involving almost half the population. Religious associations offer ways for people to donate money, receive aid, hold meetings, recruit members for other associations and learn about public issues."[34] In public policy matters, the historical development of most health, social welfare, and education programs, ideas, and institutions are inseparable from the church. In some parts of North America, notably in the older cities of the Northeast, the great bulk of social welfare services function under religious auspices.[35] "Not only are religious institutions significant players in the public realm," say Berger and Neuhaus, "but they are singularly important to the way people order their lives at the most local and concrete levels of their existence."[36]

Values and public discourse: The faith-based religious community is a primary agent for transmitting the operative values of our society. This is true not only in the sense that most North Americans identify their most important values as being religious in character, but also in the sense that the values that inform our public discourse are inseparably related to specific religious traditions.[37]

Religiously based communities supplement components of modern life that are missing. They provide stable values, ritual, substance, and direction to people's lives, fulfilling the needs of many for affiliation, connection, socialization, and ultimate purpose, which our modern society often lacks. Spirituality "is nurtured in community, the oneness with others that springs from shared vision and shared goals, shared memory and shared hope," Kurtz and Ketcham assert.[38] Faith-based communities prize mutuality, the antithesis of the giving/getting mode of being. In mutuality one gets by giving and by being open to receiving, by shared values and shared experiences in personal, face-to-face relations. Faith-based communities demonstrate ways in which the weak and strong can be related without paternalism and are often judged by their altruism, compassion, and caring.[39]

Historical remembrance: Faith-based communities offer historic remembrance that links their members to others who have gone before. "This historical consciousness consists largely in 'stories' from the perspective of the oppressed. Voices of the poor and oppressed provide the means out of which justice must be sought."[40] Remembrance helps cement people's roots and heritage, overcoming the social amnesia that is so often a part of modern organizational society.

Community building: Many faith-based communities prize justice and develop programs that "take in the stranger, assist the needy, and care for widows and orphans."[41] A 1990 study of more than 2,100 urban African American congregations found that about 70% sponsored or participated directly in community outreach activities, staffing day care facilities, offering substance abuse programs, administering food banks, building shelters, and more. A 1994 compendium showed that most urban African American churches are involved in community efforts ranging from housing and health to preschools and elementary education. In Atlanta, for example, 85% of the African American churches are engaged in some type of outreach.[42]

Faith-based communities are among the more powerful disseminators of community building today. Accountable to the vision of the prophet Jeremiah who implored, "seek therefore, the welfare of the city, for in its welfare you will find your welfare,"[43] faith-based communities are committed to enriching the vitality of the towns and cities in which they are located.

African American inner-city churches have been instrumental in initiating the community development movement. They are among the most vital centers of community organization practice today. For example, the Nehemiah Project developed by East Brooklyn Churches (EBN), affiliated with the Industrial Areas Foundation (IAF) founded by Saul Alinsky, provide a powerful image based on stories of Babylonian Jews who took on the project of rebuilding Jerusalem as a metaphor for rebuilding community, a theme replicated in community after community across the United States and Canada.

A BRIEF HISTORY OF COMMUNITY AND ITS THEORISTS

From classical Greece and before, community was the center of society continuing into the 16th century. Beginning with the Enlightenment, a new form of human-associated life gradually asserted its dominance, a phenomenon that provided an arena of study for the new discipline of sociology in the 19th and 20th centuries. Today community continues its role as the fundamental building block of human society.

Early Communal Society

In early societies people typically engaged one another on an informal, personal basis by means of communal social relationships. Community was also the way people structured their social and political life. The early Greeks, for example, did not split the life of a person into one's communal relations and one's duties as a citizen. The two were indivisible and congruent. However, members of classical Greek society were concerned that economic activities not spill over and contaminate civil society. They relegated calculative activities such as bargaining and negotiation and buying and selling for household management, or *oikonomia* (*oikos,* house; *nomia,* rule or management), from which we get the word "economy," to a physically and culturally restricted enclave called the *agora* or marketplace. Containment of economic pursuits continued to be the norm in many premodern societies. Formal economic relationships tended, in the main, to be a less important aspect of structured social existence than communal, personal relationships, which were the primary way people formed their associated life together.

The Enlightenment (1400–1700)

The Enlightenment project in Europe opened the new world to commercial exploration, created the scientific revolution, emancipated the individual and the economy, and resulted in the rise of the market society.

Commercial Exploration Beginning around 1400 and progressing with increasing speed into the 16th and 17th centuries, new economic forces were changing the way human life was structured. In the forefront were the Italian trading cities of Venice and Florence and their great merchant families.[44] By the end of the century, mercantile zeal had inspired entire nations to explore unknown regions of the globe in a quest for wealth. One explorer, Christopher Columbus (1451–1506), is credited with opening up the hitherto unknown area of North America in 1492.

Scientific Revolution On the intellectual front, scientists Nikolaus Copernicus (1473–1542), Tyco Brahe (1546–1601), and Johannes Kepler (1571–1630) challenged traditional ways of thinking about nature and the universe with their discoveries in astronomy and physics. During the 16th century, a number of other thinkers inspired by these ideas and the inevitable conflicts that they created redefined the nature of man, society, and politics based on what they increasingly understood as perennial laws that could be objectively defined, predicted, and controlled. These philosophers captured the spirit of the age of reform, hastening its speed, giving it direction, and providing it with the intellectual, social, and political ideas on which new structures and processes could be developed. Among these ideas was a new way of thinking based on mathematics and the laws of science: the view that the universe operated much as a mechanistic system and that humans also were subject to the laws of the physical universe.

Emancipation of the Individual and the Economy Among the most important events in the history of social relationships was the emancipation of the individual and the economy. The means by which this emancipation occurred was, among other things, due to the writings of Thomas Hobbes (1588–1679). Reason, asserted Hobbes, was nothing other than reckoning, a cost calculus in which individuals applied economic logic to maximize their self-interests. It soon became commonplace to view humans no longer as people "in relationship" with one another but as atomistic individuals intent on maximizing their own individual welfare, called "possessive individualism" by many today. Society was seen as being comprised of individual components, each of whom was activated by ambition and the quest for material wealth, often to the exclusion of community.

Once the basis of society was no longer comprised of community social relationships or a community structure, however, a means needed to be devised by which the conflicting ambitions of these self-interested, calculative actors could be managed. For Hobbes, the solution was a sovereign government, which established the rules, maintained the channels and boundaries, and played a role as umpire in regulating the processes by which people could achieve their goals without interfering with one another.

Rise of a Market Society Implicit in Hobbes's work, somewhat more explicitly in the writings of John Locke (1631–1704) and Jacques Rousseau (1712–1778), and later most clearly with Adam Smith (1723–1790), unfettered market economic relationships were to be the primary means by which individuals could express their freedom, meet their needs, and achieve their goals. The stage was set for the gradual but inevitable transformation of the fundamental unit of society from family and community to the individual, from intimate personal relationships to calculating impersonal relationships, and from the economy as a restricted and minor element of civil society to a market society in which public and civic affairs became components of economic structures governed by the logic of the marketplace.

Community in Early America (1600–1800)

Civic life in early North America was characterized by community solidarity primarily because people resided in small towns. These communities submerged the economy as an enclave of the larger society and engaged in consensual political discourse.

Community Solidarity Thomas Bender says, "The social experience of early 17th century Americans . . . was not divided between communal and noncommunal ways of life;" the whole of life "was framed by a circle of loved, familiar faces."[45] Each of its several hundred provincial communities was "consciously separate" and often "surprisingly different."[46] Local Puritan communities, for example, were based on a covenant that members agreed to and joined. Membership was "fundamentally spiritual and experiential, often based upon previous and long established friendship" in which "like minded people sorted themselves out among diverse towns."[47] Men and women came together to form small, intensely parochial local units of life that made up the kaleidoscopic of American social landscape.

Size and Structure

As late as 1790 there were only 24 towns in the United States with a population of more than 2,500 people, and in a village or town of this size or smaller, everyone and everyone's business was known by all. As small as they were, towns were subdivided into even smaller sections and became "redefined as a confederacy of smaller communities."[48] Within these sections, people divided themselves into even more compact neighborhoods, each of which developed their own separate identities, and in which the full range of one's social life was lived. Social networks held together by personal interaction and mutual friendship characterized these neighborhoods.

Submergence of the Economy

The local community provided a focus for the economic, political, social, and religious lives of the townspeople. Communities "were not so much segments of the larger commonwealth," claims Bender, "as they were miniature commonwealths. . . . While townspeople engaged in trade, their lives were not shaped or even touched by participation in a competitive market society. They were in the market but not of it. . . . Trade did not dominate local society; rather it was itself dominated by local society."[49]

Communal Politics

The informal and personal relationships that maintained the essential unity of the town also produced a strong impulse toward political consensus. The town, not the individual, was the basic unit of political representation. Political decisions were made through "discussion" and consensus rather than through interest-group conflict. When decisions were made, the town records indicate simply that they were reached by general agreement, which allowed the town to speak to the larger society with one political voice. Bender states that this unified expression often went beyond voting. The returns from the towns after votes on the Constitutions of 1778 and 1780, for example, include detailed criticisms and suggestions, and each of these was phrased as the sense of the town, which indeed it was.[50]

The Industrial Revolution (1800–1920)

The process of social change over the next two centuries altered all of this, however, asserts Thomas Bender. The rise of factory towns and industrialization created a bifurcation of North America into communal and noncommunal society.

Science, Technology, and Factory Towns

The power of science and technology, fed by the growth of the rational self-interested market, had a major impact on communal relationships and the structure of community in North America at the turn of the 19th century. The invention of machinery and the factory as a means of mass production gave a boost to the developing market society. Factories needed sources of material supplies and outlets for goods. Locations that favored certain factories also became the site for other manufacturing and commercial businesses. Industry attracted numbers of unskilled laborers from the countryside. Because the mode of human transportation was mostly by foot, workers needed to live close to their worksite. Sometimes factories constructed housing for workers and not only profited from their labor but from providing accommodations as well. In these "factory towns" life was often regulated and organized around the factory. In other areas densely packed cheap housing surrounded the factories. These "slums" became notorious in London and in America's large northern cities including Boston, New York, and Chicago.[51]

Communal and Noncommunal Society

The growth of industrialism, and its dislocations, transformed the structure and meaning of community, but community was not eclipsed. Communal and noncommunal spheres were gradually distinguished from each other, and the distinctions between public and private spheres were sharpened. The mass of Americans became involved in two distinct but intertwined patterns of social relations, one communal and the other not.

Community Sociology (1887–1920)

Increasingly at the end of the 19th and beginning of the 20th century, industrial society was becoming a phenomenon of interest for a group of thinkers called sociologists. Among the most prominent were Ferdinand Toennies, Émile Durkheim, Max Weber, and George Simmel in Europe, and Edward Ross in the United States.

Ferdinand Toennies (1855–1936): Gemeinschaft *and* Gesellschaft

Ferdinand Toennies explored the transformation of community in modern times more deeply than any other sociologist of his generation. In his book, *Gemeinshaft Und Gesellschaft,* published in 1887 and often translated as *Community and Society*, Toennies observed that a phenomenon was occurring in which one form of human association, or "*gemeinschaft*," was giving way to another form of social relations, which he called "*gesellschaft*."

Gemeinschaft   "*Gemeinschaft* is a type of relationship that . . . focuses around emotional commitment, loyalty, emphasizing common ties and feelings and a sense of moral interdependence and mutual obligation."[52] *Gemeinschaft* is characterized by natural, personal, face-to-face social relationships. *Gemeinschaft* relationships," asserts Hassinger and Pinkerton, are "informal, intimate, and most commonly found in families, small groups and communities."[53]

In traditional family-like community relationships, for example, a person is perceived "according to *who* he is rather than on *what* he has done, what he can produce, or the amount of wealth he can command."[54] With *gemeinschaft* relationships "ends and means are not separate. Action is based on emotion and sentiment."[55] People are seen as totalities and are appreciated for their innate qualities. Where *gemeinschaft* relationships permeate community, people encourage neighborliness, informal control, and group relations over individualism.

Gesellschaft   Toennies observed that in modern society *gesellschaft* relationships had become the dominant mode of being. *Gesellschaft* is characterized by artificial, impersonal, economic relationships designed and controlled by others. In *gesellschaft* relationships, people engage one another impersonally, as objects who can be used as a means for another person's ends. Encounters with others tend to be directed toward achievement of specific utilitarian goals rather than entered into for their own sake. A person is valued according to how useful he or she is: one who has skills that are needed, who is in command of resources, or who has power to obtain others' compliance.

Ultimately a person becomes transformed into an object, a functionary who plays a role in return for some benefit such as a salary, the hope of security, a favor, or advancing one's interests in a kind of social exchange. A person comes to view him- or herself and others as commodities.[56] *Gesellschaft* relationships result in dehumanization of human beings, and often there is little conscious awareness that this has occurred.

Two Alternative Forms of Interaction   For Toennies, the rise of industrial capitalism represented a "great transformation" from *gemeinschaft* to *gesellschaft* relations. Toennies asserts that "this change reaches its consummation in what is frequently designated as individualism. . . . A new phenomenon, in which 'capitalistic society' captures individualism and impersonal economic relationships with which it is associated, increases in power and gradually grows to ascendancy."[57] In addition, *gesellschaft* requires the universal application of rational/legal forms of control, an institutionalized power orientation, and formal contractual relationships.

By the time that Toennies observed the dominance of *gesellschaft* over *gemeinschaft,* formal impersonal relationships had become so universal that they were already the norm for European society as a whole. This transformation, however, did not mean the death of community as a social form of association. Whereas *gesellschaft* was gaining in significance in people's lives, Toennies did not say that all relationships were or would become what he called *gesellschaft*. "The force of *Gemeinschaft* persists," he wrote, "even within the period of *Gesellschaft*."[58] Toennies "used his dichotomy to denote the character of a whole society in a particular historical period, and to describe two patterns of human relationships within that society."[59] The two forms of human interaction, *gemeinschaft* and *gesellschaft,* constitute two kinds of alternative relationships available in modern society, and Toennies anticipated that both forms of interaction were likely to be permanent aspects of all social life. Even though the social space in which *gemeinschaft* relationships existed was shrinking, community continued to be and would remain an irrevocable component of the human condition.

Émile Durkheim (1858–1917) and the Division of Labor

In *The Division of Labor in Society* (1893), Émile Durkheim asserted that modernity and the Industrial Revolution resulted in an "increased division of labor in more advanced societies that leads to the interdependence of specialized parts,"[60] a structural form that was occurring not only in the market economy but was increasingly present in government, art, and science as well.[61] This new mechanistic form of society, Durkheim said, was inherently destructive of the human condition. In his classic work, *Suicide* (1897), Durkheim explored how the modern lack of associational relationships resulted in "normlessness" or anomie in mainly Protestant countries where the division of labor was most developed, leading to a higher incidence of suicide. "Durkeim, who apparently developed his concepts of 'mechanical' and 'organic' solidarity independently of Toennies, similarly believed that modern society contained both of them simultaneously. It was a historical event in modern society that produced two closely interrelated but distinct patterns of social interaction. These 'two societies,' Durkheim wrote, 'really make up only one' just as Toennies claimed. As Toennies noted that the 'town lives within the city,' Durkheim believed that there continues to be an intimate social life outside of the whole division of labor."[62]

Max Weber (1864–1920) and Bureaucracy and Instrumental Reason
In *Economy and Society*, Max Weber, the foremost and most brilliant sociologist of our time, also described societal transformation in ways virtually identical to that of Toennies.[63] However, Weber's unique contribution was his understanding of how *gemeinschaft* relationships tend give way to *gesellschaft* in modern society. In his classic article "Bureaucracy," Weber asserted that in either the economy or government, modern complex organization is *the* means of transforming informal, personal, socially oriented communal action (*gemeinschaftshandeln*) into formal, impersonal, rationally organized action (*gesellschaftshandeln*).[64] The way by which complex bureaucratic organizations change our thinking is the key to understanding how this new more impersonal society is created.

Two Ways of Thinking
On one hand, for Weber, communal social thinking (described in Chapter 3) is based on a conception of ethical "virtue" (*wertrationalitaet*) in which people attempt to apprehend what is ultimately good and insert those qualities that constituted a "good life" into their communities and society as a whole. Alberto Guerreiro Ramos claims that this "substantive" or classical reason is an authentic, inherent, and invariable quality of human consciousness.[65]

Weber asserts that modern bureaucratic organizations require a fundamentally different epistemology than is used in communal social relations. Managers of modern complex organization utilize Hobbesian functional or instrumental reasoning, devoid of values and ends (*zweckrationalitaet*), to achieve their purposes. Calculative rationality is not an inherent quality of human character but is an artificial skill that one learns by education and training. By imposing functional rationality (*zweckrationalitaet*) over social value-laden reason (*wertrationalitaet*) as a preferred way of thinking, bureaucracy wars against personal, informal communal action (*gemeinshaftshandeln*), transforming it into instrumental, rational/legal action (*gesellschafthandeln*).

Organized individuals are required to surrender their capacity to think valuationally, and instead depend on calculating the most efficient way to accomplish the goals of the owner of the organization. Once initiated, Weber asserted, the rationalization of communal relations, transforming personal relationships into impersonal ones,[66] cannot be diverted from its path. Modern complex organization "was and is a power instrument of the first order for the one who controls the bureaucratic apparatus."[67]

Dominance of Modern Bureaucratic Organization
As it acquires power, grows in size, and imposes its imperatives on more and more social space, complex organizational systems shrink the arenas where people can express communal social relations and exercise value-based social thinking in their lives. Echoing Weber, Robert Bellah and colleagues comment that

> just as individualism has contributed to the loss of self in today's society, a kind of surrogate community, modern complex organization, is the means by which natural authentic community has become undermined. In the economic sphere this new social form, capable of extending the control of a group of investors over vast resources, huge numbers of employees and, often great distances, was the business corporation.[68]

In its modern form, bureaucratic organization is unprecedented. It was seen first in industrial capitalism, beginning with the modern factory and commercial enterprises, and has expanded to become the most common form of economic structure comprising our market society, or what others call the "organization society."[69]

George Simmel (1858–1918) and the Money Economy and Urbanization

George Simmel, another sociologist at the turn of the century, observed the growing urbanization and the growth of large cities in Europe and North America and explored the link between *gesellschaft* and urbanization in the modern money economy. Simmel wrote that modern reason and the rise of a monetary market economy are "intrinsically connected. They share a matter-of-fact attitude in dealing with men and with things."[70] In the money-driven market economy, all values are reduced to price, but this change tends to be deceitful, destroying the content of what is of authentic value. "Money . . . becomes the common denominator of all values; irreparably it hollows out the core of things, their individuality, their specific value and their incomparability,"[71] claimed Simmel.

In *gesellschaft* society, the organized market economy changes the basis on which human life exists. In community, for example, where personal social relationships are the norm, we see people as having intrinsic worth. In modern society, dominated by functional social relations, a person only has utilitarian worth. A person is not valued for who he or she is but by the amount of money for which the person can sell his or her skills. Those who are unemployable by modern organizations are worthless both in social and psychological terms.

Edward A. Ross (1866–1951) and Social Control

Writing at the turn of the 19th century, Edward A. Ross, one of America's most influential social theorists during the Progressive Era, rejected Toennies's dualistic notion and offered a linear model of change. Ross saw society as progressing from particularistically oriented community to rational, mass urbanized society in an inevitable, historically determined process. In his book *Social Control,* for example, Ross argued that "powerful forces are more and more transforming *community* into *society* that is, replacing living tissue with structures held together by rivets and screws."[72] With the erosion of all traditional or communal forms of social cohesion in modern urban society, it was essential, Ross argued, to develop artificial or formal institutional mechanisms of social control.[73]

Urbanization (1920–1990)

In North America, urbanization grew with amazing speed. By the first quarter of the 20th century, Chicago was a transportation hub and a food-processing and manufacturing center that became the prototype of the industrial city. Cities were magnets that drew young people from the farms. In the national census of 1920, the urban population of the United States exceeded the rural population for the first time. Social thinkers Louis Wirth and Edward Ross began to consider urbanization as an inevitable historically determined process. Others tended to dispute that assessment, including early communitarian Robert Redfield and new community theorists.

Louis Wirth (1897–1952) and Urbanism

In 1938 Louis Wirth wrote what is "possibly the most-cited, most influential article ever written in American sociology, 'Urbanism as a way of Life.'"[74] Wirth explored how population size, density, and heterogeneity combined to create the conditions for *gesellschaft* relationships by increasing specialized division of labor, more impersonal relationships, competition, and the need for more social control. Wirth argued that "communal ways broke down and were replaced by a new pattern of life called 'urbanism,'"[75] and he insisted that urbanism is both the cause and the result of weakening kinship bonds, the declining social significance of the family, disappearance of the neighborhood, and the undermining of the traditional basis of social solidarity."[76] With the collapse of *gemeinschaft,* Wirth supposed that "competition and formal control mechanisms [would have to] substitute for bonds of solidarity that hold a communally oriented society together,"[77] and in agreement with Ross and contemporary modernization theorists, Wirth conceived of urbanization as a linear progression by which society emerged from its more communal past.

Early Communitarians

"If in American social science there was a clear tradition extending from Ross at the turn of the century to Wirth in the late 30s that emphasized one aspect of Toennies theory and denied or de-emphasized the other," says Thomas Bender, "there was also an important group of progressive social theorists including Jane Addams, at the turn of the century and continuing with Charles Horton Coolely, Robert Park, Mary Parker Follett, and John Dewey who maintained the dual perspective of Toennies."[78] Although acknowledging that the advent of modern, urban society meant increasing *gesellschaft* relations, they agreed with Toennies and Durkheim that community was still vital.

Jane Addams, for example, embraced Cooley's advice that the reinvigoration of informal and intimate groups in the city should involve "trusting democracy more, rather than less,"[79] and by means of her work she enhanced democracy while making the local neighborhood a community within the city. Mary Parker Follett, another social worker connected with the Settlement House movement, "theorized about the necessity of revitalizing the neighborhood as a social and political group that might counterbalance the modern tendency toward bureaucratization and centralization."[80]

Robert Park viewed society as "double-visioned." Rather than society replacing community, he believed each individual was involved in alternative forms of human interaction.[81] Finally, John Dewey denied the existence of any inevitable evolution of society from individualism to collectivity. "There is nothing intrinsic in the forces which have effected uniform standardization, mobility, and remote invisible relationships,"[82] he said. For Dewey, the small community remains vital. Until "local communal life can be restored, the public cannot adequately resolve its most urgent problem: to find and identify itself."[83]

Robert Redfield (1897–1958) and Folk Society

Robert Redfield exhaustively studied both communal and urban society and came to the most reliable conclusions about whether impersonal social relationships and communal relationships could exist together, or whether *gesellschaft* supplants *gemeinschaft* relationships in an inevitable linear progression. In 1941 Redfield examined small communities in his book *The Folk Culture of the Yucatan,* locating four settlements in Mexico that stood at different points on a continuum from communal to urban. Redfield's was an essentially linear model similar to that of Wirth, stressing the harmony of the pre-urban community and the breakdown of community under the impact of urbanization.[84] However, following a critique of his study by Oscar Lewis, who disputed Redfield's finding of the breakdown of community after urbanization, Redfield reformulated his ideas.

Redfield retained his original notion of sequential change associated with the process of urbanization, but he now speculated that folk (communal) and urban ways coexisted in the same society. Redfield now realized that Toennies "conceived of two imaginably distinct and contrasting aspects of all societies."[85] We need to think of local society as "an interpenetration of two opposite kinds of living, thinking and feeling": of *gemeinschaft* as "an isolated, homogenous, sacred and personal community" and simultaneously of *gesellschaft,* as "a heterogenous, secular, and impersonal society that we find in cities,"[86] Redfield concluded.

"From this perspective," says Bender, "community is not a baseline for historical change; it is a fundamental and enduring form of social interaction. Thinking of *gemeinschaft* and *gesellschaft* in terms of sequential development in which impersonal society replaces personal community is erroneous. They represent instead 'two kinds of collective living' in which all individuals are involved."[87]

Community Theorists (1990–2000)

In the 1980s and 1990s three ideas about community gained popularity: Eastern European activists and civil society, Amitai Etzioni and communitarianism, and Robert Putnam and social capital.

Eastern European Activists and Civil Society

During the 1980s, Eastern European activists were struggling against communist dictatorships. These dissidents discovered that even the most efficient police states could not stamp out all vestiges of independent social life, which survived in cafés, churches, workplaces, and families. Eastern European rebels used these enclaves of civil society to incubate the idea of free societies that eventually triumphed.[88] Their struggles created renewed interest in the idea of civil society that "offered a language of volunteerism and freedom, and those forms of communal and associational life that are organized neither by the self interest of the market nor by the coercive potential of the state."[89]

Civil society centers on the importance of strengthening the social infrastructure of local communities through civic engagement and citizen participation. Public life in a democracy depends on the social virtues of people who are willing and to give of themselves as "participators in the affairs of government," in the phrase of Thomas Jefferson.[90] Rather than self-interest, civil society is dependent on those who offer service. Instead of top-down autocratic dominance and control, democracy requires social leadership from people who work for justice, equality, and human rights.

Amitai Etzioni and Communitarianism
Communitarians, led by Amitai Etzione, present strong communities as the solution to contemporary social ills: "Our ultimate purpose is to provide an opportunity for deep human satisfaction, the kind found only when we are engaged with one another, and to strengthen the community as a moral infrastructure."[91] The communitarians focus on the value of local self-sufficiency and civic responsibility. They believe that a stable, well-functioning society is characterized by strong local communities working together to solve problems: "[A]s a rule every community ought to be expected to do the best it can to take care of its own . . . whether the problem is mounting garbage, crime, drug abuse, or any of the well known host of social problems that beset us, the first responsibility lies with those who share a community."[92]

Robert Putnam and Social Capital
The communitarian emphasis on rebuilding local capacity that began in Eastern Europe has been echoed in the writings of civil society theorists Robert Bellah, Robert Putnam, and others. Robert Putnam, for example, emphasized the importance of social capital: those products of human association that are indispensable in our common lives and without which we could not exist.[93] Community social capital is a measure of how much collaborative time and energy people have for each other, the amount of time parents have for their children, the attention neighbors give to one another's families, the quality of relationships people in congregations have with each other, and the relationships people form in associations such as PTAs and scout troops, among others. The relationships in these communal associations build trust, loyalty, and honesty, without which the foundations of many social institutions would dissolve. Kristina Smock, comments, for example, "In any comprehensive strategy for improving the plight of America's communities, rebuilding social capital is as important as investing in human and physical capital. . . . Social capital is not a substitute for effective public policy but rather a prerequisite for it and, in part, a consequence of it."[94]

Toennies Revisited: Social Work and Modernization Theory
Macro social workers must have a clear perspective on the role of community in today's modern urban society and understand the historical and theoretical ideas about community. Although each social worker may come to his or her own conclusions about the importance of community, two issues seem clear.

First, community is not disappearing, nor is it subject to eradication by the encroachment of *gesellschaft* relationships. Community exists wherever and whenever human beings exist together. Community may take a variety of forms and express itself in a variety of ways, but its persistence is part of the human condition. The question for macro social workers, then, is how to strengthen and empower people in community and in so doing help improve individual character and the qualities that enhance the self and community welfare.

Second, although the encroachment of *gesellschaft* relationships and the paraphernalia of modernity seem to be triumphant, proceeding in a linear path toward development and modernization, this perspective is tantamount to a false consciousness, and is, in part, one of the causes of social problems in our global society. Modernization theory that emerged in the 1960s represents a distorted and misleading view of society. According to its logic, the inevitable progressive movement of history involves the replacement of community and communal ways by modern ways.[95]

Those who accept modernization theory tend to applaud the change of *gemeinschaft* to *gesellschaft,* rural to urban, traditional to modern, and undeveloped to developed as an inevitable process by which history is moving, requiring individuals and entire societies to conform to its demands. Modernization theorists treat rural/urban, traditional/modern, and underdeveloped/developed as zero-sum equations in which growth in *gesellschaft* requires an equivalent reduction in *gemeinschaft,* until ultimately the society is completely transformed.[96]

Social workers must reject any evolutionary, deterministic perspective of social change and instead understand that change is never the construct of impersonal societal or historical forces beyond the reach of the individuals who compose society. Instead, humans are active and creative actors in the construction of society, and they bring with them ideals, values, visions, social consciousness, and social capital that can be used to continually inform and improve their social condition. Social workers have faith that people working together can make a difference and that each individual is an important part of making that difference. Of all the assets and tools that humans have for constructing their social environment, community is the most basic and most important.

MACRO SOCIAL WORK AND THE COMMUNITY

Generalist-based macro social workers apply varied skills, a broad worldview, inclusive methods, and a commitment to social justice and empowerment to community engagement. When working with communities, we simultaneously increase the capacity of communities to build strong social selves, improve social groups, and engage wider society. Macro social workers use three traditional approaches, each with its own theoretical model or perspective, when engaging people in community: community social work planning, community development, and community organization. A relatively new model is Mike Eichler's consensus organizing model, which approaches community improvement from a systems-based contingency model of social work.

Community Planning Approach

Community planners rely on a structural functionalist model based on a systems framework and using concepts such as equilibrium, synergy, and feedback. Structural functionalism asserts that any social system is comprised of various structures that exist to carry out a particular function. If one of those functions becomes disordered, the structure will fail. The goal of community social planners is to examine the kinds of needs that exist in a community and devise structures or plans to fill functions that are lacking. The structural functionalist model is nonconflictual, working harmoniously with all parts of the system of the community, and helps members work together in synergistic unity in which the whole is greater than the sum of its parts.

Each part of the community must be built to contribute its function, playing a particular role, and all of the various parts must work together and interrelate, providing feedback so that the community can continually adjust its structures, programs, and processes to provide those functions that the community needs. Feedback occurs when individuals take civic responsibility, participate in the democratic process, and improve their communities with concrete ideas and a vision of the future that they can implement.

Community social work planners assist members in deciding on goals, look at social needs and assets, and work to balance areas where there is inequity or lack of resources, or where the feedback system is not effective. In the structural functionalist systems model, people with low incomes need opportunity, not power, says Randy Stoecker. Cooperation between the haves and the have-nots is the best means of providing opportunity. Rational planning that produces gradual, incremental change by rearranging structural balance is an effective way of achieving a socially and economically healthy community.[97]

Community Development Approach

Community developers use entrepreneurial skills in social enterprise development, helping members use the assets of a modern community to build a strong financial base. Community development works to generate community resources that members can use to enhance their social environment. They use the assets that already exist in the community or develop new ones.

Many community developers use a sustainability framework. Macro social workers work to improve the sustainability of the community, create economic development projects, construct community development corporations, and arrange for social services, programs, and opportunities. They engage citizens in devising social, recreational, and educational, health, and other services and programs for the betterment of the community.[98]

Community Organization Approach

The community organization approach often uses an intergroup conflict model. The intergroup conflict model is based on interest group liberalism, the idea that power is up for grabs and politics is a struggle between groups to attain their interests in competition with other like-minded groups. The conflict model pits community organizations and the interests of the community members against claimants in business or government in a power struggle. These interests at times try to disempower community members by keeping wages low, appropriating their housing to build commercial enterprises, redlining their communities to prevent members from obtaining loans, shifting city revenue to suburbs and wealthy areas of the city, and leaving impoverished areas to fend for themselves.

The community organization becomes a countervailing power center that can bring contending groups to the table and prevent vested interests from destroying or exploiting the community. Community organizations often operate from the premise that people and institutions with power will never surrender it voluntarily. Conflict-oriented organizers devote themselves to orchestrating the application of force, usually in a series of events such as rallies or pickets.[99] They gather large numbers of people because the organizers believe numbers are one of the main sources of the community's strength. They develop leadership by securing "victories" over institutions with power including banks, universities, corporations, and government agencies.[100]

Macro social work community organizers work to overcome oppression, anonymity, alienation, and depression in a culture in which, Alinsky asserts, people are trained to be apathetic. We help members of the community oppose those forces that undermine and exploit the community for their own interests and assist people in mobilizing their thinking, vision, intuition, and action to attain a better life with more opportunities, better schools, health care, and jobs. In contrast to the structural functionalist approach, community organizers believe these results will not come easily out of a rational planning process or by developing community projects through community development corporations alone.

The Consensual Approach

Community social work planning, community development and community organization continue to be used as distinct ways of achieving the goals of community betterment, but it is becoming clear that none of them will work all of the time or in every situation. Instead, macro social workers must be able to understand each of them and combine them in different ways, depending on the unique situation that presents itself in any particular community. Today macro social workers must be able to think in creative ways to assess the specific issues that they confront to help community members devise the best strategies and tactics to achieve their goals.

The consensus approach combines planning, community development, and community organization models and uses the strengths of each one depending on the situation. This contingency approach is flexible. It is based on a social ecology model in which macro social workers help members achieve a healthy, sustainable community. Although Mike Eichler has developed a fairly clear-cut process, many organizers call their process "learn as you go." It more often resembles a spiral than a straight line. The members' vision will often be more useful if it is fleshed out over time, adapted, and based on what the community members learn as they proceed. It does not have to be spelled out in full before members begin to act.

The consensus approach uses social thinking, in which members apply their own ideas and perceptions, often with the involvement of a macro social worker to develop a strategy of action. Members try, regroup, and try again, learning and modifying their strategy depending on responses from those in the social environment who are the targets of activity.

The planning component of the process is a means by which members gather information and develop a strategy. Planning is not seen as an end in itself but rather is a means to develop an inventory of community assets and devise a strategy based on the results. The initial planning should not take too long, nor does it have to be perfected before members take action. It is important to get members into action projects quickly to keep people motivated and to assist them in accomplishing things.

Planning and implementation can often proceed simultaneously and concurrently. In other words, planning is a continual process rather than an isolated separate method or the first in a sequence of steps. Consensual community building tends not to engage in conflictual confrontations but instead seeks strategies in which communities can succeed while still maintaining relationships with those who are the targets of organizing.

CONCLUSION

Without healthy communities, people tend to aimless, vulnerable, and displaced, and freedom becomes simple emptiness. For citizens to be authentically free, we must experience and have available to us free communities from which we can draw strength and which act as centers of values and character. Authentic social work is nothing less than assisting people in choosing the kind of social world they decide is best, and then helping people struggle, against all odds, to make this world real. Community social workers become active in inner-city neighborhoods, inner-ring suburbs, suburbs, and rural communities. We work with associations, communities of diversity, and faith-based communities. Macro social workers engage in community planning, community development, community organization, and sometimes use a consensus approach.

KEY CONCEPTS

community

community as locality

inner cities

inner-ring suburbs

suburbs

rural communities

relational community

transcend location

transcend structure

transcend time

social action

gemeinschaftshandeln

we relations

community, civic, service associations

communities of diversity

study circles

faith-based communities

civil society

values and social discourse

historical remembrance

community building

agora (marketplace)

commercial exploration

scientific revolution

market society

Industrial Revolution

community sociology

Ferdinand Toennies

gemeinschaft

gesellschaft

Émile Durkheim

division of labor

suicide

anomie

bureaucracy

instrumental reason

gesellschafthandeln

virtrationalitaet

zweckrationalitaet

George Simmel

money economy

Edward A. Ross

social control

linear model of change

urbanization

Louis Wirth

early communitarians

Robert Redfield

Amitai Etzioni

communitarians

Robert Putnam

community planning approach

structural functionalism

systems framework

community development approach

sustainability

community organization approach

intergroup conflict theory

Mike Eichler

consensual approach

contingency

social ecology

QUESTIONS FOR DISCUSSION

1. What characterizes an ideal community? What qualities constitute a human environment that not only meets needs but inspires people to reach excellence as well?

2. This chapter explored the idea of *gemeinschaft* relationships. Sociologists tend to take two differing perspectives about *gemeinschaft* relationships. One is that modern *gesellschaft* is supplanting communal *gemeinschaft*. The other is that although *gemeinschaft* seems to be eroding, it continues to exist within the arena of *gesellschaft*. Which position do you believe is correct? Explain your position. Extend your argument into the future. If you believe *gesellschaft* will supplant *gemeinschaft*, what are the implications of this development? If you believe *gemeinschaft* exists in *gesellschaft*, what are the implications of this?

3. The theory of modernization applauds the triumph of the rationalization of social relationships, material progress, and technology. What stance should a macro social worker take toward modernization theory?

4. Some people assert that humans are irrevocably social by nature and, as such, cannot exist without community. Others believe community is an idea whose time is past and, in fact, because it emphasizes personal, irrational emotions is often the cause of strife and conflict. These individuals look to modern organizations as a means of stability, security, and power. What are the benefits of community, and what are its limitations? What are the benefits of organization, and what are its limitations?

ADDITIONAL READING

Community Building

Alliance for National Renewal. *The Kitchen Table: Newsletter of the Community-Based Renewal Movement*. Denver, CO: National Civic League. National Civic League, 1445 Market Street, Suite 300, Denver, CO 80202; Phone: 800-223-6004.

Barber, Benjamin. *A Place for Us: How to Make Society Civil and Democracy Strong*. New York: Hill and Wange, 1998.

Kemmis, Daniel. *The Good City and the Good Life*. New York: Houghton Mifflin, 1995.

Kretzmann, John, and John McKnight. *Building Communities From the Inside Out.* Evanston, IL: Northwestern University, 1993.

Fellin, Phillip. *The Community and the Social Worker.* Itasca, IL: F. E. Peacock, 1987.

Lappe, Frances Moore, and Paul Martin Du Bois. *The Quickening of America.* San Francisco, CA: Jossey-Bass, 1994.

Harker, Donald F., and Elizabeth Ungar Natter. *Beyond Voting—A Citizen's Guide to Participating in Local Government.* Berea, KY: MACED, 1991. Mountain Association for Community Economic Development (MACED), 433 Chestnut Street, Berea, KY 40403.

Program for Community Problem Solving. *Building Community: Exploring the Role of Social Capital and Local Government.* Program for Community Problem Solving, 1319 F Street NW, Suite 204, Washington DC 20004.

Rankin, Tom, and Trudy Wilner Stack. *Local Heroes Changing America.* New York: W.W. Norton/Lyndhurst Books, 2000.

Sociology of Community

Bellah, Robert N., Richard Madsen, William M. Sullivan, Ann Swidler, and Steven M. Tipton. *Habits of the Heart: Individualism and Commitment in American Life.* New York: Harper and Row, 1985.

Berger, Peter L. *Facing Up to Modernity: Excursions in Society, Politics and Religion.* New York: Basic Books, 1977.

Berger, Peter L., and Richard John Neuhaus. *To Empower People: From State to Civil Society,* 2d ed. Washington, DC: American Enterprise Institute Press, 1997.

Boyte, Harry C., and Nancy Kari. *Building America: The Democratic Promise of Public Work.* Philadelphia: Temple University Press, 1996.

Diggins, John Patrick. *The Promise of Pragmatism.* Chicago: University of Chicago Press, 1994.

Etzioni, Amitai. *The New Golden Rule: Community and Morality in a Democratic Society.* New York: Basic Books, 1996.

Haworth, Lawrence. *The Good City.* Indianapolis: Indiana University Press, 1966.

Koenig, Rene. *The Community.* London: Routledge and Kegan Paul, 1968.

Putnam, Robert D. "Bowling Alone: America's Declining Social Capital." *Journal of Democracy,* 6 (1), 1995, pp. 65–78.

Schutz, Alfred. *Collected Papers.* Arvid Brodersen, ed. The Hague: Martinus Nijhoff, 1962.

Seligman, Adam. *The Idea of Civil Society.* New York: Free Press, 1992.

Toennies, Ferdinand. *Community and Association.* London: Routledge and Kegan Paul, 1955.

Warren, Roland L. *The Community in America.* Chicago: Rand McNally, 1963.

Wolfe, Alan. *Whose Keeper? Social Science and Moral Obligation.* Berkeley: University of California Press, 1989.

Wuthnow, Robert. *Sharing the Journey: Support Groups and America's New Quest for Community.* New York: Free Press, 1994.

History of Community

Bender, Thomas. *Community and Social Change in America.* New Brunswick, NJ: Rutgers University Press, 1978.

DeToqueville, Alexis. *Democracy in America.* New York: Harper and Row, 1966.

McCarthy, Kathleen, ed. *Lady Bountiful Revisited: Women, Philanthropy, and Power.* London: Rutgers University Press, 1990.

Scott, Anne Firor. *Natural Allies: Women's Associations in American History.* Chicago: University of Illinois, 1991.

Schneewind, J. B., ed. *Giving: Western Ideas of Philanthropy.* Bloomington: Indiana University Press, 1996.

Hallie, Philip. *Lest Innocent Blood Be Shed: The Story of the Village of Le Chambon and How Goodness Happened There.* New York: Harper and Row, 1979.

Mumford, Lewis. *The City in History.* New York: Harcourt Brace Jovanovitch, 1961.

Trattner, Walter I. *From Poor Law to Welfare State: A History of Social Welfare in America.* New York: Free Press, 1984.

Shain, Barry Alan. *The Myth of American Individualism: The Protestant Origins of American Political Thought.* Princeton, NJ: Princeton University Press, 1994.

Community Research

Jones, W. Ron. *Finding Community: A Guide to Community Research and Action.* Palo Alto, CA: Freel and Associates, 1971.

Communitarianism

Etzioni, Amitai. *The Spirit of Community: Rights, Responsibilities and the Communitarian Agenda.* New York: Crown, 1993.

Coleman, James. "Social Capital in the Creation of Human Capital." *American Journal of Sociology,* 94, 1988, pp. S95–S120.

Foley, Michael W., and Bob Edwards, "Escape From Politics? Social Theory and the Social Capital Debate." *American Behavioral Scientist*, 40 (5), 1997, pp. 549–560.

Modernization Theory

Rostow, Walt Whitman. *The Stages of Economic Growth: A Non-Communist Manifesto.* Cambridge: Cambridge University Press, 1960.

McClelland, David. *The Achieving Society.* New York: Van Nostrand, 1961.

Inkeles, Charles, and David Smith. *Becoming Modern.* Cambridge, MA: Harvard University Press, 1974.

Articles Online

National Civic League's Community Assistance Team. *Building Your Community's Problem Solving Capacities.* http://www.ncl.org/ncl/cat1.htm.

National Commission on Civic Renewal. *Nation of Spectators: How Civic Disengagement Weakens America and What We Can Do About It.* http://www.puaf.umd.edu/civicrenewal/finalreport/table_of_contentsfinal_report.htm

Walsh, Joan. *Stories of Renewal: Community Building and the Future of Urban America.* New York: Rockefeller Foundation, 1997. http://www.rockfound.org/

6
The Practice of Community Planning

Visionary Planning

A vision without a plan is just a dream. A plan without a vision is just drudgery. But a vision with a plan can change the world.

Proverb

The Iron Law of Community Planning

It is better to plan for ourselves, no matter how badly, than to be planned for by others no matter how well.[1]

John Forester

Ideas in This Chapter

The planning process is one of the key means by which citizens gain access to power to meet community needs.

Provide Feedback
Present the Solution to the Community
Present the Solution to Decision Makers
Implement the Solution
Monitor and Evaluate

CONCLUSION
KEY CONCEPTS
QUESTIONS FOR DISCUSSION
ADDITIONAL READING

COMMUNITY PLANNING, ALIVE AND KICKING

In Richmond, Virginia, a Neighborhood Team Process includes 1,000 people participating in monthly meetings in nine planning districts. In Charlotte, North Carolina, 60 neighborhoods have become organizing units for local government in which citizens devise neighborhood plans whose specific conditions and priorities city officials use to orient their policy and program decisions. In Minneapolis a joint venture between residents, government, and the private sector, called Neighborhood Revitalization Program (NRP), encompasses 79 of 81 neighborhoods and uses government and private funds to leverage service delivery and revitalization initiatives.

In 1990 community residents in Sandtown-Winchester, Maryland, formed the Enterprise Founda-

tion, a joint community planning board comprised of two neighborhood organizations and staffed by professional community planners provided by the City of Baltimore, to overcome high unemployment, poverty, substandard and vacant housing, vacant lots, and an illegal dumpsite. Beginning in 1995, Portland's Target Area Designation Program (TADP), administered by the Bureau of Housing and Community Development (BHCD), donated staff assistance and awards up to $100,000 over a 3-year period to enable members of low and moderate neighborhoods to plan and implement their own revitalization strategies.

More than 1,200 community members, businesspeople, and city employees have participated in the Livable Tucson Vision Program to address the real concerns of the community, laying the groundwork for the development of new and enhanced programs and services. Insisting on developing their own community initiatives, citizens of Roxbury, Massachusetts rejected a community plan developed by 30 community agencies in 1984. The result was formation of the Dudley Street Neighborhood Initiative (DSNI), a collaboration of residents, social service agencies, businesses, and churches in the Dudley Street area.

From Seattle to Jacksonville, citizens across the country are defining a vision for themselves. They are learning that when they plan the future of their own communities, they have a chance to construct their social environment in ways that no one else could accomplish. Citizens are showing that "participatory democracy can grow and develop within the bounds of America's existing political framework . . . opening broad avenues for citizen roles in policymaking extending far beyond that which is possible through electoral politics."[2]

Planning Process

In each of these community planning initiatives, citizen planners meet together, share ideas, and with the assistance of a community planner engage in participative action research to help neighborhoods develop their own vision. In Sandtown-Winchester community residents developed a set of guiding principles that framed the design process, including the involvement of community residents in increasingly central roles in all initiative activities. In Minneapolis local neighborhood planning groups develop "Neighborhood Action Plans" in collaboration with city and county agencies. In Portland each target area is sponsored by a community-based organization that coordinates the action planning and implementation process through a paid BHCD staff coordinator. The planning coordinator provides technical assistance and support to the neighborhood planning organization throughout the planning process and can access more specialized consultants if needed. Neighborhood group members in St. Paul, Minnesota, elect a local council, which selects a chairperson.

In Tucson public forums are held in each ward to engage the community in identifying a common vision and strategies for achieving a sustainable community. Other forums target businesses, youth, and Spanish speakers. An Internet site also gives citizens the opportunity to contribute their priorities, and City Council offices established bulletin boards for community input. In other cities planning officers are elected directly by members of the community organization.

Staff of the individual district planning councils work directly with city agencies and city counselors.

Methods

Community planning organizations employ a variety of methods to assist neighborhoods and to organize groups. Their processes are invariably democratic but express a wide diversity in the way democracy is conducted. All of these organizations and methods emerged out of ideas from the people themselves. "In Atlanta," said one participant, "you have the whole spectrum of types of participation from New England town meetings to elected councils. If people can't participate in the way they feel comfortable, then the process won't work."[3] St. Paul one district planning council boasts more than 250 block associations, each with its own block captain and active members. In Portland district coalition boards and staff represent the planning process and in Dayton priority boards are utilized. San Antonio uses community representatives and a citizens' advisory board and the citywide COPS community organization; in Birmingham community resource officers do this work.

Participation

Not everyone can be expected to participate directly in a community planning process, but the numbers are impressive. Thomson and colleagues found that in Birmingham, Dayton, Portland, San Antonio, and St. Paul, 16.6% of the population have been involved in community projects and 10.7%, or 150,000 people, are active in dealing with their cities' concerns at least once a month.[4] But at the core of the participation systems in each city are small natural neighborhoods where regular, face-to-face discussion of the issues takes place by all who choose to become involved. Rules of operation are informal; people join and leave as their interest peaks and wanes, and generally everybody who attends has a chance to put in his or her 2 cents worth. The neighborhood planning associations take on any and all issues that residents bring before them. Some of these are developed informally at monthly meetings; others come out of a formal survey process. Many issues grow from individual residents' concerns; others are responses to city initiatives or to a dramatic event, such as discovery of toxic materials in the water supply.

Goals

Many planning projects define short- and long-term goals that guide them in the process. By 1987 the DSNI had developed a comprehensive 5-year strategic plan that included housing development, job creation, environmental health projects, and more. In Sandtown-Winchester, neighborhood citizen planners identified goals in health and human services, education, physical/economic development, and community building. Citizens of Tucson developed a comprehensive list of 17 goals that embody the values and aspirations of the community to maintain and improve Tucson in the future. The next phase involved holding six workshops to develop indicators of progress toward each of the 17 goals.

Implementation

The result of the planning process in each of these communities is the implementation and development of programs. Sandtown-Winchester, for example, developed housing rehabilitation, economic development, and job training projects that linked neighborhood residents to jobs created by neighborhood renewal activities and creating cooperation between service providers. DSNI was able to close several illegal trash stations, restore a rail stop to downtown Boston, cleaned up vacant lots, and they created a Community Development Corporation to provide affordable housing and economic development and a youth training and employment initiative.[5] In Portland, TADP funding awards helped implement neighborhood action plans on economic development, job creation, youth and after school services, and open space. In Tucson the overall sustainable plan included programs to develop the city's core rather than the periphery, a series of neighborhood and regional parks, community gardens, bike and walking paths, protection of the Sonoran Desert ecosystem, reduced pollution, an improved public transportation system, improved roadways, and others.

Leadership

Citizen community planning councils increase leadership. "When we get educated by city government, we learn how to get things done," asserts a Wilmington, Delaware, citizen planner. "The program brought out a whole new leadership in neighborhoods," resulting in increased community awareness and competence,

and improved relations between citizens and government.[6] One member who served as chairperson of a neighborhood planning organization asserted, "I helped meetings get more information. I was asked to help plan the community development budget. Some of my ideas were incorporated into the plan."[7] Supplemented by more formal leadership training offered by the neighborhood planning program, a number of these chairpersons have gone on to hold elected or appointed offices in the city.

Official Status

Neighborhood planning groups are acquiring official status. In St. Paul, Raleigh, Wilmington, and Cincinnati, neighborhood planning councils have been authorized by resolution of the city council. In other cites they are brought into being by executive order of the mayor; and in others they are sanctioned by city charter amendments giving community planning organizations a firm legal basis.

Political Power

Community planning organizations are gaining political power. In an unprecedented agreement with the city of Boston, for example, DSNI was given the right of eminent domain over 30 acres of publicly and privately owned land in their neighborhood. They exert their political power by speaking for their neighborhoods at council meetings, through personal contacts with the mayor or members of the council, by seeking out politicians to discuss local issues, and by using the media. This face-to-face democratic community planning is the reality of the daily experience of neighborhood associations, and it provides the essential ingredients of openness that Benjamin Barber calls "strong democratic talk," the basis for productive citizen empowerment.[8]

WHAT YOU WILL LEARN IN THIS CHAPTER

Macro social workers are vitally concerned about preserving and protecting the public good when that good is trampled by private self-interest ruthlessly pursued. It is out of this concern that macro social workers become engaged in community social planning. In this chapter, you will learn why people plan and what social work planning includes. You will explore a brief history of planning the welfare state, housing and urban renewal, mental health, planning for older Americans, and community neighborhood planning. You will explore approaches to community social work planning and learn how to do community planning and the specific techniques social work planners use.

WHY PLAN?

When you think about what you want to do in any one day, you are planning. If you have a goal that you are trying to reach or something that you want to accomplish, you begin to plan for it. Things happen when you plan. All modern social systems exist by planning. Large and small business organizations expend a great deal of energy developing marketing plans, engaging in strategic planning, and planning new products. City planning departments develop land use plans and plans for municipal services. Regional and state governments develop comprehensive health plans, water resource plans, environmental plans, and mass transportation plans. The federal government plans for national defense and space exploration.

Planning also occurs at the international level. The Marshall Plan was a means by which those nations that experienced massive destruction during WW II rebuilt themselves. Today the European Union develops cooperative economic plans, providing fiscal arrangements for its member countries. The members of the world's eight wealthiest nations hold a yearly summit to ratify plans for international economic stability. Planning even occurs at the global level. Through the World Health Organization (WHO), the United Nations develops plans to eradicate disease. The UN makes plans to ease the condition of refugees and works to eliminate slavery around the globe.

WHAT IS SOCIAL WORK PLANNING?

Macro social workers engage in the process of social planning to ensure that services are provided on behalf of those who are in most need. Social planning is a "process of selecting and designing a rational course of collective action to achieve a future state

of affairs"[9] for the social good, including "development, expansion, and coordination of social services and social policies" at both local and societal levels.[10]

Social work planners insist that communities of people who have fewer resources, less power, and little influence be given opportunity to develop plans for their welfare that compete on an equal footing for recognition, funding, and entitlement with plans developed by powerful businesses and government bureaucracies. Until relatively recently, however, many communities have been ignored in planning for their own welfare. Community members were given only token membership in the planning process. As a result, neighborhoods have sometimes been decimated so that governments could build highways, corporate office buildings, or housing projects in the name of "redevelopment." Funding has generally flowed into middle- and upper-middle-class suburbs, ignoring neighborhoods most in need of support.

The planning process is one of the key means by which citizens gain access to power to meet community needs. Macro social workers engage in three kinds of planning. We help regional and statewide social welfare agencies develop plans for their constituents, assist community social agencies in developing organizational plans, and work with local citizen planners to develop plans for their own neighborhoods.

Social Welfare Planning

A social work planner may be employed by an organization that is exclusively dedicated to social welfare planning for a specific population on a regional basis. A social welfare planner, for example, may assess needs, review and make recommendations for awarding government grants, assist in developing new services, and in some cases maintain quality control over services in their mandated arena. Social welfare planners interact with a variety of service providers, agencies, and parent organizations, as well as ancillary service systems such as universities, government agencies, businesses, and community groups, to develop comprehensive plans for their service area.

Area Developmental Disabilities Boards in California, for example, gather information and develop comprehensive welfare plans that become the basis for the provision of new services and for awarding governmental grants. They oversee the provision of services and make funding recommendations on behalf of persons with epilepsy, cerebral palsy, autism, and intellectual disabilities. Area Agencies on Aging assess needs, make recommendations, formulate plans, and oversee grants for services to maintain and enhance the welfare of persons who are elderly. Social work planners in these agencies most often have a planning background or degree in planning, policy, or public administration in addition to an MSW degree.

Social Agency Planning

Some social work planners are staff specialists working in large public and quasi-public direct service case management, casework, and clinical service agencies such as county Departments of Social Services, Human Services, Departments of Mental Health, and Housing and Human Development, among others. These social work planners work closely with the chief social work executive and use research skills to analyze needs, assess services, write grant proposals, and make recommendations to help the agency meet the needs of its clientele, adjust agency resources, and adapt services to a changing population.

Planners working in direct service agencies often begin their careers as line social workers and develop an interest in social planning as they become involved in wider issues. They may have a variety of titles, such as planning consultant, staff analyst, planning analyst, mental health or developmental disabilities specialist, or resource developer. Some analyst or planner positions require a bachelor's degree. Others require an MSW degree and some experience, particularly in the field in which the agency specializes.

Neighborhood Planning

Macro social workers engaged in generalist-based neighborhood planning work with individuals, groups, community programs, and government organizations.

Neighborhood Planning With Individuals

Macro social workers develop relationships with members of the community; helping them gain involvement and empowerment and a means to make a difference in their neighborhoods. We work closely with particular individuals to develop skills in the planning process, develop their fund of knowledge and information, increase their communication effectiveness with one another, and present themselves responsibly to the public. We help them understand the political process.

Neighborhood Planning With Groups

Social work planners work with community groups to help members strengthen leadership, obtain information, and develop new plans or strengthen existing ones.

Strengthen Leadership Macro social workers use their skills in task group leadership to assist neighborhood residents in organizing themselves into effective community planning councils, identifying potential local leaders, helping them practice group leadership, and learning how to lead the group through its stages of development. Social worker planners help planning group members learn group discussion and decision-making techniques. We assist community members in organizing neighborhood leadership training workshops.

Obtain Information One of the key tasks in neighborhood planning is to engage in community action research to discover the needs or assets in a community and use that information to help improve their neighborhoods. We help members scan the social environment of the community for gaps in service provision where services are poorly, inequitably, or ineffectively provided. We help citizen planners obtain existing data from agencies, universities, and policy groups and help them use government documents, maps, and statistics as they develop responsible plans for their neighborhoods. We help community members carry out their own primary survey research, including constructing questionnaires, selecting a sample of the population, administering the questionnaire, and analyzing the data.

Develop New Plans Macro social workers use management science techniques to help members decide among alternative planning proposals and to develop ones that are not only the most rational but also are economically, politically, and socially feasible. We assist members in testing out proposals by conducting public forums and helping members write a community plan that can be presented to public officials.

Neighborhood Planning With Community Program Development

If a plan calls for providing a new social service by means of a social organization, macro social workers use their program development skills to train members in the process of incorporating as a nonprofit organization. We help new boards of directors of social organizations write by-laws, rules of procedure, and constitutions. We assist local planning leaders in developing committees and learning how to use them effectively and assist board members in conducting meetings. We help citizens' groups raise funds and obtain grants to address local problems, develop budgets, and learn about record keeping, accounting, and the various laws that govern social organizations. We help neighborhood groups conduct evaluations of their own organizations and the programs they initiate or provide evaluations to help community groups function more effectively. We assist neighborhoods in maintaining their local planning councils so they can continue the planning process.

Neighborhood Planning With Governmental Organizations
Macro social workers engage community members in participating with local government officials to ensure that neighborhood members have input in the overall city planning process. We engage community members in advocacy and community organizing to ensure that the plans, once formulated, are not ignored.

Political Skills With Local Government We train citizens to be influential and involved in civic affairs and press local government for active participation and inclusion in planning. We teach our members about the operation of city government, explain city budgeting procedures, local, state, and federal program requirements, and agency operating procedures. We provide neighborhood planning groups with the contacts to work effectively through governmental administration and city and state bureaucracy. We help community planning councils obtain information about publicly and privately initiated plans that may affect their neighborhoods.

When community planning councils are asked to comment on city-initiated plans and public services, we help citizens develop criteria for evaluation, analyze city plans, write reports to city government, and provide input for comprehensive neighborhood plans. We use our understanding of the political process and policy making as we act as liaisons between city politicians, staff, and neighborhood organizations.

Advocacy to Mediate With Government We use our understanding of the neighborhood and its members to advocate and mediate on the behalf of citizens. We provide communication linkages to government officials and from government to the neighborhood. On one hand, macro social workers use contacts with neighborhoods to keep local government in touch with neighborhood needs. We help city planning commissions, city councils, mayors' offices, and other public officials understand the concerns and desires of neighborhood groups. We help neighborhood residents explain the position of a neighborhood to the mayor or city manager, present proposals to the city council, or provide input on neighborhood conditions to other public officials.

On the other hand, social work planners act as liaisons to local neighborhoods, communicating and informing members about the politics of city government, developing working relationships between community members and government officials, and assisting local neighborhoods in funding and implementing local initiatives. If there are misunderstandings or conflicts, we often bring conflicting parties together to discuss the issues and promote compromise and reconciliation.[11]

Community Organizing to Press for Change If the efforts of our community members in presenting rational plans to local government and businesses fall on deaf ears, we may use our organizing skills to mobilize local leaders to develop activist community organizations. We shift our role from planning to helping community members learn how to become activists in making community change.

The Real World of Planning
Community planning is never neatly organized and rarely "rational," and community social workers use a variety of skills at the micro, mezzo, and macro level to assist the planning process in the neighborhood where it really counts. Macro social workers play one of the potentially most important roles in the field of social work today.

A BRIEF HISTORY OF SOCIAL PLANNING IN AMERICA

Planning in the United States first occurred as the nation was founded. Social work planning originated during the Progressive Era. The history of social welfare planning in America continued as social workers engaged in planning the welfare state, housing and urban renewal, mental health, planning for older Americans, and community neighborhood planning.

Founding the Nation

American society is a combination of planning and freedom from planning. The founding fathers were the first people in history to plan a new nation from scratch. They were acutely aware that although plans provide a direction, once they are made and become binding these plans tend to prescribe a path that eliminates other options. The Constitution was a way of ensuring that choice would not be limited to only a few people who could impose their own plans or ideas on the populace. It was a social plan that prevented the few who hold power from planning for everyone else. We call this the "balance of power."

In the minds of the founders of our nation, people should be particularly free from oppression in these three areas. First, people should be free from political oppression. Instead of politicians holding a monopoly on power, White, male citizens would elect a few of their own to represent their interests. Second, people should have unfettered freedom to pursue wealth. Government would limit its role to setting the rules by which individuals and groups could accumulate wealth and ensure that they would not interfere with one another. Third, religion was to be forever separated from the state, preventing government from imposing a belief system on the populace and ensuring that small groups would not impose their belief system on the public at large. Liberty was conceived in political, economic, and religious terms.

Progressives and Social Work Planning

As America grew, however, defects in the principles of political and economic freedom began to appear. After the Civil War, the unfettered freedom of the economy combined with the complex modern system of interlocking corporations created huge centers of unregulated political and economic power. Gigantic monopolies and corporate trusts began manipulating the political process to their own advantage using bribery, rigging elections, buying votes, selecting candidates of their own choosing, and pouring money into political campaigns.

Social problems often remained unaddressed and social issues unattended. As a result, during the Progressive Era (1885–1915) the first social workers advocated that government develop social plans to organize and place the provision of public services on a more rational and secure basis. Social work planning in America developed along two planes. Settlement House workers advocated a welfare state that eventually included housing, mental health, and the elderly. Charity Organization Society social workers planned at the community level.

Planning the Welfare State

Settlement House workers worked to broaden the role of both state and federal governments at the end of the 19th century. Social workers were active in Roosevelt's New Deal of the 1930s, and welfare planning continued during Lyndon Johnson's Great Society.

Settlement House Workers and the Welfare State

Settlement House workers in the late 19th century envisioned an enlarged role for the federal government, advocating that the government use its power to support the welfare of society. They developed plans and policies to assist some of our most vulnerable citizens: those who lived in poverty, women, children, and immigrant laborers. Working with other professionals and citizens, settlement social workers developed plans and programs that would increase government's social involvement, including labor laws, better wages, shorter hours, and better working conditions for men, women, and children. They encouraged regulation of sweatshops and pressed for federal and state consumer protection laws and for safe food and drugs. Settlement workers successfully developed proposals for a new juvenile criminal justice system, advocating and obtaining a separate court system for juvenile offenders, with laws to protect children from overly punitive sentencing and prison conditions, and achieved provision for a Children's Bureau at the federal level of government.

1930s and the New Deal

With the New Deal of President Franklin Delano Roosevelt, "the federal government assumed a greater role in social planning"[12] and in the provision of relief and in the development of social programs. Social planning became one of the weapons in the federal government's arsenal of social programs, such as the Social Security system, which "required a projection of the number of and size of beneficiary claims and revenues"[13] and any number of federal social programs involving cooperative and coordinated effort. Since the Depression, social planning had assumed an even larger and clearer role in government social service, with the social planner becoming a more central, if technically oriented, professional.[14]

1960s Planning the Great Society   Building on the impetus of citizen participation and community-based social care established by the community mental health movement, "President John F. Kennedy's Council of Economic Advisers began working on antipoverty proposals using recommendations by the President's Committee on Juvenile Delinquency, the Ford Foundation and various cabinet-level departments."[15] Carrying forward the proposals of these groups after President Kennedy's assassination, President Lyndon Johnson undertook one of the most ambitious campaigns of social planning since the New Deal of Franklin Roosevelt. The Partnership for Health Act and the Regional Plan Act of 1966, for example, provided incentive and structures for coordination of medical services and health planning with citizen input. The Comprehensive Employment and Training Act, National Health Planning and Resources Development Act, and the Economic Opportunity Act (EOA) "carved out a role for new quasi-public bodies to assume a planning, coordinating role on a municipal or regional basis."[16]

GRAHAM ROMEYN TAYLOR (1880–1942) AND THE SURVEY

Born in Hopewell Junction, New York, on March 17, 1880, Graham R. Taylor was familiar with social planning through the work of his father, who founded Chicago Commons, one of the earliest and best-known social settlements in the country. With an AB degree from Harvard in 1903, Taylor became a reporter in Boston and then an Associated Press correspondent in Albany. In 1904 he joined the editorial staff of *The Commons,* a periodical established by his father in 1896. *The Commons* merged in 1905 with *Charities,* published in New York City. The combined publication took the name of *The Survey* in 1909 and became one of the most important and well-known journals in social work and social welfare. Taylor was responsible for many of its articles on social issues and social and industrial problems.

A series of articles on planned industrial communities such as Pullman, Illinois, and Gary, Indiana, was published in book form under the title *Satellite Cities: A Study of Industrial Suburbs* (1915). In Chicago and other cities, Taylor was active in movements to integrate

public social and recreation facilities and improve living conditions through citywide planning.

In 1916 Graham Taylor traveled to Russia as a special assistant to the U.S. ambassador to investigate the condition of German and Austrian civilian prisoners, and he was later detailed to the American Consulate General in Moscow when the Russian Revolution broke out in November 1917. He remained in Russia as head of the Leningrad office of President Wilson's committee on public information until May 1918. In April 1919 he traveled through China and India.

Upon returning to the United States, Taylor turned his attention to Chicago race relations, and in 1920–1921 he conducted a survey to determine the causes of the Chicago race riots of July 1919. The report, *The Negro and Chicago* (1922), was called one of the important documents in the history of race relation in the United States.

In this period, Taylor became the executive secretary of the American Association of Social Workers. He again went to Russia as a member of the National Information Bureau to investigate famine and recommend relief measures. He then joined the Commonwealth Fund as director of its joint committee on methods of preventing juvenile delinquency.

Taylor directed the Commonwealth Fund's division of publications until his death in 1942. In addition, he was director of the Common Council for American Unity and the National Urban League and a member of the Council on Foreign Relations of the National Conference of Social Work.[17]

Housing and Urban Planning

The history of planning for housing began in the 1930s. Citizen participation in this planning process waxed and waned but continued into the 1940s and 1950s, saw increased growth in the 1960s, and progressed with Housing and Urban Development programs into the 1990s.

Beginnings in the 1930s   During the 1930s, under the Works Progress Administration, a national effort was undertaken to attack the problem of growing inner-city slums and a lack of decent housing for people with low incomes. The Housing Act of 1937, for example, had triple objectives of slum clearance, job creation, and development of low-rent housing. Spurred by these federal initiatives, community civic organizations in many cities including Philadelphia, Cleveland, and Chicago attempted to develop plans for local neighborhood districts. Although citizens' groups were given a great deal of control, the result was generally the same: Planning commissions overrode or ignored citizen recommendations and demolished neighborhoods on behalf of large public and private organizations. Instead of housing construction in Chicago, for example, two large institutions, Michael Reese Hospital and the Illinois Institute of Technology, were able to acquire sizable acreage through wholesale clearance and redevelopment. Chicago adopted redevelopment plans that cleared another area to provide for a large campus for the University of Illinois, Chicago Circle.[18]

Redevelopment in the 1940s and 1950s

Congress gave redevelopment a major boost by authorizing federal support through the Housing Act of 1949, which encouraged community planning by means of a "community master plan," a planning concept that achieved broad public support.[19] Planning was becoming a central tool of government in assessing need and developing social programs, too important an endeavor to be left to professionals alone.[20]

After reviewing the neighborhood clearance approach, the Eisenhower administration offered recommendations for greater emphasis on housing rehabilitation. As a result the Housing Act was amended in 1954, calling for a "Seven Point Workable" program that specified seven requirements before funding for redevelopment would be approved, including planning, code enforcement, relocation of displaced residents, financing, and most important, citizen participation in the planning process.[21]

Citizen participation, however, was generally limited to the appointment of a citywide advisory committee composed of civic leaders to work with planners. Representation of the community residents who were usually most affected by renewal activities was neither mandatory nor commonplace,[22] and in practice, strong citizen participation was the exception rather than the rule. In 1959, for example, Gerda Lewis surveyed the first 91 cities with approved workable programs and found that the community advisory committees were composed most often of real estate, construction, downtown business, and civic organizations. Minority groups had limited representation, and project areas almost none. In only a few places were there separate project area committees. Even then, the citywide advisory committees were confined to the review of plans and policy recommendations.[23]

Some localities did more, however. In a special demonstration project, the Housing Association of Metropolitan Boston placed organizers in various neighborhoods to boost resident involvement in urban renewal planning. In Philadelphia's Eastwick project, the Redevelopment Authority contracted with the Citizens Council on City Planning to provide an organizer. In Detroit, staff from the City Planning Commission assisted citizens in the Concord-Mack area, but eventually the strain of working for both the neighborhoods and city hall became too great and the city withdrew its organizer. Likewise, in Baltimore an attempt to build a strong community-organizing component into a consolidated housing and urban renewal agency foundered on the issue of divided allegiance.

Planning for Housing in the 1960s

Among the many pieces of legislation in the Johnson years, the Fair Housing Act of 1968 banned racial discrimination in the sale, rental, or financing of housing. In spite of this legislation, however, "widespread housing discrimination remained, though largely covert, a symptom of the persistent racism that continued to pervade American society."[24]

The Housing and Urban Development (HUD) Act of 1968 was "the culmination of the federal government's attempts to provide housing and assistance programs for poor and moderate-income families."[25] The act, which Johnson called the "Magna Carta to liberate our cities," affected more than 700 planning grants and funds for water and sewer projects, flood insurance, model cities, and mass transit. In that same year, as residents demanded and in many localities achieved greater participation in urban renewal planning, HUD issued regulations that mandated project area committees in all renewal projects involving housing rehabilitation and permitted federal funds to be spent for that purpose. Many cities provided staff services to these committees, and some were allowed to hire their own staff.[26]

Planning Participation in the 1970s and 1980s

The Housing and Community Development Act of 1974 continued to encourage social planning at the local level by requiring citizen participation and led to greater efforts to include grassroots citizens in social planning in other social arenas as well. Requirements for citizen participation spread to other federal aid programs: education, social services, health, employment and training, economic development, transportation, water resources management, and many more. In 1978 the Advisory Commission on Intergovernmental Relations (ACIR) tallied 155 federal grant programs with statutes or regulations mandating citizen participation, more than one fourth of all grant programs, and even more significantly those requiring citizen participation accounted for more than 80% of federal grant expenditures.

ACIR reported that more than half of the programs required boards or committees to reflect the public in various ways in their membership. Compared to the degree of neighborhood involvement in public programs in the 1950s, federally mandated citizen participation marked a noteworthy advance. Although the requirements fell considerably short of the aspirations of planning activists, federal regulations and money significantly aided increased neighborhood participation.[27]

HUD Programs in the 1990s

In 1993 federal government "empowerment zones" administered by the Housing and Urban Development Department (HUD) focused attention on distressed urban and rural communities by developing comprehensive strategic plans to link the economic, physical, and human development needs of these communities. Hundreds of communities competed for federal funds. In its first year, 1994, only nine communities were selected for the empowerment zone program, but the process engaged in by ordinary citizens resulted in these plans being produced from the bottom up. In addition, HUD's HOME program was a flexible block grant requiring that localities spend a minimum amount of funding on local community development corporations engaged in housing construction, called Community Housing Development Organizations (CHDOs).[28]

Planning for Mental Health

Planning for mental health services began in the 1950s, culminated in the 1960s, declined in the 1970s, and dissipated in the 1980s.

1950s and 1960s: Community Mental Health Centers

In the 1950s and early 1960s, social work planners and community activists engaged in social reform efforts to improve the nation's mental health system. State social welfare planners "tirelessly worked as advocates to provide information about the need for mental health services and the rights of mental patients," Madelene Stoner states. "They were effective campaigners and social activists who viewed their roles as most effective when stimulating the public welfare sector to provide more and better services."[29]

Supported by President John F. Kennedy, these efforts paid off with the passage in 1963 of the Comprehensive Community Health Act, which encouraged planning and development of local community mental health centers, mental health planning boards, and community consultation.[30] More important for community-based social work and planning, the Community Mental Health Centers Act of 1963 "made it possible to employ community organizers in service delivery settings,"[31] Stoner states, providing the first major impetus for agency-based community social work practice in mental health. The door was opened to transform hospital-based psychiatric casework into psychotherapeutic social work, paving the way for government reimbursement for treatment, state licensure of clinical social workers, and private social work practice. The Community Mental Health Centers Act expanded the delivery of psychotherapy at the local level. Implicit in the philosophy of community-based mental health care was the role of advisory councils drawn from the providers and consumers of the services.

"Together with the state agency, advisory councils had the responsibility for inventorying state facilities for the mentally ill and developing state-wide plans for the creation of mental health centers,"[32] asserts Stoner. As a result, social work community organizers and planners were able to work inside the mental health service delivery system "using a non-medical model that sought to prevent mental illness through non-clinical services that reflected social goals rather than psychiatric ones."[33] According to Stoner, social workers relied on "community groups to define issues and problems and to participate in developing services. This principle of citizen participation became the rationale and basis for much community social work practice."[34]

In addition, social work planners and organizers helped mental health clients actively engage in planning and organizing services, "buttressed the individual's sense of personal control," and empowered clients by emphasizing "local and democratic control of social institutions."[35]

Decline in the 1970s and 1980s

Just as the number of community mental health centers began to peak, however, newly elected President Richard M. Nixon began dismantling social service and mental health programs. By the early 1970s, the government's interest in citizen planner participation began to diminish, and in "1973 the 'drift' became a tide race."[36] Citizen participation in the mental health movement went into remission and was relegated "toward minimal or token change,"[37] Stoner states. Never completely comfortable with citizen participation in mental health planning, powerful psychiatric and managerial professionals used community mental health legislation to consolidate and expand their interests rather than those of the citizenry at large. Mental health services became a closed system.

In 1980, at the end of President Carter's administration, the Mental Health Systems Act was passed, which would have provided for more community-based services and community involvement in coordination and development. The act was repealed, however, under the Reagan administration. The initiative for planning was taken away from local communities, and block grants were given to states for mental health, alcohol abuse, and drug abuse programs. In spite of financial reductions, however, community mental health centers continued to provide services, a testimony to advocacy-based social work planning in the field of mental health.[38]

Planning for Older Americans

Older American Act of 1965   The Older Americans Act (OAA) of 1965 and its implementation ensured that services to the elderly "became the province of the expert planner," Monk states.[39] State agencies on aging were to design programs, coordinate services, and assess needs. At the local level, the nearly 700 Area Agencies on Aging (AAAs) were required to produce 3-year plans, award grants for services, contract with local providers, and monitor the implementation and quality of services. According to Monk, the AAAs were "responsible for mounting a continuous process of planning, including definition of service priorities, and development of a comprehensive system specially designed to improve delivery of services."[40]

Although these administrative responsibilities did not openly encourage planning advocacy, "advisory boards had enough latitude to become interest group representatives," asserts Monk. "Assisted by planners with a bent toward policy analysis, they took stands on proposed legislation, lobbied on behalf of their constituents, and maintained a constant watch on trends in program funding."[41] These efforts paid off in tangible benefits to the elderly so that by 1971 OAA funding was about $30 million, and by 1980 it exceeded $500 million.

Amendments in the 1970s   With the 1973 amendments to the Older Americans Act, citizen participation in planning gained ground when the government spearheaded broad citizen participation, but 5 years later the 1978 amendment signaled the end of an expansionist era in social planning for the elderly and the beginning of a more cautious managerial mandate. Rather than focusing on advocacy and citizen involvement, says Monk, "social work planners in state agencies and local AAAs became more involved in scrutinizing program compliance, writing contracts in the language of management by objectives, measuring units of service, adjudicating purchase of service agreements, negotiating budgets, establishing quality central and quality assurance procedures and evaluating program efficiency."[42]

Community Planning

Community planning has its origins with the Charity Organization Society and continued with Councils of Social Agencies and cooperative fundraising. From the 1960s to the present, community planning has continued to expand.

Charity Organization Society   The Charity Organization Society (COS) movement pioneered in using planning as a way of developing improved services at the local level. Originating in 1877 "in response to rapid urbanization and industrialization and the effects of the Great Depression of 1873,"[43] the COS movement developed a "science of charity" based on "rationality, efficiency, foresight, and planning."[44]

Committed to the principle that "poverty could be cured and prevented if its causes could be discovered and removed,"[45] the COS attempted "to achieve rationality in social welfare by managing the entire voluntary system based on the most respected social science principles of the time."[46] The COS movement affirmed that a collective and cooperative approach to the problems of poverty could be made, avoiding duplication and ensuring collaboration, resource coordination, and efficiency. The early Charity Organizations Societies emphasis on planning and organizing services at the local level is "generally credited with being the beginning of modern social work."[47] From its inception, social work and social planning were seen as largely synonymous, having common roots and common methods.[48]

Councils of Social Agencies (1911–1928)

Francis McLean, superintendent of the Brooklyn Bureau of Charities and full-time organizer for the Russell Sage Foundation, served as the executive of the National Association of 62 charity organization societies in 1911. McLean saw the need for a new coordinating device, a citywide "Council of Social Agencies" that brought community agencies together for regular meetings for a collective review and planning of community needs and services as well as coordinating funding of social agencies and the operation of voluntary service agencies. Social services would be organized in an effective and efficient way, producing greater centralization of operations and more emphasis on professionalism.[49]

Soon, these councils sprang up in many cities throughout the country, continuing the momentum toward coordination and planning initiated by the COS movement and emphasizing "efficiency, centralization, and specialization in the planning and delivery of services by private agencies within the community."[50] So important were these councils that the influential 1939 Lane Report cited the Council of Social Agencies as the only urban community organization on the scene that organized resources to meet community needs.

Community Chests and United Way

By World War I, cooperative solicitation agencies called Community War Chests were developed to "centralize planning and administration and achieve greater efficiency in utilization of community resources."[51] These agencies emphasized rational planning for the use of funds, efficiency, and a willingness to respond to community priorities.[52] The Community Chest movement spread throughout the country as a recognized way in which individuals at the local level could contribute to the social welfare of their communities, with the confidence that the Community Chest would support and distribute the funds in an equitable, fair, and compassionate manner. Later the Community Chest developed into the nationwide United Way, which exists in virtually every community in the nation today. The Community Chest and council

movements were "early attempts to assess community needs and for rational decision-making in projecting the development and location of community agencies"[53] by citizen volunteers and professional social work planners.

Community Planning From the 1920s to the 1950s

Community planning tended to be quiescent during this period, with Community Chests and Councils of Social Agencies the major efforts of community planning for social welfare. The Great Depression of the 1930s depleted many communities of resources, limiting expansion, and WW II in the first half of the 1940s focused local and national concerns nearly exclusively on the war effort, and in the latter half of the 1940s on postwar recovery.

Community Planning in the 1950s and 1960s

Two events gave community welfare planning a boost in the 1950s and 1960s: Community Planning Boards and the community planning initiatives of Johnson's War on Poverty.

Community Planning Boards

By the late 1950s the idea of planning and political involvement at the neighborhood level began to come of age. The president of Manhattan Borough in New York City appointed advisory community planning boards, and a 1961 charter amendment applied this concept citywide. Subsequent amendments added to the role of community boards, although they have remained appointed bodies.

In 1967 the Advisory Commission on Intergovernmental Relations drew up model state legislation authorizing cities and counties to set up neighborhood subunits with advisory powers. During the next several years, bills based on this model were introduced in the legislatures of Oklahoma and Minnesota but were not adopted. Among the specific recommendations were neighborhood action task forces, neighborhood city halls, and multiservice centers.[54]

In 1968 the National Commission on Urban Problems appointed by President Johnson recommended decentralization of municipal services to the neighborhood level, and efforts were initiated to establish channels of communication. New city charters authorized neighborhood planning councils in Honolulu, Pittsburgh, the District of Columbia, New York, and Newton, Massachusetts. Similar recommendations were proposed in Los Angeles, Boston, Chicago, Detroit, and Rochester but were defeated over other issues. City councils in Birmingham, St. Paul, Wichita, Anchorage, Eugene, Salem, and Portland, Oregon, did pass ordinances creating neighborhood planning councils or officially recognized existing neighborhood associations.

Johnson's War on Poverty
Lyndon Johnson's "Great Society" programs, initiated in the 1960s as part of his "War on Poverty," particularly Community Action Agencies (CAAs) and the Model Cities programs, encouraged planning and community action at the local level.

Community action agencies: CAAs were created to improve public services, mobilize resources, and ensure the contribution of the poor in planning programs that affected them and their neighborhoods. An important requirement of CAAs in improving inner cities, Pine asserts, was "maximum feasible participation by the poor in planning, development and execution of the programs that the CAAs coordinated or sponsored."[55] While this requirement became highly controversial, the CAAs represented individuals with low incomes in dealing with bureaucracies, trained individuals for leadership, and "helped institutionalize citizen input concerning federal programs and agencies for all members of society, not just the poor."[56]

For "civil rights organizations in poor black communities, CAAs presented an opening to get some real power to force changes in the community . . . the poor were to play a major role in both planning and directing the service they selected."[57] Congress later amended the law to require that at least one third of the board of directors of a local Community Action Agency be representatives of the poor chosen by residents of the target area themselves. The redistribution of power in poverty programs meant not "simply 'helping' the poor, but empowering impoverished people to help themselves and to challenge anyone who got in their way. In the end, however, the mayors, agencies, businessmen, and unions continued to hold the reins of power . . . and maximum feasible participation in any real sense was unable to survive."[58]

Model cities: The Demonstration Cities and Metropolitan Development Act of 1966 (the Model Cities program), was intended to bring "resident groups, business interests, and social welfare agencies together in a planning network for developing the physical and social aspects of the community"[59] as well as increase

the supply of housing, enhance the social environment, and improve delivery systems. Cities that qualified for an initial planning project were provided with funds to change the social environment of the target area using benefit-cost analysis as well as the active engagement of residents in planning and executing the programs.[60]

BRADLEY BUELL

Community organizer and planner Bradley Buell (1893–1976) was born in Chicago and educated at Oberlin College and the New York School of Philanthropy, now the Columbia University School of Social Work. He assisted in the development of the American Association of Social Workers, in which he served as secretary and as associate executive.

Buell was the director of the New Orleans Community Chest and Council, field director of Community Chests and Councils, and founder and executive director of Community Research Associates. He wrote about community planning and consulted and conducted research projects in 156 communities. In 1952 he published *Community Planning for Human Services,* analyzing the work of more than 100 agencies in St. Paul, Minnesota, finding that families with multiple problems used almost 50% of all services. In 1953 he published *Let's Work Together in Community Service,* co-authored with Eloise Walton, and in 1973, *Solving Community Problems.*

Community Planning in the 1970s
During the first half of the 1970s, a number of cities set up neighborhood planning councils, defined as broad-based organizations of residents, usually elected, with official recognition by city government and assigned advisory roles on matters affecting their neighborhoods. New York City created 62 local planning councils to screen proposals for development in their respective neighborhoods or districts. Cincinnati formally recognized self-generated neighborhood organizations, and after consulting with them, drew up official boundaries for its 44 neighborhoods.

Washington, Baltimore, and other cities provided money and technical assistance to neighborhood organizations. In other locales, less formal systems developed to give quasi-official recognition to neighborhood associations. Among the most comprehensive was the plan in Dayton, Ohio, where 149 residents were elected to Dayton's five neighborhood priority boards in 1971.

They joined the 21 elected members of the Model Cities Planning Council in being responsible for the allocation of $5.2 million in federal funds under the Model Cities program. In that same year the California legislature adopted an act authorizing counties to establish municipal advisory councils in unincorporated areas, and by 1977 there were 27 of them in eight counties.[61]

By the late 1970s neighbors were becoming active participants in planning in their own communities in nearly every large city in the United States and increasingly in middle and smaller ones as well. Neighborhood planning represented a new wave of federated partnerships in which federal, state, and local governments cooperated with local planning groups at the grassroots level by providing funding and support. Many of these partnerships were based on the practical reality that this is the best way to conduct governance. More than 80% of the community planning organizations received federal money, covering most, if not all, of the administrative costs of operating neighborhood planning councils, supplemented by local planning commissions, community development agencies, and city managers' or mayors' offices that provide funding directly to neighborhood planning councils.

Community Planning in the 1980s and 1990s

During the 1980s, in spite of the retrenchment in social legislation of the Reagan and Bush administrations, community planning sponsored by local city governments continued. The city of Houston, for example, provided technical assistance through workshops, a newsletter, and consultation. In Atlanta, Raleigh, and Wilmington, local government provided staff assistance to help citizens develop local plans and analyze development proposals. Cincinnati and St. Paul provided funds directly to local groups to hire their own staff and fund projects, as well as for operating expenses and capital improvements in the neighborhood.

In the mid-1980s, the administration of Boston's Mayor Ray Flynn expanded the role of neighborhood planning, creating citizen participation organizations, including the neighborhood councils. Boston's Chinatown/South Cove Neighborhood Council's plan was adopted as the official land use plan for the area. Other advisory bodies, called Station Area Task Forces, were created in conjunction with the relocation of the Massachusetts Bay Transportation Authority's Orange Line and the disposition of the land that had been cleared for a failed highway project. Although these bodies had only advisory power, they created institutions that enhanced the ability of residents to organize and advocate their interests.

DUDLEY STREET NEIGHBORHOOD INITIATIVE

In the 1980s the Dudley Street Neighborhood Initiative (DSNI) extended the involvement of communities. The Dudley Street community developed a plan for revitalizing the community and then invited the city to participate. The DSNI was an ambitious and comprehensive approach to community planning and revitalization, an attempt to revitalize the "Dudley Triangle" neighborhood through a number of interrelated strategies and activities. Through the use of public and private resources, it has created a land trust upon which it has undertaken the construction of housing and a community center. Construction began in 1993, and currently 77 families reside in the first-phase housing. Construction is under way on another 90 units.

While the construction of housing has been a vital centerpiece, the overall plan is multifaceted and also involves a wide variety of undertakings, including the construction of a town common, a community center, and a number of social activities including neighborhood cleanups, youth activities, multicultural festivals, homeowner classes, and more. Key to much of the DSNI's success is the "bottom-up" approach that reflects the belief that community residents must be central participants in both the planning and implementation processes.[62]

Comprehensive Community Planning in the 2000s

In the decade of 2000, several major foundations, in addition to city governments, launched pilot projects in an effort to test the effectiveness of a comprehensive approach to community initiatives that included community planning, community development, advocacy, and service provision. The Ford Foundation's Neighborhood and Family Initiative (NFI), the Annie Casey Foundation's New Futures Program, the Rockefeller Foundation's Community Planning and Action Programs, and recent projects of the Pew Charitable Trust all target urban neighborhoods with comprehensive planning projects that utilize corporate and community partnerships to address neighborhood needs.

The Ford Foundation, for example, identified two principles that have guided the Neighborhood and Family Initiative: "The first is a notion of neighborhood-focused, comprehensive development. It involves the formation and implementation of strategies that harness the interrelationships among social, physical and economic development. The second principle is that it is necessary to have the active participation, in both planning and implementation, of residents and stakeholders in the neighborhood targeted for development."[63]

The Future of Social Welfare Planning

The great federal planning initiatives of the Progressive Era, the New Deal, and the Great Society provided encouragement and an infusion of hope for people at the local level. But these programs, sometimes conceived in haste to create stability out of crisis and turbulence, were vulnerable to the agenda of conservative political parties and giant corporations. Conservatives lost little time dismantling these social programs when they came to power, and planning for persons with emotional disabilities, the aging, those with housing needs, and those who have low incomes is on the decline.

On the other hand, planning at the community level by engaging citizen planners as part of an ongoing, conscientious process is increasing. Even conservative federal administrations recognize their value and are funneling dollars into local nonprofit faith-based organizations, community development corporations, and others. City governments are taking advantage of citizen participation in planning to enhance government and services.

FOUNDATIONS OF COMMUNITY PLANNING

Community planning is an important adjunct to individual self-determination, inclusion, and constructing the social environment. To allow planning professionals, government officials, politicians, and corporate managers to devise and put their plans into action without our involvement means that we are disenfranchised from creating our own dreams, making our own decisions, putting our ideas into action, and developing our own culture. Others have appropriated the most important processes at the center of our humanity.

Planning is integral with community life. If it is removed from people, the community begins to die. A plan not devised by the people is morally destructive to the people upon whom the plan is imposed. Community social work planners insist that community members are not only capable of planning for their own future betterment, but that community social welfare cannot be achieved without their personal engagement and involvement. Where people are deprived of the opportunity to plan for themselves, social work planners assist people in reclaiming their rights to self-determination. When community members are provided with only token involvement, we help press for total inclusion. Community planning is empowerment oriented, future directed, democratically aimed, advocacy based, and practically engaged.

Empowerment Oriented

Macro social workers assist members to become empowered and plan for their own futures in their own neighborhoods. We work at the individual level helping people gain skills and learning how to plan. As facilitators we help members gain access to the government and corporate power structure, provide technical assistance to members in research and in management science techniques, and train community members in the planning process. Community social work planners not only work to achieve goals but help our members make quality decisions. We use all of our social thinking functions and help community members develop and use theirs as well. While we want our plans to succeed, we understand that "more development takes place by engaging in planning than as a result of the implementation of plans," and that "it is better to plan for ourselves, no matter how badly, than to be planned for by others no matter how well."[64] This is the iron law of macro community planning.

In Raleigh, North Carolina, for example, neighborhood planning groups discovered that undesirable planning proposals were being submitted to the city by developers, and they took a stand on nine zoning amendments. The groups appeared eight times before the city's Board of Adjustment to voice their opinions. Now "developers have begun to work with the local task forces before submitting proposals to the city."[65] In part this is due to the personal relationships, communication, and trust being developed between neighborhoods and government. "Our credibility came from responsible recommendations and building a rapport with developers and the council," commented one citizen planner.[66]

Future Directed

Social work community planners are not bound to the past as are reactivists or committed to the present as are inactivists; nor do we rush into the future as do proactivists. Social work planners are "interactivists" who assist community members in learning from the past to reshape the present and work to transform the future.[67] We utilize our intuition and help community members "try to idealize"[68] the future for themselves. Together with our members "we become credible inventors of the future, designers and analysts who are also involved in selecting supporters and mobilizing the implementation of plans."[69] We learn to calculate what is possible and at the same time nurture emergent ideas. Moving beyond simple prediction and preparation, we help community members create and control their future, shaping not only its design but its internal culture and values as well.

Democratically Aimed

Representative politics tends to consist of manipulating self-interested power, resolving conflict, and adding up the sum of individual preferences to arrive at a majority. Macro social work planners believe that democracy also can be a choice worthy lifestyle in which people shape a social world that aims toward the achievement of a good society. Social work planners believe that planning must be carried out by means of a deliberative, substantive, and transformative democratic process.

Advocacy Based

Community social work planners tend to be pressured to divert our attention from addressing the needs and issues of the people. We resist subordinating social and human systems to economic, utilitarian purposes. We advocate for the community and resist the temptation to sacrifice members' interests to expediency, procedural issues, or the self-interest of others. We work to "anticipate and counteract pressures that stifle public voice, that manipulate democratic processes of consensus-building, and that ignore the many in need so that a few may prosper."[70] We use our skills to manipulate influence on behalf of those who have been manipulated by the influential.

Macro social work planners are concerned about the effectiveness of social programs, but also about welfare of all people, and the eradication of hurt, want, and need. We implement a vision of the public interest and the public good that equalizes power and service arrangements for those who are powerless, and speak for those who have little voice.

Practically Engaged

Community social welfare planning should make a difference—changing something that would otherwise not have changed. Social work planning can be considered effective to the extent that things are changed in a direction that is better. Macro social workers do the following:

Accept Different Agendas   People will want to be involved for a variety of reasons, for instance: academic enquiry, altruism, curiosity, fear of change, financial gain, neighborliness, professional duty, protection of interests, or socializing. These motives need not be a problem, but it helps to be aware of people's different agendas.

Accept Limitations   No community planning activity will solve all the world's problems. But that is not a reason for holding back. Limited practical improvements will almost always result, and community planning activity can often act as a catalyst for more fundamental change.

Accept Varied Commitments   Far too much energy is wasted complaining that certain people do not participate when the opportunity is provided. Every person has his or her own priorities in life, and these should be respected. If people do not participate, it is likely to be because they are happy to let others get on with it, are busy with things more important to them, or the process has not been made sufficiently interesting.

Agree on Rules and Boundaries   There should be a common understanding by all main interest groups of the approach you and the community planning group adopt. It is vital that everyone understands and agrees to the rules and boundaries, particularly in communities where there is fear that others may be trying to gain territorial advantage.

Avoid Jargon   Social workers use plain language. Jargon prevents people from engaging and is usually a smokescreen to hide incompetence, ignorance, or arrogance.

Are Honest   Community planners are open and straightforward about the nature of any activity. People will generally participate more enthusiastically if they know that something can be achieved through their participation, for example, or if their community may qualify for a foundation or government grant.

HOW TO PRACTICE COMMUNITY PLANNING

Working with a community or neighborhood planning group often follows a series of steps, but arriving at a plan to achieve an ideal future state cannot always be routinized. There are too many unknowns, too many variables for planning to be caught in a rigid process or method. Methods themselves need to be contingent on the particular situation that presents itself to the citizen planners. Macro social workers find, however, that most community groups use similar steps. Let's review these steps.

Build a Network of Relationships

One of the key skills of a community social work planner is the ability to bring people together around a social problem of concern to them and help them seek its resolution. Community social work planners are not mere value-neutral technicians. We plan with people and engage in a number of organizing efforts, including networking, negotiating, coalition creation, and consensus building. We bring people together to discuss difficult social issues for which answers may be unclear, opinions differ, goals may conflict, or interests may clash. Social work planners need to be good listeners and be able to relate to a variety of people, many of whom have a vested interest in the issues and may want more rather than less while contributing less to the process rather than more.

Develop a Planning Board

Developing a neighborhood planning board consists of three steps: recruit members, form them into a recognized planning board, and orient them to the process.

Recruit Members   When you develop a neighborhood planning board, consider committed community residents. Use a series of focus groups to develop interest and recruit members.

Stakeholders   In every community there are numerous individuals, vested interests, groups, organizations, and agencies that may be affected by, have information about, and have a stake in the outcomes of the problem. These are the stakeholders. The most important of these stakeholders are interested and involved community members. The planning board should be composed exclusively of these community members. Other stakeholders may be people in positions of power, such as representatives from government agencies and business corporations that operate in the community. These stakeholders can provide input, give advice, offer information, and develop support, but they should not be members of the community planning group itself who make the decisions about community plans.

Focus Groups   One way to develop a planning board is to conduct a series of focus groups. Focus groups are small groups of about 8 to 15 people who come from a particular geographical area of a community or who represent particular interests, such as local merchants. When you organize focus groups, you are beginning a process of grassroots democratic participation. Advertise the group meeting and try to arrange to hold it in a neighbor's home. Explain to the members that you are going to develop a neighborhood planning board and want to solicit ideas and interest from the neighborhood. Answer questions and engage members in a discussion of their concerns, getting to know them and their skills and strengths. Ideally, one or more participants will be willing to become members of your community planning board.

Hold as many focus groups as you need to generate community interest and involvement in the project. Ask those people who volunteer to join the planning board to report back to their focus group periodically to give information, solicit feedback, and keep the community involved in the process. If a member of your group decides to stop his or her participation, ask the member to try to recruit a replacement from the focus group.

Form the Planning Board   When you have 15 to 20 members, you can form a community planning board. This number is large enough to represent a variety of interests of the community but small enough for face-to-face meetings and for getting work accomplished. It is also large enough to break into several smaller groups that can be assigned smaller projects and report to the larger group. Make sure that the memberships represent all stakeholders and are representative of the ethnic, gender, age, cultural, and religious diversity of your community as well as inclusive of persons with disabilities.

Orient the Members   Spend time orienting members in how to perform in a task group, including using parliamentary procedure, or assist in leading the planning board until it has developed sufficient readiness to elect its own leaders. After that you play the role of staff, helping members and the group as a whole move through the group life cycle described in Chapter 4.

Define the Problem

Community members themselves should define the arena of planning. A citizen's planning council on developmental disabilities, for example, may define a problem as the lack of day programs for severely disabled adults; a neighborhood planning board may be concerned about the lack of social programs for teenagers.

Mobilize Guiding Values

A community planning group should discuss its guiding values early in the process. These values may diverge from those of the county planning commission or other governmental agencies, which are often used as tools by developers and corporations to obtain variances, policy concessions, and rulings that benefit them. Community planning groups need to clearly understand what values are most important to them, why they are important, and how to present the content of those values to others. They must also understand the values that powerful interests represent and learn how to counteract them. A community social work planner can be a valuable resource in helping the neighborhood planning board discuss and articulate the content of their values and, particularly, the interests of those in power with whom they may conflict.

Perform Assessments

The planning board should gather two kinds of information. One kind of information is the assets, strengths, and resources that exist in your community. Second are the needs that your community members have, gaps in services, or areas that may require attention. This information can give your planning board different perspectives and facilitate the generation of a community plan.

Assets or Resource Assessments   You want to energize the community so it will recognize and use its strengths. Every community has resources and assets that it can use to improve its social environment. Focus your attention on what you want to accomplish, then think of all the resources that could apply. If you track these assets, you will have an updated inventory of available community capital.[71] Kretzman and McKnight offer the following categories of items.[72]

Capacities of Individuals   Talents of individuals in the community provide the fundamental base of community assets, even those who may seem to be less capable, such as the elderly or those with disabilities.

Associations   Faith-based communities, Girl and Boy Scouts, service organizations such as Lions Clubs, Jaycees, Kiwanis, and others working together empower individuals and add to participation and social capital.

Private, Nonprofit, and Governmental Organizations   These organizations can offer information, facilities, expertise, materials, equipment, a source of volunteers, and access to power and leadership in communities.

Physical Assets   Land, buildings, streets, parks, forests, rivers, and lakes enhance the community and can be a focus of unused resources that can be developed, enhanced, or preserved.

Capacity Finders and Developers   Local community leaders, professionals, and experts can help in using and discovering assets and mobilizing, encouraging, and empowering one another in the community.

Needs Assessments   Needs assessments are surveys that focus on gaps in service and areas where people's needs are not being met. When a community cannot meet its goals or sustain itself, the community has unmet needs. Often a needs assessment is required with a grant application to fund a project because the funding source wants to ensure that your project will serve a real need. More important, a needs assessment can help you identify barriers to community economic and social capacity and raise community consciousness and commitment to action. The assessment can assist your community members in realizing that unmet community needs are a result of not using its resources effectively or, says Homan, the assessment may help members demand their fair allocation of resources from the broader community. When you perform a needs assessment, ask, "What's not here that should be here? What's not happening that should be happening?" This is quite different from asking, "What are all the bad things in this community?"[73]

Perform Research

When your planning board either assesses the strengths, resources or assets of your community, or performs a need assessment, you will be conducting research. Macro social work planners help members of neighborhood planning councils collect data, use statistics, analyze information, and prepare reports. Community planners use three methods in gathering information about assets or needs in their communities: the social indicators approach, focused interviews, and social surveys.

The Social Indicators Approach   Social indicators are "inferences of need drawn from descriptive statistics found in public records and reports."[74] They are markers by which your planning group can spot underlying social issues. Lots of information exists to help your group members discover indicators of social problems in your community. Health services both locally and nationally collect data on incidence of diseases and health of the population, including disabilities, aging, and specific diseases. The Department of Housing collects information on the need for low-income housing. Local, state, and federal justice agencies compile data on crime.

Although "using social indicators is unobtrusive and can be done quickly and inexpensively," Rubin and Babbie caution that "this must be weighed against potential problems in the reliability of a particular data base . . . and the degree to which the existing indicators can be assumed to reflect future service utilization patterns accurately."[75]

Focused Interviews   A common and simple way to gather information is by using focused interviews to talk to the key community individuals, called key actors. Look for key actors and conduct focused interviews.

Key Actors   The key actor approach is "a research activity based on information secured from those in the area who are in a position to know the community's needs and utilization patterns."[76] Interviewing key actors can help your planning group understand people's perceptions about their community, its resources, assets and needs of its members, gaps in services, or issues that need resolution. A key actor can provide detailed historical data, knowledge about contemporary interpersonal relationships, and a wealth of information about the nuances of everyday life of the population about which you are concerned. For example, a neighborhood planning board concerned with homeless persons with emotional disabilities should interview key persons from the grassroots who are homeless and can help your group understand the perceptions, difficulties, struggles, and lifestyle as well as the strengths and resources these individuals have. These key actors may not always be those who identify themselves as being community leaders, experts such as professionals, or who think of themselves as well informed. Nevertheless, they are crucial persons from whom you should gather information.

In addition, your board members may also talk with others who are knowledgeable about that population, including social workers and community leaders associated with homeless shelters, members of support groups, key members of the local mental health association, professionals employed by county mental health departments and departments of social services, friends, and family members. Be aware, however, that if you confine your discussion to those who have positions of power, who represent the ethnic majority, or who have acquired social standing in the community, you will not hear the views of those who are poor, people from ethnically diverse communities, or those who tend to be overlooked such as persons who are developmentally disabled, elderly in nursing homes, or children and youth.

How to Find Key Actors: Snowball Sampling   One way to discover the best sources of information is to simply begin asking for names of the people who have been in the community the longest, who have the greatest involvement, or who people at the grassroots identify as key figures who are well informed and are members of the population about whom you are interested. When several people give you the same names, you have probably located a key actor. As you obtain a referral for one person, ask for other names; one person will lead to others just as a snowball grows larger as it rolls down a hill.

Conduct Focused Interviews   Before you conduct focused interviews, decide on your questions and practice. Include a variety of key actors, introduce yourself, ask each question the same way, use a funneling technique, keep a notebook and journal, and develop relationships.

Decide on questions and practice: Focused interviews tend to be semistructured. They "center on selected topics but specific items are not entirely predetermined."[77] Develop a series of four or five questions you want to ask, and decide on follow-up questions for each one. The questions should be open ended and broad, allowing the person to answer in any way he or she chooses.

Usually when your members conduct focused interviews, they practice beforehand and critique each other's performance. Ask follow-up questions to get more depth, and make sure your members are alert for leads that will help them discover new areas no one has mentioned.

Include a variety of key actors: Talk to a variety of key actors to ensure that you have heard all sides of community opinion, not just people sympathetic to the issues on which you are working but those antagonistic to the problem as well. One way to ensure that you have included a variety of key actors is to ask for names of people who share opposite or different points of view, who are leaders of groups who would block or even fight against your efforts. For example, if your group is planning community housing for persons who are former criminal offenders, it is important to talk to members of local neighborhood associations, support groups for victims of assault, and families with small children. These groups may have strong feelings about locating a group home in their neighborhood or even in their town.

If your members find that certain key actors meet them with skepticism or rejection, try to discover why they feel this way. Talking with these people is crucial because they may give your planning group valuable insights about restraining forces or issues in the community of which the group may have been unaware.

Introduce yourself: Members should introduce themselves, give the name of the planning group and its sponsor, explain the purpose of the interview, and the use to which the information will be put. Tell people how many questions they will be asked and how long the interview will take. People tend to be busy and their time should be respected. Let people know that what they tell your group will be confidential and that you will not quote them or otherwise misuse their information. This will help them be open and honest with your interviewers.

Ask the same questions the same way: Have your members ask the same questions each time so that they can compare answers. If members ask different questions with different people, they will get incomplete or fragmented answers. Although you want to cover the same ground with all respondents, make sure questions are flexible enough to go into more depth, drawing people out. Focused interviewers may obtain unanticipated information that will help you define the problem better.

Use a funneling technique: Generally, use a "funneling" technique, going from the general to the specific. For example, ask whether a respondent is aware of the drug problem in the Hillcrest neighborhood. If she or he answers yes, go deeper and ask questions such as whether the person has personally been affected by the problem, if it is an important issue, or what the individual thinks might help alleviate it. Make sure your members keep their eyes open for nonverbal cues such as a raised eyebrow, an unexplained smile, a laugh that may seem out of place, tone of voice, or a hesitation about answering. All of these cues may open the door to asking for more information.

Keep a notebook and a journal: Make sure your members keep a notebook to jot down names and phone numbers of key people they meet, as well as names of key actors they may want to contact. It is frustrating to meet key people and not be able to follow up because members can't remember names or phone numbers.

Ask members to keep a journal and, as soon after the interview as possible, to write down the things they want to keep in mind, questions they want to ask, names and addresses of other people to contact, and issues to track down.

Develop relationships: As your planning group members interview people, they get information about the strengths, assets, resources or needs that people see, but they will be developing relationships with them and gathering insight into the kinds of services that exist. Let people know that your group will be using information to bring about positive changes in the community. Your members may want to ask these people to help later in your change efforts. Key community leaders can be very important in opening doors, and using their influence can help your planning group accomplish its goals. Everywhere they go, your group should build bridges, make connection, and develop relationships.

Social Surveys   Surveys give you the opportunity to quantify information and ask specific questions to which you need answers. A survey is a systematic inquiry of perceptions or attitudes about strengths, resources, assets, gaps in services, needs, or issues affecting a community or neighborhood. Surveys can be used to "explore, describe, or explain respondent's knowledge about a particular subject, their past or current behavior or their attitudes and beliefs concerning a particular subject."[78]

Because surveys ask specific questions, however, they are limited in the depth of responses you may receive. Therefore, they are best used when you want to narrow down issues, ask respondents to rank the importance of particular concerns, or give you an indicator of a range of preferences among items. This can be very important for a community because it gives specific information members can use in making decisions about the direction in which they should go. Three factors are important in designing a survey or needs assessment: when—the time frame; who—the population you wish to survey; and how—how the survey will be accomplished.

When—The Time Frame   The time frame of your research may be important. Your community group may need to meet any number of deadlines. If you are applying for a grant, the foundation or government agency may require a needs assessment. These funding sources have deadlines for submitting applications. You will have had to conduct your needs assessment by that deadline. Community planning groups are often interested in legislation. For example, a bill on gun control about which your community is interested may be scheduled for a public hearing. A survey can provide data to support your community's position, but you need to have it ready in time for the hearing.

A planning commission meeting may soon be held about a proposal to run a highway through a low-income area of your community, and you know that a survey of residents' perceptions could have an important impact on the decision. Your group needs to obtain and analyze the data before the hearing.

Who—The Survey Population   Sometimes you will survey all of the individuals involved in the issue being investigated. Often, however, the number of people that live in the area is so large that you cannot reach all of them. Your time frame or resources may be limited, and you may need to reduce the number of people you survey. In this case a portion of the population, called a "sample," must be used.

If you are surveying a sample of an entire population, it is important to select the subjects using a valid sampling procedure to ensure that the sample is representative, accurately reflecting the composition of the population surveyed. Decide on the size of the sample, and use as large a sample as possible because the larger the size of your sample, the smaller the error. Guy and colleagues, for example, recommend that "for most research endeavors, samples will be adequate if they are within the limits of 30 and 500. Samples of less than 30 are usually too small, while samples greater than 500 are seldom necessary."[79] If you want to reach a particular level of statistical accuracy, your group can use statistical formulas to help you determine a sample size that will give you a level of accuracy, say, of 99% or higher. Four kinds of sampling procedures are common: simple random sampling, systematic sampling, stratified random sampling, and cluster sampling.

Simple random sampling: Simple random sampling is similar to putting everyone's name in a hat and picking out every xth name, always replacing the name before drawing the next name. If a computerized list of an entire population is available, you can have the computer assign random numbers to each person and use those numbers to select a sample.

Systematic sampling: An even simpler, and in some ways better, method than simple random sampling is systematic sampling. First, compile a list of the names of all the people in the population you wish to sample. For example, in a population of 1,000 people, you decide that a sample of 100 people, or 10% of the population, is the number of respondents you have time and resources to survey. Randomly choose a place to begin, and count down every 10th name to obtain 100 names.

Stratified random sampling: It is important to make sure that your sample is accurate enough to include every subgroup in proportion to its actual representation in your population. For example, in a survey of a college population, there may be a small, but important number of Asian, African American, and Hispanic students. If you use a simple random sample, your group may miss some of them, and your sample may misrepresent the population. One way to make sure that your sample includes the same percentage of smaller groups as occurs in the population as a whole is to "stratify" your sample.

First, calculate the percentage of subgroups such as African American, Hispanic, and Asian persons in the population you are sampling. Then sample each of these populations separately by randomly drawing out names until you reach the proportionate amount. For example, assume you are going to sample 100 people from the total population of 1,000. You know the population is 20% Hispanic, 15% African American, and 5% Asian. Separate the names of all African Americans, Hispanics, and Asians from the total population. Out of the group of Hispanics, draw 20 random names, from the population of African Americans draw 15 names, and from the group of Asians draw 5 names. From the remaining list you draw 60 names to obtain 60%. You now have a representative sample with exactly the same proportion of African Americans, Hispanics, Asians, and Caucasians as in the total population.

Cluster sampling: Sometimes you have many different groups of people such as families, schools, or businesses from which to obtain a sample. In this case you can do a cluster sample. Assume, for example, you are conducting a survey of religious group members in your town. First, define a "religious group" for your purposes. Then cluster the groups into categories depending on the purpose of your research. Take a stratified sample of each group to ensure you get an accurate count of both large and small groups. You now have a representative list of the specific religious groups. Obtain a membership listing from each religious group selected, and take a systematic or simple random sample of names from each of these. In this way your survey will accurately represent the membership of religious groups in your town.

How—Accomplishing the Survey

When your group performs a survey, they will need to decide what kind of survey to use. They will need to consider their resources of time, energy, and money to decide whether they should administer the questionnaire by means of an interview in person, over the telephone, or by mail. They will need to prepare a questionnaire, write a letter or compose an introduction, pretest the questionnaire, and analyze the data.

Face-to-face interview: Interviewing 100 people in person is time consuming and takes a lot of energy, particularly if the people are spread out over a large geographical area. Your group may also have to deal with not finding people home. Face-to-face interviewing requires skill and training. On the positive side, doing interviews face to face ensures that you will get the information you need and often ensures accuracy. A face-to-face interview decreases the number of "don't know" answers, and the interviewer can sometimes clarify survey questions that are vague. A good face-to-face interview will allow you to obtain a completion rate of 80 to 85%, which is usually required if you are conducting a survey funded by the federal government.

Mailing questionnaires: Mail-out questionnaires are popular because they reach people living in widely disbursed geographical areas at a relatively low cost. However, a major problem with mailed questionnaires is the response rate. Rubin and Babbie state that for mailed questionnaires, "a response rate of at least 50 percent is usually considered adequate for analysis and reporting. A response rate of at least 60 percent is good and a response rate of 70 percent is very good." However, the response rate for mailed questionnaires may be "well below 50 percent."[80] A mailed questionnaire, therefore, may not give you enough data. You can overcome this by increasing your sample size, sending out reminders, or making phone calls to nonresponders.

Telephone interviews: Telephone interviews can reduce the cost and inconvenience of personally interviewing respondents. Telephone interviewing allows your members to dress as they please without affecting the answers the respondents give. Telephone interviews allow workers to operate in comfort and safety, which is particularly important if the survey is being conducted in an unsafe area of a city. A disadvantage of telephone interviewing is the tendency for people to refuse to talk because of the number of calls they get from solicitors. However, if the interviewer introduces the issue as one that is of interest or concern to the respondent, and if the questionnaire is short, telephone interviewing can be effective.

Prepare the Questionnaire

Whether your survey is face-to-face, mailed out, or by telephone, you need to prepare a questionnaire. It is important that your questionnaire helps get information about the kinds of problems your community wants to resolve. The questionnaire should be clear, easy to administer, and not too long.

Review the information you have already gathered from social indicators or focused interviews. Ask your community planning group what they need to know to decide what direction to take. For example, if your group is working on economic development in a highly industrialized community where there is a large amount of unemployment, you may need to know the number of people who are out of work, the kinds of job skills required, and the kinds of training people might need.

Brainstorming, described in Chapter 11, can help you elicit the kinds of questions you need to ask. Group members think of as many responses as they can without discussion. Write down each idea, no matter how unusual. When no more questions are forthcoming, your group looks over the responses. Some of them may be redundant, vague, or have more than one idea in them. Refine and add to the responses until you have enough questions to obtain the information you need for your survey.

When you develop questions for your questionnaire, follow these rules:

1. Don't ask for more information than you need. Keep your questionnaire short and to the point, and make sure the answers are necessary in planning action.

2. Aim your questions at the level of education and background of your respondents.

3. Try to avoid jargon. For example, you may talk about "delinquent" while your respondents may talk about "being in trouble."

4. Do not ask two questions at once. Asking a double-barreled question will cause confusion. For example, "Should the government reduce the amount it pays to welfare recipients and spend it on education instead?" is a double-barreled question. One respondent may agree with reducing welfare but not that money should be spent on education. Others may want to increase spending on education but not at the expense of reducing welfare. Another may disagree with both parts of the statement. Whenever the word "and" appears, check to see if it is a double-barreled question, and if so, break it apart into separate questions.

5. Make sure your questionnaire items are clear. Consider the question "What is your level of education?" and the possible response items: (a) grade school, (b) high school, (c) college, (d) graduate school. A person who has attained all these levels could circle every category. It is also not clear whether "level of education" means that a person graduated or simply attended at that level. A clearer instruction would read: "Circle the highest level of education which you completed."

6. Do not ask leading questions. Leading questions presuppose an answer or skew the answer in a certain direction. For example, "Delinquent teenagers should be placed in institutions. Yes___ No___" is leading because it biases the response toward a yes answer and gives only two choices.

7. Avoid long items that may confuse the respondents.

8. Avoid negative terms. In responding to the statement "Carrying guns should not be allowed on our streets," some people may overlook the word "not" and answer on that basis.

9. Try to use a mixture of "closed-ended" and "open-ended" questions.

   Closed-ended questions: Closed-ended questions are easy to quantify, but they only provide information according to your preselected answers. Closed-ended questions are those in which a respondent can answer with either (a) yes or no, (b) scales, or (c) rankings.

   a. *Yes–No.* Except for law enforcement, I believe handguns should be banned in this town.

      _____Yes _____No

   b. *Scales:* A common way to get a range of responses is to ask respondents to answer using a scale. One common scale is a Likert scale.

1	**2**	**3**	**4**	**5**
Strongly Agree	*Agree*	*No opinion*	*Disagree*	*Strongly Disagree*

   c. *Ranking:* You may ask respondents to make choices among a range of answers. For example:

   On a scale of 1 to 5 with 1 being the highest and 5 the lowest, rank the community services that are most important to you.

   _____ education _____ employment
   _____ health _____ police _____ recreation

   Open-ended questions: Open-ended questions allow flexibility in response but are harder to quantify. Often you may follow a closed-ended question with an open-ended one. For example, "In your opinion, is the President doing a good job? Yes___ No___," is a closed-ended question. If you then ask, "Why or Why not?" you are following it up with an open-ended question that gives you more information.

Write a Cover Letter and Introduction   Give your questionnaire a title and write out an opening paragraph or script that your group members will use in describing the purpose of the research. Include a statement on confidentiality. In the case of a mail-out questionnaire, this will take the form of a cover letter.

Emphasize the importance of the research and the need for accurate and truthful answers. Assure respondents that their answers will be anonymous. Tell how many questions the questionnaire contains and how long it will take to answer them. Explain how the questionnaire is to be filled out. For example, if you are using a scale, explain how it is to be scored.

Pretest the Questionnaire   It is important to pretest the questionnaire. Select a number of people from your population and try out the questionnaire on them. Pretesting helps you answer the following questions: Does the questionnaire give you the information you need? Are the questions worded correctly? Were they clear and unambiguous? Is the length of the questionnaire appropriate? Was it easy to administer? After you have pretested your questionnaire, meet with your community group and revise the questionnaire using the information from your pretest.

Analyze the Data   Count the number of responses to each question and calculate percentages of people responding to each question. If you have a large number of respondents, arrange your data in graphs or tables rather than describing the data in narrative form only. Computer programs are available that can automatically convert raw data into beautifully arrayed graphs and tables. One such program is SPSS. Follow up tables or graphs with a narrative explanation or interpretation highlighting the points you want to make. Summarize the data as you go along. Be sure that you have fully answered the question you have posed.

Every sample has some built-in error. SPSS can also perform statistical calculations if your group needs to calculate correlations between variables, statistical significance of your findings to determine the degree of confidence that a reader can have in the study, and the degree of sampling error that may exist.

Develop Alternative Solutions

The neighborhood planning group needs to look at the variety of alternative solutions and assess their effectiveness in achieving the community's goals. Social work planners use a variety of decision-making and forecasting techniques. To assist in determining which technique is best, operations research (OR) or systems analysis can be employed.

Operations Research   Operations research, often called management science, was initiated during WW II and includes such techniques as queuing, networks, difference equations, Markov models, and linear programming by which a planner or administrator may solve linear or sequential problems.

Queuing   Developed in the early 1900s, waiting line analysis, or queuing, uses formulas to reduce time lost by waiting in a line or the costs incurred by having an empty facility or station with no one waiting. This is important particularly in agencies where establishing a waiting line for services may create problems or where there are specific time limits, such as in child protective agencies.

The goal of queuing is to find an appropriate level of service that reduces the amount of time people wait in line and provides the most efficient utilization of existing resources. By calculating the average arrival time, the average time in the line, and how the lines are arranged, you can decide to hire more workers, prioritize services such as in a "triage" system used in emergency rooms, or develop strategies to reduce waiting time.

Balancing Costs   Costs to the agency by providing service stations that reduce waiting time include construction costs, operations costs, maintenance costs, insurance, rent, and other fixed costs. On the other hand, costs to the agency by not reducing waiting time include loss of business, ill will, and potential harm to the client. If the service facility is an emergency room in a hospital, the cost of waiting to the customer could be death. In a child protective service agency, the costs to the client could be the risk of continued child abuse.

Agencies must balance the monetary costs with the cost to clients. The larger the facility and the more stations, the higher the agency's cost but the less the cost to customers in time waiting. The fewer the stations, the lower the agency's cost, but the cost to the customer is higher. A queuing analysis is a means of deciding how to balance these costs. Formulas exist to help calculate the most efficient waiting line processes.

Networks   During World War I, Henry Gantt, a prominent efficiency expert, developed a model called a Gantt chart that diagrammed and simplified work flow through various departments in an organization. A manager could "tell at a glance the status of both the projects that were under way, activities and performance of the operating departments."[81] Gantt charts were predecessors of the Program Evaluation and Review Technique (PERT) and the Critical Path Method (CPM), which are now used to chart projects that involve many interrelated activities. PERT and CPM are nearly the same. However, if time estimates are certain, CPM is used. If time estimates are uncertain, PERT is used.

PERT: PERT was the major planning technique used in the Polaris missile program. "To build the Polaris missile, management developed an intricate plan that consisted of a series of interrelated steps, some of which could be implemented simultaneously, and those that needed to be completed before others could begin."[82]

CPM: The critical path method consists of "laying out or diagramming the flow of activities in a project to identify all possible sequences of steps from beginning to the end of the project. The longest sequence is the *critical path*, which determines the completion time of the project. Once it is known, managers can focus on particular activities that are likely to delay the project."[83] In using CPM, you first identify every significant event that must occur to compete the project. These events, called milestones, are arrayed in sequential order and a time is allocated to each event. All milestones are plotted on a chart. The total time is then calculated, and a model is created showing all the events with time lines so that each one is performed in order.

Difference Equations   Suppose you are asked to help assess the ability of a mental health system to successfully fund its programs over the next several years. You need to project income and expenses over that time to decide what programs to expand or reduce. A public hospital in an inner city is faced with severe overcrowding, for example. One possible solution is to build an additional facility; another is to disperse services to community clinics. A local Area Agency on Aging (AAA) is asked to fund programs for Alzheimer's patients over the next 10 years. To put together a budget, the AAA needs estimates of the number of people in day programs during the first 2 years. Each of these forecasting problems raises issues that rely on difference equations. Difference equations are tools for exploring the way events and activities change over time using rates of growth over a specific time period in the past to project growth rates during a specific period in the future.

Markov Models   Imagine you are a social work planner in a low-income community with high unemployment. You want to plan programs to deal with unemployment, and you need to know not only how many unemployed people there are now but how many people will be unemployed at any particular time in the future, and how those numbers will vary given certain conditions. If you can trace employment rates over time and within differing conditions, you can develop effective solutions to the unemployment problem.

Markov models are designed to assist in resolving such questions. Assume, for example, that you think up four different solutions to the problem of unemployment. One solution is to obtain federal funds to improve the job security of those already employed. Another is to establish a training program for the unemployed. A third is to attract new industry through tax concessions, and a fourth solution is to increase unemployment compensation. Which alternative will gain the most employment? Markov models can help you discover how employment and unemployment will vary with each of these different programs, and which solution or combination of solutions would be most effective.

Markov models can also help you understand population flows within a system. Imagine, for example, that an institution for persons with emotional disabilities in your community is operating at full capacity. The mental health planning board has decided to open a new wing. Should the facility serve long-term patients or short-term patients? What size facility will meet the needs? Markov analysis can help predict how many new persons can be admitted to the facility at 3-month intervals, for example, and how many people will be in the facility 2 years hence. This kind of information can help the board decide whether they need a short- or long-term facility, and what size the facility should be.

Linear Programming Linear programming is "a mathematical technique for deriving the optimal solutions to linear relationships. Linear programming can assist in resolving any problem concerned with maximizing or minimizing some economic factor, such as cost, that is subject to a set of constraints (e.g., human resources, materials, and capital)."[84] Because of its power, linear programming is one of the most highly developed and widely used management science techniques. It has been used with enormous success to solve a variety of planning problems such as allocating scarce resources to completing projects or objectives. It can be an invaluable aid for making policy choices that range from allocating the budget for a small library to selecting the components of a gigantic hydroelectric plant. A linear programming model of the entire Ganges-Brahmaputra river system, for example, takes into account flood control, power production, irrigation, navigation, and salinity control.[85]

Linear programming is useful because it is an optimizing model "concerned with choosing the best levels for various activities in situations where these activities compete for scarce resources."[86] Linear programming is most successful if the issues are straightforward, such as when an administrator in a child protective service agency must allocate 450 hours of a caseworker's time among various cases, when a center for the disabled must develop a work schedule to use $100,000 of staff time efficiently, or when a neighborhood house must determine expenditure level for various activities.

Often, however, the problems are such that inequalities exist. For example, a social work administrator may want to minimize the cost of a job-training program, but at the same time she may be willing to go over budget if particularly good jobs can be found or more people placed. Fortunately computer software can be obtained to perform these kinds of calculations.

Systems Analysis Systems analysis or the systems approach is used to evaluate more complex problems in which many variables interact with one another in ways that are not solvable using linear-based mathematical formulae. According to Starling, systems analysis "forces us to look at problems as systems; that is, assemblies of interdependent components"[87] that interact with one another. Systems analysis may include operations research or the management science techniques described previously, but systems analysis also employs simulations and sensitivity analysis.

Simulations An advantage of using simulations derives from the counterintuitive nature of complex social systems. *Counterintuitive* means that social systems do not react in the ways we think they should because the human brain cannot grasp the totality of relationships among all the variables that may interact together. When you simulate how a system works, however, you will often understand how the system operates and can discover what will occur when you change or manipulate the external environment. You can then use this information to improve a system or to correct a system's malfunction.

When you engage in simulation, you first define the problem by examining all the relevant steps, interactions, important variables, and their relationships. Next, you develop a miniature or simulated model of the system that replicates the system as closely as possible. Include all relevant aspects of the real situation, and keep the model simple enough so that you can manipulate it to discover how it works in the real world. Then evaluate the results and develop a strategy for resolving your problem. Simulations help you discover flaws in your solution so you can modify the solution before you expend energy and incur any expense.

Sensitivity Analysis A sensitivity analysis process consists of making very small changes in the model to show the extent to which results may be altered because of a change in one or a few factors.

Assess and Compare Alternatives

Once the planning group has developed two or three alternatives for reaching its goals, members need to compare them. Force-field analysis or rational problem solving using benefit-cost analysis (both described in Chapter 3) can give your planning group an estimated relative cost of various proposals. The least costly option, however, may not be one the community would choose. Although it is useful to calculate and rank alternatives, the community as a whole should ultimately make the final decision about a community plan.

Provide Feedback

At every step in community planning, it is vital to give feedback to officials in positions of political power. Make sure your group regularly informs those people from whom they will seek support, approval, or ask for funding. If those officials have questions, concerns, or conflicts about what your group is doing, it is better to have those issues examined earlier rather than later. If you wait until your group has finished its process and then discover your members lack support, you will have complicated or damaged your planning process.

The community as a whole on whose behalf the planning process is being conducted must be regularly apprised about its progress and expected outcomes. Individuals from the community at large can give valuable periodic feedback to the community planning group about the feasibility and utility of the planning objectives.

Including community members in the process also can ensure that those who were not initially part of the process may now become involved. Keeping community members informed may provide an army of volunteers to take on various parts of the project. The more the planning process includes and involves members of the community, the greater its impact and success may be.

Present the Solution to the Community

As soon as the planning team decides on several recommended solutions to the problem, they should present the proposal to the wider community to solicit feedback in a series of open community forums. In a forum, the community planning board gives a short history of the problem and how the committee generated its solutions. Members present all alternatives by debates, focus-group discussions, or panel discussions with audience participation. When the community as a whole has had time to reflect and consider the merits of the various alternative proposals, a general meeting should be called to help your group decide which among the various proposals they think is best. Your planning group can use buzz groups, Crawford slip writing, idea writing, or group voting to help a large audience come to a decision.

Buzz Groups   When you want to divide a large group into smaller ones and obtain feedback, use "buzz groups." There are several advantages of buzz groups. When using buzz groups, you divide the audience, give instructions, and obtain reports.

Advantages of Buzz Groups   Buzz groups give members the satisfaction of participating and engaging one another. They help your leaders tap a variety of ideas, concerns, and issues to help the larger group move forward. Individuals can engage in two-way communication by listening to one another and giving feedback.

You can also use buzz groups as listening teams. Each team listens for certain content in the speaker's presentation and reports back to the larger group. You can also use them to reflect on or to apply the ideas of the main speaker to their own situations. You can ask the groups to raise issues or ask questions to a speaker or panel.

Divide the Audience   In the classic buzz group, called Phillips 66, you divide your audience into groups of six persons and allow them 6 minutes to formulate a question for the speaker. However, you can decide how many people to include in each group yourself and how much time to spend. If your audience is larger than 30 participants, be directive and structured about the outcomes you want from each buzz group. When you give clear instructions, you will not confuse members, make them take extra time to understand their task, or interfere with their satisfaction when they give input to the larger group.

Explain the method you will use to divide the large task group into smaller units. The easiest way is to ask the large group to divide itself into groups of a specific number, such as groups of five. People who already know each other will tend to form themselves into groups. If you want to ensure that members do not choose people they know, divide the number of participants by the size of the groups you want to form. For example, if there are 100 participants and you want groups of 5, you will form 20 groups. Ask members to "count off" by that number, and ask those with the same number, such as all number ones, to form a group. You can also divide people into groups by providing name tags marked with a color, a number, or symbol. You can group people together on the basis of their particular interest, geographic area, or some other commonality that helps members facilitate the task they are to accomplish.

Give Instructions   Tell the members what kind of task they will engage in and what the outcomes should be. Explain how long they will have to complete the task and how each group's output, product, or decisions will be shared with the larger group. If groups remain together in the same room, the noise and activity of the differing units may become contagious, motivating all of the groups to work harder.

If you want the small task groups to meet in separate rooms, give everyone the instructions they need before the groups adjourn to the rooms. Have assistants guide the small groups to their location and meet with them to repeat the instructions and answer questions about the goals. Once members are clear, the assistants may leave or stay to act as recorders or facilitators.

Obtain Reports   If you have a few buzz groups, ask each one to select a reporter who will offer the conclusions, decisions, or feedback to the larger audience. If you provide flipcharts to each buzz group, each small group can use the chart to report its ideas and then display them together, so that during a break participants may view the major ideas.

If there are many groups, reports may become repetitive. In this case, ask the recorders to write the results of the buzz session on a sheet of paper and give the list to a panel. The panel members will then synthesize the reports and present the different points to the audience. Although buzz group members may loose credit for their individual ideas, they may gain satisfaction from seeing how their contributions are reflected in the total group response.

Another method is to ask the recorders of each buzz group to act as the panel and synthesize the groups' ideas before reporting them. While the recorders are assembling the information, give the audience a short break, telling them to return to their seats at a specific time. If you want to provide follow up, collect the written reports and mail them to all of the participants. Then call a meeting or meetings to continue the planning process using the information you have collected.[88]

Crawford Slip Writing   Crawford slip writing is a brainstorming session with a large task group, even one as large as 5,000 people. Slip writing will often generate up to five ideas per person and can speed up the planning process in decision making, maximize total group participation, and help your planning committee discover new solutions and ideas. The purpose is to bring out as many good ideas as possible and obtain a group consensus.

Give each person in the audience a scratch pad or a stack of 25 3×5 cards. Read the problem statement, which you leave open-ended to elicit a variety of responses. For instance, your planning group may ask: "How can we . . . ?" or "How to. . . ." Ask participants to write one idea on each slip without considering their priority or importance. After 5 to 10 minutes, ask members to stop writing and collect the statements. Ask members of your planning committee to evaluate and sort the best ideas into workable proposals.[89]

Idea Writing   Idea writing is a method that involves dividing a large task group into smaller groups for idea building. You make preparations, explain the process, divide the audience, and conduct the process.

Make Preparations   First, decide whether you will give members the same question or use a list of items. If you use one question for everyone, test it before using it with the large group. If you decide to use a list of items, print them on a sheet of newsprint and prepare it for display. Have available several large pads of paper, pencils, pens, large tables, and chairs as well as flipcharts or easels, newsprint, masking tape, and felt-tip pens.

Explain the Process   When the large task group meets, explain the importance of the task and how the results of their efforts will be used. Ask members to work silently. Identify the steps of idea writing and ask participants to complete writing their ideas in 15 to 30 minutes.

Divide the Audience   Divide the audience into small groups of three or four persons each with one person serving as a group leader. You can appoint the leaders, ask the group to choose, or choose the leader randomly.

Conduct the Process   Each member writes his or her name in the upper right-hand corner of a large sheet of paper. At the top of the paper, each member then lists triggering questions they believe the group as a whole must answer before the main issue can be resolved. The members post their list of questions so everyone can refer to them. Each participant then takes 10 to 15 minutes to quickly, silently, and independently write responses to the questions the members have listed.

Have participants from each small task group place their worksheets on a table. Each person from the small group then selects someone else's worksheet and, after reading it silently, reacts to it by writing additional comments, pointing out weaknesses, qualifying what that person said, and offering a solution of his or her own. Repeat the process until everyone has responded to everyone else in each small group.

You may either process the worksheets immediately or ask members to leave the worksheets with monitoring teams who will report back at a later time. If you process the results immediately, ask the participants to return to their small groups. Each person reads the comments on her or his pad and reports them to the other group members for discussion. After discussion, each member summarizes the issues and ideas. The group then summarizes its efforts on a single sheet of newsprint. One person reports to the large group using the newsprint for a summary of ideas. The large task group holds a discussion to refine the material further and then reaches a decision.[90]

Group Voting   If you want your larger group to help the planning committee decide which of the various solutions they believe to be best, ask them to do a group vote. Ask the audience to consider all the alternatives and rank them according to the solution that they think is best. For example, if there are three alternatives, the first choice receives a score of 3, the second a score of 2, and the last a score of 1. Calculate the total scores for each alternative and divide that score by the number of participants. This gives an accurate assessment of the rankings of each alternative.

If you have a large number of people in the audience, divide the members into small groups and ask a recorder to calculate the rankings. A panel will then combine the rankings and calculate the final score. After the voting process, ask for feedback from the audience about the rankings and why members voted the way they did. This will give your planning group some insight into the perceptions and attitudes of the audience.

Present the Solution to Decision Makers

The neighborhood planning board needs to devise its strategy for dealing with political decision makers. You provide training, help members present their proposals, and engage in political action and pressure tactics.

Provide Training   You and your group must not be naive about this political process. Many interests are competing for attention and approval. These claimants press for policy and legal concessions to further their own interests and may actively challenge and undermine the planning efforts of your community. The political process can be highly irrational, fraught with emotion, and dependent on compromise, bargaining, and negotiation.

Provide training to your group about the political process. A community planning group that assumes that dominant interests are bound by rules, rational arguments, facts, or figures will miss the point of organizational power and self-interest and be out of touch with the real operating principles of conventional politics. Your group, for example, may use forecasting or decision techniques to develop a very rational analysis, but when they present their case to politicians, developers, and citizen groups, they may find that no one seems to be listening. The merits of the case, if they are not in the interests of those in power, are beside the point. Your group must be able to communicate with and present its plans to political leaders who have the power to approve the plan in a way that will capture their attention and help your members set it in motion.

Present Proposals   Assist your members in presenting proposals and ideas in language that people can understand. An analysis not communicated well, Forester says, is "worse than useless—it can be counterproductive and damaging, just as it might also at other times deliberately serve to obfuscate important issues."[91] Help your planning group get involved, talk, and argue, especially when confronted by misinformation, misrepresentation, disparities in power, and subversion of a process that advantages some and disadvantages others. Help community members "anticipate misinformation in time to use those strategies effectively, rather than looking back and saying, 'Well, what we should have done was . . .'" A "good idea presented the week after a crucial meeting (or too late on an agenda, or on the wrong agenda) will no longer do any good."[92]

Engage in Political Action   Help your planning group and community members learn how to engage in political action by lobbying key political decision makers, networking with key leaders, negotiating and building coalitions, and creating consensus on behalf of your community plan. Try to even the scales, balancing power misalignments so that truth will win out in the end, encouraging "democratically structured, publicly aired political argument, not covert wheeling and dealing."[93]

How do you assist your community in such political action? According to Forester, by "informing the 'affected but unorganized' earlier rather than later in the planning process,"[94] as well as by helping the community in "checking, double-checking, testing, consulting experts, seeking third-party counsel, clarifying issues, exposing assumptions, reviewing and citing the record, appealing to precedent, invoking traditional values (democratic participation, for example), spreading questions about unexplored possibilities, spotlighting jargon and revealing meaning, negotiating for clearly specified outcomes and values, working through informal networks to get information, bargaining for information, [and] holding others to public commitments."[95]

Use Pressure Tactics   When necessary, your planning group may use citizen protests, including packing council meetings, forming delegations, and voting as a block to support political candidates or to propose specific referenda or initiatives. When the Public Works Department in Wilmington wanted to expand a garage for city vehicles with Economic Development Administration funds, for example, the local citizens planning council fought the proposal and were able to stop the project. In East St. Paul the city wanted to redevelop an old hospital site and put up townhouses. "The city was really pushing saying, 'Hey, we need the tax base!' but members of the community asserted, 'No, we don't want that; we want a park,' and they got what they wanted."[96]

Implement the Solution

A plan, even if it is well thought out and well designed, is of little use unless it can be implemented. Many specific projects or comprehensive neighborhood plans developed by neighborhood citizen planning councils have been successfully implemented. In St. Paul more than 80% of the neighborhood projects were funded. In Cincinnati community planning groups obtained funding for neighborhood improvement and housing programs that led to improvement in police services, crime prevention, and witness assistance programs. A district council initiated a neighborhood dispute board to address local conflicts and minor criminal acts such as vandalism, and a youth

federation to provide counseling and advocacy. In other communities, drug education and counseling for local youth, day care cooperatives, tutoring, youth recreation, emergency paramedic units, and a multiservice center have emerged out of the community planning process. In addition, neighborhood planning programs established many new neighborhood organizations in areas where they did not exist, more equitable distributed public resources, made major improvements for poorer neighborhoods, and increased the quality of life in neighborhoods.

Help the planning group itemize the steps by which the plan can be put into action by community members themselves in partnership with government and corporate leaders who may have resources that the community needs. For example, the plan may recommend that community members organize a community development corporation. The plan must help community members design and develop the corporation, described in Chapter 7. The plan may call for the development of a social program or social agency. You assist the planning group in transforming itself into a board of directors and a social organization, described in Chapter 10. The plan may call for coordination, funding, and implementation of services by existing social agencies. Social work administrators will need information on how to proceed with such implementation. You may act as a consultant to administrators or help community members facilitate administration of the plan.

Monitor and Evaluate

The planning process is not complete until a plan for monitoring and evaluation is developed. If a private agency is responsible for writing a grant and obtaining funding from a social planning organization, a program evaluation component will often be part of the grant proposal. You will be active in working with community groups to analyze the consequences of change, monitoring program effectiveness, providing consultation, specifying adjustments needed, and identifying new problems that may call for action and planning.

CONCLUSION

Planning for social welfare, social agency planning, and community social planning requires macro social workers to exercise a number of skills. Social work planning is one of the most important and potentially powerful means by which macro social work achieves its goals. It has, from the beginning of the social work profession, been a key player in the inception and implementation of social programs. Social work planning has been one of the major points of entry for macro social workers into housing, mental health, poverty, and social services with the elderly, community affairs, and empowerment.

Today many cities across America have officially designated neighborhood planning organizations in partnership with city councils, mayors' offices, and planning commissions to take responsibility for developing, monitoring, and carrying out plans in their communities. Community planning engages citizen participation in ways that have not often previously occurred. This is a substantive shift in decision making and politics, indicating a new era of grassroots democracy and local responsibility, with people planning for their own futures with centralized government as partners in that effort. Social planning has great potential for empowering people in a community to take direction over their lives.

KEY CONCEPTS

community social work planning

social welfare planning

social agency planning

neighborhood planning

Progressive Era

Graham Taylor

New Deal

Great Society

War on Poverty

housing and urban planning

Housing Act of 1937

Housing Act of 1949

Fair Housing Act of 1969

Housing and Urban Development Act of 1968

Housing and Community Development Act of 1974

Department of Housing and Urban Development (HUD)

HOME program

empowerment zones

planning for mental health

Comprehensive Community Health Act of 1963

Community Mental Health Centers Act of 1963

Economic Opportunity Act of 1964

community action program (CAP)

community action agency (CAA)

Demonstration Cities and Metropolitan Development Act, 1966 (Model Cities)

planning for older Americans

Older Americans Act, 1965

Area Agency on Aging

community planning

councils of social agencies

Francis McLean

Community War Chests

Community Chest

War on Poverty

model cities

citizen participation

Bradley Buell

Dudley Street Neighborhood Initiative (DSNI)

community planning process

comprehensive community planning

stakeholders

focus groups

planning board

resource and assets assessment

needs assessment

social indicators approach

focused interviews

key actors

snowball sampling

funneling technique

social surveys

survey population

questionnaires

sampling

simple random sampling

systematic random sampling

stratified random sampling

cluster sampling

face-to-face interviewing

mail-out questionnaires

telephone interviews

closed-ended questions

scales

Likert scale

ranking

open-ended questions

pretesting

operations research

management science

queuing

networks

program evaluation and review technique (PERT)

critical path method (CPM)

linear programming

systems analysis

simulations

sensitivity analysis

buzz groups

Crawford slip writing

idea writing

group voting

political action

pressure tactics

QUESTIONS FOR DISCUSSION

1. If planning is a normal aspect of the human condition, why has there been so much controversy over planning, particularly in the field of social welfare?

2. As you have read in this chapter, macro social work was in large part responsible for the development of clinical social work practice, yet in recent years social work planning and other community social work arenas have declined while clinical practice has boomed. If it is true that clinical practice is reactive, dealing with past hurts rather than solving current and future problems, what is your assessment of the ultimate capacity of clinical social work to survive?

3. What do you believe will be the role of activist community social work planning in the future?

4. What role should social work planning take?

ADDITIONAL READING

Medoff, Peter and Holly Sklar. *Streets of Hope: The Fall and Rise of an Urban Neighborhood.* Boston, MA: South End Press, 1994.

Forester, John. *Planning in the Face of Power.* Berkeley: University of California Press, 1989.

Gharajedaghi, Jamshid. *A Prologue to National Development Planning.* New York: Greenwood Press, 1986.

Kahn, Alfred J. *Theory and Practice of Social Planning.* New York: Russell Sage Foundation, 1969.

Lauffer, Armand. *Social Planning at the Community Level.* Englewood Cliffs, NJ: Prentice-Hall, 1978.

Mayer, Robert R. *Policy and Program Planning: A Developmental Perspective.* Englewood Cliffs, NJ: Prentice-Hall, 1985.

Mayer, Robert R. *Social Planning and Social Change.* Englewood Cliffs, NJ: Prentice-Hall, 1972.

Michael, Donald N. *On Learning to Plan and Planning to Learn.* San Francisco: Jossey-Bass, 1973.

Rohe, William M. and L. B. Gates. *Planning With Neighborhoods.* Chapel Hill: University of North Carolina Press, 1985.

Rothman, Jack. *Planning and Organizing for Social Change: Action Principles From Social Science Research.* New York: Columbia University Press, 1974.

Smith, Herbert H. *Citizen's Guide to Planning,* 3d ed. Chicago: APA Planners Press, 1993.

Walker, Alan. *Social Planning: A Strategy for Socialist Welfare.* Oxford: B. Blackwell, 1984.

Wates, Nick, ed. *The Community Planning Handbook: How People Can Shape Their Cities, Towns and Villages in Any Part of the World.* London, UK: Earthscan Publications, 2000.

Wildavsky, Aaron. *Speaking Truth to Power.* Boston: Little, Brown, 1979.

Management Science Techniques

Mishan, E. J. *Economics for Social Decisions: Elements of Cost-Benefit Analysis.* New York: Praeger, 1973.

Stokey, Edith and Richard Zeckhauser. *A Primer for Policy Analysis.* New York: W. W. Norton, 1978.

Wisniewski, Mik. *Quantitative Methods for Decision Makers.* 2d ed. London: Pitman, 1997.

General Works

Friedman, Milton. *Capitalism and Freedom.* Chicago: University of Chicago Press, 1962.

Galbraith, John Kenneth. *The New Industrial State.* 2d ed. Boston: Houghton Mifflin, 1971.

Hayek, Friedrich A. *The Road to Serfdom.* Chicago: University of Chicago Press, 1944.

Kretzman, John and John L. McKnight. *Building Communities From the Inside Out.* Chicago: ACTA, 1993.

Kretzman J. and McKnight John L. *A Guide to Capacity Inventories: Mobilizing the Community Skills of Local Residents.* Chicago: ACTA, 1997.

McKnight, John. *The Careless Society: Community and Its Counterfeits.* New York: Basic Books, 1995.

Prugh, Thomas, Robert Costanza, and Herman Daly. *The Local Politics of Global Sustainability.* Washington, DC: Island Press, 1999.

Study Circles Resource Center. *Organizing Community-wide Dialogue for Action and Change: A Step-by-Step Guide.* Pomfret, CT: Study Circles Resource Center, 2001.

Study Circles Resource Center. *Building Strong Neighborhoods for Families With Children.* Pomfret, CT: Topsfield Foundation, Inc., 2001.

Study Circles Resource Center. *Building Strong Neighborhoods: A Study Circle Guide for Public Dialogue and Community Problem Solving.* Pomfret, CT: Topsfield Foundation, Inc., 1998.

7 The Practice of Community Development

Social Change

Social change isn't going to come as quickly as any of us would like it to come. Building a community is a subtle, delicate, long-term process.

Sam Brown, community organizer[1]

Community Vision

Each person in a community must do his part. All have gifts and an area to do. Together we can accomplish great things. Where there is no vision, the people perish. If we don't continue with that vision before us then in essence our community will perish.

Margaret Kinaanen, community leader, Embarrass, Minnesota

Ideas in This Chapter

CDCs serve as vital alternatives to privately owned businesses by constructing or improving housing and creating jobs that make the market work for the poor.

COMMUNITY DEVELOPMENT FINDS ITSELF

It was clear to many leaders in Black communities in the middle to late 1960s that the Civil Rights demonstrations had been a powerful mechanism to achieve justice and restore rights, but the riots and dissention created problems in communities, both in urban ghettos and in rural America. These leaders understood that demonstrations and picketing, although effective in breaking the back of racial inequality, were not going to build communities again. Neither would stricken neighborhoods improve because of natural and spontaneous market forces nor because government agencies would eventually do something. If change was going to happen, residents in these neighborhoods would have to consciously take their destiny into their own hands and build all of the necessary resources—the institutions and social tools—that make a community work.

As communities began to "shift their perspective from an individually based legal conception of African American civil rights to the socio-economic concept of black community," asserts Stewart E. Perry, community members began to look to themselves and toward local self-determination.[2] Across the country awareness grew that the community members themselves needed to develop and control the economic institutions in their own neighborhoods.

A decisive turning point in the life of community had occurred. Members of these communities were committed to their own recovery. They would not allow the community's resources to be drained or exploited. They would not be dependent on government or on outside experts. People in impoverished communities across North America would find in themselves and in one another the power and the resources to revitalize their communities and in the process find themselves as well. Community in America would never be the same again. As a result of determination combined with ingenuity, opportunity, and talent, a number of different African American communities spontaneously invented a new social and economic tool, the community development corporation, or CDC.

In November 1980 members of Opa-locka and North Dade County, Florida, established the Opa-locka Community Development Corporation (OLCDC) to address the distressed unemployment conditions. The H Street CDC, founded in 1984, has worked to revitalize the H Street N.E. corridor of Washington, D.C., developing housing and commercial projects and facilitating bank loans for new and existing businesses. In that same year, a Catholic Bishop and a nun began doing door-to-door outreach in Detroit to rekindle their deteriorating neighborhood, resulting in the development of the Core City Neighborhoods (CCN) Corporation. Community Development Works (CDW) is using a multifaceted approach to create a community development infrastructure with residents in Central Louisiana (Cenla). Members of Leadership Arkansas/Searcy County, organized in September 2001, know that community development doesn't just happen accidentally. It begins with a willingness to see things differently and with optimism about future possibilities.

Cooperation

Businesses compete with one another and often hoard trade secrets from rivals, but the "secret" of CDC strength is their cooperative spirit, their alliances with government, and their willingness to share ideas and network with one another and with a variety of business and nonprofit groups. Through Industry Canada and FedNor, a Canadian government CDC assistance program, the Canadian federal government provides funding, advice, and support across Ontario to more than 58 community futures development corporations (CFDCs), the name for CDCs in Canada. LAMBAC, the LaCloche-Manitoulin Business Assistance Corporation, for example, formed a partnership in January of 1999 with a private corporation, Northern Communications, and FedNor with the goal of enhancing paging service and high-speed Internet access to Manitoulin Island in Canada.

Since its inception in North Dade County, Florida, more than 20 years ago, Opa-Locka CDC has worked extensively with private developers, businesses, residents, community organizations, and government agencies to build affordable housing, revitalize the business environment, and improve the quality of life. To achieve its goals, Core City Neighborhoods (CCN) in Detroit collaborates with businesses, banks, and community organizations. Its accomplishments include affordable housing rehabilitation, after-school and summer programs for children, job creation, and business counseling to local entrepreneurs.[3]

Leadership Development

Far from the beaten track of the major centers of leadership in New York, Washington, and San Francisco, CDCs provide quality leadership training rivaling some of the best programs in the nation. Leadership Arkansas/Searcy County (LASC) with the help of the University of Arkansas Cooperative Extension Service provides training to 20 community leaders each year. A goal of Community Development Works (CDW) is to develop diverse leaders from across central Louisiana (Cenla). CDW provides training seminars in community organizing and nonprofit governance, and in partnership with the LSUA Nonprofit Management Program, CDW provides experienced nonprofit executives, managers, and board members with 8 months of training and networking with regional and national speakers. In 2003 CDW concluded the third year of its Leadership for a Healthy Cenla program, bringing together more than 50 leaders in a year-long program in development, collaboration, and leadership.

Innovation

Another reason CDCs are successful is their ability to innovate. The cadre of leaders trained by Leadership Arkansas/Searcy County (LASC) have developed a 4,000-foot paved airstrip, a 90-acre industrial park with a new industry, and a new post office and bank that serves tourists stopping in Leslie and Marshall on their way to Branson, Missouri. In 2004 Community Development Works (CDW) in Central Louisiana (Cenla) developed Brokering Professional Services, providing financial management, technological assistance, legal aid, and public relations assistance to area organizations. The CDW Resource Center enables members to network and access technical assistance, information, publications, and databases that support their community development efforts.[4] Opa-Locka CDC manages the Opa-locka Airpark and is using this experience to attract other business development and to develop retail shopping in Miami Gardens.[5]

Consensual Community Organizing

Some CDCs innovate by combining community development with community organizing. The largest and best-known effort to help CDCs do community organizing is the $1.5 million Ricanne Hadrian Initiative for Community Organizing (RHICO), sponsored through the Massachusetts Association of CDCs and the Neighborhood Development Support Collaborative. The Organized Neighbors Yielding Excellence (ONYX) CDC, for example, adopted a combined organizing and development group model, where leadership and authority over the organizing effort remain vested in the CDC board of directors. A similar project to promote community organizing through CDCs is the Toledo Community Organizing Training and Technical Assistance Program sponsored through the Toledo Community Foundation. These innovative CDCs seem to display more community involvement in decision making, less fund-driven project development, and more effective CDC advocacy efforts.

Results

CDCs in the decade of 2000 are achieving remarkable results. In 1940, for example, Tupelo/Lee County, Mississippi, was one of the poorest counties in the nation. Because the Tupelo/Lee CDC conscientiously trained its members to assume leadership, its per capita income is now the second highest in the state, and its income level is near the national average. Tupelo's primary advantage is that the citizens of Tupelo/Lee County know how to work together toward common goals. The county has added more than 1,000 new manufacturing jobs a year for 13 years straight. The area has also been cited for the quality of its education and health care systems.

In 2003, 4 years of perseverance by the partners of LAMBAC paid off on Manitoulin Island. Its paging and Internet communication services are a tangible improvement in an area that did not have adequate service and where pagers did not work. This was particularly important for the medical profession, firefighters, and service and sales people covering the island from other areas. About 15,000 people benefit from this increased Internet access, which includes most of Manitoulin, Killarney, and parts of the North Shore. The upgraded communication service of LAMBAC has been a boost to the local business economy.

Community development corporations represent a direct community approach to comprehensive revitalization of a neighborhood, including businesses that create jobs and incomes, political networks, housing, schools, recreation facilities, and all of the mediating infrastructures that build a new sense of self-respect and self-determination. These efforts were the invention of African American inner-city communities, but they have now spread to Hispanic, Native American, and white neighborhoods in both the United States and Canada. In rural towns and urban cities, from Southern Florida and across the great plains of the United States and Canada to the Northwest, CDCs are a gift from African Americans to small communities throughout North America.

WHAT YOU WILL LEARN IN THIS CHAPTER

Neither corporate nor government assistance alone will provide the answer to America's depressed communities. Nor do they often have the will or the ability to solve the problems of inner-city and rural poor. Only the people of a community, in partnership with government and business, can solve their common problems. In this chapter, you will learn what community development is. You will explore a brief history of community development and learn how macro social workers help people begin a community development corporation.

Along with community organization, community development has the potential to revitalize community and to remediate social problems that have gone unsolved for generations. Community development is one of the most important arenas of community social work today.

WHAT IS COMMUNITY DEVELOPMENT?

Community development is a method by which macro social workers assist community members in developing resources and promoting networks that enable a community to become a source of economic, political, and social support to its people. Community development aims at establishing small business enterprises such as housing development, job creation, or providing financial products such as loans by means of a community development corporation (CDC). Antonia Pantoja and Wilhelmina Perry define community development as a means by which members of an economically dependent and politically disenfranchised community work together to do the following:

1. Understand the forces and processes that have made them and keep them in their state of poverty and dependency.

2. Mobilize and organize their internal strength, as represented in political awareness, a plan of action based on information, knowledge, skills, and financial resources.

3. Eradicate from individuals and from group culture the deception that makes them participants in their own dependency and powerlessness.

4. Act in restoring or developing new services and programs for the well-being of its members—starting with the economizing function.[6]

In addition, generalist macro social workers see community development as a means by which individuals can engage in individual growth and skill enhancement, learn the importance of task groups, and construct a community development corporation.

Individual Growth and Skill Enhancement

Community development provides inclusive "individual self-development of creative human capacities . . . to acquire and exercise the skills of citizenship."[7] Macro social workers help community members learn the demands of planning and carrying out business and social projects. Through their involvement with hands-on projects, residents gain valuable experience in meeting facilitation, budget preparation, strategic planning, fundraising, event coordinating, media relations, public speaking, and research. Individuals may also learn how to write proposals and developing contracts for services. When local citizen/members of CDCs monitor the policy-making process, for example, by pressing public officials to enact equitable legislation and regulations, or formulate and lobby for policy alternatives, "they gain power over development decisions in their neighborhoods."[8]

These skills not only increase the leadership capacity of the neighborhood as a whole but influence other aspects of residents' lives. For example, a welfare recipient who had never held a job became an active participant in the Target Area Designation Program, relates Kristina Smock. She began to blossom as a leader and was offered a job as a tenant organizer in her neighborhood. The self-confidence and skills that she gained in this position propelled her to enroll in college and begin planning a future career as a social service professional.[9]

The Importance of Task Groups

CDCs help community members understand the importance of using task group research and planning, implementation, and community building.

Task Group Research and Planning   CDCs that employ a macro social worker will utilize task groups of citizens to assess their community, engage in action research, and perform community planning. In some cases, these are elaborate processes, involving surveys, one-to-one meetings, small group discussions, and large community meetings over the period of a year or more. The Neighborhood of Affordable Housing (NOAH), for example, is nearing the end of one of these planning processes, which will produce a final plan addressing economic development, housing, community safety, human services, education, open/green space, health, arts/culture/heritage, and transportation. Other CDC grassroots planning processes are not so elaborate. They might focus on a single issue, such as housing, and use a more targeted, small-scale approach.

Implementation   Many CDCs, such as the Twin Cities CDC, engage citizens not only in planning but also in implementing the plan. Once residents decided on housing priorities, for example, the Jamaica Plain Neighborhood Development Corporation (JPNDC) developed project management task groups to create a design review process that gives residents an accessible and meaningful way to participate in development decisions. Members of these task groups make sure the units developed by JPNDC meet the needs of neighborhood residents and advocate for the finished project, help the CDC sell or rent units, and provide spokespeople who can respond to neighborhood critics of the project.[10]

Community Building

When community members use task groups to conduct research, develop plans, and carry out projects, they develop tangible skills in group processes and leadership and the infrastructure of community building. They learn that the core of community building is working together in groups. They form relationships and develop networks that can increase the capacity of their communities.

Constructing a Community Development Corporation

When members of a community decide to form a CDC, they have accepted the challenge of operating a business enterprise; they will gain skills in CDC administration and in CDC/community organization.

Operating a Business Enterprise

The ability to develop and manage a business is key to economic power in North America, but is a skill that has often been out of reach of many ordinary citizens. A macro social worker helps members understand how to establish a corporation, select and train a board of directors, develop an organizational structure, engage in raising capital, and recruit and hire staff. You help members acquire skills in business planning, fiscal management, budgeting, accounting, marketing, sales, and customer satisfaction. These skills of establishing and operating a business enterprise are prized and respected in American market society. Macro workers understand the importance for people in lower income neighborhoods to become skilled in using organizational systems as countervailing tools in the quest for community control and economic development. When community members, with the assistance of a macro social worker, capture a vision, develop a business enterprise, and put it to work on

behalf of the community, they develop the potential to compete with private capitalistic enterprise on an equal footing.

Community development corporations help members acquire a mentality that allows them to demystify business enterprise, learn its techniques, and marshal the rational logic of the marketplace. Members may learn that using business to make money is not complex; rather, it requires a combination of perseverance, hard work, vision, and an influx of capital. Most of all it takes the dedication of a group of people who keep their eyes squarely on the goal.

Macro social workers assist people in developing the capacity to become shrewd business entrepreneurs, but entrepreneurs with a social purpose. As they learn how to use economic assets, they learn the language and conceptual tools by which the profit motive works.

CDC Administration

CDCs, like other corporations, need skilled executive leadership. A CDC will succeed or fail based on the skills its administrator brings: to raise funds, relate to its board of directors, inspire confidence from the community it serves, and keep the organization headed in the right direction. CDCs give community members the opportunity to see one of their own in an executive leadership position and to participate with that leader in forging the organization into a strong system by serving on its board and setting policy. Macro social workers can assist the chief administrative leader as well as the board members to ensure that the CDC has a strong presence in the community.

CDC/Community Organizing

Community development in partnership with community organizing helps people collectively make real gains on issues they have identified; and it builds power for the participants. CDCs who engage in community organizing empower their members to challenge government decisions, particularly when those decisions favor large corporations or when governmental agencies give preferential treatment to companies with whom they sometimes collude.

CDC/community organizing partnerships provide citizens not only with economic but political leverage. Members learn to use that leverage to demand recognition, fair treatment, and an end to unchallenged exploitation by those who have had a free hand in milking the public cow. Building an economic power base helps members develop respect and credibility from the business community, and a political power base helps citizens gain attention in the offices of government.

WHAT IS A COMMUNITY DEVELOPMENT CORPORATION?

A community development corporation (CDC) "is a locally based, community-oriented nonprofit social organization, governed by a community based board that serves a low income community and develops commercial/industrial, business enterprise or housing projects in cooperation with private and government sponsorship for the benefit of the community."[11] In addition, some CDCs coordinate local government planning initiatives, provide a source of government subsidized capital for small businesses and cooperatives at the local level, or function as mediating structures between government and community networks. Their purpose is to reconstruct the physical, economic, and social environment in their targeted area or neighborhood.[12]

Community development corporations are dependent on citizen participation, are community based, and operate as alternatives to private businesses. They vary in both size and scope and provide a variety of programs and activities. Their funding comes from multiple sources. Today, nearly 4,000 CDCs have organized into statewide, regional, and national associations in the United States and Canada.

Citizen Participation

Citizens attend CDC neighborhood meetings, play leadership roles in project planning committees, and volunteer for hands-on CDC projects. Resident participation provides the CDC with social and political legitimacy, but it also increases residents' willingness to commit to a project. A recent General Accounting Office evaluation of several community initiatives concluded that "significant community development takes place only when residents are committed to investing themselves and their resources in the effort."[13] Dudley Street Neighborhood Initiative (DSNI), for example, has been able to unify an extremely diverse target area through the use of an inclusive participatory process designed to give all members of the community a share in decision making. And, because of the initiative's strong community support, DSNI has gained the respect and support of the Boston city government as well as numerous funders and partners.[14]

Community Based

Just as important as CDC economic projects themselves is their community-based focus, the process of neighbors getting together, making decisions, seeing a project through to the finish, and then using their finished products. The CDC builds a sense of community control and enhances individual and collective empowerment. CDCs provide community-based leadership in economic development of their communities and tailor projects and programs to the community's specific needs and situation. Their boards of directors are representative of the communities they serve, with community residents and stakeholders serving as members.[15] A well-established CDC knows community needs and can access charitable and private dollars, develop numerous interlocking successful projects, and serve as a financial stimulus for the community. It can become a means by which the community plans and develops its own economic future.

Alternatives to Private Business

CDCs serve as vital alternatives to privately owned for-profit businesses. Rather than leave the local economy dependent on outsiders, CDCs work to increase the economic power of the community and strengthen its leveraging ability. The profit accruing from various CDC ventures is kept in the community and can be used for running the CDC and stimulating other businesses and to provide additional social services.[16]

Size and Scope

In virtually every major American city with a substantial African American population, Black churches have undertaken community improvement efforts. In some cities, the African American church-associated CDC is the preeminent means by which Black residents have reformed the conditions in their neighborhoods. Nowhere is this truer than in New York City, where nine African American church-associated CDCs toil to make areas of Black settlement decent and stable.

Although the population and size of the target areas vary, most CDCs target relatively small, manageable, geographically defined inner-city neighborhoods and low-income rural neighborhoods. CDCs vary from small agencies often sponsored by one faith-based organization serving one neighborhood to organizations sponsored by coalitions of faith-based organizations that develop and administer services and represent communities to public and private institutions of power. Those that can do these things well have acquired fame beyond the limits of their cities. National political and financial elites celebrate them as among the country's best community development organizations including, for example, the Los Angeles Renaissance Development Corporation, an affiliate of the First African Methodist Episcopal Church, and Detroit's REACH, Inc., an affiliate of the Twelfth Street Missionary Baptist Church.[17]

Most CDCs, however, depend on meager resources, sparse staff, small annual budgets, have modest reputations, and receive little publicity. But all are formed by residents, small business owners, congregations, and other local stakeholders whose mission is to revitalize low- or moderate-income communities and to provide economic development for low-income residents in their neighborhoods.[18]

Programs

In spite of their relatively small size, CDCs generally have extensive records of accomplishment. They engage in housing construction and development, financial services, job creation, and commercial development services. They provide a range of social service programs, and some engage in community organizing as well.

Housing Construction and Development   CDCs
produce affordable housing. Some CDCs build and rehabilitate owner-occupied housing; others develop and manage renter-occupied housing. CDCs operate as investors, sponsors, developers, property managers, and service providers. They assist in raising funds for development and secure support for housing projects among residents. They help select sites, engage in construction, market the housing, and bear the responsibility for property and building maintenance. They provide services to the tenants of the new housing following completion of the housing project. In New York City, CDCs in primarily African American

neighborhoods, for example, have developed approximately 5,000 units of affordable housing including low- and moderate-income rental housing and moderate- and middle-income owner-occupied units. Since 1960 CDCs have produced about half a million units nationwide.

Financial and Other Services   Other CDCs
develop and own commercial property and lease the space for profit. Some offer economic development services through small or micro loans to small businesses in low-income areas and provide revolving loan funds. Others establish financial institutions such as savings and loans to ensure a supply of funding to homeowners and local businesspeople. Some create jobs for community residents and promote private investment. A few of the younger ones seem more creative in the types of services they deliver. For example, the Bridge Street Development Corporation, which operates a free neighborhood computer lab, is the only African American church-associated CDC among the nine in New York City to have computer literacy as a primary program area.

Social Programs   Once members establish their
primary program, many engage in a number of other projects. They may add subsidiaries intended to make a profit or engage in community organizing. Those that have accumulated surplus capital, such as the Harlem Congregations for Community Improvement and the Abyssinian Development Corporation, provide local community residents with shelter, jobs, counseling, day care, and groceries. These CDCs may also provide adult education, job training, and mentoring programs, deliver social and neighborhood services, promote public safety, sponsor community picnics and rallies, and strengthen local schools and health clinics.[19]

Community Organizing   Marilyn Gittell, Jill
Gross, and Kathe Newman reported in 1994 that half of the 347 CDCs they surveyed in eight states identify community organizing as one of their activities.[20] By 1999 the National Congress for Community Economic Development (NCCED), the national trade association for CDCs, reported that two thirds of CDCs responding to its national survey are involved in community organizing including resident council organizing, organizing to obtain resources, issue organizing,

political organizing, organizing community events that support development projects, and several kinds of partnership organizing.

Resident Council Organizing   Allston-Brighton CDC, Codman Square NDC, Fenway CDC, Urban Edge, and many other Massachusetts CDCs organize residents of CDC-developed buildings into resident councils. Resident councils exist in low-income housing projects with very different types of ownership arrangements, including rental housing owned by the CDC, cooperatives and condominiums owned by the residents, and mutual housing and other hybrid forms owned jointly by the CDC and the residents or a residents association. Although the degree of residents' ownership, control, and power differ, in all cases resident councils involve residents in the management of the housing project development.

Resource Organizing   Some CDCs mobilize residents to pressure public or private entities to turn over land, buildings, or money necessary for development. The Fenway CDC, for example, organized residents to convince the quasi-governmental Resolution Trust Corporation to turn over units they owned in distressed condominium buildings, which the CDC then redeveloped and converted into affordable rental housing. The Coalition for a Better Acre turned out 100 residents in a rally and convinced the City of Lowell to make federal HOME funds available for a project to convert four abandoned buildings into affordable rental housing.

Issue Organizing   Some CDCs organize around crime and police behavior, tenants rights (including landlord/tenant issues, rent control, and just cause eviction legislation), city or town services, youth issues, open space and environmental justice issues, community gardens, welfare reform, immigrant rights, jobs, community control of development, and many other issues. The Fenway CDC organized residents to stop a neighboring university from building a new dorm in a residential neighborhood. Allston-Brighton is currently organizing residents to change the disruptive business practices of a nearby seafood processing plant. NOAH has organized residents to convert asphalt school lots into green play space and to clean up polluted Chelsea Creek.

Political Organizing   Coalition for a Better Acre sponsored the first ever televised debate between Lowell city council candidates, which was a major factor contributing to the defeat of many incumbents in 1993. Codman Square CDC began a systematic voter registration and education campaign with the help of a statewide group called Voter Power. Jamaica Plain NDC, in conjunction with two other local groups, sponsored a debate among state senate candidates. In 1990 many Massachusetts CDCs worked to help defeat a statewide ballot initiative that would have drastically cut state taxes and services. In 1994 some Boston CDCs organized residents against a ballot initiative to end rent control.

Organizing Community Events and Support for Development   Many CDCs organize community events, annual meetings, ethnic or multicultural festivals, neighborhood cleanups, barbecues, picnics, and street fairs to build community ties. Sometimes CDCs use community events to teach members how to plan and run the event and develop relationships and leadership skills as part of a campaign to build power.[21] Other CDCs organize support for CDC development projects that are in danger, organize local newsletters, or plan a voter registration day.

Partnership Organizing   Sometimes CDCs increase their effectiveness by partnering with existing community organizations, called multilocal organizing. Others may develop organizing efforts on a number of fronts, called front-group organizing.

Multilocal organizing: A multilocal community organizing group is one that partners local CDCs with community organizations to accomplish mutual objectives. The Sacramento Valley Organizing Community (SVOC), for example, is a multilocal organization of nearly 30 predominantly Latino Catholic and African American Protestant faith-based CDCs in a three-county area in Northern California. The SVOC brought 1,800 members to a meeting with area health system officials, successfully demanding 200 jobs. SVOC then partnered with the Private Industry Council (PIC), the county welfare department, and a community college to do job training.

Perhaps the best-known multilocal organization, however, is the NorthWest Bronx Community and Clergy Coalition. Over its 25-year history, NWBCCC has organized 10 neighborhoods, 20 local religious communities in the Northwest Bronx area of New York City, and has developed a number of CDCs. Because of the numbers of affiliate groups, different subcoalitions can relate together and work on issues they have in common.

Front-group organizing: A CDC or community organization may develop several separate small organizations on a number of fronts to simultaneously handle different aspects of a community problem in a synchronized effort. The Cedar-Riverside neighborhood in Minneapolis, for example, was threatened with total destruction from a developer-state coalition that wanted to replace their homes with high-rise buildings. Neighborhood members waged a sophisticated battle, creating a Project Area Committee that had official government status, a CDC to develop alternative redevelopment plans, and a tenants union to challenge developer ownership because the developer had purchased all their existing housing. The community organization created an environmental defense fund to raise money for legal battles and established a cafe they used as a meeting place.

These individual organizational components were all active in the struggle at the same time, and each took on a different piece of the problem. Because not enough people were available to separately staff all the organizations, everybody got involved in everything. In a sophisticated, coordinated community effort, they eventually drove the developer from their neighborhood, took over all their housing, and turned the neighborhood housing into community-owned cooperatives.[22]

Funding

CDC funding varies depending on the location, size, and the resources available, but all are nonprofit organizations. Most CDCs put together projects with diversified financial help from government, businesses, foundations, and development intermediaries. They often receive assistance from multiple sources, and they have become astute in fiscal management so that their funding is used for maximal efficiency.

Government Funding   Government money is not the prime source of funding for many CDCs, but it is elemental to their work. CDCs utilize funding from the city, state, and federal governments.

City and State Funds   "City and state funds," comments the director of a Queens-based African American church-associated CDC, "go hand in hand in terms of our programs and projects." In New York, for example, one CDC uses New York State funds for administrative expenses through the state's Neighborhood

Preservation Development Companies program. The CDC also taps New York City for funding. Much of its funding is in contracts and fees for service, particularly with the City Department of Housing Preservation and Development, Human Resources Administration, and other city agencies.

Federal Funding   CDCs participate in federal programs including the U.S. Federal Housing Administration's Section 203(k) Rehabilitation Mortgage Insurance program and the U.S. Department of Housing and Urban Development's Section 202 Elderly Housing program. Two government programs most useful to CDCs are HOME Investment Partnership (HOME) and Community Development Block Grants (CDBG) administered by HUD.

Corporations, Foundations, and Development Intermediaries   Some CDCs develop cooperative relationships with private sector businesses including banks, real estate, insurance, and contractors. Many CDCs receive funding from national foundations such as the Ford Foundation. Increasingly, however, important sources of funding are development intermediaries such as the Local Initiatives Support Corporation (LISC) and the Federal Low-Income Housing Tax Credit program (LIHTC). The LIHTC is introducing new, and sometimes very large, sums of private, corporate dollars into low-income neighborhoods and CDCs.

Astute Fiscal Management   A mix of private and public funding gives CDCs the financial resources needed in their efforts to, in the words of Robert Clemetson and Roger Coates, "restore broken places and rebuild communities."[23] CDCs are becoming increasingly astute about managing those various funds so that their funding has multiple reinforcement, projects feed into one another, and operate in the wider marketplace as well.

Multiple Reinforcement   Many CDCs operate so that funding they receive multiplies and reinforces itself in their communities. If the CDC engages in housing, for example, it may set up its own construction company to do the work and establish a management company to administer the property. It may also act as a broker to help local businesses obtain inexpensive rentals and may even operate a revolving loan fund to assist local businesses, including its own, to establish new spin-off companies, and it may establish other community controlled financial institutions. A CDC may also move into real estate and develop shopping centers or industrial parks and use federal or foundation grants to provide job training for minority youth in the projects it runs. It might even set up its own community foundation to serve as a source of funds for community social service projects.[24]

Feed Into One Another The CDC's various subsidiaries feed into one other so that the whole becomes more than the sum of its parts. If a grant is obtained to rehabilitate housing, for example, by setting up a construction company the CDC can ensure that local people are employed and more money circulates in the neighborhood. This assists in the profitability of the new shopping center that the CDC is also trying to establish. The shopping center encourages the growth of minority businesses by renting space and creating jobs. Job training programs ensure a supply of capable and committed local employees in its various projects.[25]

Operate in the Wider Marketplace The subsidiaries of multipurpose CDCs are sometimes encouraged to operate in the wider marketplace. For example, a construction or management company can obtain contracts from organizations other than its parent body, thus contributing again to the profitability of the main CDC and reversing the normal money flow out of the deprived area.[26] Because of its diversified economic base and government support, financial institutions may be more willing to provide a wide range of loan products and guarantees to the CDC that make the market work for people who are poor in ways that have never been done before.[27]

STATEWIDE, REGIONAL, NATIONAL, AND INTERNATIONAL ORGANIZATIONS

When CDCs were first being developed in the late 1960s and early 1970s, each was an independent organization that had little experience or history to guide it. There were no infrastructures, support organizations, regional, statewide, or national associations to look to for guidance. Today that has changed. In the United States and Canada, CDCs comprise a strong network of provincial, statewide, regional, and national organizations that provide funding, technical assistance, information, support, training, and linkages to foundations, businesses, and government. In addition, CDCs have begun to spread beyond North America. Today "CDCs have a significant developmental role to play in the industrialized world and probably in the third world, a role which governments seem to have great difficulty playing directly."[28]

Statewide Organizations

Many statewide and provincewide organizations exist in the United States and Canada. Founded in 1992, the Association of Oregon Community Development Organizations (AOCDO) is a statewide association that promotes quality programming, healthy organizations, and advocates public policy for CDCs in Oregon. AOCDO coordinates training projects, centralizes information about training, and provides advocacy at the local, state, and federal level. In addition, the AOCDO coordinates the Rural Forum, a loose association of nonprofit groups that focus on rural community development issues and provide technical assistance on projects to members through its Technical Assistance Response Team.

On the opposite side of the country, the statewide South Carolina Association of CDCs (SCACDC) provides technical assistance and training to local community development practitioners through their Community Economic Development Studies Series. SCACDC provides yearly grassroots leadership training to develop skills in raising, packaging, and promoting community issues to be addressed by policy makers. The retreat also seeks to enhance the leadership skills of community economic development practitioners and community leaders. Another statewide organization, the Texas Association of Community Development Corporations (TACDC), founded in 1995 by a group of CDC executive directors, bank officers, community development officers, and leaders from public housing authorities, develops support programs and services for local CDCs by means of TACDC's board, roundtable, and staff.

Regional Organizations

In Canada CDCs are called Community Futures Development Corporations (CFDCs). Western Economic Diversification Canada (WD) was established in 1987, offering more than 100 points of service across the West, partnerships with public and private sectors, other levels of government, academic, and financial institutions, and research centers.

National Organizations

Many national support organizations assist the CDC movement today that were not on the scene even 10 years ago. Among these are the National Neighborhood Coalition, National Community Development Association (NCDA), National Congress for Community Economic Development (NCEED), National Community Development Initiative (NCDI), and the National Community Building Network (NCBN), about which you will read later.

International Organizations

Since 1991 international CDCs have been receiving assistance from the Institute for Sustainable Communities (ISC), helping communities in existing and emerging democracies by providing training, technical assistance, and grants to solve their own problems and shape their own destiny. As of 2004 the ISC had engaged in 52 international projects in 15 countries with support provided from individual donors, private and corporate foundations, and the U.S. Government. ISC community development projects are managed jointly with national nongovernmental organizations (NGOs), which take the lessons they learn to other international communities.

A BRIEF HISTORY OF COMMUNITY DEVELOPMENT

Three strands of community development provide an interwoven texture of CDC history. The first and most important strand is that of international community development, beginning with the efforts of missionaries in Africa, India, and Asia colonies. Today, international community development is a major, and increasingly important, means by which citizens in mainly rural communities worldwide are improving their lives economically, socially, and politically. You will read about international community development in Chapter 15.

A second strand of community development was the emergence of utopian communities in Britain and

the United States in the 18th and 19th centuries. The third strand is modern community development as a mode of social work engagement in rural and urban communities in Canada and the United States.

Utopian Community Development

In the 19th century in the United States, both religious and secular groups, whose intentions were to create sustainable communal living arrangements based on alternative values, economics, and lifestyles, conducted a variety of utopian communities experiments.

Religious Communities Among alternative utopian communities were those of the Anabaptists, a religious group of primarily German descent who had formed their own religious ideas during the Protestant Reformation and "re-baptized" (anabaptism) its members into that tradition. Named after the founder of this movement, Menno Simon, the Mennonites were severely persecuted during the 17th through the 19th centuries, and many fled to Russia, the United States, Canada, and Brazil where they formed insular communities to maintain their religious traditions. Mennonites no longer live in exclusive communities, but others, particularly the Hutterites and the Amish, continue to maintain their way of life in the 21st century. Other religious communities also developed utopian communities to practice their religion including the Shakers and the Quakers in the 18th and 19th centuries. Among the religious beliefs of all of these groups was a strong commitment to pacifism, communal sharing, and a simple, nonacquisitive lifestyle.

Secular Communities The 19th century in England and the United States was a time of alternative models of economic and communal experimentation. Social reformers became concerned with the problem of poverty in the slums. In his book *Progress and Poverty,* published in 1879, Henry George (1839–1897) criticized landlords for appropriating the "socially created value of land . . . [which] properly belonged to the community as a whole." George asserted that "land values were *created by the growth and needs of the community rather than by efforts of the owner"* (emphasis in the original) and described the consequences of private profit from land sales.[29] Utopian communitarians like George stimulated the development of utopian communities including the Oneida colony, Brooks Farm, and others in the United States.

Over a century later, during the turbulent era of the 1960s, an increased interest in forming cooperative associations called "communes" developed out of the so-called human potential movement, and a wide variety of alternative self-help groups emerged based on a renewed sense of community. Most of these experiments in communal living were very short lived, however.

Modern Community Development in North America

There are two main periods of community development in North America: the period of convergence from 1890 to 1960, and the era of community development corporations from 1960 to the present.

Convergence: 1890–1960   The specific method of developing communities socially and economically was the result of a convergence of a number of experiments and influences, beginning at the turn of the 20th century with the Charity Organization Societies and continuing until about 1960 with the efforts of the Cooperative Extension Services, universities, and the federal government. Each group took a slightly different approach and added to our fund of understanding.

Charity Organization Societies (COS)   Charity Organization Societies emphasized public participation and a social planning perspective and encouraged development and coordination of community-based programs and projects. The early work of the Community Chest movement, the United Community Services, and the United Fund was supported by the COS. These agencies provided a means by which many local social services, including social settlements, community and neighborhood centers, group work agencies, and family service agencies, could add to the resources and social capital of the communities in which they were located.

Cooperative Extension Services   In 1908 rural community development in the United States was initiated as a result of President Theodore Roosevelt's Country Life Commission, which encouraged the Department of Agriculture (USDA) and land grant colleges to take a more active role in the life of rural Americans.

This top-down approach resulted in the Cooperative Extension Service, begun in 1914.

One of the mechanisms by which the "Cooperative Extension Service assisted rural communities was a series of local clubs that joined with extension agents in developing and working out local programs [of community development] work."[30] Originating in the South in the 1920s, community clubs were widely used in African American communities and were based on the principle of developing projects with people, rather than for people. By 1923 more than 21,000 communities were engaged in cooperative extension community development projects at the grassroots level.[31]

Universities   Educational institutions in both Canada and the United States became involved in supporting, encouraging, and training individuals in community development work. In Canada, for example, community organizing and community economic development (CED) became a practical alternative for strengthening communities socially as well as economically as part of the cooperative movement of the early 20th century, preceding the emergence of that nation's welfare state. The Canadian cooperative movement involved groups of people, often farmers, who joined together to share resources and information and who pooled their produce to reduce costs, avoid needless competition, and cut out middlemen. One of these efforts was the Antigonish Cooperative Movement in Nova Scotia, assisted by St. Francis Xavier University. Xavier University has provided distinguished training programs in community development since about 1930. Its cooperative community development programs work within an adult education framework through group discussions aimed at identifying the causes of economic problems, empowering people, and encouraging them to organize for change.

In the United States, one of the most influential educational programs in community development was the National University Extension Association, which began in 1915 and extended through the 1960s. William Biddle, one of the field's most prolific writers, began a community development program at Earlham College in 1947. Since then, universities have continued to provide impetus for community development. Today, for example, the Center for International Education at the University of Massachusetts provides training and educational materials in international community development.[32]

Federal Government   During the Great Depression, the federal government expanded community development efforts by means of several national initiatives. One of these was the Works Progress Administration (WPA), administered by social worker Harry Hopkins, whose goal was to give unemployed people jobs working on projects of community improvement and betterment. In addition, Hopkins pioneered the development of the Civilian Conservation Corps (CCC), through which "young men whose families were on relief" were employed in improving parks and community beautification projects.[33] One of the most famous community development projects of all time was the Tennessee Valley Authority (TVA).

Community Development Corporations: 1960 to the Present

Community development corporations have their immediate origins in the turmoil of the 1960s. Since the first phase of CDCs, they have moved through a second wave in the 1970s, a third wave in the 1980s, shown expansion as a fourth wave in the 1990s, and continue with successes in the decade of 2000.

Origin of CDCs in the 1960s   Modern CDCs sprang up out of the disorder and chaos of the late 1960s, one of the most turbulent periods in U.S. history. Between 1962 and 1965, at least 12 major disorders occurred in large metropolitan centers. In 1965 a racial disorder in Los Angeles was the worst that the country had seen since 1943 when massive World War II riots took place in Detroit.[34] In the first 9 months of 1967, the nation experienced 167 outbreaks of civil disturbance. In that one year, major riots occurred in eight cities, involving damage to property, violence, and death. In Detroit, 43 people were killed; 33 cities experienced serious disturbances; and lesser disorders occurred in 123 more.[35] Twenty-five cities suffered disorders at least twice, and New York City suffered five times. Major riots in Cleveland and Rochester involved loss of life. In the spring of 1968, the evening of the day that Martin Luther King Jr. was assassinated, cities across the nation again erupted in looting and burning.

African American neighborhoods seemed to hit rock bottom. When the looting and burning stopped, however, a growing Black consciousness began to stir. It was, after all, African American citizens of all classes who were suffering most from the riots. The urge to burn was destroying their own neighborhoods. The riots mobilized middle-class and working-class Blacks in a new and different kind of struggle, joining poorer and more alienated people in reassessing the African American agenda. All over the stricken areas, independent neighborhood groups formed to work out the meaning of these events and to light a different beacon.

As neighborhoods in each city puzzled out their local scene, pieces of the answer began to fall into the same pattern. Whatever was wrong went far beyond the acts of those who set the fires, looted, and taunted the police and firefighters—or shot at them. The community itself had not taken enough responsibility to direct its own destiny or to counteract the systemic inattention, degradation, and exploitation by the larger society. The rest of society had forgotten their communities, but it seemed that the residents themselves had forgotten them as well.

President Kennedy paved the way by developing the Area Redevelopment Administration, which carried out community and area projects and required that local committees of concerned citizens and government officials make the overall economic development plans. By the mid-1960s, Rural Area Development Committees were active in more than half the counties in the country. The Kennedy/Johnson administration stimulated more than 1,000 federal programs, many of which provided funding for community programs. Expenditures for housing and community development jumped from $30 million in 1959 to $1.4 billion in 1969—a 466% increase.[36]

First Wave CDCs: 1966 to 1970   In 1966, then Senator Robert F. Kennedy made an historic tour of Bedford-Stuyvesant, stimulating the vision of New York City's Bedford-Stuyvesant activists. The subsequent Special Impact Amendment to the Economic Opportunity Act led to the formation of the nation's first CDC, the Bed-Stuy Restoration Corporation in Brooklyn.[37] The Bed-Stuy project was quickly followed by the Woodlawn Organization (TWO) in Chicago, and in 1968 the Hough area project in Cleveland. In their steps a first wave of about 100 CDCs arrived in the North Avondale neighborhood in Cincinnati; the Hillside Terrace Housing Project in Milwaukee's North Side; the Near Northwest Side of Chicago; the Mission District of San Francisco; the Lower East Side of New York City, and in Newark, New Jersey; Syracuse, New York; Roxbury, Massachusetts; and Austin, Texas.[38]

Many of these first wave CDCs discovered that the best way to cure the problems in low-income neighborhoods was to generate homegrown business activity in their own neighborhoods. The first natural activity centered around housing, a primary need for poor families,[39] and job creation.[40]

Second-Wave CDCs: Retrenchment and Expansion in the 1970s   In the first half of the 1970s the federal government attempted to restrict community development initiatives. They continued to expand, however.

Retrenchment: In 1973 in an effort to reduce community-based improvement efforts, President Richard Nixon declared a moratorium on funding for urban development programs, and in 1974 President Gerald Ford signed the Housing and Community Development Act, replacing the Johnson administration's model cities, urban renewal, and neighborhood facility grants with a single community development block grant program. "Unlike the Great Society legislation which had forced local officials to share power with neighborhood community organizations, [the act] limited citizen participation to purely an advisory role and was generally seen as a setback for community development efforts."[41]

Expansion: In the second half of the 1970s, CDCs continued to grow. They also developed an infrastructure of support. In spite of a regressive federal administration, community development expanded. Additional neighborhood organizations sprang up in Birmingham, Brooklyn, Oakland, Stockton, San Diego, Cleveland, and Wichita in the 1970s. Many of these second-wave CDCs began in the 1960s as community organizations involved in the Civil Rights movement. In the 1970s they reoriented themselves to the community development field as a new approach to improving their neighborhoods. Between 500 and 1,000 of these second-wave CDCs were formed from community organizations that had originally addressed redlining and displacement-based urban renewal, factory closings, or irresponsible landlords who abused tenant rights,[42] a 10-fold increase. Others, such as Habitat for Humanity or Neighborhood Housing Services, although not bearing the CDC label in their names, also identified themselves as CDCs.[43]

An expanded infrastructure for second-wave CDCs was built as foundations, intermediary organizations, and supportive federal legislation under Jimmy Carter occurred in the latter half of the 1970s. Many CDCs created partnerships with foundations such as the Ford Foundation's Grey Areas Program. National intermediary development organizations began to be created. Neighborhoods U.S.A. (NUSA) began in 1975 and helped develop partnerships among neighborhood residents, elected officials, and professionals by sponsoring conferences on community development issues.[44]

As the idea of community development caught on in the Carter administration, the Housing and Community Development Act was amended to allow for more citizen participation and required citizen involvement in planning, execution, and evaluation stimulating "new community organizations that became agents for citizen participation in the local community."[45] Funding from Title VII of the 1974 Community Services Act, the federal government's Community Services Administration, and the Office of Neighborhood Development provided additional assistance.[46]

Because of President Carter's commitment to community and neighborhood development, federal interest in neighborhood-based programs grew, and Carter subsequently signed into law several pieces of legislation that provided power and leverage for CDCs. The Home Mortgage Disclosure Act of 1975 and the Community Reinvestment Act (CRA) of 1977, both initiated by the community organizing efforts of Gale Cincotta and Shel Trapp of National Peoples Action (NPA), required banks to disclose how much money they invested in neighborhoods in which they were located. For example, if a bank obtained $1 million in deposits in a poor neighborhood, but loaned only $50,000 to its people, it laid itself open to pressure to lend more money in that neighborhood. The Neighborhood Reinvestment Corporation (NRC) stimulated the creation of local partnership efforts for comprehensive housing rehabilitation services.[47]

With the support of President Carter, "the tireless efforts of those involved in the neighborhood movement to bring the needs and potentialities of the nation's neighborhoods to the attention of federal policymakers" bore fruit with the passage of the National Neighborhood Policy Act of 1977.[48] The Neighborhood Self-Help Development Act of 1978, in addition, recognized "the neighborhood to be a national resource which . . . deserved to be conserved, revitalized."[49] As a result, by the late 1970s CDCs had become central components of a limited but significant federally assisted neighborhood development movement.

Third-Wave CDCs: The Reagan Years   The conservative Reagan and Bush administrations of the 1980s encouraged a shrinking tax base at the local level.

Economic support for social services and solving social problems declined. Political discourse in the nation revolved around free market solutions to all social problems, and community organizing moved into closer collaboration with CDCs.[50] The Carter administration's Community Services Administration and the Office of Neighborhood Development were dismantled. Other sources of federal funds for local initiatives were dramatically cut back.

In spite of this, however, African American communities and others were determined to support "a non-white middle class by developing highly specific and measurable development projects in which community people could work for their own economic betterment."[51] The bottom line for CDCs was economic success to "correct the market's failure to provide jobs and services to the community."[52] The new, third wave of CDCs that developed in the 1980s expanded to close to 2,000 organizations and continued to climb.[53] CDCs in the 1980s became more businesslike and produced results, but they were forced to avoid conflict.

More businesslike: In the privatization campaigns of the Reagan years, CDCs were forced to become much more businesslike than their predecessors. They were less like community organizations and more like small businesses and investment projects, evaluated by their economic success. They had to exhibit "business talent and development skills once thought to be the exclusive province of the for-profit sector," as one report put it.[54]

Produced results: In late 1988, Renee Berger conducted a study of 834 CDCs and found that CDC projects had produced some 125,000 units of owner-occupied and rental housing and repaired 275,000 additional units. They developed 16.4 million square feet of offices, retail spaces, and industrial parks in poor communities; loaned money to some 2,000 enterprises, mostly for amounts under $25,000; and created or retained nearly 90,000 jobs in the 5 years prior to the study.[55]

Avoided activism: The privatization and market mentality of the 1980s forced most third-wave CDCs to become so oriented to achieving economic success that many were not able to completely sustain their work for community empowerment. Most tended to avoid political controversy, became dominated by professionals with technical orientations, narrowed their membership bases, and rejected social action. CDCs that formed during the conservative years of

the Reagan/Bush administrations did not, however, always give up activist goals by choice. The absence of public support, newly rigid interpretations of IRS restrictions on political activity of nonprofit groups, the necessity of seeking funds from and seeking partnerships with private sector leaders, and the orientation of the CDC approach to economic investment and development decisions combined to push CDCs away from political action, " forcing them to accommodate themselves to rather than redirect the course of the free market."[56]

Fourth-Wave CDCs: The 1990s   The decade of 1990s was important for community development and for CDCs.[57] Interest in community development and volunteerism was renewed during the Clinton administration, stimulated in part by the National Service Corps, in which young people were assigned to a variety of community development projects. In the 1990s a new generation of neighborhood initiatives began emerging within the context of a growing national consensus about the importance of rebuilding communities.[58]

These advances were largely the result of an institutional revolution within most major U.S. cities during the decade of the 1990s. "By the 1990s most people engaged in community development were recognizing that the effective revitalization of deprived areas required CDC/public/private/intermediary partnerships or a 'four-legged stool.' "[59]

CDC/federal program initiatives: Public services for poor communities tend to be fragmented across multiple agencies and levels of government. CDCs are the only institution with a comprehensive and coordinated program agenda that can work creatively with and seek new solutions as the social environment changes across these different levels.[60]

During the 1990s, the U.S. Treasury took advantage of the unique position of CDCs by initiating a program called the Community Development Financial Institutions (CDFI) fund. The fund helps create CDFIs as new nonprofit, community controlled financial organizations. CDFIs provide community loans, banking services, and finance real estate development dedicated to the revitalization of poor neighborhoods. CDFI organizations undertake physical revitalization as well as economic development, social services, and organizing and advocacy activities that spur more investment by banks and other financial institutions in poor neighborhoods. Some existing CDCs used the fund to create their own CDFIs. Other communities used the fund to initiate CDCs created as CDFIs to offer access to capital for housing, small businesses, and other ventures.[61] In addition, the evolution of federal programs such as the Community Development Block Grant (CDBG) and the HOME program enabled many CDCs to become successful at improving their communities through housing by building assets that could remain a part of the community.

The Community Empowerment Program, enacted into law in August 1993, provided a long-term partnership between the federal government and rural communities. The act emphasized partnerships with federal and state agencies, local and tribal governments, private businesses, foundations, and nonprofits by insisting on broad-based citizen participation in planning and implementation. It provided for local self-determination in setting priorities and put the federal government in the role of assisting communities with the priorities they had chosen, maintaining the integrity of the program's local implementation.

Since its inception, the Community Empowerment Program has created 57 rural empowerment zones and enterprise communities, more than 100 champion communities, and 5 rural economic area partnership (REAP) zones. Altogether they have created or saved nearly 20,000 jobs and have raised an aggregate of more than $10 for every dollar granted to them at the time of their designation.

Growth of CDC/private partnerships: Because of the Community Reinvestment and Home Mortgage Disclosure Acts, initiated by the National People's Action in the 1970s, CDCs were increasingly able to attract low-interest loans, loan guarantees, and other financial assistance from private financial institutions in the 1990s. The Community Revitalization Act (CRA) of the 1990s spurred bank investment in poor neighborhoods and in CDCs. Many CDCs, in addition, developed partnership arrangements with local financial institutions to facilitate community reinvestment lending in deprived communities, and some involved government support in the form of loan guarantees, insurance, and rebate assistance to lessen the risk.

CDC/intermediary support organization partnerships: The most important development of the 1990s was development of many intermediary support organizations. Before 1991, only a few cities had operating support programs for CDCs, and many were rudimentary, ad hoc, and poorly coordinated. During the 1990s, however, community development support

systems emerged in many cities, and by the decade's end they had become more rational, entrenched, and effective. Governments, financial institutions, and philanthropic organizations came together to create new collaborative bodies to mobilize money. These intermediary organizations attracted resources from local and national sources and channeled them to CDCs as project capital, operating subsidies, and technical assistance grants. In the most advanced community development environments, local intermediary organizations emerged to mobilize funding from local financial institutions and to supply technical expertise to members of the community development industry or for special types of projects. They also linked CDCs with political support and sources of power by helping CDCs connect with civic and political leaders to support their agendas for neighborhood improvement. Among the many intermediary organizations that existed in the 1990s at the national level were the following:

National Neighborhood Coalition: Many national neighborhood organizations joined to share information and engage in joint action on common concerns, especially to lobby for positive federal legislation and shape national governmental policy.

National Community Development Association (NCDA): At the forefront in securing effective and responsive housing and community development programs for local governments since 1968, it is comprised of more than 550 local governments that administer federally supported community and economic development, housing and human service programs. The association provides information and technical support on federal housing and community development programs and serves as a national clearinghouse of ideas for government officials.

National Community Development Initiative (NCDI): Launched in 1991, NCDI has played a key role in the gains CDCs have made in 1990s through its consortium composed of national foundations, corporations, and the U.S. Department of Housing and Urban Development.[62]

National Community Building Network (NCBN): In 1993 CDCs that followed a comprehensive community initiative strategy formed the NCBN, which quickly achieved a voice in national political discussions about effective approaches to urban renewal, particularly in the design of the empowerment zone program.[63]

National Congress for Community Economic Development (NCCED): Along with the Corporation for Enterprise Development, it shares information, develops resources for poor and disadvantaged neighborhoods, and analyzes proposed federal laws and regulations,[64] operates a number of temporary and long-term projects benefiting community economic development and works with state associations. NCCED has stimulated the development of the State Community Economic Development Association, the Community Development Leadership Association (CDLA), and others.

Local Initiatives Support Corporation (LISC) and the Enterprise Foundation: Developed in the 1990s as intermediaries to assist foundations, business corporations, and government take better advantage of opportunities offered by CDCs, the LISC and the Enterprise Foundation through their network of field offices in nearly 60 U.S. cities provide technical assistance to help streamline the process when CDCs apply for funds to governments, foundations, and corporations. LISC and Enterprise networks helped CDCs obtain $250 million of working capital in the 1990s and can take major credit for the creation and growth of many new local collaborative efforts.[65]

As a result of these various partnerships, CDCs have improved their resource utilization, increased their productivity, developed greater self-sufficiency, and experienced impressive expansion and diversification.

Improved resource utilization: The affordable housing industry became more adept at using the Low-Income Housing Tax Credit (LIHTC). Private capital became easier to secure for affordable housing, federal housing resources grew, as did some local funds. National intermediaries supplied large amounts of hard-to-get development funding to CDC projects, which went partway toward helping CDCs move into new types of community development activities, most notably the development of for-sale housing, commercial centers, and community facilities.[66]

Increased productivity: CDCs substantially boosted their productive capabilities in the 1990s.

In 1993 two thirds of U.S. community development corporations had completed at least one concrete development project and had created roughly 100,000 jobs. By 1998 urban CDCs had built or renovated 435,000 units of housing, both rental and owner-occupied; developed approximately 48 million square feet of commercial and industrial space; and created 113,000 jobs. Local community development practitioners in most cities were able to identify at least one neighborhood where residential property values were rising and CDCs were most likely responsible; and in two thirds of cities, this has happened in more than one neighborhood.

Developed greater self-sufficiency: By the end of the decade, more CDCs found themselves seeking to develop business initiatives that could help them become self-sufficient, which would also serve their constituents through asset-building, job development, and other forms of revitalization rather than strictly through old-school social services alone.[67] Some CDCs were in position to take full advantage of new national sources of support for housing and commercial development.

CDC expansion and diversification: CDCs as an industry, asserts Christopher Walker of the Urban Institute, made strong gains in their numbers, size, outputs, and contributions to neighborhood revitalization throughout the 1990s. In 1993, for example, well over 3,000 CDCs existed in the United States. Five years later, according to a national census of CDCs conducted by the National Congress of Community Economic Development (NCCED), their numbers grew to 3,600 CDCs, with more in Canada. In 1999, 1,870 CDCs were located in cities and about 1,730 were located in rural areas.[68] Total value of CDC projects receiving support from intermediaries doubled between 1991 and 2000, and the overall size of CDC industries grew as well.[69]

Whereas in the 1980s organizations tended to focus on single issues such as housing or economic development, efforts in the 1990s diversified and often took a multifaceted approach. CDCs continued to create low-income housing, but they increasingly included middle-income apartments, single-family subdivisions, and homeless shelters. They also engaged in developing credit unions, retail companies, and shopping centers in major urban centers such as New York, Detroit, and Kansas City. They began to develop commercial real estate to bring retailers back into the neighborhoods, along with services that were difficult to find nearby, such as insurance agents, doctors, supermarkets, and others. Some even started loan funds to offer small businesses loans in the neighborhood when bank financing was not available.

CDCs diversified their range of community development activities, with increasing interest in adopting or expanding commercial development, workforce and youth development, and community facilities programs. This diversification took place across a variety of cities in all regions of the country.[70]

New Directions: 2000 and Beyond   In the decade of 2000, CDCs have received major attention from government and private funders as a promising way to improve urban neighborhoods and the lives of those who live in them. The network of intermediary coalitions supporting CDCs continued to expand. CDCs have showed increased leadership capacity, and a community development professional association has been established. Some CDCs developed comprehensive community initiatives, and others focused on sustainable community development.

Expansion of intermediary coalitions: As of 2000, asserts the Urban Institute, the number of statewide, nationwide, and provincewide intermediary community and economic development coalitions and associations of community development organizations has expanded. CDCs are represented in at least 31 states, including Arizona, Mississippi, Arkansas, Missouri, California, Florida, New York, North and South Carolina, Louisiana, Tennessee, Delaware, Wisconsin, Minnesota, Michigan, and Texas. By 2001, 21 cities had comprehensive support.

In addition, the new collaborative and capacity-building intermediaries provided multiyear grants, allowing CDCs to establish larger and longer term programs while simultaneously holding CDCs to stronger performance standards. In 2001, for example, the National Community Development Initiative (NCDI) committed themselves to an additional 10 years of investment. Since that time, the NCDI has expanded its activities and incorporated as a nonprofit with a new name: Living Cities: The National Community Development Initiative.

Increased leadership capacity: In the first half of the decade of 2000, because of their increased visibility and success, CDCs rose on the political agenda in many cities. Leaders across multiple sectors flowed into community development, primarily because of the new collaborations forged in the 1990s.

The first professional association of CDCs: The Community Development Society (CDS), the first national professional association of community developers and citizens, appeared. The CDS serves as an advocate for healthy communities and their importance to society. CDS members represent a variety of fields: education, health care, social services, government, utilities, economic development practitioners, citizen groups, and others. CDS integrates knowledge from many disciplines with theory, research, teaching, and practice and works actively to enhance the leadership capacity of community members, leaders, and groups within the community.

Comprehensive community initiatives (CCIs): The idea of comprehensiveness guides the direction of a new form of community development corporation called comprehensive community initiatives (CCIs). These new initiatives encourage all community stakeholders to work together collaboratively rather than in a confrontive mode and stress citizen participation in all aspects of their activities. CCIs view the problems of urban neighborhoods as interconnected and approach them in a holistic way. Unlike piecemeal approaches, CCIs address issues such as poverty, inequality, disinvestment, and unemployment as a web of interrelated problems. CCIs address these problems on multiple levels with individuals and families, and at the neighborhood and city levels as well.[71]

Sustainable community development: In the second half of 2000, many CDCs and other community groups worked to find creative, sustainable solutions to the problems facing low-income communities. Sustainable community development focuses on the whole community instead of just disadvantaged neighborhoods. It depends on the existence of a social infrastructure that provides for the basic needs of shelter, jobs/income, health, education and social support and seeks improved public health and a better quality of life for all its residents by limiting waste, preventing pollution, maximizing conservation and promoting efficiency, and developing local resources to revitalize the local economy. Sustainable community development supports a vision that includes healthy ecosystems, using resources efficiently, a pervasive volunteer spirit, and enhancing the local economy.

Supported by two national groups, the Institute for Sustainable Communities (ISC) and the International Council for Local Environmental Initiatives, sustainable community development builds partnerships between and among all of the key sectors of society, including government, the business sector, nonprofit organizations, disadvantaged groups, environmentalists, civic associations, and religious organizations. Public debate in these communities is engaging, inclusive, and constructive and enables people to share their difficulties, hopes, and challenges, face issues and seek solutions together, and build on commonalties while respecting each other's differences.[72]

HOW TO BUILD A COMMUNITY DEVELOPMENT CORPORATION

Community development corporations are among the most important community structures in Canada and the United States today. Effective community development happens through a series of deliberate steps. A macro social worker must identify with the community and its people, and the people must be willing and motivated.

Use focused interviews and focus groups to develop an action group. Help group members use a resources and assets approach, develop a resources and assets inventory, and develop the action group into a CDC. The members of the new CDC decide on a set of actions, develop a project, and establish relationships with corporations and government. You then end your involvement in the process or move into other roles such as developing social programs and services, community organizing, or helping the CDC expand its ventures.

Community Identification

When you affiliate with a community, make sure you can identify with the culture and ethnicity of its members as closely as possible. Without such identification, a community developer may find it difficult to directly engage a community in all of its history, values, symbols, language, culture, and traditions. Si Kahn says that "experiencing racism, economic deprivation and social injustice are the key relevant politicizing forces in most urban areas."[73] Rivera and Erlich have devised a three-tiered model based on contact intensity and influence that can help determine an appropriate role for community developers in ethnically diverse communities.

Primary Level   At the primary level, you must engage the community members directly, immediately, and personally. "[T]he only way of gaining entry into the community is to have full ethnic solidarity with the community . . . requiring racial, cultural, and linguistic identity with its members." Working at the primary level, for example would "not be possible for a Chinese American in a Vietnamese or African-American area."[74]

Secondary Level   At the secondary level of involvement, you function as "liaison with the outside community and institutions and serve as a resource with technical expertise based on the culturally-unique situations experienced by the community." Here, knowledge of the language, although helpful, is not absolutely mandatory such as "a Puerto Rican social worker in a Mexican-American neighborhood, for example, or a person identified as Haitian in an African American area."[75]

Tertiary Level   The tertiary level of intensity of engagement includes a nonethnically similar "outsider working for common interests and concerns of the community by using technical skills, political connections, understanding of the outside environment as advocates and brokers on behalf of the community where cultural or racial similarity is not a requirement."[76]

Willingness and Motivation

People have to be willing to come together and agree on their community's challenges, and they must be able to collaboratively decide how to solve the problems. Community members must have the optimism, determination, and ability to break up the vicious circle of impoverishment in a community.[77]

Focused Interviews and Focus Groups

Focused Interviews   When you talk to people, use semistructured focused interviews, described in Chapter 6, that center on selected topics but in which specific items are not entirely predetermined. Once you have examined the community, you are ready to gather a number of community people together in focus groups to help you identify the opportunities members can activate to improve their community.

Focus Groups   Focus groups help you confirm or elicit new information, begin generating ideas for change and, most important, engage people in forming a community development task force committed to developing a community development corporation. Focus groups help community members begin to see the power that information can give them. They will have more trust in the outcome of their effort if they have a hand in framing the issues and opportunities. Organize a series of home meetings and engage members in discussing issues that are important to them.

Organize Home Meetings   Ask one of the persons you have met to sponsor the meeting in his or her home. Generally meet with people who are homogenous in background. For example, hold a focus group for people you have interviewed from the business community. Hold others for members of local neighborhoods. One focus group could be composed of church leaders, social workers, and other community professionals.

Discuss Issues Important to Members   This can be your first opportunity to begin organizing. When people get together to talk about the issues they feel are important, they often begin to realize they are not alone. This helps take away the stigma that social problems such as unemployment or poverty bring. They begin to realize that social or economic forces beyond their control have created the conditions that cause suffering. When people share their experiences as well as their assets and resources, they begin to generate hope. You empower them to begin thinking of ways that they can change things for the better. They gain skills in problem solving and planning, reducing their reliance on technical experts.

Make sure everyone understands that the goal of the meeting is to develop a community development corporation and that all are invited to participate. Begin by introducing people to one another. As a springboard for discussion, present the findings of your focused interviews, the comments people have made, and center on issues that are of crucial importance to the group. Give everyone a chance to speak. After the discussion, engage people for the next step, such as joining the community development action group, serving on a subgroup, or helping out in some other way. Remind the group when and where the next steps will occur.

Develop an Action Group

Successful neighborhood initiatives require the involvement of all community stakeholders. Rebecca Stone says that "community building is rooted in the belief that strategies . . . must be designed around the specific assets, needs, institutional relationships and existing power structures of the target communities."[78] If some important members of the community were not included in the focus groups, recruit them now for your action group.

Use a Resources and Assets Approach

The task of a CDC action group is to select actions that offer the best prospect of reaching the specific goals of the community in general and the community development group in particular. One way to do this is by means of a resources- and assets-based approach, also known as the strengths approach. This approach is capacity based and emphasizes that communities contain a multitude of resources or have the ability to acquire them.

A resources- and asset-based approach recognizes that even the most impoverished communities can manage themselves by making use of the wealth of resources available to them. The asset-based approach is proactive. It envisions a community as its members want it to be and works to bring about the best social environment that enhances and enriches the lives of all of its members. Community residents and their allies seek and find the best points of leverage within the community for effective action. The resources and asset-based approach utilizes various kinds of community capital and capacity building tools.

Community Capital   All communities have physical, financial, human, and social capital.

Physical Capital   Every community has physical capital including buildings, land, forests, and waterways. A rural locality may, for example, have significant mineral, land, or forest resources. An inner city may have vacant lots, abandoned buildings, and unused office space.

Financial Capital   A community also has access to wealth, sometimes including a budget surplus of money or a tax base, as well as access to and a means of acquiring capital through connections with intermediaries, foundations, and those at the state and federal levels.

Human Capital   Every community has human capital including people with various talents, initiative, and leadership. Communities often include members with skills in carpentry, masonry, electronics, and computer technology or people who are willing to learn those skills. A rural area may have a surplus of people to mine, cultivate, harvest, or manufacture. Many communities include professionals, managers, some who have high levels of education, some who are in positions of power or possess wealth, and those who have connections with people of influence. Where communities lack people with special skills, those resources can be developed through training and education and by providing opportunities for enhancement.

Social Capital   Many communities are rich in social capital including goodwill, citizenship, public spirit, and a willingness to cooperate together for the good of the community. People often have abundant commitment, indigenous leadership, desire to improve the community, and a sense of shared responsibility and meaning. Members of communities display loyalty, honor, trustworthiness, responsibility, honesty, and a host of values. Communities can enhance their fund of social capital by providing character building activities and opportunities for people to work together on common projects, which not only implement the public good but also empower people as they achieve their goals.

Capacity Building Tools   While the various types of capital are important, communities also need psychological, social, and cultural capacity building tools to put together various kinds of capital that make things happen. Without those intermediary capacities, resources will be unused. Ernesto Cortes explains:

> [F]or community development to be successful, differing types of capital must be mixed with each other to be productive. The items of "physical capital" such as machines alone are not enough, but require workers with "human capital" skills to operate them. Teams of workers need not only tools and skills but the trusting relationships of "social capital" to work together. They all need "financial capital" to facilitate the exchanges and investments central to economic life.[79]

Even if it is not immediately apparent, community residents already either have the capacity building tools they need or have the ability to acquire them. They have members skilled in connecting people and resources or resources and projects, for example. Communities are composed of citizens who can teach, advise, provide consultation, train, and provide support. In addition, most communities already have intermediary groups, networks, and relationships of people that add to the strength of the community effort and many have infrastructures of support systems for its members.

As a macro social worker, you also have such tools and capacities to assist communities. You stimulate, inspire, and assist your action group to put resources together to develop a plan. You help community members utilize social tools that already exist or are under local control or stimulate members to develop those that the community must have to make use of its physical, human, and social capital.

Develop a Resources and Assets Inventory

Perry says that a resources and assets inventory is a local review of factors of production: land (and all the natural resources), labor (people and categories of skills), capital (including dollars and results of previous investments such as buildings, highways, manufacturing), and managerial and entrepreneurial resources.[80] In addition, social capital needs to be included. To have a grasp of all this information about a local area is to have a powerhouse ready to be put to use in making decisions about local development. The act of jointly inventorying assets is itself a powerful community organizing device that motivates people's collaboration and commitment to action by disclosing opportunities for change.[81] Two ways to conduct an inventory are geographically and by kinds of organizations.

Geographically   Divide the community into geographical sections and then, within each section, look at specific categories of resources. For example, if your community is rural, you may want to begin with resources in town, first looking at homes, shops, manufacturers, civic associations, and churches. Then look in the countryside, examining farms, land, homes, forests, and so forth.

Kinds of Organizations   Begin with organizations in your community that are easy to categorize such as businesses, social, religious, and civic organizations. Assume, for example, that you are examining social and civic organizations. Develop a list of all the social and civic organizations in your community or neighborhood, and subdivide them into categories such as libraries, social agencies, schools, churches, civic associations, recreation, community services, parks, and other resources. Rather than inventory physical, human, financial, and social capital separately, examine them concurrently. For example, choose the first organization on your list. Look at physical capital, then proceed to financial, human, and social capital.

Physical Capital   You list land, buildings, physical space, and the price of these structures.

Financial Capital   How much income do these sources generate? How much remains in the community? How much leaves the community? What is the extent of the assets these resources own? What salaries do people earn? For nonprofit organizations, what are their budgets, their source of income, and how much income do they generate? For profit making organizations, what is their gross and net profit?

Human Capital   What kinds of jobs, skills, and capabilities are available in your community?

Social Capital   You may need to develop indicators for such intangible items as trust, honesty, cooperation, and community spirit. What kinds of programs and services do civic and social organizations offer? What is the diversity of these community components? Are the social service networks both public and private? The number and variety of nonprofit social service organizations and agencies will tell you about the civic-mindedness of its citizens. Do churches and social agencies interact and engage one another, or are they insular and disengaged? This will give you an indication about the extent of social networks.

If you are looking at public organizations such as schools, examine how schools are maintained and where they are located. This will tell you about community pride and the importance of education to the community. What is the racial and economic balance in the schools? Do some public schools have rich resources and higher achieving students and others fewer resources and low-achieving students? This will tell you something about how the community views equality and discrimination.

Look for leaders. What are the qualities of leaders in the community, in government, and in business? Are these leaders socially engaged, working to build the community, or do they drain resources out of it?

Your community development action group must take the information about the resources in the community and put together a plan to use those assets in a positive way. Your community group then becomes a catalyst for community engagement.

Develop the Corporation

Once your group decides on a project, they will need to form themselves into a nonprofit corporation to do business. Chapter 10 describes how to develop a nonprofit organization, including developing articles of incorporation, a constitution and by-laws, filing the necessary papers with state and federal governments, selecting a board of directors, staffing, developing a budget, and structuring the corporation. You will develop a business model and identify financial capital.

Adopt a Business Model   Even though your group will incorporate as a not-for-profit organization, Alan Twelvetrees recommends that the group adopt a business model rather than a social services design for the corporation. Undertake a careful feasibility study, and make a good business plan. Hire a skilled executive who can direct the operation, one who can build a cadre of competent middle managers and a strong board familiar with operating a business, and who can oversee the operation, set clear goals, and ensure the financial stability of the project. Twelvetrees says, "Try to make sure that the manager of the business has incentives to ensure that the venture is profitable, as well as having the skill to run it. Lack of managerial expertise is one of the main reasons for business failure."[82]

Obtain Financial Capital   It is not wise to start a business unless there is sufficient capital. A large chunk of that capital needs to be equity rather than a loan, unless it is at a low rate of interest and is to be repaid over a long period. Equity means money or financial resources that you have already acquired. Few businesses make money in the first three years, and loan repayments during that time can be crippling.

Private developers are now joint venturing with CDCs because this is the only way in which they can access public money as well as invest some of their own to redevelop a deprived area. The CDC benefits from the expertise of the developer and, if it has cut a good deal, gets financial payback when the project is up and running. Some CDCs have used joint-venture arrangements to establish major schemes such as shopping malls.[83] Most successful CDCs benefit from some form of assistance from a foundation, government contracts, grants, technical advice, or a start-up loan.[84]

Decide on a Set of Actions

Visualize the goal. One way to decide on a set of actions is to visualize the end goal and then work backward. For example, at this stage the group will probably be interested in devising a project. The end goal is to decide on a project. Ask yourselves what are all the components we need to consider to make a good decision. Some things will become immediately apparent.

Research other successful projects. You have already collected information about the resources and assets in your community. You will also need to gather information about a variety of projects that are possible and feasible. Visiting successful projects will help your group get a tangible idea of what is possible. Talking to developers of successful community development projects will give you information about pitfalls to avoid. This is a also a good time to use the help of outside business experts who can provide consultation to the group on beginning business ventures and learning the language of entrepreneurial leadership, risks of new ventures, and obtaining capital.

Develop a plan to reach the goal. While there will be a strong incentive for members to jump into deciding on a specific project, it is important that the group look at the larger picture at this point. They must begin to devise a set of concrete actions by which they can see their projects to completion. Always break a set of actions into smaller components. This way you can see all of the parts that need to be done. Breaking things down also helps you chart accomplishments on each piece and makes the entire project manageable.

Develop a Project

When you decide on a specific project, brainstorm many possibilities. Aim for success. Choose a project with an assured return. Compare several projects, and convene a public forum.

Brainstorm   A number of possibilities will occur to members that can be used to help develop the economic resources of your community. Many members will have their own ideas. These need to be validated. But they must also be put into the context of the particular capacity of the community. Use brainstorming to help people think creatively and not jump to solutions or become stuck on one pet project.

Aim for Success   Building a community development corporation is a long-term process, the success of which may not become evident for many years. It took 8 years before the Chatham-Savannah Youth Futures Authority in Savannah, Georgia, began to see improvement in their neighborhood. Asked how long it took before he knew that the New Community Corporation of Newark, New Jersey, was making a real difference in its target neighborhood, founder Monsignor William Linder answered, 12 years.[85]

Choose a project with which you can have a reasonable chance of success and one that your group can achieve relatively quickly. Alan Twelvetrees says that many CDCs become involved in housing from the start. The kinds of projects they have undertaken include buying and rehabilitating housing for rent to low-income families, new housing for rent to senior citizens, new housing for sale to low- to moderate-income families, buying and relocating houses displaced by a freeway, and cooperative housing. As Twelvetrees points out, however, these projects often require massive subsidies. Unless construction is completed on time and the management company is effective at collecting rents, the finances may not work out.[86]

Start out with a modest project that your group can achieve rather quickly that has a more or less guaranteed result, and from which your group can learn and test itself. Once your group is successful, they can build on that success and slowly develop other larger projects.

Choose a Project With an Assured Return   Try a venture with an assured rather than a speculative return, at least to start with. Identify clearly the various objectives of the proposed venture, and distinguish between social and economic objectives—the need to give disadvantaged people jobs and the need to make a profit, for example. If it is not possible to make a profit and meet social objectives at the same time, then social objectives may initially have to take a second place. Try to develop a business that "captures the outside market" rather than relying only on money circulating in the local community, especially if it is very impoverished.

Compare Several Projects

Using rational problem solving, come up with various possibilities that meet the contingencies that your group has decided upon. Develop pros and cons or benefits and costs of each alternative, and try to put the benefits and costs into monetary terms so your group has a hardheaded financial basis for decision making. Rank the various possibilities using a quantitative format such as force field analysis or benefit-cost analysis, and choose the one that will give your organization the highest rate of return.

Convene a Public Forum

Present your top options to the community in a public forum. The public forum is a device to give information about what the community development group has done and what projects it is considering, and to solicit input and advice from the community as a whole. Make sure your constituents at the forum understand that this is not a decision-making meeting, but informational and to solicit input. The public forum should also have a wider purpose of engaging community members to help with the eventual project.

Develop Relationships With Corporations, Government, and Intermediaries

Community development requires reciprocal relationships between the CDC, business, government, and CDC intermediaries. CDCs, for example, need financial and technical support from government and from business. Government has public dollars that CDCs need and without which most community development projects will not get off the ground. CDCs offer government a resource by which public dollars can work for community improvement, but without the burden of having to administer those programs themselves. Corporations can also provide funding, expertise, and connections in return for the goodwill that community cooperation generates. Intermediaries can help link CDCs, business, and government so that all benefit.[87]

End the Process

There will come a time when your work as community developer is finished and you move on to other communities, other issues, and other problems. If a community developer stays in the community too long, the social worker will often inhibit the development of community leadership and independence. It is important for people in a community to become free not only of their dependence on the power structure but also of their dependence on you, the social worker. You determine when it is time to leave, and then you work through a process of termination.

Determining When to Leave

One way of determining whether it is time for you to leave is to assess the extent to which the CDC and the community members are competent, leadership has developed, the organization is established, goals have been accomplished, and political networks have been established. The CDC may not have achieved all of its goals, but if it has met a number of them in these areas, you can leave knowing that the organization you have helped develop is strong enough to move in a positive direction.

Member Competence   Do community members continue to identify themselves as victims and play a victim role, or have they gained skills, competencies, confidence, empowerment, and control over their community and the CDC?

Leadership Development   To what extent have community leaders emerged? Do these leaders act on behalf of the community, or do they use their positions to possess power for themselves? Do the leaders actively train others to take their place? Is leadership broadly shared, or is it hoarded by a few?

Organization Is Established   Is the CDC in a strong financial position? Is its board composed mainly of community residents who support and give good direction to the CDC? Do community members identify with the CDC and recognize it as "our organization"? Are community members committed to and engaged in helping the CDC grow and develop? Is the CDC in coordination with business and government capable of eliminating community problems over the long haul?

Goal Accomplishments   Has the CDC established at least one successful, ongoing business project? Has it accomplished at least one of its subsidiary goals?

Political Networks   How effectively does the CDC work with elected officials? Has the CDC established strong and permanent partnerships with major corporations inside and outside of the community?

Power   Is the community power structure responsive to the CDC and to its political strength? Does the community power structure recognize the CDC as effectively representing the needs of the community?

The Process of Terminating Your Role   When you feel that the time for you to leave is coming, you need to prepare the community. Just as engaging the community took time and was a systematic process, disengagement should also be done over a period of time and with deliberation.

Reduce the Intensity of Your Involvement   Your leadership style with the community development corporation should be a low-task/low-relationship facilitating style. You take less and less active involvement in meetings. You tell your members that you will be absent occasionally, and then more frequently. Finally, you meet with the members, board, and staff of the CDC and explain that you will be leaving and outline your strategy for disengagement.

Terminate Community Relationships   You begin to terminate the relationships you have developed in the community. You visit as many people as you can, "attend meetings of block clubs, committees and organizations in the community" to say goodbye.[88] Visit members of the power structure, both those who have supported your efforts and those who have opposed you.

Assess the CDC's Accomplishments   Meet with the CDC board and staff and present your assessment of the organization. In your assessment, explain the condition of the community when you came. Review the history of the CDC and your evaluation of its condition at present. Affirm their strengths and commend them for their victories. Let them know what areas you think they need to work on in the future to become a stronger organization.

Have a Celebration   Have a celebration in which you and the CDC can enjoy a closure experience. Members will need to express their feelings toward you, and you will have a chance to say your final goodbyes to them and share what the organizing experience has meant to you.

When you leave, the community's members should be strengthened and able to carry on its programs, implement the vision, and continue the leadership that they have begun. The community should have a sense of itself, and its members should be walking their way together. There should be a sense of victory and accomplishment, and the vision of the future should be clear and easily seen.

E-COMMUNITY DEVELOPMENT

Today e-community development is providing a number of innovations, thrusting community development into the future. Among these innovations has been original use of e-community development by Chittenden Community Television (CCTV), Playing to Win (PTW), the Institute for the Study of Civic Values, government cooperation, and community technology centers. Macro social workers are making more effective use of the Internet to assist community development projects.

Chittenden Community Television

Lewis Friedland says that "some of the most important democratic innovations have come from local and state governments in new forms of economic planning and community development."[89] E-community development saw its beginnings in Burlington, Vermont, where Mayor Bernie Sanders made economic development a central focus of his administration. Sanders initiated Chittenden Community Television (CCTV), which produced programs for nonprofit organizations in the early 1980s. By the 1990s CCTV realized that the real issue was not access but economic and community development.

CCTV began to develop job training and community computing centers in Settlement Houses, libraries, and other community settings. Through community meetings and short courses in computer literacy, electronic publishing, and the Internet, CCTV recruited and taught basic job skills. In 1994 with a grant from U.S. Department of Housing and Urban Development (HUD), CCTV established a public access telecomputing center as a model of how to move disenfranchised communities from a focus on housing development to sustainable community economic development. The project is run as a cooperative, with members who cannot afford to pay using their labor to contribute to their fee. CCTV continues to participate in the citywide telecommunications planning process, which allows the city to make legitimate claims on cable and telephone providers for both better service and a percentage of gross revenues.

Playing to Win

Begun in 1981 in Harlem in New York City, Playing to Win network (PTW) worked to get technology to those who wouldn't otherwise have access. By the end of the 1980s, as hundreds of grassroots community organizations began to experiment with computer technology, it became important to connect them. In 1991 the National Science Foundation gave PTW a $1 million grant to connect those centers together. By 1996 PTW had 56 affiliates, some outside the United States.

PTW also expanded its role in planning and community development programs by implementing a grant from the Community Networking Initiative of the U.S. Corporation for Public Broadcasting, designed to stimulate Internet partnerships between public television stations and community development organizations, as well as encourage local democratic planning using the assets-based model. The project focused on literacy with six low-income organizations in multiethnic neighborhoods that integrated computing skills into existing literacy programs.

Institute for the Study of Civic Values

The Institute for the Study of Civic Values was founded in 1992 by Ed Schwartz, together with Liberty Net, developed by the Philadelphia library, community development agencies, schools, and local public television. The institute organized a series of workshops and briefings about Liberty Net with more than 50 groups. The result was an effort to provide free accounts and training for nonprofit neighborhood groups. The institute helped neighborhood members develop neighborhood "home pages," giving residents access to learning tools that they themselves control. In addition, using the assets-based approach, the institute has developed a master citywide map of Philadelphia neighborhoods, giving each neighborhood immediate

access to the others, to tools for citizenship, and to model block contracts in which neighbors pledge specific actions to make their blocks clean and safe places to live.

Government Cooperation

Experiments in the use of the Internet to support and encourage community development efforts have drawn on government resources and its power to legitimate grassroots organizing through community economic planning and development. Beginning in 1994, the Telecommunications and Information Infrastructure Assistance Program (TIIAP) began funding projects including economic development, services to people who were homeless, and education. Focusing on local grassroots efforts, TIIAP works to create a social network of people who are thinking about community networking, link them together, help them conduct experiments, and facilitate the learning process.[90]

Community Technology Centers

Since 1995 the Department of Housing and Urban Development (HUD) has been working with local businesses, CDCs, and others to develop community technology centers in HUD housing programs. There are now more than 1,000 centers throughout the nation in both urban and rural communities. In Harlem, a small computer technology center operating in the basement of a housing development has grown into the Community Technology Centers Network (CTCNet), a network of more than 1,000 community technology centers, that provide public access hours, promote technology education in low-income communities, assist in advocacy efforts, and offer job training. These centers are also working with populations whose language and culture are underrepresented on the Internet to produce culturally relevant content.[91]

Using the Internet

Today the use of commuter technology is enhancing the work of macro social workers in community development. For example, nonprofits can participate in Community Voice Mail, a basic telecommunications system shared by an entire community of social service agencies that help their clients get the kinds of messages many of us take for granted. By using computers linked to telephone lines and Direct Inward Dials (DIDs) purchased from the phone company, agencies can provide clients with personalized seven-digit phone numbers that can be accessed from any touch-tone phone, 24 hours a day.

CONCLUSION

Community development is much like grassroots democracy, in which power is shared in an equal and open forum. It encourages the values of citizenship and citizen participation in the life of the community, promotes education in civic pride and civic consciousness, and sees in the community itself an arena where the public interest can become a living force. From its inception in the 1960s into the decade of 2000, despite barriers erected by conservative federal governmental administrations, community development has grown numerically and in its accomplishments. Community development today comprises a strong network of corporations with healthy connections with business, foundations, government, and support intermediaries both in the United States and Canada.

Social workers are learning how to create a community development organization, and the increased use of e-community development is making that process easier. Community development is strong, but there is a need for renewed community development effort by macro social workers. Community development corporations provide an exciting, fulfilling, and creative arena for macro social work practice.

KEY CONCEPTS

community development

community development corporation (CDC)

alternative to private business

financial and other services

social programs

community organization

residential council organizing

resource organizing

issue organizing

political organizing

organizing community events

partnership organizing

multilocal organizing

front-group organizing

CDC intermediaries

Local Initiative Support Corporation (LISC)

Low Income Housing Tax Credit Program (LIHTC)

fiscal management

multiple reinforcement

utopian community development

religious communities

anabaptists

secular communities

Henry George

Oneida Colony

communes

Charity Organization Society

Cooperative Extension Services

Antigonish cooperative movement

William Biddle

Harry Hopkins

Works Progress Administration (WPA)

Civilian Conservation Corps (CCC)

Bedford-Stuyvesant CDC

Community Development Society (CDS)

Tennessee Valley Authority (TVA)

first-wave CDCs

second-wave CDCs

Housing and Community Development Act

Housing Mortgage Disclosure Act, 1975

Community Reinvestment Act, 1977

National Neighborhood Policy Act, 1977

National Self-Help Development Act, 1978

third-wave CDCs

fourth-wave CDCs

community development financial institutions (CDFIs)

community development block grant (CDBG)

community empowerment program

national support organizations

Community Enterprise Program, 1993

Community Development Society (CDS)

intermediary coalitions

comprehensive community initiatives (CCI)

sustainable community development

how to create a community development corporation

resources and assets approach

physical capital

financial capital

human capital

social capital

resources and assets inventory

three-tiered model of intensity and influence

consensual community social work

e-community development

QUESTIONS FOR DISCUSSION

1. One observation about the state of macro social work today is that while it is becoming more generalist, it is at the same time becoming more specialized. For example, because the new wave of community development corporations are occurring in faith-based organizations, a macro social worker interested in community development needs not only general social work skills but specialized skills in community development, community organization, administration, and business, and an appreciation for religiously oriented communities of meaning. What does this mean for social work education at the BA level? What does it mean for social work education at the MSW level?

2. Another observation about community development is that it draws upon all of one's problem-solving functions, enhancing your growth and mastery by using your skills in a variety of ways. Think about your own needs for professional growth. How well do you think performing community development would assist you in becoming a whole, masterful individual?

3. Comment on this statement: Becoming skilled in community development allows you to expand your options for the future. For example, a social worker trained to perform psychotherapy will, for the most part, always be a psychotherapist. As a macro social worker skilled in community development, you will not only be able to work with communities but develop new programs and services, become an administrator, a community organizer, a management consultant, and engage in planning as your interests, skills, and capabilities change and develop. Do you agree or disagree with this statement? What is your perspective on the utility of becoming a community developer?

ADDITIONAL READING

Community Development Prior to Community Development Corporations

Biddle, William W. and Loureide Biddle. *The Community Development Process: The Recovery of Local Initiative.* New York: Holt, Rinehart and Winston, 1965.

Clinard, Marshall B. *Slums and Community Development.* Glencoe, IL: Free Press, 1966.

Farrington, Frank. *Community Development: Making the Small Town a Better Place to Live and a Better Place in Which to Do Business* (1915). The first book on community development published in the United States.

Mezilrow, Jack D. *The Dynamics of Community Development.* New York: Scarecrow Press, 1962.

Community Development

Berry, Jeffrey, Ken Portney, and Ken Thomson. *The Rebirth of Urban Democracy.* Washington, DC: The Brookings Institute, 1993.

Chaskin, Robert. *The Ford Foundation's Neighborhood and Family Initiative: Toward a Model of Comprehensive, Neighborhood-Based Development.* Chicago: Chapin Hall Center for Children, 1992.

Briggs, Xavier de Souza and Elizabeth J. Mueller. *From Neighborhood to Community: Evidence on the Social Effects of Community Development.* New York: Community Development Research Center, Milano Graduate School of Management and Urban Policy, New School for Social Research, 1997.

Clemetson, Robert and Roger Coates (eds.). *Restoring Broken Places and Rebuilding Communities: A Casebook on African-American Church Involvement in Community Economic Development.* Washington, DC: National Congress for Community Economic Development, 1992.

Halpern, Robert. *Rebuilding the Inner City: A History of Neighborhood Initiatives to Address Poverty in the United States.* New York: Columbia University Press, 1995.

Community and Economic Development Corporations

Berger, Renee. *Against All Odds: The Achievement of Community-Based Development Organizations.* Washington, DC: National Congress for Community Economic Development, 1989.

Campfens, Hubert. *Community Development Around the World.* Toronto: University of Toronto Press, 1997.

Ferguson, Ronald F. and William T. Dickens (eds.). *Urban Problems and Community Development.* Washington, DC: Brookings Institution Press, 1999.

Hallman, Howard W. *Neighborhoods: Their Place in Urban Life.* Vol. 154. Beverly Hills, CA: Sage Publications, 1984.

Hatry, Harry P., Elaine Morell, George P. Barbour Jr., and Steven M. Pajunen. *Excellence in Managing: Practical Experiences From Community Development Agencies.* New York: Urban Institute, 1991.

Keating, W. Dennis, Norman Krumholz, and Philip Star. *Revitalizing Urban Neighborhoods.* Lawrence: University Press of Kansas, 1996.

Mier, Robert. *Social Justice and Local Economic Development Policy.* Newbury Park, CA: Sage, 1993.

National Congress for Community Economic Development. *Community-Based Development Organizations.* Washington, DC: National Congress for Community Economic Development, 1999.

Peirce, Neil R. and Carol F. Steinbach. *Enterprising Communities: Community-Based Development in America.* Washington, DC: Council for Community Based Development, 1990.

Perry, Stewart E. *Communities on the Way.* Albany: State University of New York Press, 1987.

Shragge, E. *Community Economic Development: In Search for Empowerment and Alternatives.* Montreal: Black Rose Books, 1993.

Stoecker, Randy. *Defending Community: The Struggle for Alternative Redevelopment in Cedar-Riverside.* Philadelphia: Temple University Press, 1994.

Sullivan, Mercer. *More Than Housing: How Community Development Corporations Go About Changing Lives and Neighborhoods.* New York: Community Development Research Center, New School for Social Research, 1993.

Twelvetrees, Alan C. *Organizing for Neighbourhood Development: A Comparative Study of Community Based Development Organizations.* 2d ed. Aldershot, England: Avebury Press, 1996.

Vidal, Avis C. *Rebuilding Communities: A National Study of Urban Community Development Corporations.* New York: Community Development Research Center, New School for Social Research. 1992.

Faith-Based Community Development

Perkins, John M. (ed.). *Restoring At-Risk Communities: Doing It Together and Doing It Right.* Grand Rapids, MI: Baker Books, 1995.

Perkins, John M. *Beyond Charity: The Call to Christian Community Development.* Grand Rapids, MI: Baker Books, 1993.

Linthecum, Robert C. *City of God, City of Satan: A Biblical Theology of the Urban Church.* Grand Rapids, MI: Zondervan Publishing House, 1991.

History of Community Development

Melvin, Patricia Mooney. *American Community Organizations: A Historical Dictionary.* New York: Greenwood Press, 1986.

Fisher, Robert. *Let the People Decide: Neighborhood Organizing in America.* New York: Twayne Publications, 1994.

Halpern, Robert. *Rebuilding the Inner City: A History of Neighborhood Initiatives to Address Poverty in the U.S.* New York: Columbia University Press, 1995.

Sustainable Community Development

Hren, Benedict J. *Community Voices for Sustainability.* Gaithersburg, MD: Izaak Walton League of America, 1998.

Community Development With Specific Communities

Ellish, William. *White Ethnics and Black Power: The Emergence of the West Side Organization.* Chicago: Aldine, 1969.

Manoni, Mary H. *Bedford-Stuyvesant: The Anatomy of a Central City Community.* New York: Quadrangle/New York Times Book Co., 1973.

Related Works

Denise, Paul S. and Ian M. Harris. *Experiential Education for Community Development.* New York: Greenwood Press, 1989.

Chaskin, Robert. *The Ford Foundation's Neighborhood and Family Initiative: Toward a Model of Comprehensive, Neighborhood-Based Development.* Chicago: Chapin Hall Center for Children, 1992.

Peirce, Neal B. and Carol F. Steinbach, *Enterprising Communities: Community Based Development in America.* Washington, DC: Council for Community-Based Development, 1990.

Journal Articles

Boothroyd, Peter and H. Craig Davis. "Community Economic Development: Three Approaches." *Journal of Planning Education and Research,* 12, 1993, pp. 230–240.

Gittell, Marilyn, Kathe Newman, Janice Bockmeyer, and Robert Lindsay, "Expanding Civic Opportunity: Urban Empowerment Zones." *Urban Affairs Review,* 33, 1998, pp. 530–558.

Gittell, Ross J. and Margaret Wilder, "Community Development Corporations: Critical Factors that Influence Success." *Journal of Urban Affairs,* 21, 1999, pp. 341–362.

Stoecker, Randy, "The CDC Model of Urban Development: A Critique and Alternative." *Journal of Urban Affairs,* 19, 1997, pp. 1–22.

Stall, S. and Stoecker, R. "Community Organizing or Organizing Community? Gender and the Craft Of Empowerment." *Gender and Society,* 12, 1998, pp. 729–756.

Swanstrom, Todd, "The Nonprofitization of United States Housing Policy: Dilemmas of Community Development." *Community Development Journal,* 34, 1999, pp. 28–37.

Bill Traynor, "Community Development and Community Organizing." *Shelterforce,* 68, March/April 1993, p. 4.

Journals

Journal of the Community Development Society
International Community Development Journal
Community Development Journal: An International Forum
(Oxford University Press, Oxford, England)

8

The Practice of Community Organization

Liberation of the Oppressed

In order for this struggle to have meaning, the oppressed must not, in seeking to regain their humanity, . . . become oppressors of the oppressors, but rather restorers of the humanity of both. This is the great humanistic and historical task of the oppressed; to liberate themselves and their oppressors. Oppressors who oppress, and exploit and rape by virtue of their power, cannot find the strength to liberate either the oppressed or themselves. Only power that springs from the weakness of the oppressed will be sufficiently strong to free both.[1]

Paulo Freire

Violence

Let us not forget, when we talk of violence, that the death of a young mother in childbirth is violent; that the slow starvation of the mind and body of a child is violent; let us not forget that hunger is violent, that pain is violent, that oppression is violent, that early death is violent; and that the death of hope is the most violent of all.

The organizer brings hope to the people.[2]

Si Kahn

Dependency

Dependency, no matter how luxurious, is a form of slavery.[3]

Joan Lancourt

Ideas in This Chapter

200

Gordon Mayer, National Training and Information Center, Chicago, IL

Community organizations help neighbors gain strength in unified engagement as we encounter forces that have kept us down.

WHEN YOU HAVE TROUBLE IN SAN ANTONIO, CALL THE COPS

Mayor Henry Cisneros called the faith-based Communities Organized for Public Service (COPS) "the voice of 150,000 families." Sonia Hernandez, however, remains skeptical about the claims of politicians. "We reject expansion based on boosterism," as she put it. She defined the relationship in a different way: "We rather call upon our public officials to challenge us as well as challenge them to be reciprocal, collaborative, and consultative as we cooperatively forge a new vision and a new consensus for San Antonio." Behind this kind of exchange is a specific organizational philosophy: "Politicians work is to do our work," Hernandez explained. "When you've got somebody working for you, you don't bow and scrape. It's not meant to show disrespect. When politicians deliver, we applaud them. Not until then." The point of COPS, she continued, is not politics as usual. "COPS is about people, mainly poor people, who have decided to do something about their lives."[4]

"There isn't anyone around—not a mayor or a governor—who is going to come in and do anything for us. We are going to do it for ourselves. If we ever lost that touch, we would cease to be COPS." Explained one leader, "If one of our members is thinking of running for office, he will be asked to resign. We will never divide or dilute our numbers by endorsing particular candidates, but we will hold all elected officials responsible for their actions. We will be the conscience of public servants."[5]

In 1973 Father Edmundo Rodriguez invited community organizer Ernesto Cortes and the Industrial Areas Foundation (IAF) to help the Mexican American community in San Antonio try to get itself together. Cortes, who grew up in San Antonio in the 1940s and 1950s, brought back with him the organizing skills he had learned at the Industrial Areas Foundation and a great zeal to see his own people gain power and new dignity. Prior efforts had failed. A variety of advocacy groups had formed around specific issues such as school reform or the environment. But these issue-oriented groups often ignored communities. It wasn't that people were unconcerned; it was that they had rarely been asked what they were most concerned about.

Cortes's basic approach was to listen. "I began to interview pastors and from them got the names of lay leaders in the parishes," he remembers. "I kept records and tapes of each conversation."[6] Through the course of perhaps a thousand interviews during the first year, Cortes gained a detailed sense of what mattered most to people in the neighborhoods. It didn't turn out to be the more visible issues that politicians or Chicano militants usually talked about—things like police brutality or racial discrimination. Instead, it was the problems close to families and neighborhoods, such as housing, utility rates, and drainage. It "was like one of those lightbulbs that suddenly appears in cartoons."[7] The issues that COPS initially addressed broke the mold. So too did those who became the leadership.

COPS built around the moderates, not the activists on the left or the conservatives on the right. It didn't begin with the politicos or people in public life; it grew from the people who run the festivals, who lead the PTAs, whose lives have been wrapped up with their children, their parishes, and their jobs. "What COPS has been able to do is give them a public life, the tools whereby they can participate," observes Sister Christine Stephes, the staff director of the organization.[8] Furthermore, Cortes sought an entirely different base of organizing. For Ernie Cortes, it was hard to imagine effectively organizing the Mexican American community in San Antonio without drawing explicitly on the religious language and stories of the people or building on the Catholic Church as an institution.

Cortes saw the church as the center of strength in the community. But this did not mean that the church doled out service to people. "Our iron rule of organizing is 'never do anything for people that they can do for themselves,'" asserted Cortes.[9] In San Antonio such an approach meant that Cortes conducted dozens of training workshops on doing research, chairing meetings, keeping leadership accountable, dealing with the press, breaking down problems into manageable parts, and others.

COPS did not seek funds from any government, foundation, or corporate agency. Combining several principles of financial independence by charging dues supplemented with funds from a grant, the remaining budget was raised through sales for an ad book. In addition, COPS stressed the development of new leadership. Every individual organization is free to take on local neighborhood issues it chooses. On larger issues, it can ask for aid from the whole organization. Leadership is elected at every level, and top leaders and staff directors alike must change regularly.

COPS held its first annual convention in the auditorium of Jefferson High School on November 23, 1974. More than 1,000 delegates jammed the auditorium, adopting a constitution and a plan for seeking $100 million in city improvements in sidewalks, libraries, and parks, and strategies for fighting problems such as air pollution. To an outside observer the meetings may have seemed spontaneous and unruly at the least. But behind the events were weeks of planning, discussion, research, and role playing that taught people to express themselves in a new way, simultaneously articulating and controlling their buried anger.

The previous year the organization had drawn up a Texas-wide plan with planks such as increased aid for school districts with low student achievement scores, state money to help schools cope with immigrant students, and increased funds for bilingual education. A number of organizing efforts around the state also backed the plan, and the Democratic gubernatorial candidate pledged his support. But before the education effort was ever formulated, extensive discussion had occurred in each parish of the organization.

COPS had an educational process all its own. "It's like a university where people go to school to learn about public policy, learn about public discourse, and about public life," described Ernesto Cortes.[10] People reflected on what schools were like in biblical times. They looked at how schools had changed and at the needs of poor people for education today. Behind such discussion is a particular approach to the organization members. "Each person is an individual and you address people as individuals. . . . You make sure each person has an understanding of what we are going to do and why and what his or her role is."[11]

Treating each member as an individual, capable of making a contribution, soon generated the reputation that the organization was amazingly well prepared. People gained detailed knowledge about the educational system and its problems. As reporter Paul Burke put it in the *Texas Monthly,* it soon became apparent that the COPS rank and file knew more about the issues than did supposedly expert public officials: "The authorities weren't so smart after all."[12] The stage was now set for COPS intervention in the political process. All during this time, COPS had been evolving a positive understanding of itself and of collaborative politics as a political alternative to "politics as usual" in America. "There can be no transformation of the human spirit without development of practical wisdom and meaningful action through the practice of collaborative politics,"[13] asserts Ernesto Cortes Jr.

COPS began to encourage businesses coming into the community to pay a decent wage. Comments Beatrice Cortez, an organization leader, "We realized that you could only do so much with neighborhood improvement. We did research and found out San Antonio paid the poorest wages of any major city."[14] Indeed, according to the *Commercial Reporter,* San Antonio wages were 20 to 40% lower than those in other areas of the country. The city establishment's protestation of innocence turned sour when COPS released a copy of the secret study it had somehow obtained called the Fantus Report, commissioned by the city's Economic Development Foundation (EDF). The Fantus Report applauded the city's "relatively unorganized" labor force and concluded that San Antonio's corporate and political leaders "must be careful not to attract industries that would upset the existing wage ladder. This would tend to dissipate the cooperative and competitive advantages enjoyed by existing manufacturers." After COPS exposed this secret citywide collusion to keep the working-class Mexican American community impoverished, their plan for inner-city economic and residential development eventually proved successful, obtaining $46 million in drainage bonds and another $8 million in neighborhood improvements. Over the past two decades COPS has won more than $750 million in new streets, parks, libraries, and other services.[15]

COPS is an organization of organizations, which gives it a certain solidity: parish clubs, church societies, parent groups, youth clubs, senior citizen groups, neighborhood associations, block clubs, and any others interested in seeing nonviolent change for the betterment of their neglected neighborhoods. Pablo Eisenberg described COPS as the most effective community group in this country. A federal study of American communities commissioned by the National Commission on Neighborhoods detailed the hundreds of millions of dollars worth of improvements in streets, drainage, public facilities, and cleanup that COPS won for poorer neighborhoods in San Antonio. It described the 5,000 to 7,000 delegates who come each year to the COPS annual convention, and it concluded: "There has been a major shift in power from the wealthy blue blooded Anglos to the poor and working Mexican American families of San Antonio. COPS has been at the center of this shift."[16]

WHAT YOU WILL LEARN IN THIS CHAPTER

A quiet revolution is sweeping the country. Born in the depths of the Depression, it waxed and waned though the 1940s and 1950s, but the ferment of the 1960s gave it a new push. Since the 1960s, it has refined its methods and become a groundswell of positive action in small and large communities from Orlando, Florida, to Anchorage, Alaska; from Bangor, Maine, to Honolulu. Less flamboyant, less confrontive, and more permanent, community organizing today most often works through existing faith-based social networks of people who become involved in political and economic action to create a better life for their children, their neighbors, and themselves.

In this chapter you will explore why community organizing is important and learn what community organizers do. You will review a brief history of community organizing, explore how to practice community organizing, and use four contemporary models of community organizing. You will discover that community organizing is a fundamental part of a new wave of societal change that is gradually reforming North American society. Community is being reborn, and politics is being reshaped. Locally based community organizing is at the forefront of those changes.

WHAT IS COMMUNITY ORGANIZING?

Ordinary people in communities have always suspected something that government officials and politicians are only now beginning to realize—"Those macro, top-down solutions don't work."[17] Powerful government redevelopment agencies that tear down the slums and build high-rise corporate offices will not solve our social problems. The solution to urban social problems does not lie in destroying neighborhoods but in empowering them. Politicians passing laws will not solve them. If politics is expected to work, democracy can no longer be the privilege of the wealthy but must be the concern of ordinary people.

Trickle-down economics will not solve problems of poverty. We will wait forever before wealthy corporations trickle good jobs, good pay, or employment benefits down to us. It is becoming increasingly clear that institutional solutions generated in corporate boardrooms, in the White House, in the halls of Congress, or in state legislatures across the country are often helpless in dealing with issues that matter most to people. "The *only* thing that really works," says Harry Boyte, "is local initiative."[18]

Social change happens when ordinary people working with others make it happen. Community organizing is a process by which people in neighborhood organizations, associations, and churches join together to address social problems in their communities, develop their own solutions, and in partnership with government and corporations implement those solutions over the long term.[19] Randy Stoecker says that community organizing "is building organizations controlled by people normally shut out from decision-making power, who then go on to fight for changes in the distribution of power." Community organizing assisted by macro social workers "occurs in local settings to empower individuals, build relationships and organizations, and create action for social change."[20]

Robert Fisher says that Americans have always turned most easily to organizations at the grassroots level to build community, meet individual and collective needs, and participate in public life. This is as true today as it was one hundred years ago.[21] Macro social workers practicing generalist-based community organization enable individuals to use social reason or whole-mind thinking, facilitate task groups, and relate to the larger community and to society as a whole.

Individuals and Whole-Mind Thinking

Macro social workers understand that community organizations provide an environment in which people can engage in critical thinking, intuitive reflection, express emotions and attitudes, discuss values, and engage in action.

Critical Thinking   Community organizations use critical thinking to overcome social amnesia, help members use their analytic capabilities, and engage in research by gathering and assessing information.

Overcome Social Amnesia   Learned apathy, alienation, and anonymity are the major social problems of modern organizational society. They result in social amnesia. We forget who we are, and we forget what happened that made this happen. Macro social workers who work through community organizations challenge social amnesia, individual passivity, and apathy. As we help people forge themselves into community organizations, we encourage them to remember that they are owners of their social environment and thinkers who construct their own reality. "The struggle for authorship [of social reality] brings us into an active, intimate relationship with our world, resulting in altered perceptions of our selves,"[22] says Jane Lancourt.

Develop Analytic Capacities   Organizing heightens members' analytic capacities, so that they see the national and global forces at work in their communities and understand emerging issues in time to address them. No longer do community residents accept conventional wisdom as a substitute for truth, the prescriptions of government as the best that can be expected, or the pronouncements of public officials as correct. Instead, community members raise questions, probe more deeply to seek answers, and try to get to the bottom of what ails their communities. Community organizing promotes a culture of active critique, dialogue, and reflection that deepens the worldview of participants, transforming them into searchers after their own answers rather than accepting answers handed to them by outsiders as sufficient.

Gather Information and Learning Facts   Community members exercise their cognitive thinking to gather information and facts by means of participative action research. As members search for answers, they learn how to ask questions, how to systematically gather data by a variety of objective social science methods, and how to analyze these data to shine light on what is unknown. Empirical data give community members evidence that confirms their feelings and intuition. Facts become weapons against injustice that protestations of innocence cannot hide. Information helps us understand "not only what can or cannot be done but more importantly, what ought to be done."[23] Members use the information they have gathered to discover connections, discuss issues, take a position, come to some conclusion, and shape their concerns into tangible recommendations, programs, and actions.

Members of community service organizations (CSOs) in California, for example, learned details of registration and voting requirements, facts about housing laws and the various options available to them, the nature and consequences of urban development, their rights under the welfare laws, and on and on. A federal official at the regional level commented that the housing surveys and program development done in Hanford and Corcoran under the aegis of the local CSO had been performed more competently than in any other community he knew of. Members learned what it took to define and reach a goal. The active educational program in those CSO chapters stretched the perception and understanding of the consequences of actions and their interrelationships, says Carl Tjerandsen.[24]

Intuitive Reflection   In a process of conscientization, or consciousness raising, macro social work community organizers help people reflect together on the meaning of the experiences they have had. Members begin to experience cognitive dissonance, in which reality fails to match the beliefs they have been taught about justice, freedom, and equality, for example, or the discrepancy between the principles that are presumed to be the operative realities in a democracy and those that actually drive American politics.

Cognitive dissonance is the window of opportunity for social learning, in which we ask the question, "What is wrong here?" It is the deadly enemy of the imposed status quo of forgetfulness and denial that demands, "Don't ask, don't see, don't tell." As members name discontinuities between the ideals society espouses and what occurs in practice, they begin to remember. Their shared memories give them power.

While society may blame members for their situation, their intuition speaks at a deeper level. Community members of impoverished neighborhoods know that they have as many inherent skills, abilities, and potential as anyone else. They understand that they have not created the conditions that keep them subservient. They realize that they have been subjected to a subtle, long-term education in dehumanization, and they call upon their intuition to visualize themselves as they could be.

Emotions and Attitudes   Members feel strength in unified engagement as they encounter forces that have kept them down. Community organizing breaks the bonds of depression, helplessness, and hopelessness by bringing community members together to gain empowerment and justice. People who were formerly alienated, apathetic, and uninvolved take responsibility for themselves to ensure that government or the private sector hold to their commitments and honor their responsibilities in deprived neighborhoods.[25]

Community members, assisted by community organizers, reclaim their ability to believe, to have hope, and to see themselves in an entirely different way. They reassert their rights to have feelings other than depression, alienation, or hopelessness. They feel anger at the injustices that have been perpetrated against them, grief over what they have lost, and recognize that by uniting they can do something about their situation.

Perhaps the most significant change in community service organization (CSO) members was in their attitudes, says Tjerandsen:

> Members learned to take the initiative in the face of problems. They gained confidence from the fact of being united, that the organization would back them up. They improved their ability to cope with a situation, which led to a feeling of self-worth and of their effectiveness in the community. Perhaps this change was expressed most simply and effectively by an elderly man in a meeting I attended at Stockton. In response to a question about what the CSO had meant to him, he responded, "Senor, we are no longer afraid."[26]

Values   Community organizing is an arena of public and moral discourse in which members, assisted by macro social workers, grasp a sense of justice and moral indignation, allowing for the reflection of diverse opinion, while always engaging in dialogue with one another about the best course of action. Members learn to express the values that are most important to them, try to put those values into action, and embed them in their own communities. Members learn to think "ethically," overcoming modern calculative reason as reason "at large." Ultimately community organizing helps revitalize communities with social values and social goods, shaping the character and personalities of the people who inhabit them. Members act on the ideals that they visualize and become committed to them.

Action Skills   Macro social workers help community organizations generate opportunities for action as well as tangible programs and services that help members obtain resources they need to live healthy lives. Members of community organizations exercise their grasp of practical solutions and experience the empowerment that comes from collective action.[27]

Reporting on the community service organization, which for 15 years in California's Central Valley was the primary community organization among Mexican Americans, Tjerandsen says that members acquired many new skills, not least of which were those involved in organizing, furthering the aims of the organization and putting those skills into action. Some learned how to deal with the problem of factions, a perennial threat to popular organizations. They learned how to run their own meetings democratically, how to express themselves, and how to put facts together to make a case. They learned to hold a practice session before a hearing to identify the possible arguments and consider what their responses should be. They learned the tactics needed to negotiate.[28]

Coming Full Circle   At each turn of the spiral, members add more self-understanding, stronger collective identity, greater resolve, and deeper insights. They consciously control their emotions, are more critically conscious and more capable of thinking ethically, and are more competent in taking action. Members think whole-mindedly, putting all of their thinking functions to use. Summing up the impact of the community organization on the lives of people, Tjeranden says, "We can only begin to identify the kinds of changes in individuals that contributed so much to the improvement of civic competence among Mexican-Americans in California."[29]

Facilitate Task Groups

Macro social workers forge alliances of neighbors working together to make their neighborhoods socially healthy, positive, safe, and humane social environments. They facilitate task groups to conjointly articulate grievances against those responsible for social problems, especially business and governmental organizations.[30] Engaging groups helps foster critical dialogue among members and develops their organizing capacities; these skills are carried into the public realm as the participants meet with public officials, participate in one-on-one interviews, and conduct house meetings and actions accountability sessions. In group meetings members gradually reshape political society, which often become a primary avenue through which organizing transforms the wider political culture.

Working With Communities

Community organizations, assisted by macro social workers, help rebuild the social infrastructure of neighborhoods from the ground up, not one person at a time, but in entire communities. They press government for adequate services and corporations for economic justice. Community organizing builds an internal political culture, including a set of shared assumptions, habits, tactics, practices, and ways of interpreting and speaking about the world that helps sustain their organizing work. Community organizations help connect people to corporate power structures and governmental agencies and teach people how to use the power of the community to make their common voices heard. They provide mutual strength and cohesion in which people decide for themselves what issues are important and systematically engage government and corporate structures in an equal forum to pursue those issues.

Community organizations hold corporate and governmental structures accountable to the neighborhoods and the citizens who comprise them. Where government or business collude to undermine the social or economic capacity of neighborhoods, community organizations work to expose these practices. Where large corporations and government bureaucracies ignore, bypass, or exploit inner-city neighborhoods, community organizations become systems of political empowerment.

LOGAN SQUARE NEIGHBORHOOD ASSOCIATION (LSNA)

This is the story of a group of residents, working through the Logan Square Neighborhood Association (LSNA) in the city of Chicago who decided that enough was enough. Many of the long-time community residents felt that they were entitled to a say in the future of their neighborhood. When Cotter & Co., which had been in the community for decades, decided to sell its warehouse and office space at the intersection of Damen and Clybourn in 1996, old-time residents made up their minds to fight for a new use of the land that would continue to provide community

jobs and not drive residents out. "We were very concerned that we would not be able to afford to stay in our own community," says Liala Beukema, pastor at the Church of the Good News on Wellington Avenue and a community resident. "Transformation was happening around us, and we felt that we deserved to have a voice."

The community contacted Costco and proposed to work with them to relocate on the Cotter property. Costco agreed fairly quickly to the community's requests, but there was still a lot of work to do. "The city gave Costco the impression it would be hard to work with us. That we were antagonistic and negative thinking people. We're working very well together, in fact. And they are working with us, treating the community respectfully. And they are hiring our people."

Training was carried out in conjunction with the New City YMCA's Local Employment and Economic Development (LEED) Council, and was made available in both Spanish and English. LSNA did the recruiting. Seventy people from the immediate neighborhood went through the 4-week job readiness training, and 32 were hired. Six months later, 30 of the original 32 were still working. Another couple dozen people from Logan Square were hired who did not need the basic training. "It's great fun to go into Costco," says Aardema, "because people start calling to you. We've been in this community a long time, and we were working for this moment."[31]

Working With Society

As community organizations activate people's political and social consciousness, they make politics less intimidating, reverse top-down politics, and stimulate people's critical consciousness. They often become the building blocks of wider social movements by providing an infrastructure of organizational coalitions that combine their strength to press for policy change at the state and national levels.[32]

Less Intimidating   Politically engaged community organizations no longer simply accept dominant power arrangements or the existing culture as givens. Community organizations help us shift the balance of power and make megastructures accountable and accessible to people by providing a collective means of engaging in decision making at the grassroots. They help reduce the intimidation people often feel when they encounter massive governmental structures. They make megastructures more human, more reachable, and more responsive, and therefore less alienating, distant, and oppressive.

Reverse Top-Down Politics

People discover that political processes are not merely for those at the top but are the prerogative of those at the bottom too. Citizens learn that substantive democracy is "not synonymous with the centralized democratic state apparatus or the structure of mass representative constitutional democracy, nor will those structures be the vehicle of human liberation."[33] By providing a collective means of engaging in decision-making at the grassroots,[34] social work community organizing transforms powerlessness into empowerment, dependency into interdependence, dehumanization into human dignity.[35] Community organizations bring decision making back to the level of ordinary people, where it counts.

Critical Consciousness

Macro social work community organizers promote the active critical assessment of current reality and call for suspension of belief in modern social practices that discourage, defeat, and disillusion people. They provide a means by which personal and social redefinitions of reality are disseminated to the larger social world, reshaping the way people see themselves and others. When those redefinitions of individual identity and social reality become widespread, the result is often a social movement of society-wide proportions.

Building Blocks of Social Movements

At the broadest societal level, community organizations build constituencies that can sometimes go beyond their local communities to create a coordinated social movement. This occurs when national social networks of community organizations such as ACORN, National People's Action (NPA), or Industrial Areas Foundation (IAF) mobilize their local organizations in a united effort. ACORN, for example, has challenged home finance organizations and banks both locally and nationally to stop usurious practices. NPA has been successful in promoting several key pieces of national legislation. IAF has engaged in a number of reforms in public services, education, and health care.

WHAT ARE COMMUNITY ORGANIZATIONS?

Community organizations are local, neighborhood groups that participate together to improve their communities by pressing corporations and governments to change policies and decisions that interfere with and have an adverse impact on those communities.

Community organizations vary in scope and size. Their change efforts include a variety of issues molded from the particular issues that confront communities.

Scope and Size

Today there are thousands of community organizations based in urban neighborhoods around the country. Community organizations exist in nearly every middle to large metropolis in America, most often in poorer neighborhoods but increasingly in middle- and working-class neighborhoods as well. Today's community organizations (one of which celebrated its 65th birthday in 2005) are becoming increasingly permanent structures on the social landscape. They include millions of people nationwide in thousands of block clubs, churches, neighborhood associations, coalitions, and federations.

Change Efforts

Community organizations bring concerns to the attention of corporate and government officials and announce that their actions must end. Many of these are relatively modest efforts: pressuring the police to close down a local crack house or getting city hall to fix potholes. More ambitious organizations have formed tenant unions, built community development corporations, fought against environmental and health problems, mobilized against plant closings and layoffs, and worked to reform public education. In general, community organizations work to improve government services, practices, policies, and procedures and ensure that people have adequate housing, develop stronger education, work with local law enforcement, and help improve business practices.

Improve Government Services

In the absence of organized citizen involvement, money for repairs and improvements to a community's infrastructure tends to be spent haphazardly at best. Community organizations help restore confidence in government by making sure that government provides efficient "civic housekeeping" municipal services such as removing snow and garbage, recycling waste, or fixing potholes, and they work to help resolve parent-school problems, address consumer complaints, and provide adequate police protection—all things that touch us where we live. Blocks Together, for example, has had substantial impact on school maintenance and repair efforts in the Chicago public schools. In 1985, UNO of South East Chicago pressed the city council into declaring a moratorium on the creation or expansion of landfills on the Southeast Side of Chicago, an area already supporting too many landfills.[36]

Community organizations sometimes help citizens prioritize the real needs of a community and have a voice when funding for improvements is being allocated. Northwest Neighborhood Federation members knew that sewer improvements to prevent flooding were their highest priority, for example, and their organized pressure made these improvements happen.

Improve Government Practices   Community organizations engage government agencies to improve their practices. Organization of the North East, for example, and a number of its Mutual Aid Association members succeeded in getting the local public welfare office to convene a monitoring process (including participation of recipients and community representatives) that addresses inefficiencies and inequities in the way clients are treated. They have improved the wages and working conditions of public employees and employees of firms with municipal contracts. They have added more women and minorities to public employment and pushed private employers to do likewise.

Establish Better Policies and Procedures Community organizations work to establish new policies and procedures instituted into law and at times develop watchdog organizations to oversee those laws and be sure they are faithfully carried out. In 1999, when the Joliet Park District board planned to build a second ice rink in the wealthier West Side, JACOB, a congregation-based organization in Joliet, forced the Joliet Park District to redirect its resources toward better maintenance and improvements for parks serving the lower-income East Side instead.[37]

Housing   Faith in Action for Community Equity (FACE) obtained more than $7 million in federal money for repairs, another $200,000 for road work, and $500,000 for renovation design, a major victory for the Kalihi Valley Homes Residents Association in Honolulu in their effort to improve living conditions.[38] They have shifted spending priorities to discourage gentrification and promote rebuilding of poor neighborhoods by community-based groups.

The Jewish Council on Urban Affairs coordinated a campaign for an ordinance that saved many hundreds of units of housing for low-income single adults. West Siders whose homes were displaced by the construction of the United Center in 1991 were not scattered due to the efforts of the Interfaith Organizing Project. Replacement housing was built nearby. In the winter of 1999–2000, Chicago's gas utility company provided services as a private enterprise, shutting off gas to people who fell behind in their payments. In that year, 4,821 families were left without heat. Chicago ACORN succeeded in preventing the local utility company from continuing those practices, and in the following winter the number of families left without heat was reduced to 103.[39]

Education Services   Harkening back to the Progressive Era when school community centers pioneered in community organizing, the Logan Square Neighborhood Association (LSNA) created community centers in four local elementary schools, demonstrating that early ideas pioneered by social workers are still valuable. The LSNA created the plan, organized to get funding, and partnered with a wide variety of related organizations. Their activities led to keeping school buildings open to the community in the evening and offering academic, recreational, social–service, and leadership development activities for community residents.

During the middle and late 1990s, the Southwest Organizing Project (SWOP) initiated a major expansion of English as a second language (ESL) classes in a region of the city that is home to sizable immigrant populations. Then, after organizing to ensure permanent funding, SWOP handed off the administration and support of these classes to a community college while retaining convenient class locations in member churches.[40]

Law Enforcement   Community organizations have worked to reduce police abuses and even gotten local police departments to work more closely with neighborhood groups. The Lakeview Action Council, for example, gained the extension of police bike patrols into late-night hours, contributing to a decrease in the number of hate crimes in a neighborhood previously troubled by gay bashing and improving police-community relations. They even have worked to supplement the efforts of local law enforcement. The faith-based Queens Citizen Organization (QCO) in New York City is fighting professional arsonists who have burned down much of the Bronx. JACOB spearheaded the adoption of citywide community policing by the Joliet Police Department.[41]

Improve Business Practices   Community organizations challenge local corporations over insurance rates, housing finance, jobs, and health care. They pressure banks to stop redlining and have forced landlords to fix slum buildings and stop rent gouging. The Metropolitan Tenants Organization led a citywide campaign that resulted in passage in 1986 of the Chicago Tenants Bill of Rights, a municipal ordinance that substantially increased tenants rights in large- and medium-sized Chicago apartment buildings.

Community organizations push for specific change by pressuring corporations to pay a living wage. In 1998 a broad coalition of community organizations spearheaded by the Chicago Association of Community Organizations for Reform Now (ACORN) convinced the city council to pass an ordinance requiring city contractors to pay all of their employees at least $7.60 per hour. This work has expanded to win wage increases for state-employed home care workers, nursing home workers, and group home workers. They challenge developers who want to reclaim vacant or public property for private development. Developers in Chicago, for example, coveted a multiacre property that had been the grounds of a Tuberculosis Sanitarium. The North River Commission led a successful campaign to preserve the land as a public park, nature center, and site for senior citizen housing instead.

Community organizations work with the business community as well. Brighton Park Neighborhood Council brought a fragmented and discouraged southwest side business community together in 1999, helping them take action to rejuvenate their businesses and cope with zoning problems, blight, and crime.[42]

COMMUNITY ORGANIZING AND MODELS OF SOCIAL DEVIANCE

Community organizers often use the organizational and intergroup conflict models of social deviance to guide their efforts.

Organizational Deviance Model

Community organizers understand that both corporate and governmental organizations operate by the same bureaucratic principles that drive them toward goals that maximize their survival, induce them to follow standardized, routinized procedures, and often resist change. Corporate and governmental organizations can become power centers that override the interests of community members. When the policies, procedures, or activities of large organizational structures interfere with or threaten to undermine communities, community organizers use an organizational deviance model, described in Chapter 2, to guide their understanding and practice.

Corporate Deviance   Social work community organizers understand how large corporate organizations serve their own interests, often to the detriment of those living in small, low-income communities. When a large corporation decides to locate in one of these communities, it destroys the community's culture and local economy. The company may fail to pay a living wage, force local merchants out of business, construct massive buildings, endanger the health of residents by polluting their environment, and distort the decision-making process by dominating local government, often persuading government officials to provide special concessions such as tax breaks, subsidies, or variances from local land use laws. In 1996, for example, a large coalition of community-based and environmental organizations known as WASTE (Westside Alliance for a Safe, Toxic-free Environment) convinced the city of Chicago to close down the Northwest Incinerator, a major source of air pollution in a densely populated neighborhood. Also in Chicago, property owned by the Canadian Pacific Railroad was neither secured nor maintained and presented a real threat to the safety of children. In 1998 Blocks Together successfully pressed the railroad to secure, maintain, and monitor its right-of-way.[43]

Government Organizational Deviance　One role of government is to help community members provide a congenial, safe, and just social environment in which residents can fulfill their lives. However, in carrying out this function, government may develop control systems that flow from their own structure rather than serve their communities. Community organizers assist members in challenging local government organizations to be more responsive to neighborhoods. Cicero Police Department officers, for example, following department policy, routinely stopped drivers merely for having a foreign appearance. The Interfaith Leadership Project (ILP) of Cicero, Berwyn, and Stickney challenged this policy and won a major change to this practice. ILP also prevented the town of Cicero from selling one of its few parks to a developer and has been the force behind school board actions taken to reduce school overcrowding.[44]

Intergroup Conflict Model of Social Deviance

Interest group liberalism theory asserts that American politics is, in large part, structured to ensure that organized, often wealthy interest groups will struggle for dominance to achieve their policy preferences in competition with other like-minded groups. Each group will seek concessions from government in the form of subsidies, favorable treatment, and tax breaks. They will attempt to obtain a large market share of business and to persuade consumers to purchase their products and services. Competition is supposed to lead to a balance in which each group attains at least a portion of its goals and in which everyone benefits. In addition, by competing with one another, these interest groups are presumed to adjust their self-interested maximizing behavior to achieve a stable society. Government serves as an umpire to ensure that the rules of the game are obeyed and that the playing field remains level.

Collusion　At times, however, rather than compete, interest groups collude with one another to manipulate the market, dominate the political process, and ensure that rules are made and interpreted in their favor. Some of the more frequent targets of power extraction are local, state, and provincial governments where interest group politics can be played to their advantage. Large interests will struggle to maximize

their power and interests no matter what kind of political culture exists. To the extent that business dominates the political process, society becomes captive not only to economic exploitation but to a corporate mentality that prizes self-interest, wealth accumulation, and control as dominate societal values.

Community Organization Response　Community organizers restructure the contest. They aim for social capital, not financial wealth. They use conflict as a limited strategy, not as a political model, engage in bargaining and negotiation, and in time may reach a point of cooperation and conciliation.

Restructure the Contest　Ordinary people in their own neighborhoods are not helpless in coping with exploitative interest groups. Communities of people cannot often compete with the physical or financial resources corporate systems can command, but they can shift the context in which the game is played to tip the balance in their favor. What community members often lack in monetary wealth or institutionalized power, they far exceed in their ability to mobilize people for common action and to harness public opinion. By directing their energies at the centers of power, community members can often bring decision making to a halt to achieve their just causes. Community organizations bring corporations and government to the bargaining table to solidify changes.

Social Capital, Not Financial Wealth　Interest groups may engage in conflict for power and wealth for their own sake, but community members fight for the right to create their social environment and build civic culture. Members of community organizations struggle against exploitation not to achieve power but justice; not to accumulate monetary riches but richness of a way of life; not to acquire material resources but resources of character, relationship, and civic culture.

Strategy, Not a Political Model　Conflict is not an end in itself but a limited and specific strategy for demonstrating the determination of community members, their willingness to endure difficulty, take risks, and struggle to achieve success. Conflict shows their adversaries that people with low incomes will not be frightened, discouraged, intimidated, or seduced into surrendering their solidarity or become appeased by the powerful. Once those in power understand that community members will not concede defeat, community organization members have dissolved the strongest weapons of those in power and conflict has served its purpose. Further conflict will only become self-defeating and antagonistic.

Bargaining and Negotiation   Once the community organization has acquired power on its own terms and for its own purposes, special interests may be willing to sit down with community members as equals and negotiate on a fair and level field. Community members shift from overt confrontation to bargaining and negotiation. When negotiations take place, however, wealthy interest groups must understand that unless concessions are made with integrity and in good faith, the community members will continue to withhold consent and do it consistently.

Community members make agreements always with the implied if not explicit understanding they will not let government or corporate managers escape their responsibility or their commitments. Linthicum asserts that one of the most important tasks "is for people to hold the government, business, educational and social institutions responsible to do what the law and their agreements requires them to do."[45]

Cooperation and Conciliation   If, after a period of time, megastructures of society show that they are willing to contribute to the community and prove that they are trustworthy, there may be room for the community organization to adopt a different approach. Rather than engage special interests as enemies or competitors, community organizers and community developers may invite them to be partners in building a better society. Instead of accepting the idea that power and wealth are scarce and limited commodities over which people must conflict, bargain, and strategize, community members may take a stance that political power and economic prosperity are goods that everyone can share, and that once shared they increase in various ways that can contribute to each other's benefit. In this way various interest groups are transformed into positive assets that can cooperatively work for the good of society as a whole.

However, community members take this conciliatory approach understanding that although special interests and the organizations they command may appear to cooperate, these groups may continue to assert their exploitative interests. Community organizations operate as "watchdogs" and must be willing to continue the struggle if corporate interests betray their promises.

A BRIEF HISTORY OF COMMUNITY ORGANIZING IN AMERICA

Labor organizing has been pervasive throughout American history. During the Progressive Era, macro social workers were already organizing communities. From about 1900 to 1930, the School Community Center movement was a major source of neighborhood organizing efforts. Community organizing came into its own in the 1930s and 1940s, however, with the work of Saul Alinsky.[46] During the 1950s and 1960s, community organizing was a major reason for the success of the civil rights and welfare rights movements. Since then, community organizing has broadened its aims, often working in partnership with corporations and government. Community organizing has been an integral, ongoing, and significant factor in the civil life of the United States throughout much of its history and continuing into the 21st century.[47]

Labor Organizing

Labor organizing, among the most intensive and difficult organizing in America, has existed in this country for more than 350 years. Organizing for worker rights has occurred in blue-collar neighborhoods and adjacent factories, mines, and factory towns. The number of violent confrontations of labor with recalcitrant factory owners and managers throughout our history far exceeds the peaceful, nonviolent demonstrations of today. Many direct confrontation tactics community organizers have subsequently used, such as picketing, marching, boycotts, leafleting, and noncooperation with oppression, originated in the struggles of labor organizing. Labor unions perfected the processes of bargaining and negotiation. The struggle for workers' rights continues internationally today among the 80% of the world's population who live in poverty. You will learn more about the history of labor organizing in Chapter 14.

The Progressive Era (1880–1915)

Charity Organization Societies (COS)   As the Charity Organization Society (COS) movement evolved, it concerned itself not only with individuals but paid increasing attention to "pauperism," a social condition that seemed to keep some people poor.

It was natural for charity organizations to focus their efforts in neighborhoods where poor people lived. COS leaders modified their organizational structure to engage communities directly, dividing their operation into districts corresponding to police precincts to get charitable services closer to the people.[48] This locality approach to poverty encouraged many Charity Organization Societies to establish new community services such as antituberculosis committees, housing committees, child labor committees, and remedial loan committees, resulting in the "earliest professional community organization in social work."[49]

Social Settlements   Community organization was one of the major activities of social settlements. While other types of neighborhood organizing existed during the Progressive Era, says Robert Fisher, "the social work approach, best exemplified in the social settlements, . . . dominated the era."[50] The settlement assumed a "special responsibility for all families living within the radius of a few blocks of the settlement house [and] it sustained a general relationship to the larger district encircling the neighborhood"[51] bringing about needed changes through direct efforts, mobilization of local resources, and democratic social action.[52]

In Boston, for example, settlements helped organize sixteen district improvement societies, whose members chose delegates to the citywide United Improvement Associations (UIAs). These associations "played a positive role in delivering needed services, raising public consciousness about slum conditions, and called for collective action to ameliorate problems."[53] They developed institutional resources suited to the needs of a working-class community, including relief of distress and development of neglected recreation. Settlement workers engaged community members, pushing for municipal reforms to improve sanitation, sewage disposal, and clean water in neighborhoods. Settlement workers such as Julia Lathrop conducted research into the incidence of tuberculosis and showed its relationship to the crowded conditions of the tenements. She and others advocated for building inspections and regulation and inspection of food to prevent disease, and she became active in the consumer protection movement. Robert Fisher asserts "there is no question about the sincerity or commitment to social reform of those who made the settlement their life's work."[54]

School Community Centers (1900–1929)

Social reformers active in settlements, recreation, and adult education banded together as early as 1907 to lobby for the after-school use of school buildings as neighborhood social centers. The Rochester Board of Education appropriated funds to use 16 school buildings for civic and social purposes serving both youth and adults. It worked so well that in 1908 a citywide federation of school-based civic clubs was formed. They were used as "centers for voting, employment information, recreation, education, health services, and Americanization programs."[55] In 1909, however, ward politicians, fearful of competition, cut off funds for the school centers.[56]

In spite of its short existence, the Rochester experience attracted wide attention. By 1911, 48 cities were using 248 school buildings as community centers, and by 1919 these community centers were operating in 197 cities.[57] By 1930 New York City alone had almost 500 school community centers, with an annual aggregate attendance of more than 4 million. The school community center was "an organizing center for the life of the neighborhood."[58]

School community center workers were regarded as neighborhood leaders. They were on the job continuously, stimulating the community to develop its own activities, and showing how they could pay their way. After a while some centers developed self-governing committees consisting of a representative from each member club. In New York, through the influence of the People's Institute, for example, school centers were used as a base for forming neighborhood organizations.[59]

Although community centers were supposed to be governed from the bottom up, a tendency toward professionalization, bureaucratization, and centralization existed throughout the liberal reform movement of the early 20th century.[60] "Citizen involvement became limited to membership in clubs and participation in center activities," while planning was left primarily to professionals, who made most of the important decisions.[61] Gradually the centers came to belong to the professionals who ran them rather than to neighborhood residents. The centers evolved into "professionalized forms of neighborhood service delivery that characterized much social work community organization before and since that time."[62] The school center movement peaked in the mid-1920s and gradually disappeared. The ideal of self-governing school centers never gained widespread acceptance, and other methods were developed to organize city neighborhoods.[63]

Saul Alinsky and Grassroots Community Organizing (1935–1940)

During the depression era of the 1930s, the social work approach that had been useful at the turn of the century had much less salience and support. As capitalism collapsed, one reform solution after another failed to halt the economic depression. The political activist type of neighborhood organizing, most notably the radical efforts of the Communist party in many cities and the urban populist work of Saul Alinsky in the Back of the Yards neighborhood in Chicago, personified a new approach to grassroots organizing activity.[64]

Saul David Alinsky, born in Chicago on January 30, 1909, is America's best-known community organizer.[65] Although he was not the first to combine political activism with an emphasis on rebuilding a specific community, he was the first to do it in a number of neighborhoods across the nation by organizing existing groups into federated coalitions. He is the main bridge between the past and future of organizing, primarily because of the extent of his work and the number of his students who have influenced the movement. His work is central to a comprehensive understanding of community organizing.

After receiving his BA degree from the University of Chicago, Alinsky accepted a fellowship in the university's graduate program in criminology. He studied the Mafia organization of notorious "Scarface" Al Capone and other Italian street gangs and became a research sociologist at the Illinois State Penitentiary at Jolliet. In 1935, in the middle of the Depression, Alinsky ended his 3-year program at Jolliet and joined Clifford Shaw's Chicago Area Project to investigate the feasibility of establishing a juvenile delinquency prevention program in the Back of the Yards, a working-class neighborhood located behind Chicago's stockyards and meatpacking plants.

At the time Alinsky arrived, John L. Lewis, president of the CIO labor union, was organizing stockyard workers in Chicago's meatpacking industry, the largest employer in Back of the Yards. Alinsky became intrigued by the dedication, conviction, skill, and expertise of the union organizers, who were involved in many of the important social and political issues of the day. Labor organizers entered into the lives of the stockyard workers, convincing people that their problems were not unique but connected with the problems of poor and exploited people everywhere. They preached unity, solidarity, action, and reform.

After three years of learning how to organize mass meetings, identify and develop issues, raise money, and recruit members, Alinsky decided to apply the CIO model to organizing community members to seek justice. Beginning with groups of local residents, including neighborhood groups, ethnic clubs, union locals, bowling leagues, and an American Legion Post, Alinsky formed a coalition of neighborhood organizations. On July 14, 1939, the indigenous leaders of the Back of the Yards Neighborhood Council (BYNC) held their constitutional convention, attended by 350 delegates representing 109 local organizations. Two days later a large delegation from the council marched to a CIO rally in a show of solidarity with meatpacking workers. The rally convinced the company of the grassroots strength of the union, and they reluctantly decided to negotiate a CIO contract, launching Alinsky on a long career organizing people in poor urban communities around the country.[66] Saul Alinsky, the social researcher, had become a community organizer.

The BYNC launched new programs, including a well baby clinic, neighborhood job fairs, a credit union, and a school lunch program in which 1,400 kids were fed hot meals. These programs were important, but Alinsky was concerned about more fundamental issues that created powerlessness. Organized apathy, he asserted, is what keeps people from getting involved with one another, keeps them in a state of helplessness and hopelessness, and prevents them from taking action. The hopelessness and alienation people feel may turn them against one another in destructive ways.

Rather than programs, Alinsky wanted the residents to understand that the real objective of the council was to build collective power so that Back of the Yards residents could run their own neighborhood and make it the kind of community they wanted.[67] Alinsky believed that mass corporate dominance induces people to accept powerlessness in exchange for security, and the surrender of autonomy in return for being taken care of by those in control.[68] According to Alinsky, the Back of the Yards district, was a cesspool of hate: the Poles, Slovaks, Germans, Negroes, Mexicans and Lithuanians. Fascist groups like the German-American Bund, Father Coughlin's National Union for Social Justice, and William Dudley Pelley's Silver Shirts were moving to exploit that discontent. . . .

It wasn't because the people had any real sympathy for fascism; it was just that they were so desperate that they grabbed onto anything that offered them a glimmer of hope. Coughlin and Pelley gave them scapegoats in the Jews and the international bankers.

I knew that once people were provided with a positive program to change their miserable conditions they wouldn't need scapegoats anymore. Probably my prime consideration in moving into Back of the Yards, though, was because if it could be done there, it could be done anywhere.[69]

Alinsky's strategy was to destroy the structure of apathy by stirring up dissatisfaction and discontent; disrupting existing complacent expectations, and breaking down the individualistic orientations of community residents. After every action Alinsky made the leaders take the time to talk about what had happened. They dissected, analyzed, and criticized each event until they understood why they won or lost. Each victory was celebrated with speeches and impromptu parties. Alinsky's careful organizing paid off. The Back of the Yards Neighborhood Council grew into a vigorous organization.[70]

Later Alinsky reflected on these lessons he learned from the Back of the Yards experience:

1. To hell with charity. The only thing you get is what you are strong enough to get—so you had better organize.

2. You prove to people they can do something, show them how to have a way of life where they can make their own decisions, then you get out. They don't need a father who stands over them.

3. It comes down to the basic argument of the Federalist papers. Either you believe in people, like James Madison and James Monroe, or you don't. . . . I do.[71]

Community Organizing in the 1940s

Alinsky Expands In August 1940 Marshall Field III, who was to become one of Alinsky's closest friends, joined with Alinsky and Bishop Bernard

J. Shiel in establishing the Industrial Areas Foundation (IAF). The IAF board of trustees voted to raise $15,000 a year for five years to support Alinsky's organizing efforts, enabling him to devote himself full time to organizing and to hire additional staff. Alinsky began sending organizers to other working-class neighborhoods in northern industrial cites, to Mexican American communities in the Southwest, and to Kansas City and South St. Paul in America's heartland. Established community leaders didn't always welcome them. Sometimes they were arrested or thrown out of town.

Fred Ross and Organizing Mexican Americans

Discrimination had been practiced against Mexican Americans in California for more than a century. When Mexican American veterans returned to their homes after World War II and the Korean War, the gap between what they had learned in the armed services and what they found upon their return seemed intolerable, including unfair treatment by public agencies in voter registration, school busing, examinations for naturalization, and welfare benefits.

Concerned about the discrimination practiced against Mexican Americans in California, the American Council on Race Relations undertook to set up Councils for Civic Unity in the spring of 1946. Fred Ross had been manager of the farm labor camp at Arvin and later was put in charge of 25 camps in California and Arizona. As assistant director of Community Services for the Farm Security Administration, Ross was hired to organize Councils for Civic Unity, which eventually were to be combined into a state federation, the California Federation for Civic Unity. As a result of his organizing experience in several barrios in Southern California, Ross came to Saul Alinsky's attention. In early June 1947, after meeting with Ross, Alinsky hired him as a staff member with the Industrial Areas Foundation. It was clear to Ross that among Mexican Americans an organization would have to be built house by house, and perhaps in time several organizations could be brought together into a federation.[72]

Community Organizing in the 1950s

In the 1950s a conservative reaction occurred in the United States, particularly among neighborhood homeowner associations. Migrant Ministries organized migrant farm workers, and Alinsky continued his work in the Midwest and far West. Fred Ross and Cesar Chavez joined Alinsky in helping to organize community service organizations with Mexican Americans in California. Social work included community organizing as one of its methods.

Homeowners Organizations

Robert Fisher says homeowner associations sprang up for the purpose of protecting property values in those neighborhoods where home ownership was an economic investment and homeowners, not the government, bore the burden of maintaining and improving their investments. During the conservative eras of the 1920s and 1950s, segregationist impulses became typical of these neighborhood associations, interconnecting the protection of property values with the politics of neighborhood exclusion. Simultaneously, the conservative cold war economy stifled much of depression era social activism. Many community groups and organizations retreated from political action and concentrated instead on providing social service maintenance programs.

Slashing expressways through residential areas, razing thousands of slum buildings, and refurbishing central business districts produced resentment among the city residents whose neighborhoods were being wrecked. As early as 1953 the idea of mobilizing public opinion for more responsible urban renewal found fertile ground at the local level. Citizen participation began to be the watchword in renewal activities.[73]

In spite of the reactionary tendencies of many homeowner associations in the 1950s and in the midst of the repressive Army-McCarthy hearings that created a near paranoic fear of Communism in the United States, under Alinsky's direction in the latter half of the 1950s the IAF developed many new community organizations. The IAF established the Chelsea Community Council (CCC), a coalition of 77 organizations in 1957, the Citizens Federation of Lackawanna (CFL) in New York in 1958, the Butte Citizens Project (BCP) in Montana in 1959, and in that same year, the Organization for the Southwest Council (OSC) in Chicago. By 1963 both the Northwest Community Organization (NCO) and the Woodlawn Organization (TWO) in Chicago, one of the most famous and important of Alinsky's organizations, were in operation.[74]

Migrant Ministries

A grant made by the Emil Schwartzhaupt Foundation to the Migrant Ministry of the Division of Christian Life and Mission of the National Council of Churches stimulated citizenship education through organizing work among migrant agricultural workers who traveled from Texas to Michigan and Illinois. Organizing activities including English language proficiency, voter registration, and citizenship classes were initiated in the Texas, Illinois, and Michigan communities where organizations were started.

Alinsky and Community Service Organizations

Alinsky had been trying to raise money for an IAF organizing program in California, and in 1951 he forwarded a proposal to the Emil Schwartzhaupt Foundation, which awarded $15,000 on an interim basis to encourage and assist Mexican Americans in California in forming community service organizations, or CSOs. Fred Ross joined the IAF's Community Service Organizations, eventually being named IAF field director for California and Arizona. Unfortunately, the limited funding then available to the IAF ran out, and by 1952 Ross was back with the California Federation of Civic Unity, organizing efforts in San Jose where he met Cesar Chavez. In July 1953, however, Alinsky received an additional $150,000 grant for a 3-year period, and work of the CSOs expanded to Salinas and soon thereafter to Fresno and San Bernardino. Cesar Chavez was hired to begin organizing in Oakland. CSO programs included English and citizenship classes, voter registration, leadership development, and educational programs. They brought pressure to bear against discriminatory practices in the issuance of motor vehicle licenses, eligibility for welfare benefits, and police misconduct.

English Literacy and Citizenship Classes Throughout the 1950s, a great amount of time and effort was invested in Los Angles, San Bernardino, Hanford, Oxnard, Fresno, and San Jose by CSO members in English literacy programs and citizenship classes for Mexican Americans. Over a 10-year period, perhaps 30,000 completed CSO-sponsored classes in English and citizenship, and by November 1962 virtually all those interested in qualifying for citizenship in Spanish had gone through the program.

Voter Registration Prior to 1960, the CSO had registered 298,000 persons, providing them with eligibility to vote in the 1960 national election and making it possible for Mexican Americans for the first time to seriously consider running for office. These unprecedented registration totals were essential to reducing if not eliminating much of the discrimination practiced against Mexican Americans.

Leadership   Chavez asserted that informed and dedicated leadership in the California Mexican American community existed only in the CSO. Chavez pointed out that impoverished Mexican Americans had not known that through the simple device of the house meeting it was possible to bring people together and help move them to work for the solution of their problems. As a result of the efforts of CSO organizers, however, many citizen leaders were active up and down the state of California, and their impact was evident throughout the rest of the Southwest, especially in Texas and Arizona.

Educational Classes   The CSO's wise leadership and their ability to take a broad view made effective use of "educationals"—groups of members who discussed problem situations, shared ideas, and learned techniques and strategies, often using a Socratic method of question and answer. Educationals provided skill training, leadership training, dialoguing, critiquing community strategies, and stories of victories and successes.[75]

AN EDUCATIONAL HAS AN IMPACT

Three Blacks were refused service by a Mexican American bartender, who was a former community service organization (CSO) member. Discussion in the educational, led by Luis Zarate, came to the conclusion that it was just as wrong for a Mexican American to discriminate against Blacks as it was for Anglos to discriminate against Mexican Americans. As the CSO president, Ernest Abeytia said, "We are trying to integrate our people into the community by dispelling discrimination. How in the world are we going to accomplish that if we do the same thing?"

The CSO decided to join the local NAACP in filing a suit against the bartender. In view of the tensions existing among many in the Black and Mexican American communities toward one another, it is a tribute to the educational process, and to the persons involved, that members of the CSO and NAACP could reach such a decision.[76]

Social Work and Community Organizing
According to Hallman, by the 1950s the professionalization of social work was complete, including casework, group work, and community organization as its major divisions. Community organization was viewed as a process used by professional workers engaged in health and welfare planning and included coordination or the financing of direct service agencies. "Very few social workers engaged in grassroots neighborhood organizing. The main exceptions were settlement houses and neighborhood centers"[77] whose major activities were group and casework services. Many, however, also "studied neighborhood problems, helped organize block associations, neighborhood organizations, and tenant councils and got involved in social action."[78]

The Turbulent 1960s

The seeds of the reformist impulses of the 1960s had already been sown by social policies of the 1950s that provided low-interest government subsidized housing, the GI bill, automobiles, and the American dream to middle- and upper-income Americans while at the same time offering slums, segregated schools, public transportation, and an urban nightmare to everyone else. Proliferating community organizations inspired by Alinksy-style organizing had plowed the ground. An almost simultaneous decision was made on college campuses, in Black neighborhoods, Mexican American barrios, and in communities of single mothers on welfare that enough was enough.

Community organizing became a major tool of social change, growing into the civil rights and welfare rights movements mainly in the Northeast, Midwest, and the South. Community organizing continued with the CSO organizations and Cesar Chavez's United Farm Workers in the West, aided by Community Action Programs (CAPs) in major cities of the nation.

Civil Rights Movement   Randy Stoecker asserts that in the United States community organizing in the 1960s was exemplified by small local organizations like the Montgomery Improvement Association, which helped lead the famed Montgomery Bus Boycott and others that provided the impetus for what became a national civil rights movement. The Montgomery Bus Boycott was coordinated through local African American networks and organizations and created a model that would be used in locality-based actions throughout the South. The Student Nonviolent Coordinating Committee (SNCC) organized African American communities and stimulated community action in the South to register voters and gain voting rights.

Welfare Rights Movement   George Wiley, Chairman of the Syracuse office of the Congress of Racial Equality (CORE), helped organize the welfare rights movement out of which grew the Association of Community Organizations for Reform Now (ACORN),[79] one of the most successful and active coalitions of local community organizations today.

The Community Service Organization   The classes in English and citizenship organized by CSOs throughout California for tens of thousands of Mexican Americans was an effort unparalleled in California history, opening the doors for their effective participation as citizens. Shortly before and during 1960, the CSO followed up this effort by embarking on an intensive voter registration effort. Using more than 500 deputy registrars and "bird dogs" who went door to door to bring unregistered persons to the deputy registrars, 137,096 new registrants were recorded in 1960, bringing the grand total to more than 430,000 new voters.

In addition to conducting "get-out-the-vote" campaigns, CSO chapters held "meet-your-candidate" nights and were responsible for providing the support that gained enactment of legislation of great concern to the Mexican American community. As a result, by 1960 a number of Mexican Americans had been elected to municipal, county, state, and congressional offices.

For a period of about 15 years, the CSO did more than any other organization in California to help the Mexican American community feel a sense of *being* something, as a prerequisite to *becoming* something, reports Carl Tjerandsen. It was one of the great contributions of the CSO that it turned thousands, if not tens of thousands, of people around in their thinking. They became aware not only of their rights as citizens but of their responsibility to work for the benefit of the community.[80]

CAESAR CHAVEZ, COMMUNITY ORGANIZER

For 41 years Cesar Chavez taught the poorest people in America to stand up for their rights—and to do it without violence. His formal education ended after the eighth grade. He never owned a home or earned more than $6,000 a year. Against tremendous odds, he organized the first successful farm workers union

---

in history. He turned compliant and submissive people into courageous champions of their families and communities. He chose a life of self-imposed poverty, grueling hours, and the frequent threat of physical violence and death. Yet his deeds live on in the millions of people he inspired with an unshakable conviction that society can be transformed from within.[81]

Cesar Chavez and the United Farmworkers Union (UFW)   In 1962 Chavez resigned from the National CSO to begin organizing farm workers. Four years later, Fred Ross also left the IAF and joined Chavez. This unionizing effort took the form of direct confrontation, including national boycotts of lettuce and grapes, which many people supported, and resulted in the first farmworkers union in California.

Community Action Agencies   With the inauguration of President John F. Kennedy, the national government became more assertive in promoting and supporting new approaches to old problems and in fostering community change. Federal agencies, national organizations, and some foundations actively pushed the application of new ideas. These national entities began funding local organizers, sometimes sending them in from the outside.[82] Government called for participation by the poor and developed programs to increase it. Pressure for access was a priority, and participation became the byword.[83]

Great Society   The Great Society programs under Lyndon Johnson added a new dimension to urban community organization. As a consequence of the Economic Opportunity Act (EOA) of 1964, an Office of Economic Opportunity (OEO) as well as Community Action Agencies (CAAs) were set up to operate and oversee the various community action programs (CAPs) in local neighborhoods. As they shaped up around the nation in 1965, 90% of the CAAs took the form of private nonprofit organizations, and local government operated the rest. Most CAAs set up neighborhood units as well as resident advisory committees for programs such as Head Start.

Maximum Feasible Participation   The Economic Opportunity Act required "maximum feasible participation" of residents in areas served, which initially was interpreted to mean at least one-third representation of people who existed on low incomes on

CAA governing boards. In 1966 Congress made this amount of citizen participation a legal requirement. Most of the representatives of the poor were selected by neighborhood committees or area councils, which themselves were chosen by residents, usually in open meetings but occasionally by ballot. Hiring organizers with public funds became commonplace, and most of the urban CAAs developed neighborhood-based programs.

Reaction Community action programs (CAPs) constituted a sufficient challenge to existing ways of doing things, however, that forces of reaction set in almost immediately. A 1967 amendment to the EOA required that one third of the local community action boards be comprised of government officials, giving local government power to take over the programs. Although few governments used this power, the threat to do so, combined with tightened OEO regulations, constrained the more militant activities of CAAs. After an initial thrust of organizing, many CAAs settled into providing social service programs, spending the bulk of their funds to remedy perceived defects of individuals rather than changing institutions or social systems.[84]

Community Organizing in the 1970s

On June 12, 1972, Alinsky died in Carmel, California, leaving behind a rich legacy of local, broad-based community organizations. Alinsky had organized, in one way or another, a couple of million men and women to take control of their lives, and he made many more Americans aware of the power of organized citizen participation to make needed changes in social institutions and government regulations. The large-scale citizen mobilizations of our time—women, antiwar and antinuclear activists, consumers, environmentalists—whether they are aware of it or not, owe most of their bottom-up organizational strategy and effective nonviolent tactics to Saul Alinsky. "Along with the Rev. Martin Luther King Jr., Alinsky deserves credit for freeing American churches from suburban captivity as ghetto sanctuaries and bringing church people into the city streets and village roads where people were struggling with problems and possibilities of everyday life."[85]

National People's Action (NPA) Gale Cincotta, a community organizer for the Organization for a Better Austin, an Alinsky-style organization, joined with

Shel Trapp and others to convene a National Housing Conference in Chicago in March 1972 that drew 2,000 delegates from 74 cities in 36 states. Out of this conference came a national membership association on housing, the National Peoples Action (NPA), and a support organization, the National Training and Information Center (NTIC).

The NPA helped 13 community groups form the Metropolitan Area Housing Alliance, which led a campaign that succeeded in getting the Commission of Savings and Loan Association of Illinois to adopt an anti-redlining regulation in 1974. Turning their attention nationally, this force, supported by grassroots organizations in many other cities and some Washington-based national organizations, pushed until they got Congress to adopt the Federal Home Mortgage Disclosure Act of 1975, which gave grassroots groups one of their most important tools for uncovering redlining practices, and the powerful Community Reinvestment Act (CRA) of 1977. The CRA resulted in more than $100 billion being invested in neighborhoods and stimulated additional legislation authorizing a presidentially appointed National Commission on Neighborhoods during the Carter administration.[86]

The NPA fought for and won passage of 14 pieces of national legislation, including the 518(b) HUD payback program, which returned money to FHA homeowners when they were defrauded by sleazy realtors and mortgage bankers. The NPA, in addition, won a massive reinvestment program for targeted neighborhoods by Aetna Insurance Company and by Marriott International, which established school-to-work programs for youth.[87]

Community Organizing in the 1980s

According to Robert Fisher, economic support for social services and community organizing declined in the 1980s because of opposition from the neoconservative Reagan/Bush administrations, a shrinking tax base at the local level, and a shift in political discourse in the nation that revolved around free market solutions to most social problems. Confronting government officials became less and less productive, and even when local government officials were sympathetic with a community issue, they felt they did not have the resources to address them. Some community organizations such as IAF adapted to the conservative culture, creating working relationships between those with and without power to promote the interests of its members. One of these efforts was organizing community development corporations.[88]

In spite of this, however, many community organizations continued to press for the empowerment of people and for redress. By 1981 the number of national training centers, national support networks, and associations of community organizations had expanded to two dozen, including among others Grassroots Leadership, begun by social worker Si Kahn in the South, Direct Action and Research Training (DART), the Gamaliel Foundation, the New England Training Center for Community Organizers in Providence, Saul Alinsky's Industrial Areas Foundation (IAF), Heather Booth's Midwest Academy, Gale Cincotta and Shel Trapp's National Training and Information Center (NTIC) in Chicago, Mike Miller's Organize Training Center (OTC) in San Francisco, Fr. John Bauman's Pacific Institute of Community Organizing (PICO) in Oakland, California, and the Center for Third World Organizing, also in Oakland.[89] Three hundred newsletters and periodicals that focused extensively on community organizations existed in 1985.[90]

Community Organizing in the 1990s

Much community organizing in the 1990s and into 2000 was occurring within faith-based groups. These congregation-based organizations were modeled after the social network process developed by the Industrial Areas Foundation (IAF), Pacific Institute of Community Organizing (PICO), Direct Action Research and Training (DART), and the Gamaliel Foundation.[91] But whether community organizations are affiliated with one of these larger networks or develop independently from the grassroots, they continue to diversify and have become more innovative, consensual, and demand accountable development.

Diversity   Community organizations continue to be involved with a great diversity of issues. NTIC, for example, made important contributions to passage of the Americans With Disabilities Act of 1990, and since 1995 it has collaborated with the departments of labor and justice and 10 community groups, including the Michigan Organizing Project (MOP), Action Through Churches Together in Virginia, and Cincinnati's Working in Neighborhoods (WIN),

exploring ways to put unemployed people back to work. NTIC continues to work with organizations such as Chicago's West Humboldt Park neighborhood, the Northwest Neighborhood Federation, and the Narcotics Nuisance Abatement Partnership, among others.

Innovative and Consensual   The violence that ripped through Los Angeles in April 1992 left more than 50 people dead and $1 billion in damages, asserts Torie Osborn. Rebuilding Los Angeles would require more than government and private sector investment. Community leaders needed to step into the void, and with the support of local foundations, they did. The federal government allotted some $1.35 million, and the City of Los Angeles responded with Rebuild Los Angeles, raising $389 million before closing its doors in 1997.[92]

A few grassroots community leaders decided to take a new approach, however. Working with local foundations, they helped move philanthropy beyond its historic support for charity, bringing together community organizations from the African American, Asian, and Latino communities of South Central Los Angeles. Together with labor and religious leaders, these organizations met with developers of the Staples Center project, who agreed to hire local workers, offer job training, build affordable housing, and make room for both parks and residential parking. Most important, however, they gained passage of a "living wage" law, approved in 1997, requiring that city contractors guarantee employees a wage that keeps them above the threshold for federal assistance, raising more than 10,000 low-wage workers above the poverty line just as do the 60 other living-wage ordinances across the country.[93]

Accountable Development   Community organizations in other parts of California also began pushing for what is called "accountable development." Accountable development requires developers to provide public benefits, such as child care facilities and teen centers, and community involvement in the selection of retail tenants. For example, in the Staples Center project, Los Angeles inserted a "claw back" provision in its contract with the developer, giving the city the right to demand the return of its subsidies if the developer failed to deliver on its promises. Such provisions have been passed into law in more than a dozen states and municipalities.[94]

The Impact of Community Organizing in the 2000s

According to Randy Stoecker, in the decade 2000 community organizing is experiencing a resurgence, with an explosion of small organizing efforts and the growth of some better-publicized efforts by the Industrial Areas Foundation (IAF), ACORN, and the New Party in their efforts to obtain living wage ordinances, and by many other groups and networks including the rapidly expanding National Organizers Alliance. As a consequence, the community organizing model is providing an increasingly visible alternative to the community development model.[95]

In Chicago alone, for example, the first several years of 2000 provides an impressive array of victories. Members of Chicago community organizations have identified problems, imagined solutions, and worked to get those solutions implemented through advocacy with police departments, youth service agencies, the criminal justice system, school systems, park districts, property owners, and others. Community organizations generate candidates, ideas, support, and friendly criticism for Local School Councils (LSCs) and are now using their community organization skills to provide impetus for new school buildings, renovations for older school buildings, the introduction of curriculum improvements, and action on school safety issues. Thousands of decent, affordable housing units in Chicago today would not exist without the sophisticated action campaigns of community organizations.

South Suburban Action Conference (SSAC), through its 30-member congregations in a dozen municipalities in South Cook County, for example, mobilized to save 900-plus units of low-income housing in Calumet City and created a campaign to get the resources needed to renovate the blighted and dangerous Ginger Ridge complex of garden apartments. Developing Communities Project knew that lack of access to day care was hampering parents' efforts to support their families. DCP lobbied successfully for the creation of a substantial number of subsidized day care slots on the Far South Side of Chicago.

Workforce development resources have often been planned, supported, and funded through the efforts of community groups such as the Westside Technical Institute (pushed by United Neighborhood Organization) and the Marquette Job Development Center (which needed the support of the Southwest Organizing Project). Access to health care, one of our society's thorniest problems, was addressed by community organizing, from the establishment of small clinics to the countywide referral system for the uninsured won by United Power for Action and Justice.[96] The same sorts of victories can be viewed in many other cities across the United States.

HOW TO PRACTICE COMMUNITY ORGANIZING

Community organizing is a creative process that will never be completely perfected. It calls forth the imagination, ingenuity, compassion, and mutual engagement of the organizer and the people. You begin by understanding the people and helping them define the problem that you will work with them to address. You engage the community, empower forces of change, and build an organization.

Understand the People

People who have been forced to live in prolonged poverty or oppression are often unwilling participants in an unequal and hurtful system in which they may feel powerless. Victims of oppression will sometimes repress, minimize, ignore, or deny their circumstances. Some may not want to admit the seriousness of their problems, recognize that their condition is as bad as it is, or believe that things can ever change. They react to their dependency by adopting any number of mechanisms that enable them to survive often brutal life circumstances. People who have spent their lives in conditions of dependency and deprivation may act out, try to get out, opt out, flake out, or cop out.

Act Out People who have been forced to live in deprived conditions sometimes develop harmful behaviors that allow them to survive. Some may *act out* their pain, turning to a life of crime or joining a gang. When this occurs, Saul Alinsky reminds us, that

> the organizer's affection for people is not lessened nor is he hardened against them even when masses of them demonstrate a capacity for brutality, selfishness, hate, greed, avarice, and disloyalty. He is convinced that these attitudes and actions are the result of evil conditions. It is not the people who must be judged but the circumstances that made them that way. The organizer's desire to change society then becomes that much firmer.[97]

Get Out and Opt Out

Others may *get out*—escaping the community and going to a better environment. A very few may *opt out*—rising above poverty and oppression to become successful professionals, actors, or businesspeople.

Flake Out

There are even a few who *flake out*. Flake outs become comedians who bring the pain out into the open by focusing it on themselves so people can laugh about it. They play a therapeutic role by helping people release the pain they feel. For the overwhelming majority of people who live with cultural abuse, economic discrimination, victimization, and racism, however, these survival mechanisms are neither available nor appropriate. Many cannot get out, and acting out only adds to their problems. Neither can everyone opt out or even flake out.

Cop Out

Most victims of oppression *cop out*. Like adult survivors of abuse, they bury their pain and learn to live with an oppressive situation until they become part of the system. They unwillingly and often unwittingly perpetuate the cycle of victimization because they have few choices. A number of scholars have examined this phenomenon, among them Paulo Freire, Overmaier and Seligman, Michael Lerner, and social worker Jose Morales.

Paulo Freire says that the oppressed sometimes behave in ways that "reflect the structure of domination." The oppressed often live with an "existential duality" in which they are "at the same time themselves and the oppressor whose image they have internalized."[98]

In 1967 social psychologists Overmaier and Seligman conducted experimental studies with dogs whom they subjected to circumstances over which they had no control. The animals developed deficits in three areas of their lives. They developed emotional anesthesia, displaying dullness to emotion and numbness to pain. Their behavior changed. Rather than being active they became extremely passive. Cognitively they were unable to learn new responses to their situations even when taught many times. Overmaier and Seligman termed this condition "learned helplessness," which they later showed applies people as well.

Michael Lerner, who in 1967 observed the social movements of the 1960s, coined the term "surplus powerlessness" to capture the identical phenomenon among members of the working classes of the developed world. According to Lerner, people carry powerlessness around with them like a script for living. They exhibit the belief that they cannot change things, interpret victories as defeats, become unable to trust others, and fail to join with others in even small-scale political activity.

What was so bewildering for Lerner was his observation of the cognitive feature of learned helplessness: the incapacity to identify and, therefore, to learn coping responses even when the information is under one's very nose. Lerner asserted that many people who participated in the struggles of the 1960s did not gain a new sense of their own potential power. On the contrary, at the very moment when victories in the struggle were being won, activists redefined the criteria of success, accentuating how little they had accomplished and how overwhelming were the tasks yet to be achieved. As a result, masses of people engaged in political activity in the 1960s were reconfirmed in their powerlessness. It was as if they had learned nothing.[99]

Julio Morales, speaking of Puerto Ricans, calls this condition "self oppression" or a "colonized mentality," which they have experienced as a result of centuries of oppression and colonization. "Many Puerto Ricans have internalized stereotypes," Morales asserts, and "blame themselves for their fate, not understanding that their poverty is responsible for their alienation and feelings of helplessness or that their poverty is a function of a macro process over which they have little, if any control."[100]

Conditioned to accept their situation, many oppressed people tend to think they are not as capable, as competent, or as good as others. Some may even believe they deserve poor services and shoddy living arrangements, and that they should be grateful for anything they get. Some express "dependency or unwarranted respect for authority and authority figures, making it difficult, at times, to organize" them.[101] They may hold an expectation that leaders and experts will solve their problems.

SI KAHN

Si Kahn is one of social work's premier community organizers. He was raised in a small college town in the Pennsylvania mountains, where his father was a rabbi and his mother was an artist. He first began organizing as a volunteer with the Student Nonviolent

Coordinating Committee (SNCC). He moved on to Georgia, working with African American farmers cooperatives and voter registration, and he became a labor organizer in the North Georgia mountains. Kahn worked with the United Mine Workers as a coordinator during the Brookside strike in Harlan County, Kentucky, and then with the Amalgamated Clothing and Textile Workers Union (ACTWU).

Kahn's books, *How People Get Power* and *Organizing: A Guide for Grassroots Leaders,* both published by NASW Press, are classics in the field of community organizing. Kahn is also a folksinger and songwriter. He has recorded nine albums, plus a double album of protest folksongs with Pete Seeger and Jane Sapp. In 1980 he founded the Grassroots Leadership Organization to continue building a multiracial movement in the South.[102]

Overcome Self-Oppression

Rather than give in to this cycle of helplessness, macro social workers help people who are oppressed face issues that they would rather avoid. Recognizing and accepting the reality of the situation is the first step in recovery. The problems of the community will not be solved until and unless community members recognize them, take a stand, and resist those who exploit them. You help people who have internalized oppression rekindle their emotional responses, discard their amnesia, begin to think and remember, and stimulate them to action.

Rekindle Emotional Responses
People who are victims of self-oppression or learned helplessness may not be able or willing to look clearly at the pain they are experiencing. You fire up their anger, touch their innate sense of dignity that has been bruised, appeal to their sadness and sense of loss, tell stories about the tragedies you know that have occurred, and get members to develop emotional contagion with one another. You help members relate their own experiences to begin to reach for emotions they have buried and have nearly forgotten. You help them regain access to feelings that they have not allowed themselves to have.

Warren Haggstrom tells of a group of neighbors who, with the help of organizers, went to a district sanitation inspector to appeal for better street cleaning. During the meeting the inspector claimed that there was no point in putting more equipment into such neighborhoods because the residents didn't care whether their streets were dirty or not. When the community heard the report, they became angry at this affront, and their anger mobilized them to fight the issue.[103]

Discard Amnesia
You use social thinking to help people remember what they are often all too willing to forget. But it is often forgetfulness that oppressors rely on to continue their oppression. You ask people to remember incidents, feelings, indignities, and events that destroyed their pride, injured their spirit, blocked their successes, coerced their compliance, and ensured their unwilling cooperation. You mobilize them to gather facts, conduct research, and confirm what their particular experiences have told them.

You give training to people to facilitate their learning and to use their intellects. You conduct "educationals" to engage them in discussions to brainstorm solutions, come up with innovative and creative ideas to their problems, and devise strategies and tactics. You review what they have done to ensure that they will not forget that they are achieving victories, that their actions are making a difference, and that they are making changes. You help them confirm for themselves that the changes are occurring not by accident, luck, or external circumstances but by their own consciously thought out and orchestrated actions. You engage them in celebrating their victories, telling stories, reviewing their accomplishments, and rewarding their heroes so that they will never forget.

Stimulate Action
You help people act on their renewed feelings and recovered thoughts and ideas rather than remain compliant. You bring people together, stimulate their energies, and mobilize the "rightness" of their cause. Alinsky asserts that you must often be like a salesperson trying to convince people to do something, showing people you are credible, creating a convincing picture of what might be, relying on emotional contagion as well as on a factual account of what can be done.[104] "You pull and jolt them into the public arena," he says. "You listen and appeal to people's self-interest, work along friendship and relationship networks, as well as other formal and informal social structures,"[105] Alinsky asserts,

> Until the people recognize that it is they who must do something about their own problems, that it is only they who can be trusted to do the

right thing and until they realize that only if they organize enough power in their community that something can be done about these things, nothing will get done.[106]

Dealing With Real Life Situations   You understand that just like anyone else, people in poverty are consumed with their own private affairs, personal survival, raising families, making it on the job, and getting along until the next paycheck. Many people in poor, oppressed communities do not have the resources, support systems, education, or influence of more affluent members of society, especially the powerful whom they will be confronting. Moreover, they are made even more helpless by the poverty and stress with which they live. Julio Morales calls this the "full plate" syndrome, in which problem after problem is compounded so that the poor and oppressed have little time or energy to confront their situations. For example, he says,

> racism, violence, AIDS, drugs, crime, homelessness, alienation from the judicial system, massive underemployment or unemployment, high levels of school dropouts, rivalry among adult leadership and others are common ingredients on that crowded plate. Insufficient services to families, inappropriate foster care for Puerto Rican children, lack of school curriculum on the Puerto Rican experience, lack of curriculum aimed at building the self-esteem of Puerto Rican youngsters, and the competing and clashing of cultural values within the larger society add to the full plate. The needs leading to the migration [of many families] to and from Puerto Rico, the different perspectives and levels of acclimating to U.S. society that [people] experience, and intra-community issues such as competition for resources . . . at times fragmentize community efforts.[107]

In spite of all of this, however, the oppressed have their innate dignity and moral justice on their side.

Engage the Community

As you engage the community and its people, you obtain an understanding of the community that you will be organizing. You gain a feeling for their issues and their plight. This must be done carefully. According to Von Hoffman, the initial job of the organizer is to listen to what people have to say about what they want and do not want to happen.[108] Moreover, Alinsky says that "the organizer must learn the characteristics

of the community from a general survey of the situation, plot the power pattern of the community, and look for and evaluate local leaders."[109]

Define the Problem

You place yourself clearly on the side of the people, and you clearly state your purpose in the neighborhood. You do not define their problems for them or provide solutions.[110] Even though you may think other issues are more important and could be addressed more effectively, if the people in a low-income housing project want to begin getting their housing project repaired or their welfare checks increased, you help them act on these issues.

As a community organizer, you assist community members in pinpointing and exposing areas of oppression, intentionally focusing on one or more problem situations that are clearly visible. Neighborhood action organizations, for example, often begin with community issues: municipal services, jobs, health care, housing finance, parent-school problems, consumer action, insurance rates, police protection—all the things that touch us where we live. Alinsky says,

> The problem must be important to the welfare of the community, and one around which people can be mobilized to action. Begin where people are and help them raise issues of acute concern—lack of police protection, crime, gangs that hang out on street corners, drug abuse, poor maintenance of a housing project, or violence that creates an atmosphere of fear in the neighborhood.[111]

Build an Organization

To Alinsky, constructing an effective organization was of central importance, along with learning how to use it. He was concerned with building enough firepower, so to speak, so that those in control of it could achieve their goals. And goals were to be understood as interests of the members that were to be served.

PROTECT THE ORGANIZATION OR FIGHT FOR PEOPLE'S RIGHTS?

In a case involving the killing of a Mexican American youth by a policeman, Fred Ross reported on a discussion called to consider what the CSO should do. A stenographer member argued against diverting attention away from "building the organization" to fighting the case because the result would be that "the better element" would not come in. A grocer and a civil service employee supported this position. But another spokesman stated the principle, "We don't have to worry about protecting the organization; our job is to fight for the rights of the people. If we do what's right for them, they'll stick with us. And that's the best protection any organization can get. If we don't, before long we won't have any organization to protect."[112]

When enough people in the community are concerned about the problem, schedule a series of preliminary meetings to build an organizational structure. Make sure that people remember the meeting day and time. You may have to arrange transportation and continue to encourage people to come. At the meeting, "concentrate on moving those attending into decision and action." In principle, a community organization is "always the expression of power through the greatest number of members acting together to resolve the central problems of their lives."[113] You insist on only two things: The organization must be democratic, and it must be broadly representative of the community.

Once the structure becomes clear and a decision is made to organize, help the community members elect officers and develop preliminary committees, role assignments, strategies, and time lines.

The Role of the Staff Organizer

You develop your organizing stance, consciously use your leadership skills, assess situations, facilitate the process, provide training, and help members debrief.

Develop Your Stance   Social work staff become "handypersons" for organization members who make the decisions. The staff works for the citizen organizers, the officers and the committees of the community organization. Fred Ross asserted that as a staff organizer you need to be able to grasp the ideas and aspirations of the people, have sensitivity to their feelings, and have an ability to articulate the concept of "organization" as a frame of reference in all kinds of action. You listen and play the role of sounding board, are at ease in relating your own experiences and attitudes, and have patience, frankness, tact, and a willingness to stay in the background so as to not appear to "hog the show."

Consciously Use Your Leadership   Never impose yourself on the community. Always present yourself clearly as someone who will "help build an organization that belongs and will belong to the members." Your leadership style must fit the situation, changing according to the particular readiness levels of the members. Balance the depth and amount of your interventions so as to continually enable community members to learn skills and assume more and more responsibility. In principle, rarely intervene in the organization directly unless it is absolutely necessary, otherwise citizen community organizers will not see the victories as their victories, acquire knowledge and skills, or develop an effective organization. Continually "ally yourself with the long-term objective self-interest of the people, building an organization through which they can act effectively."[114]

Assess the Situation   You assess events and developments as they affect the organization, help members conceive possible responses, and assist members in critiquing them. Being a good staff person means getting the people to "scratch around for what they know and then spit it out so that they could see that they weren't as dumb as they thought they were." It means asking, "What are you trying to prove? What evidence do you need? Do you have it? If not, where do you get it?" says Fred Ross.[115]

Facilitate the Process   While you resist doing things for people, if the president makes a mistake in a confrontation, you step in to forestall disaster. You are available to raise questions about the real purpose of the organization whenever someone tries to divert it for his or her own uses. You arrange for someone to check on training and staffing so that the potential for building the organization will not be lost. Continually raise questions about whether the organization is serving the members' needs and see that new life is constantly being pumped in from the bottom. You build and train leaders, review and evaluate your members' strategies, celebrate victories, regroup, and move on to other issues. And, of course, you carry a certain part of the mechanics of the organizational effort.

Provide Training   You work behind the scenes and work yourself out of a job by training community members to be skilled community organizers.[116] At first, hold staff meetings daily. One question follows another in an effort to extract principles, but counsel citizen organizers to look at each situation as unique so they will not apply a principle blindly. A typical question would be: "Assume your plan works 100 percent (which it won't), what have you got when you succeed?" If the anticipated result does not seem worthwhile, you and your citizen organizers scrap the proposal. After a time, each citizen organizer will have developed his or her own plan of procedure and defended it in meetings with the rest of the staff.[117]

IAF TEACHES THE ORGANIZER TO TEACH HIMSELF

In the Industrial Areas Foundation (IAF) training is done on the job. Organizers are expected to make mistakes. But at the end of the day they are required to complete a detailed diary of their contacts and activities, not only as a record but as a basis for reflection on what they have done. A dialogue is then set up in which the individual organizer's experience is compared with the cumulative experience of the IAF.

The discussion of the day's experience in relation to analogous situations elsewhere encourages the organizer to look at his or her activities from other points of view: "We can make suggestions; we can point out aspects of things she or he has overlooked; we can broaden his or her horizons; but in the last analysis the citizen organizer must teach oneself."[118]

The method is Socratic. It is effective when staff members feel free to speak with complete candor, not only about their own individual experiences but those of other staff members as well.

Carry Out Strategies

The aim of community organizing is to develop a community power base, a democratic organization capable of broad local political participation in which ordinary people make the decisions about things that affect them. Your members engage in a series of specific and localized confrontations to achieve their goals, work to build confidence among leaders and members, and demonstrate the organization's ability to improve the quality of neighborhood life.[119] You help members solidify the changes they have made. Once the organization is functioning well, begin to spur the organization to do something about self-support and hiring its own staff on a continuing basis.

Debrief

After your organization members engage in an action, hold a postmortem to review what happened. This gives you an opportunity to raise questions about weak points, reinforce the good things that were done, assess the effect on the program, and consider what steps might be taken next.

Termination

Just as you must spend time getting to know the community and its people and developing relationships, you must likewise spend a lot of time disengaging and helping the organization assess itself. The description in Chapter 7 of how a community developer disengages from a community is essentially the same as the way in which a community organizer exits from a community organization. When this is completed, the organizer's job is done.

HOW TO USE FOUR MODELS OF COMMUNITY ORGANIZING

Four different ways of doing community organizing have been developed by community organizers. These models can give you some basic ideas, but community organizing is not a static process. Organizing emerges out of the needs of the people and out of the particular situation they confront. When deciding among these models, assess your situation based on the differences between two variables: (1) the number of local associations in the community and (2) the amount of social cohesion that exists between these organizations (see Figure 8.1).

For example, if there are few existing associations in your community and a sense of locality, cohesion, or commitment to locality is low, Cesar Chavez's linking model may work best. Fred Ross's house meeting model is useful if there are few existing associations in your community but social cohesion and commitment to the locality are high. If there are many existing associations but little cohesion among them, the Alinsky coalition model is useful. Finally, if there are many existing associations in your community and there is strong cohesion among them, the IAF/PICO social networks model might be the best model to consider.

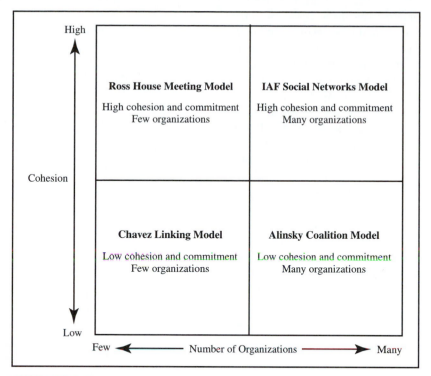

FIGURE 8.1   Four Models of Community Organizing

Chavez Organizational Linking Model

Sometimes alienation, lack of commitment and social cohesion, and few associations characterize areas dominated by large business enterprises.[120] Dominant corporate cultures often promote these conditions to keep people in subservience so they can be exploited. When you work to organize people in these communities, the amount of resistance your community will face will often be high. In California, for example, large agribusiness interests have exploited migrant farm laborers for many years, beginning at the turn of the century with Japanese and Chinese workers, and during the depression with African Americans and unemployed laborers from southwestern states, particularly Oklahoma, generically called "Okies," and Mexican Americans. Today many farmworkers are Mexican or Central American nationals who possess few legal rights or Mexican Americans who possess little education and may not speak English. They work long hours in fields where temperatures reach 110 degrees in the shade for weeks on end, for little pay, poor housing, often no medical care, and only intermittent education for their children.

They move seasonally with the crops. Beginning with oranges and avocados in the San Fernando Valley, farmworkers move north to California's great Central Valley, picking lettuce in Delano, grapes in San Benito, cotton in Fresno, artichokes in Castroville, strawberries in Watsonville, and almonds in Ukiah. They may travel north to Washington and Oregon to harvest apples or work on farms in the Midwest. They often have developed little attachment or commitment to the land or to the communities where they work and, aside from the Catholic Church, belong to few associations.

These are the conditions into which Cesar Chavez was born and which he found in California's migrant work camps in the 1940s and 1950s. Chavez realized that to organize the farm workers he would first have to provide a structure to which the laborers would feel attachment and some commitment. The workers had to be convinced that they actually had an interest in the locality and power to approach growers.

Chavez began to help build trust and a sense of community by creating farmworker food and gas buying clubs. These clubs were nonthreatening to agribusiness, but once a number of clubs were organized, they became the basis for organizing the workers. The clubs built social cohesion in the farmworker community. They gave the people a sense of solidarity, a commitment to locality, and an attachment to one another. They helped develop leadership around common issues. The clubs became a source of community strength.

Once the laborers realized that by working together they could improve their situation, Chavez linked their new associations with existing, legitimizing institutions such as the church and labor unions. They began to assert themselves over issues of low wages, long hours, and abysmal working conditions.

Chavez built even more cohesion by direct confrontation methods including picketing, marches, and boycotts, along with intensive negotiation. Immigrant farmworkers no longer saw themselves as expendable laborers who could be easily displaced or threatened with deportation. The process was neither easy nor quick. Chavez invested himself in a protracted struggle to help migrant laborers in California's Central Valley become organized.[121]

Ross House Meeting Model

Arguing that many poor people did not already have organizations representing their interests, Fred Ross of the Community Services Organization in California developed a new form of organizing in the 1960s, the house meeting model.[122] This model was perfected by the Association of Community Organizations for Reform Now (ACORN), which organized around southern African Americans who had few existing organizations but did have a sense of place and a commitment to a particular locality. The house meeting became an indispensable organizing tool.

YOU CONDUCT A HOUSE MEETING

You are meeting with a group of relatives and friends of Senor Sanchez in his house across from the church. Children are playing in and out of the house. You begin by introducing yourself and explaining what you have been doing in other towns in the valley. This soon leads to talk about what is wrong in their town. In no time, there is a list. There are many areas of concern: no school bus routes serving children in the barrio, politicians who pay no attention to Mexican Americans and their problems, no sidewalks or street lights in the barrio, and no medical clinic.

Why is this so? It is because Mexican Americans do not register and vote. So this must be changed. Before the group breaks up, you have commitments from several of those present to bring together their friends and relatives—meeting with them will keep you busy for most of the week.

It saved time, and those attending often encouraged each other. If you use the house meeting model, you need to be clear about the purpose of the house meeting, understand how to conduct the first meeting, engage in door knocking, form an organizing committee, and hold a public forum to establish the organization.

Purpose of a House Meeting   House meetings are evening sessions held in poor communities where 6 to 12 people focus on specific problems and develop a preorganizational infrastructure. Sometimes house meetings are held in a series that leads to significant growth by expanding membership into new social circles. Meeting in a member's home is ideal for getting to know people, listening to what they have to say, talking to them about issues, and encouraging them to become involved. By talking together, you advance people's understanding and their sense of commitment. These meetings are crucial for developing group solidarity and leadership skills, instilling confidence, and heightening people's spirit and willingness to struggle.

The First Meeting   In your first meeting identify contacts, find a sponsor, introduce members and the purpose of the meeting, talk about issues, and begin working on an organizing task.

Identify Contacts and Find a Sponsor   Develop as many community contacts as you can by knocking on doors, getting people's names, and talking with them in their homes. Once you find someone willing to sponsor the first house meeting, talk to the host beforehand about what may occur. This will help make the meeting go better and the host becomes a kind of assistant leader. Make sure that first house meeting is representative of the community but is limited to fewer than a dozen people. Plan for the meeting to last no more than an hour and a half.

Introduce Members and the Purpose As guests arrive, greet the members and introduce them to each other. Once everyone has arrived, lead a short "icebreaker" to help people get to know each other and feel more comfortable. Then describe the purpose of the meeting, and let people know when the meeting will end.

Talk About Issues and Work on a Task Engage people in identifying issues. Let people talk about their own personal and local concerns. Your goal is to encourage group members to continue the process and perhaps become part of the organizing committee. Draft a document detailing the concerns of the group. It should include something that the members can do right away. For example, they might go with you to talk to their friends about their concerns or host another house meeting.

Door Knocking
During the next month or so, go door to door with members you have met from your house meetings and talk to as many people as you can. "Door knocking" is perhaps the most important activity in which you will engage. It enables you to meet people and draw them out, learn about them as they learn about you, and gives them a better sense of their collective power. Talking directly with people in the informal, intimate atmosphere of their homes helps you reach them in a personal way. People may get involved not only because they are frustrated and angry over local problems that they feel powerless to correct but because they like you, trust you, or are looking for something meaningful to do.

Form an Organizing Committee
Invite people to join an organizing committee group and hold more house meetings. After talking with nearly everyone in the community, you and the organizing committee will have collected a great deal of information about the community, its people, and its problems. The issues that initially concerned the organizing committee may no longer be the dominant ones.

Hold a meeting to help your organizing committee identify the issues community members have described as most important and pressing. Members of your organizing committee should lead the meeting, and they should decide what issues to attack. The issues should galvanize people and be ones that they can win if they organize and work together. Your role is to help generate discussion, keep the discussion on track, and help the group identify criteria for deciding on issues.

Hold a Public Forum to Form the Organization
After the organizing committee has identified two or three key issues, they should set up a community-wide public meeting or forum. This is the meeting at which the organization will be born. Make this founding meeting as important an event in the neighborhood as you can. Spend a lot of time carefully planning the meeting with the organizing committee. Develop a temporary name and mission statement. Agree on who will lead the founding meeting and the agenda. Get your committee members to nominate one another for the election of temporary officers. Develop lots of publicity with telephone calls, flyers, and press releases.

Four important things should occur at this meeting: (1) members explain the purpose of the community organization, (2) the community decides on the most important of the two or three issues to work on, (3) the new organization is officially established, and (4) community members join the organization and become involved in the process.

Explain the Purpose and Decide on Issues At the meeting, an organizing committee member should explain the purpose of the organization and its temporary mission. Have community members rank the two or three issues the committee has decided on and add others that they think are relevant. Make sure everyone who attends gets a chance to speak. People have come to have their say; make a list of their comments. Use some of the large group techniques described in Chapter 6 such as buzz groups, Crawford slip writing, idea writing, or group voting to help your community decide on the issue that concerns them most.

Establish the Organization and Elect Officers Hold an election for temporary offices to provide an ongoing structure for the organization. Have a committee member explain the next community-wide action steps, which were planned roughly by the organizing committee beforehand. Get people to sign up for different jobs or roles such as writing letters or attending a city council meeting or a training session.

Sign Up Members and Assign Tasks Have people at the meeting officially join the organization by filling out a membership application and becoming dues-paying members ($1 a month). Give out membership cards.

Dues are significant not only because they provide some funding, but more important, because people relate differently to an organization that they own. Make sure everyone knows when and where the next actions will take place. The next step is to appoint committees to work on those problems of greatest concern to the group.

Alinsky Coalition Model

The coalition model assumes that a number of associations in the community can be used for organizing but that commitment and social engagement among them is lacking. Through the process of coming together, residents discover that their individual problems are also the problems of others and that the only hope for solving these problems is by pooling their efforts.

As a social worker using Alinsky's coalition model, you should become familiar with the principles of organizing. Learn about the community and develop relationships, and develop a sponsoring committee. Organize block clubs, form an organizing committee, and establish an organization. Decide on strategies, tactics, and move to action.

Organizing Principles
As a community organizer you work *with* people rather than *for* people. You target those persons who are responsible for causing the problem. Maintain steady pressure on perpetrators until the problem is resolved. To get something from politicians, voting power is required, which means you need a large organization. If people "don't want" something, it may well be because their past experience has convinced them that their situation is hopeless. It is essential to achieve some visible success quickly to sustain hope in the people.

Learn About the Community and Develop Relationships
Immerse yourself in community life to gain an understanding of members' experiences, customs, and values. Identify their self-interests and concerns, and develop relationships with existing organizations and community leaders.

Relationships With Existing Organizations A people's coalition organization is open to any association, group, or individual who is concerned about community issues such as fair housing, decent wages, good schools, neighborhood services, quality of neighborhood life, crime, drugs, and jobs. Develop relationships

with as many organizations, members, and leaders as possible. Families, employed and unemployed workers, merchants, members of ethnic, civil rights, business, civic and neighborhood associations and unions, churches, temples, and mosques should be within your realm of interest. The broader and more representative the neighborhood coalition is, the stronger the organization will become. As you develop relationships, try to identify the major patterns of the community including its customs and values.

Relationships With Community Leaders The organizer's task is to identify natural community leaders as well as those already in charge of existing organizations and associations with whom the organizer will form a coalition organization. Talk to them, discover their concerns, and get them interested in working together on common issues.[123]

Develop a Sponsoring Committee
In Alinsky-style coalition building, you develop a sponsoring committee composed of leaders of major social organizations within the community. This sponsoring committee becomes the basis for building a coalition of existing organizations as well as a resource for raising money. The sponsoring committee gets other leading groups to buy into the organizing effort and neutralizes political opponents.[124]

Organize Block Clubs
While you are organizing the sponsoring committee, also spend time establishing block clubs to ensure that as many parts of the community as possible are represented.[125] House meetings are intended to be temporary, but block clubs are more or less permanent units that represent segments of the community. A network of block clubs provides a broad foundation for the community organization. The more deeply people on a block or neighborhood become acquainted with each other, the higher the level of interactive problem solving they may achieve, and the more open they may become to new views and to one another's concerns.[126]

Hold Meetings As soon as you get to know enough people, invite them to an informal meeting in someone's home just as an organizer does with house meetings. Serve refreshments and allow plenty of time for socializing. Start off with an enjoyable activity that is appropriate to the culture or population that you are organizing, and develop a spirit of camaraderie, intimacy, and mutual trust. Encourage members to speak their minds with a spirit of acceptance, and listen carefully to their ideas, concerns, questions, and issues. Listen for patterns that you can use in helping to organize members into a group that will work toward a common goal.

At the end of the meeting or meetings, help the group come to some sort of decision, with each person saying his or her piece. "The key value in decision making within a poor people's organization is not efficiency, but participation,"[127] asserts Si Kahn:

> The time required to reach a decision should not be the shortest time required or for a small, select group to make the decision, but the amount of time it takes to educate all the members in the meaning of the decision and to involve them in understanding the decision-making process.[128]

Rotate Leadership   Give everyone a chance to gain leadership experience and status by rotating the leadership of meetings. "You play the role of an enabler by facilitating a process of problem solving, helping people express their discontents, nourishing good interpersonal relationships, and emphasizing common objectives."[129]

Form an Organizing Committee
Set up a coalition organizing committee to recruit delegations from other organizations and block clubs. When your committee members have recruited as many organizations and block clubs as they can, your organizing committee calls a Community Congress with representatives from the organizations and clubs to consider and adopt a coalition constitution and to elect officers. The Community Congress conducts a series of preliminary meetings to build an organizational structure. The congressional representatives should "concentrate on moving into decision and action." In principle, the "basic orientation should always be the expression of power through the greatest possible number of members acting together to resolve the central problems of their lives."[130]

Establish a Community-wide Coalition Organization
Congressional representatives hold a founding meeting, elect officers, and establish the purpose of the coalition organization.

Hold a Founding Meeting   Assist congressional representatives in developing a constitution and circulate it to the various organizations that will form the coalition. Your organizing committee plans a founding meeting or constitutional convention to ratify the constitution. At the founding meeting, representatives of all groups, block clubs, associations, and organizations meet to officially form the coalition organization. The coalition transforms neighborhood associations and block clubs into a broad-based, multiple-issue, permanent community organization by electing officers and establishing its purpose and mission.

Choose a Board of Directors   Help the members choose the board of directors of the coalition organization and elect its officers. These members should represent the organizations comprising the coalition and should report regularly and consult with their membership about the activities of the coalition. The board of directors will develop preliminary committees, role assignments, strategies, and time lines. An important part of the coalition's structure is to form many standing committees that can manage the several activities with which the coalition needs to engage. This committee structure permits the coalition organization to pursue multiple issues simultaneously and to mobilize the interests of many groups and segments of the community.

Develop Statements of Purpose, Mission, and Slogans   Help the board develop a statement of purpose, a mission statement, and slogans. A statement of purpose should be expressed as the long-range goals or permanent reasons for the organization to exist. A mission statement expresses the purpose of the organization in one sentence. The mission statement of ACORN, for example, is "To advocate a stronger local neighborhood voice in and power over the economic, political, and social institutions that dominate the lives of families of low and moderate income."[131] Slogans are short: one word or one phrase that sums up the organization. The slogan of the Industrial Areas Foundation (IAF) is "Power, Action, Justice."

Develop the Organization's Structure, Funding, Staff, and Goals   The first several meetings of the board members of the coalition should be to develop a preliminary organizational structure, including a budget and funding, hire staff or recruit volunteer citizen organizers, disseminate information to the coalition members, and develop goals, targets, and strategies.

Move to Action The first set of challenges your coalition organization decides to tackle is particularly important when your organization and its leaders are inexperienced, members are tentative in the commitment, or acceptance of the organization and organizers are still in question. Alinsky urges organizations to select initial issues that are highly visible, important to local residents, and easy to win but not divisive or antagonistic to other local groups.[132] Alinsky advocates the use of nonviolent confrontation tactics to achieve organization objectives. You will find a description of many of these tactics in Chapter 14.

Social Networks Model

The most recent variation of Alinsky's work is the social networks model carried on by his training school for organizers, the Industrial Areas Foundation (IAF) founded in 1940, as well as the Pacific Institute for Community Organization (PICO), Direct Action and Research Training (DART), and the Gamaliel Foundation and the Association of Community Organizations for Reform Now (ACORN).

The social networks approach often uses faith-based organizations that see part of their social mission as helping members organize themselves to provide safe, clean neighborhoods, good schools, more responsive government, and improved relationships with neighboring communities. Local clergy are more outspoken when they see the anguish of their people, and many church people today seem to understand better than their parents that a little community controversy is often a necessary price in the beginning to bring about neighborhood health and stability. As a result, "hundreds of local faith-based coalitions across the country are now reaching out to organize millions of middle class and poorer people who are frustrated by the economy, government paralysis, and anti-community corporate policies."[133]

The social networks model promotes the expectation that government will act justly by refusing to give preferential treatment to middle- and upper-class suburbs and instead recognize the importance of inner cities and working-class neighborhoods. They expect that corporations will no longer drain money from poor communities without reinvesting an equal amount in them.

The Industrial Areas Foundation (IAF) In the 1970s the IAF opted for a strategy of social network organizing rooted in the belief that institutions such

as synagogues and churches can be transformed into agents of social change.[134] The IAF mobilized large numbers of faith-based organizations, bringing about significant improvements in marginalized communities.[135]

When a local community requests assistance in organizing, IAF staff ask them to form a sponsoring committee that can raise initial funds and guarantee legitimacy for the organizing effort. IAF provides leadership training, not only in local communities but also in regular 10-day sessions in different parts of the country. In these sessions local community leaders meet other leaders engaged in similar efforts, often with similar problems,[136] and share experiences, information, and resources. As community leaders interact with a wide variety of people, they come to see power as the craft of arguing, listening, revising views, and compromising "in exchange for respect and a willingness to compromise from those who now hold power. What often matters is not arriving at a consensus, but a stake in the ongoing dynamic of controversy, resolution and change."[137]

The IAF currently has 28 organizing projects in New York, New Jersey, Maryland, Tennessee, Arizona, California, and Texas, but it is in Texas, where the IAF network includes 10 organizing efforts, that it is the strongest. Throughout the state, in San Antonio, Houston, El Paso, Austin, Fort Worth, and in the Rio Grande Valley, IAF organizers and active members struggle for utility reform, improved public education, government accountability, health care for the indigent, and basic public services, including water and sewers for the "colonias."

Most visibly they organize "get out the vote" efforts to promote bond packages to help IAF neighborhoods, hold "accountability sessions" to keep politicians publicly in line with IAF objectives, encourage voter registration, and work to improve schools by halting the dropout rate, stopping drug use and violence, and getting parents more involved. More quietly, in the day in and day out practice of community organizing they serve as "schools of public life," empowering neighborhood residents by giving them "an opportunity to do something about things that [they] have been frustrated about all their lives."[138]

The Direct Action and Research Training (DART) Network In June 1996 DART founded the Federation of DART Organizations, which works with nearly 20 faith-based community organizations

to promote justice and equality of opportunity through the empowerment of people with low to moderate incomes. The federation is rooted in an understanding that religious congregations have a role to play in political and economic systems.

The Pacific Institute for Community Organization (PICO)

In 1972 two young Roman Catholic priests, John Bauman and Jerry Helfrich, fresh out of an organizer-training program, moved to the West Coast. The success of their Oakland Training Institute brought inquiries from other clients, and the institute quickly grew. It changed its name to the Pacific Institute for Community Organization (PICO) in 1976. By 1984 PICO had affiliated organizations in Oakland, San Diego, and Orange County, California, and in Kansas City, Missouri. The group decided to use a social network, congregation-based approach for community organizing.

In October 1997 the Pacific Institute for Community Organization (PICO) celebrated its 25th anniversary, gathering more than 400 grassroots leaders, organizers, friends, and supporters from around the country.[139] One of the largest grassroots community efforts in the United States, PICO is affiliated with more than 1,000 religious congregations, schools, and neighborhood institutions and 1 million families working in 150 cities and towns.[140]

PICO goes into an area only after being asked by local pastors or congregations. It helps people form a sponsoring committee, raise seed money from local sources, and go through the legal process of incorporation. The network assists congregations in selecting and hiring a PICO-trained organizer. This initial process usually takes 1 to 3 years.

PICO helps train pastors, staff, and congregation members in organization techniques. Bauman says, "Our style of organizing is to get into the community and listen, and to train people to listen."[141] After an affiliate becomes more established, PICO continues to provide backup support. Twice a year, it holds 6-day leadership training sessions to teach the principles of the congregation-based model.

Association of Community Organization for Reform Now (ACORN)

Beginning in Little Rock as the Arkansas Community Organizations for Reform Now, ACORN has its roots in the civil rights movement, and more directly through the former

National Welfare Rights Organization activists of the 1960s. Today ACORN is the nation's largest national network of community organizations of low- and moderate-income families, with more than 175,000 member families organized in 850 neighborhood chapters in 75 cities across the United States and Canada, the Dominican Republic, and Peru.[142]

Unlike other social network organizations, ACORN finds its members by going door to door, not through institutions such as churches. The ACORN model emphasizes building organizations controlled by community leadership and collecting dues from members to make the organization as self-sustaining as possible. ACORN organizes issue campaigns not just to win the issue but also to build the organization, and it has a reputation for holding large rallies and other confrontational actions when needed. ACORN also employs a sophisticated negotiation model when possible. The organizer's role is to build local leadership and to remain in the background as support when it comes time for public actions and negotiations, which are led by community members.

ACORN presses for more investment in communities from banks and governments and for better public schools. Its members achieve these goals through direct action, negotiation, legislation, and voter participation. More recently ACORN's priorities have included obtaining a commitment for living wage laws for low-wage workers, challenging predatory lenders, and obtaining better housing for first time homebuyers and tenants.

Living Wage Law Spearheaded by ACORN, in 1998 a coalition of labor, community groups, and churches in Oakland, California, got the city council to vote unanimously to adopt the Jobs and Living Wage law, requiring companies doing business with the city to pay a living wage. On March 26 in that same year a new coalition of churches and labor organizations in Contra Costa County, California, met for the first time, bringing living wage legislation to that region.

Stopping Predatory Lending Both locally and nationally, ACORN has a long history of demanding that financial institutions deal fairly with low-income people. In the late 1990s ACORN went after predatory lending practices, and over the next several years it staged "national days of action," sponsored public information campaigns in 35 cities across the nation, staged a confrontation at a convention of the National Home Equity Mortgage Association, and instigated letter writing campaigns, held public meetings and worked directly with local and state representatives as well as local banks to stop predatory lending practices.

ACORN continued its campaign against predatory lenders, shifting its focus to Wells Fargo Bank in California. The damage done by Wells Fargo, Household, and other predatory lenders is increased by the fact that predatory loans are made in concentrated volume in poor and minority neighborhoods where better loans are not readily available, and the loss of equity and foreclosure not only hurts individuals and families but also can devastate already fragile communities. ACORN is campaigning to stop these abuses.

In April 2004 ACORN members put pressure on Wells Fargo at its annual meeting in San Francisco, and in May they protested predatory lending at the Wells Fargo offices in Louisiana, promoting legislation and regulation, putting pressure on particular offenders, and providing education and outreach.

Housing   ACORN has worked with banks and city officials to turn abandoned dwellings over to "homesteaders." Local homesteading programs have so far been set up in five cities. ACORN does rehabilitation work on these and other sites, setting up "coops" for the new occupants and acquiring deeds for abandoned housing and conducting "sweat equity" projects to put them back into shape for the new homeowners. ACORN also joins in partnerships with mainstream political and corporate funders. In its joint home acquisition and rehabilitation efforts in Chicago, for example, ACORN works with Citibank, Mayor Richard M. Daley, and the federal government.

COMMUNITY ORGANIZING FOR THE 21ST CENTURY: CONSENSUS ORGANIZING

Consensus organizing builds cooperative relationships between community leaders and business and government to improve poor communities.[143] While consensus community organizing builds relationships, it also focuses on moving people from welfare to work, improving school achievement, promoting inner-city reinvestment, and developing housing and businesses, among other things. Consensually oriented community organizing uses a triple-pronged and sometimes a four-pronged approach.

Triple-Pronged Approach

The partnership of advocacy-based community organizations, CDCs, and program development services provides a triple-pronged approach, strengthening the economic and social base of communities while at the same time ensuring that the public and private sectors do their fair share to promote and enhance the life of the communities. The result is a partnership of public, private, and voluntary or nonprofit groups who all share in the responsibility for revitalizing and restoring communities.

Four-Pronged Approach

When faith-based community organizations or community development corporations are added to the mix, their spiritual frame of reference helps members develop meaning and purpose in their personal lives. This four-pronged approach is very effective in helping mediate between the private life of self and family and the larger, more anonymous organizational structures in society.

How to Do Consensus Building Community Organizing

Steps in consensus community organizing include finding an institutional partner, building the community organization, assessing strengths, engaging in planning, developing a strategy, and participating in joint ventures and processes.

Find an Institutional Partner   Consensus community building usually begins with the identification and involvement of a local institutional partner such as a charitable foundation, business organization, social service agency, or a government agency. The partner provides financial resources and helps open doors to similar institutions. The partner can also be used as an organizing tool, giving skeptical community members a reason to believe that their efforts will lead to something tangible.

Build a Community Organization   The goal of the members is to build a permanent, self-sustaining organization that will become a means for continued community involvement, leadership development, and advocacy. Members can either build the organization from scratch or modify an existing organization's composition or mission. A broad representation of all levels and kinds of community members who live or work in the community comprise the consensual community organization, especially widely trusted individuals from every recognized group of people affiliated with the community. It is especially important to recruit local merchants doing business with the community and public housing tenants with the greatest credibility, for example. Organizations controlled from outside the community, including the project's institutional partners, should not be members of the community organization even though the organization may engage them in cooperative ventures.

Assess Strengths
Using participatory action research, citizen organizers assess the strengths of existing community groups and develop an inventory of community assets including issues and interests that unite the community. Members examine the organizations located in the community but controlled by others outside it such as banks, hospitals, local corporations, charitable foundations, and service and governmental agencies. Who supports or opposes the community's agenda? Are these organizations involved in improving the community? Do they have a history of inactivity or exploitation of community resources? Community members carefully analyze their results and use them to develop their strategy.

Engage in Planning
Planning is a means by which members gather information, develop a strategy, regroup, and plan again to revise the strategy and reorient members. Initial planning should not be prolonged, nor does it have to be perfected before members take action. It is important to get members into action projects quickly, even small ones, to keep people motivated and to help them accomplish things. Planning and implementation proceed simultaneously and concurrently in a continual process rather than as isolated or separate endeavors or the first step of a sequential procession.

Develop a Strategy
Members apply their own ideas, perceptions, values, intuition, and reflection to develop a strategy of action. Members make an effort, regroup, and try again, learning and modifying their tactics depending on responses from their targets in the social environment. Consensus community building tends to avoid confrontations; instead, it seeks strategies by which communities can succeed while still maintaining good relationships with the corporations or governments they are challenging.

Participate in a Joint Venture
Organization members often develop joint ventures between themselves and organizations controlled by interests outside the community such as community cleanups or publishing community newsletters as well as more substantive collaborations. For example, organization members may be interested in creating job opportunities and may discover that owners of a factory, while disagreeing with residents about many issues, complain about the lack of well-trained local job candidates. A consensus organizer, says Mike Eichler, may be able to turn this single point of overlapping interest into a joint venture such as a training program that brings together residents and factory owners.[144]

Eichler further states that the opportunities joint ventures create for developing relationships and interactions between the community organization and businesses may be even more important than the tangible benefits that the joint venture provides. It may help develop relationships built on trust and respect, beginning a process of developing social capital. For example, if the activities of the community organization and an external organization conflict, community organization members may draw upon the accumulated social capital developed by their relationships as a basis for cooperation and communication. Members may discover that their agendas are less in direct conflict than they at first appear, sometimes because past miscommunication and misunderstandings distorted the perceptions of the other's interests. Efforts to find niches where mutual benefit can be achieved make it possible for both sides to think creatively and discover solutions and compromises that have value for everyone.

Process
Consensus organizing is an ongoing process of seeking openings and opportunities for community members to pursue a long-term agenda rather than seeking a single victory or decision that becomes a focal point of community effort. Through a thousand small interactions in the course of a hundred relationships, the community may pursue its strategy, position its residents with respect to the entities with power, present its agenda, influence the course of events, and achieve its objectives. The entire

process may be entirely informal, diffuse, and invisible to the casual observer. The only overt manifestation may be its successful result.

This process, says Eichler, demands a great deal from community members. Traditional community organizing tends to use massive numbers to confront organizational intransigence, but participants in joint ventures must use the knowledge and skills appropriate to the particular venture. They may be required to engage in management, accounting, real estate, banking, teaching, or a variety of other disciplines. It may be necessary for some to develop new skills or enhance existing ones through training and practice. Ultimately it falls to the community members to commit their time and energy to building and applying their skills with creativity and care.

Consensus organizing is not one-sided, however. When factory owners, hospital administrators, public officials, merchants, or bankers work with a group of skilled and dedicated community members, develop relationships of respect and trust, and carry out successful ventures, they often feel tremendous enthusiasm about participating in other similar projects. They begin to feel that they have a stake in the welfare of the community in which they have developed new respect for the cadre of trustworthy, informed, and reliable resident leaders.[145]

Strengths and Limitations of Consensus Organizing

Strengths   There is little doubt that consensus organizing has become an active form of community-based organization and is likely to expand in the future. The consensus model can foster unity and harmony among participants, strengthening their commitment to work toward a common good. In *Beyond Adversary Democracy*, Jane Mansbridge argues that when participants have shared interests, a consensus-based, "unitary" democracy can motivate people to understand one another and to focus on their common goals. "While its members may initially have conflicting preferences about a given issue, goodwill, mutual understanding, and rational discussion can lead to the emergence of a common enlightened preference that is good for everyone."[146]

Social worker Michael Eichler, who pioneered the consensus organizing model, argues "by participating in the consensual approach corporate types become more active and aware of social problems,

city officials see community organizing as valuable instead of threatening, and neighborhood residents feel more empowered and get more control over community resources."[147]

Limitations   Despite its positive potential, members who are more influential and persuasive than others can dominate the consensual decision-making process by overriding the opinions of others. The emphasis on agreement can mask inherent conflicts among the interests of the different partners.

Domination by Influential Members   Effective consensus-based decision making requires that both the consensual community organization and its targets express their views and discuss their differences until agreement is reached. However, when the power dynamics between targets and the consensual organization are uneven, this process can be dominated by the most influential members. Where the interests of the groups conflict, this can be especially problematic. Mansbridge asserts: "The claim that people have common interests can . . . be a way of misleading the less powerful into collaborating with the more powerful in schemes that mainly benefit the latter."[148] The noncontentious nature of the consensus-based decision-making process may lull participants into a false sense of harmony. Unless all community stakeholders are able to assert their interests with equal force, the consensus process can become a vehicle for the imposition of dominant members' interests.

Masking Competing Interests   Consensus-based decision making often masks the fact that citizens, corporations, and government have competing interests. Not only do they have different interests, corporations and government are frequently the source of citizens' problems. Mansbridge asserts that an emphasis on consensus can obscure the important distinctions between each player's goals: "[T]he pressure for consensus suppresses information. More importantly, it suppresses information in a way that benefits the most powerful."[149] Thus, by focusing on building partnerships between groups, community organizations may be unable to address the role of corporations and government in fostering inequality and instability in the community "The new partnerships between the community, voluntary, public, and business sectors will remain problematic as long as the latter are the chief causes of the problems communities face."[150]

CONCLUSION

You have learned in this chapter that community organization offers people a chance to express their hopes and dreams and to make those dreams real in tangible policies and programs. Community organizing is fundamentally reshaping the way politics is practiced at the local level. When poor and middle-class people work together, their communities can become directly engaged in making political change.

Community organization has a long history in the profession of social work, but it has more often been practiced by non–social work professionals. Except for the Progressive Era, social work has only committed itself to active engagement in social reform since the 1960s. There are four main kinds of community organizing today. Recently, however, social worker Mike Eichler has pioneered in a new consensual model of community organizing. When community interests are joined in partnership with government and corporate interests, the results are impressive, not only because of the community improvements that are accomplished but also because of the success that people achieve in making democracy work. Community organizing enables people to actively take control of their lives, claim their own futures, and assert their own values, while at the same time concretely demonstrating their commitment to a democratic way of life.

Along with social planning and community development, community organization in the last decade has acquired power, influence, and the potential for solving social problems. If America's social problems are to be solved, they will only be solved in the social sector, by the collective effort of local people working through their own neighborhood organizations, associations, and religious centers. Social work as a profession needs to reclaim community social work as its mandate and its foundation. Only then will social work be capable of making a lasting contribution to a better social world for ourselves and for our children.

KEY CONCEPTS

community organizing

critical thinking

social amnesia

analytic capabilities

gather information

intuitive reflection

conscientization

moral discourse

action skills

community organizations

organizational deviance model

corporate deviance

intergroup conflict model

labor organizing

Progressive Era

Charity Organization Society (COS)

Social Settlements

school community centers

Saul Alinsky

Back of the Yards Neighborhood Council (BYNC)

Industrial Areas Foundation (IAF)

Fred Ross

homeowners organizations

migrant ministries

community service organizations (CSO)

Emil Schwartzhaupt Foundation

Cesar Chavez

educationals

civil rights movement

welfare rights movement

George Wiley

United Farm Workers (UFW)

Economic Opportunity Act, 1964 (EOA)

community action agencies (CAAs)

community action programs (CAPs)

Great Society

maximum feasible participation

National People's Action (NPA)

National Training and Information Center (NTIC)

Gale Cincotta

Shel Trapp

Federal Home Mortgage Disclosure Act, 1975

Community Reinvestment Act, 1977

Si Kahn

Direct Action and Research Training (DART)

Gamaliel Foundation

New England Training Center for Community Organizations

Midwest Academy

Organize Training Center

Pacific Institute for Community Organization (PICO)

Center for Third World Organizing

faith-based community organizations

living wage law

Americans With Disabilities Act, 1990

accountable development

survival mechanisms

act out

get out

opt out

flake out

cop out

Paulo Freire

Overmaier and Seligman

learned helplessness

Michael Lerner

surplus powerlessness

Julio Morales

self-oppression

colonized mentality

full plate syndrome

engage the community

define the problem

build organization

role of organizer

carry out strategy

termination

models of community organization

Chavez linking model

Ross house meeting model

Alinsky coalition model

block club

social networks model

Association of Community Organizations for Reform Now (ACORN)

consensus organizing

Mike Eichler

triple-pronged approach

four-pronged approach

QUESTIONS FOR DISCUSSION

1. How was the term *community organization* used by social workers in the 1950s?
2. How has the perception of community organizing in social work changed since the 1950s?
3. What role do you believe social work should take in grassroots organizing?
4. Should community organizing as described in this text be a major activity of social workers? Why or why not?

ADDITIONAL READING

Modern Classics in Neighborhood and Community Organizing

Alinsky, Saul. *Reveille for Radicals.* New York: Random House, 1989.

Alinsky, Saul. *Rules for Radicals: A Pragmatic Primer for Realistic Radicals.* New York: Random House, 1989.

Hallman, Howard. *The Organization and Operation of Neighborhood Councils.* Westport, CT: Praeger. 1977.

Jacobs, Jane. *The Death and Life of Great American Cities.* New York: Vintage, 1963.

Kahn, Si. *How People Get Power: Organizing Oppressed Communities for Action.* Washington, DC: National Association of Social Workers, 1991.

Kahn, Si. *Organizing: A Guide for Grassroots Leaders.* Washington, DC: National Association of Social Workers, 1991.

Delgado, Gary. 1986. *Organizing the Movement.* Philadelphia: Temple University Press, 1986.

Finks, P. David. *The Radical Vision of Saul Alinsky.* New York: Paulist Press, 1984.

Keller, Suzanne. *The Urban Neighborhood.* New York: Random House, 1968.

Kotler, Milton. *Neighborhood Government.* New York: Bobbs-Merrill, 1969.

Morris, David and Carl Hess. *Neighborhood Power.* Boston: Beacon, 1975.

O'Brien, David. *Neighborhood Organization and Interest Group Processes.* Princeton, NJ: Princeton University Press, 1976.

Piven, Frances Fox and Richard Cloward. *Poor People's Movements: Why They Succeed, How They Fail.* New York: Vintage, 1979.

Reitzes, Donald C. and Dietrich C. Reitzes. *The Alinsky Legacy: Alive and Kicking.* Greenwich, CT: JAI Press, 1987.

History of Community Organizing

Adamson, Madeleine and Seth Burgos. *This Mighty Dream.* Boston: Routledge and Kegan Paul, 1984.

Betten, Neil and Michael J. Austin. *The Roots of Community Organizing, 1917–1939.* Philadelphia: Temple University Press, 1990.

Boyte, Harry. *The Backyard Revolution.* Philadelphia: Temple University Press, 1980.

Fisher, Robert. *Let the People Decide: Neighborhood Organizing in America.* New York: Twayne, 1994.

Fisher, Robert and Peter Romanofsky, eds. *Community Organization for Urban Social Change: A Historical Perspective.* Westport, CT: Greenwood Press, 1981.

Halpern, Robert. *Rebuilding the Inner City: A History of Neighborhood Initiatives to Address Poverty in the United States.* New York: Columbia University Press. 1995.

Community Organizing: Theory and Practice

Bobo, K., J. Kendall, and S. Max. *Organizing for Social Change: A Manual for Activists in the 1990s.* Washington, DC: Seven Locks Press, 1991.

Gerlach, Luther P. and Virginia H. Hine. *People, Power, Change: Movements of Social Transformation.* Indianapolis: Bobbs-Merrill, 1970.

Ng, Roxana, Gillian Walker, and Jacob Muller, eds. *Community Organization and the Canadian State.* Toronto: Garamond, 1990.

Boyte, Harry C. *Community Is Possible: Repairing America's Roots.* New York: Harper and Row, 1984.

Boyte, Harry C. *Common Wealth: A Return to Citizen Politics.* New York: The Free Press, 1989.

Brown, Cherie R. *The Art of Coalition Building: A Guide for Community Leaders.* New York: American Jewish Committee, 1990.

Cunningham, James V. and Milton Kotler. *Building Neighborhood Organizations.* Notre Dame, IN: University of Notre Dame Press, 1983.

Dahir, J. *The Neighborhood Unit Plan: Its Spread and Acceptance: A Selected Bibliography With Interpretive Comments.* New York: Russell Sage Foundation, 1947.

Delgado, Gary. *Beyond the Politics of Place: New Directions in Community Organizing in the 1990s.* Oakland, CA: Applied Research Center, n.d.

Dillick, Sydney. *Community Organization for Neighborhood Development: Past and Present.* New York: Woman's Press and William Morrow, 1953.

Evans, Sara M. and Harry C. Boyte. *Free Spaces: The Sources of Democratic Change in America.* New York: Harper and Row, 1986.

Gittell, Ross J. and Avis Vidal. *Community Organizing: Building Social Capital as a Development Strategy.* Thousand Oaks, CA: Sage, 1998.

Gittell, Marilyn. *Limits to Citizen Participation: The Decline of Community Organizations.* Beverly Hills: Sage, 1980.

Hallman, Howard W. *Neighborhoods: Their Place in Urban Life* [Vol. 154, Sage Library of Social Research]. Beverly Hills, CA: Sage, 1984.

Hallman, Howard W. *Small and Large Together: Governing the Metropolis.* Beverly Hills, CA: Sage, 1977.

Kling, Joseph M. and Prudence S. Posner, eds. *Dilemmas of Activism: Class, Community, and the Politics of Local Mobilization.* Philadelphia: Temple University Press, 1990.

Kretzmann, John P. and John L. McKnight. *Building Communities From the Inside Out.* Evanston, IL: Center for Urban Affairs and Policy Research Neighborhood Innovations Network, Northwestern University, 1993.

Lykies, M. Brinton, Alli Banuazizi, Ramsay Liem, and Michael Morris, eds. *Myths About the Powerless: Contesting Social Inequalities* Philadelphia: Temple University Press, 1996.

Perry, Stewart E. *Communities on the Way: Rebuilding Local Economies in the United States and Canada.* Albany: State University of New York Press, 1987.

Wachter, Mary I. with Cynthia Tinsley. *Taking Back Our Neighborhoods: Building Communities That Work.* Minneapolis: Fairview Press, 1996.

Williams, Michael R. *Neighborhood Organization: Seeds of a New Urban Life* [Contributions in Political Science 131]. Westport, CT: Greenwood Press, 1985.

Social Work Community Organizing

Brager, George, Harry Specht, and James L. Torczyner. *Community Organizing,* 2d ed. New York: Columbia University Press, 1987.

Burghardt, Steve. *Organizing for Community Action.* Beverly Hills, CA: Sage, 1982.

Burghardt, Steve. *The Other Side of Organizing.* Cambridge, MA: Schenkman, 1982.

Dunham, Arthur. *The New Community Organization.* New York: Thomas Crowell, 1970.

Ecklein, Joan. *Community Organizing.* New York: Free Press, 1984.

Fisher, Robert and Joseph Kling. *Mobilizing the Community: Local Politics in the Era of the Global City.* Newbury Park, CA: Sage, 1993.

Lee, Judith A. B. *The Empowerment Approach to Social Work Practice.* New York: Columbia University Press, 1994.

Kahn, Si. *How People Get Power: Organizing Oppressed Communities for Action.* Washington, DC: National Association of Social Workers, 1991.

Kahn, Si. *Organizing: A Guide for Grassroots Leaders.* Washington, DC: National Association of Social Workers, 1991.

Rubin, Herb. *Renewing Hope Within Neighborhoods of Despair: The Community-Based Development Model.* Albany: State University of New York Press, 2000.

Staples Lee. *Roots to Power: A Manual for Grassroots Organizing.* Westport, CT: Praeger, 1984.

The Alinsky Approach

Alinsky, Saul. *Reveille for Radicals.* New York: Random House, 1989.

Alinsky, Saul. *Rules for Radicals: A Pragmatic Primer for Realistic Radicals.* New York: Random House, 1989.

Bailey, Robert. *Radicals in Urban Politics: The Alinsky Approach.* Chicago: University of Chicago Press, 1972.

Doering, Bernard, ed. *The Philosopher and the Provocateur: The Correspondence of Jacques Maritain and Saul Alinsky.* Notre Dame, IN: University of Notre Dame Press, 1994.

Finks, David. *The Radical Vision of Saul Alinsky.* Mahwah, NJ: Paulist Press, 1984.

Horwitt, Sanford. *Let Them Call Me Rebel: Saul Alinsky: His Life and Legacy.* New York: Alfred Knopf, 1989.

Lancourt, Joan E. *Confront or Concede: The Alinsky Citizen-Action Organizations.* Lexington, MA: D. C. Heath (Lexington Books), 1979.

Reitzes, Donald C. and Dietrich C. Reitzes. *The Alinsky Legacy Alive and Kicking.* Greenwich, CT: JAI Press, 1987.

Williams, Michael R. "Saul D. Alinsky, The War on Poverty: Political Pornography," *Journal of Social Issues,* 21, January 1965, p. 53.

Community Organization With Specific Communities

Boyte, Harry C. *Commonwealth: A Return to Citizen Action.* New York: Free Press, 1989.

Delgado, Gary. *Organizing the Movement: The Roots and Growth of ACORN.* Philadelphia: Temple University Press, 1986.

Kurzman, Paul, ed. *The Mississippi Experience: Strategies for Welfare Rights Action.* New York: Association Press, 1971.

Medoff, Peter and Holly Sklar. *Streets of Hope: The Fall and Rise of an Urban Neighborhood.* Boston: South End Press, 1994.

Rabrenovic, Gordana. *Community Builders: A Tale of Neighborhood Mobilization in Two Cities.* Philadelphia: Temple University Press, 1996.

Rooney, Jim. *Organizing in the South Bronx.* Albany: State University of New York Press, 1995.

Skerry, Peter. *Mexican Americans: The Ambivalent Minority.* New York: Free Press, 1993.

Stoecker, Randy. *Defending Community: The Struggle for Alternative Redevelopment in Cedar-Riverside.* Philadelphia: Temple University Press, 1994.

Faith-Based Community Organizing

Bobo, Kimberly. *Lives Matter: A Handbook for Christian Organizing.* Chicago, IL: Midwest Academy, 1986.

Coleman, John, ed. *One Hundred Years of Catholic Social Thought: Celebration and Challenge.* Maryknoll, NY: Orbis Books, 1991.

Fagan, Harry. *Empowerment: Skills for Parish Social Action.* Ramsey, NJ: Paulist Press, 1979.

Freeman, Samuel. *Upon This Rock: The Miracles of a Black Church.* New York: HarperCollins, 1993.

Linthicum Robert C. *Empowering the Poor: Community Organizing Among the City's "Rag, Tag and Bobtail."* Monrovia, CA: MARC, 1991.

McDougall, Harold. *Black Baltimore: A New Theory of Community.* Philadelphia: Temple University Press, 1993.

McMahon, Eileen. *What Parish Are You From? A Chicago Irish Community and Race Relations.* Louisville: University Press of Kentucky, 1995.

Murnion, Philip and Anne Wenzel. *The Crisis of the Church in the Inner City: Pastoral Options for Inner City Parishes.* New York: National Pastoral Life Center, 1990.

Perkins, John M. *Let Justice Roll Down.* Glendale, CA: Regal Books, 1976.

Perry, Cynthia, ed. *IAF: 50 Years: Organizing for Change.* Chicago: Industrial Areas Foundation, 1990.

Rogers, Mary Beth. *Cold Anger: A Story of Faith and Power Politics.* Denton: University of North Texas Press, 1990.

Related Works

The Rebirth of Urban Democracy. Washington, DC: Brookings Institute, 1993. The Collaboration Project. *Collaborating for Change in Chicago.* Chicago: John D. and Catherine T. MacArthur Foundation, 1993.

Articles

Dreier, Peter. "Community Empowerment Strategies: The Limits and Potential of Community Organizing in Urban Neighborhoods." *Cityscape,* 2, May 1996, pp. 121–159.

Edwards, Bob and Michael W. Foley. "The Paradox of Civil Society." *Journal of Democracy,* 7 (3), 1996, pp 38–52.

Fisher, Robert. "Community Organizing in the Conservative '80s and Beyond." *Social Policy,* 25, 1994, pp. 10–17.

Fisher, Robert. "Neighborhood Organizing: Lessons From the Past." *Social Policy,* Summer 1984, pp. 9–16.

Eisen, Arlene. "Survey of Neighborhood-Based, Comprehensive Community Empowerment Initiatives." *Health Education Quarterly,* 21, 1994, pp. 235–252.

McCarthy, J. D. and M. N. Zald. "Resource Mobilization and Social Movements." *American Journal of Sociology,* 82, 1977, pp. 1212–1241.

Stoecker, Randy. "The Community Development Corporation Model of Urban Redevelopment: A Critique and an Alternative." *Journal of Urban Affairs,* 19, 1997, pp. 1–23.

Stoecker, Randy. "Community Organizing and Community Development in Cedar-Riverside and East Toledo: A Comparative Study." *Journal of Community Practice,* 2, 1995, pp. 1–23.

Stoecker, Randy. "Community, Movement, Organization: The Problem of Identity Convergence in Collective Action." *Sociological Quarterly,* 36, 1995, pp. 111–130.

Online Articles

Russell, Dan. Roots of Social Justice Movement (1970–75), 2000. (http://www.acorn.org/history-content.html)

Tresser, Thomas. "The Work of the Industrial Areas Foundation—Building Strong Citizens Organizations for Power—Action—Justice," 1999. (http://my.voyager.net/ttresser/iaf1.htm)

Warren, Mark Russell. "Social Capital and Community Empowerment: Religion and Political Organization in the Texas Industrial Areas Foundation." Unpublished Ph.D. dissertation, Harvard University, 1995.

Wessel, Paul. message posted on COMM-ORG: The On-Line Conference on Community Organizing and Development, 2000. (http://comm-org.utoledo.edu/pipermail/colist/2000-December/001212.html)

Winkelman, Lee. "Organizing Renaissance: Twin Cities CDC Leads Exploration of Organizing by Massachusetts CDCs." *Shelterforce,* September/October, 1998. (http://www.nhi.org/online/issues/sf101.html)

Winkelman, Lee. "Organizing: An Investment That Pays." *Neighbor Works Journal,* 16 (2), Winter 1998. (http://www.nw.org/resources/pub/nwjournal/1998/vol16no2/)

Smith, Ken. message posted on COMM-ORG: The On-Line Conference on Community Organizing and Development, 2000. (http://comm-org.utoledo.edu/pipermail/colist/2000-December/001213.html)

Smock, Kristina. "Comprehensive Community Initiatives: A New Generation of Urban Revitalization Strategies." Paper presented on COMM-ORG: The On-Line Conference on Community Organizing and Development, 1997. (http://comm-org.utoledo.edu/papers.htm)

Leavitt, Jacqueline. "Public Housing Tenants Confront Deregulation." Planners Network Online, 1997. (http://www.plannersnetwork.org/126/leavitt.htm)

National Organizers Alliance, 2001. (http://www.noacentral.org/)

New Party. "Living Wage and Campaign Finance Reform Initiatives, 1997." (http://www.newparty.org/reforms.html)

Hess, Doug. "Community Organizing, Building and Developing: Their Relationship to Comprehensive Community Initiatives." Paper presented on COMM-ORG: The On-Line Conference on Community Organizing and Development, 1999. (http://comm-org.utoledo.edu/papers.htm)

Beckwith, Dave with Cristina Lopez. "Community Organizing: People Power From the Grassroots." COMM-ORG Working Papers Series, 1997 Working Papers. (http://comm-org.utoledo.edu/papers.htm)

ACORN. "Capital & Communities: A Report to the Annie E. Casey Foundation on ACORN's Work to Revitalize Low and Moderate Income Communities," 1997. (http://www.acorn.org/ACORNarchives/studies/c-and-c/capital-and-communities.html)

Callahan, Steve, Neil Mayer, Kris Palmer, and Larry Ferlazzo. "Rowing the Boat With Two Oars." Paper presented on COMM-ORG: The On-Line Conference on Community Organizing and Development, 1999. (http://comm-org.utoledo.edu/papers.htm)

COMM-ORG: The On-Line Conference on Community Organizing and Development. CO Groups and Networks, 2001. (http://comm-org.utoledo.edu/orgs.htm)

Consensus Organizing Institute, 2000. (http://www.consensusorganizing.com)

Eichler, Michael. "Organizing's Past, Present, and Future." *Shelterforce* Online, 1998. (http://www.nhi.org/online/issues/101/eichler.html)

PART Three

The Practice of Social Work With Organizations

Bureaucracy
Bureaucracy is *the* means of transforming social action into rationally organized action.[1]

Max Weber

Organizational Society
We live in a society that is an organizational society.[2]

Robert Presthus

Organizational social work is a process of developing, administering, and improving social organizations as tools for social betterment. Every macro social worker needs to understand how organizational systems work, design systems that are better, infuse those which are unethical with integrity, and fix them when they become dysfunctional. As North America enters the 21st century, you have a great challenge and opportunity to help rebuild the social framework of our organizational society and create space for an authentically *social* environment.

SOCIAL ORGANIZATIONS

Organizational social workers, in partnership with others, have been developing a new social form called *social organizations*. They are working to construct an entirely new "social" sector of society. In Chapter 9 you will learn more about these new social organizations and how organizational macro social workers are using them to reassert the social in a world of impersonality, alienation, and dehumanization. You will find that the emergence of the social sector is another indication of a vast social revolution that is accumulating strength and power in our society to usher in the postmodern era of the 21st century.

You will also explore the phenomenon of modern complex organizations, one of the most powerful and wealthiest social systems ever devised. You will discover that modern corporate organizations, for example, are wealthier than many entire nations. As corporations entrench themselves more deeply in our global society, they are also supplanting the sovereign power of many of those same nations. You will learn how macro social workers can use modern complex organizations but must also understand how these systems often shape our society to their own designs and become control systems of the first order.

PROGRAM DEVELOPMENT

In Chapter 10 you will learn how to help individuals and community groups create a new social organization, including assessing the need for a program, developing a constitution and by-laws, organizing a board of directors, hiring staff, creating a budget, and developing funding. Once a social organization or agency is established, it needs to be administered by skilled, energetic macro social workers.

SOCIAL ADMINISTRATION

In Chapter 11 you will learn how to translate your social leadership skills into helping operate an organization as a supervisor or departmental or chief social administrator. You will learn how to share the process of taking responsibility for the social organization with social work staff and the community in which it resides. You will learn how to make administrative decisions and engage in personnel administration, budgeting, and agency planning.

ORGANIZATION DEVELOPMENT

Sometimes macro social workers consult with administrators of social organizations to strengthen or improve their programs. The work of consulting with established social organizations is called *organization development*. In Chapter 12, you will learn how to help employees take ownership of the organization change process and make the social organization a more responsive system for serving its clients and the community.

ADDITIONAL READING

Perrow, Charles. *Complex Organizations: A Critical Essay.* 2d ed. Glenview, IL: Scott Foresman, 1979.

Ruitenbeek, Hendrik M., ed. *The Dilemma of Organizational Society.* New York: E. P. Dutton, 1963.

9 Social Organizations

Organization and Democracy

While we are members of a society that protects freedom of speech, choice, and the rights of the individual, we work in places that . . . view the values underlying democracy with deep skepticism, if not contempt. . . . We are still convinced that for large groups of people to get work done and succeed in the marketplace control, consistency and predictability, engineered from the top are absolute requirements.[1]

Peter Block

Bureaucracy

When fully developed, bureaucracy also stands, in a specific sense, under the principle of *sine ira ac studio* [without sympathy or compassion]. Its nature, which is welcomed by capitalism, develops the more perfectly the more the bureaucracy is "dehumanized," the more perfectly it succeeds in eliminating from official business love, hatred, and all purely personal, irrational, and emotional elements which escape calculation. This is the specific nature of bureaucracy and it is appraised as its special virtue.[2]

Max Weber

Ideas in This Chapter

ST. John Evangelist Girl Scouts

© Michael Newan/PhotoEdit

The common purpose of social organizations is to change human beings. The product of the Girl Scouts is a mature young woman who has values, skills, and respect for herself.

THE SUCCESS OF SOCIAL ORGANIZATIONS

Despite a decline of almost one fifth the number of girls of high school age between 1978 and 1988, the Girl Scouts of the USA, the world's largest women's organization, managed to maintain a membership of 3.5 million, significantly increasing its market penetration. In the state of Florida, thousands of criminal offenders sentenced to jail for the first time are paroled into the custody of the Salvation Army. These convicts are poor risks, many of them poor blacks or Hispanics, and three out of every four would become habitual criminals if actually sent to jail.

The Salvation Army rehabilitates three out of four of these parolees.

Church membership and attendance have been going down quite sharply in all denominations, but membership and attendance is growing fast in those pastoral churches, Protestant and Catholic, mainstream and evangelical, that concentrate on serving the needs, problems, and families of their parishioners. Around 1970 there were no more than 5,000 pastoral churches with a membership of 2,000 parishioners or more. By the late 1980s their numbers had grown fourfold to 20,000, and they employ more than a million volunteers as unpaid staff.

Drucker says these successes are based on greatly increased productivity. Social organizations, or at least a large number of them, get more results from their resources. The Girl Scouts saw their opportunity in demographic change. They adapted their programs and activities to married women with children who are now in the labor force. Recognizing that the career aspirations of girls are changing fast in the United States, they converted those changes into opportunities. They began to recruit aggressively among minorities, offering children and their mothers an opportunity to participate in what had up to then been considered a white, middle-class organization.[3]

By 1987 the proportion of African American girls of elementary school age enrolled in the Girl Scouts matched that of white girls. "In the war on drug abuse, the Boy Scouts and Girl Scouts of America have taken the lead. In their work with elementary school children—and one out of every four elementary school children in the United States is a scout—the two organizations try hard, with considerable success, to inculcate resistance to drugs well before the children are actually exposed to the menace."[4]

The Salvation Army used an organizational tool—organized abandonment. They assessed their efforts in crime prevention in the slums and realized that they were ineffective. The return on their investment of time and energy was close to zero. Once they examined the problem, it became clear why they were not effective. Before being caught and convicted, endangered young people in the slums are not receptive to the Salvation Army's message. Each of them thinks he or she will beat the odds. Being arrested but released on probation only confirms this belief. After young people have served even a short term in jail, it is too late. They are traumatized by their experience and corrupted by it.

However, the Salvation Army staff realized that for a very short period of time there is a window of opportunity in which pre-convicts (those who have been caught and sentenced to jail but have not yet been sent to prison) are susceptible to change. They are sufficiently frightened but not yet corrupted by the prison system. Now the Salvation Army contracts with government to keep these young people out of further trouble, and they are doing it with considerable success.

Human sector organizations work at making their governing boards effective. Many have work programs against which they regularly evaluate their boards. In the well-run social sector organization, there are no "volunteers"; there is only unpaid staff. Increasingly these people are taking over the professional and executive work in nonprofit organizations. The 1,800 local chapters of the American Heart Association, for instance, are managed and run by volunteers. A growing number of volunteers are professional men and women; 20 or 30 years ago they tended to be housewives. For a senior business executive, board membership in a nonprofit organization has almost become a "must." The number of active volunteers working for nonprofits has grown fast these past 10 years. A lot of older people, retired or semiretired, have found volunteer work to be satisfying and a way to put a lifetime's experience to work. But there is even more demand for participation on the part of affluent baby boomers.

Social sector organizations have gone heavily into training. Staff members, whether paid or unpaid, are expected in the Girl Scouts or the Salvation Army to define clearly the performances and contribution for which they are to be held accountable. They are then regularly appraised against these performance objectives. A large pastoral church runs a dozen ministries, both for its 13,000 members and in its community. Yet it has a paid staff of only 160. New members of the congregation are asked after a few months to become unpaid staff. They are thoroughly trained and given a specific assignment with performance goals. Their performance is regularly reviewed, and if it does not come up to high expectations, the volunteer is either shifted to another, less demanding assignment or asked to resign.

The Salvation Army keeps a tight rein on its 25,000 parolees in Florida. About 160 paid staffers supervise and train volunteers and take care of crises while 250 to 300 unpaid people do the work itself.

What enabled the Girl Scouts to maintain enrollment in a shrinking market was a substantial increase in the number of volunteers: from 600,000 to 730,000. Many of the new volunteers are young professional women without children of their own but with a need to be a woman in a feminine environment a few evenings a week and on weekends, and to be with children. They are attracted precisely because the job is professional; they are required to spend several hours a week being trained or working as trainers for newcomers.

One Midwestern diocese doubled its community service even though it had barely half the number of priests it had 20 years before. Its 140 priests preach, say mass, hear confession, baptize, confirm, marry, and bury people. Everything else is done by 2,000 laypeople, each of whom is expected to work at least 3 hours a week and to spend an additional 2 or 3 hours in training sessions. Each layperson's performance is appraised twice a year. "It's worse than Marine boot camp," one of these unpaid staffers said. Yet there is a long waiting list of potential volunteers. American and Canadian social sector organizations are rapidly becoming the creators of new bonds of community. They create a sphere of effective citizenship and involvement.[5]

Retired working-class and young professionals work side by side in the Salvation Army's efforts with young convicts, designing programs and training leaders in a local chapter of the YMCA, and helping disaster victims with the Red Cross. What the Girl Scouts contribute to inner-city women may be more important than what they contribute to children. These women are becoming leaders in their communities, learning skills, setting examples, and gaining recognition and status. There are now more African Americans in leadership positions in the two U.S. scouting organizations than anywhere else except in black churches. In the Scouts they are leaders in racially integrated organizations. Social organizations are creating a sphere of meaningful citizenship for their volunteers.[6]

WHAT YOU WILL LEARN IN THIS CHAPTER

You will learn that there are two major kinds of organizations in our North American society today: social organizations in the social or nonprofit sector of society and modern complex organizations in the private economic and public governmental sectors of society.

You will learn what social organizations are, why they are important for macro social work practice, and their potential for social change. You will be challenged to consider the implications of social organizations for yourself and for the field of social work.

In addition, you will learn about modern complex organizations and explore a brief history of modern organizations and their characteristics. Large organizational systems are the means by which many of our goods and services are provided today, but you will discover that they are also the reason many of our social problems exist.

SOCIAL ORGANIZATIONS

Today, macro social workers are engaging in a revolution in thinking, in government, and in the way we understand the social. At the center of this revolution is the rise of a new institutional and social form, says Peter Dobkin Hall.[7] These alternative social forms are social organizations. They are uniquely suited to promoting components of social life that large bureaucratic organizations are unable to provide, and in some cases macro social workers are at the center of bringing these new forms into being.

Many people have been unaware of the existence or strength of these social organizations. Although they lack a commonly accepted name, they comprise a new sector of society and contain a number of important components.

No Commonly Accepted Name

Social organizations have existed almost from the beginning of North American society, but they have no commonly accepted name. They have been variously called nonprofit, not-for-profit, nonbusiness, or nongovernmental organizations (NGOs). But as Peter Drucker says, these are negatives and one cannot define something by what it is not. They have also been called mediating structures, third sector organizations, human service organizations, public benefit organizations, voluntary associations, and civic organizations. The name that most closely resembles the purpose of these new social forms is *social organization*s.

Just as many people not completely aware of the rise of new social organizations, "few people," says Peter Drucker, "realize the size, let alone the importance of the [social] sector. In fact, few people are even aware of its existence."[8] Just as with social organizations, the new sector also suffers from a confusing array of names. It has been variously called the independent sector, the third sector, the voluntary sector, the human services sector, and the nonprofit sector. Lester Salamon and Helmut Anheier refer to it as the "civil society sector."[9] The name that seems to define this sector most accurately, however, is the *social sector.*

New Components

Social organizations are essential to our civil society. Nonprofits have a great diversity in scope, vary enormously in what they do, and are among the most ethnically diverse systems in North America. They provide a new form of organizational structure and offer a new social purpose to clients and staff.

The sources of revenue for social organizations follow no clear pattern, and although most are dedicated to charitable purposes and operate by community boards, they also maintain other means of governance as well. They offer multiple levels of inclusion and operate as new configurations of power affecting business and government.[10]

Essential to Civil Society
Social organizations produce social goods and capital that are essential for the economy and the government. In return, social organizations need the products that government and the economy provide.

Social Goods and Social Capital   Social organizations, along with the family, groups, and community, are one of the important means by which civil society creates social goods and social capital on which the economy and government depend, but which these sectors cannot themselves produce. Business corporations produce private goods and economic capital. Governmental organizations generate public goods such as military defense, public education, public land, and highways. Social organizations provide social goods and social capital including social welfare, cooperation and public spirit, friendship and caring, leadership and community service, responsibility and commitment, perseverance and trust, and a host of other human virtues. Charitable, civic, human service, and public benefit organizations enable people to develop close relationships, build community,

construct their social environments, and form the culture in which they find their identities.

Neither the private sector of the economy nor the public sector of government could survive without a healthy civil society of which social organizations are a key component, says Salamon and Anheier.[11] Frances Fukuyama agrees, furthermore, that the economy is dependent on and could not exist without the capacity of people to trust to be honest and thrifty. The economy depends on people's dedication to a task, willingness to contribute, and cooperation in producing goods and services.[12]

In the same way, government depends on the willingness of people to apply democratic ideals such as equality, fairness, and justice in their duties as citizens. A democratic society could not exist without people who express public spirit, civic responsibility, public service, engagement in public affairs, and carry out their ideals in the public interest and service to their communities, cities, and the nation as a whole. Without these values of citizenship and public engagement, government would be reduced to a role of monitoring and control. Coats and Santorum explain, for example, "When civil society is strong, it infuses a community with its warmth, trains it people to be good citizens and transmits values between generations. When it is weak, no amount of police or politics can provide a substitute."[13]

Social Organizations Need the Economy and Government   Civil society cannot achieve its purposes in isolation from a healthy economy or a supportive governmental sector. To the extent that government and the economy fail to support the social sector or act against it, civil society may be weakened. When economic organizations fail to pay workers a living wage while offering millions in salary to corporate executives, they not only hurt people financially but destroy their own integrity. When government proclaims allegiance to political freedom while hoarding power and preventing access to government information, it not only disempowers people but undermines citizens' trust in government.

By supporting the infrastructure of civil society, contributing to the social organizations that produce social capital and provide opportunities and social space in which communities of people construct social relationships and individual character, private industry and government strengthen and reinforce trust, cooperation, and a more equitable and more just society,[14] and in the process they contribute to strengthening people economically and politically as well.

Diversity At first glance new social sector organizations offer a bewildering array of diversity in their scope, activities, and the ethnicity of their members.[15]

Scope Social organizations come in all shapes and sizes, ranging from small locally based community and neighborhood associations with no assets and no employees to powerful multibillion dollar national foundations with many staff members. Some social organizations are relatively recently organized and virtually unknown except in the communities in which they operate. Others, including the Boy Scouts, Girl Scouts, Salvation Army, YMCA, and Red Cross are among the oldest and most respected organizations in Canada and the United States, operating in nearly every country around the world.

Social organizations are ubiquitous. They exist in every society and predate the advent of modern complex organizations by several millennia. Today, for example, even the small nation of Singapore boasts 900 institutions of public character.[16]

Activities Social organizations vary enormously in what they do, from offering traditional charitable assistance to the needy to carrying out advanced research. Far from focusing exclusively on the poor or needy in the United States and Canada, nonprofit social organizations serve a broad cross section of the population and provide a host of activities that reflect the diversity of human interests and the full scope of community life. Social organizations provide nearly all of the humanitarian and social welfare services in North America. They provide a good share of its educational, cultural, health, and religious activities. They are becoming an even stronger force internationally.[17]

Humanitarian and social services: Nonprofit social organizations deliver a larger share of publicly funded human and social services than do government agencies.[18] Social organizations consist of a wide range of direct service social work agencies that provide counseling and mental health, social case work, case management, and group work services to persons with intellectual, emotional, and physical disabilities, and social services to offenders in virtually every city, county, state, and province in North America.

Neighborhood, civic, ethnic, fraternal, sororal, and service associations, community organizations, social planning councils, and economic and community development corporations are all social organizations.

Social organizations comprise large international philanthropic organizations, smaller community foundations, and cooperative solicitation agencies such as Community Chest and the United Way, which support local charities.[19] Some social support organizations are regional and national, including training organizations and intermediary organizations that link private and public funding programs with community organization and community development corporations. Other social organizations are major providers of advocacy, social justice, social research, human rights, environmental, civil rights, activist social movements, and social policy in the United States and Canada.

Education, cultural, health, and religious activities: Social organizations include a very large part of North America's schools, and an even larger percentage of colleges and universities. Social organizations engage in an indescribable variety of cultural enterprises, from neighborhood arts programs and community theaters to hundreds of symphony orchestras and museums. They provide the majority of North America's hospitals, as well as national health care public awareness and education groups such as the American Heart Association, the American Lung Association, and the American Mental Health Association. Social organizations include the enormous diversity of religious organizations in the United States and Canada ranging from those with more than 10,000 parishioners to conventicles with fewer than 25 members.[20]

International social organizations: Although American and Canadian nonprofits have for decades been active in international relief and development, these activities have been matched or exceeded by the proliferation of indigenous nongovernmental organizations in the Third World.[21] With a collective membership of hundreds of millions of people,[22] social organizations comprise the literally hundreds of thousands of grassroots organizations (GROs), nongovernmental organizations (NGOs), transnational nongovernmental organizations (TNGOs) and nongovernmental support organizations (NGSOs) that exist globally in every nation of the world (about which you will read in Chapter 15).

Ethnic Diversity   Social organizations are among the most ethnically diverse and pluralistic social systems in Canada and the United States. Administrators of social organizations celebrate new arrivals to the table of equality, actively support their rights to full expression of ideas and perspectives, facilitate their access to all needed resources, and most important, ensure equity power in the pluralistic organization.[23]

The Equity Institute has developed categories of inclusion by which they evaluate organizations. At the highest level of ethnic diversity is the category "pluralistic organizations." Pluralistic organizations prohibit all forms of discrimination, prescribe governance policies and practices that support the value of pluralism, and develop a workforce composed of individuals and groups who subscribe to multiple cultural perspectives. Darlyne Bailey says many social organizations are moving in the direction of such genuine pluralism. The Equity Institute has designated Big Brothers, Big Sisters, and the Girl Scouts as "pluralistic organizations," the top category of organizational ethnic inclusion.[24]

New Structure

Peter Dobson Hall asserts that social organizations are a new hybrid institutional form whose employees and members are often indivisible, and who operate using a number of structural designs.[25]

Hybrids   In contrast to modern complex organizations, most of the newer social organizations are combinations of a social community *and* an organizational tool.

Community   *Gemeinschaft* community members are the "owners" of the social organization, comprising its social component and giving it purpose and direction. These members spontaneously and voluntarily form themselves into an association to accomplish their common goals and meet their mutual needs.

Organization   The organization itself is the functional component, the agent or tool that community members use to reach their goals, meet their needs, carry out their purposes, and represent the community to the external world. It is because of this unique combination of social/community and functional organization that they are called "social organizations."

Indivisible   Because the unpaid staff or volunteers who operate the social organization are often also members of the community, it is sometimes difficult to distinguish between the community and the organization. The life of the organization and the community tends to be indivisible, particularly in faith-based and community organizations.

Faith-Based Organizations   In a faith-based social organization such as a synagogue, church, or mosque, the member-owners who join together to form the religious community also make the decisions and establish the policies that guide the social organization. The paid staff may consist of a single rabbi, priest, or mullah whom the congregation hires, serves at the pleasure of the members, takes direction from them, and represents the congregation to the wider community. The members-owners of the organization are also its employees who perform the majority of the teaching, maintenance, and secretarial services. Member-owners administer the organization, lead youth groups, organize retreats, provide social and community services, and assist in worship.

Community Organizations   Likewise, in social service community organizations, there may be only one paid community organizer but hundreds of unpaid staff—the members of the community organization who carry out the work of designing strategies, carrying out direct and indirect confrontation, leadership, serving on committees, and raising funds. The paid community organizer provides consultation, support, and assistance to members in developing the community organization. In both a faith-based organization and a community organization, the members are both the community and the organization.

Social System Designs   Social organizations comprise a multiplicity of social system designs that provide for authenticity, human actualization, meaning creation, and self-expression. Their own locally elected volunteer boards govern social organizations. In the United States they are mostly run autonomously. Social organizations have their own budgets and are operated by administrators chosen by their boards.

Because community members and their organizational structures often operate inseparably, however, social organizations rarely if ever form themselves into hierarchical bureaucratic structures. Authoritarian power and control, impersonality, artificiality, uniformity, and unidimensionality have little place in social organizations and are often antithetical to them. Three common organizational structures that social organizations often adopt are the parallel model, the federal structural model, and the loose-linked model.

Parallel Model   Groups exist in parallel with each other and connect with other functions as the task requires. Structure is formed around the flow of the work process. The Girl Scouts, for example, is structured as a series of concentric circles. Information and ideas begin with the local units and pass through the circles toward the central executive group in the middle circle. The circles give emphasis to dialogue and exchange and the idea that everyone is equally important in the operation of the whole system.[26]

Federal Structural Model   According to Skocpol, from the Civil War to around 1960, the quintessential form of U.S. voluntary organizations was the federation, linking membership groups in cities and towns into networks with an organizational presence in each state, and at the same time tying the localities and states into a national organization that ran conventions and disseminated publications.

This three-tiered federal structure, paralleling that of the U.S. government, has been extraordinarily resilient and fertile. It has allowed participation and democracy to be combined with group decision making at state and national levels and has allowed voluntary groups, if they chose, to relate to all levels of U.S. party politics, public administration, and legislative decision making. It allowed for pluralism within unity because local and state groups could pursue their own purposes while at the same time cooperating for other purposes with groups in other places and in a common cause at the national level as well.[27]

Loose-Linked Model   Many faith-based organizations use a loose-linked model. In this model each congregation is a separate, independent entity that is owned and operated by its members and takes direction from them. However, the congregation is also linked by history and belief to other faith-based organizations that have a common heritage. These organizations are members of a "denomination" to which member congregations contribute funds and that establishes schools to educate future pastors, provides social services, publishes literature, and carries out overall coordination

functions. All congregations are autonomous, but they are all loosely linked with one another.

New Social Purpose

Social organizations are committed to promoting social inclusion, serving human and social purposes, and reinventing society.

Inclusion   Social organizations offer people increasing levels of inclusion as members, partners, helpers, and paid or unpaid staff.

Members   Social organizations are meant for all people in society, but they are particularly concerned with those people who are unable to compete in today's utilitarian, technological society, those who subsist at the fringe of institutional life. The doors of modern complex organizations are generally closed to people who are less advantaged, but the gates of social organizations are open and macro social workers go into the communities to meet and welcome people to come in. At the most primary level of inclusion, each person, no matter how damaged or devalued, is accepted as a valued individual with dignity, respect, and hospitality.

Partners   At the second level of inclusion, all members are welcomed to fully engage others as partners in the task of overcoming the conditions in society that may have caused personal and social problems. Social organizations eradicate the dichotomy between client and professional expert. Human change organizations invite all their members to participate in a joint venture of personal achievement in which they can exercise influence, discharge responsibility, and make decisions.[28] Those who seem the least valuable members of modern organizational society become partners with others in the process of constructing society and constructing themselves.

Helpers and Being Helped   At the third level of inclusion, many social organization members have a consciousness that they are simultaneously helpers and being helped, learners and teachers, followers and leaders. There is recognition that for true humanness to exist we give and take, serve and are served, and in the process strengthen one another and the social organization. We understand that at many levels each person is dependent on everyone else for his or her social well-being. Members of the social organization become a community of mutuality.

Staff   At a fourth level, members become staff who are dedicated to a profession of service as either paid or nonpaid employees. The social sector is the country's largest employer although neither its workforce nor the output it produces shows up in the statistics. In 1998, 56% of adult Americans, a total of 109.5 million people over the age of 18, volunteered a total of 19.9 billion hours. This is an increase of nearly 30 million people since 1987 and is the highest number ever recorded. In addition, most were also holding a paid job, asserts the Independent Sector.[29] The volunteer workforce represented the equivalent of more than 9 million full-time employees at a value of $229.5 billion in 1998, an increase of almost $80 billion from 10 years earlier, says Peter Drucker.[30] In that year 43% of seniors aged 75 and over reported volunteering, an increase from 35% in 1995. Volunteers included 46% of Hispanics, up from 40% in 1995, and 47% of African Americans, up from 35% in 1995.[31] Churches are the single largest source of volunteers, ahead of workplaces, schools or colleges, fraternal groups, and other civil institutions. George Gallup Jr. summarizes, "Churches are the major supporters of voluntary services of neighborhoods and communities. . . . Almost half of the church members did unpaid volunteer work in a given year, compared to only a third of non-members."[32]

These unpaid employees not only contribute their efforts to social organizations but raise money as well. But most important, they provide services to people and in the process add to the social capital contributing to their communities. As people volunteer, they also receive fulfillment and create social meaning in their own lives.

Human and Social Purpose   Peter Drucker says

that social organizations "all have in common, and this is a recent realization, that their purpose is to change human beings."[33] The product of a hospital, for example, is a cured patient. The product of a church is a changed life. The product of the Salvation Army, one social organization that reaches the poorest of the poor regardless of race or religion, is that the derelict becomes a citizen. The product of the Girl Scouts is a mature young woman who has values, skills, and respect for herself. The purpose of the Red Cross in peacetime is to enable a community hit by natural

disaster to regain its capacity to look after itself, to create human competence. The product of the American Heart Association is middle-aged people who look after their own health and practice preventative cardiac maintenance in the way they live. The successful resettlement of more than 100,000 Vietnam refugees in 1975 was accomplished not by setting up a government agency but by working though voluntary social agencies, mainly faith-based social organizations.[34]

Reinventing Society   Instead of erecting gigantic

economic enterprises or huge institutional structures, social organizations are tools for reinventing society, a means for re-creating our human culture and social environment. Social organizations are dedicated to reconstructing the infrastructures of society neglected by corporations and governmental bureaucracies alike. Social organizations mediate between the individual and the large economic and governmental structures of society, helping reduce alienation and providing a space where people can bear the stresses that institutionalized organizational dehumanization imposes on modern life. Social organizations orient themselves to community values, especially to compassion, caring, and the value of personal social relationships.

The success of social organizations in serving humanitarian purposes is reflected in a 1998 survey administered by the Independent Sector organization revealing that 68% of the respondents expressed a high level of confidence in human service organizations such as homeless shelters, soup kitchens, and employment programs. In addition, 62% believed that most charitable organizations were honest and ethical in their use of funds, and 76% agreed that nonprofit organizations generally played a major role in their communities.[35]

New Means of Funding

Social organizations draw their resources from an array of sources, including fees and charitable donations. Others receive support from private corporations, and some obtain funding from government fiscal arrangements. Many receive funds from several of these sources.

Fees and Charitable Support   Fee income is the

most widely used source of agency support, with nearly 7 out of 10 nonprofit agencies collecting this type of revenue. Direct individual giving is more prevalent but benefits a smaller proportion of agencies than do government and fee incomes.[36] In 1998, according to the Independent Sector survey, more than 70% of U.S. households contributed $135 billion to social organizations. What is most surprising, however, is the relatively small proportion of agencies that receive private philanthropic support. Private charitable giving ranks third among all major funding sources: 23% of social agencies receive funding from cooperative solicitation such as United Way, accounting for only 21% of social organization income, 38% of agencies receive foundation grants, and 34% receive corporate gifts.[37]

Corporate Support

One of the newer sources of income has been the increasingly cooperative and helpful social investment by major corporations. Many companies work closely with social organizations that serve persons with disabilities by providing training and employment opportunities. Ben and Jerry's ice cream and other companies invest time and funding in the communities in which they operate. Even more traditional corporate organizations heavily invest in social organizations in their communities by active participation in United Way campaigns and by making direct contributions, lending staff to these organizations, providing consultation, and giving time to such efforts as "Days of Caring."

Governmental Support

Social organizations receive more of their income from government than from any other single source. Government has created new fiscal tools to funnel funding to social organizations, creating a new federal-social organization partnership that is reshaping the public sector in the United States.

New Fiscal Tools   Some social organizations obtain purchase of service contracts; others receive government loans or loan guarantees. Many receive government grants-in-aid, and all receive tax subsidies.

Government grants: Many social organizations base their economics on grants or one-way economic transfers rather than the two-way exchange common in free market economics. Grants are gifts offered freely with no expectation of a return by the grantors of the gift. From its meager beginnings in the 19th century, Salamon says, the federal grant-in-aid program has mushroomed into a massive system of interorganizational action. Today more than 500 grant-in-aid programs exist, making federal resources available to state and local governments for everything from emergency medical services to the construction of the interstate highway system. Since 1955, grant-in-aid funding has grown three times faster than the budget as a whole and by 1979 accounted for more than 40% of all domestic federal budget outlays, and about 17% of the total federal budget.[38]

Tax subsidies: A second and even more important method of funding social organizations is by means of tax subsidies. By exempting individual and corporate charitable contributions from taxation, the federal government delivers an implicit subsidy to the social sector. This subsidy was estimated to be worth $13.4 billion in 1985. About 78% of this subsidy flows to human service organizations, including faith-based organizations.[39]

New Federal Partnerships   The federal government has emerged as a partner with social organizations, turning to a host of social organizations to carry out its responsibilities rather than expand the federal bureaucracy. So extensive are these arrangements that government in the United States today relies more heavily on nonprofit social organizations than on its own agencies to deliver government-funded human services. In recent years this partnership has expanded in scope and scale, encouraging nonprofit involvement in new fields and even creating new types of nonprofit social organizations where none existed before. The result is an elaborate pattern of nonprofit federalism linking government at all levels to nonprofit organizations across a broad front.[40]

Multiple Sources of Funding

Social organizations rarely rely on only one or two sources of funding. Although many have a chief or preferred manner of raising funds, they also diversify to capture market niches as funding sources open or move in new directions. For example, faith-based organizations continue to rely on individual contributions from members, but they are increasingly receiving funding from the federal government through service provider contracts, which offer a variety of social services to the community at large. They also raise funds through benefits, fees for service, and private charitable donations.[41]

New Configuration of Public Power

The emergence of social organizations as a central feature in society represents a new configuration of public and private power, a necessary force in American society.[42] Many social organizations have been given authority for spending federal money.

Third Party Government Restructuring the federal-social organization relationship has been so substantial, Salamon asserts, that it constitutes a qualitative not just a quantitative change in economics. Social organizations are now a third party to government. The result is a diverse and varied set of institutions connected to government at all levels through a rich network of interactions that differ markedly from place to place in response to local circumstances, traditions, and needs.

In fact, in economic terms, the nonprofit social sector in some localities equals or surpasses the role played by local governments. In the Pittsburgh metropolitan area, for example, the expenditures of private, nonprofit organizations exceed the total budget of the county government by a factor of six to one. In the Twin Cities area of Minnesota, the expenditures of the local nonprofit sector are as large as the combined budgets of Minneapolis, St. Paul, Hennepin, and Ramsey counties. In other local areas as well, the nonprofit sector is as significant an economic force as local government. Cooperation between government and the voluntary social sector is now a central financial fact of life and has become the backbone of this country's human services delivery system.[43]

Authority Over Spending Many social organizations share a basic government function: the exercise of discretion over spending of federal funds and the use of federal authority. The $6 billion to $8 billion that Congress annually appropriates for employment and training assistance, for example, does not go to the Department of Labor but to more than 450 locally organized prime sponsors. These social organizations enjoy substantial discretion in selecting the training and the trainees, and the Labor Department has only limited oversight.[44]

A BRIEF HISTORY OF SOCIAL ORGANIZATIONS

Social organizations in Canada and the United States actively provided the bulk of social, health, religious, cultural, and educational services at the turn of the 19th century. They found new roles after the Civil War and increased cooperation with government in the New Deal and after World War II. Social organizations experienced unprecedented growth in the second half of the 20th century.

The 1800s

Before the advent of the modern welfare state, says Peter Berger, almost all organizations in the social services were under the aegis of voluntary associations, usually religious in character.[45] Many of these voluntary associations launched during the 1800s have survived and continue to flourish into the 21st century. More than four fifths of associations, for example, that enrolled more than 1% or more of American adults at any point between 1790 and the present still exist today, says Theda Skocpol. Gerald Gamm and Robert Putnam assert that between 1840 and 1940 about a third of these voluntary associations were fraternal or sororal groups, which were central to North American civic society. In addition, during this period, North Americans developed churches, women's clubs, union halls, and service and professional groups, many of which were linked together into regional or even national networks of voluntary associations.[46] Many of these associations benefited from and reciprocally assisted in the development of federal initiatives in civil society sponsored by the government.

Civil War and Reconstruction

Civil War benefits stimulated the growth of the Grand Army of the Republic, which in turn promoted and helped to administer federal, state, and local support for veterans and their families. Many other private institutional settings and social service agencies were born in the period after the Civil War, including institutions for orphaned, neglected, and troubled children, societies dedicated to the elimination of poverty, those working to assist emancipated slaves, and hospitals, schools, colleges, and associations dedicated to the elimination of social problems. Early 20th century local, state, and national policies to assist mothers and children were championed by the Women's Christian Temperance Union (WTCU), the National Congress of Mothers (later the PTA), and the General Federation of Women's Clubs—groups that themselves expanded in part because of encouragement from the government.

New Deal and World War II

Even when U.S. politics became more nationally focused during major wars, the depression, and the cold war, voluntary associations did not wither away. On the contrary, many established associations added new local and state units, recruited more members, and branched into new activities, and many of these benefited from governmental support. In the first half of the 20th century, for example, state and federal efforts to support farmers and farm families were championed and administered by associations such as the Grange and the American Farm Bureau Federation. The Farm Bureau Federation later grew into a nationwide organization in conjunction with New Deal farm programs. New Deal social security legislation was originally encouraged by the Fraternal Order of Eagles and the Townsend movement, which in turn stimulated the emergence of more recent local, state, and national associations for the elderly.

Membership dipped during the depression when people could not afford dues, and some groups never recovered, but others reached membership peaks in the middle of the 20th century.[47] Numbering only 12,500 in 1940, more than 90% of social organizations currently in existence today were established after World War II: 27,000 in 1946, and 32,000 in 1950.

Many of these organizations also benefited from social sector and governmental synergy. The GI Bill of 1944, for example, would not have had the inclusive shape it did, opening up American higher education to hundreds of thousands of less privileged men, had not the American Legion taken the lead in writing generous legislation and encouraging public and congressional support for it. In turn, the GI Bill aided the postwar expansion of the American Legion.

Growth From 1950 to 2000

By 1989 just under a million social organizations existed in the United States, an 80-fold increase since 1940, finally achieving the centrality they had always claimed to hold, even though the concept of charitable tax-exempt organizations as a unified and coherent sector dated from little more than 20 years ago. Nonprofit organizations (and their grant economies) comprise the fastest growing category of organizations in the United States; they touch the lives of almost all Americans as donors, as board members, as employees, as clients, as consumers, and as citizens.[48]

MODERN COMPLEX ORGANIZATIONS

Modern complex organizations are the most common social systems in existence today, comprising the private corporate and public governmental sectors of society. These large hierarchical structures have a number of characteristics, some of which distinguish them from social organizations. They are ubiquitous and are among the wealthiest systems in the world. They have grown in size, concentration, and innovation.

Ubiquitous

For the past 100 years, Western society has been dominated by modern complex organizations. This social system is the representative of modernity and is its greatest invention. They are the defining characteristic of our age. We use modern complex organizational systems to achieve advancements in science and technology, cure disease, feed the world's population, expand our horizons into outer space, and explore the intricacies of the atom and the genetic code of life.

Formal organizations have been universally adopted as *the* structure by which people are engaged in productive activities. So marvelous are these organizational systems in helping us achieve our goals that we use them in almost every sphere of life.

You engage modern organizations, for example, when you get a driver's license, sign up for Social Security, vote, pay your taxes, or send a letter. You participate in other organizations when you watch a baseball game, go to a concert, rent a video, or watch a movie. The clothes you wear, the car you drive, the housing that provides you shelter, and the electricity that powers our society are all manufactured by complex organizations. We are born in organizations, educated in organizations, eat food that was grown, processed, packaged, transported, and sold by organizations, find our livelihood working in organizations, and when we die we will be buried by still other organizations.

Wealthy

Top American corporate organizations, by any standard, are extremely wealthy, outstripping the wealth of most of the world's nations. They generate astounding revenue, make huge profits, accumulate astronomical assets, and most have been remarkably stable in their capacity to acquire wealth.

Revenue   In 1983 Wal-Mart's sales were $4.7 billion—far below the top 200 threshold. By 1999 its sales had climbed to $166.8 billion, making Wal-Mart the second largest firm in the world. At the close of 2003, Wal-Mart's annual revenue was $258.7 billion, making it the wealthiest U.S. company. The next wealthiest was ExxonMobil, with $213.2 billion in revenue, followed by General Motors, with $195.6 billion. By the end of 2003, the 500 largest U.S. companies had "raked in a record-breaking $7500 billion in revenues."[49]

Based on a comparison of corporate sales and the gross domestic products (GDPs) of individual nations, Sarah Anderson and John Cavanagh, of the Institute for Policy Studies, report that 51 of the 100 largest economies in the world are corporations and only 49 are sovereign nations. If the gross domestic product of the four wealthiest organizations in 1995 were combined, they would have been the seventh largest economy in the world, richer than Brazil, China, Canada, India, or Russia.[50] The 1999 sales of *each* of the top five corporations—General Motors, Wal-Mart, ExxonMobil, Ford Motor, and Daimler Chrysler—was larger than the gross domestic product of 182 of the world's nations.

In 2003, for example, Wal-Mart had an economy larger than all of Russia. General Motors had more income than Denmark; Daimler Chrysler was wealthier than Poland; Royal Dutch/Shell was richer than Venezuela; IBM had more corporate sales than the gross domestic product of Singapore; and Sony earned more money than the sum of the incomes of all of the people in Pakistan.

Between 1983 and 1999 the combined sales of the world's top 200 corporations grew from 25% to 27.5% of the world's GDP, and their profits grew 362.4%. Employees of the world's top 200 corporations accounted for only 0.78% of the world's workforce, but their combined salaries were 18 times the size of the combined annual income of the 1.2 billion people living in "severe" poverty. If one excluded the gross national product of the 10 largest nations in 1999, the sales of the top 200 corporations would be greater than the combined economies of all the remaining countries on the globe.[51]

Profits   The total 2003 profits for the 10 top earners was $119.5 billion. Among the most profitable companies was ExxonMobil with $21.5 billion in profits for 2003, Citigroup was next with $17.9 billion in profits, and General Electric with $15 billion was third. At the end of 2003, the largest *Fortune* 500 companies had accumulated $445.6 billion in profits.[52]

McDONALD'S AND SOCIAL ACCOUNTABILITY

In spite of their defects, many corporate enterprises today are attempting to enhance the social environment, provide a means for developing social capital, and contribute to society. McDonald's Corporation, for example, "stung by unfavorable attention it has attracted as a symbol of rampant globalization, is touting its record of promoting animal welfare, protecting tropical rain forests and hiring disadvantaged workers."[53]

In a 45-page "social accountability" document using guidelines provided by Global Reporting Initiative, a Boston based group developing international standards for social reporting,[54] McDonald's, the largest beef buyer in the United States, asserts that it has been a key driver of change in the cattle industry, leading the charge toward more humane treatment of animals and requiring suppliers to adhere to a strict code of conduct. McDonald's is committed to protecting tropical rain forests and will not buy any beef raised on rain forest land. It uses recycled paper products, reduced packaging by switching to paper wrappers from Styrofoam packaging, and was the first food service company to phase out the use of chlorofluorocarbons in packaging in the late 1980s. The company says it buys nearly 80% of its supplies locally in the countries where its restaurants operate, with the remainder coming from bordering countries.

European corporations have historically been more open about their compliance efforts, but McDonald's joins only a few U.S. concerns that have catalogued their track records, including Ford Motor Co., Procter and Gamble, and drug maker Baxter International.

Allan White, Global Reporting Acting Executive Director, predicts that by 2006 the number of companies producing social accountability reports will grow to 5,000 from the 200 tracked in 2001 and 657 tracked in 2004.[55]

Assets The organization with the most assets in 2003 was Citigroup, with more than $1,264 billion, topping Fannie Mae, the government's largest private lending institution whose assets were $1,009.6 billion. Morgan and Chase held the third largest assets of nearly $771 billion, followed by Bank of America with $736.5 billion.[56]

Size and Stability

Not only are organizations among the wealthiest economies in the world, they are also large. A full 5% of the top 200's combined workforce is comprised of Wal-Mart employees. The discount retail giant's workforce skyrocketed from 62,000 in 1983 to 1.14 million in 1999, making it the largest private employer in the world. The next largest, Daimler Chrysler, had a workforce of 466,938—less than half the size of Wal-Mart's.[57]

The wealthiest corporations are remarkably stable in their ability to command huge revenue, profits, and assets.[58] More than half of the firms that were on the top 200 list in 1983 were still at the top in 1999, and some of them, such as General Mills, General Motors, Ford, General Electric, IBM, and Bank of America, have been among the strongest organizations for decades.

Concentrated

The wealth of the top corporations is becoming more concentrated in North America and Europe. In 1983, for example, Brazil, Israel, South Africa, and India also had firms among the top 200, but by 1999 South Korea was the only country outside North America, Japan, and Europe on the list. The merger boom of the past two decades, particularly among U.S. firms but also in Europe, further concentrated economic power in companies based in the leading industrial economies. In 1995, for example, Japanese and U.S. firms were nearly tied in the number of corporations on the top 200 list, with 58 and 59, respectively. By 1999 the United States had attained 82, or 41% of the total, of the top 200 corporations; Japan had 41, or 20.5%; Germany 20, or 10%; and France 17, or 8.5%.

Technologically Innovative

Organizations produce most of the new technology that exists today. The 10 most prolific organizations applied for and received 16,758 preliminary patents in 2001. The top applicant in 2001 was IBM, which received preliminary approval for 3,411 patents. The next 9 organizations were all Japanese firms, including NEC, Canon, Micron Technology, Samsung, Matsushita, Sony, Hitachi, Mitsubishi, and Fujitsu, which received a total of 13,347 preliminary patent approvals. The same pattern occurred in 2000. IBM was the top patent receiver with the remainder being Japanese firms.

A DEFINITION OF MODERN COMPLEX ORGANIZATIONS

Modern complex organizations are artificial, intentionally contrived tools for accomplishing the goals of their owners. Let's expand on that definition and explore some of its key components.

Artificial

Organizations are artificial systems.[59] They are both the product of and the producer of technology. Because technology can create a machine-oriented world that is efficient and productive, humans invented the organizational machine to produce more and better kinds of technology.[60] Jacques Ellul asserted that this artificial machinelike system tends to destroy, eliminate, or subordinate the natural world, however, and does not allow the natural world to restore itself or even to enter into a symbiotic relation with it. The two worlds obey different imperatives, different directives, and different laws that have nothing in common.[61]

In the natural world, for example, relationships are intimate, personal, and often compassionate and caring. All relationships in the artificial world of organizational systems are impersonal and abstract.[62] Complex organizations eliminate personal, compassionate, altruistic treatment of individuals. According to Victor Thompson, in modern organizations "compassion as exceptional, special, non-legitimate treatment is irrational in relation to the owner's goal, and it is also illegitimate—a form of theft or personal appropriation of administrative resources."[63]

Clients are "cases," not persons, and workers must conform their behavior as well as that of clients to the expectations required by the organization, often in rigidly programmed ways. Social workers are constrained from expressing or acting on altruistic feelings in making decisions for clients if those decisions contradict prescribed agency mandates. "In fact," asserts Thompson, "a caring relationship between the incumbent in a role in a modern organization and a client is regarded as *unethical*."[64]

Even administrators who attempt to "humanize" relationships within their organization's hierarchy will be seen as subverting the basic structure of the organization. They are questioning the value system of the organization and engaging in "corruption" in the true sense of the word by propagating relationships "that threaten death to rationalistically legitimated ones."[65]

Intentionally Contrived

Complex organizations are "consciously designed control machines"[66] that exact "conforming behavior in every area of organizational life."[67] Organizations have only one vision, that of the owner, and everyone is trained to envision the organizational environment through that perspective. Once the owner embeds the organization with its ends and provides it with premises and goals, decisions become inevitable and predictable. Organized and rationalized individuals will, as closely as possible, always think alike, behave in the same way, communicate with the same technical language, and in theory reach the same decisions.

The result is standardization, routinization, and uniformity over all the organization's components, clients, social workers, and administrators alike. Unidimensional rational thinking is necessary for the organization, so that all of its components behave in programmed ways, not only in complex organizations themselves but also in social systems comprised of them in politics, economics, and nearly every facet of social life. According to Peter Block, "We have implemented and perpetuated work structures, financial control systems, information systems, performance appraisal and reward systems, and other management practices that reinforce the class system and reenact in a thousand ways the primacy of consistency, control and predictability."[68]

Functional Tools

Modern organizations are unitary, unipurpose functional tools guided by one kind of reason and devised to shape the world as its owner wishes. Organizations provide the means for imposing the owner's definition of proper affairs on others and give owners power that others do not have. Peter Block says, for example, that we have given organizations and their owners responsibility for shaping and coordinating goals and the direction of our society. Modern complex organizations become a means of dominance "based on sovereignty and a form of intimate colonialism."[69] Organizational megastructures decide what is in our best interests and remove the locus of decisions far from those affected by them. Complex organizations intentionally keep us captured by dependency, chained to helplessness, and disempowered by their command and control systems.[70]

Accomplish Goals

A tool does not have a goal; it is a means to achieve a goal. Organizational tools are neutral instruments that accomplish the purposes of their owners. The owners of the organization establish its goals, and the organization carries them out. Their function is to survive in competition in a social environment composed of all other organizations. "Private organizations engage in the primary task of maximizing their control and position."[71] Product or service quality is necessary only to the extent that quality helps achieve the end of organizational survival. If quality can be sacrificed without affecting power or profit, it is only rational that an organization will do so.

Directed by Their Owners

Most modern organizations are structured as more or less hierarchical, bureaucratic systems in a pyramidal structure. At the top is the owner, who has power and control and makes the major decisions for the organization. At the bottom are line employees, who carry out the work of the organization, do what they are told, and rarely, if ever, are involved in making decisions about how the organization operates or its direction. Bureaucracies operate by a "chain of command" in which orders are passed down the hierarchy by means of one-way communication. Communication filters upward through this chain of command and may be stopped at any level. Hierarchical bureaucracies are tightly controlled systems created for efficiency, effectiveness, and speed. However, in reality, because of their size, many bureaucracies generate rigid procedures that slow their operations and create inefficiencies and lapses in communication.

A BRIEF HISTORY OF MODERN COMPLEX ORGANIZATIONS

The first profit-making corporations were invented in Britain and then imported to the United States and Canada. New technology created by the Industrial Revolution inspired a new social invention, the modern factory, resulting in an enormous growth in productivity. Corporations, meanwhile, were legally defined as "persons" and concentrated into huge monopolies. Sociologists and management theorists developed several "schools" of organization theory. Today modern business and public organizations have become global phenomena.

The First Corporations (1600–1750)

According to the New Internationalist, prior to the 17th century the first corporations were created in Europe as not-for-profit entities to construct institutions for the public good including hospitals and universities. These corporations had constitutions detailing their roles and were regulated by government. Straying outside those prescribed functions was punishable by law. In the 1600s, however, European nations used their wealth to finance colonial expansion and corporations changed into profit-making organizations. Imperial governments used corporations to maintain control of trade, resources, and territory in Asia, Africa, and the Americas.

The founders of the East India Company, for example, combined their personal stock to create the world's first commercial corporation, which was granted a Royal Charter by Queen Elizabeth in 1600. Initially this private, profit-making organization traded spices, textiles, and luxury goods from Asia, but it soon expanded into a huge imperialistic enterprise conquering and acquiring entire countries in its quest for power. The East India Company, not Great Britain, conquered India and ruled with a total monopoly on trade and the territorial powers of a government. At its height the company ruled more than a fifth of the world's population with a private army of a quarter of a million. After a mutiny in 1857, however, Britain dissolved the territorial authority of the East India Company, taking over its governance. The company continued its operations in China, however, trading in opium and leading to the opium wars of the 19th century.

In the American colonies royal charters allowed corporations such as the Hudson Bay Company to obtain monopoly powers. These corporations shipped raw material such as furs, lumber, and cotton to Britain for manufacture, after which the colonies were forced to purchase the finished goods. After the War of Independence, U.S. corporations were chartered to perform public tasks such as digging canals or building bridges. Their charters were limited to periods of 10 to 40 years, and limits were set on their commercial activities and prohibited them from participation in the political process.[72]

The Industrial Revolution and the Factory System (1750–1910)

Beginning in England about 1750, with the creation of new technology in the textile industry, production moved from the home and shop to the factory. Inventions in the textile industry were numerous—including the spinning jenny (1764), the water frame (1769), the spinning mule (1778), and the power loom (1785). Central to factory production of textiles and other products was power, which was generated by the steam engine developed by James Watt in 1769. This led to the mass production of goods. As the steam engine was reshaping the world of work and transportation, a new process for smelling ore with coke increased the production of iron, and the telegraph was speeding communication.[73] In 1853 the Bessemer converter was invented, making possible large-scale production of steel and paving the way for the huge expansion of the modern railway system.

Productivity   The modern factory combined technology, surplus capital, and organization of the workplace to accomplish large-scale production of goods. In the United States during the decade of 1850 to 1860, manufacturing increased with amazing speed. "The great packing plants at Chicago and Cincinnati, the flour mills of the Twin Cities, and breweries of

Milwaukee and St. Louis, the iron and steel mills of the Pittsburgh region, the oil refineries of Ohio and Pennsylvania, and a hundred others worked day and night to meet the orders that poured in on them."[74]

Twenty thousand miles of track were laid, most of it in the West, and transcontinental railroads pushed across the plains and the mountains with dizzying speed. Telegraph lines were strung from city to city and soon crossed the continent; cables were laid across the Atlantic. Productivity and industrial expansion increased with the need to supply the forces in battle during the Civil War, and although "the United States of Lincoln's day was still by and large a nation of small enterprises, the momentum that occurred during the Civil War went on with mounting speed after the seventies."[75]

In the 5 years after Appomattox, assert Nevins and Commager, almost every industrial record was shattered.[76] More coal, iron ore, silver, and copper were mined, more steel forged, more rails laid, more lumber sawed, more houses built, more cotton cloth woven, more flour milled, and more oil refined than in any previous 5 years in our history. In the decade from 1860 to 1870, the total number of manufacturing establishments increased by 80% and the value of manufactured products by 100%.

By 1880 industry was in full swing. Breakthroughs were being made in scientific and technological fields, particularly in electronics and communication. Between 1860 and 1900, no fewer than 676,000 patents were granted by the U.S. Patent Office, among them the radio, the phonograph, and the electric light. The gasoline combustion engine and the automobile were to revolutionize transportation as the assembly line was revolutionizing production. By the turn of the century, the organization of production and distribution was nearly complete:

> The life of the average man, especially if he was a city dweller, was profoundly changed by this development. Almost everything he ate and wore, the furnishing of his home, the tools he used, the transportation he employed were made or controlled by complex organizational systems.[77]

The Corporation as a Person and Growth of Monopolies

In 1886 a landmark decision by a U.S. court defined the corporation as a "natural person" under law, giving corporations many of the same rights and protections that the constitution guarantees to its citizens. For example, the court specifically extended the Fourteenth Amendment to commercial corporations; the original intention was to provide civil rights and liberties to former slaves. The rule that "no state shall deprive any 'person' of life, liberty or property" was adopted to defend corporations and limit regulations on them.[78]

With these new entitlements and protections, business corporations expanded even more and combined into large monopolies that threatened to usurp the political process, undermine the nation's economic health for their own interests, and institutionalize injustice and oppression in nearly every arena of public life.

> The proliferation of the great manufacturing companies and business corporations made possible large scale combination, centralized control and administration, and the elimination of less efficient units, the pooling of patents, and, by virtue of their capital resources, power to expand, to compete with foreign business enterprises, to bargain with labor, to exact favorable terms . . . and to exercise immense influence with politics, state and national.[79]

By 1906 four groups of investors controlled two thirds of the nation's railroads. One company, U.S. Steel, controlled 62% of steel production, and Standard Oil controlled 90% of oil.[80] The power and wealth of these and other conglomerates was attended by the abject poverty of millions of laborers. In the last quarter of the 19th century 1% of the population owned 47% of the nation's assets. In that same period, for a family of four to survive, everyone had to work, including the children. Those in control of the economic machinery of society esteemed child labor as beneficial. Asa Chandler, one of the founders of the Coca-Cola Company, asserted that "the most beautiful sight that we see is the child at labor; [and] as early as he may get at labor, the more beautiful and the most useful does his life get to be."[81]

Frederick Taylor and Scientific Management (1910–1920)

In the early 1900s efficiency expert Frederick Winslow Taylor investigated the influence of financial incentives, tool design, and work layout on job performance. Based on his empirical studies, Taylor applied his ideas to management and to organizational design as well. In his book, *Principles of Scientific Management,* published in 1911, Taylor asserted that scientific management could reduce "every single act of every workman to a science"[82] and develop a cooperative spirit between worker and manager while increasing productivity and control in a benign, rational, "scientific" manner.

This new approach was intended to increase efficiency and worker productivity while inducing the worker to accept the demands of management in a docile fashion.[83] It was the role of "efficiency experts" to scientifically determine, by time and motion studies, the most effective, efficient, least fatiguing, and least expensive "one best way" to perform a job.[84] Management was to get the most productivity out of workers by planning and teaching this one best way, motivating and supervising workers in using the new approach. If properly taught, functionaries would behave in a way that enhanced productivity and everyone would benefit. Working together for a common purpose, the entire organization could be scientifically converted into a rational system.[85]

The Bureaucratic Machine Tool (1900–1930)

Taylor's ideas set the tone for thinking about organizations for the next two decades and beyond. Not only could rational scientific management be applied to worker productivity but to the task of organizing as well. Scientific principles of organization were assumed to exist and were waiting to be discovered by diligent scientific observation and analysis. Organizations were seen as machine tools, composed of machinelike people, carrying out machinelike functions.

Machine Tool Metaphor   The metaphor used to describe complex organizations was adopted from the factory system. The heart of productivity was machinery. This organizational machine could not function if the parts pulled in different directions. The corporation and factory were conceived as nothing but gigantic human machines in which all the parts were to fit together smoothly and function together just like a clockwork mechanism. The organizational mechanism was to be "monocratic"—aimed in one direction with one overarching goal and one person in command, the manager or the boss.[86] The manager steered the organizational machine toward its destination by performing tasks itemized in the acronym PODSCORB—plan, organize, direct, supervise, control, order, regulate, and budget.

Decisions were made by means of linear reckoning and incremental thinking congruent with the modern scientific method. "Science," says Schuman,

> does not really attack a huge problem, it only goes after small ones. Incrementally, a step at a time, discoveries are made and techniques are developed that will eventually add up to a fantastic enterprise. ("One small step for man; one giant step for mankind.") The world gets scientized— gets rationalized—just a little bit at a time.[87]

In exactly the same way, an organization encroaches on its environment, building on past decisions and moving ahead little by little while ordering and controlling both its inputs and outputs and, ultimately, its entire social environment.

Machinelike People   To develop a machinelike organization, managers must also develop the kind of individual who will fit into, work well with, and be able carry out narrowly defined specific tasks, often in repetitive, uniform ways. Machinelike organizations need machinelike people.[88] The organizational components—the workers—must do what they are told to carry out the requirements of the system. Any functionary with the needed technical skills can be placed in most organizational roles, and people are viewed as if they are interchangeable parts, easily replaceable, making it easy to construct all the organization managers need.[89]

In a form of contractual social exchange, individual employees agree to give up an amount of time, apply their skills, and devote their energy to accomplish the organization's goals in return for an amount of security and a paycheck. What is not often understood, however, is that functionaries are induced to surrender a part of their humanity as well. Because personal feelings, ideas, values, and sentiments are, for the most part, irrelevant to carrying out a job or even antithetical to it, individuals must give up these qualities in favor of carrying out the mandates of the organization.

The organizational machine becomes a system of domination that transforms individual human beings into "things." Frederick Nietzsche asserted that such "depersonalization destroys the creative power in life. Man becomes . . . a cog in the all-embracing machine of production and consumption . . . that transforms everything into an object, a thing, a tool."[90] This process, according to Paulo Freire, is a form of oppression. "The oppressed as objects, as 'things' have no purposes except those their oppressors prescribe for them,"[91] he asserts.

The Human Relations School (1927–1940)

In 1927 Elton Mayo and Fritz Roethlisberger conducted a series of experiments called the Hawthorne studies at the Western Electric Company,[92] marking the introduction of "social science into the study of organizations,"[93] and giving birth to the human relations school of organization theory. According to human relations theorists, organizations were not only ruled by an artificial, impersonal, machinelike system, but they contained a natural social system as well. To obtain a maximum amount of productivity from employees, managers needed to understand how to motivate people by considering people's needs, utilizing the dynamics of organizational change, and using organizational politics.

Natural Social System   Mayo and Roethlisberger discovered that despite of the rules, structure, and inducements of management, people naturally formed personal relationships inside the impersonal organizational culture. A secondary informal, natural social system, formed out of the needs, interests, and feelings of the employees of the organization, and existed concurrently with the artificial, hierarchical structure of the organization. Running parallel to the formal chain of command, an informal leadership structure inevitably existed. Assembly line workers, for example, may sometimes adjust their speed and productivity to that of the slowest member of the work group. They may collude among themselves in deciding on levels of productivity based on what they perceive is fair. Sometimes they may retaliate against supervisors or others who "played favorites."[94]

In spite of attempts to create a closed system that operated automatically, theorists of the new "human relations" school began to understand that organizations could only exist as open systems that changed and adapted their social environment. A more realistic and accurate model was to view organization as an enlarged version of a human being that was "believed to have, on a large scale, all the qualities of the individual, including beliefs, modes of behaving, objectives, personality, motivations, rationality, and the capacity to grow and evolve."[95]

Motivation, Change, and Politics   Human relations theory assumed that all behavior is goal seeking, in individuals and in organizations. Improvement of the system, therefore, was aimed at increasing its effectiveness as a totality to reach its goals. Individuals were viewed as creatures who had *needs* that must be met by the organization to assure full productivity. The challenge for management was to understand what made individuals productive and what constituted contentment. Individuals were to be motivated or otherwise induced by manipulation of their needs, satisfactions, group dynamics, socialization, and a host of psychological factors to become more integral components of the organization tool. Change, for example, was considered to be appropriate under certain conditions. Conflict, too, could be expressed within certain constraints. Informal organizational politics, the "grease" that often helped employees accomplish goals by sliding around the formal, and at times dysfunctional, organizational rules, were recognized as a reality to be dealt with rather than as behavior to be suppressed or punished.

Deceitful Implications   For all its emphasis on "participatory" management and democratizing the workplace, however, organizational humanization did not extend to allowing workers to decide on organizational goals or premises. This remained firmly in the hands of the owners of the organization. What seemed to be a benign form of humanization of the impersonal organization was used by many managers as a way to appropriate sociological and psychological knowledge to motivate people to higher levels of productivity and adapt them unobtrusively but more completely to the organizational design.

Interregnum of World War II

The entry of the United States into the Second World War in 1941 greatly affected the way organizations were viewed. The recommendations of the human relations school, emphasizing group process, motivation, cultivating two-way communication, participative decision making, and being sensitive to workers' needs and feelings, were incompatible with accomplishing the goal of winning the war. A model of organization congruent with the requirements of a turbulent environment, a hierarchy of command, a closed and tight structure, and organizational control was required to shape the nation into a gigantic war machine in a single-minded drive to save the Allied nations from destruction.

Congruent with the demands of turbulence, conflict, and competition, the machine tool organizational model was dusted off and polished up to save the United States from defeat at the hands of the supremely efficient and effectively organized war machines of the Axis nations—Germany, Japan, and Italy.

In a social environment of uncertainty, the most effective leadership was authoritarian—directing and commanding. All action was directed to accomplishing a single goal, that of surviving and winning, and every unit was forged into a single organizational machine focused on that goal. Goal accomplishment required that everyone play prescribed roles in strict compliance with procedures and the orders of the one in charge. There was little room for discussion, communal interaction, dialogue, or disagreement. Structure was hierarchical and communication one-way, from the top down. Relationships were prescribed within the chain of command, and internal conflict was reduced to a minimum.

Herbert Simon and the Decision-Making School (1945–1960)

In 1945 Nobel Prize winner Herbert A. Simon developed ideas in his book, *Administrative Behavior,* that were to change the way we looked at organizations. At about the same time, Max Weber's classic work on bureaucracy was translated for the first time into English. The mechanism of bureaucracy now had two theorists who could adequately explain and expand on its principles. Simon rejected the machine tool and human relations models and intuitively grasped the embryonic field of computer technology as a more accurate and realistic metaphor of organizational systems. For Simon, humans are only "intendedly rational" beings who must be integrated into the organization by means of unobtrusive control.

Rejection of Machine Tool and Human Relations Theories
Simon, claiming to base his model on logical positivism and systems theory, challenged the rule-of-thumb "proverbs" and slogans such as PODSCORB, which tended to comprise the conventional wisdom about organization and administration of that day. Simon criticized the rational model of "one best way" of scientific management whose

decision maker was presumed to have perfect information, know all of his or her preferences, and who had "no limits on the complexity of the computation he can perform in order to determine which alternatives are best."[96] For Simon, the machine tool model of organization attributes a "preposterously omniscient rationality to man . . . that had little discernible relation to the actual or possible behavior of flesh and blood human beings."[97] On the other hand, theorists of the human relations school who based decision making on people's feelings, emotions, needs, values, and other irrational sentiments, and attempt to "reduce all cognition to affect," are likewise unrealistic, asserted Simon.[98]

Computer Metaphor
Simon contends that a more appropriate model places organization in a context of rational action and decision making "as we should expect actually to see it in real life."[99] In Simon's conceptual scheme, the organization is like a gigantic computational decision-making machine. Computers process information and solve problems faster, more efficiently, and more effectively than any human being. Just like organizations, they are highly logical, calculating, rational processing machines. Simon declared that organizations are themselves "frozen decisions."

Humans Are "Intendedly" Rational
Simon envisioned individuals as components similar to computer chips. Each individual may have a piece of information or skill and may be able to process information to a certain extent. But no one individual is fully capable of processing or retaining all of the information needed by the organization in making decisions.

For this reason, individuals, for all of their pretensions to full rationality, are only "intendedly" rational. "Human reason is *limited*." Therefore, Simon says, "administrative theory is one of intended and bounded rationality—of the behavior of human beings who *satisfice* because they have not the wits to *maximize*."[100] No individual has the capacity to rationally evaluate every potential solution because an individual cannot absorb every piece of information or calculate all the possible variables that impinge on decisions to arrive at a best solution. It "is *impossible,*" said Simon, "for the behavior of a single, isolated individual to reach any high degree of rationality" (emphasis added).[101] Humans are only capable of satisficing; that is, taking the first "good enough" solution that they find and stopping their search efforts at that point. Because individual humans are limited rationally, it is only when they are linked together in a gigantic information processing system, such as an organization, that they can approach something like full rationality and maximize their decision-making capacity.

To be fully rational, therefore, individuals must be integrated into, and take their premises from, the organizational context of which they are a part. "Organization," according to Simon, "provides much of the force that molds and develops personal qualities and habits." The organization "selects the individual's ends, trains him in skills, and . . . provides him with information" which he needs to make decisions correctly and "places organization members in a psychological environment that will adapt their decisions to the organization objectives." As a result, says Simon, "The rational individual is and must be an organized and institutionalized individual."[102]

Unobtrusive Control   There is no need to motivate individuals to behave according to organizational norms, as the human relations school would recommend. Instead, says Simon, "you change the premises of their decisions."[103] These premises are to be found in the "vocabulary of the organization, the structure of communication, rules and regulations and standard programs—in short, the structural aspects."[104] Controlling the premises of decisions allows for what Perrow calls "unobtrusive control"; namely, the control of the cognitive premises underlying action.[105] These organizational premises, says Simon,

> inject into the very nervous systems of the organization members the criteria of decisions that the organization wishes to employ. . . . It enables him to make decisions by himself as the organization *would like him to decide*.[106] (Emphasis added)

The aim of the organization is the total integration and inclusion of individuals into its premises. Organization tends to assume more and more qualities of the human character and, according to Simon, even characteristics that transcend those of humanity. Organization becomes human culture. Organization no longer is a tool serving human ends; it is itself the end, and humans are the means by which organization functions. Organization supplants individuals,

and to the extent that an organization forms a total social milieu, individuals must conform to it for their own good.

The Contingency School (1970–1980)

By the 1960s the United States had recovered from World War II and had entered an era of expansion, growth, and development. Sophisticated computers and "space age" technology progressed rapidly. At the center of this progress were complex organizations. Many of the newer organizations oriented to research and development needed to be open to change and capable of fitting new market niches. Relationships between government and the economy were closer and more integrated. Organization theorists utilized an ecological metaphor of organizations, a contingency approach to systems designed to explain and make recommendations about how to construct modern organizational systems.

Ecological Metaphor   Organizational theorists began using "ecological systems" theory of organizational design, borrowing concepts from biology to explain the organizational phenomenon. The organization was considered to be an "open" living system that obtains inputs, uses information, makes decisions, has outputs, and interacts freely with, adapts to, and finds a niche in its wider social environment. Organizations are artificial constructs, as in the machine tool model, but they also have the qualities of an organism, as in the human relations school. An organization is "rational," as in the decision-making school, but unlike the decision-making school, an organization is a growing entity that exploits resources, changes, and develops. If any part of this system becomes dysfunctional, according to this model, the entire organizational system can be expected to reflect this dysfunction. Just like other living systems, however, organizations can be treated to bring them back to effective functioning.

Contingency Theory   Organizations vary or are *contingent* on a number of factors. The answer to the question "What is the best structure, size, and leadership style for an organization?" is "It all depends." All organizations have similarities, but no two organizations are exactly alike, just as no two humans are exactly alike. Using social ecological metaphors, contingency-oriented organizational theorists developed concepts that help us understand the "anatomy" and "physiology" of organizational design. Emery and Trist for example, discovered at least four subtypes of organizational environments: placid-random, placid-clustered, disturbed-reactive, and turbulent field."[107] James D. Thompson developed a taxonomy of propositions, or what he calls "a conceptual inventory," from which one could construct an organizational organism.[108] Stephen Robbins identified 11 kinds of organizational structures, each of which has "a different combination of complexity, formalization, and centralization."[109] Rensis Likert, in his "science-based theory," lists "forty-two aspects of organizations and for each one arranged them under each of four system [designs.]"[110]

Despite initial optimism and some promising early findings, Levine and colleagues assert that contingency theorists have yet to explain why some successful organizations' structures resemble those of less successful ones that confront similar environments, or why two organizations with very different structures perform effectively in the same environment.[111] As a consequence, contingency theorists have been unable to predict what structure or strategy will work best on any except a very general basis.

Transnational Organizations in the Global Society (1990s–Present)

By the 1990s many corporations had become transnational in character. Transnational corporations (TNCs) own other companies and subsidiaries that cross national borders and operate in an international systemic web throughout the world. This new global organizational society, asserts Gary Teeple, is driven by an economy characterized by enormous conglomerates, oligopolies, and cartels, with intense competition between them, new modes of highly capital-intensive production, and vast capital funds in constant search of profitable investment opportunities. International governmental organizations (IGOs) often preempt national laws and allocate additional power to TNCs, which respond in turn by usurping the functions of nation-states and operate with little civil or criminal regulation.[112]

Preempt National Laws   International governmental organizations (IGOs) such as the World Trade Organization, the International Monetary Fund (IMF), and the World Bank, each of which is affiliated with the United Nations (UN), have tended to preempt local and national laws and standards in health and welfare, workers rights, environmental protection, food quality, capital flow, and land ownership. Smaller and less developed nations have had to sacrifice autonomy over their own national policies as the price of borrowing capital through the World Bank, invest in huge "development" projects sponsored by TNCs, or purchase military weaponry from wealthy nations. Less wealthy nations have had to subordinate a portion of their own interests, independence, national rights, and even the welfare of their own people to the regulations, demands, and requirements imposed by TNCs. In addition, their weakened condition has hampered many nations in preventing transnational corporations from decimating forests, extracting mineral wealth, polluting air and water, and destroying their natural ecosystems.[113]

Usurp the Nation-State   Since the 1990s in many less powerful countries the integrity of the nation-state as an institution has been increasingly usurped by the membership of transnational corporate organizations in trading blocs, the world market, international monetary agreements, and supranational political and military organizations. Corporate organizations whose wealth exceeds that of many of these small states have been more able than ever to play nation against nation, demanding policy concessions, tax reductions, and laws written in their favor.

The cost of being included in the global market economy has meant that many smaller nations have become increasingly powerless in deciding their own affairs, and their sovereignty as nation-states has been eroded. Less developed nations have been forced to give up control over many areas of jurisdiction to which they previously had held title. Rather than authority to determine their own goals in a global economy, for example, power to act in their own interests on the world stage, or commanding a respected international presence, their role has shifted to regulating local affairs, providing internal security, and helping facilitate domestic rather than international economic development as if they were merely regional administrations.[114]

BHOPAL AND CORPORATE CRIME

On January 26, 2003 Diane Wilson appeared in court to face charges of criminal trespass and resisting arrest that could lead to 6 months in jail. On August 26, 2002, after ending a 30-day hunger strike outside the Dow Chemical company's Seadrift plant in Port Lavaca, Texas, Ms. Wilson scaled a 90 foot tower at the plant and unfurled a banner that read, "Dow—Responsible for Bhopal."

Wilson was protesting because for 12 years Union Carbide, a subsidiary of Dow Chemical, has refused to face trial in India where it stands charged with homicide. In 1983 the world's worst industrial disaster occurred when 27 tons of poison gas escaped from a Union Carbide pesticide factory in Bhopal, India, killing 20,000 people within hours and injuring more than 500,000 others. Today, nearly 20 years after the event, chemicals continue to leak from the abandoned factory, poisoning drinking wells with carcinogens causing liver damage and birth defects to many residents of the area. In addition, 150,000 victims remain chronically ill, but physicians are helpless to save lives because Union Carbide refuses to release crucial medical data on the long-term effects of the poisons from its more than 15 studies on the grounds that they are "trade secrets."

In 1992, asserts the Common Dreams Progressive Newswire, an Indian Court published notices in the *Washington Post* declaring Union Carbide and Warren Anderson, its former CEO, as "fugitives from justice" after they avoided service of arrest warrants delivered by Interpol. Then on May 26, 2003, after widespread protests in India and elsewhere, the Indian government asked U.S. authorities to extradite Warren Anderson to face trial in India. Anderson, however, remains at large today, and Dow Chemical continues to refuse to pay for cleaning up the toxic wastes at Bhopal. Dow does not dispute that the chemicals came from the factory but asserts that the victims of the disaster should pay for the cleanup themselves from a fund established for their relief.[115]

Little Corporate Regulation "There is no *political* regulation of transnational corporations," claims Gary Teeple.[116] As early as the 1960s, a number of international organizations including the UN and the International Chamber of Commerce put forth guidelines, rules, regulations, and charters in an effort to control the extensive unethical and illicit practices of TNCs. These international nongovernmental organizations (INGOs) worked to define and control the extent of bribery, extortion, nondisclosure, restrictive practices, environmental destruction, money laundering, disregard of human and trade union rights, abrogation of national laws, and erosion of consumer health and safety that were part of the normal operating procedures of transnational corporate organizations. The efforts of these INGOs have had little effect on international corporate activities, however. There are no overall international agreements or jurisdiction, no authoritative international institutional machinery, and no agreed-upon sanctions or means of enforcement over transnational corporate organizations or the global market economy.

The financial cost to society and the harm to individuals by unethical corporate behavior and corporate crime is greater in every way than individual crime. However, organizational wrongdoing at the international level is rarely punished because the corporation is fundamental to capitalism; those who engage in corporate law breaking "sin *within* the system." Teeple says that organized corporate "activities are not perceived or treated as criminal because they are not defined as such."[117] TNCs can claim that they are operating within the boundaries of legality and avoid the real consequences of their behavior.

Increasing Control In the post World War II period, Western corporate organizations completed conquest of their own domestic markets, comodified almost every aspect of life within non-Western nation-states, controlled the system of intervention in international markets, and opened up the entire world for business. Corporate economic organizations captured larger and larger amounts of capital, expanding, diversifying, and encroaching on resource-rich but capital-poor nations. The larger and wealthier these TNCs became, the more they minimized competition and maximized control over all markets within their reach. Transnational corporate organizations bought out or suppressed their rivals, took advantage of more economic niches, controlled the affairs of less affluent and sophisticated nations, and instituted a market mentality over increasing areas of social life. By the 1990s a "free" market in which many smaller businesses competed in an open and level playing field had disappeared. Any hope for reversion to a period of robust and unfettered competition among many innovative and unique enterprises in either developed or less developed areas of the world had become unthinkable, even impossible. In this global market society, Teeple says, "there will be a continuous growth of the global system of enormous social and economic inequalities that already exists—a natural consequence of the more or less unrestrained accumulation of capitalist private property."[118]

A PENNY HIDDEN IS A PENNY EARNED

A democratic government is the only one in which those who vote for a tax can escape the obligation to pay for it.
—*Alexis de Tocqueville*

Even though Bechtel Corporation is currently facing allegations that it sold illegal weapons to Iraq during the 1980s, Bechtel is one of the favored corporations given a contract by the Bush administration to help rebuild Iraq. Iraq's oil is being pumped out of the ground, converted into U.S. dollars, and those dollars are flying right past the Iraqi people into the pockets of American businessmen who work for companies such as Bechtel. There is nothing ostensibly wrong with this, but Bechtel and others including Halliburton and the Fluor Corporation are currently hiding millions of dollars of taxable income in offshore tax havens, according to the E-Mail Activist.

These tax shelters are also called "shell companies" because they aren't real businesses; they're just paper entities that give real U.S. corporations a way to send money out of the country, where it eludes taxation. This should be illegal, but it isn't. According to Arianna Huffington, cofounder of the Bermuda Project, offshore tax havens steal more than $70 billion per year from the federal treasury. Asserts the E-Mail Activist, "the very same companies that are making millions from the invasion of Iraq are the very ones who are *not* paying taxes to the government that rewards them."[119]

MACRO SOCIAL WORK AND PERSPECTIVES OF CHANGE

Macro social workers often use a structural functional perspective to engage in organizational social work. At the societal and international level, macro social workers employ the organizational deviance perspective described in Chapter 2.

Social Work and the Structural Functional Perspective

A structural functional perspective assumes that both the functions and structures of organizations must be congruent and fit together. Social workers assist members of communities to develop new social organizations, administer social organizations, and remediate organizations when they become dysfunctional.

Develop Social Organizations   The structural functional perspective asserts that the culture, values, ways of thinking built into the design of organizational systems must complement and enhance the purposes for which it has been formed. Otherwise, an organizational system will work at cross purposes with itself and inevitably fail to effectively reach its goals. Because modern complex organizations work against and destroy the bases of human sociality and personal *gemeinschaft* relationships, social workers are often concerned when these systems are used as a means for supplying social welfare services. Allen Jedlicka asserts that if we want change to occur on a macro scale,

> we cannot expect professional bureaucrats and the bureaucratic organizations to do a good job. . . . Professional bureaucrats cannot be expected to behave without a preoccupation with bureaucratic activities and control rather than a focus on effective service for people. We cannot expect them to be anything else, no more than we would expect a leopard to lose its spots.[120]

If, therefore, we are looking for effective ways to help people use their strengths to make changes in their own lives and in their social environment, we must talk about incorporating the unique strengths of the volunteer social organization and look for ways to avoid bureaucratically dominated development approaches.[121]

Macro social workers rely on the structural functional model to help invent and create social programs and social organizations whose operating premises and structural components work together to enrich our communities, provide avenues of socialization for children and youth, and help people make connections and form relationships in a world of increasing anonymity. You will learn in Chapter 10 how social work program developers create and use social organizations to provide *gemeinschaft* relationships, social goods and social capital, ensure social justice, increase social welfare, and provide for a thriving civil society.

Administer Social Organizations

Often guided by a structural functionalist model, macro social workers keep in the forefront of their consciousness a commitment to the administration of social organizational systems where authentic leadership occurs. By means of social administration, described in Chapter 11, you will discover that social workers use their skills to develop an organizational culture that reflects self-determination, empowerment, justice, and opportunity for growth that is different from the management of corporate organizations, which aims at dominance and control of both people and society as a whole.

Provide Social Organization Development

Modern organizational systems often have built in contradictions and imperatives that create stress and burnout for employees. You will discover in Chapter 12 that macro social workers provide conventional organization development using the structural functional perspective to realign and remediate these organizational dysfunctions.

In addition, you will discover that macro social workers engage in social organization development when their functions and structures become out of sync with one another. Social organization development is a process of improving and ensuring that social organizations are congruent in their policies, procedures, and programs with the humanization, empowerment, understanding, and justice that provide the foundation of the social work profession. Social organization developers help ensure that open communication, shared decision making, authenticity and genuineness in relationships, compassion, caring, and service are modeled throughout social agencies so that they are places where people engage one another with the fullness of being and work to create a social environment that models the ethical standards that we profess.

Social Work and the Organizational Deviance Perspective

Social workers tend to be critical of modern organizational systems because they distort social reality. Complex organizations are economic tools by which their owners impose their definition of the necessary and essential bases of social life onto others. These definitions tend to elevate wealth accumulation, commodification, and the manipulation of power over all other values. Furthermore, modern corporate and governmental organizations manufacture *gesellschaft* relationships, impersonality, and operate as control systems of the first order for those who own them. Many macro social workers have adopted the organizational deviance perspective to assist in creating a social environment free of the dominance of these systems.

Social activists use the organizational deviance perspective at the societal level when large corporate or governmental organizations use their power to oppress workers. You will learn in Chapter 14 that they protest the power of military organizations such as the school of terrorism at Ft. Benning, Georgia, and corporations that destroy the environment by logging, overfishing, contributing to the greenhouse effect, producing industrial waste, or polluting the world's oceans, rivers, forests, and atmosphere.

In Chapter 15 you will discover how the dominance of corporate and government organizational alliances in the most highly developed nations of the world pose a danger to the ideals of authentic participative democracy, economic freedom, and the integrity of less developed nation-states. International social workers use the organizational deviance perspective to help people resist the encroachment of transnational corporations and international governmental organizations (IGOs) that work to extend their hegemony over the entire global society. In the process they destroy local economies, exploit natural resources, and contribute to continuing global violence, impoverishment, health problems, a weakening of sovereignty in nation-states, and the oppression of men, women, and children worldwide.

CONCLUSION

In this chapter you have explored two alternative organizational systems in our modern world. Both are relatively recent inventions, but they operate on different principles and premises and serve different functions. In some ways they are opposed to one another and at times engage in a struggle for people's loyalty and commitment.

A few prototypical social organizations existed in the colonial period of North American history, but they have only very recently come into their own, growing to comprise their own social sector along with the private and public sectors of society. Social organizations are hybrid systems whose function is to produce social goods and capital and to increase people's social welfare, health, education, and other aspects of life. Social organizations have grown rapidly, and many believe that today they constitute a new "third party government" in the United States.

Modern complex organizations also appeared at the beginning of the colonial period, and they increased rapidly before and after the Civil War. They are the most ubiquitous, powerful, and wealthy social structures that exist today, outstripping the economies of many nations. Although modern organizations are useful systems in many ways, they are tools that have tended to become the master of their owners. They often become closed social structures in which people obey their demands, operate by means of their imperatives, obey their rules, conform to the roles they demand, operate by their communication systems, think by means of their logic, and adhere to their norms and values.

In spite of their utility, modern complex organizations have generally failed to deliver successful solutions to social problems, but instead often create problems for communities as well as individuals. Macro social workers use an understanding of organizational deviance to moderate the power and influence of these systems when they distort the economy and the political process in their favor.

As you extend your skills and interests to include organizational social work, you will have the opportunity to participate in using new social organizations to develop social programs, provide leadership in social administration, and help dysfunctional organizational systems by means of organization development. You will also use your understanding of modern complex organizations to challenge organizational deviance at the societal and international levels.

KEY CONCEPTS

social organization
nonprofit
social sector
civil society

social goods
social capital
private sector
public sector

diversity
scope
activities
pluralistic organization
hybrid
faith-based organization
social systems design
parallel model
federal structures model
loose-linked model
social purpose
levels of inclusiveness
reinventing society
funding
fees
charitable support
corporate support
government support
fiscal tools
purchase of service contracts
grants-in-aid
tax subsidy
federal partnerships
third party government
modern complex organization
definition of modern organizations
artificial
intentionally contrived
functional tool
accomplish goals
owner
ubiquitous
wealthy
social accountability
concentrated
technological innovation
corporations

East India Company
Hudson Bay Company
Industrial Revolution
factory system
organization as a person
monopolies
Frederick Winslow Taylor
scientific management
organizational machine tool
human relations school
natural social system
motivation
change
organizational politics
Herbert Simon
decision-making school
intendedly rational
satisfice
rational organization
unobtrusive control
contingency school
ecological metaphor
open systems
transnational corporations (TNC)
international governmental organizations (IGO)
structural functional perspective
program development
administration
organization development
organization deviance perspective
social activism
international social work

QUESTIONS FOR DISCUSSION

1. The assertion was made in this chapter that social organizations are a relatively new and increasingly important component of our society. Do you believe this is a true statement? Why or why not? If it is true, what are the implications of this development?

2. What is the role of macro social work in the promotion and development of social organizations, if any?

3. If it is true that the new social sector is growing, to what extent do you believe this will also increase the extent of *gemeinshaft* relationships, which were described in Chapter 5?

4. Is the rise of social organizations and the new social sector an indication that we are entering a postmodern era? How would you characterize the coming postmodern era and its components?

5. To what extent do you think we control modern organizations? To what extent do they control us?

6. In the process of achieving their goals, is there a danger that modern organizations reduce people's humanity? Why or why not?

7. Modern bureaucratic organizations have enabled our society to become massive and complex. To what extent will artificial, contrived social relationships become important in human life in the future? Is this an occurrence you would welcome, or would it concern you? Explain.

8. What responsibility does a modern bureaucratic organization and those who own and operate it have to those who work for it, to the community in which it resides, and to society at large? Assuming that they have responsibility, do you believe complex organizations readily accept this responsibility? Why or why not?

9. John Forester says that we can "generally expect that organizational actors will deter cooperative, well-organized community-based organizations that might press to meet social needs to the detriment of concentrations of private capital. They distract public attention from social needs and instead focus on the promotion of individual consumption."[122] What does this statement mean? What are its implications for macro social work practice?

10. Social work is a field that prizes altruism, compassion, self-actualization, authentic personal relationships, and two-way communication. Modern complex organizations tend to eliminate altruism and compassion, require impersonal relationships, and use one-way communication. What dilemmas occur as social workers insert personal feelings and values into an impersonal organizational system? How would you cope with these dilemmas?

11. Robert Presthus claims that we live in an "organizational society." What is your understanding of that term? What are the implications of organizational society for social work as a whole and macro social work in particular?

12. Some theorists claim that our society is largely an artificial one, in contrast to premodern societies that may be considered "natural." What is the difference between an artificial and a natural society? Is this difference a real one? Why or why not? What are the implications of this for social work today?

ADDITIONAL READING

The Social Sector

Burlingame, Dwight F. et al. *Capacity for Change: The Nonprofit World in the Age of Devolution.* Indianapolis: Indiana Center on Philanthropy, 1996.

Fishman, James J. and Stephen Schwarz. *Nonprofit Organizations: Cases and Materials.* New York: Foundation Press, 1995.

Hall, Peter Dobkin. *Inventing the Nonprofit Sector and Other Essays on Philanthropy, Voluntarism, and Nonprofit Organizations.* Baltimore: Johns Hopkins University Press, 1992.

Lohmann, Roger A. *The Commons: New Perspectives on Nonprofit Organizations and Voluntary Action.* San Francisco: Jossey-Bass, 1992.

McKnight, John. *The Professional Service Business.* Evanston, IL: Center for Urban Affairs and Policy Research, Northwestern University, 1976.

Nielsen, Waldemar A. *The Endangered Sector.* New York: Columbia University Press, 1979.

O'Neil, Michael. *The Third America: The Emergence of the Nonprofit Sector in the United States.* San Francisco: Jossey-Bass, 1989.

Osborne, David and Ted Gaebler. *Reinventing Government: How the Entrepreneurial Spirit Is Transforming the Public Sector.* New York: Addison-Wesley, 1992.

Payton, Robert L. *Philanthropy: Voluntary Action for the Public Good.* Phoenix AZ: Oryx Press, 1988.

Powell, Walton, ed. *The Nonprofit Sector: A Research Handbook*, New Haven: Yale University Press, 1987.

Salamon, Lester M. *Partners in Public Service: Government-Nonprofit Relations in the Modern Welfare State.* Baltimore: Johns Hopkins University Press, 1995.

Wolch, Jennifer R. *The Shadow State: Government and Voluntary Sector in Transition.* New York: Foundation Center, 1990.

Wolpert, Julian. *Patterns of Generosity in America: Who's Holding the Safety Net?* New York: Twentieth Century Fund Press, 1993.

Social Organizations

Drucker, Peter F. *The New Realities: In Government and Politics, in Economics and Business, in Society and World View.* New York: Harper and Row, 1989.

Hall, Peter Dobkin. "Historical Perspectives on Nonprofit Organizations." In *Jossey-Bass Handbook of Nonprofit Leadership and Management,* Robert D. Herman and Associates, eds. San Francisco: Jossey-Bass, 1994.

Hasenfeld, Yeheskel. *Human Services as Complex Organizations.* Newbury Park, CA: Sage, 1992.

Herman, Robert D. and Associates. *The Jossey-Bass Handbook of Nonprofit Leadership and Management.* San Francisco: Jossey-Bass, 1994.

Wuthnow, Robert, Virginia A. Hodgkinson, et al. *Faith and Philanthropy in America: Exploring the Role of Religion in America's Voluntary Sector.* San Francisco: Jossey-Bass, 1990.

Theory of Modern Complex Organizations

Barnard, Chester I. *The Functions of the Executive.* Cambridge, MA: Harvard University Press, 1938.

Etzioni, Amitai. *Modern Organizations.* Englewood Cliffs, NJ: Prentice-Hall, 1964.

Katz, David and Robert L. Kahn. *The Social Psychology of Organizations.* New York: John Wiley, 1978.

Ott, Steven. *The Organizational Culture Perspective.* Homewood, IL: Irwin, 1989.

Simon, Herbert. *Administrative Behavior: A Study of Decision-Making Processes in Administrative Organizations,* 4th ed. New York: Free Press, 1997.

Taylor, Frederick Winslow. *The Principles of Scientific Management.* New York: W. W. Norton, 1947.

Thompson, James D. *Organizations in Action: Social Science Base of Administrative Theory.* New York: McGraw-Hill, 1967.

Thompson, Victor A. *Bureaucracy in the Modern World.* Morristown, NJ: General Learning Press, 1976.

Thompson, Victor A. *Without Sympathy or Enthusiasm: The Problem of Administrative Compassion.* University: University of Alabama Press, 1975.

Weiner, Norman. *Human Use of Human Beings: Cybernetics.* New York: Avon Books, 1967.

Critique of Modern Complex Organizations

Ellul, Jacques. *The Technological Society.* New York: Vintage, 1967.

Hummel, Ralph. *The Bureaucratic Experience.* New York: St. Martin's Press, 1977.

Parkinson, C. H. *Parkinson's Law.* London: Oxford, 1985.

Perrow, Charles. *Complex Organizations: A Critical Essay,* 2d ed. Glenview, IL: Scott Foresman, 1979.

Presthus, Robert. *The Organizational Society,* Rev. ed. New York: St. Martin's, 1978.

Ramos, Alberto Guerreiro. *The New Science of Organizations: A Reconceptualization of the Wealth of Nations.* Toronto: University of Toronto Press, 1981.

Ruitenbeek, Hendrik M. ed. *The Dilemma of Organizational Society.* New York: E. P. Dutton, 1963.

Weber, Max. *Economy and Society: An Outline of Interpretive Sociology*, 3 vols. Guenther Roth and Claus Wittich, eds., Elphraim Fischoff et al., trans. New York: Bedminster Press, 1968.

Whyte, William H., Jr. *The Organization Man.* New York: Doubleday Anchor, 1958.

Social Critique

Freire, Paulo. *Pedagogy of the Oppressed.* New York: Continuum, 1992.

Slater, Philip. *The Pursuit of Loneliness: American Culture at the Breaking Point.* Boston: Beacon Press, 1971.

Polanyi, Karl. *The Great Transformation: The Political and Economic Origins of Our Time.* Boston: Beacon Press, 1944.

Journal Articles

Drucker, Peter F. "What Business Can Learn From Nonprofits," *Harvard Business Review,* October 1989, pp. 818–893.

Drucker, Peter F. "Lessons for Successful Nonprofit Governance," *Nonprofit Management and Leadership,* 1(1), 1990, pp. 7–14.

J. R. Kimberly. "The Life Cycle Analogy and the Study of Organizations." In *The Organizational Life Cycle:*

Issues in the Creation, Transformation and Decline of Organizations, J. R. Kimberly, R. H. Miles, and Associates, eds. San Francisco: Jossey-Bass, 1980.

Max Weber. "Bureaucracy." In *From Max Weber: Essays in Sociology,* H. H. Gerth and C. Wright Mills, eds. New York: Oxford University Press, 1958.

Journals

Non-profit and Voluntary Sector Quarterly

Websites

Corporate Watch, www.corporatewatch.org

Corporate Europe Observatory, www.xs4all.nl/~ceo

Corporate Critic online, www.ethicalconsumer.org

Business and Human Rights, www.business-humanrights.org

Endgame Research Services, www.endgame.org

Multinational Monitor, multinationalmonitor.org

Transnationale, www.transnationale.org

10
The Practice of Social Work Program Development

How to Meet People's Needs

What would he say, that famous poor man the leaders of this country so often talk about, and so rarely talk with, if he were given a chance to speak?

That I needed a home, and you gave me food stamps That I needed a job, and you got me on welfare That my family was sick, and you gave us used clothes That I needed my pride and dignity as a man, and you gave me surplus beans.[1]

Si Kahn

Ideas in This Chapter

History has no more eloquent record of self-sacrifice, courage, and devoted service to humanity than that of Clara Barton, one of America's social heroes and great program developers.

CLARA BARTON, ANGEL OF THE BATTLEFIELD

Clarissa Harlowe Barton was born in North Oxford, Massachusetts, on December 25, 1821.[2] At 18 years of age, Clara Barton displayed the talents that would later distinguish her as a premier community developer by establishing one of the first public schools in the state at Bordentown, New York, and afterward developing a number of others in New Jersey. Never in robust heath, Barton went to Washington, D.C. to recuperate. There the Commissioner of Patents appointed her to the first independent clerkship ever held by a woman in the United States. She overcame opposition and antagonism that her appointment aroused by means of her tact, faithfulness, and remarkable executive ability. Newly elected President Buchanan relieved her of her position, however, and withheld a large part of her salary because of her Republican and antislavery sentiments.

Shortly after the election of Lincoln, Barton was recalled to the patent office, but when the Civil War began, she refused to draw her salary from an already overtaxed treasury. Believing that service to her country lay on the battlefield rather than in an office in Washington, she resigned her position and requested permission to nurse wounded soldiers. No woman had ever been permitted in a military hospital or on the battlefields, and both military and civil officials declined her services. In her own unequaled manner, however, she succeeded in gaining their confidence and finally made her way to the front. Barton never engaged in hospital service, but from the beginning she remained on the battlefield with the wounded and dying. Side by side with field surgeons, Barton was under fire in some of the most severe engagements of the war—at Cedar Mountain, the Second Battle of Bull Run, Chantilly, Antietam, Fallmouth, Fredericksburg, the Wilderness, Spotsylvania, and the sieges of Charleston, Petersburg, and Richmond. During the 4 years of the war, she endured the rigors of a soldier's life in action. She was exposed at all times, her clothing was pierced with bullets and torn by shot, but miraculously she was never wounded.

Supplies sent for her work poured into Washington, and at her own expense she had them forwarded to the battlefield. By her quiet self-reliance and prompt decision, Barton obtained such complete recognition that the surgeon general placed hospital supplies, a corps of assistants, and military railways at her disposal.

In a short time her courageous work, under the most distressing conditions, gained her the name "Angel of the Battlefield." Barton knew no north or south and bestowed her care indiscriminately on any wounded soldier, whether Union or Confederate. She was a great commander in army camps and on the battlefield, and she never asked for favor or aid because she was a woman.

While the Civil War was still raging in America, Jean Henri Dulant began heading a movement in Europe for relief of wounded soldiers. In 1864 a convention was held in Geneva, Switzerland, at which almost every major nation was present except the United States. Ten articles of agreement were adopted, known as the Treaty of Geneva of the Relief of Sick and Wounded Soldiers, providing that all wounded or sick soldiers and the surgeons and nurses attending them would be held neutral in time of war and not captured by either army. Twenty governments affixed their signatures on August 22, 1864. As a compliment to Switzerland, the Swiss Flag with colors reversed was adopted as the organization's insignia, and with it the Red Cross, the world's greatest humanitarian movement, was born.

After the war, while Barton was visiting Switzerland, war was declared between France and Germany.

She immediately offered her services under the Red Cross of Geneva and was present during nearly every battle of the Franco-Prussian war. During the war she helped establish hospitals, organized assistance for women and child refugees, and distributed money and clothing to more than 30,000 destitute people. Germany awarded her the Iron Cross for her services.

When Barton returned to the United States, she pledged to devote the rest of her life to introducing the Red Cross to America, and in 1882 President Chester V. Arthur signed the Geneva Treaty. Barton founded the American National Committee of the Red Cross (later the American National Red Cross) and was its president from 1881 to 1905. She extended the scope of the Red Cross in America to provide aid in any great national calamity. As the U.S. delegate to the Red Cross Conference in Geneva, she successfully proposed that the Red Cross provide relief in peace as well as in war. Known as "the American Amendment," this helped distinguish the United States as "a Good Samaritan of Nations."

During her presidency, Barton and the Red Cross engaged every major calamity that occurred in the country, assisting victims of forest fires in Michigan in 1881, floods of the Mississippi and Ohio rivers in 1882, the Louisiana cyclone of 1883, the Ohio River flood in 1884, the Charleston earthquake, and the Texas Famine of 1886. When most people were enjoying retirement, at age 66 Clara Barton supervised relief work during the Florida yellow fever epidemic of 1887, the great Johnstown flood of 1889, the Galveston hurricane and tidal wave of 1900, and the San Francisco Earthquake of 1906.

Twice she carried relief to Russia during the Russian Famine of 1891, and she was present during the Armenian massacres in Turkey in 1896, assisting the homeless and wounded. Barton was again on the battlefield in Cuba during the Spanish-American War of 1889.

During the Boer War in South Africa (1899–1902), she commanded the relief ship *Clinton,* for which the whole U.S. Navy made way. To ensure immediate action in any emergency, Barton placed $3,000 of her own money at the disposal of the American Committee of the Red Cross. Throughout her long career of developing and providing relief services throughout the United States and the world, Barton's moral courage, energy, diplomacy, and unwavering integrity were her chief characteristics.

She had two rules of action: unconcern for what cannot be helped, and control under pressure.

Her career teaches that the meaning of human life lies not in what we get but in what we give. History has no more eloquent record of self-sacrifice, courage, and devoted service to humanity than that of Clara Barton, one of America's social heroes and great program developers. She died on April 12, 1912, at age 91.

WHAT YOU WILL LEARN IN THIS CHAPTER

Every facility for elderly persons, day care program for children, sheltered workshop for adults with intellectual disabilities, treatment program for people with emotional disabilities, socialization program for youth, or shelter for battered women has been developed by a group of people who had a vision about helping their neighbors in a new way or saw an unmet need and worked to meet it. Social workers who help build such social organizations are program developers.

In this chapter you will learn how you, too, can assist people in developing a social organization. You will explore how to form an organization action group, assess social needs, set up a formal corporation, establish a board, recruit and hire staff, and obtain funding. You will discover that social work program developers are more than mere social entrepreneurs who put together social agencies like businesspeople develop businesses for making profit. Social work program developers are engaged in the task of helping people construct their own social reality, meet their own social needs, add to the store of social capital, and assist in making communities stronger and healthier.

WHO ARE SOCIAL WORK PROGRAM DEVELOPERS?

Social work program developers are often employed by social agencies serving a particular population, such as women who have experienced domestic violence, abused children, the elderly, and persons with intellectual, emotional, physical, or behavioral disabilities. We help ensure that social welfare services are in place to meet a range of needs for that population. We meet with various public and private agency staff to assess where gaps in services are occurring and assist parent groups, agency staff, and interested community leaders who want to establish a new social organization from scratch. Where services already exist, we assess the changing needs of a community and work with social organizations to improve or expand those services.

A BRIEF HISTORY OF PROGRAM DEVELOPMENT

This brief history explores the origins of program development early in the colonial period, its expansion in the first half of the 19th century, and through the Civil War and the Progressive Era.

Colonial Period and American Independence (1609–1800)

During the colonial period, citizens from a variety of national and religious groups developed America's first charitable and social organizations. One of the most prominent program developers in colonial America was Benjamin Franklin.

America's First Social Programs   The first social welfare program in the United States had its origin with the Dutch Reformed Church of New Amsterdam, a Dutch colony settled in 1609. Like early Christian groups, the colony established a voluntary collection for the poor and distributed it to the needy.[3] The first almshouse in the American colonies was established at Rensselaerswyck, New York in 1657.[4] In that same year, the Scots Charitable Society, the first and in many ways most important of many private associations that sprang up in colonial America to aid the unfortunate, was founded by 27 Scotsmen living in Boston. The society aided the poor, cared for the sick, and buried its dead. This society, still functioning today, became the model for countless others that sprang up over next 200 years.

Many ethnic groups, fraternal societies, and social organizations established such "friendly societies" to aid their neighbors. One of these was a program of relief designed by the Quakers even before the Revolutionary War broke out to "deal with the hardships likely to arise from the impending struggle."[5] Though they were persecuted by the colonists for their pacifism, the Quakers raised several thousand pounds, which they distributed without respect to religious or political ideals to those in need during the war.

A number of early societies committed themselves to establishing institutional care to those in need. The Ursuline Sisters in New Orleans, for example, founded a private institution for girls in 1729, the first institution for children in the United States, and in 1790 the Charleston Orphan House opened its doors in Charleston, South Carolina, the first publicly supported children's institution.[6]

Benjamin Franklin

Benjamin Franklin was one of the most important early program developers in colonial America. "Believing in the importance of preventing poverty rather than relieving it, he worked to increase the opportunities of people for self-help."[7] Among Franklin's efforts was a club for the mutual improvement of its members that later resulted in the establishment of a library; founding a volunteer fire company; formulating a scheme for paving, cleaning, and lighting the streets of Philadelphia; developing a plan for policing Philadelphia; leading the effort to establish the Philadelphia Hospital; and founding an academy that later became the University of Pennsylvania. More than any other American before him, Franklin established the principle of improving social conditions and opportunities for the poor through voluntary associations, and he worked to apply the principle of self-help to the community as well as to individuals.

Period of Institutional Programs (1800–1860)

In the first half of the 19th century, the main thrust of social welfare by local governments lay in constructing institutional settings. Private groups also established services to combat poverty, group work services, and child welfare services.

Government Institutions

In the first half of the 19th century, the thrust of government intervention was the development of institutions including almshouses, workhouses, poorhouses, prisons, and specialized institutions for children and for persons with intellectual and emotional disabilities.

Children's Institutions   In 1811 state governments began to help private institutions through financial subsidies, the first of which was the Orphan Asylum of New York. The House of Refuge for Juvenile Delinquents in New York City was founded in 1824 with state funds, followed 2 years later by one in Boston. In 1847 the House of Refuge for Delinquent Boys was begun in Massachusetts and operated by the state. By 1851 there were 77 children's institutions in the United States, and an additional 47 were built prior to 1860.

Institutions for Persons With Developmental and Emotional Disabilities   The first institution for persons with developmental disabilities was opened in 1848 and operated by Dr. Samuel Gridley Howe. The next decade saw institutions for people with developmental disabilities opened in Albany, Columbus, and Lakeville, Connecticut.[8]

Perhaps the most prominent program developer in U.S. history was Dorothea Dix, who nearly single-handedly paved the way for reform and establishment of facilities for the mentally ill and developmentally disabled. Beginning as a Sunday school teacher for women inmates in a Cambridge, Massachusetts, asylum, she was horrified by the treatment the women were subjected to, particularly those who had emotional disabilities. Although a number of private hospitals for persons with emotional disabilities had been established, public facilities were few in number. Working as an advocate for these persons, Dix successfully pressed the state legislature to expand its facilities. Then she carried her crusade to more than a dozen other states.

Dix began each campaign with patient, careful research and successfully established several institutions. Next, using the statistics she had gathered and direct political tactics, Dix was instrumental in introducing a bill to Congress in 1848 asking that the government appropriate 10 million acres of federal land to the states to help pay for the construction and maintenance of hospitals for persons with emotional disabilities. When the bill was ignored, she reintroduced it. Most members of Congress, however, were more interested in using land remaining in the public domain for interests of their own or for those of land speculators.

For the next 5 years, Dix lobbied representatives and senators in and out of congressional corridors until finally in 1854 her bill passed both houses of Congress. President Franklin Pierce vetoed it, however. In his opinion, the bill was illegal because no precedent had been established for the federal government to provide social services to citizens.

Private Social Services   Citizens groups established associations to overcome poverty, group work services, and child welfare and protection services.

Association for Improving the Condition of the Poor (AICP)

Private benevolent associations dealing with problems of poverty began to spring up. These societies aimed "at uplifting them through improving their character rather than merely provide material aid to the needy."[9] When a financial panic and depression occurred in 1837, causing hardship and straining existing relief agencies beyond their capacities, concerned citizens began to develop groups to coordinate the various efforts to reduce poverty on a more rational basis. In New York City, for example, a group that came together to examine the city's charities found a disjointed system of relief with overlapping and poorly coordinated services, which led them to establish the New York Association for Improving the Condition of the Poor (AICP) in 1843. Less than 90 years later, the New York AICP employed a young social worker, Harry Hopkins, providing him with experience in working with poverty that would lead him to become a leader in implementing relief during the Great Depression of the 1930s.[10]

Group Work Services

In the 1840s social group work saw its beginnings in the Jewish Center movement. Groups of young Jewish people began to establish literary societies, and today Jewish community centers continue to be an active focal point for Jewish culture in many cities. In 1851, following in the footsteps of George Williams (1821–1905), who founded the Young Men's Christian Association (YMCA) in England, a retired sea captain established the first American YMCA in Boston.[11] Like Jewish community centers, the YMCA has continued its efforts into the 21st century. In 1860 a women's church group established the first Boy's Club in Hartford, Connecticut.

Child Welfare and Child Protection

In the mid-1850s community-based approaches to institutional care of children began to be developed. In 1853, for example, the Reverend Charles Loring Brace, a 27-year-old missionary in New York's notorious Five Points District, founded the Children's Aid Society of New York, originating the idea of foster home placement for abandoned, homeless, orphaned, and runaway children. The children's aid movement quickly caught on with the development of the Church Home Society in Boston in 1855, the Henry Watson Children's Aid Society in Baltimore in 1860, and the Home for Little Wanderers in New York in 1861.

Civil War and Reconstruction (1860–1885)

After the Civil War there was a great increase in the development of social programs. In March 1865 the nation's first federal welfare agency, the Bureau of Refugees, Freedmen, and Abandoned Lands, known as the Freedmen's Bureau, was instituted in large part because of the heroic and persistent efforts of Thadeus Stevens. The agency was established to assist African Americans and others displaced by the Civil War. The program was soon abandoned due to political pressure from the South, but the spirit of program development continued on many fronts:

> So rapidly did private agencies continue to multiply that before long America's larger cities had what to many people was an embarrassing number of them. Charity directories took as many as one hundred pages to list and describe the numerous voluntary agencies that sought to alleviate misery, and combat every imaginable emergency. In Philadelphia alone, in 1878, there were some eight hundred such groups of one kind or another in existence.[12]

In 1868 the first YWCA was founded, and in 1880 the Salvation Army, founded in 1865 by William Booth (1829–1912) in England, was transplanted to the United States. The New York Society for the Prevention of Cruelty to Children established the first child protective service agency in 1875. The Reverend M. Van Arsdale founded the American Aid Association in 1883. The association's name was later changed to the Children's Home Society, the parent agency for the National Children's Home Society, a federation of children's home societies in 28 states that is still active today.[13]

Progressive Era (1885–1910)

Among the social agencies that saw their beginnings during the Progressive Era was the first Social Settlement, the Neighborhood Guild of New York City. Established in 1886 by Stanton Coit and based on the principles of Residence, Research, and Reform—the three R's of the movement—it was modeled after

Toynbee Hall, founded in England in 1884 by Canon Samuel Barnett. Although only 4 settlements were founded before 1890, their numbers increased rapidly. By 1900 there were about 100 in existence, and by 1910 roughly 400 were in operation.[14] The first Charity Organization Society was established in Buffalo, New York, by the Reverend Stephen Humphries Gurteen in December 1877.

Saint Xavier Francis Cabrini (1850–1917), the first U.S. citizen to be made a saint by the Roman Catholic Church, became involved with immigrants, primarily Italians. Through her efforts, more than 60 orphanages, schools, free clinics, hospitals, and other programs were instituted. Among these were Columbus Hospital in New York City in 1892 and Columbus Hospital in Chicago in 1905.[15] The son of William Booth, founder of the Salvation Army, established the Volunteers of America in 1896. In 1902 Goodwill Industries was formed. The Boy Scouts of America, founded in England by Lord Robert Baden-Powell (1857–1941) was established in America in 1910. That year also saw the origination of Catholic Charities, and in 1911 the Family Service Association of America opened its doors.[16]

Program Development Today

Many of these original social agencies provide services today, and the pattern of citizens establishing social welfare organizations and agencies continues in response to changing conditions and the efforts of people to create a more socially healthy society. Human and civil rights groups were established as a result of the civil unrest of the 1960s, and since then community development corporations have been created and have expanded, as have numerous community organizations. Many women's shelters have been established because the experience of domestic violence and rape has moved citizens groups to help women escape from this brutal situation. Because of the closure of large institutional settings for persons with intellectual and emotional disabilities in the past 30 years, a variety of community services, agencies, and programs for these populations have been established. As the social environment changes, more and different social programs will undoubtedly be needed. Social workers and concerned U.S. and Canadian citizens can be proud of the rich outpouring of compassion that has resulted in the establishment of so many social programs and agencies, a phenomenon that continues with vigor today.

HOW TO DEVELOP A SOCIAL ORGANIZATION

Community planning groups may recommend development of a social program that meets people's needs in some way, but more often than not, ideas for social programs come out of the involvement of ordinary citizens concerned about social problems in their communities. They meet with their neighbors informally and begin to envision a social program. Macro social workers are often creative and insightful individuals who can observe needs and quickly conceive programmatic solutions to them. These social workers sometimes become "social entrepreneurs" who energetically work to fill gaps and meet needs.

There is a danger, however, if you are inclined to develop a program or construct a social organization single-handedly. Robert Linthicum observes, for example, "a problem with professionals is that they are the perceived experts because of their degrees and body of knowledge."[17] They often believe they "know what is best" for the individual or for the community. This is the great weakness of outsiders such as legislators or city council persons who want to start programs for others. They look at social problems and come up with ideas that are intended to fix them as if they are social mechanics fixing a broken engine. One group may see the problem of drugs, for example, and say, "Let's hire more police officers." Others may read about teenage delinquency in a poor, rundown neighborhood and advise, "Those people need a youth program to get the teenagers off the streets." Some people see persons who are homeless with emotional disabilities or those suffering from alcoholism wandering the streets and they ask, " Why don't they develop a soup kitchen or a shelter?" People become concerned about children running around the vacant lots and suggest, "That neighborhood needs a playground."

These well-intentioned and concerned people have many worthwhile ideas, but the common element with these solutions is that someone else, often a person from outside the community, sees the community or its people as a problem that needs to be fixed. The assumption is that the people who have the problem are not as capable as others of seeing what needs to be done, do not have the imagination to conceive of solutions that are obvious to others, and do not have the capacity to do it themselves.

Interested outsiders may assert, for example, that if people who are alcoholics or homeless or in poverty had the ability, they would have solved their problems long ago. Shouldn't the experts who have the knowledge, skills, resources, and political connections be the ones to solve these problems? So social workers and a host of public health, mental health, recreation, and other professionals are called in to make recommendations. Politicians pass legislation and appropriate money, new programs are initiated, and well-intentioned social welfare professionals are hired. All of this, however, ignores one of the primary assumptions of social work: "The people best able to deal with a problem are the people most affected by the problem. The people best able to deal with teenagers who are running amok in their neighborhood are the people who live in that neighborhood."[18]

The concept of client self-determination is one of the most difficult insights for social workers to apply in their own professional lives. We want to get results, and because of our expertise we may think we know what is best for the community. We unwittingly teach people to be passive recipients and beneficiaries of charity. We train community members to be ancillary spectators and nonparticipants in the vital and necessary forces that shape their social world. We expect them to remain socially unresponsive and disengaged from the problems that affect their lives. As a result, community members often feel victimized and demeaned by our benevolence. They may resent social agencies deeply for making them feel so helpless.

Sometimes, however, social work agencies set up processes to encourage a sense of ownership of the community's social services. They invite two or three community residents to sit on the agency's board, set up a women's auxiliary, or develop a community advisory committee. But community members normally won't accept that offer of participation because it is not their project or even their idea. They may refuse to get involved, and the burden of leadership continues to fall on the social agency.

Agency staff and board members may become cynical about the lack of community involvement, while at the same time community members continue to feel no ownership in the project. Eventually social workers and community members burn out on the project. The fate of any program developed under such conditions is inevitable. It will function successfully only as long as others commit people, money, and materials to the program. When the well-intentioned executive can no longer raise sufficient resources, it will die. It will die because it has never been a project of the people.

Whether the concern for developing a social program comes from a planning group, community members, or elsewhere, the process should always begin with the people in a community who have the greatest stake in any resource that is developed there. Rather than independently deciding what is best for a locality, your most effective role as a macro social worker is to help community members form a program development group, identify the need, incorporate as a formal social organization, form a board of directors, develop the structure of the organization, obtain initial funding, and recruit staff and clients.[19]

Form a Program Development Group

When you form a program development group, you engage in many of the steps used in beginning a task group, described in Chapter 4. You recruit members, decide on your role, and lead the members through the first meeting.

Recruit Members   If you have been working with a community planning group that has identified an idea for a social program, they may decide to reform themselves into a program development group to implement the program. At other times you may join a group of neighbors already concerned about a common problem, or you may form a group of concerned citizens to help you work on community issues.

Your group should consist of at least seven key community people who will assess needs and, if necessary, put the organization and its programs together. While developing a social organization is the concrete task around which your group members form, they may also use the group to meet their needs for developing friendships and, with other members, becoming more involved in their community.

Try to involve members who are heterogeneous in terms of skills, personality, and personal history, but who are homogenous in terms of community membership, who desire to see the program succeed, and who have time and commitment to offer the program development process. Above all, find people who represent the particular community that the program will serve. Suppose, for example, your community is interested in establishing a day program for the elderly. These programs primarily serve people in a specific geographic location. Community members whose elderly parents or grandparents will use the services are often the best choices for the program development group. They know the needs of their relatives and the resources in the community, and they are most committed to ensuring that the program is a success.

Some social programs serve people in a wider area. Specialized residential care treatment centers for youth who are disabled emotionally, for example, may serve the needs of parents and their children from different areas of a region. Facilities for children who have severe developmental or physical handicaps may serve families from many localities. Although these families live in dispersed areas, their common problems and needs bring them together to consider ways of providing safe, well-managed facilities for the welfare of their children. Together they can form a group committed to developing a social organization that will not only meet their own needs but also the needs of many others in the region.

If possible, locate people who know something about program development. For example, members who have served on boards of social organizations, who have worked as staff members for social agencies, or who have familiarity with budgeting or fundraising, recruiting, or selecting staff would be useful members.

Decide on Your Role as a Macro Social Worker

As a macro social worker centered in the principles of generalist social work practice, keep in mind that your goal is to engage your members on a number of levels simultaneously. As you work with members on a personal level, think about and try to connect that work with their development at the group, community, and organization levels as well. At the individual level, your role is to help community members add social meaning to their lives, engage in decision making, gain control over the formation of their social world, and learn the skills to make the social program a strong and lasting one. You use the group process to help members learn skills in group interaction, communication, and leadership. You assist them in learning how to conduct action research.

Your focus is also on the community in which your group is located, and you help community members strengthen and improve their social environment. Because your members' specific interests are at the organizational level, you assist them in learning the technical skills of how to develop a social organization, including planning and administration.

Conduct the First Meeting

If you are working with an existing group or a group of neighbors who have already formed themselves into a program development group, try to meet with the leader to clarify your mutual roles. Your role is to support and assist the group leader, help with the group process, develop leadership skills, and give administrative support.

If your group is new, follow the process of leading a task group through its first meeting and explore your group members' perceptions and personal experiences about the need for this particular program.

Identify and Verify the Need

Performing a needs assessment is a critical first step in the development of any social program. Your group must first decide on the kinds of needs it wants to examine. Then it should carry out a needs assessment to verify the need for the program.

Decide on the Kinds of Needs to Examine

There are two different kinds of needs. You may define need in normative terms or in terms of demand.

Needs Determined Normatively   Rubin and Babbie state that "if needs are defined normatively, then a needs assessment would focus on comparing the objective living conditions of the target population with what society, or at least that segment of society concerned with helping the target population, deems acceptable or desirable."[20] For example, evaluating services for persons who are developmentally disabled may lead your group to conclude that some may lack equal access to educational services afforded others in a particular geographical area. The same may be true of dental care, medical care, or housing for the homeless. These populations may be in need of services whether or not they express the need or claim dissatisfaction with their current condition. When this occurs, your group members may advocate for such "underserved" populations by means of developing "precise estimates of the number and distribution of individuals or social units exhibiting the problem."[21]

Your program development group may define needs normatively by using existing data. For example, the numbers of children who are developmentally disabled who actually attend school may be compared with the number of disabled children in the population as a whole. If there is a significant difference, your members might conclude that more school programs need to be established.

Needs Determined by Demand   When needs are defined in terms of demand, "only those individuals who indicate that they feel or perceive the need themselves would be considered to be in need of a particular program or intervention."[22] Demand data are helpful when mobilizing community support for a program. However, if need is defined solely in terms of the number of individuals who press for a service or who express an interest in it, those who do not understand the service, are not aware of its benefits, or actively resist it will not be included in determining the extent of the need. Demand data should be combined with normative data to determine the extent to which those eligible for a particular program would actually use it. Normative data may show that there is a need for additional shelters for persons who are homeless, for example, whereas demand data would give an indication of the number of people who would actually use them.

Carry Out a Needs Assessments

"The purpose of a needs assessment is to verify that a problem exists within a client population to an extent that warrants the existing or proposed service."[23] Often social planning agencies will not validate or assist in funding programs for which an assessment has not been performed to verify the need. There are five approaches to performing needs assessments: (1) social indicators, (2) rates under treatment, (3) focused interview or key actor, (4) focus groups or community forum, and (5) survey.

Social Indicators   You may wish to develop your own needs assessment, but often you'll find that a needs assessment has already been performed by a social service or planning agency. Social indicators such as data on crime, abuse, housing, and health, for example, can be gathered from public and private agencies concerned with these problems.

Rates Under Treatment   The rates under treatment approach is one way of assessing needs determined by demand. Your group assesses the extent to which people utilize particular services within a community over a period of time. For example, if your group is interested in developing a shelter for battered women, the program development group can study the utilization of shelters in communities of similar size and

demographics. This will help determine whether such a facility would be used and the amount and kinds of services the facility should offer.

Key Actors   Key actors are people knowledgeable about the needs of a particular problem area. Invite potential clients to help define problem areas more specifically. Talk to people with professional, governmental, or other expertise about the need in your intended service area. Meet with providers operating similar or existing programs. The key actor approach is easy and quick and can help build connections with key community resources, but the information does not come from representatives of the entire community. The quality of information you receive will depend on the objectivity and depth of knowledge of the informants you contact.

Community Forums and Focus Groups   Community forums and focus groups can give indications of demand data, but they may be suspect from a scientific perspective. For example, people with vested interests, with a particular ax to grind, or who feel negative about or threatened by a proposed need may be overly represented in forums or focus groups. When attempting to establish the need for a home for people with emotional, behavioral, or developmental disabilities, for instance, your group may discover that many people who attend your meetings may oppose the idea because they do not want such a facility in their neighborhood—the phenomenon of NIMBY, "not in my backyard." Conversely, strong social pressures may prevent some people from speaking or from expressing minority viewpoints at community forums.

Forums or focus groups will often help you assess the political climate that a program may face, but they may not always assist in demonstrating need. "One way to overcome these threats to the validity of data is to hold closed meetings, one for each preselected homogenous group of people,"[24] allowing your program development group to control the representation of members in community forums or focus groups.

Community Surveys   A representative random sample of a community or a sample of the target group can also indicate a need. If you mail questionnaires, however, you must weigh the advantages and disadvantages of this method, given the problems in accuracy associated with low response rates. Making person-to-person contacts will often give you ideas for resources, help you recruit potential board members, and help you obtain information from key community leaders and groups who can be of assistance to you.

After the Needs Assessment

Once your group has performed research, they examine the extent to which your assessment verified the need. Then they define the target population and develop a statement of the needs and problems of that population.

Verify the Need   As a result of their research, your group members may discover that the needs or problems they intend to address are on target, or they may find them not to be what they originally thought. If your group cannot verify the need, help your members explore their initial impressions and look again at what prompted them to want to develop a particular program. Help your group review the problems it wants to address, and select one or two issues that the program realistically can work on in its first years. Ask yourselves, "Over what situations can we have a significant impact?" There may be some aspects of a problem over which you have no control or influence. If the program can make no difference over certain social problems, or will have little significant impact, it is not worthwhile to choose those problems.

Define the Target Population   Be specific in selecting and defining the target population for whom the program can make a significant impact. For example, in 1972 a community program development group in Oakland, California, targeted the neighborhood of West Oakland and issues such as vacant housing, zoning, prostitution, and junkyards. However, it was the specific issue of 1,100 vacant houses that brought leaders from the neighborhoods together and planted the seeds of the Oakland Community Organizations (OCO). In the next 5 years, OCO staff targeted four more Oakland neighborhoods, and one by one, they developed other community organizations: SAFO, 50th to 80th, and Elmhurst. Today, nearly 30 years later, by targeting a specific community and clearly identified important issues in that community, OCO has developed a federation of more than 32 church and community organizations directly involving more than 32,000 families in East, West, and North Oakland, affecting the lives of 300,000 families.[25] The better your group is able to define the target audience, the more likely it is that your program will be effective in meeting the needs of your members.

Compose a Needs, Problem, and Population Statement   Have your group develop a statement of the needs, the problem, and the defined client population. Such a statement might look like this:

Client Population: 60,000 residents including more than 1,500 homeless citizens live in West Oakland.

Needs: More than 1,500 homeless men, women, and children live in West Oakland, and there are more than 1,100 rundown, vacant houses that need to be renovated to make them habitable.

Problem: How can the needs of individuals and families who are homeless be met while at the same time utilizing the 1,100 vacant houses that exist?

Establish the Legal Corporation

After your program development group has verified the need, identified the problem, and selected the target population, it needs to establish a legal corporation. Although most social organizations become incorporated as nonprofit corporations, it is also a good idea to consider whether to establish a for-profit enterprise. Once this decision is made, the group must develop a constitution, articles of incorporation, and by-laws and file these with the state secretary general.

For-Profit Agencies

Income from a profit-making enterprise becomes the property of the owners to dispose of as they wish and is taxable. If the income earned by the enterprise (minus taxes, interest on loans, salaries, and overhead) will provide profit, then it may be to the advantage of the board to incorporate as a small business enterprise. Many board and care homes, institutions for the elderly, hospitals, intermediate care facilities, small family care facilities, as well as counseling clinics incorporate as profit-making agencies.

To become a business, the board must file a "fictitious name" (the name of the business), obtain a tax number, and apply for the licenses required to operate in the city or county. Profit-making enterprises often obtain start-up money by taking out small business loans and repaying them from income generated by the service.

Not-for-Profit Organizations

Just as profit-making organizations do, not-for-profit social organizations may obtain loans, acquire capital and other assets, own property, charge fees for services, manufacture and sell merchandise, and employ and pay staff. However, not-for-profit corporations do not pay taxes on income, property, or other assets as for-profit businesses must. Among the kinds of organizations that qualify for tax-exempt status are social organizations such as churches, labor unions, benevolent associations, foundations, private schools, and social welfare organizations.

In addition to exemption from taxes, not-for-profit social welfare organizations may apply for charitable foundation and government grants or contract with public agencies as service providers for a fee. They can accept charitable contributions from individuals or corporations that can be deducted from the donor's taxes, providing an incentive for donors to contribute to the social welfare organization, and tax-exempt social welfare organizations may become members of cooperative fundraising campaigns such as the United Way.

Social organizations that incorporate as not-for-profit social welfare agencies must meet requirements of federal and state laws for exemption from taxation. Any surplus income that the agency generates must be used for the charitable purposes for which the organization has been formed and not for the personal profit of its owners, and no substantial part of the corporation's assets may be used for partisan political purposes.

JANIE PORTER BARRETT (1865–1948)

Janie Porter Barrett was a program developer and activist during one of the most important periods of program building in America. She made her home into a place for needy people. Using her savings and contacts from the Hampton Institute in Virginia, her alma mater, Barrett led a successful fundraising campaign to develop the Locust Street Social Settlement. She provided job training for people of all ages who learned to sew, care for children, raise livestock, and cook.

In 1915, convinced that the state needed a rehabilitation center for African American girls in legal difficulties, she became superintendent at the Virginia Industrial School for Colored Girls, near Richmond. Barrett obtained regular state and philanthropic subsidies and increased the school's enrollment to 100. By the mid-1920s, the Russell Sage Foundation ranked the center among the country's five best institutions of its type. As a resident among the center's girls, Barrett fostered an atmosphere of community. The center was without locks, bars, or physical punishment, reflecting the ideals of progressive reform, and it set the standard for treatment in which humane social work was becoming increasingly important. Barrett received the William E. Harmon Award for Distinguished Achievement among Negroes in 1920, and she participated in the White House Conference on Child Health and Protection in 1930.[26]

Incorporation   If your program development group decides to become a not-for-profit social welfare organization, it must be incorporated at the state level and apply for not-for-profit status with the federal government. It must also meet local or state licensing requirements, particularly those organizations offering day programs, residential facilities, food service programs, health or medical treatment programs, and others that provide direct care to clients. A group that attempts to provide such services without incorporation and without acquiring formal licensing approval is operating illegally.

Incorporation means that your group chooses a board of directors who have legal responsibility and ownership over the organization. The board defines the purposes of the agency, sets policy, owns the assets of the program, and has ultimate authority to make decisions about services, structure, personnel, and the budget.

The process for becoming incorporated is straightforward. Apply to the Federal Internal Revenue Service to obtain a tax exemption for your new organization and provide a copy of the articles of incorporation from your state's office of the secretary of state. Compose your organization's constitution and by-laws.

Obtain Tax Exemption   Your nearest IRS office can provide your group with forms by which you can apply for federal exemption from taxation, called Section 501(c)(3) of the 1986 Internal Revenue Code. The form is easy to fill out, but you can ask for help if your group needs assistance. While your group's application is being processed by the IRS, you should continue to complete the remainder of your documents.

Articles of Incorporation   You may be tempted to hire a lawyer to draft the articles of incorporation. This is not necessary and it is expensive. Write to the secretary of state in the state where you wish to incorporate. The secretary of state will send you forms that

I

The name of this corporation is _____

_____

II

A. This corporation is a nonprofit PUBLIC BENEFIT
    CORPORATION and is not organized under the private
    gain of any person. It is organized under the Nonprofit
    Public Benefit Corporation Law for:
                ( ) public puposes.
            or ( ) charitable purposes.
            or ( ) public and charitable puposes.
B. The specific purpose of this corporation is to

_____

III

The address in the State of California of this corporation is:

Name _____
STREET address _____
City _____ State CALIFORNIA Zip _____

IV

A. This corporation is organized and operated exclusively
    for charitable purposes within the meaningof selection
    501(c)(3), Internal Revenue Code.

B. No substantial activities of this corporation shall
    consist of carrying on propaganda, or otherwise
    attempting to influence legislation, and the
    corporation shall not participate or intervene in any
    political campaign (including the publishing or
    distribution of statements) on behalf of any candi-
    date for public office.

V

The property of this corporation is irrevocably dedicated
to charitable purposes and no part of the net income or
assets of this corporation shall ever inure to the benefit
of any director, officer or member thereof or to the
benefit of any private person. Upon the dissolution or
winding up of the corporation, its assets remaining after
payment, or provision for payment, of all its debts and
liabilities of this corporation shall be distributed to a nonprofit fund, foundation or corporation which is
organized and operated exclusively for charitable
purposes and which has established its tax exempt status
under Section 501(c)(3), Internal Revenue Code.

_____
(Signature of Incorporator) (date)

_____
(Typed Name of Incorporator)

FIGURE 10.1   Articles of Incorporation, California

can be filled out by anyone familiar with your organization. By following the instructions from the secretary
of state, you and your program development group can
devise an acceptable set of articles for your organization. Articles of incorporation usually include the name
of the corporation, date of incorporation, names of
officers of the board of directors, and a statement of
purpose. Your group may adopt stock (boilerplate)
paragraphs, provided by the secretary of state, that apply
to any corporation. See Figure 10.1 for a sample of
Articles of Incorporation from the state of California.

Constitution and By-Laws   Standard language also
exists for the constitution and by-laws by which your
organization's board of directors will operate. The
constitution usually contains the name and address of
the organization, its purpose, and its originating officers. By-laws are the general rules that govern the
organization, the board's composition, and structure.
They outline how your board of directors will operate, its size, the number, kinds of officers, and their
roles, the manner in which officers and committee

members are selected, the selection and tenure of
board members, the place and times of board meetings, the financial and legal procedures, the mechanisms by which meetings are to be conducted, and
rules for making decisions. By-laws should be tai-
lored to meet the needs of your organization. Because
these rules may not always be current, however, you
should also outline the steps by which the by-laws can
be revised when it becomes necessary.

It may be helpful to obtain a sample copy of the
constitution and by-laws of an organization similar to
the one your group wants to establish to use as a
guide. Although writing a constitution and by-laws
may seem formidable, it can be a very useful process
that helps your group think through the structure of
this new organization. Your organization may use the
following format to write your constitution and by-
laws, unless your state requires a different one.

I. Purpose of the organization: Indicate that the
    organization exists exclusively for religious,
    charitable, scientific, literary, or educational

purposes and that it operates under section 501(c)(3) of Internal Revenue Code of 1986 or such other provisions of state or federal laws. Provide a description of the specific purposes of the organization.

II. **Location of the organization:** Provide the permanent, registered office address of the organization.

III. **Members:** There is a distinction between members of an organization and members of a board of directors. If your organization will not have members, the by-laws should simply state that there are no members. If the founders of your organization conclude that there is a value to having members, you should explain the classes of members, dues, qualifications, length of membership, powers of members, number of meetings they must attend, what constitutes a quorum (the smallest number who can make decisions), and rules by which meetings are to be conducted. For example, members generally meet only once a year at the organization's annual meeting. Some nonprofits provide that the members elect the board of directors, adopt or revise by-laws, and approve merges, dissolution, and the sale of assets. In other nonprofits, members are simply people who make annual contributions.

IV. **Structure of the board of directors:** Describe the size of the board, who is eligible for membership, how long and the number of terms board members may serve, how board members who resign during their terms are replaced, and if members will be compensated.

V. **Structure of board meetings:** State the minimum number of times a year the board must meet, who may call a special meeting of the board, notification requirements for meetings, the size of a quorum, the number of votes required to pass a motion, and what rules or procedures will be used to conduct meetings.

VI. **Duties of officers:** Explain what officers the board will have and the powers and duties of each officer.

VII. **Committee structure:** Committees only have authority that is specifically given to them by the by-laws or the board. If your board is small, it may prefer to deal as a body with the business of the corporation with no need for committee

work. If your board has a dozen or more members, it may choose to divide its major responsibilities among standing (ongoing) committees that report to the board as a whole. Board members with interest and expertise in specific areas are often appointed to serve on standing committees by the board's chair. In some states, all committee members must be members of the board. In other states, the board is permitted to appoint other people to committees, which it may want to do to acquire special expertise. Here are some common types of committees organizations may establish.

The *executive committee* is composed of officers of the board and chairs of the key board committees. An executive committee could be given decision-making authority in the by-laws to act on urgent business that arises during the periods between board meetings. Sometimes the duties of the executive committee are subject to the approval of the board, however, and the executive committee is only advisory.

The *finance committee* monitors fiscal operations, assists the agency's Executive Director in developing an annual budget, and ensures that an audit is performed annually. It may also be responsible for developing and overseeing fundraising campaigns.

The *nominating committee* recommends individuals to serve as board members. It may also recommend the criteria for selecting new board members, provide orientation to new members, and review the participation and performance of current members.

The *personnel committee* reviews the organization's personnel needs, determines schedules of salaries and benefits, and develops personnel policies or grievance policies.

The *community relations committee* works with staff in disseminating information about the organization through the media.

The *program committee* advises staff in service delivery, recommends service delivery policies, monitors the agency's services, and provides the board with detailed information regarding the effectiveness of services.

Ad hoc committees are temporary committees that carry out one project and are then disbanded. For example, a special committee may be formed to search for an executive director and be disbanded after that position is filled.

VIII. **Special rules of the corporation:** Explain whether the corporation will indemnify its board members from the financial consequences of liability lawsuits and judgments, the time period that constitutes the fiscal year of the corporation, and other special rules.

 IX. **Amendment of the by-laws:** Explain the procedure by which by-laws can be changed or added.

Ending the Program Development Group   With incorporation of the new organization, the work of your program development group is finished. Your team members may decide to end their involvement at this point, although it is possible that some may be willing to carry on as members of the new agency's board of directors. If so, they will take charge of recruiting and training new board members and help them become oriented to their new roles. Have a party for your program development team, celebrating the accomplishment and the hard work of your members, giving recognition to them, and welcoming those who will continue as board members of the new corporation.

WORKING WITH THE BOARD OF DIRECTORS

After the corporation is legally formed, your role will change from working with a program development team to working with the new board of directors. Members of your program development group who have decided to continue will help recruit additional board members.

Recruit Board Members

Seek people to make a full complement of board members who have the interests and skills necessary to help translate ideas into functioning services. Consider the number and personal qualities of potential members and their capabilities. After a potential board member is identified, explain what will be required, what he or she can contribute, and offer an invitation.

Number and Personal Qualities   Most boards probably function best with a dozen or so members, but new organizations might function better with only half a dozen. Board members must have the time, interest, and willingness to be of service to the agency. Individuals who serve on the board should be able to work cooperatively and tactfully with one another. They should be recognized as credible and responsible individuals. Ideally members of the board should include people with varied areas of expertise and perspectives and reflect the gender, age, and ethnic diversity of your community.

Capabilities   Members should be selected according to qualities they can offer your organization, especially competence, bridge to constituents, community leadership, and shared goals.

Competence   Board members should be capable of making sound governance decisions and, if possible, have special competencies in fundraising, budgeting, law, public relations, personnel, or social work skills. Board members should have enough expertise, experience, and good judgment to help keep the organization's mission and strategic decisions consistent with its charitable purpose.

Bridge to Constituents   The board should be composed of members of the community, the target population of the program, and other stakeholders who live or work in the community.

Community Leadership   Board members should either be or have potential to become leaders in the community, have access to resources, or possess affiliations with groups or organizations of importance to the new social welfare organization.

Shared Goals   Board members should have a sincere interest in the work of the organization, a commitment to its goals, a willingness to ask questions, and the ability to offer constructive criticism.

Ask What They Can Contribute   Ask potential board members what they feel they can contribute to the organization and how their participation can be easily and best utilized. Have members of your original

team explain the rewards members may receive by being on the board—for example, the satisfaction of serving the community, social contacts, and experience in policy making, fundraising, and other aspects of the agency.

Explain What Will Be Required   Ask your team members to clearly explain to potential board members why they were selected, in what capacity they will serve, what skills they can be expected to contribute, and committee work they may be expected to perform. Potential members need to know how much time they will need to give to meetings and other activities, the length of their term on the board, possible costs to them such as lunches, travel, time away from work, and any expectations of personal financial contributions. Your original team members should discuss with potential board members whether there are any conflicts of interest, such as business or other relationships that could affect their ability to serve the program's interests.[27]

Offer an Invitation   Once your original team members have explored all these issues with potential board members, encourage them to think about their invitation. New board members who are well informed about the organization, its problems and opportunities, and their expected role are more likely to participate well and be effective board members. [28]

CHARLES LORING BRACE, CHILD SAVER (1826–1890)

Writer, minister, free thinker, program developer, and social reformer, Charles Loring Brace was the originator of the child welfare movement in the United States, as well as foster care and child placement services. He was one of the primary organizers of the Children's Aid Society of New York City. As its executive director for almost 40 years, Brace chronicled the problems of destitute, vagrant, and homeless children and initiated many child welfare services.

Brace was born in Litchfield, Connecticut, June 19, 1826. He graduated from Yale University in 1846 with honors and entered Yale Divinity School, finishing his course at Union Theological Seminary in New York City. After traveling through Europe in 1850–1851, the Rev. Brace attended lectures at the University of Berlin and visited Hungary out of sympathy with the revolution in that country. The Austrian government, however, suspected him of being in league with Hungarian

refugees, and he was imprisoned for a month but released through the efforts of the U.S. Consul.

Brace settled in New York City and began missionary work in the notorious Five Points area and with the prisoners of Blackwells Island. Serving as a city missionary, he became aware of the many homeless children roaming the streets and made a study of the "ragged schools" and prisons, becoming convinced that reformation of the poor must begin with children.

In 1853 the chief of police issued a report calling attention to the multitude of vagrant children who almost of necessity became criminals. In that same year, a number of citizens, including Brace, began the needed work of reform by organizing the Children's Aid Society. After much hesitation, Brace, who had wanted to continue his ministry, accepted the position of executive officer. "He had every quality for philanthropic work," wrote one who knew him well, "clear insight, perfect sanity of judgment, supreme diligence and indomitable patience."

Under Brace's leadership, the Children's Aid Society developed industrial schools, reading rooms, penny savings banks, newsboy lodging houses, night schools, summer camps, sanatoriums, children's shelters, special classes for children with disabilities, and dental clinics. The first newsboy lodging house was founded in 1854, and during the first year 408 boys used its services. Brace pioneered in placing homeless children in families settling in the West. In his last report to the society in 1889, Brace stated that since 1853 more than 70,000 children had been transplanted from the slums to good homes and that through the lodging houses probably 200,000 had been helped to improve their condition. Rev. Charles Loring Brace, saver of children, died in Campofer, Switzerland, August 11, 1890.[29]

Train and Orient the Board

As a social work program developer, you help train and orient board members in the history and purpose of the new organization, role and function of a board, and how to use parliamentary procedures. This may require from one half to a full day of training. Use this opportunity not only to instruct members but also to form a strong cohesive group of members who can work well together.

History and Purpose of the Organization
Bring back some of the original team members, asking them to tell the history of the formation of the organization, provide information about the needs

assessment, and explain the vision of the original program development team. Give a copy of the organization's constitution and by-laws to each board member. Assign the task of explaining the purpose of the new organization to members of your original team.

Role and Function of the Board

You and your original team may share in training new members to the roles that board members and its officers will play. For example, all board members should know that the board of directors is the policy-making body of the organization with a legal duty to ensure that the organization's actions are consistent with its goals. Explain that members of the board give general direction to the organization, and that they share collective responsibility for the fiscal and programmatic aspects of the organization's performance. Board members should understand that boards typically fulfill the following six functions.

1. Maintain general direction and control of the agency (policy development).
2. Direct short- and long-term planning (program development).
3. Hire competent administrative staff (personnel).
4. Facilitate access to necessary resources (finances).
5. Interpret the organization to the community (public relations).
6. Evaluate operations (accountability).[30]

Parliamentary Procedures

Board members must be able to work effectively together and be able to come to decisions quickly and efficiently. One way that many boards conduct their meetings and come to decisions is by means of Robert's Rules of Order, commonly called parliamentary procedure. Parliamentary procedure has traditionally been used as the basic method for decision making in social service and other organizations, and it is especially appropriate in large groups because of its formality and structure.

One of the potentially negative consequences of using these procedures, however, is the sacrifice of member satisfaction. Over time, as some members find themselves in the minority and feel unimportant or insignificant in the group process, they may develop dissatisfaction with their participation in the group. Fatout and Rose recommend establishing as many subcommittees as possible to provide each member with a maximum amount of participation.[31]

When you train members, explain the general parliamentary procedure, how members obtain the floor, make motions, second motions, debate, put the question, and announce the vote and privileged motions.

General Procedure   The first step in making a decision by means of parliamentary procedure requires a member to "obtain the floor"; that is, to be formally recognized by the chairperson. The member who has the floor then makes a motion or a request that a particular resolution be debated and decided. The motion must be "seconded" by another person. After the second, the chairperson either rules it out of order or "states the question" so that the members will know what is before them for consideration and action. The chairperson manages the debate procedure. When the debate has reached an end, someone must "call for the question," or end the debate. Once the debate is finished, the chair calls for a vote on the motion and any amendments that have been added to it.

Obtaining the Floor   Before a member can make a motion, or address the board in debate, he or she must obtain the floor. After the floor has been yielded, the member must rise (in board meetings, members usually raise their hands) and address the chairperson, "Mr. Chairman," or "Madam Chairwoman." After a member has been given the floor, no one may interrupt except to raise a procedural point of order, request information that requires an immediate answer, raise an objection to considering the motion, request that the question be divided into different subjects, or other structural concerns.

Motions and Resolutions   A motion is a proposal that the board take certain action, or that it express itself as holding certain views. The member who has the floor announces, "I move (propose) that . . ." stating the action the member wishes the board to take such as adopt or amend a resolution, refer it to a committee, offer a vote of thanks, or other proposal. Although most board members offer motions verbally, at times it may be useful to prepare them in writing so that they are clear to everyone. If a member wishes to have the board adopt a written resolution after having obtained the floor, he or she says, "I move the adoption of the following resolution," or "I offer the following resolution," which the member then reads and hands to the chair.

Seconding Motions   To prevent time being consumed in considering a question that only one person favors, every motion should be seconded. If members are slow about seconding a motion, the chair should ask, "Is the motion seconded?" When a member wishes to second a motion, he or she says, "I second the motion," or "I second it," without obtaining the floor or raising his or her hand.

Stating the Question   After a motion has been made and seconded, the chair should state the question—that is, state the exact proposal or motion that is before the board for its consideration and action. For example: "It is moved and seconded that the following resolution be adopted [reading the resolution]"; or "It is moved and seconded to adopt the following resolution"; or "It is moved and seconded that we adjourn."

Debate   After the chair states a question, it is before the board for consideration and action. Unless a two-thirds vote of members decides to dispose of the motion without debate, all resolutions, committees reports, communications to the member, motions, and amendments may be debated before members take final action on them. In the debate each member has the right to speak twice on the same question in the same meeting but cannot make the second speech until any member who has not spoken on the question and desires the floor has a chance to speak. No one can speak longer than 10 minutes at a time without permission of the members.

Members must limit their comments to the merits of the question that is still pending. Speakers must address their remarks to the presiding officer, be courteous in their language, avoid making comments about the personalities or motives of members, or allude to the officers or other members by name.

Putting the Question and Announcing the Vote
When the debate appears to have finished, the chair asks, "Are you ready for the question?" If no one raises a hand, the chair proceeds to "put the question"; that is, to take a vote on the question, first calling for the affirmative and then for the negative vote. In putting the question, the chair should make the wording of the motion on which the members are voting perfectly clear. Unless it has been read very recently, the chair should read the motion again. For example, "The question is on the adoption of the resolution [which the chair reads]; those in favor of the resolution say aye; those opposed say no." "The ayes have it, and the resolution is adopted"; or "The noes have it, and the resolution is lost." The assembly is assumed not to know the result of the vote until announced by the chair, and

the vote does not go into effect until announced. As soon as the result of the vote is announced, the chair should state the next order of business.

Privileged Motions   Privileged motions include fixing a time to adjourn, adjourning, or take a recess. While privileged motions do not relate to the pending question, they can be made while a main motion is pending, take precedence over all other questions, and are not subject to debate.[32]

The First Board Meeting

After the board is trained and oriented, members hold their first meeting to organize themselves to conduct business. The first order of business is to conduct elections, followed by selection of committees. Explain your role to the members of the board.

Conduct Elections   One of the members of the original program development team should begin the first meeting and ask for nominations for president or chairperson of the board. The board then selects one of its members to be the chair, usually by secret ballot. As soon as the chairperson is elected, he or she immediately presides over the rest of the election process. The board should then elect other officers such as a vice chair, treasurer, or secretary.

Decide on Committees   The board decides if it will divide its work among committees or if the board will work as a committee of the whole. If the board decides to have a committee structure, it assigns members to them, and each committee then selects its own chairperson and decides how often it will meet. The board members decide on the time and place of board meetings. Small, active boards tend to have monthly meetings. Larger boards may meet only quarterly to deal with major issues, and committees of board members work on organizational concerns between the quarterly board meetings.

Role of the Macro Social Worker   Explain that until they choose a new chief administrator, you will continue to work closely with the board members, especially its officers and committee chairpersons, assisting them as they grow in their new roles, learn leadership, carry out their tasks, and function effectively as a whole.

ESTABLISH THE SOCIAL ORGANIZATION'S CULTURE AND STRUCTURE

After the board has organized itself, it is ready to get down to the business for which it was formed, including establishing the new social organization's mission, vision, values, and goals. The board then develops a plan for the agency's structure, staffing, finances, and recruiting clients.

Mission Statement

The mission statement of the social organization describes the purpose of the organization, the reason it exists. This statement generally identifies the organization's target population and the geographic area of operation. The mission statement should be short enough that staff, board, and volunteers can recite it from memory.[33] For example, the mission statement of the Pacific Institute for Community Organizations (PICO) is "to assist families build community organizations."[34] The mission of the National Training and Information Center (NTIC) is to "build grassroots leadership and strengthen neighborhoods through issue-based community organizing."[35]

Vision Statement

The vision statement sets forth the expected future of the social organization. The members should understand what is expected over the long term so they can focus on that desired outcome. Keep the vision statement as short as possible.[36] The vision statement of PICO is "Through effective community organization, to empower poor and moderate income families to participate effectively in our democratic system and to enable them to address the issues affecting their lives."[37] The vision statement of Western Economic Diversification Canada (WD) is "A stronger West. A stronger Canada"[38]

Values Statement

The program's values or guiding principles spell out the ethical framework of how things get done. They tell your stakeholders what kind of organization you are. For example, the Pacific Institute for Community Organization states "Over the years the following beliefs have guided and shaped all our decisions and actions. PICO believes (1) people are precious. (2) Because they

are precious, they deserve to live in a world that is just. (3) Justice is a product of the interaction of the spiritual and social dimensions of our lives. (4) Organizing is a tool to integrate these two pieces: the spiritual and social, and create a world of dignity and justice for all the families of our community."[39]

Goal Statement

The goals describe the intended outcomes for which the community established the organization. Goals are usually long-term aims driven by the organization's mission and vision. A goal statement does not describe the year-to-year objectives or program activities but sets forth what will result from them. Be sure your goal statements describe measurable outcomes. These outcome statements should refer specifically to those who will be affected, describe what these people are expected to do, under what conditions, and how well or to what extent. They should also include a time factor.

The Organizational Structure

Board members develop a plan for the agency's structure, staffing, finances, and client recruitment. There are a number of structural models from which board members can choose. Chapter 9 described the parallel model, the federal structural model, and the loose-linked models. For beginning organizations, the most common are the whole group and team models. Under rare circumstances social organizations may consider adopting a modified hierarchical model.

Whole Group Model   The board may decide that the organization should be a loosely structured group in which all staff have equal roles. This model is particularly useful for small organizations. The entire organization may operate as a single unit or consist of several subgroups. There may be no traditional supervision, leader, or coordinator. Instead, those roles may be rotated among some or all members of the group.

In another version of the whole group model, leadership may be based on a partnership or collaborative model in which an ad hoc (temporary) administrator facilitates carrying out tasks by the staff rather than using an authoritarian or directive leadership style. The administrator makes sure that everything necessary is available so that the group can get its business done, assumes a facilitative role, schedules meetings, makes sure everyone has a chance to contribute, and between meetings makes sure tasks are accomplished. Instead of commanding or controlling, the leader assists and pitches in to fill in gaps to support the group and its goals.

Team Model   In a social organization structured according to the team model, the staff may be broken into subgroups by program or by major organizational functions. Senior staff members coordinate the work of the various teams, making sure communication between them is effective, relationships are smooth, resources are available to accomplish tasks, and problems between team members or at the interface between teams are resolved.

Modified Hierarchical Model   Businesses and government organizations concerned with efficiency

allow their organizations to become large to decrease overhead costs. As these organizations become larger, however, relationships between units and departments become more complex, the need for communication among different groups increases, and coordination becomes more crucial. With increased size and complexity comes a need for more centralization, standardization, routinization, and control, resulting in a hierarchical organization structure (see Figure 10.2).

As you learned in Chapter 9, hierarchical organizational structures are rarely appropriate for social organizations. Social organizations are often most effective when they are small and community based. If social organizations are part of a large organizational network, however, they should be dispersed in smaller units in a modified hierarchical arrangement. It is important that they reflect and relate to the

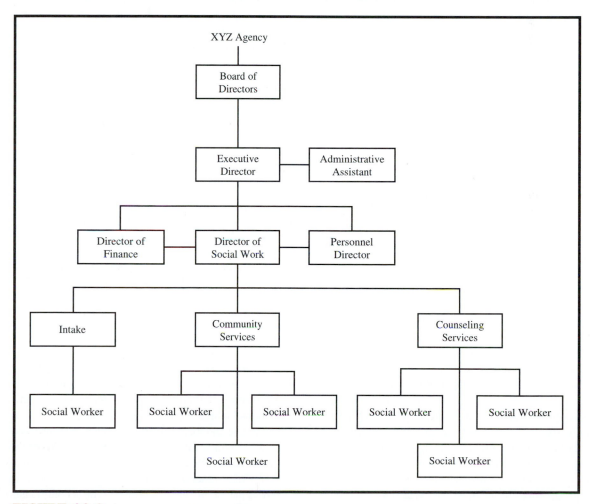

FIGURE 10.2   Organizational Chart for XYZ Agency

individual communities in which they reside rather than to a superordinate, centralized control center.

STAFF THE SOCIAL ORGANIZATION

Community members often identify the quality of the program by the ability of your paid employees and volunteers. The community looks at the staff and sees your social organization. It is important, therefore, for you to help the board take the time and energy to carefully consider staffing needs of the organization. It is more useful to work from the tasks to be performed and find the kind of people needed than to arbitrarily name a position and then assign responsibilities to people. Among the most important staffing responsibilities of the board is hiring the chief administrator, instituting fair employment practices, and decide on positions, salary, and benefits.[40]

The Administrator

Usually the first person the board hires is the executive director, the chief administrative officer of the organization. The administrator serves as long as the board has confidence that he or she is accomplishing the purposes for which he or she was hired. The executive implements board policy and guides the staff in formulating strategies designed to achieve organizational objectives. The executive draws on the energy, expertise, and resources of the board members by involving them and keeping them informed. Staff who report to the chief administrator generally should be hired and evaluated by the administrator, who should also determine their individual compensation within the overall compensation policy approved by the board.[41]

Fair Employment Practices

Equal employment practices are not only simple common sense, they are a responsibility that every organization owes to society as a whole. There are certain restrictions on the freedom of the board to hire, promote, pay, and fire people under federal and state law and often under a city's human rights statutes as well. The board should be aware of prohibited information, use statements of nondiscrimination, understand requirements of the Americans With Disabilities Act (ADA), and use an applicant register.

Prohibited Information   The Equal Employment Opportunity Commission (EEOC) prohibits asking for certain information on applications, in résumé reviews, or in interviews because they may result in illegal discrimination. Prohibited information includes birthplace, age, height and weight, race, gender, marital status, number and age of children, child care arrangements, weekend working capacity (unless part of regular work week), credit records, public assistance status, medical history, worker's compensation history, arrest and conviction records, military service record, disability, or foreign language proficiency if not required by the job.

Your board should ask for information about knowledge, skills, abilities, and experiences they are confident are necessary for effective job performance. Agencies of your state and city responsible for human rights will provide your board with guidelines about their legal responsibilities. Use caution to protect the rights of applicants during all phases of hiring. Be careful not to place unjust or unsupportable demands on applicants.[42]

Statement of Nondiscrimination   Valuing diversity or creating a pluralistic organization has increasingly become a focus of all types of employers. Many businesses, educational institutions, government agencies, and social organizations have adopted statements similar to the following:

> We will not discriminate against any employee or applicant for employment because of race, color, creed, religion, national origin, ancestry, gender, sexual orientation, age, disability, marital status, or status with regard to public assistance. We affirm the value of human diversity and manage all aspects of our agency to provide every individual with the opportunity to achieve his or her fullest potential.

Americans With Disabilities Act   The Americans with Disabilities Act (ADA) applies to employers with 15 or more paid employees, but its provisions reflect responsible treatment of people with disabilities, and some state and local laws may apply similar provisions to all organizations. Under ADA an employer must make reasonable accommodations to the known disability of an otherwise qualified employee or applicant, unless the employer can show that the accommodation will impose undue hardship.

Use an Applicant Register   For equal employment opportunity or affirmative action purposes, use an applicant register to document all aspects of your recruitment and hiring practices as a safeguard against allegations of discrimination. You can get a sample applicant register to help you document the pertinent ethnic and general information of all applicants from your Equal Employment Opportunity office. In addition, the dates and texts of ads and the publications in which the ads were placed should be recorded, and your hiring procedures should be outlined in writing.[43]

SAINT FRANCES XAVIER CABRINI (1850–1917)

Born in Italy on July 15, 1850, Maria Cabrini studied at the Convent of the Sacred Heart, and between 1868 and 1872 she ministered to the poor and sick, taught in a public school, and took charge of a home for orphans. In 1880 she founded the Institute of the Missionary Sisters of the Sacred Heart of Jesus and became the mother general of this group of young women dedicating their lives to missions.

In 1889, at the direction of Pope Leo XIII, Mother Cabrini continued her work among Italian immigrants in New York City and established an orphanage and school. Two years later she founded Columbus Hospital. Gradually her activities expanded to other cities and other countries, resulting in the opening of schools, hospitals, and orphanages in Italy, France, Spain, England, and North and South America. More than 4,000 sisters were engaged in these services.

Difficulties were always overcome by her faith, abilities, and courage. In recognition of her exceptional virtues, the Catholic Church eventually granted Mother Cabrini sainthood. As a naturalized citizen of the United States, Mother Cabrini became the first American saint.

Positions, Salary, and Benefits

The board should use the social organization's goals statement to determine the staffing pattern, salary scales, and benefits for the staff. You can be of assistance to the board as you help members accomplish the following:

1. Determine the skills needed for each task. Task functions or responsibilities should be clustered by skill areas such as administration, clerical support, counseling, education, lobbying, community relations, and fundraising.

2. Determine the length of time required for completing each task. How often must this activity be carried out? How much time will it require? Based on these skills, task, and time estimates, the board develops a list of the staff positions necessary to carry out the organization's program.

3. Develop task assignments for each position.

4. Think about various ways to obtain people to perform the tasks. There may be many possible options besides having full-time paid staff. Alternatives include part-time paid positions, temporary paid staff, paid consultants, unpaid staff (volunteers) including senior citizens, social work interns, and college and high school students.

5. Consider various staffing patterns to determine which is most workable for the organization.

Determine the Salary Range   Determine the salary ranges for each of the paid positions. Contact other nonprofit agencies with similar staff positions to find out their salaries. Develop salary ranges (e.g., $27,000–$31,000) rather than a specific salary ($29,000). This allows your board to use some discretion when hiring staff so they can pay each individual according to his or her relevant education and experience. The result should be a list of staff positions and task assignments that indicates the type of employees the agency needs: full or part time, regular or temporary, paid or unpaid, professional or intern.

Develop Job Descriptions   Job descriptions define staff positions and outline the tasks and experience, education, and personality characteristics of the people needed to perform them. A job description should be developed for each staff position, including volunteer and intern positions. Developing job descriptions forces your board to explain each position in objective, measurable terms. They help potential applicants decide whether to apply, and they are a means for recruiting, screening, and selecting staff. Job descriptions provide guidelines for job performance and employee evaluation (see Figure 10.3).

Here are some things to keep in mind as you develop job descriptions for your organization:

1. Decide the primary responsibilities or major tasks that each employee must perform. Develop

Agency: Prairie Community Organization Network (PCON)
Job Title: Community Developer
Reports to: Executive Director
Supervises: Community Development Intern

Primary Responsibilities

1. Provides community development services to the Lawndale Community.
2. Assists citizens in development of a Lawndale community-based grassroots organization including: forming community development task force, conduct needs assessments, develop nonprofit corporation, recruit and train board of directors.
3. Assists board to develop organizational structure.
4. Assists board to recruit and hire director and staff.
5. Assists board to obtain initial funding.
6. Engages new organization in business, political, educational, and religious community in Lawndale.
7. Orients agency director and staff to the board and Lawndale community.

Other Activities

1. Serves as member of PCON staff development team.
2. Assists in coordination and overall planning for PCON.
3. Meets with PCON staff and reports on work in Lawndale community.
4. Fills out financial reports and helps prepare PCON budget.
5. Gives input to other staff about Lawndale community projects.
6. Provides consultation to other staff.
7. Provides supervision to community development interns.

Skills and Knowledge

Ability to conduct needs assessments and train nonprofit corporation board of directors. Skill in writing grant applications, contracts with government, and fundraising. Ability to write job descriptions, recruit, and hire staff. Skill in providing consultation to staff and community members. Ability to relate to various segments of Lawndale community.

Education

BSW or BA degree in generalist social work required. MSW preferred with specialization in community organization or community development.

Experience

At least 2 years experience in community organization, community development, and/or community planning (up to 1 year of which can be in community practice internship).

Other

Ethnic sensitivity and compatibility with Lawndale community.

Desired but not required: Ability to speak Spanish. Ethnic identification with Hispanic or Filipino culture. Knowledge of Lawndale community. Ethnic, women, handicapped, are welcome to apply.

The Prairie County Community Organization Network does not discriminate against any employee or applicant for employment because of race, color, creed, religion, national origin, ancestry, gender, sexual orientation, age, disability, marital status, or status with regard to public assistance. We affirm the value of human diversity and work to provide all staff with the opportunity to achieve his or her fullest potential.

FIGURE 10.3 Sample Job Description

a statement of one to three sentences that answers the question: What is the primary reason this position exists?

2. Outline the specific tasks that are *essential* to the job. Give each major responsibility a distinct one-sentence statement. If there are other, secondary activities, list these also.

3. Decide the education and experience requirements for each position. What must a person know or what skills and abilities must he or she have to do those tasks? If the applicants don't have this particular knowledge or skill, will they still be able to do the job while they are acquiring the knowledge and skill?

Recruit and Select Candidates

Your board decides where to recruit, reviews applications, selects the best candidates, and finally the top candidate, and should understand the skills of recruitment.

Where to Recruit Candidates   You help the board discover the various means available to reach your target audience such as ads in the local papers (daily, weekly, business, minority, suburban), notices in college, university, and technical school placement centers, and ads at state unemployment offices. Include in your thinking public and private retraining centers, job clubs (where job seekers meet in support groups), and business and personal acquaintances via networking.

Your board can also use employment agencies. If you or your board members know the agency or know people who have had continued success with them, you may be able to save yourself time and effort. But check out an agency's reputation carefully. Do as much as you can to acquaint the employment agency representative with your organization and the job requirements. Sturgeon says, "We give a reputable employment agency an exclusive for a limited period of time (two to three weeks) to see if they are able to produce a match. If they do, fine; if not we do our own recruiting by means of ads and other postings."[44]

Review Applications   Whether your board members do recruiting themselves or work with employment agency professionals, the next steps are pretty much the same: Read the applicants' résumés or employment applications, select the most likely persons for initial interviews, interview these applicants, and narrow your field down to fewer than five final candidates for a second interview. It reflects well on your organization if, as your board members weed out applicants, the board chairperson sends them a turndown letter. It's tough for a candidate to receive a rejection letter, but even tougher to never hear back at all.

Select Candidates   In the personnel world, people are applicants until they have gone through the first screening; those who pass it become candidates. Candidates are different from applicants because any one of them could be hired. This is a "courtship" stage during which sloppy communications, neglecting to communicate with candidates for weeks at a time,

giving misinformation, or not responding to their questions can lead to losing the person your organization needs. Each serious candidate should receive a packet of information about your organization that includes a summary of benefits, vacation policy, relocation policy, and other relevant information. Add informative literature such as a copy of your organization's newsletter, the annual report, and any marketing material that describes your organization.

Ensure that whoever is in contact with the job candidates treats them with courtesy and care. Candidates are forming an impression of your organization at this time, and communication and interaction are important.

Decide on the Best Candidates   Gather together everyone who interviewed the candidates to select the top candidates. After they have ranked the candidates by preference, it is time to check references. Try to speak to people who have supervised, been peers of, or worked for the person. Describe the key elements of your job. Ask open-ended questions about the candidate's ability to perform the skills you require. Be sure to cover any important areas about which you have doubts or insufficient or ambiguous information.

Select the Top Candidate   Your board is now ready to select the top person for the position. It is time to focus on your information and your instincts about each of the candidates. In some cases the top choice will be clear, but quite often it is not. Even if your board knows which candidate you want, remember that it's never over till it's over. Do not turn loose an acceptable runner-up candidate until you've received a firm acceptance from your first choice. Hiring an employee is a little like getting married. If you suddenly feel that what you are getting is not what you think, it is better to back off than to jump in and live for a long time with the consequences. Follow up quickly on a successful offer. Be sure a sign-up and benefits orientation session is scheduled with the personnel or payroll person. Inform the unsuccessful final candidates.[45]

Important Components of Recruitment   Finding the right person for a position requires objectivity, clarity of thought, application of energy, and steady nerves. A well-written and objective job description that sets forth the basic requirements for the job is essential for legal, ethical, and practical management reasons. Narrowing the field, selecting final interviewees, discussing salary expectations, handling competing offers, checking references, and handling various employment arrangements are important as your board moves toward offering the position to the right person.

SAINT ELIZABETH ANN SETON (1774–1821)

Elizabeth Ann Bayley was born into an Episcopalian family in New York City on August 23, 1774, during the Revolutionary War. When she was 20 years old she married William Seton, a prominent banker and descendent of Lord Seton of England. Elizabeth Ann Seton was a very religious woman. Even though she traveled primarily in social circles, she devoted much of her time to the poor. In 1803 her husband's health began failing. After his death, she became involved in the Roman Catholic Church and became a member.

Having little property, she opened a school in New York City to support herself and her five children, but the venture was unsuccessful. With the encouragement of Catholic Church officials, she and her three daughters moved to Baltimore, where Seton opened a boarding school for girls, the Paca Street School, the first Catholic elementary school in the United States. In 1809, however, she felt the calling to a religious vocation in the Church. Shortly thereafter, she took religious vows and with four others founded the Sisters of Charity, modeled after the Children of Charity founded by St. Vincent De Paul in France. The Sisters of Charity became the first Catholic religious community originating in the United States.

In that same year the sisters founded a school on a farm at Emmittsburg, Maryland, where six other women soon joined them. The sisters suffered much poverty and illness during the winter, but in the spring they received several boarding and day pupils and by June the school was flourishing. In 1814 they established the Orphan Asylum of Philadelphia, the nation's first Catholic child care institution. Seton established more than 20 communities of the Sisters of Charity, and many orphanages, free schools for the poor, boarding schools, and hospitals in the United States. She died in Emmittsburg in 1821. Canonized in 1975, Elizabeth Ann Seton was the first American-born citizen proclaimed a saint by the Roman Catholic Church.

FINANCE THE SOCIAL ORGANIZATION

Three components of financing the social organization are crucial to its success: the budgeting process, the bookkeeping system, and the fundraising process.

The Budgeting Process

When your board has determined the agency's goals, outlined its programs, considered funding sources, and planned the staffing pattern, they are ready to develop the budget.[46] In established agencies the chief administrator ultimately has responsibility for developing the budget, but it is very important to use the skills and experience of staff and board members throughout the process because they must approve the final budget. Begin developing the budget 3 to 6 months before the onset of the new fiscal year, and get it approved by the beginning of the year. The budget should clearly establish what should happen in expenditures and revenues as a result of the agency's service programs. The board or the chief agency administrator first develops an expense budget and then an income budget.

Develop an Expense Budget   Expenditures include all of the costs of purchasing the services, space, and supplies necessary to operate the social agency. Include in your expense budget salaries for each regular, paid staff person, health and life insurance, retirement plans, staff development costs, rent, utilities, telephone, janitorial services, purchased equipment, leased equipment, insurance (fire, automobile, theft, workers compensation, disability, bonding, general liability, and directors and officers liability), loan repayment, supplies, postage, subscriptions, services (consultants, bookkeeper, secretarial), printing, conferences, travel, advertising, licensing, membership fees, and petty cash. Because fledgling organizations will find it more difficult to project future expenses without financial records and past experience, it may be helpful to talk to other administrators and review the budgets of programs similar to yours. An expense budget includes fixed and variable costs.

Fixed Costs   Fixed costs include items such as most salaries, insurance, and rent that occur regardless of the level of activity or service. Fixed costs are easier to determine than variable ones, although your board should try to anticipate changes such as rent increases and salary increases.

Variable Costs   Variable costs such as postage and printing costs change directly with the level of use or activity. Telephone expenses are both fixed and variable. Monthly phone service charges are fixed, but the cost of long-distance calling varies depending on the number of calls you make. Estimate variable costs as best you can. Include seasonal as well as average monthly costs. For instance, postage estimates should include the cost of postage used each month as well as the annual bulk mail permit fee and the cost of the several bulk-mailings that may be planned for the coming year.

Determine the Income Budget

Income includes earned income for which a service must be performed, such as ticket sales and fees for services; and contributed revenues, such as government or foundation grants and contributions from individuals including equipment, other goods, and services that are donated. A social organization rarely has total commitment for funding for an upcoming year at the time it begins budgeting, so it is necessary to estimate as accurately as possible the income your board members can expect from those sources upon which your agency depends for funds. Among the sources of income to include or to generate are fees, contributions from individuals, income from special events, earnings on endowment investments, and anticipated grants.

Fees   Many nonprofits obtain a significant percentage of revenues from fees for services. If your board intends to collect fees, you may be able to help them determine the kind of fees and an appropriate fee structure. Determine direct costs necessary to provide the service, such as staff costs and overhead costs, including rent, supplies, phones, and other costs. Will the agency have a sliding fee schedule based on income? What do other providers charge? Estimate how many participants the agency will serve in each of its programs and calculate the anticipated fee income.

Contributions   Your board members may have pledged to make contributions of a certain amount, or they may have gotten pledges from other individuals, groups, organizations, or businesses. Include in the income budget only amounts for which your organization has a firm pledge.

Special Events, Investments, and Grants   Estimate income your organization expects to generate from special events and benefits. Add expected earnings on endowment investments, if there are any. Estimate all the grants your board anticipates receiving. Ask the grant sources you are most sure of to confirm their interest in the program, and include the amounts of their grants in the income budget.

Next Steps

Calculate the differences between the agency's anticipated income and its expenses. The amount left over is the figure your board members still need to raise. If this figure is a large portion of the budget, your board may have set unrealistically high income goals. You should help them consider either trimming back expenses or rethinking what they will receive from undetermined sources of income. These sources may be individuals, groups, foundations, or corporations your board members have not yet approached or about whom they are not yet sure. Calling on potential funders to share the agency's vision and financial needs before the board makes a formal request from them could help them estimate more objectively the likelihood of obtaining income grants.

Engage staff and board in contingency planning. Help them think through what they will do if revenues do not develop month to month as they have planned or if some unusual expense occurs. Be prepared to outline prioritized spending decreases or increases from initial budget plans, depending on the progress the board makes with their funding sources. Your board can be of significant help in reflecting on the budget and in assisting the administrator and staff with fundraising ideas, with persons to contact, committing themselves to fundraising programs, or making contacts to meet your anticipated budget goals.

Bookkeeping System

All organizations need workable systems for recording what they do with their money, keeping track of where it originates and where it goes. A good bookkeeping system provides the means for documenting, recording, summarizing, and reporting the financial transactions of your organization. It will show where agency revenues came from and where they have been spent, and it will assist your board and administration with budgeting and calculating fundraising needs. It will also help prevent misuses of funds, save money by identifying wasteful spending, and provide information to construct financial statements. Funders, government bodies, clients, and consumer groups will ask for this information, and the organization's board or administrator must have the means of providing it.

When the board sets up its organization, help them do everything possible to commandeer the services of a willing and able accountant to set up the organization's bookkeeping system, teach them or the administrator how to use it, and advise them about the most appropriate type of financial reporting for their organization.

After the board has the books set up with the help of an accountant, they will need a bookkeeper. The agency may be able to depend on the treasurer, who is usually a member of the board, to fulfill this role on an unpaid basis. Medium-size staffed organizations often rely on paid, specially trained secretaries to do the bookkeeping. Larger agencies sometimes hire part-time or full-time bookkeepers. The future of the program may depend on the quality of the financial information generated by your organization.

Obtain Funding

Most people consider obtaining funding to be one of the more difficult aspects of beginning a new program. Joan Flanagan, a skilled fundraiser, asserts that obtaining funding needn't be difficult. She says people can "learn to raise money by doing it; they don't need any particular educational background, economic status, or writing skills. The only thing necessary to be a good fund raiser is the desire or will to raise money."[47]

The board can obtain funding in several ways. They may solicit contributions from interested people or businesses, called independent solicitation. They may use cooperative solicitation or assess membership dues. Members may hold fundraising benefits or other events, charge fees for service, contract for services with local, state, or federal government, or take out a loan. If your board operates on a nonprofit basis, you may apply for a grant. Grants are available from private foundations or from the government. Your board may also contract with the government to provide services.

Independent Solicitation
Your agency's board and administrator can ask a few wealthy individuals, many people of average income, or businesses to contribute to the agency.

Wealthy Individuals There are several advantages to approaching a few wealthy individuals for money. Unlike asking for money from foundations or the government, if board members can sell someone on the agency's program, they obtain funding immediately. They may be able to enlist wealthy individuals in their cause. In addition to money, wealthy individuals may offer services, advice, or provide the board with other funding contacts.

A potential drawback in asking individuals for money, however, is that, at times, money comes with "strings attached." It is one thing if the individual wants only recognition but quite another if the donor wants to dictate policy. Your board members need to decide what they are willing to give up in return for the money.

Persons With Middle Incomes In addition to asking a few wealthy individuals for contributions, the board and administrative staff can also ask many less wealthy persons for money. This often requires a well thought-out campaign. Professional fundraising organizations carry out these campaigns for a percentage of funds raised. Such fundraising can be very sophisticated, with slick brochures, telephone solicitations, and television advertisements.

Businesses and Corporations Other sources of contributions are businesses and corporations. Businesses obtain tax write-offs for making charitable contributions and are sometimes willing to make cash donations to worthy causes, particularly if they can obtain some publicity in return. A business may get behind a worthy project, involving its employees in fundraising efforts and providing donations of material or support services. A grocery store, for example, may donate food, and a building supply company may donate lumber. Many business people, in addition, are willing to serve on committees, give advice, or even donate services of staff to a worthy project.

Cooperative Solicitation So many charitable organizations exist today that people often become overwhelmed with requests for money. As a result, social agencies make fundraising more efficient, effective, and equitable by means of organized, cooperative solicitation agencies such as United Way. Social organizations participating in United Way are released from the burden of spending their own staff time on fundraising and can devote their energy to providing services. More money is raised collectively than if agencies competed with one another.

However, because United Way usually does not fund pilot projects or new, untested programs, they tend to include only a limited number of new programs each year, often those with an established track record. In addition, most United Way organizations have commitments to certain priorities or needs. If your agency does not meet these priorities, you may have difficulty obtaining this funding. Many United Way organizations do not guarantee funding from year to year, nor do they guarantee a given amount of funding. If a program cannot show its effectiveness or is inefficient, its funding may be reduced or eliminated entirely.

Membership Dues   If the board has decided to include members as part of the organization, the dues they provide may become an important part of funding the organization or project. Dues are a source of funds, but they also help develop community commitment and are a gauge of community support.

Source of Funds   Many membership-oriented faith-based organizations, the YMCA, YWCA, Boy Scouts, Girl Scouts, American Association of Retired Persons (AARP), Association for Retarded Citizens, Camp Fire Boys and Girls, and neighborhood associations depend primarily on membership dues and member contributions to support their efforts.

Community Commitment   When community members join and pay membership dues, they "own shares" in the project, have a stake in its outcome, and can assist the community in developing greater commitment to the agency. As the board and staff engage in a membership drive, for example, the members can educate, develop community awareness, and build support for the agency's programs. Members can provide the social organization with a strong source of social and political influence. At the local level, members often join together to press for services and just concerns. Large membership organizations such as AARP and the Association for Retarded Citizens provide advocacy for and with their members and work to influence public policy and legislation. Just as important, members can be a source of unpaid staff in the agency, can assist in serving as members of board committees, and can be a pool of potential board members. They offer a network of goodwill and strength, imbedding the goals and purposes of the social organization in the culture of the community.

Gauge Community Support   You can help the administration and board use membership as a gauge of community support. A demographic assessment of membership lists can tell the staff and board where their primary support and involvement is coming from, where it is weakest or nonexistent, and where they need to improve community relationships. In addition, the board can build community spirit, cooperation, and cohesion by sponsoring regular meetings and social activities with members and unpaid staff.

Fundraising Benefits   Members of a social organization can aid fundraising efforts by organizing benefits. Many organizations depend on fundraisers or benefits. Dinners, entertainment, dances, fairs, cookouts, raffles, auctions, theater productions, walk-a-thons, telethons, car washes, and yard sales are all ways social organizations make money for worthy projects. The Mennonite Central Committee raises most of its budget through an annual auction. The American Cancer Society and the Heart Association sponsor walk-a-thons. Lutheran Social Services sponsors boutiques and dinner dances. The Jerry Lewis Annual Telethon for Muscular Dystrophy is a national event, and the Girl Scouts are known for their annual cookie sales. There are both positive and negative aspects of fundraisers.

Positive Aspects of Fundraisers   A number of side benefits attend fundraisers. The social organization obtains publicity, and you can help staff and members engage in community education about their programs. Even the wider community becomes mobilized and involved in the project. Many times people not connected directly with the organization will help out with a benefit. The benefit is an opportunity for the project staff, membership, and board to provide a service for the community. People who hate meetings will often show up at a benefit where they can meet one another, engage in social activities, and develop relationships.

Negative Aspects   Benefits are time consuming and involve a lot of hard, detailed work. They require skill in organization and often divert staff time to the benefit. There are people, however, who are skilled in these kinds of projects and who enjoy organizing them. If the social organization is lucky enough to have some of these people on its board or as members, they can make a real contribution to the organization.

Fees for Service   Encourage your board to consider charging a fee for the services you provide. Fees are an important source of funding, but they are useful for psychological reasons as well.

Source of Funding   Counseling, family services, and adoption agencies typically charge a fee to help bear the cost of the service. Group work agencies charge fees, as do day care services, alcohol and drug treatment programs, and recovery programs. Often fees are charged on a sliding scale according to a person's ability to pay.

Psychological Benefits   People who pay a fee are more likely to respect the service and take it seriously. If a person is paying a reasonable fee, he or she will not tend to miss sessions and will be more engaged in treatment than if the service is free. If your members pay a fee, they will expect quality service from your organization and will hold the staff accountable. Staff will also feel obligated to offer high level services because their clients are customers who are paying a portion of staff salaries.

Contracting   Rather than operate their own programs, federal, state and local government agencies often contract with nonprofit social organizations to provide services. State and county departments of social services, for example, often contract with independent foster homes, small group homes, institutions, and counseling and other treatment agencies to provide clients with services, as do probation departments for juvenile offenders and departments of mental health for people with emotional disabilities. In California, regional centers for people with developmental disabilities contract with a wide variety of service providers called vendors. Regional centers contract with infant stimulation programs, speech therapists, day programs for adults, workshops, respite care programs, recreational programs, treatment centers, small family homes, group homes, intermediate care facilities, and others. A program that provides a service for a county or state agency must meet county or state licensing requirements, fulfill the specific requirements of the funding agency, and accept the fees that are part of the contract.

Obtaining a Loan   If the social organization intends to purchase property or a building, the board of directors may need to arrange for financing. For many

loans, the board must produce some collateral or proof that the organization has the capacity to repay the loan as well as have a down payment available. If your board includes a banker or real estate agent, or if one of your board members has connections with banking or real estate, you may be able to arrange for a loan at a reasonable rate of interest. Some organizations obtain a donation of land or a building that will serve their purposes.

Private Foundation Grants   Foundations are tax-exempt organizations that exclusively fund social organizations. The Russell Sage Foundation was the first modern foundation. Several thousand foundations exist in a wide variety of forms and with differing funding commitments.

Definition of Foundation   A grant is a one-way transfer of money from a donor to a recipient with no expectation that the donor will receive a benefit from the recipient. It is a free gift with no strings attached. A private foundation is an organization set up as a not-for-profit charitable trust operated by its own board of trustees or directors who manage the trust and provide grants to aid the religious, charitable, scientific, literary, or educational activities of individuals and social organizations. Many wealthy individuals use foundations to reduce their taxable income as well as to fund worthwhile philanthropic purposes. College scholarships, for example, are educational grants to individuals, many of which are administered by a foundation.

First Foundation   Credit for the first modern foundation goes to Margaret Olivia Slocum Sage, who established the Russell Sage Foundation in 1907.[48] The Russell Sage Foundation was of particular importance to the growth and development of the social work profession. In 1917 the Sage Foundation published the pioneering textbook on social casework, *Social Diagnosis,* by Mary Richmond, head of the Charity Organization Department of New York. Sage also published the first 10 volumes of the *Social Work Yearbook* and many important books in social work. The Russell Sage Foundation continues its commitment to social work and social welfare in the 21st century.

Kinds of Foundations   There are a number of kinds of foundations, each of which identifies specific purposes for which its grant money can be used, including general purpose, family, community, corporate, special purpose, social justice and operating foundations.

General purpose foundations have broad areas of interest and are often national in scope. For the most part they have been established by wealthy individuals, many of whom are deceased. They usually carry the name of the founder, such as the Carnegie Foundation, Rockefeller Foundation, Kresge Foundation, Ford Foundation, R. W. Johnson Foundation, W. K. Kellogg Foundation, and Alfred P. Sloan Foundation. General purpose foundations are managed by boards that make funding decisions and employ their own staff who administer the foundation funds. General purpose foundations are usually large and heavily funded, and there is a great deal of competition for funds from these foundations.[49]

Family foundations are controlled by the family members. Because the family members make funding decisions, people who have a personal contact or relationship with a member of the family have the best entree to these funds.

Corporate foundations usually fund organizations that provide some benefit to the company's interests such as community projects where the corporation does business, special interests of employees, or areas of corporate concern. The Crown Zellerbach Foundation in San Francisco provides funding for many local San Francisco social service organizations, for example. Company foundations often offer support by donating equipment and supplies, loaning executives, providing conferences and meeting facilities, and extending in-kind services such as printing and management consulting.

Community foundations, sometimes called a community trust, charitable trust, or community fund, are vehicles for administering a number of separate charitable and combined funds in a given geographic area. Community foundations can be found in most major cities and are often named for the locality, such as the San Francisco Foundation.

Community foundations are public charities supported by the contributions of a large number of individuals who pool their resources for the common good. These foundations may receive large as well as small gifts from people who are charitably inclined but do not have enough money to form their own foundation. Donors can designate the organization they wish to fund, designate a type of service or geographic area, or leave an unrestricted gift. An unrestricted gift gives a community foundation much more leeway in responding to emerging community issues. A community foundation must by law and by

spirit continually attract new donors to maintain its public charity status. Thus it is not unusual to see community foundations advertise for donors.

Macro social workers can assist community members in approaching wealthy and not so wealthy people to develop a community foundation that can enrich and enliven the community, equalize resources, improve neighborhoods, develop scholarship endowments for youth, assist minority businesses, and develop group services or community development corporations.

Special purpose foundations assist programs within a single field or only a few fields of interest. Over the past decade the percentage of special purpose grant dollars has increased steadily. Children and youth continue to be the single largest special beneficiaries of foundation grant dollars.[50] A number of special purpose foundations have evolved within the last decade, however, to serve women, the homeless, and people with AIDS.

Social justice foundations concentrate on social justice and advocacy and have significantly enhanced social reform. The overwhelming majority of social justice foundations are family and special interest foundations concerned with systems of change. The Arca Foundation, for example, supports a wide variety of organizations struggling for social and economic justice. The Compton Foundation has as one of its program priorities social justice, including the provision of adequate social services at the local level, with a particular interest in programs directed at youth. The Emil Schwartzhaupt Foundation was one of the most active and consistent sponsors of community organization projects in many areas of the nation and with numerous organizations from the 1940s through the 1960s.

Operating foundations are dedicated to only one project, organization, or program. An organization may set up its own private foundation, for example, which then solicits money for that organization or program. Many universities and hospitals use operating foundations. Fresno Pacific Foundation, for example, solicits funds and disburses them for scholarships, capital improvements, and other needs of Fresno Pacific University. The Bulldog Foundation supports the football team of California State University, Fresno.

Foundations Today In 1990 foundations awarded more than 12,000 grants to social welfare organizations, representing more than 21% of the giving and constituting the second largest group of recipients following education. Although more than 24,000 grant-making foundations exist today, they generally do not fund minority-controlled social services in any significant way, although they do fund a number of programs that serve people of color. This is an area in which the social work profession as a whole could provide significant advocacy.

A trend in foundation giving is funding collaborations, or partnerships between various foundations. For example, community-based organizations, businesses, universities, and public schools may establish a collaborative foundation to help low-income students gain access to college. The Pew Charitable Trusts, John D. and Catherine T. MacArthur Foundation, and the Rockefeller Foundation joined to establish the Energy Foundation. The Ford Foundation established a national initiative in 1989 that allocates funds to community foundations to assess the demographic changes occurring in areas that the community foundations serve to determine how the change may affect their programs. Today funders often work together to donate to a particular agency project, with each funder giving a specific amount to meet the budgetary need.[51]

Government Grants

Government organizations or agencies often have funds available for pilot projects, startup grants, research grants, or ongoing funding grants. Sometimes government agencies want to experiment with new and innovative approaches and will ask for proposals for such projects. Local communities have input on the specific needs and can better allocate funds and provide services.

Government agencies fund many social organizations by contracting or by means of grants. The National Institutes for Mental Health (NIMH) provides funding for pilot projects in the field of mental health. The Area Agency on Aging receives federal money to distribute to local agencies for provision of services to the elderly. Department of Housing and Urban Development (HUD), through its HOME program and empowerment zones, provides grants to community development corporations as does the Department of Agriculture.

Approaches to Grant Seeking

Your chief administrator or board must decide what approach to take and select a funding source. If the board decides to seek a private foundation grant, it must submit an idea statement. If your organization is seeking a government grant, the board must respond to a request for proposal (RFP).

Decide on an Approach and Select a Funding Source
Two different approaches to obtaining grant money are the reactive approach and proactive approach. If you wait until grant announcements come to you and then apply, you are using a reactive approach. This approach is most common with government grants. Using the proactive approach means actively searching for potential funding sources. Many boards use both reactive and proactive approaches when seeking grants.

Find a foundation or governmental grant that supports the mission of your organization's program. A number of sources of information can help you choose the right foundation. Two key sources are the Foundation Center and the Federal Register.

The Foundation Center is a national organization established by foundations to provide a single authoritative source of information on foundation and corporate giving. It provides annually updated directories and guides and other publications covering grants and nonprofit funding. A bibliography of foundation resources is found in the Additional Readings section at the end of this chapter.

The Federal Register is a daily publication that provides information on federal government legislation and guidelines for new and revised grants. If you are interested in a particular kind of government funding, you can ask the chief administrator to become a member of the government agency's mailing list or review the *Federal Register* at your public library. You can also obtain the *Catalog of Federal Domestic Assistance,* which provides basic information on federal resources, including a profile of each program, eligibility, deadlines, funding levels, and telephone numbers of places to contact.

Idea Statements When the board or staff apply for funding to a private foundation, they must write an idea statement. An idea statement gets the organization in the door of the foundation. An idea statement is two to four pages long and tells the foundation what the agency's board and staff want to do, how they intend to do it, and how much it will cost.

An idea statement usually has the following components: a *summary* or abstract of the entire proposal, an *introduction* to the idea statement, a need or *problem statement*, the *goals* of the project, and project *objectives* (if they are different from goals). Additional information includes the method by which the agency will accomplish its goals, how the chief administrative officer will evaluate the program, and a budget summary.

Make sure that the idea statement is neatly typed and is in the best writing style the organization's staff can muster. Send it with a cover letter to the foundation your board has chosen. If the foundation is interested, they will request a meeting, ask for further information, or ask for a full grant proposal.

Request for Proposals   Government agencies have a standardized application process called request for proposals (RFP). An RFP is an invitation for organizations to provide a proposal on a specific project. They are usually distributed to social organizations, professional organizations, and state or county agencies responsible for administering grants at the local level. RFPs are routinely announced in the *Federal Register* and sometimes in newspapers or newsletters.

The Association of Community Organization and Social Administration (ACOSA), the major macro social work professional association, often forwards RFPs to its members. If your organization is interested in applying for a government grant, it should respond to the RFP announcement and obtain the application forms and other information.

There may be a meeting for all applicants at which grant administrators provide specific information, distribute forms, and answer questions. Often, only applicants who attend the information session are permitted to apply for the grant.

Writing a Grant Proposal   If the idea statement is appealing to a foundation, its staff will invite your board to submit a formal proposal. Usually foundations supply an outline of the kinds of information they require that you can use as a guide to write the proposal. One of the most important components of a proposal is the budget, which provides the foundation with an indication of the board's planning and management skills. The funds the program requires must be projected clearly so that the organization's needs can be understood and accepted by potential funders.

Government agencies often choose the proposal that offers the best program ideas at the least cost. Several sources on the techniques of writing grant proposals are listed in the Additional Reading section at the end of the chapter.

Carrying Out the Project   Once your agency receives a grant, the staff must keep records and statistics on services provided, clientele, staff service hours, and other items. As the staff monitors the program's effectiveness, the board will be able to pinpoint what areas it needs to improve, where it needs to grow, and areas where it is functioning well. This information is invaluable in convincing funding agencies, foundations, constituents, members, and others who support your organization that their money has been well spent and that the program deserves continued funding.

Agencies unable to show they are effective in carrying out their goals and that cannot account for meeting needs or making an impact in the arena of their service provision cannot expect to receive ongoing support. At the end of the project period, the board will need to evaluate the overall project and report the results to the foundation or the government agency that has funded it.

A Caveat   It is sometimes difficult to secure a foundation or government grant. There are always more applicants than grant awards. For instance, according to the *Annual Register of Grant Support,* in 1993 the Ford Foundation received 30,000 proposals but funded only about 2,000 of them. The Barbara Bush Foundation for Family Literacy typically receives 600 to 700 applications annually but funds only 10 to 20 projects each year.[52] Researching and writing grant applications take skill and sometimes a great deal of work. However, if you are persistent and choose your source carefully, you can be successful.

RECRUIT CLIENTS

When board or staff whom you are assisting recruit clients, they should seek referrals from other agencies, network with organizations, and sponsor an open house.

Obtain Referrals

The best source of clientele for your social organization or its programs are referrals from other agencies in your area. Most social agencies welcome having additional resources and are interested in knowing more about your agency's services.

Networking

Assist the staff and board in getting the word out about the new program by networking. There is nothing like face-to-face contact to spread the word about a new social program. Have the agency join the local council of social agencies or other social services networks in your area. Encourage social worker staff to attend NASW meetings, go to workshops and training programs where other professionals will be present, and visit agencies that will be the most likely referral sources.

When your board members or staff network or visit, make sure they carry flyers or brochures and hand them out to people as they explain the new program. The agency's brochures should be clear and specific about its services, the kinds of clients it accepts, fees, and geographic boundaries or other service limitations. Television and radio spots are also helpful and often can be obtained free in the form of community service announcements.

Sponsor an Open House

Have an open house to announce the opening of the program to community leaders, community agencies, and referral sources. This can be a gala affair with refreshments, a short presentation, and introductions of board members and those who have been instrumental in getting the program established. Make sure that the staff and board members maintain positive relationships with all the members of the community and that everyone understands the services they are providing.

CONCLUSION

A macro social work program developer helps the community form a program development team, engages them in performing a needs assessment, assists them in establishing the corporation, helps recruit and train the board, and then works with the board to develop the organization. As a program developer, you help the board develop a statement of the organization's mission, vision, values, and goals. You also assist with deciding on an organizational structure and recruiting the staff of the organization.

You help board members set up the budget and accounting procedures, obtain funding, and find clients for the services of the organization. You and your program development group and the board of directors may feel proud that the lengthy process that began with a needs assessment has resulted in the development of a new social organization to help the members of your community.

KEY CONCEPTS

Clara Barton
Benjamin Franklin
Samuel Gridley Howe
Dorothea Dix
institutions
Association for Improving the Condition of the Poor (AICP)
Jewish Center movement
George Williams
Charles Loring Brace
Thadeus Stevens
Freedman's Bureau
Stanton Coit
Steven Humphries Gurteen
Canon Samuel Barnett
St. Francis Xavier Cabrini
needs assessment
normative needs
demand needs
social indicators
rates under treatment
key actor
focused interviews
community forum
focus groups
community surveys
board of directors
for-profit organization
not-for-profit organization
incorporation
Jane Porter Bennett
tax exemption
articles of incorporation
constitution

by-laws
board of directors
committee structure
standing committee
ad hoc committee
Roberts Rules of Order
parliamentary procedure
obtain floor
motion
second the motion
stating the question
putting the question
privileged motions
mission statement
vision statement
values statement
goals statement
whole group structure
team structure
modified hierarchical structure
fair employment practices
prohibited information
statement of nondiscrimination
Americans With Disabilities Act (ADA)
applicant register
salary range
job description
applicant
candidate
St. Elizabeth Ann Seton
budgeting process
expense budget
fixed costs
variable costs
income budget

accounting system

independent solicitation

cooperative solicitation

membership dues

fundraising benefits

fees for service

contracting

loans

private foundation

operating foundation

community foundation

general purpose foundation

family foundation

corporate foundation

special interest foundation

social justice foundation

collaborative funding

government grant

idea statement

request for proposal (RFP)

grant proposal

reactive approach

proactive approach

Foundation Center

Federal Register

recruiting clients

referral

networking

open house

QUESTIONS FOR DISCUSSION

1. What changes in purpose, structure, and roles do you think may be required of a community planning group as it shifts to developing a community program?

2. You are thinking of setting up a small group home for persons who have emotional disabilities. Discuss the benefits and disadvantages of being a profit-making organization versus a not-for-profit organization and make a decision about which is best for your program.

3. Social agencies, businesses, as well as your college or university more than likely have articles of incorporation, constitutions, by-laws, and mission statements. Collect as many of these as you can. Compare the mission statements. What are their common characteristics? What do they tell you about an organization? Do they leave out anything you think is important? How could you improve them?

4. Compare the articles of incorporation, by-laws, and constitutions that you have collected. What are the similarities and differences?

5. Obtain an organizational chart from your college or university. Examine the staffing patterns. Is the organization hierarchically structured? How many

organizational layers are there? Does it have a flat structure in which decision making is dispersed, or is it a thin vertical structure in which decision making is concentrated at the top? Would you characterize the organization as simple or complex? Would you recommend any of these structures for a social organization?

ADDITIONAL READING

Theory

Clark, Margaret S., ed. *Prosocial Behavior*. London: Sage, 1991.

Coles, Robert. *The Call of Service: A Witness to Idealism.* New York: Houghton Mifflin, 1993.

Etzioni, Amitai. *The Spirit of Community: Rights, Responsibilities and the Communitarian Agenda*. New York: Crown, 1993.

Lohmann, Roger A. *The Commons: New Perspectives on Nonprofit Organizations and Voluntary Action*, San Francisco: Jossey-Bass, 1992.

Margolis, Howard. *Selfishness, Altruism & Rationality: A Theory of Social Change*, Chicago: University of Chicago Press, 1982.

History

Addams, Jane. *Twenty Years at Hull House.* New York: Macmillan, 1910.

Addams, Jane. *The Second Twenty Years at Hull House.* New York: Macmillan, 1930.

Bremner, Robert H. *American Philanthropy*. Chicago: University of Chicago Press, 1988.

Bremner, Robert H. *Giving: Charity and Philanthropy in History*. New Brunswick: Transaction Publishers, 1994.

Davis, F. A. *Spearheads for Reform: The Social Settlements and the Progressive Movement: 1890–1914*. New York: Oxford University Press, 1967.

Walter, Trattner I. *From Poor Law to Welfare State: A History of Social Welfare in America*. New York: Free Press, 1984.

Basic Philanthropy

Bremner, Robert H. *American Philanthropy*, Chicago: University of Chicago Press, 1988.

Dwight Burlingame, F. and Dennis R. Young, eds. *Corporate Philanthropy at the Crossroads*. Bloomington: Indiana University Press, 1996.

Carnegie, Andrew. *The Gospel of Wealth*. Indianapolis: Indiana University Center on Philanthropy, 1993. (Originally published in 1889)

DeToqueville, Alexis. *Democracy in America*. New York: Harper & Row, 1966.

Martin, Mike W. *Virtuous Giving: Philanthropy, Voluntary Service, and Caring*. Bloomington: Indiana University Press, 1994.

McCarthy, Kathleen, ed. *Lady Bountiful Revisited: Women, Philanthropy, and Power*. London: Rutgers University Press, 1990.

Mollat, Michel. *The Poor in the Middle Ages: An essay in Social History*. New Haven: Yale University Press, 1986.

Monroe, Kristen Renwick. *Heart of Altruism: Perceptions of a Common Humanity*. Princeton: Princeton University Press, 1996.

Payton, Robert L. *Philanthropy: Voluntary Action for the Public Good*. Oryx Press, 1988.

Sealander, Judith. *Private Wealth and Public Life: Foundation Philanthropy and the Reshaping of American Social Policy From the Progressive Era to the New Deal*. Baltimore: Johns Hopkins University Press, 1997.

Wolpert, Julian. *Patterns of Generosity in America: Who's Holding the Safety Net?* New York: Twentieth Century Fund Press, 1993.

Wuthnow, Robert. *Acts of Compassion: Caring for Others and Helping Ourselves*. New Jersey: Princeton University Press, 1991.

Wright, Conrad Edick. *The Transformation of Charity in Postrevolutionary New England*. Boston: Northeastern University Press, 1992.

Fundraising and Giving

Anderson, Albert. *Ethics for Fundraisers*. Bloomington: Indiana University Press, 1996.

Bremner, Robert H. *Giving: Charity and Philanthropy in History*. New Brunswick: Transaction Publishers, 1994.

Burlingame, Dwight F., ed. *Critical Issues in Fund Raising*. New York: John Wiley & Sons, 1997.

Burlingame, Dwight F., ed. *The Responsibilities of Wealth*. Bloomington: Indiana University Press, 1992.

Burlingame, Dwight F. and Lamont J. Hulse, *Taking Fund Raising Seriously: Advancing the Profession and Practice of Raising Money*. San Francisco: Jossey-Bass, 1991.

Cutlip, Scott M. *Fund Raising in the United States: Its Role in America's Philanthropy*. New Brunswick: Transaction Publishers, 1990.

Duronio, Margaret A. and Eugene R. Tempel, *Fund Raisers: Their Careers, Stories, Concerns, and Accomplishments*, San Francisco: Jossey-Bass, 1997.

Kelly, Kathleen S. *Effective Fund-Raising Management*. New Jersey: Lawrence Erlbaum, 1998.

Martin, Mike W. *Virtuous Giving: Philanthropy, Voluntary Service, and Caring*. Bloomington: Indiana University Press, 1994.

Rosenberg, Claude, Jr. *Wealthy and Wise: How You and America Can Get the Most Out of Your Giving*. New York: Little, Brown, 1994.

Rosso, Henry A. et al., *Achieving Excellence in Fund-raising*. San Francisco: Jossey-Bass, 1991.

Wheatley, Steven C. *The Politics of Philanthropy: Abraham Flexner and Medical Education*. Madison, WI: University of Wisconsin Press, 1988.

Getting Started

Flanagan, Joan. *The Successful Volunteer Organization: Getting Started, and Getting Results in Nonprofit, Charities, Grassroots, and Community Groups*. Chicago: Contemporary Books, 1984.

Heskett, James L., W. Earl Sasser Jr., and Christopher W. L. Hart. *Service Breakthroughs: Changing the Rules of the Game*. New York: Freedom Press, 1990.

Crane, Jonathan D., ed., *Social Programs That Work*. New York: Russell Sage Foundation, 1998.

Working With Boards and Staff

Powers, Bradford Leland. *Making Meetings Work: A Guide for Leaders and Group Members*. San Diego, CA: Pfeiffer, 1976.

Carver, John. *Boards That Make a Difference*. San Francisco: Jossey-Bass, 1990.

Carver, John and Miriam Mayhew Carver, *Reinventing Your Board: A Step-by-Step Guide to Implementing Policy Governance*. San Francisco: Jossey-Bass, 1997.

Conrad, W. R. and W. E. Glen, *The Effective Voluntary Board of Directors*. Athens, OH: Swallow Press, 1983.

Duca, Diane J., *Nonprofit Boards: A Practical Guide to Roles, Responsibilities, and Performance*. Phoenix, AZ: Oryx Press, 1986.

Devney, Darcy Campion, *Organizing Special Events and Conferences: A Practical Guide for Busy Volunteers and Staff*. Sarasota, FL: Pineapple Press, 1990.

Emenhiser, David, *Power Funding: Gaining Access to Power, Influence, and Money in Your Community*. Rockford, MD: Fundraising Institute, 1992.

Greenleaf, Robert, *Trustees as Servants*. Peterborough, NC: Windy Row Press, 1973.

Lawson, John D., *When You Preside*, 5th ed. Danville, IL: Interstate, 1980.

Houle, Cyril O., *Governing Boards*. San Francisco: Jossey-Bass, 1990.

Whetten, Mary Bray, ed., *The Basic Meeting Manual: For Officers and Members of Any Organization*. Nashville, TN: Thomas Nelson, 1986.

Young, Dennis R. and Richard Steinberg, *Economics for Nonprofit Managers*. New York: The Foundation Center, 1995.

Management, Leadership, and Economics

Clotfelter, Charles T., ed., *Who Benefits From the Nonprofit Sector?* Chicago: University of Chicago Press, 1992.

Hamack, David D. and Dennis R. Young, eds., *Nonprofit Organizations in a Market Economy: Understanding New Roles, Issues, and Trends*. San Francisco: Jossey-Bass, 1993.

Herman, Robert D. and Richard D. Heimovics, *Executive Leadership in Nonprofit Organizations: New Strategies for Shaping Executive-Board Dynamics*. San Francisco: Jossey-Bass, 1991.

Hermann, Robert D. et al., *The Jossey-Bass Handbook of Nonprofit Leadership and Management*. San Francisco: Jossey-Bass, 1994.

Houle, Cyril O., *Governing Boards*. San Francisco: Jossey-Bass, 1990.

Foundation Fundraising Resources

Andrews, F. E., *Philanthropic Foundations*. New York: Russell Sage Foundation, 1998.

Foundation and Grant Information

The Foundation Center publishes grants directories, grants indexes, guidebooks, monographs, and bibliographies and offers a wide variety of services and information to grant seekers. The center has regional centers in New York, Washington, D.C., Atlanta, Cleveland, and San Francisco and cooperates with public libraries nationally to house its materials. The following are publications of the Foundation Center, 79 Fifth Avenue, New York, NY, 10003. Each of these sources is updated and published annually.

> *The Foundation Directory* provides information on finances, governance, and giving information. It contains profiles of the largest U.S. foundations—those that have at least $2 million in assets and disperse

$200,000. Includes information on 28,000 selected grants.

The Foundation Directory, Part 2: A Guide to Grant Programs $50,000 to $200,000. Data on more than 4,200 midsized foundations, including more than 28,000 recently awarded foundation grants.

Foundation Grants Index Annual. An index of grant subject areas within which grant descriptions are listed geographically by state and alphabetically by foundation.

The Foundation 1000. Information on the thousand largest U.S. foundations responsible for 60% of all foundation grant dollars. Foundation 1000 grant makers hold more than $100 billion in assets and award $6 billion in more than 190,000 grants to nonprofit organizations annually.

National Directory of Corporate Giving. Information on corporate foundations.

National Guide to Funding for Children, Youth and Families. Information on foundations and corporate direct-giving programs.

National Guide to Funding for the Economically Disadvantaged. Information on foundations for employment programs, homeless shelters, welfare initiatives, and others.

Foundation Fundamentals: A Guide for Grant Seekers is an exceptionally useful book for people who are new to grant seeking.

The National Network of Grantmakers is an association of individual grant makers committed to social and economic justice with a strong focus on advice. Members often describe their foundations as promoters of social change and as supporters of new approaches. The National Network publishes *The Grant Seekers Guide: Founding Sourcebook,* which identifies foundations with assets of $1 million or more that address social and economic justice issues. The guide is designed for smaller grassroots community-based organizations.

The Council on Foundations, a national organization to which foundations belong, publishes *Foundation News,* which can be helpful to grant seekers who might have an interest in the latest concerns in the foundation world.

The Independent Sector is the primary support organization of nonprofit social organizations. Composed of more than 800 organizations, its mission is to create a national forum capable of encouraging giving and volunteering. Because its membership has a significant number of foundations, social welfare organizations that belong have an opportunity to interact with other foundations and can help keep foundations current on issues and concerns. The Independent Sector publishes the *Non-Profit Almanac* and *Dimensions of the Independent Sector,* which can serve as important reference tools.

Government Funding Sources

Superintendent of Documents. *Catalog of Federal Domestic Assistance*. U.S. Government Printing Office, Mailstop SSOP, Washington, DC 20402-9328.

Federal Register and *Federal Register Index*. Superintendent of Documents, P.O. Box 371954, Pittsburgh, PA, 15250-7954.

Contracting

Alson, F. M. et al., *Contracting With the Federal Government*. New York: Wiley, 1984.

Writing Grants and Proposals

Bauer, D. G., *The "How-to" Grants Manual*. New York: Macmillan, 1984.

Foundation Center, *The Foundation Center's Guide to Proposal Writing*. New York: Foundation Center, 1994.

Hall, Mary. *Getting Funded: A Complete Guide to Proposal Writing*, 3d ed. Portland, OR: Continuing Education Publications, Portland State University, 1988.

Read, Patricia, *Foundation Fundamentals: A Guide for Grantseekers*, 5th ed. New York: Foundation Center, 1994.

White, Virginia, *Grant Proposals That Succeeded*. New York: Plenum Press, 1984.

Shellow, J. R. and N. C. Stella, eds., *The Grant Seekers Guide,* 3d ed. Mt. Kisko, NY: Moyer Bell Limited, n.d.

Grassroots Fundraising Resources

Flanagan, Joan, *The Grassroots Fundraising Book*. Chicago, IL: Contemporary Books, 1992.

Flanagan, Joan, *Successful Fundraising: A Complete Handbook for Volunteers and Professionals*. Chicago: Contemporary Books, 1991.

Klein, Kim, *Fundraising for Social Change*. Berkeley, CA: Chardon Press, 1985.

Journals

Chronicle of Philanthropy, a national newspaper published twice a month.

Grassroots Fundraising Journal, P.O. Box 11607, Berkeley, CA 94701.

11

The Practice of Social Work Administration

Management and Workers

We have grown up with the belief that control, consistency, and predictability are essential. We have separated managing the work from doing the work. We have created a class system inside our institutions. There is a management class and an employee or worker class. The management class enjoys privileges and prerogatives and is taught management skills. The worker class has fewer privileges and prerogatives and is taught operational or basic skills. The fundamental beliefs we have about how to run organizations and organize work aren't working.[1]

Peter Block

Ideas in This Chapter

© CORBIS

Harry Hopkins, public social work administrator, was one of the most dedicated heroes of World War II. He had conviction without limit and was without a doubt one of the great humanitarians of our time.

HARRY HOPKINS, SOCIAL WORK ADMINISTRATOR

He wrote no books and gave few speeches. He never earned a large salary, and when he died he was nearly penniless. Rarely in good health, he was in pain much of his life. He was never elected to public office, and he did not earn advanced degrees. Throughout much of his career politicians vilified him in the press, and yet during the 13 years that Harry Lloyd Hopkins remained in public service, he was recognized as the second most powerful man in America and had a profound impact on every major crisis from the international economic collapse to the dawn of the atomic age.

Within 5 years of coming to Washington, Hopkins spent more money and employed more people than any other person in history. He directed programs that helped mobilize the nation for one of the greatest confrontations of the century and with that productivity paved the way for the defeat of the Axis powers during World War II. Emissary to two presidents, he forged the great alliance between the United States, Russia, and Great Britain that helped win the war and set the course for the postwar era.

Harry Hopkins, public social work administrator, was born in 1890. In all his endeavors, his mother impressed upon Harry, "You were put on earth to serve others. Don't be afraid to take risks. What counts is not words but actions."[2] Hopkins attended Grinnell College, where he majored in the new field of political science, and was president of the senior class of 1912. An extrovert with acute powers of calculation, he had the ability to learn with speed and accuracy, his most remarkable attribute in later years.

Hopkins had not made up his mind about a future career when he graduated, but he was offered a summer job at a camp for poor children in New Jersey, an experience that was to change his life forever. After 2 months at the camp, he was a zealous champion of the underprivileged. Hopkins became a social worker at the Christadora House on New York's Lower East Side for room and board and $5 a month pocket money. The wrenching poverty and squalor of the city slums were to Hopkins alien and shocking. It was something he never forgot. During his first winter in

New York, he asked for a job with the Association for Improving the Condition of the Poor (AICP) and was put on the payroll at $40 a month on a training basis. During the day he worked for Christadora House, and at night went out on assignments for the AICP. Within 2 years this zealous social worker became the executive secretary of the New York City Board of Child Welfare.

He joined the Red Cross during World War I as director of the Gulf Division in New Orleans, and eventually he was overseeing all Red Cross activities in the southeastern United States. After the war, Hopkins accepted a position as director of the Health Division of the AICP. He was charged with providing research into the health conditions of New York City. From there he became administrator of the New York Tuberculosis Association.

In 1928 Franklin Roosevelt was elected Governor of New York. After the crash of 1929, Roosevelt established the Temporary Emergency Relief Administration (TERA) and offered the position of deputy to Hopkins. TERA was the largest and most daring program for the relief of unemployment that had ever been undertaken by any state. Within a year he was appointed chair, and by 1932 had given out $30 million in aid and helped more than a million destitute people.

Shortly after Roosevelt was elected president of the United States, he invited Hopkins to head the Federal Emergency Relief Administration (FERA), which meant a reduction in pay for Hopkins from $15,000 to $8,000. Roosevelt wrote of Hopkins, "Action had to be immediate." It was immediate. In his first 2 hours in office, Hopkins disbursed more than $5 million in aid to the states. But more than simply providing relief, Hopkins and Roosevelt were engineering a revolutionary change in the relationship between the American government and its citizens. Three-and-a half weeks after he had entered federal service, Hopkins spoke at the National Conference of Social Work and announced the principle that relief was an obligation of government, breaking with the tradition of nongovernmental intervention that had been in place for the preceding 70 years.

At the end of his first year, Hopkins had helped in solving the vital problems of some 17 million people and spent $1.5 billion in aid with an organization consisting of only 121 people and a payroll of only $22,000 per month. Hopkins believed in jobs, not welfare. He put together a program for putting people to work on government subsidized projects for the Civil Works Administration (CWA), one of the broadest programs ever instituted by the U.S. government, and none too soon. By 1933, 42,000 businesses had failed and 25% of the entire workforce was unemployed. The country was near revolution. Nazism and Communism were barking at the door.

"Get the money out fast, and get it out honestly," was Roosevelt's charge, and Hopkins did it with incredible zeal and at a terrific pace, putting 4 million people to work in the first 30 days of CWA's existence. In three and a half months the CWA inaugurated 180,000 work projects. It built or improved 40,000 schools, laid 120,000 feet of sewer pipe, built 469 airports and improved 529 more, built 255,000 miles of road, employed 50,000 teachers, and built 3,700 playgrounds.

Among the 4.26 million people for whom work was found, 3,000 were writers and artists, the inception of the Federal Arts Program. While compassion drove Hopkins onward, his genius for problem solving drove him upward. Administration, for Harry Hopkins, was not simply putting a policy into motion. It was deciding to do something, seeing it work, seeking new opportunities, and being willing to live in a stream of events that couldn't be predicted.

With the passage of the Work Relief Bill in 1934, Hopkins was put in charge of the Works Progress Administration (WPA). Told by Roosevelt, "Do something and do it quickly, and don't come back with problems," Hopkins was eventually to spend more than $10 billion creating jobs, mobilizing more people than the army and navy combined during World War I. By 1935 he had found jobs for over 18 million workers and reported to Roosevelt, "Well, they're all at work, just don't ask me what the hell they're doing."[3] Hopkins organized medical care, housing, education, school hot lunch programs, adult literacy programs, day care centers, rehabilitation for families, employment programs, and direct relief. The federal government became involved in almost every sector of American life.

In 1939, at the end of his second term, Roosevelt began grooming Hopkins as a presidential candidate and appointed him secretary of commerce to give him a less controversial role with more status. Hopkins developed a mysterious ailment, however, that prevented his body from absorbing nutrition. Fed intravenously and subsisting on vitamins and blood transfusions, he survived but became a semi-invalid.

Gaunt and worn after his years of 18-hour days and constant pressure, Hopkins resigned from the cabinet and left public service. Having no position, title, or salary, he was invited by his old friend Roosevelt to live as a guest in the White House.

Yet events would draw Hopkins back to even more important service to his country. When Winston Churchill became Prime Minister in May 1940, Britain was financially bankrupt and threatened with imminent destruction by Hitler's aerial attacks. Roosevelt sent Hopkins as his personal envoy to Churchill, who found in Hopkins a staunch ally. Against the cries of those who advocated U.S. neutrality, Hopkins urged that America support Britain, arguing for a "Lend-Lease" program to arm the allies. Hopkins was put in charge.

Working from a card table in his bedroom at the White House, he began the most massive undertaking this nation has ever known. With $7 billion to spend, Hopkins developed a program that exceeded the war production of Germany, Italy, and Japan combined. Because of Hopkins, when Japan attacked Pearl Harbor, bringing America into the war, American war production was near full capacity, arming and supplying not only American soldiers but the Allied forces as well.

Harry Hopkins, public social work administrator, the personal envoy of two presidents, empowered by the time he died to spend $9 billion for the relief of others and billions more in Lend Lease, who guided America out of the Great Depression, and whose foresight forged the Great Alliance, was one of the most dedicated heroes of World War II. Public service was his creed, his life, and his legacy. He had conviction without limit and was without a doubt one of the great humanitarians of our time.

WHAT YOU WILL LEARN IN THIS CHAPTER

Most social workers will have an opportunity to work in social organizations and experience the importance of administration in carrying out social work. In this chapter you will learn the differences between management and social administration. You will explore a short history of organizational laws with which administrators should be familiar. You will learn about tasks that social administrators carry out including supervision, decision making, budgeting, and personnel administration. You will learn about the role of the chief social work administrator in providing service, planning, working with the board, and program evaluation.

BUSINESS MANAGEMENT AND SOCIAL ADMINISTRATION

There is a fundamental difference between business management by which employees in corporations are directed and social administration. Management is a term that applies exclusively to private sector organizations. Managers are chosen because they can get results, exerting both unobtrusive and overt control to obtain employee compliance. Social administration is aimed at service and is staffed by social workers who use social organizations to improve the social welfare of individuals, groups, communities, and our national and global societies as well.

Business Management

Business management is the process by which owners of corporate organizations induce employees to exchange their talent, time, and energy for rewards including money, status, stability, and the opportunity to increase those benefits over time. Command-oriented hierarchical business is almost uniformly based on the idea that power, along with the capacity to dispense favors, resides at the top of an organization and imposes governance "which can best control costs, deliver quality, adapt quickly to customers, shorten the time cycle, and keep employees driving toward their markets."[4]

Who Are Managers?   Business corporations choose persons for managerial roles who seem most capable of using informational, economic, and material resources, including its human components, to reach its goals effectively. Managers are desperate to win the competitive race by having their companies succeed, and they are burdened with the continual task of squeezing more productivity out of their employees. Because human beings tend to "track all kinds of mud from the rest of their lives with them into the organization and have all kinds of interests that are independent of the organization,"[5] managers must often expend a great deal of effort to shape the behavior of employees so they operate smoothly and produce results. For this reason the process of utilizing the human resources of functional, economizing organizations is correctly called management.

Control Orientation

Corporate organizations are mechanisms of social control, and management is the means by which control is carried out. Some control is unobtrusive, built into the organizational system itself. Other forms of managerial control are more overt.

Unobtrusive Control   Management uses many unobtrusive controls to ensure that employees accept the premises of organizational decisions and behave according to them. Management exacts conformity by such mechanisms as chain of command, standard procedures, the hierarchical ordering of power relationships, and by training and indoctrination of its functionaries. Management shapes what gets communicated to whom, develops the organization's own internal language, and channels decision making.[6]

Among the most important control mechanism is authority. Authority is the power of the manager to impose decisions on employees that guide their behavior. If a person accepts an offer to work for a firm, that person also accept the manager's authority to tell the employee what, how, and when to perform his or her duties. The manager socializes the individual to the norms and culture of the organization.[7] "The superior frames and transmits decisions with the expectation that they will be accepted by the subordinate. The subordinate expects such decisions, and his conduct is determined by them."[8]

Overt Control   In addition to unobtrusive controls, managers use overt methods to induce employees to perform tasks that are sometimes boring, physically demanding, distasteful, and even dangerous. Managers motivate workers by offering positive rewards, dispensing opportunities for advancement, money, status, and other benefits. Managers use personal influence ranging from suggestion and persuasion to commanding compliance. They use negative reinforcements such as setting limits, giving warnings, using threats, coercion, and exacting punishment.[9] Paulo Freire asserts that when a manager imposes a foreclosed decision onto another and prescribes behavior to reinforce that decision, the manager participates in the dehumanization and becomes guilty of oppression.[10]

Management as a form of control may be appropriate in command structures of privately owned business firms, threat systems such as the military and police where compliance is vital, and in systems requiring speed, precision, and effective operating procedures such as emergency medical services. Inducing people to become machinery for productivity, defense, or saving lives may be acceptable in these restricted arenas so long as those who accept those roles do so with full information and consciously accept the consequences of living a functional existence. When management is presumed to be authentic leadership or a means by which people achieve access to a meaningful direction in life, management exceeds its boundaries, leads us astray, and becomes deceitful.

Social Administration

The word *administer* comes from the Latin *ad ministrare,* meaning "minister to" or "to serve." The role of a social administrator is to provide social leadership in the process of building a collaborative social organization that focuses on delivering social services and developing social programs in service to the community. Social work administrators provide assistance to members of the board, employees, and less directly to clients and members of the community by means of a nonprofit social organization.

Who Are Social Administrators?

A social administrator is an experienced generalist-based social worker rather than a narrow managerial specialist. The administrator sees the social organization as a system with responsibility to the individuals who comprise it, to the groups who help it function, to the community of which it is a part, and to the national and international social environment. Social administrators use social leadership to help others develop their own social leadership skills.

Responsibility to Individuals, Groups, and Community
A social administrator is committed to use his or her agency's assets, services, and resources from a generalist perspective to create a psychologically healthy social environment for employees and is committed to assisting individual clients as human beings to achieve their goals and the purposes for which they exist. Administrators understand how to work with a variety of task groups to assist the organization in devising agency policies, procedures, plans, and

activities to provide quality services that are useful and needed. Social administrators are sensitive to the needs of the larger community in which the social organization is located, centers the social agency in the community as a good neighbor, and uses its resources to contribute to the community.

Improve National and International Society Social work administrators are committed to improving society as a whole by aligning the culture of the social organization to provide social goods and promote the general social welfare. Social administrators are guided by social work values and ethics to work toward social justice and end oppression, discrimination, inequity, and violence. Social work administrators align themselves and their social organizations in solidarity with disempowered people everywhere, especially those in underdeveloped nations.

Social Leadership Social administration seeks liberation not control, affirms authenticity not dehumanization, prizes personal encounters rather than impersonal human relations, and seeks to make the social agency a place where people make their own choices and exert leadership for the common good.

A BRIEF HISTORY OF ADMINISTRATIVE LAW

Today all administrative organizations are mandated to adhere to a number of laws that guide the behavior of individuals and organizations. Every macro social worker should become familiar with the Equal Pay Act of 1963, portions of the Civil Rights Act of 1964, Age Discrimination Act of 1975, the employee privacy issues in *O'Conner v. Ortega* (1987), and the Americans With Disabilities Act of 1989.

Equal Pay Act of 1963

The Equal Pay Act of 1963 ensured the principle of "equal pay for equal work." Men and women working in the same establishment under similar conditions must receive the same pay if their jobs require equal or similar skills.

Civil Rights Act of 1964

The Civil Rights Act of 1964 outlawed discrimination in the United States in nearly every area of life. For administrators the act outlaws discrimination in employment as an intentional, calculated act to exclude some people from work, prohibits preferential treatment by means of quotas or other means, and defines sexual harassment as a form of discrimination.

Discrimination in Employment There are two different components of the law: equal opportunity and affirmative action regulations.

Equal Opportunity Title VII, section 703 (a) provides for equal employment opportunity and asserts that it shall be unlawful for an employer to

1. Refuse to hire, discharge or otherwise discriminate against any individual, or

2. Limit, segregate, or classify employees or applicants for employment in any way to deprive any individual of employment opportunities because of race, color, gender, or national origin.

3. Nothing shall be interpreted to require any employer, however, to grant preferential treatment to any individual or group on account of an imbalance that may exist with respect to the total number or percentage of persons of any race, color, religion, gender, or national origin employed by any employer.

Affirmative Action At his historic commencement address at Howard University in June 1965, President Johnson extended the meaning of equal opportunity.

> Freedom is not enough. You do not take a person who, for years, has been hobbled by chains and liberate him, bring him up to the starting line of a race and then say, "You are free to compete with all the others" and still justly believe that you have been completely fair. It is not enough just to open the gates of opportunity. All our citizens must have the ability to walk through those gates.
>
> This is the next and the more profound stage of the battle for civil rights. We seek not just freedom but opportunity. We seek not just legal equality but human ability, not just equality as a right and a theory but equality as a fact and equality as a result.

The outgrowth of that promise were "affirmative action" regulations. Affirmative action plans (AAPs) require employers to demonstrate good faith in their efforts to increase opportunities for deprived groups. According to affirmative action, employers may offer preferential treatment to disadvantaged or minority group members including training, selective certification, and aggressive recruitment.

What the Courts Have Said   In three lawsuits, the Supreme Court clarified how administrators were to interpret equal employment and affirmative action.

Griggs v. Duke Power Co.   In 1973 a group of African American employees challenged Duke Power's requirement of a high school diploma and satisfactory intelligence scores for certain jobs previously given only to white employees. The court found that these job requirements were not relevant for the positions, were discriminatory, and upheld the challenge. However, to avoid incessant litigation, employers were encouraged to adopt a quota system to ensure ongoing parity.

United Steelworkers of America v. Weber   Six years later an African American man was accepted into a training program that would have resulted in a better paying job, while Brian Weber and several other men of Caucasian descent who had more seniority were not. Weber sued under the Civil Rights Act. The Supreme Court decided unequivocally that the Civil Rights Act allowed racial preferences, because the purpose of the act was to break down barriers to the employment of African Americans and other people of color, and an employer could, therefore, give preference to them.

Johnson v. Transportation Agency, Santa Clara County   In 1987, in an interview for a position of road dispatcher, Diane Joyce, a woman, received a score of 73 and was hired over Paul Johnson, who scored a 75 and who had been recommended over Joyce for the position by a panel of three supervisors. Even though she had scored lower than Paul in the first round of interviews and was not recommended in the second round, Joyce was hired because the company had never employed a female road dispatcher and the agency wanted a balanced workforce. Johnson sued claiming reverse discrimination because of his sex. The Supreme Court, however, upheld the hiring, affirming employment rights for women.

Sexual Harassment   Under Title VII of the Civil Rights Act, sexual harassment in the workplace is a form of discrimination. Sexual harassment involves unwelcome sexual advances, requests of sexual favors, or other conduct of a sexual nature when such conduct is made either explicitly or implicitly a condition of employment. Sexual harassment can also occur when such conduct interferes with an individual's work performance.

Harassment can be verbal, visual, or physical. Visual harassment involves leering, suggestive ogling, making offensive signs and gestures, or openly displaying pornographic or other sexually offensive materials. Verbal harassment includes telling sexually explicit jokes, making sexual suggestions, highly personal innuendoes, and explicit propositions. Physical harassment includes brushing up against the body, patting, squeezing, pinching, kissing, fondling, forced sexual assault, and rape. The Supreme Court's interpretation of the law asserts that the law is violated when the work "environment would reasonably be perceived, and is perceived, as hostile and abusive."

Age Discrimination Act of 1975

By the year 2000, the median age for employed Americans reached 39. Between 1986 and 2000, the number of people ages 48 to 53 leaped a staggering 67%. Moreover, older Americans are politically active. Because of this, Congress passed the Age Discrimination Act of 1975, which made illegal most discrimination against people aged 40 to 70 in the workplace. Unless age is essential to the performance of a job, employers may not give preference to younger workers in hiring, firing, or granting benefits. Furthermore, in 1986 Congress eliminated mandatory retirement ages in most occupations, meaning that a worker is no longer obliged to retire by age 70.

O'Conner v. Ortega, 1987: Employee Privacy

While looking into charges of sexual harassment and malfeasance at a state hospital, investigators conducted a search of Dr. Dennis M. O'Connor's office. O'Connor sued. The Court ruled in the government's favor because its investigators had applied a standard of reasonableness when they conducted the search. Lower federal courts have also upheld the use of polygraph tests by police and prison officials for preemployment screening.

On the issue of drug testing, the operative standard for management is one of reasonableness. Are there reasonable grounds for believing an employee was impaired on the job? Can the agency demonstrate that an employee represents a clear and present danger to other workers or to the general public? For example, the Supreme Court has held that government regulations requiring drug and alcohol testing of railroad crew members involved in serious accidents are constitutional, because such tests are a reasonable and effective way to serve the government's interest in promoting public safety.

Americans With Disabilities Act of 1990

Enacted July 26, 1990, the Americans With Disabilities Act (ADA) bars discrimination and extends broad civil rights protection to many Americans with disabilities relating to private and public employment, public accommodations, transportation, and communication services.[11] This sweeping antidiscrimination measure affects 43 million Americans with physical, intellectual, and emotional disabilities. It also bars discrimination by private businesses against people with AIDS or its virus.

The act forbids all employers from making hiring decisions based on criteria that are either irrelevant to the job or inappropriately subjective, such as preferring an underqualified nondisabled person over a qualified person who has a disability. The ADA requires employers to make "reasonable accommodations" for disabled applicants and employees so that they can compete on more equal terms[12] unless that obligation places an "undue hardship" on an organization. For example, the measure mandates elevators in new commercial and public buildings of more than two stories and calls for employers to provide special devices and services for those with impaired hearing or vision.[13]

HOW TO PRACTICE SOCIAL ADMINISTRATION

Social administration includes supervising social work, administrative decision making, administering finances, administering the human side of organizations, and the role of the chief administrative social worker. Much of the success of any social work program depends on the quality of its administrative leadership.

Supervision

A supervising social worker relates individually to social workers to develop skills and assists them in working with clients. The supervising social worker engages in performance appraisal and assists members of the work unit as a group.

Individual Supervision A supervising social worker is at different times an information giver, instructor, problem solver, coach, consultant, mentor, and evaluator. The social model of administration expects social workers who engage in supervision to assist other social workers in developing skill and to collaborate with them in the provision of service to their clients. In a 1974 study of social work supervision, Al Kadushin found that "being able to share responsibility with supervisors and being able to obtain support for difficult cases was the greatest source of social work satisfaction."[14] Both supervising social workers and workers themselves believe that as a social worker gains experience, the best relationship becomes one of consultant-consultee, a form of supervision preferred by many social workers.

Shulman says that research shows that social workers often want supervising social workers to devote time to teach practice skills, discuss research information, and provide feedback on performance. When a supervisor models rapport and caring as well as offering empathy, respect, mutuality, and trust, these qualities carry over in the way many social workers assist their clients. Shulman found that "supervisees learn what a supervisor really feels about helping by observing the supervisor in action. More is often 'caught' by social workers than is 'taught' by the supervisor."[15]

Sometimes, as a social worker, you will need explicit, direct answers to a policy or procedural question. Your supervising social worker should provide answers clearly and forthrightly. As you increasingly think about and make your own decisions, the trust and support of your supervisor is important. Ongoing positive reinforcement, good communication, including active listening and giving feedback, and your supervising social worker's attempts to create a positive work environment are often essential in helping you become independent and self-directing.

Performance Appraisal In most social agencies, supervising social workers monitor and evaluate performance as an ongoing process. Performance appraisal often comes out of one's discussions with a supervisor, may be based on your own professional objectives as well as the agency's standards, and is often performed collaboratively with you confirming what has been occurring during the year's period.

Sometimes in larger, more hierarchically structured organizations, however, social workers are evaluated by means of conventional performance evaluation processes developed by human resource specialists. Such evaluation are designed to measure the extent to which you achieve the requirements of your position by means of specific, realistic, and achievable criteria in relation to standards of agency performance. These organizations evaluate staff on at least an annual basis and use these evaluations to determine pay raises, promotions, future assignments, or the need for discipline.

At times, however, performance appraisal in large bureaucratic organizations is used more for the purpose of organizational accountability, control, and compliance than for assisting social workers in their professional development or improving their work with their clients. Sometimes such control can fail to respect a social worker as a competent professional capable of self-direction, but it misuses supervisors as well. Critics find such impersonal formal procedures "no more than a vehicle for the bureaucratic surveillance of social workers."[16]

An approach that is more consistent with social work values of self-determination and respect for the ability of social workers will reverse this type of patriarchal management. Instead of measurement serving the interests of control, consistency, and predictability, administrative social workers will "let measurement and control serve core social workers," asserts Peter Block. "For example, measures should come out of conversation with clients, between workers themselves as well as supervisors."[17]

As a social worker, you and your social work team members maintain control by your commitments to your jobs and to one another. These commitments become mutual agreements, not only between workers but also between workers and supervising social workers. Because contracts are between partners, expectations go both ways, with equal demands between workers and supervising social workers and between supervising social workers and departmental administrators. The intent is to eliminate coercion as the basis for getting results.

According to Block, performance contracts would not be tied to pay or punishment but to mutual accountability, teamwork, and accomplishing the goals of serving the community, your clients, and increasing your skills and capacities for growth. "No one," asserts Block, "should be able to make a living simply planning, watching, and controlling or evaluating the actions of others." Social work administrators should "exist primarily to contribute to social workers who do the core work. Core social workers should have strong voices in determining what administrators can do to help them accomplish the common purposes of the social organization."[18]

MARY PARKER FOLLETT (1869–1933): SOCIAL ADMINISTRATOR

Born in Quincy, Massachusetts, an 1898 graduate of Radcliffe College, Mary Parker Follett was active in vocational guidance, industrial relations, civic education, settlement work, and social administration theory and practice. As a vocational counselor for Boston's Roxbury Neighborhood House, Follett became aware of poor working families in need of social, recreational, and educational facilities. In 1909 her lobbying efforts resulted in legislation that made her the initiator of the first public school community center,[19] the Boston School Centers for after-school recreation and education programs. In 1924 Follett moved to England, where she was vice president of the National Community Center Association and a member of the Taylor Society, an organization concerned with scientific management, administration, and efficiency in industry.

In an era when management was the exclusive bastion of wealthy male business leaders, Mary Parker Follett brought a new perspective to social administration, concentrating on social work values. Of all the important organizational theorists and writers, she was the only social worker, and the only theorist, to challenge the scientific management model of business. Her epistemological starting point, and the way she followed out the implications, were both daring and dazzling.[20]

Her ideas predated Martin Buber's concept of "I and Thou." Follett finds in relationships the basic dynamic that runs the world. "In human relations" she says, "this is obvious: I never react to you but to you-plus-me; or to be more accurate, it is I-plus-you reacting to you-plus-me. I can never influence 'you' because you have already influenced me; that is, in the very process of meeting, we both become something different."[21] Follett wanted an organization to draw on the kind of creative energy produced by that kind of dynamic. Her theory of "psychological interpenetrating" pioneered the concept that was later described by Alfred Schutz as "intersubjectivity." In her 1924 book, *Creative Experience,* Follett advocated administration practices in which people of different socioeconomic and occupational backgrounds understand one another's viewpoints.[22]

Follett anticipated the importance of generalist social work. "The people, it is assumed, will gladly agree to become automata when we show them all the things they can have by abandoning their own experience in favor of a superior race of men called experts."[23] She suggests that a person can become an expert not by being a specialist in one small area, but because of "his insight into the relationship of his specialty to the whole."[24]

She laid a foundation for social administration. "Individuals who participate in administration make it social," she wrote. "The process of production is as important for the welfare of society as its products. Progress," she continues, "implies respect for the creative process, not the created thing. We must allow no mechanism to come between our spiritual source and our life."[25]

Her various writings on administration are contained in *Dynamic Administration: The Collected Papers of Mary Parker Follett,*[26] and they describe her perspective on social administration. More than 100 years ahead of her time, her voice is now beginning to be recognized for its uniqueness, creativity, and advocacy of authentic social work administration. She is the greatest of our social administration thinkers.[27]

Supervising social workers are valuable people. They have special knowledge and experience, and we choose them because we believe they are the best social workers we have. We need these talented individuals who are skilled in providing caring, concerned relationships and who are capable of passing their experience on to others. We need to reorient our thinking about supervision. Instead of monitoring and controlling, we should allow our experienced social workers to coach, teach, support, and provide modeling and consultation in service of those who do social work with clients. The role that we call "supervision" should not be one of authority but rather should assist and support you in becoming the best social worker you can be.

Assisting the Work Group

In addition to working with you individually, your supervising social worker assists your entire work unit to set work priorities, goals, and work assignments. He or she acts as a buffer between your unit and administration, providing you with information and training about the agency's plans and priorities. The supervising social worker informs the department administrator about your unit's needs and performance. The ultimate objective of good supervision is to help your unit become a cohesive group of highly capable social workers who deliver the highest amount and quality of service to your clients.

Administrative Decision Making

Individual Decision Making

An administrator will often decide to make a decision alone when faced with the following constraints:

1. When time limits preclude group process
2. When the administrator has all the information needed to decide
3. When the alternatives are clear and the constraints are easily calculated
4. When intergroup coordination and cooperation is not a factor
5. When values inherent in the decision are straightforward and are not in conflict.[28]

After gathering information and reviewing the strengths and limits of each alternative solution, the administrator chooses the alternative that is cheapest, most efficient, or most effective in accomplishing a specific goal. Then the administrator will often involve others in implementing the decision. Individual decision making is fast, requires few organizational resources, and can be effective in implementing an administrator's values and in giving the organization direction.

Group Decision Making

Groups have advantages over individuals in deciding, but they have disadvantages as well. Criteria exist to help an administrator decide when to use group decision making, and a number of group decision-making techniques are also available to assist.

Advantages of Group Decision Making Several scholars support the conclusion of Paul Hare who wrote in 1976 that "When pairs or larger groups are compared in the solution of the same types of problems, groups are generally found to be more efficient than individuals."[29] Hare noted that "although the group is usually better than the average individual, however, it is seldom better than the best individual."[30]

Groups tend to be superior to individuals because they can break a complex problem into pieces and each member can assess different parts of it. Group members together often have more accumulated knowledge and information than any one individual. The diversity of experience and thinking styles present in a group can lead to more innovative solutions than an "expert" could produce by working alone. When people with different styles interact in a group, they can often stimulate each other to try new ways of approaching the problem and compensate for the weaknesses in any one member's thinking style.[31] Members working together can often see a problem from different perspectives, and because members have different skills and talents, they can tackle varying components of a problem more effectively than one person alone.[32] They form a system in which synergy operates: The group becomes more than the sum of its parts.

In addition, people may be more willing to accept, support, and implement a decision that was made by the group rather than an individual. If the solution is going to affect the group and implies changes in procedures, their involvement will often ensure a willingness to accept that change.[33] A group decision is often easier to implement because more people feel they had a say in it, and they understand the problem more thoroughly.[34]

Disadvantages of Group Decision Making   Group problem solving takes longer than an individual working alone, and as a result, it is more expensive for an agency. The dynamics of groups may lead to compromise solutions, in which members follow the ideas of the leader or the most persuasive member, overriding valuable dissenting opinions. Also, there is often no clear focus for responsibility in groups if things go wrong.

When to Use Group Decision Making   Group decision making is usually best when a problem meets the following conditions:

1. The problem requires interagency or intergroup cooperation and coordination.
2. The problem and its solution have important personal and organizational consequences for members.
3. There are significant but not immediate deadline pressures.
4. The problem is technically complex, has different facets, and requires input from different sources.
5. The problem may be valuationally or ethically complex, requiring discussion from a variety of points of view.

6. The problem may require creative solutions, and members are able to successfully resolve conflicts when they disagree.
7. Widespread acceptance and commitment are critical to successful implementation.[35]

Group Decision-Making Techniques   Administrators, particularly those in larger organizational settings, should be familiar with a variety of management science techniques, including queuing, Markov models, linear programming, operations research, and simulation (described in Chapter 6), as well as benefit-cost analysis and force field analysis (described in Chapter 3).

In addition, administrators often use decision techniques with groups of staff members to develop solutions to social and administrative problems. Three kinds of decision techniques are common in meetings: brainstorming, reverse brainstorming, nominal group technique (NGT), and, sometimes, the Delphi technique.

Brainstorming   Brainstorming allows a group to obtain the maximum amount of input in an orderly manner. Brainstorming reduces dominance by cliques and disruption by overly assertive, excessively garrulous, or domineering individuals. It also eliminates group dependency on a single authority figure and allows those who are generally silent to contribute. Brainstorming is useful when the solution to a problem requires the group's cumulative wisdom. It provides a means by which a number of ideas about a topic can be generated in a short amount of time.

When you use brainstorming, explain the purpose and rules to ensure an orderly process, especially in the early stages of a group when members are still getting to know one another. The rules for brainstorming are as follows:

Expressiveness—express any idea that comes to mind.

Nonevaluation—no criticism allowed.

Quantity—the more ideas the better.

Building—try to build on one another's ideas.

Brainstorming should be fun, exciting, and interesting. Thought will be stimulated, and members will build on one another's ideas or come up with new and different combinations. Write the issue on a blackboard or sheet of newsprint. Explain that the purpose of brainstorming is to generate as many ideas as possible, without thinking about the quality of the ideas. Any idea, no matter how far-fetched, is appropriate. In fact, the wilder and more audacious the idea the better, because one goal of brainstorming is to break through old ways of thinking and come up with new, innovative courses of action. The more ideas the members generate, the greater the likelihood they will discover a superior idea.

While members are coming up with ideas, they should not make comments, criticize, evaluate, or discuss the quality of any ideas. As members develop ideas, write them down as quickly as members can think of them. Ask participants to suggest how the ideas of others can be turned into better ideas, or how two or more ideas can be joined into still another idea. Encourage shy or reluctant members to participate. To make sure everyone has a chance and that all of the ideas are elicited, limit members to one idea at a time. After members have finished, help the group review all of the suggestions, prioritize them, and vote on those that seem worthwhile. You may improve the group's proficiency if you provide some training and practice before your brainstorming session and allow members to record ideas *after* the brainstorming session.[36]

Reverse Brainstorming Reverse brainstorming is a technique for considering negative consequences of ideas that are generated through brainstorming. After your group has generated lists of various ideas and members are narrowing the list to the best ideas, ask them "What might go wrong with this idea?" When members look at the negative consequences of ideas, they can often eliminate unworkable ones.

Does Brainstorming Work? Empirical evidence indicates that individuals working alone who are asked specifically to be creative tend to generate more solutions than brainstorming groups. When individual scores are added together to yield group scores, individuals working alone have tended to outperform brainstorming groups.

However, when nearly 50 AIDS researchers from around the world met in a Houston hotel in November 1995 to brainstorm ways to revive immune systems devastated by the human immunodeficiency virus, the fifth such meeting held over the previous 5 years, the researchers agreed that without brainstorming together many would not have taken the dramatic, often-controversial steps that may lead to important treatments for the disease.[37]

John Dwyer, from the Prince of Wales Hospital in Sydney, Australia, would never have revived the notion of transplanting tissue from the thymus without the encouragement and brainstorming that he encountered during his interaction with this group. Suzanne Illdstad, from the University of Pittsburgh, says she never would have proposed her baboon-to-human bone marrow transplant. "Brainstorming should serve as a paradigm for researchers in all diseases," urges Illdstad.[38]

Nominal Group Technique Andre Delbecq and Andrew Van de Ven developed an approach that combines group brainstorming with the benefits gained when members of a group work alone to generate ideas. They called their technique the "nominal group technique," or NGT, because the members form a group in name only—that is, a *nominal group*. NGT differs from brainstorming in that the process is not freewheeling but is controlled and structured in a series of steps to ensure that every member has equal input in the process. Members may initially feel uncomfortable using this highly structured process, but this discomfort usually diminishes after some practice.

To use the NGT process, proceed through the following steps. Before you begin, introduce the problem or issue in writing on a blackboard or newsprint pad, explain the theory of NGT and the procedure, and answer questions.

1. *Silently generate ideas in writing:* Working alone, each participant writes ideas on the problem to be discussed for about 10 to 15 minutes. These ideas usually are suggestions for a solution.

2. *Round robin sharing:* After everyone has finished generating ideas, ask each member in turn to read one idea from his or her list, and write it on the board. If members have an idea that is the same as one on the board, they move to the next new one on their list. Members continue until all of the ideas are on the board. There is no discussion of ideas until every person's ideas have been presented for general viewing.

3. *Discussion and clarification:* Ask members to look over the entire list to ensure that it is comprehensive, clear, accurate, and nonrepetitive. Refine the list, but do not comment, discuss, or debate the merits of differing ideas. Ask members to openly discuss the ideas to become clear about them, but not to evaluate them. This part of the discussion tends to be spontaneous and unstructured.

4. *Voting:* Because a large number of items may be on the board, you may want members to decide by multiple voting. Ask members to give three points for their first choice, two points for their second choice, and one point for their third choice. Each person should write his or her top three preferences on a card and pass it to the leader. Add the total points and divide by the number of group members to obtain an average. Compare and rank order the results.

5. *Discussion (optional):* If several rankings receive close scores, ask members to explain why they voted the way they did.

6. *Revoting:* Repeat the voting process among the top scoring items until a clear winner emerges.

7. *Devils advocate (optional):* Sometimes the facilitator assigns a member to play the role of devil's advocate, challenging the assumptions and assertions made by the group. The devil's advocate forces the group to rethink its approach to the problem and to avoid reaching premature consensus or making unreasonable assumptions before proceeding with problem solutions.

8. *Dialectical inquiry (optional):* Dialectal inquiry is similar to a devil's advocate approach, however in this approach you assign groups to challenge the underlying values and assumptions associated with the problem definition. For example, the facilitator might form a Red Team and a Blue Team to critically examine prevailing assumptions that underlie the issue.[39]

Assessing NGT NGT protects individuals from group pressure because anonymity is assured and discussion is not allowed. In the idea generation phase, each person is given the assurance that he or she will have an opportunity to generate as many ideas as possible. This stimulates creativity, but in a quiet atmosphere in which everyone can give the problem their full concentration and attention.

The round robin phase provides face-to-face contact and interaction at an appropriate time and in a controlled atmosphere. Each person knows that his or her ideas will receive equal and legitimate attention. The voting process provides an explicit mathematical solution that fairly weighs all members' inputs. Finally, in the discussion phase, members' subjective feelings, perceptions, and input can be factored into the final vote, and individuals understand that there will be joint group commitment to the final decision.

Delphi Technique Rand Corporation in the early 1950s developed the Delphi technique to assess current needs. The technique was given the name Delphi from the oracle of the Greek god Apollo. This technique employs expert opinion while clarifying minority opinions. Delphi is a creative, futuristic, and sometimes controversial tool that gives each participating individual equal input toward consensus, although participants may be miles apart and perhaps unacquainted with each other. Delphi "provides for an impersonal anonymous setting in which opinions can be voiced without bringing 'experts' together in any kind of face-to-face confrontation."[40] The steps in this procedure are as follows:

1. *Select the experts:* Carefully choose 15 or 20 researchers, professors, lecturers, authors, editors, or others to provide a broad range of opinion, and invite them to participate.

2. *Design the questionnaire:* Limit the number of questions and allow two to four lines for each response. Later questionnaires may be longer, so be brief in the first round. The answers you receive from your first questionnaire provide the raw data for your second round of questions.

3. *Send questionnaires and elicit brief statements from the panel.*

4. *Collect and edit the data from the first questionnaire:* You will need to use good judgment when analyzing the content from the panel respondents. This is a crucial part of the technique. Delphi administrators often use an editorial panel of persons who are familiar with the subject matter in this step. Major complications include differences in terminology and even unreadable handwriting.

5. *Design and send two additional rounds of questionnaires:* Design a second questionnaire based on the opinions you received from the first one. Mail this second questionnaire to members of the group for their feedback. Design a third questionnaire based on the material obtained from the second questionnaire, and mail the third set to further refine the opinions. In each round, the questions become more specific and refined than in the previous set. The final questionnaire usually produces the greatest respondent attrition

due to respondent burnout and, occasionally, increasingly complicated questions.

6. *Obtain consensus:* Although three rounds of questionnaires are most often used in the Delphi technique, a fourth round may be used to gain consensus. Even if you do not reach consensus, you will be able to identify differing schools of thought and develop your own opinion.

7. *Develop a summary:* As a professional courtesy, write a summary of the data, prioritizing the opinions of the members and indicating the number who disagreed with each statement. Summarize the minority opinions, and send the report to each respondent with a note of thanks for their participation.

Administering Finances

Administering an organization's finances includes developing the budget, presenting the budget to the board of directors, overseeing how money is generated and spent, and ensuring that there is good fiscal accountability. In a small agency, the chief social work administrator often takes the lead in overseeing the financial health of the agency, preparing the budget, raising funds, and assisting staff in managing the agency's finances. In a middle-sized agency that has two or three social work departments, a finance manager is often responsible for managing agency funds. In a larger agency, this job is usually delegated to a finance or accounting department.

Managing the Budget
Budgeting is a process that all administrators need to master. Social agencies have a choice of three budgeting models: line item budgeting, functional budgeting, or program budgeting.

The Budgeting Process   The budget is your agency's most basic and important organizational plan. The budget sets out the financial outcomes that you, as a finance manager, intend to accomplish during a specific period, usually a year. According to Malvern Gross, a budget is a "plan of action that represents the organization's blueprint expressed in monetary terms, a tool to monitor the financial activities [of an agency] throughout the year."[41] Budgeting is intended to be a rational process. According to Wildavsky, "Making budgetary decisions depends on calculating which alternatives to consider and to choose. Calculation involves determining how problems are identified,

get broken down into manageable decisions, how choices are made, and who shall be taken into account."[42]

However, arriving at a budget is far from perfectly rational. For one thing, people are limited in their ability to calculate, time is severely limited, and "the number of matters that can be encompassed in one mind at the same time is quite small."[43] As a result, people tend to make budgeting decisions *incrementally*. We "simplify in order to get by. We tend to make small moves, let experience accumulate, and use feedback from our decisions to gauge consequences."[44] Social work agencies, in addition, often lack a well-understood financial base. "Spending agencies do not know how much they will need; reviewing bodies do not know how much they should allocate. Requests for spending and actual appropriations fluctuate wildly."[45]

As a result, budgeting, especially in small agencies, involves making educated guesses about a future state of affairs and what the needs of the agency will be. Some budgets tend to be "wish lists" in which administrators ask for what they want, but they must work within whatever amount is allocated to them. If the agency or program is new, the problem is compounded and a negotiated struggle takes place.

Central funding sources, such as United Way, government agencies, or county or state budget departments will exert control, knowing that agencies will push for increases as hard as they can. The result is a game in which each attempts to maximize its position without regard for the other. Added to this mix is the self-interested pursuit of power by executives who see success in the budgeting arena as their "road to fortune."[46]

Line Item Budgeting   The line item budget, the most common form of budgeting in social agencies, is a description of revenue and expenditures on functional items such as salaries, rent, utilities, postage, office supplies, training, consultation, and so forth. A line item budget for an entire agency may include the following:

Personnel costs: salaries, health and life insurance, staff development

Space: rent, utilities, telephone, insurance

Equipment: purchased equipment, leased equipment, equipment maintenance

Consumable items: supplies, postage, books, subscriptions, printing, advertising

Petty cash (other): Conferences, travel, services purchased

The line item budgeting process is relatively easy to calculate and understand. Because line items may cut across departments or divisions, each department calculates how much it spent on these various items in a given year. Budget planners add up these line items, compare actual expenditures with last year's budget, and project costs on those items into the next year. Assume, for example, that last year your agency spent $100 on paper products. Allowing for 5% inflation, this year the board approved a budget allocation of $105 for paper expenditure. Because of increased demand for paperwork, however, the agency actually spent $10 more, totaling $115. Based on those figures and assuming that both demand for paperwork and inflation will continue to rise at the same rate, it would probably make sense for the board to budget at least $131.25 next year, ($115 base + $10 increased demand + $6.25 inflation).

There are advantages and disadvantages when using line item budgeting. An advantage of line item budgeting is "simplicity and expenditure control. The categories are limited and fixed over time, and increases and decreases projected in any given line are usually determined as a small increment"[47] over the previous year.

A disadvantage of line item budgeting is that it sometimes diverges from reality. At times they are developed by financial or accounting staff who may guess how costs might increase or decrease in the coming year. They ask social work professionals what increases they expect to make. Based on those figures, the budget is submitted to the board who, without further information or understanding, is asked to approve it.[48]

Line item budgeting may suffer because it is based on previous expenditures that may or may not be accurate predictors of future needs. The budget often tells nothing about the relative importance of budget items, or whether various departments or units needed them. Line item budgeting "does not depict efficiency, effectiveness, priorities, or programs of the agency,"[49] neither does it help you plan for new programs or for agency innovation.

Functional Budgeting   A functional budget places various organizational functions into categories that can be examined and monitored. As an administrator of a smaller social organization, you may divide finances into social work services and supporting or administrative services.[50] If you administer a larger organization, you may want to know whether expenditures for social service programs are growing more quickly than system maintenance (personnel, accounting) and support (clerical, facilities maintenance), and whether the amounts allocated to these various functions are appropriate. If social services programs are growing, for example, they may be outstripping system maintenance and support, putting a strain on these departments.

Program Budgeting   Administrators who use program budgeting make budgetary decisions by focusing on end products of output. As a finance administrator, for example, you may ask "What do we do (program)?" "Why do we do it (objective)?" and "How are we doing (output in relation to objectives or results)?" You define program objectives in terms that can be analyzed, establish specific time horizons for accomplishing objectives, measure program effectiveness, and develop and compare alternative ways of attaining those objectives.[51]

Assume, for example, that the goal of a program is to rehabilitate 100 persons addicted to alcohol in the coming year; the administrator and staff calculate the resources needed to accomplish this goal. The meaning of "rehabilitation" may become an issue. Is an alcoholic considered rehabilitated when he or she has been sober for 3 months, 6 months, or 1 year? Is a person addicted to alcohol considered rehabilitated if he or she is capable of holding a job and attends Alcoholics Anonymous (AA) meetings regularly?

Once you decide on a definition, social workers can arrive at some goals. It is best to make goals specific, measurable, and time limited. You assess particular treatment methods. For example, if your definition of rehabilitation includes holding a job or enrolling in AA, you will probably add a job-training program to your services as well as referrals to and monitoring of AA attendance.

You and your staff calculate how much it will cost to rehabilitate 100 persons addicted to alcohol. At various points during and at the end of the year, you can review the budget to assess the degree to which the program was successful in accomplishing its goals and whether it is within its cost projections. You and the other social workers can also assess the effectiveness of various treatment modalities, arrive at more realistic operational definitions, and improve treatment effectiveness. You and the social work staff continue to adjust your treatment goals and budgets so that they are in alignment.

Program budgeting has an advantage over line item budgeting and functional budgeting because it allows you to examine how effective services have been in the past year, and it provides a mechanism to plan a better program for the future. In addition, program budgeting involves everyone in the budgeting process who is responsible for program outcomes, particularly line social work staff. This makes budgeting an integral part of the treatment process, gives social workers increased control over their own work, and provides incentives in goal accomplishment. Program budgeting can also help evaluate treatment and program effectiveness. Because program budgeting includes complicated issues of matching treatment outcomes with budget predictions, the process of engaging in such calculation may be difficult, however.

Administering the Human Side of Social Organizations

Because social organizations are composed of people, and the agency's purpose is to enhance people's lives, the human side of organizational life ought to be one of the most, if not *the* most, important aspects of social work administration. In some agencies this role is termed "personnel administration" and in others "human resource administration."

As an administrator who engages the human side of social organizations, you may assist in recruiting and selecting potential employees. You will need to be familiar with how to administer rules relating to diversity and to people with disabilities in your agency. In addition, you may be engaged in orienting new employees, administering policies relating to sexual harassment, handling employee performance problems, terminations, and sometimes participating in collective bargaining.

Recruitment and Selection   Sturgeon believes everything the organization does depends on the quality of its employees; therefore, recruiting and selecting people is the organization's most important function.[52] Recruitment provides the agency with an adequate number of job applicants. When you perform recruitment and selection, use the following steps:

1. Develop a job description that outlines information regarding the minimum qualifications for the position in terms of education, experience, and skills.

2. Recruit employees by designing position announcements, advertising, and outreach.

3. Screen applicants using application forms, résumé reviews, references, and tests, if appropriate.

4. Conduct screening interviews.

5. Select the person and notify other applicants.

The details of how to carry out these functions are described in Chapter 10.

Administering Diversity   Sturgeon says that equal employment opportunity is common sense. Ethnic diversity should be significantly represented in the workforce of every social organization, and every social organization has a responsibility to support the community that sustains it. One of the striking features of North Americans is the strength of the belief held by people at all levels of society that achieving the "American dream" is really possible for many citizens. When American and Canadians come to believe that they cannot better their lot through their own merit and efforts, society stands at risk. Equal employment opportunity is a responsibility that every social organization owes not only to its community but also to society as a whole.[53]

Affirmative Action   Affirmative action is voluntary, allows for increased value for those with protected characteristics, and gives preference to members of protected groups in hiring and promotion. Affirmative action involves taking steps to ensure proportional recruitment, selection, and promotion of qualified members of groups formerly excluded, such as ethnic groups and women. Many employers' unions and employment agencies are required to plan and document the steps they are taking to reduce underrepresentation of various groups through written affirmative action programs (AAPs).

Equal Employment Opportunity (EEO)   The Civil Rights Act of 1964 mandates equal employment opportunity. EEO is neutral with respect to protected characteristics, and it prohibits discrimination in promotions and hiring. Equal Employment Opportunity Commission (EEOC) guidelines explain the types of questions that can be asked on an employment application or in an interview and require screening or interviewing committees to be composed of a mix of males, females, and ethnic group members.

EEOC guidelines prevent an agency from selecting candidates that may have an adverse impact on any social, ethnic, or gender group unless the procedure is validated through job analysis or employee selection research. *Adverse* impact means an employee selection rate for any race, sex, or ethnic group that is less than 80% of the rate of the groups with the highest rate of selection. Proscriptions against discrimination in employment mandate that employment decisions based on standard criteria such as education and experience must have a specific relationship to the job.[54]

Orienting Staff   When you hire someone, it is important to take time to introduce the employee to other staff members, explain his or her particular role, and review the important policies and procedures, including state and federal regulations or agency by-laws. Have copies of the organizational charts available, and introduce the new social worker to the organization as a whole. In hierarchically oriented organizations, it is also important to orient the worker to the responsibility and authority structure.

Most often you will accomplish the basic components of such an orientation over several working days and follow it up by additional on-the-job orientations. In a case management agency, for example, you provide policy for recording and documentation of files and how to perform social case histories or other work-related procedures. If you are orienting social work students for internships, go through the same process as with any other professional social worker to replicate what they will experience when they get their first job.

Handling Employee Performance Problems   It is important to distinguish between social worker and agency performance problems. Employee performance problems are often assumed to be due to lack of knowledge or skills, poor attitude, need for more supervision, or poor work habits such as carelessness, lack of attention to detail, lack of personal organization, or poor use of time. Be sensitive, however, to the possibility that personal factors such as a social worker's health problems, family pressures, emotional difficulties, or external stress may be contributing to poor performance.

A social worker's performance difficulties may also be a result of a host of nonworker factors, including stress due to unclear or inconsistent agency policies, resource limitations, and vague or shifting work priorities or vague performance standards. Performance problems can result from unsupportive or punitive supervision, excessive workload demands, and assignment of inappropriate cases. As an administrator of the human side of an organization, before you decide on a course of action, make sure you understand fully the source of a social worker's difficulties and can distinguish among those due to the worker's lack of ability, to personal problems, or to agency factors. You will find more ideas about work- and non-work-related personal problems and possible solutions in Chapter 12.

Sexual Harassment   Sexual harassment is increasingly recognized as one of the most sensitive employee issues you may be called on to handle. Local and federal courts have held agency supervisors, administrators, as well as entire organizations liable in cases of sexual harassment. Pecora reports that in a study of 23,000 randomly selected male and female civilian employees conducted by the Federal Merit System between May 1978 and May 1980, approximately 42% of the women and 15% of the men reported being harassed, and 1% reported the most severe form of harassment (actual or attempted rape). Sexual harassment is often widespread and occurs regardless of a person's age, marital status, appearance, ethnicity, occupation, or salary.

Because of the seriousness and extent of this kind of behavior, make sure that your social organization has clear written standards of behavior in place. Help your staff understand what constitutes appropriate behavior, and ensure that everyone knows his or her rights and obligations. Train your supervising social workers in how to handle complaints promptly and fairly.[55]

Termination   Discharging someone can be one of the most difficult and unpleasant tasks in working with employees. You should develop explicit policies that describe the conditions under which an employee can be disciplined or terminated. Termination involves a host of legal issues, and nearly all groups of employees have protections under the law enforced by local courts, state human rights agencies, the EEOC, and in the case of unions, the National Labor Relations Board (NLRB). Be sure your social work staff and supervising social workers know the conditions under which termination may be considered and the process by which it may occur. Just as with any other sensitive issue, help your supervising social workers understand how to handle termination fairly, objectively, and honestly.[56]

Collective Bargaining

Collective bargaining is the process by which an employer and employees arrive at agreements governing compensation and working conditions. Social workers and social work administrators should follow principles of good collective bargaining. Three stages in collective bargaining usually occur: election, developing a contract, and administering the contract.

Principles of Collective Bargaining To a large extent, building a tradition of harmonious employee relations depends on developing an organizational culture of fair and workable arrangements for resolving disputes. Although negotiation is adversarial at times, it is important for both parties to reach for the source of labor peace; that is, mutual respect between employees and management based on good day-to-day working relationships and concern for the legitimate interests of both sides.

Both parties should agree to and follow the principles of good collective bargaining. To bargain in good faith means that the parties make an earnest effort and act meaningfully to help bring an agreement into being. Both employers and employees should be willing to sit down at reasonable times and exchange nonconfidential information, views, and proposals on subjects that are within the scope of bargaining. Authorized spokespersons should represent both sides. When social workers and administrators cannot reach agreement by bargaining, they should be able to justify their differences with reasons. The parties must be ready to put their agreement into writing. Most important, they must be willing to keep an open mind, consider compromise solutions to their differences, and make an effort to find a mutually satisfactory basis for agreement.

Election Employees must decide what constitutes the definition or boundaries of their bargaining unit, the kinds of employees who will join together for collective bargaining purposes. Members of the bargaining unit may either create their own bargaining organization or select an already existing union outside the agency to represent them for labor relations activities. Existing union organizations may try to win the support of employees by holding an organizing

campaign, distributing literature, soliciting membership, and holding discussion meetings. Members of the bargaining unit select a bargaining organization by means of secret ballot, monitored by an NLRB official.

Developing a Contract Developing an employer-employee agreement is a process that begins with negotiation. If members cannot reach an agreement by negotiation, they may engage in progressively more formal steps of mediation, fact-finding, and arbitration.

Negotiation: Employer and the employee representatives negotiate issues to reach an agreement. The agreement should be one that both can "live with" in relation to working conditions, salary, benefits, grievance procedures, and so forth. The most desirable situation is for both social administrators and social workers to bargain until they reach a satisfactory agreement.

Mediation: If the parties are unable to reach an agreement by themselves, they can ask a neutral third party mediator to conciliate the dispute. A mediator will facilitate the negotiation process but does not have the power to enforce a settlement.

Fact-finding: If the social workers' union and the administrators cannot agree by means of mediation, they may ask the NLRB to conduct a fact-finding process. Fact-finding is a formal proceeding, conducted by a neutral third party individual or a panel of fact-finders who hear the cases presented by each side and make specific recommendations for resolving the dispute.

Arbitration: An arbitrator is a neutral third party who goes beyond fact-finding to decide in favor of one side or the other. In binding arbitration, the decision of the arbitrator is final. In last-offer arbitration, the arbitrator must find in favor of the last offer presented by each of the parties. Last offer arbitration encourages each side to bargain seriously, because an unreasonable offer will result in adoption of the other side's proposal.

Seventeen states now provide for arbitration of collective bargaining impasses, but compulsory and binding arbitration is typically opposed by managers who fear that these mechanisms give power to bind them to costly settlements to a third party who is unfamiliar with local conditions.

Contract Administration Contract administration is the heart of labor relations; it involves putting the collective bargaining agreement into practice on a day-to-day basis. No matter how hard a negotiator works to write a clear and understandable agreement, disputes inevitably arise about the true meaning of the written agreement and the intent of the parties when they agreed to particular provisions. These disagreements occur even among reasonable and well-intentioned people. Disagreements are handled through grievance procedures, a vital part of contract administration.

THE ROLE OF THE CHIEF ADMINISTRATIVE SOCIAL WORKER

A chief administrative social worker helps create conditions by which people's welfare can be improved by means of a social organization. An administrative social worker will have an attitude of service rather than power and control. In addition to overseeing the budget and personnel issues, the chief social work administrator is directly responsible for much of the planning for the agency, relates to the social organization's board of directors, and sees to it that the agency is periodically evaluated.

Service

As a chief administrative social worker, your leadership style, the way in which you disseminate decision making, your approach to the community in which your organization is located, and the manner in which you relate to social work staff and the board will be reflected in many ways throughout the social agency. You work to maximize choice for social workers who do the day-to-day work with clients rather than hoard decision making as the exclusive prerogative of the top administrative team. You maintain an attitude of service toward the social workers doing the work rather than a presumption that social workers are servants of the administration in carrying out its plans, programs, goals, or directions.[57] As much as possible, you involve social workers in the design of the governance systems by which the social organization operates. You encourage a climate of personal responsibility, individual choice, humanization, and independent action on the part of social workers and clients.

Planning

Planning is one of the most important tasks of an administrative social worker. As an administrative social worker, you plan the direction of the social agency and develop polices and procedures.

What Is Administrative Planning?   Weinbach says that planning includes "those structures and activities that are used to shape future events in organizations."[58] Planning involves setting *goals* and *objectives* for the social organization and developing "work maps" such as programs and budgets that show how these goals and objectives can be accomplished.[59]

Social organizations are always in a state of change. There are new services to consider, new problems to solve, new issues in the agency's environment, and new political and economic factors with which to contend. As a result, a good deal of social administrative effort goes into planning. In fact, planning is probably one of the major tasks that you accomplish as a social administrator.

Planning the Organization's Direction   As a responsible social work administrator, you continually sift through the many issues confronting you and develop plans to deal with those issues. In partnership with the agency's board, social workers, and clients, you scan the organization's environment for "major discontinuities . . . that might provide opportunities or constraints" and monitor "gradual changes in environmental indicators"[60] to plan for client needs, and for ways that the social agency can meet those needs. Rarely will you be caught off guard or unaware of problems in the agency's internal processes or in its external social environment.

Planning Policies and Procedures   The agency board of directors sets overall agency policy and direction, but the chief administrative social worker is responsible for developing internal organization policies and procedures. Agency policies are the fundamental assumptions, rules, or understandings that guide the organization's culture and stance. Sometimes social workers develop policies in the form of goals and objectives. Usually plans are written in a form that helps social workers and clients orient themselves toward those goals and objectives.

Procedures flow from internal policies. Procedures are work plans that help people work in a coordinated fashion and facilitate communication. Procedures are specific steps that help social workers carry out tasks or implement goals. It is important for you to work closely with all staff to fashion internal agency policies and procedures because they shape the culture of the agency.

Relating to the Board of Directors

Social organizations need both an effective board of directors and an effective administrative social worker. Both must be clear about their respective roles. The board and chief administrative social worker relate in a milieu of shared power. One way of sharing power is by means of the double-bridge team model.

Role of the Board of Directors

Despite the almost limitless diversity in their missions and size, the majority of North American social organizations have the same governance structure. They have an unpaid, outside, part-time board of directors. An effective board composed of independent but committed community members can help the social organization keep a clear focus on its mission, ensure that it gets results, and maintain accountability for the money entrusted to it. Without these, warns Peter Drucker, any social agency will soon decline into nonperformance.[61]

In an effective nonprofit social organization, every board committee—indeed, every board member—accepts a number of duties with specific achievement goals. The agency's by-laws invest the community board with the power and authority to make overall agency policy. The ultimate responsibility for the agency functioning and for your performance and that of the agency staff resides with the board.[62]

Role of the Administrative Social Worker

As chief administrative social worker, you are delegated authority for the agency's day-to-day operations and for handling most personnel matters. You play a critical role in determining the nature and extent of the relationship between yourself and your board. You serve as an advocate for employees with the board members, but you also stimulate board members to advocate for the social organization in the broader society.

You also accept duties assigned by the board. For example, one work assignment from the board may be to raise so many dollars in contributions in the coming year. You may be asked to recruit a given number of new volunteers the next year, successfully introduce two new programs,[63] and conduct an overall evaluation of the effectiveness of the social organization's performance.

You provide your board of community members with statistics, interpret client, consumer, or patient needs, discuss program options, and provide information on funding possibilities. Because your board members are dependent on you for information, you are an integral part of the policy-making process. You establish a balance in your role. The relationship between policy formation and administration is never settled for all time but involves a continuous process of negotiation.[64]

Power Sharing

As long as respect exists and the give-and-take is roughly equal, most relationships between you and the members of your board involve elements of power and dependency that develop a creative tension that can work to the advantage of your organization. Although board members can draw on your expertise and knowledge, they cannot allow their legal responsibility to be diluted or coopted by overdependence on you. You need to develop a collegial working relationship with the board members, but you remain an employee of the board, no matter how seasoned you become.[65]

Double-Bridge Team

The board and the chief administrative social worker must be colleagues. Their tasks are complementary. Peter Drucker recommends the double-bridge team as a model for the board executive team in social organizations. In the double-bridge team, neither player is more important; they work as one team of equals and are equally indispensable. The stronger player adjusts to the style, strengths, and personality of the weaker partner. The executive officers in nonprofit organizations are often the stronger players. It is their job to adjust both what they do and how they do it to the personalities and strengths of their board chairpersons and board members.

Evaluating the Social Organization

Every chief administrative social worker should ensure that the social organization is periodically evaluated. As a chief administrator, you need to understand what program evaluation is, why you do it, and how to accomplish it. If you hire an external program evaluator, you obtain the final report and ask the evaluator to present it to the board.

What Is Program Evaluation?

Carol Weiss says that program evaluation measures the effects of a program against its goals to help make decisions about your organization's future direction.[66] According to Rossi and Freeman, the purpose of program evaluation is to assess and improve the "conceptualization, design, planning, administration, implementation, effectiveness, efficiency, and utility of social interventions, and human service programs."[67]

Why Do You Evaluate?

Program evaluation today "has become ubiquitous in the planning and administration of social welfare policies and programs."[68] Government agencies and foundations want to know how much impact your program has had on the problems that it was established to remediate. As a chief administrative social worker, if you can show that your program did what you intended, you may be able to make a case to continue or even expand it. If the program your social work organization operates is successful, others may want to know about and replicate it elsewhere.

Your clients want to be assured that they are receiving the best services that can be provided.[69] "Politicians demand that programs demonstrate their cost effectiveness and be accountable to the public."[70] More and more program evaluation is automatically built into the process of obtaining funding from either government or private foundations.

How to Conduct a Program Evaluation

Program evaluation is most useful when an objective outsider conducts it, one whose skills you and your community board can trust. Two ways that a program evaluator may assess your agency's effectiveness are internal process analysis and outcome or impact analysis.

Process Analysis Process analysis is one way to assess the internal processes by which services are carried out in the social organization. A program evaluator will conceptualize the internal system state of a social organization by means of "systems fit." The evaluator examines the extent to which (1) the organization's members, (2) processes, (3) structures and technologies, (4) goals, strategies, and culture, and

(5) funding and clientele fit together smoothly. The evaluator makes recommendations where there are gaps, conflicts, or discontinuities.

Members: As a program evaluator, you monitor organizational members' skills, attitudes, and values by asking these questions: Do employee skills and training fit the job requirements? Does the organization attract and retain the best people? Are professionals and others who seek autonomy and challenge assigned to less structured and less closely controlled jobs? Do work-related organizational problems create undue stress or employee health problems? Your assessment may lead you to recommend improved recruitment and selection, counseling, stress management, and health maintenance programs.

Processes: Look at processes of organizational decision making, leadership, and communication. Does the decision-making process use all available resources and arrive at decisions that further organizational goals? Does organizational leadership create a sense of mission and identity among members? Is communication effective and efficient, or does it result in mixed messages, misunderstanding, or delay? You may recommend team building, process consultation, third party interventions, or survey feedback techniques (see Chapter 12).

Organizational structures and technologies: Are people who work together closely grouped in units or otherwise linked structurally? Are procedures for coordinating work and information flow appropriate to the tasks and technology? Do members regard the rules and procedures as fair and sensible? As a result of your assessment, you might recommend techniques such as job redesign, revised administrative procedures, reward mechanisms, redesigned divisions of labor, or new work procedures to improve effectiveness.

Organizational goals, strategies, and cultures: You examine whether procedures are supported by the organization's culture and norms. Do power struggles or interunit rivalries prohibit achieving organizational objectives? Your recommendations may include promoting goal clarification, coping with change through workshops, or improving the organizational culture.

Funding and clientele: Which fundraising strategy yields the most funds? What proportion of the target population is being served? What types of individuals is the program not reaching? Do targeted individuals refuse services? Do clients drop out of the program prematurely? You may recommend different funding possibilities, ways of recruiting clients, or ways to help clients stay with the agency's services.[71]

Outcome or Impact Analysis   Outcome or impact analysis is a process by which a program evaluator assess the organization's effectiveness according to the goals that it is intended to achieve. It includes deciding on the (1) agency's goals, (2) developing criteria to measure effectiveness, (3) choosing measurements, and (4) employing an evaluation research design.

Agency Goals   To evaluate the extent to which the program is achieving its goals or outcomes, the program evaluator must understand the program's goals.[72] Often, however, program goals are vague and nonspecific. For example, an organization may state that its goals are to reduce crime, assist the homeless, or support victims of domestic violence. These are worthy endeavors, but they are not goals that you can easily assess. Your first task, therefore, is to assist the organization's key stakeholders, including clients and the community in general, social workers, and other staff, and the board and administration, in stating their goals in clear, specific, and measurable terms,[73] and help them decide which are the most practical and important. Other stakeholders are funding agencies and other social organizations and governmental agencies that partner with the social organization. Involve these stakeholders not only in the selection of goals and the evaluation design but also at every step by "sharing mutual incremental feedback throughout all phases of the evaluation."[74]

Develop Effectiveness Criteria   Put goals in operational or measurable terms. To assess *quantity,* determine the volume, speed, or rate of services. For example, the goal of a probation department may be to maintain a certain rate of recidivism (the number of repeat offenses) made by offenders. An effectiveness criterion is the specific number of offenses per offender in a period of time. Other effectiveness criteria may be number or hours of services provided, percentage of target group reached, number of people served, and number of people rehabilitated.

You may also assess the effectiveness of a program by the *quality* of the services it provides. How good were the services? For example, the goal of an in-home support service to the elderly may be to provide food preparation, visitation, and transportation services. Evaluating the quality of the in-home support

program would include determining how well food was prepared, the friendliness of the visitors, and the efficiency of transportation. Quality may be measured by assessing client satisfaction with services, the length of time treatment was effective, and the impact of services on the problem.

Choose Measurements   Measurements are indicators of success or effectiveness. A number of scales, indices, tests, instruments, and measures exist that you can use for measuring organizations and groups. Among these are the Michigan Organizational Assessment Questionnaire, the Organizational Assessment Inventory, Group Effectiveness Survey, Organizational Diagnosis Questionnaire, and Job Diagnostic Survey.[75] Try to use multiple measures to develop a more rounded and truer picture of program outcomes[76] as well as multiple means of collecting data.

The number and mix of sources of data are limited only by your ingenuity and imagination. Possible sources include interviews, questionnaires, observation, ratings (by peers, staff, experts), psychometric tests (of attitudes, values, personality, preferences, norms, and beliefs), institutional records, government statistics, tests of information, interpretation, and skills, physical evidence, clinical examinations, financial records, and documents (minutes of meetings and newspaper accounts).

Designing the Evaluation   Three kinds of designs most useful in program evaluation research are pure experimental research, quasi-experimental research, and benefit-cost analysis.

Pure experimental research: Pure experimental research typically uses randomly selected subjects in controlled settings. If you are evaluating a new treatment program in an outpatient facility for juveniles addicted to drugs, for example, randomly select a group of typical drug users from all the facility's clients. Divide this number into two subgroups. One is the control group and the other is the experimental group. Next, assess the levels of drug abuse of each group to get a baseline before treatment begins. The control group receives conventional treatment. The experimental group receives the new treatment. When the treatment is completed, retest each group and compare the results. If the rate of drug use in the experimental group is considerably less than that of the control group, you might conclude that the new treatment approach is effective.

Experimental research is fairly straightforward, but you may already see why this "pure" experiment might not work in actual practice. Because the offenders know who is receiving a treatment program, they may collude to interfere with its results. Any number of external factors that have nothing to do with treatment, such as the home, school, and peer relationships, may affect the outcomes. Clients enter programs and leave them without notice. Staff come and go. Clients change and grow independently of treatment in ways that may affect results.

Quasi-experimental research: Quasi-experimental research allows you to assess program effectiveness in settings where you cannot control many of the variables. There are many kinds of quasi-experimental research designs.[77] The two that are useful in program evaluation are time series and nonequivalent control group designs.

Time series designs account for events that give false indicators of success over time, such as changes in the program's environment, the life cycle of a program, or shifts in personnel. For example, heaviest drug users may drop out of the program, giving a false impression that the treatment program was successful. Staff may gradually gain skill in providing treatment, or less capable staff may have been replaced with more competent people, giving a misleading picture of effectiveness of the program itself.

Collect data at regular intervals over a period of time before the program is implemented to obtain a picture of normal changes in the program's service pattern. When you institute the new treatment program, measure it over time to allow for maturation of staff, adjusting to the new program routine, and changes in clients or staff. When enough evaluations have been conducted to give a comprehensive picture of the new treatment's success rate, compare the pattern of program changes before and during the treatment to assess whether the new service is effective.

Nonequivalent control group designs are useful if it is impossible to divide a population into two random groups for an experiment. Instead of dividing a population, find another group with similar characteristics against which you can compare the experimental group. For example, if you want to evaluate a new treatment program for youth in a residential facility, use a randomly selected control group of similar residents of another facility who are receiving no treatment or a conventional treatment. Use a time series design to obtain a baseline on both the experimental group and the control group. Then, implement the treatment program with the experimental group while continuing to take measurements on both groups. After the treatment is over, test both groups and compare the results. If the experimental group improved in comparison to the control group, you may have some confidence that the outcome was the result of the treatment and not due to extraneous factors.

Benefit-cost analysis: Benefit-cost analysis, briefly described in Chapters 3 and 6, is an extension of rational problem solving. It is a way of looking at various program alternatives and estimating the benefit in dollars that each alternative will provide in comparison to its potential dollar costs.[78] Establish a benefit-cost ratio for each program and compare them.

For example, if program A provides benefits of $200 and costs only $100, the benefit-cost ratio is 2:1, or 2. The program owners obtain twice as much benefit as the program costs. If program B provides the same benefits of $200 but costs $300, its benefit-cost ratio is 2:3, or 0.667. This program will only achieve a two-thirds return for the money and other resources the owners put into the project. Assuming that services in two programs are of equal quality and meet program objectives at about the same level, you would normally give the highest rating to the program that costs less.

Benefit-cost analysis tends to be most useful when you can easily obtain information about the degree of the program's impact, when its benefits can be reduced to dollar terms without extraordinary guesswork, and when you can easily identify the program's indirect costs.

The major difficulty in benefit-cost analysis is accounting for all of the costs and benefits of a program and converting often highly intangible results into dollar figures. For example, what are the costs to a community if a child is abused or the benefits in dollars when the cycle of abuse is broken? How much dollar benefit accrues when community members make decisions for themselves? Community empowerment may not be considered by some to be a benefit, because powerful groups may have a vested interest in keeping community members dependent on them. Some argue that trying to place dollar amounts on social costs is inappropriate because activities such as educating a child with an intellectual disability ought to be done for humanitarian reasons even though the costs far outweigh any monetary benefits that will result, for example. In spite of these difficulties, there are ways to develop measurable criteria for the purposes of benefit-cost analysis. Hornick and Burrows recommend that you do the following:

1. Compare only services or agencies with similar objectives and similar clients.

2. Use the same cost criteria for all services or agencies being compared.

3. Calculate the costs in as many ways as possible, such as cost per case, cost per client, and cost per hour of direct service to the client, and compare them to those of other agencies.

4. Use the same outcome criteria for all agencies to obtain an accurate indicator of benefits.[79]

Write the Evaluation Report   After you evaluate the program, write a report describing the agency's goals, the criteria used to measure the organization, the results of the research, and your recommendations. Present the report to the chief social work administrator and to the agency's board, review it with them, answer questions, and help the organization understand your recommendations.

CONCLUSION

Social work organizations are rich in resources for providing assistance and for empowering clients. The role of social work administration is to utilize this human capacity to create social organizations that are models of leadership, innovation, and compassion.

Social work administration involves supervising, decision making, administering to the employees in the organization, and administering the organization's finances. In addition, the chief administrative social worker must relate to the organization's board of directors and see to it that the organization is evaluated periodically.

Social work administration is one of the most important arenas of macro social work practice. As a social worker administrator, you can assist in reducing dependency on management practices and instead find ways to implement authentic social administrative leadership in social work organizations.

KEY CONCEPTS

business management
unobtrusive control
authority
overt control
social administration
administrative law
Equal Pay Act, 1963

Civil Rights Act, 1964
Age Discrimination Act, 1975
Griggs v. Duke Power Company
O'Connor v. Ortega, 1987

Americans With Disabilities Act, 1990
supervision
performance appraisal
Mary Parker Follet
administrative decision making
individual decision making
group decision making
brainstorming
reverse brainstorming
nominal group technique (NGT)
Delphi technique
administering finances
budget
incremental budgeting
line item budget
functional budget
program budget
administering to human side of organizations
recruitment
selection
orienting
performance appraisal
administering diversity
affirmative action
affirmative action programs (AAPs)
equal employment opportunity (EEO)
Equal Employment Opportunity Commission (EEOC)
sexual harassment

termination
collective bargaining
bargaining in good faith
bargaining unit
National Labor Relations Board (NLRB)
negotiation
mediation
fact-finding
arbitration
binding arbitration
last offer arbitration
contract administration
chief administrative social worker
board of directors
agency planning
agency policy
agency procedures
double-bridge team
program evaluation
internal process analysis
impact or outcome analysis
effectiveness criteria
measurements
evaluation research design
pure experimental research
quasi-experimental research
time series design
nonequivalent control group design
benefit-cost analysis

QUESTIONS FOR DISCUSSION

1. Charles A. Rapp and John Poertner, in their book *Social Administration: A Client-Centered Approach*, assert that clients are "resources to be acquired" but that administrators are to "promote

the idea that clients are heroes." In what sense can clients be considered "resources"? In what sense can they be considered "heroes"? Is there an inherent contradiction in these terms, or can clients be considered both resources and heroes?

2. This chapter has referred to both social administration and functional management. What are the differences between administration and management?

3. What is your understanding of "generalist" social work administration?

4. Human resources management assumes that social workers are resources who need to be managed. In what sense can social workers be considered organizational resources? In what sense do social workers need to be managed?

5. Recall that affirmative action is voluntary, allows for increased value for those with protected characteristics, and gives preference to members of protected groups in hiring and promotion. Equal employment opportunity, on the other hand, is a legal obligation, neutral with respect to protected characteristics, and prohibits discrimination in promotions and hiring. What are the strengths of affirmative action? What are its limitations? What are the strengths of equal employment opportunity? What are its limitations?

6. Affirmative action assumes that there are times when discrimination in employment is warranted. Equal employment opportunity assumes that discrimination in employment is rarely warranted. Which is correct? Can both be correct? Which is congruent with social work values and principles?

7. Since 1883, the U.S. Civil Service Commission has required all nonpolitical public employment decisions be made strictly on the basis of "job relatedness," preventing public officials from giving preferential treatment to friends or relatives. This is called the "merit principle." Aside from ethnicity, should government ever abrogate the merit principle and offer preferential treatment to certain groups of people over others in public employment? If not, why not? If so, why and under what circumstances? Has government ever done so?

8. Aside from ethnicity, should government ever provide public employment to people regardless of merit? If not, why not? If so, why and under what circumstances? In the past 100 years has government ever done so?

ADDITIONAL READING

Federal Regulations Dealing With Administration

Executive Order No. 11246.

Title VII of the Civil Rights Act of 1964 as amended in 1991.

Age Discrimination in Employment Act, 1967, as amended in 1978 and 1986.

Americans With Disabilities Act, 1990.

Equal Opportunity Act, 1972.

Equal Pay Act, 1963.

Fair Labor Standards Act.

Immigration Reform and Control Act, 1985.

Rehabilitation Act, 1973, especially handicap sections (sections 503 and 504).

Vietnam Veteran Era Veterans Readjustment Assistance Act of 1974 (veteran status).

Veterans Reemployment Rights Act.

1972 Amendments to the 1964 Civil Rights Act.

Classics in Administration Theory

Weber, Max. "Bureaucracy." In *From Max Weber: Essays in Sociology,* H. H. Gerth and C. Wright Mills, eds. New York: Oxford University Press, 1958.

Taylor, Frederick Winslow. *The Principles of Scientific Management.* New York: W. W. Norton, 1947.

Simon, Herbert. *Administrative Behavior: A Study of Decision Making Processes in Administrative Organization,* 4th ed. New York: Free Press, 1997.

Bellone, Carl J. *Organization Theory and the New Public Administration.* Boston: Allyn and Bacon, 1980.

Harmon, Michael M. *Action Theory for Public Administration.* New York: Longman, 1981.

Elliot M. Fox and Luther Urwick. *Dynamic Administration: The Collected Papers of Mary Parker Follett.* New York: Hippocrene Books, 1977.

General Administration

Berk, Joseph and Susan. *Managing Effectively: A Handbook for First Time Managers.* New York: Sterling, 1991.

Carter, R. *The Accountable Agency.* Beverly Hills, CA: Sage, 1983.

Schuman, David. *Bureaucracies, Organizations, and Administration: A Political Primer.* New York: Macmillan, 1976.

Social Administration

Austin, David M.. "Management Overview." In *Encyclopedia of Social Work,* 19th ed. Washington, DC: NASW Press, 1995, pp. 1642–1659.

Block, Peter. *Stewardship: Choosing Service Over Self-Interest.* San Francisco: Berrett-Koehler, 1993.

Edwards, R. L. and David M. Austin. "Managing Effectively in an Environment of Competing Values." In *Skills for Effective Human Services Management,* R. L. Edwards and J. A. Yankey, eds. Washington, DC: NASW Press, 1991, pp. 5–22.

Garner, Leslie H., Jr. *Leadership in Human Services: How to Articulate and Implement a Vision to Achieve Results.* San Francisco: Jossey-Bass in collaboration with the National Child Welfare Leadership Center, School of Social Work, University of North Carolina, Chapel Hill, 1989.

Glisson, C. A. "A Contingency Model of Social Welfare Administration," *Administration in Social Work,* 5, 1981, pp. 15–30.

Gummer, Burton. *The Politics of Social Administration: Managing Organizational Politics in Social Agencies.* Englewood Cliffs, NJ: Prentice-Hall, 1990.

Keys, P. R. and L. Ginsberg, eds. *New Management in Human Services.* Silver Spring, MD: NASW, 1988.

Oster, Sharon M. *Strategic Management for Nonprofit Organizations: Theory and Cases.* New York: Oxford University Press, 1995.

Quinn, R. E. *Beyond Rational Management: Mastering the Paradoxes and Competing Demands of High Performance.* San Francisco: Jossey-Bass, 1988.

Rapp, Charles A. and John Poertner. *Social Administration: A Client Centered Approach.* New York: Longman, 1992.

Shorris, Earl. *Scenes for Corporate Life: The Politics of Middle Management.* New York: Penguin, 1981.

Rex Skidmore. *Social Work Administration: Dynamic Management and Human Relationships,* 2d ed. Englewood Cliffs, NJ: Prentice-Hall, 1990.

Slavin, Simon, ed. *Social Administration: The Management of the Social Services.* New York: Haworth Press, 1978.

Spencer, Sue. *The Administration Method in Social Work Education.* New York: Council on Social Work Education, 1959.

Weinbach, Robert. *The Social Worker as Manager: Theory and Practice.* New York: Longman, 1990.

Weiner, M. E. *Human Services Management: Analysis and Applications.* 2d ed. Belmont, CA: Wadsworth, 1990.

Weisbord, Marvin R. *Productive Workplaces: Organizing, and Managing for Dignity, Meaning, and Community.* San Francisco: Jossey-Bass, 1987.

Young, Dennis, Robert M. Hollister, and Virginia Hodgkinson, eds. *Governing, Leading and Managing Nonprofit Organizations.* San Francisco: Jossey-Bass, 1992.

Supervision

Austin, M. J. *Supervisory Management for the Human Services.* Englewood Cliffs, NJ: Prentice-Hall, 1981.

Bolton, R. *People Skills.* New York: Simon and Schuster, 1986.

Bramson, R. M. *Coping With Difficult People.* New York: Ballantine Books, 1981.

Holloway, S. and George Brager. *Supervision in the Human Services: The Politics of Practice.* New York: Free Press, 1989.

Kadushin, Al. *Supervision in Social Work,* 4th ed. New York: Columbia University Press, 1992.

Middleman, Ruth and G. Rhodes. *Competent Supervision: Making Imaginative Judgments.* Englewood Cliffs, NJ: Prentice-Hall, 1985.

Decision Making

Janis, Irving. *Victims of Groupthink.* Boston: Houghton Mifflin, 1972.

Kaner, Sam et al. *The Facilitator's Guide to Participatory Decision Making.* Gabriola Island, BC, Canada: New Society Publishers, 1996.

Kaner, Sam et al. *Decision-Making: A Psychological Analysis of Conflict, Choice, and Commitment.* New York: Free Press, 1977.

Rosehead, J., ed. *Rational Analysis for a Problematic World.* New York: Wiley, 1989.

Tropman, John E. *Effective Decisions in Meetings.* Beverly Hills: Sage, 1995.

Tropman, John E. *Effective Meetings: Improving Group Decision Making,* 2d ed. Beverly Hills, CA: Sage, 1996.

Budgeting

Wildavsky, Aaron. *Budgeting: A Comparative Theory of Budgetary Processes.* Boston: Little, Brown, 1975.

Wildavsky, Aaron. *Politics of the Budgetary Process,* 3d ed. Boston: Little, Brown, 1979.

Finance

Olenick, Arnold J. and Philip R. Olenick. *Making the Nonprofit Organization Work: A Financial, Legal, and Tax Guide for Administrators.* Englewood Cliffs, NJ: Prentice-Hall, 1983.

Administering to People

Brown University. *The American University and the Pluralist Ideal: A Report of the Visiting Committee on Minority Life and Education at Brown University.* Newport, RI: Brown University Press, 1986.

Coulson, R. *The Termination Handbook*. New York: Free Press, 1981.

Crul, P. *The Implications of Sexual Harassment on the Job: A Profile of the Experience of 92 Women*. Research Series Report No. 3. New York: Working Women's Institute, 1979.

Equity Institute. *Renewing Commitment to Diversity in the 90s*. Paper presented at the 16th Annual Nonprofit Management Conference, Cleveland, Ohio, June 1990.

Girl Scouts of the United States of America. *Valuing Differences: Pluralism*. New York: Author, 1990.

Johnston, W. B. and Alfred E. Packer. *Workforce 2000: Work and Workers for the Twenty-First Century*. Indianapolis: Hudson Institute, 1987.

Klinger, D. E. and J. Nalbandian. *Public Personnel Management: Contexts and Strategies*. Englewood Cliffs, NJ: Prentice-Hall, 1985.

National Association of Social Workers. *NASW Standards for Social Work Personnel Practice*. Washington, DC: NASW Press, 1990.

Merit Systems Protection Board. *Sexual Harassment in the Federal Workplace: Is It a Problem?* Washington, DC: U.S. Government Printing Office, 1981.

Pecora, Peter J. "Personnel Management." In *NASW Encyclopedia of Social Work*, 19th ed. Washington, DC: NASW Press, pp. 1828–1837.

Chief Administrative Social Work

Clifton, R. L. and A. Dahms. *Grassroots Administration: A Handbook for Staff and Directors of Small Community Based Social Service Agencies*. Prospect Heights, IL: Wavelin Press, 1983.

Herman, Robert D. and Richard D. Heimovics. *Executive Leadership in Nonprofit Organizations: New Strategies for Shaping Executive-Board Dynamics*, San Francisco: Jossey-Bass, 1991.

Hermann, Robert D. et al. *The Jossey-Bass Handbook of Nonprofit Leadership and Management*, San Francisco: Jossey-Bass, 1994.

Nutt, P. C. and R. W. Backoff. *Strategic Management for Public and Third Sector Organizations: A Handbook for Leaders*. San Francisco: Jossey-Bass, 1992.

Waldo, C. N. *A Working Guide for Directors of Not for Profit Organizations*. New York: Quorum, 1986.

Program Evaluation

Bennett, Carl A. and Arthur A. Lumsdaine, eds. *Evaluation and Experiment*. New York: Academic Press, 1975.

Posavac, Emil J. and Raymond G. Carey. *Program Evaluation: Methods and Case Studies*. Englewood Cliffs, NJ: Prentice-Hall, 1985.

Rossi, Peter H. and Howard E. Freeman. *Evaluation: A Systematic Approach*. Beverly Hills, CA: Sage, 1982.

Tripodi, T. *Evaluative Research for Social Workers*. Englewood Cliffs, NJ: Prentice-Hall, 1983.

Weiss, Carol. *Evaluation Research*. Englewood Cliffs, NJ: Prentice-Hall, 1972.

Benefit-Cost Analysis

Thompson, M. S. *Benefit-Cost Analysis for Program Evaluation*. Beverly Hills, CA: Sage, 1983.

Journals in Administration

Administration in Social Work, National Network for Social Work Managers.

Administrative Science Quarterly.

Social Work Administrator, Society for Social Work Administration in Health Care.

Public Administration Review, American Society for Public Administration (ASPA).

12

The Practice of Organization Development

Can a Leopard Change its Spots?

You cannot solve [organizational] problems by using the same management strategies that created the problem. The very system that has patriarchy as the root problem uses patriarchal means to try to eliminate its symptoms.[1]

Peter Block

Ideas in This Chapter

Conflict is common in organizations, especially when there is a great deal of interdependency creating rivalry, communication, and performance problems. An organization developer helps manage conflict constructively.

JEAN CARLYLE TAKES A STAND

For the past 10 years, Wells County has experienced a high level of growth, which was welcome. But along with that growth has come traffic congestion, increased gang activities, drug use, and crime, and as a result, a rise in the caseloads of the Wells County Probation Department. As some areas grew more rapidly than others, boundary shifting became necessary. The East Side, with large Spanish-speaking immigrant and low-income populations, experienced rapid growth and a greater degree of crime as well. Not only were caseloads in the East Side unit growing more rapidly, but

the crimes were of a different nature, necessitating additional work. A vicious cycle developed. With more work to be done, there was less time to monitor cases, and probationers were more likely to repeat offenses. Not only was the work more difficult and the caseloads higher, but worker success rates were far lower than those of other units whose workloads were lighter and whose probationers were far less difficult.

The East Side unit had younger, less experienced workers and some who were older and near burnout. It also had acquired some of the less competent workers. Many more assertive and capable workers obtained valuable experience at the East Side unit and then transferred out or were promoted to specialist positions.

Being isolated from Central, the East Side unit was out of the loop of information and power. As a result, the unit began to think of itself as the Siberia of the probation department, full of less competent workers and victims of an unjust system. On the other hand, because East Side was located physically away from the central office, the East Side staff had some status and privilege, resulting in greater cohesion. In addition, officers had private offices, unlike workers at Central, who were all located in one large pool with workers separated only by 5-foot-high partitions.

In an effort to balance caseloads, Jean Carlyle, supervisor of the East Side unit, changed assignments often. With each change, workloads backed up even more. Jean did everything possible to develop equity, but many members of the unit did not feel they could adequately supervise their wards.

The six supervisors in other geographical areas, where there was less growth, resisted shifting boundaries because they did not want to absorb more work for themselves and their workers, cause confusion in their units, or risk their success rates. Supervisory meetings often ended in heated arguments in which supervisors of units with smaller caseloads defended their territory against Jean, who staged what she considered a one-person battle and often felt discriminated against. Jean did not give up, however, because she wanted to make the East Side unit into one of the best units in the agency, and she was committed to serving the Spanish-speaking and African American populations on the East Side.

Because of agency growth, the entire agency moved to new headquarters, and the East Side unit was merged into the new building. The members of the East Side office lost what little special status they had, and what is worse, in the new arrangement they were deprived of their individual offices. Arthur Thompson, a new probation chief, began putting pressure on all units to meet demands from the state for accountability. His style was simply to apply pressure and weed out workers who were incompetent.

Farthest behind and with low success rates, Jean was under the gun to get more work from staff already overwhelmed, with more difficult loads and more change and now having to travel farther to visit clients. The members of the unit blamed Jean for what they believed was her inability to adequately represent the needs of the unit in agency meetings, and for the increased workload. They were angry about losing their private offices and stressed because of the increased pressure from which Jean had sheltered them in the past.

Stress levels in the unit rose even higher. Everyone now heard conversations previously held in private. Members had little opportunity to blow off steam with one another. As a result, East Side unit members began to take longer lunches, sometimes leaving on prolonged visits to clients' homes and not returning until the next day. Meeting behind closed doors, members of Jean's unit became openly hostile to her. "Wimp" could be heard whispered in corridors when she came by. Morale in the unit plummeted.

Distrust, miscommunication, and conflicts were developing. One day, in the middle of a conversation, one of Jean's workers started shouting at her. Jean was stunned, as were the rest of the probation officers, as the worker's screaming voice echoed throughout the agency. Jean went to Arthur Thompson, who berated her for being ineffective. Despite what she considered to be heroic measures to advocate for her workers, even they had turned on her. Jean felt helpless, alone, and stressed.

The county had recently hired Kathy Herbert, a social work organization developer, who had visited the probation department and explained her services. With no one else to turn to, Jean called Kathy. Meeting over coffee, Jean for the first time poured out her frustrations built up over years of being a buffer between her unit and the rest of the agency. Her feelings were deep and painful, and it was embarrassing for her to express her grief. She felt that her battles to help her unit, her concern for their good, and her compassion were being thrown back at her in the form of resentment and anger. She felt blamed for the very situation she had fought against.

Kathy provided a listening ear and over the course of several weeks helped Jean work through her anger, loss, and hurt. Together they began to problem solve, working on different approaches to the unit. Kathy met with Jean and her unit together, engaging in mutual problem solving and team building to increase cohesion and work through unitwide problems. Gradually, the unit began to see that they were in a self-defeating cycle. They were under stress and blaming Jean, but their own attitudes and work habits were contributing to their low morale and lack of self-esteem. Jean also realized that she needed to be much more directive, and she began to make some changes in how she related to her unit. Her self-confidence began to return, and she began to feel in control once again, developing a proposal for redistributing workloads on a more equitable basis.

As the East Side members began to take responsibility for themselves rather than blaming the supervisor for issues beyond her control, Jean and her unit began to work together as a team once again. Jointly, they began to strategize for solutions. Although the external pressures of work did not ease up, Jean and her unit were communicating on a regular basis and reworking their relationships.

WHAT YOU WILL LEARN IN THIS CHAPTER

It is probably safe to say that no organization is without defects. Individuals in organizations may sometimes lack motivation, display decreased morale, or be prone to stress and burnout. A work group may lack cohesion or have poor productivity. Dysfunctions may show up in interunit rivalry, miscommunication, or conflict. Symptoms may manifest themselves in lessened organizational effectiveness, inefficiency, or poor adaptability to the organization's environment and affect the provision of quality services to customers and clients.

In this chapter you will learn that organization development (OD) is the practice of helping people restore dysfunctional organizations to become socially compatible with the human beings who work in them. You will learn who organization developers are. You will discover that there are two types of organization development—conventional OD and social organization development—and you will explore a brief history of organization development.

You will learn how to practice generalist-based conventional organization development step by step, including diagnosing and applying a variety of treatment tools at the individual, group, intergroup, and organization level. Then you will learn how to use social organization development to assist other social workers to improve the effectiveness and quality of life in social organizations.

WHAT IS ORGANIZATION DEVELOPMENT?

Harvey and Brown define organization development as "a set of methodologies for systematically bringing about organizational change, improving the effectiveness of the organization and its members."[2] French and Bell add that "organization development is a long-range effort to improve an organization's problem solving and renewal processes . . . through a more effective and collaborative management . . . with the assistance of a change agent, and the use of . . . action research."[3] Organization developers help employees plan for and carry out change to create a healthier, more productive work environment. Because organizations affect people's lives in so many ways, macro social workers are increasingly turning their attention to these important social systems, finding that the methods and skills we use in assisting families, groups, or communities are also effective in helping dysfunctional organizations.

Social workers often work as "internal" organization developers. Some may also become "external" organization developers, and still others may combine the two approaches. For example, French and Bell assert that many times organization developers use "outside consultants who work with an inside team to diagnose the organization's internal environment and then design and then implement a program of team development, intergroup relations, and structural changes."[4]

Internal Organization Development

OD specialists work as staff members for private corporations, the military, hospitals, or government-sponsored social agencies. Staff members employed to help improve the organization's effectiveness are called "internal" organization developers. They often assist administrators in diagnosing and resolving areas of organizational dysfunction, help improve organizational communication, conduct workshops in conflict management, train employees in interpersonal relationship skills, and engage in survey feedback research.[5]

External Organization Development

An "external" organization developer works either as a private management consultant or as a member of an organization development firm. Management consultants contract with and provide consultation, training, and problem solving to many different organizations and agencies. Because external consultants are not members of the organization with whom they consult, they provide an objective perspective to organizational difficulties, but because they do not have an intimate understanding of the history, culture, goals, and procedures of the organization, the solutions they offer may be limited in their effectiveness.[6]

MACRO SOCIAL WORK AND ORGANIZATION DEVELOPMENT

Organization development can be a very rewarding but complex social work endeavor. It is a field of practice well suited for and requiring a full range of generalist social work skills, from working with individuals to engaging the wider organizational systems. As an organization developer, for example, you will use active listening, perception checking, and accurate feedback as you relate to employees or administrators who consult with you about organizational problems. You may be called on to use your skills in assessing and making referrals for employees whose personal problems are affecting their work performance.

You may be asked to facilitate agency task groups and decision-making and problem-solving groups. You may develop and implement groups to help improve organizational effectiveness such as quality circles or project management teams. If conflicts or communication problems arise between units or departments, you may be asked to work at the intergroup level to restore smooth working relationships between groups. You may also work with the organization as a whole, helping employees cope with organizational change, reduce organizational stress, or develop a better working environment. You may even be asked to help your agency relate to the wider community in which it is located or network other agencies and organizations to develop strategies and plans to improve the social environment.

Although your generalist skills are crucial, organization development requires particular skills and familiarity with complex organizations, so you will need to acquire experience in these systems and education in organization development beyond the BSW degree. Many social workers who aspire to internal organization development find it useful to obtain an MSW degree, with training in administration or organization development.

If you wish to become a private management consultant or work with a management consulting firm, you will find it helpful to gain experience in a large organizational system in an employee assistance program (EAP) or a training department, for example, as well as obtain additional education at the master's or preferably at the doctoral level in administration, applied organization behavior, or organization development.

A BRIEF HISTORY OF ORGANIZATION DEVELOPMENT

The Origins of Organization Development: 1940s and 1950s

According to French and Bell, organization development originated as a result of a convergence of three strands of work by a diverse group of organizational psychologists, researchers, and practitioners. These strands are laboratory training, action research, and survey research and feedback.[7]

Laboratory Training   In 1945 Kurt Lewin, a prolific theorist, researcher, and practitioner, founded the Research Center for Group Dynamics (RCGD) staffed by social science researchers Leon Festinger, Ronald Lippitt, and Dorwin Cartwright. A year later Lewin and several members of this group conducted a workshop using unstructured small groups in which participants learned from their own interaction. At the end of each day, trainers gave feedback to members about their individual and group behavior, which stimulated great interest and appeared to produce more insight and learning than did lectures and seminars.

Although Lewin died in early 1947, Benne, Bradford, and Lippitt of RCGD continued his work and in the summer of that year organized a 3-week workshop in Bethel, Maine, called the National Training Laboratory in Group Development. Participants met with a trainer and an observer in workshops known as Laboratory Training using Basic Skill Training Groups, later called training or T-groups. This initial workshop evolved into the National Training Laboratory (NTL), later called NTL Institute for Applied Behavioral Science.

In addition to the original staff at RCGD, researchers and practitioners Robert Tannenbaum, Douglas McGregor, Herbert Shepard, and Robert Blake, as well as Richard Beckhard, Chris Argyris, Jack Gibb, and Warren Bennis, each of whom had been T-group trainers at NTL, would subsequently make significant contributions to the field of organization theory, leadership, and development.

In 1952 and 1953, for example, Robert Tannenbaum conducted sessions subsequently called "team building" at the U.S. Naval Ordnance Test Station at China Lake, California, dealing with "personal topics and organizational topics such as deadlines, duties and responsibilities, policies and procedures, and interorganizational group relations."[8] Douglas McGregor, working with Union Carbide in 1957 as a professor-consultant, helped apply T-group skills to complex organizations and established a small internal consulting group later called an "organization development group," helping line managers and their subordinates learn how to be more effective in groups.

In 1958 and 1959 Herb Shepard, who was to have a major impact on the emergence of OD, launched three experiments in organization development at major Esso (now Exxon) refineries. At Bayonne, New Jersey, Shepard administered an interview survey, arrived at a diagnosis, which he discussed with top management, followed by a series of 3-day laboratories for all members of management. At Baton Rouge, Robert Blake joined Shepard in a workshop that emphasized T-groups, organizational exercises, and lectures in intergroup as well as interpersonal relations. At Bayway, Texas, rather than members of different organizations, Shepard, Blake, and Murray Horwitz used team development, consultation, and intergroup conflict resolution with members from the same organization, "triggering real OD." In addition, they experimented with the instrumented laboratory, which Blake and Jane Mouton later developed into the managerial grid approach to organization development described in Chapter 4. Richard Beckhard worked with McGregor at General Mills in 1959 in an attempt to facilitate "a total organizational culture change program," a forerunner of "quality of work life," and in 1960 influenced MacGregor's book, *The Human Side of Enterprise*.

Action Research   Action research is a collaborative, client–consultant process in which both client and consultant develop a tentative diagnosis about the problem together. The consultant assists members of the group in constructing a survey research instrument. The group members then administer the questionnaire and collect and analyze the information. The client group members use the information to develop an action plan that they implement.

Action research also emerged at Tavistock Clinic in England from attempts to give practical help to families, organizations, and communities. Today action research is used by macro social workers in community social work in which community residents and the social worker develop a social survey that residents administer and then use to make changes in their communities.

Survey Feedback Research   Survey research and feedback, a specialized form of action research, was developed by staff members at the Survey Research Center of the University of Michigan, which was founded by Rensis Likert in 1946. In 1947 Likert experimented with improving management performance at Detroit Edison Company using data collected from a survey. Likert and his colleagues found that little change occurred if the survey data were reported to a manager or supervisor who tried to improve the task group without discussing the results or planning with members. However, substantial favorable changes did occur when the manager not only discussed the results of the survey with subordinates and but also planned with them to bring improvement. This led to the development and use of the survey feedback method in which survey information about individual interaction is fed back to task group members who then try to use that information to improve their performance in a work team.

Organization Development in the 1960s and 1970s

Organization developers in the 1960s and 1970s experimented with community development strategies, developed a professional organization, and saw OD become incorporated in the curriculum of a number of universities.

OD and Community Development   Some "community development" strategies have elements in common with organization development, such as the use of action research, the use of a change agent, and an emphasis on facilitating decision-making and problem-solving processes. Some of this commonality may stem from OD practitioners working in community development. In 1961, for example, Herbert Shepard conducted community development laboratories at China Lake, California, sponsored by the

Naval Ordnance Test Station. Outcomes included the resolution of some community and intercommunity issues.

Organization Development Network   The Organization Development Network (ODN), the first professional organization of OD theorists and practitioners, began in 1964 and was originally called the Industrial Trainers Network as a part of NTL. In 1975 ODN included approximately 1,400 members. In that same year the OD Network became independent of NTL and by late 1981 claimed a membership of about 2,100. Most members either maintained a major role in the OD effort of their organizations or were scholar-practitioners in the OD field.

An OD Division of the American Society for Training and Development (ASTD) was established in 1968 and had more than 4,000 members by the summer of 1981. It is also significant that the Academy of Management, whose members are mostly professors in management and related areas, established a Division of Organization Development within its structure in 1971, and this unit identified approximately 1,100 members in late 1983. The Division of Industrial and Organizational Psychology of the American Psychological Association has, in addition, held workshops on organization development at the annual APA conventions.

Education in Organization Development   The first doctoral program devoted to training OD specialists was founded by Herbert Shepard in 1960 at the Case Institute of Technology. This program is now part of the Department of Organizational Behavior, School of Management, Case Western Reserve University. Master's degree programs in organization development or master's programs with concentrations in OD were offered by several universities in the 1970s, including New York University, Brigham Young, Pepperdine, Loyola, Bowling Green, Columbia, Case Western Reserve, and Sheffield Polytechnic in England. Today most major universities have graduate courses directly bearing on organization development, including UCLA, Stanford, Harvard, University of Southern California, Hawaii, Oklahoma, Colorado, Indiana, and Purdue; and in England, such courses are found at the University of Manchester Institute of Science and Technology and the University of Bath.

Organization Development in the 1980s

In the 1980s the U.S. Army, Navy, and Air Force began utilizing OD as a training method. The U.S. Army opened an Organizational Effectiveness Center at Fort Ord, California, in the mid-1970s, and between 1975 and late 1981 they had trained about 1,200 organization development consultants. In 1981 the U.S. Army authorized 388 positions at the officer rank, 100 newly created OD positions at the noncommissioned officer level, and 24 consultant positions in the National Guard and the Reserves.[9]

In 1980 the Navy was using approximately 700 officers and noncommissioned officers full time in its Human Resource Management (HRM) OD Program. OD consultants were trained in a 12-week program and then assigned to one of five HRM centers having detachments throughout the world.

In 1981 the Management Consulting Program of the U.S. Air Force, part of the Leadership and Management Development Center at Maxwell Air Force Base, Alabama, included 44 consultants who developed job enrichment programs as well as team building, intergroup development, feedback, and third party peacemaking.

Organization Development: 1990s to the Present

By the 1990s many of the innovations of the 1970s and 1980s had taken root. OD specialists developed theories and strategies to help organizations modify their organizational culture. The field of organization development continued to expand.

Solidifying Changes   By the 1990s the notion of the work group or team and team building had become accepted and commonplace in many organizations throughout the United States. Team building interventions evolved from being seen as an end in itself to having a clear task focus of improving how the team accomplishes its tasks.

In the mid- to late-1970s, quality of work life (QWL) came to be seen by many as a social movement, and by the 1990s QWL had become increasingly popular as defining an area for study by social scientists as well as an arena for social action and organizational change. T-groups, or encounter groups, however, had passed out of common use in both OD and therapy.

The Organization Culture and OD   It had become clear to many organization development specialists that when top management decided on an organizational change strategy without a commensurate plan to modify the organization's culture, those efforts tended to fail. OD practitioners, therefore, immersed themselves in understanding and assessing the organization's culture and designed change strategies to assist managers in modifying the culture. In addition, OD consultants devised strategies to assist organizations and employees affected by corporate acquisitions or mergers, helping to align the previous organization culture as the newer culture emerged.[10]

The Growth of Organization Development

Organization development has spread to Canada, Britain, Japan, Norway, Sweden, Finland, Australia, New Zealand, the Philippines, and others. In the United States organization development efforts have been used by major corporations, many of them *Fortune* 500 companies. A random sample of half of the *Fortune* 500 companies, yielding 71 respondents, found 46% (33 firms) of the responding firms to be using organization development techniques. At TRW, for example, organization development included team building, intergroup team building, interface laboratories' between departments and between company and customers, laboratory training, career assessment workshops, and organization redesign and restructuring for improved productivity and quality of working life.

In addition, OD applications have been made in public school systems, colleges, and medical schools; social welfare agencies; police departments; professional associations; governmental units at the local, county, state, and national levels; various health care delivery systems; churches; and American Indian tribes well as the U.S. military.[11]

Organization Development Today   OD is healthy and stable, entering a period of slow but steady and productive growth in which its primary task is refinement and consolidation. OD practitioners realize that they cannot work miracles, but they have come to better understand that their effort can make a difference. Some of the most generally useful bits and pieces of OD practice have become widely integrated in organizational life. OD has demonstrated strength, substance, and persistence.[12]

CONVENTIONAL ORGANIZATION DEVELOPMENT

Conventional organization development was created by organizational psychologists and management consultants to improve the effectiveness of modern complex organizations, particularly business corporations, the military, and public organizations. Richard Beckhard asserts that conventional organization development is "(1) planned, (2) organization wide, (3) managed from the top, (4) to increase organization effectiveness and health, (5) through interventions in the organization's processes (6) using behavioral science knowledge."[13]

Studies suggest that conventional OD is not only effective but has sustained considerable popularity as both a theory and a practice in administration.[14] An analysis by Robert Golembiewski, for example, shows that conventional OD is about 85% successful with both business and government organizations. However, as is often the case with social science research, definitive proof is difficult to establish in part because of methodological difficulties. In spite of this, Levine and colleagues assert that conventional "OD, and the human relations philosophy upon which it is based, will continue to be a major part of public administration theory in the years ahead."[15]

CONVENTIONAL ORGANIZATION DEVELOPMENT AND CHANGE

The environment of the organization developer is change. A number of factors impel modern complex organizations toward change, and other factors cause these organizations to resist change. As a conventional organization development consultant, you must understand both of these forces to assist organizational members in responding positively to the need for change.

Forces Impelling the Need for Change

Stephen Robbins tells us that at least six forces are "increasingly creating the need for change: the changing nature of the work force, technology, economic shocks, changing social trends, the 'new' world politics and the changing nature of competition."[16] According to Harvey and Brown, because of the world's "increasingly complex environment, it becomes even more critical for management to identify and respond to forces of social and technical change."[17] Those organizations that adapt to changing circumstances will survive; those that fail to adapt will not.

Barriers to Change

In spite of the need for change, a number of factors create complications for managers who try to create change in their own organizations. Among the forces that cause organizations to resist change are organizational inertia, size, and structure. In addition, organizational chain of command, bureaucratic surveillance, employee dependence, patriarchal organizational culture, the disruptive nature of change, and managerial reluctance may contribute to an organization's resistance to change.

Organizational Inertia

"Organizations," as Robbins says, "by their very nature are conservative. They actively resist change."[18] It is a paradox that change and innovation are at the heart of organizational survival, yet "organizations are not necessarily intended to change."[19] According to systems theory, there is a tendency for an organization to exhibit inertia. An organizational system will tend to maintain a stable state that works against change. All organizations have inherent mechanisms to maintain homeostasis or stability.[20]

Organization Size

Smaller systems are more malleable and adaptable to change. In larger organizational systems, it is more difficult to shift direction because more people are involved in change, any one of whom can cause resistance. More subsystems must be integrated, coordinated, and linked together.

Organization Structure

More important than size, however, are the organization's structural aspects. Modern complex organizations, almost without exception, are based on a hierarchical structure, unitary command, and one-way communication in which subordinates do what they are told. Each of these organizational components becomes entrenched in a self-reinforcing organization culture that resists change at every level. According to Charles Perrow, the top-down hierarchy

> promotes delays and sluggishness; everything must be kicked upstairs for a decision either because the boss insists or because the subordinate does not want to take the risk of making a poor decision. All this indecision exists at the same time that superiors are being authoritarian, dictatorial, rigid, making snap judgments which they refuse to reconsider, implementing on-the-spot decisions without consulting with their subordinates, and generally stifling any independence or creativity at the subordinate levels. . . . Hierarchy promotes rigidity and timidity.[21]

Chain of Command

In modern hierarchical governance systems, change must proceed up and down the chain of command. In general, it will be resisted at each level, particularly when organizations are composed of highly trained professionals.[22]

Bureaucratic Surveillance

Subordinates are under constant surveillance from superiors; thus they often give up trying to exercise initiative or imagination and instead suppress or distort information. Finally, because everything must go through channels and because these channels are vertical, two people at the same level in two different departments cannot work things out by themselves but must involve long lines of superiors.

Employee Dependence

When managers see their role as making decisions from the top, a model of obedience and dependency is established. Organizational problems that may be obvious to line workers go unrecognized by management for long periods of time. Because workers are functionaries who do what they are told, they may think it inappropriate to suggest changes and even self-defeating for them to do so. Individuals at lower levels of the organization may be reluctant to complain to their supervisors out of fear of causing trouble. They may not want to appear disgruntled because this could reflect badly on their performance evaluations. Those who call attention to problems may even be subject to reprisal. "Subordinates are afraid of passing up bad news, or of making suggestions to change. (Such an action would imply that their superiors should have thought of the changes and did not.) They are also more afraid of new situations than of familiar ones, since with the new situations, those above them might introduce new evils, while the old ones are sufficient."[23]

Patriarchal Organization Culture   Organization culture naturally shapes human character to conform to the premises of organization decisions. According to Herbert Simon, "organizational environment provides much of the force that molds and develops personal qualities and habits."[24] People tend to be very malleable; therefore, if the organization culture is patriarchal, people will adapt to those organization patterns. Patriarchy and resistance to change become self-reinforcing.

Disruptive Nature of Change   Organizational change becomes very difficult because "in changing old patterns, people must alter not only their behavior, but also their values and their view of themselves [while at the same time] the organization structure, procedures and relationships continue to reinforce prior patterns of behavior and to resist the new ones."[25] As a result, "almost any change will be psychologically painful,"[26] sometimes bringing with it personal "upheaval and dissatisfaction."[27]

Managerial Reluctance   Organization managers are often faced with a dilemma. "In a monocratic administrative system—a bureaucracy—the external owner has all the rights. He alone can innovate," asserts Victor Thompson. "[I]nnovation will depend upon the psychology of the owner—his mood, confidence, faith in the future and so forth."[28] Managers may not want to hear about problems or may themselves have contributed to them. Even though the boss may realize that change is needed, he or she may be reluctant or even unable to change the hierarchical, patriarchal organization culture that the manager has created.

APPROACHES TO CONVENTIONAL ORGANIZATION DEVELOPMENT

Most conventional organization development "seeks to improve the ability of the organization to adapt to changes in its environment. It seeks to change employee behavior."[29] Organization developers have many different ways to engage in organizational change. Conventional organization developers, for example, may take a systems, social ecology, levels of analysis, subsystems, contingency, or therapeutic approach to making organizational change.

Systems Approach

In the systems approach, the organization developer sees the system as a process of inputs, system maintenance, outputs, and feedback. A change strategy could occur at any point within the system. A change in one part of the system process could create changes in other parts of the system.

Social Ecology Approach

In the social ecology approach, the organization developer views an organization as an open system that is continually interacting with and adapting to its environment. A dysfunctional organization system is one that has failed to adapt. A system design that may at one time have been appropriate or workable has become outmoded or incongruent with new conditions.

The organization may become rigid, its members unable to scan its environment or cope with tensions or stresses that the environment presents. As a conventional organization developer, you try to help management and staff anticipate changes and initiate strategies to adapt to them.

Levels of Analysis Approach

In the levels of analysis approach, the organization developer might focus on the level of individual effectiveness, examining morale, absenteeism, or productivity. You could focus at the level of the group or unit, helping work groups cooperate more effectively together. You help resolve conflicts, communication problems, or coordination difficulties at the intergroup level. You could concentrate on the effectiveness of the organization as a whole, making sure its overall goals are being met and that the organization's culture is healthy.[30]

Subsystems Approach

In the subsystems approach to organizational change, the organization developer focuses on one or more subsystems in the organization. For example, you could begin by improving the reward system in hopes that improving compensation or benefits will increase organization effectiveness. You might examine the communication system, improving information flow between units. You might work with the decision-making system to improve the decision quality and quantity. You could focus on the fiscal budgeting system, improving efficiency and cost-effectiveness and reducing waste.[31]

Contingency Approach

In the contingency approach, the organization developer may view the corporation as a system composed of a variety of components, each of which must fit together harmoniously for the system to function effectively. You look at the relationship between all parts of the company and attempt to discover which of the parts do not fit well with the others. Once the dysfunctional components are located, you adjust them so that the parts of the organization work smoothly together.

Therapeutic Approach

In the therapeutic approach to organizational change, you assume the role of a therapist whose client is a dysfunctional organization. Just as a social work clinician uses personality theory to diagnose psychopathology, you use organization theory and a variety of theories of human behavior, group dynamics, and organization behavior to diagnose organizational problems. You look at different components of the system to determine where pain is located, and at which level of analysis dysfunctions are occurring. You develop a treatment plan and provide interventions to restore the system to better functioning, and you evaluate the treatment to ensure its success.

HOW TO PRACTICE CONVENTIONAL ORGANIZATION DEVELOPMENT

The steps in conventional OD described here combine the various approaches to organization development. As a conventional organization developer, you meet with the owner, the board of directors, and the chief executive officer (CEO) of the organization and negotiate a contract, identify the organizational problem, gather information about it, develop a tentative diagnosis, carry out a treatment plan, and evaluate the results.

Negotiate a Contract

As an organization developer, you meet with the corporation's manager for a preliminary interview. After listening to the manager's perception of the problem, you talk to the organization's board of directors and assess whether the problems they have identified are ones that you have the skills and capabilities to address. Explain your philosophy, and be clear about your own professional and personal commitment to bringing about a better social environment. This may include empowering staff or ensuring that the company is fully a part of the community in which it resides, for example.

Give the managers and board members an idea of the time, resources, and cost to bring about the changes that they want to achieve so they can decide whether they are able and willing to undertake the process. Ultimately you must decide whether you can be of help to the organization and the extent to which management is serious about wanting to change.

Be clear about the methods you plan to use and the extent to which you may need access to employees, company records, and files. Stress the need for confidentiality and your expectation that the organization will protect employees, clients, and management from reprisal or breaches of trust that would irreparably damage the change process. Should you decide to proceed, make sure you, management, and the board agree on your mutual expectations for the project, and formalize a contract specifying payment, the timing, and the nature of your activities.

Identify the Problem

Your first task is to clearly identify the problem. One way to assess an organization's health is to look at how effectively its components work together. You look at the company's outputs, its internal system state, and its adaptation to the social environment.[32]

Outputs   You examine the quantity and quality of the organization's outputs. An effective casework agency, for example, will process a sufficient number of clients per month. One that is less effective will have a waiting list or backlog of clients. A recent study of child care programs in the United States found that only one in seven were "of good quality where children enjoyed close relationships with adults and teachers focused on the individual needs of the children."[33] The study concluded that most child care centers, and especially infant/toddler rooms, did not meet children's needs for health, safety, warm relationships, and learning. In this case, the quality of output goals of many child care centers would be considered poor.

Internal System State   The internal system state is the capacity of the people in the organization to carry out their tasks effectively, interact well together, and engage in productive problem solving, planning, and service provision. You might explore these questions: What is the ratio of service units to their cost? How much waste or downtime occurs in service provision? How effectively are problems resolved, plans carried out, or services provided?

Corporations need people who have effective interpersonal relationships, agree on goals and procedures, and express a level of work satisfaction. Examine how satisfied the employees are. You will be on the lookout for the extent to which members of an organization experience emotional pain and discomfort related to work stress. Employees may be absent or late more often than seems warranted, morale may be low, and work-related injuries may be high. The organization may experience a great deal of employee turnover.

Examine internal relationship processes by asking these questions: What is the extent to which the members of the firm are engaged in destructive conflicts? How cohesive and cooperative are workers? Is there a smooth flow of information among people? How high is employee participation in decision making?[34]

Adaptation   Adaptation of a company in relation to its wider environment is an important indicator of organizational health. Is there adequate financial support for the corporation? Does it have enough human resources at its disposal? How proactively does it scan its environment and anticipate problems? How positive are its relationships with private, public, and not-for-profit agencies in its environment? What is its reputation in its wider community? What is its ability to use resources available to it?

Gather Information

There are a number of ways to gather information about the output, internal system state, adaptation, or culture of an organization. Talk with people using semistructured interviews. You may observe the corporation's milieu as a participant observer, gather information by means of questionnaires, or examine agency records.

Talk to People   You formally or informally interview the board of directors, chief executive officer (CEO), key staff, and company employees.

Begin with the board of directors. Board members are the ones who must accept your findings and treatment plan. Next talk to the CEO and his or her key staff. They will implement changes and are the gatekeepers who give you permission to investigate key components of the organization. You may ask, for example, for their perceptions of the problem: Where in the organizational system does it seem to be located? How is the problem manifesting itself? What kinds of effects does the problem cause? How effective is the organization's output, its internal system state, its ability to adapt, and its culture?

Then gather information from organization members. Just as a social work therapist offers an opener to a client, you may offer, "Tell me your story." Establish rapport and communicate a caring attitude. Make sure that you cover as many people in the organization as you can. Even if you are concerned only with one unit or part of an organization, reach out beyond that unit's boundaries, because what affects one unit will often affect other units in the organization.

Participant Observation   In addition to interviewing people directly, use yourself as a research instrument by means of participant observation. Engage the day-to-day life of the organizational system, observing its culture and interactions. Participate in staff meetings, talk with employees as they gather around the coffeepot, and chat with the receptionist and secretaries. Immediately after you make an observation, take time to record the details as objectively as possible. A good participant observer will watch for signs of stress, tension, conflict, avoidance, poor performance, and communication problems.

Questionnaires   Talking individually to people and using yourself as a participant observer will help you pinpoint specific questions. You can devise a questionnaire and distribute it to all employees or, if the company is large, to a random sample of them. Questionnaires can be helpful because of their anonymity, the speed by which information can be collected, their ability to reduce bias, and the ease by which data can be tabulated.

Existing Data   Existing data from the organization's files, records, budgets, and personnel information can help you obtain a clearer picture of the problem. Personnel information, for example, can give you a picture of employee turnover, an indication of how much sick time employees take, grievances, and other issues.

Diagnose and Treat the Problem

Examine the information you have collected from formal and informal interviews, participant observation, questionnaires, and existing data for patterns, themes, and common indicators that will tell you where in the system the problem is located and what the sources of the problem are. This becomes a tentative diagnosis.

Organizational diagnosis and treatment is often complex and involves intensive work. Organization developers have devised numerous kinds of interventions, and the range of solutions is still in the process of development. A solution developed for one organization may not fit another. Adjust any prescriptive solution to the particular situation with which you are faced. This may mean developing an entirely new and innovative solution. Depending on your diagnosis of what the problem is and where it is located, you may treat systems at the individual level, the group level, the intergroup level, or the organization level.

At the Individual Level   Sometimes people bring personal problems, called work-related personal problems, into a company that affect their performance. At other times the organization itself causes personal problems for employees, called systemwide personal problems.

Understanding Work-Related Personal Problems

Work-related personal problems may occur as a result of life stress, emotional disorders, or addictions. One of the most common addictions is workaholism.

Life stress and emotional disorders: Many people experience stress during personal life crises such as divorce, death, marriage, or giving birth. The stresses of these events often affect individual job performance. Some people are victims of emotional disorders such as chronic depression, bipolar psychosis, obsessive-compulsive disorders, or phobias that affect their ability to carry out their jobs. Life stress or chronic emotional disorders may be expressed in lowered job performance and effectiveness, erratic attendance, increasing tardiness, or excessive absenteeism. An employee may develop a negative attitude, become physically ill or accident-prone. At times the symptoms of emotional disability may increase.

Addictions: Sometimes employees and managers bring dysfunctions into their position carried over from their childhood. People who come from abusive, alcoholic, or addictive homes may use the organization as a source of their own addictions. Personal behavior problems such as alcohol, drug abuse, compulsive eating disorders, or gambling can have an impact on work effectiveness.

Workaholism: Overworking because of a compulsion rather than enjoyment is a common addiction in organizations. People who are workaholics or who work under a workaholic boss are ultimately less rather than more productive. Driven workaholics inevitably induce stress in the workplace and, because they don't take care of themselves, they frequently feel a lot of anger and resentment, eventually displaying physical symptoms such as irritable bowel syndrome, headaches, or ulcers. Exhibiting denial, they operate by "don't think, don't feel, don't talk" rules. According to Rebecca Jones, while "work addiction can be just as unhealthy as substance abuse, the majority of U.S. corporations not only tolerate it, they actually reward it."[35] When work-related problems are of a purely personal nature, make an assessment, and either provide short-term counseling or make a referral to a clinical social worker, usually one practicing in an employee assistance program (EAP). Employee assistance programs provide diagnosis, counseling, and referral for individuals under personal or job-related stress.

Diagnosing Systemwide Individual Problems

Organization developers are concerned with how organizations interfere with individual well-being. Stress is one of the most common systemwide problems individuals experience in organizations.

Everyone experiences stress. In fact, a certain amount of stress is necessary for life. There are two kinds of stress. *Positive stress* includes experiences that are perceived as challenging, exciting, and stimulating. For some people, speaking in front of a group is a personally affirming and enhancing opportunity. *Negative stress* is physically and emotionally damaging. Speaking in front of a group can be so painful and threatening that the person may become physically ill, forget what she or he was to say, and afterward have a feeling of shame or embarrassment. Among the negative stressors that organizations create are excessive change, overspecialization, and overwork.

1. *Excessive change:* Excessive changes in organizational rules and procedures over a long period of time can lead to stress as well as lack of control over one's job environment. A study by the California Worker's Compensation Institute states that the "increase in work-related mental stress claims in the 1980s was phenomenal."[36] Claims of mental stress resulting in lost work time increased from 1,178 incidents in 1979 to 9,368 in 1988, a total of 540%. Job pressures caused employees mental stress 69% of the time, followed by harassment 35%, firing 15%, discrimination 7%, demotion 2%, and other grievances 11%.

2. *Overspecialization:* Stress caused by overspecialization, rigid rules and roles, and formalized procedures can make jobs routine, boring, and lacking in challenge. Overspecialization combined with lack of opportunity to use all of one's abilities, and the pressure of trying to please often-conflicting demands of managers and clients is a situation ready-made for major health problems. A 1988 study by the American Medical Association revealed that "jobs causing the most problems were not those with a great deal of pressure to work hard and fast. Instead, the types of jobs causing increases in blood pressure were lower-level jobs that required high psychosocial demands coupled with little control over the workplace and little use of skills."[37] An employee who is experiencing stress from overspecialization coupled with high interpersonal demands, for example, may develop high blood pressure, irritability, difficulty in making routine decisions, and loss of appetite.[38]

3. *Overwork:* Kathy Slobogin reports on a survey indicating that nearly half of U.S. workers feel overworked or overwhelmed. About one quarter of U.S. employees work 50 or more hours a week, and the same percentage do not take vacations to which they are entitled. Overworked employees are more likely to have work and family conflict, negative health effects, and sleep loss. They are also prone to making mistakes on the job.[39]

Treating Systemwide Stress   When systemwide patterns of organizational dysfunction cause stress, interpersonal conflicts, or emotional and health problems, you should become personally involved in the treatment process. Many programs are available for helping employees with generalized stress. However, stress due to underused skills, high interpersonal demands, and overspecialization may require changes in the quality of work life (QWL) of the organization.

Generalized stress: A number of techniques such as stress reduction, biofeedback, meditation, stress management training, and physical exercise are available to treat individual stress. Companies sometimes provide counseling services, memberships to fitness clubs, and even on-site exercise rooms to help employees cope with job-induced stress. Johnson and Johnson, for example, has developed a Live for Life (LFL) program, a "total immersion approach including fitness, smoking cessation, moderation of drinking, nutrition, weight control, blood pressure control, and stress management."[40] By the third year of the program involving 8,000 employees, LFL showed enough profit in the time and money saved by reducing absences and illnesses to pay back the expenses incurred the first year of the program.

Overspecialization: Quality of work life programs help you consider redesigning jobs, helping employees enhance and use their skills, and increase worker participation in decision making. QWL programs that increase the variety and number of operations of a job by means of job rotation, work modules, and job enlargement can make work more meaningful and increase worker motivation. Job enrichment increases personal control and autonomy in a job.

1. *Job Rotation:* One way to provide increased skill variety for employees who are no longer challenged with their assignments is through job rotation. By diversifying employee activities, workers learn new skills and managers obtain more flexibility in scheduling work, adapting to change,

and filling vacancies. Drawbacks to rotating jobs include increased training costs, job disruption, and increased inefficiency due to lag time in job changeover.

2. *Work Modules:* Work modules spread undesirable jobs among everyone in a unit rather than assigning them permanently to a few people. At the beginning of a workday, employees may request a set of job modules that constitute a day's work, rotating jobs as often as three or four times per day. Work modules allow individuals greater autonomy over work, take into account their own particular job preferences, and build skill variety into the workday.

3. *Job Enlargement:* Job enlargement increases the number of different operations required in a job, thereby increasing its diversity. When you expand assignments by adding a variety of interesting, meaningful tasks, you help employees identify with and make projects their own. If, however, you merely add more boring or meaningless jobs to existing ones, your workers will lose the value of job enlargement.

4. *Job Enrichment:* Job enrichment not only increases responsibility but also autonomy, independence, self-reliance, and self-esteem. You trust the worker to perform an entire job. You provide feedback so the worker can correct his or her own performance.

Diagnosing and Treating Burnout   Another problem, especially for persons in the helping professions, is burnout. Burnout is an occupational hazard that leaves people "vulnerable to doubt, disillusionment, and leads to eventual exhaustion."[41] People who are experiencing burnout may also have physical symptoms such as backaches, frequent colds, or sexual dysfunction. Edelwich says that although burnout can occur in any kind of employment, "it does not occur with anything like the same regularity or carry with it the same social costs in business as it does in the human services where it takes on a special character and special intensity."[42] Burnout may occur due to either individual or system deficiency. Edelwich has developed a four-stage system for diagnosing burnout in the helping professions.

Stage 1: *Idealistic Enthusiasm.* Many who enter social work do so with a sense of altruism and idealism. As a social worker, you may lose yourself in your helping role, leading to unrealistic expectations in your work. For example, you may expect that your presence will make all the difference in the world to your clients, that the job will work a miracle in your own life, and that success and its rewards will be immediate, automatic, and universal. You may expect that every client will be highly motivated and respond with appreciation to your omniscience and omnipotence.

Stage 2: *Stagnation.* When the expectations of Stage 1 go unrealized, social workers may lose momentum. The job does not meet all of your personal needs, such as the need to earn a decent living, to be respected, to have satisfying family and social relationships, or the leisure to enjoy them. If you give all of your energy to clients during the day and have little left over, you may retreat from family or from the sources of rejuvenation that are available. You may expect the small world of the agency to provide identity and meet your social needs, but in reality the agency sucks you dry.

Stage 3: *Frustration.* When you feel bogged down and lose your energy and enthusiasm, you may become frustrated, disappointed with yourself and others, and disillusioned about your role and about the social work profession. You may display symptoms of frustration such as emotional outbursts, exhaustion, or depression.

Stage 4: *Apathy.* If these stages go unrecognized and untreated, frustration may lead to apathy, the final stage of burnout. Apathy exhibits itself in detachment, boredom, indifference, and retreat. The job is no longer exciting or fulfilling.

Agencies can treat burnout by reducing the amount of time a social worker spends working directly with clients each day, each year, or over the course of a career. After a number of years in direct individual service, the worker could shift to an administrative or educational role, work with support groups or peer counseling groups, or engage people at the community level.

The best way to deal with burnout, however, is prevention. Help workers establish realistic expectations at the beginning of their career. Provide education in the stages of burnout. If burnout does occur, assist the social worker to assess his or her goals and expectations and make personal or job-related changes.[43]

At the Group Level   Groups are powerful systems for accomplishing work, but they can also create difficulties if they become dysfunctional. Communication problems, interpersonal relationship problems, poor leadership, undefined tasks or roles, and intraunit rivalry or conflict are all issues you may confront. Organization developers and theorists have developed a number of techniques for improving group effectiveness. Among these are integrated work teams, project management, quality circles, and team development and group conferences.

Integrated Work Teams   One way to increase job satisfaction among individuals is to transform functional work groups into integrated work teams. Instead of several groups performing a single role independently of one another, assign several tasks to each team. Team members decide on specific member assignments and are responsible for rotating jobs as tasks require. Many work crews operate as integrated teams. For example, in cleaning a large building, a supervisor will identify tasks but allow workers as a group to choose how the tasks will be allocated. Roadwork crews, outside maintenance crews, or construction crews often distribute work this way.[44]

Project Management   Project management is another way to structure teams for effective work accomplishment. Managers may pull together specialized workers from several departments or units and assign them to work on a specific project. Because project teams are generally temporary, a leader needs to know how to build a team quickly, adapt his or her leadership style to the situation, and help the group become a functioning unit. The leader must help members understand and accept their new role assignments.

If not organized correctly, a project management team has potential for role or task conflict. You can assist the new project team leader to think through these issues before the project team is developed and assist the leader to help the group through its life cycle.

Quality Circles   A quality circle is a voluntary group of workers, often a normal work unit that has a shared area of responsibility. They meet together weekly on company time and on company premises to discuss their quality problems, investigate causes of problems, recommend solutions, and take corrective action. Members not only take responsibility for solving problems but generate and evaluate their own feedback.

Part of a quality circle's success rests on developing trust, sharing, and good communication skills.[45]

Team Development and Group Conferences   A team is a "group of individuals who depend upon one anther to accomplish a common objective."[46] You can use team building or team development to assist work group members who are either unfamiliar with one another or who are experiencing difficulty in working together. Your goal is to increase the communication, cooperation, and cohesiveness of units to increase their effectiveness.

The team development process is also appropriate for engaging two departments that are experiencing interunit rivalry. A meeting of two or more units is called a group conference. There are six steps in the team development or group conference process:

1. Establish the need for a team or a team development process.

2. Diagnose the problem. Hand out questionnaires and meet with the team to formulate a diagnosis of the level of team development and to establish an agenda of issues.

3. Develop a group contract. Provide feedback to the team members on the issues, establish a set of objectives, and develop a group contract with the team asking for a commitment to work on specific issues over a span of time.

4. Decide on problems. Ideally have the team meet for several days away from the office. Restate the objectives and lay out the issues. Ask members to develop an agenda and rank the issues in order of priority. Ask them to write down five problems they consider detrimental to the group's functioning and task accomplishment. Rank the problems from 1 to 5, 1 being the most serious problem. Make five columns, ranking each column in order of importance or urgency, the first column being most urgent or important and the last column not urgent:

   Most Urgent—needs immediate response

   Very Urgent—needs response within the week

   Urgent—needs response within the month

   Less Urgent—can wait more than one month

   Not Urgent—can be put off for the immediate future

Place the problem issues that members ranked 1 or most serious under the heading "most urgent," those ranked 2 under "very urgent," and so on. Once group members are satisfied with the completeness of the listing, ask them to determine the "ease" and "speed" of arriving at solutions. For each problem, weigh ease of solution: E for easy, MD for moderately difficult, and H for hard. Indicate the amount of time it will take to reach resolution: Q for quick, M for moderate speed, and L for lengthy. Members can now see which issues are most important and most urgent, and how difficult and long it will take to resolve them. With this new information, group members can decide which problems to tackle first. Sometimes a very important problem may appear to have a fairly easy solution. On the other hand, the team may decide to address shorter term, more immediate solutions even though they may not be the most important.

5. Devise a resolution process. Help members reach agreement to work in new ways, restructure roles, and develop time lines to test new processes. The means by which the group works on its own internal problems can be a beginning for restructuring the group's internal dynamics. For example, if leadership is identified as a major problem, assign the unit supervisor, foreman, or division chief to observe or record the process, and appoint someone else to lead the group. This will enable the manager to be objective and involved and ensure that she or he hears what is said about management without the need to be defensive.

If there are subgroup rivalries within the group, break the subgroups apart and place individuals in different groups to promote interaction with others. If communication problems or conflicts exist between particular members, form them into triads. Ask each triad to choose a problem to focus on. One member tells his or her perceptions of the problem while the listener reflects back. Message senders and receivers exchange roles so each practices communication and listening while an observer gives feedback. During these exchanges, work closely with each subgroup, listening, facilitating, modeling, coaching, giving feedback, and structuring activities to help members work more closely together.

Once members have resolved an interpersonal issue, they may be ready to deal with task-related issues. The goal is to arrive at specific action plans to which all members can commit themselves. Before the meeting ends, the team should list action items to be dealt with, who will be responsible for each item, and a time schedule.

6. Develop criteria for evaluating whether the team has been effective, provide training in the new processes, and, if needed, make periodic reassessments and adjustments.[47]

Treating Problems at the Intergroup Level

Organizational problems often exist at the boundaries between subunits in an organization where different groups, units, or departments interact, communicate, and relate. You may consider using problem-solving task forces, boundary spanning, or conflict resolution techniques.

Problem-Solving Task Forces   A problem-solving task force is a short-term conference group made up of two departments that are having trouble coordinating their work. The following process is a modification of a technique called intergroup team building, which was developed by Robert Blake, Herbert Shepard, and Jane Mouton.[48]

1. Bring both units together. Elicit as many symptoms as possible to get a clear picture of the performance problems and uncover their dynamics. Have each unit go to separate rooms. Using information developed in the discussion phase, ask them to develop a list of problems that interfere with performance between the units.

2. After the lists are complete, the units meet together and record their lists on a board for all to see. Facilitate a process of narrowing the lists to specific underlying issues or causes. Divide the larger group into several subgroups comprised of equal representation from each of the two units. Ask them to arrive at solutions to the problems they have identified.

3. Have the subgroups return to the larger group to report on solutions and reach a consensus. Develop a mutual contract in which both units commit themselves to the joint solution, agree to assess its effectiveness, and report back to evaluate on a specific date.

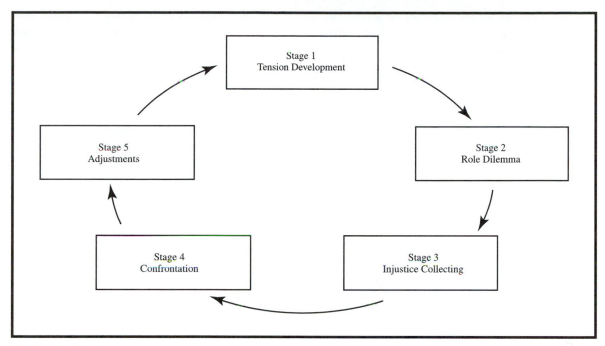

FIGURE 12.1   The Conflict Cycle

Problem-solving task forces are useful in solving problems that have reached a crisis point. For longer term solutions, however, you may need to develop ongoing coordination task forces composed of representatives from various units whose role is to monitor, assess, and propose solutions to continuing interunit coordination problems, resolve disputes, and facilitate planning or production between units.

Boundary Spanning   Boundary spanners are staff troubleshooters who are on the lookout for problems and work to ensure that the relationships between units are smooth. Boundary spanners coordinate efforts between units, teams, or task forces by bringing them together for problem solving. They help resolve conflicts between supervisors, forepersons, or department heads, facilitate integration and work flow, listen to complaints, and in general make sure that communication and integration of the units occur.

Conflict Resolution   The Chinese word for change contains two symbols, one meaning danger, the other opportunity. Change can create opportunity, but it is not without risk. One of the darker aspects of change is conflict in which some attain their goals at the expense of others who perceive themselves as being blocked. Conflict is common in organizations, especially when there is a great deal of interdependency creating rivalry, communication, and performance problems.[49] One of your roles as an organization developer is to help manage conflict constructively. When you work to resolve conflicts, you should understand the stages of conflict development, take a stance of unconditional commitment, and choose one of three processes to help resolve the conflict. Most conflicts follow predictable stages or steps (see Figure 12.1).[50]

Stage 1: *Tension Development.* A minor conflict occurs. The issue may seem insignificant, but it creates discomfort. This is the best time to deal with the irritation, but people tend to avoid recognizing or confronting the situation, hoping it will pass or not repeat itself.

Stage 2: *Role Dilemma.* As conflicts continue, a dilemma is created and tension builds. Parties may feel that this situation should not have occurred, and they may experience increased powerlessness and helplessness to resolve it. To resolve their confusion and reach equilibrium, parties may try to understand who is at fault, pinpoint the cause of the problem, and attach it to an incident, issue, event, or person.

The injured parties try to get out of the dilemma by asking themselves, "What am I doing to cause this tension?" "What is the other person doing?" "What went wrong?" "What is happening here?" Because individuals often struggle alone with the issue, their questions may remain unanswered, perceptions may become entrenched, and dilemmas continue. Issues become more urgent, and it may become difficult for the parties to break the cycle on their own.

Stage 3: *Injustice Collecting.* If the cycle is not broken, people begin to attach blame. Hurts multiply, piling up with each new confrontation. Individuals nurse their wounds, inventory injustices, and dwell internally on their own injuries. Each party feels justified in his or her anger, actively blaming the other party. The parties involved unconsciously prepare for battle.

At this point, it is still possible to break the cycle by having the parties face each other and talk about the issues. But because individuals have withdrawn into their hurts, dialoguing with themselves and cataloging their own injuries, communication will tend to be tense and difficult.

Stage 4: *Confrontation.* The original problem may have been forgotten or swallowed up in each person's accumulated hurts. The focus of the conflict is now on getting even, obtaining revenge, or restitution. Trading hurts, however, only exacerbates injuries, further damaging relationships, blocking communication, and separating the parties from understanding or resolving the issue. Conflict at this stage is often destructive. If people remain inflexible at this stage, conflict may escalate into a fight, or the parties may refuse to interact at all. If the parties are able to stop trading verbal punches and can open themselves to one another, you may be able to trace the conflict back to the original problem and work toward resolution.

Stage 5: *Adjustments.* If the parties have chosen to either fight or withdraw, they will have locked themselves in a standoff. In families this leads to separation and divorce; in international conflict it leads to a battle or a "cold war." In organizations, an employee may ask for a transfer or quit, rival units may refuse to work on common

projects, and labor unions may go on strike. If the parties have been able to engage one another, however, you may be able to assist them to make adjustments using intensive third party peacemaking, mediation, or arbitration. Remember that jumping into the content of a dispute without laying groundwork will often only escalate the conflict and produce negative results.

Unconditional commitment: The best resolutions come about when both parties have made an unconditional commitment to be constructive and to do only those things that will be good for the interunit groups' relationship. Work to help both parties agree to the principles of unconditional commitment:[51]

1. I will commit myself to make things right, even if I may not be sure of how that may occur or how committed others may be at the moment. I will declare my intention to resolve the conflict and work toward reconciliation even if others' commitment seems to waver.

2. I will work at expressing and owning my negative as well as positive feelings so that what caused them can be worked through and resolved.

3. I will balance reason and emotion even if other parties are acting only emotionally or only logically.

4. I will work at understanding. Even if they misunderstand me, I will try to understand them.

5. I will work at good communication. Even if others are not listening, I will listen to them and consult with them on matters that affect them.

6. I will be reliable. Even if others are trying to deceive me, I will neither offer blind trust nor will I try to deceive them.

7. I will use persuasion rather than coercion. Even if they are trying to coerce me, I will be open to persuasion, and I will try to persuade them.

8. I will work at acceptance. Even if others reject me and my concerns as unworthy of their recognition, I will accept others as worthy of consideration.

9. I will be open to learning. Even if others seem to be unbending, I will be accessible and committed to my own growth and learn from this experience.

10. I will relate with respect. I will respect ideas, feelings, and perceptions even if they differ from my own. Likewise I will uphold respect for my own perceptions and expect that others will offer me the same respect.

Three different processes can be used in resolving conflicts: mediation if the problem involves healing an injury or injustice that has broken a personal relationship; negotiation when the issue is external to each party, or to reach agreement in a dispute or arrive at a settlement to which both parties must agree; and mutual problem solving to resolve a breach in a working relationship.

Resolving conflict through mediation: Mediators are advocates for both parties in a disagreement. Mediators help those involved recognize injustice, restore equity, regain relationships, and commit to future resolution.

Explain that this stage is to restore what was broken or bring balance back to the relationship. Ask each party to use the following "four R's," and suggest what would be needed to restore equity: (a) relate to the hurt, (b) reasonable, (c) respectful, and (d) restorative.

Have both parties describe how they became involved in the conflict. Ask party A to describe the conflict, including both facts and feelings while party B listens and takes notes. When party A is finished, ask party B to summarize the main facts and feelings until party A can say, "Yes, that is what I said." Repeat the process with party B describing the conflict while A listens, takes notes, and summarizes what party B said. If there are still unspoken or unresolved hurts, these need to be expressed.

Ask both parties to what behaviors or actions they will commit to prevent future conflicts. What agreements need to be made to build trust? How will accountability be dealt with? Ask both parties to contract with one another to implement the mutually arrived upon solutions. Write a summary and have each party sign an agreement. Schedule a follow-up meeting to check what each party is doing to keep the contract, follow their agreements, or make adjustments.

Resolving conflict through negotiation: Negotiation is a universal process in which an issue or dispute affecting two parties is settled so that a mutual agreement is reached. People negotiate every day over many issues.[52] The most successful negotiation is one that ends in a win-win situation, in which both parties get something they want and each is willing to negotiate again. However, there are also win-lose and lose-lose outcomes. Negotiators work hard to prevent one or both sides from losing. Negotiation occurs in several stages:

1. Preparation: Examine the situation in which both parties find themselves, including the background, culture, and reasons each side takes the position it does. Ask for or gather information from both parties about their positions, what each is willing to give up, and the demands that each party is making. You cannot negotiate what the other side is not capable of or authorized to give. Asking what is impossible for the other side will only result in a deadlock or a lose-lose situation.

2. Presentation of Demands: Meet with both parties. Choose a neutral setting in which both parties are comfortable and at a time when neither will be rushed. Ask each party to present his or her position and formally lay out demands. The demands should be specific, clear, and measurable. Plan an agenda.

3. Negotiating Rounds: (Round 1): You meet with party A, the least flexible party, and obtain as many concessions as you can that will come close to what you know party B will accept. Explain what you think the chances of success are. Point out the areas and to what extent party A may need to give ground.

    (Round 2): Meet with party B and present the concessions of party A. Depending on your assessment of B's position, you may offer only part of party A's demands. Try to come to agreement on as many issues as possible. On those areas where party A's concessions are not acceptable, extract from party B a compromise that will come as close as possible to what you know A will accept.

    (Round 3): As party B considers its position and strategy, meet again with party A and present the items on which you have obtained agreement, pressing A to make concessions on the remaining issues to obtain as much of B's demands as possible.

    (Continuing Rounds): Negotiate in continuing rounds until a compromise is reached. If either party becomes inflexible, try to understand why and problem solve, helping to arrive at creative solutions. Then present those solutions to the other party, asking each party to consider alternative solutions until an acceptable compromise is reached.

Resolving conflict through mutual problem solving: Mutual problem solving relies on "seeking fundamental points of difference rather than on determining who is right, who is wrong, who wins or who loses."[53] This technique requires you to bring the conflicting parties together and encourage them to face the underlying causes for their conflict. The purpose is to solve the problem through collaboration rather than merely accommodate different points of view as with negotiation. The steps are as follows:

1. Define the Problem: Have each party define the problem and commit to a resolution. Ask each party to privately make a list of its concerns and the reasons for taking a particular position. Combine each party's listings, taking one item from one group and one from the other, rewording the concerns in a positive manner. For example, "I don't want to have to put up with your reneging on our agreements" becomes "Keeping our agreements is important." Write the reworded lists in full view on a board or sheet of newsprint.

2. Adopt a Solution: Each party silently writes down possible solutions to the problems that have been listed. Place all of the suggested solutions in plain view. Participants assess the solutions in terms of their particular interests and goals. Modify, shape, combine, adapt, or change the solutions until both groups adopt one or possibly a series of solutions.

3. Adjust the Solution: If a solution does not work because one or the other violates the contract, bring the parties together again to air grievances and renegotiate the contract. If each side tries the solution in good faith, but it does not work, have the parties join together to review why the approach did not work and adjust the solution to accommodate the issues that continue to get in the way.

At the Organizational Level
When problems affect all or almost all employees in an organization, you listen for common patterns or themes that reflect organization-wide problems. Treating organization-wide problems may involve developing a better fit between the structure and function of the organization, assisting members in adapting to its social environment or in restructuring the culture of the organization.

Diagnosing Organization Problems As you listen to organizational members' stories, observe them in action, and review interviews with them, you may observe members expressing one or more of the following diagnostic patterns or themes. When you see these indicators, you may be able to label particular problems and pinpoint their source.

The Sound of "If Only": People are expressing hopelessness, alienation, and powerlessness in an organization when you hear things like this: "If only I could work with so and so." "If only this could be changed." "If only people would listen to me."[54]

Dualism: When a company operates on the basis of either-or dichotomies, organizational managers will demand that employees commit themselves by asking "Are you for it or against it?" The implied message is acquiescence to the manager's ideas or policies. Employees understand that they need to "toe the line." Questioning decisions or offering alternative ideas is seen as disloyalty or disagreement.

Unchallenged Ambiguity: If employees leave things vague enough, they can't be challenged or held accountable. "We'll do that as soon as possible," "We're working on it," or "I'll get around to it" are typical responses to problems that are never resolved.

Inconsistencies: Supervisors or workers are given double messages, which leaves them in a position of trying to second-guess managers. When this happens, workers or supervisors either take literally what managers say and risk making a mistake, or they ignore the administration, using their own better judgment but risk going against the manager's demands. For example, a manager tells supervisors to tighten services because of budget problems but gives no guidelines. Attempting to comply, a supervisor applies rules more strictly, but fairly, angering a client who complains to the director. The supervisor is threatened with termination if the client complains again.

Let George Do It: People in the organization see things going wrong and do nothing about it. Nobody volunteers. Mistakes and problems are habitually hidden or shelved.[55]

No Problem Here: One level of organization dysfunction occurs when ambiguities or inconsistencies cannot be discussed. A sign of greater dysfunction is when the fact that they can't be discussed cannot be discussed. "Don't talk, don't feel, don't think" becomes unspoken policy. People begin to say, "This is a place that's not prepared to address the issues" or "We can't challenge statements, decisions, or assumptions." Instead of confronting discrepancies directly, people begin to express their feelings indirectly by complaining, griping, and sniping in the break room.[56]

Too Hot to Handle: Workers will tend to stay away from conflicts when the source is their own supervisor or interaction between supervisors. If those in authority demand that workers take sides in these disputes, workers are caught in the middle and are in an untenable position.

Unresolved Conflicts: Conflicts remain unresolved when they are covert or are managed by office politics and other games. Arguments may be interminable and irreconcilable. In a crisis, staff members withdraw or blame each other.

Triangulation: Triangulation occurs when people refuse to take responsibility for their feelings or avoid direct communication with others about issues. Instead they complain to a supervisor, who gets stuck with the problem. If the supervisor can solve the problem, he or she becomes a hero. If not, he or she becomes the stuckee. Stuckees tend to be rescuers who cannot say "no." They perpetuate triangulation by encouraging people to air grievances with them rather than talk directly to one another.

The Sorry Circle: Sometimes triangulation expands to include several people. One person, for example, is offended or blocked by another worker. Instead of talking to the offender, the staff member goes to his or her manager. Rather than bring together the two who are in conflict, the manager continues the process, complaining to the manager of the offender. Instead of bringing everyone together, the second manager assumes the offender is guilty and reprimands him or her. If enough time is allowed to lapse before the offender is made aware of the problem, he or she may have completely forgotten the incident and be totally confused. A perpetrator of the sorry circle may operate even more subtly by sending a formal memo of complaint to the manager and the CEO without copying the victim. Left out of the communication loop, the victim is presumed guilty, without knowing he or she has been accused.

Overcontrol: Robert Weinbach says, "people at the top try to control as many decisions as possible."[57] Supervisors or managers can become bottlenecks. They may make decisions without adequate information or advice. They may tightly control small expenditures and demand excessive justification. They may allow little freedom for staff to make mistakes.

Nero Fiddled While Rome Burned: During times of great organizational stress, managers may work hard at solving insignificant issues while the agency is crumbling about them. For example, in one agency the director was being accused of incompetence, its board was under siege, and the state was threatening to take over the agency's operation. Workers were demoralized, services had nearly ground to a halt, clients were up in arms, and the budget was in shambles. A crucial strategy meeting of management was held with all top management staff. It dealt with a procedure on how to answer phone calls from clients.

Scapegoating: Agency anger, frustration, and anxiety may get pinned onto one individual or subunit of the organization as a convenient target. The unit or individual ends up with the most difficult assignments, usually with fewer resources, and then is blamed when things go wrong. Ultimately, these scapegoats bear the pain and become vehicles for system dysfunction. "One more mistake and you're out."

Get No Respect: When managers are under stress, they may sometimes demand blind allegiance based on their position in the organization rather than on their leadership style or the quality of their decisions. Staff is expected to support and offer deference to shore up the manager's sagging self-esteem, compromising their own integrity in the process.

Do as I Say, Not as I Do: In this dysfunctional game, managers assume that they are a species apart, not liable for the same behaviors or procedures for which they hold others accountable. Dispensing favors or punishment with impunity, they set in motion a culture of favoritism. Double standards become the norm. People are treated progressively as objects the farther they are positioned down the hierarchy.

I'm All Alone Here: The ultimate result of "I get no respect" and "Do as I say and not as I do" is that managers try to get things done by themselves without relying on others. Orders, policies, and procedures don't get carried out as intended. The manager becomes increasingly isolated, frustrated, and without support.

The Party Line: Overly stressed managers stop listening to internal and external organizational reality, failing to adequately scan the organization. Instead, they fall back on rules, roles, and procedure manuals rather than what is required to meet changing conditions. When in doubt, they pull out the procedures manual as an authority to buttress their decisions.

Lack of Trust: Lack of trust may flow into the culture of the entire organization. "The judgment of people lower down in the organization is not respected outside the narrow limits of their jobs. People compete when they need to collaborate. They are very jealous of their area of responsibility. Seeking or accepting help is felt to be a sign of weakness. Offering help is not thought of. They distrust each other's motives and speak poorly of one another,"[58] asserts Weinbach.

Playing Politics: If organization politics becomes the normal way of operating, the organizational culture operates not on "what you know, but who you know." Those who are "in" are listened to rather than those who raise disquieting questions; supervisors do what will best protect themselves, and the agency may be seen as a place by which maneuvering to get ahead or covering oneself is the norm.

We Have Always Done It This Way: People may be reluctant to admit that things are not going well because it may reflect on them and on their own performance. Because they are immobilized and cannot change, they resist seeing that current practices no longer fit changing circumstances and display blindness to problem situations. Instead of adaptability,

they fall back on the adage, "We have always done it this way."

Helplessness: "People swallow their frustrations: 'I can do nothing. It's their responsibility to save the ship,'" says Weinbach.[59]

Burnout and Get Out: "People feel locked into their jobs. They feel stale and bored but constrained by the need for security. Their behavior in staff meetings is listless and docile," says Weinbach.[60] Ultimately people become so burned out, they end up getting out of the organization.

Treating Organization Problems   When you as an organization developer assist in resolving problems that affect the entire organization, you may decide to work at the level of structural functional change, use management by objectives, or help the organization improve its culture.

Structural functional change: When you engage in structural functional change, you look at the fit between what the organization members want to do (its functions) and the way they have decided to accomplish them (structures). You form a problem-solving task group that examines the problem, arrives at alternative solutions, chooses the best solution, presents it to the organization as a whole, and works with management to implement the solution.

1. Form a Problem-Solving Task Group: Discuss with top management which employees should be chosen as members of the problem-solving task group. Because organizational change involves the entire organization, the process should be inclusive, democratic, and participative. One way is for each staff group or work unit to recommend a member to join the task group, including a member from the top management team and at least one member of the board. In a large organization you may form several groups, each representing a section of the organization.

2. Examine the Problem: Ask the task group to brainstorm a list of all the functions that the organization or their section performs and group them into categories. Next, list the ways that the section or organization fulfills these functions. Compare the functions and the structures and ask members to match the functions with structures. If there are gaps, discrepancies, or weaknesses, note where they occur. For example, there may be gaps or

ineffectiveness in service provision, poor communication, lack of accountability, ineffectiveness in meeting objectives, or no objectives at all.

3. Arrive at Alternative Solutions: The problem-solving task group should compare pros and cons of alternative proposals and devise one that they believe will help the organization develop a better structural functional fit. If several groups have been used, ask a representative from each one to join a final problem-solving task group. Each representative will present that group's best solution to the problem-solving group. Together representatives will compare the pros and cons of each alternative solution and choose one to present to the organization.

4. Present the Solutions to the Organization as a Whole: In an organization-wide meeting, a panel of problem-solving group members should briefly describe the history of the process and present the solution to the organization members including the board. A moderator should then solicit ideas and opinions from organization members using buzz groups, slip writing, idea writing, or other techniques described in Chapter 9. The panel will then assimilate the feedback from the organization members and refine its solutions. The panel may perform a second round of discussion and feedback from the organization. When everyone is satisfied with the final solution, it is presented to the chief administrative officer to discuss with the board of directors.

5. Implement the Solution: Upon approval by the board of directors, the chief administrator will develop a process of implementation.

Management by objectives: Sometimes the social environment of an organization changes so that it needs to adapt its goals to the new situation. When the organization's goals lack effectiveness, one way to examine and change those goals is by means of management by objectives (MBO). MBO is a process whereby each unit of an organization develops long-range goals and short-term objectives, action plans, and behavioral reinforcements.[61]

1. *Establish Long-Range Goals and Short-Term Objectives:* The manager establishes long-range goals and strategic plans for the organization and breaks them down into specific overall organization objectives for each department. Objectives are statements of measurable results the organization is to achieve within a specific time period. Each department head breaks down the departmental objectives for each subunit. Then, within each work unit, line supervisors develop specific job objectives for each worker.

2. *Develop Action Plans:* Managers develop actions plans that contain the sequence of tasks, key activities, and budgets required to accomplish the objectives as well as methods for ensuring the accomplishment of the objectives for which they have responsibility. Managers implement the action plans and assign individuals responsibility for specific tasks.

3. *Provide Behavior Reinforcements:* Usually managers develop a series of behavior reinforcements and motivational incentives to strengthen performance through training, compensation, or other techniques. They build feedback by means of periodic progress reviews, adjusting objectives, action plans, and control methods in the process.[62]

Improve the organization's culture: When the morale throughout an organization is low, turnover is high, personal conflicts are common, and productivity is low and of poor quality, there may be problems in the organization's culture. The organization's culture is composed of the meanings that people attach to the organization and the underlying premises that an organization represents.[63] The culture is "shared values, beliefs, assumptions, perceptions, norms, artifacts, and patterns of behavior. It is the unseen and unobservable force that is always behind organizational activities. Culture is to the organization what personality is to the individual—a hidden, yet unifying theme that provides meaning, direction and mobilization."[64]

A company with a weak culture may have only a vague sense of its purpose, and often there is a discrepancy between what it says about itself and what it actually does. There may be an underlying sense that what people do or think doesn't matter. Firms with weak cultures give unclear or conflicting messages about what is important or how to succeed. For example, an organization in which the implicit message is "it's not what you know, but whom you know" encourages people to spend time appeasing others rather than getting the job done. The culture of an organization is weak or fragmented when employees from some units or worksites are given preferential treatment or when different classes of employees are treated differently. Employees lose sight of who the heroes of the corporation are and the values those heroes represent. Management spends little time recognizing employee achievements and organizational successes.

When a culture is weak or in trouble, people get frightened. This shows up in emotional outbursts such as denouncement of an agency policy in the workplace and visible displays of anger or through personal problems such as a wave of divorces or drinking problems. People lack idealism, energy, and a sense of enthusiasm about the agency and what it does. Employees simply "put in their time" because they know that their efforts will not pay off, will not be recognized, or may be discouraged. In a weak corporate culture, staff members have little idea about the history or philosophy of the agency.

Mark Homan says that the culture of the organization is its "single, most powerful force affecting change."[65] He provides the following suggestions for strengthening the culture of the organization:

1. Engage in purposeful and open discussion about the weaknesses in the organization's culture, its effects on the organization's functioning, and engage in a clear agreement with the board, administration, and staff to change it. Over time minor alterations of the culture of an organization can be made, but they must occur steadily and consistently.

2. Create an awareness of the problems that exist in the organization's culture. For example, people in the organization may be working at cross purposes because the mission of the organization is not clear or has changed so rapidly that people have not had time to adjust. Give examples of how the vagueness of the mission creates a lack of strong commitment on the part of employees, lack of motivation, and low morale, or cite other symptoms of a weak culture.

3. Present your change as being culturally consistent and relevant to the goals of improving the milieu of the organization for employees and customers or clients, and link your recommendations for change to the existing values of the organization. Rather than suggesting radical change, build on the existing values and help employees strengthen them.

4. Hold a workshop to help members examine the organization's culture and its problems. Brainstorm ways to improve the culture, and then along with the board and administration take steps to implement the ideas.

Once the membership of the organization becomes aware that its culture is in need of strengthening, are committed to its improvement, and work consistently to institute gradual changes over time, the cohesion and commitment of employees to the mission may steadily improve.

SOCIAL ORGANIZATION DEVELOPMENT

Social organization development was specifically created to improve the working environment of social work agencies and programs. Because a social organization is accountable to the stakeholders that established and supports it, its effectiveness is important to its clients, employees, and the wider network of social programs and services. Macro social workers have the skills and should provide internal organization development to their social organizations in a process of ongoing, mutual problem solving in collaboration with their colleagues, administrators, clients, and community members. This process should be proactive, consensual, voluntary, and aimed at strengthening, empowering, and enhancing the service environment of the agency as well as its goals of improving its social environment.

Social organization development is designed to help employees of social organizations create and maintain systems that are congruent with social work values of respect, self-determination, authenticity, genuineness, freedom, choice, and opportunity for growth, autonomy, and self-management. Social organization development places a high priority on creating an organization culture that produces social capital of service, improves people's social welfare, creates social opportunities, is less concerned about efficiency, and overtly rejects management and control of people. For social agencies that have fallen into the trap of emulating structures of private corporations and their values, social organization development offers an opportunity to realign the social organization to become more faithful to foundational values of the social work profession. For newer agencies that are faced with a choice, social organization development offers a way to develop an organizational culture in which social workers are in control of the systems they construct.

HOW TO PRACTICE SOCIAL ORGANIZATION DEVELOPMENT

When you perform social organization development, you begin with engagement, develop a contract, renegotiate control and responsibility, offer an invitation to change, create a desired future, form improvement teams, change work practices, redesign the organization, offer learning opportunities, and expect administration to trust the social workers. Keep in mind that you follow the lead of the people you are assisting. You do not rigidly follow a process, but you become familiar enough with the various steps so you can apply them when they are called for.

Engagement

Helping people choose autonomy, partnership, and service is difficult. When core social workers and administrative social workers choose to create their own experiment, it is like walking into an unlit room, says Peter Block.[66] For this reason, a partnership or social model of organization development often begins as an act of faith in people and in the principles of social work, and it gets built when responsibility and commitment are widely shared.

The partnership model asserts that "creating our own practice is the basis of ownership and responsibility," and claims that change can start from wherever a person happens to be. As a social organization developer, you present these challenges to administrators and to members of the organization as a means of transforming social organizations from control and threat systems into an authentic means of service and social liberation. When social administrators as well as social workers accept this challenge for themselves and their social organizations, they can begin to assist clients to do the same.

You must be clear at the outset that the partnership approach is unlike conventional organization development, but you need to be equally clear that it will improve organizational functioning, effectiveness, and service in ways that will ensure genuine congruence with social work principles and values.

Develop a Contract

Try to determine how ready and able the board, administration, and members of the social organization are in following through on a project of self-determination and mutual responsibility in taking charge of their futures together. Your goal is to help the social organization build its community component, which can be used for transformative purposes. You want to help board members, social workers, and clients empower themselves so that they control the organization, instead of the organization controlling people.

You invite the entire membership of your social organization to jointly consider your expectations for the project and formalize them in a written contract specifying the timing and nature of their mutual activities. The joint contract includes the difficult issues, such as a commitment to improved quality and service, and concludes with the principles for the redesign effort.

Renegotiate Control and Responsibility

You renegotiate control and responsibility with core social workers, administrative social workers, and staff. With each group you ask for exemptions from business as usual to provide space for engaging in change.

Core Social Workers   Your discussion with core social workers is about purpose and responsibility and includes self-management.

Purpose and Responsibility   Social organization development shifts the emphasis from top-down planning and puts responsibility and choice in the hands of ordinary core employees of the organization. They are the ones who do the organization's work, who experience its failures and dysfunctions, and who must endure being deprived of full humanity in complex organizations. It is they who must survive the impersonality that organization imposes on daily existence, which robs them of creativity and keeps them dependent.

All employees join in designing the kind of unit in which they will function. They exercise more choice and control, and in return they claim ownership and real responsibility for the work process and outcomes. One way to talk to workers and staff about change is through self-management.

Self-Management Everyone has doubts and fears. Even though history may be on the side of the doubtful and their wounds are real, people can choose to have faith in the face of that experience. You affirm their version of history and support them in their doubts by acknowledging the part of you that agrees with their position. You acknowledge their perceptions of reality, while you affirm your faith and commitment in the face of your own reservations and invite the same choice from others. You replace unobtrusive control, persuasion, or coercion with an invitation to choice and opportunity.

What is critical in this whole process is that people make choices in spite of the doubts they have. Social organization development asks: What will it take for me to claim my own freedom and create an organization of my own choosing? What is it I uniquely have to offer and what do I wish to leave behind here? When will I finally choose adventure and accept the fact that there is no safe path? When will I decide that my underlying security comes from counting on my own actions or from some higher power rather than with the decisions of others or the supererogatory power of an organizational tool?

When you pose these challenges to core workers, you are asking them to say yes to questions of freedom, service, and adventure and for them to open up the possibility of beginning their own experiment in partnership and service. It only takes one instant to decide for freedom and autonomy, one moment of decision to affirm one's life and move in another direction. Social workers only have to choose it and have the courage to live with the consequences. Along with challenging others, you affirm the choice that you have made. You speak to those who are cynical about change, to those who have been victimized by organizational threat systems, and to bystanders.

Cynics For the cynics you, too, can name other programs that have started and resulted in nothing of value. But you can also own the risks of the path you are choosing. For example, say to the cynics, "I understand what you say. In some ways, I share the doubts and perhaps bitterness you express. I, though,

have decided to have faith that this time we can do something here that will matter, and I hope you will make the same choice and join in this effort." This may not be persuasive and may not change a cynic's position, but it neutralizes the power he or she has over the organization. While cynics have a right to their own stance, they do not have a right to hold back others.

Victims and Bystanders For the victims, you acknowledge their feelings of helplessness and their wish that people in power will not disappoint them. You have the same desire and the same doubt. For the bystanders, support their desire for more data, more proof that this story has been written elsewhere and will have a happy ending. You, too, may have searched for reassurance and wanted more, but you continue in spite of the unknown.

Administrative Social Workers

Social organization development presents a challenge to administrative social workers who genuinely value service, individual dignity, personal self-determination, and freedom of choice. Social organization development is for social workers and administrators who have a vision of transforming social organizations into authentic tools of social service, not control; of social change, not conformity; and making them congruent with the principles of social work.

The stakes are high, however, when people in key staff positions are skeptical about what you want to do. They often want to maintain tight control and consistency even after your best arguments have been made. Despite the risk, you approach these people in generally the same way as you do core social workers and staff.

Make the case for reform. State the results you are seeking and the harsh realities they may face. Be clear about the principles you want to reach toward and the constraints you have established. Affirm the choice you have made for responsibility, organizational service, quality, and empowerment, and ask administrative social workers to support what you are trying to do. You ask to be given a chance, as an experiment. In return for an exemption from normal procedures, you promise better work outcomes.

Ask to Be Treated as a Pilot Project When administrators lack faith or commitment, don't argue or negotiate. All you can do as a social organization developer is communicate understanding to them. In a sense, take their side, acknowledge the risks, and ask to be treated as an exception, a human pilot project. You have to be willing to absorb all the risk. You will deliver results to administration, and if you do not, you expect to pay a price. All you want from those in charge is tolerance or indifference. You do not require sponsorship, commitment, or even deep interest. If you get enthusiasm, take it, but don't set it up as a requirement.

Ask for an Exemption   Acknowledge that you want an exemption to normal requirements for control and consistency. Let administration know that you understand the problem your request creates for them. The discussion with administrators is about their giving up control in exchange for a promise. You ask them to yield on their wish for consistency and let you and the core workers conduct an experiment.

Deliver Better Outcomes   In return for the exemption, you are committing to delivering specific results. Along with core workers, you are promising certain operational outcomes in return for the freedom to pursue a unique path. You are promising that clients will be better served and that the organization will function better. You promise that core workers will honor the requirements of the organization, that you will keep the administrators fully informed, and that you will live with the consequences.

Staff   Staff members hold specialized positions in management functions. Their jobs were created to ensure consistency and control in personnel administration, financial operations, and information systems technology. Discuss with agency staff the need for an exception. In return you agree to give them what they require in terms of accountability, paperwork, time limits, and formal processes so that their work is not hampered. But explain that core social workers and their work units will operate internally in ways of their own choosing. Let staff know that you understand the risks of deviating from the standard ways of operating. The chief administrative social worker may mediate or advocate for you in getting this exception.

Offer an Invitation to Change

Invite members to make a choice. There is no promise in this invitation, nor is there an immediate demand for acceptance. You only ask to keep doubts and excuses in the background where they belong. Workers have a right to say no to your invitation. They may want a boss

who will take care of them in return for hard work and loyalty. Their choice needs to be acknowledged, but it also has consequences. In the longer run, they will have a hard time getting what they want from the organization, and the organization may not have a place where their skills can make a contribution.

Despite this, you do not need to force the issue at this moment. People need to be given time and support to make fundamental choices about faith and responsibility. Block asserts that "we do not need everyone to chose partnership and service. All you need is about 25% to commit and the way the organization operates will start to shift. Over time this 25% will pull the others along and another 20% will usually move on out of their own discomfort."[67]

Create a Desired Future

Partnership is created as each board member, social worker, staff member, and administrative member defines a vision for the area of his or her responsibility. Partnership offers hope that freedom, opportunity, and service can be rediscovered in the renunciation of organizational dependency. According to Block, social organization development offers this affirmation: "I discover my freedom through the belief that my security lies within and is assured by acts of congruence and integrity. I can be of real service only when I take responsibility for all my actions, and when the choices I make are mine which is the only safety I have. Service out of obligation is co-dependency and a disguised form of control. Service that fully satisfies is done with no expectation of return, and is freely chosen."[68]

Focus on the future the members of your group want to create for the organization. Ask members to participate in expressing a joint vision of the organization, its purpose, governance, and structure for the future. What is the best way of including the organization as part of the community? How do you create partnership? How does the organization engage in mutual empowerment of members and clients? How is accountability to be provided? How can clients be part of the organization and community building?

Form Improvement Teams

Encourage each unit to begin a dialogue about what values are important to each person at this stage of life and how these can be lived out more deeply in this workplace. Dialogue is key. The hallmark of partnership in action, says Block, is to ask people to talk about what matters to them, not ask people to support what matters to you or those in authority.

Have groups meet regularly to discuss improvement ideas. Several organizations have been engaging core workers in developing self-determination in this way. General Electric, for example, has a process called a workout in which departments meet to discuss and decide on how to streamline the business. It is their vehicle for creating a more entrepreneurial mindset. Quality circles were an early version of improvement teams. Many improvement teams cross functions and levels. Their focus is usually on cost cutting, quality enhancement, reducing cycle time, and satisfying customers.

Change Work Practices

Teams of core social workers, board members, clerical workers, custodial and other staff meet together to rethink questions of service provision, meeting client expectations and needs, ways of approaching social problems, arranging for services, delivering services, or new ways of making social change. Procedures in budgeting, funding, structuring the work, hiring, and evaluations all come under the umbrella of changing management and work practices.

You may also set up steering committees and task forces that include clients, community members, and board members along with agency employees to shape this activity. Steering committees guide the whole effort, setting priorities, establishing study groups, making final decisions on changes, and monitoring the effort. Task forces get set up to address specific changes and make recommendations.

You can share your experiences about how to implement particular improvements about which you may be familiar such as techniques of work redesign, ecology of work, implementing high-performance work teams, total quality management (TQM), reinventing the workplace, and others. This step is where the idea of service and partnership begins to get institutionalized.

Redesign the Organization

As a social organization developer, you help administrative social workers and members redesign the structure or architecture of the organization. Partnership

acknowledges that we social workers are capable of defining for ourselves the rules and yardsticks by which we live and work. If you want the middle and core social workers to treat the organization as their own, they have to steer the reform efforts with their own hands. Help people at the bottom gain more control over how the change happens. The substantive work of redesign has to be done by self-managing teams of social work and staff groups.

Each team of core social workers designs what is right for its own unit. Members must struggle with how much of the traditional supervising social worker's tasks to take on themselves. How does the team reassign roles, administer discipline, schedule work, hire and train new members, monitor outcomes, and relate to other units and to the top administrative team? There is no one answer.

Offer Learning Opportunities

If you want social workers in each unit to design their own experiments, they also should define their learning requirements. The partnership model of social organization development puts choice in the hands of the learner. If training is needed, those who require it define it, choose it, and manage it. Let different units choose their own ways and places for learning.

Let the agenda and environment for learning emerge rather than be a cornerstone of the change strategy. For example, offer management training to core workers in team skills, conflict management, communication skills, quality tools, and work process improvement. Most social organizations create a menu that teams can choose from. Each team chooses its own agenda, and team members attend sessions together.

Trust the Social Workers

With your assistance, core social workers, office workers, and other staff implement the plans they have devised. If you want social work staff to take ownership and responsibility, they will have to define and create the means for successfully living out those responsibilities on their own. You, the administrative social workers, and the board of directors must trust that mature social workers have the skills, training, and capabilities to take control of their work, their workplaces, and their futures.

CONCLUSION

There is probably no modern complex organization in existence that does not have problems at some level: employees with stress-related personal problems, units or teams that do not function effectively, departments experiencing interunit rivalries, or entire organizations whose workers are dissatisfied and in conflict with management. Conventional organization development can be a very exciting and rewarding arena of social work practice. Macro social workers can find a great deal of challenge and satisfaction in helping organization members develop healthier, more satisfying and productive work environments.

Social organization development workers help reconstruct the culture of social organizations to embody the values and principles that social workers honor, help social workers create social organizations that practice empowerment and self-determination, and treat organization members as mature adults who can and should chart their own future.

KEY CONCEPTS

organization development

internal organization development

external organization development

management consulting

laboratory training

Kurt Lewin

T-groups

National Training Laboratories (NTL)

action research

survey feedback research

Rensis Likert

Organization Development Network (ODN)

Herbert Shepard

Association for Training and Development (ASTD)

conventional organization development

need for change

barriers to change

systems approach

social ecology approach

levels of analysis approach

subsystems approach

contingency theory approach

therapeutic approach

steps in conventional OD

outputs

internal systems state

adaptation

participant observation

questionnaires

existing data

work-related personal problems

employee assistance programs (EAP)

quality of work life (QLW)

life stress

addictions

workaholism

systemwide individual problems

positive stress

negative stress

excessive change

overspecialization

overwork

job rotation

work modules

job enlargement

job enrichment

burnout

stages of burnout

integrated work teams

project management

quality circles

team building

group conferences

problem-solving task force

boundary spanning

conflict cycle

conflict resolution

mediation

negotiation

mutual problem solving

structural functional change

management by objectives (MBO)

changing the organizational culture

social organization development

steps in social organization development

steering committees

task forces

improvement teams

redesigning the workplace

offer learning opportunities

trust the social workers

QUESTIONS FOR DISCUSSION

1. How are the role, skills, and process of an organization developer similar or different from those of a psychotherapist?
2. How is the role of an organization developer similar or different from that of a community developer?
3. Organization developers are charged with improving the effectiveness of the organization with which they have contracted. Are there situations in which an organization developer may find his or her social work values in conflict with helping the organization become more effective? What are some ethical conflicts organization developers might encounter?

4. Modern organizations are tools for implementing the predetermined ends of the owners. Does an organization developer have a right to question those ends? Why or why not? Would it be easy for you to find work if you questioned the ends to which client organizations were directed?

5. Social organization development asserts itself to be fundamentally different from conventional organization development. What are its similarities and differences? Are those differences "fundamental" or only technically different?

6. It has been asserted that it is impossible and deceptive to presume to "humanize" modern bureaucratic organizations because their very nature is to dehumanize people. Do you agree or disagree with that assertion. Is it appropriate or even possible for a conventional organization developer to attempt to humanize a rational/legal organizational system? Is it possible for a social organization developer to try to humanize a social organization?

ADDITIONAL READING

Block, Peter. *Stewardship: Choosing Service Over Self-Interest.* San Francisco: Berrett-Koehler, 1993.

Brager, George and Stephen Holloway. *Changing Human Service Organizations: Politics and Practice.* New York: Free Press, 1978.

Redburn, Ray et al. *Confessions of Empowering Organizations.* Cincinnati, OH: Association for Quality and Participation, 1991.

Weisbord, Marvin R. *Discovering Common Ground: How Future Search Conferences Bring People Together.* San Francisco: Berrett-Koehler, 1992.

Conflict Resolution and Negotiation

Fisher, Roger and Scott Brown. *Getting Together: Building a Relationship That Gets to Yes.* Boston: Houghton Mifflin, 1988.

Fisher, Roger, Scott Brown, and William Ury, with Bruce Patton, ed. *Getting to Yes: Negotiating Agreement Without Giving In,* 2d ed. New York: Penguin Books, 1991.

Organization Development

Beckhard, Richard. *Organization Development: Strategies and Models.* Reading, MA: Addison-Wesley, 1969.

Bennis, Warren et al. *The Planning of Change,* 4th ed. New York: Holt, 1985.

French, Wendell and Cecil H. Bell Jr. *Organization Development: Behavioral Science Interventions for Organization Improvement,* 2d ed. Englewood Cliffs, NJ: Prentice-Hall, 1978.

Gould, Gary M. and Michael L. Smith, eds. *Social Work in the Workplace: Practice and Principles.* New York: Springer, 1988.

Kanter, Rosabeth Moss. *The Change Masters.* New York: Simon and Schuster, 1983.

Peters, Tom and R. Waterman. *In Search of Excellence: Lessons From America's Best Run Companies.* New York: Harper and Row, 1982.

Management Consultation

Block, Peter. *Flawless Consulting: A Guide to Getting Your Expertise Used.* San Diego: Pfeiffer, 1981.

Goodstein, L. *Consultation With Human Service Systems.* Reading, MA: Addison-Wesley, 1978.

Lippitt, G. and R. Lippitt. *The Consulting Process in Action.* La Jolla, CA: University Associates, 1978.

Schein, Edgar A. *Process Consultation: Its Roles in Organization Development.* Reading MA: Addison-Wesley, 1969.

Articles

At Work: Stories of Tomorrow's Workplace (bimonthly). Berrett-Koehler Publishers, 155 Montgomery St., San Francisco, CA 94104-4109.

Lippitt, G. L. "A Study of the Consultation Process," *Journal of Social Issues,* 15, 1959, pp. 43–50.

PART Four

Social Work Practice at the National and International Levels

---

Difficulties in Making Change

It must be considered that there is nothing more difficult to carry out, or doubtful of success, or more dangerous to handle than to initiate a new order of things. The reformer has enemies in all those who profit by the old order, and only lukewarm defenders in those who would profit by the new.[1]

Niccolo Machiavelli

In its drive to power and wealth before the turn of the 20th century, the organized market economy threatened to overwhelm the American political apparatus. Not only was the national government relatively small, but it was also philosophically constrained against regulating or controlling the economy, providing a milieu ripe for exploitation. Corporations formed political machines and manipulated local, state, and even national elections, deciding on candidates for public office in "smoke-filled rooms" and virtually assuring their election by bribery, graft, and corruption. The result was a nation in which the corporate economy engineered public policy and ate at the public trough for its own profit.

"Only when mass unrest arose—the massive and threatening social movements of the poor—that awareness of the crisis was forced on the middle class," says John Ehrenreich.[2] "Large numbers of middle class Americans added their sympathy for the lot of the poor and anger at what untrammeled capitalism was doing to small town America in which they had grown up at the turn of the 20th century," and once aroused, "the mix of fears and concerns, drove growing middle America including social workers toward Progressivism and the reforming programs, movements and ideologies that gave their name to the entire historical period."[3]

369

In the last half of the 20th century, the modern free market found an expanded and even more vulnerable arena as more than 100 small nations with rich natural and human resources struggled to enter the arena of modernity. Today's market society continues its expansion into nearly every corner of the globe. Transnational corporations dominate and overwhelm entire nations, control governments, and determine the fate of their citizens.

The result is vast poverty for 80% of the world's population, decimation of the environment, disenfranchisement of people, and the subterranean operation of power that is out of reach of the vast majority of the world's citizens. What is clear to most of these people and to many macro social workers is that the military power, economic might, political control, and cultural hegemony of modernity cannot correct the disparities that these systems have created. Modernity is helpless in resolving the dilemmas on which it is based and can only exacerbate those inequities as it proceeds along the path of its rational self-interest. It is impossible for the global market to reform, restrain, or reshape itself into a kinder and gentler system.

What is even more obvious to the poor people of the earth is that the natural capacity of this planet cannot be contained by the perpetual rapacious consumption that these economic systems demand. The billions of the earth's people who live under conditions of inhumanity, trauma, deprivation, upheaval, and decimation forced upon them by the demands of the self-interested global market system cannot endure.

Economic exploitation and usurpation of the political process in the United States 100 years ago led to efforts of national reform. Mass unrest at the accumulated oppression experienced by the impoverished members of developing nations at the turn of the 21st century is driving the poor people of the earth not toward reform but to a rejection of the excesses of modernity and toward a new society. Some members of the middle classes of developed nations are growing in awareness that the problems faced by the majority of the world's population are their problems as well, and many macro social workers see clearly that we are at the dawn of a new era.

This new era has been called by many names: the information age, the age of technology, the postindustrial age, and the postmodern era. As pressures build for change, a paradigm shift is required. We need to rethink what society should be like, the relationship between people, and the relationship between people and the natural environment. Already some macro social workers and others have taken steps in the direction of forging a new postmodern world that rejects modern premises and forges completely new ones. In Part Four you will learn the role of macro social work in making social change by means of social policy advocacy and politics and social activism, and how to assist in making changes at the international level. You will learn how you can be a participant with the impoverished ones in forging a new society.

SOCIAL POLICY ADVOCACY AND POLITICS

In Chapter 13 you will learn how macro social workers engage themselves in social policy and practice social policy advocacy. You will learn a definition of social policy and read a brief history of social policy in the United States. You will explore various ideas about how social policy is assumed to originate. You will also learn that these theories ignore the most important arena where social policy ought to originate. You will learn components of a normative social policy. You will learn step by step how to form a social policy advocacy group and how the Internet is helping ordinary people become aware of and involved in policy formation.

SOCIAL MOVEMENTS

Macro social workers understand that many of our social problems are rooted in the common culture of our North American society, the way we think, our values, and our heritage. Although there are many positive aspects to that culture, there are also endemic defects that, as Coleman asserts, are tantamount to a "permanent blindness" in our modern society.

Macro social work activists have often participated in mass modern social movements to advocate for labor reform, civil rights reform, and disabilities reform. You will discover in Chapter 14 that social work activists also engage in new "postmodern" social movements that shift our values and explore alternative ways of being. You will learn how to become involved in such movements and discover that these new social movements may be among the most powerful means to bring about a better society.

INTERNATIONAL SOCIAL WORK

Macro social workers work not only to develop a better society but to develop a better world. Macro social workers are especially drawn to the developing nations where poverty, violence, disease, famine, and oppression continue to steal the lives of men, women, and children. In Chapter 15 you will learn about global social problems, and you will find out how macro social workers help communities engage in planning, community development, and community organization at the international level. You will see how new social organizations called nongovernmental organizations (NGOs) are revolutionizing our global society.

Rather than exploit the world's resources, international social workers advocate for sustainable development in which humans live in a cooperative relationship with the environment, protecting and preserving its irreplaceable biological treasures. Instead of dominance by a hegemony of the global market society, macro social workers press for a global human society. You will find that societal and international social work are among the most personally rewarding kinds of social work, and you will discover that this work can help bring about a better world.

13

The Practice of Social Work Policy Advocacy

Illusions

If anyone else still has illusions about this country, it's not the poor. They know that this country will spend $20 billion to put a man on the moon, but will not spend $20 to put a man on his feet. They know it will spend more to keep weevils from eating the cotton than to keep rats from eating the fingers of a baby in Harlem. They know it will pay a U.S. Senator over $100,000 a year not to plant cotton, but will not pay $1 to the families on his plantation not to raise hookworms in the stomachs of their own children.

Si Kahn[1]

Costs of Conflict

Every gun made, every warship launched, every rocket fired signifies, in the final sense, a theft from those who hunger and are not fed, those who are cold and not clothed. This world in arms is not spending money alone. It is spending the sweat of its laborers, the genius of its scientists, the hopes of its children.

Dwight D. Eisenhower

Ideas in This Chapter

Macro social worker Barbara Mikulski, the 16th woman to serve in the U.S. Senate and the first Democratic woman to have served in both Houses of Congress, was reelected to a second term in 2003.

JOAN CLAYBROOK: SOCIAL POLICY ADVOCATE

The tall, bespectacled woman at a makeshift lectern in a Capitol Hill hearing room doesn't look particularly fierce. Her face is scrubbed, her shoes sturdy, her smile ready. In a brightly colored suit and pearls, she looks like an aging version of the Junior Leaguer she once was. But make no mistake, consumer policy advocate Joan Claybrook is no pussycat.[2]

As president of Public Citizen, the consumer advocacy group founded by Ralph Nader in 1971, Claybrook has a point of view on just about every issue affecting the public good, from health care to insurance, from legal rights to banking. But there are two things that really get to her: automobile safety and campaign finance. In 1992 she hammered away at how much public money former President Bush took in during his presidential and vice presidential campaigns ("over $420 million by the end of 1992," she says), while he said he would veto any campaign finance reform bill that provided for public funding of congressional elections or restricts spending on them. In early May 1992, a bill doing just that landed on his desk, and Joan Claybrook was one of the people who pushed it there. As she sees it, she represents the interests of the people, and the people deserve to win.

"It's important to approach people in the best way that you can," says Claybrook. "We think very hard about that. What is the best way to communicate the message?" She goes about it by studying the issues and learning their history, including previous congressional votes. She also works the media by staging press conferences, writing opinion pieces, and sending letters to the editor.

Claybrook was reared to be a social policy analyst. At her parents' house, dinner conversations were about politics. Her father, a bond attorney and Baltimore City Council member, stalwart of the local civil rights movement in the 1950s, was a founder of the Maryland Americans for Democratic Action. Her mother, a homemaker, was a natural organizer who believed that their three children ought to be encouraged to do anything they wanted, even if they failed.

After her parents died, Joan's attitude changed. "I never thought about having to achieve either before or after their deaths, but I realized that I was the older generation now, and that I had a lot to give." One of the original Nader's Raiders, Claybrook became a consumer advocate even earlier. She came to Washington in 1965 as a fellow of the American Political Science Association, the first time the program included women. Required to work for a member of Congress, Claybrook signed on with James MacKay, a Southern Liberal Democrat who asked her to work on auto safety. She had just read an amazing book, *Unsafe at Any Speed*, by Ralph Nader. When MacKay decided to introduce an auto safety bill, the first regulatory bill for the auto industry, he asked Claybrook to draft it. As Claybrook followed the bill through Congress, she was introduced to lobbying Nader-style. "I saw Ralph in operation, how he manipulated, maneuvered, pushed and pulled, how he used disclosures to shock people," she recalls. "It was an incredibly fast education." The following September, the bill, which established safety standards for motor vehicles, was enacted into law. At the end of her fellowship, Claybrook moved to the National Traffic Safety Bureau (NTSB), where she became assistant to the director. She stayed there until 1970, when she joined Nader.

In 1973 she founded and directed Congress Watch, Public Citizen's congressional lobbying group, and when Jimmy Carter was elected president, she was asked to head the NTSB. She pushed to require automobile makers to provide air bags or at least passive seat belts. In 1980 she was back in the trenches of the consumer movement as president of Public Citizen. "I have a love of battle," she says. "I work on issues I care deeply about and get paid enough to live on. Who could ask for anything more?"

WHAT YOU WILL LEARN IN THIS CHAPTER

Macro social workers practice in the arena of social policy and politics. In this chapter you will learn what social policies are and explore who decides on policies in the United States and Canada. You will critique conventional policy making and learn about community-centered policy. You will explore how to apply community-based policy making step by step, conduct policy research, apply critical thinking to policy questions, decide among various policy alternatives, and learn how to implement public policy.

WHAT ARE SOCIAL POLICIES?

Policies, according to Herbert Simon, are the premises of decisions.[3] Koontz, O'Donnell, and Weinrich define policies as "general statements . . . which guide or channel thinking and action in decision-making."[4] They include ways of thinking and values implicit in decisions.[5] Public policies are operating principles by which government systems carry out their goals in foreign and domestic affairs. Foreign policy, for example, guides government action in international relations. Domestic policy is the stance government takes to national, state, and local issues. Social policies are a category of national domestic policy that provides direction to government in the resolution of social problems. Social policies also are devised at the provincial or state and local levels. Many social policy advocacy organizations become involved in pressing government to decide on policies in their favor.

Federal Social Policies

Federal social policy issues raise some of the most important and fundamental questions about people's rights and the meaning of social justice: Should U.S. or Canadian citizens have inalienable rights to health care or to possess handguns? Should women have a right to abortion, and should the federal government subsidize abortions for poor women who cannot afford them? Should people who are gay be afforded the same legal rights and protections as other citizens, including the right to marriage? Should government be permitted to execute certain criminals? Should people in poverty be provided with financial assistance? Answering policy questions such as these provides positions that guide us in problem resolution. Social workers, often through the National Association of Social Workers (NASW), the Canadian Association of Social Workers, and other social work associations, are often involved in advocating for better social policies.

State and Local Social Policies

In addition to questions of social policy at the national level, social policies are also considered at both state and local levels of government. At the state level, watchdog commissions often act to oversee the application of public polices. In California, for example, the California Coastal Commission oversees and implements policies intended to protect the California coastline from indiscriminate development.

At the local level, in 2004 the Mayor of San Francisco decided to allow residents who were gay to marry. In addition, citizens are sometimes called upon to offer their input on mental health commissions, human rights commissions, planning commissions, and others or are elected to the governing boards of special districts such as a community college district or the board of education, which guides the policies of educational institutions.

Social Policy and Social Organizations

Government institutes rules and decisions about public social policies, but many independent, private, nonprofit organizations perform policy research, disseminate information on policy questions, develop policy proposals, and advocate for progressive social policy. Organizations such as Save the Children, the National Coalition Against Domestic Violence, the National Alliance to End Homelessness, and Human Rights Watch advocate policies in favor of child welfare, women who have been physically abused, people who are homeless, or those who have suffered human rights abuses, pressuring government for policy outcomes in their favor.

A BRIEF HISTORY OF POLICY MAKING AND ADVOCACY

During the 1800s many individual policy advocates pushed for action for specific populations. By the time of the Progressive Era, however, organized policy advocacy on many fronts became a compelling social force in America, and it was often led by social workers. A second surge of social policy advocacy occurred during the Depression years of the 1930s. During the 1940s and 1950s social policy concentrated on urbanism and control of the labor force, but it exploded during the 1960s as social policy advocates developed social legislation on many fronts. The neoconservative political climate from the early 1970s to the early 1990s and for much of the first decade of 2000 has restricted progressive social policy in the United States and, at times, in Canada as well.

Individual Policy Activists of the 1800s

The earliest social policy advocacy can be traced to the individual effort of many early North American pioneers of social betterment including Horace Mann, advocate for better education; Thomas Gallaudet, advocate for the deaf; John Howard, advocate of prison reform; Frederick Douglass and Sojourner Truth, advocates for civil rights; along with the many abolitionists and abolitionist societies of the pre-Civil War period. In the later half of the 1800s, social policy advocates included Samuel Gridley Howe and Dorothea Dix, advocates on behalf of persons with emotional and developmental disabilities; Charles Loring Brace, advocate for abandoned and neglected children; Mother Jones, advocate for workers' rights; Susan B. Anthony and Carrie Chapman Catt, advocates for woman's suffrage; and Clara Barton, advocate for victims of war and natural disasters.

The Progressive Era: 1885–1915

During the Progressive Era, the United States was a country in crisis, and not a few feared outright revolution. Many people joined together to advocate for favorable legislation on many fronts. Among the largest and most influential of these groups were social workers who pressed for better social welfare policies.

Social Work and Social Welfare   The growing "middle class," including social workers, began to see a way to rationalize and reform societal, economic, and political processes.[6] As Edward A. Ross, a leading sociologist, and key progressive ideologue wrote in 1907, "Social defense is coming to be a matter for the expert. The rearing of dikes against faithlessness and fraud calls for intelligent social engineering. If in this strait the public does not speedily become far shrewder, . . . there is nothing for it but to turn over the defense of society to professionals."[7]

JEANNETTE RANKIN (1880–1973)

Jeannette Pickering Rankin was born June 11, 1880, and attended Montana State University at Missoula, graduating in 1902. Looking for some work to which she could commit herself, she was inspired by slum conditions to take up the new field of social work, became a resident in a San Francisco Settlement House for 4 months, then entered the New York School of Philanthropy (later to become the Columbia School of Social Work). She returned to the West to become a social worker at a children's home in Spokane, Washington.

Rankin studied at the University of Washington in Seattle and became involved in the woman's suffrage movement in 1910. Visiting Montana, Rankin was the first woman to speak before the Montana legislature; she worked for the New York Women's Suffrage Party and in 1912 became the field secretary of the National American Woman Suffrage Association. Rankin returned to Montana where she helped organize the successful Montana suffrage campaign in 1914. As war in Europe loomed, Rankin turned her attention to working for peace, and in 1916 she ran for one of the two seats in Congress from Montana as a Republican, becoming the first woman elected to the U.S. Congress and the first woman elected to a national legislature in any western democracy.

Only 4 days after taking office she voted against U.S. entry into World War I. Violating protocol by speaking during the roll call before casting her vote, she announced, "I want to stand by my country, but I cannot vote for war." In 1917 she opened the congressional debate on the Susan B. Anthony Amendment, which became the Nineteenth Amendment when ratified by the states. During her tenure in office, Congresswoman Rankin worked for political reforms including civil liberties, suffrage, birth control, equal pay, and child welfare, but her first antiwar vote sealed her political fate. When her congressional colleagues gerrymandered her out of her district, she ran for the Senate, lost the primary, launched a third party race, and lost overwhelmingly.

After the war ended, Rankin worked for the National Consumers' League, the American Civil Liberties Union, and became Field Secretary of the Women's International League for Peace and Freedom (WILPF). She formed the Georgia Peace Society and lobbied for the Women's Peace Union, American cooperation with the World Court, and labor reforms and an end to child labor.

By 1939 she had returned to Montana and was running for Congress again, supporting a strong but neutral America in yet another time of impending war. Elected with a small plurality, Jeannette Rankin arrived in Washington in January as one of six women in the House, two in the Senate. After the Japanese attack on Pearl Harbor, the U.S. Congress voted to declare war against Japan, but Jeannette Rankin once again voted "no" to war, and once again violated tradition and spoke before her roll call vote, this time saying: "As a woman I can't go to war, and I refuse to send anyone else." She voted alone against the war resolution. Denounced by the press and her colleagues, she barely escaped an angry mob. Rather than run for Congress again (and surely be defeated) in 1943, Rankin went back to Montana.

At the age of 88, stirred by the atrocities of the War in Vietnam, Rankin emerged from retirement, and in 1968 she led more than 5,000 women in a protest in Washington, D.C., demanding that the U.S. withdraw from Vietnam and heading up the Jeannette Rankin Brigade. She continued to be active in the antiwar movement and was often invited to speak or was honored by young antiwar activists and feminists until her death in California in 1973 at the age of 93.

Social worker Jeannette Rankin, the first woman to serve in the United States Congress, the only Representative who voted against the nation's entry into World Wars I and II, a lifelong pacifist, and one of the country's earliest women suffragists, was inducted into the National Women's Hall of Fame in 1993.[8]

It was the social workers of the Charity Organization Society and the Settlement Houses who were the professional experts applying rational planning and policy techniques to engineer the social machinery of the emerging modern American society. "Modern American social policy advocacy and the social work profession emerged as more or less conscious efforts to deal with the economic, political and social crises facing American society," notes John Ehrenreich.[9] Social workers went about their work with reformist zeal to lay the foundations for a welfare state, enlarge the role of government, provide for a renewed democratic process, and regulate a growing market economy that threatened to crush the common person in its path toward power.

Origin of the Welfare State   Many of the reforms advocated by progressive social workers "are the origins of the modern welfare state and of both social policy and social work as we know them today."[10] Charity Organization, for example, was active in the arena of social planning and scientific rationalization of charity aided, says Ehrenreich, "by a huge economic surplus that increasingly collected and concentrated in private foundations and the public sector that became available for use in regulating and managing civil society."[11]

Larger Role for Government   Settlement House social workers encouraged government to play a larger role in providing for the public welfare through policies, programs, and regulatory efforts. Progressive policy advocates pressed for consumer protection, enforcement of pure food and drugs laws, and advocated for regulatory agencies such as the Food and Drug Administration. They lobbied for better working conditions for women and laws regulating child labor rights by means of a strengthened Interstate Commerce Commission. At the state level, Settlement House workers initiated a reformed criminal justice system by obtaining a separate juvenile court that protected the rights of children and teenagers.

Renewed Democracy   Progressive social workers advocated for renewed commitment to America's democratic principles and succeeded in initiating a new form of city government called the city manager system, changing state constitutions to provide direct citizen legislation by means of initiatives and referendum and recalling politicians who failed to carry out the will of the people. At the federal level, social work policy advocates called for reformed political institutions including the direct election of U.S. senators, the direct primary, and extending the political franchise to include women.

Reduction in Power of Corporate Interests   Many social workers saw the problems of the time as originating with the size and power that large corporations had assumed. They pressed for policies that would break these systems into smaller units to prevent them from usurping the public interest and restore a more level and competitive playing field for business. Social workers lobbied for government to begin to modify its laissez-faire (hands off) policy toward a market economy dominated by giant transportation, mining, power, manufacturing, and financial monopolies. For example, they lobbied government to forge legislation preventing these conglomerates from fixing prices, destroying competition, and controlling the political process. They also advocated for a Federal Trade Commission to enforce those laws. In addition, many Settlement House workers advocated for an end to war and for the prohibition of alcohol consumption.

Principles of Progressive Social Policy   The goal of progressive social workers was nothing less than to create a rational, stable, efficient, and self-reproducing social order. Rather than using confrontational strategies, however, the new social work professionals saw their role as that of harmonizers, mediators, and planners. They embraced the value neutrality of knowledge, the benefits of science, technological expertise, and the desirability of efficiency and order in all things. Social workers intended to carry out the task of reform on a uniform statewide or nationwide basis by applying impartial rules of governance, rational decision making, interest group liberalism, social control and amelioration, organizational imperatives, and mechanistic systems thinking to social policy.[12]

Impartial Rules   Reformers based their ideas on the principle that efficiency could be improved by instituting professional nonpartisan administration in government and policy making. Government would apply its policies fairly, neutrally, and without favor or "compassion," according to universal rules that applied equally to all rather than on the basis of nepotism (in favor of relatives) or amicism (in favor of friends). Civil servants themselves, who were to carry out those policies, were chosen according to the principle of the most qualified candidate who best fit the requirements of the job. Government employees were to be protected from pressure exerted by politicians to bend the rules in favor of special interests or those with influential connections. The public's interest as a whole, rather than those of special individuals or groups was, above all, to be served and protected.[13]

Rational Decision Making   The reformers of the Progressive Era imposed rational decision making and bureaucratic functional reasoning on all aspects of public governance. Individuals would adopt a rational, impersonal, and objective approach to decision making, and government organizations would operate as unitary actors in the public realm, balancing claimants needs, dispensing judgments, and creating rules on a fair and impartial basis to achieve effectiveness and efficiency.

Decisions would be made by gathering facts, comparing alternatives, and choosing solutions that best served the public good, guided by an understanding of the public interest arrived at by an open and democratic process. If otherwise equally rational individuals were presented with the same information and were motivated by clearly articulated values and goals, rationality meant that each decision maker would arrive at the same logical decision. The goal of

rationality was to maximize, if not optimize (find the one best way), solutions to social problems.

Interest Group Liberalism   Where interests conflicted, government would seek a balance by means of bargaining and negotiation. Each contender in the policy arena could then meet at least a portion of its needs.

Social Control and Social Amelioration   "Social control and social amelioration were central to American social policy from its beginnings," says John Ehrenreich.[14] Progressives intended for government to accept at least a minimum role in regulating and keeping business honest, and that government was obligated to control itself as well. Above all, it was in the public's best interests that social and economic life should be at least partially constrained by some ideal of the public good.

IDA B. WELLS-BARNETT (1862–1931)

Ida Bell Wells-Barnett was born July 16, 1862 in Holly Springs, Mississippi. Both of her parents were slaves. Education was important to Wells's parents. She began attending school at an early age. In her teens she was educated at Shaw University, a school for freedmen, where the religious training she had received at home was reinforced.

In 1878, when she was 16, both of her parents died of yellow fever. Rather than allow her five younger siblings to be split up, she took on the responsibility of raising them herself. In 1881, after three of her siblings were old enough to live on their own, Wells and her two younger sisters moved to Memphis, Tennessee. While in Memphis, Wells became editor and co-owner of a local African American newspaper called the *Free Speech and Headlight,* writing editorials under the pen name "Lola."

Wells's crusade for justice began when she was removed from her seat on a railroad coach after refusing to give it up and sit in the "colored only" car. She challenged Jim Crow Laws in Tennessee and brought a successful lawsuit against the Chesapeake and Ohio Railroad in the Circuit Court. However, the Tennessee Supreme Court overruled the lower court in 1887. Wells completed her studies in 1888 at Rust College, passed an examination, and obtained a job teaching at a country school.

Wells continued her pursuit for justice. In 1891 under the pen name Lola, Wells wrote newspaper articles criticizing the educational resources available to

African American children. When her teaching contract was not renewed, Wells continued her writing career. She worked as a journalist for the *Memphis Free Speech* and also acquired an ownership interest in it.

After three of her friends were lynched by a mob in 1892, Wells began an antilynching crusade. While attending an editor's convention in New York, her newspaper office was destroyed, and her friends advised Wells not to return because her life was in danger. She took her crusade to England, returned to Chicago, and formed the Women's Era Club, the first civil rights organization for African American women, later changed to the Ida B. Wells Club in her honor.

In 1895 Wells published *A Red Record*, a history of lynching in America, and in that same year she married Ferdinand Barnett, a prominent Chicago attorney and devoted herself to raising two sons and two daughters. Wells was asked to become a member of the "Committee of 40," which laid the groundwork for the NAACP, the oldest civil rights organization in the country, and she continued her crusade for equal rights for African Americans until her death on March 25, 1931.[15]

Organizational Imperative Just as progressives depended on the institution of bureaucratic organizations, commissions, and governmental offices to rationalize political processes and the economy, they also used the control function of bureaucracy to induce workers, consumers, and the public at large to become acculturated to the values, ideals and behaviors of a rationally organized society.

According to John Ehrenreich, social control included the gradual indoctrination of workers to the demands of organizational life including objectivity, impersonality, obedience to the norms and values of the organization, subservience to its processes and rules, allegiance to the decisions made by those at the top, application of one's energy to the task, and upholding the right of the organizational managers to scrutinize, shape, and modify the behavior of the employee according to the organizational goals.[16]

Mechanistic Systems Thinking Implicit in this orientation was a mechanistic systems thinking approach to social change and social policy. Expert social work professionals were charged with the task of harmonizing, stabilizing, and arranging for decisions that produced a homeostatic balance in government and the economy. What was wanted was growth and progress, but growth that occurred without conflict and that responded as automatically as possible to stimuli in the nation's social environment.

It was the role of government managers and planners as well as social workers to achieve reconciliation between the goals and needs of the public, the requirements of the economic and social systems, and the regulation of their growth. Schools, for example, were to help students become good citizens and incorporate values that would make them into good workers, and businesses were to provide opportunities for employment. Factories were to inculcate hard work, thrift, efficiency, and effectiveness in production. Government was to at least minimally ensure that large corporations did not overly exploit workers or distort the economy in their pursuit of wealth and power. Universities were to train students to become specialists in applying rational thinking to their professional activities.[17]

Social Policies of the 1930s

During the Great Depression of the 1930s, Franklin Roosevelt initially shared former President Herbert Hoover's belief that the economic system of the United States was fundamentally sound. He proposed initiatives that were intended to be temporary, emergency efforts to lift the nation out of its economic collapse. These measures of the "First New Deal," tentative as they were, represented a major break with the social policies of both the 1920s and the Progressive Era.

For the first time, for example, the federal government embraced a direct role in financing and organizing relief for citizens who were destitute in a time of financial crisis. In addition, Roosevelt and his advisers embraced large corporations and approved their imperatives to collaborate in pursing wealth and power, policies progressive social workers would have opposed. "We are no longer afraid of bigness," announced presidential adviser Rex Tugwell. "We are resolved to recognize openly that competition in most of its forms is wasteful and costly; that larger combinations must in any modern society prevail."[18] Rather than limiting corporate size, as occurred during the Progressive Era, government would play a more cooperatively interventionist role in balancing large business and consciously engage in more centralized planning. Just as economic organizations were encouraged to grow, government would also need to become large to manage and coordinate the often conflicting interests of consumer and producer, employee and employer, and to promote the establishment of large-scale public organizations to implement these purposes.

CONGRESSWOMAN BARBARA LEE

Born in El Paso, Texas, Barbara Lee came to California in 1960. After receiving the Bank of America Achievement Award and the Rotary Club Music Award, she went on to Mills College, graduating in 1973, and earning a master's degree in social welfare from the University of California, Berkeley in 1975. While working toward her graduate degree, Lee founded a community mental health center in Berkeley.

Barbara Lee began her political career by working as an intern in the office of social worker Congressperson Ron Dellums and later became his chief of staff. In 1990 she was elected to the California State Assembly where she served for 6 years. In 1996 Lee was elected to the California State Senate. While in public office in California, Lee served as a board member of the California State World Trade Commission, the California State Coastal Conservancy, and the District Export Council, and was a member of the California Defense Conversion Council. She created and presided over the California Commission on the Status of African American Males, the California Legislative Black Caucus, and the National Conference on State Legislatures Women's Network, and served as a member of the California Commission on the Status of Women.

Barbara Lee was first elected to the House of Representatives for the 9th District of California in a 1998 special election to fill the seat of retiring Congressman Ron Dellums. Since then, Lee has worked with teachers and counselors to craft legislation to provide schools with the means to hire much needed counselors and other mental health and social work professionals. She is currently the co-chair of the Progressive Caucus, chair of the Congressional Black Caucus (CBC) Task Force on Global HIV/AIDS, whip for the CBC, and a member of the CBC Minority Business Task Force.

Temporary relief and economic encouragement, Roosevelt quickly learned, were not enough to stem the rising tide of unemployment and economic malaise. A further shift in policy was needed. Massive agitation on the left from such figures as Huey Long of Louisiana, the Lafollette brothers from Wisconsin, Upton Sinclair, and Francis Townsend of California insisted that government take even more responsibility for managing the nation's economic system and provide for the economic security and well-being of its citizens.

This "Second New Deal" brought an enormous and permanent strengthening of government with establishment of a centralized and unprecedented Executive Office of the President to oversee the administration of the many new government agencies that had been created. Roosevelt moved to create a "Welfare State," taking the initiative from Townsend, Sinclair, and Long, and established the Social Security Act of 1935, which permanently cemented the federal government's role and responsibility in caring for certain categories of the poor. The Second New Deal also established the Works Progress Administration (WPA), a massive work relief program putting a third of unemployed Americans to work by 1936; the Fair Labor Standards Act, establishing a national minimum wage and the 40-hour work week; national child labor laws; and the National Labor Relations Act, providing authority for employees to bargain collectively with management.[19]

Social Policies of the 1940s and 1950s

American social policy of the 1940s and 1950s was built around two concerns: urbanization and the resulting urban crisis, and government efforts to manage and control the labor force.

Urbanization   Policies of urbanization included urban renewal, housing for middle-income families, and growth of the automobile industries.

Urban Renewal   After World War II the federal government promoted a policy of constructing hundreds of thousands of low-income housing units, but little public housing was actually built. In reality, "urban renewal" of the 1950s meant tearing down acres of slum housing and replacing that with commercial industrial construction, hospitals, museums, and universities. Little provision was made for the people whose housing, however substandard, was destroyed in the process. In fact, asserts Ehrenreich, the Housing acts were used to *reduce* housing opportunities in the cities.[20]

Middle-Class Housing   The federal government did subsidize enormous amounts of new home construction, but it was suburban housing for the middle class, not urban housing for the poor. "The net effect of federal housing policies in the postwar years was to strongly and systematically encourage the growth of new suburban areas while ignoring, or contributing to the destruction of, housing in the inner city."[21]

Automobile Industry   The federal government embarked on a massive campaign to subsidize the automobile by providing funds for road building. The Interstate Highway Act of 1956 provided billions of dollars a year for highway construction, but not mass transit. In the 1960s federal subsidies for road building rose to $4.3 billion a year, while subsides for urban mass transit ranged from zero to $103 million, and that amount only at the end of the decade. Fuel was also subsidized by the government by means of the oil depletion allowance, which provided billions of dollars to oil companies and enabled them to keep the price of gasoline artificially low. Public mass transit and long-distance passenger railroads stagnated while the automobile and trucking industries prospered.

CONGRESSWOMAN SUSAN A. DAVIS

Susan A. Davis was born in Cambridge, Massachusetts, and grew up in Richmond, California. Davis graduated from the University of California at Berkeley with a degree in sociology and earned her MSW degree from the University of North Carolina. From 1983 to 1992 Davis served on the San Diego City School Board—serving as president or vice president for 5 of those years—and from 1990 to 1994 Davis was the executive director of the Aaron Price Fellows Program, a program designed to teach multiethnic high school students leadership and citizenship skills.

In1994 Davis was elected to the California State Assembly where she served three terms. In 2000 she was elected to the United States Congress where she is proud to serve on the House Armed Services Committee, the Education and the Workforce Committee, and the Veterans Affairs Committee.

Urban Crisis   Agricultural policies of the 1940s and 1950s contributed to expanded agribusiness and to the "urban crisis" of the 1960s. These policies included price supports and acreage limitations for farmers, which kept the price of farm products artificially high. Farmers used these supports to increase the quantity and quality of nonsubsidized crops while reducing the acreage for which government paid a subsidy. Government also subsidized research that underwrote the development of new high-yield seeds, fertilizers and pesticides, and new machinery, and provided training for farmers in the application of new capital-intensive technologies, all of which primarily benefited larger farmers. Some farmers in the South with larger landholdings rented their vacant acreage to tenant farmers, often African Americans, who were unable to profit by governmental benefits, and provided even more capital to wealthier farmers. In addition, smaller farmers were not often able to benefit by government subsidies.

Fewer farmers were needed for unsubsidized crops, the prices of which remained artificially low. As a result, millions of small farmers were forced to leave their farms. Acreages were consolidated, and the remaining farms increased in size as agribusinesses bought up farmland at depressed prices. From 1940 to 1970 the number of American farms declined by more than half. African American tenant farmers, who could not compete with the larger, more efficient farms, were especially hard hit. Between 1940 and 1969 the number of African American owned or operated farms declined 87%, from 680,000 to 90,000.

Many African Americans in rural areas of the South who were pushed out of farming headed toward the larger cities of the South and the North, lured by the hope of better jobs. Middle-class homeowners and businesses, encouraged by government subsidized housing in the suburbs and increased utility of the automobile, fled central inner cities just as millions of unskilled African American and Hispanic Americans began pouring in.

When they arrived, however, African Americans often found that the jobs they were seeking had moved to the suburbs along with the city's tax base that was needed to provide social services for these newcomers. Instead of prosperity, the cities offered unemployment, increased segregation, deteriorated housing, lack of recreational space, and lack of services. African American unemployment had exceeded that of whites by 20% in the 1940s, but by 1955 it had soared to more than twice that level.

Management and Control of the Labor Force
Officials of the Eisenhower administration of the 1950s were afraid that another severe depression

would occur when unemployed veterans returned at the end of the Korean War. Government responded by encouraging women to leave the workforce by means of public media and by outright firings. Returning veterans were offered the "GI Bill," which made it possible for millions to attend college instead of immediately entering the labor market.

At the same time government reduced the pool of private sector civilian workers, simultaneously keeping demand high by maintaining a large standing army, expanding government civilian employment, and offering government contracts to the private sector, largely for military purposes. According to one estimate, these policies generated more than one quarter of all jobs in the U.S. economy, few of which, however, benefited the poor urban African or Hispanic Americans that populated the inner cities of the North and the South in increasing numbers.[22] In addition, many Whites insisted on segregating and overtly discriminating against African, Hispanic, and Native Americans in services, jobs, and facilities, and in the South and Southwest African Americans were denied the political franchise.

Seedtime of Reform

Although the late 1940s and 1950s were a period of relative calm, the seeds of radical protest were being planted by the very social policies intended to provide stability and prosperity. Masses of students were flooding universities, many of whom had been schooled in war and racial division, providing the foundation for a student movement.

Government policies that had undermined the careers of university-trained women, forcing them to remain at home as housewives, provided women with a lesson in injustice and sensitized them to their own powerlessness, inadvertently stimulating their readiness to engage in a feminist movement.

The huge influx of African and Hispanic Americans who were increasingly concentrating themselves in the inner cities of the North and South, where combinations of inequitable economic and social policies, political disenfranchisement, and segregation were demonstrating the disparity between their lives and those of prosperous, White middle-class suburbanites. The times were ripe for concerted civil rights activism.

The policies of the government in promising but not delivering on housing, and its reluctance to fund mass transit for inner-city dwellers while providing massive subsidies for highway, gasoline, and the automotive industries, contributed to inner-city decline and raised people's consciousness of the disparities in policies, all of which worked against the urban poor. Combined with inadequate financial assistance and welfare services, these conditions provided the glaring contrast in government policies that favored one group of people while simultaneously disadvantaging another, paving the way for the welfare rights movement. Students, women, African Americans, and the urban poor were poised to challenge the inequitable government policies that had kept them locked in an unjust and inferior position.

Social Policies of the 1960s

Sparked by massive social movements, nonviolent protests between 1955 and 1973 were among the most significant of the century. The resulting social policies of the 1960s, including landmark legislation in civil rights and the War on Poverty, led to major improvements in people's social welfare.

Civil Rights Policies

John Kennedy initially attempted to "temporize on black rights and sought solutions to social problems through a simple application of New Deal-style social policy,"[23] but it quickly became apparent that these measures were insufficient. In June 1963 he sent a bill to Congress to "ban discrimination in all places of public accommodation, in employment, and to strengthen the Attorney General's authority to speed up school desegregation."[24]

Lyndon Johnson continued these efforts to destroy segregation and discrimination through passage of the Civil Rights Act of 1964, the Voting Rights Act of 1965, and the 1968 Affirmative Action Order. The Voting Rights Act resulted in the registration of almost a million southern African Americans within 3 years, and by the mid-1970s in the South, African Americans and Whites were registered in proportion to their population. Southern sheriffs and judges, representatives of institutional repression, became vulnerable to the African American vote, and the use of terror as a means of social control was diminished.

The War on Poverty

The Economic Opportunity Act (EOA) passed in 1964, often called the War on Poverty, linked individual change to social reform, changing institutions, community patterns, and the "structure of opportunity." The War on Poverty included antipoverty programs, community action programs (CAPs), and model cities programs.

Antipoverty Programs   The EOA initiated a series of programs that provided for training and career development for young people: the Neighborhood Youth Corps for jobless teenagers, the Job Corps program for school dropouts, the New Careers programs for paraprofessionals, and college work-study programs and Volunteers in Service to America (VISTA), the domestic peace corps.

Community Action Programs (CAPs)   Community action programs attempted to engage community residents directly in the development of locally based programs, funding inner-city projects of public and private agencies. Programs included neighborhood health centers; Operation Head Start, a project of preschool training for children; Upward Bound, a program encouraging slum children to go to college; Neighborhood Legal Services; Adult Basic Educational Services; family planning services; and addiction services. Community action agencies (CAAs) provided "advocacy for welfare recipients, establishment of day care and health care, and pressured welfare public housing and other agencies to respond more effectively and equitably to the poor."[25]

CONGRESSMAN EDOLPHUS TOWNS

Edolphus "Ed" Towns was born on July 21, 1934, in Chadbourn, North Carolina. He served in the U.S. Army from 1956 to 1958 and received his BS degree from North Carolina A&T State University and his MSW degree from Adelphi University in New York. Towns taught in the New York City public school system and, as a social worker, became assistant administrator at Beth Israel Medical Center. He was appointed professor of social work at Medger Evers College and at New York's Fordham University. In addition to his other accomplishments, Towns is an ordained Baptist minister.

Towns has the distinction of being the first African American to serve as Deputy Borough President of Brooklyn, and in 1982 was elected to the U.S. House of Representatives. The Congressman and his son, NYS Assemblyman Darryl Towns, became the first African American father/son to serve simultaneously in public office in New York State.

Congressman Towns is currently serving his 11th term in the U.S. House of Representatives. He is chair of the Congressional Black Caucus and a member of the exclusive Energy and Commerce Committee where he is on the Commerce, Trade and Consumer Protection Subcommittee, the Health Subcommittee, and the Telecommunications and Internet Subcommittee. He also serves on the Government Reform Committee's Subcommittee and the Government Efficiency and Financial Management Committee, where he is the ranking member.

Model Cities   At the beginning of the decade of the 1960s, President John F. Kennedy attempted to develop a number of initiatives "based on a new relationship between the federal government and localities, in which money from the federal government went directly to service programs, circumventing city and state governments."[26] During the Johnson years, the federal government enlisted communities of the poor in solving their own problems. The Demonstration Cities and Metropolitan Development Act of 1966, often called the Model Cities program, provided for a concentrated and coordinated attack on the economic, social, and physical problems of selected slum neighborhoods. The poor themselves were asked to provide information and other input for planning the new programs, participate on the boards that planned and administered the programs, and perform some of the jobs that traditionally had been held by professionals.

Significance of the Kennedy and Johnson Initiatives   The Kennedy and Johnson social reforms had a significant effect in reducing poverty, increasing civil rights, expanding the arena of citizen participation, and providing empowerment of previously underrepresented groups in employment, political engagement, and educational opportunity. The Civil Rights Act shifted the culture of the nation toward acceptance of African, Hispanic, and Native Americans as full-fledged citizens. The Voting Rights Act enormously expanded the entry of African Americans and other ethnic minorities into the political process. Improved legal and social status both stemmed from and led to a greater assertiveness on the part of African, Hispanic, and Native Americans and others.[27] "Virtually all of the reduction in poverty since the mid-1960s," asserts Nathan Glazer, "came about through the expansion of social insurance and income transfer programs, such as welfare, food stamps, social security, and rent supplement programs initiated during the Kennedy/Johnson Administrations of the 60s."[28]

Public Policies in the 1970s and 1980s

The Nixon and Ford administrations (1969–1977) lost little time dismantling much of the social legislation that the Kennedy and Johnson administrations had enacted, initiating a retrenchment in progressive social policy during the 1970s. The Reagan and Bush administrations (1981–1993) did the same for the legislation of President Jimmy Carter (1977–1981), who had promoted a number of policies and initiatives for local community and neighborhood development. The Reagan and Bush administrations fostered a neoconservative policy agenda, resulting in economic recession and federal cutbacks. These policies shifted responsibility from the federal government to states and local government, saw a rescission of democratic processes, and encouraged a shift in emphasis from the public to the private sphere.

Neoconservative Policy Agenda

The 12 years of Reagan/Bush policy, spanning the decade of the 1980s and on into 1993, promoted a neoconservative agenda grounded in right-wing programs, policies, and political discourse. Under Reagan, legal services and the human rights commissions were severely restricted in the United States, a direction that was replicated in several Canadian provinces and in the Thatcher administration in Britain in the early 1990s. According to Gary Teeple, the goal of the Reagan and Bush administrations was to redistribute wealth upward, away from those with little. Their policies emphasized "looking out for Number One" and tended to ignore the concerns of the needy or the long-term general welfare of the American people. Declaring that government social programs cause dependency and increased poverty, Reagan and Bush dramatically decreased the federal government's financial commitment to urban programs. Confrontational tactics by neighborhood groups became less and less productive, and local government officials argued that, although they were sympathetic to the issues, cities did not have the resources to address them.[29]

Economic Recession and Federal Cutbacks   The immediate impact of Reagan's presidency was a severe recession with increased unemployment, a rapid increase in the cost of necessities, and serious economic hardship for those at the lower end of the income scale. As community development corporations and organizations responded to federal cutbacks and the privatization of public services, neighborhood organizations, including the IAF, tended to focus more on partnerships and collaboration than on demanding reforms from local government.

Many shifted to partnership-based initiatives and consensus-oriented strategies to accomplish their goals. This contrasted dramatically with the political empowerment tradition of the 1930s, 1960s, and to some degree the 1970s. Community development corporations, for example, tended to be pushed away from politics, forcing them to accommodate themselves to rather than redirect the course of the free market. In conjunction with this shift, many social welfare organizations began to emphasize the importance of professionalism, strong management, and effective administration of programs. Grassroots neighborhood groups often developed into professional organizations that took a businesslike rather than an activist approach to neighborhood improvement.[30]

Shift Responsibility to State and Local Governments   Reagan also set about changing the shape of American politics by taking important responsibilities away from national control and placing them at the state and local levels. Tax cuts, vastly increased defense spending, and dramatic cuts in social spending saddled state and local governments with severe economic and social problems. Meanwhile, the federal government piled up unheard-of budget deficits.[31]

Rescission of Democratic Processes   The Reagan and Bush administrations progressively restricted citizens' access to information about government in practice or in law, creating a culture in which government officials operated in relative secrecy from their own citizens, contradicting the ideal of democracy as an open and accessible forum for the exchange of ideas and the engagement of citizens in public affairs.[32]

Shift From Public to Private Sector   Responding to the heightened demands of an emerging global economy and the challenged status of U.S. corporations, neoconservatives sought to cut social costs. Corporations went after labor unions, government programs, and social movements. They shifted even the limited political dialogue about human needs to concern for corporate needs and delegitimized social action.[33]

The role of public service and the public sector as a whole was disparaged by the Reagan and Bush administrations, dissolving interest in public issues while emphasizing matters of private, often individualistic economic pursuits. People were pushed from interest in the ideals of public affairs and public life to increasingly private spheres and private conceptions of the good life.[34] Even mundane local government services shifted from the public to the private sector. For example, as Kristina Smock asserts, "public services such as garbage collection and street repair, which in previous eras had been frequent targets of neighborhood organizing efforts, were transferred to the private sector. As a result, neighborhood organizations' ability to hold public service providers accountable to citizens' needs was undermined."[35]

Social Polices in the 1990s

Social policies in the 1990s included a return to interest in community affairs, increased military spending, and reforms in welfare.

Community Affairs   At the federal level, in the 1990s the Clinton administration (1993–2001) based its urban policy agenda on the concept of government serving as a catalyst to develop strong networks of citizens, community organizations, and businesses in inner-city neighborhoods. Unlike the administrations of the 1960s that saw the federal government as a partner and funder of local initiatives, or the 1970s and 1980s policies that limited federal government to a minimal role in local initiatives, Clinton's approach emphasized the role of government in creating and sustaining strong, self-sufficient communities. Empowerment Zone and Enterprise Zone community projects, for example, provided tax incentives and block grants to target areas to encourage private sector investment, local collaboration, and comprehensive service provision, reflecting a commitment to the same strategies that characterize comprehensive community initiatives.[36]

Military Spending   Nearly 20 years after the end of the Cold War, the United States had still not significantly reduced its military spending, in part because much of the private economy continued to be dominated by military research and production. The Pentagon's priorities in the 1990s helped undermine key industrial sectors in the cities where they were located.

In 1990 alone, for example, 18 of the 25 largest cities suffered a total loss of $24 billion in their balance of payments with the Pentagon.

A study by two Harvard economists found that most big cities send more to Washington each year in federal taxes than they get back in social programs, defense spending, or public works projects. New York City contributed $9 billion more to the federal government than it got in return. Even in those metropolitan areas that won the Pentagon sweepstakes, asserts Peter Dreier, the bulk of those dollars were allocated in the suburbs, not in the central cities.[37]

In 2000 the number of active military personnel was 1.4 million, down from a "peacetime" peak of 2.2 million in 1987, but still making the military the single largest employer in the United States. In 2001 the House Armed Services Research and Development Subcommittee approved more than $8.1 billion for missile defense, part of its $37.7 billion authorization for military research and development programs.[38]

GUNS OR BUTTER

The financial burden of the arms industry on U.S. citizens is astronomical, according to Alice Slater, director of Economists Allied for Arms Reduction (ECAAR). From 1945 to 1995 the estimated costs to U.S. taxpayers for nuclear weapons was $4 trillion. From 1974 until 1990 the United States spent more than $11 trillion on the military, asserts H. Henderson. The costs of building only one aircraft carrier could feed several million of the poorest, hungriest children in America for 10 years.[39]

Greater sums have been budgeted for development of the Navy's submarine-rescue vehicle than for U.S. occupational safety, public libraries, and day care centers combined, and according to Michael Parenti, the cost of military aircraft components and ammunition kept in storage by the Pentagon is greater than the combined costs of pollution control, conservation, community development, housing, occupational safety, and mass transportation.[40]

The New Internationalist claims the United States spends more on its armed forces than the rest of the world put together. In 2002 the U.S. military accounted for $343 billion of the total federal budget of $1,900 billion, and since September 11, 2002, the military budget has jumped by $46 billion. In that same year, the so-called rogue nations of Cuba, Iraq, Iran, Libya, North Korea, Sudan, and Syria combined spent only $14.4 billion on their military. NATO, Australia, Japan, and South Korea, combined, spent $212.6 billion. Russia spent $56 billion, and China $39.5 billion.[41] According to Michael Parenti, "The total expenses of the legislative and judiciary branches of government and all of the U.S. regulatory commissions combined constitute little more than one half of 1% of the Pentagon's yearly budget.[42]

Welfare Reform   In the 1994 federal elections, Republicans won both houses of Congress. The 104th Congress initiated a number of welfare reforms, which limited the time people could remain on welfare, imposed stringent work requirements, and restricted the rights to welfare of single mothers below the age of 18. When the legislation was finally passed, the Personal Responsibility and Work Opportunity Act of 1996 assigned responsibility for providing financial assistance to the states, changed the name of AFDC to Temporary Assistance for Needy Families (TANF), gave few guidelines, and limited federal funding to the program. The thrust of the TANF was to move recipients of assistance off welfare and into jobs by providing them with work training and education to develop employable skills.

Social Policies in the First Decade of 2000

Social policies in the decade of 2000 present the nation with even greater social retrenchment than occurred during the earlier Reagan and Bush administrations. These policies display greater restrictions in the democratic process, resistance to international global social cooperation in criminal justice or the environment, and further the hegemony of transnational corporations in controlling the global economy.

Social Retrenchment   The George W. Bush administration in the first decade of 2000 invigorated the restriction of citizen access to government information. Rather than encourage domestic policies to improve the infrastructure of the cities, engage in the eradication of poverty, or encourage basic biological research to cure disease at the genetic level, the nation saw a retrenchment in each of these areas. The Tokyo accords, which would have provided a needed incentive to reduce greenhouse gas emissions, was rejected.

According to Jeremy Brecher, the second Bush administration has been totally hostile to attempts to deal with global warming and other forms of environmental destruction.

U.S. Power and Control   Jeremy Brecher asserts that officials who control the second Bush administration seek direct, unilateral world domination for the United States. The Bush National Security Strategy document of September 20, 2002, states, for example, that there is "a single sustainable model for national success: freedom, democracy and free enterprise. . . . We will actively work to bring the hope of democracy, development, free markets, and free trade to every corner of the world. . . . We will not hesitate to act alone, if necessary, to exercise our right of self-defense by acting preemptively and by convincing or compelling states to accept their sovereign responsibilities."[43] In short, says Brecher, the second Bush administration intends to use its military and economic might to make sure that no other world is possible.[44]

Opposition to the International Criminal Court The United States aligned itself with a handful of dissident nations opposing creation and implementation of the International Criminal Court and has determined that it will not allow the court to interfere with the second Bush administration's efforts to use military force to conquer its perceived enemies. According to the National Security Strategy document, the second Bush administration will ensure that the efforts of the United States to "meet its global security commitments . . . are not impaired by the potential for investigations, inquiry or prosecution by the International Criminal Court (ICC) whose jurisdiction . . . we do not accept. We will work . . . to avoid complications in our military operations . . . [to] protect U.S. nationals from the ICC."[45] The Bush administration will not be impeded in its efforts to use military force to protect its interests regardless of charges of human rights abuses or be dissuaded even if its military personnel are accused of criminal behavior. In its efforts to ensure global security, the United States has placed itself above the law.

Policy Implications for 2000 and Beyond Social worker Phyllis Day summarized the policy stance of U.S. government administrations in the decade of the 1990s and the first half of the decade of 2000.

> The 104th Congress and Presidents Bush, Clinton and G. W. Bush legitimized control by the wealthy in the legislative, judicial and administrative branches of government, undercutting the promises of the nation for equal opportunity and equal treatment under the law. In addition, they have reinvested patriarchy—control of women, children and workers—with a new "morality" that defies humankind's vision of social morality.... We have created a "Third-World citizenry" within the United States, a neo-colonialism of our disadvantaged. With wage labor controlled, a segment of our population walled off in urban ghettos killing one another and being killed in "drug wars" and social programs limited, proscribed and deteriorated, a small group of moneyed elite nevertheless continues to increase profits and reap rewards in the destruction of lives.[46]

INTERNATIONAL CRIMINAL COURT

On July 1, 2002, the International Criminal Court (ICC) became active with 76 nations ratifying it and another 139 still in the ratification process. Under the Bush administration, however, the United States and 7 other nations, including some its most notorious enemies—North Korea, Iraq, Cuba, and Libya—rejected the ICC and, according to the Email Activist, is "working very hard so that it doesn't work even for the nations that want to participate."

The ICC was established as a court of last resort to bring to justice to soldiers or political leaders who have committed war crimes, crimes against humanity, or genocide. The International Court of Justice in The Hague only settles disputes between governments, but the ICC has jurisdiction over groups and individuals. The ICC takes cases only when a government that should have jurisdiction over a crime is either unable or unwilling to prosecute offenders, such as occurred in Bosnia where heinous crimes were committed but no effective government was in place to round up and prosecute offenders.

The Email Activist asserts that the United States government has agencies that regularly commit crimes against humanity, and it wants to keep it that way. The Bush administration sees the ICC as a major obstacle in carrying out its policies. For example, the Central Intelligence Agency (CIA) has admitted to Congress that it typically commits 100,000 acts per year that in most countries would be considered to be very serious crimes, including overthrowing democratically elected governments that aren't friendly to U.S. corporations.

At its infamous School of the Americas at Ft. Benning, Georgia, the United States trains guerilla fighters, mostly from Latin America, in torture, false imprisonment, kidnapping, and assassination. In 1993 in retaliation for an assassination attempt on former President Bush, the United States fired 23 cruise missiles into Baghdad and committed another retaliation attack in 1996 in which 27 more missiles were fired at Iraq for its attack on the Kurds. America's armed forces have created additional damage in developing countries such as a 1998 cruise missile attack on an alleged "terrorist base" in Sudan that turned out to be a pharmaceutical plant, the only one in that desperately poor nation.

"One of the most durable features of the US culture is its inability or refusal to recognize crimes its military commits," says Edward S. Herman. While the media has long been calling on the Japanese and Germans to admit guilt, the idea that this country has committed huge crimes and that the World Trade Center attack may be rooted to those crimes is close to being inadmissible."[47]

WHO DECIDES: MODELS OF POLICY MAKING

As a macro social worker, before you can have an impact on social policy, you need to have a grasp of who makes social policy. Several models of policy making are described in the following sections. Use your critical thinking skills to assess these models. At the end of this section you will be asked to consider whether any important areas of political engagement have been left out and to decide what kind of model would provide the best social policies.

Elite Model

In the elite model, policy is presumed to be in the hands of a few individuals who pull the strings of government and business and decide on the rules according to their preferences and values. Elites use government as a resource to exact policy preferences in their favor and have influence on and access to policy arenas far beyond others who lack such resources. Economist John Kenneth Galbraith asserts, for example, "the president of General Motors has a prescriptive right, on visiting Washington, to see the President of the United States. The president of General Electric has a right to see the Secretary of Defense and the president of General Dynamics to see any general."[48]

Many of these corporate elites are appointed to high-level policy-making or cabinet-level posts in government. Elites often shift from managing large business corporations to directing federal bureaucracies, and vice versa. They exert enormous influence, imposing their own policy preferences on the agencies they direct.[49] Elitists tend to believe "the masses are largely passive, apathetic and ill-informed," Thomas Dye asserts. Public policy, therefore, does "not reflect demands of 'the people' so much as it does the interests and values of elites."[50]

Institutional Model

In the institutional model, policy is seen as the purview of the formal institutions of government, particularly legislatures. Legislatures of provincial, state, and federal governments make policy, and the ministries or executive branch have the responsibility to carry out these policies. The U.S. Congress and the Canadian Parliament, for example, develop laws governing services to people in poverty, those without health care, the elderly, child welfare, people with disabilities, and criminal offenders and their victims, among many others. Likewise, state and provincial legislatures mandate policies for departments of social services, education, transportation, health, and others. In the United States county boards of supervisors set policies regulating departments of social services, mental health, probation, and public health. At the local level, policy is developed by city councils for city agencies.

Interest Group Model

Although the legislative process may be the means by which policy becomes legitimized, William Morrow asserts that "government institutions have accepted interest-group liberalism as the official public philosophy"[51] by which policy is actually said to be conceived. Government institutions operate within a milieu of intersecting interest groups and a political culture of pluralism, both of which determine the direction of public policy in America.

Policy making occurs as various interest groups press for policy outcomes on both the institutional and agency structures of government. Social problems,

Morrow asserts, are supposed to "work their way to decision-making arenas for action. Involvement in interest-group politics helps generate loyalty to the system with the result that society remains relatively stable. Policies that ultimately emanate from group interaction represent a consensus of diverse opinion."[52]

According to Morrow, pluralism is "a mutual balance of power among religious, ethnic, economic and geographical groups, with overlapping membership, all of which participate in policy-making through mutual adjustment of conflicting goals within policy arenas."[53] James Madison, for example, one of the framers of the Constitution, wrote that a democratic state contains a multiplicity of interests, among which are "landed interests, a manufacturing interest, a mercantile interest, a moneyed interest." Because the natural propensity of these interests "is to vex and oppress each other rather than co-operate for the common good,"[54] government offices should be divided and arranged "in such a manner that each may be a check on the other that the private interest of every individual may be a sentinel over public rights."[55]

Government carries out its conflict management function by establishing rules of the game, enacting and enforcing compromises in the form of public policy,[56] the outcome of which is equilibrium in which "ambition must be made to counteract ambition."[57] Business corporations, for example, continually lobby government for favorable legislation and bargain for preferential policy treatment in the form of subsidies, price supports, tax breaks, tariff protection, interest-free loans, contracts, or the free or below-cost use of public land, water, and other benefits. Social policy advocates may work for or against various interest groups, all of which compete with one another for the attention of policy decision makers and planners. Policy making is a reflection of the success or failure of these groups in having their particular preference schedules enacted in legislation.

WHO GETS WELFARE IN AMERICA?

House Republicans took a hard look at corporate welfare in 1995—and liked what they saw. Rather than slashing special interest tax loopholes, corporate subsidies, and promotional programs, House Republicans chose to preserve many of those programs and in some cases increased their funding. "One of the lessons we've learned," said Stephen Moore, director of fiscal policy studies at the Cato Institute, "is that the corporate lobby is extraordinarily powerful in this town."[58] Corporate welfare, in general, includes tax breaks, subsidies, direct purchases, and interest-free loans that provide benefits to a particular company or industry.

In 1994 the federal government spent an estimated $51 billion on direct subsidies to industries and provided $53 billion more in tax breaks. In contrast, the total amount of money spent on social welfare in 1994 by federal and state governments combined was a little more than $22.5 billion, less than one fourth the amount spent by the federal government subsidizing business corporations. Although Congress cut billions in social programs in 1995, it provided corporate subsides to 129 private industries totaling $87 billion. In that same year a Washington watchdog group found that the federal government provided $167.2 billion in welfare for wealthy corporations.[59]

The situation may even be worse at the state level. In 1995, for example, of concern was what one newspaper termed "the festering pile of special interest tax bills moving through the California State Legislature. What smells worse than hundreds of millions of dollars in tax breaks to multinational corporations at a time when the state's treasury is so empty that lawmakers must cut grants to the blind and disabled?"[60]

One bill sponsored by Pepsico would redefine restaurants and coffee shops as "manufacturers," entitling them to California's 6% investment credit on equipment. A bill sponsored by the Air Transport Association would restore a loophole that exempted airlines from sales tax on fuel and petroleum products. The worst case is Sony, which has paid no corporate taxes in California for years and still wants to take advantage of the new manufacturing investment tax credit. A bill was written to make the credit refundable to Sony alone, entitling them to a huge government gift. As the *Fresno Bee* noted, "Writing tax legislation company by company, to put it mildly, doesn't pass the smell test."[61]

Interest groups exert their influence by means of political action committees (PACs). PACs sponsor particular viewpoints and perspectives on legislation and funnel campaign contributions to candidates they hope will favor legislation benefiting them. Wealthy PACs such as the National Rifle Association (NRA), for example, have been able to influence legislation allowing nearly anyone in the United States to own handguns and various kinds of military-style weapons.

The corporate sector establishes many PACs, but the social sector including social action, environmental, and social welfare advocacy groups establishes other PACs, although these are not nearly as prolific or as wealthy. For example, the National Association of Social Workers established Political Action for Candidate Election (PACE), which makes contributions to candidates who profess positions similar to and are endorsed by the membership.

Critique of Interest Group Liberalism Model

A problem with the pluralist paradigm of policy making is that interest group politics does not result in equally contending actors, each of which operates on a level playing field, but rather in unequal struggles of organized groups to press for policy prizes. E. E. Schattschneider once remarked, "the flaw in the pluralist heaven is that the heavenly chorus sings with a strong upper-class accent."[62] Powerful, organized interests headed by well-educated, experienced leaders in control of special interests that have access to policy makers win out in the struggle over resources.[63]

Public life in the United States becomes a subsidiary component of private affairs, and government an arena of imperialistic enterprise or "marketplace politics" in which private interests seek preferential treatment in the form of policy concessions. Morrow calls this a "bazaar" model of politics in which organized interest groups bargain in the public arena for goods, services, and policy concessions. Government provides arenas of opportunity for those who exploit its resources to increase their power and influence at public expense. Absent in marketplace politics is the notion of the "common good" or the "public interest" as a whole. The interest group model reduces U.S. politics to conflict resolution between contending actors, which in the opinion of Frank Coleman, "is corrupt, sterile and deprived of purpose."[64]

Rational Model

Those who claim that policy making is a primarily rational process assume that interest groups as well as local, state, and national governments operate as unitary actors who attempt to maximize their interests by means of a set of value preferences. "The person making the decision is required to decide upon a goal or hierarchy of goals, determine the path of reaching the goal, and analyze the paths and their consequences, assign a value to each of the consequences, and select the path most likely to lead to the desired goal at a minimum cost. Decision makers are assumed to be optimizers of their own or the government's utility."[65] This "concept of rationality is important mainly because, if a government, like a person acts rationally, its behavior can be *fully* explained in terms of the goals it is trying to achieve," says John Harsanyi.[66]

Governments compete for scarce resources or attempt to reach prescribed goals in an environment of other like-minded, competitive, maximizing, self-interested rational actors. Why nations engage in seemingly "irrational" activities such as war can, therefore, be understood in terms of rational action. Each governmental actor is in competition with every other actor to maximize its national interest. These interests have to do with appropriating resources, maintaining the integrity of boundaries, developing "spheres of influence," and obtaining markets for goods, as well as such intangibles as maintaining national pride and honor.

Limitations of the Rational Model   Although the rational model is theoretically very appealing, there are difficulties in practicing it. First, goals are not always completely clear, especially in government where there are many conflicting interests as well perspectives on what is the best course to take. Second, the capacity of policy makers to consider all the possible courses of action and then choose the best course is a nearly impossible task. Third, it is difficult to project the outcomes of any course of action, and the outcomes some people consider desirable, others consider undesirable.[67]

As a result, sometimes social planners or social policy analysts become confused when their arguments to convince political actors about the necessity of policies based on needs, facts, human concern, or compassion fall on deaf ears. As a social policy analyst, you need to understand that political actors often operate primarily out of their own particular self-interests, which may not be those you or your policy group believe are desirable.

Administrative Model

Legislatures or parliaments may set broad policies, but it is the organizational actors and agencies that interpret, implement, and decide on policy at the local level where it really counts,[68] says William Morrow. Public organizations come into being as a result of

problem arenas and policy agitation on the part of claimants for a voice in policy making, a response by government to regulate and mediate conflicting interest groups, provide access to government processes, and act as spokespersons for interpreting government policy. Often there are overlapping jurisdictions, and mandates reflecting a multiplicity of interests and policy arenas. Power is not only fragmented among the branches and levels of government, therefore, but also among this "fourth branch" of government. These administrative actors often engage in "bureaucratic politics" in the environment of other bureaucratic organizations to ensure their own survival. They plot strategies, build coalitions, bargain, and compromise among the various actors with whom they must contend. These large bureaucratic organizations are often impervious to political control, and they may engage in alliances and collusion with the special interests they are established to serve.

Impervious to Political Control   Administrative organizations typically move ahead in small, incremental steps, scanning the horizon of the political environment, responding marginally to pressures. They build on past decisions on a short-term, yearly basis from a budget that has past program commitments. The staff of these organizations have watched politicians come and go while they continue to exert influence and carry out their routines at the grassroots level. They collect an immense amount of experience, wisdom, and information over the years with which to address problems, much of which is extremely useful in policy debates on one or another solution to problems. As a result, these organizations are often impervious to the demands of politicians, who may attempt to divert or utilize the agency's resources on behalf of their constituents, their own interests, or ideology. As a result, Graham Allison asserts, "Government behavior relevant to any important problem reflects the independent output of these agencies. Government leaders can substantially disturb, but not substantially control, the behavior of these organizations."[69]

Alliances With Special Interests   According to William Morrow, as "administrative agencies are established, the expectation is that the structure and jurisdiction of these agencies will facilitate the legitimization of some values at the expense of others."[70] They constitute "intra-bureaucratic lobbies for certain biases" or particular value preferences. Public agencies relate to their constituents, provide services, address needs, bargain with claimants for the organization's resources, develop expertise on the policy arena they are mandated to address, arrange interorganizational alliances, scan their environment for resources, and predict the consequences of current conditions. They give policy concessions, impose rules, and propose laws in favor of claimants and their constituents.

Public organizations become targets of vested interest groups who seek to maximize their value preferences by capturing agencies or by influencing the policy outcomes expressed by those agencies. At times public agency staff become accomplices to special interests and those who control resources in the private marketplace by helping extend the private marketplace to public arenas. Interest groups that achieve the establishment of an administrative agency mandated to allocate resources and carry out policies on their behalf, therefore, have a powerful tool in their hands to extract additional policy concessions. The Department of Agriculture, for example, reflects and responds to the particular needs and preferences of agribusiness, particularly the American Farm Bureau Federation. So successful has the federation been that in 1995 it won $10 billion per year in federal crop subsidies for farmers.[71] In the same way, the Department of the Interior reflects voices of conservationists. The Defense Department "is subjected to claimant pressure from the various branches of the armed forces, as well as powerful corporations of the defense industry, each of which seeks to amplify its own role within the defense establishment."[72]

Bargaining and Negotiation

The Environmental Protection Agency (EPA) was established as a result of intense lobbying by environmentalists who wanted to protect public and private land from exploitation by private interest groups. The Bureau of Land Management was established on behalf of miners, loggers, and ranchers to protect their private access to mineral, forest, and grazing rights on public lands. Often these groups conflict. The outcome is determined by bargaining among these groups and their supporters in legislatures and administrative agencies. This bargaining "nearly always results in compromise among the numerous interests, with each making concessions in the interests of

securing at least a portion of its goals."[73] According to its advocates, Morrow asserts, bargaining or negotiation represents the most practical view of the common good or public interest.

CONGRESSMAN CIRO D. RODRIGUEZ

Born December 9, 1946, Ciro D. Rodriguez attended San Antonio College and received his BA in political science from St. Mary's University in San Antonio. He received his MSW from Our Lady of the Lake University.

From 1975 to 1987 Rodriguez served as a board member of the Harlandale Independent School District, worked as an educational consultant for the Intercultural Development Research Association, and served as a caseworker with the Department of Mental Health & Mental Retardation. From 1987 to 1996, he taught at Our Lady of the Lake University's Worden School of Social Work.

He was elected to the Texas House of Representatives in 1987 and chaired the important Local and Consent Calendar Committee. Rodriguez served on the Public Health and Higher Education Committees and as vice chairman of the Legislative Study Group, a coalition of progressive Texas House members.

Congressman Rodriguez began his service in the U.S. House of Representatives in 1997. He joined the Armed Services Committee and serves as the ranking member of the House Veterans' Affairs Subcommittee on Health. In 2003 he became a member of the House Resources Committee and currently serves as the chair of the 20-member Congressional Hispanic Caucus, an organization that advocates on issues of particular importance to the fast-growing Hispanic community in the United States. In addition, Congressman Rodriguez has joined the Missing and Exploited Children's Caucus, Education Caucus, Mental Health Caucus, Human Rights Caucus, and Child Care Caucus.

Systems Model

The systems model is possibly the most comprehensive model available because it includes many of the models previously described. The policy process is seen as a total system in which the variety of political actors including wealthy corporate executives and governmental elites, legislatures, administrative agencies, political parties, and interest groups operate in various ways to determine policy.

This model suggests that the policy-making process is a closed system in which claimants to policy preferences provide inputs to the policy process. These inputs are processed in the political decision-making arena, resulting in outputs that then have an impact on the political, social, and economic environment. A feedback loop is created in which the subsystems in the political environment react to policy outputs and generate new inputs. The outputs of one policy decision create material for the inputs to a new decision.

The systems model of policy making assumes a self-contained, self-regulatory, automatically self-adjusting process. Several policy processes work together to form a complex intermixture of activities, each of which plays a role in the ultimate formulation of a policy. Politics, according to those who advocate a systems perspective, becomes much like a mechanism that moves of its own volition. Social policy analysts, however, who are concerned about the health of our civil society and who are familiar with systems thinking, can intervene at salient points in the systems process and use the system to achieve policy ends for the public good and in the public interest.

Garbage Can Model

The garbage can model asserts that at times policy making results when policy claimants who jointly experience particular problems grasp a window of opportunity and press government with their solutions. This often happens during a crisis period when events occur for which there is little precedent, providing little time to plan or decide. Certain individuals with ideas about solutions and problems happen to come together at a particular time when the opportunity for decision presents itself. Chance and luck have a lot to do with what happens. Often, policy results from action rather than from well-thought-out plans. Policy theorists who have studied the piecemeal policy making during the Progressive Era and the Roosevelt and Kennedy and Johnson administrations often characterize them as a garbage can approach to social policy.

EXERCISE 13.1

Critiquing Policy-Making Models

Models are representations. Several models have been presented in the preceding description, but they may not be completely accurate in presenting

---

the operative realities of modern politics. Moreover, models are not normative. They do not explain how politics *ought* to work.

Before reading on, exercise your critical sensibilities and decide if any important areas of political engagement have been left out of these policy-making models. What would you include in an ideal model of democratic politics and policy making? After you have developed your own critique, read the critique that follows.

A CRITIQUE OF CONVENTIONAL POLICY-MAKING MODELS

The various policy-making models described previously comprise individuals, groups, organizations, and systems that political scientists generally concur influence policy making. These conventional policy models tend to reflect the extent to which the thinkers and leaders of today's mass society have diverged from recognizing authentic grassroots democracy as a living reality. Immersed in the ambiguities of mass political processes, these leaders and thinkers reinforce how modern Western society has developed a politics of patriarchy, disengagement, powerlessness, and exclusion, as well as a politics of persuasion and inequality.

Politics of Patriarchy

One institution tends to be ignored in virtually every compendium of policy making. Policy making is almost never seen by policy theorists or practitioners as a process located at the level of ordinary citizens as policy makers in their *neighborhoods,* the communities where people live and have the opportunity to express their most vital interests. This oversight demonstrates the extent to which policy making is seen by many observers as a top-down, patriarchal process pursued exclusively by those few who are in positions of power, and how completely the idea of politics and modern political processes has been captured by a few institutions and individuals removed from the people at large.

Politics of Disengagement

Except for those communities where community planning and community organizations engage people directly in grassroots democracy, people in many communities in the United States, Canada, and other developed nations are not directly engaged in modern politics and policy. Thomson et al., assert that "For all the value that citizen involvement is said to possess, the role of citizens is very limited in America's formal public structures. Citizens are expected to spend five minutes in the voting booth once every year or two or four. And they are expected to do little more."[74]

Ernesto Cortes asserts, furthermore, that "focusing on the least important elements of political action—voting, elections and turnout—trivializes our citizens by disconnecting them from the real debate and power of public life. We fail to recognize that voter participation is the wrong measure of the health of our politics. Voter turnout was high in Pinocet's Chile nor was it ever a problem in totalitarian countries. Becoming mere voters rather than citizens renders people incompetent," converting people who have the capacity for thinking and acting into mere spectators.[75]

Professional politicians and political scientists, moreover, tend to assume that a deeper role for the average citizen is impractical and cannot be sustained. This assumption is often affirmed; even during elections when the majority of those eligible to vote do not exercise their franchise, leaving elections in the hands of a minority of voters. "One of the greatest incentives for increasing participation in American government, therefore, is the pervasive sense of alienation that has settled upon American politics."[76]

DEMOCRATIC NONPARTICIPATION

By almost any standards, democratic participation has dramatically declined in the last 15 years. "Voter turnout has dwindled. Political party identification is rare. Those with money almost completely dominate electoral politics and the policy making process. . . . Citizens distrust politicians. Most are deeply cynical about and alienated from public life. Civic culture has devolved into a brutish individualism. Only the private—personal and family issues—seem to matter."[77]

Politics of Powerlessness

Another result of the debilitating political effects of modernization is a "feeling of powerlessness in the face of institutions controlled by those whom we do not know, whose values we often do not share,"[78] and whose motives we may question. The result is a citizenry that does not have a deep sense of political involvement or control over decisions that matter to them and a tendency for people to become apathetic in public affairs.

It is somewhat ironic that the original meaning of the words *politics* and *policy* are derived from the Greek word *polis,* a small unit of governance like a community or small town where people engage in mutual decision making and construct the rules and processes that guide their lives. It is even more disconcerting that although the United States is generally conceived by Americans to be a government "of the people," the people are rarely, if ever, engaged as direct actors in the policy-making process.

Politics of Exclusion

Many people tend to be generally content with social noninvolvement in public affairs as long as political systems allocate resources and provide decision-making arrangements that do not diverge significantly from their interests. Those in power who actively assert their own policy preferences also tend to be content with such public apathy and uninvolvement because it provides them with a free field in which to operate.

There are, however, other groups of people who know what the powerful have forgotten, and what most North American citizens rarely reflect upon: That to be fully human and for democracy to survive, the populace can no longer afford to leave the machinery of politics to the wealthy, the professionals, the influential, or the government officials. These groups and others, more often than not, are the large number of citizens who do not share equally in the benefits society offers. They comprise many ordinary citizens in working-class and poor neighborhoods, the marginalized, and the handicapped, people who have routinely been kicked out, left out, and kept out of the policy-making system.

Rather than universal political inclusion, which remains a pervading American myth, the reality of American political history is much the opposite. According to Harry Boyte, citizens in the American political process are "permanent outsiders, detached from the actual practices of decision making and action in solving the problems of social reproduction."[79] African Americans, Native Americans, and women, for example, were legally excluded from decision making prior to emancipation and suffrage. Even after emancipation, African Americans and

Native Americans continued to be prevented from voting by regulations explicitly designed to keep them out. Political disenfranchisement has also included Hispanic Americans, Japanese Americans, people convicted of crimes, and those with intellectual and emotional disabilities.

Politics of Persuasion

In their attempt to influence policy, citizens must struggle to appeal to the sensibilities of elected officials in government and to their commitment to a higher public good. Unable to influence policy directly, citizens are reduced to capturing a representative's attention by phone calls, letters, or e-mail to urge him or her to act according to the preferences of the voters. Others may express their concerns by demonstrations, picketing, and marches. There is little assurance, however, that these efforts, even if they persuade a politician, will result in a consensus of the will of the people.

Politics of Inequality

Social policy carried out by those involved in the policy system may reflect the "assumptions about the human condition that may be reasonable to the upper socioeconomic groups who make them, but bare little resemblance to the reality of the lower socioeconomic groups that are supposed to be beneficiaries." The policy-making process in the United States, says Karger and Stoesz, often tends, therefore, to be not only "irregular and irrational, it is also unrepresentative."[80]

NORMATIVE SOCIAL POLICY

A theory of policy and politics that resists taking the assumptions of conventional policy making as inevitable is called a *normative* theory. Normative policy theory is less concerned with describing how policy actually takes place than with exploring how it ought to occur.[81] Self-perpetuating political systems may be difficult to change, but many macro social workers believe it is nevertheless possible and above all necessary to change them. By conceiving of a normative process of politics and social policy, macro social workers may be able to work toward substantive political change.

Allen Jedlicka's recommendations are to develop a secular, humanistic renaissance in which we all equally share in a spirit "of humans having a serious, direct, and continuous say in all matters that affect their lives. (This spirit) would be characterized less by a 'me first' attitude . . . and more by a spirit of mutual assistance toward shared goals."[82] A normative model of social policy making includes substantive politics, character and value education, community politics, grassroots democracy, and creating a good society.

Substantive Politics

Substantive politics, in contrast to mass, representative democracy, places the political process as an integral and necessary component of human life for every citizen who exercises his or her judgment about what is the best way to guide our society. Substantive politics recognizes that people are by nature political animals, that politics is a role for ordinary citizens, amateurs rather than professionals, and centers itself in praxis.

Humans as Political Beings

Aristotle said that we are political beings. A fundamental part of a person's humanity emerges only to the extent that individuals participate in public life, exercise their sense of what is good and excellent, and institute these values into communities by the decisions and actions of every citizen. Politics is where our moral dimension can emerge, the arena in which people exercise ethical reason that infuses a person's commitment to social virtue. Virtue comes from the Latin *virtus,* whose root, just as in virile, means strength and power.[83] "Politics is people exerting the power of what they conceive to be good and right, enabling citizens to disagree, argue, clarify, and negotiate, and through this process of debate and conversation forge a compromise and consensus that enables us to act."[84]

Politics by Amateurs

For the Greeks politics was a role for "amateurs," ordinary citizens who engaged in deciding and acting because it was part of their way of being rather than an endeavor left in the hands of a few, often wealthy, paid professionals. When politics is relegated to professionals, people have surrendered a birthright that calls forth the most necessary dimensions of our humanity—the right to decide what is important and the capacity to act on those decisions.

To the extent that social policy becomes divorced from us, and politics becomes the purview of mass political processes in control of the influential, we are disallowed from making crucial choices that determine the shape of our social environment. People abdicate their right and responsibility to create their own society.

U.S. SENATOR BARBARA MIKULSKI

Born in Baltimore, Maryland on July 20, 1936, Barbara Ann Mikulski is the great-granddaughter of Polish immigrants and the oldest of three daughters. Her parents, William and Christine Mikulski, operated a neighborhood grocery store in East Baltimore where she worked during her high school years.

Mikulski was educated at local parochial schools in Baltimore. She received her BA from Mount St. Agnes College in Baltimore in 1958, and her MSW from the University of Maryland School of Social Work in 1965. Mikulski worked in Baltimore as a social worker for a local Catholic charities organization and later for the Baltimore City Welfare Department. It was while working with these organizations, on cases of child abuse and child neglect, that Mikulski developed her deep concern for the rights of children and families.

Although child saving and family social work was important, Mikulski was drawn into the struggle to save communities as well. In the late 1960s, the City of Baltimore announced plans to locate a 16-lane highway through the city's historic Fells Point neighborhood. In addition to destroying areas of Fells Point, the proposed highway would have destroyed the first Black homeownership neighborhood in the city.

Mikulski used her social work skills in community organizing to help stop the proposed highway, and she soon became one of its key leaders and spokespersons. At one major rally of supporters, the feisty Mikulski told those in attendance: "We didn't let the British take Fells Point; we didn't let termites take Fells Point; and we're not going to let the State Roads Commission take Fells Point."[85]

By 1970 the antiroad forces had won their fight. Social worker Mikulski then decided that rather than being on the "outside" knocking on City Hall's door, it would be better to be "inside," letting the people in. So she announced her candidacy for the Baltimore City Council. Campaigning as an outsider taking on established political machines, Mikulski used the summer of 1971 to go door to door throughout her council district. "I knocked on 15,000 doors that summer, wore out 5 pair of shoes and got mugged by 14 Chihuahuas," she later recalled.[86] But it was worth it. On election day when she claimed success in her first bid for elective office.

Mikulski served on the Baltimore City Council for 5 years. In 1976, when Congressman Paul S. Sarbanes announced his candidacy for the U.S. Senate, Councilwoman Barbara Mikulski was one of six people to throw her hat into the race to take his place in the U.S. House of Representatives. Using a vast network of community volunteers and 110% of her own energy, Mikulski won the Democratic primary and went on to beat the Republican nominee in the general election in 1977.

After 10 years in the House, more than 10,000 votes, and thousands of hours of committee work, town hall meetings, and visits with constituents, Congresswoman Mikulski announced on October 28, 1985, that she would seek the U.S. Senate seat being vacated by retiring Senator Charles Mc. Mathias Jr. Mikulski was elected to the Senate in November 1986, winning 61% of the vote against her Republican challenger. After being sworn in on January 6, 1987, Senator Mikulski became the 16th woman to serve in the U.S. Senate. She was the first Democratic woman to hold a Senate seat not previously held by her husband; the first Democratic woman ever to have served in both Houses of Congress; and the first woman ever to win a statewide election in Maryland.

After 6 years in the Senate, Mikulski was reelected to a second term in 2003, and she has already become deputy minority whip and serves on the Appropriations and Labor and Human Resources Committees.

The political power that ordinary people are alleged to possess becomes deprived of content, and we lack control over the premises and social contexts by which we live. "The domain of political action," says Abe Kaplan, "is itself one of the loci of increasing depersonalization and dehumanization. The political leader, furthermore, is not a person, but an image, and to him ordinary citizens are not even that, only a vote, or at best, a constituent."[87]

Praxis   Sheldon Wolin describes as our birthright a political identity to collaboratively debate, decide, and initiate collective ethical action with other human beings who have engaged in public discourse. Political discourse, therefore, is dependent on practical wisdom, or what the Greeks called *praxis* or good judgment: action based on informed discussion by which people decide on policies infused with higher purpose that they themselves put into action.

"In praxis the most important part of action is the reflection and evaluation afterward. The experience of action when people engage in planned activities to move on a particular issue often creates a reaction that is unanticipated," says Ernesto Cortes Jr.[88] This reaction produces the material for real teaching of politics and how to engage in social thinking, reflection, discussion, and more planning. Praxis enables us to shape our community, mold the content of our schools, produce our culture, and build associations and social programs that reflect our deepest and most cherished ideals about who we are and the kind of people we want to become.

SENATOR DEBBIE STABENOW

Born on April 29, 1950, Debbie Stabenow grew up in the small town of Clare, Michigan. She received her BA in 1972 and her MSW in 1975 from Michigan State University. She was first elected to the Ingham County Board of Commissioners in 1974, becoming from 1977 to 1978 the youngest person and first woman to chair the board. She was elected to the Michigan House of Representatives where she served for 12 years (1979–1990) and rose in leadership, becoming the first woman to preside over the House. She served in the State Senate for 4 years (1991–1994) and was elected to Congress in 1996 where she served two terms representing Michigan's Eighth Congressional District.

Debbie Stabenow made history in 2000 when she became the first woman from the State of Michigan elected to the United States Senate. She has been recognized nationally for her leadership on issues such as domestic violence, child support and visitation enforcement, drunk driving, Alzheimer's disease, mental health, child abuse prevention, and foster care reform. She has been a leading advocate for small businesses, a leader on property tax and school finance reform, and instrumental in several important environmental reforms.

Senator Stabenow has become one of Michigan's most influential and accomplished leaders. As a state legislator, she was acclaimed one of Michigan's most passionate advocates for children and an expert in family law. Senator Stabenow's leadership and experience were rewarded with four key Senate committee assignments including the powerful Budget Committee; Banking, Housing and Urban Affairs; Agriculture, Nutrition and Forestry; and the Special Committee on Aging. She also heads the Senate Health Care Task Force.

Character Education

Early in its history, social workers understood the role of character education as a vital component of democracy. *Character Education in a Democracy,* by social worker S. R. Slavson, who later became the father of American group psychotherapy, laid the foundation for the character-building role in social group work. Professional social group work was identified as a method of character building and citizenship,[89] and Slavson pioneered character-building programs of the YMCA, YWCA, Boy and Girl Scouts, and Boys and Girls Clubs as a means of building a democratic society in which involvement in citizenship is a key characteristic.

Value Education

Values are the substance of politics and policy. Public education systems, however, do not generally emphasize skills in value-oriented decision making, depriving students of an important tool for graduation into adult citizenship. Having reduced politics to the possessive pursuit of self-interest and decision making to the pragmatic compromise between contending actors, ethical political discourse tends to be a diminished arena of thought and action in American public affairs. Local communities, social organizations including community and faith-based organizations, and community planning and policy making groups, among others, are value-generating, value-bearing, and value-transmitting agencies of society.

In neighborhood social structures, the process of social valuation occurs continually as we communicate, engage, and relate face to face. The values that infuse each community's history and culture reproduce those same social values in the lives of community members.[90] Neighborhood social organizations that involve us in community-building projects, social service, and direct grassroots political engagement are important components of civic and social consciousness. People become political beings by actively engaging one another in community organizing, social planning, and policy making by making informed value decisions in areas that affect their lives and incorporating those values in the life of the community.

Community Politics

Berger and Neuhaus assert that human beings in their own communities understand their needs better than anyone else. Neighborhood and ethnic associations and community, social, and religious organizations exist where people are, and that is where sound public policy should originate. Neighborhood politics aims at empowering ordinary people to do the things that the more affluent can already do. Politics at the neighborhood level spreads the power around a bit more—and they do so where it matters, in people's control over their own lives. It is at the level of community neighborhoods that people can "generate principled expression of the real values and the real needs of people in our society."[91]

Community political structures are essential for a vital democratic society. Government needs to support community political involvement by designating policy-making structures at the community level. We should learn to ask about the effects of public policies on community structures and at the very minimum put in place policies that prevent government and corporate power from damaging neighborhood communities. For example, we should work against the flight of people from inner cities, which has created wastelands of abandoned buildings and businesses, and against decimating neighborhoods in the name of "redevelopment."

Grassroots Democracy

Representative democracy was practical and efficient in early America when distance and lack of instantaneous communication meant that direct democracy was impossible. Because of the small size and homogeneity of most towns, politicians were often truly "representative" of the culture and values of the communities that elected them. Thomas Bender says that in 1790 there were only 24 places in the United States with a population of more than 2,500 people. Most people lived in a town or village of that size or smaller,

and politics was embedded in social relations, which promoted political consensus.[92]

Today, however, there is such a mixture of groups in many locales that no one representative can adequately speak for all. The massive size of many cities and the pluralistic and complex nature of our society make representative democracy increasingly ineffective and dysfunctional. Modern technology, on the other hand, has made politics accessible to each person in ways never before conceived as possible. Computers, television, and the "information highway" make distance or time no barrier to communication and decision making.

As social work policy advocates utilize creative thinking, a "populist" or people's orientation to democracy, often termed "grassroots" democracy, may become possible. Politics and policy making may begin to become a daily and normal role of all citizens who exert their sense of what is good and right in mutual interaction at the level of the community, not in back rooms of legislative chambers, in the corridors of power, or in the board rooms of multinational corporations. Government would become truly "of the people, by the people, and for the people" rather than "of the elites, by the Congress, and for special interests."

Creating a Good Society

A normative perspective on social policy would view the state as a good society comprised of a variety of pluralistic communities, each of which develops its own cultural milieu by means of value education and interaction with other communities. The ethnic, historical, and cultural diversity of these communities would be recognized and honored as building blocks of the social order.

Society would not be seen merely as an aggregation of conflicting individual interests, tastes, or opinions, each of which competes in the policy arena on an equal level. Instead, certain overarching ideals would be recognized toward which the society ought to move. Within the policy arena, some values will be subordinated to those ideals. Where the two conflict, the public interest ought to generally supersede purely private self-interest, for example. Privilege and position will give way to equalizing opportunity of the less privileged and less powerful. Rewarding accumulation of wealth, for example, would receive less policy recognition than assisting those who lack the means of survival.

KINDS OF POLICY ANALYSIS

Two kinds of policy analysis exist in today's political circles: top-down policy analysis and community policy making.

Top-Down Policy Analysis

Most modern policy analysis occurs today at high levels of government and results in lengthy reports on specific social problems. Professional experts skilled in policy research provide policy makers with pragmatic, action-oriented recommendations for alleviating social problems.[93]

Sometimes a policy analysis is commissioned by the President or Prime Minister or by a congressional committee. Sometimes an interest group concerned about the policy question performs policy analysis. For example, *The State of America's Children,* a report by the Children's Defense Fund, provides information, analysis, and recommendations on many issues concerning child welfare. These policy assessments are often very valuable, and many times the policy recommendations they contain are implemented.

At times, however, worthwhile recommendations that are not politically "correct," according to a governmental administration, are never implemented. A policy analysis commissioned by one national administration may be ignored by a succeeding administration whose policy preferences are different. Policy analysis generated by experts may offer recommendations for, rather than with, people and miss the mark of what is most important or helpful. At other times, policy decisions may be manipulated to serve the interests of those in power rather than assist victims of social problems.

Community-Centered Policy Analysis

Community-centered policy analysis is performed at the local level by people who are directly affected by social issues and concerns, not by a professional analyst who acts alone or as part of an independent policy research group. Often coalitions or federations of community organizations engaged in a policy issue combine local policy recommendations at the regional or national levels into a unified proposal.

Community-centered policy analysis uses rational problem solving and action research, an investigation conducted by people who are themselves part of the research population and who then use their results to develop solutions to the problems they are examining.

HOW TO DO COMMUNITY-CENTERED POLICY ANALYSIS

Community-centered policy analysis includes developing a policy-making group, defining the policy problem, finding the real problem, relabeling, getting the facts, developing alternative solutions, choosing among alternative solutions, deciding on the best solutions, developing a policy proposal, gaining acceptance of the sponsoring organization, and implementing the policy.

Develop a Policy-Making Group

Developing community public policy may come as an offshoot of community organizing, community development, or community planning. Members of these community-based organizations may want to propose changes in city ordinances or zoning laws, propose new laws governing the allocation of city services, or ask for watchdog commissions that have authority to investigate police brutality, discrimination, or human rights violations.

Community-based organizations may ask for neighborhood authority to participate in the city budgeting process or for new police procedures regarding use of tactical squads or firearms that may endanger innocent citizens. They may work for local neighborhood-based government, laws governing the use of drugs, gun control, rent control, requirements for paying living wages, laws against redlining, restrictions on dumping waste on community land or in rivers and streams, or any of a host of other issues that will lead to a better community and a more responsive local government.

SOCIAL WORKERS IN ELECTIVE OFFICE

In 1991 a NASW survey revealed that 113 social workers held elected offices. In 1993, 165 elected officeholders were identified, a 50% increase in 2 years. In 1992 an unprecedented number of social workers ran for Congress, 10 in all. At that time there were

5 social workers in Congress, 9 serving in state legislatures, 26 in county or borough governments, 47 in city or municipal offices, and 11 in other elected capacities. Among the social workers in elected office, 132 were women and 72 were men, 154 were White, 28 African American, 17 Hispanic, and 5 Asian American. In 2003, 6 social workers were elected to national office, 2 social workers in the Senate, and 4 in the House of Representatives.[94]

When a community organization, community development corporation, or neighborhood planning board decides to engage in policy advocacy, its members form a community policy-making group. The group should represent the values of the organization and the culture of the community on whose behalf the organization is proposing policy change. Individual members of the policy-making group may be chosen because they represent particular segments of the community population, its various interests, and its values. Members of any policy-making group should be members of the community and the organization that is sponsoring the process. Out of a pool of potential representatives, members could be asked to volunteer or could be democratically elected. A macro social worker can assist the policy-making group as consultant, trainer, information gatherer, liaison to local government, group facilitator, advocate, or technical adviser.

Define the Problem

To develop policy alternatives, your community policy-making group needs to define the policy issues in ways that they can be solved,[95] and at the same time you help your policy group avoid pitfalls in defining the problem.

Ask Questions   You assist your group members in asking themselves these questions: What part of the policy problem do we want to resolve? Are we interested in certain aspects of the issue, or should we try to tackle the problem as a whole? How do we define a policy problem in such a way that it is solvable, given the limitations on our resources—time, manpower, funding, and expertise?

Pitfalls in Defining the Problem   Solutions may seem very obvious. It is tempting for members to pull

solutions out of the air. However, your group needs to be able to work through the policy definition process systematically. As you assist members in defining the problem, you help them navigate through a number of initial pitfalls including premature labeling, fitting preconceived solutions to a policy issue, accepting the leader's definition, or giving in to group pressure.

Premature Labeling   Labeling helps you see the policy in a clear way, restricts the range of choices, and identifies what is, as well as what is not to be considered. Labeling a problem too early in the process may prevent the group from considering the problem completely. Premature labeling may lead group members to be concerned with symptoms rather than causes, with causes when symptoms are all that realistically can be treated, or with the wrong problem. At the beginning of policy analysis, leave all options open until the real problem emerges clearly.

The Solution in Search of a Problem   Sometimes people come to the policy table armed with a full repertoire of solutions gleaned from articles, journals, meetings, research, and their own experience and values. As soon as they encounter a condition that one of these ready-made solutions might fix, they may phrase the problem to fit their preconceived solution, so that their answers are the best and most logical remedies. Each of these solutions may appear correct and, to the individuals proposing them, necessary. If they are lucky, their solution will fit the problem, but more than likely the situation is more complicated and, having already made up their minds, they may have foreclosed other possibilities. In the battle of solutions that ensues, each group member attempts to persuade the group that his or her idea is best.

This process is almost always destructive. It rarely leads to effective solutions because the problem has not been clearly defined based on its characteristics. Moreover, the group may accept a statement with which most, if not all, are uncomfortable. While those whose ideas prevailed may "win," it is at the expense of those who may feel they were forced to capitulate or compromise. They may go along but not be really committed to the issue. If your policy-making group seems to focus on solutions before clearly examining the problem, you need to recognize that they are playing the "solutions in search of a problem" game and help members disengage themselves from this process.

Accepting the Leader's Definition   As a macro social worker, you may have a highly developed intuitive sense and a knack for putting your finger on the crux of the problem. Allowing your own intuitive sense to dominate the problem identification process may work for you some of the time, but it won't work all of the time. The community policy-making group may accept your version of the problem because of your expertise, track record, or power position. None of these is a valid reason for deciding on a problem definition.

If you happen to be wrong, you will have wasted valuable time and tarnished your own reputation. If you have a hunch about what the real problem is, it is best to wait, watch, and use the group process to confirm your intuition rather than make a pronouncement. Keep in mind that you need to help the whole group work through a process in which all can learn. You are not helping if you move too far ahead of your policy group.

Personal Influence   Be careful about those who tend to be most persuasive, influential, or assertive. Often the group may initially accept their version, parts of different problem perceptions may be pieced together, or a compromise may be reached among dominant members. None of these may reflect the ideas of the group as a whole. The result is a problem statement based on personalities and personal influence of the members and not centered on the real problem itself.

How to Avoid Pitfalls   There are two ways to help your group avoid pitfalls. One is to help the group be objective by asking themselves questions. A second way is to use focus groups.

Ask Questions   Help your group explore questions such as when, who, what, where, why, and how in relation to the problem.

Ask when: Explore the origins and history of the problem arena. When did the problem first appear? Through what historical events or circumstances has the social problem evolved to the present state of affairs? Did it come about suddenly, or does it have a long history? Knowing these antecedents will help your group understand the variety of factors that have led to the present situation, the length of time the problem has been in existence, its scope, and its severity.

Ask who: Who are the major actors? These may be decision makers, agency or organizational administrators, various interest groups, community leaders,

or legislators. Who has contributed to the problem? Are there groups of perpetrators or potential targets that may have caused or potentially may have added to the policy issue? Who are the prime victims of the policy problem? Who has the most to gain, and who has the most to lose by solving the problem?

Ask why: Why did the policy problem come about? What events or conditions have led to the current state of affairs? Are there particular cycles or trends that tell you which factors may be causally related to the problem?

Ask what: What questions include consequences, solutions, and what aspect of the problem is important.

1. Consequences. What are some of the major consequences of the policy problem? This question deals with symptoms of the problem. What are the economic, social, and political affects of the problem? What social situations or social conditions have contributed to the problem's continuance or added to its complexity?

2. Solutions. What kinds of policy solutions have been tried in the past? How effective were these policy solutions? Knowing what has been tried in the past will help avoid dead-end solutions or blind alleys, and understanding what has worked will help prevent your group from reinventing the wheel. Alice Kitchen says, however, simply because a policy recommendation did not work in the past does not mean that a similar action won't work this time. The wrong people may have been in leadership roles, receptivity to the proposal may not have been strong, or the urgency may not have been felt. The time may now be ripe for your group to try again.[96]

3. Aspects: Your group might ask themselves what part of the policy problem do we want to resolve? Are we interested in certain aspects of the issue, or should we try to tackle the problem as a whole?

Ask where: Where is the problem located? Is the problem generalized throughout the community or are particular areas affected more than others? Obtaining an idea of where the problem is located will give your group an idea of where to start.

Ask how: How important is the problem? How widespread is it? How many people are affected by it? How do we define a policy problem in such a way that it is solvable, given the limitations on our resources such as time, manpower, funding, and expertise?

Focus Groups　Bring together those representatives who have a stake in the problem to help define the problem from their perspective, and ask them questions your community policy-making group has prepared. Focus group participants may be politicians, planners, community leaders, agency administrators, victims, and service providers. As members of the policy-making group meet with focus groups, be alert for persons who may want to work with you on the solution after the group has identified the problem.

Define the "Real" Problem

After the community policy-making group has gathered, asked themselves questions, and engaged focus groups of key actors, your members' perceptions of the problem may bear little resemblance to the issue they initially formulated. Your group should welcome this because the members' perceptions of the problem will have been refined, clarified, and shaped by the new information they have developed.

Even though there may be many perspectives on the problem, your policy-making group has control over the way they define the problem. There is no one best problem statement, nor is there only one real problem. "Each problem situation contains within its boundaries—however vague and fuzzy those boundaries might be—numerous potential 'real' problems."[97] As you assist your members, help them explore their own perceptions about what issues are important, whether the problem is meaningful, whether it is of sufficient size, and whether it is resolvable.

Look for Member Perceptions　Most social problems are laden with subjective perceptions and values. For example, if your group explores its concern about violence in your neighborhood, any number of issues may occur to them. Does the problem concern the availability of handguns, assault rifles, or hunting weapons? Is the problem the number of shop owners or dealers who sell guns? Does the problem lie in the laws that permit easy access to weapons? Is your group interested in violence on television or about specific kinds of violence such as domestic violence, rape, or violence used in the commission of robberies? Are they concerned about youth-oriented violence such as gang violence?

Meaningful　Help your members choose a problem that is meaningful and valid for the community.

Certain problems will intuitively speak to the policy-making group members. The problem should be important and be one that will mobilize the community to action.

Problem Scope　Look at the scope of the problem. Some problems may seem so large or unwieldy that they appear unsolvable. The group may have to break them down into smaller, more manageable pieces. On the other hand, members may see patterns of smaller problems that they want to group together into a larger one.

Solvable　The problem should be one that the community members can actually do something about. It doesn't make sense to try to solve elder abuse in general, for example. But you can help your group choose the individual aspect (elder abuse hurts individuals), the family aspect (elder abuse is on the rise in families containing an elderly member), or the institutional aspect (elder abuse occurs frequently in institutional settings). The group could narrow its focus to a particular neighborhood (Northside) or location (Northside Gardens Elder Village).

Relabel the Problem

Help your group relabel the problem and come up with a working problem statement from which they will continue the problem-solving process. For example, using the hypothetical problem of elder abuse, your group may redefine the problem to focus on family and institutional elder abuse in Northside.

Gather Information

When your policy group gathers information about a policy problem, they are conducting research. Two ways to approach policy research are focused synthesis and epical research.

Focused Synthesis　A focused synthesis pulls together information from a variety of sources in support of a policy position, including published articles, discussions with experts and stakeholders, focus interviews, reports from congressional hearings, anecdotal stories, experience of researchers, unpublished documents, staff memoranda, and existing research data. One Agency for International Development (AID) study of rural water supply problems, for example, used available literature, the researchers' own field experiences in the past 5 years, and discussions with individuals at several agencies and organizations.

Epical Research

Epical research involves formulating specific research questions, operationalizing variables, and collecting and analyzing data.

Formulate Specific Research Questions   The process of formulating specific research questions should include those aspects of the problem that your group can change. People's attitudes, for example, cannot generally be changed easily, but social conditions that affect those attitudes can be changed. Look for those aspects of the problem that the community can do something about. Then formulate research questions around those areas in which change is possible. For example, it is impossible to know where elder abuse will occur, but your group can develop some policy proposals that may help prevent elder abuse at home or in residential facilities. The members of your group can develop proposals that will require welfare agencies to investigate allegations of elder abuse and provide treatment.

Select questions that address an important aspect of the problem given the financial and manpower limits of the policy group. Questions should provide information that will be useful for current and future decision making and address issues in a manner that will help policy makers act on the social problem. For example, you can ask how much elder abuse is occurring in your community, the kinds of elder abuse that occurs, and what government is currently doing to either prevent or cope with the problem.

Operationalize Variables   To operationalize means to define the variables or the particular aspects of the policy problem as specific, measurable indicators. If your group is exploring elder abuse, for example, age is a variable that you may need to define. You may define elderly as anyone above the age of 65, for example. You may need to define what your group means by abuse. You may need to define and devise some ways of measuring physical abuse. Physical abuse, for example, is often measured by the presence of a broken bone, bruises, cuts, scrapes or burn marks.

Some variables may not be directly measurable. For example, it may be difficult to measure verbal abuse or emotional abuse. You may need to give a questionnaire to an elderly person that asks about his or her relationship with a caregiver and focuses on patterns of interaction that may indicate verbal or emotional abuse.

On the other hand, a number of indicators to measure such variables as crime, unemployment, or poverty may be available from which your group may choose. You can help the policy-making group find proxy or substitute indicators for those variables that are not directly measurable. Proxy indicators are measures that reasonably substitute for the issue about which your group wants information. For example, suppose your group is examining ethnic intolerance. You may look at unemployment rates of different ethnic groups, a racial attitude survey of randomly selected citizens, or the affirmative action practices of corporations. Even though none of these separately or together measure racial tolerance, they can provide a partial substitute.

Collect and Analyze Data   Epical research involves collecting factual information by means of using existing data, social surveys, performing case studies about specific problem situations, and using a mixed approach.

Existing data: Using existing data, also called secondary research, such as that acquired by universities, government agencies, and policy research institutes is the most cost-efficient method for answering policy research questions. Existing data can provide answers more quickly than information your group collects itself.[98] Secondary or existing information about elder abuse, for example, comes in many forms, such as large statistical studies provided by the federal government and other government bodies, government reports, industry studies, traditional books, and journals found in libraries, as well as the observations of knowledgeable observers such as nurses, social workers, care workers, or doctors. If your policy-making group wants to use existing research information, however, they will need to ask their own questions about the data and subject it to their own statistical analysis.

Social surveys: A survey is a systematic inquiry of perceptions or attitudes about problems affecting an entire population or a sample of that population. Surveys are ways your group can follow up on issues raised from focus groups, focus interviews, or examination of secondary data. Your policy group can make good use of surveys, described in Chapter 6, when you want to narrow issues, ask respondents to rank the importance of particular concerns, or give you an indicator of a range of preferences among items.

Case studies: Many people use case studies in policy research because they are quick, cost-efficient, and allow room for impressionistic analysis of a situation. They often provide a relatively complete understanding of a situation's complexity and promote examination of the process by which intervention or policy actions have been implemented. In studying the problem of elder abuse, a person could follow one example of elder abuse and look at it from several perspectives, such as its medical, social, emotional, and financial aspects. A case study might focus on elder abuse in one particular residential facility for the elderly. Case studies also promote examination of the process by which intervention or policy actions have been implemented. For example, one might examine the effectiveness of policies of a particular city or county in dealing with elder abuse. Case studies are particularly useful for developing recommendations about the future.

Mixed approach: Combine a number of different research methods, such as a survey with focused synthesis or case studies with secondary analysis. An ideal combination is to use qualitative methods such as participant observation and quantitative methods such as a social survey. If your group uses several different combinations, they will increase the perceived validity of the study if both methods corroborate one another, and they can give your group additional insight that one method alone could not provide.[99]

Develop Alternative Solutions

Your community policy group devises possible solutions or interventions. They examine issues they cannot change and those that they can. Members make a list of change points and then develop and rank the alternative solutions they have developed.

Issues You Cannot Change Eliminate those issues about which you can do nothing. For example, in considering the problem of elder abuse, your policy-making group may decide that eradicating the cause of elder abuse is an issue they cannot change. However, try to be conservative when deciding what the group cannot change. Things that at first appear unchangeable may turn out to be amenable to change

after all. For example, the stress of caring for a frail elderly parent may be reduced by developing policies that allow for homemaker assistance, respite care, day programs, counseling, and other services.

Issues You Can Change After your group has eliminated those components of the policy problem they cannot change, your members are left with those elements of the problem over which it has some control. If your group discovered, for instance, that some elder abuse is caused by care workers, your policy group might recommend better screening of care workers and create better standards for care workers, medical personnel, and social workers. Your group may examine the quality of care worker training or the ratio of care workers and other staff to elderly clients in a facility.

They could assess the system of reporting elder abuse. They could make recommendations about how to handle specific incidents of abuse or provide ideas about a variety of services to prevent elder abuse. These are windows of opportunity where changes can bring about different consequences for people.

List Change Points List your group's "change points" on a board to make them explicit. Help your members analyze the change points to eliminate or ameliorate the problem by asking the following questions.

1. Who will be affected?
2. What action will be taken?
3. Who will pay and by what means?
4. Who will implement the policy?
5. Who will have jurisdiction over policy?
6. How will the policy be regulated?

Consider the problem of elder abuse in Northtown. For each category, list as many items as your group can think of. For example, assume your group wants to examine the quality of caretaker training. Those affected would be the elderly person, siblings, children, doctors, nurses, social workers, and caretakers. Actions might include screening caretakers, giving examinations, tests, or internships. The issue of who will pay would include citizens, businesses, and others. Financial measures include taxes, grants, contracts, loans, rewards, incentives, subsidies, and compensation for loss. Jurisdiction could be with the

Department of Social Services, the county sheriff's department, or the city police. Regulation may occur by means of standards, licenses, codes, warnings, fines, probation, or incarceration. Place each of these lists in separate columns and, using iteration, take the first item from the first column and add one item from each additional column to it, putting together different combinations of items. For example, an item may look like "screen caretakers paid for by taxes, monitored by welfare department, implemented by Area Agency on Aging, regulated by fines." Then move to the second item on the first column and repeat the process until you have worked through every item. Some combinations will make no sense, but using this technique will open your group to thinking of alternatives they may not have visualized.

Examine and Rank Alternative Solutions
Your group examines the lists of alternatives and eliminates those that are obviously not workable. Then the group ranks the viable alternatives in order. Leaving things just as they are is an option that your group should always consider.

Convene a public forum or arrange for focus groups to get input from the community on the issues and on the various alternatives that your group is now considering. The community forum or focus groups are intended to present the alternatives and to solicit input. Out of these community gatherings your community policy group may be able to sharpen their perspective, discover issues they have not previously considered, obtain a clear sense of the community's interests, and understand the power of its concern about the issues. Decide on a final ranking of the alternatives using input from the community forum.

Choose Among Alternative Solutions

In the best of all worlds the policy-making group would chose the policy alternative that members consider the best one. The best solution, however, may not be feasible. Your group, therefore, needs to assess which of their most highly ranked alternatives have the best chance of being implemented. There are three ways to consider which of the alternative solutions your community has agreed on are the most feasible. You can assess political feasibility, economic feasibility, and social feasibility.

Assess Political Feasibility
If your community policy-making group intends to implement a policy proposal, political actors—those who hold power—and their influence are important for you to consider. Many political actors will have a stake in the outcome of any policy. Each of these individuals or groups may have preferred solutions that will compete with your solution in the political arena. Politicians may be interested in your group's policy solution only to the extent that it enhances or detracts from their chances for reelection or affects their constituencies. Think of the most important political decision makers who will influence the choice of a policy. Consider the issue position, power, and salience that a policy commands for these decision makers.

Issue Position Issue position indicates the strength of support an actor expresses for this particular alternative solution. Score each of the decision makers who you believe support your policy with a +1 to a +3. Score those who oppose your policy with a −1 to a −3, and assign 0 to those who are neutral.

Power The power variable estimates the amount of power possessed by the actor to decide on the alternative. If the actor has maximum influence to decide, assign a 3, moderate influence a 2, and low influence a 1. Assign a 0 to those who have no influence at all.

Salience The third variable is salience, the degree to which the actor cares about and pays attention to the issue. Salience measures how high the issue stands on the actor's list of concerns, in contrast to issue position, which indicates the strength of the actor's preference for this particular alternative solution. Score a 3 for actors who feel strongly about the policy issue, a 2 for decision makers who are moderately concerned about the issue, a 1 for those who have low interest, and a 0 for those who give no importance at all to the issue.

Calculate the Political Feasibility Calculate the political feasibility for each of your top alternatives by multiplying the three variables for each decision maker and then adding the scores. The larger the positive number, the more likely that support for this alternative will be strong. The closer the net score is to zero, the more likely the alternative will be politically contentious. The larger the negative score, the more likely it is this particular alternative will not be feasible.[100]

Assess Economic Feasibility There are three ways to assess economic feasibility: benefit-cost analysis, cost-effectiveness analysis, and decision analysis.

Benefit-Cost Analysis Benefit-cost analysis, introduced in Chapter 3 and amplified in Chapter 11, is a method by which your group compares costs and benefits to society of alternative policy options. Given two proposals, each of which will meet your goals, the one with the highest benefit-cost ratio will often be more appealing to decision makers. Generally speaking, a benefit-cost ratio that equals or exceeds 1 will attract attention because the benefits of that alternative will equal or exceed its costs.

Add all of the benefits in dollars that will be incurred by implementing the alternative. Divide these benefits by a sum of all of the costs to obtain a benefit-cost ratio. For example, in considering a problem of gun control, suppose your group decided on the three most politically feasible alternatives to control access to guns in Northside. Assume that the cost of a child's life is $500,000 and that each alternative has equal benefits; that is, the life of one child will be saved for every 10,000 guns immobilized. The hypothetical benefit-cost ratios for three alternatives are as follows:

1. Require all guns to have a special child-proof safety device at $10 additional cost, to be born by the buyer. Assuming 10,000 guns, the estimated total cost of saving the life of one child is $10 × 10,000 = $100,000. The benefit-cost ratio is 500,000/100,000 = 5.

2. Require anyone owning a gun to have special training in safety, paid by the gun owner. Training costs $100 per gun owner. Total cost for 10,000 owners is 100 × 10,000 = $1,000,000 to save one child's life. The benefit-cost ratio is 500,000/1,000,000 or 0.5.

3. Institute an amnesty program in which guns would be accepted by the local government for destruction in return for a $200 rebate per gun, paid for by taxpayers. The total cost for alternative 3 for 10,000 guns recaptured for each life saved is $2,000,000. The benefit-cost ratio is 500,000/2,000,000 or .25.

Given these three proposals, the most favorable benefit-cost ratio is to provide guns with safety devices. It is also the most politically feasible because the cost is born by the buyer rather than by taxpayers. The amnesty program is least cost-beneficial, not only because it is most expensive but also because the cost is born by all taxpayers. A limitation of benefit-cost analysis is the difficulty in assigning monetary costs to such intangibles as a human life and the difficulty of calculating future unknowns with any accuracy.

Cost-Effectiveness Analysis Sometimes costs and benefits of different policy options cannot be clearly identified to allow for analysis. When this occurs, benefit-cost analysis is often replaced by cost-effectiveness analysis. Cost-effectiveness analysis expresses the actual monetary cost per unit of benefit or expected outcome. Examples of costs effectiveness include the following:

The amount of money needed to reduce the number of incidents of elder abuse by a certain number.

The amount of money needed for an alcohol abuser to achieve abstinence over a period of time.

The amount of money needed for a former convict to not recidivate.

The amount of money needed to achieve a certain percentage increase in the literacy rate of the population.

The amount of money needed to reduce infant mortality by a certain percentage.

The amount of money needed to reduce child abuse by a particular number.

By themselves, cost-effectiveness dollar amounts say little about whether a policy should or should not be implemented. Therefore, policy makers often compare the cost-effectiveness of several different options. For example, the cost to the county of rehabilitating an alcoholic convicted of drunk driving ($10,000) may be compared to the costs of incarcerating the driver for a particular period ($200 per day × 30 days = $6,000), withholding the driver's license and imposing a fine ($300 administrative costs minus $300 fine = 0), mandating community service and driver training courses borne by the offender (30 days community service at $60 wages per day = $1,800 cost savings to the county), or doing nothing = $2,000 per offense. The costs of doing nothing may be determined by the average cost of property damage, injuries, and deaths incurred per alcoholic. Policy makers can then judge which of these alternatives is the best use of taxpayers' money.

An advantage of cost-effectiveness analysis is the ease by which expenses of one alternative can be calculated in comparison to other alternatives. Policy makers can judge whether a policy option is sufficiently effective to warrant its cost.

Decision Analysis   Decision analysis requires a panel of experts to assign a numeric score on an agreed-upon common denominator to all benefits and costs. For example, the cost of the abuse of a child or the benefits of preventing or rehabilitating abuse would be calculated. With such numeric scores, statistically expected values of each alternative policy solution can be computed. Comparing these values for each policy alternative will then yield the optimal policy.

Assess Social Feasibility   Social feasibility estimates the impact on people, groups, organizations, and communities that will result from one or more policy options. Social feasibility is measured by means of a Social Impact Assessment (SIA). For example, in developing an SIA for a Crosstown Expressway in Northtown, a policy analysis group first studied a variety of costs including aesthetics, traffic, and directness of route in addition to construction and maintenance costs. Then they assessed potential beneficial impacts of the expressway on employment, urban renewal, property values, and impact on community life. Each variable was assigned a subjective score (from 0 to 10) of acceptability.

While SIA acceptability scores cannot be used to calculate social benefits in monetary terms, by considering a range of costs and benefits, SIAs do consider less tangible but important aspects of social concern. Because SIAs help policy makers assess the extent to which an alternative will have an adverse impact on the public, they give some indication of public acceptability of an alternative.[101]

Decide on the Best Solution

Your policy-making group now has four different measures they can use to gauge their alternatives: the rankings that express your community group's preferences, and the political, economic, and social feasibility scores. If your group believes that some of these measures should be give higher or lower preference,

they can assign "weights" to them. For example, assume that in your community economic factors far outweigh social acceptability. Your group decides that economic concerns are twice as important as social concerns. Therefore, your group doubles the score of the economic ranking.

After your group considers weighing the different categories, they multiply each of these to get a score for each alternative. Compare the final scores of each alternative. The alternative with the highest score should have the best chance of being implemented successfully.

Develop a Policy Proposal

In a written report, set forth the policy-making group's recommendations for resolving the social problem. Describe the policy issue your group is considering and the three or four top policy alternatives that the group recommends, including the feasibility measures for each solution. Explain why each received its ranking. Offer short- and long-term recommendations, as well as strategies for implementation.

When issuing a statement or report, help your group present the results as simply as possible so the report is easily understood. Present the conclusion and major caveats first. Be concise. Use examples and anecdotes. Avoid jargon. Discuss the effectiveness of several of the group's alternatives, and reduce your proposal to its essential elements.

Present the Proposal

Present the policy proposal to the members of the community organization, community development corporation, or community planning council who sponsored the policy board, to other community organizations and agencies, and to community members as a whole in a public forum or series of forums. These meetings should be informational but also should seek advice and changes and solicit assistance from community members. Make these meetings open to all members of the community. Break the group into smaller buzz groups or use large decision techniques described in Chapter 6 to solicit opinions, advice, or changes to the proposal. After the public forum, the policy-making group should revise the policy proposal to reflect any additions or changes recommended by those persons attending.

Gain Acceptance by the Sponsoring Organization

The policy-making group, with the assistance of the macro social worker, has struggled through an often arduous and long process, considered questions that are of importance to the organization and the community as a whole, and produced a document that the board of the sponsoring organization can now use to make specific and needed changes in the foundational principles on which the community depends for its guidance and direction.

The policy-making group should request a special meeting with the sponsoring organization or its board to present the proposal to the organization. The board should make this special meeting into a celebration to bring closure to this part of the process. At the celebration, the committee members should formally submit the final proposal to the organization's members, ask for its formal adoption, and propose that the board devise a mechanism for its implementation.

Once the board accepts the proposal, the board gives members of the policy-making group recognition for their hard and dedicated work. Members of the planning group should be congratulated, and the sponsoring organization and board should offer its thanks and give a tangible or symbolic reward to the members for their achievement. The entire sponsoring organization should feel a sense of victory and success as well for having accepted a challenge from the policy board to turn its recommendations into a reality.

Implement the Policy

When the sponsoring organization accepts the policy proposal in its original or adapted form, they now have responsibility to implement it. Implementing policy occurs in the "real world" of politics. Your role as an adviser to the policy-making group shifts. As a macro social work policy advocate, you now work with the organization as a whole to help devise ways of getting the policy proposal accepted by government leaders and to encourage them to either put it into action themselves or provide your sponsoring social organization with the authority and means to do so.

The board of the social organization forms a group of members to engage the implementation process. The members of this group should be different from those who helped develop the policy proposal. They can engage the proposal with new energy and see the proposal with fresh perspectives, and they should not be hampered by the vested interests original policy group members may have acquired. You assist members of the policy implementation group by means of case conferences, fact gathering, position taking, committee work, petitions, media campaigns, e-advocacy, consensus policy advocacy, or working directly through politicians by means of lobbying, political pressure tactics, initiative and referendum, or legal action.

The Case Conference   Hold a conference with agencies that have responsibility in your policy initiative's area. Your goal is to help agency administrators realize that the policies or procedures that are dysfunctional for your social organization and community may also be problematic for others. Raising the issue in a case conference may assist in getting the policy changed.

Fact Gathering   Having the right information in a form that can be used properly gives you leverage and influence for change. You can use the facts that your policy group has developed to urge leaders in positions of authority to make needed changes, or your implementation group can continue to obtain more facts that cement your recommendations more firmly.

Position Taking   Issue a public statement or report that puts your social organization on public record as a participant in a change process. Taking a position informs people about where you stand, clarifies your objectives, and provides a point of identification. You put agencies and politicians on notice that your organization is fighting for change, and you make clear what you want to accomplish.

Committee Work   Government policy committees provide a public forum for the discussion of ideas and publicize potential alternative solutions. Social workers can often help the community by recommending community citizens to government officials to serve as committee members or consultants to governmental policy committees, or a macro social worker may participate, on behalf of the social organization and the community, on such committees.

Petitions   Petitioning can indicate public support for a particular solution to a problem. Petitioning is a useful way your social organization can both publicize your community's proposal and develop public awareness. "It informs decision-makers that there are people 'out there' who have a stake in the decision."[102]

Media Campaigns   The implementation group can use public information campaigns including television, talk radio, newspaper articles or stories, and letters to the editor as important parts of the policy change process. Publicity, stories, and pictures bring issues to public attention and create a climate in which change is possible.

Consensus Policy Advocacy   Your organization can link up with other advocacy, public policy organizations, and special interest policy groups that advocate similar concerns in your area of interest. By combining forces, you can increase your power, range of options, and access to resources.

Lobbying   Lobbying is a fundamental part of the American system of government.[103] Large corporations continually work for their self-interest, and you and your members can lobby governmental officials in the public interest, equalizing the power balance and ensuring that individuals, groups and communities who cannot lobby for themselves are represented in the political bargaining process.

You and your group can lobby face to face, by telephone, letter, or by giving testimony. When lobbying face to face keep in mind that a legislator needs information and assistance. Be honest and factual. Know your issue thoroughly. Anticipate the opposition's claims and formulate persuasive counterarguments. Acknowledge the merits of competing proposals. If your group members are unwilling to acknowledge the strengths of alternative proposals or the weaknesses of the organization's own proposal, your members may be seen as propagandists and damage their credibility.

Straightforward presentations with data are generally the most persuasive. Be able to answer two critical concerns of legislators: What will the proposed legislation cost? and What will be the bill's social impact? Provide succinct supportive documents. Thank legislators for their time and for being open-minded. Follow up with a thank-you letter that includes a synopsis of the position taken by that legislator

during the meeting and with anything that you have agreed to do.

Letter Writing   Letters to legislators are an effective way to get your point across. Make them short, to the point, and credible, one or two pages at most. Describe your position succinctly and provide documentation. Avoid form letters or those that look like form letters. The more personal the letters are, the more persuasive they will be. Clearly handwritten letters on a member's own stationery are the most effective. End your letter with a short thank-you for considering the proposal or request.

Telephoning   Phone calls, usually 48 hours before a legislative vote, will signal a legislator which way the wind is blowing on a piece of legislation and may swing those who are undecided. When calling, state who you are and the message you wish to convey. For example, "I would like to urge Representative Smith to vote yes on Bill 33 because . . ." Leave your name, address, and phone number to confirm that you are a constituent.

Testifying   Legislative committees gather as much information as possible from a wide variety of viewpoints. You or your members may be asked to testify on behalf of the social problem about which your organization has been advocating. The key to offering successful testimony is preparation. Keep your presentation to 10 minutes or less. Never read a statement, but make your testimony interesting and conversational.[104]

Briefly introduce yourself. If you are giving testimony, tell who you are, what program you are representing, how many people you represent, and your qualifications. State your goal and outline your main points. Talk about the problem. Discuss the significance of the issue, and try to relate it to the district represented by the legislators before you. Talk about current efforts to resolve the problem—what solutions have been tried, which ones have worked, which have failed. Explain why current efforts are insufficient and how they can be improved.

Offer specific recommendations. In a few sentences summarize the process by which your organization has developed its proposal and why it is important. Outline the recommendations proposed by your policy group. Explain why these recommendations will be effective, how much they will cost, and how legislators can help implement them. Offer the panel a model law or policy that will achieve your goals, and place the social organization and its resources at the disposal of the legislative committee in helping implement the policy should they ask.

Conclude. Summarize your main points, thank the panel or committee, and tell them you would be happy to answer questions.

Political Pressure Tactics Your group may consider the variety of political pressure tactics described in Chapter 14, including exposure of perpetrators and direct confrontation to achieve your policy goals.

Initiative and Referendum Social workers were among the originators of initiative and referendum laws, which allow citizens to place issues on statewide ballots. In states where initiative and referendum is permitted, your group may be able to develop a campaign to collect enough signatures on petitions to qualify for voting on your proposal.[105]

Legal Action Encouraging your group to seek redress by means of legal action is one way to set precedents and secure change. Class action lawsuits against cigarette smoking, for example, have had a major impact on public health. Others have been employed in protecting consumer rights and preventing environmental contamination by industries.[106]

SOCIAL POLICY AND THE INTERNET

Grassroots social policy advocacy has taken a leap forward by means of the Internet. The Internet enables people to engage in politics and policy making through electronic democracy (e-democracy), e-government, e-journalism, and e-advocacy.

E-Democracy

Lewis A. Friedland asserts that "much as the 'information society' implies a rupture with industrial capitalism, electronic democracy suggests new citizenship practices. New communications technologies are being used in ways that can extend democratic communication practices as wider publics gain access to

them, dissolving control of information as a discreet, privatized commodity."[107]

Social worker John McNutt says, in addition, that one of the trends that creates a basis for e-democracy is devolution. The trend to decentralize government authority, first to states and later to lower levels, is creating a decentralized and diffused decision-making structure that makes electronic democracy more compelling. McNutt asserts that citizen participation in the democratic process is becoming more accepted, including virtual town meetings, forums, and eventually, online elections. Direct democracy—that is, citizens voting on every issue—is probably years away, if at all, but electronic elections should be easier to implement more immediately.[108] There are two approaches to e-democracy: the plebiscitary approach and the deliberative approach.[109]

Plebicitary Approach The plebicitary approach to e-democracy provides citizens with capacity to directly express their opinions through an expanded "electronic marketplace" similar to the advertising marketplace, in which advocacy and social action groups mobilize mass media including e-mail and information networks to immediately capture public attention and mobilize people for action. For example, MoveOn.org was able to generate a huge number of citizens in protest to the Iraq war via Internet and e-mail, bombarding the federal government with their messages. In addition, e-democracy using the plebecitary approach is capable of developing strengthened neighborhood assemblies, televised town meetings, national civic communications cooperatives, a service to equalize access to information and promote full civic education of all citizens, and electronic balloting.

Deliberative Approach The deliberative approach argues for a "communitarian" framework, in which dialogue rooted in identifiable communities takes precedence over direct voting, and in which a concept of the public good goes beyond individual and group interests. One of the key organizations using the deliberative approach is the Institute for Global Communications.

Institute for Global Communications The deliberative approach has been pioneered by the Institute for Global Communications (IGC), a loose coalition of Free-Net groups including HandsNet, PeaceNet,

EcoNet, ConflictNet, LaborNet, and Women'sNet. IGC helps them make use of computer and communications technology to further their own agendas and provides resources for individuals, groups, and organizations engaged in advocacy for social justice, human rights, and the environment. Each of these groups shares information resources, giving people a sense of community and a feeling of membership. In 1996 IGC had about 13,000 members, including 300 to 500 organizations, and incorporated other specialized networks under its umbrella, including UNICEF, the Advocacy Institute, and the Playing to Win network, discussed in Chapter 7.

HandsNet   In its first year HandsNet gave computers to 100 organizations, primarily those on the state level working on hunger and housing issues. By 1989 HandsNet included 500 additional members and had developed a "distributed" database, parceling out information gathering to specialized organizations, some of whom became facilitators managing the flow of policy and program information from Washington D.C., collecting and gathering information for redistribution to other members of the network. The facilitators also managed ongoing electronic discussions, keeping group discussions focused on issues to lead to practical problem solving.

As of 1995, 50 forum managers provided support for nine separate top level forums including 5,000 member organizations across the United States in areas of children and families, community and economic development, rural issues, poverty, youth, community organizing, welfare, and others as well as digesting and abstracting 300 to 400 articles a day for network members.

PeaceNet and EcoNet   PeaceNet hosts more than 1,000 conferences in which members post newsletters, news releases, legislative alerts, and news services. EcoNet hosts the Greenpeace conference and news service. During the Gulf War, the peace and human rights organizations on PeaceNet converged with Greenpeace on EcoNet to offer a virtual worldwide alternative news service.

E-Government

Electronic government (e-government) is the process of delivering government services through technology. There is a move to put a large portion of available government information on the Internet. This will increase the capacity of government to respond electronically and encourage citizens to think of cyberspace as an arena of government action, making e-policy and e-advocacy more acceptable to decision makers.

E-Journalism

Public electronic journalism (e-journalism) seeks to engage in a dialogue with citizens and provides avenues to participate in public life and civil society. It focuses on projects centered either around developing citizen agendas for elections or around specific community problems and issues. Online Wisconsin (OLW), an electronic news journal begun at the University of Wisconsin School of Journalism, organizes debates on issues such as immigration or welfare in a new format that allows many sides to be expressed. In the welfare reform section, for example, the statements of the governor, a conservative advocate of punitive reform, are juxtaposed with welfare mothers describing their own experience of the system. The state's own documents, including studies, are posted online. Multiple viewpoints critical of state welfare reform sits alongside a photo essay exploring life in the welfare system, framing the debate from a more complex perspective than would normally be found in newspapers.[110]

E-Advocacy

Electronic advocacy (e-advocacy) refers to advocacy techniques that use communications technology to support policy change efforts. A policy advocacy group may generate a wide spectrum of interest at little cost by communicating with decision makers, stakeholders, and the community at large by e-advocacy.

John McNutt says that Internet-based technologies are changing the way policy advocacy is practiced. Traditional media-based advocacy involves the use of television, direct mail solicitation, and other methods to change policy and public opinion. By means of e-advocacy, community members use Internet-based technologies including web pages, electronic e-mail, discussion groups, newsgroups, and faxes to provide information to stakeholders, decision makers, and the general public as well as to coordinate policy change. Community members find that e-advocacy is relatively inexpensive and easy to use. It allows advocacy groups to reduce costs and extend their reach, and it is most useful when combined with traditional media techniques.

McNutt anticipates that changes in technology will increase the effectiveness of e-advocacy. Among these will be more elaborate web technologies and more sophisticated geographic information systems, which will enable campaigns to target potential supporters and identify needs. Webcasting technology provides advocates with a means to communicate with supporters on a consistent basis with a wide variety of media. In addition, video teleconferencing that combines the ability to talk with another party with picture and data enables people to simultaneously examine documents and slide presentations.

The growth of e-commerce has created a technology base that facilitates online fundraising for social causes and the use of secure systems for credit card information. The ability to do survey research has been enhanced by the growth of the Internet and tools facilitating research through e-mail and websites. Wireless communications makes portable communication possible even in remote areas and can assist advocates in rural areas, inner-city settings with poor infrastructure, or overseas. The development of personal assistants, small computers called palmtops, can link a worker to the organizational headquarters and assist with the huge amount of information generated through the organizing process.[111]

Blending Approaches

Rather than rely on only one technique, encourage your policy advocacy group or organization to blend political pressure, legal tactics, and confrontation along with e-advocacy approaches. If the goal of the organization is to increase the city's commitment to open housing, representatives of the organization might generate general community interest and provide information by e-advocacy. They can lobby to get a strong open-housing ordinance on the books (a political pressure tactic), simultaneously seeking a court injunction to halt the city's receipt of state development funds until its housing profile improves (a legal tactic), while conducting demonstrations in the plaza in front of city hall to publicize the difficulties facing the poor in finding housing (a confrontation tactic).

CONCLUSION

Social policy occurs as institutional political actors, competing interest groups, government agencies, and business corporations bargain for policy concessions in an interlocking system of decision making. Macro social workers help community groups, community organizations, community development corporations, and community planning boards propose policies that can improve communities and society as a whole. To abdicate this role inevitably means leaving the field of policy and politics to those who wield power at the highest levels of influence.

We need to understand theories of policy making and how to decide on, propose, and get policy implemented. We need to have a normative vision of politics and social policy that helps move the United States and Canada toward what they could become in today's highly technological, fast-paced world. One such model of community policy advocacy provides an understanding of the necessity for locating policy at the community level. It includes a vision of the self as a political actor, a belief in the value of mediating structures, grassroots democracy, community politics, value-based education, and a vision of the state as a good society.

KEY CONCEPTS

public policy

social policy

Jeannette Rankin

policy-making models

laissez-faire

principles of progressive social policy

Ida Wells-Barnett

first New Deal

second New Deal

Barbara Lee

urbanization

urban crisis

Susan A. Davis

civil rights policies

War on Poverty

Edolphus Towns

neoconservative policy

Temporary Assistance for Needy Families (TANF)

military spending

International Criminal Court

models of policy making

elite model

political action committees (PACs)

institutional model

interest group liberalism model

pluralism

rational model

administrative model

fourth branch of government

bazaar politics

marketplace politics

bargaining and negotiation

systems model

Ciro Rodriguez

garbage can model

critique of policy-
making models*polis*

normative policy
making

substantive politics

Barbara Mikulski

praxis

character education

value education

communal politics

grassroots democracy

state as good society

Debbie Stabenow

top-down policy process

community-centered
policy

policy analysis process

operationalize

proxy indicators

secondary research

change points

political feasibility

economic feasibility

benefit-cost analysis

cost-effectiveness

decision analysis

social impact analysis

case conference

fact gathering

position taking

committee work

media campaigns

petitions

lobbying

letter writing

telephoning

testifying

political pressure
tactics

initiative and
referendum

legal action

e-democracy

plebicitary approach

deliberative approach

Institute for Global
Communication
(IGC)

Free-Net groups

HandsNet

PeaceNet

EcoNet

QUESTIONS FOR DISCUSSION

1. In this chapter the point was made that modern technology is making politics accessible to each person in ways never before conceived possible. E-democracy, e-journalism, e-government, and e-advocacy make distance no barrier to political decision making. How will technology make politics and social policy processes more accessible to people, increasing the quality and representativeness of policy solutions?

2. A proposal was made in this chapter for direct citizen access to policy and politics rather than leaving politics to professionals such as elected and appointed officials and lobbyists. What are the advantages of this proposal? What are its disadvantages?

3. Given the fact that often less than 50% of those eligible to vote actually exercise this right, is it realistic to expect that citizens will want to become more directly involved in politics even if they have the opportunity?

4. DiNitto and Dye assert that social policy is a *continuing political struggle* over "conflicting goals and objectives, competing definitions of problems, alternative approaches and strategies, multiple programs and policies, competing proposals for reform, and even different ideas about how decisions should be made."[112] If this is an accurate statement about social policy, can decisions that are good in themselves ever be made about social issues?

5. Can policies be made on any other basis than conflict resolution or on a set of majoritarian decision rules? Explain your answer.

6. If resolving policy disputes by bargaining or voting are the only options available, what assurance is there that policies will be developed that rise above dominance by those groups that have the most power or the most votes?

7. Can you think of a different model of politics that would be more appropriate for our highly mobile, technological society than those discussed in this chapter?

8. John McNutt of the Boston College School of Social Work asserts that the information divide—access to computers and computer information—between haves and have-nots is the policy problem of the new century. What do you think of McNutt's assertion? (For more information, you can obtain a PBS series on the *Information Divide* that discusses this policy issue.)

9. Does social work have a responsibility to help correct market failures and help people meet needs, accomplish life tasks, and realize their aspirations? What solutions can you recommend?

10. The National Rifle Association has successfully carried the battle of upholding the right of people to bear arms. The result has been little gun control legislation in this country. Some people assert that the Second Amendment provides a moral, if not a legal, right to own handguns. Are there ethical values that override this moral and legal right? If so, what does that higher good consist of?

ADDITIONAL READING

Policy

Alliance for Justice. "Worry-Free Lobbying for Nonprofits: How to Use the 501(h) Election to Maximize Effectiveness." Washington, DC: Alliance for Justice, 1999.

Bratt, Rachel G. *Rebuilding a Low-Income Housing Policy.* Philadelphia: Temple University Press, 1989.

Politics

Goetz, Edward. Shelter Burden: Local Politics and Progressive Housing Policy. Philadelphia: Temple University Press, 1993.

Hula, Richard, Cynthia Jackson, and Marion Orr. "Urban Politics, Governing Nonprofits, and Community Revitalization." *Urban Affairs Review,* 32, 1997, pp. 459–489.

Green, Charles and Basil Wilson. *The Struggle for Black Empowerment in New York City: Beyond the Politics of Pigmentation.* New York: McGraw-Hill, 1992.

Howard, Christopher, Michael Lipsky, and Dale Rogers Marshall. "Citizen Participation in Urban Politics: Rise and Routinization." In *Big City Politics, Governance, and Fiscal Constraints,* George E. Peterson, ed. Washington, DC: Urban Institute Press, 1994.

Imbroscio, David L. *Reconstructing City Politics: Alternative Economic Development and Urban Regimes.* Thousand Oaks, CA: Sage, 1997.

Jennings, James. *The Politics of Black Empowerment: The Transformation of Black Activism in Urban America.* Detroit: Wayne State University Press, 1992.

Judd, Dennis R. and Todd Swanstrom. *City Politics: Private Power and Public Policy.* New York: Longman, 1998.

Boris, Elizabeth T. and C. Eugene Steuerle, eds. *Nonprofits and Government: Collaboration and Conflict.* Washington, DC: Urban Institute Press, 1999.

History of American Social Policy

Sealander, Judith. *Private Wealth and Public Life: Foundation Philanthropy and the Reshaping of American Social Policy from the Progressive Era to the New Deal.* Baltimore, MD: Johns Hopkins University Press, 1997.

Chambers, C. *Seedtime of Reform: American Social Services and Social Action, 1918–1933.* Minneapolis: University of Minnesota Press, 1963.

Ehrenreich, John. *The Altruistic Imagination: A History of Social Work and Social Policy in the United States.* Ithaca, NY: Cornell University Press, 1985.

Social Policy Critique

Bartlett, Donald L. and James B. Steele. *America: What Went Wrong?* Kansas City, MO: Andrews and McMeel, 1992.

Cetron, Marvin and Owen Davies. *American Renaissance: Our Life at the Turn of the 21st Century.* New York: St. Martin's Press, 1989.

Greider, William. *Who Will Tell the People: The Betrayal of American Democracy.* New York: Simon and Schuster, 1992.

McKnight, John. "Do No Harm: Policy Options That Meet Human Needs," *Social Policy,* Summer 1989, pp. 5–15.

Osborne, David and Ted Gaebler. *Reinventing Government: How the Entrepreneurial Spirit Is Transforming the Public Sector.* New York: Addison-Wesley, 1992.

Phillips, Kevin. *The Politics of Rich and Poor.* New York: Random House, 1990.

Center for Urban Affairs and Policy Research. *Politics of the Helping Professions.* Evanston, IL: Northwestern University, n.d.

Wildavsky, Aaron. *Speaking Truth to Power: The Art and Craft of Policy Analysis.* Boston: Little, Brown, 1979.

Elite Model

Domhoff, William G. *The Power Elite and the State: How Policy Is Made in America.* Hawthorne, NJ: Aldine De Gruyter, 1990.

Domhoff, William G. *The Powers That Be: Processes of Ruling-Class Domination in America.* New York: Random House, 1979.

Domhoff, William G. *The Higher Circles: The Governing Class in America.* New York: Random House, 1970.

Domhoff, William G. *Who Rules America?* Englewood Cliffs, NJ: Prentice-Hall, 1967.

Parenti, Michael. *Power and the Powerless,* 2d ed. New York: St. Martin's Press, 1978.

Parenti, Michael. *Democracy for the Few,* 5th ed. New York: St. Martin's Press, 1988.

Galbraith, John Kenneth. *Economics and the Public Purpose.* Boston: Houghton Mifflin, 1973.

Mills, C. Wright. *The Power Elite.* New York: Oxford University Press, 1956.

Institutional Model

Truman, David B. *The Governmental Process.* New York: Knopf, 1971.

Rational Model

Allison, Graham T. *The Essence of Decision: Explaining the Cuban Missile Crisis.* Boston: Little, Brown, 1971.

Edwards, George C. III and Ira Sharkansky. *The Policy Predicament: Making and Implementing Public Policy.* San Francisco: W. H. Freeman, 1978.

Stokey, Edith and Richard Zeckhauser. *A Primer for Policy Analysis.* New York: W. W. Norton, 1978.

Interest Group Model

Lowi, Theodore. *The End of Liberalism.* New York: W. W. Norton, 1969.

Smith, V. "How Interest Groups Influence Legislators," *Social Work,* 24(3), 1979, pp. 234–239.

Walker, J., Jr. *Mobilizing Interest Groups in America: Patrons, Professions, and Social Movements.* Ann Arbor: University of Michigan Press, 1991.

Administrative Model

Kerwin, C. *Rulemaking: How Government Agencies Write Law and Make Policy.* Washington, DC: Congressional Quarterly Press, 1994.

Morrow, William L. *Public Administration: Politics and the Political Process.* New York: Random House, 1975.

Systems Model

Easton, David. *A Framework for Political Analysis.* Englewood Cliffs, NJ: Prentice-Hall, 1965.

Easton, David. "An Approach to the Analysis of Political Systems," *World Politics,* 9, 1957, pp. 383–400.

Social Policy and Social Work

Dye, Thomas R. *Understanding Public Policy*, 2d ed. Englewood Cliffs, NJ: Prentice-Hall, 1975.

Gilbert, Neil and Harry Specht. *Dimensions of Social Welfare Policy,* 2d ed. Englewood Cliffs, NJ: Prentice-Hall, 1986.

Glazer, Nathan. *The Limits of Social Policy.* Cambridge, MA: Harvard University Press, 1988.

Harrington, Michael. *The Other America: Poverty in the United States.* New York: Macmillan, 1962.

Meenaghan, Thomas M. and Robert O. Washington. *Social Policy and Social Welfare.* New York: Free Press, 1980.

Miringoff, M. and S. Opdycke. *American Social Welfare Policy Reassessment and Reform.* Englewood Cliffs, NJ: Prentice-Hall, 1986.

Pierce, Dean. *Policy for the Social Work Practitioner.* New York: Longman, 1984.

Prigmore, Charles S. and Charles R. Atherton. *Social Welfare Policy Analysis and Formulation,* 2d ed. Lexington, MA: D. C. Heath, 1986.

Rican, W. *Beyond Altruism: Social Welfare Policy in American Society.* New York: Haworth Press, 1988.

Tropman, John E. et al. *Strategic Perspectives on Social Policy.* New York: Pergamon Press, 1976.

Politics and Social Work

Addams, Jane. "Pragmatism in Politics," *The Survey,* 29(12), 1912.

Albert, R. "Social Work Advocacy in the Regulatory Process," *Social Casework,* 1983, pp. 473–481.

Davis, A. "Settlement Workers in Politics, 1890–1914," *Review of Politics,* 26(4), 1964, pp. 505–517.

Dear, R. and R. Patti. "Legislative Advocacy: Seven Effective Tactics," *Social Work,* 26(4), 1981, pp. 289–296.

Fisher, R. "Political Social Work," *Journal of Social Work Education* 31(2), 1995, pp. 194–203.

Galper, Jeffrey H. *Politics of Social Services.* Englewood Cliffs, NJ: Prentice-Hall, 1975.

Giles, K. *Flight of the Dove: The Story of Jeannette Rankin.* Beaverton, OR: Touchstone Press, 1980.

Haynes, K. and J. Mickelson. *Affecting Change: Social Workers in the Political Arena,* 3d ed. New York: Longman, 1997.

Mahaffey, M. and J. Hanks, eds. *Practical Politics: Social Work and Political Responsibility.* Silver Spring, MD: NASW Press, 1982.

Mahaffey, M. and J. Hanks. "Lobbying and Social Work," *Social Work,* 17(1), 1972, pp. 3–11.

Mandell, Betty Reid and Ann Withorn. *Keep on Keeping On: Local Politics in the Era of the Global City.* [Urban Affairs Annual Review 41]. Newbury Park: Sage, 1993.

Patti, R. and R. Dear. "Legislative Advocacy: A Path to Social Change," *Social Work,* 20(2), 1975, pp. 108–114.

Rees, S. *Achieving Power: Practice and Policy in Social Welfare.* North Sydney, Australia: Allen and Unwin, 1991.

Ribicoff, A. "Politics and Social Workers," *Social Work,* 7(2), 1962, pp. 3–6.

Richan, A. *Lobbying for Social Change,* 2d ed. New York: Haworth, 1996.

Salcido, R. and E. Seck. "Political Participation Among Social Work Chapters," *Social Work,* 37(6), 1992, pp. 563–564.

Wolk, J. "Are Social Workers Politically Active?" *Social Work,* 25(5), 1981, pp. 283–288.

Social Policy Advocacy

Jansson, C. *Becoming an Effective Policy Advocate: From Policy Practice to Social Justice,* 3d ed. Pacific Grove, CA: Brooks/Cole, 1999.

Other

Finn, Janet and Maxine Jacobson. *Just Practice*. Peosta, IA: Eddie Bowers, 2003.

Klein, Naomi. *No Logo*. London: Flamingo, 2001.

Ehrenreich, Barbara. *Nickel and Dimed.* New York: Metropolitan Books, 2001.

Shipler, David K. *The Working Poor: Invisible in America*. Westminster, MD: Adolph Knopf, 2004.

Websites

Institute for Global Communications: http://www.igc.org

Institute for Study of Civic Values: http://www.libertynet.org/~edcivic/

LibertyNet: http://www.libertynet.org

National Public Telecomputing Network: http://www.nptn.org

National Telecommunications and Information Administration: http://wwww.ntia.doc.gov/tiiap/

Playing to Win: http://www.ign.apc.org/intercambios/appeal.html

14

The Practice of Social Work With Social Movements

Limits of Tyranny

Those who profess to favor freedom, and yet deprecate agitation are men who want crops without plowing up the ground. They want rain without thunder and lightning. They want the ocean without the mighty roar of its many waters. This struggle may be a moral one; it may be a physical one; or it may be both moral and physical; but it must be a struggle.

Power concedes nothing without a demand. It never did and it never will. Find out just what people will submit to and you have found the exact amount of injustice and wrong that will be imposed upon them; and these will continue until they are resisted with either words or blows, or with both. The limits of tyrants are prescribed by the endurance of those whom they oppress.

Frederick Douglass

Ideas in This Chapter

Social action is a process by which people attempt to realize the democratic dream of equality, justice, peace, full opportunity, and express values that give meaning to life.

MARTIN LUTHER KING JR. AND THE WAR IN VIETNAM

On January 14, 1967, Martin Luther King Jr. bought a copy of *Ramparts* magazine and read the illustrated story "The Children of Vietnam." This event was to be a turning point in the history of social movements.[1] Many photos showed the burn wounds suffered by youngsters who had been struck by American napalm.

As he looked at the pictures from Vietnam, King's attention froze. He saw a picture of a Vietnamese mother holding her dead baby, a baby killed by the U.S. military. He pushed the plate of food away from him. His friend Bernard Lee looked up and said, "Doesn't it taste any good?" King answered, "Nothing will ever taste any good for me until I do everything I can to end that war." The antiwar protests and other postmodern social movements of the 1960s were watershed events in the history of social protest, but more important, for perceptive observers of American society they marked a turning point in our modern era as well. There is no clearer indicator of this change than the little understood shift by Martin Luther King Jr. from protests against segregation to protests against the war in Vietnam. Many people considered this shift a dilution of the civil rights movement. Others considered it subversion of national policy. Even more thought it an effort to exploit the protest against the war to boost the waning influence of King's Southern Christian Leadership Conference (SCLC).

King's inclusion of the protest against the war in Vietnam in the civil rights struggle was a matter of conscience that deepened the meaning of nonviolence and called America to face its commitment to freedom and justice. Even more important, in choosing that path King confronted the ideals and values of modernity and began to lead America into the postmodern era. He saw that the struggle for equal opportunity was not only about jobs but about human dignity; that nonviolence on the streets of Selma, Birmingham, or Chicago was meaningless when children were slaughtered in My Lai; and that racism and colonialism at home could not be defeated unless America repudiated racism and colonialism abroad.

In the early days of the civil rights movement, like most civil rights activists before him, King pursued political and economic freedom for African Americans. King articulated the essence of modern social movements. "Gentlemen," he said to those who were trying to prevent a protest march, "you know we don't have much. We don't have much money. We don't really have much education and we don't have political power. . . . We are not trying to overthrow you. We're trying to get in. We are trying to make justice a reality." For civil rights leaders, and for most African Americans, the goal of civil disobedience was to "get in" to make justice real for all Americans. Getting in has been the goal of all modern social movements. The goal of the suffrage movement was for women to get in; of the labor movement, for workers to get in; now for African Americans, the goal was also to get in.

King realized that unless he took a stand against the war, however, his years of struggle for African Americans meant participating in the very things he had fought against: racism, violence, injustice, and oppression. Unless he worked to change the foundations of American culture that promoted paternalism

and racism, getting in might be worse than staying out. He saw that racism was only part of the modern system built on domination, exploitation, privilege, and power; that racism was violent, no matter how distant; that colonialism was violent, no matter how benevolent; that exploitation was violent, no matter how profitable. The struggle to get in to the benefits of the American dream also meant to get into this world of violence, not as a victim but as a perpetrator, as a prosperous American who benefited by the suffering, oppression, and even death of others. It was something he could not accept.

"I spent a lot of time in prayerful meditation," King said. "I came to the conclusion that I could no longer remain silent about an issue that was destroying the soul of our nation." Later King said to a *New York Times* correspondent, "We are merely marking time in the civil rights movement if we do not take a stand against the war." King clearly announced his intention not merely to reform but to change society. "It is out of this moral commitment to dignity and the worth of human personality," King said, "that I feel it is necessary to stand up against the war in Vietnam. If we are to get on the right side of the world revolution, we as a nation must undergo a radical revolution of values. We must rapidly begin the shift from a thing-oriented society to a person-oriented society." King began to lead America out of the wilderness of modernity and into the promised land of the new postmodern era.

WHAT YOU WILL LEARN IN THIS CHAPTER

Social work is called to transform society and to create a more just social order. In fact, says Gustavo Gutierrez, "to do nothing in favor of those who are oppressed is to act against them."[2] Macro social workers ought to be "building a world where every man, regardless of race, religion, or nationality can live a fully human life, free of the servitude that comes from other men and from the incompletely mastered world about him."[3]

In this chapter you will learn that social action is for those social workers who "are deeply troubled by our present world, seek a vision of a society which supports life,"[4] and are committed to a process of social change and an end to violence and human misery. Social action has nothing less as its goal than making fundamental changes in social structures that foster oppression and injustice.

You will discover that there are two forms of social movements with which macro social workers engage in social action: modern social movements and postmodern social movements.

Modern Social Movements

You will learn that macro social workers often join modern social movements and engage in social action struggles against injustice, economic inequalities created by the free market system, power imbalances endemic to mass representative democracy, and the tendency of those in authority to use the systems they control for purposes we may be unaware of or disapprove of but are powerless to stop through normal political processes. You will also discover that modern social action differs significantly from community organization, even though the two are connected and often use similar tactics and techniques. You will learn that modern social activists use organizational, institutional, systems, and social cultural models of social problems to frame their understanding of the world (see Chapter 2). You will explore the heritage of modern social action and learn how social workers were among the foremost champions of freedom and equality for all Americans.

You will learn how to conduct a campaign of modern social action, unfreeze inequitable systems, move to action, and establish ways that are more just. You will explore the process, tactics, and techniques by which social activists brought the nation's attention to their just causes and how social activists have, for the most part, brought to completion the social promise of modernity.

Postmodern Social Movements

You will learn about postmodern social movements and social action. You will discover how social activists have laid a foundation for the emergence of the postmodern social era in which we now live. You will learn that postmodern social action is engaged not in social reform but in a revolution that is even now slowly changing the premises upon which modern society exists. You will explore the process by which social activists engage in postmodern social action and learn how postmodern social activists are generating new social movements in the United States and

around the world. You will discover how you, too, can become involved in constructing the new society of the future.

You will come to understand that social action deals with the most pressing and important issues of our time. Some of the most impressive and long-standing social victories in the human struggle for justice and equality have come from social action. Many of these, such as the peace movement, regulating nuclear arms, protecting the environment, and ending racism and human exploitation, affect us all.

MODERN SOCIAL ACTION

The United States was founded in the fires of protest and revolution by those who sought an end to tyranny and a nation of liberty and justice. It was peopled by many who were disaffected—outcasts, protestors, idealists, visionaries, seekers, true believers, and religious dissidents—who fled their homeland because of persecution and wanted to make their dream of opportunity and freedom a reality. When those ideals failed to materialize or the basic premises of economic freedom and political democracy became distorted by those in power, many North Americans continued to press government for redress by means of modern social action. Social action occurs when an oppressed, disadvantaged, or injured people engage in mutual action against an oppressor, aim for a redistribution of power at the political or economic levels, reorder organizational alliances at the top levels of the bureaucratic apparatus, and ultimately change public policies.

Modern social action is not seriously opposed to modernity or to the premises of the modern market system and mass representative democracy. Modern social movements, in fact, are determined to preserve and restore those systems so they function effectively for the good of all. The goal of modern social movements is to correct the defects in societal systems so that both the economy and the government will deliver on their promises, provide opportunity, and enable ordinary people to pursue their self-interests. Social action tries to achieve those goals by slowing down or stopping practices that many citizens perceive as politically unjust, socially harmful, economically inequitable, and destructive to the human condition or to the global ecosystem.

Rather than radical societal change or revolution, modern social action is aimed at remediation and reform, restoring the ideals of a good society that have become damaged. It is a process by which people attempt "to realize the democratic dream of equality, justice, peace, cooperation, equal and full opportunities for education, full and useful employment, health and the creation of those circumstances in which man can have the chance to live by values that give meaning to life."[5] Modern social action has been practiced under many names. It has been variously called social reform, social protest, and resistance. It occurs by means of social movements under the labels of war resistance, cultural resistance, civil disobedience, and even civil insurrection.

COMMUNITY ORGANIZATION AND MODERN SOCIAL MOVEMENTS

Community organization and modern societal action share some similarities, and at times use similar tactics. Sometimes people, even social workers, confuse these two kinds of social work practice and see them as synonymous. However, community organizing and societal action are different in scope, purpose, permanence, and numbers.

Community Organization

Community organization is a process by which macro social workers and others work with people in their own neighborhoods to address local issues that community members want to change, including better police protection, stopping the city from building a highway through the neighborhood, preventing a corporation from locating a shopping mall in the community, or exposing a bank that is redlining the neighborhood. Community organizations are local, are aimed at immediate threats to a community, and seek community betterment and enhanced opportunities for their citizens. Community organizations are more or less permanent structures that work on a variety of issues that affect the community in which they are located. Today, at the age of 60, the nation's oldest community organization, the IAF, begun by Saul Alinsky in 1945, shows increasing vigor. Rather than coming to an end, the IAF is expanding and finding new communities and issues with which to work.

Their goals are not only the achievement of successful confrontations but development of local leadership, engagement of local people in the political process, and development of social goods and social capital in the community. Local community organizations often work with one another on joint issues that affect them all. They join together into formal or informal coalitions to press for larger societal change. When this occurs, they may form a social movement.

Social Movements

Modern social movements are not limited to one community or locality. Social movements are mass, action-oriented processes, often on a societywide or even global scale, that seek to change national policies or shift the direction in which society is moving. They are open to and, in fact, must mobilize as many people as possible from all walks of life to effect societal change. Members of community organizations are important but not exclusive members of social movements.

Modern social movements most often focus on a single issue such as civil rights, suffrage, labor rights, or the environment. Social movements may take a long time to win the struggle in which they are engaged, but they are often time limited. For example, the women's suffrage movement progressed with increasing vigor over a period of about 50 years. Once the constitutional amendment was passed giving women the vote, the movement had achieved its purpose and disbanded. The abolitionist movement began in the 1830s and ended with the Emancipation Proclamation 60 years later. Once the struggle for adoption of public policy has generally been won, the movement slows and shifts to a watchdog role.

MODELS OF SOCIAL CHANGE

Modern social activists use a variety of theories and models in their work to eradicate social problems and make social change. Among these are the organizational, institutional, social systems, and social cultural premises models of social change.

Organizational Deviance Model of Social Change

As part of a larger strategy of bringing public awareness to the plight of endangered old-growth forests, ecological activists, for example, may target a particular lumber company that has been notorious for destroying endangered trees. This strategy allows activists to not only publicize their cause but to fight a battle in their own time, on their own terms, and to confront an organization against which they have a reasonable chance of winning. Movement activists choose large organizations, often conglomerates, that engage in the exploitation of workers, manufacture and sell firearms, or produce cancer-causing tobacco products. Activists also target public organizations that abuse people's rights as is occurring at the Western Hemisphere Institute for Security Cooperation, (WHISC) at Ft. Benning, Georgia.

U.S. SCHOOL FOR TERRORISM

On January 26, 2004, 27 human rights activists went on trial for trespassing on the property of the Western Hemisphere Institute for Security Cooperation (WHISC) in Ft. Benning, Georgia, a combat training school for Latin American soldiers, more popularly known as the "U.S. School for Terrorism." The activists, who faced up to 6 months in federal prison and $5,000 in fines, were among 10,000 protesters who gathered in November to call for a closure of the training school, claiming that the school's graduates are consistently involved in human rights atrocities and coups, including the El Mozote Massacre of more than 900 civilians and the failed coup of 2002 in Venezuela.

Several of the defendants stated that the Latin American military trainees do not exist primarily to defend one nation against another but to protect the unjust and inequitable distribution of resources within each country against movements for social and political change. This accusation gained credibility when the Pentagon was forced in 1996 to release school training manuals that advocated torture, extortion, and execution.[6]

Institutional Deviance Model of Social Change

Social activists also engage larger governmental and corporate systems that have institutionalized socially harmful values and premises in their policies and actions. Social activists working against institutionalized social deviance range from protesting a single policy decision to challenging broad global issues. Social activists, for example, sometimes take on a single governmental decision such as the refusal of the

Bush administration to sign the international Tokyo environmental protocols to prevent global warming. Activists work to change the institutionalized corporate exploitation of laborers, such as with the struggle of migrant laborers against agribusiness in California, or institutionalized polices of governmental violence, as in the movement to end the war in Vietnam or the movement to end the war in Iraq. Others work to institutionalize broader human rights into the framework of government policy including civil rights, gay rights, women's liberation, and the rights of labor.

Systems Deviance Model of Social Change

When social activists take a systems perspective to social change, they may see the interlocking system of the market economy as being in collusion with government to prevent people in underdeveloped nations from obtaining economic justice. Social activists may see economic and political systems in one or several countries as creating the conditions for trafficking of persons, drug trafficking, or proliferation of international weapons sales.

A BRIEF HISTORY OF MODERN SOCIAL MOVEMENTS

Modern social protest has occurred over the entire course of American experience, but it has been most visible in four major social movements: the labor movement (1636–1940), the abolitionist movement (1830–1865), the progressive movement (1885–1910), and the many social movements that occurred in the 16 years between 1955 and 1973.

Modern social movements in the United States have, to a large degree, made strides in eradicating systemic injustice and oppression and have broadened the benefits of political liberty and economic opportunity for all Americans. They ended the scourge of child labor, sweatshops, and 12-hour workdays and have given laborers the legal right to bargain collectively with management. They extended democracy, expanded suffrage to every citizen, and opened voting booths to those citizens who were prevented from voting on the basis of race. Modern social movements have broken the back of slavery and segregation and destroyed numerous barriers to opportunity. They have been responsible, in large part, for ending the war in Vietnam, for bringing an end to institutionalized discrimination in the United States, and for guaranteeing equal civil rights to every citizen.

Labor Movement: 1636 to 2000

Within two decades of the landing of the first settlers in the new land, workers began agitating for their rights, beginning a struggle that would last for 300 years on U.S. soil. For the first 250 years, labor struggled to find a way to organize, eventually founding the American Federation of Labor (AFL). Although legislation was passed to support the rights of workers, it was not until 1935 that legislation finally secured the rights of U.S. laborers to bargain collectively with management. Even after that time, however, corporations continued to harass labor and agitated for legislation restricting its activities. Today the rights of workers continue to be in jeopardy as transnational corporations work actively to withhold workers rights internationally.

The Early Labor Movement (1636–1800)

The struggle of North American laborers for decent working conditions, fair wages, and decent hours began as early as 1636 when a group of fishermen in Maine mutinied when their wages were withheld.[7] Unions of craftsmen first appeared a little over 200 years ago when shoemakers organized in Philadelphia and Boston in 1793, and printers in New York in 1794.[8]

Sowing the Seeds of Organizational Forms (1800–1865)

During much of the 1800s, laborers tried to strike a balance between organizing for direct economic gains and for political redress, trying to find an organizational model that would be the most effective in furthering their action agenda. They also made attempts to expand from local shops to national federations.

Economic and Political Action During economic expansion, unions engaged in direct economic action, seeking higher wages and better working conditions. In 1806 the Journeymen Cordwainers (shoemakers) of Philadelphia struck for higher wages and were indicted for criminal conspiracy. This was the first American court case involving the right of workers to join a union and engage in collective bargaining.

During recession, however, unions were unable to survive the economic turndown, and many simply disintegrated and disappeared. Many laborers switched to political or social action by joining reform movements to seek justice. The first labor party was formed in 1828 in the midst of a recession, as a union reorganized itself into the Republican Political Association of the Workingmen of Philadelphia. The following year a Working Men's Party was formed in New York City. With the return of prosperity, however, workers became more interested in immediate goals of higher wages and better working conditions. Unions revived or reorganized and reengaged direct economic pressure on employers, and the whole cycle began again.

Vertical Expansion Unions were experimenting with vertical as well as horizontal growth. In 1827, for example, 15 unions formed the first citywide federation in Philadelphia, and by 1836 city federations existed in 13 cities, mostly along the eastern seaboard. Between 1834 and 1837, carpenters, shoemakers, printers, and others formed national unions, but they all collapsed and disappeared during the depression of 1837. A preliminary attempt to bring together all local, national, and city central unions into a national federation of craft unions, the National Trades Union, occurred in 1834, but like other efforts to form national unions it too was wiped out in the depression of 1837. Even though these beginning unionizing efforts did not result in permanent organizations, they sowed the seeds of all later organizational forms.[9]

Reconstruction (1865–1889)

In the period of reconstruction, labor agitation became violent, and the National Labor Union and the Knights of Labor made their appearance.

Violence The struggle of laborers began to get the attention of people as miners, railroad workers, steel workers, and others engaged in illegal strikes and fought sometimes bloody battles with armed guards hired by the companies, often killing workers as well as women and children.[10] Violence continued as rent strikes were held, and riots occurred in cities over undue profits and exorbitant prices.

National Labor Union After the Civil War, some 30 craft unions were active. The National Labor Union was formed in 1866 and survived until 1872. It was converted into a political party and subsequently collapsed, but it set a record for longevity of a national federation.

Knights of Labor   The most successful short-term effort was the Noble Order of the Knights of Labor. Founded as a secret society in 1871, the Knights came out into the open as a national organization in 1878. They attempted to unite farmers and lower-middle-class wage earners into one organization. The Knights prohibited national trade associations, were opposed in principle to strikes, and instead of economic gains were dedicated to reform and education.

The Knights "were successful in spite of themselves, winning a strike in 1885 against Jay Gould, one of the most powerful industrialists of the period."[11] A year later they claimed a membership of 700,000, an all-time high in labor history. The Knights quickly disintegrated, however, in part due to the appearance of the American Federation of Labor (AFL) a year later and in part due to anti-union sentiment resulting after a bomb was thrown during a strike at the McCormick Reaper Plant in Chicago, causing the Haymarket Riot. By 1890 the membership of the Knights of Labor had declined to 100,000.

The cause of the Knights was not helped when one of the worst strikes of all, the Great Pullman Strike, occurred in 1886. Pullman laid off more than 3,000 of its 5,800 Chicago employees and cut the wages of the others 25 to 40% without reducing the rents workers paid for living in company housing. The consequences were economically disastrous, and thousands of people were left completely destitute. "In one instance, an employee found that after payment for rent was taken out, his paycheck came to two cents."[12]

Increased Violence: 1890–1905   The fight for decent working conditions and fair pay, and against exploitation of workers, continued through the early 1900s, prompting confrontations with the paid henchmen of wealthy business owners and their cohorts in law enforcement. In company after company, activists and organizers fought for worker rights. At times the struggle was brutal and bloody. Workers at the Carnegie-owned Homestead steel plant in Pennsylvania, for example, refused to accept wage cuts, instigating the Great Homestead Strike of 1892. General manager Henry Clay Frick shut the plant down and hired special deputy sheriffs to guard the buildings. The striking workers ran them out of town, whereupon Frick called in 300 Pinkerton detectives armed with rifles to subdue the workers. A battle ensued as the workers opened fire on Frick's private army and attempted to sink their barges with a small brass cannon. Eventually the detectives ran up a white flag of surrender. Infuriated that seven of their number had been killed, the workers again attacked the detectives, who escaped but had to run the gauntlet of an angry mob of men and women. Six days later the governor of Pennsylvania mobilized a militia of 8,000 men to take over Homestead and place it under martial law. Frick then brought in scabs—nonunion workers hired to take the jobs of the striking workers—reopening the plant with militia protection.

MOTHER JONES: THE MINERS' ANGEL (1830–1930)

Mary Harris "Mother" Jones was born in Cork, Ireland, on May 1, 1830. Her father was forced to flee to Toronto, Ontario, with his family in 1835. In 1861 she met and married George E. Jones, an iron molder and staunch member of the Iron Molders Union. When she was 37, she lost her husband and their four small children within one week to a yellow fever epidemic, and 4 years later in 1871 she lost everything she owned in the great Chicago fire.

The early Knights of Labor, with their ideals and sense of fraternity, fulfilled her need to dedicate herself to a cause. Jones began traveling across the country from industrial area to industrial area, living with the workers in tent colonies or shantytowns, tending to men's spirits, buoying them and goading them to fight even though the battle seemed hopeless. When there was a strike, Mother Jones organized and helped the workers; at other times she held educational meetings. In 1877 she helped in the Pittsburgh railway strike, and during the 1880s she organized and ran educational meetings.

After 1890 Jones became involved in the struggles of coal miners. In 1898 she helped found the Social Democratic Party and became an organizer for the United Mine Workers, attending her first convention in 1901. She was a lecturer for the Socialist Party for several years. In 1903 she led a "children's crusade" of striking children from the textile mills of Kensington, Pennsylvania, to President Theodore Roosevelt's home on Long Island to dramatize the case for abolishing child labor.

Mother Jones was, in 1905, one of the founders of the Industrial Workers of the World—the Wobblies. In 1911 she left the Socialist Party to return to the payroll of the United Mine Workers as an organizer. She came to national attention during the Paint Creek-Cabin Creek strike in West Virginia when, on September 21, 1912, she led a march of miners' children though the streets of Charleston. In February 1913, at the age of 83, she led another protest at which she was arrested, convicted by a military court, and sentenced to 20 years in prison. The newly elected governor pardoned Mother Jones, but in a short time she was in Colorado participating in the miners strike in Cripple Creek where she was evicted, arrested, and twice imprisoned. On April 20, 1914, 20 miners and their families were machine-gunned in a tent colony at Ludlow, Colorado. Mother Jones traveled across the country telling the story.

Jones participated in the garment workers and streetcar workers strikes in 1915 and 1916 in New York, and in the steel workers strike in Pittsburgh in 1919. In January 1921, as a guest of the Mexican government, she traveled to Mexico to attend the Pan-American Federation of Labor meeting. Her last public appearance was at her 100th birthday party on May 1, 1930, where she made a fiery speech for the motion picture camera. Mary Harris Jones died in Silver Spring, Maryland, on November 30, 1930, 7 months after her 100th birthday, and was buried in the Union Miners Cemetery in Mt. Olive, Illinois, near victims of the Virden Illinois mine riot of 1889.

Metal miners in Coeur d'Alene, Idaho, switchmen in Buffalo, and coal miners in Tennessee walked off their jobs in defiance of their employers. Workers in the minefields of the western states had established the Western Federation of miners in 1897 and engaged in a series of strikes in the gold, silver, lead, and copper mines of the West. In each instance, the strikes were forcibly broken through the intervention of the state militia. In 1903–1904, miners in the Cripple Creek area of Colorado attempted to go on strike and were attacked by strikebreakers. The miners fought back. Mine owners escalated the violence, hiring vigilantes and calling in the state militia against the striking miners. Miners sabotaged trains and exploded mines; in retaliation they were murdered or arrested and imprisoned. Miners' meetings were machine-gunned. Vigilantes, deputized sheriffs, police, and militia finally crushed the strike.[13]

The American Federation of Labor: 1890–1929

The American Federation of Labor (AFL), organized at the turn of the 19th century and continuing today, was the beginning of modern union activity. In 1914 the Clayton Act was passed, but violence continued. In 1926 Congress passed the Railway Labor Act.

Growth of the AFL   The AFL, founded in 1886 by Samuel Gompers who was only 36 when he assumed the presidency, was the fruit of more than 50 years of trial and error for union organizing and marks the beginning of modern unionism as it exists today. The AFL was a craft union, a federation of specific crafts or skills such as carpenters or machinists regardless of the particular industry with which they were affiliated. Among the innovations devised by the AFL was the guarantee of "trade autonomy" to AFL affiliated national unions who were afforded "exclusive jurisdiction" over their particular craft or occupation. The policy of exclusive jurisdiction was the labor union counterpart of the exclusive business franchise.

The AFL, however, did not confer autonomy on the national unions. The national unions already had autonomy. The federation simply recognized their independent decision-making power. Estey asserts, for example, that the "AFL was in the position of the United Nations in its early years—trying to attract membership with assurances that their sovereignty would not be impaired by joining it."[14]

Clayton Act of 1914   In 1914 mine laborers secured a victory with the passage of the Clayton Act, Section 6 of which specified that "nothing . . . shall be construed to forbid the existence and operation of labor . . . organizations . . . nor shall such organizations or the members be held or construed to be illegal combinations or conspiracies in restraint of trade."[15] However, when the law was tested in 1921, the Supreme Court founded that strikes in single industries such as the railroads as well as entire industries including manufacturing and coal mining were a restraint of trade and illegal.

Continued Violence   Labor unrest continued. In 1919 an enormous wave of strikes swept the nation. In Seattle a general strike of 60,000 workers overtook the city for several days, commandeering all public services. Strikes for the 8-hour day stormed through the industrial heartland, succeeding in the meatpacking houses but failing in the steel industry, where an epic strike of 365,000 workers was crushed by force. On Memorial Day 1919 in South Chicago, police fired on a peaceful demonstration of strikers, supporters, wives, and children, killing some 30 people, most of whom were shot in the back.[16]

Railway Labor Act of 1926 In 1926 the Railway Labor Act was passed by Congress, affirming that railroad "employees shall have the right to organize and bargain collectively through representatives of their own choosing, prohibited employers from interfering in any way with the organization of its employees, and requiring them to bargain with the unions they selected."[17] In 1930 the Supreme Court upheld the act. Although it applied only to railroads and not to interstate commerce generally, a precedent had been established by the highest court in the land, an indication that sentiment was building on behalf of labor rights. Events were speeding to a conclusion.

The Depression Years (1930–1940) During the decade of the 1930s, three events turned the tide of collective bargaining in the United States: the Norris-LaGuardia Act of 1932, the National Labor Relations Act of 1935, and formation of the Congress of Industrial Organizations (CIO).

Norris-LaGuardia Act In March 1932, Congress passed the Norris-LaGuardia Act, freeing union activity from court interference. Federal courts were forbidden to issue temporary or permanent injunctions in labor disputes. No peaceful or nonfraudulent union activity, including strikes and picketing, was subject to injunction, and where court injunctions were not forbidden outright, they were subject to specific and limiting criteria. The act made illegal the "yellow dog contract," in which an employee agreed to refuse to join a union on penalty of discharge.[18] The Norris-LaGuardia Act was a powerful legislative effort, dealing a major blow to the efforts of management and owners of corporate enterprise. The tide had clearly turned.

On to Victory In spite of this positive labor legislation, however, workers were still prevented from collective bargaining in many organizations. Realizing that the battle was being lost, corporations put up a furious last-ditch effort. In desperation, workers fought back, and as early as 1933 wildcat strikes broke out in the auto, steel, rubber, and textile industries. In 1934 general strikes broke out in Toledo, Minneapolis, and San Francisco, and a nationwide textile strike led to martial law in Georgia. In 1934 alone, says Ehrenreich, some 40 workers were killed

in strike-related violence, and in the 18 months between late 1933 and 1934 troops were called out in 16 states. Corporations stocked arsenals of weapons and spent hundreds of thousands of dollars spying on union activities.[19]

In the face of powerful industrial interests and an unsympathetic administration, by 1935 labor leaders were "almost in despair of making headway toward union recognition."[20] Although the existence of unions and the right of workers to join unions and bargain collectively had already been legalized, these labor rights were of little value as long as an employer was free to fire a worker for exercising those rights. In their desperation, labor leaders did not realize that these tactics were management's final futile efforts and that victory was near.

The National Labor Relations Act of 1935 In July 1935 Congress passed the National Labor Relations Act (NLRA), also known as the Wagner Act, making it illegal for employers to interfere in the exercise of a laborer's right to organize, prohibiting unfair labor practices, and establishing a regulatory agency. This finalized the victory labor had struggled to achieve for hundreds of years.

Interfering with unions: The act prohibited employers from interfering with unions or refusing to bargain collectively and upheld the rights of workers to negotiate on an equal basis with management. It declared illegal a laundry list of anti-union activities on the part of employers and established procedures by which unions could gain recognition.

Unfair labor practices: The act spelled out in detail "unfair labor practices" including preventing employers from interfering, restraining, or coercing employees in their union activities, subverting legitimate unions by setting up "puppet" unions controlled by the employer, discriminating against an employee by demotion or firing because of joining a union, preventing employers from discriminating against employees who bring charges against the employer, and refusing to bargain collectively. The act afforded unions a new method of organizing—a secret ballot election. This mechanism democratized the workplace and provided an orderly way for workers to agree on a bargaining unit.

National Labor Relations Board: The NLRA put teeth into the policy by establishing a regulatory agency, the National Labor Relations Board (NLRB), which had sole authority to enforce the law including the power to determine bargaining units, to supervise secret-ballot elections, adjudicate complaints of unfair labor practices, issue cease and desist orders, and petition the court for enforcement of its orders.[21]

Congress of Industrial Organization (CIO)

The AFL and craft unions were preeminent until 1935 when a new organization, the Committee for Industrial Organization (CIO), and its model of industrial unionism arrived on the scene. Craft unions organized all workers with a particular skill, such as all electrical workers or steel workers, but industrial unionism organized all workers, regardless of type of craft or skill, who were employed in a particular industry such as the mining, automobile, rubber, or steel industries.

CIO's entrance into the labor field was especially dramatic. Within a 3-week period in early 1937, the CIO brought to terms two of the largest corporations in the nation: General Motors in the automobile industry and United States Steel in the steel industry. By penetrating to the very heart of the mass production industries, they paved the way for their subsequent virtually complete organization. The CIO proceeded to organize the electrical and radio manufacturing, rubber, men and women's clothing, textiles, meatpacking and other industries. By the end of 1937, 33 national unions had affiliated with the CIO. The success of the CIO was reflected in the power of numbers. When a single plant, such as Ford Motors Rouge plant in Detroit, employed 40,000 workers, for example, it made little difference if the workers were skilled, semi-skilled or unskilled. Their numbers made their replacement virtually impossible during a strike.[22]

Economic Expansion (1941–1954)

For the next 12 years, despite passage of the NLRA, corporations continued to harass workers and agitate for passage of legislation that would place restrictions on union activity.

Corporate Harassment   An intransigent corporate community continued to harass and intimidate workers. Violence against strikers was not to become uncommon until World War II, says Eyerman and Jamison,[23] and Jedlicka states that as late as the 1940s labor leaders were still being blacklisted and beaten for exercising their right to organize workers.[24] During the economic expansion of World War II, union membership increased from 3.6 million to 13.9 million.

Encouraged by employers anxious to keep unions from threatening their power, Estey asserts that many people felt that labor had become too big and too powerful. Building on those sentiments, management lobbied for legislation that would dilute the gains labor had made.

Taft-Hartley Act of 1947   Responding to the anti-union sentiment of the 1940s, the Taft Hartley Act of 1947 attempted to constrain unions by requiring them to abide by rules limiting their activities. It prohibited a union from engaging in "unfair union practices" including coercing employees to join a union. It outlawed the "closed shop" industry, which requires employees to become union members before they are hired. The act prohibited unions from refusing to bargain with an employer, engaging in secondary boycotts by using innocent third parties as tools in disputes, and causing an employer to pay for services not performed, called featherbedding.[25]

Consolidation (1955–2000)

The last half of the 20th century saw the AFL and CIO merge in the United States. It also witnessed a weakening of unions internationally and rampant joblessness.

AFL and CIO Merger   On December 5, 1955, after 20 years of separate organizing, the AFL and CIO merged into a single federation, consisting of 138 national and international unions with a combined membership of 16.1 million workers. In the merger each national and international union was to remain completely autonomous with sole control over its actions. The AFL-CIO, like the United Nations, became a voluntary association composed of free and autonomous labor unions. The AFL-CIO was not all embracing, but it did include the great majority of national and international unions with a smattering of locals.

AFL-CIO Today   The AFL-CIO is a union of unions, not individuals. The federation exists at the wish of the national and international unions rather than the other way around. The federation has neither the formal authority nor the power to dictate the behavior of its constituent unions. It is not directly involved in the fundamental union function of collective bargaining, which is reserved for local and national unions. Instead, the AFL-CIO serves a political function. It is to organized labor what the U.S. Chamber of Commerce is to business. The union engages in lobbying, public relations, research, and education. It presents labor's views on a wide range of issues, including wages, hours, and working conditions, as well as performing functions necessary to the smooth working relationships between unions.[26]

International Labor: 1990 to Present

Because transnational corporations (TNCs) operate across the boundaries of potentially hundreds of nations, many of which are small and poor, they can impose their economic leverage to their own advantage. They use many tactics, including violence, to ensure that their freedom to reap profits is not restricted. The result has been that even in the developed nations of Europe workers are left in largely powerless positions and face increasing joblessness worldwide.

Repressive Business Tactics   From the point of view of TNCs in our global society, the rights of trade unions, even the very existence of unions, including safe and healthy working conditions and high standards of employment are viewed as so many barriers restricting the "freedom of the market" and capital accumulation. Through "global strategic management," including multiple sourcing, international subcontracting, blackmail, bribery, political pressure, and financial manipulation, TNCs pressure local and national governments to restrict union rights, reduce the quality of working conditions, limit benefits, and prevent higher employment standards.

Violence   At times TNCs even resort to violence as has occurred in the United States. In its annual survey of violations of global trade union rights, in 1992 the International Confederation of Free Trade Unions reports, for example, that 260 activists were killed and 2,500 arrested for carrying out legitimate trade union activity. This compares with 200 deaths and 2,000 arrests in the previous year. The reported deaths were the result of repression by government, security services, and death squads. Most of these crimes remain unpunished. When intimidation tactics are unsuccessful, in their efforts to avoid complications that restrict their freedom, TNCs often move their operations to escape legislation or simply refuse to obey national laws.

Worker Powerlessness   Because unions often are local or at best are limited to the boundaries and laws of the nation in which they exist, unions have little real strength to confront transnational corporations.

There is, furthermore, no supranational labor organization with international jurisdiction to which TNCs are subject or by which local or national unions can exercise leverage. TNCs can exert pressure on individual governments and unions separately, often exacting compliance with their demands.

TNCs have used these tactics with success even in developed nations. During the formation of the European Common Market, for example, claiming that they could not operate with restrictions or barriers imposed by unions, transnational corporations spent considerable effort to ensure that labor's attempt to establish a regulatory system for transnational collective bargaining and union activities would not occur. European corporations fought common employment standards and trade union rights, resulting in only minimum standards for workers. Laborers were left without the right to unionize or strike and without a mechanism to enforce labor rights at the international level.[27]

Joblessness   The International Labor Organization estimates that 1 billion people worldwide are unemployed or underemployed. Joblessness affects individuals and families in North America, but unemployment around the world hurts the United States as well. By reducing the capacity of consumers in other countries to purchase U.S. products, unemployment can lead to social instability with international ramifications.[28]

Abolitionist Movement: 1830 to 1865

In the early 19th century, modern social activists observed with rising concern the horrors that slavery and racism brought to the American nation.[29] Described in Chapter 2, they worked in many ways and in increasing numbers to establish the beginnings of the abolition movement, forming antislavery societies and escalating their activities after 1850, resulting in a Civil War that nearly destroyed the nation.

HARRIET TUBMAN (1820–1913)

In about 1821, Araminta Ross was born into slavery in Dorchester County, Maryland. When she was 13, a plantation overseer struck her on the head so severely that Araminta's skull was fractured, leaving her physically handicapped for the rest of her life. In 1844 she married Samuel Tubman, a free black man, and changed her name to Harriet, renouncing her former life of slavery. In that same year she fled to Philadelphia with her husband but clandestinely returned to Baltimore a year later and helped several members of her family escape from bondage.

Encouraged by her success, Tubman devoted all of her energy to guiding runaway slaves to freedom from the plantations of Maryland through the Underground Railway. When the fugitive slave law was rigidly enforced in Maryland, she moved her fugitive refugees at first to New York and afterward to Canada, aiding in the escape of more than 300 slaves. Her activity became so obnoxious to the southern states that a reward of $40,000 was offered for apprehending the "Negro Moses." During the Civil War, Tubman served as a spy for the Union Army and as a nurse in Union Army hospitals.

Progressive Movement: 1885 to 1910

Progressivism began convulsively in the 1880s and waxed and waned in the years that followed. To ensure the survival of democracy in the United States, progressives advocated for an enlarged government that could control and offset the power of private corporations over the nation's institutions and life. One of the foremost groups of progressives was the emerging profession of social workers. Progressive social workers became involved in nearly every issue of the times in an era rife with social movements, including the charities and corrections movement, the temperance movement, the women's suffrage movement, and social settlements.

Charities and Corrections Movement   The charities and corrections movement was a response of idealistic reformers to the misery and despair that accompanied industrialization in the United States in the years following the Civil War. The movement was based on a powerful belief in the perfectibility of society. The major arm of the charities and corrections movement was establishment of the Charity Organization Societies (COS), but its aims were much broader. Charities and corrections people were concerned with every corner of darkness, despair, and deprivation on earth. They sought to aid criminals, alcoholics, the poor, children, and people suffering from mental or physical disabilities. They worked to

improve food and drug safety, sanitation, playgrounds, and slums. Many of the reforms they sought—the 40-hour workweek, social security, child labor laws, disaster relief—have become institutionalized, and we now take them for granted. In the 19th century, however, these ideas were considered radical.

Temperance Movement   Encouraged by the inexpensive production of corn in the Midwest after the Revolutionary War, whiskey drinking became something of a national pastime for men, women, and children. Between 1800 and 1830, whiskey consumption increased to more than 5 gallons per person per year. Many people were concerned about the relationship of alcoholism to unemployment, poverty, and family breakdown. Alcoholism caused loss of time from work and physical abuse within families. Ultimately its eradication was seen as a matter of women's and family rights.

In 1826 the American Society for the Promotion of Temperance was founded, motivated by a spirit of religious and humanitarian reform. So successful was this movement that the annual consumption of whiskey dropped from 5 gallons to less than 2 gallons per person per year. In the 1830s and 1840s, thousands of local temperance societies were formed to prohibit the sale of liquor altogether. By 1860 the temperance movement boasted a membership of more than a million individuals. The members of the movement became more and more politically active. Even though women lacked the right to vote, they entered the political arena. In 1869 women formed the Prohibition Party, the Women's Christian Temperance Union (WCTU), and the Anti-Saloon League. Frances Willard, the militant leader of the prohibition forces, carried the battle into the enemy territory of the saloons, where women sang hymns, prayed, and at times engaged in acts of symbolic protest, destroying bottles of whisky and kegs of beer.[30]

ELIZABETH CADY STANTON (1815–1902)

When Elizabeth Cady married abolitionist Henry Brewster Stanton in 1840, she'd already observed enough about the legal relationships between men and women to insist that the word "obey" be dropped from the ceremony.

An active abolitionist herself, Stanton was outraged when the 1840 World's Anti-Slavery Convention in London denied official standing to women delegates, including Lucretia Mott. In 1848 she and Mott called for a women's rights convention to be held in Seneca Falls, New York. That convention, and the Declaration of Sentiments written by Stanton which was approved there, is credited with initiating the long struggle toward women's rights and woman suffrage.

After 1851 Stanton worked in close partnership with Susan B. Anthony. Stanton often served as the writer and Anthony as the strategist in this effective working relationship. After the Civil War, Stanton and Anthony were among those determined to focus on female suffrage when only voting rights of freed males were addressed in Reconstruction. They founded the National Woman Suffrage Association, and Stanton served as president. When the NWSA and the rival American Woman Suffrage Association finally merged in 1890, Stanton served as the president of the resulting National American Woman Suffrage Association.

In her later years she wrote a history of the suffrage movement, her autobiography, *Eighty Years and More,* and a controversial critique of women's treatment by religion, *The Woman's Bible.* Stanton is best known for her long contribution to the woman suffrage struggle, but she was also active and effective in winning property rights for married women, equal guardianship of children, and liberalized divorce laws so that women could leave marriages that were abusive of the wife, the children, and the economic health of the family. Elizabeth Cady Stanton died in New York on October 26, 1902, nearly 20 years before the United States granted women the right to vote.

Women's Suffrage Movement   Women have been involved at the center of every major social movement in the United States, "moving from concern for rooting out individual imperfections that would lead to unhappy family living to a demand for explicit political recognition and power, and then to larger social issues."[31] In 1848 the first Women's Rights Convention was held in Seneca Falls, New York. Women's suffrage was demanded, and a Declaration of Independence was adopted. In 1900 the National American Woman's Suffrage Association was founded, along with a number of other women's groups, among them, the National Consumer's League, the National Women's Trade Union League, and the Young Women's Christian Association.

These organizations "were at once concerned with matters affecting women as women and the potential of the vote for righting wrongs."[32] Social activists such as Susan B. Anthony, Carrie Chapman Catt, Elizabeth Cady Stanton, and social workers Jane Addams, Florence Kelly, Sophonisba Breckenridge, and others led the fight for women's rights—writing pamphlets and tracts, lobbying state legislatures and Congress, demonstrating, marching, and picketing. The Nineteenth Amendment to the Constitution, giving women the right to vote, was approved by Congress on June 4, 1919, and ratified by the states on August 26, 1920. The National American Women's Suffrage Association dissolved but later was revived as the League of Women Voters.

By the beginning of the 20th century, seven states had voted to prohibit alcohol and by World War I, two thirds of the U.S. population lived in areas where drinking was outlawed. In 1919 the Eighteenth Amendment to the Constitution was passed, completely outlawing manufacture, sale, import, or export of alcoholic beverages in the United States. Social protests by women against drinking were overwhelmingly effective, but implementation proved to be another matter.

Enforcement of prohibition by interdiction and criminalizing the use of alcohol consumption ultimately proved to be impossible. Bootlegging, speakeasies, smuggling, and the manufacture of "bathtub gin," and "white lightning" in homemade stills (distilleries) proved that the human predisposition to alcohol was more potent than government enforcement. In 1933 the Eighteenth Amendment was repealed.

CARRIE CHAPMAN CATT (1859–1947)

Born Carrie Clinton Lane in Ripon, Wisconsin, and raised in Iowa, Catt trained as a teacher, briefly studied law, and was appointed a high school principal a year after graduation from Iowa State College. Two years later in 1883 she became Superintendent of Schools in Mason City. Catt married newspaper editor and publisher Leo Chapman, but in 1885, just after moving to California, he died, leaving his new wife to make her own way. She found work as a newspaper reporter.

Catt soon joined the woman's suffrage movement as a lecturer, moved back to Iowa and joined the Iowa Woman Suffrage Association, and in 1890 was a delegate at the newly formed National American Woman Suffrage Association. In 1890 she married wealthy engineer George W. Catt whom she had originally met in college and then met again during her time in San Francisco. They signed a prenuptial agreement that guaranteed her 2 months in the spring and 2 months in the fall for her suffrage work. Her husband supported Catt in these efforts, considering that his role in the marriage was to earn their living and hers was to reform society. They had no children.

Catt's effective organizing work brought her quickly into the inner circles of the suffrage movement. She became head of field organizing for the National American Woman Suffrage Association (NAWSA) in 1895, and in 1900, having earned the trust of the leaders of that organization including Susan B. Anthony, she was elected to succeed Anthony as president. Four years later she resigned the presidency to care for her husband, who died in 1905. She was a founder and president of the International Woman Suffrage Association, serving from 1904 to 1923 and until her death as honorary president.

In 1915 Catt was reelected to the presidency of the NAWSA and led the organization in fighting for suffrage laws at both the state and federal level. Her leadership was key in the final passage of the Nineteenth Amendment in 1920. She pioneered in obtaining an increased number of states in which women could vote in primary elections and regular elections, without which the 1920 victory could not have been won.

Catt was also one of the founders of the Women's Peace Party during World War I, she helped to organize the League of Women Voters after passage of the Nineteenth Amendment, and she served the league as honorary president until her death. She also supported the League of Nations after World War I and the founding of the United Nations after World War II. Between the wars, she worked for Jewish refugee relief efforts and for child labor protection laws. When her husband died, she went to live with a long-time friend, suffragist Mary Garrett Hay. They moved to New Rochelle, New York, where Catt died in 1947.

Settlement House Movement
Settlement workers were at the forefront of every major social movement in an era that was filled with reform efforts. They were tireless fighters for social justice, helping to mobilize people who were desperate for social change. Settlement activists engaged in municipal reform, worked on behalf of labor, child welfare, progressive politics, and pacifism, seeking social reform, not revolution.

Municipal Reform   When New York City politicians in collusion with construction companies proposed an elevated loop connecting the Brooklyn and Williamsburg bridges as a way to skim money from the public treasury, Settlement workers of the Henry Street and University Settlements in New York City organized mass meetings, sent out letters to influential people, persuaded newspapers to present their point of view, and bombarded the city council with letters and petitions.

Settlement workers at the Chicago Commons, including Allen T. Burns and Raymond Robins, "made surveys, filed reports, checked for voting frauds, organized political rallies and torch parades, and distributed posters and handbills."[33] They also served as campaign managers, advisers on policy, statistics gatherers, and "brain trusters" for reform political administrations.

Labor   Florence Kelly was instrumental in obtaining the constitutionality of the 10-hour workday. Settlement workers fought for laws to protect employed women, helped organize the National Women's Trade Union, and picketed with women workers in strikes against sweatshop owners. Jane Addams was instrumental in the creation of the State Boards of Conciliation and Arbitration in Illinois. In 1902 Lillian Wald and Florence Kelly mobilized 32 Settlement Houses in New York City to abolish the horrors of child labor, stimulating the 1903 Conference of Charities and Corrections, which built opposition to child labor at the national level. In 1904 the National Child Labor Committee was organized, including founding members Jane Addams, Florence Kelly, and Lillian Wald.[34]

Child Welfare   Settlement workers were prime advocates in the child welfare movement, pushing for child welfare legislation. Lillian Wald and Florence Kelly organized the first White House Conference on Child Dependency in 1909, bringing the issue of dependent children before the entire nation. The White House conference was instrumental in developing the Children's Bureau, established in 1912, the first Child Welfare agency of the federal government. Settlement workers helped organize the juvenile criminal justice movement, agitating for a separate juvenile court system, and provided leadership in establishing the first probation service in Chicago and the Juvenile Protective Association. Hull House workers organized the Immigrant Protective League, easing immigrants' adjustment to their new country and helping to prevent political exploitation of immigrants by corrupt political machines.[35]

Progressive Politics Settlement workers formed the Municipal Voters League, provided national leadership to the General Federation of Women's Clubs, and were in the forefront of passage of the woman's suffrage amendment to the Constitution in 1919. Settlement House staff were active in the progressive political movement. Jane Addams, for example, contributed to the platform and the organizational work of the Progressive party in 1912. She was a delegate to the first national convention of the Progressive party and seconded the nomination of Theodore Roosevelt as a presidential candidate.[36]

Pacifism A number of Settlement workers became active in the pacifist movement during World War I, among them Jane Addams. In 1915 she founded the Women's International League for Peace and Freedom and continued to press for peace during the war. Social workers who were members of religious groups including Quakers, Mennonites, and Seventh Day Adventists held pacifist and nonviolent beliefs and were jailed for their resistance to the war. Out of those efforts, however, conscientious objection to war became recognized as a legitimate right.

Social Reform, Not Revolution Progressive social work activists did not oppose the premises of modern American society. They worked to reform society, not revolutionize it. They wanted a society that carried out in practice the social principles of justice and opportunity that the Constitution in theory guaranteed to all our citizens. They struggled to create a level playing field, to make society more just and equitable, to seek out those who had been excluded and seat them in the banquet hall of the American dream. Progressive social workers and other modern activists promoted "economic growth and prosperity, social security and social control, individual freedom and self-interest, private consumption and material progress"[37] for all people, and they worked against the powerful who distorted these components of opportunity.

Period of Quiescence: 1920 to 1955

Even though social movements had already accomplished a great deal, a reaction set in through much of the 1920s to the late 1950s. Social movements tended to be conceptualized as potentially dangerous to the stability of established ways of life. Between World War I and World War II, social movements became identified with fascism, communism, anarchism, and subversion of the social order, and to most people, such movements posed enormous threats to enlightened reason, liberty, democracy, and capitalistic free enterprise, which they believed were central to Western civilization.

Protests were seen as resulting in disruptive strikes, demonstrations, and riots. As a result, mass social movements of any kind were often tinged with a fear of tyranny, accusations of un-Americanism, distaste for irrational behavior, and concern about mob violence.

The period between 1920 and the late 1950s silenced minorities, women, and the least skilled. This period saw the suppression of the African American population in the South—through lynching, beatings, and a massive reign of terror—ultimately as part of an effort to discourage forever any possibility of unity between poor African Americans and poor Whites. In 1948 President Truman ordered the desegregation of the Armed Forces, but his attempt at passing a civil rights bill in Congress was defeated. Two years later, the Korean War itself seemed to be a symbol in which young African American men fought side by side with young White men against oppression in an Asian nation, only to face segregation, discrimination, and oppression in their own land.

Social protest went underground during this period. But a process was covertly being generated out of sight of the mainstream that would bring about a convulsive outburst to end discrimination and begin a new era of social movements.[38]

BERTHA CAPEN REYNOLDS (1885–1978)

Bertha Capen Reynolds, social worker, educator, and activist, advocated for working-class and oppressed groups and stressed the importance of working together for a more humane world. Born in 1885 and raised in Stoughton, Massachusetts, she graduated from the Boston School of Social Work in 1914. She participated in the first course in psychiatry ever offered to social workers at Smith College in 1918, and in 1925 she was appointed associate director of Smith College School of Social Work.

In 1938 Reynolds was asked to resign from the college because she encouraged social workers to unionize to improve their working conditions and the lives of their clients. After her dismissal, she continued to write extensively in *Social Work Today,* the journal of the rank and file movement, on the need for social workers to become more politically active and concerned about the civil rights of their clients. In 1942, she published *Learning and Teaching in the Practice of Social Work*. Despite her background and scholarship, she found it difficult to obtain employment either in schools of social work or social agencies, coming to the conclusion that she had been blacklisted for her union activities. In 1943, however, the National Maritime Union hired her.

After her retirement in 1948, Reynolds wrote three more books, *Social Work and Social Living* (1951), *McCarthyism Versus Social Work* (1954), and her autobiography, *An Uncharted Journey* (1963). Although she did not stand alone in her perspectives, Reynolds has come to symbolize the historic tradition of progressive social work. What distinguished her was her serious and lifelong commitment to understanding the forces behind oppression, war, and human degradation. Reynolds died in 1978 at the age of 92.

In 1985 progressive social workers, compelled to resist the conservative drift of the social work profession and their increasing marginalization, rallied around the centennial celebration of her life and legacy and formed a national organization, the Bertha Capen Reynolds Society (BCRS).

Period of Protest: 1955 to 1973

The period before, during, and several years after the 1960s is generally recognized as the era of protest in U.S. history. The Kennedy and Johnson administrations were a watershed in the history of social movements. Many social movements were born during the 1960s, including human potential, student free speech, counterculture, environmental, and women's liberation movements, and the movement to end the war in Vietnam. Those affecting social work most directly were the civil rights and the welfare rights movements.

Watershed Era of the Kennedy and Johnson Administrations   The thrust of the Kennedy and Johnson administrations was, in many respects, the last great attempt to bring the modern Enlightenment project to fruition, including not only the triumph of modern reason and science but individual freedom and liberty, economic self-determination, and democracy. The ideals they championed included the virtues of the

welfare state and a desire to bring the poor and racially excluded groups, especially African Americans, into full political, economic, and social equality. The great contradictions of discrimination and segregation could no longer stand the combined pressure that the civil rights and welfare rights movements exerted in an age that celebrated progress, justice, and the democratic way of life as a model for the world.

Civil Rights Movement   The early civil rights movement had its origin in the Progressive Era. Modern civil rights movement began in the 1940s, but it was not until the late 1950s, when Thurgood Marshall and the NAACP began to use legal action, that events began to escalate. The turbulent period of 1955 to 1964 witnessed a major thrust of grassroots social action and the work of several civil rights organizations, culminating in the Civil Rights Act of 1964.

Early Civil Rights Activism   The civil rights movement began as far back as the Progressive movement with the formation of two major civil rights organizations. The National Association for the Advancement of Colored People (NAACP) came into being in 1910 as an embodiment of the political and legal activism advocated by W. E. B. Dubois. A year later the National Urban League was established to help southern migrants adjust to urban living conditions in the North, expressing Booker T. Washington's view that African Americans should concentrate on economic progress.[39]

Modern Civil Rights Movement   The modern civil rights movement can be traced to 1941, when A. Philip Randolph, president of the International Brotherhood of Pullman Workers, and the NAACP used the threat of a march on Washington to force President Roosevelt to sign Executive Order 8802, creating a temporary Committee on Fair Employment Practice to give African Americans equal treatment in jobs. Although southern conservatives in Congress killed the committee in 1946, this political victory demonstrated the power African Americans could wield by using collective action and inspired the vision that social justice could be attained when African Americans refused to endure injustice any longer.

Congress for Racial Equality and Civil Rights Activism Shortly after Randolph's victory, A. J. Muste, James

Farmer, and others founded the Congress for Racial Equality (CORE), an offshoot of the Quaker-sponsored Fellowship of Reconciliation, and began to use techniques of nonviolent direct action to fight racial discrimination at the University of Chicago. In 1943 members of CORE used sit-in demonstrations to successfully desegregate a Chicago restaurant, and in April 1947 CORE and its allies sent African American and White freedom riders into the South to test compliance with federal court decisions on interstate bus routes, tactics that would later be used all over the South. In 1948 President Truman ordered the desegregation of the U.S. Armed Forces, and momentum was beginning to build among champions of civil rights that segregation could be ended.

National Association for the Advancement of Colored People and Legal Action   Although the legislative and executive branches of federal government had been largely resistant to racial segregation, civil rights groups, especially the NAACP, had been pressing their cause through the judicial process. Thurgood Marshall, one of the NAACP's chief litigants and later a Supreme Court justice, used legal action to build precedent after precedent in court victories against segregation in higher education, including *Sweatt v. Painter, McLaurin v. Oklahoma State Regents,* and *Henderson v. United States.* Direct grassroots action by CORE and precedents established by the NAACP began to pay off when in 1953 the Supreme Court banned segregation in restaurants in Washington, D.C.

A year later, in the landmark rulings in *Brown v. Board of Education of Topeka* and *Bolling v. Sharpe,* the U.S. Supreme Court ruled that segregated schools were a violation of the Fourteenth Amendment and ordered desegregation with "all deliberate speed." The Supreme Court made clear its determination to prohibit government-sanctioned forms of racial discrimination and marked the beginning of hope that the stranglehold by which one group of people were able to impose a series of policies to enforce institutional inequality, unfairness, and disadvantage on others could not stand.

The Supreme Court decision was dramatically tested in September 1957 when Governor Orval Faubus used the Arkansas National Guard to prevent nine African American children from attending school in Little Rock. Defying Governor Faubus, President Eisenhower enforced the Supreme Court decision by sending federal troops into the South for the first time since the end of Reconstruction.

Grassroots Social Action   The tide was clearly beginning to turn against segregation in the United States, but many civil rights activists realized that the battle against discrimination could not be won by the courts or by government intervention alone. The real struggle to end racism would be won on the streets and playgrounds, in classrooms and churches, in stores and restaurants, in factories and offices, and it would have to be won by African Americans themselves.

Beginning with the historic Montgomery Bus Boycott of 1955, African Americans from all over the South took to the streets in the great Selma to Montgomery March and in demonstrations in Birmingham and a host of other cities. In February 1961 students in Greensboro, North Carolina, staged the first sit-in of the 1960s at a segregated lunch counter. Sit-ins spread like a prairie fire, asserts Ehrenreich, and within one year no less than 25% of all students in Black colleges of the South had participated in at least one sit-in; one in six had been arrested; and students had demonstrated in more than 100 cities.

By 1963 rent strikes were occurring in Harlem and East Harlem, demands for desegregation of schools were heard in Boston and New York, and demonstrations demanding jobs for African American workers took place at construction sites in Chicago and New York. Supporters of sit-ins picketed Woolworth stores and Greyhound terminals, and Black and White student activists initiated community organizing projects in northern ghettos. In Detroit, New York, and other cities, the Black Muslims were a growing force; Malcolm X the militant Muslim minister drew ever-larger crowds. By one count during the summer of 1963 "no less than 1,412 civil rights demonstrations occurred including the 300,000 strong March on Washington of late summer."[40]

Civil Rights Organizations   Throughout the 1960s, the principle civil rights organizations—the National Association for the Advancement of Colored People, National Urban League, Congress of Racial Equality, Southern Christian Leadership Conference, and the Student Nonviolent Coordinating Committee—promoted mass, nonviolent resistance to segregation by means of sit-ins, boycotts, picketing, marches, and legal action all over the South.

WHITNEY M. YOUNG JR. (1921–1971)

Born in 1921, Whitney Moore Young Jr. served in the segregated U.S. Army in Europe during World War II, where he acted as a liaison between White officers and African American enlisted men. He later referred to his experience as the inspiration for his subsequent career as an expert in race relations. With a MSW degree from the University of Minnesota School of Social Work, Young worked for the Urban League of St. Paul and later become executive secretary at the branch office in Omaha, Nebraska.

At age 33 he was named dean of the Atlanta University School of Social Work, acquiring a formidable reputation as an administrator and fundraiser. In 1961 Young returned to the National Urban League, where he served for 10 years as executive director. During his tenure, he successfully secured jobs and training for African Americans in areas traditionally closed to them. "Selective placement" was the name he gave to this pioneering employment program responsible for moving African American professionals into well-paid white-collar jobs in major businesses and industry.

Young's innovative plan was considered a major inspiration for the War on Poverty of the Johnson administration. He was an adviser on race relations to Presidents Kennedy, Johnson, and Nixon. Macro social worker Whitney M. Young Jr. served as president of NASW from 1969 until his death in 1971 at the age of 50, He is considered one of the principal pioneers in community organization, demonstrating its use in advocacy for oppressed people, and he pioneered the development of social work in industrial settings with both union and management.

National Urban League: In 1961 the new executive director of the National Urban League, social worker Whitney M. Young Jr., proselytized for a "decade of discrimination" in favor of African Americans by means of racial preferences in employment.

Southern Christian Leadership Conference (SCLC): After the Montgomery, Alabama, bus boycott of 1955–1956, the SCLC was organized by Martin Luther King Jr. and Ralph Abernathy, becoming the largest and most active civil rights group. The SCLC-affiliated Student Nonviolent Coordinating Committee (SNCC) organized by Stokely Carmichael in 1960 was the most vocally militant of the major civil rights organizations and was instrumental in developing the organizational infrastructure for SCLC in a number of southern states, including Alabama and Mississippi.

Congress of Racial Equality (CORE): Although fading in the 1950s, CORE revived when James Farmer returned as national director in 1961. CORE fought southern segregation with Freedom Rides and other tactics, and in the North it increasingly relied on the boycott as a weapon to force racial quotas on targeted corporations. Between 1960 and 1962, CORE inspired boycotts, coordinated by almost 400 religious leaders, that brought 24 corporations including Pepsi-Cola, Esso, Gulf Oil, and Sun Oil to an agreement to hire African Americans in specific numbers. Completely committed to racial quotas by 1962, CORE disseminated the strategy of boycotts for quotas in New York, Boston, and Detroit and continued to be involved in issues affecting African Americans in northern urban centers, particularly housing and job discrimination.

Increased Tension Throughout these years of turbulence, members of activist civil rights organizations, Blacks and Whites, Rabbis and ministers, Christians and Jews, social workers and social activists were vilified, spat on, yelled at, threatened, beaten, tear-gassed, jailed, and some even murdered in the cause of civil rights. The vision of these events on television and in newspapers and magazines captured the nation's attention. But opposition was also mounting, and the forces of racism used every tactic at their disposal to intimidate civil rights activists.

The Civil Rights Act of 1964 While each victory added to the groundswell of momentum, A. Phillip Randolph, who had used the threat of a march on Washington in 1941 to gain the first major civil rights victory, believed that if civil rights organizations acted together, they could give a final push to obtain passage of the civil rights bill that was pending in Congress. Using his influence with organized labor, Randolph persuaded the unions to jointly sponsor a mammoth March on Washington with the civil rights organizations in 1963. The "I Have a Dream" speech of Martin Luther King captured the nation's moral consciousness, and at that moment the tide turned.

Less than a year later, the Civil Rights Act of 1964 was passed, prohibiting racial, sexual, or ethnic discrimination in employment or public accommodations in the United States. It established an enforcement mechanism, the Equal Employment Opportunity Commission, to implement the law. In short order

Congress passed the Voting Rights Act of 1965 and in 1968 the Fair Housing Act. Later, aware that as late as World War II, 30 of 48 states outlawed Black-White marriage, the Supreme Court struck down miscegenation laws, the most offensive apartheid measures of all.

Welfare Rights Movement

During the late 1960s and early 1970s, the National Welfare Rights Organization (NWRO), founded by Syracuse CORE chairman George Wiley, provided the structure for a powerful welfare rights movement. All around the country, but especially in the North, poor women organized to stop what they saw as ill treatment from welfare workers. Then they organized to change rules that made it impossible for them to survive and began demanding more benefits at the local and state levels. By the early 1970s the role of the NWRO became more pronounced, and local organizing efforts began to follow a national strategy.

Their efforts were instrumental in leading Congress to consider a guaranteed national income and to reject President Nixon's Family Assistance Plan. Nevertheless, organizing became more difficult as state and county welfare departments learned better how to routinize benefits and limit worker discretion, so that one critical focus of early organizing—its attacks on the arbitrary allotment of benefits—was reduced.

With the death in 1973 of NWRO founder George Wiley, and the defeat of the Family Assistance Plan, the national focus of the welfare rights movement quickly collapsed. The movement splintered into remnants, with some areas losing any organizational form and others maintaining small organizations that struggled to retain at least a watchdog role in regard to state programs to organize around particularly offensive polices.

Modern Social Activism Today

Since the mid-1970s, progressive activists have made significant headway in urban politics. They have generally used three, often overlapping, strategies: labor organizing, electoral politics, and engagement in social movements often at the international level.

Labor Organizing   Urban activists also sank their roots in the labor movement, focusing their organizing efforts among workers in low-wage industries such as hospitals, hotels, and janitorial services. This work has primarily been among women, immigrants, and people of color. Unions that have made the most headway in recent years have drawn on the tactics and themes of civil rights crusades and grassroots organizing campaigns that emphasize dignity and justice and that forge alliances with community and church groups. Recently, unions and community groups in several cities have run "living wage" campaigns to require private firms with municipal contracts or subsidies (such as tax breaks) to pay their employees wages that exceed the poverty line and to provide decent benefits.

Electoral Politics   Over the past 20 years, modern progressive grassroots activists have created lasting networks to support electoral work, such as the Conference on Alternative State and Local Policy, the Planners Network, and the New England Citizen Action Resource Center.

International Social Movements   Social activists have made significant progress to end pollution and create an ecologically sustainable environment. They have protested the Iraq War, the arms race, and continued the efforts to achieve world peace. International women's rights have become an issue in many nations, and indigenous peoples throughout the world have been active in challenging the International Monetary Fund (IMF) and the hegemony of modern development.[41]

HOW TO ENGAGE IN MODERN SOCIAL ACTION

To bring about change, we first must unfreeze the systems that are locked into patterns of oppression. After we unfreeze the system, we help move it in a better direction by engaging in a cycle of social change. Then we refreeze the system to solidify change by initiating laws and policies that institutionalize the system in its new pattern.[42]

Unfreeze the System

Modern social activists understand that strong forces will resist social change. They use a number of action strategies and tactics to unfreeze dysfunctional systems of oppressive structures.

Resistance to Change

Resistance can be seen as the enemy against which you are working. Among these enemies are inertia and homeostasis, fear of the unknown, disruption of routine, threats to security, and threats to power.

Inertia and Homeostasis   At the simplest and most mechanistic level, any social system manifests strong forces that tend to keep it moving in one direction. This is called inertia. It is very difficult to derail a system once it is moving along a prescribed path. Another tendency that keeps the system from changing is homeostasis. Systems have built-in mechanisms for self-correction that keep them stable; they resist external forces that would disturb their equilibrium.

Fear of the Unknown   On a more personal level, change creates anxiety. It is often less threatening to keep something old and familiar, even if it is dysfunctional, than to trade it in for something that is new, unknown, and filled with potential risk and uncertainty.

Disruption of Routine   People are creatures of habit and routine. Change in the social system tends to upset this routine, disturbing lifestyles, often requiring us to change behaviors, ways of thinking, and attitudes that have served us over the years. It is sometimes difficult for us to adjust to new ways of being.

Threats to Security   Our livelihood or job security frequently depends on and is a result of fitting into a system, learning the rules and procedures, and becoming socialized to that organizational setting. We establish security by building a family, putting down roots, and investing time and energy in that effort. Social change may disrupt or threaten our jobs, families, social situations, or place in a community.

Threats to Power   Entrenched powers want to keep things the way they are, often because they have developed a system that benefits them at the expense of others. They have a vested interest in maintaining the systems over which they have control. Control means that they have freedom to mobilize values, influence policy, pursue their own interests, and develop social tools such as organizations to create wealth and more power. Social action develops new countervailing power bases that threaten to usurp this power. Perhaps more than anything else, it is the struggle for social, political, and economic power that motivates people in influential positions to resist social change.

Strategies   Strategies are broad plans to break up an oppressive system. Some of the strategies by which social action organizations unfreeze oppressive systems are non-cooperation with oppression, exposure of perpetrators, information campaigns, public

relations, legal action, *satyagraha* or nonviolent resistance, e-activism, and direct confrontation.

Active Non-Cooperation With Oppression   One of the key strategies in breaking cycles of victimization is to resist participating in self-defeating oppression, not cooperating with required behaviors, and refusing to accept laws, policies, and procedures that are demeaning. For African Americans in the South, this meant sitting in White-only sections of public transportation, using White-only restrooms in defiance of existing practices, and using sit-ins at restaurants that would not serve them.

Refusal to be a victim: Non-cooperation with oppression may also include not acting in the role of a victim. A victim may act in stereotyped ways that reinforce the perception of oppressors that the victim is inferior. Retraining oppressed individuals to develop skills, habits, dress, appearance, and language helps overcome demeaning, stigmatizing behavior. During the civil rights movement, African Americans mounted campaigns emphasizing "Black pride" and education in African American studies. Many African Americans adopted African names, African dress, and "natural" hairstyles.

Inner social presence: Education means acquiring cognitive skills and changes in outward appearance as well as the inner social presence and self-presentation skills that stimulate others to treat the oppressed with respect and dignity. To the extent that oppressed and stigmatized persons no longer act the role of victim, oppressors will have difficulty relating to them as victims.

Exposure of Perpetrators   We make every effort to expose perpetrators to the victims of their oppression and acts of oppression to public scrutiny by personalizing an abstract organizational system and targeting specific individuals.

Personalize an abstract organizational system: We often put impersonal, distant, and sanitized oppression where it belongs—at the personal level. Victims gain power as they see their oppressors as real people, not shadowy processes, procedures, rules, or policies. They learn that behind the seemingly impenetrable maze of rules and norms are individuals. This places the victims, often for the first time, on an equal footing with those who have taken advantage of them. You publicly disclose the plight of the disadvantaged, showing who is responsible for their situation.

Target specific individuals: Your campaign members target specific individuals rather than institutions. "Who can attack the telephone company or the government? It is far easier to attack the callousness of the president of the company, Mr. Smith, who won't let shut-in elderly people have affordable phones, while he has a telephone in his limousine."[43] You challenge oppressors by making demands, giving ultimatums, and delivering messages to them personally. They may be shielded by layers of bureaucracy, networks of interlocking relationships with others in power, the right of protection from self-incrimination, and skillful use of evasion, but you demand to have your members meet those in charge face to face. Saul Alinsky puts the point this way: "Pick the target, freeze it, personalize it and polarize it."[44]

Information Campaigns Expect that your opponents will use deceptive tactics and distortions. We anticipate misrepresentations of people who are oppressed and challenge misinformation.

Deceptions and distorted information: Don't be so naive as to believe that oppressors will play fairly. You can expect that forces of oppression will "make a mockery of the democratic . . . process by misrepresenting cases, improperly invoking authority, making false promises, or distracting attention from key issues," says John Forester.[45] Some oppressors will very selectively inform and misinform citizens. They may call attention to particular needs and obscure others. They may appear to welcome legitimate, open discussion and public education while simultaneously ignoring the need for affected populations to join in those discussions. They may omit a careful analysis of legitimate alternatives and thus misrepresent actual options. Sometimes officials of a government agency or corporate managers will give in during a demonstration but then renege on agreements after everyone has gone home.

Anticipate attempts to misrepresent the oppressed: Forester recommends that your activist organization "anticipate the attempts of established interests to shape the perceived needs of citizens . . . and work against such needs-shaping rhetoric."[46] Activists counter those who shape information to keep people in subservient positions. We confront misrepresentations and stereotyping of the poor by gathering facts and presenting them in newspapers, magazines, and on television. Activists demand that reports and information about victims of oppression be intelligible to the public and actively explored at public hearings, not simply noted and passed over. We confront misrepresentations of costs, risks, and available alternatives to

social problems by those in power, temper exaggerated claims, demystify organizations and bureaucratic or corporate processes, and encourage mobilization and action of affected citizens.[47]

Challenge misinformation: Information campaigns actively challenge misinformation and distortions of truth where they occur and dig up facts and data that oppressors would rather hide to keep power and domination. For decades the tobacco industry consistently denied and suppressed research that indicated smoking caused cancer. Once evidence was shown to be irrefutable, they resisted facts that secondhand smoke was likewise cancer causing. The exposure of tobacco company disinformation and evidence of the dangers of tobacco smoke have led to laws banning smoking in public places and requiring warning labels on cigarette packages, as well as lawsuits by state and federal governments on behalf of people addicted to nicotine.

Public Relations As your organization strategizes and maneuvers, you gain media attention. You use TV investigative reporters to help you expose injustice. Your group obtains exposure though newspapers and journalists.

TV media: Exposure may mean finding a vulnerable spot and exploiting it. One of the most powerful tactics of the civil rights demonstrators, for example, was the television exposure of the brutality, anger, and hate aimed at nonviolent resisters as they sought equal rights and access guaranteed in the Constitution. The media captured national attention by showing that civil rights was a compelling moral cause that could not be denied.

Newspapers and journalism: A group of journalists and novelists called "muckrakers" exposed oppressors in the early 20th century, aiding social activists in their cause. Carey McWilliams exposed discrimination with such books as *Brothers Under the Skin,* and John Steinbeck publicized the story of migrant workers in California in his novel *Grapes of Wrath*. Like the muckrakers, your members can use public relations by giving speeches, making personal appearances, and writing articles, pamphlets, books, newsletters, and flyers.[48]

Legal Action Legal tactics are a way of forcing a solution by using the court system and existing laws to command those in power to live up to their own rules and agreements.[49] By using the legal process, social movement organizations can ask judges to clarify the responsibility of governmental agencies in cases where vaguely written legislation makes implementation difficult. You can force government officials to faithfully and responsibly carry out laws in situations where they have been pressured by particular interest groups to dilute or not comply with existing laws. For example, courts can order slum landlords to stop evicting people from their homes, order school districts to provide equal educational opportunities, or mandate compensation for damages caused by toxic waste. There are several kinds of legal action: injunctions, discovery, and lawsuits.

Injunctions: An injunction can help your organization stop practices that are damaging. Injunctions are court orders to stop possibly harmful action until additional facts are gathered. The instant papers have been served, the recipient must cease actions or risk being in contempt of court. Such tactics place the full weight of the government behind your organization, giving your members time to rally their forces, gather information, and plan their next tactic.

If your organization gets an injunction against the builder, construction is delayed, costing the builder money on the loans incurred. To avoid these expenses, as well as those of a potential court battle that could drag on for months or years, a developer might be willing to negotiate, giving in to your organization's demands.

Discovery: Discovery is a legal tactic that allows lawyers to examine an opponent's documents. Through discovery, for example, movement organizations found internal reports of the Department of Interior showing that public water was being sold far below market costs to large-scale commercial farmers.

Lawsuit: A lawsuit is another major legal action that movement organizers can take against perpetrators of oppression. A lawsuit can be filed to "right a wrong, claim compensation for harm done, or make a party perform as agreed."[50] Because legal tactics can be expensive, the mere threat of a lawsuit often leads oppressors to the bargaining table. Builders, for example, can only make a profit when houses are sold and loans paid off. Social activists have used performance lawsuits, class action lawsuits, and procedural lawsuits.

1. Performance Lawsuits: A performance suit forces individuals or corporations to live up to a contract.

2. Class Action Lawsuits: Sometimes advocacy groups or regulatory agencies whose legal role is to protect the public will file a class action suit. Class action suits are helpful when the overall societal damage is large but the damages suffered by any single person are relatively small, making individual suits prohibitively expensive. Consumer activists have filed class action suits on behalf of citizens who have been overcharged by utility or insurance companies or who have purchased defective products.

3. Procedural Lawsuits: If regulatory agencies do not follow their own procedures, your organization can file a procedural suit. You greatly improve your bargaining power if you can show that government agencies do not follow rules or adjudicate claims fairly. During the Reagan administration, for example, many people were wrongly denied Social Security benefits because policies were interpreted too narrowly. Many of these people sued to obtain aid.

   Consumer movement activists file procedural suits against the Food and Drug Administration for ignoring scientific evidence and force them to regulate food additives. In addition, sometimes city councils illegally hold closed hearings, planning commissions give preferential treatment to developers, or general services agencies do not use sealed bids but give favored treatment to certain contractors. These agencies may begin to follow correct procedures if challenged with a lawsuit.

Advantages of lawsuits: Using the legal process enhances your organization's legitimacy. Legal action places your movement organization on an equal level with business or governmental organizations, forcing them to recognize the rights of migrant workers for redress, the legitimate grievances of the homeless poor, and the just cause of victims of discrimination.

Disadvantages of lawsuits: Court processes are slow and expensive, and suits filed in one state are not valid in other states. Lawsuits may stimulate opponents to file a countersuit against your organization. Even when the courts give a social movement the victory, this may only be temporary. Laws may be repealed or past legal actions revoked.

Satyagraha Mahatma Gandhi remains one of the foremost movement activists of our time. A diminutive man, he challenged the weight of the entire

British Empire and nearly single-handedly mobilized colonial India into a massive effort to gain independence. In doing so, he pioneered one of the most compelling principles of social action. This is the principle of *satyagraha*. It has been described as "soul force" or "truth force." Ferguson says that satyagraha has been misunderstood in the West as "passive resistance" or "nonviolent resistance." Gandhi disavowed these terms because they suggest weakness, nonaction, or passivity in the face of violence and oppression. Timothy Flinders asserts, "to call satyagraha passive resistance is like calling light non-darkness: it does not describe the positive energy of the principle."[51]

Satyagraha is a combination of two opposite forces: fierce autonomy and total compassion. It asserts the following:

> I will not coerce you. But, neither will I allow you to coerce me. While I will not allow you to behave unjustly toward me, I will not oppose you by violence (physical force), but by the force of the truth and the right—by the integrity of my beliefs and by my commitment to what is just and good.
>
> My integrity shines forth because I will not compromise my commitment by acting unjustly or falsely or try to overturn violence with violence, humiliation, injury, or subjugation. Instead I will show my integrity by my willingness to suffer, to pour myself out for my community, to place myself in danger, go to prison, and die if necessary. But I will not condone, cooperate, or allow by inaction injustice, oppression, or violence to continue. Ultimately the moral force of my restraint, seeing my intention, sensing my compassion and openness, and by treating myself with intense respect and dignity, you must also treat me with respect and dignity. By my unrelenting commitment to justice, you too must also begin to respect justice.

Satyagraha opens the heart of the adversary and stirs the conscience of the indifferent. Satyagraha removes social action from the arena of confrontation or threat, bargaining or negotiation, deal making, game playing, or pleading. Satyagraha requires heroic restraint and courage to forgive. Martin Luther King Jr. used oppression of African Americans as a moral force with which to confront oppressors. He resisted being oppressed, and he even submitted to imprisonment and death. To his Atlanta congregation he said,

> I choose to give my life for those who have been left out of the sunlight of opportunity. I choose to live for and with those who find themselves seeing life as a long and desolate corridor with no exit sign. This is the way I'm going.
>
> If it means suffering a little bit, I'm going that way. If it means sacrificing, I'm going that way. If it means dying for them, I'm going that way. Because I heard a voice saying, "Do something for others."[52]

King demonstrated that oppressors could imprison his body but could not imprison his self or break his spirit. He challenged injustice with just demands, demonstrating justice in every action, and he did not let himself be treated unjustly. He demonstrated to the oppressor that injustice would not be accepted, and he challenged America to live up to the values it espoused, to become a just nation in its actions as well as its words.

E-Activism

Today e-activism is being used with more and more success. E-activism is the use of the Internet to support, engage, and provide information about social causes that reach people worldwide. E-activism was used effectively with the anti-Iraq War movement, supporting and organizing demonstrations all over the world. America Coming Together, the Media Fund, and the MoveOn.org voter fund sponsored the current 527 IRS code definition for nonprofit organizations that raise money to espouse political causes but not candidates. The use of e-activism has been so effective that in China there has been a major effort to crack down on unrestricted computer use.[53]

Direct Confrontation

"Direct action campaigns must not be undertaken lightly," assert Rubin and Rubin, "they require people's time and moral commitment to the issues, and sometimes they involve risk. Only try direct action after a conventional approach has failed, and then do so cautiously by engaging in testing actions."[54] Plan the confrontation carefully. Prepare and train participants well. Anticipate retaliation and strategize for it in advance.

Planning the Confrontation Take into consideration the abilities of the participants, their commitment to the issues, and the effectiveness of the tactic you are using. If you use picketing, for example, your group needs to know whether your city has laws about the materials with which pickets signs can be made to prevent them from being used as weapons. Picketers should be located where they get attention, but if they obstruct traffic or violate private property, you may anger the public and risk arrest. Your members need to work out a plan to get picketers out of jail.

Likewise, an enormous amount of planning is required for a successful march. For example, when Martin Luther King Jr. led marches in Chicago in 1966, "months of negotiation were required to determine which groups would participate and to ensure that King's overall philosophy of nonviolence would be observed. The choice of which streets to march down were argued over for weeks because some streets showed the deterioration of housing but other streets better illustrated the effects of discrimination."[55]

Training   Confrontation tactics must be "planned with an awareness of how far members of the action organization are willing to go in a campaign."[56] They must be rehearsed and participants trained in their use, especially for nonviolent tactics. "Few people can be beaten and arrested without wanting to defend themselves. People who by temperament are not non-violent must be kept out of the actions. During the Montgomery Bus Boycotts, there were training schools in nonviolence, and only people trained and experienced in nonviolence were allowed to become Freedom Riders."[57] Training is also crucial for pick-eting and marching. Picketers, for example, "must be trained not to respond to taunts or unpleasant distractions. Giving in to taunts, the picketers look disorderly and thereby lose legitimacy."[58]

Threats and Reprisals   Gaining power for people who are oppressed cannot be resolved without negative consequences for those who must give up power. Whenever your movement organization stimulates social action, you will inevitably generate conflict. Retaliation can range from mild to brutal. When your organization conducts direct confrontation, anticipate and plan for retaliation. Sometimes retaliation can provide advantages for your group.

Forms of Retaliation   In its mildest form, the response of targets may only be an attempt to deny the legitimacy of protests. They may charge that the protest is un-American or mount their own campaign against social change. Phyllis Schlafly established a national movement called STOP ERA to prevent adding the Equal Rights Amendment to the Constitution, and Jerry Falwell of the religious right established the Moral

Majority to counteract abortion rights and gay rights activists.

Sometimes the opposition "will turn one group against another, exploiting tensions between groups." They may use slander and personal defamation. "Opponents may accuse the group's leader of being a communist, homosexual or lesbian, an embezzler, or a philanderer."[59] Retaliation efforts against African American and Native American militants included eavesdropping, propaganda, disinformation, harass-ment, infiltration, and manufacturing evidence that some activists were police informers.

Sometimes, however, counterstrikes are brutal and may decimate the membership. Your members can be threatened with intimidation, insults, arrests, physical attacks, or even death. The Ku Klux Klan attempted to intimidate civil rights activists by their own counterdemonstrations. During the civil rights movement of the 1960s, police officials raided homes of African American militants and killed them, allegedly in self-defense. Union organizers have also been fired, threatened, beaten, and murdered.

Anticipate Retaliation   Always expect and try to anticipate counterattacks. Rubin and Rubin alert orga-nizations to expect that "opponents will try to seize the organization's books, records, and mailing lists. They will search for financial irregularities . . . and try to taint the organization with scandal."[60] Make sure your organization's books are squeaky clean, be aware of skeletons in the closet of organizational lead-ers, keep books and mailing lists in a secure place, and watch what is put in writing that might give the appearance of slander. Your movement organization must be "very cautious to avoid the appearance of impropriety" because it is trying to take the high moral ground.[61]

Plan Your Response   Plan what you will do in the face of massive assaults such as imprisonment of your movement's leaders, attempts to demoralize your membership, and threats or bribes. The more aware and prepared your organization is, the better it will resist counterattacks. Try not to play in a game you don't think you can win, and never take on more than your organization can handle.

Advantages of Retaliation   There are tactical advan-tages to being retaliated against. "Overt repression," for example, "denies the enemy legitimacy and often grants it to protesters. . . . Evoking a response (even a high negative response as with the use of excessive force) from the opposition is a sure indication that a direct action organization has reached and scared its target."[62]

TOYOHIKO KAGAWA, RENEWER OF SOCIETY (1888–1960)

Toyohiko Kagawa was born in 1888 in Kobe, Japan. Orphaned early, he lived first with his widowed stepmother and then with an uncle. He enrolled in a Bible class to learn English, and in his teens he became a Christian and was disowned by his family. In his late teens, he attended Presbyterian College in Tokyo for 3 years.

Kagawa decided that he had a vocation to help the poor, and that in order to do so effectively he must live as one of them. Accordingly, from 1910 to 1924 he lived for all but 2 years in a shed 6 feet square in the slums of Kobe. In 1912 he unionized the shipyard workers. He spent 2 years (1914–1916) at Princeton studying techniques for the relief of poverty. In 1918 and 1921 he organized unions among factory workers and among farmers. He worked for universal male suffrage (granted in 1925) and for laws more favorable to trade unions.

In 1923 he was asked to supervise social work in Tokyo. His writings began to attract favorable notice from the Japanese government and abroad. He established credit unions, schools, hospitals, and churches, and he wrote and spoke extensively on the application of Christian principles to the ordering of society. He founded the Anti-War League, and in 1940 was arrested after publicly apologizing to China for the Japanese invasion of that country. In the summer of 1941 he visited the United States in an attempt to avert war between Japan and the United States.

After the war, despite failing health, he devoted himself to the reconciliation of democratic ideals and procedures with traditional Japanese culture. He died in Tokyo April 23, 1960. A day of remembrance has been set aside for this hero of social work and Christianity in the Christian Church Year.

Tactics   Tactics are shorter-term actions designed to carry out a strategy. Macro social work activists need to know how to combine tactics in an overall strategy to achieve a desired effect. For example, your group can uses variations in tactics to overcome resistance, lessen resistance, or move in both directions at once. A number of tactics are available for your group to use.

Overcome Resistance   To overcome resistance, different tactics may be required in each campaign for social justice, depending on the unique situation your group is confronting. One way is to begin your campaign "with a confrontation to attract media attention," say Rubin and Rubin, "then proceed to political pressure tactics to make long-term changes. Or, it may begin with mild pressure tactics, and if success is not forthcoming, gradually apply more power, using first legal, and finally, confrontation tactics."[63]

Lessen Resistance   Another approach is to lessen resistance so that the forces for change can prevail by using media, moral demonstrations, and nonviolent resistance. Your movement organization can overpower resistance by direct action, including rallies, marches, sit-ins, vigils, slowdowns of services, and traffic blockages.

Move in Both Directions at Once   Your organization can move in both directions at once, overcoming resistance and strengthening the driving forces that promote change. Informational campaigns, for example, can mobilize people while pressuring the opposition. Use education programs that inform citizens followed by community forums on the issue. "A frequent side effect is that when confronted by knowledgeable opponents, the opposition shows itself to be ignorant of technical details, which makes them look foolish and denies them legitimacy."[64] Public disruptions can place a social issue on the public agenda by gaining media coverage and implying the potential for violence. The change forces may gain support if opponents react belligerently. Or the campaign may run several tactics simultaneously.

Kinds of Direct Confrontation Tactics   Direct confrontations include rallies, moral demonstrations, picketing, marches, sit-ins, boycotts, and symbolic demonstrations.

Rallies: Rallies mobilize numbers of people for a cause and provide supporters and potential supporters with information and a sense of unity. They also attract media attention and make a statement about the issues you are raising. One of the most impressive rallies in the history of protest was the 1963 March on Washington for Civil Rights. The rally was seen on national television with a crowd of between 200,000 and 500,000 participants. Louis Farrakhan's "Million Man March" is another example.

Moral demonstrations: Moral demonstrations include voluntary jailing, fasts, and prayer vigils. In these kinds of demonstrations, individuals often become the focus of attention. For example, Gandhi placed himself at the center of attention by going on hunger strikes in his efforts to free India from British rule. Cesar Chavez's fast during the grape boycott in California gained national attention. This demonstration solidified the strikers and brought Senator Robert Kennedy onto the side of the farm workers. Prayer vigils, in which demonstrators silently light candles, demonstrate both moral and spiritual nonviolence. Some anti-abortion protesters use peaceful prayer walks rather than militant tactics.

Picketing: Picketing focuses attention on the targeted oppressor and is intended to achieve an immediate political solution. Protesters have picketed corporations, nuclear reactors, government offices, governors, and presidents, among other real or symbolic targets.

Marches: Marches demonstrate the power of the activist organization, provide an arena of media attention, and bring together other organizations in a show of solidarity.

Sit-ins: Sit-ins inconvenience the opponent, bring media attention, and avoid violence by taking over offices, highways, lunch counters, stairways, lobbies, or other public places. A sit-in puts protesters on the opponent's turf and often leads to arrest because those involved are trespassing. Sometimes sit-ins seek immediate gains, such as when welfare rights activists demand services to which they are legally entitled. Others aim at broader issues, such as the Native American "capture" of Alcatraz that publicized the abnegation of Indian Treaty Rights.

Boycott: A boycott is an economic pressure campaign designed to force an immediate solution to a problem by advocating that people refuse to purchase a particular product, or all products from a particular company. For example, Cesar Chavez initiated a national boycott of table grapes to force commercial farmers to yield to union demands. Environmentalists organized a boycott of tuna fish caught with nets that endanger dolphins. Another kind of boycott is renter strikes in which people refuse to pay rent until landlords take responsibility for repairs or provide services such as adequate heat. Sometimes, however, such boycotts are illegal. In some states it is illegal to withhold rent no matter what the landlord does. In other states, tenants can place funds in an escrow account until the problem is settled.

Symbolic demonstrations: Symbolic demonstrations are powerful ways of demonstrating goals and values. For example, students protesting apartheid in South Africa constructed shantytowns on the lawns of universities to show the living conditions of black South Africans. When Greenpeace protesters surround nuclear naval vessels with small dinghies, or place themselves between a whaling ship and whales to protest their destruction, they engage in a symbolic action of David taking on Goliath. Demonstrators advocating awareness for AIDS research have developed a huge quilt, each section of which has the name of a person who died from AIDS sewn into it by a friend or relative. The quilt is unrolled at demonstrations and rallies, symbolizing in graphic detail the number of people who have died as their names are read into a microphone.

Other tactics: Other tactics include leafleting, disrupting services, slowing traffic, and creating congestion. For example, the National Training and Information Center (NTIC) created congestion on the streets of a major city in which groups of persons with disabilities in wheelchairs tried to use mass transportation, to cross streets while trying to negotiate curbs, to maneuver around barriers or enter stores whose doorways were too small, and to move through narrow aisles or obtain products beyond their reach. These tactics demonstrated the difficulties persons with disabilities encounter in having access to public services.

What If the Strategy Fails   You will not win every battle. When difficulties set in, consider debriefing and helping people in the social movement cope with burnout and demoralization.

Debrief: If your social action strategy fails, spend time debriefing to figure out what happened and why. What tactics could have been changed? Was the timing of the campaign poor? Did the opponents capture the symbols that garner public support? Was there too much fragmentation in the movement organization to bring about a coherent effort? What could be done differently the next time?

Cope with burnout and demoralization: Because of the stress of confrontation, the long-term nature of the issues, and the strength of the opposition, your members may burn out and demoralization may occur. How do you cope with burnout?

Keep in mind that capacity building, rectification of social injustice, strengthening community, and empowerment are long-term issues. There will always be ups and downs, victories and defeats. Prepare for the long haul. Be careful not to take on too much too soon.

Pace yourselves so that you or your organization does not become overwhelmed. Take on issues that will motivate and energize your organization. When you or your organization begin to become weary of the struggle, it may be time to take a break. Saul Alinsky says, "A tactic that drags on too long becomes a drag. A good tactic is one your people enjoy."[65]

Give yourself time to step away from the conflict and assess how far you have come. Then celebrate your successes together. Let yourselves enjoy what you have accomplished, and allow yourselves to feel renewed in one another's presence. Share your feelings of accomplishment and affirm one another's importance. Give recognition and reflect on your victories. Have fun and find rejuvenation in the relationships you have developed.

Move to Action

When your group moves to action, you manage the change process and move through a life cycle of social change.

Management of Social Change
Your social movement group understands that it has control over the strategies, timing, and where you apply your efforts. Your group can work in small increments, measure your progress, and predict eventual victory.[66] Two factors that affect managing social change are the magnitude of the problem and its time frame.

Magnitude of the Problem The greater the extent and pervasiveness of the social problem, the more resistance there will be and the greater the forces will be that oppose any change effort. The greater the degree of change that needs to be made, the more difficult it will be to make successful changes.

Time Frame Another important factor is the time frame. The longer the history of the problem, the more likely that change will need to proceed slowly toward victory. Often the more gradual the change process, the more successful it will be. Sometimes, however, rapid changes are indicated. The massive social changes that were instituted during the Great Depression and the urgency to end the war in Vietnam are examples of the necessity for speedy change.

The Life Cycle of Social Change
Your group may be encouraged by the realization that social movements are often cyclical, "having their own life cycles and their own internal dynamics."[67] You can use the cycle to decide on and change your strategies, understand where your group is in the process, and where you must go next. Most change efforts move through all the phases of the change cycle, but every change effort is unique. Some phases may be shortened or omitted, or there may be regression to previous phases. Inevitably the process is a slow one. The life cycle of social change includes entrenchment, recognition, confrontation, shifting gears, and moving toward victory.

Phase 1: Entrenchment At the beginning of the change effort, the existing state of affairs—the status quo—is solidly entrenched. The status quo benefits those in power, has evolved over time, or has become part of the system's culture and way of operating. Keeping the system going is accepted as the way things are or even should be. Sometimes the oppressed have been socialized to accept their situation, or have developed a mentality in which they perpetuate the very systems that oppress them.

Prophetic stance: In the beginning stage of change, therefore, social workers and other social movement activists take a prophetic stance. Like a "voice in the wilderness," you are in the minority, alone, and isolated. You can expect to be openly criticized, ridiculed, scapegoated, or persecuted by whatever means the entrenched interests have at their disposal.

Attacks and resistance: Personal attacks on your character or attacks on members of your organization in the form of harassment, intimidation, threats, and even physical violence may be used to force you to conform to the norm and not disturb the system's equilibrium. Resistance to the change effort appears to be massive. Unless you and your members understand, prepare for, and are willing to encounter this phase of resistance, the change effort may be overwhelmed. Harvey and Brown describe, for example, how the environmental movement began with a small group of concerned conservationists, scientists, and young people in the 1960s. Rachel Carson's book *Silent Spring* raised the nation's consciousness about the dangers of pesticides, and the first Earth Day was held in 1970.

However, opposing political forces emerged during the late 1970s and throughout the 1980s, and commitment to environmental concerns waned. Environmentalists were portrayed as alarmists and radicals who were concerned about saving insignificant species at the expense of jobs and progress. Because resistance will be massive at the beginning of a change effort, Rubin and Rubin suggest that before commencing, you and your members consider the following issues.

1. How can you obtain the power you need to either overcome opponents or to reduce the forces that resist change?

2. How can your organization achieve legitimacy?

3. What kinds of symbols can you design that will allow the organization to get its issues high on the agendas of those who can influence change?

4. What strategies can the organization develop to increase chances of victory?

5. What can the organization do to maintain people's morale until victories occur?[68]

Phase 2: Recognition   As the movement for change grows, forces for and against change become more clearly defined. Your members gather facts, and patterns begin to emerge. As your members and others become more aware of the issues and the consequences, what at first may have been perceived as being an insignificant issue begins to be recognized as a legitimate social problem that concerns everyone. When you engage and sensitize people to the problem, the initial threat that exposure posed begins to lessen, and your forces for change gain understanding and recognition.

During the 1980s, for example, growing bodies of evidence on a number of fronts supported the position of the environmentalists, who persisted through court actions and pressure on elected officials. Research confirmed that pollution was destroying the ozone layer in the atmosphere and that the greenhouse effect was a reality. Data on the harmful effects of pesticides, not only on wildlife but also on humans, was documented. Information showed that shrinking habitats and decimation of wilderness areas resulted in the extinction of numerous species of plants and animals. Massive oil spills brought home to people the dangers of technology. The inability to process

raw sewage and dispose of nuclear waste became national concerns. The dangers to the environment could no longer be ignored. In fact, they were becoming an international problem.

Phase 3: Confrontation   In the third phase of change, lines have been drawn and there is direct confrontation between the forces battling for change and those struggling to maintain the status quo. Those fighting against change marshal all of their forces, realizing that they need to take the activists seriously. The stakes are raised, and an all-out attempt is made to destroy the change effort once and for all. When this occurs, you refine your strategies, sometimes using direct confrontation tactics such as sit-ins, marches, leaflets, demonstrations, and rallies. You make use of the media, attacking specific perpetrators and gaining publicity.

In the early 1980s, for example, the environmental movement became increasingly well organized, vocal, and active on a number of fronts. Numerous environmental groups began agitating for change locally as well as nationally. Specific companies that engaged in pollution were targeted. James Watt, secretary of the interior, one of the most vocal and visible opponents of environmental concerns, became a lightning rod for pro-environmental forces such as the Sierra Club and the Wilderness Society. Demonstrations occurred. People boycotted environmentally insensitive companies or specific products that harmed the environment. Media attention increased.

Phase 4: Shifting Gears   If you and your social movement organization are successful at persuasion and have won decisive battles, those who continue to resist are seen as stubborn, ignorant, and obstructionist. However, resistance forces can still mobilize enough power to regain their momentum. This is a time for you to shift gears, use tact, patience, and wisdom, keep your balance, and persuade those who are not openly opposed to change but may not yet be completely convinced about the need for change. Your change strategies move from direct confrontation to legal action, negotiation, and policy development. You shift from a confrontive to a visionary stance.

In the environmental movement, for example, the struggle moved from confronting lumber, mining, and oil corporations to the development of policy culminating in the Endangered Species Act, Clean Air Act, creation of the Environmental Protection Agency, and development of the Environmental Super Fund. Each piece of legislation meant compromise and bargaining with agribusiness, miners, and oil interests, who continued to press for concessions favoring their interests. With each successive victory, however, the environmental movement gained strength and power.

Phase 5: Toward Victory   In the final phase, those who resist change are as few and as alienated as you and your organization were in Phase 1. Even those who were opposed to change jump on the bandwagon and try to show how they too are part of the forces for change. Corporations that were major opponents of the environmental movement, for example, began to take out advertisements showing how they contribute to cleaning the environment. Being environmentally sensitive is now "politically correct."

Battles for social change are never finished once and for all, but must be refought again and again. The forces against change may still be mobilized to undermine changes that have been so hard won. The congressional elections of 2000 saw the Republican party not only win a majority of House and Senate seats but capture the Executive office as well. Conservative forces of the second Bush administration lost no time in establishing strategies to dismantle as much environmental, social welfare, and other progressive social legislation as possible, just as had occurred during the Nixon and Ford, and Reagan and Bush administrations.

Refreeze: Solidify Change

If your movement organization is successful in your social action efforts, the unjust, harmful, dehumanizing systems or processes that have been exposed and broken up now need to be replaced with ones that are just, helpful, and humanizing. This is the refreezing or solidifying stage of the change process. Your organization turns to the political process to change laws, works on policies, establish an agency, and ensure that monitoring and enforcement occur.

Politics
Political pressure is intended to change laws and enforce regulations that preserve the short-term victories. Tenants can't demonstrate each time a landlord turns off the heat in a building. Instead, a tenant's organization needs to have a city code adopted and enforced that guarantees warm apartments.

Political tactics require detailed knowledge of laws and regulations, the power structure, interest groups, and the political process. Macro social work activists become involved in the political arena, obtaining the political support of elected officials such as local, county, and state legislators, judges, lawyers, lobbyists, and administrators of public agencies.

Policy
The ultimate goal of modern social action is to institute new social policies that widen the scope of justice, equality, and freedom, that bring more and more people under the umbrella of opportunity and prosperity and keep the power and influence of the wealthy from usurping the rights of others. One way to obtain policy concessions is to negotiate and bargain with public officials. If the issues are large enough, you may have to move the political process in your favor by petitioning or developing referendums and initiatives. You can form an interest group that can lobby for changes in the law, or propose new laws. For example, the civil rights movement resulted in the passage of the Civil Rights Act, the environmental movement in the Clean Air Act, and the labor movement in the National Labor Relations Act.

Establish an Agency
If your organization has been successful in obtaining policy concessions, try to obtain a public agency that will operate programs and propose legislation on your behalf. Educators have a Department of Education to represent their interests, defense contractors the Department of Defense, farmers the Department of Agriculture, veterans the Veterans Administration, and small business owners the Small Business Administration, and so on.

Monitoring and Enforcement
Even with laws, policies, and agencies in place, however, the social action process is still not complete. There is no guarantee that the same social or cultural forces will not continue to work to undermine the new structures you have created. For example, even though the Emancipation Proclamation freed the slaves and the Fourteenth Amendment guaranteed equality and gave African Americans the right to vote, racism continued to be practiced even more virulently by means of the Black Codes, racist organizations such as the Ku Klux Klan, and the *Plessy v. Ferguson* Supreme Court decision, which institutionalized "separate but equal" facilities in the United States.

A mechanism of monitoring, enforcement, and imposing consequences needs to be instituted to ensure that social systems abide by the new behavioral constraints. Clear sanctions or punishments for those who refuse to live by the new, non-oppressive standards must be established. An agency, usually a regulatory commission, must be authorized as a watchdog to ensure compliance with standards. The Civil Rights Act established the Equal Employment Opportunity Commission (EEOC) to ensure compliance with nondiscrimination in employment. The National Labor Relations Act established the National Labor Relations Board to enforce compliance with labor laws. The California Coastal Commission was established to ensure laws protecting the California coastline are enforced.

The governor or the president must establish those regulatory agencies and follow through in a way that meets the spirit and intent of the law. Commitment on the part of the executive branch of government to enforce the laws must be obtained. Appropriations of funds must follow the establishment of advocacy agencies and regulatory commissions so that the executive branch of government has resources to enforce the law.

An unsympathetic executive can easily undermine all of your efforts to change social policy by not enforcing the regulations. In a more subtle fashion, the composition of the regulatory commission can be so arranged that the very perpetrators of injustice and oppression become the regulators, and regulatory agencies are transformed into systems that reinforce oppression.

Finally, enforcement of the laws can be twisted, loopholes found, exceptions made, delays granted, and a host of obfuscating processes developed that destroy the gains you and other social activists have worked hard to achieve. While the main outlines of these issues may already have been won for most people, the battle is never over once and for all. Macro social work activists need to be continually vigilant when the megastructures of society attempt to extend their domain at the expense of others.

LIMITATIONS OF MODERN SOCIAL ACTION

Modern issue-oriented social movements may be one of the few means of resisting the defects of an increasingly centralized, organized, technological society. Modern social action slows down injustice and brings society closer to the values inherent in the Constitution. Modern social movements have worked to expand democracy to more than half the population of the United States, which had been legally disenfranchised, banished institutionalized racism, mandated corporations to provide workers with rights to bargain on an equal basis with management, forced industries such as the tobacco industry to pay damages to customers, sensitized an entire nation to the effects of ecological damage, and brought an end to the war in Vietnam. These are by no means insignificant matters, and much good can be accomplished and has been achieved by means of modern social movements.

Critics of the activist perspective, however, argue that social action is essentially reactive rather than proactive. Modern social activists tend to become engaged where oppression and injustice have become fully entrenched, using confrontation tactics to fix a system that is broken rather than to prevent injustice in the first place. Modern social movements seek to reform society's defects rather than reconstitute the premises on which modernity itself has been founded.

In today's interrelated global society, by attacking organizational or institutionalized injustices one by one, activists may win battles but lose the war. The global market society in the 21st century perpetuates a modern culture of control, exploits the biological and social environment, and applies the combined power of government and the wealth of transnational corporations to extend the hegemony of the free global market economy. According to President Bush, for example, because "free trade and free markets have proven their ability to lift whole societies out of poverty, so the United States will work with individual nations, entire regions, and the entire global trading community to build a world that trades in freedom," which he then clarifies as meaning economic freedom. "The United States," he says, "welcomes our responsibility to lead in this great mission."[69]

Social activists who want to make long-term, fundamental changes in the premises and structures of society must go beyond reforming one corporation, one government agency, or one social policy at a time. Social activists must assert the power to change the premises on which the modern Enlightenment project operates. This is the challenge of postmodern social movements and social action.

POSTMODERN SOCIAL MOVEMENTS

"Some time between 1965 and 1973," says Peter Drucker, "we passed over a divide and entered the 'next century.' We are in political *terra incognita* with few landmarks to guide us."[70] Members of modern North American civilization, whether or not they are fully aware of it, are living in a transition period between the modern world of the Enlightenment, which is passing away but is still much with us, and the new postmodern era, the outlines of which remain to be fashioned.

It is the contention of many thinkers today that the postmodern era cannot be constructed from the combined ideology of free enterprise capitalism, mass representative democracy, individualism, modern instrumental reason, complex organization, science, or technology. Instead, groups of socially conscious people are creating new social movements that will shape a new era unlike anything that has been seen before. Eyerman and Jamison assert that society is "continuously being recreated through complex processes of interaction and innovation in particular contexts"[71] by means of a variety of new social movements. By 1983, for example, the major media were reporting a new kind of social action around the country, or what John Herbers of the *New York Times* called a "new wave of citizen initiatives." Women's liberation, the movement to end the nuclear arms race, the environmental movement, the new consumer movements, gay rights, and animal rights represent a new kind of citizen involvement in which ordinary people became knowledgeable about the most complex issues.[72] These movements reached beyond issues of economics to include issues of collective identity, new modes of consciousness, and a reconsideration of the basic premises upon which modern Enlightenment culture is founded.

SOCIAL CULTURAL MODEL OF SOCIAL CHANGE

Social critics such as Anthony Diggins, Amilcar Cabral, and others link the second class status of women, America's propensity toward violence, and the compulsion to destroy the environment by economic exploitation to a unified dominant culture in which a scientific control orientation, organized power relations, rational self-interest, and possessive individualism dominate the modern worldview. Postmodern social thinkers challenge the premises of this dominant culture and, along with social activists, engage themselves in understanding and building "new social movements" to bring about a society freed from captivity to the modern mind.

The shared logic of the new movements is the demand that society should be structured so that people themselves working together ought to be able to shape the conditions of their lives. The feminist or women's liberation movement, for example, is not just about gender equality; it aims at a fundamental restructuring of power relations between the sexes. The peace movement is not simply "anti-war," nor is the environmental movement merely an attempt to preserve the ozone layer or save rain forests. These movements are fundamentally efforts to make public decision making fully accountable to those affected, and to give people in their communities the chance to control their own futures[73] rather than have those futures determined by the activities, intentions, and decisions of others.

Women's Liberation Movement

In the late 1960s, the women's movement took on renewed vigor with the National Organization for Women (NOW), the effort to pass the Equal Rights Amendment (ERA) to the Constitution, promotion of equal pay for equal work, and the right of women to obtain an abortion on demand. While the ERA did not obtain the approval of two thirds of the states needed for ratification, it heightened the consciousness of America to women's issues. Women were elected to public office in increasing numbers. Even more important, the women's movement worked at redefining the role of women in society, searching for a way for self-expression and a new identity that did not depend on modern stereotypes.

The new identity was encapsulated in the term "feminism." Feminism was not merely an attempt to reach parity with males, nor was it merely a rejection of male dominance. Feminism was a rejection of dominance itself as a framework on which human relationships were based. It was a rejection of the mentality of paternalism. Women were reaching for a new way of being. They rejected the premise that some people have an innate claim to superiority based on membership in a racial, gender, or sexual-orientation category.

Such claims always deny others the right to their own self-determination, to control their lives, and to decide who they want to become.

Peace Movement

The civil rights movement created an atmosphere of ferment that became translated into the protest movement against the war in Vietnam in the mid 1960s, a general sense of disenchantment with government, large complex organizations, and the values of the "establishment." The movement to end the war in Vietnam decisively rejected the American colonialist mentality and imperialist national policy of modern politics that used war as a way of defending America's hegemony of power. It revealed the misunderstanding of authentic democracy by those who believed that democracy could be unilaterally imposed on a small, underdeveloped nation "for their own good," and the utter futility of thinking that modern rationality and weaponry could make any difference against a communally based culture of defiance.

The peace movement was not merely "anti-war"; it was a challenge to the presumption that a powerful nation, under the pretense of democracy or "freedom," had a right to interfere with the self-determination of a weaker nation and use military violence toward that end. Today the same issue faces the world in even more blatant form. The second Bush administration has determined to "exercise our right of self defense by acting preemptively"[74] against Iraq, a small underdeveloped nation, in spite of the reality that Iraq has never verbally threatened the United States, attacked this country or its citizens, maintained weapons of mass destruction (WMD), engaged in terrorism, or harbored terrorists.

Environmental Movement

The miracles and benefits of science and technology have been the hallmarks of modernity since the Enlightenment, but in the 1960s the relationship between the general public and those who create, manage, and profit from technology soured. The litany of ecological disasters and technical failures from Love Canal, the space shuttle *Challenger* explosion, the Chernobyl nuclear meltdown, the pesticide poisoning from the Dow Chemical Plant in Bhopal, India, numbers of massive oil spills, acid rain, the devastation of vast ecosystems in oceans and on land,

destruction of the ozone layer, and endemic industrial and agricultural pollution turned many Americans away from technological optimism. The environmental movement that resulted involved people of every age and station in life around the issue of preserving a sustainable environment.

People realized that they could do little to influence major environmental problems caused by ineptitude, corruption, and greed at the highest levels of business and government. But they could often limit the dangerous side effects of technological miscalculations in their own neighborhoods. The result was a reaction against the most cherished ideals of the modern era: rejection of technological progress for its own sake. This reaction was seen not only in the people whose impoverished neighborhoods were often used to dump hazardous wastes but also in intellectuals, professionals, and the middle class.

CHARACTERISTICS OF POSTMODERN SOCIAL MOVEMENTS

Postmodern social movements attempt to forge a new construction of social reality.[75] They are concerned with self-determination rather than dominance, the right to choose and decide rather than have others decide for us, and the necessity to shape our own future with friends and neighbors in our own communities. Postmodern social movements "are distinct from modern protest organizations or mobilization campaigns. They are characterized by self-conscious awareness that the very foundations of society are at stake or in contest."[76] New social movements provide a new structure, reject possessive individualism in the creation of human meaning, advocate for new ways of thinking, a revitalized sense of community, a redefined role of government and public affairs, and expanded opportunities for each citizen to participate in the construction of social reality.

New Structure

Postmodern social movements arise around communities of mutual interest or geography, not necessarily using protest against companies, factories, or wealthy executives as their focus as did many modern social movements.[77] They tend to be made up of heterogeneous groups of people across the spectrum of social life. A postmodern movement on behalf of a woman's right to choose, for example, may include people of different economic and social status and different cultural identities, such as Whites, African Americans, and other ethnic groups, working women and professionals, the poor and the wealthy, the young and the old.[78]

Modern social movements were large, single-issue, highly organized mass movements. Postmodern social movements are often small, loose, and open, tap local knowledge and resources, and respond to problems rapidly and creatively. They have deeper and more complex channels, often remaining underground for long periods of time as new identities are forged. These hidden networks are composed of small, separate groups in a circuit of exchanges. Information circulates through the networks, and specific agencies ensure a certain amount of unity and allow multiple membership.[79] They function as social laboratories, experimenting with new ways of understanding, new kinds of communally based social relationships, new organizational forms, and new ways of conceiving politics and of devising policy.

Rejection of Individualism

Postmodern social movements reject passive, atomistic individualism in which people are treated as components, objects, or functions of social systems. Michel Foucault argues that postmodern social movements "assert the right to be different and underline everything which makes individuals truly individual."[80] They encourage us to resist forfeiting our individuality for individualism. Instead of being forced back on ourselves, we fall back into community. Postmodern movements attack everything that separates us from one another, alienates us, or splits up community life.

New Ways of Thinking

New social movements are cognitive processes that develop new ways of social thinking and new understandings about the world. They attempt to broaden unidimensional modern reason, which limits thinking to instrumental means, accepts preprogrammed ends as valid, or reduces thinking to mere calculation. When complex organizations restrict people's actions, values, or ideas to narrow operational arenas, postmodern social movements encourage consideration of social reason, multiple ways of thinking, the exploration of

rival ends or goods, the value of creativity, and new ways of meaning creation arrived at by means of social interaction. The result is the creation of arenas of social space for the consideration of new ideas that differ from the programmed ideas and functional thinking of systems processes.

Just as modern reason was born out of the Enlightenment and shaped our institutions and mentality, social thinking is being born out of community and those structures that support community, including community organizations, social organizations, community development corporations, and postmodern social movements. Social thinking is reciprocally shaping the frameworks and structures that are emerging from them. It is precisely in the creation, articulation, and formulation of new thoughts and ideas that a postmodern social movement defines itself in society. New social movements create new types of knowledge as well as recombine or connect previously separate types of knowledge. They are "cognitive movements" that seek entirely new approaches to understanding.

Social knowledge is not the "discovery" by an individual genius, nor is it the determined outcome of systemic interactions within an established research and development system. Knowledge is primarily a social creation, and the postmodern social movement is the source and model of this way of understanding and thinking socially. Postmodern social understanding is the product of a series of social encounters within movements and between movements and their established opponents. Knowledge creation is seen as the collective creation of social groups. The collective articulation of movement identity can be likened to a process of social learning in which movement organizations act as structuring forces, opening a space in which creative interaction between individuals can take place.

Community Based

Of most importance, however, postmodern social movements develop new conceptualizations and associational forms that can serve as social laboratories for trying out new ways of thinking and being.[81] The new forms of consciousness discovered in new social movements provide something crucial in the constitution of postmodern society. They focus on community self-help and empowerment. For example, emerging postmodern social movements of the 1960s brought about a new awareness of the power of community as the locus where social problems need to be solved. Community building thus becomes the natural focus of the new social movement efforts—not necessarily community as mere locality but as a center of political and social action.

New social movements redefine community as a form of social relationship not restricted to time or place, generating a flexible group that transforms society internally. Community is increasingly seen as assuming responsibility for itself and is envisaged as the center of a new conception of grassroots politics and problem solving. The ideology of community participation is sustained by the belief that the power of the state has extended too far, diminishing the freedoms of ordinary people and their rights to control their own affairs.

Redefined Role of Government

Richard Flacks says that postmodern social movements fundamentally reconceptualize the nature of the state. The top-down solutions and centralized welfare state solutions to social problems are seen as a dead end. The rejection of the welfare state and the substitution of community suggest a radically redefined role of government in society. The state is not seen as the source of social welfare but as a vehicle for community empowerment and local control. The state is the source of capital and law that enables people to solve their problems at the level of the community.[82] Government validates new community-generated solutions, provides institutional legitimization of community, and acts as a financial sponsor of community projects either directly or by means of third party social organizations.

Transformation of Public Life

Postmodern social movements challenge the "closed and settled" questions of modern liberal politics and the "frozen decisions" that constitute complex organizational megastructures. Postmodern social movements are "transforming agents of political life,"[83] allowing for new understanding. New postmodern social movements struggle against interlocking megastructures that override the public interest. Megastructures assert that their solutions are the only ones possible, and they often hide their specific interests and their core of arbitrary power and oppression. New social movements reveal "what the system does not say about itself." They unmask the deception, paternalism, and violence that are often covert in modern society.

Culture Building

Postmodern social movements support the rights of people to frame and develop their own cultures and the need for people everywhere to construct their own social reality. Some see postmodern social movements as nonideological because they dismiss the old ideologies of capitalism and socialism, nationalism and imperialism, paternalism and colonialism. Participants engage in the process of defining new historical projects by reflecting on their own identities and by articulating values such as respect for the environment as an end in itself. They encourage people to resist becoming trapped in commodifying, dehumanizing social systems, and reject technological progress as an unqualified social good.[84]

THE POSTMODERN SOCIAL MOVEMENT PROCESS

The postmodern social movement process includes cognitive dissonance, shared perceptions and meanings, envisioning a new future, collective identity and submerged networks, and moving to action.

Cognitive Dissonance

Social learning begins with experience. We all seek positive, harmonious experiences, but our negative experiences tend to be the most important and valuable. Negative experiences are those in which some injury occurs, an injustice is felt, a trust is betrayed, or a loss is sustained. We are shaken out of our everyday routines. Our normal way of thinking becomes disturbed. Something altogether new enters the picture that requires our understanding and integration. It is out of socially negative experiences that personal growth, social learning, and value choices often occur.

More important, however, when we encounter betrayal, loss, and deceit in our engagement with the megastructures of the modern project, we experience discontinuities out of which postmodern social movements form. These discontinuities are called cognitive dissonance. Cognitive dissonance is the perception that current ways of thinking, belief systems, and structures are not congruent with the way things ought to be, the feeling that "there is something wrong here." For example, if we expect to be treated personally in our encounters with modern organizations and experience dehumanization and impersonality instead, our experience of social reality becomes problematic and begs for resolution. When such experiences are compounded daily, they add up to a generalized disenchantment with the premises on which modernity rests and eventually promote a need to change our social environment. Over time we may generate a feeling that modernity has outlived its usefulness, that it overextended itself and is becoming destructive to the human condition.

Shared Perceptions and Meanings

In a social movement, the "personal grievances that we experience in our everyday lives become translated into a collective sense of injustice."[85] This commonality forms an arena of opportunity to restructure the social world and align it more closely with a new perception of the human condition. As we collectively talk about our common experiences of alienation and apathy, the dissonance caused by passive individualism becomes the tool for its own correction.

We link the structured practices of social life with the collective action of a social movement through the intermediate step of face-to-face interaction and meaning construction. We define the social discontinuities that we experience. We attach them to concepts. We give them names and labels. As we articulate our feelings, we often ask one another, "What do these experiences mean?" While we may not have all of the facts, we intuitively reach for deeper meaning and come to some consensus. When we explore our understanding of social policies in relation to our new understanding of truth and congruence with meaning, we intuitively recognize that certain policies are basically wrong and in need of correction. We assert our common refusal to accept such policies or the premises on which they are based.

Envisioning a New Future

New visions, hopes, dreams, and the values they embody begin to become real. Envisioning future possibilities begins a process of understanding and conceptualizing a different worldview and the construction of a new social reality. Imagination produces alternative possibilities that may not currently exist, but if we stretch our perceptions, we can see beyond present reality. We imagine a future that is different, more congruent, and more aligned with the truth of the human condition.

Collective Identity and Submerged Networks

From the initial experience of injustice to the perception of cognitive dissonance, reflection, and agreed-upon shared meanings in close face-to-face interaction, we develop a strong emotional investment that encourages us to share in a collective identity. These new collective identities are formed during an incubation period by means of submerged networks out of view of the public eye. The submerged network is a system of small groups of people who experiment with new definitions of their situation, alternative perceptions of the world, different societal truths and cultural norms, and new ways of thinking.

These postmodern movement groups are not special interest groups like modern social movements that compete in the political arena for policy consideration. They are like a cognitive territory or a new conceptual space filled with dynamic interaction. As groups and organizations interact in those conceptual spaces, they form the collective identity of a postmodern social movement organization.[86]

Leaders and members work to give permanence to this collective identity. At a certain point, however, movement organizations take on a further dimension as different forms of association carve out an actual societal space together. They transform what began as interpersonal interests into interorganizational concerns and then define themselves in wider social terms.

Action

Social engagement in new social movement organizations is ultimately action oriented. It includes a goal and tactics and a strategy for collective action to resolve shared grievances. It is action that cements social thinking into new social forms. When postmodern groups come out into the open, they confront political authority and proclaim opposition against the decision-making logic and values that result in specific policies.[87] Postmodern movements act as a medium that reveals to the rest of society the connection between a specific problem and the logic that dominates the system. Members proclaim that alternative cultural models are possible, specifically those that they already display and practice by means of their collective action.

CONCLUSION

Social activism has a long, rich, and successful history in the United States and Canada. It continues to be a strong and viable means of social change as social problems become entrenched in the economic and political institutions of our society. Modern social movements, often assisted by macro social workers, have helped bring many collective groups of people to share in the benefits of modernity: immigrants, people of color, women, laborers, children, and others. However, just as macro social workers at the turn of the 20th century engaged in major social reform, macro social workers at the turn of 21st century face another challenge.

We are in the early stages of an entirely new and unprecedented era, the outlines of which are still not entirely clear. But what is becoming increasingly understood is that the new postmodern era will not merely reform modernity—it will supercede it. It will usher in new ways of social thinking, new forms of communality, new social identities, and new forms of social consciousness. New postmodern social movements will be one of the major means by which this new era will be born, and macro social workers such as yourselves who are perceptive social actors will have an opportunity to be at the center of these changes.

KEY CONCEPTS

modern social
  movements
postmodern social
  movements
modern social action
postmodern social
  action
community and social
  movements

models of social change
organization deviance
  model of social
  change
U.S. school for
  terrorism
institutional deviance
  model of social
  change

systems deviance model
  of social change
labor movement
Knights of Labor
American Federation
  of Labor (AFL)
Samuel Gompers
Great Homestead
  Strike
Henry Clay Frick
Clayton Act of 1914
Mary Harris "Mother"
  Jones
Railway Labor Act of
  1926
Norris LaGuardia Act of
  1932
National Labor
  Relations Act of 1935
National Labor
  Relations Board
  (NLRB)
Congress of Industrial
  Organizations (CIO)
Taft Hartley Act of 1947
AFL-CIO
international labor
abolition movement
Anti-Slavery Society
Frederick Douglass
Harriet Tubman
Fugitive Slave Act
Dred Scott decision
John Brown
Civil War
progressive movement
charities and corrections
  movement
temperance movement
Women's Christian
  Temperance Union
  (WCTU)
Anti-Saloon League

Eighteenth Amendment
  to the Constitution,
  1919
prohibition
woman's suffrage
  movement
Elizabeth Cady
  Stanton
Susan B. Anthony
Carrie Chapman Catt
National American
  Women's Suffrage
  Association
  (NAWSA)
Nineteenth Amendment
  to the Constitution,
  1920
Settlement House
  movement
Betha Capen Reynolds
civil rights movement
National Association for
  the Advancement of
  Colored People
  (NAACP)
W. E. B. Dubois
National Urban League
Booker T. Washington
Congress of Racial
  Equality (CORE)
freedom riders
sit-in demonstrations
James Farmer
A. Philip Randolph
Executive Order 8802
Thurgood Marshall
*Brown v. Board of
  Education of Topeka*
Whitney M. Young Jr.
Southern Christian
  Leadership
  Conference (SCLC)
Montgomery Bus
  Boycott of 1955

Martin Luther King Jr.

Malcolm X

Student Nonviolent
    Coordinating
    Committee (SNCC)

Civil Rights Act of 1964

welfare rights
    movement

George Wiley

National Welfare Rights
    Organization (NWRO)

unfreezing

resistance to change

strategies

active non-cooperation

exposure of perpetrators

information campaigns

public relations

legal action

injunctions

discovery

lawsuits

satyagraha

e-activism

direct confrontation

tactics

rallies

marches

picketing

symbolic
    demonstrations

prayer vigils

boycotts

threats and reprisals

Toyohiko Kagawa

move to action

management of social
    change

life cycle of social
    change

refreeze: solidify change

modernity

limitations of modern
    social action

postmodernity

social cultural model of
    change

women's liberation
    movement

feminism

Equal Rights
    Amendment (ERA)

National Organization
    for Women (NOW)

peace movement

environmental
    movement

characteristics of
    postmodern social
    movements

postmodern social
    action process

cognitive dissonance

shared perceptions and
    meanings

envision the future

collective identity

submerged networks

action

QUESTIONS FOR DISCUSSION

1. What is the modern era, and what are some of its
   leading ideologies, prominent values, and most
   important structures?

2. What is the postmodern era? What are some of
   its leading ideologies, values, and most prominent structures?

3. What is the difference between modern social
   movements and postmodern social movements?

4. Describe two of the most notable modern
   social movements. Why do you consider them
   "modern"?

5. Describe two postmodern social movements.
   Why do you consider them "postmodern"?

6. The opening narrative asserts that the turning
   point in the history of social movements was the
   shift in thinking by Martin Luther King Jr. as he
   broadened his vision from wanting African
   Americans to "get in" on the benefits of modernity to protesting against modernity's fundamental defects. Comment on this assertion and its
   implications for the future of social work.

7. Chose a social movement that occurred in the
   decade of the 1960s and answer these questions
   about it:

   Who were some of the major figures associ-
      ated with the movement?
   What issues caused people to engage in mass
      action?
   What were the goals of the movement?
   What major events or activities are identified
      with the movement?
   What kind of social action did those sup-
      porting the movement use to achieve its
      goals?
   To what extent was the movement either suc-
      cessful in reaching its goals or in mak-
      ing an impact and shifting our values
      and ways of thinking?

ADDITIONAL READING

Verba, Sidney, Kay Lehman Schlozman, and Henry E.
    Brady. *Voice and Equality: Civic Voluntarism in
    American Politics*. Cambridge, Mass.: Harvard Uni-
    versity Press. 1995.

Theory of Social Movements

Eyerman, Ron and Andrew Jamison. *Social Movements: A
    Cognitive Approach*. Cambridge: Polity Press, 1991.

Larana, Enrique, Hank Johnston, and Joseph R. Gusfield,
    eds. *New Social Movements: From Ideology to Iden-
    tity*. Philadelphia: Temple University Press, 1994.

Lowe, Stuart. *Urban Social Movements: The City After
    Castells*. London: Macmillan, 1986.

Lyman, Stanford M., ed. *Social Movements: Critiques, Concepts, Case-Studies.* Washington Square, NY: New York University Press, 1995.

McAdam, Doug, John D. McCarthy, and Mayer N. Zald. *Comparative Perspectives on Social Movements: Political Opportunities, Mobilizing Structures, and Cultural Framing.* New York: Cambridge University Press, 1996.

Morris, Aldon and Carol McClung Mueller, eds. *Frontiers of Social Movement Theory.* New Haven and London: Yale University Press, 1992.

Moyer, B. *The Movement Action Plan: A Strategic Framework Describing the Eight Stages of a Successful Social Movement.* San Francisco: Social Movement Empowerment Project, 1987.

Oberschall, Anthony. *Social Movements: Ideologies, Interests, and Identities.* New Brunswick, NJ: Transaction, 1993.

Tarrow, Sidney. *Power in Movement: Social Movements, Collective Action, and Politics.* Cambridge, UK and New York: Cambridge University Press. 1994.

Teske, Nathan. *Political Activists in America: The Identity Construction Model of Political Participation.* Cambridge, UK and New York: Cambridge University Press, 1997.

Zald, Mayer N. and John D. McCarthy. *Social Movements in an Organizational Society.* New Brunswick, NJ: Transaction, 1987.

Zirakzadeh, Cyrus Ernesto. *Social Movements in Politics: A Comparative Study.* New York: Longman, 1997.

Practice of Social Activism

Reeser, L. *Professionalism and Activism in Social Work.* New York: Columbia University Press, 1990.

Bobo, Kim, Jackie Kendall, and Steve Max. *Organizing for Social Change: A Manual for Activists in the 1990s,* 2d ed. Santa Ana, CA: Seven Locks Press, 1996.

Boyte, Harry, Heather Booth, and Steve Max. *Citizen Action and the New American Populism.* Philadelphia: Temple University Press, 1986.

Huenefeld, John. *The Community Activist's Handbook: A Guide to Organizing, Financing, and Publicizing Community Campaigns.* Boston: Beacon, 1970.

Civil Rights Movement

Carmichael, Stokely and Charles V. Hamilton. *Black Power: The Politics of Liberation in America.* New York: Random House, 1967.

Garrow, David J. *Bearing the Cross: Martin Luther King Jr. and the Southern Christian Leadership Conference.* New York: William Morrow, 1986.

King, Martin Luther, Jr. *Stride Toward Freedom: The Montgomery Story.* New York: Ballantine, 1958.

Morris, A. *Origins of the Civil Rights Movement.* New York: Free Press/Macmillan, 1984.

Parris, G. and L. Brooks. *Blacks in the City: A History of the National Urban League.* Boston: Little, Brown, 1971.

Whitman, Alden. *American Reformers.* New York: H. W. Wilson, 1985.

X, Malcolm. *Autobiography of Malcolm X.* New York: Ballantine Books, 1981.

Environmental Movement

Carson, Rachel. *The Silent Spring.* Boston: Houghton Mifflin, 1962.

Piller, Charles. *The Failsafe Society: Community Defiance and the End of American Technological Optimism.* New York: Basic Books, 1991.

Labor Movement

Bernstein, Irving. *The Turbulent Years: A History of the American Worker, 1933–1941.* Boston: Houghton Mifflin, 1971.

Gordon, David M., Richard Edwards, and Michael Reich. *Segmented Work, Divided Workers: The Historical Transformation of Labor in the United States.* New York: Cambridge University Press, 1982.

Seidman, Joel. *American Labor from Defense to Reconversion.* Chicago: University of Chicago Press, 1953.

Taft, Philip. *Organized Labor in American History.* New York: Harper and Row, 1964.

Ware, Norman J. *The Labor Movement in the United States, 1860–1895.* New York: Vintage, 1964.

The Progressive Movement

Hofstadter, Richard. *The Age of Reform.* New York: Knopf, 1965.

Lasch, Christopher. *The New Radicalism in America, 1889–1963.* New York: Knopf, 1965.

Weinstein, James. *The Corporate Ideal in the Liberal State, 1900–1918.* Boston: Beacon, 1968.

Kolko, Gabriel. *The Triumph of Conservatism.* New York: Free Press, 1963.

Student Protest Movement

Miller, James. *Democracy Is in the Streets: From Port Huron to the Siege of Chicago.* Cambridge, MA: Harvard University Press, 1994.

Tenant Movement

Lawson, R. and M. Naison, eds. *The Tenant Movement in New York City, 1904–1984.* New Brunswick, NJ: Rutgers University Press, 1986.

Welfare Rights Movement

Delgado, Gary. *Organizing the Movement: The Roots and Growth of ACORN.* Philadelphia: Temple University Press, 1986.

Diamond, J. *For Crying Out Loud: Women and Poverty in the U.S.* New York: Pilgrim, 1986.

Hertz, S. H. *The Welfare Mothers Movement: A Decade of Change for Poor Women.* Nadham, MD: University Press, 1981.

Kurzman, Paul A. *The Mississippi Experience: Strategies for Welfare Rights Action.* New York: Association Press, 1971.

Piven, Frances Fox and Richard A. Cloward. *Poor People's Movements.* New York: Pantheon, 1977.

Pope, J. *Biting the Hand That Feeds Them: Organizing Women on Welfare at the Grass Roots Level.* New York: Praeger, 1989.

Women's Movement

Colt, Nancy F. and Elizabeth H. Pleck, eds., *A Heritage of Her Own.* New York: Simon and Schuster, 1979.

Evans, Sara. *Personal Politics: The Roots of Women's Liberation in the Civil Rights Movement and the New Left.* New York: Random House, 1980.

Flexner, Eleanor. *Centuries of Struggle.* New York: Atheneum, 1972.

Kaplan, Temma. *Crazy for Democracy: Women in Grassroots Movements.* New York: Routledge, 1997.

History of Social Movements and Social Protest

Allen, Robert. *Reluctant Reformers: Racism and Social Reform Movements in the United States.* Washington, DC: Howard University Press, 1983.

Anderson, Terry H. *The Movement and the Sixties: Protest in America from Greensboro to Wounded Knee.* New York: Oxford University Press, 1995.

Anderson, Walter. *The Age of Protest.* Pacific Palisades, CA: Goodyear, 1989.

Goldberg, Robert A. *Grassroots Resistance: Social Movements in Twentieth Century America.* Belmont, CA: Wadsworth, 1991.

Sinclair, Upton. *The Cry for Justice: An Anthology of the Literature of Social Protest.* New York: Lyle Stuart, 1964.

Walters, Ronald G. *American Reformers: 1815–1860.* New York: Hill and Wang, 1978.

Progressive Social Work

Davis, Allen F. *Spearheads of Reform: The Social Settlements and the Progressive Movement, 1890–1914.* New York: Oxford University Press, 1968.

Simon, B. "Rethinking Empowerment." *Journal of Progressive Human Services*, 1(1), 1990, pp. 27–39.

Simon, B. *The Empowerment Tradition in American Social Work.* New York: Columbia University Press, 1994.

Related Works

Freire, Paulo. *Pedagogy of the Oppressed.* New York: Continuum, 1992.

Ingram, Catherine. *In the Footsteps of Gandhi: Conversations With Spiritual Social Activists.* Berkeley, CA: Parallax Press, 1990.

Schaper, Donna. *A Book of Common Power: Narratives Against the Current.* San Diego, CA: Lura Media, 1989.

Timmon, Milne Wallis. *Satyagraha: The Gandhian Approach to Nonviolent Social Change.* Northampton, MA: Pittenbrauch Press, 1995.

Journal Articles

Epstein, Barbara. "Rethinking Social Movement Theory." *Socialist Review*, 90, January–March 1990, pp. 35–66.

Kitschelt, Herbert P. "Political Opportunity Structures and Political Protest: Anti-Nuclear Movements in Four Democracies." *British Journal of Political Science*, 1986, pp. 16, 57–85.

Meyer, D. S. "Protest Cycles and Political Process: American Peace Movements in the Nuclear Age." *Political Research Quarterly,* 46(3), 1993, pp. 451–479.

Meyer, D. S. and S. Staggenborg. "Movements, Countermovements, and the Structure of Political Opportunity." *American Journal of Sociology,* 101(6), 1996, pp. 1628–1660.

15

The Practice of Social Work at the Global Level

Exploitation

When one third of the world's population consumes two thirds of the world's resources and then exhorts others to do as they, it is little short of a hoax. Development, it turns out, is all too often a euphemism for exploitation, another form of colonialism.

Norberg-Hodge[1]

Power

Our awesome power is deployed to defend the rights of capital and commerce, but not human rights and people exploited by the global system.

William Greider[2]

Ownership

Just because you own the land doesn't mean you own the people.

Philippine land reform saying[3]

Ideas in This Chapter

In the arms trade, developed nations that sell the weapons are the only ones who win. In 2001, more than 300,000 children under 18 were fighting in conflicts in 41 countries around the world.

OUR GLOBAL SOCIETY IN PERSPECTIVE

If we could shrink the earth's population to a village of precisely 100 people, with all the existing human ratios remaining the same:

57 Asians

21 Europeans

14 from the Western Hemisphere, both north and south

8 Africans

52 would be female

48 would be male

70 would be non-White

30 would be White

70 would be non-Christian

30 would be Christian

89 would be heterosexual

11 would be homosexual

6 (all from the United States) would possess 59% of the world's wealth

80 would live in substandard housing

50 would suffer from malnutrition

1 would have a college education

1 would own a computer

70 would be unable to read or write

If you have food in the refrigerator, clothes on your back, a roof overhead, and a place to sleep, you are richer than 75% of the world's people. If you have money in the bank, in your wallet, and spare change in a dish someplace, you are among the top 8% of the world's wealthy. If you woke up this morning with more health than illness, you are more blessed than the million who will not survive this week. If your parents are still alive and still married, you are very rare, even in the United States and Canada. If you have never experienced the danger of battle, the loneliness of imprisonment, the agony of torture, or the pangs of starvation, you are more fortunate than 500 million people in our global society.

WHAT YOU WILL LEARN IN THIS CHAPTER

On every continent and in virtually every nation, international macro social workers engage the most difficult social problems people face. In this chapter you will explore the practice of macro social work in the poorest nations of the world. You will explore a brief history of social work at the international level, and you will learn about global social problems. You will discover that modern development, which has produced affluence, political liberty, and technological advances in North America, Japan, and Europe, has failed to replicate those achievements in many of the world's more impoverished nations.

You will learn how indigenous people are using grassroots social movement organizations to shape their own identities, construct their cultures, and take ownership of their lives. You will discover that this worldwide movement is comprised of tens of thousands of new social organizations, spread throughout almost every nation of the world, and on an immensely wider scale than is occurring in North America. You will explore how you, as an international macro social worker, can assist members of the world's poor and destitute nations strengthen their communities, overcome poverty, and engage in social change on a global scale. You will learn, however, that social workers in North America have tended to neglect international social problems and ignore our global interconnections.

WHAT IS THE PRACTICE OF MACRO SOCIAL WORK AT THE GLOBAL LEVEL?

The South African term "ubuntu" refers to the spirit of community. It is a shortened version of a Xhosa saying that means, "I am a person through other people. . . . My humanity is tied to yours." This is probably the single most important aspect of living in a highly connected planet: Our lives, whether we are aware of it or not, are tied together. We must respect each other, and we must always keep our interconnection in mind.[4]

Globalization means that actions in one part of the world affect people in other areas. Macro social workers are one among many other professions including teachers, health professionals, ecologists, and employees of international NGOs who work to improve the global social environment. International social workers may assist with community and economic development projects in underdeveloped nations, although indigenous community members themselves conduct much of this grassroots work today. We work in the area of international refugee and relief services with the Red Cross, CARE, and others. We assist numbers of child welfare and other human service organizations that struggle against particular social problems such as child slavery, trafficking in persons, violence, and oppression of women. We work with international social justice organizations such as Amnesty International to combat torture, imprisonment, and other human rights violations. We become engaged at the policy level to help bring about humane international cooperation among nations to help reduce pollution, end international conflict, and reduce weapons production and sales. We are active in social movements aimed at creating a sustainable natural and social environment, and we work to end exploitation and economic injustice.

A BRIEF HISTORY OF INTERNATIONAL SOCIAL WORK

The history of international social work has been most prominent in international community development, work with international NGOs, refugee and relief social work, and social work education.

Origins of International Community Development and Relief: 1800–1899

Ward Goodenough says that the earliest international community development efforts were church related.[5] The first international community developers were Christian, Hindu, and Buddhist missionaries.[6] Western missionaries have been criticized for trying to destroy tribal culture by superimposing Western values, culture, and religion on traditional communities, but this criticism has often been too extreme, asserts Roland Oliver.[7] Although the major aims of missionaries were evangelism and conversion, many soon realized that improving the living conditions of their converts was inseparable from their religious goals. Missionaries pioneered in establishing experimental pilot community development projects to discover appropriate methods of assisting indigenous people. One of the earliest community development efforts, for example, was a mission program begun in 1838 that organized and conducted day schools, model farms, and normal schools for emancipated slaves in the British West Indies.[8]

Gradually, however, Chau and Hodge report, "community development efforts of the missions became intertwined with community development efforts of the colonial government."[9] In this combined effort, the British "set up in each territory a pilot project to experiment with a comprehensive and intensive program of rural betterment and experiment with a team of technical offices and missionaries to try to combine efforts in a single unified program."[10]

International humanitarian organizations including the Foreign Anti-Slavery Society in London (1823), the World Evangelical Alliance, (1846), and the World Alliance of Young Men's Christian Associations (1855) contributed to early international concern, assistance, and understanding,[11] and the numbers of these organizations continued to increase in the second half of the 19th century. The International Red Cross (1863–1880), for example, sponsored the first relief and refugee services to victims of international conflict and natural disasters. Clara Barton of the American Red Cross offered her services under the Red Cross of Geneva and was present during nearly every battle of the Franco-Prussian War. During the war she helped establish hospitals, organized assistance for women and child refugees, and distributed money and clothing to more than 30,000 destitute people. Barton carried relief to the people of Russia during the Russian Famine of 1891 and to Turkey during the Armenian massacre of 1896.

Social Work Education and Community Development: 1900–1945

International Social Work Education   At the turn of the 20th century, social work education began in England, Germany, the United States, and Canada as social agencies and charities created local training programs with the goal of meeting the agencys' local personnel needs. Some local schools of social work were established in the United States, but most of these were aimed mainly at dealing with the immediate needs of urban immigrants and those in poverty. Only Jane Addams and her associates in the social settlement movement believed that world peace and disarmament were suitable goals for social work, a view shared by some of Addams's European counterparts. By 1914 there were fewer than 30 schools or training programs in social work worldwide, but an upsurge in social welfare development in industrialized countries occurred to assist with refugees and victims of World War I and as social welfare legislation in European countries expanded.[12]

International social work education struggled for a foothold in the decade of the 1930s. In 1935 the first school of social work in India opened its doors. It was founded by Clifford Manshardt, an American protestant missionary, with financing from the Sir Doraabji Taqta Trust.[13] German state schools of social work were begun in Berlin under the leadership of social worker Alice Solomon during the 1920s and 1930s, but they were decimated or destroyed when the Nazis came to power.

International Community Development

During this same period, the experiences of British, German, French, and American missionaries in third world colonial regions resulted in a growing understanding of community development work. In 1923 an international missionary conference brought together missionaries from several countries to share information and explore community development principles. The result was a report by the Advisory Committee on Native Education in tropical Africa, "often regarded as the original foundation of modern community development."[14] This committee recommended that community development should

> render the individual more efficient in his or her condition of life, . . . and promote the advancement of the community as a whole through the improvement of agriculture, development of native industries, improvement of health, training of people in management of their own affairs, and the inculcation of true ideals of citizenship and service. It must include the raising up of capable, trustworthy, public-spirited leaders of the people.[15]

The term "community development" was first used in 1928 by the International Missionary Council. The council defined its methods, its focus, and its principles, which continue to be relevant today. They included the following: (1) preserving all of the permanent values of indigenous family systems; (2) renewing and giving major attention to the role of women; (3) fellowshipping, building, and ministering to the whole life of the community; (4) assisting in education by means of local schools; (5) developing economic and social voluntary organizations and training in self-government; and (6) promoting relationships with government.[16]

Nongovernmental Organizations

By 1920 about 1,000 international nongovernmental organizations (NGOs) had been founded. In addition, between 1921 and 1945 the League of Nations created a number of organizations to help resolve the increasingly important international refugees problem.[17]

The Rise of the Global Market: 1945–1970

The period between World War II and the 1970s was qualitatively different from previous postwar periods, an interregnum between the age of competing imperial powers and the coming of the global economy. The United States emerged as the leading world power, and a surge of interest in international social concerns resulted in the formation of the United Nations and its involvement in community development and refugee and relief services. Developed nations inserted international governmental organizations (IGOs) into the affairs of former colonies, including the World Trade Organization, the International Monetary Fund (IMF), and the World Bank. The world market society became a confirmed reality. Nongovernmental organizations achieved recognition that was long overdue. International social work education continued to expand.

Supremacy of the United States

The United States was the only nation strengthened as a result of World War II. The other industrial powers emerged either defeated, economically exhausted, or indebted to the United States. U.S. corporate interests, whose production increased dramatically during the war, were poised to continue their growth internationally by "opening new markets for themselves and laying the groundwork for a single world economy of competing capitals."[18] The U.S. goal was to export its version of "modern development" to conquered and colonized nations alike, particularly but not exclusively on behalf of its own corporate interests, and to remake the entire global civilization in its own image. Modern development included rationalizing and modernizing "backward" underdeveloped nations and inducing them to accept a capitalistic economy and a representative democratic style of government, or at the very least be willing to cooperate economically and politically with the United States as its chief spokesperson and sponsor.

The United Nations

The United Nations, "dominated by the United States, was formed as a supranational quasi-government that provided the political, economic and to less extent, the social foundation for the new internationalism."[19] While the World War II allies worked to create a global community of nations, they also ensured that they would control the new system, limit the role of nongovernmental organizations, engage in refugee and relief work and, most important, establish a global economic network.

Control Instead of equal power sharing and dispersal of power among all nations, the United States and the other victorious powers determined that the poor nations would have no say in how the world was run. Britain, Russia, France, China, and the United States—all permanent members of the UN security council—each has the power of veto not only over decisions concerning peace and war but also over all attempts to amend or review the UN charter. Even if every other nation in the world demanded change, the United States or any one of the other four permanent members could block it.[20]

Limited Role of Nongovernmental Organizations At the Founding Conference of the United Nations in San Francisco on April 25, 1945, 42 U.S. humanitarian NGOs participated as official advisers and 240 others enjoyed "observer status," far outnumbering the delegations from national states. Despite this level of interest, the Soviet Union preferred that NGOs restrict their role to social and economic concerns rather than becoming involved in central political or security issues.[21]

The "most developed" nations of the world, supported by the United Nations, understood that nations emerging from colonization would be critical strategic political and economic resources in the new economic world order. Rather than permit independent religious and human service NGOs to assist those developing nations create their own political and economic cultures, the developed industrial powers assumed major responsibility for national and community development of poorer nations. This ensured that their progress conformed to the interests of Western democratic politics and the emerging free global market.

Refugee and Relief The ravages of World War II increased the need for refugee and relief services. Large numbers of persons were displaced, primarily children who lacked shelter, food, and clothing. In 1947 the UN established the International Children's Emergency Fund (UNICEF) to help displaced children and the International Refugee Organization (IRO) to protect the 21 million refugees scattered over Europe. In 1951 the United Nations High Commissioner for Relief (UNHCR) replaced the IRO with the mandate to coordinate refugee protection worldwide as one of the main functions of the UN.

International Governmental Organizations In 1944 under U.S. auspices, the future permanent members of the UN held a conference at Bretton Woods and established the basis for an international monetary system. They created an exchange rate mechanism by setting the parities of national currencies against the U.S. dollar.[22] Three major global economic networks, also known as international governmental organizations (IGOs), affiliated with the United Nations were established: the World Trade Organization (WTO), the International Monetary Fund (IMF), and the World Bank. By 1970 the IGOs had developed structural adjustment programs (SAPs) to ensure compliance by less developed nations with their rules.

World Trade Organization: The World Trade Organization, by means of the General Agreement on Trade and Tariffs (GATT), worked to improve the general world economy by increasing the flow of capital between nations, reducing protective trade barriers between nations, stimulating open trade, and reducing national debt.

International Monetary Fund: The world's major industrial nations assumed that economic development in their former colonies was compatible with their economic interests and enterprises. The IMF was created to promote world commerce by stabilizing foreign exchange, fostering international trade agreements, and serving the interests of expanding transnational corporations.[23] It was and continues to be responsible for monitoring exchange rates, setting the terms for nations that in the IMF's judgment require economic stabilization, and applying economic pressure on nations to change failing economic policies.[24]

World Bank: The World Bank provides long-term, low-interest loans exceeding $15 billion annually to build dams for power and irrigation, develop industry, build roads and utilities, and engage in agriculture projects in less developed nations. Catherine Caulfield explains that the bank is the biggest single lender to the third world. It holds more than 11% of the third world's long-term foreign debt, public and private. The bank also decides how loans will be spent. It proposes, designs, and oversees implementation of projects it funds, and the bank requires its borrowers to adopt economic and other domestic policies it considers conducive to successful development.[25]

Structural adjustment programs: As a condition of refinancing, maintaining their credit, and assuring that their currency is internationally acceptable, World Bank and IMF impose a variety of demands on debtor nations. They may ask that nations in debt to the World Bank make loan repayment their national priority. The IMF may demand that debtor nations increase foreign currency reserves by eliminating restrictions on their imports and exports,[26] use their land and capital to produce goods for export rather than for their own consumption, import Western products for their own use, or raise prices for domestic goods and services while reducing wages for labor.

By the early 1970s the three major international government organizations had broadened their powers. IMF and World Bank, for example, developed mandatory austerity requirements called structural adjustment programs (SAPs), which require that debtor nations provide tax breaks and incentives to corporations who want to relocate in their territories while terminating the land rights of peasant and indigenous peoples. They may demand that borrowing nations limit rules that require transnational corporations (TNCs) to protect workers health, safety, or the environment while simultaneously requiring governments to cut back on health services, education, housing, nutrition, and income maintenance for their citizens.[27] Structural adjustment programs also often require underdeveloped nations to devalue their currency, which may lead to rising prices on imports, lower wages, more unemployment, and even eventual bankruptcy. SAPs, asserts social worker Arline Prigoff, "are truly genocidal for indigenous and other subsistence cultures whose identity and way of life is based on relationship with the land."[28]

The policies of the IMF and World Bank, particularly their austerity programs, have met with resistance by those nations who are forced to conform to them. A report by the World Development Movement, for example, lists massive demonstrations in 23 nations in 2001 against the IMF's austerity programs and forced privatizations. In spite of this pressure, however, IGOs are powerless to unilaterally change the policies by which they operate. According to George Monbiot, altering the constitution of the World Bank or the IMF requires an 85% vote of member nations of the UN. The United States alone possesses 17% of the votes: It can stop any measure proposed by other nations, however desperately needed. Unsurprisingly, the rich nations use this power to run other countries for the benefit of their merchant banks.[29]

The Rise of Transnational Corporations and International Nongovernmental Organizations

As the three IGOs proceeded to develop a Western economic mentality in third world nations, decolonization neared completion. Except for socialist nations such as the U.S.S.R. and China, the entire globe was opened to free markets, and the world became subject to the capitalist mode of production. National corporations became multinational corporations (MNCs) as they shifted profits and operations to less developed nations where the advantages of taxation, wages, or state support were greatest. Increasing numbers of these multinational corporations transformed themselves into transnational corporations (TNCs), in which a parent organization may own and operate many multinational corporations around the globe, carrying out business in different forms and across several nations.[30]

Business-oriented international nongovernmental organizations (INGOs) including commercial, trade, agricultural, and professional coalitions, increased about threefold. By the end of the 1970s, there was hardly an aspect of national life in industrial countries that was not addressed in some way by a supranational body,[31] including IGOs, TNCs, and business-oriented INGOs. The system of highly integrated world trade was an irreversible fact, confirmed and hastened by the increased speed of transportation and the electronic revolution of computers in communication.[32]

CORPORATE SLASH AND BURN

At a workshop Dara Silverman showed how globalization affects people locally. She described how a rural family from the Dominican Republic in Central America ended up in Worcester, Massachusetts. Several years before, a U.S. company, Converse Industries, having exhausted its opportunities for cheap labor at home, relocated to a small town in the Dominican Republic where labor was cheaper, destroying the local agrarian economy in the process. When the company left for greener pastures a few years later, the result was a mass migration to the United States due to a lack of employment opportunities in their hometown. The acquisitive self-interest of Converse, having caused economic disruption in the Dominican Republic, has also changed the community of Worcester.

Nongovernmental Organizations   Independent countries in Africa and Asia tended to share the distrust many socialist countries had for nongovernmental organizations until the watershed period of the early 1970s. As attitudes toward NGOs began to change, NGOs received increased informal acceptance in the United Nations. In the 1970s the U.S. Congress promoted a "new directions" humanitarian image for its foreign aid programs and espoused a basic human needs approach to development assistance to counteract the negative image of U.S. activities abroad. Congress asserted that NGOs were the ideal conduit for delivering humanitarian aid and development assistance.[33]

International Social Work Education   Social work education resumed its growth after World War II. Schools of social work began to be established in economically advanced countries as well as in the newly decolonized countries of the world. Japan, which had a few missionary-established schools of social welfare before 1941, increased their number. After the Korean War ended in 1953, South Korea began to open schools of social work. By 1960 about 800 schools of social work existed worldwide. During the decade of the 1960s, Taiwan established its first schools, 20 more schools of social work were established in South Africa, and social work education in North African countries began. Social work education, which had made a beginning in Eastern Europe before 1939 and immediately after 1945, was virtually eliminated, however, by the Communist regimes that took over after 1949 in Hungary, Czechoslovakia, and the Baltic states.

Increasing Growth of the Global Economy: 1980s

In the 1980s earlier trends toward the growth of the free market continued. The role of the IMF and World Bank continued to exert pressure on third world nations on behalf of transnational corporations, resulting in disastrous economic consequences including a weakening of national sovereignty for many developing countries. Social work education expanded.

Growth of the Free Market   The development of a world capitalist economy expanded. Markets in capital, commodities, and foreign exchange consolidated. Common markets and free trade areas embraced most of the countries of Europe and the less developed world. The hegemony of the world capitalist economy was given a boost with the demise of the Soviet Union and the entry of its member nations into the global free market.

Role of the IMF and World Bank   The IMF and the World Bank continued their goals of stabilizing world economies, preserving a balance of payments structure, and protecting the interests of wealthy nations for the benefit of large multinational corporations at the expense of third world debtor countries with weak market economies.[34] The World Bank and the International Monetary Fund lifted controls on investment in banking, telecommunications, and other services, opening new markets for global giants in these businesses. General Motors, for example, obtained liberal trade and investment policies. Global firms had a new freedom to pursue profits internationally. They convinced governments to take a general hands-off approach to corporate monopolies because they claimed megamergers were needed so that firms could compete in global markets.[35]

BLOOD FOR FOOD, BLOOD FOR DEATH

In the 1980s poor farmers in some parts of China were so desperate for income that they were reduced to selling their blood to companies who manufacture plasma and other health products from it. To increase their blood plasma productivity, many villagers transfused red blood cells back into their bodies after the plasma was separated. Entire towns entered into agreements to sell blood, but in an ironic but tragic twist their effort to survive has resulted in death for many. In the early 1990s, some of the blood became contaminated with AIDS as it was mixed and recycled back to donors. Entire villages were unknowingly infected, and AIDS spread from village to village. Those who became infected in the mid-1990s have now entered the peak of symptoms and death. However, the number of AIDS cases of blood sellers continues to grow in regions previously regarded as not seriously affected, and still other areas exist where HIV-positive blood sellers remain undiscovered.[36]

China is finally recognizing the problem. In 2004 the Health Ministry asked provinces to carry out a comprehensive search to "fully grasp" who sold blood, test them for HIV, and present a report by April 15, 2005. But for many of the estimated 170,000 AIDS infected blood donors, out of the total 840,000 AIDS patients in China, time may be running out.[37]

Effects of IMF and World Bank Policies

Gary Teeple asserts that income disparities, external debt, and rates of poverty, illiteracy, morbidity, and mortality grew throughout most of the nonindustrialized world in the 1980s.[38] Rural peasant groups as well as urban dwellers lost the traditional resource bases of their economies, a prelude to cultural and physical genocide leading to forced migration and displacement of these vulnerable populations.[39] There is incontrovertible evidence, asserts Prigoff and Teeple, that these trends were the consequences of the Western approach to "development," particularly the lending policies of the World Bank and the IMF,[40] which contributed to financial losses and a long-term drain on the economic potential of impoverished nation-states. Prigoff claims that "it would be difficult to overestimate negative outcomes of IMF and World Bank's international economic development projects especially in agricultural regions in Africa, Latin America and Asia."[41]

Weakening of Nation-States

The dominance of the global market has led to the transformation of power and sovereignty in poorer nation-states. Multilateral treaties, military pacts, economic control imposed by the three IGOs, and the interrelated dominance of business-oriented INGOs has influenced almost every aspect of economic activity as well as significant aspects of social and political life across the globe. Because of the increasing control of IGOs and INGOs in the global economy, and the economic strength and independence of TNCs, the power of individual underdeveloped nation-states to control their own interests was diluted. Many of these smaller, economically dependent states lost and continue to lose much of their sovereignty to international global powers. Increasingly during the 1980s, in fact, Gary Teeple says, multinational and transnational corporations assumed the powers of sovereign entities, ignoring and interfering in the interests of nation-states, particularly those with smaller and weaker economies.[42]

Social Work Education

During the decades of the 1970s and 1980s, schools of social work proliferated in Europe, Canada, and the United States, reaching 1,200 by the 1970s. By the mid-1980s India boasted 43 schools of social work.[43]

Increasing Influence of Nongovernmental Organizations: 1990s

During the 1990s NGOs achieved increased growth, influence, and recognition in policy making, becoming increasingly important actors on the world stage. Social work continued to expand internationally.

Growth of NGOs

As of 1996, 22,000 NGOs existed worldwide, promoting national or international social development,[44] and these NGOs are an accepted and increasingly integrated part of the international policy network. According to Anheier and Cunningham, they comprise the "basic ingredients of an emerging international society of social organizations."[45]

Influence In the last decade of the millennium and into the 21st century, the UN and many Western governments began to recognize the role NGOs play. They contribute to energizing civil society and strengthen democratic traditions in third world countries. Increasingly, the UN and Western governments are turning to NGOs rather than working directly through third world governments to promote local reforms, to institute building and engagement in the community, and to promote economic development.

Recognition in Policy Making In spite of this, NGOs continue to remain on a level of consultative status with specialized UN organizations only, and they have little substantive role within the UN in general. In this role, about 130 NGOs are linked with the World Health Organization (WHO), for example, and several hundred are tied into the UN news and information system.

In spite of these limitations, NGOs have made their influence felt outside the centers of UN decision making. NGOs "together with governmental and intergovernmental representatives, are part of a global inter-organizational network in which policies are discussed and formulated."[46] Nongovernmental organizations, and not the regular political channels of UN member states, brought most of the important global social and political issues of the 1990s to the attention of the UN and other international bodies. NGOs, for example, kept social and economic development, participative democracy, human rights, and the environment in the forefront of policy discussions during the 1990s. The 1992 United Nations Conference on Environment and Development (the first Earth Summit), in Rio De Janeiro, Brazil, was a direct result of NGO lobbying efforts. The summit included not only the largest ever gathering of heads of state (118) but more than 1,000 accredited member NGOs, the largest participation of NGOs ever in an international intergovernmental conference.

Social Work Education   Social work education continued to grow in the 1990s. By 1995, 1,600 schools of social work were listed in the International Association of Schools of Social Work (IASSW) directory, including more than 100 schools in the People's Republic of China and 50 schools in Russia.

Domination of the Free Global Market: 2000s

During the first 5 years of 2000, developed nations and transnational corporations cemented their dominance in the free global market and made new rules for economic trade, creating new markets in currency and foreign exchange. Except for a few nations, international social work education became nearly global in scope.

Cemented Dominance in the Global Market

Reforms to protect the environment and uphold health, safety, and employment standards brought by trade unions and social movements continued to be eroded or were completely eliminated as national jurisdictions succumbed to the demands of international corporations, commissions, and agencies. Laborers experienced greater structural and long-term unemployment, lower standards of living, increasing rates of poverty, restricted social security, weakened trade unions, and an ecosystem that had become pervasively degraded.[47]

Made New Rules   During the first decade of 2000, economies of developing countries continued to depend on labor-intensive products that can command high prices. Wealthy nations, however, make the rules, imposing duties, taxes, or tariffs on products from developing nations, thereby increasing their cost and reducing profit. Even though the United States imported 12 times more products in dollar terms from France than from Bangladesh in 2001, for example,

the United States charged Bangladesh more in import duties ($331 million) for its largely indigenous, handmade products than it charged France ($330 million).

Agriculture is another area in which developed nations impose inequitable and unfavorable rules on less developed nations. Agriculture in developing nations typically comprises between 17 and 35% of the entire gross domestic product (GDP) and is one of the major means by which indigenous citizens can sustain themselves. In contrast, agriculture in rich nations commands less than 3% of GDP and is primarily conducted by large, government-subsidized agribusinesses. When high-income countries tax imported food and subsidize their own farmers' production, they destroy markets in developing countries and hurt poor farmers who lack such protection.

At the September 2003 World Trade Organization (WTO) Conference in Cancún, Mexico, an alliance of developing countries challenged the agricultural subsidies and tariffs that were hurting them. A coalition of rich nations led by the United States, Japan, and France refused to reduce their agricultural tariffs in spite of the relatively small effect that such reduction would have had on their economies. Their refusal also destroyed a 2002 agreement to permit poorer countries to import "generic" copies of patented pharmaceuticals that would have opened the door to cheaper AIDS drugs for Africa.[48]

Currency and Foreign Exchange Markets   In the first 5 years of 2000, TNCs developed international markets in capital and foreign exchange, becoming the dominant force in economic relations between nations. These private international foreign exchange and currency markets allowed international businesses increased freedom from national government regulation. In fact, independent corporate markets, not national governments, were establishing rules over credit, money supply, exchange and interest rates, debt management, investment policies, and taxation,[49] usurping roles that had been the exclusive domain of sovereign nation-states.

Social Work Education   Today social work education exists on every continent and in almost all North and South American and European nations. Japan now maintains nearly 100 undergraduate and graduate programs in social welfare, including many at the doctoral level. In 2003 the Japan University of

Social Work opened Japan's first MSW program, ushering in the profession of social work in Japan. Social work education, however, continues to be absent in large parts of sub-Saharan Africa, several Southeast Asian nations including Thailand and the South Pacific Islands, and in some of the Asian republics of the former Soviet Union.[50]

BRAVE NEW MILLENNIUM: SOCIAL PROBLEMS IN OUR GLOBAL SOCIETY

Over the past several centuries, the forces of modernity have become international and now global in character, bringing wealth to many developed nations in Europe, North America, and Japan.[51] While people in developed nations have prospered, those in third world developing nations, which comprise 80% of the world's population, have not. People in many of these countries confront a seemingly endless list of social problems, including the population explosion, epidemic health problems, ethnic violence, political instability, corruption, lack of education and health care, and now AIDS.[52] Among the most important of these social problems are endemic poverty, slavery, the manufacturing of violence and international conflict, and destruction of the global ecosystem.

Poverty

Most of the people in developing nations face poverty as a consequence of international development. The few wealthy nations of the world are surrounded by many others that remain poor. The living standards of many people in impoverished nations are below the threshold of basic needs, and many lack purchasing power. They also lack clean water, medical care, and housing. Everyone in poor nations suffers, but the world's children are most severely affected by poverty.

Consequences of Development
For nearly half a millennium, indigenous peoples throughout the world have lived as aliens in their own land, as subjects of developed nations including Britain, Portugal, Spain, the Netherlands, Belgium, France, Germany, Japan, and the United States. Overt colonization generally came to an end after World War II, but economic exploitation continues unabated as the fabric of many former colonies continues to erode. "The past half-century of development has not profited the poorest people, nor the poorest countries," says C. Caulfield. "Rather, they have paid dearly—and their descendants will continue to pay dearly—for the disproportionately small benefits they have received."[53] The developmental paths of modern industrialized societies, in either their socialist or capitalist variants, have destroyed the economies of less developed nations, bringing massive and pervasive poverty to four fifths of the world's population.

AIDS

As many as 48 million workers may be killed by AIDS by 2010, and the toll could rise to 74 million by 2015, inflicting a body blow to national economics, the UN International Labour Organization (UNILO) warned July 11, 2004, the opening day of the 15th and largest International AIDS Conference in Bankok. The analysis, "'HIV/AIDS and Work: Global Estimates, Impact and Response" covers 50 countries.

In 2001, 40 nations had an estimated HIV prevalence of more than 2% of their population. By the end of 2001, India had an estimated 3.8 million HIV carriers. Today, five countries, including South Africa, China and India, each have a million people or more infected with HIV. It is estimated that by 2010 China alone will have a population of 10 million HIV-positive citizens.[54]

The worst situations are in African countries south of the Sahara where the highest concentration of AIDS exists: 70% of world's total, with an estimated total of nearly 30 million people infected by the virus. In 2002 the number of people HIV-positive increased by 5 million throughout the world and by 3.5 million in Africa alone.[55]

In addition, a 2004 report titled *Children on the Brink 2004,* co-authored by the United Nations AIDS agency, UNICEF, and the U.S. Agency for International Development (USAID), asserted that AIDS orphans in sub-Saharan Africa will top 18 million in 2010, up from 15 million in 2003, and 11.5 million in 2001. By 2010 it will also have orphaned an additional 5 million children elsewhere in the world. AIDS threatens a "tidal wave" of death, affecting children worldwide. In sub-Saharan Africa, 3.8 million children have lost one or both parents to AIDS since 2000. In the region's 11 worst hit countries, one in seven children are orphans, and by 2010, 6% of all children in Africa will have lost at least one parent to AIDS. Even if by some miracle the spread of HIV is stopped today, the number of orphans would still rise because parents who are HIV-positive will continue die in the next few years.

HIV/AIDS is not only a human crisis, it is "a threat to sustainable global, social, and economic development" asserted Juan Somavia, Director general of the UN International Labour Organization. "The loss of life and the debilitating effects of the illness will lead not only to a reduced capacity to sustain production and employment, an increase in poverty, but will be a burden borne by all societies rich and poor alike."[56] AIDS orphans are not receiving the attention and treatment that would help them cope. Global efforts are reaching only a fraction of those in need.

The Wealthy Few, the Many Poor
The top fifth of the population on the global economic ladder enjoyed 30 times the goods and services of the lowest fifth in 1960, and by 1994 the wealthiest 20% of the world's people consumed 78 times more than the remainder of humanity.[57] In 2003 the United States contained 4.65% of the world's population, but its members used nearly one third of the entire global gross domestic product, 7 times its share of the world's goods. Japan has 2% of the world's population, but its citizens consumed 13.4 % of the global domestic product, 6.2 times more than other nations. In contrast, China has more than 20% of the world's people, but they survive on only 3.7% of the world's domestic product, about one fifth that of people in other nations.[58]

Standard of Living
The 1997 United Nations Development Programme (UNDP) Human Development Report asserted that "in the past 15–20 years more than 100 developing and transition countries have suffered disastrous failures in growth and deeper and more prolonged cuts in standards of living than any experienced in the industrial countries during the Great Depression of the 1930s"[59] Today more than 1.5 billion people live beneath the threshold of basic needs, and this number is increasing by 25 million people per year.[60] In most third world cities, 35 to 75% of the population is poor. In 19 countries per capita income is lower than it was in 1960, and as of 1997 as many as 1.6 billion people were worse off than they were 15 years ago.[61]

Purchasing Power Parity
In 1995 the gross domestic product (GDP) per person in the poorest 15 countries of the world was $200 or less per year, yet citizens of the 15 richest countries had GDPs above $21,000 per person per year.[62] In 2003 the annual purchasing power parity (PPP) of an average person in Iran was $1,540, a little more than $4 a day, and in Turkey a citizen had to survive on $2,780 a year. In India an individual had $2,540 a year on which to live. In contrast, in 2003 the yearly PPP of the average Canadian citizen was $29,400, or about $80.50 a day. In Japan it was $28,000, and in the United States the average American took home $37,600 in 2003, about $103 per day.[63]

Water, Health and Housing
About 800 million people lack access to health services, and more than 1.2 billion have no access to safe water.[64] In Bombay, India, a million people live in a slum built on a giant garbage heap. On the other side of the Indian subcontinent, between 500,000 and 750,000 Bengali live their entire lives on the streets of Calcutta—never once to experience a roof over their heads. In Lagos, Nigeria, 75% of families live in one-room shacks.

PRIVATIZING WATER IN BOLIVIA

Cochabamba, Bolivia, lies in a semidesert region where the minimum wage is less than $100 a month and water is a scarce but necessary commodity. In 1999 Bechtel Corporation, in collusion with the World Bank, forced the Bolivian government to privatize Cochabamba's municipal water supply company (SEMAPA) by passing a Drinking Water and Sanitation Law, which eliminated government water subsidies to citizens, began private ownership of the community's water resources, and even going so far as to forbid Bolivians from drawing water from their own local wells.[65] Water prices skyrocketed in a country already desperately poor, hitting $20 a month, nearly the cost of feeding a family of five for 2 weeks.

In protest, citizens formed La Coordinadora de Defensa del Agua y de la Vida (Coalition in Defense of Water and Life) and shut down the city for 4 days. Within a month millions of Bolivians marched to Cochabamba, held a general strike, stopped all transportation, and issued the Cochabamba Declaration, calling for universal water rights.

The government, however, reneged on its promise to reverse the price hike, and in February 2000 La Coordinadora organized a peaceful march demanding the repeal of the law, termination of the water contract, and participation of citizens in drafting a water resource law. The people's demands were violently rejected. In early April the Bolivian government shot hundreds of protesters in the streets to protect itself and its corporate benefactor and tried to silence the water protest by arresting activists and censoring media. On April 10, however, Bechtel left Bolivia, and the government was forced to revoke the hated privatization legislation. The water company was handed over to the people, who began to hold public hearings to decide its policies.

Bechtel's reprisals have not ended. It is now suing the Bolivian government for $25 million in damages and potential lost profits while the Bolivian government continues to harass the activists of La Coordinadora.[66]

More than a million people—half the population of Nairobi, Kenya—live in the giant slums of Mather, Korogocho, and Kibura. In Guayaquil, Ecuador, 60% of the people live in shantytowns amid garbage-strewn mud flats and polluted water.[67]

Poverty and the World's Children   The burden of poverty falls most heavily on the shoulders of the world's children. In 1997 nearly 160 million children under age 5 were malnourished, and more than 110 million children were out of school.[68] In the summer of 1999, according to the World Food Program, 1.2 million people were in danger of starving in the southern part of the African nation of Sudan in a famine caused by civil war, drought, and displacement, four times the estimate just 2 months earlier.[69]

Across the globe, poor care for newborns, malaria, diarrhea, malnutrition, and even measles can snuff out lives before a child's fifth birthday. In October 2004 the *New Zealand Herald* reported that 1 in 12 children worldwide does not make it to their fifth birthday, and half of these occur in sub-Saharan Africa. Twenty-five percent of babies in Sierra Leone and 10% of toddlers in Iraq die before the age of 5. The 2003 UNICEF report asserted that there is "alarmingly slow progress on reducing child deaths."[70] Even those children who avoid early death must continue to struggle. Manila's street children survive through prostitution, and many more are prostitutes in Thailand, Cambodia, and Laos. In Sao Paulo, Brazil, 700,000 street children, abandoned by their parents,[71] face a daily struggle to outrun death by starvation, disease, or police extermination squads.

Our Impoverished Globe   It is evident that society as a global marketplace does not provide all of its members with the basic elements of life: employment, housing, food, water, and health care. As the welfare state declines, says Teeple, those people who are "marginalized will increasingly become dependent on the purported benevolence or good will of others, and this in a society that looks on altruism as abnormal."[72]

Slavery

For North Americans slavery is a problem of the past, eradicated with the Emancipation Proclamation during the Civil War. What many people in our global society fail to realize, however, is that the problem of human slavery has not ended. When compared to estimates of slavery at the end of World War II, in fact, the number of slaves today has increased 10-fold.

The *New Internationalist* reported in 2001, for example, that a conservative "estimate of 27 million people, many of whom are children in developing nations, were enslaved around the world, a little short of the population of Canada, and higher than during the heyday of the colonial slave trade."[73] The value of global slavery is estimated at $12.3 billion a year, including a significant amount of international trade in slave-produced goods. Six kinds of slavery exist in our modern world: trafficking in persons, child slavery, debt bondage, forced labor, marriage as slavery, and traditional slavery.

Trafficking in Persons   Trafficking occurs when people are transported from their homes, often with a promise of a better life, or forced through violence, threats, and deception to work in conditions of slavery.[74] The U.S. Department of State in its 2002 "Trafficking in Persons Report" asserts that "traffickers use threats, intimidation, and violence to force victims to engage in sex acts or to labor for the trafficker's financial gain."

In 1997 the Central Intelligence Agency (CIA) estimated that more than 50,000 persons a year are trafficked into the United States alone, and 700,000 persons, mainly women and children, are trafficked across national borders worldwide each year. Educated young women from Ghana and Cameroon, for example, lured with a chance of further study in the United States, have been enslaved as domestics. Large numbers of Nigerian women have been forced into prostitution in Italy.[75] With the cooperation of the Japanese government, Filipino, Romanian, and Russian women are brought to Japan on "entertainment visas," often by the Yakuza or Japanese Mafia to service its many bars and brothels. Trafficking is not only common but very profitable. National instability creates the conditions for trafficking.

Profitable The UN Centre for International Crime Prevention says trafficking is now the third largest money earner for organized crime after drugs and guns.[76] The profit that slavers make, particularly for young girls in prostitution, can be as high as 800%, even though the girls will rarely see any of that money. Slaves used for prostitution are cheaper today than at any other time in history, and they are easier to procure, do not require a large capital investment, and often involve little risk of discovery. Unlike drugs, victims can be re-sold and re-used repeatedly,[77] and because she is so cheap, a girl can easily be replaced. If she becomes ill, injured, or troublesome, she's disposable.[78] The low status of women and girls in some societies contributes to the growing trafficking industry by not valuing their lives as highly as the male population.[79]

National Instability Civil unrest, internal armed conflict, and natural disasters destabilize and displace populations, increasing their vulnerability to exploitation and abuse.[80] The U.S. State Department asserts, for example, that economic and political instability as well as chronic unemployment, widespread poverty, and a lack of economic opportunities greatly increases the likelihood that a country will become a source of trafficking victims.[81] Economic change and globalization tend to drive rural people in poor countries into the cities and into debt, and they become a bumper crop of potential slaves.

Child Slavery Children are increasingly forced into slavery within and across national borders. UNICEF estimates that in West and Central Africa more than 200,000 children are trafficked,[82] and across Asia tens of thousands of children are peddled into slavery each year. Some children toil with their families as bonded laborers on farms. Others are sold by their parents or tricked by agents into servitude as camel jockeys, fisher boys, or beggars. Some children are kidnapped by the state and forced to become soldiers. In 2001 more than 300,000 children under the age of 18 were estimated to be fighting in conflicts in 41 countries around the world, and of those 120,000 are fighting in sub-Saharan Africa.[83] In the race to escape deprivation, whole villages are sometimes complicit in the sale of their own children into prostitution.

According to the International Labor Organization, at least 1 million children are prostitutes, with the greatest numbers in Thailand, India, Taiwan, and the Philippines. At least 60,000 children are prostitutes in Thailand although some estimates go as high as 200,000. An estimated 7,000 Nepalese children are smuggled into India each year to join the sex industry.[84] Procurers of these children might be the wives of village heads, says Sompop Jantraka, a leading Thai activist who has saved thousands of girls from being sold into brothels. Teachers know which children are vulnerable, and some inform procurers for a fee. Even those responsible for law and order can be made to turn a blind eye through bribes, leaving slave-makers to operate undisturbed.[85] Jantraka himself has seen pickup trucks full of girls sold to brothels leaving from schools . . . often with a police officer at the wheel.[86]

Debt Bondage Poor villagers fall into debt to a landlord because of marriage or the need for medical treatment. They are forced to slave from morning to night to repay debts of as little as $10 or $20, with usuriously inflated interest, or use their labor as collateral, making repayment virtually impossible. Sometimes their wives and children also end up working for the landlord.

SHRAMAJEEVI SANGATHANA

In 1979 a young couple, Vivek and Vidyullata Pandit, who began working in Bombay's slums, decided to focus their energies in the rural areas. Discovering that his uncle, with whom they were staying, kept bonded laborers, Vivek began demanding their release. Only after being attacked by his own uncle's men did the Pandits gain the trust of the people they wanted to help. They knew that India had outlawed bonded slavery and also that no one was being paid the minimum wage, so in 1982 they demanded the landlords pay up. They called a local official who threatened the landlords with police action. Strengthened by this approach, bonded adivasi laborers in 15 villages united to go on strike. For 24 days the adivasis survived by gathering wild vegetables in the forests as the agitation continued. When the landlords' unattended crops began dying, the landlords started fighting among themselves, and some became willing to pay the minimum wage. Their unity was broken.

Two decades later the Shramajeevi Sangathana organization begun by the Pandits has freed 450 villages from bonded slavery. They keep the police force in check by protesting its excesses. Today numerous farms operate cooperatively, special schools are opening to help children who cannot attend regularly, savings groups are beginning, and in a strange reversal, landlords are turning to the Sangathana for advice on farming methods.

It has not been an easy struggle, however. The Pandit's guiding principle is that power is never given freely; it must be taken. The Sangathana prepares bonded laborers to face conflict and backs them 100%. Despite death threats, assaults, false imprisonment, and vilification in the press; despite the malaise of Indian politics, a police system over friendly with the rich, and gangster rule in many areas where they work, the Sangathana has come through.[87]

Today, according to the *New Internationalist,* debt bondage is the major form of slavery in the world. In Pakistan and India, Northern Africa, Southeast Asia, and in Central and South America, debt bondage enslaves up to 20 million people. Ten million debt slaves, who may be in their third or fourth generation of bondage, live in India despite the fact that debt bondage has been illegal there since 1976.[88] Police are often ignorant of these laws, or as in Brazil and Thailand, they may be profiting from bonded labor themselves.[89]

Forced Labor   Forced labor often occurs through government or paramilitary coercion. In Sudan women and children captured as war booty enter into forced labor. Forced labor exists for minority groups in Burma, for prison camp slaves in China, and for exploited migrant workers in many Western nations. Forced laborers work against their will in construction, road maintenance, and building railroads and bridges, often under threat of violence.

Marital Slavery   Marital slavery occurs in situations in which a woman, without the right to refuse, is given in marriage as payment of money or in kind. In some nations girls as young as 10, unable to give informed consent and without choice, are compelled to enter into marriages where they are forced into domestic servitude, often accompanied by physical violence. In parts of rural China and the Central Asian republics, women are sometimes abducted and forced to marry men from neighboring villages. In other situations, to atone for an offence committed by a family member, girls are pledged to priests in Ghana, Togo, Benin, and Nigeria, becoming domestic and sexual slaves.[90]

YANAR MOHAMED, WOMEN'S ADVOCATE

Yanar Mohamed, a 43-year-old Iraqi-Canadian woman whose grandmother was forced as a teen into marital slavery with a cleric 40 years her senior, is often the advocate of last resort for women in Iraq. Last year a group of 47 women bank clerks were accused of theft by their supervisor. After days of waiting to plead her case, Mohamed lost her patience and began shouting at the Iraqi clerks and the American military officials. "I had bad manners," she said, "but they listened to us." Three weeks later all 47 women were released and the supervisor was arrested.

In the summer of 2004, the Organization of Women's Freedom in Iraq, which she founded, opened the country's first two women's shelters with facilities for 10 women. In addition, she runs a newspaper, organizes lobbying campaigns, and employs a lawyer who offers legal services to women. She is fighting against "honor killings" in which a man murders a female relative who has violated the family honor and often is given a much-reduced sentence. A book written by Iraqi Rega Rauf, for example, detailed 400 cases of honor killings in the Northern Iraqi district of Sulaimaniya in 1998 alone. "I don't want to take us back to the time of my grandmother," Mohamed said. "It depends on us whether we resist or not."[91]

Traditional Slavery   People continue to be bought and sold as commodities. Although this is the least common form of slavery, it still exists in Sudan where women and children from villages in the south are abducted by pro-government militia and sold to households in the north. In Mauritania and Niger, nomad and seminomadic tribes have slave castes. Even among slaves who have managed to become free and earn money, tribute must often be paid to their family's former master who also maintains inheritance rights over any property the free slave may have accrued.[92]

Manufacturing Violence and International Conflict

Two thirds of the arms trade in our global society is conducted between developed and developing countries,[93] but the only nations who win are the developed nations that sell the weapons. Developing countries can least afford to spend their capital on the military, weaponry, or armed conflict, which destroys their country's infrastructure, kills its citizens, and burdens the nation with debt to developing nations.[94]

INTERNATIONAL ARMS SALES

Once he was elected, reports the MoJo Wire, rather than insert human rights concerns into the arms sales equation, President Bill Clinton aggressively continued the sales policies of former President Bush, requiring our diplomats to shill for arms merchants to their host countries. In his first year in office, arms sales more than doubled. From 1993 to 1997 the U.S. government sold, approved, or gave away $190 billion in weapons to virtually every nation on earth. The arms industry meanwhile has greased the wheels. It filled Democratic coffers to the tune of nearly $2 million in the 1998 election cycle.

The United States sells arms to its NATO allies and others, such as Japan and South Korea. But it also arms both sides in a conflict, such as Greece and Turkey who have been threatening to go to war with one another over the island of Cyprus. The United States also supplies arms to nations with dismal human rights records, including Indonesia, Colombia, and Saudi Arabia. Under a Defense Department policy initiated in 1993, Congress created the Defense Export Loan Guarantee program to finance U.S. weapons sales to foreign countries. If a country defaults on its payments for arms, the company gets paid anyway and U.S. taxpayers are left holding the bag.[95]

The United States isn't the only arms dealer in this lucrative market. Robert Grimmet of the Congressional Research Service in his report "Conventional Arms Transfers to Developing Nations—1993–2000" reports that in 2000 Britain sold $5.1 billion in arms, Russia ranked third with $3.5 billion deliveries to developing nations, and France was fourth with $2.38 billion. The United States, the global arms sales leader, ranked first with $14.3 billion in sales. Determined to improve its performance, in 2002 Russia's President Putin put the final figure at $4.4 billion in arms sold to developing nations, including tanks and MIG fighters to India and China.[96]

A 1997 UNDP Human Development Report points out the leaders of developing nations continue to squander their limited budgetary resources in their obsession with military might. In 1995, for example, South Asia spent $15 billion on weaponry, more than what it would cost annually to achieve basic health and nutrition for its entire population. Sub-Saharan Africa spent $8 billion on arms, about the same as the estimated annual cost of achieving universal access to safer water and sanitation in all developing countries; and East Asia spent $51 billion, nine times the annual amount needed to ensure basic education for all children in that region.[97]

Not only do some third world nations waste their resources by purchasing weaponry from wealthy nations, but they are the chief targets of military campaigns from those same industrialized nations as well. "Since 1945, for example, armed conflicts between developed and underdeveloped nations have taken 21 million lives most of whom have occurred in the third world, and of these lives, where a meaningful distinction could be made, three out of every five were civilians."[98] Of the 21 countries that the United States has bombed since World War II, all have been third world nations,[99] and these interventions "have been fueled not by devotion to any kind of morality, but to the necessity of making the world safe for American corporations, profiting arms manufacturers, extending the political and economic hegemony over as wide an area as possible,"[100] concludes William Blum.

THE U.S. GOVERNMENT HAS BOMBED 21 COUNTRIES SINCE WORLD WAR II

China	1945–1946, 1950–1953
North Korea	1950–1953
Guatemala	1954, 1960, 1967–1969
Indonesia	1958
Cuba	1959–1961
Congo	1964
Peru	1965
Laos	1964–1973
Vietnam	1961–1973
Cambodia	1969–1970
Lebanon	1983–1984
Grenada	1983
Libya	1986

El Salvador	1980s
Nicaragua	1980s
Panama	1989
Bosnia	1985
Sudan	1998
Former Yugoslavia	1999
Iraq	1991–present
Afghanistan	1998, 2001–2002[101]

Refugees

According to Rodreck Mupedziswa, "the refugee problem is perhaps the most serious crisis facing humankind today," particularly in developing nations.[102] There are a number of causes of displacement. The number of refugees is growing, and many nations are experiencing "refugee fatigue."

Causes of Displacement   People become refugees because of environmental disruptions including sudden natural disasters such as earthquakes and floods, as well as gradual changes in the environment including desertification, deforestation, over fishing, and the destruction of rivers, lakes, and the ocean. People also become displaced because of ethnic conflicts, armed conflicts between opposition groups in a nation, governmental oppression, human rights violations, and invasion by external forces. Armed conflict, furthermore, often leads to homelessness and economic disruption, creating masses of refugees. After the Gulf War, for example, 1.8 million Iraqi Kurds fled to the border region of Turkey and Iran. Recently more than 400,000 refugees flooded into Kenya from Somalia, Sudan, and Ethiopia, and more than 1.2 million victims of violence in Yugoslavia sought refuge in Croatia, Montenegro, Slovenia, and Macedonia.

The Extent of the Refugee Problem   The more than 1 billion people in underdeveloped countries who live near or under the poverty level deteriorate further when their way of life is disrupted or destroyed. When faced with displacement, they become destitute, often becoming victims of massive starvation and famine. The numbers of refugees who have been displaced has reached unprecedented proportions, and nearly all of these people are in developing countries. In 1964 there were 1.4 million international refugees in the world. In 1970, the number grew to 2.5 million

and by 1980 it stood at 5 million. In 1990 refugees exceeded 14 million; in 1993 the number was estimated to have reached 17 million; and in 2005 there were 27.4 million refugees around the world.[103] In the industrial nations a staggering figure of some 3.7 million applicants for sanctuary was recorded in the period from 1983 to 1992 alone. Mupedziswa claims that at least one in every 130 people in the world today has been forced into flight and exile.

U.S. FOREIGN AID

U.S. foreign aid is given in six categories: military assistance, bilateral development assistance, economic support, humanitarian assistance, and aid to Eastern Europe and former states of the Soviet Union. Since World War II, U.S. foreign aid has been used primarily as a policy tool for political and security purposes rather as a way to alleviate suffering in the world's most desperate nations. For example, the Middle East, mainly Israel and Egypt, shared nearly half of the $14 billion U.S. AID budget in 1997, including gifts of $3.4 billion in military assistance, $1.5 billion on private enterprise, education, agriculture, and health, and $2 billion in economic support. In that year $1.4 billion went to Eastern European and former Soviet Union nations, and about $1.7 million for humanitarian aid including emergency food programs for refugees and to alleviate conditions in natural disasters.[104]

The real impact of U.S. aid on developing nations is less bountiful than it seems because it is tied to the procurement of goods and services manufactured in the United States. Rather than sending money, more than any other donor nation America sends aid in the form of surplus food, which not only has high transaction costs but disrupts local food markets.

Official U.S. aid of $10.9 billion in 2001 was down from $14 billion in 1997. Jean Claude Faure of the OECD said that the United States continued to be the world's largest aid donor because of the size of its economy, but it has the lowest ratio of aid to gross national income of any developed country. The United States gives only 0.11% of its income in official aid, against a UN target of 0.7 percent.

In 2002 U.S. aid dropped again to $8.5 billion. In that year, Andrew Natsios, head of the U.S. Agency for International Development (US AID), reported that a new policy of the Bush administration would apply to all future aid. About one quarter of the $8.5 billion aid budget will be dedicated to just two countries: Egypt and Israel. The United States will restrict the remainder of about $6.4 billion to countries that provide good governance, the rule of law, free markets, and respect for contracts. Asked if countries not fitting that description were exactly the ones that needed foreign development assistance, Natsios replied that the aim was to identify those nations that were about to take off and accelerate their process. The policy of helping those who help themselves was intended to promote competition. By giving countries left out of the aid programs a transparent set of reasons for their exclusion, they would be encouraged to change their policies, he said.[105]

These numbers however, only account for those who have crossed international borders. The U.S. Committee for Refugees estimated that in 1993 about 24 million internally displaced people fled violence and persecution but had not crossed international borders,[106] and in 1997 UNDP asserted that more than 40 million refugees and internally displaced people[107] were still living outside their homeland. The *New Internationalist* reported in October 2002 that in 2001 many thousands of refugees returned to countries where conditions have improved but remain unsafe, and the UN High Commissioner for Refugees (UNHCR) estimates that a further 22 million, not protected by international refugee law, may be "internally displaced" and may be at even greater risk.[108]

Refugee Fatigue   Because of the numbers of refugees some nations have become "refugee fatigued" and are less accommodating to people seeking asylum. In 2002, for example, Australia refused asylum to Indonesian refugees. The UNHCR has "found itself in the unenviable position of pleading for permission to shelter refugees with unwilling leaders."[109] Mupedziswa asserts that increasingly African governments are becoming ambivalent and even hostile to accepting refugees from other nations.[110]

Destruction of the Global Ecosystem

Rich countries are the primary users of scarce global resources, but poor countries are the most likely to be hurt by ecological deterioration and are least capable of adapting. Underdeveloped countries typically have weak infrastructures and less than adequate social services, making them particularly vulnerable to the floods, droughts, and spread of infectious diseases that global climate change could bring.[111]

The international policies of wealthy nations implemented by global economic IGOs, such as the IMF and World Bank, are part of the problem, says Kevin Danaher. "It is now generally recognized that the environmental impact of the IMF-World Bank on the South has been as devastating as the economic and social impact on peoples and societies."[112] C. Caulfield asserts, furthermore, that the Bank's decades-long series of grant experiments in poverty reduction have required the sacrifice of vast areas of productive forests, soils, rivers, and coastlines,[113] and "have created environmental deterioration or even permanent environmental degradation in many third world nations."[114] Five years after the historic 1992 Earth Summit in Rio de Janeiro, the Worldwatch Institute provided an assessment of the progress of the world's nations in reducing environmental destruction.

THEIR DAY IN COURT

In December 2002 a Nicaraguan judge, asserting that Dow Chemical, Shell Chemical, and Standard Fruit, an affiliate of Dole Foods Company violated Law 634, ordered the transnationals to pay $489 million to 468 banana workers allegedly poisoned by DBCP, a pesticide agent that causes sterility in men and is now widely thought to increase cancer rates. The United States government banned DBCP in 1979, but it is still being used on Nicaragua's banana plantations, especially in Chinandega. Health problems are rampant in Chinandega including sterility, cancer, and birth defects in children. A third of the women tested in Chinandega's Profamilia clinic in mid-2001 were found to have breast or uterine cancer.

Attorney Walter Gutierrez sued the TNCs that allegedly sold or used pesticides containing the chemical in Nicaragua. "The companies' obligation was to let the workers know that DBCP was potentially harmful so that they could protect themselves," asserts Gutierrez. "This stuff was dumped on them." The transnationals refused to recognize the judge's ruling, however, arguing on May 6, 2003, before the Securities and Exchange Commission that Law 634 is "unconstitutional and violates international due process."

Gutierrez then attempted to get the Nicaraguan judgment enforced in the United States, but, rather incredibly, translation errors led to an initial dismissal. While efforts are under way to have that decision reversed, the plan is to try to get this ruling, and a further one delivered in March 2004, executed in other countries, such as Venezuela and Ecuador, where the companies have assets, says Megan Rowling.

Shell says it "sympathizes with those people in Nicaragua who are claiming they have 'been affected,'" but it continues to assert that its product "was not sold to Nicaragua" despite court rulings to the contrary. Gutiérrez argues: "We have a judgment that is enforceable in any country. The companies can't hide from the facts."

Unsurprisingly, the TNCs are fighting back hard. Rather than pay the compensation awards, the transnationals are placing a string of legal obstacles in the workers' way. The Office of U.S. Trade has already identified Law 634 as an obstacle to investment, and U.S. officials began negotiating the Central America Free Trade Agreement to establish rules preventing workers from suing multinational corporations. Dole is now trying to sue some of the workers and their lawyers for allegedly falsifying evidence.

For now, thousands of impoverished banana workers remain stuck in legal and medical limbo. Gutierrez says that three Nicaraguan banana workers die a month from DBCP-related diseases, unable to pay for medical treatment. With government assistance lacking, the workers risk being run over by cash-rich transnationals able to keep bringing their cases back before the courts.[115]

During the last 5 years, the nations of the world have fallen short of attaining an environmentally sustainable global economy. Much of the earth's biological riches have been rapidly and irreversibly diminished. Huge areas of old-growth forests have been degraded or cleared in temperate as well as tropical regions—eliminating thousands of species of plants and animals. Biologically rich wetlands and coral reefs are suffering similar fates. Annual emissions of carbon that produce carbon dioxide, the leading greenhouse gas, have climbed to a new high, altering the very composition of the atmosphere and earth's heat balance.

Brown and colleagues conclude that governments still pursue economic growth as an end in itself, neglecting the long-term sustainability of the course they chart,[116] and adds Teeple, "governments minimize their import, mouthing concern but doing little to clean up or prevent further destruction; and corporations resist the idea of accepting responsibility for the external costs of their industrial processes."[117]

INTERNATIONAL SOCIAL ORGANIZATIONS

Multitudes of new social organizations are springing up in nearly every impoverished nation.[118] Hubert Campfens reports "there has been a rapid growth in grass roots organizations (GROs) that contrast sharply with state-initiated or administered programs that were so prominent across the developing world during the 1950s and 60s."[119] They include broad-based and single-focus grassroots organizations, nongovernmental organizations (NGOs), nongovernmental support organizations (NGSOs), transnational NGOs (TNGOs), and the United Nations.

Broad-Based Grassroots Organizations

Broad-based GROs originated in Brazil, experienced submergence, then experienced a period of consolidation and secularization, and developed further in other nations in which they designed new structures, offer programs and activities, and have developed influence.

Origination   In the 1960s Catholic priests in Central America and Brazil were impressed with the way that people who lived in poverty survived by helping each other. They generated their own perspective on biblical interpretation, known as liberation theology, and began organizing grassroots communities called *Communidades Ecclesiales de Base,* or base ecclesial communities. These *communidades* defined themselves as base or basic because they were composed of the simplest and poorest of people, but also because they were the most basic and foundational structures of the church. Being from the base, these new social organizations intended to take care of the whole of human life, its spiritual as well as its worldly aspects. They called themselves "Church of the Poor" or "Popular Church" because they were "of the people." *Communidades* also grew under the auspices of Popular Education Centers, Social Promotion Centers, and Advice and Support Centers in Brazil, and it was in those centers that the work of Paulo Freire germinated.[120] These grassroots *communidades* were small, unobtrusive, low-profile, nonhierarchical groups within submerged networks in villages, barrios, and neighborhoods that raise people's consciousness about social problems.

Submergence *Communidades* often remained underground because Brazil was ruled by an authoritarian regime after a right-wing military coup in 1964, and the *communidades* needed time to develop creativity and flexibility, which allowed them to survive and grow.[121] Because of their small size and community orientation, the *communidades* were able to maintain their space in a civil society dominated by oppression. Evans and Boyte assert that their roots in community define these free spaces, the dense, rich networks of daily life "that nurture values associated with citizenship and a vision of the common good."[122]

During this period of submergence, *communidades developed* their collective identity, communal culture, and a vision of what might constitute a new society. Their unity and values became an integral part of the self-understanding of each of their members.[123] Poor people realized that oppression and poverty are not "givens" in the nature of things. They worked to understand their situation, not to accommodate to it but to change it.

Consolidation The "work of the ants" consolidated into a wide range of submerged groups in cities and in the country.[124] The communal culture that emerged rejected the premises of modernity that had brought indigenous people nearly 400 years of oppression, poverty, and genocide. They refused self-interested market economies, top-down decision making, impersonal liberal democratic politics, and self-serving "development." This new awareness energized them for social, ecclesial, and political action that would have been unthinkable in the past. Vatican Council II empowered the faithful of the estimated 80,000 *communidades* in Brazil to perform the sacraments in remote areas lacking priests, and entrusted to the faithful the conduct of priestly functions within *communidades* in Panama, Guatemala, Argentina, and Peru. This is why Gustavo Gutierrez has characterized these new expressions of community as "an irruption of the poor" into the mainstream of church and society. The "absent ones" were making their presence felt.[125]

Secularization Gradually, many *communidades* secularized. They consolidated to engage in decision making without becoming a political party. They concentrated on participatory education, active social learning, and participant action research without being a university. They created small economic projects, experimented with self-help, and formed an economic base with the community's own resources without becoming market-centered corporations. They continue to be known as *communidades,* but they are also called grassroots organizations or GROs.

Generation of other BBGROs At the same time *communidades de base* were emerging in Latin America, similar GROs began developing autonomously and spontaneously in Africa, India, and Asia. People came together in villages, neighborhoods, and shantytowns around the world in response to modern forces that endanger their communities and the planet.[126] They not only emerged independently of one another but diffused transnationally more rapidly than has any other social movement.[127] In Indonesia, for example, in the late 1960s and 1970s only a handful of these organizations existed. Less than two decades later more than 3,000 had been formed.[128]

What is remarkable about these new BBGROs is "the speed with which the masses in each country converged on particular strategies, coordinated their operations, and successfully executed their plans."[129] In the Bhoomi Sena (land army) movement in Maharastra, India, for example, poverty-stricken villagers spontaneously formed a people's GRO called *Tarun Mandals,* whose membership includes all the people in the village. In three years the Bhoomi Sena movement spread to 120 villages, with *Tarun Mandals* GROs in about 40 of them. Functioning systematically and holding weekly meetings, they have managed to free villagers who were virtually enslaved as bonded laborers. A minimum wage is now in effect in Bhoomi Sena villages and in many others. *Tarun Mandals* are spontaneously creating people's institutions to settle disputes, provide education, sponsor elections, and develop a labor union.[130]

Structure Many BBGROs are located in rural villages or in the slums of larger cities, and they are characterized by their lack of official corporate status. They are informally structured and range in size from three-member groups to communities of 20 to 30 members. The members carry out all the functions of the social organization, including common education, self-help projects, and political action. Just as decision making, tasks, learning, and participation are shared, leadership is also shared. They respond to the circumstances, issues, and concerns of their members.

Programs and Activities   Some BBGROs devote themselves to charitable work. Others engage in conscientization (consciousness raising) and discussion of social and political problems, and still others become actively involved in social outreach, social action, and social services. Members of GROs who identify themselves as base ecclesial communities gather for Sunday Liturgy of the Word, engage in Bible reading and reflection, and discuss the social conditions that affect their lives. They help organize community social events such as festivals and celebrations.

BBGROs in larger cities organize literacy classes and neighborhood crime watches, build and maintain community centers, provide aid for those most in need of economic assistance, and petition the local government for better municipal services.[131] Often they join with others to obtain training and develop joint strategies for community improvement. By the end of 1984, for example, 2,000 GROs with more than 60,000 participants in the diocese of Machakos, Kenya, were actively involved in tree planting, cooperatives, savings groups, water projects, enterprise development, and consumer shops.

Influence   According to Mansour Fakih, by 1985 the lives of more than 100 million peasants in Latin America, Africa, and Asia had become directly affected by the activities of BBGROs, and no doubt their influence has increased since then.[132] The picture shows an expanding latticework covering the globe. At the local level, particularly among the close to 4 billion humans in developing lands, it appears that the world's people are better organized today than they have been since European colonialism disrupted traditional societies centuries ago. Fisher asserts, "The proliferation of grassroots efforts is in fact a hallmark of our era."[133]

Single-Focus Grassroots Organizations

Some GROs form single-issue organizations around women's issues, ecology, or social action. Each single-issue GRO has its own separate clan of activists with its guiding truths and ideology. They are composed entirely of volunteer members who carry out all the functions of the organization, and they have devoted themselves to such diverse and specific areas as defense of flora and fauna, organic agriculture, alternative medicine, alternative journalism, agricultural communities, esoteric knowledge, meditation, defense of indigenous communities, antinuclear struggles, and alternative physical therapies.[134]

Nongovernmental Organizations

When larger GROs become formally structured and incorporated by the state, they are generically labeled nongovernmental organizations, or NGOs, just as their counterparts in the United States are called nonprofit or social organizations. In the Philippines the name NGO was rejected, however, and the term Self-Reliance Promoting Organization was adopted instead.[135] In Indonesia they are called Community Self-Reliance Organizations. In India they are called voluntary agencies or nonparty political formations. In Singapore they are Institutions of Public Character.

Smaller NGOs rarely have paid staff and almost never have any structure resembling a hierarchy except at the most formally organized levels. NGOs nearly always comprise members who organize themselves with full participation and engagement of all. They represent a "bewildering mix of ideologies, objectives, working styles, social composition, funding and support sources."[136] NGOs are single issue, broad-based, and exist at the urban, rural, and regional levels.

Single-Issue NGOs   Some NGOs operate as freestanding organizations with a single-issue focus in ecology, health, economic development, or social policy. In India, for example, women-led NGOs (WNGOs), particularly those assisting in the empowerment of women and social development, women's health, and advocating for women's rights, are breaking the gender gap as well as providing needed services. These WNGOs are highly organized and effective. They "have a clear idea of their activities as well as scheduling of services provided and tasks for paid personnel and volunteers."[137]

Broad-Based NGOs   Other NGOs are the multimember organizational coalitions composed of hundreds of GROs such as the broad-based Six-S Movement in Burkina Faso, which covers nearly two thirds of the country's villages and has become a regional movement spreading to a number of other countries, including Senegal, Chad, Niger, and Mali. These broad-based NGOs operate in ways that reflect the different needs, cultures, and situations of the great variety of their members.

Urban NGOs   In the 1970s, larger and more urban-oriented NGOs in Brazil engaged in reorganizing and restructuring the unions, and organized neighborhood associations, cooperatives, consumer groups, small trades, and peasant associations of all kinds. They took on projects in economic action, communication, human rights, participant research, health, and education,[138] as well as relief, training, social service, and political action.[139]

Rural NGOs   Many NGOs concentrate in rural areas. In 1980, for example, a group of concerned persons in Matabeleland, one of the most depressed areas in Zimbabwe with acute poverty and the highest rate of illiteracy in the country, decided to help people understand their poverty, question its causes, regain their dignity, and take collective initiatives for their self-development. They structured themselves as the Organization of Rural Associations for Progress (ORAP) and formally registered as an NGO in 1981. Six years later, ORAP included 500 grassroots village groups with an average membership of about 75, as well as 30 to 40 umbrella organizations and 10 associations.

ORAP uses the local cultural tradition of people working together to help themselves (*amalima*) and rural mutual help groups (*ilima*). People's groups in the villages grew out of the village committees formed during liberation and some out of existing women's clubs. After a great deal of discussion about their problems and needs, they took action, mobilizing their labor and skills with the help of external donors. Assisted by professional and semiprofessional staff, village groups federated into "umbrellas," and the umbrellas federated into "associations." Each association elects representatives to the ORAP advisory board. Ordinary villagers form themselves into mass community associations called development centers to consolidate and plan their mutual efforts.[140]

Regional NGOs   In addition, many direct-service NGOs are forming permanent networks at the regional and national level to debate common problems and perspectives and to develop policy initiatives, much like national federations of community organizations in the United States and Canada.

HOW TO ELIMINATE A SOCIAL PROBLEM

"Everyone is afraid," he said as he fiddled with a piece of plastic tape, keeping his eyes on the table. Sister Beatriz Semiano and a social worker, Wolmer Nascimento, a coordinator for the National Movement for Street Boys and Girls, listened as A. G., a thin, dark boy, one of the ragged legion of street kids who live by their wits in Sao Paulo, Rio, and Reclife, told how death squads hired by local merchants roam the streets exterminating homeless children. "He was sleeping," A. G. said, "and they filled his face with bullets." Cleiton, 12, used to steal from stores in a shopping gallery near the center of Duque de Caxias, Brazil, one of the grimy, violent suburbs only a few miles from the swaying palms, elegant hotels, and white sand beaches of Rio de Janeiro. Cleiton's death was not an isolated incident.

Hundreds of children are murdered each year by bands of private security guards, many of them off duty or former police officers, the very people who should safeguard the children. A. G. said that he had known "a heap" of youngsters killed in Duque de Caxias. One was Luciano, 16, picked up by his killers and shot in the head. "He robbed stores," A. G. said of Luciano. Two weeks after Luciano's death, gunmen killed his friend Ademir, 16. "He also robbed," A. G. said. There is no doubt, A. G. insisted, about who the killers work for. "The store owners pay them to kill us." A. G. has slept on the streets for 11 of his 16 years. He said the killers almost got him when he was 13. The merchants treat the children like rats. Kill them and the problem goes away. Sometimes, in a shrewd if twisted scheme, they pay members of street gangs to exterminate children in rival gangs.

Sr. Beatriz confirmed the dangers A. G. described. "He lives in the street, he sleeps in the street, and he is threatened with death," she said. "It is a terrible problem in Brazil." The problem, she and others say, has its roots in urban poverty, antiquated laws, police corruption, and ineffective systems for providing child welfare and criminal justice.[141]

Nongovernmental Support Organizations

Special NGOs called nongovernmental support organizations (NGSOs) provide resources, education and training, staff, and technical support for indigenous NGOs. Some of these NGSOs maintain linkages with international social work organizations in

North America and Europe or with the United Nations. Oxfam, Africares, World Vision, Lutheran World Relief, the Mennonite Central Committee, the International Red Cross, the Christian Children's Fund, CARE, and many other international humanitarian organizations operate as NGSOs, providing assistance in community development and community organization, relief, immigration, human rights, advocacy, funding, and other services.

The Save the Children Federation, for example, organized a network of women's clubs in Colombia to promote small enterprise development and health education. Technoserve has provided assistance in agrarian reform cooperatives in Peru and El Salvador.[142] The Inter-American Foundation and the African Development Foundation fund international grassroots support organizations. All of these international social welfare organizations are important sources of assistance, support, direct involvement, coordination, and information that would not otherwise be available. They are also a means by which social workers from North America and Europe can find a way of direct involvement in international social work.

Transnational Nongovernmental Organizations

Transnational NGOs (TNGOs) have members in two or more nation-states and an international office that coordinates or facilitates their transnational activities. Amnesty International, for example, is a TNGO that operates around the world, mobilizing an international base of human rights advocates who question individual states about their human rights practices and provide material resources and legal services for victims of human rights abuse.[143] The International Red Cross has an international office in Geneva that coordinates its many member affiliates in most of the world's nations.

Many TNGOs operate at the people-to-people level, providing educational campaigns, citizen exchanges, information sharing, or services that increase pubic awareness. They maintain international solidarity networks,[144] educate the public about development issues, provide training for new social movement organizations, or act as advocates for specific groups. TNGOs often work to bring policies of individual states in line with international standards by lobbying delegates at international meetings and monitoring compliance with international agreements. The International Red Cross, for example, has negotiated agreements for the care of wounded soldiers called the Geneva Conventions. A few TNGOs such as International Social Service have a strong social work presence, but most do not.

The United Nations

The United Nations, founded in 1945, is the world's largest, oldest, and most important international support and advocacy organization.[145] The UN provides community programs and is a repository of social data. Among its community programs are the UN Development Program (UNDP), UNICEF, the High Commissioner for Refugees (UNHR), and the UN Disaster Relief Organization (UNDRO).

Community Programs and Social Data   Operating under the auspices of its Economic and Social Council, the United Nations provides community development programs and services to developing nations worldwide through information, technical assistance, and a variety of specialized programs. Information is an important resource in community development efforts. The United Nations is a central collection repository for social data and statistics from all member nations, and it publishes its own *World Economic Survey*, a *Report on the World Social Situation*, and the *State of the World's Children* compiled by UNICEF. These data are complemented by periodical statistical collections such as the *UN Statistical Yearbook* and the monthly *Statistical Bulletin*.[146]

UN Development Program   The UN Development Program (UNDP) is a major UN vehicle for community development. The Development Program provides expert assistance to developing countries, regional training centers, scholarships, and planning projects for investment.

UN International Children's Emergency Fund (UNICEF)   One of the best-known UN community development programs is UNICEF. Initially established to provide aid to children who had suffered during World War II, UNICEF now develops long-term programs for health, social welfare, and teaching.

UN High Commissioner for Refugees   The UNHCR has established a strategy with five elements:

prevention, preparedness, response, protection, and solution. The UNHCR tries to prevent displacement of people by resolving the causes, such as political conflict, poverty, and environmental disasters, and works to protect refugees by ensuring them safe passage and security. The UNHCR enforces international agreements to provide asylum, sometimes using peacekeeping forces.[147] The UNHCR struggles to find durable, long-term solutions to the refugee problem. Sometimes the solution includes repatriating refugees to their homeland. Where this is not possible, they work to integrate refugees into the host society or to aid resettlement in a third nation. In each case, however, the immediate solution includes the provision of services to enable refugees to cope with their situation and minimize the problems they face.

UN Disaster Relief Organization
The UN continues to provide assistance and protection to refugees who are displaced due to political reasons, war, famine, floods, and other disasters through the UN Disaster Relief Organization (UNDRO). This agency "is on the scene first to protect the human rights of people outside their own countries and to offer material assistance where forced migrations occur."[148]

Other Humanitarian UN Programs
The UN provides a variety of specialized programs that complement its community development efforts. For example, the UN recruits a corps of volunteers who do community development work. In 1991, for example, the corps consisted of more than 2,200 volunteers worldwide. The UN Fund for Population Activities (UNFPA) assists communities in applying knowledge of population dynamics to family planning services and training, and the UN Capital Development Fund (UNCDF) provides grants and low-interest loans for community development in the least developed countries. The World Food Program distributes agricultural surpluses or gifts in kind to developing countries. The UN is also involved in health issues, mainly by means of its affiliated World Health Organization (WHO). WHO coordinates research, provides a system for notification of infectious diseases, and helps developing countries organize their own public health services and control health-related problems such as poor sanitation.[149]

The UN and Social Work
More social worker involvement in the United Nations is needed. Social workers have provided some leadership in UNICEF, UNHCR, and the WHO, but this involvement has been limited to a small number of individuals. Currently the organized social work presence at the UN is minimal and needs to be both expanded and better coordinated.

International Social Work Organizations

Several international organizations provide an identity for social work, including the International Federation of Social Workers (IFSW), the International Association of Schools of Social Work (IASSW), and others.

International Federation of Social Workers
The IFSW, founded in 1956, has associations in 59 different countries with more than 430,000 members. The IFSW is active in promoting human rights and protesting human rights violations, developing policies on social issues, and advancing international ethical standards for social work.[150]

International Association of Schools of Social Work
The IASSW is the principle international organization for social work education. With its affiliated regional organizations, it serves about 1,600 educational programs around the world. It sponsors a biennial international congress and represents social work education at the UN and other international organizations and cosponsors the journal, *International Social Work*. Fewer than a quarter of all programs and about 2% of all social work educators are now paying members of IASSW.[151] The IASSW and IFSW developed a manual on human rights and social work and a range of policy papers on social issues, often linked to those produced by the UN.[152] However, according to Hokenstad and Midgley, except for their annual conferences, few social workers tend to be in contact with the programs of IFSW and IASSW.[153]

Other International Social Work Organizations
Other international organizations such as the International Council on Social Welfare (ICSW) and the Inter-University Consortium on International Social Development (IUCISD) have close ties with social work, but they are little known to most social workers. These organizations need increased involvement

and support from national social worker organizations as well as from rank and file social workers to become more of a force on the global scene.

ARENAS OF INTERNATIONAL SOCIAL WORK

Macro social workers concerned about specific arenas can use their compassion, dedication, and skills to provide programs and develop facilities to protect street children and orphans, rescue children who have been forced into prostitution, war, and labor, and engage in policy making to change laws to improve social conditions. All of these are important areas of social work intervention. In this section, you will discover how international social work becomes engaged in international refugee and relief services, sustainable human economic and community development, social action, and political advocacy. You will also find, however, that the profession of social work, particularly in North America, has failed to extend itself wholeheartedly into the international arena.

International Relief and Refugee Social Work

Generalist-based social workers have a composite blending of skills that can provide help to individual refugees, but especially to groups, and communities. However, the profession of social work, at least in the United States, has tended to neglect the field of refugee assistance.

Composite Blending of Skills   Macro social workers whose historical commitment, background, and generalist-based training involves helping at multiple levels are in a unique position to be of service in assisting people needing refugee and relief services. Vera Mehta asserts for example, that

> Relief work with individuals and families involves intensive counseling; physical, medical and psychological rehabilitation; tracing missing family members across borders and reunifying them; and repatriating and resettling refugees. It also includes empowering victims to exercise their rights and organize collaborative enterprises. Because there are ever-increasing numbers of civilian war victims to be reached and relatively few social work professionals available, group and community

methods must be used to provide these services and a new cadre of personnel must be created by training community aides and using indigenous leadership. . . . War zones demand a multifocal social work practitioner equipped with generic and integrated methods and skills.[154]

Individuals   At the micro level, international social workers can provide counseling services to those people who have experienced emotional and social trauma. Many refugees have lost families, homes, their livelihood, friends, and a sense of belonging. Many have been victims of violence, human rights abuses, and physical and emotional trauma. Often they experience posttraumatic stress disorder, depression, loss, and grief. Social workers can train volunteers in communication and listening skills so that refugees become capable of helping one another in a therapeutic community of friends helping friends.

Group Work   Many refugees live in camps or locations where they are in close proximity to one another for lengthy periods of time. Social workers can assist people in these camps form support groups for those who have gone through trauma and loss and for women who have been victims of sexual assault. We can train group leaders among those who are on the road to recovery to lead groups of others. In addition, we can help members of the community develop self-help groups in which they begin to utilize their resources and strengths to come to terms with their situation and begin to rebuild their lives. Adult volunteers, for example, may be recruited to form a primary or high school and become schoolteachers. Others may form self-help groups to engage in community development projects providing medical, construction, agricultural, childcare, or economic development help.

Community Social Work   Macro social workers can use their community skills to form planning groups to assess resources and assets and help members of the refugee communities cope with rebuilding their communities. They can help develop a community structure of organizations in which refugees come together to consider their situation and make decisions about what needs to be done to strengthen their community. Social workers can assist in building leadership among refugees, providing consultation and training in developing resources, advocating on their own behalf, even forming refugee NGOs whose members can reach out beyond the refugee camp to communicate with other refugee or NGO support organizations to obtain assistance.

When refugees are returned to their homes, social workers can be a resource to people in rebuilding their communities and engaging in economic development projects. Macro social workers can also sensitize the social work profession about the plight of refugees, provide advocacy, and mobilize efforts on their behalf by working through and with the United Nations and existing relief and refugee NGOs.

Social Work and Relief Efforts   There are great opportunities and challenges for international relief and refugee social work, but our profession has not been actively involved in contributing to the resolution of the issues and crises in this field, says Rodrick Mupedziswa. Moreover, he asserts that the social work profession has not demonstrated its willingness to respond to the needs and concerns of refugees.[155] International relief and social development agencies such as Cooperative for American Relief Everywhere (CARE) and Oxfam have little social work involvement in spite of having many programs directly related to social work functions.[156]

Mupedziswa asserts, "social work's major professional associations have not organized on behalf of refugees or made effective representation to those in positions of power and influence who are able to bring about improved conditions for refugees."[157] He also claims that social work has not yet developed a specialized body of knowledge in relation to practice with refugees, nor is there a great deal of curriculum content in social work education in this area. He says, "Millions of desperately needy people among the world's refugees deserve the profession's attention. The crisis is too severe—and the needs of refugees are too great—for social work to neglect this field any longer."[158]

Sustainable Human Development

Macro social workers concerned about the effects of modern political and economic systems on individual lives, communities, and societies of people must begin to think about alternative ways of thinking and living. One of these ways is through sustainable human development. According to the United Nations Development Programme, "sustainable human development . . . is

concerned with models of material production and consumption that are replicable and desirable. It does not regard natural resources as a free good to be plundered at the will of any nation, any generation or any individual."[159] Sustainable human development

> puts people at the center of development and points out forcefully that the inequities of today are so great that to sustain the present (modern) form of development is to perpetuate similar inequities for future generations. . . . Sustainable human development means that we have a moral obligation to do at least as well for our successor generations as our predecessors did for us . . . that current consumption cannot be financed for long by incurring economic debts that others must repay. It also means that sufficient investment must be made in the education and health of today's population so as not to create a social debt for future generations. And it means that resources must be used in ways that do not create ecological debts by over exploiting the carrying and productive capacity of the earth.[160]

Prigoff asserts "social workers . . . in partnership with community organizations can be effective in building public awareness and community based coalitions which will hold the economic and political power groups publicly accountable for the costs of their actions, expose the bankruptcy of their leadership and build alternative systems that support sustainable human development."[161]

Community Economic Development

Community economic development is one of the more important areas in which NGOs become active. Local people develop alternative cooperative models, engage in housing and other projects, build social capital, reject dependency, and develop empowerment.

Alternative Cooperative Models   Many NGOs work to develop alternatives to capitalistic industrial models, state-controlled social programs, or centralized hierarchical, top-down institutionalized structures of decision making. In some ways they resemble North American asset-based community development projects, helping communities become economically sustainable, using the communities' resources, and building on their strengths in ways that are compatible with the ecology and with their own culture.

DEVELOPMENTSPACE: A NEW WAY OF GIVING

DevelopmentSpace was created by Dennis Whittle and Mari Kuraishi, two former world bank employees, and it is devoted to pairing small-scale entrepreneurs in developing countries with donors elsewhere, rather like an eBay of international aid. DevelopmentSpace focuses entirely on projects that require thousands of dollars, not millions.

It opened in February 2002, and by April of that year it already had more than 500 registered donors and 78 projects seeking funds. The company, says Meitamei Ole Dapas, director of a project seeking funds, is very efficient and responsive in building rapport and establishing a personal connection. Accountability is its most important challenge, and its creators say they have safeguards in place to ensure integrity. Entrepreneurs who approach the company are screened by a third party, business plans are screened by volunteers, many products have been endorsed by established organizations, and an eBay-style rating system lets entrepreneurs and contributors rate one another.[162]

Changing its name to Globalgiving, its mission is to become the world's richest marketplace in international aid and philanthropy, according to the *Free Dictionary*. The philosophy underlying Deveopmentspace/Globalgiving is that market-based mechanisms can provide increased access and help ensure that aid flows to its best use. Some of the world's leading NGOs, including Ashoka, World Neighbors, IDEX, and Women's Funding Network, use Globalgiving to load projects that they stand behind.[163]

In Latin America a majority of the estimated 20,000 squatter settlements have created their own community economic development organizations. In the Lima squatter settlement Villa El Salvador, nearly 350,000 people have constructed hundreds of thousands of neatly designed homes. Mostly community volunteers built the nearly 200 nursery, primary, and secondary schools. Virtually everyone knows how or is learning to read and write.

Residents piped in water, and desert areas that were once barren now yield tons of oranges, vegetables, sweet potatoes, papayas, and corn. What most impresses visitors is organization. Every block and every activity is intensely organized through crisscrossing neighborhood associations, women's groups, youth groups, artisan associations, and production cooperatives. An estimated 2,000 organizations are nestled within federations of larger federations, and these confederations largely control the democratically elected local government.[164]

Housing Construction   Just as in North America, many community economic development NGOs emphasize housing. In Colombia there are more than 700 public nonprofit community housing organizations. A grassroots community organization in Costa Rica built 1,300 houses in 2 years at final construction costs that were 40 to 50% lower than houses of comparable quality built by either government or the private sector. Ordinary people learned to erect prefabricated walls and used computers for accounting, planning, and compiling data.[165]

Other Projects   Many community economic development NGOs engage in a wide variety of other self-help projects, including carpentry, sewing, building, basketry, wood carving, livestock grazing, school uniform making, vegetable gardening, poultry keeping, cement sheet making, knitting, mat making, ox-yoke making, baking, grinding mills, food storage, water, and sanitation.[166]

Some economic development NGOs help provide needed programs of assistance. In Peru, urban social movement organizations developed popular kitchens. In 1986, 625 kitchens existed in Lima and by 1990 the number had grown to 1,500 community kitchens averaging 50 members each. One hundred thousand people, mostly mothers, are organized into barrio, zonal, and district organizations that raise funds for 7,500 *Vaso de Leche* (glass of milk) committees that work through community kitchens to distribute powdered milk as well as participating in developing popular libraries and health projects.[167]

Develop Social Capital   The common goals of all these projects foster individual and communal self-reliance, help people control their own futures, and provide a forum by which members can express and discuss ideas and projects. Community economic development NGOs promote solidarity and foster self-management while working to improve the life chances and well-being of their residents They work to construct their communal reality out of their values, history, culture, and traditions, and by their own action regardless of and often in spite of those in authority.

Reject Dependency   Many times community economic development NGOs resist accepting government assistance. Imported capital and technology can be helpful, but assistance must be based on people's ability to use credit productively, on accurate perceptions of need, and on their own initiative. External assistance can be supplementary if it is not dependency creating, and it must be under the control and planning of community members themselves.

Although poor people in villages cannot prevent governments from accepting development money that benefits the rich, they can decide whether dependence on outside funds is in their own interest. Residents of Kujupukur village in India, for example, considered the question of accepting government aid in developing their agriculture, health, and literacy: "We have realized that ours is a country of villages and if villages want money from the government, either the government has to take from us and give back, or beg for us from other countries. So we decided not to ask anything from anybody."[168]

Empowerment   The answer to poverty will never come from top-down solutions, capital investment, or gigantic corporate or government development projects. The cure to poverty will not come by converting local economies into high-powered market systems, or by inducing people to accept the premises on which modern market economies are based. Economically developed nations cannot create wealth in poor nations when they appropriate people's land for their benefit or exploit citizens as cheap sources of labor.

Poverty will only be eradicated as people in their own local communities take charge of their lives. It will begin when people reject an image of themselves, often imposed by the "developmental" mentality, that impoverishment is due to their inability, laziness, and lack of intelligence, or a desire to be dependent on others. The forest dwellers of India, for example, report that

> We lived with the forest as one organic whole—there was no separation between the trees and us physically, culturally, or emotionally in daily living and growing together. Then you came, with your notion of "development," and separated us. To you the forest was just a "resource," but you could not even develop this resource because now the forest is disappearing. Even we did not count to you.
>
> The path of your "development" did not lead us to mansions but to the slums. Because of "development" we had to give up our lifestyle, and our culture. You deprived us of our habitat and deprived our country of its environment. We feel cheated and our country has been cheated too. It is strange that what is good for us has been decided by those who have cheated our country and us. To us real development is not a negation of nature and its forces, but being a part of it. Our consensus is that we have to preserve what we have and develop a new perspective based on the flowering of our own eco-regions.[169]

The economic capacity of people will continue to grow as they work together on common projects for the benefit of all. It will come to fruition as they develop self-sufficiency, using primarily their own resources, guided by their own ideas, engaging in their own common effort to better the lives of their children and their communities.

International Social Activism: New Social Movements

By means of new activist social movements, 80% of the world's population, comprising the poor people of the earth, is disarming the modern developmental worldview by disassociating themselves from its methods, abandoning belief in its promises, refusing to accept its goals, and ignoring its premises. In 2002 at the Second World Social Forum (WSF) in Porto Alegre, Nicola Bullard, deputy director of Focus on the Global South, a Bangkok-based think tank, reported, "there are strong social movements in Asia. We have a vibrancy that I believe is important." In Indonesia former President Suharto, for example, was driven out of office in 1998 by public outrage and in the Philippines a popular uprising in 2001 by people tired of corruption ousted then-President Joseph Estrada. Marwaan Mancan-Makar says, "These two episodes . . . show that despite all the ill effects of market-driven development models and policies, Asia has a healthy record of public protest that reminds the world that people's power does work."[170]

Bullard asserts, furthermore, that we need to build such social movements against the ill effects of the neoliberal economic order found in many parts of the world. The Porto Alegre conference and its affirmation of new social movements, reports Mancan-Makar, is sending a powerful message to the mandarins of the World Bank, the IMF, and the WTO that the critics of neoliberalism and corporate-driven globalization have by no means disappeared from Asia.[171]

Activist GROs engaged in new social movements are qualitatively different from earlier movements against colonialism and for liberation, land reform, or labor unions.[172] New social movements do not aim at overthrowing governments or seizing the assets of the world's global corporations, but they represent a rupture with authoritarian political cultures[173] in South America, Africa, and Asia, a rejection of market-centered thinking, and repudiation of the developmentalist worldview of the West. The new social movements engage in critical consciousness raising, reject the culture of oppression, regain identity, reconstitute their culture, and promote strategies including popular resistance, cooperative alliances, political action, environmental protection and women's rights.

Critical Consciousness Raising

Like community organizations in North America, international social movements in poor nations of the world work to promote people's "critical consciousness" that names and denounces the philosophies of dominance.[174] They reject the modern developmentalist hegemony as a "false consciousness." New social movements struggle against the dominant modernization worldview. Their main concern is to develop a collective "critical consciousness" that will bring about human liberation and create diverse grassroots structures in which people construct their own social reality.

Reject the Culture of Oppression

Amilcar Cabral, one of the foremost leaders and thinkers about globalization, asserts that there is an inseparable gulf between the economic and political domination brought about by modernity and the preservation of the cultural identity of an oppressed people, and it is impossible to harmonize the two. This is not only because of the tremendous differences in the history and culture of those who are dominated and the culture of the oppressor. It is also because it is impossible for the oppressor and the oppressed to move along the same path simultaneously. A modern oppressor may claim to work for progress, growth, and development, but these assertions can only occur on the oppressor's own terms, within the framework of his dominant mentality, and at the expense of the indigenous people. Indigenous people, however, are continually in a state of maintaining and spreading their culture, developing their identity, and seeking ways to crack the domination of their oppressors.

BOLIVIA'S POOR SAY "NO" TO GLOBALIZATION

America, labor unions, student and civic groups, and a new wave of leaders are expressing doubts about who actually benefits from a free flow of international trade and investment. "Globalization is just another name for submission and domination," said Nicanor Apaza, an unemployed miner, at a demonstration denouncing the International Monetary Fund. Protestors see an unbroken line from Bolivia's colonial history to the failed economic experiments of the late 20th century in which Bolivia was one of the first Latin American countries to open itself to the modern global economy.

The Indians of Bolivia got a foretaste of globalization centuries ago with the age of exploration and the arrival of European colonizers. Silver from the mines of Potosi provided Spain with the wealth that allowed it to forge a global empire, and in modern times tin made a few families fabulously wealthy. "But the wealth always left the country and enriched foreigners, rather than staying here to improve our lives," claimed Pascuala Velazuez, an egg vendor, "but we cannot allow that to happen this time."

Starting with the end of a military dictatorship at the beginning of the 1980s, Bolivia embraced the free market model. State-owned companies were sold off; foreign investment was courted; and government regulation was reduced—all in the name of a new era of growth and prosperity. After a few years it became clear, however, that the policies urged by the United States, the IMF, and the World Bank were not working. Exports declined; growth stalled; and unemployment soared. Bolivia sunk to being the poorest country in South America with a per capita income of less than $900. After 21 years the economic model in place has not solved the problems of poverty and social exclusion, said Carlos Toranzo, of the Latin American Institute for Research.

Rather than export gas and other resources, Bolivian protesters are determined to use them to build an industrial base. The protesters are giving a powerful message: No to the export of gas and other natural resources; no to free trade with the United States; no to globalization in any form other than solidarity among the downtrodden peoples of the developing world. They plan to force the government to abandon a plan to export natural gas to the United States. But freedom from powerful interests does not come without a price. Protests in only one month in 2003 have already left more than 80 people dead.[175]

Regain Identity   The goals of new social movements are often modest and simple. Indigenous people seek to reclaim their lives and the cultures that modernity has taken from them. The forest people of India speak for many: "The major interest [of first world leaders] is the development of the forest as a resource rather than as a habitat of people. This basic difference distinguishes 'us' [the forest dwellers of India] from 'you.' You believe that we should reap the dubious benefits of 'development,' and become like you or your serfs. We reject your notion of development and we want back our lives."[176]

Reconstitute Their Culture   If people are to be authentically free and liberated, says Ponna Wignaraja, "they must be the final arbiters of their lives. They need to form their own organizations and through their own organizations to counter the socio-economic reality that keeps them in poverty."[177] Cabral believes that a new social movement must base itself on the people's own popular culture. In this effort indigenous people must reconstitute their history-making and culture-building capacities in a nation-wide movement to oppose the colonizers cultural hegemony with the colonized counterhegemonic culture. For Africans this means the re-Africanization of minds, including reclaiming the nation's suppressed history and culture from both colonialism and neo-colonialism, building a popular, democratic and collectively oriented political process, and educating people who have been denied the possibilities of fully learning their own indigenous culture.

Strategies   New social movements promote strategies of popular resistance, support cooperative alliances, engage in political action, and promote environmental protection and women's rights.

Popular Resistance   New social movements engage in popular resistance and social change worldwide. Multiple and varied activist projects range from the struggle of members of a Caracas barrio to prevent the removal of a tree to the armed defense of their culture by ethnic groups in Guatemala. They range from efforts of small, politically oriented *communidades ecclesiales de base* that engage in social action in local villages to global social movements that help bring about social justice, equality, and equal rights to people who have been oppressed and exploited.[178]

In 1973, in the midst of Brazil's military dictatorship, for example, mothers' clubs in south Rio de Janeiro initiated a neighborhood movement against the high cost of living and denounced the high levels of pollution in the water supply, mobilizing 20,000 in a street demonstration that remains a landmark in the struggle for democracy.[179] Tens of thousands of students in Mexico City led mass demonstrations to eliminate obstacles to university entry, and in Buenos Aires grandmothers and mothers continue their daily march around the Plaza de Mayo, protesting the disappearance of their children and grandchildren.[180]

Cooperative Alliances   Not only do social movement GROs work on behalf of their own particular concerns, but they also form alliances with one another. In Mexico, neighborhood organizations systematically join with independent workers, peasants, and teachers in their struggle for housing, clean air, education, a decent environment, solidarity, and democracy. Economic development Glass of Milk committees in Peru became integrated with broad-based community organizations, with the workers movement, and with women's movement organizations.

Political Action   New social movements mobilize around a vision of people-centered development policy and political reforms. The cumulative effect of direct political action by these new social movements has begun to change the political climate in many impoverished nations, says Camacho.[181] Voluntary associations in urban areas in Africa have promoted social change by spearheading struggles for independence. New democracy movements and people's struggles in the Philippines, Pakistan, Bangladesh, and some Latin American countries have been dramatic responses to repressive regimes and military dictatorships. By 1991 political reform in 25 countries in Asia, Africa, and Latin America now allows for wide voter participation in free elections with multiple candidates.[182]

Environmental Protection   Many new activist movements have begun to involve thousands of people to protect the endangered ecosystems in their countries. In 1976 Mexican activist GROs joined to agitate for the defense of nature,[183] and ecological movements in India and people's movements against the commercial destruction of rain forests in Brazil and other kinds of predatory development projects built countervailing political power.

A Brazilian congressman, for example, asserted that legislation against deforestation of the Amazon had been passed not because of international pressure or because congress understood the greenhouse effect, but because it was facing intense, organized pressure from Brazil's environmental movement and networks of Indian tribes.[184]

Women's Rights   Social movement organizations raise special questions of human development for women in developing nations where women often have a doubly subhuman status. Social movement organizations help women think and act independently of the men to whom they are often held to be subordinate.[185] Landless women's groups assert, for example, that

> We know that there is no easy or quick solution to our problem of food and clothing. As women did not even have the right to speak, in our organization we can now meet and speak, and share and discuss our problems. We feel that we are now human beings. We look forward to our weekly meetings where we stand up and speak—we can release ourselves as we have never been able to do before, and we now have the courage to speak the truth.[186]

MAKE TRADE FAIR

On March 15, 2004, Oxfam brought together human rights leaders, farm workers, and others in Immokalee, Florida, as part of its Make Trade Fair campaign, calling corporations, government, and consumers to action. A study released the same day by Oxfam America, titled "Like Machines in the Fields Workers Without Rights in American Agriculture," exposes how global business trends are occurring not only in underdeveloped countries but in the United States as well.[187]

Global brand name industries such as Yum Brands, the largest fast food company in the world, which owns Taco Bell, Kentucky Fried Chicken, Pizza Hut, and others, undermine labor standards by squeezing their supply chain to provide cheaper products. Producers in turn must substantially reduce their labor costs or be forced out of business. Instead of receiving their fair share of increased global trade, laborers often pay the price by working harder for less money under more hazardous conditions. It is not only "unacceptable that huge profits are being made off the backs of the hardest working and lowest paid workers in the world, but it is unconscionable that this is happening right here in the United States," said Oxfam America President Raymond C. Offenheiser. "In the United States, just as in underdeveloped nations, farm workers are systematically excluded from basic core labor rights which other American workers enjoy; the right to organize, rights to overtime pay as well as labor rights protecting children."[188] Said former UN High Commissioner for Human Rights, Mary Robinson. "This is discrimination and it must be corrected."[189]

Nearly 2 million farm workers in the United States, mainly immigrants, according to the Common Dreams Progressive Newswire, toil without rights, are excluded from most federal labor law protections, including the right to organize and bargain collectively, and suffer from poor sanitation and below poverty wages. In the fields of Florida, California, North Carolina, and other states, 1 million farm workers earn less than $7,500 per year. They earn no overtime pay, no health benefits, have insufficient water, and suffer from violence and abuse as a daily reality.

Companies such as Yum Brands, a *Fortune* 500 company, with $8.38 billion in revenues including $617 million in profits in 2003,[190] use their dominant market position to drive cost and risk down their supply chains. Global institutional buyers, Oxfam says, are the ones with the power and profits to ensure that workers get a fair share. Mary Robinson's "message to Yum Brands is: you can't pass the buck. You are profiting by exploitation and you have the power to change what is happening in the fields. So, pay this penny a pound more for workers rights and assume your fair share of responsibility."[191]

The Role of Social Work in International Social Activism   Macro social workers can align themselves in the struggle for emancipation with the oppressed people of the world by understanding that oppression inevitably carries within it the seeds of its own demise, and by joining new social movements that protect the environment, oppose corporate greed, and work against international conflict.

HOW TO PRACTICE INTERNATIONAL SOCIAL WORK

Practicing international social work depends on the history and culture of the people with whom you are working, the issues you are facing, the arena of your service, and the organization with which you are affiliated. However, some general principles can be applied to many situations. You will need to find a position, orient yourself, engage people, develop trust, develop empowerment, encourage decision making, develop plans, provide training, develop leadership, and evaluate your accomplishments.

Find a Position

The easiest and most accessible way to become involved in international social work is to become a volunteer, social work intern, or obtain a paid position in an international social welfare organization such as Oxfam, CARE, World Vision, or Church World Service that provide relief or promote community development; an international refugee service organization such as Refugees International; a child welfare organization such as Save the Children or Children's Aid International; a research and policy advocacy organization such as Worldwatch; a human rights organization such as Amnesty International; or with an indigenous child welfare agency or human service NGO or agency working with street children or orphans. You may also find employment in one of the United Nations organizations such as UNICEF, UN Development Program (UNDP), UN Disaster Relief Organization (UNDRO), or the High Commission for Refugees (UNHCR), or as a volunteer for the UN.

Orient Yourself

When you perform international social work, you often need to learn the language and understand the culture, customs, and history of the people with whom you are working. In addition, only with a mind freed from the presumption that Western ideas are superior can prevent you from unintentionally reinforcing the conditions you intend to change. You may, for example, come with a sincere intention to help develop people in an impoverished nation. Social workers who come from Canada or the United States,

however, cannot develop people who live in poverty. The only person you can develop is yourself, and the only people who can develop people who are impoverished are the people themselves.[192]

Modern developmental models represent top-down, rational, market-orientated ideas of "progress." You cannot be a representative of these ideas. Instead, you honor the ideals of human potential, self-determination, self-development, and the necessity for people to construct their own social reality and community culture. Self-reliant action by the people will not be determined by others' knowledge but by the knowledge and action of the people themselves. You cannot assist in the process of liberation if you are not first liberated yourself. *Tarun Mandals* (poor people's village organizations) give you this advice:

> We need outside help for analysis and understanding our situation and experience, but not for telling us what we should do. Initially we had genuinely thought that outsiders had our good at heart and knew better. We did not think much of ourselves and did not have ideas of our own.
>
> An outsider who comes with ready-made solutions and advice is worse than useless. He must first understand *from us* what our questions are, help articulate the questions better, and then help *us* to find solutions. An outsider also has to change. He alone is a friend who helps us to think about our problems *on our own*. The principle should be minimum intervention.[193]

Engage People

One of the hallmarks of an international social worker is your ability to engage people. No matter whether you are working in communities, NGOs, NGSOs, TNGOs or the UN, in the early stages of social work your main job is simply to get to know people and make friends with them. Talk to members about their lives, about the life of their community, organization, or program. Share with them who you are, and be as real and genuine as you can. Express real interest in people, their surroundings, their hopes and fears, and their personal situations. Relate their lives to something in your own life. When you develop common ground or rapport, real understanding and communication can begin. The more you talk with people and get to know them, the closer to them you will become, and the more you will become one of them.

Develop Trust

Relationships and communication develop trust. Trust is essential in all international social work. Your influence will depend on the extent to which the community, NGO, or social program members trust you. The fastest way to develop trust is visibility. Go to places where people congregate. Go to religious celebrations and traditional festivals. Try to become close to several key citizens. Once you have done this, you will more than likely be able to expand to other subgroups, because most communities, NGOs, and social organizations have overlapping networks of relationships. When you meet with a group of community members, listen to the issues, gather information, and take time to talk to key community leaders, or simply act as a participant-observer in the community itself.

Develop Empowerment

When you work to develop empowerment, you help people break the bonds of external and internal oppression, raise consciousness, challenge perceptions, and stimulate reflection.

External and Internal Oppression

One of the overriding tasks in an underdeveloped nation is helping its members break the bonds of oppression that hold them in chains. While overt oppression continues to plague people who are homeless, slaves, women, and children, the oppressed people's perception of their situation and their internalization of that oppression can also become a persistent and insidious enemy.

After centuries of conditioned helplessness, many people are trapped in "self-colonization." Freire calls this "playing host to the oppressor." In the United States this process has been called "learned helplessness," described in Chapter 8. Impoverished people may participate in their own self-oppression. They sometimes accept their role as an oppressed people and act in helpless and dependent ways rather than reject those roles. They may internalize the opinions that the oppressor holds of them as if they are true. They often believe themselves to be nothing more than "things" owned by oppressors.[194] People who have lived in destitution often blame themselves for the conditions that oppressors have placed on them.

Raise Consciousness

You help raise the consciousness of these people and assist them in developing a new attitude of empowerment. One way to do this is by using Paulo Freire's model of education of critical awareness and critical evaluation. Conscientization is a deepened consciousness of one's situation that leads people to understand their situation as a historical reality susceptible to transformation.[195] You help members by means of dialogue, simulation exercises, consciousness raising, and critical assessment exercises in which members examine their situation and self-perceptions.

Challenge Perceptions

You ask your members: "Who are we? For what reason do we exist? Why are we poor?" You help them understand that they are no different from the rich and the powerful and that poverty is not inherent in them but lies in situations that they can change.[196]

Stimulate Reflection

Stimulate people's reflection and analysis, assisted but not dominated by the knowledge and considerations you may have. Help each person to speak his or her mind with a spirit of acceptance, and listen carefully to his or her ideas, concerns, questions, and issues. As you listen, try to develop commonality, and look for patterns you can use in helping them organize in a common direction. Clarify objectives and help develop a sharper direction for their work. Ask people to deliberate on what they want to do long range and how the social movement organization can help them.

Encourage Decision Making

Your goal is to help members of communities make their own decisions, not judge whether the direction is the right one. The strength of your method is your conviction that ordinary working people are capable of social inquiry and analysis, and this capability can be enhanced by practice. Liberating education is more than the transfer of information; it is the practice of freedom. You affirm that even impoverished villagers have the capacity to direct their own development and discover a "truth" of their community that becomes as valid for them as scientific truth is to technologically minded members of the West.

Develop a Plan

At the end of the meeting or meetings, assist the group to come to some sort of decision. The key value in decision making is not efficiency but participation.

The time required to reach a decision should not be the shortest time required, nor should a small, select group make the decisions. Only those directly involved have the right to decide whether to implement or refuse an idea. You may provide information and support, but the ultimate strategy must remain the possession of those affected by the consequences.[197]

Involve members in understanding the principles of good decision making, and help members organize around their decision and come up with a plan. When they are ready, help them move toward implementation. Implementation of change in a community, or economic development, may include initiating a community project or volunteer effort, coordinating efforts with other communities, or developing a project that the community members agree will benefit them. Because those who dominate and exploit people control most of the material and financial resources in less developed nations, your members may decide to work toward justice and equity in the use of public resources.

Provide Training

Depending on the kinds of projects or issues with which your community group is confronted, you may need to arrange for training in legal rights, government policy, or process. You help people obtain their rightful share of normal public resources, learn how to use them, and engage in this process on their own. For example, it does not make sense to help members who are impoverished depend on voluntary agencies or special donors to obtain financial help for their projects when public resources are available. You help people who are poor understand that they have a right to receive credit from the banking system just as others do. You help your citizens use an NGO to obtain a loan for a brief period to establish themselves as good credit risks. Once they have a credit history and have gained confidence and skill in using credit wisely, you help them through a process of obtaining financing through regular financial lending agencies.

You help them learn how the banking system works, how to negotiate for a loan at favorable interest rates, and how to utilize their combined strength. When a system unjustly discriminates against the people with whom you are working, you help them affirm their rights. You train them in direct action tactics and strategies and help your members organize themselves to exercise their collective power.

Develop Leadership

One of your most important goals is to help move members toward leadership. You liberate members from the need for a trainer so that they become self-educators in their own learning. You help train members as facilitators who assist one another or consult with other grassroots organizations or NGOs in cultural, political, and economic self-reliance and decision making.

Evaluate

Assist your members to periodically evaluate their own experience and review their progress collectively and draw lessons from successes and failures. Help develop a consciousness among citizens so they see short-run failures as a learning process upon which subsequent strategy is to be built. A struggle is never lost if constructive lessons are drawn from its failure. After your members have reviewed their own work, ask an NGO to do a more systematic and formal assessment based on the members' own objectives.

USING THE INTERNET IN INTERNATIONAL SOCIAL WORK

Networks of grassroots women's groups and indigenous peoples have discovered that several powerful tools formerly used to achieve conquest of land and labor may now be used to construct a more caring world. Electronic communications, including the Internet and the World Wide Web, which were initially introduced for military surveillance and continue to serve as a means to control populations, have now become tools for liberation. The World Wide Web is now being used as a tool in international social activism that provides services, empowerment, and community development.

International E-Activism and E-Services

The Internet is a tool ideally suited for networking by international activists. Because goals of transformation are often urgent, you may empower working people and youth to use the Internet to gain worldwide access to sources of liberating information that can be freely shared. You help local people organize their communities and beyond by sending messages of protest that are heard around the world.[198]

NGOs and individuals are beginning to use the Internet to assist in providing services. For example, Mark Homan observes that although most of the library books and documents have been destroyed at Kabul University in Afghanistan, a country devastated by 23 years of war, a grant from UNESCO has provided a cyberspace connection to an Internet café located inside the main library with nine computers.[199]

In Bangladesh, many doctors and health workers lack the expertise to recognize an illness at its early stages. A private company called Bangladesh Telemedicine Services (BTS) has set up telemedicine centers to help doctors identify diseases early. The centers will be linked to a network of 200 specialists on hand to offer their expert opinion.

In South India, 5 to 10 fishermen died each year due to drowning. An NGO called MS Swaminathan Research Foundation established a telecenter to collect data from a U.S. Navy space satellite that measures wave heights to predict storms at sea. Pakkialouchme, a 24-year-old Dalit woman in India, translates this data on the Internet in Tamil, and every afternoon while fishermen sit on the beach to mend their nets, storm warnings pour out through a series of loudspeakers planted along the shoreline. Since installation of the telecentre 2 years ago, there have been no additional deaths.

E-Empowerment

The Asian Women's Resource Exchange (AWORC), an Internet-based women's information service and network, increases access and application of communication technologies for women's empowerment. Its goal is to enhance Internet literacy and social activism among women and women's organizations. The website includes a keyword search engine in English, Korean, and Japanese and links to participating organizations.

E-Development

Two international organizations, One World, an online sustainable development and human rights network, and Benton Foundation, founder of the Digital Divide Network, have created the Digital Opportunity Channel, an online community that focuses on the use of information and communications technologies for sustainable development, bringing greater equality and international understanding by news and information pieces, success stories in development, and search capabilities on information and communication technology.[200]

CONCLUSION

In the 500 years since European explorers first encountered indigenous people in the Americas, India, and Asia, the Enlightenment has increased the wealth of European and North American nations, but it has created poverty for much of the remainder of the world's population. Modernity continues to destroy communal identity and negates the freedom, self-determination, and humanity fundamental to indigenous cultures of non-market-centered nations. The modern project generates violence, creates hopelessness, breeds dependency, and undermines the human spirit. It has contributed to human bondage, slavery, and trafficking in persons. It has fomented war and international conflict, resulting in the displacement of people. It endangers the land and decimates wildlife, forests, rivers, lakes, and oceans.

Members of the least developed nations are beginning to exercise their right of refusal to accept the market-centered, rational, goal-maximizing Enlightenment tradition and to reject colonial mentality and patriarchal rule. They are autonomously and spontaneously reasserting their prerogative as humans to choose new social forms worldwide that provide room for the social, renewed communal relations, and recognition of the value of their indigenous cultures. Where windows of opportunity emerged, they began to create small *communidades de base* and other GROs. As they acquired experience and strength, they began joining forces in an amazing variety of processes through NGOs, expressing the ingenuity, diversity, and creativity that people generate when they solve problems together. They have become a global social movement of momentous proportions.

Generalist-based macro social workers, trained in a variety of methods, who think creatively and broadly about how to remediate or prevent social problems, and who are motivated to empower and strengthen our social environment, may be able to engage people in sustainable human development projects by means of community social planning, community organization, and economic and community development. Social workers can use skills in advocacy, policy, and political intervention to help shift the extent to which the global market society has created a hegemony of exploitation and oppression in developing nations.

Macro social workers dedicated to eradicating economic, political, and social injustice can help indigenous people claim the right to their own culture and way of life, free of the encroachments of global corporations. By working with larger social movements, they can help establish economic justice, eradicate slavery, prevent the arms trade and armed conflict, protect the environment, and prevent human rights abuses. Enormous challenges and opportunities await the social work profession and macro social workers who help orphans, refugees, street children, families who are living in poverty, and victims of disasters and war.

Macro social workers are among those professionals best suited for the complicated social issues facing people in our global society, but relatively few social workers have accepted the challenge to become engaged in international social work efforts. The social work profession in both the United States and Canada is far from active in helping people in developing nations who are on the path to true cultural and social autonomy. Often concerned with conducting private psychotherapeutic practice, many social workers in the United States have ignored the misery of the 80% of the world's population that lives in poverty and oppressive conditions.

Working at the international level is the "conquest of a small piece of humanity for the common heritage of human kind," asserts Amilcar Cabral.[201] When you engage in international social work, you participate in an emancipatory project with people in one of the most important and vital arenas of social work. Those of you who become involved in international social work will no doubt play an increasingly important role in shaping the future. Helping people build a new social world, create their own communities, and in the process construct themselves is what social work is all about. The new global social revolution and practice of international social work waits for you to accept its challenge.

KEY CONCEPTS

international social
   work
international community
   development
International Red Cross

international social
   work education
International Missionary
   Council
global market

United Nations (UN)
modern development
most developed nation
developing nation
underdeveloped nation
Bretton Woods
international
   governmental
   organizations (IGOs)
World Trade
   Organization (WTO)
UN Security Council
General Agreement on
   Trade and Tariffs
   (GATT)
International Monetary
   Fund (IMF)
World Bank
structural adjustment
   programs (SAP)
multinational
   corporation (MNC)
transnational
   corporation (TNC)
international
   nongovernmental
   organizations (INGO)
international social
   work education
AIDS
World Health
   Organization (WHO)
decolonization
First Earth Summit
free market
currency and foreign
   exchange markets
global poverty
standard of living
gross domestic product
   (GDP)
purchasing power parity
   (PPP)
slavery

trafficking in persons
child slavery
debt bondage
forced labor
marital slavery
traditional slavery
international conflict
manufacturing
   violence
international arms
   sales
refugees
refugee fatigue
foreign aid
global ecosystem
international social
   organizations
grassroots organization
   (GRO)
broad-based grassroots
   organization
   (BBGRO)
communidades
   ecclesiales de base
communidades de base
conscientization
submergence
convergence
secularization
generation
single-focus GRO
broad-based GRO
urban GRO
rural GRO
regional GRO
nongovernmental
   organization (NGO)
nongovernmental
   support organization
   (NGSO)
transnational
   nongovernmental
   organization (TNGO)

United Nations Development Program (UNDP)

UNICEF

United Nations High Commissioner for Relief (UNHCR)

United Nations Disaster Relief Organization (UNDRO)

United Nations Fund for Population Activities (UNFPA)

United Nations Capital Development Fund (UNCDF)

World Food Program (WFP)

World Health Organization (WHO)

International Federation of Social Workers (IFSW)

International Association of Schools of Social Work (IASSW)

international relief and refugee services

sustainable human development

CARE

Oxfam

international community economic development

international social action

international social movements

colonialism

critical consciousness

culture of oppression

regain identity

reconstitute culture

popular resistance

cooperative alliances

political action

environmental action

false consciousness

practice of international social work

international e-activism

international e-services

international e-empowerment

international e-development

QUESTIONS FOR DISCUSSION

1. What are some of the premises, ideas, and characteristics of modern developed nations? How do they affect people in developing and least developed nations?

2. What is meant by "development"? What positive benefits has development provided? What negative consequences has it had? Can development be used to help poor people in developing nations enter modernity?

3. What would happen if the entire world were to become completely modern? Would this be an event that you would welcome? Why or why not?

4. The point was made that because of modernity, the developed nations of Europe and North America have prospered economically and politically. Critique this assertion. In your critique, consider the comment of Alberto Ramos, a Brazilian scholar and politician, who asserts that modernity has won a phyrric victory. In what sense has modernity benefited Europe and North America? In what sense is the triumph of modernity a phyrric victory?

5. David Beckman asserts that foreign aid to developing nations contributes to combating hunger, disease, and poverty. Critique his assertion. Is foreign aid the answer to helping people in developing countries? Under what circumstances should it be used? When should it not be used?

6. It was asserted that U.S. and Canadian social workers individually and as a profession are often not active at the international level. Do you agree with this statement? If so, what are its implications for the field of social work and for our global society?

ADDITIONAL READING

Base Ecclesial Communities

Barreiro, Alvaro. *Basic Ecclesial Communities: The Evangelization of the Poor.* Barbara Campbell, trans. Maryknoll, NY: Orbis, 1982.

Boff, Leonardo. *Ecclesiogenesis: The Base Communities Reinvent the Church.* Robert R. Barr, trans. Maryknoll, NY: Orbis, 1986.

Cook, Guillermo. *The Expectation of the Poor: Latin American Basic Ecclesial Communities in Protestant Perspective.* Maryknoll, NY: Orbis, 1985.

Gutierrez, Gustavo. *The Power of the Poor in History.* Maryknoll, NY: Orbis, 1983.

Hewitt, W. E. *Base Christian Communities and Social Change in Brazil.* Lincoln: University of Nebraska Press, 1991.

Kleissler, Thomas A., Margo A. LeBert, and Mary McGuinness. *Small Christian Communities: A Vision of Hope.* Mahwah, NJ: Paulist Press, 1991.

Torres, Sergio and John Eagleson, eds. *The Challenge of Basic Christian Communities.* John Drury, trans. Maryknoll, NY: Orbis, 1981.

Vandenakker, John Paul. *Small Christian Communities and the Parish: An Ecclesiological Analysis of the North American Experience.* Kansas City, MO: Sheed and Ward, 1994.

International NGOs and Nonprofit Organizations

Clark, John. *Democratizing Development: The Role of Voluntary Organizations.* West Hartford, CN: Kumarian Press, 1990.

Fisher, Julie. *The Road From Rio: Sustainable Development and the Nongovernmental Movement in the Third World.* London: Prager, 1993.

Fisher, Julie. *Non-Governments: NGOs and the Political Development of the Third World.* West Hartford, CN: Kumarian Press, 1998.

James, Estelle, ed. *The Nonprofit Sector in International Perspective: Studies in Comparative Culture and Policy.* New York: Oxford University Press, 1989.

McCarthy, Kathleen D. et al., eds. *The Nonprofit Sector in the Global Community: Voices From Many Nations.* San Francisco: Jossey-Bass, 1992.

Salamon, Lester M. *The Global Associational Revolution: The Rise of the Third Sector on the World Scene.* Johns Hopkins University Occasional Paper Series, No. 15. Baltimore, MD: Shriver Hall, April 1993.

Wuthnow, Robert, ed. *Between States and Markets: The Voluntary Sector in Comparative Perspective.* Princeton: Princeton University Press, 1991.

International Social Work

Hokenstad, M.C., S. K. Khinduka, and J. Midgley, eds. *Profiles in International Social Work.* Washington, DC: NASW Press, 1992.

Development Planning

Chowdhury, Anis and Colin Kirkpatrick. *Development Policy and Planning: An Introduction to Models and Techniques.* London: Routledge, 1994.

Singh, Abhimany. *Planning for Developing a Backward Economy.* New Delhi: Vikas, 1991.

Development Policy

Apthorpe, Yamond and Des Gasper, eds. *Arguing Development Policy: Frames and Discourses.* London: Frank Cass, 1966.

Friedman, John. *Empowerment: The Politics of Alternative Development.* Cambridge, MA: Blackwell, 1992.

Kempe, Hope. *Development in the Third World: From Policy Failure to Policy Reform.* Armonk, NY: M. E. Sharpe, 1996.

Kurer, Oskar. *The Political Foundations of Development Policies.* Lanham, MD: University Press of America, 1997.

International Development Practice

Campfens, Hubert. *Community Development Around the World.* Toronto: University of Toronto Press, 1997.

Jedlicka, Allen. *Volunteerism and World Development: Pathway to a New World.* New York: Praeger, 1990.

Lappe, Frances Moore and Joseph Collins. *World Hunger: Twelve Myths.* New York: Grove Press, 1986.

La Pierre, Dominque. *The City of Joy.* Garden City, NY: Doubleday, 1995.

McMichael, Philip. *Development and Social Change: A Global Perspective.* Thousand Oaks, CA: Pine Forge Press, 1996.

Rapley, John. *Understanding Development: Theory and Practice in the Third World.* Boulder, CO: Lynne Rienner, 1996.

Subbarao, K. et al. *Safety Net Programs and Poverty Reduction: Lessons From Cross-Country Experience.* Washington, DC: World Bank, 1997.

World Bank. *Liveable Cities for the 21st Century.* Washington, DC: World Bank, 1996.

Development Theory

Escobar, Arturo. *Encountering Development. The Making and Unmaking of the Third World.* Princeton, NJ: Princeton University Press, 1995.

Hettne, Bjorn. *Development Theory and the Three Worlds,* 2d ed. Edinburgh Gate, England: Addison Wesley Longman, 1995.

McClelland, David. *The Achieving Society.* New York: Van Nostrand, 1961.

Osterhammel, Juergen. *Colonialism a Theoretical Overview.* Princeton, NJ: Marcus Weiner, 1997.

Rostow, W. W. *The Stages of Economic Growth.* Cambridge: Cambridge University Press, 1960.

Seabrook, Jeremy. *Victims of Development: Resistance and Alternatives.* London: Verso, 1993.

Liberation Theology

Bonino, Jon. *Doing Theology in a Revolutionary Situation.* Philadelphia: Fortress, 1975.

Gutierrez, Gustavo. *Theology of Liberation.* Maryknoll, NY: Orbis, 1973.

Gutierrez, Gustavo. *The Power of the Poor in History.* Maryknoll, NY: Orbis, 1983.

Modernization

Black, Cyril E. *The Dynamics of Modernization.* New York: Harper, 1967.

Brown, Richard D. *Modernization: The Transformation of American Life, 1600–1865*. New York: Hill and Wang, 1976.

Dube, S. C. *Modernization and Development: The Search for Alternative Paradigms*. Tokyo: United Nations University, 1988.

Inkeles, Charles and David Smith. *Becoming Modern*. Cambridge, MA: Harvard University Press, 1974.

Social Critique

Amin, Samir. *Unequal Development*. New York: Monthly Review Press, 1976.

Freire, Paulo. *Pedagogy of the Oppressed*. New York: Herder and Herder, 1970.

Freire, Paulo. *Education for Critical Consciousness*. New York: Seabury Press, 1973.

Gramsci, Antonio. *Selections From the Prison Notebooks*. New York: International Publishers, 1971.

Habermas, Jurgen. *Knowledge and Human Interest*. Jeremy Shapirs, trans. Boston: Beacon, 1983.

Luke, Timothy. *Social Theory and Modernity: Critique, Dissent, and Revolution*. Newbury Park, CA: Sage, 1990.

International Social Problems

Bales, Kevin. *Disposable People: New Slavery in the Global Economy*. Berkeley, CA: University of California Press, 1999.

Environment

"The World Directory of Environmental Organizations Online: Who's Doing What to Protect the Earth's Resources." California Institute of Public Affairs. (http://ww.interenvironment.org)

Internet

Hick, S. and J. McNutt, *Advocacy, Activism and the Internet: Community Organizing and Social Policy*. Chicago, IL: Lyceum Books, 2002.

Websites

Canadian International Development Agency (CIDA): http://www.acdi-cida.ge.ca/index.htm

Organization for Economic Co-operation and Development (OECD): http://www.oecd.org/

Peace Corps: http://www.peacecorps.gov/

International Committee of the Red Cross (ICRC): http://www.icrc.org/

International Council on Social Welfare: http://www.icsw.org

International Federation of Social Workers: http://www.ifsw.org

Inter-University Consortium for International Social Development (IUCISD): http://www.iucisd.org

ReliefWeb: http://www.reliefweb.int/

United Nations Children's Fund (UNICEF): http://www.unicef.org

United Nations Educational, Scientific, and Cultural Organization (UNESCO): http://www.unesco.org

United Nations High Commissioner for Refugees (UNHCR): http://www.unhcr.ch/

United Nations Volunteers: http://www.unv.org/

United Way International: http://www.uwint.org/

U.S. Department of State Bureau of Population, Refugees and Migration: http://www.state.gov

U.S. Agency for International Development (USAID): http://www.usaid.gov/

World Food Program: http://www.wfp.org/

World Health Organization (WHO): http://www.who.int

Epilogue

Macro Social Work: A Profession of Heroes

The Categorical Imperative

We ought always and in every way treat mankind and every other rational being as an end and never merely as a means only.

Immanuel Kant, Groundwork of the Metaphysic of Morals

Encircled by Love

The woman who took care of my daughter when she was little was a Greek Jew. She was very young, nine, ten, eleven when the war broke out, and was lying on the crematorium door when the American troops came through. So she has a number tattooed on her arm.

And it was always like being hit in the stomach with a brick when she would take my baby and sit and circle her with her arm, and there was the number. So encircled by love and suffering shared, we are no longer in the "giving-getting" mode. We know ourselves as social selves, parents and children, members of a people, inheritors of a history and a culture that we must nurture through memory and hope.[1]

Robert Bellah et al., Habits of the Heart

Ideas in the Epilogue

Macro social workers such as Dorothy Day show compassion in a world that is often uncaring, altruism in a world of selfish consumption, sacrifice in a world of self-interest, and humanity in a world rife with dehumanization.

IRENA SENDLER: SOCIAL WORK RESCUER

In 1940 Nazis confined 500,000 Polish Jews in the Warsaw Ghetto to await their deaths. Most people in Warsaw turned their backs, but not Irena Sendler.[2] A Warsaw social worker, Sendler decided to invest herself in this community and wangled a permit to check for signs of typhus, a disease that the Nazis feared. Sendler decided to do something about what she saw. Joining Zegota, a tiny underground cell dedicated to rescuing the Jews, she took on the code name "Jolanta." Because the deportations of Jews had already begun, it was impossible to save the adults, so Sendler began smuggling children out in an ambulance.

Over the next 3 years Sendler successfully transported more than 2,000 Jewish children to safety, giving them temporary new identities. To keep track of the children's real names, she placed information about their identities in bottles, which she buried in her garden. It was difficult for Sendler to find people willing to help these children. However, after much effort, she did find families and developed a network of churches and convents that were willing to help. "I have clothing for the convent," she would write, and the nuns would come and pick up the children.

In 1943 the Gestapo arrested and tortured Sendler and sentenced her to die. At the last minute, her colleagues in the Polish underground bribed a prison guard to free her, listing her as "executed" on the official form. In hiding Sendler continued her work of rescuing children. After the war, she dug up her bottles and began searching for the parents of the children she had rescued. She could find only a few of the parents because most had died in Nazi concentration camps. Years later, when Irena Sendler was honored for her rescue work and her picture appeared in a newspaper, "a man, a painter, telephoned me," Sendler said. "I remember your face," he said. "It was you who took me out of the Ghetto." Sendler had many calls like that.

MACRO SOCIAL WORKERS AND HEROES OF SOCIAL JUSTICE

Macro social work is a field in the profession of social work that aims at community betterment; developing, administering, and improving social organizations, engaging in social policy and social movements, and helping construct a better global society. We need social workers of vision, commitment, and courage who see a future in which social relationships among people are as important as technological advancement; in which community solidarity and engagement are prized as much as organizational efficiency and effectiveness; in which heroes of social justice are revered as much as flamboyant entertainment celebrities or sports figures.

The trend in social work for the last several decades, however, has been away from macro social concerns and toward micro social work practice.[3] Counseling and psychotherapy are needed, and there are many rewards in treating individuals, couples, and families and helping people change their lives and overcome personal troubles. Much good is being done helping people break cycles of abuse, codependency, and addictions as well as treating depression, anxieties, and other emotional and behavioral disorders. As important as micro social work is, however, the extent to which we focus our professional energies on individual problems rather than the social conditions that may have brought them about, the more we tend to ignore our wider and more fundamental social problems.

It would be tragic, asserts Noam Chomsky, if those who are fortunate enough to live in the advanced societies of the West were to forget or abandon the hope that our society can be transformed to an environment in which the creative spirit is alive, and in which life is an adventure full of hope and joy, based on the impulse to construct rather than seize what is possessed by others or the desire to hold onto what we possess.[4]

In this book you have explored how the poor people of the earth, who have often been exploited by unjust economic and political systems of the modern age, are reinventing society and helping to bring about a new postmodern era. Ordinary people in their own communities are creating new planning councils, faith-based community organizations, community development corporations, social organizations, new social movements, and *base communidades,* which are transforming the way we think about social problems, leadership, social relationships, and the nature of the human condition. You have discovered how macro social workers align themselves with those who seem to be the least significant but who, in reality, are the only ones who have the power to change our modern dominance and control-oriented society into a more just and humane world.

You have learned how the reactive social problem-solving approach is giving way to social change. Instead of weaknesses, you have discovered how macro social workers are looking at people's strengths. Instead of relying exclusively on modern rational problem solving, you have discovered that macro social workers are using whole-mind social thinking. Rather than patriarchal control, macro social workers exemplify social leadership. Instead of impersonal *gesellschaft* relationships, macro social workers work to enrich society with personal and communal *gemeinschaft* relationships.

Unlike corporate executives or business entrepreneurs who accumulate private capital for their own use, you have discovered how macro social workers help communities of people generate social capital and social goods for the benefit of all. Macro social workers pioneer in engaging social organizations, not large modern complex organizations. Instead of management of people, macro social workers excel in social administration, providing service instead of servitude. Macro social workers are not reactivists who look to the past, inactivists who hold onto the present, or proactivists who rush toward technological progress, but interactivists who take a sustainable, holistic approach to inventing society. You have found that macro social workers want to reform society, but more important, they seek to transform it through postmodern movements that work to place society on a new basis of social opportunity for all. You have explored how macro social workers oppose the modern, exploitative developmental model and engage in authentic international community development in which people take charge of their own lives.

It is my hope that you have learned how you can be part of bringing the new postmodern era into existence, and I hope you will want to be a participant with those who are the least likely, the poor ones of the earth, in that effort. If so, you will become a member of a group of outstanding macro social workers. You will join social workers of the stature of Saint

Elizabeth Ann Seton, Clara Barton, Charles Booth, Dorothea Dix, Canon Samuel Barnett, Reverend Charles Loring Brace, Homer Folks, Graham Taylor, Clara Barton, Sojourner Truth, Mary Parker Follett, Mary Simkhovitch, Grace and Edith Abbott, Clifford Beers, Harriet Tubman, Lord Robert Baden-Powell, Sophonisba Breckenridge, Sir George Williams, Lillian Wald, Dorothy Day, Reverend William Booth, Jane Addams, Harry Hopkins, Mary McLeod Bethune, Saint Frances Cabrini, W. E. B. Du Bois, Wilbur Cohen, Toyohiko Kagawa, Si Kahn, Jeanette Rankin, Michael Harrington, Whitney M. Young Jr., Florence Kelly, Josephine Shaw Lowell, and Bertha Capen Reynolds.

You will become partners with these heroes of social justice in the United States as well as around the world who want to bring an end to oppression, inhumanity, and injustice: Ida B. Wells–Barnett, Marian Wright Edelman, Frederick Douglass, Carrie Chapman Catt, Senator Thadeus Stevens, Mary Harris "Mother" Jones, A. Phillip Randolph Jr., Ida Tarbell, Rev. Walter Rauschenbusch, Mary B. McDowell, Susan B. Anthony, Rev. Dr. Martin Luther King Jr., Lucretia Mott, George Wiley, Roy Wilkins, Alice Paul, Rev. John Perkins, Elizabeth Stanton Cady, Cesar Chavez, Saul Alinsky, and many others. The contributions of these macro social workers and workers for social justice have changed the direction of our nation and improved the quality of our lives.

We need to remember these heroes and their accomplishments. They form a "cloud of witnesses" whose vision and dedication support our efforts today and on whose shoulders we ride. From these heroes we can learn compassion in a world that is often uncaring, altruism in a world of selfish consumption, sacrifice in a world of self-interest, and humanity in a world rife with dehumanization. Not only are the accomplishments of these macro social workers impressive, but the writing by and about them is prodigious. Read about some of these macro social workers and the books they have written. You will be inspired and come to a better understanding of what macro social workers have accomplished. You will learn about the challenges that await you and discover how you, too, can become a hero for others.

Edith Abbott (1876–1957)

Edith Abbott. *Democracy and Social Progress in England.* Chicago: University of Chicago Press, 1918.

Edith Abbott. *Historical Aspects of the Immigration Problem.* New York: Arno, 1969.

Edith Abbott. *Immigration. Selected Documents and Case Records.* New York: Arno, 1969.

Edith Abbott. *The One Hundred and One County Jails of Illinois and Why They Ought to Be Abolished.* Chicago: 1916.

Edith Abbott. *Public Assistance: American Principles and Policies.* NY: Russell and Russell, 1966.

Edith Abbott. *The Real Jail Problem.* Chicago: Juvenile Protective Association of Chicago, 1915.

Edith Abbott. *Social Welfare and Professional Education.* Chicago: University of Chicago Press, 1942.

Edith Abbott. *Some American Pioneers in Social Welfare.* New York: Russell and Russell, 1963. (Original work published 1937)

Edith Abbott. *The Tenements of Chicago, 1908–1935.* New York: Arno, 1970. (Original work published 1936)

Edith Abbott. *Truance and Non-attendance in Chicago Schools.* New York: Arno, 1970. (Original work published 1916)

Edith Abbott. *Women in Industry: A Study in American Economic History.* New Salem, NH: Ayer, 1969. (Original work published 1910)

Grace Abbott (1878–1939)

Grace Abbott. *The Child and the State, Select Documents.* New York: Greenwood, 1968. (Original work published 1938)

Grace Abbott. *From Relief to Social Security: The Development of the New Public Welfare Services and Their Administration.* New York: Russell and Russell, 1966. (Original work published 1941)

Grace Abbott. *The Immigrant and the Community.* New York: J. S. Ozer, 1971. (Original work published 1917)

Grace Abbott. *The Juvenile Court and a Community Program for Treating and Preventing Delinquency.* Chicago: 1936.

Grace Abbott. *The Social Security Act and Relief.* Chicago: 1936.

Grace Abbott. *Ten Years Work for Children.* Washington, DC: Government Printing Office, 1923.

Lela B. Costin. *Two Sisters for Social Justice: A Biography of Grace and Edith Abbott.* Urbana: University of Illinois Press, 1983.

Jane Addams (1860–1935)

Jane Addams. *Democracy and Social Ethics.* Cambridge: Belknap Press of Harvard University, 1964.

Jane Addams. *Jane Addams on Peace, War, and International Understanding, 1899–1932.* Allen F. Davis, ed. New York: Garland, 1976.

Jane Addams. *A New Conscience and an Ancient Evil.* New York: Arno, 1972.

Jane Addams. *Newer Ideas of Peace.* New York: J. S. Ozer, 1972.

Jane Addams. *Peace and Bread in Time of War.* New York: J. S. Ozer, 1972.

Jane Addams. *Philanthropy and Social Progress.* Montclair, NJ: Patterson Smith, 1970.

Jane Addams. *The Social Thought of Jane Addams.* Christopher Lasch, ed. New York: Irvington, 1982.

Jane Addams. *The Spirit of Youth and the City Streets.* Urbana: University of Illinois Press, 1989. (Original work published 1909)

Jane Addams. *Twenty Years at Hull House.* New York: Penguin Books, 1998.

Jane Addams. *The Second Twenty Years at Hull House.* New York: Macmillan, 1930.

Frank E. Aloise. *Jane Addams.* New York: Crowell, 1971.

Allen F. Davis. *American Heroine: The Life and Legend of Jane Addams.* Chicago: Ivan Dee, 2000.

Mary Jo Deegan. *Jane Addams and the Men of the Chicago School, 1892–1918.* New Brunswick, NJ: Transaction Books, 1988.

John C. Farrell. *Beloved Lady: A History of Jane Addams' Ideas on Reform and Peace.* Baltimore, MD: John Hopkins Press, 1967.

Mary Kittredge. *Jane Addams: Helper of the Poor.* New York: Chelsea House, 1988.

Daniel Levine. *Jane Addams and the Liberal Tradition.* Westport, CT: Greenwood, 1980.

James Linn. *Jane Addams: A Biography.* Urbana: University of Illinois Press, 2000.

Eleanor J. Stebner. *The Women of Hull House: A Study in Spirituality, Vocation, and Friendship.* Albany: State University of New York Press, 1997.

Margaret Tims. *Jane Addams of Hull House, 1860–1935.* New York: Macmillan, 1981.

Lord Robert Baden-Powell (1857–1941)

Robert Baden-Powell. *Scouting for Boys.* London: C. A. Pearson, 1910.

Howard Fast. *Lord Baden-Powell of the Boy Scouts.* New York: J. Messner, 1941.

Tim Jeal. *The Boy-Man: The Life of Lord Baden-Powell.* New York: Morrow, 1990.

Duncan W. Grinnell-Milne. *Baden-Powell at Mafekin.* London: Bodley Head, 1957.

William Hillcourt. *Baden-Powell: The Two Lives of a Hero.* New York: G. P. Putnam's Sons, 1964.

Ernest Edwin Reynolds. *Baden-Powell: A Biography of Lord Baden-Powell of Gilwell.* London: Oxford University Press, 1943.

Canon Samuel Barnett (1844–1913)

Samuel Barnett. *Religion and Progress.* New York: Macmillan, 1907.

Samuel Barnett and Henrietta Barnett. *Towards Social Reform.* New York: Macmillan, 1909.

Henrietta Barnett. *Canon Barnett: His Life, Work, and Friends,* 2 vols. Boston: Houghton Mifflin, 1919.

Clara Barton (1821–1912)

Clara Barton. *The Story of the Red Cross: Glimpses of Field Work.* New York: Airmont, 1968. (Original work published 1904)

Clara Barton. *The Red Cross in Peace and War.* Meriden, CT: Journal Publishing, 1912.

Clara Barton. *The Story of My Childhood.* New York: Arno, 1980.

William E. Barton. *The Life of Clara Barton: Founder of the American Red Cross.* New York: AMS Press, 1969.

David Burton. *Clara Barton: In the Service of Humanity.* Westport, CT: Greenwood, 1995.

Jeannette Covert. *The Story of Clara Barton of the Red Cross.* New York: J. Messner, 1941.

Leni Hamilton. *Clara Barton.* New York: Chelsea House, 1988.

Stephen B. Oates. *A Woman of Valor: Clara Barton and the Civil War.* New York: Free Press, 1994.

Elizabeth Pryor. *Clara Barton: Professional Angel.* Philadelphia: University of Pennsylvania Press, 1987.

Susan Sloate. *Clara Barton: Founder of the American Red Cross.* New York: Fawcett, 1990.

Clifford Beers (1876–1943)

Clifford Beers. *A Mind That Found Itself: An Autobiography.* Pittsburgh, PA: University of Pittsburgh Press, 1981.

Clifford Beers. *The Aftercare of the Insane.* New Haven, CT: Bradley and Scoville, 1909.

Clifford Beers. *A Society for Mental Hygiene as an Agency for Social Service and Education.* New Haven, CT: 1910.

Norman Dain. *Clifford W. Beers: Advocate for the Insane.* Pittsburgh, PA: University of Pittsburgh Press, 1980.

Mary McLeod Bethune (1875–1955)

Mary McLeod Bethune. *Building a Better World: Essays and Selected Documents.* Audrey McCluskey, ed. Bloomington: Indiana University Press, 1999.

Olive Burt. *Mary McLeod Bethune.* Indianapolis IN.: Bobbs-Merrill, 1970.

Rackham Holt. *Mary McLeod Bethune: A Biography.* Garden City, NY: Doubleday, 1964.

Milton Meltzner. *Mary McLeod Bethune: Voice of Black Hope.* New York: Viking, 1987.

Catherine O. Peare. *Mary McLeod Bethune.* New York: Vanguard, 1951.

Beth P. Wilson. *Giants for Justice: Bethune, Randolph, and King.* New York: Harcourt, Brace, Jovanovich, 1978.

Ruby Radford. *Mary McLeod Bethune.* New York: Vanguard Press, 1951.

Rinna Wolfe. *Mary McLeod Bethune.* New York: F. Watts, 1992.

Charles Booth (1840–1916)

Charles Booth. *Life and Labour of the People of London*, 9 vols. New York: Macmillan, 1892–1897.

Charles Booth. *Pauperism: A Picture.* London: Macmillan, 1892.

Charles Booth. *Old Age Pensions and the Aged Poor: A Proposal.* London: Macmillan, 1899.

T. S. Simey and M. B. Simey. *Charles Booth: Social Scientist.* Westport, CT: Greenwood Press, 1980.

William Booth (1829–1912)

William Booth. *In Darkest England and the Way Out.* London: International Headquarters of the Salvation Army, 1890.

William Booth. *Training of Children.* London: Salvation Army, 1888.

William Booth. *The Vagrant and Unemployable.* London: Salvation Army, 1909.

Richard Collier. *The General Next to God: The Story of William Booth and the Salvation Army.* New York: Dutton, 1965.

Ervine St. John. *God's Soldier: General William Booth.* New York: Macmillan, 1935.

Norman E. Nygaard. *Trumpet of Salvation: The Story of William and Catherine Booth.* Grand Rapids, MI: Zondervan, 1961.

Harold C. Steele. *I Was a Stranger: The Faith of William Booth: Founder of the Salvation Army.* New York: Exposition, 1954.

Charles Loring Brace (1826–1890)

Charles Loring Brace. *The Best Method of Disposing of Our Pauper and Vagrant Children.* New York: Wynkoop, Hallenbeck and Thomas, 1859.

Charles Loring Brace. *The Dangerous Classes of New York and Twenty Years Among Them.* Silver Spring, MD: National Association of Social Workers, 1978. (Original work published 1880)

Charles Loring Brace. *The Life of Charles Loring Brace.* Emma Brace, ed. New York: Arno, 1976.

Sophonisba Preston Breckenridge (1866–1948)

Sophonisba Breckenridge and Edith Abbott. *The Delinquent Child and the Home.* New York: Survey Associates, 1912.

Sophonisba Breckenridge and Edith Abbott. *The Housing Problem in Chicago.* Chicago: University of Chicago Press, 1910–1915.

Barr, Nancy Ellen. *A Profession for Women: Education, Social Service Administration, and Feminism in the Life of Sophonisba Preston Breckenridge, 1886–1948.* Ph.D. Thesis, Emory University, 1993.

St. Frances Cabrini (1850–1917)

Lucille Papin Borden. *Francesca Cabrini.* New York: Macmillan, 1945.

Pietro Di Donato. *Immigrant Saint: The Life of Mother Cabrini.* New York: St. Martin's Press, 1991.

Dorothy Day (1897–1980)

Dorothy Day. *From Union Square to Rome.* New York: Arno Press, 1978.

Dorothy Day. *Little by Little: Selected Writings of Dorothy Day.* Maryknoll, NY: Orbis Books, 1992.

Dorothy Day. *Loaves and Fishes.* Maryknoll, NY: Orbis Books, 1997.

Dorothy Day. *The Long Loneliness: Autobiography of Dorothy Day.* San Francisco: Harper, 1981.

Dorothy Day. *On Pilgrimage.* Grand Rapids, MI: W. B. Eerdmans, 1999.

Dorothy Day. *On Pilgrimage: The Sixties.* New York: Curtis Books, 1972.

Dorothy Day. *Selections From Her Writings.* Michael Garvey, ed. Springfield, MD: Templegate, 1996.

Michele Teresa Aronica. *Beyond Charismatic Leadership: The New York Catholic Worker Movement.* New Brunswick, NJ: Transaction Books, 1987.

Robert Coles. *Dorothy Day: A Radical Devotion.* Reading, MA: Addison-Wesley, 1989.

David R. Collins. *Got a Penny? The Story of Dorothy Day.* Boston: Pauline Books and Media, 1996.

Marie Dennis. *A Retreat With Oscar Romero and Dorothy Day: Walking With the Poor.* Cincinnati, OH: St. Anthony Messenger Press, 1997.

James S. Forest. *Love Is the Measure: A Biography of Dorothy Day.* Maryknoll, NY: Orbis Books, 1994.

Deborah Kent. *Dorothy Day: Friend to the Forgotten.* Grand Rapids, MI: W. B. Eerdmans, 1996.

William D. Miller. *Dorothy Day: A Biography.* San Francisco: Harper and Row, 1982.

June O'Connor. *The Moral Vision of Dorothy Day: A Feminist Perspective.* New York: Crossroad, 1991.

Nancy Roberts. *Dorothy Day and the Catholic Worker.* Albany: State University of New York Press, 1984.

Dorothea Lynde Dix (1802–1887)

Dorothea Lynde Dix. *Asylum, Prison, and Poorhouse: The Writings and Reform Work of Dorothea Dix in Illinois.* David L. Lightner, ed. Carbondale: Southern Illinois University Press, 1999.

Dorothea Lynde Dix. *The Lady and the President: The Letters of Dorothea Dix and Millard Fillmore.* Charles M. Snyder, ed. Lexington: University Press of Kentucky, 1975.

Dorothea Lynde Dix. *On Behalf of the Insane Poor: Selected Reports.* New York: Arno Press, 1971.

Dorothea Lynde Dix. *Remarks on Prisons and Prison Discipline in the U.S.* Montclair, NJ: Patterson Smith, 1984.

Thomas J. Brown. *Dorothea Dix: New England Reformer.* Cambridge, MA: Harvard University Press, 1998.

Penny Colman. *Breaking the Chains: The Crusade of Dorothea Lynde Dix.* White Hall, VA: Shoe Tree Press, 1992.

David Gollaher. *Voice for the Mad: the Life of Dorothea Dix.* New York: Free Press, 1995.

Frederick Herrmann. *Dorothea L. Dix and the Politics of Institutional Reform.* Trenton NJ: New Jersey Historical Commission, 1981.

Helen E. Marshall. *Dorothea Dix: Forgotten Samaritan.* New York: Russell and Russell, 1967.

Charles Schaifer and Lucy Freeman. *Heart's Work: Civil War Heroine and Champion of the Mentally Ill, Dorothea Lynde Dix.* New York: Paragon House, 1991.

Francis Tiffany. *Life of Dorothea Dix.* Ann Arbor, MI: Plutarch Press, 1971.

Dorothy Clarke Wilson. *Stranger and Traveler: The Story of Dorothea Dix, American Reformer.* Boston: Little, Brown, 1975.

W. E. B. Du Bois (1868–1963)

W. E. B. (William Edward Burghart) Du Bois. *The Autobiography of W. E. B. Du Bois.* New York: International Publishers, 1968.

W. E. B. Du Bois. *Against Racism: Unpublished Essays, Papers Addresses 1887–1961.* Herbert Aptheker, ed. Amherst: University of Massachusetts Press, 1985.

W. E. B. Du Bois. *In Battle for Peace.* Millwood, NY: Kraus-Thomson, 1976.

W. E. B. Du Bois. *Black Reconstruction in America 1860–1880.* New York: Atheneum, 1992.

W. E. B. Du Bois. *The Correspondence of W. E. B. Du Bois.* Herbert Apthecker, ed. Amherst: University of Massachusetts Press, 1973.

W. E. B. Du Bois. *Darkwater: Voices From Within the Veil.* Mineola, NY: Dover, 1999.

W. E. B. Du Bois. *Dusk of Dawn: An Essay Toward an Autobiography of a Race Concept.* New Brunswick: Transaction Books, 1984.

W. E. B. Du Bois. *The Emerging Thought of W. E. B. Du Bois: Essays and Editorials From the Crisis.* New York: Simon and Schuster, 1972.

W. E. B. Du Bois. *The Gift of Black Folk.* Millwood, NY: Kraus-Thomson, 1975.

W. E. B. Du Bois. *The Negro.* Mineola, NY: Dover, 2000.

W. E. B. Du Bois. *The Negro American Family.* Cambridge: MIT Press, 1970.

W. E. B. Du Bois. *The Oxford W. E. B. Du Bois Reader.* New York: Oxford University Press, 1996.

W. E. B. Du Bois. *W. E. B. Du Bois: A Reader.* David Lewis, ed. New York: Holt, 1995.

W. E. B. Du Bois. *Souls of Black Folk.* Las Vegas, NV: Classic Americana, 1997.

W. E. B. Du Bois. *The Writings of W. E. B. Du Bois.* New York: Crowell, 1975.

Herbert Aptheker. *The Literary Legacy of W. E. B. Du Bois.* White Plains, NY: Kraus International, 1989.

Francis L. Broderick. *W. E. B. Du Bois: Negro Leader in a Time of Crisis.* Stanford, CA: Stanford University Press, 1959.

Seamus Cavan. *W. E. B. Du Bois and Racial Relations.* Brookfield, CT: Millbrook Press, 1993.

Joseph DeMarco. *The Social Thought of W. E. B. Du Bois.* Lanham, MD: University Press of America, 1983.

Virginia Hamilton. *W. E. B. Du Bois: A Biography.* New York: Harper-Row, 1972.

Gerald Horne and Mary Young, eds. *W. E. B. Du Bois: An Encyclopedia.* Westport CT: Greenwood, 2000.

Melissa McDaniel. *W. E. B. Du Bois: Scholar and Civil Rights Activist.* New York: Franklin Watts, 1999.

Kwadwo O. Pobi-Asamani. *W. E. B. Du Bois: His Contribution to Pan Africanism.* San Bernardino, CA: Borgo Press, 1994.

Marian Wright Edelman (1936–)

Marian Wright Edelman. *Guide My Feet: Prayers and Meditations for Our Children.* Boston: Beacon, 2000.

Marian Wright Edelman. *I'm Your Child, God: Prayers for Our Children.* New York: Hyperion, 2002.

Marian Wright Edelman. *Lanterns: A Memoir of Mentors.* Boston: Beacon, 1999.

Marian Wright Edelman. *Families in Peril: An Agenda For Social Change.* Cambridge, MA: Harvard University Press, 1987.

Susan Skog, ed. *Embracing Our Essence: Spiritual Conversations With Prominent Women.* Deerfield Beach, FL: Health Communications, 1995.

Mary Parker Follett (1868–1933)

Mary Parker Follett. *Creative Experience.* New York: Longmans, Green, 1924.

Mary Parker Follett. *Dynamic Administration: The Collected Papers of Mary Parker Follett.* Henry Metcalf and Luther Urwick, eds. London: Hippocrene Books, 1973.

Mary Parker Follett. *Freedom and Coordination: Lectures in Business Organization.* New York: Garland, 1987.

Mary Parker Follett. *The New State: Group Organization: The Solution of Popular Government.* University Park: Pennsylvania State University Press, 1998.

Pauline Graham, ed. *Mary Parker Follett—Prophet of Management: A Celebration of Writings From the 1920s.* Boston: Harvard Business School Press, 1995.

Homer Folks (1867–1963)

Homer Folks. *The Care of Destitute, Neglected and Delinquent Children.* New York: Arno, 1971.

Homer Folks. *The Human Costs of War.* New York: Harper and Brothers, 1920.

Walter I. Trattner. *Homer Folks: Pioneer in Social Welfare.* New York: Columbia University Press, 1968.

Michael Harrington (1928–1989)

Michael Harrington. *The Other America: Poverty in the United States.* New York: Collier Books, 1994.

Michael Harrington. *The Accidental Century.* New York: Macmillan, 1965.

Michael Harrington. *Decade of Decision: The Crisis of the American System.* New York: Simon and Schuster, 1980.

Michael Harrington. *Fragments of the Century.* New York: Simon and Schuster, 1977.

Michael Harrington. *The Long Distance Runner: An Autobiography.* New York: Holt, 1988.

Michael Harrington. *The New American Poverty.* New York: Holt, 1984.

Michael Harrington. *The Next America: The Decline and Rise of the United States.* New York: Holt, 1981.

Michael Harrington. *The Vast Majority: A Journey to the World's Poor.* New York: Simon and Schuster, 1976.

Loren Okroi. *Galbraith, Harrington, Heilbroner: Economics and Dissent in an Age of Optimism.* Princeton, NJ: Princeton University Press, 1988.

Harry L. Hopkins (1890–1946)

Harry L. Hopkins. *Spending to Save: The Complete Story of Relief.* Seattle: University of Washington Press, 1972.

Henry Hitch Adams. *Harry Hopkins: A Biography.* New York: Putnam, 1977.

Searle F. Charles. *Minister of Relief: Harry Hopkins and the Depression.* Westport, CT: Greenwood, 1974.

June Hopkins. *Harry Hopkins: Sudden Hero, Brash Reformer.* New York: St. Martin's Press, 1999.

Paul Kurzman. *Harry Hopkins and the New Deal.* Fairlawn, NJ: Burdick, 1974.

George McJimsey. *Harry Hopkins: Ally of the Poor and Defender of Democracy.* Cambridge, MA: Harvard University Press, 1987.

Robert Sherwood. *Roosevelt and Hopkins: An Intimate History.* New York: Harper, 1950.

Dwight Matthew B. Wills. *Wartime Missions of Harry L. Hopkins.* Raleigh, NC: Pentland, 1996.

Toyohiko Kagawa (1888–1960)

Toyohiko Kagawa. *Behold the Man.* New York: Harper and Brothers, 1941.

Toyohiko Kagawa. *Brotherhood Economics.* New York: Harper and Brothers, 1936.

Toyohiko Kagawa. *The Challenge of Redemptive Love.* New York: Abingdon Press, 1940.

Toyohiko Kagawa. *Living Out Christ's Love: Selected Writings of Toyohiko Kagawa.* Nashville, TN: Upper Room Books, 1998.

Toyohiko Kagawa. *Meditations on the Cross*. Chicago: Willett, Clark, 1935.

Toyohiko Kagawa. *Songs From the Slums: Poems by Toyohiko Kagawa*. Nashville, TN: Cokesbury Press, 1935.

William Axling. *Kagawa*. New York: Harper and Brothers, 1946.

Emerson Bradshaw. *Unconquerable Kagawa*. St. Paul, MN: Macalester Park, 1952.

Cyril J. Davey. *Kagawa of Japan*. New York: Abingdon Press, 1961.

Masao Takenaka. "The Impact of Kagawa and his Movement," *The Study of Christianity and Social Problems*, vol. 6, July 1993, pp. 55–99.

Robert Schildgen. *Toyohiko Kagawa: Apostle of Love and Social Justice*. Berkeley, CA: Centenary Books, 1988.

Jessie M. Trout, ed. *Kagawa: Japanese Prophet: His Witness in Life and Word*. New York: Association Press, 1960.

Florence Kelley (1859–1932)

Florence Kelley. *On the Inside*. New York: Sanford, 1890.

Florence Kelley. *Minimum Wage Laws*. New York: National Consumers League, 1912.

Florence Kelley. *Modern Industry in Relation to the Family, Health, Education, Morality*. Westport, CT: Hyperion, 1975.

Florence Kelley. *Some Ethical Gains Through Legislation*. New York: Arno, 1969.

Florence Kelley. *A Privileged Industry*. New York: National Consumers League, 1912.

Florence Kelley. *Wage-Earning Women in War Time: The Textile Industry*. New York: National Consumers League, 1919.

Florence Kelley. *The Working Child*. Chicago: Hollister, 1986.

Dorothy Rose Blumberg. *Florence Kelley: The Making of a Social Pioneer*. New York: Augustus M. Kelley, 1966.

Josephine Goldmark. *Impatient Crusader: Florence Kelley's Life Story*. Westport, CT: Greenwood, 1976.

Katherine Kish Sklar. *Florence Kelley and the Nation's Work*. New Haven: Yale University Press, 1995.

Martin Luther King Jr. (1929–1968)

Martin Luther King Jr. *Strength to Love*. New York: Harper and Row, 1968.

Martin Luther King Jr. *Stride Toward Freedom: The Montgomery Story*. New York: Harper and Brothers, 1958.

Martin Luther King Jr. *The Trumpet of Conscience*. New York: Harper and Row, 1968.

Martin Luther King Jr. *Where Do We Go From Here: Chaos or Community?* New York: Harper and Row, 1967.

Martin Luther King Jr. *Why We Can't Wait*. New York: New American Library, 1964.

John J. Ansbro. *Martin Luther King Jr.: The Making of a Mind*. Maryknoll, NY: Orbis, 1982.

David J. Garrow. *Bearing the Cross: Martin Luther King Jr. and the Southern Christian Leadership Conference*. New York: William Morrow, 1986.

Lerone Bennett Jr. *What Manner of Man: A Biography of Martin Luther King Jr.* Chicago: Johnson Publishing, 1968.

Thomas C. Clemens. *Martin Luther King: Man of Peace*. Washington, DC: USIA, 1965.

Bennie E. Goodwin. *Dr. Martin Luther King Jr.: God's Messenger of Love, Justice and Hope*. Jersey City, NJ: Goodpatrick, 1976.

James P. Hanigan. *Martin Luther King Jr. and the Foundations of Nonviolence*. Lanham, MD: University Press of America, 1984.

Walton Hanes Jr. *Political Philosophy of Martin Luther King Jr.* Westport, CT: Greenwood, 1971.

William D. Watley. *Roots of Resistance: The Nonviolent Ethic of Martin Luther King Jr.* Valley Forge, PA: Judson Press, 1985.

Jeannette Rankin (1880–1973)

Judy Rachel Block. *Jeannette Rankin: First Woman in Politics*. New York: CPI, 1978.

Sue Davidson. *A Heart in Politics: Jeannette Rankin and Patsy T. Mink*. Seattle, WA: Seal Press, 1994.

Kevin Giles. *Flight of the Dove: The Story of Jeannette Rankin*. Beaverton, OR: Touchstone Press, 1980.

Hanna Geffen Josephson. *Jeannette Rankin: First Lady in Congress*. Indianapolis: Bobbs-Merrill, 1974.

Barbara Kramer. *Trailblazing Women: First in Their Fields*. Berkeley Heights, NJ: Enslow, 2000.

Norma Smith. *Jeannette Rankin, America's Conscience*. Helena, MT: Montana Historical Society Press, 2002.

Bertha Capen Reynolds (1885–1978)

Bertha Capen Reynolds. *Between Client and Community: A Study in Responsibility in Social Case Work*. New York: Oriole, 1973.

Bertha Capen Reynolds. *Learning and Teaching in the Practice of Social Work*. Silver Spring, MD: NASW Press, 1985.

Bertha Capen Reynolds. *Social Work and Social Living: Explorations in Philosophy and Practice.* New York: Citadel Press, 1951.

Bertha Capen Reynolds. *An Uncharted Journey: Fifty Years of Growth in Social Work.* Silver Spring, MD: NASW Press, 1991.

St. Elizabeth Ann Seton (1774–1821)

Elizabeth Ann Seton. *Collected Writings.* Regina Bechtle and Judith Metz, eds. Hyde Park, NY: New City Press, 2000.

Joseph I. Dirvin. *Mrs. Seton: Foundress of the American Sisters of Charity.* New York: Farrar, Straus and Giroux, 1975.

Leonard Feeny. *Mother Seton*: *Saint Elizabeth of New York.* Cambridge, MA: Ravengate Press, 1991.

Sr. Mary Celeste. *The Intimate Friendships of Elizabeth Ann Bayley Seton, First Native-Born American Saint.* Lanham, MD: University Press of America, 2000.

Alma Power-Waters. *Mother Seton: First American-Born Saint.* New York: Pocket Books, 1976.

Lord Shaftesbury (Anthony Ashley Cooper) (1801–1885)

Georgina Battiscombe. *Shaftesbury: The Great Reformer: 1801–1885.* Boston: Houghton Mifflin, 1975.

Barbara Blackburn. *Noble Lord: The Life of the Seventh Earl of Shaftesbury.* London: Home and Van Thal, 1949.

Mary Kingsbury Simkhovitch (1867–1951)

Mary K. Simkhovitch. *The City Worker's World in America.* New Salem, NH: Ayer, 1971.

Mary K. Simkhovitch. *The Church and Public Housing.* New York: Department of Christian Social Service, National Council, 1934.

Mary K. Simkhovitch. *Group Life.* New York: Association Press, 1940.

Mary K. Simkhovitch. *Neighborhood: My Story of Greenwich House.* New York: Norton, 1938. Reprint. New Salem, NH: Ayer, n.d.

Mary K. Simkhovitch. *Quicksand: The Way of Life in the Slums.* Evanston, IL: Row, Peterson, 1942.

Mary K. Simkhovitch. *The Red Festival.* Milwaukee, WI: Morehouse, 1934.

Graham Taylor (1851–1938)

Graham R. Taylor. *Chicago Commons Through Forty Years.* Chicago, IL: University of Chicago Press, 1936.

Graham R. Taylor. *Pioneering on Social Frontiers.* New York: Arno Press, 1976.

Graham R. Taylor. *Religion in Social Action.* New York: Dodd, Mead, 1913.

Louise C. Wade. *Graham Taylor: Pioneer for Social Justice.* Chicago: University of Chicago Press, 1964.

Sojourner Truth (1797–1883)

Catherine Bernard. *Sojourner Truth: Abolitionist and Women's Rights Activist.* Berkeley Heights, NJ: Enslow, 2001.

Jacqueline Bernard. *Journey Toward Freedom: The Story of Sojourner Truth.* Reprint. New York: Feminist Press, 1990. (Original work published 1967)

Arthur H. Fauset. *Sojourner Truth: God's Faithful Pilgrim.* New York: Russell and Russell, 1971.

Suzanne P. Fitch. *Sojourner Truth as Orator: Wit, Story and Song.* Westport, CT: Greenwood Press, 1997.

Carleton Mabee. *Sojourner Truth: Slave, Prophet, Legend.* New York: New York University Press, 1993.

Olive Gilbert. *Narrative of Sojourner Truth: A Bondswoman of Olden Time With a History of Her Labors and Correspondence.* New York: Penguin, 1998.

Nell Irvin Painter. *Sojourner Truth: A Life, a Symbol.* New York: W. W. Norton, 1996.

Hertha Ernestine Pauli. *Her Name Was Sojourner Truth.* New York: Appleton-Century-Crofts, 1962.

Erlene Stetson. *Glorying in Tribulation: The Lifework of Sojourner Truth.* East Lansing: Michigan State University Press, 1994.

Margaret Washington. *The Narrative of Sojourner Truth.* New York: Vintage Books, 1993.

Harriett Tubman (1820–1913)

Sarah H. Bradford. *Harriet Tubman: The Moses of Her People.* Magnolia, MA: Peter Smith, n.d.

Dan Elish. *Harriet Tubman and the Underground Railroad.* Brookfield, CT: Millbrook Press, 1993.

Ann Petry. *Harriet Tubman: Conductor on the Underground Railroad.* New York: Crowell, 1955.

Lillian Wald (1867–1940)

Lillian Wald. *The House on Henry Street.* New Brunswick, NJ: Transaction, 1991. (Original work published 1915)

Lillian Wald. *Windows on Henry Street.* Boston: Little, Brown, 1934.

Clare Coss. *Lillian D. Wald: Progressive Activist.* New York: Feminist Press at the City University of New York, 1989.

Doris Daniels. *Always a Sister: The Feminism of Lillian D. Wald.* New York: Feminist Press at the City University of New York, 1989.

Robert Duffus. *Lillian Wald: Neighbor and Crusader.* New York: Macmillan, 1938.

Alberta Eiseman. *Rebels and Reformers: Biographies of Four Jewish Americans.* Garden City, NY: Zenith Books, 1976.

Beatrice Siegel. *Lillian Wald of Henry Street.* New York: Macmillan, 1983.

Sir George Williams (1821–1905)

J. E. Hodder-Williams. *The Life of Sir George Williams: Founder of the Young Men's Christian Association.* New York: Association Press, 1915.

E. G. Lentz. *George Williams: A Tribute to the Founder of the Red Triangle.* Carbondale: Illinois Area YMCA, 1959.

Cecil B. A. Northcoat. *Sir George Williams: Founder of the YMCA.* London: Religious Tract Society, n.d.

Others

Clarke A. Chambers. *Paul U. Kellogg and the Survey: Voices for Social Welfare and Social Justice.* Minneapolis: University of Minnesota Press, 1971.

Gisela Konopka. *Eduard Lindeman and Social Work Philosophy.* Minneapolis: University of Minnesota Press, 1958.

CONCLUSION

While devotion to the individual has grown in professional social work, its active participation in solving social problems has tended to shrink, diverting "social work from its original mission and vision of the perfectibility of society."[5] In spite of these trends away from macro-oriented practice, the field of macro social work has a unique opportunity to reclaim its heritage as the profession committed to community enrichment and conceiving a society that is ethically good as well as economically prosperous. You, too, can add your name to the list of those social workers who saw a better future and gave their lives to bring hope and possibility, and to defeat oppression and injustice.

ADDITIONAL READING

Heroes of Social Work

McKown, Robert. *Pioneers in Mental Health.* New York: Dodd, Mead, 1961.

Stroup, Herbert. *Social Welfare Pioneers.* Chicago: Nelson-Hall, 1986.

VonHoff, Heinz. *People Who Care: An Illustrated History of Human Compassion.* Philadelphia: Fortress Press, 1971.

Whitton, Mary Ormsbee. *These Were the Women: USA, 1776–1860.* New York: Hastings House, 1954.

Altruism and Caring

Bach, George and Laura Torbet. *A Time for Caring.* New York: Delacourte, 1982.

Luks, Allen and Peggy Payne. *The Healing Power of Doing Good.* New York: Fawcett, 1992.

Oliner, Samuel P. and Pearl M. Oliner. *The Altruistic Personality: Rescuers of the Jews in Nazi Europe.* New York: Free Press, 1988.

Meltzer, Milton. *Who Cares? Millions Do: A Book About Altruism.* New York: Walker, 1994.

Zimmerman, Richard. *What Can I Do to Make a Difference? A Positive Action Source Book.* New York: Plume, 1991.

Lubove, Roy. *The Professional Altruist: The Emergence of Social Work as a Career, 1880–1930.* New York: Atheneum, 1969.

NOTES

Chapter 1: Overview of the Practice of Macro Social Work

1. Abraham Kaplan, "Perspectives on the Theme." In *Individuality and the New Society,* Abraham Kaplan, ed. (Seattle: University of Washington Press, 1970), pp. 19–20.
2. Adapted from Alex Pulaski, "A Difficult Death in a Strange Land," *Fresno Bee,* February 16, 1993, pp. A1, A18. Used with permission.
3. Jack Rothman and John E. Tropman, "Models of Community Organization and Macro Practice Perspectives: Their Mixing and Phasing." In *Strategies of Community Organization,* 4th ed., Fred M. Cox, John L. Erlich, Jack Rothman, and John E. Tropman, eds. (Itasca, IL: Peacock, 1987).
4. See Harry Specht and Mark E. Courtney, *Unfaithful Angels: How Social Work Abandoned Its Mission* (New York: Free Press, 1994).
5. John Ehrenreich. *The Altruistic Imagination: A History of Social Work and Social Policy in the United States* (Ithaca: Cornell University Press, 1985), p. 173.
6. Dara Silverman. "Struggling Forward: Organizing as a Building Block of Resistance." *Znet Magazine.* May 8, 2003. (http:www.zmag.org/content/print_article.cfm?itemID=3587 &sectionID=41)
7. Peter Berger and Richard John Neuhaus, *To Empower People: From State to Civil Society,* 2nd ed., Michael Novak, ed. (New York: AEI Press, 1996).
8. Robert Presthus, *The Organizational Society,* rev. ed. (New York: St. Martin's Press, 1988); and Hendrik M. Ruitenbeek, ed., *The Dilemma of Organizational Society* (New York: E. P. Dutton, 1963).

Part 1: Solving Social Problems and Making Social Change

1. Adapted from F. A. Hayek, *The Counter-Revolution of Science: Studies on the Abuse of Reason* (New York: Free Press of Glencoe, 1964), pp. 32–33.
2. Paulo Freire, *Pedagogy for the Oppressed* (New York: Continuum, 1992), pp. 28, 42.
3. Michael M. Harmon, *Action Theory for Public Administration* (New York: Longman, 1981), pp. 4, 5.

Chapter 2: Social Problems: The Challenge of Macro Social Work

1. Si Kahn, *How People Get Power: Organizing Oppressed Communities for Action,* rev. ed. (Washington, DC: NASW Press, 1994), p. 132.
2. Pope John Paul II, San Antonio, Texas, September 13, 1987.
3. Genaro C. Armas, "Number of Poor, Uninsured Rose in 2003" AP Press, August 27, 2004.
4. Ibid.
5. Children's Defense Fund, November 2003. (familyincome@ childrensdefense.org).
6. http://www.aflcio.org/corporateamerica/paywatch/pay
7. Children's Defense Fund, November 2003.
8. Ibid.
9. Ruth Leger Sivard, *World Military and Social Expenditures* (Washington, DC: World Priorities, 1991), pp. 33.
10. Ronald C. Frederico, *Social Welfare in Today's World* (New York: McGraw Hill, 1990), p. 294.
11. H. Wayne Johnson, *The Social Services: An Introduction,* 3d ed. (Itasca, IL: F. E. Peacock, 1990), p. 24.
12. Harry Specht and Mark Courtney, *Unfaithful Angels: How Social Work Has Abandoned Its Mission* (New York: Free Press, 1994), p. x.
13. Thomas J. Sullivan and Kenrick S. Thompson, *Introduction to Social Problems* (New York: Macmillan, 1988), p. 3; and Charles Zastrow, *Social Problems: Issues and Solutions* (Chicago: Nelson Hall, 1988), p. 6.
14. Robert K. Merton and Robert Nisbet, *Contemporary Social Problems,* 2d ed. (New York: Harcourt, Brace, and World, 1966), p. 799.
15. Soroka and Bryjak assert, "Social problems . . . are perceived as unacceptable by an influential segment of a society's population." In *Social Problems: A World at Risk,* Michael P. Soroka and George J. Bryjak (Boston: Allyn and Bacon, 1995), p. 22.
16. Fox Butterfield. "2 Economists Give Far Higher Cost of Gun Violence," *New York Times,* September 15, 2000, p. A24.
17. C. Wright Mills, *The Sociological Imagination* (London: Oxford University Press, 1959), p. 187.
18. Ibid.
19. Joseph M. Kling and Prudence S. Posner, eds., *Dilemmas of Activism: Class, Community, and the Politics of Local Mobilization* (Philadelphia: Temple University Press, 1990), p. 40.
20. Alan Nevins and Henry Steele Commager, *A Pocket History of the United States,* 5th ed. (New York: Washington Square Press, 1966), pp. 5, 6.
21. Beulah Compton, *Introduction to Social Welfare and Social Work:* (Homewood, IL: Dorsey Press, 1980), p. 178.
22. Nevins and Commager, A Pocket History, pp. 180.
23. Ibid., p. 181.
24. Ibid.
25. Ibid.
26. Ibid.
27. Roger A. Lee, "The History Guy: The Mexican-American War," 1998. (http:www.historyguy.com/Mexican-American _War.html)
28. Compton, *Introduction,* pp. 221, 227.
29. Clinton Rossiter, *The First American Revolution* (New York: Harcourt Brace and World, 1956), pp. 148–149.
30. Ibid., p. 181.
31. Ronald G. Walters, *American Reformers* (New York: Hill and Wang, 1978), p, 80.
32. Ibid., pp. 78, 80, 85.
33. Charles D. Garvin and Fred M. Cox, "A History of Community Organizing Since the Civil War With Special Reference to Oppressed Communities." In *Strategies of Community Organization,* Fred M. Cox et al., eds. (Itasca, IL: F. E. Peacock, 1987), p. 30.

34. Royce Delmatier, Clarence McIntosh, and Earl G. Waters, *The Rumble of California Politics 1848–1970* (New York: Wiley, 1970), p. 59.

35. Ibid., p. 33.

36. William R. Brock, *Conflict and Transformation: The United States, 1844–1877* (New York: Penguin Books, 1973), p. 436.

37. Garvin and Cox, "A History of Community Organizing," p. 30.

38. Brock, *Conflict and Transformation*, p. 438.

39. Delmatier, McIntosh, and Waters, *The Rumble of California Politics*, pp. 71, 72, 87.

40. Garvin and Cox, "A History of Community Organizing," p. 30.

41. Delmatier, McIntosh, and Waters, *The Rumble of California Politics*, p. 184.

42. Ralph P. Hummel, *Bureaucratic Experience* (New York: St. Martin's, 1977), p. 42.

43. Alberto Guerreiro Ramos, "A Substantive Approach to Organizations." In *Organization Theory and the New Public Administration,* Carl J. Bellone, ed. (Boston: Allyn and Bacon, 1980), p. 158.

44. Allen Jedlicka, *Volunteerism and World Development: Pathway to a New World* (New York: Praeger, 1990), p. 36.

45. Max Weber, "Bureaucracy." In *Economy and Society: An Outline of Interpretive Sociology,* 3 vols., Guenther Roth and Claus Wittich, eds. (New York: Bedminster Press, 1968), p. 987.

46. Charles Perrow, *Complex Organizations: A Critical Essay,* 2d ed. (Glenview, IL: Scott, Foresman, 1979), p. 6, 13f.

47. Victor A. Thompson, *Without Sympathy or Enthusiasm: The Problem of Administrative Compassion* (University: University of Alabama Press), p. 67.

48. Alberto Guerreiro Ramos, *The New Science of Organizations: A Reconceptualization of the Wealth of Nations* (Toronto: University of Toronto Press, 1981), p. 147.

49. Hummel, *Bureaucratic Experience,* p. 42.

50. Alasdair MacIntyre, *After Virtue,* 2d ed. (Notre Dame, IN: University of Notre Dame Press, 1984), pp. 23–24.

51. Max Weber, "Politics as a Vocation," in *From Max Weber: Essays in Sociology,* H. H. Gerth and C. Wright Mills, eds. (New York: Oxford University Press, 1946), p. 95.

52. Victor A. Thompson, *Bureaucracy and the Modern World* (Morristown NJ: General Learning Press, 1976), p. 113.

53. Ramos, *The New Science,* p. 158.

54. Paul Tillich, "The Person in a Technical Society." In *Social Ethics: Issues in Ethics and Society,* Gibson Winter, ed. (New York: Harper and Row, 1968), pp. 150–151.

55. Thompson, *Without Sympathy,* p. 28.

56. Hummel, *Bureaucratic Experience,* pp. 42–43.

57. Max Weber, "Bureaucracy." In *From Max Weber: Essays in Sociology,* H. H. Gerth and C. Wright Mills, eds. (New York: Oxford University Press, 1946), pp. 215–216.

58. Hummel, *Bureaucratic Experience,* p. 42.

59. Perrow, *Complex Organizations,* p. 194.

60. Ibid., p. 196.

61. Alex Taylor III, "GM Gets Its Action Together Finally," *Fortune* 149 (6), April 5, 2000, p. 67.

62. Karl Polanyi, *The Great Transformation* (Boston: Beacon Press, 1971), p. 71.

63. Ramos, "A Substantive Approach to Organizations," p. 146.

64. Marcel Mauss, in *Primitive, Archaic, and Modern Economies: Essays of Karl Polanyi,* G. Dalton, ed. (Boston: Beacon Press, 1971), p. ix.

65. Ibid., pp. 6, 13; see also Hummel, *Bureaucratic Experience,* pp. 45–50, 83–88.

66. Robert Presthus, *The Organizational Society* (New York: St Martin's Press, 1978).

67. James Madison, Alexander Hamilton, and John Jay. "Federalist No. 10" in *The Federalist Papers,* Introduction by Clinton Rossiter (New York: New American Library, 1961), p. 76.

68. Soroka and Bryjak, *Social Problems,* p. 15.

69. James M. Henslin, *Social Problems* (Upper Saddle River, NJ: Prentice-Hall, 1996), pp. 42, 46.

70. Stanley Eitzen and Maxine Baca-Zinn, *Social Problems,* 6th ed. (Boston: Allyn and Bacon, 1994), p. 9.

71. Ibid., p. 6.

72. Ibid., p. 5.

73. Ibid., p. 6.

74. Peter M. Berger and John Neuhaus, *To Empower People: From State to Civil Society* 2d ed. (Washington, DC: American Enterprise Institute Press, 1996), p. 159.

75. Patricia Yancey Martin and Gerald G. O'Connor, *The Social Environment: Open Systems Applications,* (New York: Longman, 1989), p. 37.

76. K. Berrien, *General and Social Systems* (New Brunswick, NJ: Rutgers University Press, 1968), pp. 14, 15.

77. Martin and O'Connor, *The Social Environment,* pp. 37, 38.

78. Charles Zastrow, *The Practice of Social Work,* 3d ed. (Homewood, IL: Dorsey Press, 1989), p. 217.

79. Augustus Y. Napier with Carl A. Whitaker, *The Family Crucible: One Family's Therapy—An Experience That Illuminates All Our Lives* (Toronto: Bantam Books, 1978), p. 47.

80. Herbert Blumer, *Symbolic Interactionism: Perspective and Method* (Englewood Cliffs, NJ: Prentice-Hall, 1969), p. 145.

81. Martin and O'Connor, *The Social Environment,* p. xi.

82. Ibid., p. 38.

83. Eitzen and Baca-Zinn, *Social Problems,* p. 4.

84. Ritchie P. Lowry, *Social Problems* (Lexington, MA: D. C. Heath, 1974), p. 205.

85. Stewart E. Perry, *Communities on the Way: Rebuilding Local Economies in the United States and Canada* (Albany: State University of New York Press, 1987), p. 33.

86. Ibid.

87. Ibid., p. 34.

88. Perrow, *Complex Organizations,* p. 13.

89. Ibid., p. 190.

90. Thompson, *Without Sympathy,* pp. 90–94.

91. Gibson Winter, *Elements for a Social Ethic: The Role of Social Science in Public Policy* (New York: Macmillan, 1966), p. 15.

92. Michael M. Harmon, *Action Theory for Public Administration* (New York: Longman, 1981), p. 37.

93. Jerome G. Manus, *Analyzing Social Problems* (New York: Praeger, 1976), p. 16.

94. Thomas P. Holland, "Organizations: Contest for Social Services Delivery." In *Encyclopedia of Social Work,* 19th ed. (Washington, DC: NASW Press, 1995), p. 1789.

95. Frank Coleman, *Hobbes and America: Exploring the Constitutional Foundations* (Toronto: University of Toronto Press, 1977), p. 6.

96. Ibid., p. 16.

97. Richard Hofstadter, "Woodrow Wilson: Democrat in Cupidity." In *The Progressive Era: Liberal Renaissance or Liberal Failure,* Arthur Mann, ed. (New York: Holt, Rinehart and Winston, 1963), p. 71.

98. Coleman, *Hobbes and America,* p. 16.

99. Mansour Fakih, *NGOs in Indonesia* (Amherst, MA: Center for International Education, University of Massachusetts, 1991), p. 11.

100. Thomas Bender, *Community and Social Change in America* (New Brunswick, NJ: Rutgers University Press, 1978), pp. 23–24, 28–29.

101. Walt Whitman Rostow, *The Stages of Economic Growth: A Non-Communist Manifesto* (Cambridge: Cambridge University Press, 1960); see also David McClelland, *The Achieving Society* (New York: Van Nostrand, 1961); and Charles Inkeles and David Smith, *Becoming Modern* (Cambridge, MA: Harvard University Press, 1974).

102. Hubert Campfens, *Community Development Around the World* (Toronto: University of Toronto Press, 1997), pp. 16–17.

103. Ponna Wignaraja, "Rethinking Development and Democracy," *New Social Movements in the South: Empowering People* (London: Zed Books, 1993), p. 8.

104. Campfens, *Community Development,* p. 17.

105. Fakih, *NGOs in Indonesia,* p. 3.

106. Wignaraja, "Rethinking," p. 8.

107. Except where noted this section relies on Jamshid Gharajedaghi in collaboration with Russel L. Ackhoff, *A Prologue to National Development Planning* (New York: Greenwood Press, 1986), pp. 27–30, 35–37.

108. Wignaraja, "Rethinking Development and Democracy," p. 8.

109. Ibid.

110. Ibid.

111. Ibid.

112. Robert R. Mayer, *Social Planning and Social Change* (Englewood Cliffs, NJ: Prentice-Hall, 1972), p. 17.

113. Ibid.

114. Ibid.

115. Ibid.

116. Ann Weick and Dennis Saleeby, "Postmodern Perspectives for Social Work." In *Postmodernism, Religion and the Future of Social Work,* Roland G. Meinert, John T. Pardeck, and John W. Murphy, eds. (New York: Haworth Pastoral Press, 1998), p. 29.

117. Mel Gray, "Developmental Social Work: A 'Strengths' Praxis for Social Development," *Social Development Issues* 24 (1) 2002, pp. 8, 9.

118. Weick and Saleeby, "Postmodern Perspectives for Social Work," p. 29.

119. John Forester, *Planning in the Face of Power* (Berkeley: University of California Press, 1989), p. 28.

120. Coleman, *Hobbes and America,* p. 21.

121. Peter Breggin cited in Eileen Gambril, *Social Work Practice: A Critical Thinkers Guide* (New York: Oxford University Press, 1997), p. 11.

Chapter 3: Rational Problem Solving and Social Thinking

1. Thomas Hobbes, *Leviathan: Or the Matter, Forme, and Power of a Commonwealth Ecclesiastical and Civil,* Michael Oakeshott, ed. (New York: Collier Books, 1962), chap. 5, p. 41.

2. Ibid., chap. 13, p. 100.

3. Hobbes begins his great work by describing his new model of such an artificial social system, initiating the idea of systems theory. "For what is the *heart* but a *spring;* and the *nerves* but so many *strings;* and the *joints,* but so many *wheels,* giving motion to the whole body. . . . Therefore, if God can create nature, which is nothing, *but a system* composed of a 'motion of limbs,' is it not also possible for humans by following the same creative process or art, to make an artificial animal? Thus [is created] the great Leviathan called a Commonwealth, or State, which is but an artificial man . . . in which the *sovereign* is an artificial *soul* . . . the *magistrates* [are] artificial *joints; reward* and *punishment* . . . are the *nerves.*" Hobbes, Leviathan, Introduction, p. 19.

4. Michael Oakeshott, "Introduction to," Hobbes, *Leviathan,* p. 11.

5. Hobbes, *Leviathan,* chap. 5, pp. 41, 42, 45.

6. Ibid. p. 41.

7. Ibid.

8. John Locke, *Two Treatises of Government,* Peter Laslett, ed. (Cambridge: Cambridge University Press, 1988); Adam Smith, *An Inquiry Into the Nature and Causes of the Wealth of Nations,* Edwin Cannan, ed. (New York: Modern Library, 1994); Alexander Hamilton, James Madison, and John Jay, *The Federalist Papers,* Clinton Rossiter, ed. (New York: Mentor, 1999).

9. There are other labels for rational problem solving. For example, it is called "public choice theory" by political scientists and public administrators, "neoclassism" and "rational choice theory (RCT)" by economists, "expected utility theory" by psychologists, "rational choice theory" by sociologists, the "systems approach" by systems analysts, and the "generalist social work method" by social workers.

10. Mary Zey, *Rational Choice Theory and Organizational Theory: A Critique* (Thousand Oaks, CA: Sage, 1998), p. 2.

11. The closer a benefit-cost ratio is to or exceeds 1 (B/C ≥ 1), the more attractive it becomes. Furthermore, this is the same definition of efficiency. E = I/O, the more efficient (E) decision is one where inputs (I) are equal to or less than the outputs. If we receive more output than we put into a project or work, we have achieved efficiency. If a decision gives us more benefits than it costs, we have profit.

12. Graham T. Allison, *The Essence of Decision: Explaining the Cuban Missile Crisis* (Boston: Little, Brown 1971).

13. Karl Polyani, *The Great Transformation* (Boston: Beacon Press, 1971), p. 149.

14. Mary Zey, "Criticisms of Rational Choice Models." In *Decision Making: Alternatives to Rational Choice Models,* Mary Zey, ed. (Thousand Oaks, CA: Sage, 1992), pp. 9–10.

15. Gary Becker, *A Treatise on the Family* (Cambridge, MA: Harvard University Press, 1981), p. ix.

16. "Curriculum Policy Statement for Baccalaureate Degree Programs in Social Work Education," and "Curriculum Policy Statement for Master's Degree Programs in Social Work Education" (Alexandria, VA: Council on Social Work Education, 1992).

17. Richard M. Grinnell Jr., *Social Work Research and Evaluation,* 3d ed. (Itasca, IL: F. E. Peacock, 1988), p. 15.

18. Michael B. Fabricant and Robert Fisher, *Settlement Houses Under Seige: The Struggle to Sustain Community Organizations in New York City* (New York: Columbia University Press, 2002), p. 24.

19. Max Weber, "Bureaucracy." In *Economy and Society: An Outline of Interpretive Sociology,* 3 vols., Guenther Roth and Claus Wittich, trans. (New York: Bedminster Press, 1968), p. 975.

20. John Dewey, *How We Think,* rev. ed. (Lexington, MA: D. C. Heath, 1933).

21. Herbert Simon, *Administrative Behavior,* 4th ed. (New York: Free Press, 1997), pp. 92–95.

22. Helen Harris Perlman, *Social Casework: A Problem-Solving Process* (Chicago: University of Chicago Press, 1957).

23. Allison, *The Essence of Decision,* pp. 10–36.

24. Ibid.

25. Simon, *Administrative Behavior,* pp. 92–95.

26. C. West Churchman, *The Systems Approach* (New York: Dell, 1968), pp. 146–176.

27. Edith Stokey and Richard Zeckhauser, *A Primer for Policy Analysis* (New York: W. W. Norton, 1978), pp. 3–44.

28. Ronald Lippitt, Jeanne Watson, and Bruce Westley, *The Dynamics of Planned Change* (New York: Harcourt, Brace and World, 1958), pp. 131–143.

29. Simon, *Administrative Behavior,* p. 75.

30. Kurt Lewin, "Frontiers in Group Dynamics: Concept, Method and Reality in Social Science, Social Equilibria, and Social Change," *Human Relations,* 1(1), June 1947, pp. 5–41.

31. Ralph Brody, *Problem-Solving: Concepts and Methods for Community Organization* (New York: Human Sciences Press, 1992), p. 107.

32. Hubert Campfens, *Community Development Around the World* (Toronto: University of Toronto Press, 1997), p. 33.

33. Dara Silverman, "Struggling Forward: Organizing as a Building Block of Resistance." *Znet Magazine,* May 8, 2003. (http://www.zmag.org/content/print_article.cfm?itemID=3587&sectionID=41)

34. Harry C. Boyte and Nancy Kari, "The Good Work in Community" [Rebuilding Civil Society. A Symposium], *The New Democrat,* 7 (2), March/April 1995.

35. John McKnight "Regenerating Community" CPN, Sept. 30, 2001. (http://www.cpn.org/cpn/sections/topics/community/civicpersectives/regencomm.html)

36. Michael M. Harmon, *Action Theory for Public Administration* (New York: Longman, 1981), p. 126.

37. Carl Tjeransen, "Education for Citizens: A Foundation's Experience," Emil Schwartzhaupt Foundation, 1980. (http://www.comm-org.utoledo.edu/papers97)

38. Campfens, *Community Development,* p. 33.

39. Michael Heus and Allen Pincus, *The Creative Generalist: A Guide to Social Work Practice* (Barneveld, WI: Micamar, 1986), pp. 47–65, 108–126, 271.

40. Chris Valley, "One Community Organizer's Career Path in Program Development, 2000" [unpublished manuscript]. Families First, Atlanta, GA, p. 6.

41. Campfens, *Community Development,* p. 34.

42. Ibid., pp. 34–35.

43. Ibid., p. 35.

44. Alberto Guerreiro Ramos, *The New Science of Organizations: A Reconceptualization of the Wealth of Nations* (Toronto: University of Toronto Press, 1981), p. 111.

45. Ibid.

46. Ibid., p. 110.

47. Peter L. Berger and Thomas Luckman, *The Social Construction of Reality* (Garden City, NY: Anchor Books, 1967), p. 189.

48. Campfens, *Community Development,* p. 37.

49. Ibid. p. 38.

50. Robert H. Lauer and Warren T. Handel, *Social Psychology: The Theory and Application of Symbolic Interactionism* (Englewood Cliffs, NJ: Prentice Hall, 1983), p. 23.

51. Ibid.

52. Berger and Luckmann, *The Social Construction of Reality,* p. 188.

53. Harry Blumer, *Symbolic Interactionism: Perspective and Method* (Englewood Cliffs, NJ: Prentice Hall, 1969), p. 14.

54. Mark R. Warren, "Connecting People to Politics: The Role of Religious Institutions in the Texas Industrial Areas Foundation Network" n.d. Paper presented on COMM-ORG: The On-Line Conference on Community Organizing and Development. (http://comm-org.utoledo.edu/papers.htm)

55. Lauer and Handel, *Social Psychology,* p. 23.

56. Walter Kaufman, ed., *Existentialism From Dostoevsky to Sartre* (New York: Meridian, 1956), p. 136.

57. Blumer, *Symbolic Interactionism,* p. 14.

58. David L Miller, *Individualism: Personal Achievement and the Open Society* (Austin: University of Texas Press, 1967), pp. 19–20.

59. Lauer and Handel, *Social Psychology,* p. 25.

60. Blumer, *Symbolic Interactionism,* p. 15.

61. Ibid., p. 15.

62. George Herbert Mead, cited in Lauer and Handel, *Social Psychology,* p. 25.

63. Ramos, *New Science*, pp. 4, 82.

Chapter 4: Leadership: The Hallmark of Macro Social Work

1. Mark R. Warren, "Connecting People to Politics: The Role of Religious Institutions in the Texas Industrial Areas Foundation Network," http://www.comm-org.utoledo.edu/papers.htm.

2. This section summarized from Daniel Levine, Jane Addams and the Liberal Tradition (Westport, CT: Greenwood Press, 1971).

3. Ibid., p. x.

4. Ibid., p. xi.

5. Ibid., p. 42.

6. Ibid., p. 129.

7. Ibid., p. 179.

8. Ibid., p. 181.

9. Robert C. Kennedy, HarpWeek, http://www.impeach-andrewjohnson.com/11biographieskeyindividuals/thaddeusstevens.htm.

10. Chris Crass, "But We Don't Have Leaders: Leadership Development and Anti Authoritarian Organizing," *Znet Magazine,* May 2, 2003. (http://www.zmag.org/content/print_article.cfm?itemID=3557&sectionID=5)

11. Carl Tjerandsen, "Education for Citizens: A Foundation's Experience." The Emil Schwarzhaupt Foundation, 1980. (http://www.comm-org.utoledo.edu/papers97)

12. Ibid.

13. Ibid.

14. David C. McClelland, *Power: The Inner Experience* (New York: Irvington, 1975), p. 260.

15. Peter Block, *Stewardship: Choosing Service Over Self-Interest* (San Francisco: Berrett-Koehler, 1993), p. 36.

16. Ibid., p. 37.

17. Tjerandsen, "Education for Citizens."

18. Paul H. Ephross and Thomas V. Vassil, *Groups That Work: Structure and Process* (New York: Columbia University Press, 1988), p. 2.

19. Alissi, quoted in Marian Fatout and Steven R. Rose, *Task Groups in the Social Services* (Thousand Oaks, CA: Sage, 1998), p. 6.

20. Ibid., p. 4.

21. Ibid.

22. Ibid.

23. *Cyclopedia of American Biography,* 23, 1925, pp. 111–112.

24. Ephross and Vassil, *Groups That Work,* p. 4.

25. Fatout and Rose, *Task Groups in the Social Services,* p. 7.

26. Ephross and Vassil, *Groups That Work,* p. 4.

27. Ibid., p. 6.

28. Eugene Jennings, quoted in Grover Starling, *Managing the Public Sector,* 5th ed. (Ft. Worth, TX: Harcourt Brace, 1998), pp. 361–362.

29. James T. Patterson, *America's Struggle Against Poverty: 1900–1980* (Cambridge, MA: Harvard University Press, 1981), pp. 44, 57–77.

30. Fatout and Rose, *Task Groups in the Social Services,* pp. 5, 6, 10.

31. Charles Perrow, *Complex Organizations: A Critical Essay,* 2d ed. (Glenview, IL: Scott, Foresman, 1979), p. 102.

32. Ephross and Vassil, *Groups That Work,* p. 4.

33. Fatout and Rose, *Task Groups in the Social Services,* pp. 7, 8, 10.

34. Wendel L. French, and Cecil H. Bell Jr., "A History of Organization Development." In *Organization Development and Transformation: Managing Effective Change,* Wendel L. French, Cecil H. Bell Jr., and Robert A. Zawacki, eds. (Burr Ridge, IL: Irwin, 1994), p. 25.
35. Fatout and Rose, *Task Groups in the Social Services,* p. 11.
36. Ibid., p. 12.
37. Ibid.
38. Ephross and Vassil, *Groups That Work,* p. 7.
39. Fatout and Rose, *Task Groups in the Social Services,* p. 13.
40. Ibid.
41. French and Bell, "A History of Organization Development," p. 35.
42. Douglas MacGregor, *The Human Side of Enterprise* (New York: McGraw-Hill, 1960).
43. Ibid., pp. 33–57.
44. Perrow, *Complex Organizations,* p. 98.
45. Paul Hersey and Kenneth H. Blanchard, *Management of Organizational Behavior: Utilizing Human Resources,* 5th ed. (Englewood Cliffs, NJ: Prentice Hall, 1988), p. 93.
46. Ibid.
47. Paul Hersey and Kenneth H. Blanchard, "Changing Patterns of Leadership: 3-D Leader Effectiveness Theory." Paper presented at the Leadership Workshop Conference, U.S. Military Academy, June 25–27, 1969.
48. Robert R. Blake and Jane S. Mouton, *The Managerial Grid* (Houston, TX: Gulf, 1964).
49. Hersey and Blanchard, "Changing Patterns," pp. 6–9.
50. Abraham Korman, "Consideration, Initiating Structure and Organizational Criteria—A Review," *Personnel Psychology,* 19 (4), 1966, pp. 340–361.
51. Fred E. Fiedler, *A Theory of Leadership Effectiveness* (New York: McGraw-Hill, 1967).
52. Perrow, *Complex Organizations,* p. 106.
53. Hersey and Blanchard, *Management of Organizational Behavior,* p. 142.
54. Edgar Shein, *Organizational Psychology,* 3d ed. (Englewood Cliffs, NJ: Prentice Hall, 1980), p. 116.
55. Charles H. Levine, B. Guy Peters, and Frank J. Thompson, *Public Administration: Challenges, Choices, Consequences* (Glenview, IL: Scott Foresman/Little Brown, 1990), p. 270.
56. Hersey and Blanchard, *Management of Organizational Behavior,* pp. 116–122.
57. Ibid., pp. 177–181.
58. Fatout and Rose, *Task Groups in the Social Services,* p. 14.
59. See, for example, Harry Specht and Mark Courtney, *Unfaithful Angels: How Social Work Has Abandoned Its Mission* (New York: Free Press, 1994).
60. Elenore Brilliant, "Social Work Leadership: A Missing Ingredient?" *Social Work,* 31 (5), September–October 1986.
61. Burton Gummer, *The Politics of Social Administration: Managing Organizational Politics in Social Agencies* (Englewood Cliffs, NJ: Prentice Hall, 1990), p. 122.
62. Chauncey Alexander, "Professional Social Workers and Political Responsibility." In *Practical Politics: Social Work and Political Responsibility,* Maryann Mahaffey and John W. Hanks, eds. (Silverspring, MD: National Association of Social Workers, 1982), p. 15.
63. Gummer, *The Politics of Social Administration,* p. 123.
64. Fatout and Rose, *Task Groups in Social Services,* p. 14.
65. Ibid.
66. Ibid., p. 15.
67. Ibid.
68. Ibid.
69. Crass, "But We Don't Have Leaders."
70. Tjerandsen, "Education for Citizens."
71. James M. Kouzas and Barry Posner, *The Leadership Challenge: How to Get Extraordinary Things Done in Organizations* (San Francisco: Jossey-Bass, 1987), p. 115.
72. Ibid., p. 113.
73. Tjerandsen, "Education for Citizens."
74. Ibid.
75. Kouzas and Posner, *The Leadership Challenge,* p. 7.
76. Gummer, *The Politics of Social Administration,* p. 187.
77. Edgar Schein, quoted in Kouzas and Posner, *The Leadership Challenge,* p. 83.
78. Gummer, *The Politics of Social Administration,* p. 132.
79. Edgar Schein, quoted in Kouzas and Posner, *The Leadership Challenge,* p. 19.
80. Ibid., p. 83.
81. Tjerandsen, "Education for Citizens."
82. Theodore Hesburgh, quoted in Rapp and Poertner, *Social Administration: A Client Centered Approach* (New York: Longman, 1992), p. 281.
83. Kouzas and Posner, *The Leadership Challenge,* p. 83.
84. Crass, "But We Don't Have Leaders."
85. Warren, "Connecting People to Politics."
86. Warren Bennis and Burt Nanus, *Leaders: The Strategies for Taking Charge* (New York: Harper and Row, 1985), p. 3.
87. Tjerandsen, "Education for Citizens."
88. Kouzas and Posner, *The Leadership Challenge,* p. 222.
89. Warren. "Connecting People to Politics."
90. Tjerandsen, "Education for Citizens."
91. Ronald W. Toseland and Robert F. Rivas, *An Introduction to Group Work Practice* (Boston: Allyn and Bacon, 1984), p. 126.
92. Fatout and. Rose, *Task Groups in Social Services,* p. 36.
93. Ibid., p. 40.
94. Ephross and Vassil, *Groups That Work,* pp. 41, 42.
95. Fatout and Rose, *Task Groups in Social Services,* p. 41.
96. Ibid., p. 36.
97. Ibid., p. 73.
98. Ephross and Vassil, *Groups That Work,* p. 74.
99. Fatout and Rose, *Task Groups in Social Services,* p. 73.
100. Ibid., pp. 68, 70.
101. Tjerandsen, "Education for Citizens."
102. Fatout and. Rose, *Task Groups in Social Services,* p. 70.
103. Ibid., p. 69.
104. Ibid., p. 73.
105. Ephross and Vassil, *Groups That Work,* p. 10.
106. Bruce Tuchman, "Developmental Sequences in Small Groups," *Psychological Bulletin,* 63, 1965, pp. 384–399. Linda Yael Schiller places the norming stage before storming based on her research in women's groups. Schiller's perspective also tends to confirm the leadership research described here and is congruent with Hersey and Blanchard's situational leadership theory.
107. Adapted from Tuchman, "Developmental Sequence in Small Groups."
108. Fatout and Rose, *Task Groups in Social Services,* pp. 66, 70.
109. Ibid., p. 70.
110. Ibid., p. 71.
111. Toseland and Rivas, *An Introduction to Group Work Practice,* p. 307.
112. Fatout and Rose, *Task Groups in Social Services,* p. 71.
113. Ibid., p. 71.
114. Ibid., pp. 72–73.
115. Kouzas and Posner, *The Leadership Challenge,* p. 162.
116. Ibid.
117. Ibid., p. 184.
118. Brilliant, "Social Work Leadership," p. 326.

Part 2: Social Work Practice with Communities

1. Hans Falck, *Social Work: The Membership Perspective* (New York: Springer, 1988), p. 6.
2. William A. Schambra, "All Community Is Local." In *Community Works: The Revival of Civil Society in America,* E. J. Dionne Jr. ed. (Washington DC: Brookings Institution Press, 1998), p. 49.
3. Harry Specht and Mark E. Courtney, *Unfaithful Angels: How Social Work Has Abandoned Its Mission* (New York: Free Press, 1994), p. 27.

Chapter 5: Community

1. Eric Voegelin, *The New Science of Politics* (Chicago, IL: University of Chicago Press, 1952), p. 183.
2. From Winthrop's sermon "A Model of Christian Charity," delivered aboard the *Arabella* in Salem harbor just before landing in the new land, 1630, as quoted in Robert N. Bellah, Richard Madsen, William M. Sullivan, Ann Swidler, and Steven M. Tipton, *Habits of the Heart: Individualism and Commitment in American Life* (New York: Harper and Row, 1985), p. 28.
3. *Weapons of the Spirit,* a film by Pierre Sauvage Productions and Friends of Le Chambon, Inc., 1988. See also Philip Hallie, *Lest Innocent Blood Be Shed: The Story of the Village of Le Chambon and How Goodness Happened There* (New York: Harper and Row, 1979).
4. Ibid.
5. Patricia Martin and Gerald G. O'Connor, *The Social Environment: Open Systems Applications* (New York: Longman, 1989), p. 230.
6. Hallie, *Lest Innocent Blood Be Shed,* p. 20.
7. Colin Bell and Howard Newby, *Community Studies: An Introduction to the Sociology of the Local Community* (New York: Praeger, 1971), p. 24.
8. Edward W. Hassinger and James R. Pinkerton, *The Human Community* (New York: Macmillan, 1986), p. 10.
9. Harry Boyte, "Reconnecting Power and Vision," Community Practices Network, September 30, 2001. (http://www.cpn.org/cpn/sections/topics/community/stories-studies/e_Brooklyn.html)
10. Peter Dreier, "The Struggle for Our Cities," 1997. (http://comm-org.utoledo.edu/colist.htm)
11. Ibid.
12. Myron Orfield, *Metropolitics: A Regional Agenda for Community and Stability* (Cambridge, MA: Brookings Institution, Lincoln Institute of Land Policy, 1997).
13. Dreier, "The Struggle for Our Cities."
14. Hassinger and Pinkerton, *The Human Community,* p. 4.
15. Ibid., pp. 4, 12.
16. Martin and O'Connor, *The Social Environment,* p. 238.
17. Acts 2:44–46, 4:32–35, 5:12b.
18. Max Weber, *Economy and Society: Outline of Interpretive Sociology,* 3 vols. Guenther Roth and Claus Wittich, eds. (Berkeley, CA: University of California Press), p. 987.
19. Roland Warren, *Social Change and Human Purpose: Toward Understanding and Action* (Chicago, IL: Rand McNally, 1977), p. 207.
20. Ibid.
21. Alfred Schutz in Ralph P. Hummel, *The Bureaucratic Experience* (New York: St. Martin's Press, 1977), p. 32.
22. Ibid., p. 36.
23. Paul Tillich, *Systematic Theology,* Vol. 1. (Chicago, IL: University of Chicago Press, 1951), p. 176.
24. Bellah et al., *Habits of the Heart,* p. 116.
25. Vu-Duc Vuong and John Duong Huynh, "Southeast Asians in the United States: A Strategy for Accelerated and Balanced Integration." In *Community Organizing in a Diverse Society,* Felix G. Rivera and John L. Erlich, eds. (Boston: Allyn and Bacon, 1992), p. 217.
26. Harry Specht and Mark E. Courtney, *Unfaithful Angels: How Social Work Has Abandoned Its Mission* (New York: Free Press, 1994), p. 27.
27. Martha L. McCoy and Robert F. Sherman, "Bridging the Divides of Race and Ethnicity." *National Civic Review,* Spring-Summer 1994, p. 111.
28. Ibid., pp. 113–114.
29. Julio Morales, "Community Social Work With Puerto Rican Communities in the United States: One Organizer's Perspective." In *Community Organizing in a Diverse Society,* Felix G. Rivera and John L. Erlich, ed. (Boston: Allyn and Bacon, 1992), p. 98.
30. Peter L. Berger and Richard John Neuhaus, *To Empower People: From State to Civil Society,* 2d ed. (Washington, DC: American Enterprise Institute Press, 1997), pp. 185–186.
31. Ibid.
32. Wynetta Devore, "The African American Community in 1990: The Search for a Practice Method." In *Community Organizing in a Diverse Society,* Felix G. Rivera and John L. Erlich, eds. (Boston: Allyn and Bacon, 1992), p. 84.
33. John M. Perkins, *With Justice for All* (Ventura, CA: Regal Books, 1982), p. 35.
34. William A. Galston and Peter Levine, "America's Civic Condition: A Glance at the Evidence." In *Community Works: The Revival of Civil Society in America,* E. J. Dionne Jr., ed. (Washington, DC: Brookings Institution Press, 1998) p. 33.
35. Berger and Neuhaus, *To Empower People,* p. 187.
36. Ibid., p. 185.
37. Ibid., p. 189.
38. Ernest Kurtz and Katherine Ketcham, *The Spirituality of Imperfection: Storytelling and the Journey to Wholeness* (New York: Bantam, 1992), p. 82.
39. Ibid., p. 85.
40. Karen Lebacqz, *Justice in an Unjust World: Foundations for a Christian Approach to Justice* (Minneapolis: Augsburg, 1987), p. 59.
41. Deuteronomy 14:29b; James 1:27.
42. John J. DiIulio Jr., "The Lord's Work: The Church and Civil Society." In *Community Works: The Revival of Civil Society in America,* p. 54.
43. Ernesto Cortes Jr., "Reweaving the Fabric: The Iron Rule and the IAF Strategy for Power and Politics." Community Practices Network, 1993. (http://www.cpn.org/cpn/sections/topics/community/civic_perspectives/cortes-reweaving.html)
44. Hassinger and Pinkerton, *The Human Community,* p. 7.
45. Thomas Bender, *Community and Social Change in America* (New Brunswick, NJ: Rutgers University Press, 1978), p. 60.
46. Ibid.
47. Ibid.
48. Ibid., p. 64.
49. Ibid., p. 68.
50. Ibid., pp. 73–75.
51. Hassinger and Pinkerton, *The Human Community,* pp. 7, 17.
52. Warren, *Social Change and Human Purpose,* p. 207.
53. Hassinger and Pinkerton, *The Human Community,* p. 17.
54. Ibid.
55. Ibid.
56. Ibid.
57. Ferdinand Toennies, *Community and Society,* C. P. Loomis ed. (New York: Harper Torchbook, 1957), p. 258.
58. Ibid., p. 232.

59. Bender, *Community and Social Change*, p. 34.
60. Bell and Newby, *Community Studies*, p. 24.
61. Hassinger and Pinkerton, *The Human Community*, p. 13.
62. Bender, *Community and Social Change*, p. 35.
63. Larry Lyon, *The Community in Urban Society* (Lexington, MA: D. C. Heath, 1989), p. 19.
64. Max Weber, "Bureaucracy." In *Economy and Society: An Outline of Interpretive Sociology*, 3 vols., Guenther Roth and Claus Wittich, eds., Elphraim Fischoff et al., trans. (New York: Bedminster, 1968), p. 987.
65. Alberto Guerreiro Ramos, *New Science of Organizations* (Toronto, Ontario: University of Toronto Press, 1983).
66. Max Weber, "Politics as a Vocation." In *From Max Weber: Essays in Sociology*, H. H. Gerth and C. Wright Mills, eds. (New York: Oxford University Press, 1946), p. 95.
67. Weber, "Bureaucracy, " p. 987.
68. Bellah et al., *Habits of the Heart*, p. 42.
69. Robert Presthus, *The Organizational Society*, rev. ed. (New York: St. Martin's, 1978).
70. George Simmel, "The Metropolis and Mental Life, 1902–3." In *Community in Urban Society*, p. 20.
71. Ibid.
72. Edward A. Ross, *Social Control: A Survey of the Foundations of Order* (Cleveland: Case Western Reserve University, 1969), p. 432.
73. Bender, *Community and Social Change*, p. 35.
74. Lyon, *Community in Urban Society*, p. 21.
75. Bender, *Community and Social Change*, p. 20.
76. Lewis Wirth, "Urbanism as a Way of Life." In *Community and Social Change*, p. 20.
77. Ibid.
78. Bender, *Community and Social Change*, p. 36.
79. Charles Horton Cooley, *Social Process* (New York: Scribner's, 1918), p. 149.
80. Bender, *Community and Social Change*, p. 37.
81. Ibid., p. 38.
82. John Dewey, *The Public and Its Problems* (New York: Hold, 1927), p. 215.
83. Ibid., p. 216.
84. Bender, *Community and Social Change*, p. 41.
85. Robert Redfield, *The Little Community* (Chicago: University of Chicago Press, 1955), p. 70.
86. Ibid., pp. 146–177.
87. Bender, *Community and Social Change*, p. 43.
88. Dionne, *Community Works*, p. 1.
89. Alan Wolfe, "Is Civil Society Obsolete?" in *Community Works*, p. 17.
90. Cortes, "Reweaving the Fabric."
91. Amitai Etzioni cited in Kristina Smock, "Comprehensive Community Initiatives: A New Generation of Urban Revitalization Strategies," 1997. (http://comm-org.utoledo.edu/colist.htm)
92. Smock, "Comprehensive Community Initiatives."
93. Alan Wolf, *Whose Keeper? Social Science and Moral Obligation* (Berkeley, CA: University of California Press, 1989); and Robert D. Putnam, "Bowling Alone: America's Declining Social Capital." *Journal of Democracy*, 6 (1), January 1995, pp. 65–78.
94. Smock, "Comprehensive Community Initiatives."
95. Bender, *Community and Society*, p. 23.
96. Ibid., p. 29.
97. Randy Stoecker, "Power or Programs? Two Paths to Community Development." Address Delivered to the International Association for Community Development Conference, Rotorua, New Zealand, 2001.
98. Ibid.
99. Mike Eichler, "The Consensus Organizing Model and the Consensus Organizing Institute," Civic Practices Network, 1993. (http://www.cpn.corg/cpn/COI/coi_model.html)
100. Ibid.

Chapter 6: The Practice of Community Planning

1. John Forester, *Planning in the Face of Power* (Berkeley: University of California Press, 1989), p. 28.
2. G. Thomas Kingsely, Josephy B. McNeely, and James O. Gibson, "Community Building: Coming of Age." Community Projects Network. 1997. (http://www.cpn.org/cpn/sections/topics/community/civic_perspectives/cb_coming_of_age1.html)
3. William M. Rohe and Lauren B. Gates, *Planning With Neighborhoods* (Chapel Hill: University of North Carolina Press, 1985), p. 80.
4. Ken Thomson, Jeffery M. Berry, and Kent E. Portney, "Kernels of Democracy." Community Projects Network (CPN), 1994. (http://www.cpn.org/topics/community/kernels.html)
5. Kristina Smock, "Comprehensive Community Initiatives: A New Generation of Urban Revitalization Strategies," 1997. (http//.comm-org.Toledo.edu/papers97/smock/.htm)
6. Rohe and Gates, *Planning With Neighborhoods*, p. 107.
7. Ibid., p. 108.
8. Thomson et al., "Kernels of Democracy."
9. Robert R. Mayer, *Policy and Program Planning* (Englewood Cliffs, NJ: Prentice-Hall, 1985), p. 4.
10. Armand Lauffer, "The Practice of Social Planning." In *Handbook for Social Services*, Neil Gilbert and Harry Specht, ed. (Englewood Cliffs, NJ: Prentice-Hall, 1981), p. 583.
11. Rohe and Gates, *Planning With Neighborhoods*, p. 82.
12. Jack Rothman and Mayer N. Zald, "Planning Theory and Social Work Community Practice." In *Theory and Practice of Community Social Work*. Samuel H. Taylor and Robert W. Roberts, ed. (New York: Columbia University Press, 1985), p. 142.
13. Ibid., p. 131.
14. Ronald L. Simons and Stephen M. Aigner, *Practice Principles: A Problem Solving Approach to Social Work* (New York: Macmillan, 1985), p. 208; and Neil Gilbert and Harry Specht, "Who Plans?" In *Strategies of Community Organization*, 3d ed., Fred. M. Cox, John L. Erlich, Jack Rothman, and John E. Tropman, eds. (Itasca, IL: Peacock, 1979), p. 347.
15. Linda Ruth Pine, "Economic Opportunity Act (E0A) 1964." In *American Community Organizations*, Patricia Mooney Melvin, ed. (New York: Greenwood Press, 1986), p. 54.
16. Paul A. Kurzman, "Program Development and Service Coordination as Components of Community Practice." In *Theory and Practice of Community Social Work*, Samuel H. Taylor and Robert W. Roberts, eds. (New York: Columbia University Press, 1985), p. 100.
17. *Cyclopedia of American Biography* (New York: American Historical Society, 1932), vol. 31, pp. 79–80; and *Social Work Encyclopedia*, 19th ed. (Washington, DC: NASW Press, 1995), p. 2576.
18. Howard W. Hallman, *Neighborhoods: Their Place in Urban Life* (Beverly Hills, CA: Sage, 1984), pp. 116–118.
19. Gilbert and Specht, "Who Plans?" p. 347.
20. Hallman, *Neighborhoods*, p. 118.
21. Simons and Aigner, *Practice Principles*, pp. 208–209.
22. Gilbert and Specht, "Who Plans?" p. 347.
23. Hallman, *Neighborhoods*, p. 118.
24. Charles F. Casey-Leininger, Sixth National Conference on American Planning History, Knoxville, Tennessee, October 15, 1995.

25. Kurzman, "Program Development," p. 98.
26. Hallman, *Neighborhoods,* p. 125.
27. Ibid., p. 126.
28. "Repairing the Breach," Community Projects Network, September 30, 2001. (http://www.cpn.org/cpn/sections/topics/community/stories-studies/repairing_breach. html)
29. Madelene R. Stoner, "The Practice of Community Social Work in Mental Health Settings." In *Theory and Practice of Community Social Work,* Samuel H. Taylor and Robert W. Roberts, eds. (New York: Columbia University Press, 1985), p. 285.
30. Rothman and Zald, "Planning Theory," p. 131.
31. Stoner, "The Practice of Community Social Work in Mental Health Settings," p. 290.
32. Ibid., p. 299.
33. Ibid.
34. Ibid., p. 303.
35. Ibid.
36. Gilbert and Specht, "Who Plans?" p. 348.
37. Stoner, "The Practice of Community Social Work," p. 305.
38. Ibid., pp. 305–308.
39. Abraham Monk, "The Practice of Community Social Work With the Aged." In *Theory and Practice of Community Social Work,* Samuel H. Taylor and Robert W. Roberts, eds. (New York: Columbia University Press, 1985), p. 268.
40. Ibid., p. 270.
41. Ibid., p. 272.
42. Ibid.
43. Kurzman, "Program Development," p. 97.
44. Walter I. Trattner, *From Poor Law to Welfare State: A History of Social Welfare in America,* 4th ed. (New York: Free Press, 1989), p. 88.
45. Margaret E. Rich, *A Belief in People: A History of Family Social Work* (New York: Family Service Association of America, 1956), p. 13.
46. Beulah H. Compton, *Introduction to Social Welfare and Social Work: Structure, Function, and Process* (Homewood, IL: Dorsey, 1980), p. 162.
47. Ibid.
48. Kurzman, "Program Development," p. 97.
49. Hallman, *Neighborhoods,* p. 108.
50. Kurzman, "Program Development," p. 99.
51. Diana M. DiNitto and C. Aaron McNeece, *Social Work: Issues and Opportunities in a Challenging Profession* (Englewood Cliffs, NJ: Prentice-Hall, 1990), p. 72.
52. Kurzman, "Program Development," p. 98.
53. Rothman and Zald, "Planning Theory," p. 130.
54. Hallman, *Neighborhoods,* pp. 132–133.
55. Pine, "Economic Opportunity Act (E0A) 1964," p. 54.
56. Ibid., p. 55.
57. Ibid., p. 56.
58. John Ehrenreich, *The Altruistic Imagination: A History of Social Work and Social Policy in the United States* (Ithaca, NY: Cornell University Press, 1985), pp. 170–171.
59. Neil Gilbert, "The Design of Community Planning Structures," *Social Service Review,* 53, 1979, p. 647.
60. Linda Ruth Pine, "Demonstration Cities and Metropolitan Development Act, 1966." In *American Community Organizations,* Patricia Mooney Melvin, ed. (New York: Greenwood Press, 1986), pp. 45–46.
61. Ibid.
62. Janice K. Tulloss, "Transforming Urban Regimes—A Grassroots Approach to Comprehensive Community Development: The Dudley Street Neighborhood Initiative." Annual Meeting of the American Political Science Association, San Francisco, California, August 31, 1996.
63. Smock, "Comprehensive Community Initiatives."
64. Forester, *Planning in the Face of Power,* p. 28.
65. Rohe and Gates, *Planning With Neighborhoods,* p. 107.
66. Ibid.
67. Guy Benveniste, *Mastering the Politics of Planning: Crafting Credible Plans and Policies That Make a Difference* (San Francisco: Jossey-Bass, 1989), pp. 263, 264.
68. Forester, *Planning in the Face of Power,* p. 35.
69. Benveniste, *Mastering the Politics of Planning,* p. 264.
70. Alan Walker, *Social Planning: A Strategy for Socialist Welfare* (Oxford: B. Blackwell, 1984), p. 137.
71. Mark S. Homan, *Promoting Community Change: Making It Happen in the Real World.* 3d ed. Belmont, CA: Thomson/Brooks Cole, 2004, pp. 163–164.
72. John Kretzman and John McKnight, quoted in Homan, *Promoting Community Change,* pp. 164–165.
73. Homan, *Promoting Community Change,* p. 160.
74. George J. Wahrheit, Robert A. Bell, and John J. Schwab, "Selecting the Needs Assessment Approach," In *Tactics and Techniques of Community Practice,* 2d ed., Fred M. Cox, John L. Erlich, Jack Rothman, and John E. Tropman, eds. (Itasca, IL: Peacock, 1984), p. 49.
75. Allen Rubin and Earl Babbie, *Research Methods of Social Work* (Belmont, CA: Wadsworth, 1979), p. 503.
76. Wahrheit, Bell, and Schwab, "Selecting the Needs Assessment Approach," p. 41.
77. Harvey L. Gochros, "Research Interviewing." In *Social Work Research and Evaluation,* 3d ed., Richard M. Grinnell Jr., ed. (Itasca, IL: Peacock, 1988), p. 275.
78. Rebecca F. Guy, Charles E. Edgley, Ibtihaj Arafat, and Donald E. Allen, *Social Research Methods: Puzzles and Solutions* (Boston: Allyn and Bacon, 1987), p. 220.
79. Ibid. pp. 191–197.
80. Rubin and Babbie, *Research Methods of Social Work,* p. 320; Guy et al., *Social Research Methods,* p. 243.
81. Martin Gannon, *Management: An Integrated Framework,* 2d ed. (Boston: Little, Brown, 1982), p. 145.
82. Ibid., p. 146.
83. Ibid.
84. Grover Starling, *Managing the Public Sector,* 5th ed. (Ft. Worth: Harcourt Brace, 1998), p. 273.
85. Gannon, *Management,* p. 142.
86. Edith Stokey and Richard Zeckhauser, *A Primer for Policy Analysis* (New York: Norton, 1978), p. 177.
87. Starling, *Managing the Public Sector,* pp. 267–270.
88. Marian Fatout and Steven R. Rose, *Task Groups in the Social Services* (Thousand Oaks, CA: Sage, 1995), pp. 130–133.
89. Ibid., p. 133.
90. Ibid., pp. 134–135.
91. Forester, *Planning in the Face of Power,* p. 5.
92. Ibid.
93. Ibid., p. 28.
94. Ibid., p. 40.
95. Ibid., p. 41.
96. Rohe and Gates, *Planning With Neighborhoods,* p. 107.

Chapter 7: The Practice of Community Development

1. Marilyn Ferguson, *The Aquarian Conspiracy* (Los Angeles: J. P. Tarcher, 1980), p. 207.
2. Stewart E. Perry, *Communities on the Way: Rebuilding Local Economies in the United States and Canada* (Albany: State University of New York Press, 1987) p. 6.
3. Kristina Smock, "Comprehensive Community Initiatives: A New Generation of Urban Revitalization Strategies,"

1997. (http://www.comm-org.utoledo.edu/papers97/smock.htm)

4. "Community Development Works," 2004. (http://www.communitydevelopmentworks.org/)

5. OLDC Online, April 11, 2005. (http: oldc.org/home.htm)

6. Antonia Pantoja and Wilhelmina Perry, "Community Development and Restoration: A Perspective." In *Community Organizing in a Diverse Society*, Felix G. Rivera and John L. Erlich, eds. (Boston: Allyn and Bacon, 1992), p. 240.

7. Michael Leo Owens, "Political Action and Black Church-Associated Community Development Corporations." Urban Affairs Association, Los Angeles, California, May 3–6, 2000.

8. Ibid.

9. Smock, "Comprehensive Community Initiatives."

10. Lee Winkelman, "Massachusetts Community Development Corporations and Community Organizing. Massachusetts Association of CDCs, December 1997. (http://www.comm-org.utoledo.edu/papers98/winkleman.htm)

11. Lewis Friedland, "Electronic Democracy and the New Citizenship." Community Practices Network, 1996. (http://www.cpn.org/crm/contemporary/electronic.html)

12. Owens, "Political Action."

13. Smock, "Comprehensive Community Initiatives."

14. Ibid.

15. Calvert Social Investment Foundation, Bethesda, Maryland, 2001.

16. Thand Williamson, "Church-Based Community Economic Development: Perspectives and Prognosis," *Religious Socialism,* Fall 1997, p. 8.

17. Owens, "Political Action."

18. Smock, "Comprehensive Community Initiatives."

19. Owens, "Political Action."

20. Ibid.

21. Winkelman, "Massachusetts Community Development Corporations."

22. Randy Stoecker, "Power or Programs? Two Paths to Community Development." International Association for Community Development Conference, Rotorua, New Zealand, 2001. (http://www.comm.-org.utoledo.edu/drafts/twopathsb2.htm)

23. Owens, "Political Action."

24. Williamson, "Church-Based Community Economic Development," p. 8.

25. Robert Fisher, *Let the People Decide: Neighborhood Organizing in America* (New York: Twayne, 1994), p. 182.

26. Williamson, "Church-Based Community Economic Development," pp. 8–9.

27. Alan C. Twelvetrees, *Organizing for Neighbourhood Development: A Comparative Study of Community Based Development Organizations,* 2d ed. (Aldershot, England: Avebury, 1996), pp. 148–149.

28. Ibid., p. 151.

29. Henry George in Beulah R. Compton, *Introduction to Social Welfare and Social Work: Structure, Function and Process* (Homewood, IL: Dorsey, 1980), p. 279.

30. Bryan M. Phifer, with E. Frederick List and Boyd Faulkner, "History of Community Development in America." In *Community Development in America,* James A. Christenson and Jerry W. Robinson Jr., eds. (Ames: Iowa State University Press, 1980), p. 13.

31. Ibid., pp. 18–20.

32. Fisher, *Let the People Decide,* p. 23; and Hubert Campfens, ed., *Community Development Around the World: Practice, Theory, Research, Training* (Toronto: University of Toronto Press, 1997), pp. 18–19.

33. Compton, *Introduction to Social Welfare and Social Work,* p. 418.

34. Perry, *Communities on the Way,* pp. 6–8.

35. Howard W. Hallman, *Neighborhoods: Their Place in Urban Life,* Vol. 154, Sage Library of Social Research (Beverly Hills, CA: Sage, 1984), pp. 130–131.

36. Phifer et al., "History of Community Development in America," pp. 26, 35.

37. Randy Stoecker, "Crossing the Development-Organizing Divide: A Report on the Toledo Community Organizing Training and Technical Assistance Program" May 2001. (randy.stoecker@utoledo.edu)

38. Robert Fisher, "Neighborhood Organizing: The Importance of Historical Context." In *Revitalizing Urban Neighborhoods,* W. Dennis Keating, Norman Starr, and Phillip Krumholz, eds. (Lawrence: University of Kansas Press, 1996), pp. 39–49.

39. J. Reymundo Ocañas, *History of Community Economic Development* (Austin, TX: Texas Association of Community Development Corporations, 2004).

40. Fisher, *Let the People Decide,* p. 181.

41. Susan Redman-Rengstorf, "Neighborhood Reinvestment Corporation (NERC) 1978." In *American Community Organizations: A Historical Dictionary,* Patricia Mooney Melvin, ed. (New York: Greenwood Press, 1986), p. 129.

42. Neil R. Peirce and Carol F. Steinbach, *Enterprising Communities: Community-Based Development in America* (Washington, DC: Council for Community Based Development, 1990), pp. 15–16; and Stoecker, "Crossing the Development-Organizing Divide."

43. J Ocañas, *History of Community Economic Development.*

44. Susan Redman-Rengstorf, "Neighborhoods U.S.A. (NUSA) 1975." In *American Community Organizations: A Historical Dictionary,* Patricia Mooney Melvin, ed. (New York: Greenwood Press, 1986), pp. 131–132.

45. Robert R. Fairbanks, "Housing and Community Development Act (HCDA) 1974." In *American Community Organizations: A Historical Dictionary,* Patricia Mooney Melvin, ed. (New York: Greenwood Press, 1986), pp. 81–83.

46. Fisher, *Let the People Decide,* pp. 157, 181.

47. Redman-Rengstorf, "Neighborhood Reinvestment Corporation (NERC) 1978," p. 129.

48. Patricia Mooney Melvin, "National Neighborhood Policy Act 1977." In *American Community Organizations: A Historical Dictionary,* Patricia Mooney Melvin, ed. (New York: Greenwood Press, 1986), pp. 127–129.

49. Lynne Navin, "Neighborhood Self-Help Development Act, 1978." In *American Community Organizations: A Historical Dictionary,* Patricia Mooney Melvin, ed. (New York: Greenwood Press, 1986), p. 130.

50. Fisher, "Neighborhood Organizing."

51. Neil R. Peirce and Carol F. Steinbach, *Enterprising Communities: Community-Based Development in America* (Washington, DC: Council for Community Based Development, 1990), p. 26.

52. Stoecker, "Crossing the Development-Organizing Divide."

53. Ibid.

54. Fisher, "Neighborhood Organizing."

55. Renee Berger, *Against All Odds: The Achievement of Community-Based Development Organizations* (Washington, DC: National Congress for Community Economic Development, 1989), p. 4.

56. Fisher, "Neighborhood Organizing."

57. Christopher Walker, *Community Development Corporations and Their Changing Support Systems* (Washington, DC: The Urban Institute, 2002), p. 1.

58. Smock, "Comprehensive Community Initiatives."

59. Williamson, "Church-Based Community Economic Development," p. 3.

60. Ibid., p. 1.
61. J Ocañas, *History of Community Economic Development.*
62. Walker, *Community Development Corporations,* pp. 1, 4.
63. Smock, "Comprehensive Community Initiatives."
64. Hallman, *Neighborhoods,* p. 137.
65. Walker, *Community Development Corporations,* p. 1.
66. Ibid., p. 2.
67. Ocañas, *History of Community Economic Development.*
68. Owens, "Political Action."
69. Walker, *Community Development Corporations,* pp. 2, 4.
70. Ibid., p. 3.
71. Smock, "Comprehensive Community Initiatives."
72. Sustainable Communities Network, revised March 9, 2004. (http://www.sustainable.org/)
73. Si Kahn, *How People Get Power: Organizing Oppressed Communities for Action* (New York: McGraw Hill, 1970), p. 5.
74. Felix G. Rivera and John L. Erlich (eds.), *Community Organization in a Diverse Society* (Boston: Allyn and Bacon, 1992), p. 10.
75. Ibid., p. 11.
76. Ibid., p. 12.
77. Perry, *Communities on the Way,* p. 37.
78. Stone, Rebecca, *Comprehensive Community-Building Strategies: Issues and Opportunities for Learning* (Chicago: Chapin Hall for Children, 1994).
79. Ernesto Cortes Jr., "Reweaving the Fabric: The Iron Rule and the IAF Strategy for Power and Politics," Community Practices Network, 1993. (http://www.cpn.org/cpn/sections/topics/community/civic_perspectives/cortes-reweaving.html)
80. Perry, *Communities on the Way,* p. 35.
81. G. Thomas Kingsley, Joseph B. McNeely, and James O. Gibson, *Community Building: Coming of Age* (St. Paul, MI: Development Training Institute and Urban Institute, 1997), p. 7.
82. Twelvetrees, *Organizing for Neighbourhood Development,* p. 174.
83. Ibid., p. 149.
84. Williamson, "Church-Based Community Economic Development," p. 3.
85. Joan Walsh, *Stories of Renewal: Community Building and the Future of Urban America* (New York: Rockefeller Foundation, 1997), pp. 2, 35.
86. Twelvetrees, *Organizing for Neighbourhood Development,* p. 174.
87. Stoecker, "Power or Programs?"
88. Kahn, *How People Get Power,* pp. 116, 120–121.
89. Friedland, "Electronic Democracy."
90. Ibid.
91. Mark S. Homan, *Promoting Community Change: Making It Happen in the Real World,* 3d ed. (Belmont, CA: Thomson-Brooks Cole, 2004), p. 114.

Chapter 8: The Practice of Community Organization

1. Paulo Freire, *Pedagogy of the Oppressed* (New York: Continuum, 1992), p. 28.
2. Si Kahn, *How People Get Power: Organizing Oppressed Communities for Action,* rev. ed. (Washington DC: NASW Press, 1994), p. 132.
3. Joan E. Lancourt, *Confront or Concede: The Alinsky Citizen-Action Organizations* (Lexington, MA: D. C. Heath, 1979), pp. 156–157.
4. Harry Boyte, *Community Is Possible: Repairing America's Roots* (New York: Harper and Row, 1984), p. 127.
5. Ibid., p. 128.
6. Ibid., p. 133.
7. Ibid., p. 135.
8. Ibid., p. 140.
9. Ibid., p. 143.
10. Ibid., p. 145.
11. Ibid., p. 147.
12. Ibid., p. 148.
13. Ernesto Cortes Jr., "Reweaving the Fabric: The Iron Rule and the IAF Strategy for Power and Politics." Community Practices Network, 1993. (http://www.cpn.org/cpn/sections/topics/community/civic_perspectives/cortes-reweaving.html)
14. Ibid., p. 151.
15. David Moberg, *All Together Now,* 27(3), Oct. 7, 1997, n. p.
16. Boyte, *Community Is Possible,* p. 152.
17. Ibid., p. 25.
18. Ibid., p. 26.
19. Robert Linthicum, "Partners in Urban Transformation, Los Angeles, CA." Memorandum to the author, July 22, 1998, p. 1.
20. Randy Stoecker, "Crossing the Development-Organizing Divide: A Report on the Toledo Community Organizing Training and Technical Assistance Program." COMM-ORG Working Papers Series, May 2001. (http://comm-org.utoledo.edu/drafts/cdcorgnew.htm)
21. Robert Fisher, "Neighborhood Organizing: The Importance of Historical Context." COMM-ORG Working Papers Series, 1996. (http://comm-org.utoledo.edu/papers96/fishercon.htm)
22. Joan E. Lancourt, *Confront or Concede: The Alinsky Citizen-Action Organizations* (Lexington, MA: D. C. Heath, 1979), pp. 156–157.
23. Michael R. Williams, *Neighborhood Organization: Seeds of a New Urban Life* (Westport, CT: Greenwood Press, 1985), p. 227.
24. Carl Tjerandsen, *Education for Citizens: A Foundation's Experience.* Emil Schwarzhaupt Foundation, 1980. (http://www.comm-org,utoledo.edu/papers97)
25. Alan C. Twelvetrees, *Organizing for Neighbourhood Development: A Comparative Study of Community Based Development Organizations,* 2d ed. (Aldershot, England: Avebury Press, 1996), p. 139.
26. Tjerandsen, *Education for Citizens.*
27. David Finks, *The Radical Vision of Saul Alinski* (New York: Paulist Press, 1984), p. xi.
28. Tjerandsen, *Education for Citizens.*
29. Ibid.
30. Saul Alinsky, *Reveille for Radicals* (New York: Random House, 1989), p. 103.
31. Judy Hertz, "Cotter and Co. Decide to Leave," *Organizing for Change: Stories of Success.* Paper presented on COMM-ORG: The On-Line Conference on Community Organizing and Development, 2002. (http://comm-org.utoledo.edu/papers2002/hertz/hertz.htm)
32. Stoecker, "Crossing the Development-Organizing Divide."
33. Samuel Bowles and Herbert Gintis, *Democracy and Capitalism* (New York: Basic Books, 1987), p. 179.
34. Peter L. Berger and Richard John Neuhaus, *To Empower People: From State to Civil Society,* 2d ed. (Washington DC: American Enterprise Institute Press, 1996), p. 159.
35. Richard L. Wood, "Faith and Power." Working Papers series for COMM-ORG: The On-line Conference on Community Organizing and Development, 1998. (http://comm-org.utoledo.edu/papers98/warren/faith/Wood.html)
36. Peter Dreier, "The Struggle for Our Cities," Working Papers series for COMM-ORG: The On-line Conference on Community Organizing and Development, 1997. (http://comm-org.utoledo.edu/papers97/dreier.htm)

37. Ibid.
38. Walter Wright, "Church Coalition Leads Way for Renovation of Kalihi Housing Project," *Honolulu Advertiser,* February 2, 1998.
39. June Beckett, "20 Additional Victories," *Organizing for Change: Stories of Success.* Paper presented on COMM-ORG: The On-Line Conference on Community Organizing and Development, 2002. (http://comm-org.utoledo.edu/papers2002/hertz/hertz.htm)
40. Ibid.
41. Ibid.
42. Ibid.
43. Ibid.
44. Ibid.
45. Linthicum, "Partners in Urban Transformation," pp. 3, 4.
46. Harry Boyte, *The Backyard Revolution: Understanding the New Citizen Movement* (Philadelphia: Temple University Press, 1980), pp. 49–50.
47. Fisher, *Neighborhood Organizing.*
48. Howard W. Hallman, *Neighborhoods: Their Place in Urban Life.* Sage Library of Social Research (Beverly Hills, CA: Sage, 1984), vol. 54, p. 108.
49. Williams, *Neighborhood Organization,* p. 227.
50. Fisher, *Neighborhood Organizing.*
51. Sidney Dillick, *Community Organization for Neighborhood Development, Past and Present* (New York: William Morrow, 1953), pp. 34–35.
52. Arthur Dunham, *The New Community Organization* (New York: Crowell, 1970), p. 74.
53. Robert Fisher, *Let the People Decide: Neighborhood Organizing in America* (New York: Twayne, 1994), p. 14.
54. Ibid.
55. Ibid., p. 16.
56. Hallman, *Neighborhoods,* p. 109.
57. Dillick, *Community Organization for Neighborhood Development,* pp. 58–66.
58. Fisher, *Let the People Decide,* p. 16.
59. Dillick, *Community Organization for Neighborhood Development,* pp. 61, 63.
60. Fisher, *Let the People Decide,* p. 19.
61. Dillick, *Community Organization for Neighborhood Development,* p. 61.
62. Fisher, *Let the People Decide,* p. 20.
63. Hallman, *Neighborhoods,* p. 110.
64. Fisher, *Neighborhood Organizing.*
65. Donald C. Reitzes and Dietrich C. Reitzes, *The Alinsky Legacy Alive and Kicking* (Greenwich, CT: JAI Press, 1987), pp. 3–9.
66. Stoecker, "Crossing the Development-Organizing Divide."
67. Finks, *Radical Vision,* pp. 21, 23.
68. Saul Alinsky, *Rules for Radicals: A Pragmatic Primer for Realistic Radicals* (New York: Vintage Books, 1974), p. xx.
69. Alinsky, *Revellie for Radicals,* p. 7.
70. Ibid., p. 72.
71. Ibid., p. 116.
72. Tjerandsen, *Education for Citizens.*
73. Fisher, *Neighborhood Organizing.*
74. Williams, *Neighborhood Organization,* pp. 31, 11, 12.
75. Tjerandsen, *Education for Citizens.*
76. Ibid.
77. Hallman, *Neighborhoods,* p. 119.
78. Ibid.
79. Randy Stoecker, "Crossing the Development-Organizing Divide."
80. Tjerandsen, *Education for Citizens.*
81. Arturo Rodriguez in Felix G. Rivera and John L. Erlich, *Community Organizing in a Diverse Society,* 3d ed. (Boston: Allyn and Bacon, 1988) p. vi.
82. Hallman, *Neighborhoods,* p. 121.
83. Marilyn Gittell with Bruce Hoffacker, Eleanor Rollins, Samuel Foster and Mark Hoffacker, *Limits of Citizen Participation: The Decline of Community Organizations* (Beverly Hills, CA: Sage, 1980), p. 30.
84. Hallman, *Neighborhoods,* pp. 122–124.
85. Finks, *Radical Vision,* pp. 274, 267.
86. Ibid., pp. 134–135.
87. National Training and Information Center, *Disclosure: The National Newspaper of Neighborhoods* (Chicago: National Training and Information Center, 1998), p. 7.
88. Fisher, *Neighborhood Organizing.*
89. Hallman, *Neighborhoods,* pp. 135–136.
90. Williams, *Neighborhood Organization,* p. 77.
91. Twelvetrees, *Organizing for Neighbourhood Development,* pp. 151–152.
92. Torie Osborn, "Rebuilding a City One Block at a Time." *New York Times,* April 29, 2002. (http: www.nytimes.com/2002/04/29.../20OSBO.html)
93. Ibid.
94. Ibid.
95. Stoecker, "Crossing the Development-Organizing Divide."
96. Beckett, "20 Additional Victories."
97. Alinsky, *Reveille for Radicals,* p. 90.
98. Freire, *Pedagogy of the Oppressed,* p. 47.
99. James G. Barber, *Beyond Casework* (London: Macmillan Press, 1991), pp. 30–34.
100. Julio Morales, "Community Social Work With Puerto Rican Communities." In *Community Organizing in a Diverse Society,* Felix G. Rivera and John L. Erlich, eds. (Boston: Allyn and Bacon, 1992), p. 96.
101. Ibid., p. 97.
102. Kahn, *How People Get Power.*
103. Warren G. Haggstrom, "The Tactics of Organization Building." In *Strategies of Community Organization,* 4th ed., Fred M. Cox, John L. Erlich, Jack Rothman, and John E. Tropman, eds. (Itasca, IL: Peacock, 1987), p. 49.
104. Ibid. p. 408.
105. Alinsky, *Rules for Radicals,* p. 3.
106. Saul Alinsky in Haggstrom, "The Tactics of Organization Building," p. 409.
107. Morales, "Community Social Work With Puerto Rican Communities," pp. 101.
108. Nicolas Von Hoffman in Haggstrom, "The Tactics of Organization Building," p. 410.
109. Saul Alinsky in Tjerandsen, *Education for Citizens.*
110. Haggstrom, "The Tactics of Organization Building," p. 408.
111. Tjerandsen, *Education for Citizens.*
112. Ibid.
113. Haggstrom, "The Tactics of Organization Building," p, 411.
114. Ibid.
115. Tjerandsen, *Education for Citizens.*
116. Fisher, *Let the People Decide,* p. 53.
117. Tjerandsen, *Education for Citizens.*
118. Ibid.
119. Reitzes and Reitzes, *The Alinsky Legacy,* pp. 36, 37.
120. Gary Delgado, *Organizing the Movement: The Roots and Growth of ACORN* (Philadelphia: Temple University Press, 1986), p. 22.
121. *Western Organizing Review,* February 1998, n. p.
122. Fisher, *Let the People Decide,* pp. 149–150.
123. Williams, *Neighborhood Organization,* p. 226.
124. Delgado, *Organizing the Movement,* p. 22.

125. Reitzes and Reitzes, *The Alinsky Legacy,* p. 35.
126. Williams, *Neighborhood Organization,* p. 226.
127. Kahn, *How People Get Power,* p. 48.
128. Ibid., p. 49.
129. Jack Rothman with John E. Tropman, "Models of Community Organization and Macro Practice Perspectives: Their Mixing and Phasing." In *Strategies of Community Organizing,* 4th ed., Fred M. Cox, John L. Erlich, Jack Rothman, and John E. Tropman, eds. (New York: Free Press, 1989), p. 34.
130. Reitzes and Reitzes, *The Alinsky Legacy,* p. 36.
131. "About ACORN." (http://www.acorn.org/index.php?id=2757)
132. Alinksy, *Rules for Radicals,* pp. 114, 159.
133. Finks, *Radical Vision,* p. 273.
134. Delgado, *Organizing the Movement,* p. 28.
135. Twelvetrees, *Organizing for Neighbourhood Development,* pp. 151–152.
136. Delgado, *Organizing the Movement,* p. 28.
137. Fisher, *Let the People Decide,* pp. 194–195.
138. Fisher, *Neighborhood Organizing.*
139. Oakland Community Organizations Profile, *PICO: 25 Years Reweaving the Fabric of America's Communities* (Oakland, CA: PICO, 1997), p. 25.
140. PICO National Network. http://www.piconetwork.org/
141. Oakland Community Organizations Profile, *PICO,* p. 25.
142. "Who is ACORN?" (http://www.acorn.org/index.php?id=2703)
143. Randy Stoecker, "Power or Programs: Two Paths to Community Development?" Working Papers Series for COMM-ORG: The On-line Conference on Community Organizing and Development, 2001. (http://comm-org.utoledo.edu/drafts/twopathsb2.htm)
144. Mike Eichler, "The Consensus Organizing Model and Consensus Organizing Institute," Civic Practices Network, 1993. (http://www.cpn.org/cpn/COI/coi_model.html).
145. Ibid.
146. Jane Mansbridge in Kristina Smock, "Comprehensive Community Initiatives: A New Generation of Urban Revitalization Strategies," 1997. (http://www.comm.-org.Toledo.edu/papers97/smock/.htm)
147. Eichler, "The Consensus Organizing Model and Consensus Organizing Institute."
148. Mansbridge in Smock, "Comprehensive Community Initiatives."
149. Ibid.
150. Smock, "Comprehensive Community Initiatives."

Part 3: The Practice of Social Work With Organizations

1. Max Weber, "Bureaucracy." In *Economy and Society: An Outline of Interpretive Sociology,* Guenther Roth and Claus Wittich, eds. (New York: Bedminster, 1968), p. 987.
2. Robert Presthus, *The Organizational Society,* rev ed. (New York: St. Martin's, 1978).

Chapter 9: Social Organizations

1. Peter Block, *Stewardship: Choosing Service Over Self-Interest* (San Francisco: Berrett-Koehler, 1993), p. 186.
2. Max Weber, "Bureaucracy." In *From Max Weber: Essays in Sociology,* H. H. Gerth and C. Wright Mills, eds. (New York: Oxford University Press, 1946), pp. 215–216.
3. Peter F. Drucker, *New Realities in Government and Politics, in Economics and Business, in Society and World View* (New York: Harper and Row, 1989), p. 200.
4. Ibid., p. 201.
5. Ibid., p. 202.
6. Ibid., pp. 203–104.

7. Peter Dobkin Hall, "An Historical Perspective on Nonprofit Organizations." In *The Jossey-Bass Handbook of Nonprofit Leadership and Management,* Robert D. Herman and Associates, eds. (San Francisco: Jossey-Bass, 1994), p. 4.
8. Drucker, *New Realities,* p. 198.
9. Lester M. Salamon and Helmut K. Anheier, "The Civil Society Sector," *Society* 34(2), January–February, 1997, pp. 60–65.
10. Hall, "An Historical Perspective," p. 3.
11. Lester Salamon and Helmut K. Anheier, "The Civil Society Sector." In *Community Works: The Revival of Civil Society in America,* E. J. Dionne Jr., ed. (Washington DC: Brookings Institution Press, 1998), p. 55.
12. Francis Fukuyama, *Trust: The Social Virtues and the Creation of Prosperity* (New York: Free Press, 1995), p. 3.
13. As quoted in Fukuyama, *Trust,* p. 4.
14. Ibid., p. 3.
15. Hall, "An Historical Perspective," pp. 3–4.
16. Wong Sher Maine and Theresa Tan, "Who Takes From the Givers?" *The Straights Times* [Singapore], November 15, 2004, p. 25.
17. Lester M. Salamon, *Partners in Public Service: Government-Nonprofit Relations in the Modern Welfare State* (Baltimore: Johns Hopkins University Press, 1995), pp. 54, 65.
18. Ibid., p. 89.
19. Ibid., p. 117.
20. Drucker, *New Realities,* pp. 195–196.
21. Hall, "An Historical Perspective," p. 30.
22. Alan B. Durning, "Poverty and the Environment: Reversing the Downward Spiral," Worldwatch Paper No. 92 (Washington, DC: Worldwatch Institute, 1989). (http://www.worldwatch.org/pubs/paper/92/)
23. Salamon, *Partners in Public Service,* p. 117.
24. Darlyne Bailey, "Management: Diverse Workplaces," *Encyclopedia of Social Work,* 19th ed. (Washington, DC: NASW Press, 1995), pp. 1659–1660.
25. Hall, "An Historical Perspective," pp. 3–4.
26. Drucker, *New Realities,* pp. 196–197.
27. Theda Skocpol, "Don't Blame Big Government: America's Voluntary Groups Thrive in a National Network." In *Community Works,* Dionne, ed., p. 41.
28. Drucker, *New Realities,* p. 205.
29. Independent Sector Survey Series, The Independent Sector, 2003. (http://www.independentsector.org/GandV/s_volu.htm)
30. Drucker, *New Realities,* pp. 197–198.
31. Independent Sector Survey Series, 2003.
32. John J. DiIulio Jr. "The Lord's Work." In *Community Works,* Dionne, ed., p. 57.
33. Drucker, *New Realities,* p. 199.
34. Block, *Stewardship,* pp. 104, 200.
35. Independent Sector Survey Series, 2003.
36. Salamon, *Partners in Public Service,* p. 5.
37. Independent Sector Survey Series, 2003.
38. Salamon, *Partners in Public Service,* pp. 15–19.
39. Ibid., pp. 33–34.
40. Ibid., pp. 60–64.
41. Ibid., pp. 65–69.
42. Hall "An Historical Perspective," p. 4.
43. Salamon, *Partners in Public Service,* p. 91.
44. Ibid., p. 94.
45. Peter L. Berger and Richard John Neuhaus, "Voluntary Association." In *To Empower People: From State to Civil Society,* 2d ed., Michael Novack, ed. (Washington, DC: AEI Press, 1996), p. 195.
46. Skocpol, "Don't Blame Big Government," p. 41.
47. Ibid., pp. 38–41.

48. Hall, "An Historical Perspective," pp. 3, 19, 30–31.
49. Janice Revell, "The Year of Comeback—Fortune 500 Largest U.S. Corporations," *Fortune Magazine,* April 5, 2004, p. F-1.
50. Sarah Anderson and John Cavanagh, "Top 200: The Rise of Corporate Global Power." Institute for Policy Studies, 2003. (http://www.ips-dc.org/reports/top200text.htm); and "Fortune's Global 500: The World's Largest Corporations," *Fortune Magazine,* August 7, 1995.
51. Anderson and Cavanagh, "Top 200."
52. Revell, "The Year of Comeback," p. 106.
53. "McDonald's Touts Record on Social Issues," *Japan Today,* April 15, 2002. (http://www.japantoday.com/e/tools/print.asp?content=news&id=211467)
54. Global Reporting Initiative. (http://www.globalreporting.org/guidelines/reports/search.asp)
55. "McDonald's Touts Record," and Global Reporting Initiative.
56. Revell, "The Year of Comeback," pp. 105–106.
57. Ibid.
58. Anderson and Cavanagh, "Top 200."
59. Victor A. Thompson, *Without Sympathy or Enthusiasm: The Problem of Administrative Compassion* (Alabama: University of Alabama Press, 1977), p. 28.
60. Alberto Guerreiro Ramos, *The New Science of Organizations: A Reconceptualization of the Wealth of Nations* (Toronto: University of Toronto Press, 1981), p. 158.
61. Thompson, *Without Sympathy or Enthusiasm,* pp. 1–7.
62. Ralph P. Hummel, *Bureaucratic Experience* (New York: St. Martin's Press, 1977), p. 13.
63. Thompson, *Without Sympathy or Enthusiasm,* p. 117.
64. Ibid.
65. Hummel, *Bureaucratic Experience,* p. 16.
66. Victor A. Thompson, *Bureaucracy in the Modern World* (Morristown, NJ: General Learning Press, 1976), p. 10.
67. Herbert Simon, *Administrative Behavior: A Study of Decision-Making Processes in Administrative Organizations,* 4th ed. (New York: Free Press, 1997), pp. 92, 112.
68. Block, *Stewardship,* p. 7.
69. Ibid.
70. Ibid., p. 51.
71. Allen Jedlicka, *Volunteerism and World Development: Pathway to a New World* (New York: Praeger, 1990), p. 27.
72. New Internationalist, "A Short History of Corporations," Report No. 347. (Adelaid Australia: New Internationalist Publications, July 2002), p. 24.
73. Edward W. Hassinger and James R. Pinkerton, *The Human Community* (New York: Macmillan, 1986), pp. 7–8.
74. Alan Nevins and Henry Steele Commager, *A Pocket History of the United States,* 5th ed. (New York: Washington Square Press, 1966), p. 168.
75. Ibid., pp. 247–248.
76. Ibid., p. 258.
77. Ibid., p. 270.
78. New Internationalist, "A Short History of Corporations," p. 24.
79. Nevins and Commager, *A Pocket History,* p. 268.
80. John Ehrenreich, *The Altruistic Imagination, History of Social Work and Social Policy in the United States* (Ithaca, NY: Cornell University Press, 1985), p. 23.
81. As quoted in Philip Foner, *History of the Labor Movement in the United States* (New York: International, 1964), vol. 111, p. 17.
82. Frederick Winslow Taylor, *The Principles of Scientific Management* (New York: Norton, 1967), p. 64.
83. Ehrenreich, *The Altruistic Imagination,* p. 30.
84. Charles Levine, B. Guy Peters, and Frank J. Thompson, *Public Administration: Challenges, Choices, Consequences* (Glenview IL: Scott Foresman/Little Brown, 1990), p. 269.

85. Taylor, *The Principles of Scientific Management,* pp. 60, 70.
86. Thompson, *Bureaucracy in the Modern World,* p. 10.
87. David Schuman, *Bureaucracies, Organization and Administration: A Political Primer* (New York: Macmillan, 1976), p. 72.
88. Ibid., p. 57.
89. Thompson, *Without Sympathy or Enthusiasm,* p. 28.
90. As quoted in Paul Tillich, "The Person in a Technical Society." In *Social Ethics: Issues in Ethics and Society,* Gibson Winter, ed. (New York: Harper and Row, 1968), p. 107.
91. Paulo Freire, *A Pedagogy of the Oppressed* (New York: Continuum, 1992), p. 46.
92. F. J. Roethlisberger and W. I. Dickson, *Management and the Worker* (Cambridge, MA: Harvard University Press, 1947).
93. Schuman, *Bureaucracies,* p. 86.
94. Charles Perrow, *Complex Organizations: A Critical Essay,* 2d ed. (Glenview IL: Scott, Foresman, 1979), p. 93.
95. The Conference Board, *Behavioral Science: Concepts and Management Applications* (New York: National Industrial Conference Board, 1969), p. 8.
96. Herbert Simon, *Administrative Behavior: A Study of Decision-Making Processes in Administrative Organization,* 4th ed. (New York: Free Press, 1997), p. xxii.
97. Ibid., p. xxviii.
98. Ibid.
99. Ibid., p. xxxvii.
100. Ibid., p. xvi.
101. Ibid., p. 78.
102. Ibid., pp. 79–80.
103. Ibid., p. 103.
104. Ibid.
105. Perrow, *Complex Organizations,* pp. 55, 56.
106. Simon, *Administrative Behavior,* p. 112.
107. Fred E. Emery and Eric L. Trist, "The Causal Texture of Organization Environments," *Human Relations,* February 1965, pp. 21–23.
108. James D. Thompson, *Organizations in Action* (New York: McGraw-Hill, 1967), p. 3.
109. Stephen F. Robbins, *Organization Theory: The Structure and Design of Organizations* (Englewood Cliffs, NJ: Prentice-Hall, 1983), p. 61.
110. Perrow, *Complex Organizations,* pp. 115–116.
111. Charles Levine, B. Guy Peters, and Frank J. Thompson, *Public Administration: Challenges, Choices, Consequences* (Glenview IL: Scott Foresman/Little Brown, 1990), p. 245.
112. Gary Teeple, *Globalization and the Decline of Social Reform* (New Jersey: Humanities Press, 1995), pp. 71–72.
113. Ibid., p. 81.
114. Ibid., p. 119.
115. "Texan Fisherwoman's Bhopal Protest Ends in Criminal Case—Dow Chemical Making a Mockery of the Law," Common Dreams Progressive Newswire, January 2004. (http://www.commondreams.org/cgi-bin/newsprint.cgi?file=/news2004/0126-02.htm); and Neil Hodge, "The Legacy of Bhopal" *New Internationalist Magazine.* (http://www.newint.org/features/bhopalzo/index.htm)
116. Teeple, *Globalization and the Decline of Social Reform,* p. 123.
117. Ibid., p. 124.
118. Ibid., pp. 126–127.
119. "New Carpetbaggers," The E-Mail Activist. (http://www.theemailactivist.org/Carpetbaggers.htm)
120. Allen Jedlicka, *Volunteerism and World Development: Pathway to a New World* (New York: Praeger, 1990), pp. 28.
121. Ibid., p. 29.

122. John Forester, *Planning in the Face of Power* (Berkeley: University of California Press, 1989), p. 79.

Chapter 10: The Practice of Social Work Program Development

1. Si Kahn, *How People Get Power: Organizing Oppressed Communities for Action* (New York: McGraw-Hill, 1978), p. 124.

2. National *Cyclopaedia of American Biography* (Clifton NJ: J. T. White, 1903), vol. 15, pp. 314–315; and Jean K. Quam, *Encyclopedia of Social Work,* 19th ed. (Washington, DC: NASW Press, 1995), p. 2573.

3. Walter I. Trattner, *From Poor Law to Welfare State: A History of the American Response to Need* (New York: Free Press, 1989), p. 17.

4. Beulah R. Compton, *Introduction to Social Welfare and Social Work: Structure, Function and Process* (Homewood, IL: Dorsey Press, 1980), p. 197.

5. Trattner, *From Poor Law to Welfare State,* p. 33.

6. June Axinn and Herman Levine, *Social Welfare: A History of the American Response to Need,* 2d ed. (New York: Longman, 1982), pp. 58–59.

7. Compton, *Introduction,* p. 176.

8. Ibid.

9. Trattner, *From Poor Law to Welfare State,* p. 60.

10. Ibid., pp. 60–65.

11. Compton, *Introduction,* pp. 287–288.

12. Trattner, *From Poor Law to Welfare State,* pp. 84–85.

13. Compton, *Introduction,* pp. 287, 298, 358.

14. Trattner, *From Poor Law to Welfare State,* pp. 154, 158.

15. Matthew A. Fitzsimons and Fulton J. Sheen, "Saint Frances Xavier Cabrini," *World Book Encyclopedia,* Vol. 3 (Chicago, IL; World Book, 1985), p. 9.

16. Compton, *Introduction,* p. 288.

17. Robert C. Linthicum, *Empowering the Poor: Community Organizing the City's "Rag, Tag and Bobtail"* (Monrovia, CA: MARC, 1991), pp. 22–23.

18. Ibid., p. 45.

19. Ibid., pp. 45–46.

20. Allen Rubin and Earl Babbie, *Research Methods for Social Work* (Belmont, CA: Wadsworth, 1989), p. 500.

21. Joseph P. Hornick and Barbara Burrows, "Program Evaluation," in *Social Work Research and Evaluation,* 3d ed., Richard M. Grinnell Jr., ed. (Itasca, IL: Peacock, 1987), p. 403.

22. Rubin and Babbie, *Research Methods for Social Work,* p. 500.

23. Hornick and Burrows, "Program Evaluation," p. 142.

24. Rubin and Babbie, *Research Methods for Social Work,* p. 502.

25. Oakland Community Organizations Profile, *PICO: 25 Years Reweaving the Fabric of America's Communities* (Oakland, CA: PICO, 1997), p. 6. Hereinafter referred to as *PICO: 25 Years.*

26. "African American Pioneers in Social Work," *Encyclopedia of Social Work,* p. 117.

27. Joan M. Hummel, *Starting and Running a Nonprofit Organization,* 2d ed. (Minneapolis: University of Minnesota Press, 1996), pp. 12–18.

28. Ibid. pp. 21–24.

29. *Encyclopedia of Social Work,* p. 2573; and *National Cyclopaedia of American Biography* (New York: The Press Association Compilers, 1907), pp. 166–167.

30. Hummel, *Starting and Running a Nonprofit,* pp. 24–26.

31. Marian Fatout and Steven R. Rose, *Task Groups in the Social Services* (Thousand Oaks, CA: Sage, 1995), pp. 128–129.

32. http://www.rulesonline/#9F1.

33. Hummel, *Starting and Running a Nonprofit,* pp. 4, 13, 15.

34. *PICO: 25 Years,* p. 2.

35. Gordon Mayer, *National Training and Information Center—25 Years: Neighborhood Dreams, Neighborhood Issues, Neighborhood Organizing* (Chicago: NTIC, 1997).

36. Hummel, *Starting and Running a Nonprofit,* p. 41.

37. *PICO: 25 Years,* p. 2.

38. Western Economic Diversification Canada, (http://www.wd.gc.ca/default_e.asp).

39. *PICO: 25 Years,* p. 5.

40. Hummel, *Starting and Running a Nonprofit,* pp. 11–12.

41. Sheldon R. Gelman, "Boards of Directors." In *Encyclopedia of Social Work,* p. 309.

42. Hummel, *Starting and Running a Nonprofit,* p. 110; and M. Sue Sturgeon, "Finding and Keeping the Right Employees." In *Jossey-Bass Handbook of Nonprofit Leadership and Management,* Robert D. Hermann et al., eds. (San Francisco: Jossey-Bass, 1994), p. 540.

43. Hummel, *Starting and Running a Nonprofit,* pp. 110–111.

44. Sturgeon, "Finding and Keeping the Right Employees," p. 544.

45. Ibid.

46. Hummel, *Starting and Running a Nonprofit,* pp. 51–59, 73–74.

47. Joan Flanagan, "How to Ask for Money. " In *Tactics and Techniques of Community Practice,* 2d ed., Fred M. Cox, John L. Erllich, Jack Rothman, and John E. Tropman, eds. (Itasca, IL: Peacock, 1984), p. 310.

48. Peter Dobkin Hall, "Historical Perspectives on Nonprofit Organizations." In *Jossey-Bass Handbook of Nonprofit Leadership and Management,* Hermann et al., eds., p. 16.

49. Ione D. Vargus, "Charitable Foundations and Social Welfare." In *Encyclopedia of Social Work,* pp. 342–343.

50. Ibid., p. 343.

51. Ibid.

52. Hummel, *Starting and Running a Nonprofit,* pp. 52, 342.

Chapter 11: The Practice of Social Work Administration

1. Peter Block, *Stewardship: Choosing Service Over Self-Interest* (San Francisco: Berrett-Koehler, 1993), pp. 50–51.

2. Robert E. Sherwood, *Roosevelt and Hopkins: An Intimate History,* Rev. ed. (New York: Harper and Brothers, 1950), p. 32.

3. Ibid., p. 281.

4. Peter Block, *Stewardship,* p. 21.

5. Charles Perrow, *Complex Organizations,* 2d ed. (Glenview, IL: Scott, Foresman, 1979), p. 4.

6. Herbert A. Simon, *Administrative Behavior,* 4th ed. (New York: Free Press, 1997), p. 112. Simon asserts, for example, that "training prepares the organization member to reach satisfactory decisions himself without the need for the constant exercise of authority or advice. . . . Training procedures are alternatives to the exercise of authority or advice as a means of control over the subordinate's decisions." (p. 13)

7. Simon asserts that "authority refers to the *acceptance* by the subordinate of the decisions of the superior and not the power of the superior to apply sanctions in case of noncompliance." (p. 196)

8. Ibid., p. 9.

9. Ibid., pp. 179–180.

10. Paulo Freire, *Pedagogy of the Oppressed* (New York: Continuum, 1992), p. 31.

11. Peter J. Pecora, "Personnel Management." In *Encyclopedia of Social Work,* 19th ed. (Washington, DC: NASW Press, 1995), pp. 1830–1831.

12. M. Sue Sturgeon, "Finding and Keeping the Right Employees." In *Jossey-Bass Handbook of Nonprofit Leadership and Management* (San Francisco: Jossey-Bass, 1994), p. 543.

13. Wright Davis and Tremaine Law Firm, "Special Summary of the ADA Prepared for the Casey Family Program," in Pecora, "Personnel Management," p. 1831.

14. Al Kadushin in Lawrence Shulman, "Supervision and Consultation." In *Encyclopedia of Social Work*, p. 2373.

15. Ibid., p. 2374.

16. Hugh England, *Social Work as Art: Making Sense for Good Practice* (London: Allen and Unwin, 1986), p. 41.

17. Block, *Stewardship*, p. 65.

18. Ibid., p. 66.

19. David M. Austin, "Management Overview." In *Encyclopedia of Social Work*, p. 165.

20. David Schuman and Dick W. Olufs III, *Public Administration in the United States*, 2d ed., (Lexington, MA: D. C. Heath, 1993), p. 121.

21. Ibid.

22. Maryann Slyers, "Mary Parker Follett." In *Encyclopedia of Social Work*, p. 2585.

23. Ibid.

24. Ibid.

25. Ibid.

26. Elliot M. Fox and L. Urwick, *Dynamic Administration: The Collected Papers of Mary Parker Follett* (New York: Hippocrene Books, 1977).

27. Schuman and Olufs, *Public Administration*, p. 122.

28. Grover Starling. *Managing the Public Sector*, 5th ed. (Ft. Worth: Harcourt Brace, 1998), p. 274.

29. Marian Fatout and Steven R. Rose, *Task Groups in the Social Services*. (Thousand Oaks, CA: Sage, 1998), p. 31.

30. Ibid.

31. Starling, *Managing the Public Sector*, p. 274.

32. Fatout and Rose, *Task Groups*, p. 31.

33. Ibid., p. 32.

34. Starling, *Managing the Public Sector*, p. 274.

35. Ibid.

36. Donelson R. Forsyth, *An Introduction to Group Dynamics* (Monterey, CA: Brooks/Cole, 1983), pp. 166–167.

37. Starling, *Managing the Public Sector*, p. 275.

38. Ibid., pp. 275–276.

39. Ibid., p. 275.

40. Fatout and Rose, *Task Groups*, pp. 138–139.

41. Malvern J. Gross, "The Importance of Budgeting." In *Social Administration: The Management of the Social Services*, Simon Slavin, ed. (New York: Haworth Press, 1978), p. 233.

42. Aaron Wildavsky, *Budgeting: A Comparative Theory of Budgetary Processes* (Boston: Little, Brown, 1975), p. 5.

43. Ibid.

44. Ibid.

45. Ibid., p. 6. See also Herbert Simon, *Administrative Behavior*, 4th ed. (New York: Free Press, 1997), pp. xxviii, xxx.

46. Wildavsky, *Budgeting*, p. 7.

47. Charles A. Rapp and John Poertner, *Social Administration: A Client-Centered Approach* (New York: Longman, 1992), p. 219.

48. Roderick K. Macleod, "Program Budgeting in Nonprofit Institutions." In *Social Administration: Management of the Social Services*, Simon Slavin, ed. (New York: Haworth Press and Council on Social Work Education, 1968), p. 251.

49. Rex Skidmore, *Social Work Administration: Dynamic Management and Human Relationships*, 2d ed. (Englewood Cliffs, NJ: Prentice-Hall, 1990), p. 69.

50. Rapp and Poertner, *Social Administration*, p. 219.

51. Wildavsky, *Budgeting*, p. 297.

52. Sturgeon, "Finding and Keeping the Right Employees," p. 535.

53. Ibid., pp. 541–542.

54. Pecora "Personnel Management," pp. 1830–1831.

55. Ibid., p. 1834.

56. Ibid., pp. 1833–1834.

57. In *Social Administration*, Rapp and Poertner advocate for a "new metaphor" in which the traditional organizational chart is inverted so that "the pinnacle of the chart is the client and all organizational personnel are subservient. In fact, supervisors are subservient to frontline workers, and the executive is subservient to supervisors and frontline workers." (p. 277)

58. Robert Weinbach, *The Social Worker as Manager: Theory and Practice* (New York: Longman, 1990), p. 75.

59. Paul Hersey and Kenneth H. Blanchard, *Management of Organizational Behavior: Utilizing Human Resources*, 5th ed. (Englewood Cliffs, NJ: Prentice-Hall, 1988), p. 6.

60. Robert H. Miles, *Macro Organizational Behavior* (Santa Monica, CA: Goodyear, 1980), pp. 322–323.

61. Peter Drucker, *Management: Tasks, Responsibilities, Practices* (New York: Harper and Row, 1973), p. 217.

62. Ibid., p. 220.

63. Ibid., pp. 221–223.

64. A. Gurin, "Conceptual and Technical Issues in the Management of Human Services." In *The Management of Human Services*, R. C. Sarri and Y. Hasenfeld, eds. (New York: Columbia University Press, 1978), pp. 289–308.

65. Sheldon R. Gelman, "Boards of Directors." In *Encyclopedia of Social Work*, pp. 309–310.

66. Carol H. Weiss, *Evaluation Research: Methods of Assessing Program Effectiveness* (Englewood Cliffs, NJ: Prentice-Hall, 1972), p. 4.

67. Peter H. Rossi and Howard E. Freeman, *Evaluation: A Systematic Approach* (Beverly Hills, CA: Sage, 1982).

68. Gurin, "Conceptual and Technical Issues," p. 482.

69. Joseph P. Hornick and Barbara Burrows, "Program Evaluation." In *Social Work Research and Evaluation*, 3d ed., Richard M. Grinnell Jr., ed. (Itasca, IL: Peacock, 1988), p. 402.

70. Allen Rubin and Earl Babbie, *Research Methods for Social Work* (Belmont, CA: Wadsworth, 1989), p. 482.

71. Michael I. Harrison, *Diagnosing Organizations: Methods, Model, and Processes* (Newbury Park, CA: Sage, 1987), pp. 77–78.

72. Ibid., p. 34.

73. Weiss, *Evaluation Research*, p. 26; and Rubin and Babbie, *Research Methods for Social Work*, p. 496.

74. Weiss, *Evaluation Research*, p. 30.

75. Harrison, *Diagnosing Organizations*, pp. 139–140.

76. Weiss, *Evaluation Research*, p. 36.

77. See, for example, Donald T. Campbell and Julian C. Stanley, *Experimental and Quasi-Experimental Designs for Research* (Chicago: Rand-McNally, 1963), for a description of 3 pre-experimental designs, 3 true experimental designs, and 10 quasi-experimental designs.

78. E. J. Mishan, *Economics for Social Decisions: Elements of Cost-Benefit Analysis* (New York: Praeger, 1972), p. 88. I use the term "benefit-cost" analysis because ratios of benefits to costs are normally expressed benefit/cost rather than the reverse.

79. Hornick and Burrows, "Program Evaluation," p. 416.

Chapter 12 The Practice of Organization Development

1. Peter Block, *Stewardship: Choosing Service Over Self-Interest* (San Francisco: Berrett-Koehler, 1993), pp. 239–240, 251.

2. Donald F. Harvey and Donald F. Brown, *An Experiential Approach to Organization Development,* 4th ed. (Englewood Cliffs, NJ: Prentice-Hall, 1992), p. ix.

3. As quoted in Charles H. Levine, Guy Peters, and Frank J. Thompson, *Public Administration: Challenges, Choices, and Consequences* (Glenview, IL: Scott Foresman/Little Brown, 1990), p. 272.

4. Levine et al., *Public Administration,* p. 272.

5. Stephen Robbins, *Essentials of Organization Behavior,* 3d ed. (Englewood Cliffs, NJ: Prentice-Hall, 1992), p. 276.

6. Ibid.

7. Wendell L. French and Cecil H. Bell Jr. "A History of Organization Development." In *Organization Development and Transformation: Managing Effecting Change,* Wendell L. French, Cecil H. Bell Jr., and Robert Zawacki, eds. (Burr Ridge, IL: Irwin, 1994), pp. 25–36.

8. Ibid.

9. Ibid., p. 35.

10. Marshall Sashkin and W. Warner Burke, "Organization Development in the 1980's." In *Organization Development and Transformation,* French et al., eds., pp. 55–56.

11. French and Bell, " A History of Organization Development," p. 34.

12. Sashkin and Burke, "Organization Development in the 1980's," p. 57.

13. Richard Beckhard, *Organization Development: Strategies and Models* (Reading, MA: Addison-Wesley, 1969), p. 9.

14. Levine et al., *Public Administration,* p. 272.

15. Ibid.

16. Ibid., p. 270.

17. Harvey and Brown, *An Experiential Approach,* pp. 13, 39.

18. Stephen P. Robbins, *Organization Theory: The Structure and Design of Organizations* (Englewood Cliffs, NJ: Prentice-Hall, 1983), p. 266.

19. Harvey and Brown, *An Experiential Approach,* p. 10.

20. Robbins, *Organization Theory,* pp. 13–14.

21. Charles Perrow, *Complex Organizations: A Critical Essay,* 2d ed. (Glenview, IL: Scott Foresman, 1979), p. 34.

22. Victor A. Thompson, *Bureaucracy and the Modern World* (Morristown, NJ: General Learning Press, 1976), p. 96.

23. Perrow, *Complex Organizations,* p. 34.

24. Herbert A. Simon, *Administrative Behavior: A Study of the Decision-Making Processes in Administrative Organizations,* 3d ed. (New York: Free Press, 1976), p. xvi.

25. Ibid., p. 9.

26. Thompson, *Bureaucracy and the Modern World,* p. 96.

27. Harvey and Brown, *An Experiential Approach,* p. 41.

28. Thompson, *Bureaucracy and the Modern World,* p. 84.

29. Robbins, *Essentials of Organization Behavior,* p. 276.

30. Harvey and Brown, *An Experiential Approach,* pp. 57–59.

31. Robbins, *Essentials of Organization Behavior,* pp. 288–295.

32. Ibid., pp. 33–35.

33. Barbara Vobejda, "Most Child-Care Centers Inadequate, Study Says," *Fresno Bee,* February 6, 1995, p. A1.

34. Michael I. Harrison, *Diagnosing Organizations: Methods, Models, and Processes* (Newbury Park, CA: Sage, 1987), p. 35.

35. Rebecca Jones, "Workaholic Women Suffer When They Put Boss First," *Fresno Bee,* May 14, 1991, p. A10.

36. Harvey and Brown, *An Experiential Approach,* pp. 306.

37. Ibid., p. 307.

38. Robbins, *Essentials of Organization Behavior,* p. 286.

39. Kathy Slobogin, "Stress in the Workplace." CNN.com/ Transcripts, May 17, 2001. (http://asia.cnn.com/chat/transcripts/ 2001/05/16/Slobogin/index.html)

40. Harvey and Brown, *An Experiential Approach,* pp. 308–312.

41. Except where noted, this section is adapted and summarized from Jerry Edelwich with Archie Brodsky, *Burn-out: Stages of Disillusionment in the Helping Professions* (New York: Human Sciences Press, 1980), pp. 114, 143–182.

42. Ibid., p. 5.

43. Robbins, *Essentials of Organization Behavior,* pp. 65, 286; and Robbins, *Organization Theory,* pp. 252, 254.

44. Robbins, *Essentials of Organization Behavior,* p. 67.

45. Harvey and Brown, *An Experiential Approach,* pp. 452–458; and Robbins, *Essentials of Organization Behavior,* pp. 68–69.

46. Ibid., p. 336.

47. Ibid., p. 351.

48. Robert R. Blake, Herbert Shepard, and Jane S. Mouton, *Managing Intergroup Conflict in Industry* (Houston: Gulf, 1964). See also Robert R. Blake and Jane S. Mouton, *Solving Costly Organizational Conflicts: Achieving Intergroup Trust, Cooperation, and Teamwork* (San Francisco: Jossey-Bass, 1984).

49. Robert H. Miles, *Macro Organizational Behavior* (Santa Monica, CA: Goodyear, 1980), pp. 131, 339–348, 131.

50. Louis Kriesberg, *The Sociology of Social Conflicts* (Englewood Cliffs, NJ: Prentice-Hall, 1973). A form of the conflict cycle appeared in Jerry Robinson and Roy Clifford, *Managing Conflict in Community Groups* (Champaign-Urbana: University of Illinois, 1974); and in Norman Shawchuck, *How to Manage Conflict in the Church: Understanding and Managing Conflict* (Indianapolis: Spiritual Growth Resources, 1983).

51. Adapted from the "Unconditionally Constructive Strategy" developed by Roger Fisher and Scott Brown of the Harvard Negotiating Project. Roger Fisher and Scott Brown, *Getting Together—Building a Relationship That Gets to Yes* (Boston: Houghton Mifflin, 1988), p. 37, 40.

52. Freda Gomes, "How to Be a Winning Negotiator," *Toastmaster,* June 1984, pp. 15–19.

53. Robbins, *Organization Theory,* p. 303.

54. Tom Jones, Organization Developer, Worx, Inc., personal interview, December 22, 1993, Fresno, California.

55. Robert W. Weinbach, *The Social Worker as Manager: Theory and Practice* (White Plains, NY: Longman, 1990), p. 316.

56. Tom Jones, personal interview.

57. Weinbach, *The Social Worker as Manager,* p. 317.

58. Ibid.

59. Ibid., p. 318.

60. Ibid., p. 319.

61. Robbins, *Organization Theory,* p. 24.

62. Harvey and Brown, *An Experiential Approach,* pp. 417–423.

63. Terrence E. Deal, *Corporate Culture* (Reading, MA: Addison-Wesley, 1982), pp. 130–139.

64. J. Steven Ott, *The Organizational Culture Perspective* (Homewood, IL: Irwin, 1989), p. ix.

65. Mark S. Homan, *Promoting Community Change: Making It Happen in the Real World* (Belmont, CA: Brooks/Cole– Thomson Learning, 2004), p. 476.

66. Block, *Stewardship,* p. 182.

67. Ibid., p. 225.

68. Ibid., p. 237.

Part 4: Social Work Practice at the National and International Levels

1. Niccolo Machiavelli, *The Prince,* George Bull, trans. (London: Penguin, 1961), p. 51.

2. John Ehrenreich, *The Altruistic Imagination: A History of Social Work and Social Policy in the United States* (Ithaca, NY: Cornell University Press, 1985), p. 27.

3. Ibid.

Chapter 13: The Practice of Social Work Policy Advocacy

1. Si Kahn, *How People Get Power: Organizing Oppressed Communities for Action* (New York: McGraw-Hill, 1978), p. 124.
2. This section is adapted and summarized from Judith Weinraub, "Consumer Advocate Doesn't Back Down From a Good Fight," *Fresno Bee,* June 21, 1992, p. F5.
3. Herbert Simon, *Administrative Behavior: A Study of Decision-Making Processes in Administrative Organization,* 3d ed. (New York: Free Press, 1976), pp. xvii, xxxvii.
4. Harold Koontz, Cyril O'Donnell, and Heinz Weinrich, *Essentials of Management* (New York: McGraw-Hill, 1986), p. 79.
5. Ibid, pp. 48–52. See also John P. Flynn, *Social Agency Policy Analysis and Presentation for Community Practice* (Chicago: Nelson-Hall, 1987), pp. 133–172.
6. John Ehrenreich, *The Altruistic Imagination: A History of Social Work and Social Policy in the United States.* Ithaca, NY: Cornell University Press, 1985.
7. As quoted in Ehrenreich, *The Altruistic Imagination,* pp. 33–34.
8. Weismiller and Rome, *Encyclopedia of Social Work,* 19th ed. (Washington, DC: NASW Press, 1995), p. 2309; and NASW, *Social Workers Serving in Elective Office* (Washington, DC: NASW, PACE, 1997).
9. Ehrenreich, *The Altruistic Imagination,* p. 30.
10. Ibid., p. 42.
11. Ibid.
12. Ibid., pp. 40, 36.
13. Charles Levine, B. Guy Peters, and Frank J. Thompson. *Public Administration: Challenges, Choices, and Consequences* (Glenview IL: Scott Foresman/Little Brown, 1990), p. 221.
14. Ehrenreich, *The Altruistic Imagination,* p. 32.
15. Stephanie Tolliver. "Ida B. Wells Barnett," Women in History, Lakewood Public Library, April 22, 2000. (http://www.lkwdpl.org/w1hoh1o/barn-ida.htm)
16. Ehrenreich, *The Altruistic Imagination,* p. 39.
17. Ibid., p. 40.
18. Ibid., p. 89.
19. Ibid., pp. 95–97.
20. Ibid., pp. 143–145.
21. Ibid., p. 146.
22. Ibid., pp. 147–149.
23. Ibid., p. 160.
24. Ibid., p. 161.
25. Beulah H. Compton, *Introduction to Social Welfare and Social Work: Structure, Function, and Process* (Homewood, IL: Dorsey, 1980), p. 460.
26. Ehrenreich, *The Altruistic Imagination,* p. 163.
27. Ibid., pp. 167–169, 181.
28. Nathan Glazer, "The Limits of Social Policy," *Commentary,* 52(3), September 1971, pp. 51–59.
29. Gary Teeple, *Globalization and the Decline of Social Reform* (New Jersey: Humanities Press, 1995), p. 111.
30. Smock, Kristina, "Comprehensive Community Initiatives: A New Generation of Urban Revitalization Strategies." Paper presented on COMM-ORG: The On-Line Conference on Community Organizing and Development, 1997. (http://comm-org.utoledo.edu/papers.htm)
31. Association of Community Organizations for Reform Now (ACORN). *ACORN History: The Reagan Years.* (http://ACORN.org.)
32. Teeple, *Globalization and the Decline of Social Reform,* p. 111.
33. Smock, "Comprehensive Community Initiatives."
34. Robert Fisher, "Neighborhood Organizing: The Importance of Historical Context" 1995. (http://comm-org.utoledo.edu/papers96/fishercon.htm)
35. Smock, "Comprehensive Community Initiatives."
36. Ibid.
37. Peter Dreier, "The Struggle for Our Cities," *Social Policy,* Summer 1996. (http://socialpolicy.org)
38. "US Approves Missile Defense Funds," *Japan Today,* August 1, 2001. (http//www.japantoday.com/e/?content=news&id=49034)
39. H. Henderson, *Building a Win-Win World: Life Beyond Economic Global Warfare* (San Francisco: Berett-Koehler, 1996), p. 295.
40. Michael Parenti, *The Sword and the Dollar: Imperialism, Revolution and the Arms Race* (New York: St. Martin's Press, 1989), p. 79.
41. *The New Internationalist,* No. 351. (Adelaide, Australia, November 2002), p. 19.
42. Parenti, *The Sword and the Dollar,* p. 79.
43. George Bush, "Introduction." In *National Security Strategy of the United States of America, September 2002* (Washington, DC: The White House, September, 17, 2002), p. 6.
44. Jeremy Brecher, "Globalization: A Coalition to Contain Economic Aggression?" World Social Forum, *Z Magazine,* 2003. (http://www.zmag.org/brecherglobo.htm)
45. Bush, "National Security Strategy," p. 31.
46. Phyllis J. Day, *A New History of Social Welfare,* 4th ed. (Boston: Allyn and Bacon, 2003), pp. 455–456.
47. *The United States v. the International Criminal Court.* The Email Activist, December 13, 2002. (http://www.theemailactivist.org/icc.html)
48. John Kenneth Galbraith, *Economics and the Public Purpose* (Boston: Houghton Mifflin, 1973), pp. 46.
49. Ibid., p. 66.
50. Thomas R. Dye, *Understanding Public Policy,* 2d ed. (Englewood Cliffs, NJ: Prentice-Hall, 1975), p. 25.
51. William L. Morrow, *Public Administration: Politics, Policy, and the Political System,* 2d ed. (New York: Random House, 1980), p. 50.
52. Ibid., p. 51.
53. Ibid., p. 83.
54. James Madison, "Federalist No. 10." In *The Federalist Papers,* Alexander Hamilton, James Madison, and John Jay (New York: New American Library, 1961), p. 79.
55. Ibid., "Federalist No. 51," p. 322.
56. Dye, *Understanding Public Policy,* p. 21.
57. Madison, "Federalist No. 51," p. 322.
58. Eric Planin, "The Stench of the Tax Giveaways," *Fresno Bee,* September 2, 1995, p. B10.
59. Phillis J. Day, *A New History of Social Welfare,* 2d ed. (Boston: Allyn and Bacon, 1997), pp. 429–430.
60. Planin, "The Stench of the Tax Giveaways."
61. Ibid.; and [Editorial] *Fresno Bee,* August 21, 1995, p. A6.
62. E. E. Schattschneider, *The Semi-Sovereign People* (New York: Holt, Reinhart, and Winston, 1960), p. 40.
63. Morrow, *Public Administration,* p. 51.
64. Frank E. Coleman, *Hobbes and America: Exploring the Constitutional Foundations* (Toronto, Ontario: University of Toronto Press, 1977) p. 38.
65. Levine et al., *Public Administration,* p. 81.
66. John Harsanyi, "Some Social Science Implications of a New Approach to Game Theory." In *The Essence of Decision: Explaining the Cuban Missile Crisis,* Graham Allison, ed. (Boston: Little, Brown, 1971), p. 31.
67. Levine et al., *Public Administration,* p. 82.
68. Morrow, *Public Administration,* pp. 63–66.
69. Allison, *The Essence of Decision,* p. 67.
70. Morrow, *Public Administration,* p. 79.

71. Michael Doyle and Jim Boren, "Dooley Harvested Subsidies," *Fresno Bee,* March 29, 1995, p. A1.

72. Morrow, *Public Administration,* pp. 63, 64, 83.

73. Ibid., p. 90.

74. Ken Thompson, Jeffrey M. Berry, and Kent E. Portney, "Kernels of Democracy," Community Practices Network (CPN), 1994. (http: www.cpn.org/topics/community/kernels.html)

75. Ibid.

76. Ibid.

77. Robert Fisher, *Let the People Decide: Neighborhood Organizing in America* (New York: Twayne, 1994), p. xii.

78. Peter L. Berger and Richard John Neuhaus, *To Empower People: From State to Civil Society,* 2d ed. (Washington, DC: American Enterprise Institute Press, 1996), pp. 163–164.

79. Harry C. Boyte, "The Pragmatic Ends of Popular Politics." In *Habermas and the Public Sphere,* C. Calhoun, ed. (Cambridge, MA: MIT Press, 1992), p. 341.

80. Howard J. Karger and David Stoesz, *American Social Welfare Policy: A Structural Approach* (New York: Longman, 1990), pp. 63–64.

81. For a critique of modern political and policy theory, see Eric Voegelin, *The New Science of Politics* (Chicago: University of Chicago Press, 1952); and Sheldon Wolin, *Politics and Vision* (Boston: Little, Brown, 1960).

82. Allen Jedlicka, *Volunteerism and World Development: Pathway to a New World* (New York: Praeger, 1990), p. 47.

83. For a discussion of a politics of virtue see Stephen Salkever, "Virtue, Obligation, and Politics," *Political Science Review,* 68, 1976, pp. 78–91.

84. Ernesto Cortes Jr., "Reweaving the Fabric: The Iron Rule and the IAF Strategy for Power and Politics," Community Practices Network (CPN), 1993. (http://www.cpn.org/cpn/sections/topics/community/civic_perspectives/cortes-reweaving.html)

85. Office of U.S. Senator Barbara Mikulski, "Senator Barbara Mikulski." (http://mikulski.senate.gov/SenatorMikulski/biography.html)

86. Ibid.

87. Abraham Kaplan, "Perspectives on the Theme." In *Individuality and the New Society,* Abraham Kaplan, ed. (Seattle: University of Washington Press, 1970), p. 15.

88. Cortes, "Reweaving the Fabric."

89. Kenneth E. Reid, *Social Work Practice With Groups: A Clinical Perspective* (Pacific Grove, CA: Brooks/Cole, 1991), pp. 26–27; and *From Character Building to Social Treatment: The History of the Use of Groups in Social Work* (Westport, CT: Greenwood Press, 1981).

90. For an alternative educational model, see Paulo Freire, *Pedagogy of the Oppressed* (New York: Continuum, 1991).

91. Berger and Neuhaus, *To Empower People,* p. 164.

92. Thomas Bender, *Community and Social Change in America* (New Brunswick, NJ: Rutgers University Press, 1978), pp. 74–75.

93. Ann Majchrzak, *Methods for Policy Research.* Applied Social Research Methods Series, vol. 3 (Newbury Park, CA: Sage, 1984), p. 12.

94. NASW, *Social Workers Serving in Elective Office* (Washington, DC: NASW, PACE, 1997, 2004).

95. This section is summarized from Christopher Bellavita and Henrik L. Blum, "An Analytical Tool for Policy Analysts and Planners." Unpublished manuscript, 1981, pp. 5, 6, 12, 13.

96. Personal communication with Alice Kitchen, MSW, June 2004.

97. Bellavita and Blum, "An Analytical Tool for Policy Analysts and Planners," p. 14.

98. David W. Stewart, *Secondary Research: Information, Sources, and Methods.* Applied Social Research Methods Series, vol. 4 (Newbury Park, CA: Sage, 1984), pp. 11, 12, 59, 63.

99. Majchrzak, *Methods for Policy Research,* pp. 47, 52, 57–63, 66.

100. William D. Coplin and Michael K. O'Leary, *Everyman's PRINCE: A Guide to Understanding Your Political Problems,* 2d ed. (North Scituate, MA: Duxbury Press, 1972).

101. Ibid. p. 65.

102. Charles S. Prigmore and Charles R. Atherton, *Social Welfare Policy: Analysis and Formulation,* 2d ed. (Lexington, MA: D. C. Heath, 1986), pp. 195–196.

103. Karen S. Haynes and James S. Mickelson, *Affecting Change: Social Workers in the Political Arena,* 2d ed. (New York: Longman, 1991), pp. 64, 72–76.

104. Child Welfare League of America, "Washington Workbook for Child Advocates." In *Affecting Change,* Haynes and Mikelson, pp. 76–77.

105. Alice Kitchen, personal correspondence, July 2004.

106. Ibid.

107. Lewis A. Friedland, "Electronic Democracy and the New Citizenship." Community Practices Network (CPN) 1996. (http://www.cpn.org/crm/contemporary/electronic.html)

108. John McNutt, "Coming Perspectives in the Development of Electronic Advocacy for Social Policy Practice" *Critical Social Work,* 1(1), Spring 2000, pp. 6, 7. (http://www.criticalsocialwork.com00_1_coming_mcn.html)

109. The following sections rely heavily on Lewis Friedland, "Electronic Democracy."

110. Ibid.

111. McNutt, "Coming Perspectives," pp. 1–6.

112. Diane DiNitto and Thomas Dye, *Social Welfare: Politics and Public Policy,* 3d ed. (Englewood Cliffs, NJ: Prentice-Hall, 1991), p. xiv.

Chapter 14: The Practice of Social Work With Social Movements

1. Summarized and adapted from David J. Garrow, *Bearing the Cross* (New York: William Morrow, 1986), pp. 513, 536–553.

2. Gustavo Gutierrez, "Notes for a Theology of Liberation." In *Theological Studies* (Baltimore, MD: Waverly Press, 1970), p. 254.

3. Ibid., p. 247.

4. George Lakey, *Strategy for a Living Revolution* (San Francisco: W. H. Freeman, 1973), p. xiii.

5. Saul D. Alinsky, *Rules for Radicals: A Pragmatic Primer for Realistic Radicals* (New York: Vintage Books, 1974), p. 3.

6. "Federal Trial for Human Rights Activists Facing Federal Charges for Civil Disobedience Begins Today in Georgia." Common Dreams Progressive Newswire. (http://www.commondreams.org/cgi-bin/newsprint.cgi?file=/news2004/0126-04.htm)

7. June Axinn and Herman Levin, *Social Welfare: A History of American Response to Need,* 2d ed. (New York: Longman, 1982), p. 248.

8. Marten Estey, *The Unions: Structure, Development and Management* (New York: Harcourt, Brace and World, 1967), p. 12.

9. Ibid., p. 13.

10. Ibid., p. 14.

11. Foster Rhea Dulles, *Labor in America: A History,* 3d ed. (New York: Crowell, 1966), p. 22.

12. Ibid., pp. 166–172.

13. Ibid., pp. 209–210, 263–275.

14. Estey, *The Unions,* pp. 15–18.

15. Ibid., p. 97.

16. John H. Ehrenreich, *The Altruistic Imagination: A History of Social Work and Social Policy in the Untied States* (Ithaca: Cornell University Press, 1985), p. 45.
17. Estey, *The Unions,* p. 99.
18. Ibid.
19. Ehrenreich, *The Altruistic Imagination,* p. 93.
20. "Labor Breaks With New Deal," *New York Times,* February 3, 1935, as quoted in Ehrenreich, *The Altruistic Imagination,* p. 91.
21. Allen Jedlicka, *Volunteerism and World Development: Pathway to a New World* (New York: Praeger, 1990), p. 45.
22. Estey, *The Unions,* pp. 22–25.
23. Ron Eyerman and Andrew Jamison, *Social Movements: A Cognitive Approach* (Cambridge: Polity Press, 1991), pp. 10, 49.
24. Jedlicka, *Volunteerism and World Development,* p. 45.
25. Estey, *The Unions,* pp. 107–109.
26. Ibid., p. 29.
27. Gary Teeple, *Globalization and the Decline of Social Reform* (New Jersey: Humanities Press, 1995), pp. 115–116.
28. Institute for Policy Studies, (http://www.ips-dc.org/downloads/Top_200.pdf).
29. Ronald G. Walters, *American Reformers 1815–1860* (New York: Hill and Wang, 1978), p. 78.
30. Axinn and Levin, *Social Welfare,* p. 47.
31. Ibid., p. 48.
32. Ibid., pp. 141–143.
33. Allen F. Davis, "Settlement Workers in Politics, 1890–1914." In *Practical Politics: Social Work and Political Responsibility,* Maryann Mahaffey and John W. Hands, eds. (Silver Spring, MD: NASW), pp. 36–38.
34. Axinn and Levin, *Social Welfare,* p. 147.
35. Jane Addams, *Twenty Years at Hull House* (New York: New American Library, 1938), pp. 227–229.
36. Ibid., pp. 126–127.
37. Claus Offe, "Challenging the Boundaries of Institutional Politics: Social Movements Since the 1960s." In *Changing Boundaries of the Political,* Charles Maier, ed. (New York: Cambridge University Press, 1987), p. 73.
38. Ehrenreich, *The Altruistic Imagination,* p. 41.
39. Robert Fisher and Joseph Kling, *Mobilizing the Community: Local Politics in the Era of the Global City.* Urban Affairs Annual Review, No. 41 (Newbury Park: Sage, 1993), p. 127.
40. Ehrenreich, *The Altruistic Imagination,* pp. 156–157, 162.
41. Peter Dreier, "The Struggle for Our Cities." *Social Policy,* Summer 1996. (http://www. socialpolicy.org)
42. Kurt Lewin, "Frontiers in Group Dynamics: Concept, Method and Reality in Social Science, Social Equilibria and Social Change," *Human Relations,* 1(1), June 1947, pp. 5–41.
43. Alinsky, *Rules for Radicals,* p. 24.
44. Ibid., p. 130.
45. John Forester, *Planning in the Face of Power* (Berkeley: University of California Press, 1989), p. 45.
46. Ibid., p. 46.
47. Ibid., p. 47.
48. Herbert J. Rubin and Irene S. Rubin, *Community Organizing and Development,* 2d ed. (New York: Macmillan, 1992), p. 313.
49. Ibid., pp. 296–298.
50. Ibid., p. 298.
51. As quoted in Marilyn Ferguson, *The Aquarian Conspiracy* (Los Angeles: Tarcher, 1980), p. 199.
52. Garrow, *Bearing the Cross,* p. 524.
53. Alice Kitchen, personal communication, April 2004.
54. Except where noted this section is drawn from Rubin and Rubin, *Community Organizing,* pp. 89–90, 264–265, 302, 309, 312–318. 320.
55. Ibid., p. 313.
56. Ibid., p. 314.
57. T. Branch, *Parting the Waters: America in the King Years, 1954–1963* (New York: Simon and Schuster, 1988), p. 438.
58. Ibid.
59. Rubin and Rubin, *Community Organizing,* p. 89.
60. Ibid.
61. Ibid., p. 90.
62. Ibid.
63. Ibid., p. 266.
64. Ibid.
65. Alinsky, *Rules for Radicals,* p. 127.
66. Except where noted, this section has been summarized and adapted from Donald F. Harvey and Donald R. Brown, *An Experiential Approach to Organization Development* (Englewood Cliffs, NJ: Prentice-Hall, 1991), pp. 199–200.
67. Eyerman and Jamison, *Social Movements,* p. 79.
68. Rubin and Rubin, *Community Organizing,* p. 245.
69. George Bush, "Introduction." In *The National Security Strategy of the United States of America, September 2002* (Washington, DC: The White House, September 17, 2002).
70. Peter F. Drucker, *New Realities in Government and Politics, in Economics and Business, in Society and World View* (New York: Harper and Row, 1989), pp. 3–4.
71. Eyerman and Jamison, *Social Movements,* p. 162.
72. Harry C. Boyte, *Community Is Possible: Repairing America's Roots* (New York: Harper and Row, 1984), pp. 26, 28.
73. Richard Flacks, "The Party's Over." In *New Social Movements: From Ideology to Identity,* Enrique Larana, Hank Johnston, and Joseph R. Gusfield, eds. (Philadelphia: Temple University Press, 1994), p. 347.
74. Bush, *The National Security Strategy,* p. 6.
75. Except where noted, this section is adapted and summarized from Carol Mueller, "Conflict Networks and the Origins of Women's Liberation." In *New Social Movements: From Ideology to Identity,* Larana, Johnston, and Gusfield, pp. 234–239.
76. Eyerman and Jamison, *Social Movements,* p. 27.
77. Ibid., p. 161.
78. Robert Fisher, *Let the People Decide: Neighborhood Organizing in America* (New York: Twayne, 1994), p. 217.
79. Alberto Melluci, "A Strange Kind of Newness." In *New Social Movements: From Ideology to Identity,* Larana, Johnston, and Gusfield, p. 127.
80. Michel Foucault, "The Subject and Power." In *Michel Foucault: Beyond Structuralism and Hermeneutics,* Hubert I. Dreyfus and Paul Rabinow, eds. (Chicago: University of Chicago Press, 1983), p. 211.
81. This section is adapted and summarized from Eyerman and Jamison, *Social Movements,* pp. 26–27, 43–59, 93, 161.
82. Flacks, "The Party's Over," p. 348.
83. Eyerman and Jamison, *Social Movements,* p. 27.
84. Ibid., pp. 27, 164–166.
85. Eyerman and Jamison, *Social Movements,* p. 55.
86. Ibid.
87. Melluci, "A Strange Kind of Newness," p. 127.

Chapter 15: The Practice of Social Work at the Global Level

1. H. Norberg-Hodge, "Learning From Ladakh: A Passionate Appeal for 'Counter-Development.'" *Earth Island Journal,* 1997, p. 28.
2. "New Carpetbaggers," E-Mail Activist. (http://www.theemailactivist.org/Carpetbaggers.htm)
3. Peter Block, *Stewardship: Choosing Service Over Self-Interest* (San Francisco: Berrett-Koehler, 1993), p. 17.

4. Julian Hewitt, "When A Superpower Sneezes, We Shudder," *International Herald Tribune,* August 1, 2004, p. 4.

5. Ward H. Goodenough, *Cooperation and Change: An Anthropological Approach to Community Development* (New York: Russell Sage Foundation, 1963), pp. 19–20.

6. Kenneth L. Chau and Peter Hodge, "The Practice of Community Social Work With Third World Countries." In *The Theory and Practice of Community Work,* Samuel H. Taylor and Robert W. Roberts, eds. (New York: Columbia University Press, 1985), p. 388.

7. Roland Oliver, *The Missionary Factor in East Africa* (London: Longmans, 1952), p. 180.

8. Chau and Hodge, "The Practice of Community Social Work," p. 389.

9. Ibid., p. 388.

10. Ibid., p. 392.

11. Helmut K. Anheier and Kusuma Cunningham, "Internationalization of the Nonprofit Sector." In *Jossey-Bass Handbook of Nonprofit Leadership and Management,* Robert D. Herman and Associates, ed. (San Francisco: Jossey-Bass, 1994,) p. 102.

12. Ralph Garber, "Social Work Education in an International Context: Current Trends and Future Directions." In *Issues in International Social Work: Global Challenges for a New Century,* M. C. Hokenstad and James Midgley, eds. (Washington D.C.: NASW Press, 1997), pp. 160–161.

13. Lynne Healy, "International Social Work Curriculum in Historical Perspective." In *All Our Futures: Principles and Resources for Social Work Practice in a Global Era,* Chathapuram S. Ramanathan and Rosemary Link, eds. (Belmont, CA: Brooks/Cole Wadsworth, 1999), p. 28.

14. Chau and Hodge, "The Practice of Community Social Work," p. 392.

15. Colonial Office, *Education Policy in British Tropical Africa* (London: HMSO, 1925) in Chau and Hodge, "The Practice of Community Social Work," p. 392.

16. International Missionary Council, "Report of the Jerusalem Meeting of the International Missionary Councils." In *The Christian Mission in Relation to Rural Problems,* vol. 6 (London: Oxford University Press, 1928) in Chau and Hodge, "The Practice of Community Social Work," p. 420.

17. Anheier and Cunningham," Internationalization of the Nonprofit Sector," p. 102.

18. Gary Teeple, *Globalization and the Decline of Social Reform* (Atlantic Highland, NJ: Humanities Press, 1995), p. 57.

19. Ibid., p. 58.

20. George Monbiot, "The Rich World's Veto," *Znet Magazine,* October 17, 2002. (http://www.zmag.org/content/print_article .cfm?itemID=2495&sectionID=13)

21. Anheier and Cunningham, "Internationalization of the Nonprofit Sector," pp. 102–103.

22. Teeple, *Globalization,* p. 57.

23. Arline Prigoff, "Global Social and Economic Justice Issues." In *All Our Futures: Principles and Resources for Social Work Practice in a Global Era,* Ramanathan and Link, eds., p. 157.

24. Arline Prigoff, *Economics for Social Workers: Social Outcomes of Economic Globalization With Strategies for Community Action* (Pacific Grove, CA: Brooks/Cole Wadsworth, 2000), p. 119.

25. C. Caulfield, *Masters of Illusion: The World Bank and the Poverty Nations* (New York: Henry Holt, 1996), pp. 1, 2.

26. Prigoff, "Global Social and Economic Issues," p. 158.

27. Prigoff, *Economics for Social Workers,* p. 120.

28. Prigoff, "Global Social and Economic Issues," pp. 157–159.

29. Monbiot, "The Rich World's Veto."

30. Teeple, *Globalization,* pp. 62, 64.

31. Ibid., p. 65.

32. Garber, "Social Work Education in an International Context," pp. 162–164.

33. Anheier and Cunningham, "Internationalization of the Nonprofit Sector," p. 103.

34. Prigoff, *Economics for Social Workers,* p. 119.

35. Institute for Policy Studies. May 2004. (http://www.ips-dc .org/reports/top200.htm)

36. "Officials Say Most China Provinces Could Have AIDS From Blood Supply," Wednesday, *UK News,* March 3, 2003. (http:// uk.news.yahoo.com/040303/323/enipe.html)

37. Agence France-Presse, "China Plans AIDS Survey Linked to Blood Sales," *International Herald Tribune,* Singapore, October 15, 2004, p. 2; and "China HIV/AIDS Blood Supply Chronology," *China AIDS Survey,* Monterey, CA, 2005. (http://www.casy.org/chron/BloodSupply.htm)

38. Teeple, *Globalization,* pp. 137–138.

39. Prigoff, *Economics for Social Workers,* p. 119.

40. Teeple, *Globalization,* p. 138; and Prigoff, *Economics for Social Workers,* p. 119.

41. Prigoff, "Global Social and Economic Issues," pp. 157–159.

42. Teeple, *Globalization,* pp. 60, 68–69.

43. Lynne Healy, "International Social Work Curriculum in Historical Perspective." In *All Our Futures: Principles and Resources for Social Work Practice in a Global Era,* Ramanathan and Link, eds., p. 28.

44. *Encyclopedia of Associations* (Detroit, MI: Gale Publishing, 1966).

45. Anheier and Cunningham, "Internationalization of the Nonprofit Sector," p. 104.

46. Ibid., pp. 104 –105.

47. Teeple, *Globalization,* p. 141.

48. Institute for Policy Studies.

49. Teeple, *Globalization,* p. 60.

50. Garber, "Social Work Education in an International Context," p. 165.

51. Doug McAdam, "Culture and Social Movements." In *Social Movements: Perspectives and Issues,* Steven M. Buechler and F. Kurt Cylke Jr., eds. (Mountain View, CA: Mayfield, 1997), p. 481.

52. Julie Fisher, *The Road From Rio: Sustainable Development and the Nongovernmental Movement in the Third World* (Westport, CT: Praeger, 1993), p. 15.

53. Caulfield, *Masters of Illusion,* p. 338.

54. "74 M workers to die of AIDS by 2015: ILO," *Manila Bulletin,* Manila, Philippines, July 12, 2004, p. A1.

55. "Worlds HIV Carriers Rise to 42 Mil in 2002," *Japantoday,* November 2002. (http://www.japantoday.com/e/tools/print .asp?con4ent=news&id=240350)

56. "AIDS Orphans to Surge to 18 M in Africa by 2010—UN," *The Philippines Star,* July 14, 2004, p. 12.

57. United Nations Development Programme (UNDP), *Human Development Report 1997* (New York: Oxford University Press) p. 25.

58. Institute for Policy Studies.

59. UNDP, *Human Development Report* 1997, p. 7.

60. United Nations, Department of Public Information (UNDPI) Report, 1995.

61. Hokenstad and Midgley. *Issues in International Social Work,* p. 3.

62. Tom Johannesen "Social Work as an International Profession: Opportunities and Challenges." In *Issues in International Social Work,* Hokenstad and Midgley, eds., p. 149.

63. Institute for Policy Studies.

64. UNDP, *Human Development Report 1997,* p. 24.

65. "The New Carpetbaggers"; and Kathryn Ledebur and Sandra Edwards, "Ring of Fire," *New Internationalist,* 374, December 2004. (http://www.newint.org/issue374/)

66. Vandana Shiva, "Terrorism as Cannibalism," *Znet Update,* January 2002. (znetupdates@zmag.org); and Marcela Lopez Levy, "The Damn Water Is Ours," *New Internationalist,* 338, September 2001.

67. Robert C. Linthicum, *Empowering the Poor: Community Organization Among the City's 'Rag, Tag and Bobtail'* (Monrovia, CA: MARC, 1991), p. 6.

68. UNDP, *Human Development Report 1997*, p. 25.

69. John Daniszewski, "Severe Famine in Sudan Surpassing Relief Efforts," *Fresno Bee,* July 15, 1998, p. A7.

70. "Child Mortality," *New Zealand Herald,* October 9–10, 2004, p. B12.

71. Linthicum, *Empowering the Poor,* p. 6.

72. Teeple, *Globalization,* p. 108.

73. "Slavery in the 21st Century," *New Internationalist,* 337, August 2001. (http://www.newint.org/issue337/facts.htm)

74. Ibid.

75. U.S. Department of State, "Trafficking in Persons Report," June 5, 2002. (http://www.state.gov/g/tip/rls/tiprpt/2002/10653.htm)

76. "Slavery in the 21st Century."

77. U.S. Department of State, "Trafficking."

78. "Going Cheap," *New Internationalist,* 337, August 2001. (http://www.newint.org/issue 337/cheap.htm)

79. U.S. Department of State, "Trafficking."

80. Alex Perry, "The Shame," *Time Magazine,* February 4, 2002, pp. 23, 24.

81. U.S. Department of State, "Trafficking."

82. "Going Cheap."

83. "300,000 Child Soldiers Fighting Worldwide," *Japantoday,* June 13, 2001. (http://www.japantoday.com/e/?content=news&id=34469)

84. Perry, "The Shame," pp. 23, 24.

85. "Going Cheap."

86. Perry, "The Shame," pp. 23, 24.

87. "Of Human Bondage," *New Internationalist,* 337, August 2001. (http: //www.newint.org/issue337/keynote.htm)

88. Ibid.

89. "Going Cheap."

90. "Slavery in the 21st Century."

91. Sabrina Tavernise with Mona Mahmoud, "Protector of Iraq Women Faces a Tough Fight," *International Herald Tribune,* Neuilly-sur-Seine, France, October 15, 2004, p. 3.

92. Ibid; and "Women's Rights, What Price Freedom," *New Internationalist,* 373. (http://www.newint.org/issue373/freedom.htm)

93. G. Sen and C. Grown, *Development Crises, and Alternative Visions: Third World Women's Perspectives* (New York: Monthly Review, 1987), p. 68.

94. Prigoff, *Economics for Social Workers*, p. 127.

95. "US Arms Sales: Arms Around the World," Mojo Wire. (http://motherjones.com/arms/)

96. Marat Kenzhetayev and Lyuba Pronina, "Moscow Rocketing Up Arms Sales Charts," *Japantoday,* April 16, 2002. (http://www.japantoday.com/e/tools/print/.asp?content=news&id=211680)

97. UNDP, *Human Development Report 1997*, p. 102.

98. Sen and Grown, *Development Crises,* p. 67.

99. http://www.newint.org/bombing.htm.

100. William Blum, "A Brief History of US Interventions: 1945 to Present," *Bulatlat,* 2(5), March 10–16, 2002. (http://www.bulatlat.com/news/2-5/2-5-reader-blum.html)

101. http://www.newint.org/bombing.htm.

102. Rodreck Mupedziswa, "Social Work With Refugees: The Growing International Crisis." In *Issues in International Social Work,* Hokenstad and Midgley, eds., p. 110.

103. UNHCR, *The State of the World's Refugees: In Search of a Solution* (New York: Oxford University Press, 2005).

104. Eric J. Labs, "The Flow of Foreign Aid and Private Capital to Developing Countries," *The Role of Foreign Aid in Development* (Washington, DC: Congressional Budget Office, May, 1997), chap. 2. (http://www.cbo.gov/showdoc.cfm?index=8&sequence=3)

105. Barry James, "US Outlines Shift in Criteria for Providing Development Aid," *International Herald Tribune,* October 25, 2002, p. 3.

106. Mupedziswa, "Social Work With Refugees," pp. 111–115.

107. UNDP, *Human Development Report 1997*, p. 24.

108. United Nations High Commissioner for Refugees, *Global Report, 2002: UNHCR: An Overview-Global Programs* (Geneva: UNHCR, June 2002). (http://www.unhcr.ch/cgi-bin/texis/vtx/publ)

109. Ibid.

110. Mupedziswa, "Social Work With Refugees," p. 115.

111. Institute for Policy Studies.

112. Kevin Danaher, ed. *Fifty Years Is Enough: The Case Against the World Bank and the International Monetary Fund* (Boston: South End Press, 1994), p. 22.

113. Caulfield, *Masters of Illusion,* p. 338.

114. Prigoff, *Economics for Social Workers,* p. 119.

115. Megan Rowling, "Their Day in Court: Nicaraguan Banana Workers May Finally Get Justice," *In These Times,* August, 11, 2003 (http://www.inthesetimes.com/print.php?id=308_0_2_0); and Megan Rowling, "Banana Benders: Transnationals Do Legal Gymnastics to Avoid Compensating Banana Workers," Currents@newint.org. October 2004. (http://www.newint.org/newint/.issue372.htm)

116. L. R. Brown, C. Flavin, H. French, et al., *State of the World, 1997: Worldwatch Institute Report on Progress Toward a Sustainable Society* (New York: Norton, 1997), p. 3.

117. Teeple, *Globalization,* p. 73.

118. John Paul Vandenakker, *Small Christian Communities and the Parish: An Ecclesiological Analysis of the North American Experience* (Kansas City, MO: Sheed and Ward, 1994), p. 98.

119. Hubert Campfens, *Community Development Around the World* (Toronto: University of Toronto Press, 1997), p. 16.

120. Daniel Comacho, "Latin America: A Society in Motion." In *New Social Movements in the South: Empowering People,* Ponna Wignaraja, ed. (London: Zed Books, 1993), p. 50.

121. Leilah Landim, "Brazilian Crossroads: People's Groups, Walls and Bridges." In *New Social Movements in the South,* Wignaraja, ed., p. 219.

122. Sara M. Evans and Harry C. Boyte, *Free Spaces* (New York: Harper and Row, 1986), p. 20.

123. Guillermo Cook, *The Expectation of the Poor: Latin American Basic Ecclesial Communities in Protestant Perspective* (Maryknoll, NY: Orbis, 1985), p. 91.

124. Anisur Rahman, *People's Self-Development: Perspectives on Participatory Action Research* (London: Zed Books, 1993), p. 26.

125. Vandenakker, *Small Christian Communities and the Parish,* p. 103.

126. Alan Durning, "Action at the Grassroots: Fighting Poverty and Environmental Decline," *Worldwatch Paper,* 88, January 1989, p. 5.

127. Sidney Tarrow, "A Movement Society." In *Social Movements: Perspectives and Issues,* Buechler and Cylke, eds., p. 570.

128. Mansour Fakih, *NGOs in Indonesia* (Amherst, MA: Center for International Education, University of Massachusetts, 1991), p. 2.

129. Tarrow, "A Movement Society," p. 578.

130. Rahman, *People's Self-Development,* p. 128.

131. Fisher, *The Road From Rio,* p. 81.

132. Fakih, *NGOs in Indonesia,* pp. 1, 6–7.

133. Robert Fisher, *Let the People Decide: A History of Neighborhood Organizing* (Boston: G. K. Hall, 1984), p. xiii.

134. Landim, "Brazilian Crossroads," p. 224.

135. Rahman, *People's Self-Development,* p. 162.

136. Harsh Sethi, "Action Groups in the New Politics." In *New Social Movements in the South,* Wignaraja, ed., p. 231.

137. Meenaz Kassam, Fedmida Handy, and Shree Ranade, "Understanding NGO Impact: The Case of Women NGOs in India," *Social Development Issues,* 23(3), 2001, pp. 27–35.

138. Landim, "Brazilian Crossroads," p. 222.

139. Fisher, *The Road From Rio,* p. 216.

140. Rahman, *People's Self-Development,* p. 128.

141. Anthony Swift, "Scared of Our Kids," *New Internationalist,* 276, November 22, 2001. (http: www//newint.org/issue276/scared.htm)

142. Campfens, *Community Development Around the World,* p. 32.

143. Ibid. p. 54.

144. Jackie Smith, "Transnational Political Processes and the Human Rights Movement." In *Social Movements: Perspectives and Issues,* Buecher and Cylke, eds., p. 541.

145. Campfens, *Community Development Around the World,* p. 16.

146. Peter R. Baehr and Leon Gordenker, *The United Nations in the 1990s,* 2d ed. (New York: St. Martin's Press, 1994), pp. 130–131.

147. Mupedziswa, "Social Work With Refugees," p. 118.

148. Baehr and Gordenker, *The United Nations in the 1990s,* pp. 133–136, 142.

149. Evan Luard, *The United Nations: How It Works and What It Does* (New York: St. Martin's Press, 1979), p. 57.

150. Tom Johannesen, "Social Work as an International Profession: Opportunities and Challenges." In *Issues in International Social Work,* Hokenstad and Midgley, eds., p. 154.

151. Garber, "Social Work Education in an International Context," p. 165.

152. Johannesen, "Social Work as an International Profession," p. 154.

153. M. C. Hokenstad and James Midgley, "Realities of Global Interdependence: Challenges for Social Work in a New Century." In *Issues in International Social Work,* Hokenstad and Midgley, eds., p. 5.

154. Vera Mehta, "Ethnic Conflict and Violence in the Modern World: Social Work's Role in Building Peace." In *Issues in International Social Work,* Hokenstad and Midgley, eds., p. 102.

155. Mupedziswa, "Social Work With Refugees," p. 123.

156. Hokenstad and Midgely, "Realities of Global Interdependence," p. 5.

157. Mupedziswa, "Social Work With Refugees," p. 123.

158. Ibid.

159. United Nations Development Programme (UNDP), *Human Development Report* (New York: Oxford University Press, 1994), pp. 13–19.

160. Ibid.

161. Prigoff, *Economics for Social Workers,* p. 12.

162. Brian Kennedy, "Buy a New Car or Build a Village?" April 11, 2002. (RaceMatters.org/buynewcarorbuildvillage.htm); and "Globalgiving," the free dictionary.com, http://encyclopedia.thefreedictionary.com/developmentspace.

163. "Globalgiving," the free dictionary.com.

164. Fisher, *The Road From Rio,* p. 64.

165. Ibid., p. 164.

166. Rahman, *People's Self-Development,* p. 128.

167. Fisher, *The Road From Rio,* pp. 21, 23, 30.

168. Rahman, *People's Self-Development,* pp. 180–181.

169. Ibid. p.168.

170. Marwaan Macan-Markar, "Focus on the World Social Forum," *Grassroots Online,* February 5, 2002. (http://www.grassrootsonline.org/gol_0202_bullard.html)

171. Ibid.

172. Ponna Wignaraja, "Rethinking Development and Democracy," In *New Social Movements in the South: Empowering People,* Ponna Wignaraja, ed. (London: Zed Books, 1993), p. 6.

173. Comacho, "Latin America: A Society in Motion," p. 39.

174. Fakih, *NGOs in Indonesia,* p. 11.

175. Larry Rohter, "Bolivia's Poor Proclaim Abiding Distrust of Globalization," *New York Times,* October 17, 2003 (http://www.nytimes.com/2003/10/17international/americas/17GLOB.html); and *New Internationalist,* 364, January 2004.

176. Rahman, *People's Self-Development,* pp. 168, 181.

177. Wignaraja, "Rethinking Development and Democracy," p. 12.

178. Vandenakker, *Small Christian Communities and the Parish,* p. xii.

179. Camacho, "Latin America: A Society in Motion," p. 47.

180. I. Queiro-Tajalli and C. Campbell, "Resilience and Violence at the Macro Level." In *Resiliency: An Integrated Approach to Practice, Policy, and Research,* R. R. Greene, ed. (Washington, DC: NASW Press, 2002), pp. 217–240.

181. Comacho, "Latin America: A Society in Motion," pp. 47–48.

182. Jeff Dumtra, "Power to the People," *World View,* Winter 1991–1992, pp. 8–13.

183. Comacho, "Latin America: A Society in Motion," pp. 46–47.

184. Wignaraja, "Rethinking Development and Democracy," pp. 6, 19.

185. Rahman, *People's Self-Development,* p. 68.

186. Ibid., p. 182.

187. "Farmworkers Call for Corporations to Respect Their Rights," Oxfam America, 2005. (http://www.oxfamamerica.org/news and publications/news_updates/art7003.html/2005)

188. "Like Machines, Nearly Two Million US Farmworkers Labor Without Rights: Oxfam Brings Together Human Rights Leaders in Fla," *Common Dreams Progressive Newswire,* March 15, 2004. (http://www.commondreams.org/cgi-bin/newsprint.cgi?file=/news2004/0315-04.htm)

189. Ibid.

190. *Fortune Magazine,* "Index to the Fortune 500," April 23, 2004, p. F-34.

191. "Like Machines, Nearly Two Million US Farmworkers Labor Without Rights."

192. Rahman, *People's Self-Development,* pp. 46–48.

193. Ibid., pp. 68–72.

194. Paulo Freire, *Pedagogy of the Oppressed* (New York: Continuum, 1992), p. 46.

195. Ibid., p. 73.

196. William A. Smith, "Concientizacao and Simulation Games," Technical Note 2 (Amherst, MA: Center for International Education, University of Massachusetts, 1972), p. 9.

197. Si Kahn, *How People Get Power: Organizing Oppressed Communities for Action* (New York: McGraw-Hill, 1972), pp. 48–49.

198. Prigoff, "Global Social and Economic Justice Issues," p. 169.

199. Mark S. Homan, *Promoting Community Change: Making It Happen in the Real World,* 3d ed. (Belmont, CA: Brooks Cole Thomson, 2004), p. 111.

200. Ibid., p. 112.

201. Amilcar Cabral, *Return to the Source: Selected Speeches of Amilcar Cabral* (New York Monthly Review Press, 1973), p. 51.

Epilogue: Macro Social Work: A Profession of Heroes

1. Robert Bellah et al., *Habits of the Heart: Individualism and Commitment in American Life* (New York: Harper and Row, 1985), p. 138.

2. This section is summarized and adapted from *U.S. News and World Report,* March 21, 1994, p. 58.

3. Harry Specht and Mark Courtney, *Unfaithful Angels: How Social Work Has Abandoned Its Mission* (New York: Free Press, 1994), p. 27.

4. Noam Chomsky, *Problems of Knowledge and Freedom: The Russell Lectures* (New York: Vintage Books, 1971). In *Community Organizing in a Diverse Society,* Felix G. Rivera and John Erlich, eds. (Boston: Allyn and Bacon, 1992), p. 64.

5. Specht and Courtney, *Unfaithful Angels,* p. 27.

NAME INDEX

A

Abbott, Edith, 85, 87, 498
Abbott, Grace, 85, 87, 498
Abernathy, Ralph, 434
Abeytia, Ernest, 217
Addams, Jane, 39, 40, 79–80, 109, 129, 429, 430, 431, 459, 498–499
Alinsky, Saul, 6, 97, 123, 212, 214–216, 219, 220, 221, 223, 224, 230–232, 420
Allison, Graham, 61, 390
Anderson, Sarah, 257
Anderson, Warren, 267
Anheier, Helmut, 249, 464
Anthony, Susan B., 85, 376, 429
Argyis, Chris, 342
Aristotle, 394
Arthur, Chester V., 276

B

Babbie, Earl, 155, 282
Baca-Zinn, Maxine, 39
Bacon, Roger, 58
Baden-Powell, Robert, 280, 499
Bailey, Darlene, 251
Barber, Benjamin, 139
Barnett, Ida Wells, 85
Barnett, Samuel, 79, 280, 499
Barrett, Janie Porter, 285
Barton, Clara, 85, 275–277, 376, 459, 499
Bauman, John, 220, 233
Beckhard, Richard, 342, 343, 345
Beckman, David, 492
Beers, Clifford, 499
Bell, Cecil H., Jr., 341, 342
Bell, Colin, 117
Bellah, Robert, 119, 127, 130, 495
Bender, Thomas, 124, 125, 128, 129, 397
Bennis, Warren, 88, 342

Berger, Peter, 44, 73, 74, 122, 255
Berger, Renee, 184
Berle, Adolph A., 87
Berrien, K., 40
Bethune, Mary McLeod, 500
Beukema, Liala, 207
Biddle, William, 181
Blake, Robert, 88, 89, 90, 342, 343, 354
Blanchard, Kenneth, 89, 92
Block, Peter, 83, 245, 259, 311, 319, 338, 363, 365
Blumer, Henry, 73, 75
Booth, Charles, 500
Booth, Heather, 220
Booth, William, 279, 280, 500
Boyte, Harry, 69, 204, 393, 475
Brace, Charles Loring, 85, 279, 289, 376, 500
Brahe, Tyco, 58, 124
Brecher, Jeremy, 386
Breckenridge, Sophonisba, 85, 429, 500
Brilliant, Elenore, 109
Brock, William, 33
Brown, Donald, 341, 346
Brown, John, 32
Brown, L. R., 474
Brown, Sam, 169
Brueggemann, William, 109
Buber, Martin, 73, 319
Bucholz, Marjorie, 97–98
Buell, Bradley, 149
Bullard, Nicola, 483
Burke, Paul, 203
Burns, Allen T., 430
Bush, George H. W., 374
Bush, George W., 386, 446

C

Cabral, Amilcar, 447, 484, 491
Cabrini, St. Francis, 280, 295, 500

Campfens, Hubert, 474
Carlyle, Jean, 339–341
Carson, Rachel, 443
Carter, Jimmy, 183, 384
Cartwright, Dorwin, 342
Catt, Carrie Chapman, 85, 376, 429–430
Caulfield, Catherine, 461, 466, 473
Cavanagh, John, 257
Chandler, Asa, 261
Chau, Kenneth, 459
Chavez, Cesar, 82, 216, 217, 218, 226, 227–228, 442
Chomsky, Noam, 497
Churchill, Winston, 314
Churchman, C. West, 61
Cincotta, Gale, 183, 219, 220
Cisneros, Henry, 202
Clague, Ewan, 86
Claybrook, Joan, 374
Clemetson, Robert, 178
Clinton, Bill, 471
Coates, Roger, 178
Cohen, Wilbur J., 87
Coit, Stanton, 279
Coleman, Frank, 44
Columbus, Christopher, 124
Commager, Henry, 261
Cook, Philip J., 27
Cooley, Charles, 86, 129
Copernicus, Nikolaus, 58, 124
Cortes, Ernesto, 190, 202, 203, 393, 396
Cortez, Beatrice, 203
Courtney, Mark, 111
Coyle, Grace, 86, 87, 88
Cunningham, Kusuma, 464
Custer, George, 33

D

Dahrndorf, Ralf, 38
Davis, Susan A., 381
Day, Dorothy, 496, 500–501

SUBJECT INDEX